U.S. Master™ Auditing Guide

Third Edition

D. Larry Crumbley
Zabihollah Rezaee
Douglas E. Ziegenfuss

CCH INCORPORATED
Chicago

A WoltersKluwer Company

Production editors: Holly J. Porter and Diana Roozeboom

Graphic design: Laila Gaidulis

Cover design: Craig Arritola

This publication is designed to provide accurate and authoritative information in regard to the subject matter covered. It is sold with the understanding that the publisher is not engaged in rendering legal, accounting, or other professional service and that the author is not offering such advice in this publication. If legal advice or other expert assistance is required, the services of a competent professional person should be sought.

ISBN 0-8080-1191-X

©2004, CCH INCORPORATED

4025 W. Peterson Ave.
Chicago, IL 60646-6085
1 800 248 3248
http://tax.cchgroup.com

No claim is made to original government works; however, within this Product or Publication, the following are subject to CCH's copyright: (1) the gathering, compilation, and arrangement of such government materials; (2) the magnetic translation and digital conversion of data, if applicable; (3) the historical, statutory and other notes and references; and (4) the commentary and other materials.

All Rights Reserved
Printed in the United States of America

To our families:

My wife, Donna, and Stacey, Dana, and Heather

                                                                                     D. Larry Crumbley

My wife, Soheila, and Nick and Rose

                                                                                           Zabi Rezaee

My wife, Mary, and Doug Jr. and Greta

                                                                      Douglas E. Ziegenfuss

Preface

The wave of corporate and accounting scandals in the early 2000s have raised serious concerns regarding the effectiveness of corporate governance, reliability and quality of financial reports, and the credibility of audit functions. These scandals eroded public trust and investor confidence in audited financial statements. Several initiatives were taken by legislators (passage of the Sarbanes-Oxley Act of 2002 and creation of the Public Company Accounting Oversight Board (PCAOB)), regulators (implementation rules issued by the Securities and Exchange Commission (SEC)), the accounting profession (Enterprise Risk Management (ERM) and Statement on Auditing Standards (SAS) No. 99), and national stock exchanges (corporate governance guiding principles) to restore public trust and investor confidence in corporate governance, financial reports, and audit functions. These initiatives are fully incorporated in the third edition of the book to inform readers regarding changes in the regulatory and business environment that affect the auditing profession. The accounting and auditing landscape has been changed forever as a result of the Enron and WorldCom debacles. The moment that President George Bush signed the Sarbanes-Oxley Act of 2002 into law, the way public companies engage in business and how the accounting profession performs its auditing functions have been changed radically.

The era of self-regulation for the accounting profession is over. On April 16, 2003, the PCAOB began setting auditing, attestation, quality control, and ethical standards for public auditing companies. The Sarbanes-Oxley Act changed the auditing profession's self-regulatory environment under the American Institute of Certified Public Accountants' (AICPA) peer review system to the regulatory framework under the PCAOB and the SEC oversight function for public accounting firms that audit financial statements of public companies. We cast no stones in this book, but covered topics in a straightforward fashion. We kept away from social commentary, but deeds often speak for themselves. Even those new to auditing will understand from coverage in our book that auditors have no shortage of rules and principles that ought to be followed. Even if only half the news reports on recent audit failures are true, our readers will see quite clearly that many of the rules and principles have been violated. We have quoted reports and stories that add context to the hard information and analysis provided. First and foremost, we wanted to cover the discipline of auditing substantively.

Suddenly, from Congress to the Caymans, auditing is on everyone's list of hot topics. Auditing has become a dangerous profession as more and more plaintiffs sue the company's accounting firm rather than the company itself. Of course, the accounting firm has much deeper pockets than a bankrupt business.

We believe the third edition of our book, by focusing on an analytical perspective of teaching auditing and the emerging initiatives in (1) regulatory framework of the auditing profession post-Sarbanes-Oxley Act and the creation of the PCAOB, (2) the financial reporting process post-financial scandals, (3) technological advances such as Extensible Business Reporting Language (XBRL) based financial reports and related continuous auditing, and (4) ethical considerations and corporate governance principles will provide a useful reference and teaching tool to obtain a better understanding of audit functions and the auditing profession. The substantial changes in the third edition reflect the intent of the book to connect auditing to the needs of business. In achieving this goal, we have (1) made refinements in the content, style, and clarity of materials in all chapters; (2) made further refinements in the organization of the text to enhance its adoptability by financial auditors, internal auditors, governmental auditors, and fraud examiners; and (3) provided relevant and timely coverage of emerging initiatives in corporate governance, the financial reporting process, and audit functions.

We all know that the subject of auditing is, now more than ever with the PCAOB, a moving target, and now that we have published a comprehensive guide, we intend to do our part writing new editions as practicable. Send us your comments, favorable or critical, and we pledge our best efforts to see that this book keeps evolving to serve your changing needs and interests.

HIGHLIGHTS OF CHANGES FROM THE SECOND EDITION

The following changes are made in the third edition to achieve the book's aforementioned goals.

1. A new Chapter 26 entitled "Ethics and Corporate Governance" is added to discuss the important role that corporate governance and corporate codes of conduct can play in improving reliability, transparency, and integrity of the financial reporting process, and the credibility and effectiveness of audit functions.

2. Chapter objectives are provided for each chapter to draw readers' attention to the main themes of each chapter.

3. A chapter summary is presented for each chapter to summarize readers' understanding of each chapter.

4. All of the chapters are updated to address emerging initiatives affecting the auditing profession (the Sarbanes-Oxley Act and SEC related implementation rules, auditing standards issued by the PCAOB, technological advances, and globalization).

Preface vii

5. The third edition provides flexibility in presenting the amount and order of materials on financial auditing, assurance and attestation services, internal auditing, operational auditing, environmental auditing, compliance auditing, fraud examination, and forensic accounting.

6. The third edition exposes readers to highly relevant auditing concepts, standards, tools, and techniques facing the accounting and auditing profession.

7. New material on general ethics and on ethical decision-making as suggested by the Ethics Education Task Force of AACSB International is provided in preparing business leaders and responsible auditors for the twenty-first century.

8. All chapters containing material on auditors' reports are updated to conform to PCAOB Auditing Standard No. 1 regarding audits and other engagements relating to public companies.

9. All chapters, including material on internal controls, are updated to conform to PCAOB Auditing Standard No. 2 on internal control over financial reporting (pertaining to Act Sec. 404 of the Sarbanes-Oxley Act regarding management reports on internal controls and auditors' attention of and report on management's assessment of the effectiveness of internal controls).

10. Increased attention is given to corporate governance and its role in improving audit effectiveness and reliability of financial reports.

11. International Standards on Auditing (ISA) issued by the International Auditing and Assurance Standards Board (IAASB) are incorporated into several chapters.

12. Supplemental teaching aids are available to assist teachers who adopt the third edition as a textbook in making a self-assessment of their understanding of key points and chapter materials. The supplements consist of (1) a student study guide and (2) a testbank. The student study guide includes for each text chapter 10-15 learning objectives, 10-15 essential terms (chapter highlights), and 10-15 review questions. Solutions are included at the end of each chapter of the study guide. The testbank is available in hard copy and electronic format. The test questions for each text chapter consist of 10-15 objective (multiple choice) questions and 10-15 discussion (short essay and analysis) questions. Suggested solutions are included.

INTENDED AUDIENCE

This book is designed for anyone wishing to obtain an understanding and knowledge of auditing, including financial auditing, internal auditing, governmental auditing, operational auditing, comprehensive auditing, environmental auditing, systems auditing, fraud examination, forensic accounting, and corporate governance. This book should be beneficial to the following groups.

1. *Corporations, their board of directors, and executives:* Provisions of the Sarbanes-Oxley Act of 2002 and related SEC implementation rules pertaining to corporate governance, the financial reporting process, and audit functions discussed throughout the third edition should help public companies and their board of directors and executives to effectively discharge their responsibilities.

2. *Auditors:* Auditors in general-including internal, external, governmental, fraud, and environmental auditors-should find the material relevant and useful to their audit functions.

3. *Business schools and accounting programs:* The third edition of the book, along with supplementary materials and the testbank for each chapter, can serve as the core for an introductory course in auditing either at the undergraduate or the graduate level. Refinements are made in the third edition to integrate corporate governance, ethics, and internal controls with auditing theory, concepts, methodology, and practice.

4. *Other professionals and training programs:* Professionals such as internal auditors, management accountants, corporate legal counsel, and financial analysts who provide accounting auditing, legal, and financial services to corporations should find this book relevant and helpful to their professional activities and services.

5. *International audience:* Chapter 24 of the third edition is devoted to international auditing standards. In addition, increased attention is given to international accounting and auditing issues, including international standards on auditing (ISAs), ISO 9000 for quality control, and ISO 14000 for environmental auditing. These and other international auditing issues incorporated throughout the book can be very useful as an educational and reference source for business schools and professionals worldwide.

D. Larry Crumbley

Zabi Rezaee

Douglas E. Ziegenfuss

July 2004

About the Authors

D. Larry Crumbley, Zabihollah (Zabi) Rezaee, and Douglas E. Ziegenfuss are well-known accounting professors with substantial practice experience and have maintained a solid working relationship with accounting firms and accounting organizations.

Dr. Larry Crumbley, CPA, Cr.FA, is the KPMG Endowed Professor of Accounting at Louisiana State University. He is an extremely prolific writer, having authored more than 300 major articles and many newspaper columns covering auditing, accounting, tax, and other technical subjects. He is also the the author, co-author, editor, or contributor to more than a hundred other publications.

Dr. Zabihollah (Zabi) Rezaee is the Thompson-Hill Chair of Excellence and professor of accounting at the University of Memphis. He is a CPA, CMA, CIA, CFE, and CGFM. Dr. Rezaee has authored two books and contributes to several other books. He has published more than 150 articles and received numerous research awards. Dr. Rezaee has more than 30 years of teaching and practice experience in auditing and currently serves on the Standing Advisory Group (SAG) of the Public Company Accounting Oversight Board (PCAOB).

Dr. Douglas E. Ziegenfuss is a Professor of Accounting at Old Dominion University in Norfolk, Virginia where he teaches auditing. He is a CPA, CMA, CIA, CFE, CGFM, and CISA and has eight years of auditing experience. His areas of expertise include operational, fraud, and information technology audits. Dr. Ziegenfuss has authored and contributed to several books and a great number of articles and research papers, and he has received numerous teaching awards.

Collectively these authors have contributed much to accounting literature and education. In addition, their continued involvement in professional accounting organizations allows them to bring a valuable practical dimension to their writing.

Acknowledgements

We'd like to thank Lars Kiertzner at the Aarhus School of Business (Handelshoejskolen at Aarhus, Denmark) for his technical review of the international auditing chapter. We'd also like to acknowledge organizations, such as NALGA, ACFE, ISACA, AICPA, IIA, PCAOB, IAAS, and others that gave permission to use their materials. We thank the members of the CCH team for their hard work and dedication, including Holly J. Porter and Diana Roozeboom for managing the third edition of the book through the production process, Laila Gaidulis and Craig Arritola for graphic and cover design, and Larry Norris for editorial guidance.

Table of Contents

	Paragraph
Chapter 1—The Professional Auditing Context	
Introduction	101
Standards of Professional Conduct	102
Legal Liability	103
Quality Control Standards	104
Planning the Financial Audit	105
Performing Fieldwork	106
Reaching Conclusions	107
Reporting Considerations	108
Reviews and Compilations	109
Special Reports and Other Selected Attestation Reports	110
New or Proposed Assurance Services	111
Forensic Accounting Services	112
IRS Auditing—Indirect Methods of Reconstructing Income	113
The Internal Auditing Function	114
Managing the Internal Auditing Department	115
Reporting Internal Audit Assignment Results	116
Operational Auditing	117
Compliance Audits	118
External Auditor's Responsibilities Regarding Fraud	119
Environmental and Quality Audits	120
Integrating Analytical Procedures and Sampling Into Audit Tests	121
IT and the Auditor	122
Government Auditing	123
Summary	124
Chapter 2—Standards of Professional Conduct	
Introduction	201
Ethical Principles: The Cornerstone	202
AICPA Rules of Conduct	203
General Standards—Rule 201	204
Responsibilities to Clients	205
SEC Enforcement Rules	206
The Oversight Organization	207
SEC on Independence	208
Independence Standards Board	209
Interpretation of AICPA Independence Rule	210
Other Standards of Professional Conduct	211
Possible Future Initiatives	212

	Paragraph

Chapter 2—continued

Strengthening Auditor Independence Post-Sarbanes-Oxley Act	213
PCAOB's Standard-Setting Process	214
COSO Enterprise Risk Management Framework	215
Summary	216

Chapter 3—Legal Liability

Introduction	301
Frequency and Severity of Claims	302
Liability to Clients	303
Third-Party Liability	304
Statutory Civil Liability	305
Statutory Criminal Liability	306
Biased Jurors	307
Federal Sentencing Guidelines	308
Summary	309

Chapter 4—Quality Control Standards

Introduction	401
AICPA Quality Assurance	402
Peer Review for Small Firms	403
Inspection of Registered Public Accounting Firms	404
Internal Auditing Quality Control	405
ISO 9000 and 14000 Standards	406
Summary	407

Chapter 5—Planning the Financial Audit

Introduction	501
Pre-Planning Stage	502
Audit Preparation Stage	503
Audit Staff Supervision	504
Summary	505

Chapter 6—Performing Fieldwork

Introduction	601
Auditor Responsibility for Detecting Misstatements	602
Management Assertions	603
The Link Between Management Assertions and Audit Objectives	604
Audit Risk and Materiality	605
Substantive Tests	606
Auditing Procedures	607
Sufficiency of Evidence	608
Competence of Evidential Matter	609
Internal Controls and Audit Objectives	610
Testing the Internal Controls	611
Using the Work of the Internal Auditor	612

	Paragraph
Chapter 6—continued	
Final Assessment of Control Risk and Risk of Material Misstatement Due to Fraud, and Their Effect on Detection Risk	613
Applying Substantive Tests Prior to the Balance Sheet Date	614
Audit Programs	615
Audit Workpapers	616
Evaluation of Evidential Matter	617
Fraud Implications Arising During the Evaluation of Audit Results	618
Illegal Acts by Clients	619
Final Review of Audit	620
The Sarbanes-Oxley Act of 2002 and the Auditor's Attestation of Internal Controls	621
Summary	622
Chapter 7—Reaching Conclusions	
Introduction	701
Auditing the Cash Account	702
Auditing Accounts Receivable	703
Auditing Accounts Payable	704
Other Procedures in the Financial Audit	705
Reviewing for Contingent Liabilities	706
Reviewing for Subsequent Events	707
Related Party Transactions	708
Reviewing the Company's Ability to Continue as a Going Concern	709
Final Fieldwork Assessment of the Risks of Material Misstatement Due to Fraud	710
Conducting a Final Analytical Review	711
Management Report on Internal Controls	712
Obtaining a Management Representation Letter	713
Summary	714
Chapter 8—Reporting Considerations	
Introduction	801
Auditing Standards	802
Categories of Audit Opinions	803
Special Reporting Considerations	804
Report of Independent Registered Public Accounting Firms	805
Summary	806
Chapter 9—Reviews and Compilations	
Introduction	901
Compilations, Reviews, and Audits	902
Compilations	903
Special Compilation Circumstances	904
Reviews	905

	Paragraph

Chapter 9—continued

Additional Review Issues	906
Review Report According to PCAOB Standards	907
Summary	908

Chapter 10—Special Reports and Other Selected Attestation Reports

Introduction	1001
Reports Using Comprehensive Basis of Accounting Other than GAAP	1002
Audits of Specified Elements, Accounts, or Items of a Financial Statement	1003
Compliance with Aspects of Contractual Agreements or Regulatory Requirements	1004
Financial Presentations Prepared to Comply with Contractual Agreements or Regulatory Provisions	1005
Financial Information Presented in Prescribed Forms or Schedules that Require a Prescribed Form of Report	1006
Prospective Financial Statements	1007
Attestation of and Report on Internal Control (Public Companies)	1008
Summary	1009

Chapter 11—New or Proposed Assurance Services

Introduction	1101
SSAE No. 10	1102
Risk Assessment	1103
Business Performance Measurements	1104
Information Systems Reliability	1105
Electronic Commerce (WebTrust)	1106
Health Care Providers	1107
Eldercare Assurance	1108
Seven Other Opportunities	1109
Trends in Internal Auditing	1110
Summary	1111

Chapter 12—Forensic Accounting Services

Introduction	1201
Defining Forensic Accounting Services	1202
Some Early History	1203
Expert Witnessing Becomes Popular	1204
The Evidence Phase of Forensic Accounting	1205
The Term "Forensic Accounting" Is Born	1206
Judicial Procedure	1207
Evidence and Computer Technology	1208
Computer Forensics	1209
Forensic Accounting Practices	1210
Federal Rules of Evidence	1211

Paragraph

Chapter 12—continued
Courtroom Etiquette 1212
Measuring Damages 1213
AICPA's Consulting Guidelines 1214
Risk Management 1215
Forensic Accounting and Fraud Deterrence Certifications 1216
Future Trends in Forensic Accounting 1217
Summary 1218

Chapter 13—IRS Auditing—Indirect Methods of Reconstructing Income
Introduction 1301
Forensic Audit Approaches Used by IRS Agents 1302
Minimum Income Probes 1303
Lifestyle Probes 1304
IRS's Financial Status Audits 1305
Indirect Methods 1306
Tracing Assets 1307
Current State of Tax Compliance 1308
Summary 1309

Chapter 14—The Internal Auditing Profession
Introduction 1401
The Modern Internal Auditing Function 1402
The Institute of Internal Auditors 1403
Future Trends in Internal Auditing 1404
Summary 1405

Chapter 15—Managing the Internal Auditing Function
Introduction 1501
Authorizing and Organizing the Internal Auditing Function 1502
Coordinating the Internal Auditing Function with Organizational Policies 1503
Interactions with the Organization's External Auditor 1504
Quality Assurance 1505
Outsourcing 1506
The Audit Committee 1507
Summary 1508

Chapter 16—Scheduling and Performing the Internal Auditing Engagement
Introduction 1601
Traditional Risk Assessment and Audit Scheduling 1602
Risk-Based Audit Planning 1603
The Individual Audit Assignment 1604
Fact-Finding Interviews 1605
Summary 1606

Paragraph

Chapter 17—Reporting Internal Audit Assignment Results
Introduction	1701
The Reporting Process	1702
The Report Format	1703
Individual Audit Findings	1704
Editing and Proofreading the Report	1705
Sample Report	1706
Summary	1707

Chapter 18—Operational Auditing
Introduction	1801
Operational Auditing Defined	1802
The Demand for Operational Auditing	1803
Necessary Knowledge, Skills, and Abilities	1804
The Typical Operational Audit Engagement	1805
Government Performance Audits	1806
Developing Performance Measures	1807
Summary	1808

Chapter 19—Compliance Audits
Introduction	1901
Organizational Policies and Procedures	1902
Control Self-Assessment	1903
Enterprise Risk Management	1904
Sarbanes-Oxley Treatment of Internal Control	1905
Laws and Regulations	1906
Contracts	1907
Summary	1908

Chapter 20—Fraud Auditing
Introduction	2001
Some History of Fraud Detection	2002
The Fraud Investigation Process	2003
External Auditor's Responsibilities	2004
Fraudulent Financial Reporting	2005
Detecting Cooked Books	2006
Financial Statement Fraud Risk Factors	2007
Horizontal and Vertical Analysis	2008
Other Forensic-Type Audit Procedures	2009
Ratio Analysis	2010
Misappropriation of Assets Fraud Risk Factors	2011
Some Asset Misappropriation Schemes	2012
Selected Indicia of Fraud	2013
Corporate Fraud Task Force	2014
Summary	2015

Paragraph

Chapter 21—Environmental and Quality Audits

Introduction	2101
U.S. Environmental Statutes	2102
The Environmental Protection Agency (EPA)	2103
Accounting Guidelines	2104
Principles and Framework	2105
ISO 14000	2106
Certifications	2107
The Role of the Environmental Auditor	2108
New Approach Systems	2109
Information Needs	2110
Organizational Responsibilities for Environmental Auditing	2111
ISO 14000 Guidelines	2112
Summary	2113

Chapter 22—Integrating Analytical Procedures and Sampling into Audit Tests

Introduction	2201
Analytical Procedures	2202
Basic Sampling Concepts	2203
Risks of Sampling	2204
Audit Testing Decisions	2205
Conducting an Attribute Sampling Test	2206
Conducting a Variable Sampling Test	2207
Tips for Accurate Sampling	2208
Summary	2209

Chapter 23—IT and the Auditor

Introduction	2301
Historical Background	2302
IT Controls	2303
IT Control Frameworks	2304
Variety of IT Systems	2305
The Computer and the Auditor	2306
IT Auditing Organizations	2307
Academic Preparation for Becoming an IT Auditor	2308
Summary	2309

Chapter 24—International Auditing Standards

Introduction	2401
International Auditing Standards and Audit Planning (ISA 300)	2402
International Auditing Standards and Performing Fieldwork	2403
International Auditing Standards and Audit Reports	2404
Global Convergence of Auditing Standards	2405
Summary	2406

	Paragraph
Chapter 25—Government Auditing	
Introduction	2501
Professional Organizations	2502
Professional Certifications	2503
Professional Standards	2504
Summary	2505
Chapter 26—Ethics and Corporate Governance	
Introduction	2601
Ethics Considerations	2602
Ethics and Corporate Governance Education	2603
Corporate Governance	2604
Causes and Effects of Financial Scandals	2605
Corporate Governance After the Sarbanes-Oxley Act	2606
Future of the Accounting Profession	2607
Summary	2608

	Page
Appendix 1: Ethics Vocabulary	901
Appendix 2: The Institute of Internal Auditors—Code of Ethics	905
Appendix 3: International Standards for the Professional Practice of Internal Auditing	909
Appendix 4: Possible Performance Measures	917
Appendix 5: Forensic Accounting and Expert Witness Vocabulary	921
Index	925

Chapter 1

The Professional Auditing Context

¶101 Introduction
¶102 Standards of Professional Conduct
¶103 Legal Liability
¶104 Quality Control Standards
¶105 Planning the Financial Audit
¶106 Performing Fieldwork
¶107 Reaching Conclusions
¶108 Reporting Considerations
¶109 Reviews and Compilations
¶110 Special Reports and Other Selected Attestation Reports
¶111 New or Proposed Assurance Services
¶112 Forensic Accounting Services
¶113 IRS Auditing—Indirect Methods of Reconstructing Income
¶114 The Internal Auditing Function
¶115 Managing the Internal Auditing Department
¶116 Reporting Internal Audit Assignment Results
¶117 Operational Auditing
¶118 Compliance Audits
¶119 External Auditor's Responsibilities Regarding Fraud
¶120 Environmental and Quality Audits
¶121 Integrating Analytical Procedures and Sampling Into Audit Tests
¶122 IT and the Auditor
¶123 Government Auditing
¶124 Summary

¶101 Introduction

The U. S. Master Auditing Guide frames the context of what auditors do and examines the important concepts, rules and procedures that make up the auditing craft. In other words, the Guide focuses on the "what" as well as the "how." While covering topics at an appropriate depth for a guide, the book often references the underlying sources and authority upon which the auditing profession depends. Like other Master Guides produced by CCH, the idea behind the guide is to provide one reference that can serve as a first source of information on an issue and a constant companion to the professional.

This chapter serves to describe the important issues in a summary fashion and is therefore written in general terms without extensive footnotes to authority. It should serve to create a context for discussion in the rest of the book, as well as provide some solid information on the most important issues. The rest of the book focuses on topics in much greater detail.

Chapter 1 objectives:

- To understand the role of auditors in society (see ¶ 102-103).
- To become familiar with the regulatory, legal, and professional environment of auditing (see ¶ 103-104).
- To learn various types of auditing and assurance services including financial, internal, governmental, and forensic auditing (see ¶ 111-123).
- To understand an overview of an audit engagement (see ¶ 105-110).

¶ 102 Standards of Professional Conduct

A professional is one who performs tasks ethically and responsibly at a high level. For the accounting professional who is an auditor, this high level is defined by standards of professional conduct. The cornerstone of profession standards are rules of ethics that come from the Securities and Exchange Commission (SEC), the American Institute of Certified Public Accountants (AICPA), the state accounting societies, the Institute of Internal Auditors (IIA), and more recently the Public Company Accounting Oversight Board (PCAOB).

The wave of corporate and accounting scandals encouraged Congress to pass the Sarbanes-Oxley Act of 2002. Provisions of the Sarbanes-Oxley Act of 2002 as related to corporate governance, financial reporting, and particularly audit functions are thoroughly integrated into all chapters. Below is a summary of some of the provisions of the Sarbanes-Oxley Act of 2002, and Table 1.1 summarizes sections of the Act.

1. Establishes PCAOB.
2. Prohibits auditors from performing non-audit services contemporaneously with audit services.

¶ 102

3. Requires publicly traded companies to have an audit committee composed of independent members of the board of directors.

4. Requires CFO & CEO to certify that financial reports do not contain any untrue statements, and they fairly present the company's financial condition and results of operations.

5. Requires CFO & CEO to be responsible for establishing, maintaining, and reporting on internal controls.

6. Requires auditors to attest to and report on management's assessment of the effectiveness of internal control over financial reporting.

7. Requires corporate executives to repay any bonus or compensation received if the company is required to prepare an accounting restatement due to material misstatements caused by fraud.

8. Increases the prison sentences for wire and mail fraud and a new category of crime for securities fraud to a 20-year maximum sentence.

9. Makes document shredding unlawful and a crime subject to prison.

10. Ensures that corporate fraud is punishable regardless of when it is discovered.

11. Requires the lead partner in charge of the audit and the audit partner responsible for reviewing the audit be replaced every five years.

12. Directs the SEC to conduct a study of securities professionals who have been found to have aided and abetted a violation of Federal Securities laws.

13. Authorizes the SEC to recognize any generally accepted accounting principles that are issued by a standard-setting body (e.g., the FASB) that is a private entity, governed by a board of trustees, and funded in a manner similar to the PCAOB.

14. Requires financial analysts to certify that their reports accurately reflect their personal views and whether or not they receive compensation or other payments in connection with the specific recommendation.

15. Requires corporate legal counsel to report evidence of a material violation of securities laws or fraudulent financial activities to the audit committee or possibly to authorities.

¶ 102

Table 1.1

Corporate Governance, Accounting, and Auditing Provisions of the Sarbanes-Oxley Act of 2002

Sect.	Provisions
101	**Establishment of PCAOB** 1. The PCAOB will have five financially literate members. 2. Members are appointed by the SEC for five-year terms and will serve on a full-time basis and may be removed by the SEC "for good cause." 3. Two of the members must be or have been CPAs and the remaining three must not be and cannot have been CPAs. 4. The chair may be held by one of the CPA members, who must not have been engaged as a practicing CPA for five years.
103	**Duties of the PCAOB** 1. Register public accounting firms (foreign and domestic) that prepare audit reports for issuers. 2. Establish, or adopt, by rule, auditing, quality control, ethics, independence, and other standards relating to the preparation of audit reports for issuers. 3. Conduct inspections of registered public accounting firms. 4. Conduct investigations and disciplinary proceedings and impose appropriate sections. 5. Enforce compliance with the Act, the rules of the Board, and other applicable rules and regulations. 6. Establish the budget and manage the operations of the Board and its staff.
107	**Commission Oversight of the Board** 1. The SEC shall have oversight and enforcement authority over the PCAOB. 2. The SEC can, by rule or order, give the PCAOB additional responsibilities. 3. The PCAOB is required to file proposed rules and proposed rule changes with the SEC. 4. The SEC may approve, reject, or amend such rules. 5. The PCAOB must notify the SEC of pending investigations and coordinate its investigation with the SEC Division of Enforcement. 6. The PCAOB must notify the SEC when it imposes any final sanction on any accounting firm or associated person. 7. The PCAOB findings and sanctions are subject to review by the SEC which may enhance, modify, cancel, reduce, or require remission of such sanction.
108	**Accounting Standards** 1. The SEC may recognize as "generally accepted" any accounting principles that are established by a standard setting body that meets the Act's criteria. 2. The SEC shall conduct a study on the adoption of a principles-based accounting system.
201	**Auditor Independence: Services Outside the Scope of Practice of Auditors** 1. Registered public accounting firms are prohibited from providing any non-audit services to an issuer contemporaneously with the audit including but not limited to (a) bookkeeping or other services related to the accounting record or financial statement of the audit client; (b) financial information systems design and implementation; (c) appraisal or valuation services; (d) actuarial services; (e) internal audit outsourcing services; (f) management functions or human resources; (g) broker or dealer, investment advisor, or investment banking; (h) legal services and expert services unrelated to the audit; and (i) any other services that the PCAOB determines, by regulation, is impermissible. 2. The PCAOB may, on a case-by-case basis, exempt from these prohibitions any person, issuer, public accounting firm, or transaction, subject to review by the SEC. 3. Non-audit services not explicitly prohibited by the Act, such as tax services, can be performed upon pre-approval by the audit committee and full disclosure to investors.
203	**Audit Partner Rotation** The lead audit or coordinating partner and reviewing partner of the registered accounting firm must rotate off of the audit every five years.

¶ 102

The Professional Auditing Context

204 Auditor Reports to Audit Committees
The registered accounting firm must report to the Audit Committee:
1. All critical accounting policies and practices to be used.
2. All alternative treatments of financial information within generally accepted accounting principles, ramifications of the use of such alternative disclosures and treatments, and the preferred treatment.
3. Other material written communication between the auditor and management.

206 Conflicts of Interest
The registered accounting firm is prohibited to perform audits for an issuer who is CEO, CFO, controller, chief accounting officer, or a person in an equivalent position employed by the accounting firm during the one-year period preceding the audit.

207 Study of Mandatory Rotation of Registered Public Accounting Firms
The Comptroller General of the United States will conduct a study on the potential effects of requiring the mandatory rotation of public accounting firms.

301 Public Company Audit Committees
1. Each member of the audit committee shall be an independent member of the board of directors.
2. To be considered independent, the member of the audit committee should not receive any compensations other than for service on the board, not accept any consulting, advisory, or other compensatory fee from the company, and not be an affiliated person of the issuer, or any subsidiary thereof.
3. The SEC may make exemptions for certain individuals on a case-by-case basis.
4. The audit committee shall be directly responsible for the appointment, compensation, and oversight of the work of any registered public accounting firm associated by the issuer.
5. The audit committee shall establish procedures for the receipt, retention, and treatment of (a) complaints received by the issuer regarding accounting, internal accounting controls, or auditing matters, (b) confidential, anonymous submissions by employees of the issuer, or (c) concerns regarding questionable accounting or auditing matters.
6. The audit committee shall have the authority to engage independent counsel and other advisors necessary to carry out its duties.
7. The audit committee shall be properly funded.

302 Corporate Responsibility for Financial Reports
1. The signing officers (e.g., CEO, CFO) shall certify in each annual or quarterly report filed with the SEC that (a) the report does not contain any untrue statement of a material fact or omitted material facts that cause the report to be misleading and (b) financial statements and disclosures fairly present, in all material respects, the financial condition and results of operations of the issuer.
2. The signing officers are responsible for establishing and maintaining adequate and effective controls to ensure reliability of financial statements and disclosures.
3. The signing officers are responsible for proper design, periodic assessment of the effectiveness, and disclosure of material deficiencies in internal controls to external auditors and the audit committee.

303 Improper Influence on Conduct of Audits
It shall be unlawful for any officer or director of an issuer to take any action to fraudulently influence, coerce, manipulate, or mislead auditors in the performance of financial audit of the financial statements.

304 Forfeiture of Certain Bonuses and Profits
1. CEOs and CFOs who revise company's financial statements for the material noncompliance with any financial reporting requirements must pay back any bonuses or stock options awarded because of the misstatements.
2. CEOs and CFOs shall reimburse the issuer for any bonus or other incentive-based or equity-based compensation received or any profits realized from the sale of securities during that period for financial restatements due to material noncompliance with financial reporting and disclosure requirements.

306 Insider Trades During Pension Fund Blackout Periods
1. It shall be unlawful for any directors or executive officers directly or indirectly to purchase, sell, or otherwise acquire or transfer any equity security of the issuer during any blackout periods.

¶ 102

2. Any profits resulting from sales in violation of this section shall inure to and be recoverable by the issuer.

401 **Disclosures in Periodic Reports**
1. Each financial report that is required to be prepared in accordance with GAAP shall reflect all material correcting adjustments that have been identified by the auditors.
2. Each financial report (annual and quarterly) shall disclose all material off-balance sheet transactions and other relationships with unconsolidated entities that may have a material current or future effect on the financial conditions of the issuer.
3. The SEC shall issue final rules providing that pro forma financial information filed with the Commission (a) does not contain an untrue statement of a material fact or omitted material information and (b) reconciles with the financial condition and results of operations.
4. The SEC shall study the extent of off-balance sheet transactions including assets, liabilities, leases, losses, and the use of special purpose entities and whether the use of GAAP reflects the economics of such off-balance sheet transactions.

402 **Extended Conflict of Interest Provisions**
It is unlawful for the issuer to extend credit to any directors or executive officers.

404 **Management Assessments of Internal Controls**
1. Each annual report filed with the SEC shall contain an internal control report which shall (a) state the responsibility of management for establishing and maintaining an adequate internal control structure and procedures for financial reporting and (b) contain an assessment of the effectiveness of the internal control structure and procedures as of the end of the issuer's fiscal year.
2. Auditors shall attest to, and report on, the assessment of the adequacy and effectiveness of the issuer internal control structure and procedures as part of audit of financial reports in accordance with standards for attestation engagements.

406 **Code of Ethics for Senior Financial Officers**
The SEC shall issue rules to require each issuer to disclose whether it has adopted a code of ethics for its senior financial officers and the nature and content of such code.

407 **Disclosure of Audit Committee Financial Expert**
The SEC shall issue rules to require each issuer to disclose whether at least one member of its audit committee is a "financial" expert as defined by the Commission.

409 **Real Time Issuer Disclosures**
Each issuer shall disclose information on material changes in the financial condition or operations of the issuer on a rapid and current basis.

501 **Treatment of Securities Analysts**
Registered securities associations and national securities exchanges shall adopt rules designed to address conflicts of interest for research analysts who recommend equities in research reports.

601 **SEC Resource and Authority**
SEC appropriations for 2003 are increased to $776 million from which $98 million shall be used to hire an additional 200 employees to provide enhanced oversight of audit services.

602 **Practice Before the Commission**
1. The SEC may censure any person or temporarily bar or deny any person the right to appear or practice before the SEC if the person does not possess the requisite qualifications to represent others, has willfully violated Federal Securities laws, or lacks character or integrity.
2. The SEC shall conduct a study of "Securities of Professionals" (e.g., accountants, investment bankers, brokers, dealers, attorneys, investment advisors) who have been found to have aided and abetted a violation of Federal Securities laws.
3. The SEC shall establish rules setting minimum standards for professional conduct for attorneys practicing before the commission.

¶ 102

The Professional Auditing Context

701 **GAO Study and Report Regarding Consolidation of Public Accounting Firms**
The GAO shall conduct a study regarding consolidation of public accounting firms since 1989 and determine the consequences of the consolidation, including the present and future impact and solutions to any problems that may result from the consolidation.

802 **Criminal Penalties for Altering Documents**
1. It is a felony to knowingly alter, destroy, falsify, cover up, conceal, or create documents to impede, obstruct, or influence any existing or contemplated federal investigation.
2. Registered public accounting firms are required to maintain all audit or review workpapers for five years.

903 **White Collar Crime Penalty Enhancements**
904
1. Maximum penalty for mail and wire fraud is 10 years.
2. The SEC may prohibit anyone convicted of securities fraud from being a director or
906 officer of any public company.
3. Financial reports filed with the SEC (annual or quarterly) must be certified by the CEO and CFO of the issuer. The certification must state that the financial statements and disclosures fully comply with provisions of Securities Acts and they fairly present, in all material respects, financial results and conditions of the issuer. Maximum penalties for willful and knowing violations of these provisions of the Act are a fine of not more than $500,000 and/or imprisonment of up to five years.

1001 **Corporate Tax Returns**
The federal income tax return of public corporations should be signed by the CEO of the issuer.

1105 **Authority of the SEC**
The Commission may prohibit a person from serving as a director or officer of a publicly traded company if the person has committed securities fraud.

The Sarbanes-Oxley Act created a new five member board called the Public Company Accounting Oversight Board (PCAOB) to oversee the audit of public companies that are subject to the securities laws. This nonprofit corporation is to protect the interests of investors and further the public interest in the preparation of informative, accurate, and independent audit reports. The PCAOB has stated that it (and not the AICPA) will set auditing, attestation, quality control, and ethical standards for accounting firms that audit public companies.

One of the greatest influences on accountants' practice is the AICPA Code of Professional Conduct, which consists of two sections—principles and rules. When one acts on principle, one acts in accordance with a set of beliefs that can help determine the best course of action in even the most difficult of circumstances. Only a CPA who understands and adheres to ethical principles can cut though the morass of a particular circumstance and make the timeless judgment required to honor the profession and the individual practitioner. The Ethics Code says that the accountant must exercise responsibility, act in the public interest, act with integrity, act objectively and independently, and act with due care. The AICPA Rules of Conduct are the enforceable minimum standards of ethical conduct stated as specific rules.

SEC Enforcement Rules are also an important influence on accounting practice. SEC rules focus on audits of publicly traded companies. For example, SEC Rule 102(e) addresses misconduct of auditors and other professionals in order to protect investors. This expansive rule attempts to

¶ 102

ferret out accountants who (1) don't have the prerequisite qualifications to represent others, (2) lack character or integrity or engage in unethical or improper conduct, and (3) willfully violate or aid and abet the violation of any provision of the federal securities laws, rules and regulations. Both the AICPA and the SEC have issued rules on auditor independence, which is a huge concern today when accounting firms can be involved in both auditing and non-audit services to the same firm thereby creating potential conflicts of interest.

Special standards of professional conduct for internal auditors are issued by the IIA. The IIA has created a special professional practices framework that helps map out actions for auditors engaged in audit departments.

¶ 103 Legal Liability

Standards adherence helps ensure professional results and is linked to liability risk for those in professional practice. While standards help the accountant produce good results, controlling liability risks can help ensure accountants' ability to continue to practice.

Accountants' liability extends beyond clients to many other stakeholders in the auditing process. Financial statement users such as creditors, stockholders, suppliers and taxing authorities may take legal action against auditors. While many observers suggested that the Enron bankruptcy represented a whole new strata of potential damages, large settlements and awards are not new. Accountants face exposure from liability to clients, third parties, statutory civil liability and statutory criminal liability.

Most client liability involves either breach of contract or negligence. However, steps can be taken to reduce these risks. The importance of a proper engagement letter is not only good practice for the accountant, but also important for managing liability risk—especially risks from breach of contract. The client and auditor agreeing to just what the engagement involves is obviously an important step in reducing or eliminating any misunderstanding during or after the assignment. There are many important aspects of the engagement that should be spelled out in the engagement letter, such as the purpose of the engagement, responsibilities, standards applicable, procedures, management representations, scope restrictions, responsibility for detecting fraud, fees, billing, timing and more.

Negligence claims from a client involve a failure to inform a client of information discovered during the audit, professional malpractice and negligent misrepresentation. Rules of conduct can provide an objective roadmap against which an auditor's actions can be measured to determine if such conduct meets the minimum level required for the profession. An obvious preventative measure against a claim for malpractice is strict adherence to the standards. Of course, the malpractice attorneys may look at much more than the standards, but such standards are likely to garner much attention in the courts.

Most accountants know that not all prospects make good clients. Another risk management approach is to avoid risky clients and assignments. There are warning signs that help identify risky clients such as past problems with other practitioners, excessive expectations, employee turnover, internal control problems, and more.

A popular risk management technique used by many national accounting firms is organizing themselves as limited liability partnerships. If an accounting firm is an LLP, partners are not liable for negligence, errors, omissions, incompetence and malfeasance of other partners or the employees supervised by other partners. In the event that a judgment is obtained against an LLP, partners are not liable in excess of their partnership interest.

Clearly there is a gap between client and third party expectations and the products that independent auditors deliver. The Statement on Auditing Standards (SAS) No. 82 clearly stated that the detection of material misstatement in financial statements is central to an audit. The Panel on Audit Effectiveness states that auditors should perform some forensic-type procedures on every audit. SAS No. 99 increased the auditors need to search for financial statement fraud and asset misappropriations. The public and today's Congress look for accountants to uncover fraud and defalcation in audits. However, the practitioner might ask, "What audit client is willing to pay for the work required for a thorough fraud audit in the typical financial audit engagement?" Most audits look at selected transactions. The current situation creates a great deal of liability risk for the auditor to third parties—those who are not party to the engagement agreement.

The Securities and Exchange Commission brings civil actions against companies and individuals that break securities laws, and auditors may incur liability to third parties under the federal securities laws such as the Securities Act of 1993 and the Securities Exchange Act of 1934. These laws generally involve liability issues that may arise from disclosures to investors, SEC filings, and the like. Many of the civil liability statutes have criminal penalties.

¶ 104 Quality Control Standards

Accountants, who adhere to professional standards, and work to control liability risks, also focus on quality. Quality in the performance of external and internal auditing engagements is paramount. A CPA firm must be sure that generally accepted auditing standards (GAAS) are followed during every audit and in order to accomplish this, quality control procedures must be in place. CPA firms that audit publicly traded companies are subject to high quality control standards and must undergo peer reviews.

Peer reviews are conducted by CPAs and look at the subject firm's quality control system and how it stacks up in terms of key elements.

The Institute of Internal Auditing seeks to maintain and improve the quality of internal auditing organizations. Standards, research projects, publications, and conferences are devoted to quality control of internal auditors. The IIA offers guidance on a system of performance measures that can be adopted by the chief auditing executive to help track the performance of his or her departments.

On the international front, the International Organization for Standardization (ISO) develops common international standards for many disciplines and industries. The ISO quality assurance and quality management standards are referred to as IS 9000. Many organizations have shown an interest in developing a quality control system that meets these quality developments.

¶ 105 Planning the Financial Audit

The practice of auditing financial statements began in 1903 when U.S. Steel Corporation hired Price Waterhouse & Co. to certify the accuracy of their 40 page annual report. Today before any audit begins, the auditor must determine whether the client is acceptable. The auditor and potential client must come to agreement on what is involved in the engagement. Normally the agreement is formally spelled out in an engagement letter. At this "pre-planning" phase of the process, there are auditing standards that must be considered and followed; research that must be done to investigate the client; good business judgment and risk assessments that need to be made; and there must be excellent legal compliance and communication skills used to frame the engagement.

Once the accountant accepts the engagement, the practitioner must acquire knowledge about client matters, the industry in which the client competes, and the client's external environment as well. Analytical procedures must then be undertaken to get a better understanding of the client's business, to identify areas of audit risk, and more. Brainstorming and skepticism are important. The auditor must understand the implications of various risk factors to plan the financial audit and must also determine whether any specialists are needed to assist the audit (e.g., forensic accountants). Client facilities are toured to view processes first hand and to meet with operational and supervisory personnel. Documents must be gathered for the permanent file. A planning memo must be issued to provide evidence of the planning performed. Proper supervision and communication with audit staff is paramount and guided in part by auditing standards and firm standards.

¶ 106 Performing Fieldwork

The bulk of the auditing evidence is gathered during the two fieldwork stages: (1) the internal control testing phase and (2) the account balance-testing phase. During the internal control testing phase, the auditor gathers evidence while testing the internal controls to determine if reliance can be placed upon the controls. Auditors apply auditing procedures to obtain reasonable assurance that the financial statements are free of material misstatement. Auditing procedures also must include procedures to detect fraud.

The primary objective of the auditor's examination of financial statements is to express an opinion about whether the financial statements present fairly, in all material respects, values of assets and liabilities in terms of GAAP. Proper application of GAAP should support management assertions. Management assertions can serve as guidelines for the audit objectives.

Since auditing decisions are based on the significance of accounts and transactions, materiality is a prime consideration in how the audit is conducted. Materiality refers to information that is important enough to change an investor's decision and is the basis for the auditor to discriminate among the various accounts contained in the financial statements. Materiality must be seen from the viewpoint of the financial statement user.

Control risk is the risk that material error in a balance or transaction class will not be prevented or detected on a timely basis by internal controls. Inherent risk is the risk that an account or transactions contain material misstatements before the effects of the controls. If internal controls are weak, then controls cannot be relied upon to prevent or detect material misstatements, and the control risk is set at a maximum.

Detection risk is the risk that audit procedures will lead to a conclusion that material error does not exist, when in fact such error does exist. The more quantity and competence of audit evidence that an auditor obtains, the less the detection risk. Because every account and transaction cannot be examined, an auditor plans for a level of detection risk in an audit based on control and inherent risks. In other words, when control or inherent risk is high, the auditor must plan on gathering more and better evidence because the auditor is less willing to accept a high level of detection risk.

Substantive tests are auditing procedures in which auditors seek account balance misstatements. Substantive tests include time-consuming and expensive tests of details of account balances, which focus on documentation support such as vouching and confirming. Substantive tests also include analytical procedures that use the plausible relationships among data and accounts to determine the reasonableness of balances. Substantive tests also include tests of transactions such as vouching individual transactions and tracing them through the accounting system. Substantive tests can be broken down into specific auditing procedures.

The auditor satisfies auditing objectives by gathering evidence provided by the underlying accounting data and all other available corroborating information. Underlying accounting data includes the general ledger, general and special journals, subsidiary ledgers, details of general ledger account balances, and more. The auditor tests underlying accounting data by retracing the transactional and adjustment process through the accounting process. The auditor prepares worksheets that analyze allocations involved in account valuation, analyze recalculations used in the accounting process, and reconcile accounts to its details and activities. Corroborating evidence is gathered through inspection, observation, inquiry, confirmation and other means.

No specific guidelines exist for quantifying evidence; rather, the auditor must obtain enough evidence to form an opinion on the financial statements. The auditor will consider time and economics as well as the strength of the client's internal control and the inherent risk of the audit. Evidence needs to be competent—it needs to be relevant and believable.

If the internal controls are designed properly, the auditor can test those controls to determine if procedures have been implemented and are functioning properly. If procedures are functioning properly, the audit also will make a determination if the work of the internal auditor can be used to make the audit more efficient and save costs. The auditor will look at certain criteria to determine if the internal auditor's work can be used and the auditor also will evaluate the quality of the work.

Auditors prepare a written audit program, which represents the detailed audit procedures of obtaining evidence to accomplish the audit objectives. The program takes into account preliminary estimates of inherent and control risks and materiality—tempered by the results of internal control testing. Audit program steps are mapped out and team members track and document what steps are completed and by whom. Modifications to the program may be required. Workpapers document evidence gathered and support conclusions. The auditor must obtain sufficient evidence to eliminate any substantial doubt about any of the assertions. Any misstatements are scrutinized and appropriate actions taken. Specific steps are involved in reacting to any detection of fraud. The final review stage of the financial audit requires the auditor in charge of the engagement to use analytical procedures on the audit work to determine whether the conclusion reached is supported by evidence in the workpapers. Once the auditor determines that enough evidence has been gathered to support the audit opinion, the audit report can be issued.

¶ 106

¶ 107 Reaching Conclusions

There are specific procedures surrounding the financial audit of selected accounts and related transactions. Typical controls for a cash account are normally instituted to maintain accurate records for cash. These controls are categorized by management assertions. Along with each control is a common test for that control. For specific accounts such as cash, cash receipts, and cash disbursements, different management assertions such as the existence, completeness, posting to subsidiary ledgers such as corresponding customer accounts, valuation, classification (recorded in proper account) and more are all examined and tested. Specific auditing procedures are followed in this process. Year-end detailed testing takes place.

Forms are used to solicit confirmation of account balance information from financial institutions. Letters are sent out to client customers to confirm accounts and analytical procedures and calculations are used as well. After the last day of fieldwork, if a subsequent event occurs, additional audit evidence is required when the auditor becomes aware of these events prior to the audit report issuing.

Auditors are required to evaluate whether there is substantial doubt about a client's ability to continue as a going concern for at least one year beyond the balance sheet date. There are specific indicators that can alert the auditor about such potential trouble. This requirement will receive a great deal of attention in light of the collapse of financial giant Enron and WorldCom.

¶ 108 Reporting Considerations

An auditor's report contains an audit opinion and is the highest level of assurance that an auditor can provide in an attestation of financial statements. An auditor's opinion issued at the completion of an audit states the degree to which financial statements conform to generally accepted accounting principles (GAAP). The method used to gather evidence for the auditor's report is governed by generally accepted auditing standards (GAAS). Recently, the SEC has approved the PCAOB's Auditing Standard No. 1 pertaining to auditors' reports. PCAOB Auditing Standard No. 1 requires, as of May 24, 2004, that auditors' reports on audits and other engagements of publicly traded companies include a reference that the engagement was performed in accordance with the standards of the PCAOB rather than GAAS.

The auditor's objective is to obtain reasonable assurance that financial statements conform to GAAP and are free of material misstatements and fraud. Fraud can be craftily concealed through forgery and collusion so that a reasonably competent auditor may not detect such fraud.

There are four major categories of opinions issued in audit reports. The unqualified opinion is a clean opinion stating that the auditor has found the

¶ 108

financial statements to conform to GAAP. The qualified opinion is a report stating that financial statements contain positive conformity to GAAP, but there is some nonconformity or there were difficulties gathering sufficient evidence to support some of the amounts and disclosures in the financial statements. A disclaimer of opinion represents no opinion, meaning that either not enough evidence or no evidence was accumulated by the auditor to render an opinion on the financial statement's conformity to accounting principles. An adverse opinion states that the auditor has found the financial statements do not conform to GAAP. Language used for these opinions is provided in the AICPA Statements on Auditing Standards.

¶ 109 Reviews and Compilations

Audited financial statements are not the only ones that require substantial discipline and involve risk for the auditor. The AICPA Accounting and Review Services Committee sets forth guidelines for the preparation of unaudited financial statements for nonpublic companies. The standards established by the Accounting and Review Services Committee apply only when CPAs provide services to nonpublic companies. A CPA can accept different levels of responsibility for financial statements. First, there is a compilation, where the CPA takes the least responsibility for the financial statement based on the fact that no auditing procedures are performed. The second level of responsibility is review. When a CPA uses limited procedures to review financial statements, the CPA states that based upon these limited procedures, nothing came to his or her attention that indicates that the financial statements need modification in order for them to be in conformity with GAAP. The third or strongest level of responsibility is audited financial statements.

GAAP requires that financial statements be expressed by using the accrual basis of accounting. These financial statements and their notes comprise the balance sheet, income statement, statement of cash flows, and statement of retained earnings. These titles are reserved exclusively for GAAP financial statements.

Rather than using GAAP, in some circumstances financial statements are prepared in accordance with other comprehensive basis of accounting, referred to as OCBOA. OCBOA financial statements can be compiled or reviewed and as such AICPA Statements on Standards for Accounting and Review Services (SSARS) would apply.

¶ 110 Special Reports and Other Selected Attestation Reports

Auditing standards enable CPAs to provide other services not covered by audit report literature. There are several types of special reports. Accountants can perform audits of financial statements prepared in conformity with a comprehensive basis of accounting, other than generally accepted accounting principles (OCBOA). They also can perform audits of specified elements, accounts or items of a financial statement. There also are audits of compliance with aspects of contracts or regulatory requirements related to audited financial statements, as well as audits of financial presentations prepared to comply with contractual agreements, regulatory requirements, and prescribed forms. These different reports represent the great variety of reporting engagements for auditors today.

¶ 111 New or Proposed Assurance Services

The AICPA Special Committee on Assurance Services, often called the Elliot Committee, identified additional opportunities for accountants to serve the needs of today's clients and developed business plans for six assurance services. These large growth assurance services comprise risk assessment, business performance measures, information systems reliability, electronic commerce, health care performance measurement, and eldercare. Assurance services are special services that focus on improving the quality of information for decision-makers. Statement on Standards for Attestation Engagements (SSAE) No. 10 was revised to allow CPAs to provide assurance on subject matters other than financial statements. In general terms, in an attest engagement an auditor issues an examination, review, or procedures report on a subject that is the responsibility of another party. After Sarbanes-Oxley, eight non-audit services have been prohibited for their audit clients.

Internal auditors, like their public accounting counterparts, also have developed new services for their companies. Internal auditors may be able to design assurance services tailored to the unique needs of their organizations.

¶ 112 Forensic Accounting Services

Fraud prevention and detection were once an accountant's main duty, but reporting issues have been the focus for a long time. The external auditor is responsible for finding only deliberate material misstatement of financial statements, although recently some have called for the applications of forensic-type techniques as an integral part of the external audit. Auditors are likely to see an expanded role in fraud prevention in light of Sarbanes-Oxley, Enron, and other developments that have shaken the confidence of securities markets in financial reporting. Auditors must learn to audit like forensic accountants with a suspicious mind.

There is a growing demand for and interest in the three areas of forensic accounting: practice-litigation support consulting, expert witnessing, and fraud detection and deterrence. The forensic accountant must use additional investigative techniques. This specialist needs a strong accounting background, a basic understanding of the law, and a thorough knowledge of auditing. The forensic accountant also needs to understand risk assessment and control and fraud detection. Communication skills are paramount if the accountant is going to be able to deal effectively with others and properly disseminate findings.

.01 Litigation Support

The forensic accountant, like other professional specialists, is sometimes called on as an expert witness. As an expert witness an accountant must be able to make a credible appearance in the witness box, give evidence clearly before the Court, and support the view that is being expressed. The accountant must understand the client's case as well as the opposition's and must be able to maintain facts, arguments, and opinions under cross-examination. The accountant should avoid inferences from unjustified facts, avoid unfair examples or improper emphasis, and exaggeration.

The modern forensic accountant in litigation support may provide pretrial support, trial support, expert witness, and settlement support. When dealing with civil actions involving contract disputes, a forensic accountant generally must deal with three elements: proximate cause, reasonable certainty, and foreseeability. When dealing with fraud issues, the forensic accountant deals with misrepresentation of material fact made knowingly and with intent to defraud and reliance on the misrepresentation by the victim, resulting in damage from such reliance.

.02 Judicial Procedure

The forensic accountant needs to understand the judicial procedures. There are three major categories of government law: legislative laws (which takes precedence), executive (regulations), and judicial law (a referee). Federal Rules of Civil Procedures (FRCP) governs U.S. district courts. Trial courts function primarily as triers of fact and appellate courts review the law applicable to the facts, but they may not redetermine the facts. Expert witnesses testify in trial courts where issues of facts are normally determined.

There are basically three types of evidence: Testimony, writings, and objects. Evidence other than oral testimony is sometimes referred to as "real" evidence. This term represents mere terminology and does not express a superiority of tangible over oral evidence. The burden of proof in civil cases is usually by a "preponderance of the evidence," meaning in substance "more likely than not" (more than 50 percent).

Pleadings are a fundamental part of litigation. There are basically two forms of pleadings: the complaint and the answer. The plaintiff files the complaint. The defendant's answer must admit or deny the allegations. The terms used to designate the parties may vary with the type of court and case.

After the pleadings, the discovery phase starts. Discovery enables parties to obtain information, narrow the issues, and, promote settlement.

¶ 112.01

Methods of discovery include interrogatories, request for production of documents, depositions, subpoenas duces tecum, physical examination, and production of tangible things and entry upon land. An expert witness will often be deposed.

Embedded in forensic accounting is the concept of evidence. Forensic simply means belonging to the courts, and forensic science uses scientific principles or techniques to identify, recover, reconstruct, or analyze evidence during a civil or criminal investigation. In the court of law, all relevant evidence is admissible, unless inadmissible due to another rule of evidence. Evidence should be relevant and objective.

Technology issues are often important in law. Auditors must evaluate their ability to audit certain technologies and obtain the necessary training or hire a specialist for areas they are not competent to audit. Electronic documents are now dealt with in investigations and the courtroom. SAS No. 80 states that substantive tests may not be sufficient for a system predominantly consisting of electronic evidence. Thus, an auditor must perform tests of system control to determine that they are strong enough to mitigate the risks with electronic evidence.

An accountant's testimony can be testimony as to facts or an expert opinion. When testifying about his or her own bookkeeping entries or accounting procedures, an accountant is not an expert. However, when testifying as to the effect of certain bookkeeping entries or accounting procedures the accountant gives his or her expert opinion, and the accountant is strictly an expert witness. Generally, nonexpert witnesses are not permitted to give opinions, but expert witnesses may. Experts must be qualified. The trial court acts as a gatekeeper to ensure the scientific validity of the expert's testimony.

A forensic accountant is often called upon to measure damages. In order to win, a plaintiff must prove that 1) the defendant violated a legal right of the plaintiff, 2) this violation harmed the plaintiff, and 3) the harm caused the plaintiff to suffer damages. There are various approaches to calculating damages.

Litigation service offered by accountants is any professional assistance to lawyers in litigation. A CPA should follow the Code of Professional Conduct, especially Article IV which states that he or she should be impartial, intellectually honest and free of any conflicts of interest. The consultant should follow Rule 201 of the AICPA Code as well as general standards for consulting services.

.03 Risk Management

There is an emerging trend of increased expert witness liability. The general rule is immunity to a witness from civil liability from testimony and communication made in the course of litigation. However, there is no immunity for communication outside the context of the lawsuit.

¶ 112.03

.04 Alternative Dispute Resolution (ADR)

Alternative Dispute Resolution (ADR) has gained increasing importance in recent years as a means to control cost and save time. Other advantages of using ADR include privacy, flexibility, and sometimes, but not always, minimum disruption of existing relationships. ADR also comes in many forms. A forensic accounting expert is advised to look into the practical opportunities of ADR.

¶ 113 IRS Auditing—Indirect Methods of Reconstructing Income

IRS agents were some of the earliest and most successful forensic accountants in the United States. Whereas other law enforcement agencies tried to pin a crime on 1930s gangster Al Capone and failed, a Criminal Investigation (CI) agent, an IRS forensic accountant, penetrated the organized racketeering gangs resulting in the tax evasion conviction of Capone and other reigning gangsters. IRS agents use forensic techniques to catch other taxpayers not paying their proper taxes.

Forensic accountants working in the private sector also can learn much from their public sector counterparts in the IRS. Some techniques used by IRS agents may be useful in the private sector. Although private sector forensic accountants lack some of the access to tax return information and the authority to summons third-party records available to IRS agents, many of the techniques used by the IRS may be used by forensic accountants to indirectly calculate net income, expenditures, and net worth.

To prove unreported income and fraud, IRS agents use both direct and indirect methods. The direct methods (or transaction methods) involve probing missing income by pointing to specific items of income that do not appear on the tax return. A taxpayer may have omitted sales, a large real estate transaction, or stock sale from his or her tax return. In direct methods, the agents use conventional auditing techniques such as looking for canceled checks of customers, deed records of real estate transactions, public records, and other direct evidence of unreported income.[1]

When conventional direct methods prove unproductive and the IRS has a reasonable indication that there is a likelihood of unreported income, indirect methods may be employed. Indirect methods use economic reality and financial status techniques in which the taxpayer's finances are reconstructed through circumstantial evidence. Some indirect methods include the cash T method, source and application of funds, net worth method, and bank deposit method.

The IRS's authority to use an indirect method is contained in Code Sec. 446(b). The Code Section provides that "if no method of accounting has

---

[1] For a detailed discussion of IRS practices, see Robert E. Meldman and Richard J. Sideman, *Federal Taxation: Practice and Procedure*, 6th ed. (Chicago: CCH Incorporated, 2001).

been regularly used by the taxpayer, or if the method used does not clearly reflect income, the computation of taxable income shall be made under such method as, in the opinion of the Secretary, does clearly reflect income."[2]

Just like an IRS agent, a forensic accountant should be aware of the lifestyles of employees of companies as well. The lifestyle of a taxpayer or employee may give clues as to the possibilities of unreported income. Jack Bologna and Robert Lindquist[3] refer to this approach of looking at events, transactions, and environments in their covert aspects. They believe that fraud auditing is like an iceberg with many of the behavioral, covert aspects of the fraud below the water line.

¶ 114   The Internal Auditing Function

The internal auditing function provides value-added assurance and consulting services to an organization. In an organization, this critical function should report to the audit committee of the board of directors. Internal auditors view the entire organization, and their work requires the highest quality technical, analytical, communication, and interpersonal skills.

Internal auditing is an activity or process, and internal auditors can be directly employed by the organization or supplied by a third party. Some companies outsource their internal auditing. Internal auditing is an independent, objective assurance and consulting activity. The purpose of the internal auditing function is to add value and improve an organization's operations by evaluating and improving the effectiveness of risk management, control, and governance processes. After Sarbanes-Oxley, forensic and fraud audits will become more important.

The IIA is the primary international professional association dedicated to the promotion and development of the practice of internal auditing. The IIA provides professional development, standards, certification, and research. The group also provides an opportunity for internal auditors to participate in a community of professionals. Recent research studies have examined the future role of the internal auditing, competencies, global perspectives, challenges to the profession and much more. The IIA helps improve the quality of services delivered by its members through the issuance of professional standards and protects the interests of parties affected by those services through its code of ethics.

The professional competence of internal auditors is usually demonstrated by obtaining professional certification. The first and chief professional certification maintained by the IIA remains the Certified Internal Auditor (CIA) which deals with all aspects of the internal auditing profes-

---

[2] Code Sec. 446(b).
[3] G.J. Bologna and R.J. Lindquist, *Fraud Auditing and Forensic Accounting*, 2d ed. (New York: John Wiley, 1995), 36-37.

sion and in many respects the CIA may be the only truly global professional accounting designation.

The IIA in partnership with the Board of Environmental Auditing Roundtable established the Board of Environmental Auditor Certifications (BEAC). The BEAC subsequently began offering the Certified Professional Environmental Auditor (CPEA). The IIA also offers the Certification in Control Self-Assessment (CCSA) designation and the Certified Government Auditing Professional (CGAP) designation for governmental auditors.

Internal auditing professionals are expected to uphold and apply the fundamental principles of integrity, objectivity, confidentiality, professionalism and competency. The Code of Conduct describes the expected behaviors that would come about following these principles.

¶ 115 Managing the Internal Auditing Department

The Chief Auditing Executive (CAE) manages the internal auditing function with the assistance and oversight of management and the audit committee. The CAE must organize the internal auditing function, perform risk assessment and schedule audits, coordinate the internal auditing function and organize policies, coordinate audit work with the organization's external auditors, maintain a quality control system, and prevent the outsourcing of the internal audit function.

Research shows that there are certain knowledge, skills and abilities that the successful CAE should possess. In general terms, the CAE must be a strategic thinker, show good judgment, have good personal skills, and possess a good understanding of the organization.

Successful CAEs reach an understanding with management and the board of directors (or audit committee of the board of directors) concerning the internal auditing department's role within the organization documented in the form of a written "Charter."

Numerous studies document the inability of internal audits to uncover fraud for various reasons. Internal auditors cannot be expected to uncover all instances of fraud, but when fraud is uncovered, the internal auditing department conducts a full investigation to aid in the recovery of lost assets. The department also aids in the prosecution of perpetrators and also designs controls to prevent future instances of fraud from occurring.

Sarbanes-Oxley now requires that annual reports filed with the SEC must be accompanied by a statement by management that they are responsible for creating and maintaining internal controls. Further, the external auditors must report on and attest to management's assessment of the internal controls.

.01 Outsourcing

Outsourcing is the performance of internal auditing services by a party external to the organization. In the past, outsourcers performed audits that were beyond the ability of the internal auditing function to perform. However, during the past five to ten years, outsourcers have taken over entire internal auditing functions to the point that the threat of outsourcing must be recognized and met by CAEs. Usually this means meeting the needs of management and the audit committee by performing value added audits and consulting engagements, for example, much of the internal auditing was outsourced at Enron.

.02 Audit Committee

The audit committee is the subcommittee of an organization's board of directors charged with overseeing the organization's financial reporting and internal control processes. To be effective, the audit committee should be composed of outside directors (not employed by the organization), and Sarbanes-Oxley mandates that committee members must be independent. Further, the audit committee must have at least one financial expert. Audit committees are the key ingredient in establishing the overall "tone at the top" or attitude towards internal controls.

.03 Scheduling and Performing the Internal Auditing Engagement

The CAE divides the organization into audit units, which may be organizational units (such as departments), functions, systems, policies and procedures, contracts, or accounts. Units are then ranked in terms of risk or the likelihood that an event or action may adversely affect the organization.

Some CAE's place differing weights on the risk factors they choose. The CAE then ranks the auditable units using the first risk factor, then the second risk factor, until all the auditable units have been ranked according to all the risk factors. The CAE then estimates the resources (time and expenses) to complete the audit of each unit. A cut-off based on the total amount of resources available to the internal auditing department is established, and audits are performed for those units ranked above the cutoff. Then the CAE prepares an audit plan scheduling those audits above the cutoff.

.04 Risk Based Audit Planning

The traditional risk assessment can cause an undue focus on the risk factors rather than the underlying risks. The resulting risk assessment may not stay in tune with changes in the risks. Traditional risk assessment only focuses on risk during the organizational planning phase and does not filter down to the individual audit assignments where the emphasis becomes controls. For these reasons, many internal auditing functions adopted risk based planning and audits. Internal auditors principally rely on three approaches to risk based audit planning: the asset approach, the external

¶ 115.04

environment approach, or the threat scenario approach. Under the asset approach, the internal auditor identifies each of the organization's assets and then determines what could cause the asset to be lost or materially impaired. The external environment approach looks at the risk that economic, financial, physical, government regulation, technology, markets, customers/constituents, suppliers, and other similar forces may pose to the organization's ability to reach its objectives. The threat scenario approach relies on the internal auditor to develop a narrative of likely scenarios for specific threats, like natural disasters or illegal acts. Threat scenarios may be particularly beneficial in evaluating the risk posed by events that are infrequent, but catastrophic, such as the terrorist attack on September 11, 2001. Any or all of these approaches can and should be adapted and integrated into the traditional risk assessment procedures. Additional tools for measuring risks include direct probability estimates, normative tables, and comparative risk ranking.

Once risks are identified, strategies should be employed to mitigate their effects. Auditors should choose the mix of strategies that are the most cost effective. Auditors should work with appropriate members of management and members of the audit committee throughout this entire progress.

¶ 116 Reporting Internal Audit Assignment Results

The audit report is the principle product of the internal audit assignment and the only item seen by the party being audited. The audit report must be objective, clear, concise, constructive, and timely. It must be well crafted to initiate change with as little organizational ill will as possible.

.01 The Reporting Process

Audit reports are a product of the internal auditing function, and a CAE should constantly evaluate the impact the entire internal auditing process has on them. The CAE, in performing the annual risk assessment and audit schedule, influences the subsequently written audit reports in terms of audience (auditee management), size (auditee size), and timing (schedule). Finally, the audit team in performing the individual audit assignment, influences the audit reports in terms of content (audit findings), style (initial draft), and initial reception by the auditee.

The reporting process begins when an initial finding is uncovered. The auditor uncovering the finding should draft a complete description of the finding both in the area of the workpapers pertaining to the area being audited and in the part of the workpapers controlling all the comments from the audit. The auditor should discuss each audit finding with the in-charge and other members of the audit team if appropriate. Following this discussion, the audit finding will be either accepted as is, dropped because it is weak and unsupportable, revised, or investigated further. The finding also should be discussed with the auditee on an informal basis.

At the completion of fieldwork, the in-charge should review all the audit findings produced during the audit and write a final report draft. The CAE then should review the final report. The in-charge should formally present the final report draft to the auditee in an exit interview. The in-charge should send the final report draft to the auditee several days before the exit meeting to allow the auditee time enough to prepare a response.

Once the exit interview is completed, the in-charge should revise the report one last time and submit it to the CAE, who will then formally issue the final report to the appropriate officials within the organization. The auditee should be given a reasonable amount of time to reply to the final report. The CAE and in-charge should review the response by the auditee for reasonableness.

.02 The Report Itself

The CAE should determine the overall appearance and organization for reports issued by the internal auditing function. The organization of the report can take many forms, but in general, should begin with an executive summary followed by a more detailed presentation of the audit findings followed by supporting material such as appendices, tables, and graphs.

Audit findings generally have five components: criterion, condition, effect, cause, and recommendations. Criterion represent the standards used in evaluating the auditee. The condition component should present the auditee's current state of affairs as found by the auditor. The effect is the result or possible result of the current condition. The cause component of the audit finding is almost as important as the effect. The cause component represents the reason why the current condition exists. Recommendation(s) address the cause(s) and represent the auditor's prescribed actions for the auditee.

Typographical errors, poor writing, or other mishaps can kill a report's effectiveness. Therefore, the CAE must establish the most stringent quality assurance process possible to prevent such mishaps.

¶ 117 Operational Auditing

Operational auditing is the systematic process of gathering evidence to ascertain whether a process or operation is effectively and efficiently run. Operational auditing is the best manner in which auditors can assist organizations in allocating and using their limited resources. Some organizational resources are wasted by unintentional poor decision making rather than by intentional misuse (fraud). Constituents or donors of government/nonprofit organizations need the results of operational audits (or performance audits as they are referred to in the government sector) in lieu of net income or another measure of effectiveness or efficiency in determining whether resources are properly used.

¶ 117

Often, the operational audit is performed as part of a complete engagement, which includes financial and compliance audits. Auditors need a firm grasp of operational auditing whether they are in public accounting, management accounting, internal auditing, or government accounting.

.01 Government Performance Audits

Performance audits are the public sector versions of "Operational Audits" that are conducted to determine if an entity's operations, programs, or projects are run according to goals, effectiveness, and efficiency.

A performance audit has two parts: an economy and efficiency review and a program review. The economy and efficiency review determines if resources have been used efficiently. The program review, on the other hand, determines whether the resources were used effectively, that is, for the purpose intended by the grantor of resources. Thus, the two reviews compliment each other in providing a complete picture of an agency's performance.

The operational audit of a for-profit entity is similar to the performance audit of a government entity in terms of efficiency, but differs in terms of effectiveness. Effectiveness is usually measured in terms of meeting the entity's mission, goals, and objectives. However, aside from this minor difference, performance and operational audits share a common methodology and are virtually interchangeable.

.02 Phases of the Operational Audit

The typical performance and operational audit, in the same way as all audits, has three phases: planning, fieldwork, and reporting. The planning phase of a performance audit tends to involve more professional judgment and business commonsense than the planning phase of a financial audit that is limited to a review of the financial statements. In planning the audit, the auditor should first determine specific objectives for the audit. After determining the specific objectives for the audit, the auditor conducts a preliminary survey to obtain information needed to write an audit program and estimate a budget.

Fieldwork in a performance audit consists of performing the audit tests listed in the audit program. If the preliminary survey was done successfully, then the fieldwork portion of the audit should proceed to confirm the tentative conclusions drawn from the preliminary survey.

Once the audit tests are completed, the auditor reaches a final conclusion concerning the entity's performance that is presented to interested parties in a draft of the audit report. The draft is then discussed with the entity's management and revised accordingly before it is issued to the appropriate parties.

Internal auditors are hired by organizations to assist management in effectively and efficiently operating an organization. Internal auditors help by reviewing the effectiveness of the organization's internal control process and making suggestions for improving it. In conducting their internal control reviews, the internal auditor should identify the potential risks faced by the organization and then ensure that the most effective and efficient controls are present to address the risks. An internal control review can take many forms, from simply ensuring that controls are present and functioning to an operational audit involving the review of an organization's mission, goals, objectives, and operating procedures.

¶ 118 Compliance Audits

Auditors perform compliance audits to provide assurance that an entity is operating in conformity with its internal policies and procedures, external laws and regulations, or to the terms of contracts. Recently, audit committees, upper management, and Chief Auditing Executives (CAEs) are becoming more selective and realize that internal auditing resources can be effectively spent reviewing the actual policies and procedures themselves. In this way, the process can help identify the strategically important policies and procedures, and then the audit can test compliance only with those important ones.

The CAE should identify those internal policies and procedures of strategic importance to the organization as part of the internal auditing department's annual risk assessment and audit scheduling process. The CAE also should identify laws and regulations having significant impact on the organization because many of the organization's policies and procedures exist to ensure compliance with those laws and regulations. Once the significant policies and procedures are identified, the CAE should determine if compliance with them is tested as part of an audit integrating financial, operational and compliance audits, or as a stand-alone compliance audit.

Individual provisions of the policy being tested should be used to produce steps in the compliance audit program. Reporting the results of these types of compliance audits remains problematic, because generally only negative findings are reported because of the reluctance of most auditors to give positive assurance.

.01 Control Self-Assessment

The issuance of the COSO and CoCo control models in 1992 and 1995, respectively, gave auditors two valuable tools with which to evaluate controls. Auditors began allowing auditees to identify risks and design controls for the auditee's operations. This process became known as "Control Self-Assessment (CSA)." Under CSA, the auditor becomes a facilitator, holding workshops that educate auditee personnel on risk and controls. The auditee personnel then design controls appropriate for identified risks.

Auditors can implement CSA either at the overall organizational level or the department or functional level or both. The results of an overall

¶ 118.01

organizational level CSA provides excellent information for the internal auditing function's annual risk assessment and to guide the department level CSA efforts.

All organizations in the United States and many other countries face a bewildering array of laws with which they must comply. Auditors can provide a much-needed service by ensuring that the organization is in compliance with at least the laws and regulations that significantly affect the organization's ability to meet its objectives. The CAE works closely with the organization's legal counsel to identify laws and regulations that apply to the organization, the impact on the organization of the laws and regulations, and any policies and procedures relating to the laws and regulations.

.02 GAGAS and the Single Audit Act

Entities receiving over $300,000 in funds from the U.S. Federal Government must comply with the Single Audit Act and generally accepted government auditing standards (GAGAS).

The Single Audit Act was adopted to eliminate the need for multiple audits of recipients of U.S. Federal government aid. In completing an audit under the Single Audit Act, the organization may choose between a program-specific audit and a single audit, depending on the type of aid received. If the organization receives funds under one grant, and the grant does not require a financial statement audit, then the organization may elect to have a program-specific audit. Single audits are much more complex.

.03 Contracts

Both internal and external auditors can perform contract audits either as part of a comprehensive internal auditing function or as a stand-alone engagement. The first step in performing contract audits is to gain an understanding of the organization's policies and procedures for awarding contracts. The auditor should ensure that the proper controls are in place concerning the awarding of contracts. These controls might require contracting and legal departments to execute all contracts, vendor financial conditions reviews, potential vendor list maintenance for currency, and the like.

There are two basic types of contracts—fixed fee and cost-plus contracts. Each type has its strengths and weaknesses. The auditor should approach each contract differently. The contract department's records are used as a starting point in developing a list of the organization's contracts, but additional procedures should be performed to ensure that there are not other parts of the organization that have executed contracts without notifying the legal or contracts departments.

¶ 118.02

Once a universe of contracts is developed, the auditor can identify the more important contracts. The auditor can often resolve simple misunderstandings between the terms of the contract and actual vendor performance with an informal discussion with the vendor. However, significant disagreements should be referred to the organization's legal department for advice on gathering the evidence needed to sustain a claim against the vendor.

¶ 119 External Auditor's Responsibilities Regarding Fraud

Independent auditors are required to assess the risk of material misstatements of the financial statements due to fraud, and they must consider that assessment in designing the audit procedures to be performed. SAS No. 82 provides risk factors that the auditor should consider, and provides that the auditor must have a questioning mind and critical assessment of the audit evidence.

The risk assessment tells the auditor how to respond. If there is a significant risk of fraud, the auditor should consider withdrawing from the engagement and communicating the reasons to the audit committee (or equivalent authority). The disclosure of fraud to parties other than senior management and/or audit committee is not the auditor's responsibility.

The auditor should document in the workpapers evidence of the performance of the risk assessment. Documentation should include any risk factors identified and the auditor's responses to the risk factors. The risk factors in SAS No. 82 are broken into fraudulent financial reporting and misstatements arising from misappropriation of assets. These factors are difficult to assess, and they may exist where there is no fraud. Where the risk factors are present, the standard does not suggest a response.

In response to the research and recommendations made by the Public Oversight Board's Panel on Audit Effectiveness in 2000, the AICPA issued Statement on Auditing Standards (SAS) No. 99, Consideration of Fraud in a Financial Statement Audit. The main points of this standard are as follows:

- Increased Emphasis on Professional Skepticism—Members of the audit team must exchange ideas or brainstorm how fraud could occur so that they might design audit tests responsive to the risks of fraud.

- Discussions with Management—Auditors must ask the client's management and other employees about the risk of fraud and whether they know of its existence in the organization.

- Unpredictable Audit Tests—Auditors should design tests that would be unpredictable and unexpected and should test areas, locations, and accounts that otherwise might not be tested.

¶ 119

- Responding to Management Override of Controls—The engagement team must test for management override of controls.

SAS No. 99 superseded SAS No. 82. However, accountants still do not accept the responsibility of finding fraud, but the PCAOB may force accountants to look for fraud.

.01 Fraudulent Financial Reporting

There is legitimate and illegitimate earnings management. In general, legitimate earnings management involves conducting business in order to attain controlled, disciplined growth. And generally, illegitimate earnings management involves deliberate manipulation of the accounting in order to create the appearance of growth when it does not exist. The demise of many e-commerce companies and the highly publicized adjustments to earnings made by a number of large companies have led to a crisis in public trust of accounting, financial reporting and investment, and the management of public corporations. The Securities and Exchange Commission (SEC) is working closely with criminal prosecutors to attack financial statement fraud.

.02 Detecting Cooked Books

Financial statements may be wrong, and some companies use creative accounting techniques to disguise damaging information. Forensic auditors should adopt a healthy skepticism when reading and evaluating financial reports. Accountants get bogged down in detail and forget to look at the overall picture.

Management fraud can often be detected by interviewing senior staff members and recently departed employees. Ask the simple question: Do you suspect anyone in management who might be committing fraud or secretly stealing from the company?

Certain clues or red flags may suggest that a company is engaging in financial shenanigans. Companies that are affected by management fraud may have earnings problems, reduced cash flow, excessive debt, and overstated inventories. They may make a sudden change of auditors, hyped sales, and artificially reduce expenses. The auditor must learn to spot the red flags that can lead to prudent actions.

.03 Horizontal and Vertical Analysis

Many red flags arise during percentage analysis (both horizontal and vertical) and ratio analysis. Many auditors forget how these simple techniques allow them to spot dangerous financial situations. Horizontal analysis (or trend analysis) assists in the search of inequalities by using the financial statements of some prior year as the base and expressing the components of a future year as percentages of each component in base year. This technique may be used for balance sheet and income statement comparison, but it is used less frequently in the analysis of the statement of

¶ 119.01

cash flow because of the lack of regularity with which items recur in this statement.

Vertical analysis (often referred to as common-size statements) presents every item in a statement as a percentage of the largest item in the statement. When vertical analysis is used to compare financial statements from several periods, changes in the relationships between items can be easily determined.

There are other forensic-type audit procedures, which can include extended procedures or analytics. Analytics will tell you where to go to audit and for what to search. Analytical procedures are often less expensive than tests of details.

¶ 120 Environmental and Quality Audits

The environmental audit is the systematic examination of the interactions between any business operation and its surroundings. It is a strategic approach to the organization's activities and includes emissions to air, land, and water; legal constraints; the effects on the neighboring community, landscape and ecology; and the public's perception of the operating company in the local area. The environmental audit does not stop at compliance with legislation or regulations. Nor is it a superficial public relations exercise.

.01 *The Environmental Protection Agency (EPA)*

The EPA was established in 1970 to consolidate into one agency a variety of federal research, monitoring, standard-setting and enforcement activities to ensure environmental protection. The EPA's mission is to protect human health and to safeguard the natural environment—air, water, and land—upon, which life depends. Much of the environmental auditing that takes place today is targeted towards compliance with environmental laws and regulations enforced by the EPA. Today's environmental audit tracks compliance with regulatory requirements, and spots and corrects problems before the enforcement agencies learn what has transpired.

.02 *Accounting Guidelines*

Once environmental risks are identified, an auditor must be aware of numerous accounting standards applicable to environmental problems. Accounting pronouncements that relate to environmental auditing include various FASB Emerging Issues Task Force (EITF) Issues, Statement of Financial Accounting Standards (SFAS) No. 5 and 19, Interpretation No. 14, AICPA Statement of Position (SOP) 96-1, Staff Accounting Bulletin (SAB) No. 92, and FASB Exposure Draft 158-B.

¶ 120.02

.03 Environmental Management System

Many companies respond to environmental challenges by creating an environmental management system. Such a system is created to protect the environment and manage environmental issues. Environmental auditing does require a number of skills and expertise: auditor, engineer, scientist, and regulatory specialist. Some argue that an internal auditor can provide vital services in the environmental areas.

Principles of Environmental Management System (EMS) have been developed, and standards for evaluating compliance have been produced. A key concept in these principles and standards is sustainable development, which involves equilibrium in the use of renewable natural resources, preservation of wildlife habitat and diversity, plus conservation of nonrenewable natural resources.

.04 International Standards

The International Standards Organization (ISO) developed ISO 14000 as an environmental management standard (EMS). EMS is a comprehensive environmental quality standard that provides a basis for society to compare a firm's sensitivity to environmental issues. EMS offers flexible guidelines for maintaining a management system that will ensure external compliance while promoting continuous improvement in performance. To obtain ISO 14000 certification, organizations must maintain an environmental management system. These systems are monitored with environmental auditing. Auditors use the standards as guidelines in assessing the sufficiency and effectiveness of the organization's environmental management system. ISO 14000 also provides guidance in attesting information contained in environmental reports and ensuring efficiency, effectiveness, and economy of environmental operations and performance.

.05 Role of the Environmental Auditor

A CPA can develop an auditing niche certifying and auditing environmental management systems under ISO 14000. However, an auditor's role in environmental management includes a number of functions besides compliance considerations. The auditor may perform calculations and accounting to determine penalty costs, cost recovery, various benefits involved, settlement costs, deductibility, capital budgeting, and pollution prevention costs/ savings.

.06 New Approach Systems

Companies have found that regulatory compliance in itself does not necessarily mitigate environmental risk. Risks not covered by legislation include public perception and the sustainability of raw materials. The primary role of an auditor is to assess how effectively organization systems identify the process points that impact the environment, measure the potential for damage, and mitigate the risks represented by such potentials.[4]

Compliance assessment is increasingly performed by line personnel using automated self-assessment tools.[5] This shifting of duties allows the auditor to remain in an office studying reports generated by the compliance self-assessment software and determining whether problems were addressed in a timely manner. This leaves line personnel to struggle with new software, production schedules, machine breakdowns, unexpected absences, arrogant staff, useless management, drug problems, and late deliveries.

An auditor's broad investigative skills provide other essential support to an environmental management system, as the focus of many corporate programs has shifted from compliance to the ongoing reduction of the overall environmental impact. Environmental auditing is now more properly described as a risk-management tool for taking a systematic and objective inventory of a company's environmental assets and liabilities.

¶ 121 Integrating Analytical Procedures and Sampling Into Audit Tests

Auditors use analytical procedures and sampling because they are efficient. Analytical procedures are simple to calculate and provide a reasonableness or reality check on audit results. Sampling allows the auditor to reach a conclusion about a population without having to test each item in the population.

.01 Analytical Procedures

In general, analytical procedures compare two or more measures to determine the reasonableness of each one. Analytical procedures help auditors identify unexpected differences, the absence of expected differences, possible errors or fraud, and other unusual or rarely occurring events. Auditors must fully investigate all unusual trends or relationships uncovered by analytical procedures because this may be the only sign that fraud has occurred. There are five major types of analytical procedures:[6]

1. Comparison with prior periods—for example, examining the trend for sales over a 10-year period, or comparing the balance sheet accounts from one period to another (also referred to as horizontal analysis). The auditor should examine the gross amount and percentage changes for proper analysis.

2. Comparison within period—for example, presenting each account in the balance sheet as a percentage of total assets and then comparing the percentages for two or more periods to determine the relative changes in accounts (whole dollar

---

[4] Ron Black, "A New Leaf in Environmental Auditing," *Internal Auditor* (Vol. 55, June 1998): 24.

[5] *Ibid.*

[6] SAS No. 56, *Analytical Procedures* (AICPA, Professional Standards, vol. 1, AU sec. 329.05).

¶ 121.01

financials or vertical analysis). This analysis will show individual accounts with abnormal changes relative to the other accounts, which could indicate fraud.

3. Comparison with expectations—for example, variance analysis.

4. Comparison with industry averages—for example, ratio analysis or benchmarking.

5. Comparison with other operating information—for example, comparing the amount of revenue recorded to amount of gas used by the organization's delivery fleet.

Analytics can be used at anytime during the audit. During the planning phase, analytics can be used to identify abnormal trends for follow-up during the audit. They also can be used during the internal auditing function's annual risk assessment to identify high-risk auditable units. Analytics can be used during fieldwork as corroboration of other audit tests. Finally, auditors can use analytics as a quality assurance procedure in wrapping-up an audit.

.02 Basic Sampling Concepts

Sampling is the application of an audit test to less than one hundred percent of an account balance or class of transactions (sample) for the purposes of reaching a conclusion about the entire account balance or class of transactions. The process of reaching a conclusion about an entire population based on a sample is called extrapolation. For extrapolation to be successful two conditions must be met: (1) the sample must be representative of the population and (2) the results must be quantitatively evaluated.

.03 Risks of Sampling

The ultimate risk in sampling for auditors is drawing an invalid conclusion. Invalid conclusions can arise from the sample itself (sampling risk) or from without the sample (nonsampling risk). Examples of nonsampling risk include the following: (1) a poorly designed or irrelevant audit test, (2) an incorrectly applied audit test, or (3) an incorrectly drawn conclusion.

.04 Audit Testing Decisions

An auditor makes certain decisions in designing audit tests. The first decision is whether to sample. Once the decision to sample is made, the auditor chooses an attribute test if control testing is being done, and variable sampling for account balance testing. Next, the auditor determines if statistical or nonstatistical sampling is appropriate. Finally, for statistical sampling there exists some additional choices. Attribute statistical sampling can take the form of fixed sample size sampling, stop-n-go or sequential sampling, or discovery sampling. Of the three sampling techniques, stop-n-go is overwhelmingly preferred to the other two.

.05 Important Sampling Concepts

The auditor should know and manage the risks associated with sampling. The auditor must remain objective and professionally skeptical in planning, and conducting the audit test and particularly when evaluating the sample results. The auditor should know as much as possible about the data being examined and should be sensitive to the presence of underlying patterns that could bias sample results. Large or significant items should be separately examined. Finally, the auditor must fully investigate all exceptions even if the overall exception rate is acceptable, because the one exception can uncover a major fraud and may be the only chance the auditor gets to catch the perpetrator.

¶ 122   IT and the Auditor

Despite the rapid and far-reaching changes in Information Technology (IT), the auditor's role remains the same: ensure that the organization has adequate controls in place to mitigate risks that could prevent the organization from fulfilling its objectives. In an IT context, the auditor must first understand the organization's IT system well enough to (1) identify the risks significant enough to impact the organizations ability to fulfill its objectives, and to (2) design tests to ensure controls function to mitigate those risks.

.01 IT Controls

IT controls have traditionally been classified as either general (system-wide) controls or application (specific) controls. The auditor would review and examine the general controls operating over the hardware and its components and then review and examine controls for a sample of applications. Due to the complex arrangement of hardware and components, the current IT environment causes auditors to focus almost exclusively on the system-wide issues. The auditor's review of an IT system can provide valuable information to upper management concerning unforeseen risks if the auditor can objectively evaluate the organization's IT system from a strategic perspective in terms of the organization's objectives.

.02 General Controls

General or system wide controls should address the organization's strategic risks. These include overall system vision and governance, use of resources, personnel issues, business-continuation, and security.

The organization's information technology vision should be in line with the organization's vision. The organization should appoint a chief information officer (CIO) with enough authority, visibility and prestige to ensure that these two visions are aligned. The CIO should establish a strategic planning process with input from key user constituents such as an IT

¶ 122.02

Steering Committee. The CIO should adopt procedures to ensure that changes to the system proceed in a business-like manner and do not compromise the IT system's integrity.

Many organizations employ the life-cycle approach in which changes to the system go through the following clearly defined steps: problem identification, feasibility study, design, implementation, and post-implementation review. Auditors should review the overall strategic planning efforts, and the functioning of the IT Steering Committee to ensure that the IT System vision is in line with the organization's vision, and that changes to the system make good business sense and are in line with the IT system vision. Auditors should become involved as consultants early in the development life cycle to ensure key internal controls are designed into the IT system. Auditors should evaluate whether the managers of the organization's IT system are able to learn from past mistakes. In addition, most changes to the IT system will take the form of packages developed by outside vendors. Hence, auditors should spend a good deal of resources reviewing the compliance of these outside vendors with the terms and conditions of their contracts.

Evaluating IT systems performance is a key management issue. Organizations that fail to evaluate the performance of their IT systems could be wasting large amounts of resources. The IT system should not be any different than other assets in that their performance should be evaluated to allow improvements to be identified and implemented.

Organizations should effectively and efficiently use their IT resources. This use is especially challenging given the current circumstances in which personal computers may be obsolete after two years and program changes may occur monthly. Most organizations are forced to build a larger IT system than needed, and others shift large data processing and record updating projects to off-peak evening hours, thus freeing up critical peak capacity for inquiry and decision support data processing. Organizations should ensure that employees use the IT system solely for organization related tasks. Clear and explicit policies should be promulgated and released stating that personal use of the organization's IT system for personal business is prohibited and offending employees will be properly disciplined.

Organizations face several important human resource challenges. Foremost among these is obtaining and keeping an IT staff that possesses the knowledge, skills and ability to run the IT system. Paying competitive wage, developing and nurturing IT personnel can help to reduce key turnover. An above normal turnover rate among IT personnel may be a sign of additional management problems.

Ergonomics, or the interaction of human beings and computers, has recently become a serious issue in most organizations. Auditors should

¶ 122.02

ensure that the CIO has implemented sensible policies and procedures to safeguard workers from the safety hazards of interacting with computers.

Organizations need to ensure that they can survive when their IT systems fail. Business continuation plans should take into account software needs through off-site backup procedures, hardware needs either through agreements with other users, manufacturers, or with secure sites; and even missing personnel. Such plans also need to be periodically tested in conditions that closely resemble an actual emergency.

Organizations must ensure that employees are given access to the IT system based on the information required to perform their job-related duties. Privacy, or rather the protection of privacy, is very important as well. Organizations should first ensure that individuals outside the organization cannot access their IT. A CIO should ensure that an organization has a proactive privacy policy that protects employees', customers', and vendors' personal information and the trade secrets of the organization.

.03 Application Controls

Application controls address the risks implicit in running individual routines or applications such as payroll, general accounting, marketing, billing, etc. More and more of these applications are integrated in large applications called Enterprise Resource Planning or ERP's. Organizations sometimes delegate responsibility for running applications to end-user departments, and auditors should be concerned with end user environments. The biggest exposure relative to an application's output lies with ensuring that its distribution is strictly controlled to those individuals with a job-related need for the output.

Numerous detailed IT control frameworks offer additional detailed guidance. The COBIT control framework developed by the Information Systems Audit and Control Association (ISACA) and the SysTrust control framework developed by the American Institute of Certified Public Accountants (AICPA) are two of the more recognized control frameworks. COBIT stresses the importance of aligning IT governance with the organization's governance through strategic planning. The AICPA with the Canadian Institute of Chartered Accountants (CICA) developed "SysTrust" services to provide assurance that IT systems were reliable.

Specific systems and applications that need special attention include batch systems, online systems, database systems, datawarehousing, networks, personal computers, service bureaus, end-user systems, and e-commerce.

.04 The Computer and the Auditor

Auditors can generally interact with IT systems to ensure that controls are adequate, account balances are fairly stated, and programs are running as designed and intended. Auditors interact with IT systems in one of three

¶ 122.04

ways: (1) auditing around (without) the computer, (2) auditing through (with) the computer, and (3) continuous (electronic) auditing.

.05 IT Auditing Organizations

The Information Systems Audit and Control Association (ISACA) remains the principal professional organization dedicated to IT auditing. ISACA is a global professional organization headquartered in the Chicago Metropolitan area and provides a range of services similar to other professional accounting bodies. ISACA develops and administers the Certified Information Systems Auditor (CISA) designation. The CISA designation is well recognized and worth pursuing for individuals interested in a career as an IT Auditor.

¶ 123 Government Auditing

Government entities lack a standardized performance measure that for-profit companies have in "Net Income" or "EPS." Nevertheless, constituents demand accountability from their government officials. Specifically, legislators, other government officials, and the public want to know whether government resources are properly managed and used in compliance with laws and regulations, government programs are achieving their objectives and desired outcomes, and government programs are being provided efficiently, economically, and effectively.[7] Government officials for their part rely on auditors to assist them in the discharge of their stewardship responsibility. The scope of government audits run the full range of audits: financial, operational, and compliance.

.01 U.S. Generally Accepted Government Auditing Standards (GAGAS)

The government entity that uses the auditor's report specifies the performance standards that the audit must meet. In the United States, most government entities are audited according to Generally Accepted Government Auditing Standards (GAGAS) published by the U.S. General Accounting Office (GAO).

GAGAS apply to audits and attestation engagements of government entities, programs, activities, and functions, and of government assistance administered by contractors, nonprofit entities, and other nongovernmental entities.

Auditors need to observe the principles of serving the public interest and maintaining the highest degree of integrity, objectivity, and independence.

---

[7] Comptroller General of the United States, *Government Auditing Standards*, 2003 Revision, paragraph 1.11.

¶ 122.05

.02 Types of Government Audits and Attestation Engagements

Types of government audits and attestation engagements include financial audits, attestation engagements, performance audits, and nonaudit services provided by audit organizations.

Audit organizations also may perform nonaudit services that do not impair the audit organization's independence as defined by the general standards of GAGAS. Nonaudit services differ from financial audits, attestation engagements, and performance audits in that auditors perform tasks requested by management that directly support the entity's operation, or provide information or data to a requesting party without providing verification, analysis, or evaluation of the information or data, and therefore, the work does not usually provide a basis for conclusions, recommendations, or opinions on the information or data. Nonaudit services may or may not result in a report and are synonymous with consulting services. GAGAS does not cover nonaudit services, and auditors should not report that these services were conducted according to GAGAS.[8]

.03 GAGAS General Standards

GAGAS general standards cover the independence of the audit organization and its individual auditors, the exercise of professional judgment in the performance of work, and the preparation of related reports; the competence of audit staff; and the existence of quality control systems and external peer reviews. The general standards provide the underlying framework for effectively applying the fieldwork and general standards.[9]

.04 GAGAS Standards for Financial Audits

GAGAS standards for financial audits include fieldwork standards and reporting standards (in addition to the GAS fieldwork and reporting standards. The financial audit fieldwork standards include auditor communication; considering previous results of audits and attestation engagements; detecting material misstatements from violations of contract or grant provisions; pursuing indications of fraud, illegal acts, violations of contract or grant provisions; developing elements of a finding for a financial audit; and audit documentation.

.05 GAGAS for Attestation Engagements

GAGAS for attestation engagements in addition to AICPA Statements on Standards for Attestation Engagements (SSAE) cover auditor communication, considering the results of previous audits and attestation engagements, internal control, detecting fraud and illegal acts, developing elements of findings for attestation engagements and attest documentation. In performing an attestation engagement, auditors issue an examination, a

---

[8] Comptroller General of the United States, *Government Auditing Standards*, 2003 Revision, paragraphs 2.14–2.15.

[9] *Ibid.*, paragraph 3.02.

¶ 123.05

review, or an agreed-upon procedures report on a subject matter, or an assertion about a subject matter that is the responsibility of another party.

.06 GAGAS for Performance Audits

GAGAS for performance audits include fieldwork and reporting standards. The GAGAS fieldwork standards deal with the following issues: planning the audit; supervising staff; obtaining sufficient, competent, and relevant evidence; and preparing audit documentation.

.07 The Single Audit Act

Entities receiving over $300,000 in funds from the U.S. federal government must comply with GAGAS and the Single Audit Act. An organization should monitor the amount of aid it receives from the U.S. federal government especially if the amount is close to the $300,000 Single Audit Act threshold.

An organization should have the same audit firm perform both the normal financial audit and the single audit, which permits the audit firm to work efficiently by using the same tests for both engagements. Internal auditors can perform much of the additional compliance testing required by GAGAS and the Single Audit Act.

¶ 124   Summary

This chapter defines the context of what auditors do and examines the important concepts, rules, standards, and procedures that make up the auditing framework. This chapter introduces important accounting issues discussed in greater detail in the following chapters and provides an overall outline of the book. The issues in this chapter are summarized and are therefore written in general terms.

This chapter introduces the various regulatory and standard-setting bodies that influence the auditing profession: the SEC, the AICPA, the IIA, and the PCAOB. This chapter also discusses the legal liabilities of the auditor, the planning of the financial audit, and the implementation of fieldwork. Also, the three types of audit risk (inherent, control, and detection risks) are introduced. It is important to note that the auditor's objective is to obtain reasonable assurance that financial statements conform to the GAAP and are free of material misstatements and fraud. In addition, this chapter also discusses the four major categories of opinions (unqualified opinion, qualified opinion, disclaimer of opinion, and adverse opinion) and introduces fraud investigation and forensic accounting services.

In addition to the external auditing function, this chapter introduces internal auditing, operational auditing, compliance audits, environmental and quality control audits, and government auditing. Analytical procedures and sampling are defined, and the impact of IT on the audit profession is emphasized.

¶ 123.06

Chapter 2
Standards of Professional Conduct

¶ 201 Introduction
¶ 202 Ethical Principles: The Cornerstone
¶ 203 AICPA Rules of Conduct
¶ 204 General Standards—Rule 201
¶ 205 Responsibilities to Clients
¶ 206 SEC Enforcement Rules
¶ 207 The Oversight Organization
¶ 208 SEC on Independence
¶ 209 Independence Standards Board
¶ 210 Interpretation of AICPA Independence Rule
¶ 211 Other Standards of Professional Conduct
¶ 212 Possible Future Initiatives
¶ 213 Strengthening Auditor Independence Post-Sarbanes-Oxley Act
¶ 214 PCAOB's Standard-Setting Process
¶ 215 COSO Enterprise Risk Management Framework
¶ 216 Summary

¶ 201 Introduction

One of the characteristics of a profession is its members' adherence to a professional code of ethics. In general, professionals are expected to operate at a higher level of conduct than other members of society. At least five groups are involved (at least for a transitional period) with the determination of ethical rules for accountants: The Securities and Exchange Commission (SEC), the Public Company Accounting Oversight Board (PCAOB), the AICPA Professional Ethics Executive Committee (PEEC), the appropriate state society, and the U.S. Department of Labor. Another group, the Independence Standards Board, went out of existence in 2001, and some of their standards and interpretations apply to auditors of public companies. Although the SEC has the statutory authority to establish accounting principles, for more than 60 years the SEC has looked to the private sector for leadership in establishing and improving accounting standards.

¶ 201

The Sarbanes-Oxley Act changed this relationship with the creation of the PCAOB. The PCAOB is a private-sector, nonprofit corporation created to oversee the audits of public companies in order to protect the interests of investors and further the public interest in the preparation of informative, fair, and independent audit reports. On April 16, 2003, the PCAOB announced plans to begin setting auditing, attestation, quality control, and ethical standards for accounting firms that audit public companies. PCAOB member Daniel Goelzer said that the accounting firms subject to the PCAOB's oversight should consider the AICPA and ISB rules to be "written in disappearing ink."[1] Prior rules apply for an interim term until they are reviewed and revised by the PCAOB. The once powerful AICPA will become a networking, social trade association only.

Chapter 2 objectives:

- To become aware of the Public Company Accounting Oversight Board and its purpose (see ¶ 201 and ¶ 207).

- To become familiar with both sections of the American Institute of Certified Public Accountants (AICPA) Code of Professional Conduct (Code) (see ¶ 202–205).

- To understand the three major functions of the SEC and how the SEC administers and enforces laws related to the accounting profession (see ¶ 206).

- To recognize the SEC's auditor independence rules (see ¶ 208).

- To understand how the AICPA has interpreted auditor independence (see ¶ 209–210).

- To become familiar with other standards of professional conduct and some of the possible future initiatives (see ¶ 211–212).

- To understand the present state of the accounting profession and the PCAOB's role in the future auditing standard-setting process (see ¶ 213–214).

- To understand how the COSO Enterprise Risk Management Framework can help auditors fulfill their standards of professional conduct (see ¶ 215).

.01 Public Company Accounting Oversight Board

The Sarbanes-Oxley Act created a new five member board called the Public Company Accounting Oversight Board (PCAOB) to oversee the audit of public companies that are subject to the securities laws. The stated purpose of the PCAOB (peek-ah-boo) is to protect the interests of investors

---

[1] Rosemary Schlank, "PCAOB Unveils Plans to Take Over Setting of Auditing Standards," *Tax Notes* (April 28, 2003): 535.

and further the public interest in the preparation of informative, accurate, and independent audit reports. The PCAOB is a corporate body operating as a nonprofit corporation in the District of Columbia.

The PCAOB has five full-time members with no more than two members who are or have been a CPA. Serving no more than two terms, a PCAOB member shall serve for five years. William J. McDonough, formerly president of the Federal Reserve Bank of New York, was unanimously selected as the first chairperson of the PCAOB with a $556,000 salary (more than the combined pay of the U.S. President and the Head of the SEC). Aside from McDonough, other board members are Daniel L. Goelzer, Kayla J. Gillan, Willie D. Gradison, Jr., and Charles D. Niemeier. The PCAOB established a Standing Advisory Group (SAG) to assist the board in establishing auditing standards for registered auditors who audit financial statements of public companies. The SAG consists of 30 members from the business community and the accounting profession appointed for a two-year term. The SAG advises the board on policy implementations of existing and proposed auditing standards and reviews the existing auditing standards to identify ways to improve these standards.

Douglas Carmichael, former professor at Baruch College in New York City, was named the chief auditor of the PCAOB. Carmichael said that the AICPA failed to aggressively implement recommendations in the 2000 Public Oversight Board. This report recommended many forensic techniques, calling for more "test of details" instead of relying so heavily on "test of controls."

Carmichael says that "auditing firms seem to find ways not to go out on locations, and to do less of the type of work that involves actually counting things, observing, physical inventory, and doing test counts," especially when these are multiple locations. Carmichael said that even "when auditors do test transactions, they frequently only sample above a certain dollar amount, and are too predictable in their approach."[2]

The PCAOB has decided to take over the responsibility of setting auditing standards for registered public accountants. Pursuant to Act Sec. 101(d) of the Sarbanes-Oxley Act, the PCAOB is organized and given proper authority to register public accounting firms and monitor their activities. The PCAOB release No. 2003-006 describes the establishment of "Interim Professional Auditing Standards" according to Act Sec. 103(a) of the Sarbanes-Oxley Act.[3] Interim auditing standards were originally issued by the AICPA and are adopted by the PCAOB on a transitional basis to ensure continuity and certainty in the standards that govern the audits of public companies. Upon further review and consideration of the standards, the PCAOB may permanently modify, repeal, replace, or adopt these interim standards.

---

[2] Kris Frieswick, "How Audits Must Change," CFO (July 2003): 42-50.

[3] The PCAOB Release No. 2003, available at http://www.pcaobus.org.

¶ 201.01

Public accounting firms must register with the PCAOB, and the PCAOB is responsible for overhauling auditing standards, inspecting accounting firms, and disciplining bad accountants. The PCAOB wishes foreign accounting firms to register as required by the SEC. Doug Carmichael says the PCAOB will take over the peer-review process once handed by the AICPA. Essentially, the PCAOB supplanted a 60-year self-regulation system.

Full inspections of accounting firms will begin in 2004 on a regular basis, with limited review of the Big Four auditing firms in 2003. The PCAOB took an active role in the peer review of PricewaterhouseCoopers which is undergoing under the prior peer-review system.[4] The inspections will occur annually for those accounting firms that audit 100 or more public-company clients a year. Firms with fewer clients will be audited every three years.

The inspection reports will be furnished to the accounting firms, but any potential problems will not be made public if the accounting firm corrects the problems within a year. The PCAOB will issue summary reports highlighting problems and issues discovered without disclosing firm names.

The PCAOB can censure, fine, suspend, or bar from practice registered accounting firms and accountants for violating any provisions of the Sarbanes-Oxley Act. Disciplinary procedures are outlined in Act Sec. 105. This choice of an accountant between self-incrimination or job forfeiture may be a form of compulsion of testimony in violation of the Fifth Amendment. Also, if the PCAOB coerces testimony, criminal authorities may be prohibited from using this testimony in criminal proceedings.[5]

.02 Registration System

Both domestic and foreign public accounting firms that prepare or issue audit reports must register with the PCAOB. Domestic firms must register by October 22, 2003, and foreign firms must register by April 19, 2004. Public accounting firms that play "a role in the preparation or furnishing of an audit report" are covered by this registration requirement.

PCAOB Rule 1001(p)(ii) defines "plays a substantial role" to "mean (1) to perform material services that a public accounting firm uses or relies on in issuing all or part of its audit report with respect to any issuer, or (2) to perform the majority of audit procedures with respect to a subsidiary or component of any issuer the assets or revenues of which constitute 20 percent or more of the consolidated assets or revenues of such issuer

---

[4] Cassell Bryan-Low, "McDonough's Modest Digs Belie Tough New Job," *Wall Street Journal*, July 23, 2003, pp. C-1 and C-9.

[5] Michael Perils and Wrenn Chais, "The Board's Investigative Authority—Does the Threat of Job Forfeiture Jeopardize Criminal Investigations," *PCAOB Reporter* (May 27, 2003): 1 and 10.

necessary for the principal accountant to issue an audit report" on the issuer.

"Material services" means services for which the engagement hours or fees constitute 20 percent or more of the total accounting in connection with the issuance of all or part of its audit report with respect to any issuer. "Subsidiary or component" includes any subsidiary, division, branch, office, or other component of an issuer, regardless of its form of organization and/or control relationship with the issuer. For both definitions, the PCAOB believes that a quantitative, as opposed to a qualitative, test imposes less of a burden on accounting firms in determining whether or not they fall into this category. The PCAOB uses a threshold of 20 percent since this threshold is consistent with accounting literature on "significance" tests.

Individual accountants associated with public accounting firms are not required to register. PCAOB Form 1 for public accounting firms consists of general instructions and nine parts, subdivided into various items requiring the disclosure of particular information concerning the applicant and its associated accountants, and the applicant's audit clients. The nine parts include:

1. Identity of the applicant.
2. Listing of applicant's public company audit clients and related fees.
3. Applicant's financial information.
4. Statement of applicant's quality control policies.
5. Listing of criminal, etc. proceedings involving the applicant.
6. Listing of filings disclosing accounting disagreements with public company audit.
7. Roster of associated accountants.
8. Consent of applicant.
9. Signature of applicant.

Firms may register online at *www.pcaobus.org*.

.03 Funding Rules

The PCAOB is authorized to collect an accounting support fee from public companies to cover its annual budget. The accounting support fee is equal to the PCAOB budget for the year, as approved by the SEC, less the amount of registration and annual fees received during the prior year from public accounting firms.

This support fee is to be collected from public companies called issuers. Issuers are divided into four classes:

1. Equity issuers: Those issuers whose average, monthly U.S. equity market capitalization during the preceding calendar year, based on all classes of common stock, is greater than $25 million and whose share price on a monthly, or more frequent, basis is publicly available.

2. Investment companies issuers: Registered investments companies and issuers that have elected to be regulated as business development companies whose average, monthly market capitalization (or net asset value) during the preceding calendar year is greater than $250 million and whose share price (or net asset value) on a monthly, or more frequent, basis is publicly available. An allocation formula scales market capitalization (or, for investment companies whose securities are not traded on an exchange or quoted on NASDAQ, net asset value) of investment companies down by 90 percent, such that a $250 million investment company would be allocated a share equal to that of a $25 million operating company.

3. All issuers that, as of the date the accounting support fee is calculated under Rule 7100, (1) have a basis, under a Commission rule or pursuant to other action of the Commission or its staff, not to file audited financial statements, (2) are employee stock purchase, savings, and similar plans, interests in which constitute securities registered under the Securities Act of 1933, as amended (the "Securities Act"), or (3) are subject to the jurisdiction of a bankruptcy court and satisfy the modified reporting requirements of Commission Staff Legal Bulletin No. 2.

4. All other issuers who do not fall in the above three classes.

The PCAOB budget for 2003 was $68 million and $103 million for 2004; the PCAOB expects to receive fees from about 5,200 publicly traded companies and about 3,300 investment companies. "About 62% of the issuers will pay $1,000 or less in support fees, with the largest 1,000 insurers paying about 87% of the total fees due."[6]

.04 Interim Rules for Public Companies

The PCAOB has released interim rules to be followed by public accounting firms:

1. SAS No. 95 (as of April 16, 2003), AU sec. 150.

2. SAS No. 10 (as of April 16, 2003), AT sec. 101.01.

---

[6] Jacquelyn Lumb, "SEC Approves PCAOB's Funding Rules," *PCAOB Reporter* (August 18, 2003): 2 and 8.

¶ 201.04

Standards of Professional Conduct   45

3. Statement on Quality Control Standard, QC secs. 20-40 (as of April 16, 2003).

4. SEC Practice Section's Requirements of Membership (d), (f), first sentence, (l), (m), (n), (i), and (o) (as of April 16, 2003).

5. Code of Professional Conduct Rule 102, interpretations and rulings thereunder (ET secs. 102 and 191) (as of April 16, 2003).

6. AICPA's Code of Professional Conduct Rule 101, interpretations and rulings.

7. Standards Nos. 1, 2, 3 and interpretations 99-1, 00-1, and 00-2 of the Independence Standards Board.

8. SEC's Rule 2-01 of Reg. S-X.

.05 Some PCAOB Definitions

The PCAOB employs the following definitions of some important terms:

Accountant—a natural person, including (1) those who are certified public accountants, (2) those who hold a college, university, or higher professional degree in accounting, or a license or certification authorizing him or her to engage in the business of auditing or accounting, and (3) those who hold a college, university, or higher professional degree in a field, other than accounting, and who participate in audits. The definition does not include persons engaged only in ministerial or clerical tasks.[7]

Associated entity—(1) any entity that directly, indirectly, or through one or more intermediaries controls or is controlled by, or is under common control with, such public accounting firm, or (2) any "associated entity," as used in Rule 2-01(f)(2) of Regulation S-X, 17 CFR 210.2-10(f)(2), that "would be considered part of that firm for purposes of the Commission's auditor independence rules."[8]

Audit—an examination of an issuer's financial statements by an independent public accounting firm in accordance with the rules of the Board or the Commission for purposes of expressing an opinion on such statements.[9]

Audit report—"a document or other record (1) prepared following an audit performed for purposes of compliance by an issuer with the requirements of the securities laws; and (2) in which a public accounting firm either (i) sets forth the opinion of that firm regarding a financial statement, report or other document; or (ii) asserts no such opinion can be expressed."[10]

---

[7] Rule 1001(a)(ii).
[8] Rule 1001(a)(iv).
[9] Rule 1001(a)(v).
[10] Rule 1001(a)(vi).

¶ 201.05

Audit services—"professional services rendered for the audit of an issuer's with annual financial statements and (if applicable) for the reviews of an issuer's financial statements included in the issuer's quarterly reports."[11]

Foreign public accounting firm—a "public accounting firm that is organized and operated under the laws of a non-U.S. jurisdiction, government or political subdivision thereof."[12]

Issuer—"any public company, regardless of the jurisdiction of its organization or operation, that is required to file reports with the Commission or that has filed a registration statement for a public offering of securities."[13]

Non-audit services—"all other services other than audit services, other accounting services, and tax services."[14]

Other accounting services—"services that are normally provided by the public accounting firm that audits the issuer's financial statements in connection with statutory and regulatory filings or engagements and assurance and related services that are reasonably related to the performance of the audit or review of the issuer's financial statements, other than 'audit services' which includes audit-related fees."[15]

Public accounting firm—"proprietorship, partnership, incorporated association, corporation, limited liability company, limited liability partnership, or other legal entity that is engaged in the practice of public accounting or preparing or issuing audit reports (but not natural person). An individual accountant that prepares or issues an audit report in his or her name would be a "proprietorship" and therefore fall under this definition."[16]

Tax services—"professional services rendered for tax compliance, tax advice, and tax planning."[17]

.06 Independence After Sarbanes-Oxley

After Sarbanes-Oxley, an auditor must be an auditor, and not an auditor and a consultant. In order to be independent, an accounting firm should not:

- Audit ones own work.
- Function as part of management or an employee.
- Act as an advocate.

The lead audit partner and concurring review partner must be rotated every five years (five years on and five years off). Other audit partners, who

---

[11] Rule 1001(a)(vii)(i).
[12] Rule 1001(f)(i).
[13] Rule 1001(i)(iii).
[14] Rule 1001(n)(ii)(2).
[15] Rule 1001(o)(i)(1).
[16] Rule 1001(p)(iii).
[17] Rule 1001(t)(i).

are part of the audit engagement team if they provide 10 or more hours of audit services to the client or serve as the lead auditor on a subsidiary whose assets or revenues are 20 percent or more of the client's consolidated assets or revenues, must be rotated after seven years and stay off the client's audit engagement for two years (seven years on and two years off). Furthermore, partners' compensation should be linked to audit quality and effectiveness rather than to fees collected for audit and non-audit services from their clients.

Eight types of services are now outlawed:

1. Bookkeeping.
2. Information systems design and implementation.
3. Appraisals or valuation services, fairness opinions, or contributions-in-kind-reports.
4. Actuarial services.
5. Internal audit outsourcing.
6. Management and human resources services.
7. Broker/dealer, investment adviser, and investment banking services.
8. Legal or expert services related to audit services.

No limitations are placed upon accounting firms in providing non-audit services to public companies they do not audit or any private companies. Audit services and non-audit services (e.g., tax) must be pre-approved by the audit committee, if not prohibited by the Act (before the non-audit service commences).

The auditor is to report in a timely manner to the company's audit committee certain items:

- Critical accounting policies and practices to be used.
- Alternative treatment of financial information within generally accepted accounting principles (GAAP) that have been discussed with management.
- Accounting disagreements between management and the auditor.
- Any other material written communication between the auditor and the management team.

There is now a one-year cooling off period for employees of an audit firm. An auditing firm may not perform any auditing service for a company whose CEO, Controller, CFO, or CAO participated in any capacity in the audit of the company within the past year.

¶ 201.06

.07 Auditing Internal Controls

Act Sec. 404 of the Sarbanes-Oxley Act and SEC-related implementation rules require management of public companies to annually issue a report of the effectiveness of the company's internal controls over financial reporting. Act Sec. 404 also requires registered auditors to attest to and report on management assertions regarding the effectiveness of internal controls. The PCAOB is authorized by the Sarbanes-Oxley Act to issue auditing standards to guide auditors as to how to conduct attestation of internal controls. On October 7, 2003, the PCAOB issued proposed auditing standards dealing with the audit of internal controls over financial reporting performed in conjunction with an audit of financial statements (with an effective date for fiscal years ending on or after June 15, 2004). The PCAOB finally adopts its PCAOB Auditing Standard No. 2 entitled, "An Audit of Internal Control over Financial Reporting Performed in Conjunction with an Audit of Financial Statements."[18] This standard is already approved by the SEC, which requires auditors to attest to and report on management's assessment of internal controls by expressing an opinion that management's conclusion is correct and thus fairly stated. The auditor's report must include the auditor's opinion on both the management's assessment of the effectiveness of internal control over financial reporting and fair presentation of financial statements in conformity with GAAP.

The PCAOB believes that an attestation is an expert's communication of a conclusion about the reliability of someone else's assertion (e.g., a financial statement audit is a form of attestation). Act Sec. 404(b) of the Sarbanes-Oxley Act of 2002 states that an auditor's attestation of management's assessment of internal controls is not a separate engagement. Instead, the PCAOB states that an "integrated audit results in two audit opinions: one on internal control over financial reporting and one on the financial statements."

The PCAOB states that internal controls over financial reporting include company policies and those procedures "designed and operated to provide reasonable assurance—a high, but not absolute, level of assurance—about the reliability of a company's financial reporting and its process for preparing financial statements in accordance with generally accepted accounting principles." Also included are those policies and procedures for "the maintenance of accounting records, the authorization of receipts and disbursements, and the safeguarding of assets." Even the PCAOB believes that internal controls "cannot provide absolute assurance of achieving financial reporting objectives because of inherent limitations (e.g., a process that involves human diligence and compliance can be

---

[18] PCAOB Auditing Standard No. 2, An Audit of Internal Control Over Financial Reporting Performed in Conjunction with an Audit of Financial Statements (PCAOB Bylaws and Rules, June 18, 2004), p. 131. Available at http://www.pcaobus.org.

intentionally circumvented)." Although evaluating internal controls are costly, such evaluations have far-reaching benefits.

The audit of internal controls includes these steps:

1. Planning the internal control audit.

2. Evaluating the effectiveness of both the design and operation of the internal controls.

3. Forming an opinion about whether internal controls over financial reporting are effective.

These steps are explained in Chapter 6.

The PCAOB suggests that the starting point for an audit of the internal controls is an evaluation of management's assessments of the controls. The purpose of the internal control audit is to form an opinion "as to whether management's assessment of the effectiveness of the registrant's internal control over financial reporting is fairly stated in all material respects."[19] Further, Act Sec. 103 of the Sarbanes-Oxley Act of 2002 requires an auditor's report to contain an evaluation as to whether the internal control structure provides reasonable assurance that transactions are necessary. The PCAOB's audit standards allow auditors to incorporate some of the work performed by internal auditors or other third parties. However, auditors must assess the competence and objectivity of the persons who performed the work. An auditor must perform "company-wide anti-fraud programs and controls and work related to other controls that have a pervasive effect on the company, such as general controls over the company's electronic data processing." Further, the auditor must "obtain directly the 'principle evidence' about the effectiveness of internal controls."

An auditor must perform "walkthroughs" of a business' significant processes. The PCAOB suggests that an auditor should "confirm his or her understanding by performing procedures that include making inquires of and observing the personnel that actually perform the controls; reviewing documents that are used in, and that result from, the application of the controls; and comparing supporting documents (for example, sales invoices, contracts, and bills of lading) to the accounting records." According to the PCAOB, in a walkthrough an auditor traces "company transactions and events—both those that are routine and recurring and those that are unusual—from origination, through the company's accounting and information systems and financial report preparation processes, to their being reported in the company's financial statements." Auditors should perform

---

[19] Final Rule: Management's Reports on Internal Control Over Financial Reporting and Certification of Disclosure in Exchange Act Periodic Reports (Securities and Exchange Commission Release No. 33-8238, § 210.2-02(f), June 5, 2003).

¶ 201.07

their own walkthroughs which provides auditors with appropriate evidence to make an intelligent assessment of internal controls.

The PCAOB provides several strong indicators that material weaknesses exist in internal controls:

- Ineffective oversight of the company's external financial reporting and internal control over financial reporting by the company's audit committee.

- Material misstatement in the financial statements not initially identified by the company's internal controls.

- Significant deficiencies that have been communicated to management and the audit committee but that remain uncorrected after a reasonable period of time.

.08 Transparency

The proper functioning of the U.S. capital markets is dependent upon the transparency and reliability of financial statements. Transparency refers to information about a company being visible and understandable to users. The AICPA does not consider a member's independence to be impaired if the member complies with less restrictive SEC independence rules. The AICPA Code of Professional Conduct (Code) provides guidance and rules for its members (whether in public practice, in industry, in government, or in education) in the performance of their professional responsibilities. The Professional Ethics Executive Committee promulgates the rules, but they must be approved by the AICPA memberships. This Code consists of two sections—principles and rules. Interpretations and ethical rulings support and help illustrate the rules for members.

The principles provide the framework for the rules that govern the performance of professional services by AICPA members. All members must agree to abide by both AICPA bylaws and the Code. If a member violates the Code, the individual may be expelled from membership in the AICPA.

Table 2.1

Major Sections of the AICPA Code of Professional Conduct

Principles	Philosophical underpinnings for the rules
Rules of conduct	Enforceable minimum standards of ethical conduct that are very broad in scope
Interpretations	Interpretations of the rules of conduct that help members understand their scope and application. A member has the burden of justifying and departing from such interpretations in a disciplinary hearing
Ethical rulings	Published responses in the *Journal of Accountancy* to questions about the rules to the AICPA from members and other parties. These rulings are not enforceable, but a member must justify departure from the rules

.09 Objectives of the AICPA Code of Professional Ethics

First, the AICPA Code of Professional Ethics assures AICPA stakeholders, i.e., the public, fellow members, and clients of the Institute, that AICPA members acknowledge their professional responsibilities. Second, the Code guides AICPA members on the tenets of professional behavior and performance. Lastly, the Code completes the circle of public trust by requiring the complete commitment of its members to the stated responsibilities.

.10 State Licensing Rules

Each state has rules of conduct that are required for certified public accountant (CPA) licensing by that state, but most states follow the same independence requirements. The AICPA and most of the state societies are members of the Joint Ethics Enforcement Program (JEEP), which permits joint enforcement of their Codes of Professional Conduct.

¶ 202 Ethical Principles: The Cornerstone

When one acts on principle, one acts in accordance with a set of beliefs that can help determine the best course of action in even the most difficult and challenging circumstance. Auditing services are often required under situations and circumstances that seemingly require the wisdom of Solomon, the courage of David, and the patience of Job. The CPA who understands and adheres to the ethical principles can often cut through the morass of an individual circumstance and make the timeless judgment required to honor the profession and the individual practitioner.

The AICPA ethical principles form the cornerstone of successful professional practice. There are essentially five fundamental beliefs or principles that make up the cornerstone of proper professional practice for AICPA members. A sixth principle builds on all of the first five.

.01 Exercising Responsibility

When a CPA accepts membership in the American Institute of Certified Public Accountants that individual assumes obligations beyond the requirements of laws and regulations.[20] The principles of the *AICPA Code of Professional Conduct* are the expression of the individual member's recognition of responsibility to the public, clients and colleagues. These principles guide members in the performance of their professional responsibilities and express the basic tenets of ethical and professional conduct. The principles call for an unswerving commitment to honorable behavior.[21] By accepting membership, one accepts the first precept of the practice—responsibility—and thereby accepts all the following principles as well.

.02 Acting in the Public Interest

Like the roles of other professionals, the role of the CPA is essential to society and the collaborative efforts of CPAs are required to maintain and enhance the traditions of the profession.[22] Much of the public relies on the objectivity and integrity of CPAs to maintain the orderly functioning of commerce.[23] This is certainly key in auditing engagements. Conflicts often surface when the CPA is engaged in practice and members should act with integrity, knowing that when they fulfill their responsibility to the public, they serve the best interests of clients and employers.[24]

.03 Acting with Integrity

Integrity is uncompromising adherence to values and is the quality from which the public trust derives and the benchmark against which a CPA tests all decisions.[25] It can survive the inadvertent mistake and the honest difference of opinion, but cannot accept deceit or subordination of principle.[26]

---

[20] Principle 51, Preamble (AICPA, Professional Standards, vol. 2, ET sec. 51.01).

[21] Ibid., 51.02.

[22] Principle 52, Article I—Responsibilities (AICPA, Professional Standards, vol. 2, ET sec. 52.01).

[23] Principle 53, Article II—The Public Interest (AICPA, Professional Standards, vol. 2, ET sec. 53.01).

[24] Ibid., 53.02.

[25] Principle 54, Article III—Integrity (AICPA, Professional Standards, vol. 2, ET sec. 54.01).

[26] Ibid., 54.02.

¶ 202.01

.04 Acting Objectively and Independently

Integrity also requires a CPA to be objective and independent.[27] The CPA must operate objectively and view facts without distortion, feelings or personal bias. The CPA must also be impartial, honest, and free of conflicts of interest. Independence precludes relationships that may appear to impair a member's objectivity in rendering attestation services.[28]

CPAs must act objectively whether in public practice rendering attest services, performing internal auditing, educating and training, or government service. They must avoid any subordination of their judgment.[29]

Those in public practice must continually assess client relationships and public responsibility to maintain their objectivity and independence. Those who provide auditing and other attestation services should be independent in fact and appearance.[30]

CPAs who are not in public practice cannot maintain the appearance of independence, but must be scrupulous in their application of generally accepted accounting principles (GAAP) (and generally accepted auditing standards (GAAS)) and candid in all their dealings with members in public practice.[31]

.05 Acting with Due Care

For CPAs, the quest for excellence is the essence of due care. Due care requires CPAs to competently perform professional services consistent with the profession's responsibility to the public for the best interest of those for whom the services are performed.[32] The quality of competence requires knowledge, judgment, skill and capability. Maintaining competence requires a commitment to life-long learning and improvement. For the CPA, competence begins with the mastery of the common body of knowledge required for designation. CPAs must achieve a level of competence to assure that the quality of services meets the level of professionalism required by these principles.[33] Each CPA is responsible for evaluating whether education, experience, and judgment are adequate for the responsibility to competently perform each engagement.[34]

CPAs must also be diligent in discharging their responsibilities. CPAs must render services promptly. They must be careful and thorough to observe applicable technical and ethical standards.[35] Due care also requires the CPA to plan and supervise adequately any professional activity.[36]

Properly determining the nature and scope of services. In the public interest, certified public accountants' services should be consistent

---

[27] Ibid., 54.04.
[28] Principle 55, Article IV—Objectivity and Independence (AICPA, Professional Standards, vol. 2, ET sec. 55.01).
[29] Ibid., 55.02.
[30] Ibid., 55.03.
[31] Ibid., 55.04.
[32] Principle 56, Article V—Due Care (AICPA, Professional Standards, vol. 2, ET sec. 56.01).
[33] Ibid., 56.02.
[34] Ibid., 56.03.
[35] Ibid., 56.04.
[36] Ibid., 56.05.

with acceptable professional behavior. Integrity requires that service and the public trust not be subordinated to personal gain and advantage. Objectivity and independence require that members be free from conflicts of interest in discharging professional responsibilities. Due care requires that services be provided with competence and diligence.[37]

In determining the scope and nature of services to be provided, each of these principles should be considered by members when deciding whether or not to provide specific services. In some instances, they may represent an overall constraint on the nonaudit services that might be offered to a specific client. No hard and fast rules can be developed to help members reach these judgments, but they must be satisfied that they are meeting the spirit of the principles.[38]

Good internal quality-control procedures can help to ensure that services are competently delivered and adequately supervised. Individual judgments must be made to determine whether the scope and nature of other services provided to an audit client would create a conflict of interest in the performance of the audit function. CPAs may be called on to assess, in their individual judgments, whether an activity is consistent with their role as professionals.[39]

Most of these principles should be equally applicable to other professions (for example, medical or legal). The major exception would be independence; for example, a lawyer most often is an advocate for his or her client. Users of financial statements, however, expect CPAs to be unbiased, so independence is a critical principle for auditing practitioners. These users (investors, creditors, and other stakeholders) make financial decisions with the expectation that the company providing attestation services did the work without an unacceptable risk of outside influence or bias. Some rules on independence have the force of law, such as the SEC rules applying to audits; other rules are set by the profession itself.

.06 Ethics Vocabulary

One must understand certain definitions in order to accurately interpret the Code and the rules imposed by the SEC. These terms will be used throughout this book and can be found as Appendix 1 in the back of the book.

---

[37] Principle 57, Article VI—Scope and Nature of Services (AICPA, Professional Standards, vol. 2, ET sec. 57.01).

[38] *Ibid.*, 57.02.

[39] *Ibid.*, 57.03.

¶ 203 AICPA Rules of Conduct

The Rules of Conduct are the enforceable minimum standards of ethical conduct stated as specific rules. They are outlined as follows:[40]

Rule 101—Independence. A member in public practice shall be independent in the performance of professional services as required by standards promulgated by bodies designated by Council.

Rule 102—Integrity and Objectivity. In the performance of any professional service, a member shall maintain objectivity and integrity, shall be *free of conflicts of interests,* and shall not knowingly misrepresent facts or subordinate his or her judgment to others.

Rule 201—General Standards. A member shall comply with the following standards and with any interpretations thereof by bodies designated by Council.

- A. *Professional Competence.* Undertake only those professional services that the member or the member's firm can reasonably expect to be completed with professional competence.

- B. *Due Professional Care.* Exercise due professional care in the performance of professional services.

- C. *Planning and Supervision.* Adequately plan and supervise the performance of professional services.

- D. *Sufficient Relevant Data.* Obtain sufficient relevant data to afford a reasonable basis for conclusions or recommendations in relation to any professional services performed.

Rule 202—Compliance with Standards. A member who performs auditing, review, compilation, management consulting, tax, or other professional services shall comply with standards promulgated by bodies designated by Council.

Rule 203—Accounting Principles. Discussed later in detail.

Rule 301—Confidential Client Information. A member in public practice shall not disclose any confidential client information without the specific consent of the client. Discussed later in detail.

Rule 302—Contingent Fees. This rule prohibits contingent fees *for any professional service performed for a client* when the member in public practice (or member's firm) also performs for that client:

- An audit or a review of a financial statement
- An explanation of prospective financial information or

---

[40] Rule 101–505 (AICPA, Professional Standards, vol. 2, ET sec. 101—505).

- A compilation of a financial statement expected to be used by third parties except when the compilation report discloses a lack of independence

This rule also prohibits a member in public practice from preparing for a contingent fee an original or amended tax return, or a claim for a tax refund. This restriction includes giving advice on determining some portion of a return or claim for refund for events that have occurred at the time the advice is given.

Rule 501—Acts Discreditable. A member shall not commit an act discreditable to the profession.

Rule 502—Advertising and Other Forms of Solicitation. A member in public practice is prohibited from engaging in the following when soliciting clients:

- False, misleading, or deceptive advertising
- Coercion or
- Overreaching or harassing conduct

A member may engage in the following forms of advertising as long as they are not false, misleading, or deceptive:

- Testimonials or endorsements
- In-person solicitation of clients
- Comparative advertising or
- Self-laudatory advertising

Rule 503—Commissions and Referral Fees. A member in public practice may not receive a commission or referral fee from a client when the member or member's firm performs for that client these disqualifying services:

- An audit or a review of a financial statement
- An examination of prospective financial information or
- A compilation of a financial statement expected to be used by third parties except when the compilation report discloses a lack of independence

Further, any member who performs these disqualifying services may not receive a commission for recommending or referring:

- Any product or service *to a client* or
- Any product or service supplied *by a client*

¶ 203

Rule 505—Form of Organizations and Name. A member may practice public accounting only in a permitted form of organization that is allowed by law or regulation, and that meets the requirements set by the AICPA Council.

¶ 204 General Standards—Rule 201

As previously noted, there are four AICPA general standards: professional competence, due professional care, planning and supervision, and sufficient relevant data. Rule 201 applies to all types of services (i.e., audit, tax, consulting). Notice that requirements A and B of Rule 201 are quite similar to the general auditing standards 1 and 2, and C and D of Rule 201 are similar to field work standards 1 and 3.

.01 Professional Competence

As a professional, an auditor should undertake only those professional services that can be completed with professional competence, according to professional standards, applying his or her knowledge and skill with reasonable care and diligence. But Interpretation .02 201-1 states that a covered member does not assume a responsibility for infallibility of knowledge or judgment.

This standard refers both to the technical qualifications of the auditor and the covered member staff and the ability to supervise and evaluate the quality of the work performed. Competence involves both the knowledge of the profession's standards, techniques, and the technical subject matter involved, and the capability to exercise sound judgment in applying this knowledge. Probably the most important aspect of GAAS is that an auditor must understand his or her client's business. Obviously, engaging in non-attest service helps a firm to understand the client's business, but the SEC disagrees with these statements.

Although additional research or consultation may be necessary, this does not represent lack of competence but rather a normal part of the performance of professional service. If an auditor is unable to gain sufficient competence through research and consultation, he or she should not do the work.

.02 Due Professional Care

Rule 201 provides that an auditor must exercise due professional care by discharging his or her professional responsibilities with competence and diligence to the best of the member's ability, considering the best interest of the client and the public. The auditor must have a mastery of the CPA's common body of knowledge. The auditor must render service with facility and acumen, render services promptly and carefully, be thorough, and observe applicable technical and ethical standards. A proper engagement letter will go a long way in outlining the terms of the engagement and defining each party's responsibilities. An engagement letter should set forth the firm and client's understanding of the terms of the engagement as well as limitations. The letter should define each party's responsibilities. See Figure 3.1.

Due professional care assumes that an auditor maintains an attitude of professional skepticism and maintains a questioning mental attitude. AU sec. 230 suggests that the auditor assume an attitude that includes a questioning mind and a critical assessment of audit evidence. This approach does not mean you believe that everyone is dishonest, but one must question and critically assess audit evidence. SAS No. 99 defines professional skepticism as "an attitude that includes a questioning mind and critical assessment of audit evidence."[41] This attitude is especially important because of the increasing litigation against accounting firms for failing to detect fraud in the post-Enron enviroment (see Chapter 20).

.03 Planning and Supervision

An auditor must plan and supervise the performance of any professional service. A firm must have in place internal quality control procedures to ensure that services are competently delivered and adequately supervised. The auditor should document in the permanent file what he or she is doing.

A firm should establish a quality control system in accordance with Statement on Quality Control Standards (SQCSs). SQCS No. 1 outlines nine elements of quality controls: six engagement controls and three practice controls. The six engagement controls are independence, assignment of personnel, consultation, supervision, acceptance and continuance of clients, and inspection. The three practice controls are hiring, professional development, and advancement. The firm must monitor the compliance with the system and not wait for a negative peer review (see Chapter 4).

.04 Sufficient Relevant Data

An auditor must obtain sufficient relevant data to afford a reasonable basis for conclusions and recommendations.

.05 Compliance with Standards

Rule 202 provides that a covered member who performs auditing, review, compilation, management consulting, tax, or other professional services must comply with standards promulgated by the Financial Accounting Standards Board (FASB). The AICPA Accounting and Review Services Committee, Auditing Standards Board, and Consulting Services Executive Committee are authorized to promulgate attestation standards in their respective areas of responsibilities. If an accountant violates an auditing standard, the rules of conduct also are violated.

---

[41] Statements on Auditing Standards (SAS) No. 99, *Consideration of Fraud in a Financial Statement Audit* (AICPA, Professional Standards, vol. 1, AU secs. 316.50).

.06 Accounting Principles

Rule 203 stipulates that an AICPA member shall not express an opinion or state affirmatively that the financial statements or other financial data of any entity conform to GAAP. A member also must not state that he or she is unaware of material modifications that should be made to financial statements or data in order to bring them into conformity with GAAP, if such statements or data contain any departure from an accounting principle promulgated by bodies designated by the council to establish such principles that has a material effect on the statements or data taken as a whole. However, if the statements or data contain such a departure and the member can demonstrate that because of unusual circumstances such documents would otherwise have been misleading, the member can comply with the rule by describing the departure, its approximate effects, and the reasons why compliance with the principle would result in a misleading statement.

Interpretation 203-1 states that adherence to the established principles will result in financial statements that are not misleading. But on occasion the literal application of an accounting principle may render the financial statements misleading, so an auditor must follow the accounting treatment that does not render the financial statements misleading. New legislation or the evolution of a new form of business transaction are examples of a situation in which a departure could be appropriate.

A client must prepare financial statements in conformity with GAAP, and an auditor may not state affirmatively that financial statements are presented in conformity with GAAP if such statements contain any departure from accounting principles.

¶ 205 Responsibilities to Clients

An auditor has certain responsibilities to his or her client. One such major responsibility is maintenance of the confidentiality of client data and records. Rule 301 of AICPA's *Professional Standards* spells out this responsibility. Rule 302 details the pitfalls of contingent fees. Rule 501 enumerates discreditable acts auditors might commit, whereas Rule 502 prohibits deceptive advertising of services for attest clients. Finally, Rule 505 lists requirements for the type of organization and name for professional practices.

.01 Confidential Client Information

Rule 301, *Confidential Client Information,* provides as follows:

> A member in public practice shall not disclose any confidential client information without the specific consent of the client. This rule should not be construed (1) to relieve a member of his or her professional obligations under rules 202 [*ET sec. 202.01*] and 203 [*ET sec. 203.01*], (2) to affect in any way the member's obligation to comply with a validly issued and enforceable subpoena or summons, or to prohibit a member's compliance with applicable laws and government regulations, (3) to prohibit review of a member's profes-

sional practice under AICPA or state CPA society or Board of Accountancy authorization, or (4) to preclude a member from initiating a complaint with, or responding to any inquiry made by, the professional ethics division or trial board of the Institute or a duly constituted investigative or disciplinary body of a state CPA society or Board of Accountancy.[42]

Members of any of the bodies identified in (4) above and members involved with professional practice reviews identified in (3) above should not use to their own advantage or disclose any member's confidential client information that comes to their attention in carrying out those activities. This prohibition does not restrict members' exchange of information in connection with the investigative or disciplinary proceedings described in (4) or the professional practice reviews described in (3).

Rule 301 applies not only to audits but also to other services provided by an accountant (e.g., tax preparation and consulting). An auditor obtains much information of a confidential or sensitive nature while auditing a client that must not be divulged to outsiders or client employees (who may be denied access to certain information). An auditor must have a system in place to protect physical access to the client information and prevent the unauthorized dissemination of any confidential information. Although audit workpapers belong to the auditor, he or she must protect the content of the workpapers from unauthorized access and dissemination.

This rule does not prohibit, however, a peer review of an auditor's professional practice under AICPA and state CPA society authorization. In order to be admitted to or retain their membership in the AICPA, practitioners must be enrolled in an approved practice monitoring program.

Likewise, in case of a prospective purchase, sale, or merger of an auditor's practice, a review of his or her professional practice is possible. The auditor must take appropriate precautions, such as through a written confidentiality agreement, so that the prospective purchaser does not disclose any information obtained during the course of the review.

Following are some ethical rulings on client information:

- A covered member may use an outside service to process tax returns.

- An auditor must obtain the client's permission to supply profit and loss percentages to a trade association.

- If an auditor discovers irregularities in a client's tax return and withdraws from the engagement, a successor auditor may ask about the withdrawal. In order to put the successor accountant on notice, the auditor should encourage the successor to ask the client for permission to discuss the problem freely.

---

[42] Rule 301, *Confidential Client Information* (AICPA, Professional Standards, vol. 2, ET sec. 301.01).

¶ 205.01

- An auditor may use a records-retention agency to store client records.

- In general, an auditor may disclose the name of a client, unless the engagement involves bankruptcy issues.

- A covered member may release confidential client information to his or her liability insurance carrier solely to assist the defense against an actual or potential claim against the member.

.02 Contingent Fees

Rule 302, *Contingent Fees,* regulates the use of contingent fees in client services as follows:

> A member in public practice shall not
>
> (1) Perform for a contingent fee any professional services for, or receive such a fee from a client for whom the member or the member's firm performs,
>
> a. an audit or review of a financial statement; or
>
> b. a compilation of a financial statement when the member expects, or reasonably might expect, that a third party will use the financial statement and the member's compilation report does not disclose a lack of independence; or
>
> c. an examination of prospective financial information or
>
> (2) Prepare an original or amended tax return or claim for a tax refund for a contingent fee for any client.[43]

Prohibition (1) applies during the period in which a covered member or the member's firm is engaged to perform any of the services listed in (a) through (c) and the period covered by any historical financial statements involved in any such listed services.

A contingent fee is one established for the performance of any service pursuant to an arrangement in which no fee will be charged unless a specified finding or result is attained, or in which the amount of the fee is otherwise dependent upon the finding or result of such service. However, fees are not regarded as being contingent if fixed by courts or other authorities, or, in tax matters, if determined based on the results of judicial proceedings or the findings of governmental agencies. Such a fee may vary depending, for example, on the complexity of services rendered.

Interpretation 302-1 provides some examples in which a contingent fee is permitted with tax services:

- Representing a client in an examination by a revenue agent of the client's federal or state income tax return.

- Filing an amended federal or state income tax return claiming a tax refund based on a tax issue that is either the subject of a

---

[43] Rule 302, *Contingent Fees* (AICPA, Professional Standards, vol. 2, ET sec. 302.01).

test case (involving a different taxpayer) or with respect to which the taxing authority is developing a position.

- Filing an amended federal or state income tax return (or refund claim) claiming a tax refund in an amount greater than the threshold for review by the Joint Committee on Internal Revenue Taxation or state taxing authority.

- Requesting a refund of either overpayments of interest or penalties charged to a client's account or deposits of taxes improperly accounted for by the federal or state taxing authority when the taxing authority has established procedures for the substantive review of such refund requests.

- Requesting, by means of "protest" or similar document, consideration by the state or local taxing authority of a reduction in the "assessed value" of property under an established taxing authority review process for hearing all taxpayer arguments relating to assessed value.

- Representing a client in connection with obtaining a private letter ruling or influencing the drafting of a regulation or statute.

A contingent fee is *not* permitted when the auditor prepares an amended federal or state income tax return for a client claiming a refund or taxes because a deduction was inadvertently omitted from the return originally filed. There is no question about the propriety of the deduction; rather, the claim is filed to correct an omission.

An auditor may receive a contingent fee for nonattest services as long as the firm is not also performing attestation services for the same client.

.03 Discreditable Acts

Rule 501, *Discreditable Acts,* provides descriptions of several discreditable acts of an auditor:

- Retention of a client's records after a demand is made for them is a violation. However, an auditor's workpapers, including, but not limited to, analyses and schedules prepared by the client at the request of the auditor, are the practitioner's property and not considered to be client records. Thus, they are not required to be given to the client. Sometimes an auditor's workpapers contain information that is not reflected in the client's books and records, with the result that the client's financial information files are incomplete. This includes:

    – Adjusting, closing, combining, or consolidating journal entries

- Information normally contained in books of original entry and general ledgers or subsidiary ledgers
- Tax and depreciation carry forwarded information

When an engagement has been completed, such information should also be made available to the client upon request. The information should be provided in the medium in which it is requested, provided it exists in that medium. The auditor is not required to convert information that is not in electronic format to an electronic form. The auditor may require that all fees due the member, including the fees for the above services, be paid before such information is provided.

- An accounting firm may not discriminate on the basis of race, color, religion, sex, age, or national origin.
- If auditing a governmental unit, an auditor must follow both GAAS and the government agency procedures, unless the audit report states otherwise.
- The auditor violates Rule 501 if by his or her negligence the auditor:
  - Makes, or permits or directs another to make, materially false and misleading entries in the financial statements or records of an entity
  - Fails to correct an entity's financial statements that are materially false and misleading when the practitioner has the authority to record an entry or
  - Signs, or permits or directs another to sign, a document containing materially false misleading information
- An auditor must follow requirements of government bodies, commissions, or other regulatory agencies.
- An auditor must not solicit or knowingly disclose uniform CPA examination questions.
- An auditor must file tax returns and pay tax liabilities.

.04 Advertising and Solicitation

Rule 502, *Advertising and Other Forms of Solicitation,* indicates the following:

A member in public practice shall not seek to obtain clients by advertising or other forms of solicitation in a manner that is false, misleading, or deceptive. Solicitation by the use of coercion, over-reaching, or harassing conduct is prohibited.[44]

---

[44] Rule 502, *Advertising and Other Forms of Solicitation* (AICPA, *Professional Standards,* vol. 2, ET sec. 502.01).

Prior to 1978, advertising in any format was not available to an auditor: direct solicitation, advertising, competitive bidding, contingent fees, commissions for obtaining clients, and referral fees were prohibited. Today all of these activities are available for nonattest clients, but the last three are violations of the attest clients. False, misleading, or deceptive acts in advertising and solicitation are prohibited, including:

- Creation of false or unjustified expectations of favorable results;

- Implying the ability to influence any court, tribunal, regulatory agency, or similar body or official;

- Representing that specific professional services in current or future periods will be performed for a stated fee, estimated fee, or fee range when it was likely at the time of the representation that such fees would be substantially increased and the prospective client was not advised of that likelihood; or

- Representing services that would be likely to cause a reasonable person to misunderstand or be deceived.

A firm must be careful that its marketing material (e.g., advertising brochures) does not promise more than the firm can deliver, resulting in a malpractice suit.

.05 Commissions and Referral Fees

Rule 503, *Commissions and Referral Fees,* provide the following guidance:

A. *Prohibited commission.* A member in public practice shall not for a commission recommend or refer to a client any product or service, or for a commission recommend or refer any product or service to be supplied by a client, or receive a commission, when the member or the member's firm also performs for that client:

(a) an audit or review of a financial statement; or

(b) a compilation of a financial statement when the member expects, or reasonably might expect, that a third party will use the financial statement and the member's compilation report does not disclose a lack of independence; or

(c) an examination of prospective financial information.

This prohibition applies during the period in which the member is engaged to perform any of the services listed above and the period covered by any historical financial statements involved in such listed services.

B. *Disclosure of permitted commissions.* A member in public practice who is not prohibited by this rule from performing services for or receiving a commission and who is paid or expects or to be paid a commission shall disclose that fact to any person or entity to whom the member recommends or refers a product or service to which the commission relates.

C. *Referral fees.* Any member who accepts a referral fee for recommending or referring any service of a CPA to any person or entity or who pays a referral fee to obtain a client shall disclose such acceptance or payment to the client.

A firm may sell such things as real estate, securities, and businesses on a commission basis as long as the transaction does not involve a client receiving attest services from the accounting firm. Commissions from an attestation client are prohibited so that a CPA can maintain objectivity in conducting an audit.[45]

.06 Form of Organization and Name

Rule 505, *Form of Organization and Name,* states:

> A member may practice public accounting only in a form of organization permitted by law or regulation whose characteristics conform to resolutions of Council.
>
> A member shall not practice accounting under a firm name that is misleading. Names of one or more past owners may be included in the firm name of a successor organization.
>
> A firm may not designate itself as "Members of the American Institute of Certified Public Accountants" unless all of its CPA owners are members of the Institute.[46]

Firms may now operate in any organizational structure permitted by state laws (e.g., limited liability company, limited liability partnership, professional corporation, or partnership). Accounting firms should pick a structure that shields the owners from the liabilities of the firm, such as an LLC.

A Council resolution provides that the majority of the ownership of a firm in terms of financial interests and voting rights must belong to CPAs. The nonCPA owners must be actively engaged as firm members in providing accounting services as their principal occupation. Ownership by investors or commercial enterprises not actively engaged as firm members in providing services to the firm's clients as their principal occupation is against the public interest and is prohibited.

The resolution also provides the following requirements:

- A CPA must be ultimately responsible for all services provided by the firm.

- NonCPAs becoming owners after May 15, 2000, have to possess a baccalaureate degree and, beginning in the year 2010, must have obtained 150 semester hours of education at an accredited college or university.

- NonCPA owners are permitted to use the title "principal," "owner," "officer," "member" or "shareholder," or any other title permitted by state law, but not to hold themselves out to be CPAs.

- NonCPA owners have to abide by the AICPA Code of Professional Conduct. AICPA members may be held responsible under the Code for acts of co-owners.

---

[45] Rule 503, *Commissions and Referral Fees* (AICPA, *Professional Standards,* vol. 2, ET sec. 503.01).

[46] Rule 505, *Form of Organization and Name* (AICPA, *Professional Standards,* vol. 2, ET sec. 505.01).

¶ 205.06

- NonCPA owners have to complete the same work-related continuing professional education (CPE) requirements as CPAs.

- Owners must at all times own their equity in their own right and shall be the beneficial owners of the equity capital ascribed to them. Provision would have to be made for the ownership to be transferred within a reasonable period of time, to the firm or to other qualified owners if the owner ceases to be actively engaged in the firm.

- NonCPA owners are not eligible for membership in the AICPA.

¶ 206 SEC Enforcement Rules

The SEC performs three major functions:

1. Regulates public companies and establishes the qualifications of their independent auditors
2. Enforces the Securities Act of 1933 and the Securities Exchange Act of 1934
3. Administers these acts and specifies the basic independence policy in Rule 2.01 and other guidance

The SEC through federal legislation has basically granted a monopoly to the accounting profession to audit and report on the financial statements of publicly traded companies. Issuers seeking to register securities with the SEC must file financial statements that have been certified by independent public accountants.[47] The SEC has expressed authority to regulate the form and content of financial statements required to issue stocks and securities.

.01 SEC Rule of Practice 102(e)

SEC Rule 102(e) addresses misconduct of auditors and other professionals in order to protect investors. This expansive rule allows the SEC to impose sanctions in any case when, after giving notice and an opportunity for a hearing, auditors are found:

- Not to possess the requisite qualifications to represent others,
- To be lacking in character or integrity or to have engaged in unethical or improper professional conduct, or
- To have willfully violated, or willfully aided and abetted the violation of any provision of the federal securities laws or the rules and regulations thereunder.[48]

A violation occurs if an auditor acts with a bad intent knowingly or recklessly. *Recklessly* is defined as an "extreme departure from the standards of ordinary care."[49]

---

[47] 15 U.S.C. § 77s(a).
[48] 17 CFR § 201.102(e).

[49] *Sunstrand Corp. v. Sun Chemical Corp.*, 553 F.2d 1033 (7th Cir. 1977).

Three types of conduct apply specifically to accountants in determining improper professional conduct:

1. Intentional or knowing conduct, including reckless conduct, that results in a violation of applicable professional standards;
2. A single instance of highly unreasonable conduct that results in a violation of applicable professional standards in circumstances in which the accountant knows, or should know, that heightened scrutiny is warranted; or
3. Repeated instances of unreasonable conduct each resulting in a violation of applicable professional standards.

During the period from 1987 through 1997, the SEC alleged fraud deficiencies in auditors performing audit engagements. All of the situations involved public companies; most involved fraudulent financial reporting (rather than misappropriation of assets). The top 10 alleged deficiencies claimed by the SEC during this period are listed in Table 2.2.

Table 2.2

Fraud Deficiencies Claimed by the SEC for 1987–1997

Problem Area	Percentage (Number of cases)
1. Gathering sufficient audit evidence.	80% (36)
2. Exercising due professional care.	71% (32)
3. Demonstrating appropriate level of professional skepticism.	60% (27)
4. Interpreting or applying requirements of GAAP.	49% (22)
5. Designing audit programs and planning engagement (inherent risk issues, nonroutine transactions).	44% (20)
6. Using inquiry as form of evidence (relying too much on this method).	40% (18)
7. Obtaining adequate evidence related to the evaluation of significant management estimates (failing to gather sufficient evidence).	36% (16)
8. Confirming accounts receivable.	29% (13)
9. Recognizing/disclosing key related parties.	27% (12)
10. Relying on internal controls (rely too much/failing to react to known control weaknesses).	24% (11)

Source: M.S. Beasley, J.V. Carcello, and D.R. Hermanson, "Top 10 Audit Deficiencies," *Journal of Accountancy,* April 2001, p. 65. Copyright 1999, 2001 American Institute of Certified Public Accountants, Inc. Opinions of the authors are their own and do not necessarily reflect policies of the AICPA. Reprinted with permission.

¶ **206.01**

Track SEC enforcement action on the internet at *www.gov/enforce.htm.*

Firms that audit SEC-registered companies have three alternatives if any of its audit engagement partners are investigated in connection with litigation alleging deficiencies in auditing:

1. Terminate or retire the partner

2. Remove the partner from performing or supervising public company audits until the AICPA has completed its ethics enforcement process

3. Subject the partner to additional oversight for at least one year on all public company audit engagements in which he or she is involved

If another firm hires the partner, that firm must assume the disciplinary responsibility.

In June 2001, the SEC fined Arthur Andersen a $7 million civil penalty for false and misleading audits of Waste Management Inc. from 1992 through 1996. In addition, Arthur Andersen settled the first antifraud injunction in more than 20 years against an accounting firm. The SEC asserted that the accounting firm issued a clean opinion on the trash hauler's financial statements that overstated pretax income by more than $1 billion. SEC's Richard Walker commented at the outcome of the suit that the SEC "will not shy away from pursuing accountants and accounting firms when they fail to live up to their responsibilities to ensure the integrity of the financial reporting process.[50] The SEC is one of only a few federal agencies to use its disciplinary rule routinely and aggressively.

With respect to Waste Management, the SEC said that the CPA firm knew that the company was exaggerating its profits throughout the early and mid-1990s but continued to certify their financial statements. A civil fraud complaint against three Arthur Andersen partners, fined each $30,000 to $50,000 and banned them from auditing public companies for up to five years.

The problem is that GAAP and GAAS do not constitute a clear and simple "Bible" for auditing purposes. As pointed out by Judge Randolph in 1994:

> The complexity of generally accepted accounting principles and generally accepted auditing standards is belied, and perhaps obscured, by their familiar acronyms.... *Accounting principles must be interpreted. Judgments must be made about specific transactions.* [R]easonable preparers of financial statements—often management—and auditors can disagree about those interpretations and judgments.[51]

---

[50] "Arthur Andersen Fined $7 Million by SEC," *http://biz.yahoo.com,* June 19, 2001.

[51] *Checkosky I,* 23 F3d 452 (D.C. Cir. 1994).

¶ 206.01

PricewaterhouseCoopers made the following comment to Proposed Amendments to Rule 102(e):

> [GAAP and GAAS] are not cookbook recipes, where reading words and following directions result in a uniform outcome. Resolutions of many auditing and accounting issues require judgment. Even where there is written guidance, there is often ambiguity. The accountant must attempt to synthesize practice and different pronouncements that may speak ambiguously or indirectly to the issue and that many have changed over time. What the proposed amendment labels as a "violation of professional standards" is apt to be, in practice, a difference of opinion between the Commission's staff and the respondent accountant over how a particular pronouncement or pronouncements should be applied.[52]

Although some authorities believe that the SEC lacks the legal authority to adopt a negligence standard under Rule 102(e),[53] the SEC can destroy the practice of auditors. A comment from a judge indicates the damage that a Rule 102(e) disciplinary proceeding can do to an auditor:

> A proceeding under Rule 2(e) threatens "to deprive a person of a way of life to which he has devoted years of preparation and on which he and his family have come to rely ... It is of little comfort to an auditor defending against such charges that the Commission's authority is limited to suspending him from agency practice. For many public accountants such work represents their entire livelihood. Moreover, when one jurisdiction suspends a professional it can start a chain reaction.[54]

Even an ultimate vindication can still have a career-crippling effect upon an auditor.

An example of the SEC using Rule 102(e) as an intimidating device to police accountants occurred in 2000. An SEC order alleged that PricewaterhouseCoopers violated the SEC's independence rules by certifying its independence while certain of its professional personnel owned securities of some of its publicly held audit clients (8,000 violations). Although the SEC has no authority to impose a fine or penalty under Rule 102(e), the firm had to establish a $2.5 million fund to use within 12 months to further the awareness and education throughout the profession relating to independence.[55]

In 1999, the SEC imposed severe penalties against an auditing team of Coopers and Lybrand because they gave California Micros Services Corporation a clean bill of health, even though the company wrote off about one-half of its accounts receivable because of product returns. The SEC took action to bar the engagement partner and the engagement manager from signing off on public audits. They were accused of conducting the audit in a vacuum and recklessly ignoring unmistakable red flags.

---

[52] *Comment Letter 116 to Proposed Amendment to Rule 102(e),* 1998, p. 6.

[53] Norman S. Johnson and Ross A. Albert, "Déjà vu All Over Again: The SEC Once More Attempts to Regulate the Accounting Profession Through Rule 102(e) of Its Rules of Practice," *Utah Law Review* (1999 No. 2): 555.

[54] *Checkosky I,* 23 F.3d 479 (D.C. Cir. 1994).

[55] Exchange Act Release No. 40, 945 (January 14, 1999).

¶ 207 The Oversight Organization

As a result of the Enron debacle, Harvey Pitt, the head of the SEC, proposed a new industry organization to oversee disciplinary reviews of accountants. This new private-sector body was supposed to replace the current disciplinary oversight function performed by both the AICPA and the Public Oversight Board. To be funded by fees from corporate audit clients, the members were supposed to be independent of the accounting profession.[56]

On news of the proposed oversight organization, the existing Public Oversight Board (POB) voted itself out of existence in protest to Mr. Pitt's position. The POB was created to oversee and report on the self-regulatory programs of the AICPA's SEC Practice Section, which consisted principally of the AICPA's peer review and quality assurance programs. Critics maintain that the peer-review process has been a failure, citing the fact that days before Arthur Andersen shredded thousands of pages involving the Enron audit, Deloitte & Touche gave Arthur Andersen a glowing peer-review report.[57]

A special study by the Dean of the University of Texas Law School reported that Arthur Andersen was paid $5.7 million to review and approve the setup of the special purpose entities that were used by Enron to increase shareholder equity by $1.2 billion. And so Andersen auditors may have been called upon to scrutinize financial dealings that other Andersen accountants had helped create. Auditors, of course, must be extremely careful in all of their audits and must not allow a supervisor or client to force any unethical or illegal acts or omissions. No matter what the outcome for Andersen or its partners, the Enron situation has taken its toll on the accounting community as a whole.

The following statement from an article in Fortune magazine describes the environment in which the accounting profession finds itself:

> Fudged numbers. Off-balance-sheet rigamarole. Perpetual nonrecurring items. Funny business with the numbers is what I'm talking about. That is a huge issue that is only getting huger. Fact: The balance sheets and income statements of American companies have become like so many rotten apples, which is a crying shame. We used to have the best, most transparent system of financial reporting in the world. That may still be the case (a sad commentary on the rest of the planet), but our 10-Ks and 10-Qs ain't what they used to be. Will there be another Enron this year? I wouldn't be at all surprised.[58]

---

[56] Michael Schroeder, "SEC Proposes Accounting Disciplinary Body," *Wall Street Journal*, January 17, 2002, p. C-1.

[57] Jonathan Weil and S.J. Paltrow, "Peer Pressure: SEC Exposes Accountants," *Wall Street Journal*, January 29, 2002, p. C-1.

[58] Andy Serwer, "Why 2002 is Looking Good," *Fortune* (January 21, 2002): 119.

¶ 208 SEC on Independence

A zealous SEC heavily regulates public companies auditing by its influence over GAAS and GAAP, which apply to publicly traded companies. On February 5, 2001, the SEC adopted a number of strict rules with respect to non-audit services that impacts the auditor's independence. Of course, it is often difficult to distinguish between attest work and non-attest services. Although these rules tend to apply to accounting firms with SEC clients, many of the rules may be used against all auditors in malpractice situations. Keep in mind that non-audit services may be an important part of many smaller practices.

SEC Rule 2-01 (a) of Regulation S-X provides that an accountant must be in good standing and entitled to practice in the state of the auditor's residence or principal office. An accountant will not be recognized as independent if the accountant is not (or if a reasonable investor would conclude that the accountant is not) capable of exercising objective and impartial judgment on all issues encompassed within the accountant's engagement.

Effective February 5, 2001, the SEC adopted a Rule 2-01 revision that provides stricter auditor independence rules. On January 16, 2001, the SEC issued preliminary guidance to certain questions. The SEC believes that if investors do not believe that an auditor is independent of the company being audited, they will obtain little confidence from the auditor's opinion and will be unlikely to invest in that company. The SEC refers to independence as a mental state of objectivity and lack of bias. The first prong of the standard is independence in fact. The second prong states that independence can be assessed only by the observation of external factors. These independence rules apply only to public companies and other entities registered with the SEC or otherwise required to file audited financial statements with the SEC.

The SEC is trying to determine whether a relationship or the provision of a service (a) creates a mutual or conflicting interest between the accountant and the client, (b) places the accountant in a position of auditing his or her own work, (c) results in the accountant acting as management or an employee of the audit client, and (d) places the accountant in the position of being an advocate for the audit client. The SEC's bright-line test assesses these factors: an auditor is not independent if he or she maintains the relationship, acquires the interest, or engages in the transactions specified by the rule.

.01 Five Violations

The SEC lists five situations in which an accountant violates the independence rule:

1. Financial relationship

2. Employment relationship

3. Business relationship

4. Transactions or situations involving non-audit services

5. Transactions or situations involving the receipt of contingent fees

.02 Direct Financial Interest

An auditor is not independent if during an audit or professional engagement period, the accountant (or close family member) has a direct financial interest or a material indirect financial interest in the audit client (that includes some affiliates of the client). A professional engagement period begins at the earlier of when the accountant either signs an initial engagement letter (or another agreement) or begins review, audit, or test procedures. A close family member is a person's spouse, spouse equivalent, parent, dependent, nondependent child, or sibling. The following constitute a financial interest:

- A covered person in the firm or an immediate family member has a direct investment (such as stock, bonds, notes, options, or other securities) in the audit client.

- Any loan, including a margin loan, to or from an audit client, or an audit client's officers, directors, or beneficial owners of more than 10 percent of the audit client's equity securities.

- Any savings, checking, or similar account is maintained in a bank, savings and loan, or similar institution that is an audit client, if the account has a balance that exceeds the amount insured by the FDIC.

- Any brokerage or similar accounts are maintained with a broker-dealer that have assets other than cash or securities.

- Futures, commodity, or similar accounts are maintained with the futures commission merchant.

- Outstanding credit card balances exceed $10,000.

- Individual life insurance policy is maintained by a company that may become insolvent.

- A financial interest is maintained in an entity of an investment company.

- Any inheritance or gift that is not disposed of in fewer than 30 days.

.03 Employment Relationship

An employment relationship between the accountant (or family member) and an audit client shows a lack of independence. Some examples provided by the SEC include the following:

- A partner serves as a member of the board of directors of an audit client.
- The sibling or spouse of a covered person is employed by an audit client as the internal auditor.
- A former professional employee of an accounting firm who resigned from the accounting firm two years ago is employed by an auditor's practice in an accounting role, and the former employee receives a pension from the firm tied to the firm's revenue or profits.
- A former partner of an accounting firm accepts the position of chief accounting officer at a client, and the former partner continues to maintain a capital balance with the accounting firm.
- A former director of a client becomes a partner of the accounting firm and that individual participates in the audit of the financial statements of the client for a period during which he or she was a director of the client.

.04 Business Relationship

An auditor's independence is impaired when the accounting firm or covered person has a direct or material indirect business relationship with the client or any person associated with the client in a decision-making capacity (e.g., client's officers, directors, or substantial shareholders). Joint ventures, limited partnerships, investments in supplier or customer companies, certain leasing interests and sales by the accountant of items other than professional services are examples of business relationships that may impair an accountant's independence.

.05 Non-audit Services

An accountant is not independent if he or she also provides any of these non-audit services:

- Bookkeeping and other services related to the audit client's accounting records or financial statements. Independence is impaired if an auditor has participated closely, either manually or through its computer services, in maintenance of basic accounting records and preparation of financial statements.
- Financial information system design and implementation. An auditor must not directly or indirectly operate, or supervise the

¶ 208.05

operation of the audit client's information system, or manage the audit client's local area network. Designing or implementing a hardware or software system that aggregates source data underlying the financial statements or generates information that is significant to the audit client's financial statement may impair independence.

- Appraisal or valuation services and fairness opinions. There are restrictions on appraisal and valuation services, but there are exceptions for valuations conducted as part of tax planning or tax compliance services.

- Actuarial services, except in four situations, including services for federal income tax purposes.

- Internal auditing services. An auditor's independence is impaired by performing more than 40 percent of a client's internal auditing work that relates to internal controls, financial systems, or financial statements, unless the client has $200 million or less in assets. In both situations the auditor must comply with six conditions, including that management must not rely on the auditor's work as the primary basis for determining the adequacy of internal controls. Operational internal auditing is not included in this prohibition.

- Acting as management.

- Certain human resources services.

- Investment decisions for the audit client, discretionary trading authority over a client's account, execution of transactions for an audit client, or possession of their assets.

- Legal services for a client (i.e., a service for which the person providing the service must be admitted to practice before the courts of a U.S. jurisdiction). This rule does not prohibit an auditor from being an expert witness.

Accounting critics argue that Arthur Andersen failed to detect financial problems at Enron because the accounting firm played a double role: independent auditor and internal auditor. Enron began outsourcing its internal auditing work to Arthur Andersen around 1985, so, in effect, the auditing firm was auditing its own work. In 2000, Enron paid Andersen $25 million for audit fees and $27 million for other services, including consulting and tax services. Enron was Arthur Andersen's second largest U.S. client.[59] In early February 2002, Walt Disney stated that the company would no longer purchase consulting services from the same accounting firm

---

[59] Jonathan Weil, "Double Enron Role Played by Andersen Raises Questions," *Wall Street Journal*, December 14, 2001, p. A-4.

¶ 208.05

that audits its books. Other large public corporations have followed. At about the same time the AICPA Board announced they support prohibitions on auditors of public companies from providing financial systems design and implementation, and internal auditing outsourcing.

.06 Contingent Fees

Contingent fees from audit clients are prohibited, except for fees fixed by the courts or other public authorities, in tax matters, and fees based on the results of judicial proceedings or the findings of government agencies. Value-added fees are allowable.

.07 Engagement Team Approach

The SEC uses an audit engagement team approach for determining a covered person for independence purposes. An audit engagement team includes those people who are more directly in a position to influence an audit. Persons in the chain of command are also considered to be covered persons. The chain of command includes those person who (a) supervise or have direct management responsibility for the audit, including at all successively senior levels through the accounting firm's chief executive; (b) evaluate the performance or recommend the compensation of the audit engagement partner; or (c) provide quality control or other oversight of the audit.

A covered person also includes any other partner, principal, shareholder, or managerial employee who is involved in providing any professional service to the audit client (or affiliate). Any other partner, principal, or shareholder from an office of an accounting firm in which the lead audit engagement partner primarily practices in connection with the audit is a covered person. This engagement team approach means that fewer employees are covered by the independence rule.

¶ 209 Independence Standards Board

Between 1997 and 2001, a special board, the Independence Standards Board (ISB), worked as a change agent and official communication conduit on the independence issue. The independence issue itself is so important to the accounting profession and the task of establishing rules so daunting a task that in 1997 the Independence Standards Board was created through an agreement between the SEC and the AICPA. The purpose of the ISB was to initiate research, develop standards, and engage in a public analysis and debate on auditor independence issues.

During its existence, the ISB issued three pronouncements: Statement No. 1—*Independence Discussions with Audit Committees,* Statement No. 2—*Certain Independence Implications of Audits of Mutual Funds and Related Entities,* and Statement No. 3—*Employment with Audit Clients.* The ISB also issued Interpretations, Staff Interpretations, Discussion Memos and Exposure Drafts. Much of the ISB's work was incorporated into the SEC's new auditor independence rules already addressed in this chapter. With the adoption of the SEC's new rules and the strengthening of the AICPA's Professional Ethics Executive Committee it was determined that the ISB had largely fulfilled its mission. The ISB was disbanded on July 17, 2001, by the SEC and the AICPA with the agreement of members of the ISB. As we go to press, the ISB website can still be accessed at *www.cpaindependence.org.*

¶ 210 Interpretation of AICPA Independence Rule

Independence is the cornerstone of the accounting profession, and the AICPA also has adopted an engagement team approach to the independence rule, rather than a firmwide approach. Interpretation No. 101-1, "Interpretation of Rule 101," [60] provides that an auditor is not independent where the individual who participates in the attest engagement knows that his or her close relative (e.g., parent, sibling, nondependent child) has a material financial interest in the attest client.

For example, suppose an audit manager's spouse were hired as a CFO of one of the firm's audit clients. Under the firmwide approach the spouse would have to resign from the firm, or the firm would have to terminate its relationship with the audit client. However, if the employee were a tax manager rather than an audit manager, the firm might have been able to insulate the tax manager from the audit.

Interpretation 101-1 states that independence is impaired if, during the period of the attest engagement, a covered employee:

- Has or is committed to acquire any direct or material indirect interest in the client;

- Is a trustee of any trust or executor or administrator of any estate, if such trust or estate has or is committed to acquire any direct or material indirect financial interest in the client;

- Has any material joint, closely held business investment with the client, any officer, or director of the client, or any shareholders thereof who has the ability to exercise significant influence over the audit client; or

- Has any loan to or from the client, any officer, or director of the client, or any shareholder who has the ability to exercise significant influence over the client. Independence is also impaired if any partner or professional employee of the firm or immediate family has a financial interest that resulted in the ability to exercise significant influence over the audit client.

---

[60] Interpretation No. 101-1, "Interpretation of Rule 101," of ET section 101, *Independence* (AICPA, Professional Standards, ET secs. 101.02 and 101.11).

Similarly, an impairment occurs if a partner in the firm, or a professional employee in the office in which the lead attest engagement partner primarily practices also is associated with the client as a director, officer, or employee, or in any capacity equivalent to that of a member of management. If a member does not have and could not be expected to have knowledge of a relationship or financial interest, the member's independence is not impaired.

An auditor can exercise significant influence under the Code over the operating, financial, or accounting policies of another entity, if for example, the person or entity:

- Is connected with the entity as a promoter, underwriter, voting trustee, general partner or director (other than an honorary director as defined in the AICPA Code of Professional Conduct);

- Is connected with the entity in a policy-making position related to the entity's primary operating, financial, or accounting policies, such as chief executive officer, chief operating officer, chief financial officer, or chief accounting officer; and

- Meets the criteria established in Accounting Principles Board Opinion No. 18, The Equity Method of Accounting for Investments in Common Stock [AC section I83], and its interpretations to determine the ability of an investor to exercise such influence with respect to an entity.

.01 Former Employee

If a former officer, director, or employee of a client or an individual formerly associated with the client as a promoter, underwriter, voting trustee, or trustee for a pension or profit-sharing trust of the client is in a position to influence the attest engagement or participated on the attest engagement team, independence may be impaired. However, a former employee providing 10 or more hours of nonattest service to the client or the partner in the office is not considered to be impaired if he or she ceases to participate or liquidates the interest in any retirement plan.

.02 Financial Interest of a Next of Kin

Independence is impaired if a partner or professional employee of an audit firm or his or her immediate family has a financial interest in the client company. Such an interest may result in the ability to exercise significant influence over the audit client. Alternatively, the client may influence the auditor's conclusions if his or her financial interst would be damaged from a negative report.

Independence is not impaired if the person is employed by the client in a non-key position. Also exempted is a family member who participates in a retirement, savings, compensation, or similar plan that is sponsored by a client or that invests in a client, provided the plan normally is offered to all

¶ 210.02

employees in a similar position. However, if the close relative has a key position with the client (of which the attest engagement team member has knowledge) or a financial interest (enabling the close relative to exercise significant influence), independence is impaired.

The independence of an auditor or a firm may be impaired by a nondependent close relative. Close relatives are nondependent children, grandchildren, stepchildren, brothers, sisters, grandparents, parents, parents-in-law, and their respective spouses. Close relatives do not include the brothers and sisters of the covered employee's spouse. If a nondependent has a material financial interest or could exercise a significant influence over the operating, financial, or accounting policies of the client, independence is impaired.

.03 Former Practitioner

A former practitioner is defined as a proprietor, partner, shareholder, or equivalent who leaves by resignation, termination, retirement, or sale of all or part of the practice. Such a former practitioner in a position of influence with the client should not be provided with office space and related amenities by his or her former firm. A former practitioner now related to a client should not participate in the firm's business or professional activities or appear to participate in the activities of, or associated with his or her former firm.

.04 Loans

In general, a covered employee's independence is impaired if he or she has any loans to or from the client or any officer, director, or principal shareholder of the client. There are exceptions to this rule, including grandfathered home mortgages, automobile loans, and loans fully collateralized by cash deposits at the same financial institution and unpaid.

.05 Other Services

A number of non-attest services prepared for an audit client may impair independence. An accounting firm must not perform management functions or make management decisions for the attest client. The Code outlines some responsibilities that suggest that an auditor has such a managerial position:

- Continuing responsibility for the overall planning and supervision of engagements for specified clients

- Authority to determine that an engagement is complete subject to final partner approval (if required)

- Responsibility for client relationships (for example, negotiating and collecting fees for engagements and marketing the firm's services)

¶ 210.03

- Existence of profit sharing as a significant feature of total compensation

- Responsibility for overall management of the firm, development, or establishment of firm policies on technical matters, and implementation of or compliance with the following five elements of quality control:

    1. Independence, integrity and objectivity
    2. Personal management
    3. Acceptance and continuation of clients and engagements
    4. Engagement performance and
    5. Monitoring

Before performing these other services, a firm should establish an understanding in an engagement letter with the client regarding the objectives of the engagement, the services to be performed, management's responsibilities, the member's responsibilities, and the limitations of the engagement. See Chapter 3 for a discussion of an engagement letter. Also, the auditor should be satisfied that the client is in a position to have an informed judgment on the results of the other services and that the client understands its responsibility to:

- Designate a management-level individual or individuals to be responsible for overseeing the services being provided

- Evaluate the adequacy of the services performed and any findings that result

- Make management decisions, including accepting responsibility for the results of the other services

- Establish and maintain internal controls, including monitoring ongoing activities

The AICPA Code gives the following examples that would impair an auditor's independence:

- Authorizing, executing, or consummating a transaction, or otherwise exercising authority on behalf of a client, or having the authority to do so

- Preparing source *documents* or originating data, in electronic or other form, evidencing the occurrence of a transaction (for example, purchase orders, payroll time records, and customer orders)

- Having custody of client assets

¶ 210.05

- Supervising client employees in the performance of their recurring activities
- Determining which recommendations of the member should be implemented
- Reporting to the board of directors on behalf of management
- Serving as a client's stock transfer or escrow agent, registrar, general counsel, or its equivalent

.06 Illustration of Non-Attest Services that Impair Independence

Interpretation 101-3 provides a table, adapted here as Table 2.3, which identifies the impact that other services for an attest client can have on a firm's independence:

Table 2.3

Other Services Performed for Clients That Impair Auditor's Independence

Actions That Do Not Impair Independence	*Actions That Impair Independence*
Bookkeeping	
Record transactions for which management has determined or approved the appropriate account classification, or post coded transactions to a client's general ledger.	Determine or change journal entries, account codings or classification of transactions, or other accounting records without obtaining client approval.
Prepare financial statements based on information in the trial balance.	Authorize or approve transactions.
Post client-approved entries to a client's trial balance.	Prepare source documents or originate data.
Propose standard, adjusting, or correcting journal entries or other changes affecting the financial statements to the client.	Make changes to source documents without client approval.
Provide data processing services.	

¶ 210.06

Standards of Professional Conduct

Actions That Do Not Impair Independence	Actions That Impair Independence
Payroll and other disbursement	
Using payroll time records provided and approved by the client, generate unsigned checks, or process client's payroll.	Accept responsibility to authorize payment of client funds, electronically or otherwise, except as specifically provided for with respect to electronic payroll tax payments.
Transmit client-approved payroll or other disbursement information to a financial institution, provided the client has authorized the member to make the transmission and has made arrangements for the financial institution to limit the corresponding individual payments as to amount and payee. In addition, once transmitted, the client must authorize the financial institution to process the information.	Accept responsibility to sign or cosign client checks, even if only in emergency situations.
Make electronic payroll tax payments in accordance with U.S. Treasury Department or comparable guidelines provided the client has made arrangements for its financial institution to limit such payments to a named payee.	Maintain a client's bank account or otherwise have custody of a client's funds or make credit or banking decisions for the client.
	Sign payroll tax return on behalf of client management.
	Approve vendor invoices for payment.

¶ 210.06

Actions That Do Not Impair Independence	Actions That Impair Independence
Benefit plan administration	
Communicate summary plan data to plan trustee.	Make policy decisions on behalf of client management.
Advise client management regarding the application or impact of provisions of the plan document.	When dealing with plan participants, interpret the plan document on behalf of management without first obtaining management's concurrence.
Process transactions (e.g., investment/benefit elections or increases/decreases of contributions to the plan; data entry; participant confirmations; and processing of distributions and loans) initiated by plan participants through the member's electronic medium, such as an interactive voice response system or Internet connection.	Make disbursements on behalf of the plan.
Prepare account valuations for plan participants using data collected through the member's electronic or other medium.	Have custody of assets of a plan.
Prepare and transmit participant statements to plan participants based on data collected through the member's electronic or other medium.	Serve a plan as a fiduciary as defined by ERISA.

¶ 210.06

Investments—advisory or management

Actions That Do Not Impair Independence	Actions That Impair Independence
Recommend the allocation of funds that a client should invest in various asset classes, depending upon the client's desired rate of return, risk tolerance, etc.	Make investment decisions on behalf of client management or otherwise have discretionary authority over a client's investments.
Perform record-keeping and reporting of client's portfolio balances, including providing a comparative analysis of the client's investments to third-party benchmarks.	Execute a transaction to buy or sell a client's investment.
Review the manner in which a client's portfolio is being managed by investment account managers, including determining whether the managers are (a) following the guidelines of the client's investment policy statement; (b) meeting the client's investment objectives; and (c) conforming to the client's stated investment styles.	Have custody of client assets, such as taking temporary possession of securities purchased by a client.
	Transmit a client's investment selection to a broker-dealer or equivalent provided the client has authorized the broker-dealer or equivalent to execute the transaction.

¶ 210.06

Actions That Do Not Impair Independence	Actions That Impair Independence
Corporate finance—consulting or advisory	
Assist in developing corporate strategies.	Commit the client to the terms of a transaction or consummate a transaction on behalf of the client.
Assist in identifying or introducing the client to possible sources of capital that meet the client's specifications or criteria.	Act as a promoter, underwriter, broker-dealer, or guarantor of client securities, or distributor of private placement memoranda or offering documents.
Assist in analyzing the effects of proposed transactions including providing advice to a client during negotiations with potential buyers, sellers, or capital sources.	Maintain custody of client securities.
Assist in drafting an offering document or memorandum.	
Participate in transaction negotiations in an advisory capacity.	
Be named as a financial adviser in a client's private placement memoranda or offering documents.	
Appraisal, valuation, or actuarial	
Test the reasonableness of the value placed on an asset or liability included in a client's financial statements by preparing a separate valuation of that asset or liability.	Prepare a valuation of an employer's securities contained in an employee stock ownership plan (ESOP) to support transactions with participants, plan contributions, and allocations within the ESOP, when the client is not in a position to have an informed judgment on the results of this valuation.
Perform a valuation of a client's business when all significant matters of judgment are determined or approved by the client and the client is in a position to have an informed judgment on the results of the valuation.	Prepare an appraisal, valuation, or actuarial report using assumptions determined by the member and not approved by the client.

¶ 210.06

Standards of Professional Conduct

Actions That Do Not Impair Independence	Actions That Impair Independence
Executive or employee search	
Recommend a position description or candidate specifications.	Commit the client to employee compensation or benefits.
Solicit and perform screening of candidates and recommend qualified candidates to a client based on the client-approved criteria (e.g., required skills and experience).	Hire or terminate client employees.
Participate in employee hiring or compensation discussions in an advisory capacity.	
Business risk consulting	
Providing assistance in assessing the client's business risks and control processes.	Make or approve business risk decisions.
Recommend a plan for making improvements to a client's control processes and assist in implementing these improvements.	Present business risk considerations to the board or others on behalf of management.
Information systems—design, installation, or integration	
Design, install, or integrate a client's information system, provided the client makes all management decisions.	Supervise client personnel in the daily operation of a client's information system.
Customize a prepackaged accounting or information system, provided the client makes all management decisions.	Operate a client's local area network (LAN) system when the client has not designated a competent individual, preferably within senior management, to be responsible for the LAN.
Provide the initial training and instruction to client employees on a newly implemented information and control system.	

Source: Interpretation No. 101-3, "Performance of Other Services," of ET section 101, *Independence,* (AICPA, *Professional Standards,* vol. 2, ET sec. 101.05) copyright 1990, 1999, 2001 by the American Institute of Certifed Public Accountants, Inc., used with permission.

¶ 210.06

.07 Litigation

Independence may be impaired for the current audit as a result of litigation or the intent to commence litigation between a CPA firm and a client. If a client sues an accountant alleging deficiencies in the previous audit, the auditor is not independent for the current audit. Likewise, if a firm sues an audit client alleging management fraud or deceit, the auditor is not independent for the current audit. Litigation as a result of disputes as to billings for services, tax, or other nonaudit services does not impair independence (see Chapter 3).

Litigation by security holders against management and an accounting firm does not necessarily result in impaired independence. Also, a third-party suit, such as might be brought by an insurance company, against management and the auditor does not necessarily result in lack of independence.

.08 Some Internet Sites About Independence

Following are websites offering information and rules about maintaining independence in an auditing practice.

- **AICPA:** www.aicpa.org/members/div/ethics/ethicdiv.htm
- **IFAC:** www.ifac.org/Members/Source_Files/Exposure_Drafts/EXD-Eth-Final_Independence.pdf
- **SEC:** www.sec.gov/rules/final/33-7919.htm

¶ 211 Other Standards of Professional Conduct

The Institute of Internal Auditors (IIA) has a Professional Practices framework, which includes three categories of guidance: mandatory Ethics and Standards, nonmandatory Practice Advisories, and Development & Practice Aids. The new standards are effective January 1, 2002, and the so-called Red Book is in effect until the adoption of these new standards. The IIA's Code of Ethics are in Appendix 2, and the *Standards for the Professional Practice in Internal Auditing* appear in Appendix 3.

¶ 212 Possible Future Initiatives

As a result of the Enron affair, Chairman Harvey L. Pitt of the SEC discussed many new initiatives that may address accounting problems. His suggested improvements are summarized as follows:[61]

- More current disclosure, including "real-time" disclosure of unquestionably material information

---

[61] Testimony of R.K. Herdman "Testimony Concerning Recent Events Relating to Enron," U.S. House of Representatives, December 12, 2001.

- Disclosure of significant trend data and more "evaluative" data
- Financial statements that are more clear and informative for investors
- Disclosure of the accounting principles that are most critical to the company's financial status and that involve complex or subjective decisions by management
- Private sector standard setting that is more responsive to the current and immediate needs of investors
- A regulatory environment that continues, as always has been the case, to encourage public companies and questions so that they may "get it right the first time" and avoid restatements and the possibility of enforcement proceedings
- A comprehensive and effective self-regulatory process for the accounting profession, as discussed above, with effective oversight by the Commission and its staff
- More involvement by audit committees with management and the auditors regarding the selection and application of accounting principles used by the company
- Analysts not expressing views or recommendations when they do not have an adequate data foundation or when confused by company presentations

Many leaders in the accounting profession announced their intention to assist the SEC in these efforts. However, on April 16, 2003, the Public Company Accounting Oversight Board basically announced that they would set auditing, attestation, quality control, and ethical standards for public accounting firms.

¶ 213 Strengthening Auditor Independence Post-Sarbanes-Oxley Act

Strengthening auditor independence post-Sarbanes-Oxley Act of 2002 requires proactive actions on the part of the audit committee, management, and registered auditors.

.01 The Audit Committee

The Sarbanes-Oxley Act requires that the audit committee be in charge of hiring, retaining, firing, compensating, and overseeing the function of auditors. Thus, the audit committee should develop a working relationship with registered auditors that promotes effective cooperation and candid communication and discussion. The audit committee is also authorized to approve audit services and permissible non-audit services. The audit committee must ensure the enforcement of registered auditors' partner rotation and compensation requirements. The audit committee

¶ 213.01

should also spend quality and quantity time with registered auditors to preserve their independence and promote audit effectiveness.

.02 Management

Management should recognize and accept the changes in the balance of power-sharing with the audit committee, particularly the changes in the reporting relationship of the auditor with the audit committee. Management should establish a proper disclosure system to collect all necessary information for fees paid to auditors for both audit and non-audit services in four categories: (1) audit fees for an annual audit of financial statements and a quarterly review of financial statements, (2) audit-related fees for attestation on internal control and assurance services, (3) tax services fees (for compliance, planning, and advice), and (4) other fees (advisory, consulting, services, and non-audit research). Management should also comply with the requirement of the Sarbanes-Oxley Act by observing a one year cooling-off period and not hire any member of an audit team for a financial reporting oversight position. Management must comply with Act Sec. 303(a) of the Sarbanes-Oxley Act and to SEC related rules that prohibit directors and executives from coercing, manipulating, misleading, or fraudulently influencing the auditor who audits financial statements.

.03 Registered Auditor

Registered auditors, in preserving their independence according to the requirements of the Sarbanes-Oxley Act and new standards of the PCAOB, should revise their system of quality control with the following provisions:

- Inform and educate partners and staff about the importance of auditor independence, both in fact and in appearance, and its impact on audit quality and credibility.

- Develop direct communication, professional working relationships, and reporting practices with the audit committee.

- Obtain audit committee preapprovals for audit services as well as permissible non-audit services.

- Comply with the partner compensation, partner rotation, and the audit team (staff and partners) cooling-off period requirements of the Sarbanes-Oxley Act.

- Observe the emerging PCAOB standards on ethics, quality control, attestation, and auditing.

¶ 214 PCAOB's Standard-Setting Process

Act Sec. 103 of the Sarbanes-Oxley Act of 2002 authorizes the PCAOB to establish auditing, attestation, quality control, ethics, and independent standards for registered accounting firms. The PCAOB, in April 2003, adopted Interim Professional Standards (IPS) during the transition period to assure continuity in compliance with standards governing audits of public companies. The adopted Interim Professional Standards are existing standards promulgated by the AICPA and are classified by the PCAOB into the following five categories:[62]

1. Rule 3200T—Interim Auditing Standards
2. Rule 3300T—Interim Attestation Standards
3. Rule 3400T—Interim Quality Control Standards
4. Rule 3500T—Interim Ethics Standards
5. Rule 3600T—Interim Independence Standards

Table 2.4 presents these five categories of interim standards and related guides, interpretations, and rules.

Table 2.4

Interim Standards and Related Guides, Interpretations, and Rules

Rule	Standards	Professional Guides, Interpretations, and Rules
3200T	Interim Auditing Standards	1. Generally Accepted Auditing Standards (GAAS) previously issued by the AICPA 2. Statements on Auditing Standards (SAS) as of April 16, 2003 3. Auditing interpretations 4. AICPA Accounting and Auditing Guides 5. Auditing Statements of Position
3300T	Interim Attestation Standards	1. Attestation Standards 2. Attestation Interpretations 3. Attestation Statements of Position
3400T	Interim Quality Control Standards	1. Statements on Quality Control Standards 2. SEC Practice Section Membership Requirements
3500T	Interim Ethics Standards	1. AICPA's Code of Conduct, Rules 102 and 191 2. AICPA's Related Interpretations

---

[62] Establishment of Interim Professional Auditing Standards, PCAOB Release No. 2003-006, April 18, 2003. Available at *http://www.pcaobus.org*.

¶ 214

3600T	Interim Independence Standards	1. SEC's Auditor Independence Rules 2. AICPA's Code of Conduct Rules 101 and 191 3. Interpretation of these rules 4. Independence Standards Board's Standard Nos. 1, 2, and 3; and recent interpretations 99-1, 00-1, and 002

.01 Rule 3200T—Interim Auditing Standards

Auditing standards in the United States, better known as the U.S. Generally Accepted Auditing Standards (USGAAS), were published by the AICPA. The ten GAAS are classified into the general standards, the three field work standards, and the four reporting standards. The Auditing Standards Board (ASB) of the AICPA has issued 101 Statements on Auditing Standards (SASs), which provide guidance for auditors to comply with the 10 GAAS. The PCAOB has decided to take the responsibility of issuing professional auditing standards for registered public accounting firms by reviewing the existing GAAS and deciding to adopt, change, or establish new GAAS. Meanwhile, the PCAOB has decided to adopt as interim auditing standards all of the 101 SASs issued by the ASB of the AICPA as they existed on April 16, 2003. These GAAS will continue to have the same authority and registered public accounting firms should comply with them unless and until the PCAOB supercedes them. The PCAOB has already established three Professional Auditing Standards as of this writing (June 2004): (1) PCAOB Auditing Standard No. 1, References in Auditor's Reports to the Standards of the Public Company Accounting Oversight Board;[63] (2) PCAOB Auditing Standard No. 2, An Audit of Internal Control Over Financial Reporting Performed in Conjunction with an Audit of Financial Statements;[64] and (3) PCAOB Auditing Standard No. 3, Audit Documentation and Amendment to Interim Auditing Standards.[65]

.02 Rule 3300T—Interim Attestation Standards

The PCAOB has decided to adopt the existing Statements on Standards for Attestation Engagements (SSAE) and related interpretations issued by the ASB of the AICPA as of April 16, 2003 as the PCAOB's Interim Attestation Standards. Thus, registered auditors should comply with SSAEs when performing attestation services unless and until the PCAOB superceded them.

---

[63] PCAOB Auditing Standard No. 1, References in Auditor's Reports to the Standards of the Public Company Accounting Oversight Board (PCAOB Bylaws and Rules, June 18, 2004), p. 126.

[64] PCAOB Auditing Standard No. 2, An Audit of Internal Control Over Financial Reporting Performed in Conjunction with an Audit of Financial Statements (PCAOB Bylaws and Rules, June 18, 2004), p. 131.

[65] PCAOB Release No. 2004-006, June 9, 2004.

Standards of Professional Conduct

.03 Rule 3400T—Interim Quality Control Standards

The PCAOB is authorized by the Sarbanes-Oxley Act to establish quality control standards for registered auditors. However, during this transition period, registered public accounting firms should comply with the ASB's SQCS. Thus, the PCAOB adopted existing SQCS as of April 16, 2003 as the Interim Quality Control Standards that registered auditors must comply with unless the PCAOB supercedes them. These Interim Quality Control Standards address the following matters that will be discussed in depth in this chapter:

- Continuing professional education for personnel of registered public accounting firms.
- Concurring partner review of the audit report and financial statements filed with the SEC.
- Written communication of the firm's policies, procedures, and quality control standards to all professional personnel of the registered public accounting firm.
- Written policies and procedures to comply with applicable ethics and independence requirements.
- Elements of the Interim Quality Control Standards are independence, integrity, objectivity, personal management, acccptance and continuance of clients' engagements, engagement performance, and monitoring.

.04 Rule 3500T—Interim Ethics Standards

The PCAOB has decided to adopt the provisions of the AICPA's Code of Professional Conduct, which will be discussed in detail in this chapter as Interim Ethics Standards. Thus, registered public accounting firms should continue to observe the adopted Interim Ethics Standards unless and until the PCAOB supercedes them.

.05 Rule 3600T—Interim Independence Standards

The PCAOB adopted the AICPA's Independence Rules as Interim Independence Standards with which registered auditors are required to comply in connection with the audit of financial statements of public companies. Furthermore, the SEC, in January 2003, adopted final rules to strengthen requirements regarding auditor independence. All registered public accounting firms must also observe the SEC's rule on Auditor Independence when practicing before the Commission. The PCAOB requires that during this transition period, registered public accounting firms comply with the more restrictive independence requirements as set forth by either the AICPA's code of professional conduct or the SEC's final rules on auditor independence.

¶ 214.05

.06 Auditing Standard-Setting Process

The Sarbanes-Oxley Act of 2002 authorizes the PCAOB to establish auditing standards for registered public accounting firms. The PCAOB is also responsible for issuing quality control and ethics standards to be used by registered public accounting firms. The PCAOB has decided to establish new Professional Auditing Standards and to amend the adopted interim auditing standards. The PCAOB will also consider proposed new or amended Professional Auditing Standards (PAS) recommended by its appointed SAG or other persons or organizations. Any new PAS or changes to these PAS may be initiated as follows:

- The PCAOB with the advice of its staff may propose a new PAS or changes in the existing PAS.
- The SAG or appointed task force may recommend to the PCAOB new PAS or changes in the existing PAS.
- Another person, group, or organization may petition the PCAOB to consider a new PAS or changes in the existing PAS.

The PCAOB Auditing and other related professional standards-setting processes are started with a proposal received from its staff, SAG, other organizations, or individuals followed up with round tables, task forces and working groups, proposed standards issues for public comments, final PCAOB adopted standards, and finally approval by the SEC. The PCAOB has already adopted three PAS. The PCAOB Adopted Auditing Standards will not take effect unless approved by the SEC pursuant to Act Sec. 107 of the Sarbanes-Oxley Act of 2002.

¶ 215 COSO Enterprise Risk Management Framework

In late 2003, the Committee of Sponsoring Organizations of the Treadway Commission (COSO) issued a draft copy of their conceptually sound framework, providing integrated principles, common terminology, and practical implementation guidance supporting entities' programs to develop or benchmark their enterprise risk management process.[66] Internal control is an integral part of enterprise risk management, and the report talks about control activities, including preventive controls, detective controls, manual controls, computer controls, and management controls.

The Enterprise Risk Management framework is based on eight key components: internal environment, objective setting, event identification, risk assessment, risk response, control activities, information and communications, and monitoring. These eight components can help management to identify and assess the information risk of possible financial misstatements and design proper control activities to prevent, detect, and correct such misstatements. Auditors then attest to and report on the adequacy and

---

[66] COSO, Enterprise Risk Management Framework, draft, *www.erm.coso.org*.

¶ 214.06

effectiveness of the designed internal controls, monitoring activities, and information and communication systems.

The draft report suggests that two broad groupings of controls are especially needed for information systems. First, general controls should apply to many if not all application systems and help ensure the continued, proper operation. "General controls include controls over information technology management, information technology infrastructure, security management and software acquisition, development and maintenance. These controls apply to all systems—from mainframe to client/server to desktop computer environments."[67]

Second, application controls are designed to ensure completeness, accuracy, authorization, and validity of data capture and processing. The report suggests that "individual applications may rely on effective operation of controls over information systems to ensure that data is captured or generated when needed, supporting applications are available and interface errors are detected quickly."[68]

Overall, this report is not practical and offers little help for stopping fraud. Fraud is an annual $600 billion gorilla, yet fraud, abuse, occupation fraud, or forensic techniques are not even mentioned in the glossary. Forensic techniques are not mentioned in the report. When giving the responsibilities of the risk officer, looking for fraud is not listed.

¶ 216 Summary

At least five groups are involved with the determination of ethical rules for accountants. These groups are the SEC, the PCAOB, the AICPA PEEC, the appropriate state society, and the U.S. Department of Labor. The SEC for many years looked to the private sector for leadership in establishing and improving accounting and auditing standards. The Sarbanes-Oxley Act now authorizes the PCAOB to establish auditing, attestation, quality control, independence, and ethical standards for registered public accounting firms that audit public companies. Prior rules apply for an interim term until they are reviewed and revised by the PCAOB.

The AICPA Code of Professional Conduct (Code) provides guidance and rules for its members in the performance of their professional responsibilities. This code consists of two sections: principles and rules. The AICPA ethical principles form the cornerstone of successful professional practice. The six principles a CPA should follow are exercising responsibility, acting in the public interest, acting with integrity, acting objectively and independently, and acting with due care. The Rules of Conduct are the enforceable minimum standards of ethical conduct stated as specific rules.

The SEC has expressed authority to regulate the form and content of financial statements of public companies. When the SEC identifies im-

---

[67] *Ibid.*, pp. 63-65.   [68] *Ibid.*, p. 65.

proper professional conduct on the part of a CPA, the SEC has the power to take enforcement action. Until recently, the accounting profession was largely self-regulated. As a result of the recent accounting scandals, the SEC created the PCAOB to oversee, inspect, and discipline registered public accounting firms.

¶ 216

Chapter 3

Legal Liability

¶ 301 Introduction
¶ 302 Frequency and Severity of Claims
¶ 303 Liability to Clients
¶ 304 Third-Party Liability
¶ 305 Statutory Civil Liability
¶ 306 Statutory Criminal Liability
¶ 307 Biased Jurors
¶ 308 Federal Sentencing Guidelines
¶ 309 Summary

¶ 301 Introduction

During the past several decades accountants have been so hammered with lawsuits, judgments, and settlements that the profession itself has often been at risk. Juries are awarding multimillion dollar recoveries to plaintiffs who are "harmed" by accountants. The firm of Laventhol and Horwath became insolvent because of legal problems. This litigation trend toward increased liability affects most professionals. But accountants' liability extends not only to clients, but to many other stakeholders (financial statement users such as creditors, stockholders, suppliers, and taxing authorities). By the end of the past century, there was a trend to narrow the scope of liability to nonclients for negligence of an auditor as a result of legislative reform.[1]

Because Americans tend to sue first and ask questions later, auditors must be aware of such legal terms as the privity standard, foreseeability standard, restatement standard, RICO, negligence, aiding and abetting, injunctive relief, and willful understatement of liability. Further, accountants must be aware of the U.S. Sentencing Commission's guidelines. These guidelines comprise complex formulas intended to standardize federal sentences based upon the types of crimes committed.

---

[1] For historical details, see Epstein M. J. and A. D. Spalding, *The Accountant's Guide to Legal Liability and Ethics* (Homewood, IL: Irwin, 1993). *See also* Carl Pacini, M. J. Martin, and Lynda Hamilton, "At the Interface of Law and Accounting," *American Business Law Journal* (Vol. 37, 2000): 171—235.

Chapter 3 objectives:

- To list the areas in which practitioners may have liability exposure (see ¶ 301–302).

- To be aware of the two types of lawsuits brought by audit clients (see ¶ 303).

- To understand approaches courts use to determine whether an auditor is subject to liability to third parties who read and rely on audit reports (see ¶ 304).

- To be aware of the statutory civil liability to which auditors are exposed and be familiar with the acts related to it (see ¶ 305).

- To understand the statutory criminal liability to which auditors are exposed (see ¶ 306).

- To recognize how biased jurors serve as a disadvantage to the auditor in a court of law (see ¶ 307).

- To be familiar with federal sentencing guidelines (see ¶ 308).

¶ 302 Frequency and Severity of Claims

Tax claims to Camino Mutual Insurance Company, the national provider of CPA malpractice insurance, were 57 percent of all claims for the period 1986 through June 2000, taking 34 percent of the total claim dollars. Audit claims were 7 percent of total claims, taking 22 percent of the total claim dollars. But for small and mid-sized CPA firms, the average dollar amount per claim for audit work was significantly higher than that for other claims, running about $341,000 per claim. The leading cause of loss in audit claims involved fraud and defalcation, probably because of the expectation gap. Claims involving creditor decisions were less frequent, but they tended to be large (about $668,000).[2] As a result of increased premiums, many accounting companies are turning to captive insurance companies—an insurance company owned by the organizations they insure.

A high-profile case involved Dallas Cowboy owner Jerry Jones suing Arthur Andersen. The owner alleged that bad tax advice by the firm cost him more than $4 million in back taxes, penalties, and interest. At issue was advice from Arthur Andersen that for tax purposes Texas Stadium Corporation (TSC) could report long-term leases of luxury suites as sales to be paid in installments, rather than as leases. Texas Stadium Corporation (owned by Jerry Jones) leased the Cowboys' stadium from the city of Irving. TSC made cash payments to the Dallas Cowboys Football Team for luxury-suite tickets, which lowered TSC's income for the year, allowing Mr. Jones

---

[2] J. F. Raspante and Ric Rosario, "Understanding and Minimizing CPA Liability," *The CPA Journal* (May 2001): 19–21.

to take nontaxable cash dividends. Four years later the IRS said TSC could not take a deduction, and Jerry Jones had taxable dividends.

Practitioners generally may have liability exposure in several broad areas:

- Liability to the client
- Liability to third parties
- Statutory civil liability
- Statutory criminal liability

This chapter shall cover these areas of exposure and discuss ways to reduce liability risk to an audit firm.

¶ 303 Liability to Clients

Lawsuits brought by audit clients generally involve breach of contract (for not performing services or rendering advice) or negligence. A claim for a breach of contract is generally brought in a state court using state laws, but under certain circumstances a breach of contract dispute may be brought to a federal court (e.g., in situations of diversity of citizenship and a claim amount exceeding $75,000). Sometimes the claim from the client is that the auditor failed to exercise the degree of care reasonably expected from an accountant. This negligence-type claim is brought as a breach of contract dispute because the statute of limitations for a negligence or malpractice claim is shorter than for a breach of contract claim.

Breach of contract covers several areas, such as whether the auditor failed to perform according to the explicit terms of the service contract, or breached an implied duty to perform in good faith, or violated an implied or express warranty. A majority of the courts require these implied duty and care disputes to be brought as negligence claims rather than breaches of contract.

A client may win a breach of contract dispute by showing that the auditor failed to (a) perform a specific contracted service, (b) perform the service in a timely fashion, (c) perform in a satisfactory manner, or (d) comply with professional standards.[3] Examples of specific service performance would include engagements such as a review of a client's internal control system or conducting a complete audit.

.01 Engagement Letter

The engagement letter between an auditor and client is critical evidence of the accountant's responsibilities and rights. When the letter is in dispute, a court often construes the written engagement letter against the auditor as the drafter of the document.[4] The engagement letter should

---

[3] "Breach of Contract" (New York Practicing Law Institute, January 2000), Ch. 3.2[B].

[4] Restatement (Second) of Contracts § 206.

indicate what services are to be performed, for whom they are to be performed, time frame of the term of services, and the amount of the fee to be charged. If the accountant does not perform the contracted services, the client may hire a replacement practitioner and sue for compensatory damages. The damage would be the difference between the amount paid to the replacement accountant and the amount that would have been paid to the original accountant. If deadlines are not met, the accountant may be held liable for damages.[5]

Although the AICPA Code of Professional Conduct does not require a written engagement letter, such a written document should outline a clear understanding of the services to be performed and the responsibilities of both the auditor and the client. Absent an engagement letter, the odds increase that the court will accept the client's position as to the duties assumed by the auditor. For accounting and review services, AR Section 100.8 states that an "accountant should establish an understanding with the entity, preferably in writing, regarding the services to be performed."[6] AR Sections 100.53 and 100.54 provide examples of engagement letters. See Chapter 5, "Planning the Financial Audit," for a discussion of engagement letters for audits.

The AICPA Audit and Accounting Manual (AAM) provides a discussion of information that should be in an engagement letter, along with illustrative forms of letters appropriate for audits, compilations and reviews in various situations.[7]

AccountingMalpractice.com suggests the following sequence of contents for an engagement letter:[8]

1. Purpose of the letter
2. Purpose of the engagement
3. Responsibilities of Management and Auditor
4. Standards that are applicable
5. Procedures
6. Management representations
7. Scope and/or restrictions
8. Responsibility for detecting illegal acts
9. Report on internal controls and deficiencies

---

[5] In the case of an expert witness, such expert would probably not be held liable for failure to testify as originally intended. *Griffith v. Harris*, 116 N.W. 2d 136 (Wisc. 1962).

[6] Statement on Standards for Accounting and Review Services (SSARS) No. 1 (AICPA, *Professional Standards*, vol. 2, AR Sec. 100.05).

[7] AICPA Audit and Accounting Manual, AAM sec. 3000, 2001.

[8] Adapted with permission from *AccountingMalpractice.com/epr/primer*. The authors of the sample are M.L Chetter, C. Renda, and J.R. Bourassa.

¶ 303.01

10. Management letter
11. Identification of intended recipients
12. Printer's proof
13. Tax services
14. Engagement staffing
15. Client assistance
16. Fees
17. Billings
18. Timing
19. Appreciation
20. Closing paragraph referencing the letter as a contract
21. Printer's proof

The New York CPA Society provides some excellent sample contents of engagement letters online at the website of The New York CPA Society, as adopted in Figure 3.1.

Figure 3.1 ──

Contents of Engagement Letter

Purpose of the letter. This letter will confirm our understanding of the arrangements for our audit of the financial statements of [company name] for the fiscal year ended [data].

Engagement purpose. We will audit the company's balance sheet at [date], and the related statements of income, retained earnings, and cash flows for the year then ended. In all circumstances, our responsibility for this engagement will be limited to this period. The purpose of the engagement will be to express an opinion on the fairness of the presentation of these financial statements in conformity with generally accepted accounting principles [or other comprehensive bases of accounting].

Responsibilities. The accuracy and completeness of the financial statements, including the related footnotes, are the responsibility of the company's management. Management also is responsible for selecting sound accounting principles and for maintaining an adequate internal control structure. Our responsibility is to express an opinion on the financial statements based on our audit.

Standards applicable to engagements. We will conduct our audit in accordance with generally accepted auditing standards. Those standards require that we plan and perform the audit to obtain reasonable assurance about whether the financial statements are free of material misstatements. The term *reasonable assurance* implies a risk that material monetary misstatements may remain undetected and precludes our guaranteeing the accuracy and completeness of the financial statements. An audit includes examining on a test basis, evidence supporting the amounts and disclosures in the financial statements. An audit also includes assessing the accounting principles used and significant estimates made by management, as well as evaluating the overall financial statement presentation. We believe our audit will provide a reasonable basis for our opinion.

Audit procedures. Our procedures will include obtaining an understanding of the company's internal control structure and testing those controls to the extent we believe necessary. We also will physically examine the fixed assets and inventories (if applicable), and will confirm receivables and certain other assets and liabilities by corresponding with selected customers, suppliers, attorneys, and banks. In addition, we will read the other information included in the annual report to stockholders and consider its consistency with the financial statements.

Management representations. At the conclusion of our audit, we will request from you a letter attesting to the completeness and truthfulness of representations and disclosures made to us during the course of our work.

¶ 303.01

Scope restrictions. If you are aware of any restrictions that might limit the scope of our testing, we ask that you bring them to our attention as soon as possible. Such restrictions, if significant, may preclude us from issuing an unqualified opinion.

Responsibility for detecting fraud. Generally accepted auditing standards require us to design our audit to detect errors and irregularities that would have a material effect on the financial statements. However, because we will not examine all the transactions that occurred during the preceding year, our audit cannot provide absolute assurance that such errors and irregularities, including fraud or defalcations, will be detected. We will inform you of irregularities that come to our attention during the course of the audit unless they are clearly inconsequential.

Responsibility for detecting illegal acts. In performing our audit, we will be aware of the possibility that illegal acts have occurred. We will design our audit to detect illegal acts that have a direct and material effect on the financial statements. Again, we will inform you of violations of government laws and regulations that come to our attention unless they are inconsequential.

Report on internal control deficiencies and management letter. In connection with our obtaining an understanding of the company's internal control structure, should we encounter any reportable conditions, we will so notify you along with our recommendations for correcting them. (Reportable conditions represent significant deficiencies in the design or operation of the internal control structure, which could adversely affect the organization's ability to record, process, summarize, and report financial data consistent with the assertions of management in the financial statements.) In addition, we will advise you of any opportunities to improve the effectiveness or economy of operations that we observe during our fieldwork. We will deliver a letter describing these matters to you at the conclusion of our audit.

Identification of intended recipients. We will be pleased to deliver to you the four copies of our audit report you require. We understand you intend to distribute copies of the company's financial statements, with our report attached, to [names of third-party recipients].

Printer's proofs. If you intend to publish or otherwise reproduce the financial statements and make reference to our firm, you agree to furnish us with printer's proofs for our review and approval before printing. You also agree to provide us with a copy of the final reproduced material for our approval before you distribute it.

Tax services. At your request, we will prepare [review] the company's federal and state [identify states] income tax returns for the year ended [date]. (These returns, we understand, will be prepared by the controller.) In addition, we will be pleased to advise you concerning any income tax

¶ 303.01

matters you bring to our attention, including the tax effects of proposed transactions or changes in business policies.

Engagement staffing. You may expect a staff senior from our firm and [number] assistant auditors to be present in your office during the course of our fieldwork. [For repeat engagements:] To promote continuity, we will make every reasonable effort to assign the same audit personnel from previous years to the current examination.

Client assistance. You agree that your accounting personnel will assist our staff by locating vouchers, contracts, minutes, and other documentation necessary to complete our tests. In addition, you agree they will help us through the timely preparation of analyses and schedules. [Attach a list of such schedules.]

Fees. We will base our fees on the amount of staff time required at the different levels of responsibility, plus travel and other out-of-pocket costs. Assuming adequacy of records and internal controls, and the assistance of your personnel, we estimate that our fee for all services will be [specify amount]. We will notify you immediately of any circumstances we encounter that materially affect that figure.

Billing. We will invoice you for our services and expenses monthly; invoices are payable on presentation. Unpaid fee balances will bear interest at [percent] per annum.

Timing. We anticipate the following timetable for the performance of our audit and delivery of requested reports and will promptly notify you of any necessary changes:

[Date] We will begin our field work.
[Date] We will observe the physical inventory.
[Date] You agree to provide us with a year end trial balance.
[Date] We will complete our field work.
[Date] We will deliver our audit [and other] reports as well as your tax returns.
[Date] We will deliver our report on your internal control structure.

Appreciation. We appreciate your confidence in retaining our firm to perform these services and are happy to have this opportunity to serve you.

Request for client signature. If this letter correctly expresses your understanding, please sign the enclosed copy and return it to us at your earliest convenience. If you have further questions concerning the engagement, including any of the detailed contents of this letter, or questions about additional services we might provide, do not hesitate to call us.

Source: nysscpa.org/prog__lubrg. The New York CPA Society.

A properly written engagement letter is an excellent way to defend against a lawsuit that is based upon the failure to perform an audit or other services. Auditors should process the engagement letter with the client *before* commencing the service. If a prospective client refuses to sign the letter, an auditor probably should not risk auditing the client's records. See Chapter 5, "Planning the Financial Audit," for a discussion of whether an engagement should be accepted or not accepted.

.02 Negligence

A lawsuit against an auditor for negligence is a tort action, which is a private wrong against a person or company (i.e., a wrongful act). The three types of negligence claims are (a) a failure to inform a client of information discovered during the audit, (b) professional malpractice, and (c) negligent misrepresentation by the auditor. A negligence claim has a shorter statute of limitation than a breach of contract action. The failure to inform a client of discovered information occurs often when an auditor is performing nonauditing services for a company.

However, an auditor may be faced with a negligent misrepresentation action if the accountant is in the business of supplying information. Here the accountant provides false information and communicates the information without reasonable care, and a client relies on the false information and suffers damages. Professional malpractice involves a claim that an auditor did not perform his or her services with a professional standard of care. Negligent misrepresentation often involves a third party (who is not a client) who is not in privity of the contract with the auditor.

A breach of a fiduciary duty claim may occur when there is a conflict between a fiduciary accountant and a client. Also, the auditor may violate a client's confidentiality, resulting in breach of duty.

In order to prove negligence, a plaintiff must show (a) a duty was imposed on the auditor in favor of the plaintiff, (b) the auditor violated a material duty, (c) this breach was the proximate cause of the harm, and (d) the plaintiff suffered damages. The duty of the auditor is to perform his or her services with care, skill, reasonable experience, and faithfulness. Because an auditor possesses special auditing skills, he or she must meet a minimum standard of care by an ordinary prudent member of the accounting profession. These factors are covered under liability for third parties.

One example of this type of litigation was in the news. In Phoenix on August 28, 2000, the Baptist Foundation of Arizona (BFA) filed a lawsuit charging its former auditor, Arthur Andersen, with negligence in conducting the annual audits of BFA's financial statements for a 15-year period beginning in 1984. BFA went bankrupt in 1999, and investors lost many millions of dollars as a result of BFA's bankruptcy. On May 30, 2001, about 50 investors in the Arizona Foundation picketed an Arthur Andersen office in Phoenix.

¶ 303.02

The lawsuit alleged that in its annual audits, the Big-5 CPA firm ignored many red-flag indications that BFA had been transformed by its former senior management team from a legitimate investment into a Ponzi scheme. In a Ponzi scheme new investors' money is used to pay off existing investors. BFA's massive losses were hidden from investors through the transfer of nonperforming assets to undisclosed related entities. Illustrating the expectation gap, attorney Alan Schulman said that the CPA firm failed to investigate the non-arm's length transactions. "The tragedy of BFA is an all too familiar example of accounting professionals failing to do their job, with innocent investors left holding the bag once the misconduct is disclosed."[9]

Figure 3.2

Levels of Conduct

- Ideal Level → Principles of Conduct
- Varying Levels of conduct
- Minimum Level → Rules of Conduct (enforceable)
- Substandard conduct

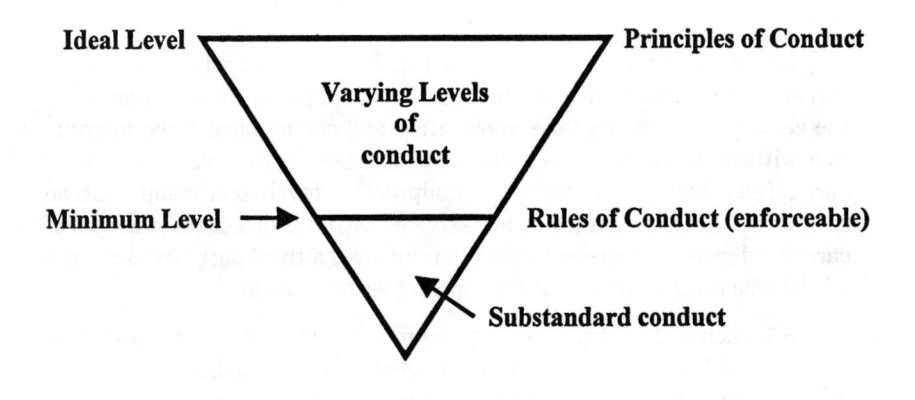

Rules of conduct can provide an objective roadmap against which an auditor's actions can be measured to determine if such conduct meets the minimum level required for the profession. Figure 3.2, Levels of Conduct, represents the universe of auditing activity. This figure suggests that most auditors go well beyond the minimum level of professional conduct into the broader section of the inverted pyramid and by so doing, presumably reduce liability risk. Of course, the malpractice attorneys and their expert witnesses may look at much more than the standards, but measuring professional conduct against such standards is often used in the Courts for many types of professional liability cases. An obvious preventative measure would be strict adherence to the standards. However, a breach of ethical standard may support a civil liability claim.[10]

---

[9] "Baptist Foundation of Arizona Files Accounting Malpractice Lawsuit Against Arthur Andersen LLP," *Business Wire*, (August 28, 2000), from http://www.businesswire.com.

[10] *Wagenheim v. Alexander Grant & Co.*, 482 N.E.2d 955 (Ohio Ct. App. 1983).

¶ 303.02

An auditor's failure to follow generally accepted auditing standards (GAAS) may be grounds for a cause for negligence. Suppose, however, an auditor does follow GAAS and generally accepted accounting principles (GAAP) in reaching an opinion on the fairness of the financial condition of a client. Do GAAS and GAAP define the duty of care of an auditor? Does meeting the Standards of Conduct protect a practitioner?

An auditor may fail in the courtroom even if he or she has followed all of the AICPA guidelines, possibly because of the expectation gap (discussed later). For example, in *Bily v. Arthur Young & Co.*, the Sixth Appellate Division in California held that GAAP and GAAS did not define the duty of care for accountants. GAAP and GAAS merely codify the standards of the profession and were *only evidence* of such duty. Expert testimony and accounting firms' manuals and procedures may be used to determine a breach of the duty of care. Basically, compliance with professional standards is only helpful to the trier of facts, but determining the standard of care is to be decided by the jury.[11]

.03 Suing for Audit Fees

An auditor faces a dilemma when a client refuses to pay accounting fees. In some states (e.g., New York) a client does not have to pay for defective professional services. Often when a CPA firm sues for payment of audit fees the client's attorney will file a counter suit for malpractice. Because malpractice claims are fact intensive, they are expensive to litigate. The auditor will have to defend his or her work product against possible unrealistic standards. Thus, even if the auditor finally wins the initial suit for payment of audit fees, the costs to defend the malpractice suit may offset any gains from the original action. Often professional liability insurers suggest that lawsuits for audit fees be avoided at all costs. Certainly, the auditor must carefully analyze the professional services performed for the client to make sure the work met GAAS and GAAP.

Prevention techniques and controls should be used to avoid unpaid bills. Over-risky clients and services should not be accepted. Investigating clients on the front end is essential; much information can be obtained on the Internet and from newspapers and magazines about clients. Does the client have a history of late payments or malpractice suits? A thorough investigation and conflict check are essential. Review the predecessor accountant's workpapers and talk with the prior accountant to weed out the bad apples.

As Elizabeth Danziger says, "just say no to costly clients." They are the ones who do not pay their bills or pose high litigation risk. These unpleasant clients detract from the auditing firm's productivity, take a toll on the staff's morale, and tend to refer others like them to the firm.[12]

---

[11] *Bily v. Arthur Young & Co.*, 271 Cal. Rptr. 470 (Cal. Ct. App. 1990), rev'd 11 Cal. Rptr. 2d 51, 834 P.2d 745 (1992).

[12] E. Danziger, "Just Say No to Costly Clients," *Journal of Accountancy* (June 1999): 45.

The best time to avoid these costly clients is before they become clients. *Accounting Malpractice Primer* gives some warning signs of a possible troublesome client:[13]

- Problems with the predecessor practitioner
- Excessive expectations of the accountant
- Excessive client staff turnover
- Prospective client's staff unhappy or replaced often
- Excessive interest in fees
- Prospective client is secretive, paranoid, or prone to irrational outbursts
- Prospective client's industry has reputation for corruption
- Less than outstanding reputation of the client
- Turnover of senior management
- Departures from the client's ordinary business
- Recent turnover of the board of directors
- Excessive delays in receiving information
- Management's unwillingness to turn over information
- Sudden change in accounting policies and procedure
- Books and records are disorganized
- Lack of adequate internal controls
- Substantial volatility in client's revenue, income, or share price
- Overly optimistic
- Competitive structure in the industry
- Volatility within the industry
- Economic climate within the industry
- Technological obsolescence
- Client appears to be "shopping" for a firm
- Client that is known to sue accountants or is constantly changing accountants
- Client is engaged in material related-party transactions
- Client is entwined in litigation

---

[13] Adapted with permission from *AccountingMalpractive.com/epr/primer* Chapter 10, p. 2.

¶ 303.03

Starting with the engagement letter, fees should be monitored and controlled. The engagement letter should include a sentence which reserves the practitioner's right to suspend or terminate work for the client if an interim invoice is not paid. Billing and fee collection must be strict. The auditing firm should (a) collect payments in advance, (b) immediately suspend services for delinquent clients, (c) obtain promissory notes for unpaid balances, and (d) collect interest on past due amounts.

.04 Limited Liability Partnerships

If an accounting firm is organized as a partnership, each partner or owner of the firm is liable generally for the entire judgment against the company until it is paid in full. Known as the joint and several liability doctrine, each tortfeasor is liable to the client for the total damages until paid. (A tortfeasor is a person who is guilty of a tort.)

All states and the District of Columbia have adopted limited liability partnership (LLP) statutes to buttress litigation because of the "deep pocket syndrome." All of the Big-4 accounting firms and many other national accounting firms have become LLPs. If an accounting firm is a LLP, partners are not liable for negligence, error, omission, incompetence, and malfeasance of other partners or the employees supervised by other partners. Many states extend this protection to liabilities chargeable to the LLP or another partner arising in contract as well as tort.

Advantages of the LLP are obvious. If an audit partner and his employees of a national accounting firm with headquarters in Detroit, Michigan were to be found liable for failure to perform a proper audit, partners in the firm located in New Orleans, Louisiana, who had no involvement in the Detroit audit, would be not liable for any damages resulting from the lawsuit.

The LLP organizational form does not protect partners from their own negligence or negligence by anyone under their direct supervision. The statutes vary according to state law. For example, in Texas a partner is protected from negligence or incompetence of other partners (i.e., tort claims), but the Texas partner is not absolved from contractual debts (commercial liability) or other liabilities incurred by the LLP. However, some states (e.g., Minnesota and New York) offer broad protection, including protection against contractual claims. Thus, negligent partners may be abandoned and forced to bear the costs alone.

Large firms should certainly operate under the LLP form to obtain this limited liability. The LLP organization form is easy to initiate and offers the additional advantage of single taxation. In states such as Minnesota and New York, the contractual liability protection is extremely beneficial. There are no uniform LLP laws, but except for extremely small firms (where most of the partners are likely to be exposed) and in states where

¶ 303.04

limited liability company (LLC) format is available, auditing firms should opt for the LLP organization form. Few states allow an accounting firm to organize as a LLC.

¶ 304 Third-Party Liability

The public, jury members, SEC, courts, and lawyers place a high professional standard on all accountants. Known as the "expectation gap," the public imposes an elevated level of accountability on auditors, especially in the area of fraud and defalcation (the leading causes of loss in audit claims).[14] The public expects auditors to find the fraud in companies even though an audit rarely examines all accounting transactions in the records of an entity. Auditing is not a routine, detailed checking of the records, primarily because the exercise of judgment is inherent in an auditing engagement.

Robert Sack, former chief accountant of the SEC Enforcement Division, indicated in 1992 that the major contributor to an auditor's failure to detect fraud is the lack of skepticism.[15] The profession expanded the auditor's responsibility in detecting fraud and illegal acts with Statement on Auditing Standards (SAS) No. 82 by clearly stating that the detection of material *misstatement in financial statements* is central to an audit. Yet paragraph 10 states the difficulties of detecting fraud when collusion and/or falsified documents are present:

> An auditor cannot obtain absolute assurance that material misstatements in the financial statements will be detected. Because of (a) the concealment aspects of fraudulent activity, including the fact that fraud often involves collusion or falsified documentation, and (b) the need to apply professional judgment in the identification and evaluation of fraud risk factors and other conditions, even a properly planned and performed audit may not detect a material misstatement resulting from fraud. Accordingly because of the above characteristics of fraud and the nature of fraud evidence, the auditor is able to obtain only reasonable assurance that material misstatements in the financial statements, including misstatements resulting from fraud, are detected.[16]

The Panel on Audit Effectiveness states that auditors should perform some "forensic-type" procedures on every audit to enhance the prospects of detecting material financial statement fraud. During this forensic-type fieldwork phase, an auditor should modify the otherwise neutral concept of professional skepticism and presume the possibility of dishonesty of various levels of management, including collusion, override of internal controls, and falsification of documents.[17]

Chapter 19 explores fraud auditing in more detail; basically, GAAP audit standards are not designed to catch instances of fraud other than

---

[14] Raspante and Rosario, "Understanding and Minimizing CPA Liability," p. 21.

[15] R. J. Sack, "The Anatomy of a Fraud," in *Curriculum Innovation: Excellence in Audit Education* (Sarasota Fla: AAA and Coopers & Lybrand Foundation, 1992). See SackR@darden.gbusvirginia.edu.

[16] SAS No. 82, *Consideration of Fraud in a Financial Statement Audit* (AICPA, *Professional Standards*, vol. 1, AU secs. 110, 230, 312, and 316). Note that SAS No. 82 was superseded by SAS No. 99.

[17] "The Panel on Audit Effectiveness: Report and Recommendations," (Stamford, Conn.: Public Oversight Board, August 31, 2000), 88.

¶ 304

financial statement fraud. Independent auditors are not charged with finding asset fraud, but merely material misstatement of financial statements.[18] Clearly, there is a gap between client (not to mention shareholder) expectations and the product that independent auditors deliver. The typical audit client is probably unwilling to pay for the time that a thorough fraud audit would require, so the expectation gap will not disappear. But the typical juror believes that the purpose of an audit is to uncover any type of fraud or wrongdoing.[19] For Example, in May 2001, Arthur Andersen agreed to pay Sunbeam shareholders $110 million to settle a securities lawsuit, and shortly thereafter, Andersen had to pay $20 million to Waste Management shareholders for accounting problems.[20] Enron could end up being even much more expensive for the firm.

Consider one of the largest embezzlements in U.S. history. Between 1990 and 1997, Yasuyoshi Kato, the CFO at Day-Lee, Inc., obtained off-book loans from U.S. affiliates of Japanese banks and issued checks to himself and his wife totaling about $63 million. This fraud was caught by the IRS, possibly as a result of an anonymous tip. Kato's opulent lifestyle gave him away: he possessed two $10,000 macaws and a zoo size aquarium containing sharks and other exotic fish.

Kato forged daily accounting entries. He started to steal when he agreed to pay his wife and two daughters $50,000 a month for support as part of his divorce settlement. He made only $150,000 a year. He later was sentenced to 63 months imprisonment and ordered to repay the embezzled funds at a rate of $100 per year.

In order to recover in a negligence lawsuit, a plaintiff must establish that the negligence of an auditor is the proximate or legal cause of his or her damage.[21] Proximate cause generally includes two elements: (a) cause in fact, and (b) foreseeability.[22] In order for a third party to prevail there must be privity to the contract (e.g., one of the parties to the contract). There are generally four approaches for determining whether an auditor is subject to liability to third parties who read and rely on audit reports: the restrictive privity of relationship and near-privity approaches (about 17 states), Restatement Second approach (about 21 states) and the reasonably foreseeability approach (Mississippi, Wisconsin). The liability of an auditor to third parties depends upon the jurisdiction of the lawsuit. The jurisdiction of a lawsuit is determined by a number of factors, such as the residence of the plaintiff or the place of business of the client. However, the Enron and WorldCom collapses have increased the liability of accountants.

---

[18] H. A. Davia, *Fraud 101* (New York, John Wiley & Sons, 2000), 27.

[19] Raspante and Rosario, "Understanding and Minimizing CPA Liability," p. 21.

[20] Vanessa O'Connell, "Arthur Andersen Confronts its Enron Role," *Wall Street Journal*, January 17, 2002, p. B-4.

[21] *Kemin v. KPMG Peat Marwick LLP*, 578 N.W 2d 212 (Iowa 1998).

[22] *Greenstein, Logan, & Co. v. Burgess Marketing, Inc.*, 744 S.W. 2d 170 (Tex. Ct. App. 1987).

¶304

.01 The Privity of Relationship Approach

The most favorable rule for auditors is the strict privity rule that requires a direct connection between the auditor and another party. First established in *Landell v. Lybrand*,[23] today only Pennsylvania and Virginia follow this standard.[24]

.02 Near-privity Rule

The next more favorable approach for auditors is the *Ultramares* approach, which denies recovery to third parties for auditor negligence in the absence of a third-party relationship to the auditor that is similar to privity. A substantial number of jurisdictions find that auditors owe no duty to third-party stakeholders for an erroneous opinion. A famous quote from *Ultramares* is instructive:

> If liability for negligence exists, a thoughtless slip or blunder, the failure to detect a theft or forgery beneath the cover of deceptive entries, may expose accountants to a liability in an indeterminate amount for an indeterminate time to an indeterminate class. The hazards of a business conducted on these terms are so extreme as to enkindle doubt whether a flaw may not exist in the implication of a duty that exposes to these consequences.[25]

Here the New York Court of Appeals did not release auditors from liability for fraud to third parties, but merely for honest blunders.

In subsequent decisions the New York Court of Appeals has found for plaintiffs using an equivalent privity of relationships between the auditor and third parties.[26] This court stated that three requirements must be met before accountants can be held liable for negligence to noncontractual parties who rely to their detriment on inaccurate financial statements:

> (1) the accountant must have been aware that the financial reports were to be used for a particular purpose or purposes; (2) in the furtherance of which a known party or parties was intended to rely; and (3) there must have been some conduct on the part of the accountants linking them to that party or parties, which evinces the accountants' understanding of that party or parties' reliance.[27]

.03 Restatement Second Approach

Most jurisdictions use a middle-of-the-road approach based upon Restatement Second of Torts, Section 552, which tends to impose liability on suppliers of commercial information to third parties who are the intended beneficiaries of the information. This user approach is a compromise between the privity approach and the unlimited liability of the foreseeable approach. Section 522 states that a party who negligently supplies false information for the guidance of others is liable for any economic loss suffered by the recipients in justifiable reliance on such information.

---

[23] 107 A. 783 (Pa. 1919). See *PNC Bank, Kentucky, Inc. v. Housing Mortgage Corp.*, 899 F. Supp. 1399 (W. D. Pa 1994).
[24] *Ward v. Ernst & Young*, 435 S. E. 2d 628 (VA. 1993).
[25] *Ultramares Corp. v. Touche*, 255 N.Y. 170 (1931).
[26] *White v. Guarente*, 43 N.Y. 2d 356 (1977).
[27] *Credit Alliance v. Arthur Andersen & Co.*, 483 N.E. 2d 118 (1985). See *Security Pacific Business Credit v. Peat Marwick Main*, 597 N.E. 2d 1080 (N.Y. 1992).

Importantly, however, the liability amount is limited to any loss suffered, and the liability of a negligent information supplier is more narrowly constructed than that for an intentionally fraudulent supplier.

Suppose an auditor is retained to conduct an annual audit and to furnish an opinion for no particular purpose. The auditor is not informed of any intended use of these financial statements, but the auditor does know that his or her audit opinion is normally used in a wide variety of financial transactions (lenders, investors, shareholders, creditors, etc.). The client does use the financial statements and the unqualified favorable opinion to obtain a loan from a bank. Because of the auditor's negligence misstating the financial condition of the audited company, the bank suffers a loss. Under the second restatement appoach, the auditor is not liable to the bank.

The difficulty of finding a satisfactory legal solution to liability to third parties is summarized by Dean William L. Prosser, the Reporter for the restatement:

> The problem is to find language which will eliminate liability to the very large class of persons whom almost any negligently given information may foreseeably reach and influence, and limit the liability, not to a particular plaintiff defined in advance, but to the comparatively small group whom the defendant, expects and intends to influence. Neither the Reporter, nor, it is believed, the Advisers nor the Council, is entirely satisfied with the language of Subsection (2); and if anyone can do better, it will be most welcome.[28]

The Restatement Second provides the following rule for auditors:

(1) One who, in the course of his business, profession or employment, or in any other transaction in which he has a pecuniary interest, supplies false information for the guidance of others in their business transactions, is subject to liability for pecuniary loss caused to them by their justifiable reliance upon the information, if he fails to exercise reasonable care or competence in obtaining or communicating the information.

(2) Except as stated in Subsection (3), the liability stated in Subsection (1) is limited to loss suffered

    a. By the person or one of a limited group of persons for whose benefit and guidance he intends to supply the information or knows that the recipient intends to supply it; and

    b. Through reliance upon it in a transaction that he intends the information to influence or knows that the recipient so intends or in a substantially similar transaction.

(3) The liability of one who is under a public duty to give the information extends to loss suffered by any of the class of persons for whose benefit the duty is created, in any of the transactions in which it is intended to protect them.

Essentially, under this approach an auditor is liable to a third party for negligence in an audit report only if the third person relied on the misrepresentation in a transaction that the auditor intended to influence.

---

[28] William L. Prosser, *Restatement of the Law Second Torts*, Tent. Draft No. 11 (April 15, 1965)

§ *552* p. 56. Cited in *Robert R. Bily v. Arthur Young & Co.*, footnote 27, p. 59.

¶ 304.03

In a dissent, one judge said that the effect of this approach is to give negligent auditors broad immunity from professional malpractice in rendering audit opinions.[29] This rule does enlarge the number of parties to whom the auditor may be liable.

Importantly, however, under Section 552(b) an auditor is not liable to third parties to whom he or she had no reason to believe that such information would be made available. For example, there is no liability to third parties if there is no communication between the auditor and client about the intended use of the audit report, and the auditor must actually supply the material to the party (or group of people).[30]

An auditor must limit access to client statements to a select group of third parties. For example, in a recent North Carolina decision the court used an internal memorandum of a firm's partner to support an inference that the firm knew a creditor. This memorandum was initiated by a partner and said that the firm "has historically reported on the financial statements of . . . , and vendors and factors are accustomed to receiving the company's financial statements."[31] This decision illustrates the importance of limiting access to client statements to a select group of partners

.04 Foreseeability Approach

The most harmful approach to an auditor is the foreseeability theory, which is a minority view among jurisdictions. Basically, this view states that auditors should be subject to liability to third parties on the same basis as other tortfeasors. Based upon the expectation gap, an auditor performs a public function in expressing opinions about the financial health of public companies:

> an independent certified public accountant performs a different role [from lawyers]. By certifying the public report they collectively depict a corporation's financial status, the independent auditor assumes a public responsibility transcending any employment relationship with the client. The independent public accountant performing this special function owes ultimate allegiance to the corporation's creditors and stockholders, as well as the investing public. This "public watchdog" function demands that the accountant maintain total independence from the client at all times and requires complete fidelity to the public trust.[32]

The foreseeability principle states that auditors are liable for all reasonably foreseeable injuries caused by any negligent performance of their professional duties. An innocent third party who foreseeably relies on a auditor's unqualified opinion should not be forced to bear the burden of the auditor's malpractice. The court said that "the risk of such loss is more appropriately placed on the accounting profession which is better able to pass such risk to its customers and the ultimate consuming public."[33]

---

[29] *Robert R. Bily v. Arthur Young & Co.*, 11 Cal. Rptr. 2d 51, 834 P. 2d 745 (1992).
[30] *Badische Corp.*, 356 S.E. 2d 199 (Ca. 1987).
[31] *Marcus Brothers Textiles, Inc. v. Price Waterhouse, LLP*, 498 S.E. 2d 196 (N.C. App. 1998).
[32] *U.S. v. Arthur Young & Co.*, 465 U.S. 817 (1984).
[33] *International Mortgage Co. v. John P. Butler Accountancy Corp.*, 177 Cal. App. 3rd 806 (1986).

A foreseen party is a specifically identified person or entity who is known by the auditor to be an intended recipient, directly or indirectly, of his or her audit opinion for the purpose of reliance in a particular business transaction known to the auditor. Foreseeable parties may be a large group, not identified to the auditor, who may be foreseeably expected to receive the financial statements when distributed by the intended client, and in some way the person acts or relies upon the statements.[34] Foreseeability is endless because it is like light, traveling in a vacuum.[35]

There are a number of arguments against the foreseeability approach:

- The auditor is a watchdog and not a bloodhound. An audit is conducted in a client-controlled environment with the company preparing the financial statements and having direct control over and assuming primary responsibility.[36]

- Although the auditor's role in the financial statements is secondary, the liability in a negligence suit by a third person is personal and can be devastating. Often the client, its promoters, and managers have left the scene, and the auditor may be the last remaining solvent party.

- An auditor may not have been aware of the existence of the third parties, and this factor raises the spectre of a huge number of lawsuits and limitless financial exposure.[37]

- Because of the labor-intensive nature of auditing, audits probably cannot be done economically enough to catch all fraud and abuse.

- Expanding liability of an auditor would cause dislocation of resources, including increased expenses and decreased availability of auditing services.[38]

.05 Negligent Misrepresentation

Although a third party may not be able to win a negligence suit under the restatement second and privity of relationship approaches, an auditor may be vulnerable for negligent misrepresentation. Negligence is a conduct that falls below the standard established by law for the protection of others.[39] Negligent misrepresentation is a species of the tort of deceit where a party makes false statements, honestly, believing they are true but without having reasonable grounds for such a belief. The party breaches a duty to exercise reasonable care in arriving at the incorrect statement.

---

[34] R. James Gormley, "Accountants Professional Liability- A Ten-Year Review," *Business Lawyer* (Vol. 29, 1974): 1207.
[35] *Thing v. La Chusa*, 771 P. 2d 814 (1989).
[36] *In re Interstate Hosiery Mills, Inc.*, 4 S.E.C. 721 (1939).
[37] *Raritan River Steel v. Cherry, Bekaert & Holland*, 367 S.E. 2d 609 (N.C. 1988).
[38] *Ibid.*
[39] Restatement 2nd, § 282.

¶ 304.05

Often an incorrect audit report may fall within this definition of negligent misrepresentation. However, the restatement second approach defines a narrow class of parties that may sue.[40] The supplier of the information (the auditor) must receive notice of any potential third-party claims. The third party must establish a close connection between the auditor's negligent act and the third party's injury. If the auditor merely knows of the possibility of third parties relying on the audit report but has no communication with the third party, the auditor probably does not have legal responsibility.[41]

How much conflict with an auditor is enough to create negligence liability to a third party? At least one court [42] has said that more than one phone call to an auditor is necessary from a potential user of financial statements to meet the privity requirement. Here a lender had a conversation with the auditor, announcing his intended reliance on the pencil draft of the financial statements. The court did not explain what would constitute sufficient conduct to meet the privity requirement under New York law.

Auditors should be aware that sophisticated third parties may try to create this requisite link to negligence liability through telephone calls and letters. Banks and other creditors regularly notify their borrower's auditor of their intentions to rely on the audit report. Auditors must be careful to preserve this privity defense by avoiding direct contact with third persons by phone and letters. If response is necessary, the auditor should call the third person's attention to the limitations of the auditing process (e.g., auditors do not audit to catch fraud). A flat statement might be made that the audit report was not prepared for the third party's purpose. Because oral communication is often subject to memory loss and confusing, auditors should avoid meeting with creditors and other third parties.

.06 Intentional Misrepresentation

There is no authority that will immunize an auditor from liability to third parties for intentional misrepresentation. An auditor who makes a fraudulent misrepresentation is subject to liability to the person or class of persons whom he or she intends or has reason to expect to act in reliance upon the misrepresentation, for pecuniary loss suffered by them through their justifiable reliance on the financial statements. See Restatement Second of Torts, § 531.

¶ 305   Statutory Civil Liability

Auditors may incur liability even to third parties under the federal securities law, specifically, the Securities Act of 1993 and the Securities Exchange Act of 1934. The 1933 Act regulates the initial offering and sale

---

[40] Restatement 2nd, § 552 (b).
[41] Restatement 2nd, § 552, com. (h).

[42] *Security Pacific Business Credit, Inc. v. Peat Marwick Main & Co.*, 79 N.Y. 2d 695 (1992).

¶ 304.06

of securities through the mail and other forms of interstate commerce, whereas the 1934 Act deals generally with previously issued securities.

Annually, the SEC brings between 400 to 500 civil actions against companies and individuals that break securities laws. At the end of 2000, 60 percent of the litigation was accounting fraud allegations, and the most frequent form of accounting allegation was improper revenue recognition. The settlement in one dispute alone, Cendant Corporation, was $3.525 billion.[43]

Accountants may get bogged down in detail and forget to look at the overall picture. On August 4, 1994, California Micro Services Corporation, a high-flying computer chip maker, disclosed that it was writing off half of its accounts receivable, primarily because of product returns. Its stock plunged 40 percent after the announcement and shareholders filed suit alleging financial shenanigans. Despite these events, the auditors of Cal Micro, Coopers and Lybrand, gave the company's books a clean bill of health the following month. Shortly thereafter, it became clear that Coopers and Lybrand had failed to detect an accounting scam. An internal Cal Micro investigation uncovered "preposterous" revenue numbers "almost immediately," says Wade Meyercord, Cal Micro's current chairman.[44]

Five years later, severe penalties were imposed upon the auditing team representing Coopers. The SEC took action to bar the "engagement partner" and the "engagement manager" from signing off on public company audits. They were accused of "conducting the audit in vacuum" and "recklessly ignoring unmistakable red flags." A hearing on the allegation was conducted by an SEC administrative law judge.

Class action lawsuits are becoming commonplace when a company falls short of its consensus earnings estimates or whisper earnings,[45] and the stock value falls sharply. These free whisper earnings on the Internet often are closer to a company's real earnings figures than are published analysts' reports. Stock prices are increasingly responding to comparisons between reported and whisper earnings rather than the difference between reported earnings and earnings estimated by analysts.[46] Louis Rukeyser says that these unpublished calculations are regarded by their favored recipients as "what we really think." This kind of hanky-panky leads us to the Orwellian world in which there is one set of truths for the elite and another for all us peons.[47]

A cottage industry among lawyers is developing when earnings fall radically. Federal securities class actions create huge settlements of $1

---

[43] From Stanford Law School Securities Class Action Clearinghouse, http://securities.stanford.edu.

[44] Elizabeth MacDonald, "Auditors Miss a Fraud and SEC Tries to Put Them Out of Business," The Wall Street Journal, (January 6, 2000), p. 1

[45] www.earningswhisper.com; www.whispernumbers.com; streetIQ.com. See D. Sinason and C. Pacini, "An Empirical Analysis of the Role of Fraud in Client Firm Market Reaction to Auditor Lawsuits," Journal of Forensic Accounting (Vol. 1, No. 2, 2000): 215-240.

[46] Ed Leefeldt, "How Can Whispers Help You?" Bloomberg (January/February 2000): 66-72.

[47] Louis Rukeyser, Louis Rukeyser's Wall Street (February 2000): 2.

¶ 305

billion to $3 billion each year. More than 500 legal cases are pending or resolved at any one time, and shareholders are urged to get their piece of the class action settlements.[48] Diligent investors can locate more and more information about class action cases on the Internet.

Lynn Turner, former chief accountant of the SEC, suggests that investors have lost more than $100 billion because of financial fraud and the resulting earnings restatements since 1995.[49]

The Stanford Securities Class Action Clearinghouse (securities.stanford.edu) provides detailed information relating to the prosecution, defense, and settlement of federal class action securities fraud litigation. The number of securities fraud cases went from 216 in 2000 to 471 in 2001. Many of these involved complaints about IPO practices. Milberg, Weiss, Bershad, Hynes & Lerach is the dominant law firm in the class action securities process. Litigation has slowed with 225 filings in 2002 and 175 filings in 2003. But even in 2003, the loss in market capitalization is $540 billion.

.01 The Securities Act of 1933

The purpose of the 1933 Act was to give complete and full disclosure to investors about new securities being offered for sale. Sections 11, 12, and 15 may have an impact on auditors.

Section 11 of the 1933 Act provides that if any part of a registration statement (as of the effective date) contains an untrue statement of a material fact (or failed to state a material fact required to be stated therein or necessary to make the statements therein not misleading), any person acquiring such security may sue every accountant, etc., who has with his consent been named as having prepared or certified any part of the registration statement, or report used in connection with the registration statement.

The U.S. Supreme Court states that Section 11 allows purchasers of a registered security to sue certain parties in a registered offering when false or misleading information is included in a registration imposing a stringent standard of liability on the parties who play a direct role in a registered offering. If a person purchased a security issued pursuant to a registration statement, he or she need only show a material misstatement or omission to establish a prima facie case. Liability against the issuer of a security is virtually absolute, even for innocent misstatements. Other defendants bear the burden of demonstrating due diligence. The purchaser does not have to prove that the auditor was negligent or fraudulent. Basically, auditors are assumed guilty and must prove themselves innocent.[50] Also the victims do not have to prove that they relied on the information furnished by the auditor (i.e., no proof of justifiable reliance is necessary).

---

[48] Michael Craig, "Class Acts," *Online Investor* (January/February 2000): 96-97.
[49] Jeremy Kahn, "One Plus One Makes What?" *Fortune* (January 7, 2002): 89.
[50] *Herman & Maclean v. Huddleston*, 459 U.S. 375 (1983).

¶ 305.01

An auditor's liability is limited to situations where he or she prepares or certifies the accuracy of a portion of a registration statement. Thus, the auditor is aware of creating part of a communication to the public, but the liability to the auditor is limited to third persons who actually purchased securities. Also, any damage exposure is limited to the out-of-pocket loss suffered by the buyer and cannot be greater than the amount of the offering. Disputes arising from violations of securities are often filed on behalf of many plaintiffs in class action suits, and damage awards can be huge.

An auditor can escape liability for false or misleading statements by proving due diligence. Due diligence means after a reasonable investigation the auditor acquires reasonable ground (as of the effective date of the registration statement) to believe and did believe that the statements were true and not misleading.[51] The auditor should comply with professional standards, including GAAS and GAAP, and show that there was no failure to state a material fact.[52] Additional procedures include reviewing interim financial information, subsequent events, and reports of predecessor auditors.

Consider the following example:

> John R. was a recent accounting graduate who knew little about auditing liability. Because of a heavy workload, John's accounting firm provided him with minimal guidance—especially the risks involved in auditing and reviewing the financial statements of a large corporation with significant accounts receivable. The accounting firm also failed to instruct him on the Statement on Auditing Standards (SAS) 82 in regards to the consideration of fraud in financial statement audits that had been released.
>
> While auditing the financial statements of a new wireless telephone company that had recently gone public, John failed to confirm several large accounts receivable. Most of the accounts he failed to confirm turned out to be fraudulent. These accounts exceeded $4 million and provided the company with a positive net worth. As a result of the unsupervised work performed by John R., the accounting firm issued an unqualified opinion. The client subsequently used the opinion, along with the fraudulent financial statements, to obtain a $3 million loan from a local Miami-Dade bank.
>
> Three months later, the wireless telephone company filed for Chapter 11 bankruptcy protection and the fraudulent accounts were discovered. The bank and the company's shareholders sued the accounting firm for accounting malpractice. The suit was ultimately settled for $2.5 million, not including attorney's fees and costs.[53]

Section 12 of the Securities Act of 1933 imposes civil liability penalties for misleading information in prospectuses. Although Section 12(2) technically applies only to "offerors" and "sellers," some courts have used aiding and abetting to hold auditors responsible.[54]

---

[51] 15 U.S.C.S. § 77K(b)(3); *Escott v. Bar Chris. Const. Corp.*, 283 F.Supp. 643 (S.D.N.Y. 1968).

[52] *See*, for example, *Straus v. Holiday Inns, Inc.*, 460 F. Supp. 729 (S.D.N.Y. 1978); *Escott v. Barchris Const. Corp.*, 283 F. Supp. 643 (S.D.N.Y. 1968).

[53] Manuel A. Garcia-Linares, "Avoiding Accounting Malpractice," *Camping Magazine* (July 2000).

[54] *See Sandusky Land, Ltd. v. Uniplan, Inc.*, 400 F. Supp. 440 (N.D. Ohio 1975).

¶ 305.01

Section 15 imposes liability on those parties who control or influence organizations or other persons and who are in effect culpable participants in the Sections 11 and 12 violations perpetrated by the controlled entities.[55]

.02 Securities Exchange Act of 1934

Both Sections 18 and 10(b) and Rule 10b-5 of the 1934 Act impose an implied liability on auditors. Section 18 stipulates that an auditor will be liable for misstatements contained in documents filed with the SEC. Any liability is limited to third parties who rely on the auditor's statements and purchased or sold a security at a price that was affected by the statement, when damages were caused by such reliance. An auditor may successfully defend the dispute by proving that he or she acted in good faith and had no knowledge that such statements were false or misleading.[56]

Although neither Section 10(b) nor Rule 10b-5 expressly subjects accountants to liability, both create an implied liability for the auditor. The plaintiff has to prove:

- Materiality of the representation
- Reliance by the plaintiff
- Actual damages sustained
- Scienter

In 1976 the Supreme Court in *Ernst & Ernst v. Hochfelder* ruled that the plaintiff must prove scienter.[57] Scienter refers to the mental state of mind embracing an intent to deceive, manipulate, or defraud. For example, in a case upholding disciplinary sanctions against an accountant under Rule 102(e), the accountant knowingly participated in the fraud practiced by the insurer (e.g., egregious scienter-based misconduct).[58] Likewise, in another situation the SEC charged a large CPA firm with committing or aiding and abetting securities fraud.[59] Here the Ninth Circuit made a strong defense of auditors:

> To accept the SEC's position would go far toward making the accountant both an insurer of his client's honesty and an enforcement arm of the SEC. We can understand why the SEC wishes to so conscript accountants. Its frequently late arrival on the scene of fraud and violations of securities laws almost always suggests that had it been there earlier *with the accountant* it would have caught the scent of wrong doing and, after an unrelenting hunt, bagged the game. What it cannot do, the thought goes, the accountant can and should. The difficulty with this is that Congress has not enacted the conscription bill that the SEC seeks to have us fashion and fix as an interpretive gloss on existing securities laws.[60]

Since *Central Bank v. First National Bank*,[61] there is no private right of action for aiding and abetting under § 10(b) and Rule 106-5.

---

[55] *See*, for example, *Bernstein v. Crazy Eddie, Inc.*, 702 F.Supp. 962 (E.D. New York, 1988).
[56] 15 U.S.C. § 78r (A).
[57] 425 U.S. 185 (1976).
[58] *Davy v. SEC*, 792 F. 2d 1418 (9th Cir. 1986).
[59] *SEC v. Arthur Young & Co.*, 590 F. 2d 785 (9th Cir. 1979) p. 785.
[60] *Ibid.*, p. 788.
[61] *Central Bank v. First Interstate Bank of Denver*, 114 S. Ct. 1439 (1994).

¶ 305.02

.03 Private Securities Litigation Reform Act of 1995 (PSLRA)

This legislation revised both the 1933 and 1934 Acts. The purpose of this reform was to decrease the frivolous securities litigation suits while improving the quality of information provided to users. Although there was a significant drop in the number of federal cases from 1995 (188 cases) to 1996 (110 cases), by year 2000 there were 211 disputes. Because PSLRA did not have a safe harbor for material misstatements contained in the audited financial statements, GAAP violations continue to increase (60 percent of all violations in 2000). Accounting violations in 1995 were only 25 percent of the total.

PSLRA added Section 10A(a) to the 1934 Act, which requires three fraud requirements for an audit. First, procedures must be designed to provide reasonable assurances of detecting illegal acts that would have a direct and material effect on the determination of financial statement amounts. An illegal act is an act of omission that violates any law, or any rule or regulation having the force of law. Second, each audit must include procedures to identify related-party transactions. Third, each audit must include an evaluation of the ability of the entity to continue as a going concern.

If fraud is discovered and is not inconsequential, an auditor must notify management and the audit committee. If the fraud is material, senior management does not take remedial action, and such failure warrants a departure from a standard opinion, the auditor must report the matter to the client company's board of directors, which in turn should notify the SEC within one day (for publicly held companies). If the board of directors does not report the matter to the SEC within one day, the auditor should report the matter to the SEC. The auditor will not be liable in a lawsuit for any findings in such reports.

PSLRA added Section 21D(g) to the 1934 Act, replacing the rule of joint and several liability with a fair share proportionate liability. Joint and several liability can be imposed against an auditor only if he or she knowingly committed a violation of the securities laws or if the auditor met some wealth and loss conditions. In other words, an auditor must not act with intent or with recklessness. This allocation process is complex, but the liability corresponds to the percentage of responsibility of the defendants.[62]

Other sections were added or amended, as summarized here:

- A plaintiff must clearly state why any statement is misleading or why omitted information is material.
- The plaintiff must state with particular facts that the auditor acted with the required state of mind.
- The plaintiff must show that the auditor's actions caused the loss in the value of the security.

---

[62] R.R. King and R. Schwartz, "The Private Securities Litigation Reform Act of 1995: A Discussion of Three Provisions," *Accounting Horizon*, Vol. 11, No. 1 (March 1997): 94-96.

¶ 305.03

.04 Securities Litigation Uniform Standards Act of 1998

After the passage of PSLRA in 1995, plaintiffs began to take securities disputes to state courts. Congress amended the 1933 and 1934 Acts so that securities class actions are permitted only in the federal courts and are governed by federal law where a lawsuit alleges:

- An untrue statement or omission of a material fact in connection with the purchase or sale of a covered security or

- The defendant used or employed any deceptive device or contrivance in connection with the purchase or sale of the covered security

Also, a plaintiff may not bring a pending state lawsuit on fraud and breach of fiduciary duty allegations where the claims involve misrepresentations and omissions. A covered security is one that is listed on a national exchange.

.05 Defense in Securities Disputes

In the courtroom, plaintiffs' lawyers will try to undermine an auditor's integrity by preserving facts as lack of independence, pecuniary gain, technical violations of rules, and a close relationship between management and the auditor. The lawyers will try to show that the financial statements were wrong, the auditors failed to perform their duties, and the auditors should have found the problems.[63]

Kelly and Young provide the four following strategies of a defendant auditor:

1. Show that the numbers in the financial statements are correct.

2. Show that the plaintiff did not justifiably rely on the incorrect numbers in such a way to cause harm (no justifiable reliance).

3. Show that others were at fault, not the auditor.

4. Show that the auditor spoke the truth based upon the audit statement opinion itself. Point out that the standard audit opinion does not state that the numbers in the financial statements are correct.[64]

.06 Foreign Corrupt Practices Act (FCPA)

Since 1977, it has been a crime for United States companies to bribe foreign officials in an effort to win or retain business. The FCPA requires companies to develop and maintain an adequate internal control system. Clients often rely on auditors to monitor internal control weakness and spot

---

[63] H.R. Kelly and M.R. Young, "Accountant Liability," in *Litigation Services Handbook: The Role of the Financial Expert*, 3d ed., (New York: John Wiley & Sons, 2001), 33:8—33:11. *See also In re Health Management, Inc.*, sec. Litig., 970 F. Supp. 192 (E.D.N.Y. 1997).

[64] *Ibid.*, pp. 33:11-33:16.

fraud. According to Statement on Auditing Standards (SAS) No. 54, *Illegal Acts by Clients,* an auditor is not required to expand the consideration of internal controls as a result of the FCPA, but the auditor is required under both SAS Nos. 53 and 54 to notify the audit committee (or management) of any suspected fraud and illegal acts. Likewise, under SAS No. 82 when an auditor discovers fraud, he or she must bring the matter to the attention of the appropriate level of client company management.

.07 Civil RICO Liability

The Racketeer-Influenced and Corrupt Organizations (RICO) statute has been used against auditors. The purpose of RICO is to prevent and prosecute criminal activity under the guise of a legitimate business. A successful civil RICO plaintiff is entitled to damages equal to three times the amount of actual damages and attorney fees.

Because RICO prohibits the participation in or profiting from racketeering activities, auditors are drawn into the RICO net through mail, wire, telephone, or securities fraud. Violations of securities laws often involve many plaintiffs in a class action, and the damages can be huge. The Supreme Court in 1993 limited the right of a plaintiff to sue auditors under RICO absent a showing that the auditor participated in the conduct of the enterprise.[65] However, plaintiffs are including a cause of action for aiding and abetting under RICO to increase chances of winning. The Private Securities Litigation Reform Act of 1995 eliminated most RICO claims based upon alleged securities fraud by requiring a prior criminal conviction in connection with the securities fraud.

¶ 306 Statutory Criminal Liability

Many of the civil liability statutes discussed previously have criminal penalties. Auditors may be fined and imprisoned, lose their CPA certificates, and licenses to practice.

.01 Securities Act of 1933

Section 24 of the 1933 Act provides the following penalties for untrue statements or omission of material facts in registration statements:

> Any person who willfully violates any of the provisions of this title, or the rules and regulations promulgated by the Commission under authority thereof, or any person who willfully, in a registration statement filed under this title, makes any untrue statement of a material fact or omits to state any material fact required to be stated therein or necessary to make the statements therein not misleading, shall upon conviction be fined not more than $10,000 or imprisoned not more than five years, or both.

---

[65] *Reves v. Ernst & Young,* 507 U.S. 170 (1993).

.02 Securities Exchange Act of 1934

Section 32(a) of the 1934 Act prohibits any willful violations of a provision of the Act and any rules and regulations of the SEC. Auditors may be fined no more than $100,000 or imprisoned not more than five years, or both. The plaintiff, either the U.S. Justice Department or a state attorney general, need not establish damage, but only that the statute is violated. The plaintiff must show beyond a reasonable doubt that the auditor knew he or she was acting criminally. The auditor will argue that the audit complied with GAAS and GAAP, and he or she had no knowledge of any criminal acts.

The Federal False Statements Statutes, Section 1001, subjects auditors to penalties for false statements made to Federal Governmental Agencies such as the SEC or Department of Defense:[66]

(a) Except as otherwise provided in this section, whoever, in any matter within the jurisdiction of the executive, legislative, or judicial branch of the Government of the United States, knowingly and willfully-

   i. Falsifies, conceals, or covers up by any trick, scheme, or device a material fact;

   ii. makes any materially false, fictitious, or fraudulent statement or representation; or

   iii. makes or uses any false writing or document knowing the same contain any materially false, fictitious, or fraudulent statement or entry; shall be fined under this title or imprisoned not more than 5 years, or both.

Auditors may be subject to the criminal sanctions in Section 1343, Fraud by Wire, Radio, or Television:

> Whoever, having devised or intending to devise any scheme or artifice to defraud, or for obtaining money or property by means of false or fraudulent pretenses, representations, or promises, transmits or causes to be transmitted by means of wire, radio, or television communication in interstate or foreign commerce, any writings, signs, signals, pictures, or sounds for the purpose of executing such scheme or artifice, shall be fined under this title or imprisoned not more than five years, or both. If the violation affects a financial institution, such person shall be fined not more than $1,000,000 or imprisoned not more than 30 years, or both.

Similarly, auditors may be subject to Section 1027, False Statement and Concealment of Facts By the Employee Retirement Income Security Act of 1974.

Finally, auditors may be subject to criminal sanctions under RICO. Review the material describing Civil RICO liability.

.03 Sarbanes-Oxley Act of 2002

Act Sec. 105 of the Sarbanes-Oxley (SO) Act empowers the Public Company Accounting Oversight Board (PCAOB) to investigate registered accounting firms, their partners, and employees. The PCAOB is to conduct disciplinary proceedings if it discovers violations of the Act, any PCAOB

---

[66] 18 U.S.C. 1001.

rules, professional accounting standards, or the federal securities laws. The PCAOB can compel testimony and the production of documents, including workpapers and other documents and information. Sanctions are available for failing to cooperate with any investigation. These sanctions include:

- Temporary suspension or permanent revocation of registration.
- Temporary or permanent suspension or bar of a person from further association with any registered public accounting firm.
- Temporary or permanent limitation on the activities, functions, or operations of such firm or person.
- Civil money penalty for each violation (e.g., not more than $100,000 for an individual or $2 million for any other entity).
- Requiring additional professional education or training.

The Sarbanes-Oxley Act made criminal misconduct in the two following broad areas:

- Executive (CEO and CFO) certificate requirements.
- Destruction, alteration, or falsification of audit evidence.

Act Sec. 906 requires that all financial reports filed with the SEC must be accompanied by a written statement from the executives (CEO and CFO) certifying that the report complies with applicable rules and regulations (SEC) and that the information contained therein fairly presents, in all material respects, the financial condition and results of operations of the company. Knowingly certifying no compliance reports may result in a fine of up to $1 million and imprisonment for up to 10 years. Willfully false certifications will be an offense courting a fine of up to $5 million and imprisonment for up to 20 years. Willfully destroying, altering, or falsifying any corporate audit records, audit evidence, audit workpapers, or any other documents related to an audit of financial statements will be subject to a maximum penalty of 10 years in prison. This requires registered auditors to maintain all audit evidence and review workpapers for five years.

The Act made other changes relevant to auditors:

- Crime to corruptly alter, destroy, mutilate, or conceal any document with the intent to impair the object's integrity or availability (up to 20 years).
- Statute of limitations for the discovery of fraud is now two years from the date of discovery and five years after the Act.
- Maximum penalty for mail and wire fraud is increased from 5 to 10 years.

In December 2002, the SEC changed its enforcement approach with respect to audit firms. Now accounting firms are to be held responsible for

¶ 306.03

the actions of their partners. This new approach reversed the previous approach of not suing auditing firms. On May 22, 2003, the SEC announced a settled enforcement action against Smartalk TeleServices. Here PwC's audit partners failed to comply with GAAPs *and* Smartalk filed an annual report containing *materially* false and misleading financial statements. PwC made undocumented changes to their workpapers and discarded some relevant documents. PwC agreed to pay $1 million.[67]

¶ 307 Biased Jurors

Jurors have high expectations of the accounting profession and accountants that can work to the disadvantage of auditors in malpractice disputes. Auditors are perceived to be experienced, knowledgeable, honest, competent and law abiding. However, jurors believe that auditors have a moral duty to be accurate and dig beneath the surface. They expect auditors to be bloodhounds, as well as watchdogs, because they have little personal experiences with accounting practices and procedures. Louis Genevie provides the following advice for attorneys in the courtroom to overcome this expectation gap:[68]

- Develop compelling demonstrative evidence to illustrate the chain of responsibility for financial information

- Since escaping responsibility entirely will be difficult, focus on the de-selection of possible punitive jurors during voir dire

- Most jurors are not interested in learning technical auditing and accounting terms and will ignore them during deliberations

- Simplify technical language in opening, and minimize technical explanations during testimony by focusing on the purpose of accounting and auditing standards

¶ 308 Federal Sentencing Guidelines

Federal Sentencing Guidelines are used for restitution, probation, and fines. Chapter 8, known as *The Federal Sentencing Guidelines for Organizations*, makes all organizations liable for criminal conduct of its employees and agents. The purposes of these guidelines are to promote uniformity in sentencing, abolish parole, and allow a judge to measure the seriousness of a defendant's offense and the extent of his or her criminal history in order to determine the appropriate sentence. The SEC, for example, is increasingly referring accounting fraud cases to federal prosecutors. Richard Walker, the SEC's director of enforcement, stated in a speech that the SEC plans to bring more enforcement cases against "weak-kneed auditors" and auditors

---

[67] Jacquelyn Lamb, "SEC Applies New Enforcement Paradigm In Action Against Accounting Firms" *PCAOB Reporter* (June 9, 2003): 2 and 12.

[68] Louis Genevie, "Hidden Biases Among Jurors in Accounting Malpractice Cases," *The CPA Journal* (March 1995): 63.

who provide consulting services to corporate audit clients and have become soft on the companies books.[69]

The *Guidelines* are made up of three tables. The first table gives a base fine for criminal offenses (e.g., fraud has a base offense level of 6). The base number is increased based upon the amount of fraud. Table two evaluates a level of culpability (e.g., low equals five points). Table three gives a multiplier. Using this mechanical system, a judge can determine the amount of the fine. There is a "good news" table that allows an organization to reduce the culpability score (e.g., self-reporting reduces the score by 5).[70]

For example, a CPA pleaded guilty to two counts of making false statements on returns in connection with a scheme to skim funds from his accounting firm's S corporation. He was given a sentencing range of 12 to 18 months under the federal guidelines. The District Court used the base offense level from the total monies skimmed, even though the CPA said that the senior partner also received skimmed income. Because the senior partner was not involved, the CPA received enhancement points for total amount skimmed, for special skills of being a CPA, and for a criminal history for a previous battery conviction. He received a point reduction for acceptance of personal responsibility.

¶ 309 Summary

During the past several decades, accountants have been so hammered with lawsuits, judgments, and settlements that the profession itself has often been at risk. Practitioners generally may have liability exposure in several broad areas: liability to the client, liability to third parties, statutory civil liability, and statutory criminal liability. These exposures are covered in this chapter in order to discuss ways auditors can reduce liability risk to the audit firm.

An expectation gap now exists between what users of financial statements expect—particularly in the area of financial statement fraud prevention and detection—and what auditors are responsible to provide in compliance with their professional standards (reasonable assurance that financial statements are free of material misstatements due to error or fraud). Lawsuits brought by audit clients generally involve breach of contract or negligence. The auditor must be aware of arguments that the prosecution will use and possible defenses that auditors can use in response. Large firms usually operate under the limited liability partnership form so that partners are not liable for negligence, error, omission, incompetence, and malfeasance of other partners or the employees supervised by other partners.

---

[69] Elizabeth MacDonald, "SEC to Boost Accounting-Fraud Attack, Work More With Criminal Prosecutors," *The Wall Street Journal*, (December 8, 1999), p. A-4.

[70] *See* Tamar Sittenfeld, "Federal Sentencing Guidelines," *Internal Auditor* (April 1996): 58-62.

The PCAOB is empowered by Act Sec. 105 of the Sarbanes-Oxley Act to investigate registered accounting firms, their partners, and their employees. The purposes of federal sentencing guidelines is to promote uniformity in sentencing, abolish parole, and allow a judge to measure the seriousness of a defendant's offense and the extent of his or her criminal history in order to determine the appropriate sentence.

¶ 309

Chapter 4
Quality Control Standards

¶ 401   Introduction
¶ 402   AICPA Quality Assurance
¶ 403   Peer Review for Small Firms
¶ 404   Inspection of Registered Public Accounting Firms
¶ 405   Internal Auditing Quality Control
¶ 406   ISO 9000 and 14000 Standards
¶ 407   Summary

¶ 401   Introduction

Maintaining the quality of the auditing of both external and internal auditors is a major goal of the AICPA, PCAOB, and the Institute of Internal Auditors. The AICPA's Statement on Auditing Standards No. 25, The Relationship of Generally Accepted Auditing Standards to Quality Control Standards,[1] requires CPA firms to maintain quality control policies and procedures. The Public Oversight Board (POB) was created to oversee and report on the self-regulatory programs of the AICPA's SEC Practice Section, which includes the AICPA quality assurance programs. An increasing number of corporate and accounting scandals (e.g., Enron, WorldCom, Global Crossing, Adelphia, and Qwest), highly-publicized financial statements (e.g., Tyco and Xerox), and perceived audit failures and ineffectiveness caused changes in the self-regulatory framework of the auditing profession. The POB voted itself out of existence and the Public Company Accounting Oversight Board was created to establish a new regulatory framework for registered public accounting firms.

Chapter 4 objectives:

- To become familiar with the recent quality control policies and programs affecting the accounting firms (see ¶ 401).

- To understand the nature of the AICPA Quality Assurance (see ¶ 402).

- To be aware of the review requirements of the AICPA (see ¶ 402).

---

[1] SAS No. 25, *The Relationship of Generally Accepted Auditing Standards to Quality Control Standards* (AICPA, *Professional Standards*, vol. 1, AU sec. 161).

- To recognize the elements of a quality control system evaluated in a peer review (see ¶ 402).

- To be able to explain the three types of peer reviews (see ¶ 403).

- To be familiar with inspection requirements of the PCAOB and the PCAOB's composition, responsibility, and operating procedures (see ¶ 404).

- To recognize approaches to quality control in the internal auditing function (see ¶ 405).

- To become familiar with ISO 9000 and 14000 standards (see ¶ 406).

.01 Regulatory Framework of Auditors

The Sarbanes-Oxley Act changed the landscape of the auditing profession by charging the Public Company Accounting Oversight Board (PCAOB) with monitoring the quality of auditing work. The Federal Revenue Board is working with the PCAOB to improve the quality assurance of auditing services. Beginning in 1991, the Federal Deposit Insurance Corporation Improvement Act has required the CEO and the CFO of all SEC bank registrants to report on the quality of internal controls.[2]

The Sarbanes-Oxley Act changed the self-regulatory environment of registered public accountants under the AICPA peer review system to regulatory framework under the oversight and monitoring system of the PCAOB. Table 4.1 describes the regulatory framework for registered auditors who audit the financial statements of public companies pursuant to the passage of the Sarbanes-Oxley Act of 2002.

Table 4.1

Regulatory Framework for Registered Auditors

Regulatory Organization	Primary Activities
Securities and Exchange Commission (SEC)	Established qualifications for accountants to practice before the SEC and punish violators of securities laws.
Public Company Accounting Oversight Board (PCAOB)	Oversee, investigate, and discipline auditors of public companies. Establish auditing, quality controls, ethics, independence, and other standards relating to the preparation of audit reports.

---

[2] James Hamilton, "Fed to Work with PCAOB to Assure Quality Audits," *PCAOB Reporter* (July 7, 2003): 4 and 6.

State and Federal Courts	Resolve litigation against auditors pertaining to substandard work and impose monetary damages for violations of law.
State Board of Accounting	Establish qualifications for taking the Certified Public Accounting (CPA) examination and issue, suspend, and revoke CPA licenses and establish and/or enforce code of ethics.

Charles Niemeier, a member of the PCAOB, said that the AICPA's quality control standards "have not adequately focused on such matters as the 'tone at the top' of accounting firms, partner compensation plans, and the business context in which audits are performed and decisions made as to which clients should be accepted and retained."[3]

On April 25, 2003, the SEC agreed with PCAOB interim quality control standards in Rule 3400T (T stands for temporary). Furthermore, a registered public accounting firm, and its associated persons, shall comply with quality control standards, as described in:

1. The AICPA's Auditing Standards Board's Statements on Quality Control Standards, as in existence on April 16, 2003;[4] and

2. The AICPA SEC Practice Section's Requirements of Membership (d), (f) (first sentence), (l), (m), (n) (1) and (o), as in existence on April 16, 2003.[5]

Note: The second sentence of requirement (f) of the AICPA SEC Practice Section's Requirements of Membership provided for the AICPA's peer review committee to "authorize alternative procedures" when the requirement for a concurring review could not be met because of the size of the firm. This provision's standards apply to public accounting firms that would be required to be registered after the mandatory registration date and to associated persons of those firms, as if those firms were registered public accounting firms.

Each of the interim standards remains in effect until modified or superseded, either by PCAOB action approved by the Commission or by Commission action pursuant to its independent authority under the federal securities laws and the rules and regulations thereunder.

---

[3] Rosemary Schlark, "PCAOB Unveils Plans To Take Over Setting of Auditing Standards," *Tax Notes* (April 28, 2003): 535-536.

[4] AICPA Professional Standards, QC secs. 20-40 (AICPA 2002).

[5] AICPA SEC Practice Section Manual sec. 1000.08 (d), (f), (j), (m), (n) (1) and (o).

¶ 401.01

Doug Carmichael says the PCAOB will take over the peer-review process once handed by the AICPA. Essentially, the PCAOB supplanted a 60-year self-regulation system. Full inspections of accounting firms will begin in 2004 on a regular basis, with limited review of the Big Four auditing firms in 2003. The PCAOB is taking an active role in the peer review of PricewaterhouseCoopers which is undergoing under the prior peer-review system.[6] The inspections will occur annually for those accounting firms that audit 100 or more public-company clients a year. Firms with fewer clients will be audited every three years.

The inspection reports will be furnished to the accounting firms, but any potential problems will not be made public if the accounting firm corrects the problems within a year. The PCAOB will issue summary reports highlighting problems and issues discovered without disclosing firm names.

Directors of internal auditing departments must establish and maintain a quality assurance program to evaluate the operations of internal auditing departments. This quality assurance program should include three elements: supervision, internal review, and external review. The Institute of Internal Auditors (IIA) works to maintain and improve quality control of internal auditors. The IIA through its Global Auditing Information Network (GAIN) program gathers and distributes information to participating internal auditing organizations on numerous benchmarking measures.

¶ 402   AICPA Quality Assurance

Quality in the performance of auditing and accounting engagements is the goal of the AICPA. Accounting and auditing practice includes all audit, attest, and accounting and review services for which professional standards have been established by the Auditing Standards Board or the Accounting and Review Services Committee under AICPA Rules 201, General Standards, and 202, Compliance with Standards. A CPA firm must be sure that generally accepted auditing standards (GAAS) are followed during every audit. In order to accomplish this objective an auditing firm must establish quality control procedures to help its members meet the GAAS consistently on every engagement. Therefore, GAAS are applicable for the individual members of the firm, and quality controls are applicable for the entire firm. A member of the firm has a responsibility to comply with the professional standards and with the firm's quality control policies and procedures.

The AICPA established the Quality Control Standards Committee in 1978 to help accounting firms develop and implement quality control standards. Quality control comprises the methods used by an auditing firm to help meet its professional responsibilities to its clients. Admission and

---

[6] Cassell Bryan-Low, "McDonough's Modest Digs Belie Tough New Job," *Wall Street Journal*, July 23, 2003, pp. C-1 and C-9.

¶ 402

Quality Control Standards

continued membership in the AICPA requires that each member engaged in the practice of public accounting must practice as a partner or employee of a firm enrolled in an approved practice-monitoring program. If the firm is not eligible to enroll, then the member individually must enroll in such a program.

The nature and extent of a firm's quality control policies and procedures depend upon five overall factors:

- The firm's size and number of offices
- The degree of autonomy of personnel and practice offices
- Knowledge and experience of its employees
- Nature and complexity of the firm's practice
- Costs of developing and implementing the quality control policies and procedures in relationship to the benefits provided

.01 Review Requirement

There are two divisions of the AICPA: the Security and Exchange Commission (SEC) Practice Section and the Private Company Section. A firm may choose to belong to one, both, or neither depending upon its engagements. If a CPA firm audits one or more publicly held companies, the firm is required to belong to the SEC Practice Section, which imposes higher standards. The CPA firms that are members of either of these sections must be reviewed at least once every three years. Only those firms that satisfactorily pass the peer review can be members of one or both of the two sections.

Peer reviews are administered in cooperation with the state CPA society for those CPA firms whose main offices are located in the state. A firm may ask another firm, an association of which it is a member, or a state CPA society administering its review to appoint a review team. AICPA members can obtain a reviewer resume form from Teresa William at 201-938-3025 or they can visit *www.adobe.com/prodindex/acrobat/readstep.html*.

A CPA firm that does not have a peer review is required to have a quality review every three years. A quality review is less extensive than a peer review. Both the peer review and quality review seek to achieve their goal of quality improvement through education and remedial corrective action. Basically, Statement on Quality Control Standards (SQCS) No. 2, *Systems of Quality Control for a CPA Firm's Accounting and Auditing Practice*, requires every firm, regardless of size, to have a system of quality control for its accounting and auditing practices.

Peer review. Both firms and individuals in the AICPA peer review program must:

¶ 402.01

- Establish and maintain appropriate quality control policies and procedures, and comply with them to ensure the quality of their practices
- Have independent peer reviews of their accounting and auditing practices at least once every three years
- Take remedial, corrective actions as needed

A peer review is essentially a review by CPAs of an accounting firm's compliance with its quality control system. If a firm performs the audit of one or more SEC registrants during the year and at least one such audit engagement is not selected for review, the review team must justify *why not* in the Summary Review Memorandum that they prepare.

.02 Elements of Quality Control

SQCS No. 2 states that the quality control system should encompass these five elements:

1. Independence, integrity, and objectivity
2. Personnel management
3. Acceptance and continuance of clients
4. Engagement performance
5. Monitoring[7]

A peer review team should obtain a sufficient understanding of the reviewed firm's system of quality control with respect to the five elements to plan the review. The nine elements in the previous SQCS No. 1 were combined into the new five SQCS No. 2 elements.

Independence. Although independence is a bedrock principle for auditing and accounting services of a CPA (see Chapter 2), it is not required in all situations. However, a CPA firm is required to establish policies and procedures to ensure that employees perform all responsibilities with integrity and maintain objectivity while fulfilling those responsibilities. Independence refers to an impartiality that recognizes an obligation for fairness. Integrity refers to being honest and candid; service and public trust should not be subordinated to personnel gain. Objectivity involves being impartial, intellectually honest, and free of conflicts of interest.[8]

Personnel management. The quality of a CPA firm's performance depends upon the knowledge, skills, and abilities of the personnel who perform, supervise, and review the accounting, auditing, and attestation assignments. See SQCS No. 5., *The Personal Manangement Element of a*

---

[7] Statement on Quality Control Standards (SQCS) No. 2, *Systems of Quality Control for a CPA Firm's Accounting and Auditing Practice* (AICPA, Professional Standards, vol. 2, QC sec. 20.07).

[8] *Ibid.*, 20.10.

Firm's System of Quality Control, Competencies Required by a Practitioner in Charge of an Attest Engagement. The appropriate personnel should participate in general and industry-specific continuing professional education to satisfy the continuing professional education requirements. The personnel selected for engagements should have the necessary characteristics to enable competent performance. They should have the necessary technical training and proficiency. The person in charge of the engagement must possess the type of competencies that are appropriate to that engagement.[9]

SQCS No. 1 suggests that the acceptance/continuance decision should consider the integrity of the client's management. SQCS No. 2 adds that an accounting firm should accept only those accounting and auditing engagements that can be finished with professional competence. Further, the auditor must obtain an understanding with the client as to the nature, scope and limitations of the services to be performed.

Engagement performance. Any work performed must meet the applicable professional standards, regulatory requirements, and the firm's standard of quality.[10] Personnel should refer to authoritative literature and consult, on a timely basis, with the appropriate individuals when dealing with complex, unusual, or unfamiliar issues.

Monitoring. This standard provides guidance for implementing these proactive monitoring procedures:

- Inspection
- Pre- and post-issuance review of selected engagements
- Review of selected administrative and personnel records pertaining to the quality control elements
- Interviews of firm personnel
- Determination of quality control corrective actions
- Communication of weaknesses
- Follow-up by appropriate personnel[11]

Monitoring in SQCS No. 3 provides:

- Relevance and adequacy of policies and procedures
- Appropriateness of guidance and practice aid
- Effectiveness of professional development activities
- Compliance with policies and procedures[12]

---

[9] *Ibid.*, 20.13.
[10] *Ibid.*, 20.14.
[11] *Ibid.*, 30.03.
[12] *Ibid.*, 30.02.

¶ 403 Peer Review for Small Firms

Effective January 1, 2001, new peer review standards were applied to firms that do not audit SEC registrants. Members practicing in organizations not eligible to enroll in an AICPA practice-monitoring program (e.g., a nonCPA-owned entity) must enroll individually in a peer review program. Individual AICPA members who are practicing with a firm that is eligible to enroll in an AICPA approved practice-monitoring program may not enroll in such a program individually. The individual could elect to have a higher-level peer review.

There are three types of peer reviews: system, engagement, and report (high to low). Under previous AICPA rules there were only two types of reviews: on-site and off-site. The old on-site peer review was renamed system review. An accounting and auditing practice is defined as all of a CPA firm's engagements that are covered by AICPA's statements on auditing standards (SASs), statements on standards for accounting and review services (SSARSs), statements on standards for attestation engagements (SSAEs), and *Government Auditing Standards* (the Yellow Book).

A firm can always move up to a higher type of review. An accounting firm required to have a report review may decide to have an engagement or system review. Likewise, a firm required to have an engagement review may decide to have a system review.

.01 System Review

This review is for auditing firms that perform engagements under SASs, the Yellow Book (government), and examinations under Statements on Standards for Attestation Engagements (SSAEs). About 15,000 firms will likely have a system review over a three-year period (the highest review). The purpose of this review is to inform the reviewer whether the reviewed firm (1) has designed its system of quality control in accordance with the AICPA quality control standards, and (2) is complying with its quality control policies and procedures in such a way that should give the auditing firm reasonable assurance that auditors are conforming to professional standards.[13]

A system review should include the following procedures:[14]

1. Plan the review, as follows.

    - Obtain a sufficient understanding of the nature and extent of the firm's accounting and auditing practice to plan the review.

---

[13] Gary Freundlich and Walter H. Webb, "Peer Review Changes for Small Firms," *Journal of Accountancy* (August 2000): 58.

[14] *Standards for Performing and Reporting on Peer Reviews* (AICPA, Professional Standards, vol. 2, PR sec. 100.30). Copyright 1990, 1999, 2001 by the America Institute of Certified Public Accountants, Inc. Reprinted with Permission.

Quality Control Standards   **135**

- Obtain a sufficient understanding of the design of the firm's system of quality control, including an understanding of the monitoring procedures performed since the prior review.
- Assess the peer review risk.
- Use the knowledge obtained from the foregoing to select the offices and the engagements to be reviewed, and to determine the nature and extent of the tests to be applied in the financial areas.

2. Perform the review, as follows.

- Review compliance by the firm with its system of quality control. The review should cover all the organizational or functional levels within the firm.
- Review selected engagements, including the relevant working paper files and reports.
- Reassess the adequacy of the scope of the review based on the results obtained to determine whether additional procedures are necessary.
- Have an exit conference with senior members of the reviewed firm and at least the team captain to discuss the review team's findings and recommendations and the type of report it will issue.
- Prepare a written report on the results of the review and, if applicable, a letter of comments.
- Review and comment to the reviewed firm on the firm's response to the letter of comments, if any.

A review should cover a firm's accounting and auditing practice and should be directed to the professional aspects of the firm's accounting and auditing practice, not the business aspects of that practice. Review team members should not have contact with or access to any clients of the reviewed firm in connection with the review.[15]

A review should encompass a current period of one year to be mutually agreed upon by the reviewed firm and the review team captain. Generally, the review should be conducted within three to five months following the end of the year chosen. Client engagements subject to selection for review should be those with periods ending during the year under review. For attestation engagements (including a financial forecast or projection) the selection for review ordinarily should be one with report dates during the year under review. If the current year's engagement is not completed and a comparable engagement within the peer review year is not available, the prior year's engagement should be reviewed. If the subsequent year's

---

[15] *Ibid.*, 100.32.

¶ 403.01

engagement has been completed, the reviewing team should consider, based on its assessment of peer review risk, whether the more recently completed engagement should be reviewed instead.[16]

Interpretation No. 1 involving a system review performed at a location other than the practitioner's office suggests the following items be given to the reviewer prior to the review:[17]

- All documentation related to the resolution of independence questions (1) identified during the year under review with respect to any audit or accounting client, or (2) related to any of the audit or accounting clients selected for review, no matter when the question was identified if the matter still exists during the review period.

- The most recent independence confirmations received from other firms of CPAs engaged to perform segments of engagements on which the firm acted as principal auditor or accountant.

- The most recent representations received from all professional staff concerning their conformity with applicable independence requirements.

- Documentation, if any, of consultations with outside parties during the year under review in connection with audit or accounting services provided to any client.

- A list of relevant technical publications used as research materials, as referred to in the quality control policies and procedures questionnaire (see AICPA *Peer Review Program Manual*).

- A list of audit and accounting materials, if any, identified in response to the questions in the "Engagement Performance" section of the quality control policies and procedures questionnaire (see AICPA *Peer Review Program Manual*).

- Continuing professional education (CPE) records sufficient to demonstrate compliance by the CPAs in the firm with state and AICPA CPE requirements.

- The relevant working paper files and reports on the engagements selected for review.

- Any other evidential matter requested by the reviewer.

---

[16] *Ibid.*, 100.33.
[17] Interpretation No. 1, "System Reviews Performed at a Location Other than the Practitioner's Office" (AICPA, Professional Standards, vol. 2, PR sec. 9100.02). Copyright 1990, 1999, 2001 by the American Institute of Certified Public Accountants, Inc. Reprinted with permission.

¶ 403.01

The AICPA Peer Review Board suggests that these specific types of engagements should be selected for review from time to time:[18]

- Governmental—if a firm performs an audit of an entity subject to Government Auditing Standards and the peer review is intended to meet the requirements of those standards, at least one engagement conducted pursuant to those standards should be selected for review.

- Employee Benefit Plans—if a firm performs the audit of one or more entities subject to the Employee Retirement Income Security Act of 1974 (ERISA), at least one such audit engagement conducted pursuant to ERISA should be selected for review.

- Depository Institutions—if a firm performs an audit of a federally insured depository institution subject to the FDIC Improvement Act of 1991 and the peer review is intended to meet the requirements of the Act, at least one engagement conducted pursuant to the Act should be selected for review. Such a review should include a review of the reports on internal control or compliance with the laws and regulations, since those reports are required to be issued under the Act.

.02 Engagement Review

This review is for accounting firms that are not required to have a system review and are not eligible to have a report review. This review cannot express an opinion on the firm's compliance with its own quality control policies and procedures or with AICPA quality control standards. Instead: the reviewer's objectives are to provide a basis for expressing an opinion as to whether:

- Financial statements information, and related reports conform in all material aspects with professional standards

- Firm's documentation conforms with the requirements of the SSARs and SSAESs

At least 10,000 firms are likely to have engagement reviews during the next three years.

.03 Report Review

A firm performing only compilations that omit substantially all disclosures must have a report review. The purpose of this report review is to help an auditing firm that performs omit-disclosure compilation engagements to improve the overall quality of its accounting practice. The peer reviewer

---

[18] Adapted from Interpretation No. 2 "Engagement Selection in System Reviews," (AICPA, Professional Standards, vol. 2, PR sec. 9100.06).

selects a sample of engagements and provides the reviewed firm a report listing comments and recommendations.

.04 Panel on Audit Effectiveness

An important Panel made a number of suggestions and recommendations to the SEC Practice Section (SECPS) Peer Review Committee for peer reviewers to:

- Evaluate firms' methodology, guidance and training materials relating to analytical procedures

- Determine whether firms have carried out the requisite training and evaluate the effectiveness of the firms' implementation of their methodology related to analytical procedures on audit engagements

- Consider the adequacy of firms' policies, guidance, and training (and any changes in them) in the area of auditing revenue recognition

- Evaluate firms' policies, training and guidance materials on auditing estimates and judgments

- Evaluate the effectiveness with which engagement teams implement SAS No. 89 and SAB No. 99 and determine whether additional guidance or training is needed

- Review and evaluate firms' policies, if any, for understanding the entity's policies and processes for communicating information to analysts; obtaining analysts' reports and forecasts, and considering them when assessing risks and evaluating important issues and the materiality of potential adjustments; and becoming aware of the information management provides to analysts

- Evaluate the effectiveness with which engagement teams implement their firm's policies and determine whether additional guidance or training is needed

- Evaluate the adequacy of firms' guidance and training (and any changes in them) in the area of going concern considerations

- Address the adequacy of firms' policies, procedures, and guidance on the testing of internal audit work and the documentation of auditors' considerations and work related to internal audit

- Address the adequacy of firms' guidance on reporting to audit committees [19]

---

[19] *The Panel on Audit Effectiveness: Report and Recommendations* (Stamford, Conn.: Public Oversight Board, August 31, 2000).

¶ 404 Inspection of Registered Public Accounting Firms

The Sarbanes-Oxley Act of 2002 created the PCAOB to register, monitor, and inspect auditors of public companies. Table 4.2 summarizes the PCAOB's composition, responsibility, and operating procedures. The PCAOB was organized in April 2003 and started to register public accounting firms that audit financial statements of public companies. Table 4.3 presents registration components and requirements of the PCAOB. In October 2003, the PCAOB adopted its final rules for inspection of registered accounting firms:

1. Annual inspections for firms that do the largest volume of audit work (more than 100 public clients) are required.

2. Triennial inspections for firms that do some volume of audit work (less than 100 public clients) are required.

3. Special inspections are not subject to a schedule and would be conducted as necessary.

4. The PCAOB is also authorized to:

    - Report information indicating possible violations of law or professional standards to the SEC, other regulators, or law enforcement authorities and appropriate state regulatory authorities.

    - Commence its own investigation or disciplinary proceeding based on relevant information.

5. Registered inspected accounting firms may submit written comments on a draft inspection report before the Board issues a final report.

6. The Board may make portions of a final inspection report that deal with criticisms or potential defects in a firm's quality control systems if the firm fails to address those issues to the Board's satisfaction within 12 months after the issuance of the final inspection report.

7. Public accounting firms that audit publicly traded companies are required to register with the PCAOB, which on average costs about $300,000 to register.

8. As part of its annual inspections, the PCAOB requires disclosure of the criminal backgrounds of the audit staff.

9. As of June 2004, 977 public accounting firms have registered with the PCAOB, from which 813 registered firms are domestic and 164 foreign registered firms are from 53 countries.

10. These registered public accounting firms audit more than 16,500 public companies.

Table 4.2

Public Company Accounting Oversight Board—Composition, Responsibility, and Operating Procedures

Composition	Responsibilities	Operating Procedures
1. A nonprofit organization funded by the SEC registrants and registered public accounting firms.	1. Prepare its budget and manage its operations.	1. Operate under the SEC oversight function.
2. Consists of five members, two of which are CPAs.	2. Register and inspect public accounting firms that audit public companies (registered firms).	2. File an annual report with the SEC.
3. Members serve full-time for a five-year staggered term, with a two-term limit.	3. Establish, adopt, and modify auditing, independence, quality control, ethics, and other standards for registered firms.	3. Register public accounting firms that intend to audit publicly traded companies.
4. The chair may be held by a CPA who has not been in practice for at least five years prior to the appointment.	4. Enforce compliance with applicable laws and regulations including securities laws, professional standards, SEC rules, and PCAOB standards by registered firms.	4. Issue auditing standards for registered firms.

¶ 404

5. The first group of members consists of:
  a. William J. McDonough (chair)
  b. Charles D. Niemeier
  c. Kayla J. Gillan
  d. Daniel L. Goelzer
  e. Willis D. Gradison, Jr.
	5. Investigate registered firms for potential violations of applicable laws, regulations, and rules.	5. Establish audit workpaper retention rules.

6. Douglas R. Carmichael (Chief Auditor and Director of Professional Standards)	6. Impose sanctions for violations.	6. Establish procedures to investigate and discipline registered firms and their personnel for violations of applicable rules and regulations.
7. Thomas Ray (Deputy Chief Auditor)	7. Perform other duties or functions as deemed necessary.	7. Form a Standing Advisory Group to assist the PCAOB in its standard-setting process.

Source: http://www.pcaobus.org.

Table 4.3

Registration Components and Requirements of the PCAOB

Registration Components	Registration Requirements
Firm identity	• Legal name • Primary contact and signatories • Form of organization • Office locations • Licenses
List of public company audit clients	• List issuers for which applicant prepared audit reports during the preceding and current calendar year. • List issuers for which applicant expect to prepare audit reports during the calendar year. • List issuers for which applicant played a substantial role in audit or expects to play a substantial role.
Statement of quality control policies	• Describe policies established to monitor compliance with the independence rule of conduct.
List certain proceedings involving the applicant	• List certain criminal, civil, and administrative actions. • List pending private civil actions. • Provide discretionary statement regarding proceedings involving the audit practice.
List filings disclosing accounting disagreements with public company audit clients	• List existence of disagreements with issuers, including name, date, and a copy of the filing.
Roster of associated accountants	• List accountants associated with applicants. • Provide profile of firm personnel, including: — Total number of accountants — Total number of CPAs or accountants with comparable licenses from non-U.S. jurisdictions — Total personnel employed by the applicant
Consent of applicant	• Provide consent to cooperate with the Board and its statement of acceptance or registration condition.

Source: http://www.pcaobus.org

¶ 404

¶ 405 Internal Auditing Quality Control

Just like that of the AICPA, a central function of the Institute of Internal Auditing (IAA) is to maintain and improve the quality of internal auditing organizations. Research projects,[20] numerous books and articles, and member conferences have been devoted to quality control of internal auditors. The IIA's Global Auditing Information Network (GAIN)[21] program (see ¶ 1505) has accumulated a vast amount of data. The hope is that by refining this database firms may select key measures that can be combined into an index to measure audit quality. These measures should allow chief auditing executives (CAEs) to more easily track the performance of their audit departments.

For the function to be successful, the CAE must establish a system to control the quality of the services performed by the internal auditing function. The traditional approach to quality control stressed supervision, internal review, and external review. Supervision entailed explaining to subordinates the task to be performed, evaluating their progress and giving appropriate feedback as the task was performed. Internal and external reviews were done periodically to ensure the internal auditing function complied with professional standards and that individual audits were performed correctly. The disadvantage with this system—and especially with the internal and external reviews—is that they occurred *after* the delivery of services.

Many internal auditing groups later adopted a Total Quality Management (TQM) approach to controlling the quality of audits. Under TQM, audit quality is defined in terms of customer satisfaction, and performance measures are identified to measure customer satisfaction. Progress is measured in steady improvement in the performance measures over time. Most internal auditing functions today track some performance measures. Appendix 4, "Possible Performance Measures," lists 81 possible performance tools for auditors. This number of measures is obviously too many to apply to every audit situation and must be reduced. In addition, the CAE should adopt measures for each major aspect of the internal auditing function namely input, process, output and overall management. This is shown in Figure 4.1.

---

[20] See, for example, J.C. Lampe, and S.G. Sutton, *Developing Productivity in Quality Measurement Systems for Internal Auditing Departments* (Altamonte Springs, Fl.: The Institute of Internal Auditors Research Foundation, 1994).

[21] Institute of Internal Auditors, Global Auditing Information Network, 1997 report based on 1996 data.

Figure 4.1

Internal Auditing TQM Process Model

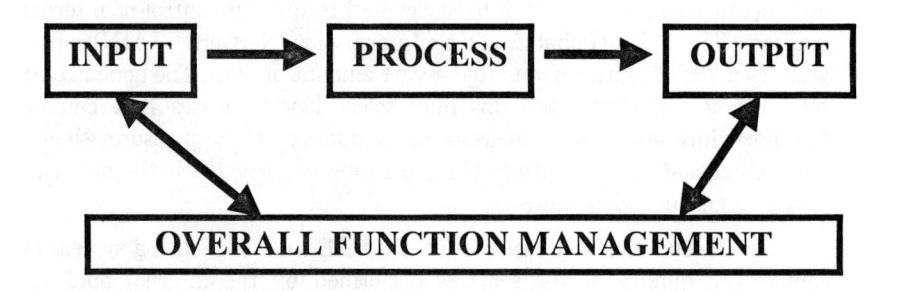

```
INPUT  →  PROCESS  →  OUTPUT
         ↕
OVERALL FUNCTION MANAGEMENT
```

Under the system suggested by IIA, a CAE would adopt one or more performance measures for each of four areas. For instance to measure input, the CAE could choose average years of auditing experience for the audit staff or educational levels or certification. Process could be measured using auditee satisfaction survey results. Likewise, output could be measured in terms of significant findings or time to release the report. Audit committee and management surveys could be used to measure overall audit function management.

CAEs should keep the following points in mind when he or she adopts performance measures:

- Performance measures should not be selected and evaluated individually; rather they should be tied to the internal auditing department's mission and goals.

- Internal auditing department performance should be evaluated based on four perspectives—input, process, output, and overall function management.

- Internal auditing department missions and goals should be stated as an integrated set of objectives and measures that describe long-term drivers of success.

- Key parties both outside and inside the internal auditing department should participate in the process of selecting performance measures.

Finally, the CAE should note that failure to adopt performance measures may lead others to impose them for the internal auditing function.

¶ 405

¶ 406 ISO 9000 and 14000 Standards

In 1947, the International Organization for Standardization (ISO) located in Switzerland was established to develop common international standards for many disiplines and industries. Members come from the standards bodies in more than 90 countries.

The ISO published its quality assurance and quality management standard in 1987 (republished as an updated version in 1994) referred to as the "ISO 9000 Standards." ISO's purpose was to facilitate international commerce by providing a single set of standards that would be recognized and respected by people everywhere. These ISO 9000 Standards apply to all types of organizations (e.g., manufacturing, processing, printing and banking).

Organizations develop quality systems that meet the ISO 9000 Standards in order to control and improve the quality of their products and services in order to reduce the costs associated with poor quality or to become competitive. Organizations develop a quality system that meets the quality requirements specified in ISO 9001, ISO 9002 or ISO 9003.

Companies then invite accredited external auditors (registers) to evaluate the system's effectiveness. If companies pass, the auditor certifies that the quality system has met all of the ISO requirements. Official certificates are issued and the achievment is recorded in their registry.

Chapter 20, "Enviromental and Quality Audits," covers ISO 14000, which deals with an enviromental management standard. ISO 14000 requires conformity of an organization's enviromental policies and systems.

¶ 407 Summary

Before the Enron scandal, the Public Oversight Board (POB) was created to oversee and report on the self-regulatory programs of the AICPA's SEC Practice Section, which includes the AICPA quality assurance programs. Quality in the performance of accounting and auditing engagements is the goal of the AICPA. There are two divisions of the AICPA: SEC Practice Section and the Private Company Section. If a CPA firm audits one or more publicly held companies, the firm is required to belong to the SEC Practice section, which imposes higher standards. In the past, the CPA firms that were members of either of these sections had to be reviewed at least once every three years. A CPA firm that did not have a peer review was required to have a quality review every three years.

As a result of the Enron scandal, the Sarbanes-Oxley Act of 2002 changed the public accountants' self-regulatory environment into a regulatory framework under the oversight function of the PCAOB. The Sarbanes-Oxley Act authorized the PCAOB with monitoring the quality of auditing work. The SEC approved the PCAOB interim quality control standards. Furthermore, a registered public accounting firm, and its associated persons, shall comply with certain existing quality standards of the AICPA. Each of the interim standards remains in effect until modified or superseded by PCAOB quality control standards.

The purpose of the ISO 9000 standards is to facilitate international commerce by providing a single set of standards that would be recognized worldwide.

Chapter 5

Planning the Financial Audit

¶ 501	Introduction
¶ 502	Pre-Planning Stage
¶ 503	Audit Preparation Stage
¶ 504	Audit Staff Supervision
¶ 505	Summary

¶ 501 Introduction

The wave of corporate and accounting scandals and Congressional responses encourage auditors to be more proactive in audit planning and be more skeptical in conducting a financial statement audit. The Sarbanes-Oxley Act of 2002 authorized the Public Company Accounting Oversight Board (PCAOB) to issue auditing standards for registered auditors who audit financial statements of public companies. PCAOB auditing standards will affect all three phases of an audit engagement: planning, evidence-gathering, and reporting. For example, PCAOB Auditing Standard No. 2 requires that during the planning phase of an audit engagement, auditors obtain understanding with the client that their attestation of and reporting on internal control is an integral part of an audit of financial statements.

With the current heightened sensitivity towards fraud issues (e.g., Enron, WorldCom) and its impact on financial statement audits, the Auditing Standards Board issued SAS No. 99, Consideration of Fraud in a Financial Statement Audit, in January 2003. The new standard expands the audit treatment of fraud in many ways; however, the new resulting procedures are meant to be incorporated into the existing standards in a seamless fashion. The planning phase of the financial audit contains some of the new requirements and are footnoted where applicable.

Chapter 5 objectives:

- To become familiar with the terms "pre-engagement and planning" and "audit preparation" and learn the benefits derived from good audit planning (see ¶ 501).

- To understand the client investigation and continuation during the planning stage of the audit engagement (see ¶ 502).

- To understand the importance of obtaining an understanding with the client during the pre-planning stage (see ¶ 502).

¶ 501

- To understand the audit preparation stage and its various steps (see ¶ 503).
- To understand the importance of audit staff supervision (see ¶ 504).

.01 Overview of an Audit Engagement

When a client approaches a practitioner to perform an audit, either as a continuing client or as a new client, the accountant cannot simply accept the engagement. Many issues must first be considered as part of the preplanning stage of the planning phase. Auditor independence, client industry knowledge, staffing ability, client integrity, and adequacy of records are but some of the issues that must be resolved before an audit engagement is accepted. If the audit engagement is accepted, the audit preparation stage of the planning phase can begin. Figure 5.1 shows the planning phase in the context of the financial audit.

Figure 5.1

Time Line for Planning the Financial Audit

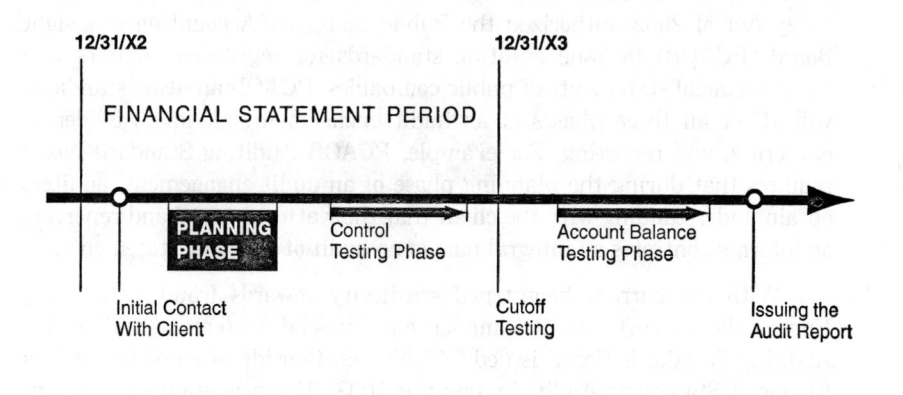

12/31/X2 — 12/31/X3

FINANCIAL STATEMENT PERIOD

PLANNING PHASE — Control Testing Phase — Account Balance Testing Phase

Initial Contact With Client — Cutoff Testing — Issuing the Audit Report

Chapter 5 presents two stages of the planning phase for a financial audit:

1. Pre-planning—During this stage, the auditor investigates whether to accept a client's request for an audit. If the audit engagement is accepted, this stage culminates with the preparation and signing of the audit engagement letter.

2. Audit preparation—This stage includes all the preparation and investigation needed to plan the audit so that it might proceed efficiently and effectively.

Auditing standards require adequate planning. The American Institute of Certified Public Accountants (AICPA) auditing standard for field-

¶ 501.01

work[1] states that the audit is to be adequately planned, and assistants, if any, are to be properly supervised. Although the standards require planning, many benefits are derived from good audit planning:

- Audit costs are minimized.
- Misunderstandings with the client are decreased.
- The auditor more effectively obtains sufficient evidence to support the audit opinion.

Figure 5.2

The Pre-Planning Stage

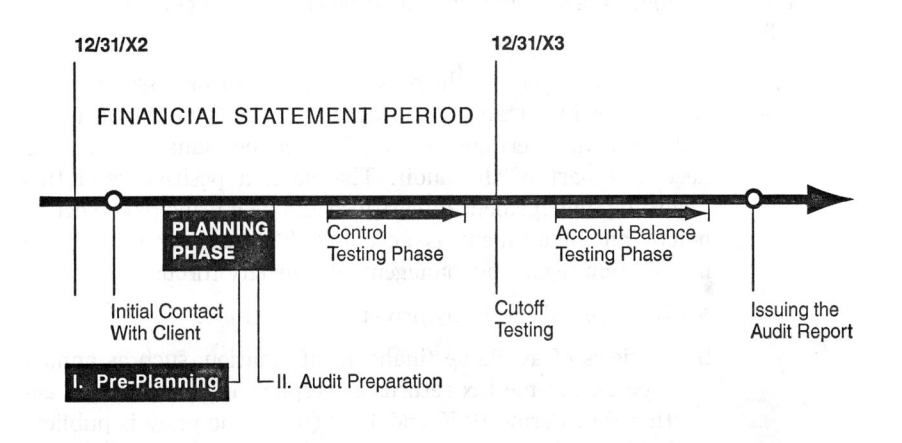

¶ 502 Pre-Planning Stage

.01 Client Investigation

A potential audit engagement can be initiated in a number of ways. A client may have contacted the auditor directly or the auditor may have submitted to the client an audit proposal. To minimize business risk to the auditing firm it is a good policy that the auditor only accept those clients engaged in legitimate pursuits. Clients with a history of involvement in litigation and other controversial matters may not be good audit candidates. Before accepting an audit engagement, the auditor should conduct an investigation to determine whether the engagement should be accepted. This investigation is contained in the "pre-planning stage" or "pre-engagement activities" (Figure 5.2). This stage involves obtaining information regarding the prospective client, the company's operations and the auditor's capabilities.

---

[1] Statement on Auditing Standards (SAS) No. 1, Codification of Auditing Standards and Procedures (AICPA, Professional Standards, vol. 1, AU sec. 310.01).

SAS No. 99 re-emphasized the need for auditors to maintain a level of professional skepticism throughout the audit. Because management is in a unique position to perpetrate fraud through their ability to override existing controls and manipulate accounting information, the auditor must be constantly vigilant against such actions.

SAS No. 99 defines professional skepticism as an "attitude that includes a questioning mind and a critical assessment of audit evidence. The auditor should conduct the engagement with a mindset that recognizes the possibility that a material misstatement due to fraud could be present, regardless of any past experience with the entity and regardless of the auditor's belief about management's honesty and integrity." Beginning with client investigation procedures, professional skepticism is needed. With this in mind, information that should be obtained about the prospective client includes:[2]

1. Background regarding the prospective client's professional reputation. It is important to consider the integrity of management. Management assertions and inquiries of the management are a necessary part of the audit. Therefore, a positive resolution regarding management integrity should be a principal objective before an engagement is accepted. The auditor can obtain information regarding management integrity through:

   a. Background checks by private investigators.

   b. Reviews of available financial information, such as annual reports, income tax returns correspondence with taxing authorities, Forms 10-K and 10-Q (if the company is publicly held), reports with any other regulatory agency.

   c. Reviews of newspaper articles, professional journals, and Form 8-K (if the company is publicly held) including any disagreements with previous auditors over accounting principles or audit scope.

   d. Inquiries of local bankers, attorneys, underwriters.

   e. Management responses to auditor suggestion for improvements to internal controls.

   f. Evaluation of the autonomy of the board of directors and the composition of the audit committee.

   g. Assessment of an internal audit staff, including their:

      i. Competence

      ii. Objectivity

      iii. Areas of audit coverage

---

[2] SAS No. 99, Consideration of Fraud in a Financial Statement Audit (AICPA, Professional Standards, vol. 1, AU sec. 316.13).

¶ 502.01

Planning the Financial Audit 151

    h. If another auditor had an engagement with the company in the previous year (a predecessor auditor), the successor auditor should make specific inquiries of the predecessor auditor. The successor auditor is responsible for contacting the predecessor auditor. Because of confidentiality matters, the successor auditor should obtain prior permission from the prospective client before contacting the predecessor auditor. Issues that the predecessor should discuss with the successor auditor include:

        i. The predecessor's understanding about the reasons for the change of auditors.

        ii. The predecessor's opinion regarding management integrity.

        iii. A discussion of any disagreements that the predecessor had with management regarding accounting principles or any other important matters.

        iv. A discussion of any predecessor communications with the audit committee or board of directors regarding fraud, illegal matters, or significant issues of internal controls.

        Under normal conditions the predecessor auditor should respond promptly and fully to the successor's request. However the successor auditor should be aware that the predecessor may need to restrict or withhold information entirely because of unusual circumstances such as litigation. Under those circumstances the predecessor should inform the successor of the limited response.

        Additionally, as part of the evidence-gathering process of the audit, the successor may request a review of the predecessor's workpapers. Again, under normal conditions the successor may provide this information.[3]

  2. Understanding of the purpose for the audit as well as who will be relying upon the audit report. It is important to obtain a complete understanding as to what is involved in the engagement. Regulatory reports, tax return preparation, and additional financial statement disclosure may be considered by the client as part of the audit. The additional work that these

---

[3] SAS No. 84, Communications Between Predecessor and Successor Auditors (AICPA, Professional Standards, vol. 1, AU sec. 315.10).

¶ 502.01

matters may entail could affect the nature, timing, and extent of the audit work.

3. Knowledge of the internal control structure to determine whether the records and controls are sufficient to support an audit. The records and internal controls may be in such disarray that an audit is not feasible.

4. Determining to what extent the prospective client is willing and able to pay the audit fee.

5. Consideration of the significance of the additional risk (engagement risk) associated with this potential new client. This additional risk emanates from various sources. Some are business risk issues; other risk comes from issues inherent to audit risk. Some of the business risk issues cited by the AICPA that may apply to the client are:

   a. Risky business ventures
   b. Controversial activities
   c. A limited number of client suppliers or customers
   d. A deteriorating financial condition
   e. An industry experiencing a deteriorating economic condition
   f. An industry saturated with competitors
   g. A large number of lawsuits
   h. Doubt about the client's going concern
   i. Disregard for regulatory compliance and
   j. Lack of cooperation with audit

Audit risk is the probability that the auditor will render the wrong audit opinion. Auditors may fail to modify their opinion when clients' financial statements are misstated. Certain conditions unmask potential problems with financial statement valuation and/or presentation. Audit risk issues that the auditor should consider before accepting a prospective client are:

1. Undue pressure on management to meet budgetary or forecasted results
2. Significant related party transactions
3. A significant number of material transactions occurring at year end
4. Operations dominated by one individual
5. A history of aggressive accounting that enhances company earnings or financial position
6. Company affiliates that are not subject to audit

¶ 502.01

The auditor's judgment of the combined effect of business and audit risks associated with the prospective client should be integral in determining whether to accept the engagement:

1. Reviewing the auditor's own staffing capabilities. According to general auditing standards, professional care must be exercised in the performance of an audit engagement. The additional audit hours that a new engagement would entail should be factored into the current working schedule of the audit staff. In this manner the feasibility of the audit can be reviewed.

2. Determining auditor and staff experience in the prospective client's industry. Only persons who have adequate technical training and proficiency as auditors should perform audits. They will serve as the technical resource for questions and problems arising during the audit. Generally accepted accounting principles (GAAP) can be industry-specific, as are internal controls and record-keeping methodologies. Those auditors applying generally accepted auditing standards (GAAS) must take this into consideration. Therefore, it is important that there are individuals assigned to the audit engagement who have the technical expertise in the client's industry or related industries.

3. GAAS require auditors to maintain independence in all matters relating to the audit assignment.[4] The independent audit is important to readers of financial statements because it involves the objective examination of, and reporting on, management-prepared statements. The auditor must be without bias with respect to the client under audit. Objectivity is enhanced if the auditor retains independence in mental attitude. Staff assigned to an audit engagement should also reflect independence with respect to the client. For this reason it is important to inform staff about the particulars of new clients. For example, many firms circulate new client lists to all personnel, requesting that staff who have any potential independence issues regarding a new client contact their supervisor. Also, any potential independence conflict that could result from acceptance of the engagement should be reviewed.

.02 Obtaining an Understanding with the Client

Once the aforementioned issues are satisfied, the auditor is in a better position to accept the audit engagement. If auditors feel that they have a clear understanding of the engagement, auditing standards require that the

---

[4] Principle 54, Article III—*Integrity* (AICPA, Professional Standards, vol. 2, ET sec. 54.01).

staff document the understanding in the workpapers. Auditors should not accept engagements they do not clearly understand.

An engagement letter should then be prepared. Although not mandatory, this letter is recommended as a means of documenting the understanding of the engagement, including the engagement's objectives, the responsibilities of the auditor and management, and the limitations of the audit. Typically, two copies of the letter are prepared and signed by both the client and the auditor. Each party receives a copy.

The engagement letter affects the planning of the audit by defining those responsibilities necessary for the audit to be completed in an effective manner. Defining responsibilities benefits both the auditor and the client by pinpointing what to expect from the engagement.

The engagement letter serves the *auditor* because it:

1. Details resources needed from the client:
    a. Records
    b. Supporting documentation
    c. Client personnel assistance
2. Clearly states the auditing fees
3. Provides a reminder that management is responsible for proper internal controls and financial statements

The engagement letter serves the *client* because it:

1. Details time frames of auditor action
2. Details what the objective of the engagement is including the preparation of:
    a. Regulatory reports
    b. Tax returns
    c. Management letters

The content of the engagement letter generally includes statements regarding:

1. The objective of the audit, which is to provide an unqualified opinion on the financial statements as specified.
2. The fact that an audit is not a guarantee of the accuracy of the financial statements.
3. Responsibility of management for the fair presentation of the financial statements as well as the establishment and maintenance of the internal controls. Management should make adjust-

¶ 502.02

ments to the financial statements to correct material misstatements.

4. Errors and fraud, which are less likely to occur or remain undetected if internal controls are effective.

5. The effectiveness of the internal controls, which will be considered in determining the nature, timing, and extent of the auditing procedures.

6. The testing of the internal controls is not detailed, however, if significant matters are noted during the course of the review or testing of the internal controls they will be communicated to the client together with any suggestions for improvement.

7. The scope of the audit, including reference to generally accepted auditing standards.

8. The auditor's responsibility in the detection of fraud.

9. The timing of the audit, which will be scheduled for performance and completion as follows:

    a. Internal control testing

    b. Inventory observation

    c. Cutoff testing

    d. Tests of account balances and

    e. Auditor report completion

10. Fee amount or means for its calculation. Other fee-related statements could include:

    a. Interest charges for late payments

    b. Additional out-of-pocket expenses to be added to the base fee

    c. The potential withdrawal from the engagement if billings become delinquent

Other possible items in the engagement letter include the following:

- Names of auditors and staff involved in the engagement.

- Arrangements concerning the involvement of experts in some aspects of the audit.

- Assistance supplied by client personnel regarding:

    a. Preparation of schedules and analyses of accounts

    b. Names of client personnel to assist the auditors as well as timeframes in which they will work

¶ 502.02

- The engagement letter should not refer to any ongoing services because doing so may preclude the initiation of the statute of limitations that may occur when a client seeks damages from the auditor. A reference to a statute of limitation with respect to pursuing damages as well as a limited damages provision in the engagement letter may be appropriate. Auditors should consult with their attorney for the propriety of such statements. [5]

- The AICPA Code of Professional Conduct requires auditors to keep client matters confidential.[6] However, legal situations may arise that force auditors to release confidential materials to legal authorities. The auditor may want to disclose this fact to the client in the engagement letter. The auditor may find it appropriate to reference those client confidential matters that may be released when the auditor receives discovery requests and subpoenas for client information. [7]

- Litigation, even if successful, can have adverse effects on the client and auditor. One option available to auditors is inserting an arbitration clause in their engagement letters. The arbitration process, as an alternative to litigation, could decrease the cost of resolving disputes between client and auditors. Auditors should consult with their attorney for the propriety of such clauses. [8]

Each engagement letter must be tailored for the situation and must be specific as to the services provided. Figure 5.3 provides an example of an engagement letter.

---

[5] Frances McNair, "Updating Your Audit Engagement Letter for the 1990s," *The CPA Journal Online*, July 1990 (http://www.nysscpa.org/cpajournal/old/08658872.htm).

[6] Rule 301, Confidential Client Information (AICPA, Professional Standards, vol. 2, ET sec. 301.01).

[7] Bruce M. Bird, Steven M. Platau, and Steven Busby, "Engagement Letters as a Risk Management Tool," *The CPA Journal Online*, 1998 (http://www.nysscpa.org/cpajournal/1998/0198/dept/d540198.htm).

[8] McNair, "Updating Your Audit Engagement Letter."

¶ 502.02

Figure 5.3

Sample Engagement Letter

April 20, 20X2
Mr. Richard Smith
Pilgrim Printing Company
71 Warren Drive
Boston, Massachusetts 02139

Dear Mr. Smith:

    This letter is to confirm our understanding with you regarding the terms and objectives of our audit and tax services engagement as well as the nature and limitations of the service we will provide to Pilgrim Printing Company.

    As agreed, we will audit the company's financial statements for the year ended December 31, 20X2. The management of Pilgrim Printing Company is responsible for the fair presentation of the financial statements for their agreement or reconciliation to company records. Management is also responsible for financial statement revision should any material misstatements become known as a result of the audit. Our responsibility is to express an opinion at the conclusion of our audit as to the fairness, in all material respects, of the financial position, results of operations, and cash flows of the Pilgrim Printing Company financial statements in conformity with generally accepted accounting principles.

    We will conduct our audit in accordance with generally accepted auditing standards. Those standards require that we obtain reasonable, rather than absolute, assurance that the financial statements are free from material misstatement. The audit is not intended as a guarantee of the accuracy of the financial statements. Additionally, audit procedures are designed to detect material misstatement, and as such, immaterial misstatements due to errors or fraud may remain undetected. Furthermore, it is not possible to examine evidence supporting all transactions. Much evidence will be obtained on a test or sample basis. Accordingly, even a material misstatement may remain undetected.

    Management is responsible for making all financial records and related information available to us. If, as dictated by the situation, we cannot complete the audit or cannot render an opinion, we may decline to issue a report.

    The management of Pilgrim Printing Company is responsible for the effective internal controls over the safeguarding of assets and the recording of transactions. During the audit we may perform limited testing on those internal controls. The objective of the testing is not to discover weaknesses in the controls but to assist us in determining the nature, timing, and extent of our audit procedures. However, if we become aware of any significant deficiency in the design or internal control that could have an adverse effect on recording, processing, summarizing, or reporting financial data, we will bring it to the attention of the audit committee of Pilgrim Printing Company.

    At the conclusion of our audit, management must provide to us a representation letter confirming that:

    1. Fair presentation of the financial statements in conformity with generally accepted accounting principles is management's responsibility, and the effects of any uncorrected misstatements aggregated by the auditor during the current engagement and pertaining to the latest period presented are immaterial.

¶ 502.02

2. Management has made available to us all books, records, and minutes of the board of directors.

3. Management has provided complete and accurate answers to all of our audit inquiries.

In addition to the audit of the financial statements, we will prepare the federal and all state income tax returns for Pilgrim Printing Company.

In performing our audit we will be at the company premises during various time frames. Our planned schedule is as follows:

	Begin	Complete
Preliminary tests	9/15/X2	10/15/X2
Cutoff tests	12/20/X2	1/7/X3
Account balance tests	2/15/X3	3/10/X3
Corporate tax returns prepared	3/12/X3	
Audit report issuance	3/20/X3	

Our quoted fees contemplate assistance from your personnel. Prior to our account balance testing, the attached schedules and analyses of accounts must be completed. Timely completion of this work will facilitate the conclusion of our audit. In addition, we will need 10 hours of assistance per week while we are on premises from the chief accountant as well as the accounts payable clerk.

Our fees will be billed as work progresses and will be based on the amount of time required for each service. In addition to the fees, you will be charged for all costs associated with the services rendered. These costs include, but are not limited to, travel expenses, delivery and courier services, and document reproduction. We will notify you immediately of any circumstances we encounter that could significantly affect our initial estimate of total fees, as follows:

Audit of financial statements	$45,000
Income tax returns (federal and state)	7,000
Total	$ 52,000

If the foregoing correctly sets forth your understanding of the terms of our engagement, please so indicate by dating, signing, and returning the duplicate copy of this letter.

We appreciate this opportunity to serve you.

Sincerely,

Singer & Cantor P.C.

Accepted by: Richard Smith, CEO

date: _____

Figure 5.4

Audit Preparation Stage

```
12/31/X2                          12/31/X3

      FINANCIAL STATEMENT PERIOD

         PLANNING    Control              Account Balance
         PHASE       Testing Phase        Testing Phase

         Initial Contact            Cutoff              Issuing the
         With Client                Testing             Audit Report

    I. Pre-Planning     II. Audit Preparation
```

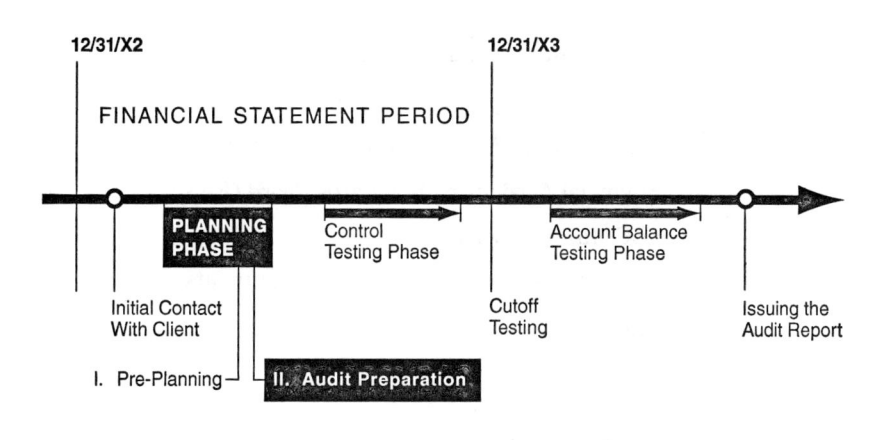

¶ 503 Audit Preparation Stage

The audit preparation stage noted in Figure 5.4 begins once the auditor accepts the audit engagement. Not only must audits be adequately planned as required by GAAS, but planning is critical because it helps ensure that the audit resources are directed in an efficient, timely, and effective manner.

.01 Obtaining Knowledge About the Client

In order to begin planning the audit, practitioners must gain knowledge about client matters, the external environment, and the industry in which the client operates. In fact, this is required by SAS No. 99 because, in order to discover risks of material misstatement due to fraud, the auditor needs this type of knowledge about the client.[9] To assist auditors in such matters, industry accounting and audit guides such as those prepared by the AICPA and the Institute of Internal Auditors (IIA) should be reviewed. Also Chapter 19, "Fraud Examinations," provides a checklist of risk factors associated with material misstatement due to fraud. All of these risk factors should be reviewed to assess risks of material misstatement due to fraud. (See Chapter 6 for more information on risk assessment and fraud.) Adequacy of auditor technical training would also include:

1. Industrial statistical knowledge obtained through:

---

[9] SAS No. 99, Consideration of Fraud in a Financial Statement Audit (AICPA, Professional Standards, vol. 1, AU sec. 316.19); *see also,* SAS No. 22, Planning and Supervision (AICPA, Professional Standards, vol. 1, AU secs. 311.06–311.08).

¶ 503.01

a. Industrial journals and regional newsletters prepared by organizations representing interests in the client industry

   b. Financial information services such as Moodys and Standard & Poors

   c. Online data services

2. A review of recently promulgated:

   a. Statements on Auditing Standards (SAS)

   b. Financial Accounting Standards Board (FASB)

   c. SEC staff bulletins

   d. Industry regulatory agency pronouncements

3. Formal training programs and continuing education courses offered by professional organizations such as the AICPA and IIA, as well as local universities and colleges.

4. An insight about client operations obtained by an in-depth study of the nature of the client's products. This should include the likelihood of the products' technological obsolescence and future salability, and information that assists the auditor in evaluating lower-of-cost-or-market calculations.

The auditor acquires the information by:

1. Reviewing last year's workpapers to determine:

   a. Prior year's audit approach

   b. Significant accounting issues

   c. Areas that affect audit logistics

2. Conducting an audit planning conference with the client. At this meeting much on-site information can be gathered and processed, such as:

   a. Reading client policy and procedure manuals, especially for those departments whose operations have direct impact on the financial statement:

      i. general accounting

      ii. accounts payable

      iii. accounts receivable

      iv. payroll

   b. Inquiring about management's policies regarding the development of accounting estimates and principles used. It is possible that the client may seek the services of outside consulting services to derive account valuations.

¶ 503.01

Planning the Financial Audit

  c. Reviewing client organization charts to understand:
    i. reporting responsibilities
    ii. departmental structure
    iii. management span of control
  d. Understanding how record-keeping is accomplished. Topics on which to focus attention are:
    i. extent of computerization
    ii. extent of outside service usage (i.e., payroll preparation)
    iii. output generated and to whom it is distributed
  e. Types of products and services.
  f. Geographical locations of production, storage, and distribution centers.
  g. Obtaining and reading any current interim financial statements.

3. Discussing with the client the following document preparation requirements and who is responsible for their preparation:
  a. A trial balance that agrees with the general ledger
  b. Account reconciliation and detailed schedules of various accounts

4. Determining the need for computer-assisted audit techniques.

5. Inquiring of the client the following:
  a. Related-party transactions
  b. New business developments
  c. Any matters emanating from the analytical procedures performed on the financial statements
  d. The audit budget by classification of audit activity as well as classification of audit staff
  e. The extent of involvement of internal auditors

.02 Analytical Procedures

Auditing standards require auditors to employ analytical procedures during the audit planning phase. Analytical procedures are "evaluations of financial information made by a study of plausible relationships among both financial and nonfinancial data."[10] Analytical procedures can provide:

---

[10] SAS No. 56, Analytical Procedures (AICPA, Professional Standards, vol. 1, AU sec. 329.02).

¶ 503.02

- A better understanding of a client's business.

- Identification of areas of audit risk and as such assist the auditor in determining the nature, timing, and extent of the auditing procedures.

- Identification of risks of material misstatement due to fraud.

Analytical procedures include:

- Trend analysis, which uses disaggregated data (i.e., by individual account) and analyzes the change in the account balance over time. Trend analysis focuses the auditor's attention on those accounts showing volatility.

- Ratio analysis, or the comparison of the relationships between financial statement accounts and/or nonfinancial data, or the comparison of the client company with other companies operating within the same industry.

- Regression analysis, which is a statistical method whereby the activity of an account is used to develop a model to predict an outcome.

SAS No. 99 requires that proper audit planning includes analytical procedures that identify unusual or unexpected relationships involving revenue and revenue-related accounts such that material misstatement due to fraudulent financial reporting might be highlighted. These analytics may include comparisons of revenue with production capacity and trend analysis of revenue and returned goods so as to determine the reasonableness of such accounts.[11]

.03 Tour of the Facilities

Touring the facilities during the planning phase allows auditors to better understand operations through observation. Some of the objectives in touring the facilities may include meeting with operational and supervisory personnel to determine:

1. Their attitudes toward internal controls.

2. Terminology used at the facilities that will enable the auditor to communicate better with the client.

3. Observing the physical safeguards over plant assets and inventory.

4. Observing the characteristics of inventory and fixed assets. This will assist the auditor with the identification of:

---

[11] SAS No. 99, Consideration of Fraud in a Financial Statement Audit (AICPA, Professional Standards, vol. 1, AU sec. 316.29).

Planning the Financial Audit 163

   a. Inventory obsolescence.
   b. Plant asset age and maintenance. Recently installed assets should appear in the records as new acquisitions. Large expenditures for maintenance should accompany assets that appear to be old. Inquiries could be made about the disposition of apparent idle assets.

During the tour of a manufacturing plant the auditor should attempt to relate the cost accumulation system of record-keeping to the flow of materials and processes including points where:

- Scrap is generated
- Spoilage occurs
- Additional material is added to the process
- The finished product emerges
- Shipping occurs
- Receiving occurs
- Finished goods are stored
- Raw materials are stored and
- The flow of documents, such as material requisitions

.04 Preliminary Judgment of Materiality

Once auditors accrue the knowledge of client operations, other tasks on which they should focus include:

- Developing a preliminary judgment about materiality and tolerable misstatement, and
- Establishing the preliminary materiality and tolerable misstatement levels to assist in discerning how to direct audit resources.

More importantly, the auditor must design audit procedures to detect material misstatements in the financial statements.[12] The preliminary level of materiality based upon the auditor's judgment is applied to the financial statements taken in total.

In addition, although the materiality level relates to the financial statements, materiality at the account balance level must also be considered. To differentiate materiality at the financial statement level from the account level, a different term is used for materiality at the account level: tolerable misstatement. During the planning phase, auditors establish a preliminary materiality level as well as the tolerable misstatement values

---

[12] SAS No. 1, Codification of Auditing Standards and Procedures, (AICPA, Professional Standards, vol. 1, AU sec. 110.02).

¶ 503.04

based upon the auditors' understanding of the business. If the materiality level for the financial statements is $1 million, that same amount cannot be used to determine what is material for an individual account balance. For instance, the auditor may use $50,000 as the tolerable misstatement level in auditing the cash account. The $50,000 material misstatement value will dictate how much evidence the auditor will need to gather for the cash account, not the $1 million materiality value.

During the planning phase, auditors should establish the tolerable misstatement level for each account balance. One method of establishing the tolerable misstatement is to allocate the materiality value to each account based upon the auditors' judgment of resources needed to audit the account.

.05 The Impact of Material Misstatement Due to Fraud on the Planning Phase

Auditors must gather enough evidence so as to build reasonable assurance that the financial statements are free of material misstatements.[13] Because many types of fraud cause the financial statements to be materially misstated, auditors must consider the impact of fraudulent financial reporting and material misappropriation of assets during the audit engagement. Chapters 12 and 19 discuss risk factors for forensic accounting services and fraud examinations, respectively. The auditor should understand the implications of these risk factors to better plan the financial audit.

Beginning with the planning phase, an assessment of risk of material misstatement due to fraud should occur continually throughout the audit engagement Evidence should be evaluated from a professional skepticism point of view. Of particular concern would be: transactions not recorded in a timely manner or improperly recorded, discrepancies or unsupported transactions, unexplained reconciliation or vague responses to auditor queries, unusual relationships between management and auditor such as the denial of access to records or customers, or undue time pressures on or intimidation of audit team members.

With SAS No. 99 there is a new requirement that the audit team conduct a meeting to discuss the potential for material misstatement due to fraud. The purpose of the meeting is to create the proper environment to approach client fraud issues. The discussion should include:[14]

1. A "brainstorming" session whereby audit team members can express where they feel the risks for material misstatement of the financial statements might lie. It is required that the

---

[13] *Ibid.*
[14] SAS No. 99, Consideration of Fraud in a Financial Statement Audit (AICPA, Professional Standards, vol. 1, AU sec. 316.14).

¶ 503.05

auditor with final responsibility for the audit attend this meeting.

2. That professional skepticism must be maintained throughout the engagement. That it is important to be continually on the lookout for information or conditions that may indicate material misstatements due to fraud.

3. An identification and discussion of the known external and internal factors affecting the company that creates the environment for fraud. This should include the three conditions that are generally present when fraud occurs:

   a. A reason to commit fraud by management, usually due to some incentive or pressure.

   b. Because of an absence of or the ineffectiveness of controls, an opportunity for fraud exists.

   c. Management is able to rationalize committing the fraud.

4. How management could override the existing controls.

5. In what manner could the auditors respond to the susceptibility of material misstatement due to fraud.

6. An emphasis that communication should continue throughout the audit among the audit team members about the risks of material misstatement due to fraud.

Also during the planning phase other information needed to identify the risks of material misstatement due to fraud should be obtained, much of this in the form of inquiries. Management should be asked if they:[15]

1. Have any knowledge of fraud, suspected fraud, or allegations of fraud.

2. Understand what risks of fraud might exist for the entity, including specific fraud risks identified at the account balance or transaction level.

3. Have established any programs or control to mitigate specific fraud risks identified above.

4. Have reported to the audit committee or others with equivalent authority and responsibility on how the entity's internal control serves to prevent, deter, or detect material misstatements due to fraud.

---

[15] *Ibid.*

¶ 503.05

Inquiries should be directed to the audit committee about their views about the risks of fraud and their knowledge of fraud or suspected fraud and how the audit committee exercises oversight activities.

Internal auditing should also be asked about their views about the risks of fraud or knowledge of fraud or suspected fraud. It is also important for the CPA to determine if the internal auditor performed any procedures to identify or detect fraud during the year and whether management has satisfactorily responded to any findings resulting from these procedures.

In addition to the above, inquiries should be made of anyone who may be able to provide information that will be helpful to the auditor in identifying fraud, suspected fraud, or risks of material misstatement due to fraud. This could include anyone with a bookkeeping function, an operating function or staff function, as well as the in-house counsel. These individuals might provide information that corroborates responses already received or how management might override existing controls. In any event after this discussion the auditor will be in a better position to determine how well management communicates standards of ethical behavior to individuals throughout the organization.

If during the audit planning fraud risk factors are identified, it is important to:

1. Document the factors identified,

2. Record the auditor's response to the fraud risk factors, and

3. Consider communicating the factors as reportable conditions to senior management and the audit committee.

4. Acquire additional evidence where applicable.

5. Consider discussions with experts in the field.

.06 Planning Model for Judging Risk

According to auditing standards, "A sufficient understanding of the internal control structure is to be obtained to plan the audit and to determine the nature, timing, and extent of tests to be performed." [16] The auditor is assuming risk when auditing. In performing an audit the auditor is using sampling techniques to obtain reasonable assurance that the internal controls are functioning as thought, and that financial statements are free of material misstatements. Audit risk is the risk that auditors face when, based upon evidence gathered, they render an unqualified opinion when the financial statements contain a material misstatement. This risk leads to auditor legal liability for audit negligence if financial statement users suffer loss as a result of their reliance upon the auditor's assurance.

---

[16] SAS No. 1, Codification of Auditing Standards and Procedures (AICPA, Professional Standards, vol. 1, AU sec. 150.02).

Figure 5.5 depicts the relationship of various risks associated with financial statement audits.

Figure 5.5

Relationship of Risks

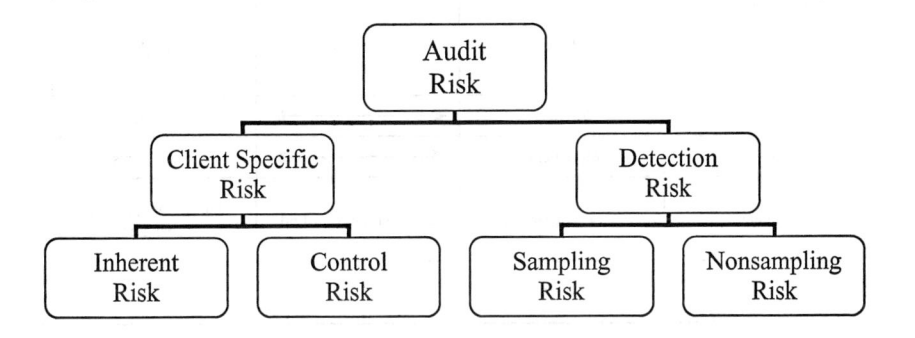

```
                        Audit
                        Risk
              ┌───────────┴────────────┐
       Client Specific             Detection
            Risk                      Risk
        ┌─────┴─────┐            ┌──────┴──────┐
    Inherent     Control      Sampling    Nonsampling
      Risk        Risk          Risk         Risk
```

Audit risk: The risk of issuing inappropriate audit opinion.

Client Specific risk: The risk that misstatements caused by errors and frauds entered into the accounting system and were not prevented, detected, and corrected by the internal control system.

Inherent risk: The susceptibility of financial items or assertions to material misstatements.

Control risk: The failure of the internal control system to prevent, detect, and correct material misstatements that have already entered into the accounting system.

Detection risk: The risk that audit procedures fail to discover material misstatements that entered into the accounting system and were not detected by the internal control system.

Sampling risk: The risk that auditor's selected sample is not representative of the entire population of classes of transactions or account balances.

Nonsampling risk: The risk of selecting inappropriate audit procedures and/or mistakes in the execution of audit procedures.

¶ 503.06

Figure 5.6

Detection Risk vs. Audit Procedures

$$\text{Planned Detection Risk} = \frac{\text{Acceptable Audit Risk}}{\text{Inherent Risk} \times \text{Control Risk}}$$

Planned Detection Risk / Audit Procedures	Low	Medium	High
Nature	Stronger	←——————→	Less Strong
Extent	More Items	←——————→	Fewer Items
Timing	Close to Year-End	Interim Near Year-End	Interim Well Before Year-End

There are three main components of audit risk: inherent risk, control risk, and detection risk. These three components show the relationships among the risk that internal controls are not functioning well and risk that the auditor does not find that a material misstatement exists in the financial statements.

Audit risk = Inherent risk × Control risk × Detection Risk

Inherent risk is the susceptibility of an assertion to a material misstatement, assuming that there are no related internal control structure policies or procedures. [17]

Control risk is the risk that a material misstatement that could occur in an assertion will not be prevented or detected on a timely basis by the entity's internal control structure policies or procedures. [18]

Detection risk is the risk that the auditor will not detect a material misstatement that exists in an assertion. [19]

For example, using a manual payroll system a payroll clerk makes an error every 10 checks that, if not detected, will produce a material misstatement in the salary expense account. This is an example of inherent risk. Continuing with the example, 90 percent of the errors are detected by the payroll supervisor, but 10 percent are not. This leads to a material misstatement in the salary expense account. This is an example of control risk. If the auditor fails to detect the material misstatement, that is an example of detection risk. Given these circumstances, the auditor who missed the material misstatement could render a clean opinion despite the fact that

---

[17] SAS No. 47, Audit Risk and Materiality in Conducting and Audit (AICPA, Professional Standards, vol. 1, AU Sec. 312.27a).

[18] *Ibid.*, AU sec. 312.27b.

[19] *Ibid.*, AU sec. 312.27c.

¶ 503.06

the salary expense account is misstated. These errors compound to create an example of audit risk.

During the planning phase of the audit, the auditor reviews the relationship of detection risk to control risk in the following model:

if:

Audit risk = Inherent risk × Control risk × Detection risk

then:

Planned detection risk = Acceptable audit risk ÷ (Inherent risk × Control risk)

As is seen in this model, the amount of detection risk the auditor is willing to accept is inversely proportional to control risk; the less the control risk, the greater the acceptable detection risk. Stated differently, strong internal controls lead to less testing of the account balances than if weak controls are detected.

The planned detection risk estimated during the planning stages of financial statement audit affects three aspects of audit procedures: nature, extent, and timing. Nature of audit procedures determines the types of evidence-gathering procedures planned by the auditor (inspections, observations, inquiries, and calculations). Extent of audit procedures determines the amount of audit evidence gathered (how many items from each account or class of transactions are selected for examination). Timing determines when audit procedures are performed (interim or close to year-end). Figure 5.6 shows the relation between planned detection risk and audit procedures.

.07 Specialists

During the audit preparation phase it is important for auditors to determine whether there is a need for specialists to assist in the audit. Typically, specialists are brought in to assist the auditor in fulfilling certain audit objectives, such as:

- Valuation and existence of investments in precious metals and gems.

- Reviewing inventories for obsolescence and lower-of-cost-or-market valuations such as apparel.

- Valuation of pension plans. The auditor may consider using the services of an actuary to serve as an objective valuator of the underlying assumptions of pension costs.

- Determining fair value of long-lived assets for possible impairment adjustment.

¶ 503.07

- Determining the existence of chemical, pharmaceutical, or technologically complicated inventories such as computer components or those for military applications.

.08 Permanent File

Many documents can assist auditors in the preparing for the audit. The process of gathering documents for inclusion in the permanent files of the workpapers will help auditors understand the business better. Permanent files are those files not only prepared for this year's audit but ones useful on a continuing basis. Documents included in the permanent files can prove useful to future engagements as well as this year's audit. The permanent file contains data of a historical and continuing nature as well as being pertinent to the current year's audit. Examples of items included in this file are:

1. Articles of incorporation
2. Corporate bylaws
3. Contracts, such as:
   a. Automobile leases
   b. Building leases
   c. Equipment rental
   d. Union contracts
   e. Employment contracts
4. Bond indentures
5. Loan commitments
6. Information about internal controls:
   a. Flowcharts
   b. Internal control questionnaires
   c. Descriptive memoranda
7. Copies of the minutes of board of director's meetings as well as subcommittee minutes. The minutes provide important information about authorizations for:
   a. Dividends
   b. Officer compensation
   c. Mergers
   d. Long-term commitments
   e. Pledges of securities

¶ 503.08

Minutes also provide information on the discussion of:

f. Related-party transactions

g. Litigation

8. Analyses of accounts and data that have a continuing importance to the auditor in future audits:

a. Operating loss carryback and carryforward information

b. Deferred income tax calculations

c. Pension cost calculations

d. Capitalized interest information on self constructed assets

e. Results of prior years' analytical procedures that are of continuing importance

.09 Planning Memorandum

At the culmination of the planning process the audit team should prepare a planning memorandum (sometimes referred to as a strategy memorandum). This memorandum provides evidence of the planning performed by the auditor, including the auditor's consideration of fraud:

1. Purpose of the audit as well as other reports required

2. Business and audit issues

3. Client reputation issues

4. Audit staffing

5. Discussions held with audit staff regarding the susceptibility of the client's financial statements to material misstatement due to fraud. The documentation of this meeting is required and must include audit team members who participated and dates of participation.[20]

6. Auditor independence review

7. Scope of work

8. Research findings regarding:

a. Client operations

b. Industry statistics

c. Industry accounting issues

d. Auditing procedures applied to industry operations

9. References to prior year's audit approach and differences in this year's approach

10. Resources necessary to perform the audit (need for specialists)

---

[20] SAS No. 99, Consideration of Fraud in a Financial Statement Audit (AICPA, 2003).

11. Special cut-off testing

12. Results of inquiries of predecessor auditors

13. Results of the tour of the facilities

14. Results of inquiries of the client regarding:

    a. Related-party transactions

    b. Results of auditor-applied analytical procedures

    c. Management policies

15. Preliminary judgment of materiality

16. Preliminary judgment of risk

¶ 504   **Audit Staff Supervision**

According to auditing standards, assistants used in the audit process must be properly supervised.[21] The purpose for the standard is to require that when assistants are used in the audit engagement, the accuracy and competency of the audit is unaffected. Delegation of audit responsibilities is a necessary component to the timely completion of the audit. The delegation of work to staff should be such that a competent, independent person performs the component functions. Staff members to whom audit responsibilities were delegated should be continually supervised by the auditor beginning with the pre-planning stage and continuing to the conclusion of the engagement. The staff member should be reminded throughout the audit engagement of the importance of maintaining professional skepticism and not be satisfied with less than persuasive client evidence. The amount of supervision required of staff is inversely related to the level of experience and capabilities possessed by the staff personnel as well as the complexity of the auditing engagement's subject matter.

Supervision involves directing individuals to accomplish the objectives of the audit. It also involves determining whether the audit objectives have been accomplished. The objectives of audit staff supervision are:

- Ensuring that the staff performance is in accordance with generally accepted auditing standards

- Overseeing that the staff performance is in accordance with firm standards

- Evidence gathered by staff supporting the audit opinion

- Resolving all significant audit matters

---

[21] SAS No. 22, *Planning and Supervision* (AICPA, Professional Standards, vol. 1, AU sec. 311.11).

Communication of audit objectives is a necessary component of supervision. It is important that staff understand the audit objectives so they are attuned to matters that affect the audit's nature, timing, and extent. To assist in this process, communication with the staff should include:

1. The nature of the client's business and its relationship to:
   a. The staff's assignments
   b. Accounting and auditing problems that may arise
2. The risks of material misstatement due to fraud and be alert for information and other conditions that indicate a material misstatement due to fraud has occurred.
3. Specific audit procedure objectives;
4. What procedures to follow when differences of opinion arise between audit personnel regarding accounting and auditing issues; and
5. Evidence-gathering techniques and documentation. Documents that contain this information and should therefore be read by the staff auditors are:
   a. A written audit program
   b. The audit time budget
   c. The planning memorandum

Other important roles of the supervising auditor are:

- Coordinating staff assignments and ascertaining that the work is being performed by staff with appropriate capabilities
- Assigning work to staff
- Monitoring the progress of the engagement to determine whether the staff appear to have the necessary skills and competence to complete their tasks
- Determining whether staff understand the audit directions
- Determining whether the audit has been carried out in accordance with the audit program
- Reviewing all documentation of evidence gathered during fieldwork to conclude that the engagement has been satisfactorily completed
- Conducting on-the-job training
- Resolving any differences of opinion among audit personnel on professional matters that arise during the course of the audit

¶504

¶ 505 Summary

The ASB issued SAS No. 99, Consideration of Fraud in a Financial Statement Audit, in January 2003 due to the current sensitivity towards fraud issues. When a client approaches a practitioner to perform an audit, the accountant cannot simply accept the engagement anymore. The auditor must consider many issues such as auditor independence, client industry knowledge, staffing ability, client integrity, effectiveness of corporate governance, and adequacy of records before accepting a client. These issues are discussed in this chapter.

There are two stages to the planning phase of a financial audit. The first one is the pre-planning stage, during which the auditor investigates whether to accept a client's request for an audit. If the audit engagement is accepted, this stage culminates with the preparation and signing of the audit engagement letter. The second stage in the planning phase is the audit preparation stage, which includes all the preparation and investigation needed to plan the audit in order to insure its effectiveness and efficiency.

The objectives of audit staff supervision are ensuring that the staff performance is in accordance with generally accepted audit standards and/or auditing standards issued by the PCAOB, overseeing that the staff performance is in accordance with firm standards, making sure that evidence gathered by staff supports the audit opinion, and resolving all significant audit matters.

Chapter 6
Performing Fieldwork

¶ 601	Introduction
¶ 602	Auditor Responsibility for Detecting Misstatements
¶ 603	Management Assertions
¶ 604	The Link Between Management Assertions and Audit Objectives
¶ 605	Audit Risk and Materiality
¶ 606	Substantive Tests
¶ 607	Auditing Procedures
¶ 608	Sufficiency of Evidence
¶ 609	Competence of Evidential Matter
¶ 610	Internal Controls and Audit Objectives
¶ 611	Testing the Internal Controls
¶ 612	Using the Work of the Internal Auditor
¶ 613	Final Assessment of Control Risk and Risk of Material Misstatement Due to Fraud, and Their Effect on Detection Risk
¶ 614	Applying Substantive Tests Prior to the Balance Sheet Date
¶ 615	Audit Programs
¶ 616	Audit Workpapers
¶ 617	Evaluation of Evidential Matter
¶ 618	Fraud Implications Arising During the Evaluation of Audit Results
¶ 619	Illegal Acts by Clients
¶ 620	Final Review of Audit
¶ 621	The Sarbanes-Oxley Act of 2002 and the Auditor's Attestation of Internal Controls
¶ 622	Summary

¶ 601 Introduction

The primary objective of a financial statement audit is for the auditor to express an opinion about the fair presentation of the financial statements. The opinion can only be expressed once enough evidence is gathered and assimilated. According to auditing standards:

> Sufficient, competent evidential matter is to be obtained through inspection, observation, inquiries, and confirmations to afford a reasonable basis for an opinion regarding the financial statements under audit.[1]

Although the auditor gathers some evidence during the planning phase, the bulk of the evidence is obtained during the two fieldwork stages at the client's premises: the internal control testing phase and year-end substantive account balance testing (see Figure 6.1). During the internal control testing phase, the auditor gathers evidence while testing the internal controls to determine if reliance can be placed upon the controls. Secondly, and depending upon the results of the internal control testing phase, evidence is obtained while testing the year-end account balances.

Figure 6.1

The Two Fieldwork Stages

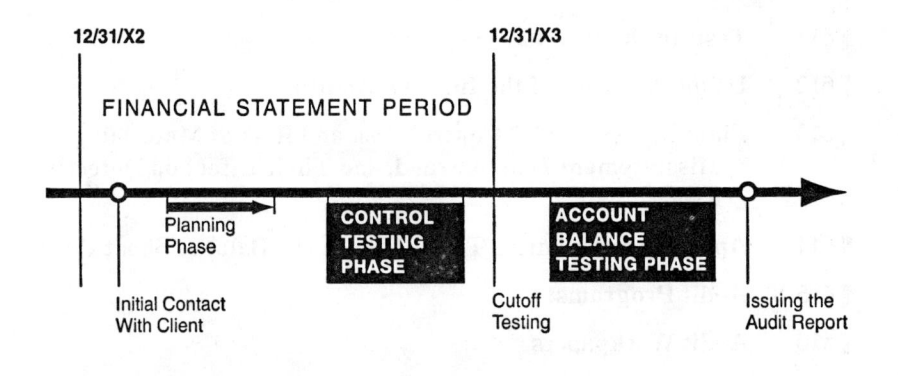

```
12/31/X2                          12/31/X3
|                                  |
|    FINANCIAL STATEMENT PERIOD    |
|                                  |
●────────┬──────[CONTROL──┬──[ACCOUNT─────────────●────────►
         Planning TESTING    BALANCE
         Phase   PHASE]      TESTING PHASE]
|                                  |                    |
Initial Contact              Cutoff              Issuing the
With Client                  Testing             Audit Report
```

Chapter 6 objectives:

- To understand the five management assertions, how they relate to audit objectives, and the auditor's responsibility for detecting misstatements (see ¶ 601–604).

- To recognize the importance of audit risk, the concept of materiality, how the detection risk can be controlled via the extent of

---

[1] Statements on Auditing Standards (SAS) No. 1, Codification of Auditing Standards and Procedures (AICPA, Professional Standards, vol. 1, AU sec. 150.02, "Generally Accepted Auditing Standards").

substantive tests, and the auditing procedures that make up the substantive tests (see ¶ 605–607).

- To define sufficiency of evidence and competency of evidential matter (see ¶ 608–609).

- To understand internal controls, how they are tested, and the audit objectives related to internal control testing (see ¶ 610–611).

- To discover how to use the work of the internal auditors and how to do a final assessment of control risk (see ¶ 612–613).

- To become familiar with audit programs, audit workpapers, and when to apply substantive tests prior to balance sheet date (see ¶ 614–616).

- To understand how to evaluate evidential matter and the fraud implications that arise during evaluation of the results (see ¶ 617–618).

- To consider illegal acts of clients and understand the final review of the audit (see ¶ 619–620).

- To understand the Sarbanes-Oxley Act's influence on attestation of internal controls and audit of internal control over financial reporting (see ¶ 621).

¶ 602 Auditor Responsibility for Detecting Misstatements

Auditors apply auditing procedures to obtain reasonable assurance that the financial statements are free of material misstatement. (See Chapters 3 and 12.) There are three types of misstatements that are of significant interest to auditors: (1) errors, which are unintentional misstatements in the financial statements (i.e., mistakes in estimating depreciation expenses or pension liabilities, mathematical errors, and incorrect recording of financial transactions); (2) fraud, which is intentional misappropriation in financial statements to deceive investors and users of financial statements (i.e., misappropriation of assets and fraudulent reporting); and (3) illegal acts, which are violations of applicable laws, rules, and regulations (i.e., violations of SEC rules). The term *reasonable assurance* implies that the auditor does not (and cannot) obtain absolute assurance. Therefore, the auditor is accepting a certain amount of risk. During this process, the auditor makes many assumptions and estimates. However, assumptions about evidence and internal controls can be wrong even when generally accepted auditing standards (GAAS) are applied. Here are some possibilities:

- Documents relied upon as competent evidence can contain forged authorizations.

- Internal controls that appeared effective may have been compromised by collusion and fraudulent transactions may have taken place, thus creating a material misstatement on the financial statements.

- Management override of the internal controls may have allowed fictitious accounts receivable to be recorded.

- Undisclosed related-party transactions may have produced a recorded value for land that is substantially greater than fair market value.

Even with an attitude of professional skepticism, the auditor may not find material misstatements produced by such scenarios. However, if a reasonably competent auditor would not have found misstatements produced by one of these scenarios, the audit was not performed negligently.

Auditing procedures are planned around the auditor's assessment of potential errors that may exist in the accounting records. Auditing standards require the auditor to specifically assess the risk of material misstatement due to fraud on every audit engagement (as described for the planning process in Chapter 5).[2] These auditing procedures must also include procedures to detect fraud. However, fraud is characterized by the intent to deceive for personal benefit. Fraud is by its very nature usually more difficult to uncover than an error in recording because the perpetrators are trying to "cover their tracks."

The unique aspects of misstatements contained in financial statements due to fraud are discussed at greater length later in this chapter.

¶ 603 Management Assertions

The financial statements are management's representations of the company's financial position and operations. If, for example, a financial statement values inventory at $5 million, the user should be able to believe certain assertions about that inventory. Although it is not expressly stated, the user should be able to believe that the inventory actually exists and that it has been correctly valued. The user should be able to believe that the company owns the inventory and intends to sell it. These inferred beliefs result from implied representations made by management and are referred to as *management assertions*.

The assertions can be either explicit or implicit. Auditing standards divide the management assertions into the following categories:[3]

- Existence or occurrence
- Completeness

---

[2] SAS No. 99, Consideration of Fraud in a Financial Statement Audit (AICPA, Professional Standards, vol. 1, AU sec. 316).

[3] SAS No. 31, Evidential Matter (AICPA, Professional Standards, vol. 1, AU sec. 326.03, "Nature of Assertions").

¶ 603

- Rights and obligations
- Valuation or allocation
- Presentation and disclosure
- Compliance

Except for presentation and disclosure, which are concerned only with the financial statements, the rest of the management assertions apply to both the financial statement account balance level as well as the transactions that comprise the account balances.

.01 Existence or Occurrence

This assertion refers to those representations made by management that the assets or liabilities on the company's balance sheet actually existed as of the balance sheet date and that recorded transactions actually occurred during the period of the operating statements. If, for example, accounts receivable appears on the balance sheet, the financial statement user should be able to believe that actual accounts receivable exist. Similarly, if sales are shown on the income statement, the financial statement user should be able to believe that the sales actually occurred to bonafide customers.

.02 Completeness

Completeness is the management assertion that states that all transactions and accounts that should be presented in the financial statements have been presented. The cash account can be used as an example of the completeness assertion at the account level. The completeness assertion would state that a complete set of financial statements would contain all cash accounts; that is, that there are no slush funds or "off-the-record" cash accounts. When a financial statement user reads the cash balance in the balance sheet they should be able to believe that all the cash accounts have been included and that there were no slush funds. Similarly, at the transaction level, management asserts that all cash receipts and disbursements have been recorded.

.03 Rights and Obligations

The assertion conveys rights that the company can use all of the assets (rights), and obligations refers to whether liabilities represent actual debt of the company. For example, if an inventory value is shown on the balance sheet, the rights assertion implies that the company owns the inventory and has the right to sell it, that is, that the inventory is not consigned and therefore owned by another party. Liabilities represent required future outflows of resources based upon past transactions. The obligations assertion implies that the company does have the liabilities that management intends to pay with future outflows of company resources, typically cash. For instance, a liability such as "payable to owner" should represent an

¶ 603.03

actual obligation to the owner that the company management intends to pay.

.04 Valuation or Allocation

This assertion means that assets, liabilities, revenues, and expenses have been valued on the financial statements at proper amounts. Generally accepted accounting principles (GAAP) govern the valuation and allocation process. The value of capital leases as shown on the balance sheet should be the present value of the minimum lease payments because that is the proper valuation method according to GAAP. The depreciation expense amount (the allocation of the original cost) shown on the income statement should have been calculated using one of the prescribed GAAP methods. At the transaction level, an example of the application of the valuation assertion is cost of goods sold. The value of an individual cost-of-sales transaction should represent the value of the cost of inventory expended to earn the sale. The cost of inventory should be determined using a GAAP method, such as "first-in, first-out" or "weighted average."

The allocation assertion refers to the amount of revenue or expense apportioned to the operating period of the financial statements. The amount of accrued expenses represents how much more expense should be incurred for the operating period. An example of an accrued expense is the salary expense accrual. Depreciation expense is another example of the allocation assertion. Depreciation expense is an allocation of the original cost of a fixed asset to represent the use of the asset for the benefit of the company.

.05 Presentation and Disclosure

Presentation refers to what should be included in the format of the financial statements, whereas disclosure refers to what should be included in the notes to the financial statements. GAAP governs how the company's financial statements should look and what should be included in the notes to the financial statements. For instance, the presentation assertion mandates that current assets are typically shown separately from the long-lived assets on the balance sheet. Disclosure requires that certain information, such as assets held as collateral and preferred stock dividends in arrears, be included in the notes to the financial statements. The types of financial statement presentations and disclosure notes can vary among different industries.

.06 Compliance

Compliance with applicable laws, rules, and regulations are becoming extremely important for public companies in the post-Enron era, particularly after the passage of the Sarbanes-Oxley Act of 2002. Compliance with applicable laws and regulations—especially the SEC rules related to the implementation of the provisions of the Sarbanes-Oxley Act—is now required for all publicly traded companies under the SEC jurisdiction. Fur-

¶ 603.04

thermore, listed companies should comply with corporate governance guiding principles and other rules adopted by national stock exchanges (NYSE, NASDAQ, and AMEX). Compliance with IRS tax rules is also required for corporations.

¶ 604 The Link Between Management Assertions and Audit Objectives

As stated earlier, the primary objective of the auditor's examination of the financial statements is to express an opinion about whether the financial statements present fairly, in all material respects, values of assets and liabilities in terms of GAAP. Proper application of GAAP should support management assertions. The auditor, in considering what the auditing procedures should accomplish, can use the relationship between GAAP and the management assertions. The management assertions can serve as guidelines for the audit objectives. The audit objectives can be viewed as the mirror image of each management assertion for each material account in the financial statements.

.01 Management Assertions

For each of the management assertions just described, the auditor can request that management provide evidence to support the assertion for each material account contained in the financial statements—the audit objective being to obtain evidence to support or refute the management assertions. In this manner the management assertions provide the link to the audit objectives and thus to the actual audit procedures providing evidence for the financial statement audit opinion.

.02 Audit Objectives

The following shows the correspondence to audit objectives:

- (Existence or occurrence) That the account actually exists or that the transaction actually occurred.

- (Completeness) That all of the details have been included in the account. That all the transactions surrounding the account have been recorded.

- (Rights and obligations) That the client has the rights to use the recorded assets and that recorded liabilities represent actual obligations.

- (Valuation or allocation) That the value shown for the account on the financial statements is correct. Included in this objective is:

    a. That there is a proper cutoff of transaction recording. That 2002 transactions were recorded in 2002 and only in 2002 and 2003 transactions were recorded in 2003 and only in 2003.

¶ 604.02

b. Where applicable, that the account is shown at net realizable value. For those accounts that GAAP requires to be valued at net realizable value be shown as such on the financial statements. Accounts receivable should be shown at net realizable value. Therefore, it is reasonable to expect that an allowance for doubtful accounts be included in the balance sheet or disclosed in the notes to the financial statements.

- (Presentation and disclosure) That the accounts and transactions be properly presented in the financial statements. That all disclosures necessary to make an informed judgment about the financial statements be contained in the basic financial statements or appear in the notes to the financial statements.

Table 6.1 shows this correspondence.

Table 6.1

Relationship Between Management Assertions and Audit Objectives

Management Assertion	Can Assertion Also Serve as a Transaction-Related Audit Objective?
Existence and occurence	Yes
Completeness	Yes
Valuation	Yes
Rights and obligations	Yes
Presentation and disclosure	No

An example using the cash account will illustrate the link between management assertions and audit objectives. When the auditor requests that management prove the existence of the cash balance, management probably would provide a bank reconciliation as of the balance sheet date. The auditor would also confirm the cash balance with a financial institution. In this manner the auditor obtains evidence of the existence of the cash account.

For those audit engagements whereby the auditor concludes that it is necessary to respond to identified risk of material misstatement due to fraud, the nature, timing, and extent of auditing procedures may be revised.[4]

- Nature of the audit procedures—more competent evidence may need to be obtained. For example, if there is related party involvement in the purchase of property by the client, the auditor may seek to obtain an independent appraisal of the property.

- Timing of evidence—more substantive testing may be needed closer to the balance sheet date. For example, confirmations of accounts receivable may be obtained for year-end balances as opposed to an interim period.

- Extent of audit procedures—more items may need to be sampled for testing purposes.

¶ 605 Audit Risk and Materiality

The auditors' opinion provides reasonable assurance that the financial statements are free of material misstatements. However, the auditor cannot guarantee that the financial statements are absolutely accurate. Auditing decisions are based upon the significance of accounts and transactions, individually or in the aggregate. Materiality refers to information that is important enough to change an investor's decision. Materiality is the basis for the auditor to discriminate among the various accounts contained in the financial statements. The concept of materiality is used to determine how significant an account is in the context of the financial statements. The assessment of materiality is a matter of professional judgment and includes consideration of the amount as well as the nature of the misstatements. Misstatements due to fraud have more complicated consequences than those that are the result of error (see ¶ 613). Errors are unintentional in nature. Errors are mistakes made in the application of GAAP, recording transactions, summarizing transactions, or possibly the omission of information such as financial statement disclosure. Fraud is intentional and when involved in the audit has more far-reaching implications regarding the nature, timing, and extent of auditing procedures needed. Management representations, internal control reliance, and documentary evidence could all be tainted when fraud is involved.[5]

Additionally and assuming misstatement due to unintentional mistakes, the materiality at the financial statement level and account balance level must both be considered. To differentiate between the two, a different term is used for materiality at the account level: tolerable misstatement. If the materiality level for the financial statements is $1 million, that same

---

[4] Statement on Auditing Standards No. 99, Consideration of Fraud in a Financial Statement Audit (AICPA, Professional Standards, vol. 1, AU sec. 316.52).

[5] Statement on Auditing Standards No. 47, Audit Risk and Materiality in Conducting an Audit (AICPA, Professional Standards, vol. 1, AU sec. 312).

amount cannot be used to determine what is material for an individual account balance. For instance, the auditor may use $50,000 as the tolerable misstatement level in auditing the cash account. The $50,000 material misstatement value will dictate how much evidence the auditor will need to gather for the cash account, not the $1 million materiality value.

During the planning phase a preliminary materiality level and a tolerable misstatement value are established based upon the auditor's understanding of the business. (See Chapter 5, "Planning the Financial Audit," for a more detailed explanation.) These preliminary materiality and misstatement levels, however, may be revised as the audit progresses.

Inherent in the concept of materiality and its effect on the auditing process is the fact that only a sample of transactions can be tested. Thus, some errors may not be discovered. The auditor is assuming an audit risk anytime he or she renders an opinion on the financial statements. Cognizant of this risk, during the planning phase of the audit the auditor develops a preliminary judgment of this and other associated risks. During the planning phase, the auditor makes a preliminary judgment regarding the control risk based upon an understanding of the business, the existing accounting systems, and how the various control procedures relate. Control risk was introduced in Chapter 5. Control itself in a broad sense is any management action taken to see that established goals are reached. It involves proper planning, organizing, and directing by management. There is a tendency of the internal control system to lose effectiveness over time and to expose, or fail to prevent exposure of, the assets under control. Control risk is the risk that material error in a balance or transaction class will not be prevented or detected on a timely basis by internal controls. Control risk is in sharp contrast to inherent risk, which is the risk that an account or class of transactions contains material misstatements *irrespective* of the effects of the controls.

For internal controls that appear weak or not functioning in an effective manner, control risk is set at a "maximum." In other words, the controls cannot be relied upon to prevent or detect material misstatements. In this situation the auditor will not test the internal controls.

In another situation, after an evaluation of the company's internal controls the auditor may determine that it would be inefficient to test the controls even when the controls appear to be designed and functioning properly. This decision may be due to the complexity of testing or some other issue that would make it impractical to audit the internal controls. When it is impractical to test the controls, the control risk is also considered at "maximum."

Detection risk is the risk that audit procedures will lead to a conclusion that material error does not exist when in fact such error does exist. Detection risk is the only risk of the audit risk components that the auditor

¶ 605

can control. The nature, timing, and extent of the audit procedures that the auditor applies affect detection risk. The more quantity and competence of audit evidence that the auditor obtains, the less the detection risk.

Audit risk is a combination of the risk that material errors will occur in the accounting process and the risk the errors will not be discovered by audit tests. The audit risk and its components assist the auditor during the planning phase to determine how much, what type, and when audit evidence should be obtained. The audit risk equation restated, solving for detection risk, is considered the audit planning model.

There is an inverse relationship between detection risk and inherent and control risks. As the auditor's combined assessment of inherent and control risk that material misstatements may exist and not be effectively prevented or detected by the internal controls increases, the planned level of detection risk decreases. The planned level of detection risk is the risk that the auditor is willing to accept. If the planned level of detection risk is low, the auditor is unwilling to accept much risk and there will be an increased need to gather reliable evidence.

Application of this concept helps the auditor to make a preliminary judgment of what type of evidence should be obtained, when it should be obtained, and how much should be obtained for the various account balances and transactions.

The auditor must also consider audit risk in the context of fraud. A discussion of what happens when there is risk of material misstatement due to fraud begins at ¶ 610. However, in general terms, risk of fraud requires more experienced personnel on the audit engagement and more substantive testing. In other words, it affects the overall audit strategy. It may even be the case that the auditor concludes that it is not practicable for auditing procedures to address the risk of fraud and may require that the auditor withdraw from the engagement.[6]

¶ 606 Substantive Tests

Substantive tests are auditing procedures whereby the auditor is searching for account balance misstatement. These types of tests are used to substantiate the account balances. There are three types of substantive tests:

1. Tests of details of account balances—tests that focus on documentation supporting the account balances. These are time consuming and expensive tests to conduct. Examples of this type of test are vouching and confirming.

2. Analytical procedures—tests that use the plausible relationship among data and accounts to determine the reasonableness of

---

[6] Statement on Auditing Standards No. 99, Consideration of Fraud in a Financial Statement Audit (AICPA, Professional Standards, vol. 1, AU sec. 316.49).

balances. These tests are typically more efficient than tests of details of account balances. An example of this type of test is a regression analysis applied to supplies expense to determine reasonableness of the financial statement account balance.

3. Substantive tests of transactions—tests that are transaction-oriented. They include vouching individual transactions and tracing transactions through the accounting system.

Because the auditor will be expressing an opinion on the financial statements, it is necessary that the auditor be satisfied that no material errors exist in the ending account balances. As such, depending upon the inherent and control risks, there is an optimal mix of substantive tests that the auditor will use. According to the planning model:

Planned detection risk = Acceptable audit risk ÷ (Inherent risk × Control risk)

The amount of detection risk the auditor is willing to accept is inversely related to the inherent and control risks. If the auditor is willing to accept a high detection risk, fewer tests of details of account balances are necessary when compared to acceptance of a low detection risk. When the auditor is willing to accept a high detection risk, more analytical procedures can be used compared to the acceptance of a low detection risk. In other words, if the controls are strong, more analytical procedures can be used and the audit is less costly. However, the auditor must remain flexible in the course of the audit. As evidence is obtained, there may be a need to modify the nature, timing, and extent of other planned procedures. (As discussed in ¶ 610, Internal Controls and Audit Objectives, there are additional audit requirements for risks of material misstatements due to fraud.)[7]

¶ 607 Auditing Procedures

The substantive tests previously discussed (tests of details of accounts, analytical procedures, and substantive tests of transactions) can be further broken down into specific auditing procedures. The financial statements produced by a well-designed and properly maintained system of accounting records should reflect a company's financial position, results of operations, and cash flows in conformity with GAAP. The auditor satisfies audit objectives by gathering evidence provided by the underlying accounting data and all other available corroborating information. The underlying accounting data includes:

1. The general ledger

2. The general journal, all special journals, and all other books of original entry

---

[7] *Ibid.*

3. All subsidiary ledgers, such as accounts receivable and accounts payable
4. The detail of all applicable general ledger account balances, for example:
    a. Short-term investments
    b. The perpetual inventory records
    c. Equipment detail
    d. Common stockholders
5. Management calculations supporting cost and revenue allocations, such as:
    a. Depreciation schedules
    b. Accrued expense calculations for wages, interest, and utilities
    c. Prepaid expenses
    d. Accrued revenues
6. Reconciliations of accounts, such as:
    a. Bank reconciliations
    b. Retained earnings
7. Calculations supporting:
    a. Bond premium and discount amortization
    b. Interest capitalization for self-constructed assets
    c. Pension costs
    d. Deferred income tax
    e. Earnings per share

The auditor tests underlying accounting data by retracing the transactional and adjustment process through the accounting process and by preparing worksheets that:

- Analyze allocations involved in account valuation.
- Analyze recalculations used in the accounting process.
- Reconcile accounts to its details and activities. For example, the account, inventory should be reconciled to its details, the perpetual inventory listing, whereas a worksheet reconciling the professional fees expense should indicate analysis of the activity of that account.

These accounting data and tests of the data taken alone are not sufficient support for the auditor's opinion. The auditor must gather addi-

¶607

tional evidence that supports the accounting data. Corroborating evidence comes in many forms. One of the fieldwork auditing standards[8] refers to evidence gathered through inspection, observation, inquiry, and confirmation. This reference is the basis for the auditing procedures necessary to gather corroborating evidence.

Inspection refers to the examination of documents underlying a transaction or account. A common auditing term for this type of examination is *vouching*. Additionally, inspection includes tracing transactions or amounts throughout the bookkeeping system.

Observation refers to the auditor actually seeing or watching some aspect of the client's operation, assets, processes, or internal control function.

Inquiry refers to a process of obtaining client responses to auditor questions. Through the interviewing process the auditor elicits responses from client personnel and management. Most inquiry responses are either verbal or in writing. Although this type of evidence is considered weak, it can be a starting point in obtaining other corroborating evidence, such as cancelled checks, invoices, contracts, and minutes of the board of directors, or confirmations and other written representations by third persons. Examples of client inquiry are client responses to the internal control questionnaire and responses to analytical review procedure questions.

Confirmation occurs when the auditor requests evidence directly from a third party. The auditor communicates directly with the third party to obtain corroborating evidence about a specific assertion or a number of assertions. The confirmation process can support one or more of the five financial statement assertions and is typically considered a highly reliable source of evidence for the existence assertion. However, confirmations are less effective in testing for the completeness and valuation assertions. For example, confirmations of accounts receivable are typically reliable evidence supporting the claim that the customer exists, but are less effective in addressing the completeness assertion that all accounts receivable have been recorded. This in part, is due to the potentially understated population from which the account receivable has been selected.

Evidence is also gathered in other manners: Staff scan the various records for unique information. An example is a review of the general journal for unusual journal entries, especially those entries made near year-end. Analytical review procedures represent the reviews and analyses of relationships among financial and nonfinancial data. These substantive tests rely on the expected interrelationships among data. For example, gross margin (sales less cost of goods sold) as a percentage of sales should not radically alter between years because of market forces influencing both the

---

[8] SAS No. 1, Codification of Auditing Standards and Procedures (AICPA, Professional Standards, vol. 1, AU sec. 150, "Generally Accepted Auditing Standards").

¶ 607

Performing Fieldwork

retail and cost values. If there was a significant change, there should be an accompanying unusual event. Unexpected findings will prompt further investigation. Analytical procedures are substantive procedures to provide evidence to corroborate or refute other findings. Analytical procedures are a valuable source of corroborative evidence, but they are not required in the fieldwork stage. The auditing standards suggest the following five general forms of analytical procedures:[9]

1. Comparison of the current year account balances to balances of one or more comparable years. For example, auditors may compare the supplies expense account over the last few years. In this manner the auditor may determine whether the current year's balance appears reasonable.

2. Comparison of the current year account balances to anticipate results found in the company's budgets and forecasts. The auditor may determine whether the current balance of repairs and maintenance is reasonable compared to the predicted figure.

3. The evaluation of the relationships of the current year account balances to other current year account balances for reasonableness. For example, a comparison of interest expense to interest-bearing debt should yield an amount comparable to the recorded interest expense. The auditor can use this relationship to determine whether the comparison is reasonable.

4. The comparison of current-year account balances and financial relationships with similar information for the industry in which the company operates. For example, the doubtful account expense as a percentage of sales for the company in comparison to the industry statistics could be an indicator of the reasonableness of the expense.

5. The study of relationships of current year account balances with relevant nonfinancial information. For example, there should be a plausible relationship between the occupancy rate percentage for a hotel and its revenue.

When comparing data, the auditor should assess the reliability of the data. Audited data and data from an independent source are more reliable than non-audited, non-independent sources.

SAS 96 requires that when analytical procedures are used as the principal substantive test for an account or a group of accounts, the auditor should document the following:[10]

---

[9] SAS No. 15, Analytical Procedures (AICPA, Professional Standards, vol. 1, AU sec. 329.05).
[10] Statement on Auditing Standards No. 96, Audit Documentation, amending Statement on Auditing Standards No. 56, Analytical Procedures (AICPA, Professional Standards, vol. 1, AU sec. 329).

¶ 607

1. What was to be expected as the results of the analytical testing. For instance, if salaries increased three percent during the audit period with little change in the number of personnel, there is an expectation that salary expense should increase about three percent.

2. Results of the application of the analytical procedures.

3. Response, if the results do not meet the expectations; in other words, what additional auditing procedures were necessary to address the difference.

Another means of gathering evidence is to use specialists. Auditors generally are not trained in a profession other than auditing and, therefore, do not hold themselves out to be experts in another profession or occupation. Thus, in the course of an audit it may be necessary to employ the services of a specialist to help fulfill one or more of the audit objectives. For example, a geologist may be needed to estimate quantities of mineral reserves for depletion calculations, or a precious metals expert may be called upon to determine that investments in gold coins are valued properly.

If a specialist assists the auditor in obtaining corroborating evidence, it is important for the auditor to verify the qualifications of the specialist to do so. The auditor should review the specialist's credentials to ensure that the specialist has the necessary knowledge and expertise. This background check may include reviewing the expert's:

- Certifications and licenses
- Professional reputation among peers
- Experience and special training

It is important for there to be an understanding between the auditor and the specialist regarding the objective and scope of the specialist's work. Additionally, if the specialist assisting the auditor is affiliated or otherwise has a relationship with the client, the auditor should consider whether the objectivity of the specialist's judgment is impaired. If there is such a concern, the auditor should perform additional evaluative procedures, such as testing some or all of the specialist's assumptions, methods, and findings. This will help the auditor to gauge the reasonableness of the findings. An alternative is for the auditor to engage another specialist for this assessment.

¶ 608 Sufficiency of Evidence

Sufficiency of evidence involves the amount of competent evidence gathered. The amount of evidence as well as the types of evidence the auditor needs to support an audit opinion is a matter of professional judgment and becomes clear only after a careful study of the client's circumstances. The nature of evidence is such that the auditor will probably not be convinced beyond all doubt of its support for some aspect of the financial statements under examination; rather, the evidence probably will be only persuasive.

No exacting guidelines exist for quantifying evidence. The auditor simply must obtain enough evidence to form an opinion on the financial statements. Sufficient evidence must be gathered to fulfill the audit objectives, thus reducing the detection risk to a level acceptable to the auditor. Certain factors must be taken into consideration to determine how much evidence is necessary:

- The concept of sufficient evidence is tempered by the reality of time and economics. Confirming all accounts receivable is more persuasive evidence than confirming a sample. However, the cost and time involved in confirming 100 percent of the accounts receivable may make the time constraints and budgetary considerations untenable.

- The strength of the client's internal control.

- The inherent risk of the audit.

- The levels of materiality for the audit.

- The existence of related-party transactions.

- The quantity of evidence needed to support the auditors' opinion, which varies inversely with the quality of the available evidence.

¶ 609 Competence of Evidential Matter

Auditors gather evidence to support their opinion on the financial statements. As just stated, evidence cannot be obtained that is absolutely persuasive but only reasonably persuasive in fulfilling the audit objectives. Therefore, there are different *degrees* of persuasiveness, and the auditor attempts to gather the most persuasive and effective evidence in the most economical manner.

Evidence is said to be *competent* if it is relevant to the audit objective and is also believable, the latter attribute being referred to in auditing literature as validity. *Relevant evidence* is evidence that relates to fulfilling the audit objectives. Relevance implies that the evidence has a direct bearing upon a management assertion that the auditor is considering. For example, the process of confirming accounts receivable relates to the existence assertion. In other words, confirmations provide evidence that the individual accounts in accounts receivable are real. However, confirming accounts receivable does not address valuation of accounts receivable in the sense of setting their net realizable value. A customer may confirm that his or her company owes an amount, but that does not mean that the customer

¶ 609

will *pay* the receivable. The auditor must gather other evidence to address the net realizable value of accounts receivable.

There are many levels of believability or validity of evidence. Whenever accounting data and documents have been developed within a system of strong internal controls, they are more reliable than comparable data and documents developed within a weaker control system. Also, documentary evidence obtained directly from the client usually is less believable than evidence received from third persons. General forms of upholding the validity of documentary evidence are:

- *External evidence*—confirmations are a form of documentary evidence obtained directly from independent sources. Of the documentary evidence, confirmations are typically considered the most valid.

- *External-internal evidence*—evidence that originated outside the client's data processing system but that has been received and processed by the client is the next most valid type of documentary evidence. Invoices, contracts, and bank statements are examples of external-internal evidence.

- *Internal evidence*—documents that are produced within the client's information system are considered the weakest form of documentary evidence. Examples of internal documentary evidence are:

    – Written representations given by the client's officers, directors, owners

    – Sales orders

    – Receiving reports

    – Purchase orders

Evidence obtained through the auditor's direct knowledge is quite often more believable than that obtained from others. For example, an auditor obtains strong evidence about a building's existence through direct knowledge—physically inspecting the premises. The evidence obtained through the auditor's direct knowledge varies in validity, however. An auditor may recompute interest expense as a source of corroborating evidence. However, what the auditor uses as the basis for the calculations affects the validity of the evidence. When this auditor recomputes interest expense to determine its reasonableness, he or she applies an effective interest rate to the recorded amount of debt. The recomputation is more valid if the debt is an audited amount rather than an unaudited amount.

Sometimes the competence of audit evidence depends more on its source than on the judgment of the auditor. If an auditor were to physically examine inventory items of a technical nature, such as computer hard

¶ 609

drives, he or she would gain direct knowledge that the inventory exists, but confirmation by an expert might be needed to determine whether the disk drives worked properly and thus represented salable inventory.

Another factor in respect to competence is the economic and time constraints of the audit. For example, an auditor could confirm with a title insurance company that a client owned a building as of the balance sheet date. This confirmation would typically produce what would be considered strongly persuasive evidence supporting the "rights" assertion. However, this process might be inefficient compared to economic and time constraints of the audit engagement, especially when other types of more economical, corroborative evidence are available.

¶ 610 Internal Controls and Audit Objectives

The Sarbanes-Oxley Act of 2002 requires each annual report of an issuer (public company) to contain an internal control report. This required internal control report must (1) state the responsibility of management for establishing and maintaining an adequate and effective internal control structure and procedures for financial reporting and (2) contain an assessment, as of the end of the issuer's fiscal year, of the effectiveness of the internal control structure and procedures over financial reporting. Furthermore, each issuer's auditor must attest to and report on the assessment made by management regarding the effectiveness of internal controls. The attestation engagement should not be the subject of a separate engagement and should be performed in accordance with PCAOB Auditing Standard No. 2.

Auditing standards require that the auditor understand the internal controls of the client. The purpose of this knowledge is to assist the auditor in identifying risks of misstatements as well as designing tests of controls and substantive tests. If the auditor finds that the internal controls are effectively designed, then the auditor may test the controls in order to substantiate that the controls have been properly implemented. Depending upon the results of the testing, the auditor may determine that less substantive testing is necessary for an effective audit, thereby a more efficient audit.

One of the purposes of internal controls, when properly designed and implemented, is to prevent and detect material misstatements in the financial statements. If the internal controls have been properly designed and implemented, in other words, it is unlikely that there are material misstatements in the financial statements, the audit team can fulfill some of their audit objectives during the internal control testing phase. In this manner the audit can be completed more efficiently. Internal controls usually are only tested during a financial statement audit if the controls appear to be designed properly. Generally if the controls are not effective, they will not be tested and most of the audit objectives will be accomplished during the year-end substantive testing phase.

Of particular importance and to be treated with utmost care are material misstatements due to fraud, because they pose more difficult problems to the auditor than mere mistakes. Management concealment of such fraud will complicate discovery of these types of misstatements.

The intent of the AICPA with SAS 99 is to integrate review for risks of material misstatement due to fraud into the audit in a "seamless" fashion. As such, it is appropriate to review for these risks during the overall internal control review phase.

Certain conditions can exist that exacerbate the susceptibility for fraud to occur. Auditing literature and SAS 99 cite three conditions that commonly occur in most frauds (see Chapter 20):

1. Management or the employees have an incentive to commit fraud
2. The circumstances exist to commit fraud
3. The individuals involved in the fraud are able to rationalize the fraud

As with all existing controls, management is responsible for establishing programs and controls to prevent and detect fraud. However it is management who may be committing the fraud, and thus it is imperative for the auditor to maintain a manner of professional skepticism while auditing, even if past experience with the client indicated the client to be honest.

SAS 99 requires the auditor, as part of developing an understanding of the internal controls, to evaluate if the client's programs and controls address identified risks of material misstatement due to fraud sufficiently. The auditor should also consider if specific control deficiencies exasperate the risk.[11]

During the planning and internal control testing phases, the auditor may become aware of significant deficiencies in the design or operation of the client's internal control system. (Information technology has a profound effect on the internal control structure as well as the initiating, processing, and reporting of transactions. See Chapter 23 for more detail.) These deficiencies are referred to as *reportable conditions* and may include those deficiencies that create the risk of material misstatement due to fraud. Auditing standards require that the client's audit committee or its equivalent be apprised of all reportable conditions, either verbally or in

---

[11] Statement on Auditing Standards No. 99, Consideration of Fraud in a Financial Statement Audit (AICPA, Professional Standards, vol. 1, AU sec. 316.44).

¶ 610

writing.[12] Written communication is preferable, but if the communication is verbal, it should be documented in the auditor's workpapers.

The auditing literature also refers to a more serious type of reportable condition—a material internal control weakness. "A material weakness is a reportable condition in which the design or operation of one or more of the internal control components does not reduce to a relatively low level the risk that misstatements caused by error or fraud in amounts that would be material in relation to the financial statements being audited may occur and not be detected within a timely period by employees in the normal course of performing their assigned functions."[13] Because a material weakness is a reportable condition, the auditor must communicate the material weakness to the audit committee, but there is no requirement for the auditor's report to differentiate a material weakness from other reportable conditions.

Auditing standards require that the auditor understand the internal control structure in order to plan the audit as well as determining the nature, timing, and extent of tests to be performed.[14] The framework for understanding the internal control structure was developed on behalf of the Committee of Sponsoring Organizations (COSO) of the Treadway Commission. The framework was later incorporated into the auditing standards. These standards define internal controls as:

> "a process, effected by an entity's board of directors, management and other personnel, designed to provide reasonable assurance regarding the achievement of objectives in the following categories:
>
> 1. Effectiveness and efficiency of operations
> 2. Reliability of financial reporting
> 3. Compliance with applicable laws and regulations"

Internal controls consist of five interrelated components:[15]

1. Control environment sets the tone of an organization, influencing the control consciousness of its people. It is the foundation for all other components of internal control, providing discipline and structure. This component includes management operating philosophy, integrity, organizational structure as well as audit committee participation, and human resource policies.

2. Risk assessment is the entity's identification and analysis of relevant risks to achievement of its objectives, forming a basis for determining how the risks should be managed. This includes how management identifies risks, especially in the preparation

---

[12] SAS No. 60, Communication of Internal Control Related Matters Noted in an Audit (AICPA, Professional Standards, vol. 1, AU sec. 325.15, "Reporting—Form and Content").

[13] Ibid.

[14] Statements on Auditing Standards (SAS) No. 1, Codification of Auditing Standards and Procedures (AICPA, Professional Standards, vol. 1, AU sec. 150).

[15] SAS No. 94, The Effect of Information on the Auditor's Consideration of Internal Control in a Financial Statement Audit (AICPA, Professional Standards, vol. 1, AU sec. 319.07).

¶ 610

of the financial statements. Risks arise when there is a change in personnel, rapid growth of the client, or new technology.

3. Control activities are the policies and procedures that help ensure that management directives are carried out. These include segregation of duties and functions and the physical control over assets.

4. Information and communication systems support the identification, capture, and exchange of information in a form and time frame that enable people to carry out their responsibilities. These include the recordkeeping system and software and communications within the organization.

5. Monitoring is a process that assesses the quality of internal control performance over time. This includes how management assess the internal controls through internal auditing, customer communications systems, and communications with the external auditor.

The context above is provided to assist the auditor in understanding the client's internal control system.

Management creates procedures in order to direct employees to accomplish the aforementioned objectives. These procedures are the internal controls. Once the auditor understands the internal control structure, their understanding should be documented in the workpapers through the use of flowcharts or memoranda. The next step is for the auditor to develop a preliminary assessment of the control risks attached to the many management assertions contained in the financial statements. This also includes an evaluation of the identified risks of material misstatement due to fraud. Auditing standards require the documentation of the preliminary assessment in the workpapers (see Chapter 5, "Planning the Financial Audit").

If the internal controls prove ineffective or testing the internal controls proves inefficient, the auditor assesses the control risk at a maximum for all financial statement assertions. The focus of evidence to be gathered in fulfilling the audit objectives will be set during the detailed testing of the account balances. Using the audit planning model and setting the control risk at maximum or 100 percent, the amount of detection risk the auditor is willing to accept is at its minimum. Evidence must be accumulated during the year-end substantive testing phase.

However, in many cases some of these internal control procedures are designed and implemented properly so that material misstatements in the financial statements have a higher probability of prevention and detection. The control risk of those internal controls that appear to be designed properly is referred to as "less than the maximum level." If the control risk is less than maximum, controls can be tested to determine whether they are

¶ 610

functioning properly and at the same time fulfill some of the audit objectives. The objective of testing the internal controls during this period is to decrease the substantive audit work.

Additionally and incorporated into this same process, the auditor should evaluate if the identified risks of material misstatement due to fraud can be related to specific financial-statement account balances or classes of transactions and related assertions, or whether they relate more pervasively to the financial statements as a whole. This will need to be addressed subsequently when the audit program is prepared.[16]

¶ 611 Testing the Internal Controls

Auditor's assessment of internal control risk is made after the study and evaluation of the client's internal control structure and the performance of tests of controls. The estimate of control risk is based on an assessment of the internal control structure and the auditor's intention to rely on those controls in determining the nature, extent, and timing of substantive tests. Estimate of control risk is made through inquiry of client personnel, observation, and performance of tests of controls. Registered auditors are required by Act Sec. 404 of the Sarbanes-Oxley Act and in compliance with PCAOB Auditing Standard No. 2 to (1) obtain an understanding of their client's internal control system, (2) evaluate how the system is functioning, and (3) test internal controls for effectiveness.

Table 6.2

Registered Auditor's Consideration of Internal Controls

	Pre-Sarbanes-Oxley Act	Post-Sarbanes-Oxley Act
Purpose	Obtain understanding of the internal control structure to determine timing, nature, and extent of audit test procedures.	Express an opinion on management's assessment of internal control over financial reporting.
Standards	AICPA Statement on Auditing Standards No. 78, Consideration of Internal Control in a Financial Statement Audit.	PCAOB Auditing Standard No. 2, An Audit of Internal Control Over Financial Reporting Performed in Conjunction with an Audit of Financial Statements.

---

[16] Statement on Auditing Standards No. 99, Consideration of Fraud in a Financial Statement Audit (AICPA, 2003).

Extent	Auditor's decision to rely or not to rely on client's internal control structure.	Auditor's attestation of and report on client's internal control structure as an integral part of audit of financial statement.
Nature	Optional tests of controls to determine adequacy and effectiveness of the internal control structure.	Required tests of controls to determine management's assessment of the effectiveness of the internal control structure as the audit of internal controls over financial reporting.
Timing	Primarily internal work.	Primarily at or near balance sheet date.
Applicable Audit Procedures	Inquiries, observations, and inspections.	Inquiries, observations, inspections, walk-throughs, and review of corporate governance mechanisms.

If the auditor determines that the internal control structure is designed effectively, the auditor must determine whether it is efficient to test the internal controls. If it is, some of the audit objectives can be fulfilled during the internal control testing phase, thus decreasing some of the substantive account balance testing. In this manner the auditing procedures can be applied more efficiently, spread out and not concentrated in the year-end substantive testing phase.

Likewise, the auditor can test to determine if the client's programs and controls that address identified risks of material misstatement due to fraud have been suitably designed and placed in operation; the auditor is then in a better position to assess these risks and can respond accordingly.[17]

For management assertions that the control risk has been determined to be less than maximum, the auditor must:

- Identify which are the specific controls that are likely to prevent or detect a material misstatement in the financial statements, and

- Test the controls to determine that the procedures have been implemented and are functioning properly.

The auditing literature refers to this latter type of testing as a *test of controls*. Tests of controls help the auditor determine whether the internal control procedures are functioning properly to support that the assessed control risk is less than maximum. A second type of test is also used during this testing phase: the substantive test of transaction. In this test the

---

[17] *Ibid.*

auditor determines whether the procedures are producing accurate transactions by classifying, recording, and summarizing all transactions properly and, if applicable, entering the transaction into the subsidiary ledger accounts properly.

To audit the control testing phase, audit objectives must be developed. However, during the control testing phase the audit objectives must be transaction-oriented. At this stage, account balances have not been finalized.

To develop audit objectives for the internal control testing phase the auditor can use the management assertions. In this case the management assertions can also be viewed as internal control objectives for the company, as described earlier in the chapter.

Management wants to establish procedures so that:

- Only authorized, actual transactions are recorded (Occurrence)
- All transactions were recorded (Completeness)
- All transactions are valued correctly (Valuation or allocation), assuming that:
  - The transaction is properly classified.
  - The transaction is recorded in the proper period.
  - Where applicable, the transaction is recorded in both the subsidiary account as well as the control account in the general ledger.

Specific control procedures that are implemented by a client will vary with the nature of the client's processing, but the basic control objectives and types of control procedures are applicable for many companies.

¶ 612 Using the Work of the Internal Auditor

The internal auditor monitors the company's internal controls. As such, the internal audit function can be an integral part of the internal control structure. Although Chapter 14 details the relationships between external and internal audit functions, this chapter's discussion focuses on ways the external auditor can adopt financial research for the external audit report. Auditing standards require the auditor to understand the internal control structure and, therefore, understand the internal auditing function. Under certain circumstances the external auditor or consultant practitioner can use the work of the internal auditor. This can make the audit more efficient, resulting in cost savings to the auditor and client.

Before using the work of the internal auditor, the external auditor must determine the following:

¶ 612

1. That the internal auditor reports to an organizational level to ensure internal auditor objectivity and broad audit coverage.

2. That the internal auditor is competent to assist the external auditor. These background elements help in reviewing an internal auditor's competence:

   a. The internal auditor's educational background

   b. Certifications and licenses held by the internal auditor

   c. The internal auditor's experience with the internal auditing department

   d. The results from recent external quality reviews of the internal auditor

3. That the internal auditor's work can be coordinated with the external auditor's engagement.

4. That the type of work that the internal auditor is performing is appropriate to the financial statement audit.

5. If the internal auditor:[18]

   a. Has knowledge of any risks of material misstatements due to fraud for the client

   b. Has knowledge of any fraud or suspected fraud

   c. Performed any procedures that identified or detected fraud

   d. Felt that management had satisfactorily responded to any findings resulting from the above procedures

6. That using the work of the internal auditor makes the financial statement audit more efficient.

Based upon these criteria, if the auditor determines that the financial audit team can use the work of the internal auditor, then past work by the internal auditor may assist the external auditor. For instance, the external auditor may be able to use these elements of the internal auditor's past work:

1. For understanding the internal control system—flowcharts and descriptive memoranda previously prepared by the internal auditor

2. As pertinent tests of controls—recent testing of controls by the internal auditor that address transaction classification, recording, summarizing and reporting and

---

[18] *Ibid.*

3. For substantive testing of transactions and account balances—recent substantive tests performed by the internal auditor for the same time frame as the financial statement audit

However, before using any work of the internal auditor, the external auditor must evaluate the *quality* of the work. The external auditor must determine:

- That the internal auditor's workpapers adequately document evidence obtained
- That the scope of the internal auditor's work met the audit objectives
- That the internal auditor's audit programs were adequate
- That the evidence obtained adequately supported the internal auditor's report

It is also possible for the internal auditor to provide direct assistance to the auditor. The internal auditor can provide an understanding of the internal control system, test it, and perform various substantive testing and account analysis, all under the direction of the external auditor. Figure 6.2 shows a flowchart of uses for work of the internal auditors by the external audit team.

¶612

Figure 6.2

Using the Work of the Internal Auditor

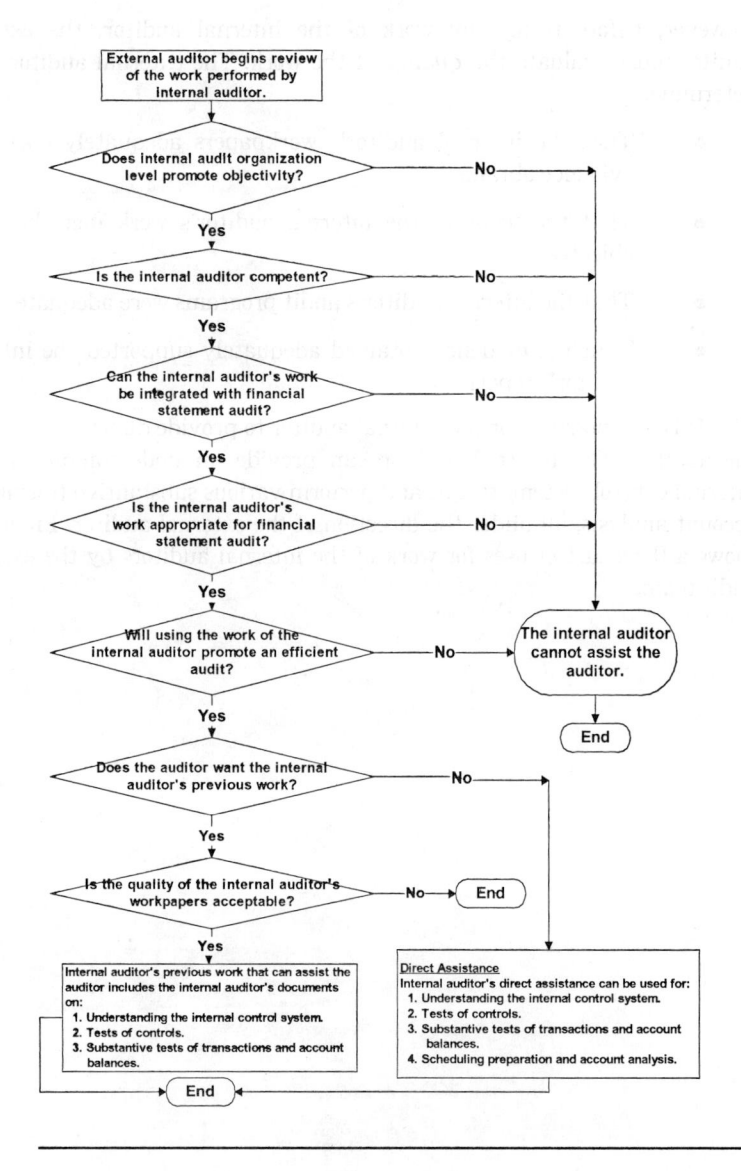

```
External auditor begins review of the work performed by internal auditor.
    ↓
Does internal audit organization level promote objectivity? ──No──┐
    │Yes                                                           │
    ↓                                                              │
Is the internal auditor competent? ──No───────────────────────────┤
    │Yes                                                           │
    ↓                                                              │
Can the internal auditor's work be integrated with financial      │
statement audit? ──No─────────────────────────────────────────────┤
    │Yes                                                           │
    ↓                                                              │
Is the internal auditor's work appropriate for financial          │
statement audit? ──No─────────────────────────────────────────────┤
    │Yes                                                           │
    ↓                                                              ↓
Will using the work of the internal auditor promote an       The internal auditor
efficient audit? ──No──────────────────────────────────→     cannot assist the auditor.
    │Yes                                                          ↓
    ↓                                                            End
Does the auditor want the internal auditor's previous work? ──No──┐
    │Yes                                                           │
    ↓                                                              ↓
Is the quality of the internal auditor's workpapers acceptable? ──No──→ End
    │Yes
    ↓
```

Internal auditor's previous work that can assist the auditor includes the internal auditor's documents on:
1. Understanding the internal control system.
2. Tests of controls.
3. Substantive tests of transactions and account balances.

→ End

Direct Assistance
Internal auditor's direct assistance can be used for:
1. Understanding the internal control system.
2. Tests of controls.
3. Substantive tests of transactions and account balances.
4. Scheduling preparation and account analysis.

¶ 612

¶ 613 Final Assessment of Control Risk and Risk of Material Misstatement Due to Fraud, and Their Effect on Detection Risk

As was shown in the planning model described in Chapter 5, the amount of detection risk the auditor is willing to accept is inversely proportional to control risk; the less the control risk, the greater the acceptable detection risk. Stated differently, strong internal controls lead to less detailed testing of the account balances than if weak controls are present.

When the external auditor tests control procedures, he or she is looking to corroborate or possibly revise the preliminary assessment of control risk. If the control procedures are not operating effectively, there is a increased risk that material misstatements exist in the financial statements. The increased risk of material misstatements should be reflected in the audit program. If the final assessment of control risk remains low, the auditor can conduct substantive testing accepting a higher level of acceptable detection risk.

Additional complications arise when risks of material misstatement due to fraud are validated. SAS 99 suggests responses to these identified risks affect the nature, timing, and extent of subsequent audit procedures. Certainly more substantive testing will be necessary. Tests of operating effectiveness of the entity's programs and controls could be tainted by the fact that management can override the controls. It will be necessary to obtain more reliable and corroborating evidence as well as performing more of the substantive tests at or near the end of the reporting period.[19]

The control testing phase validates the nature of the internal control system, what controls have been implemented, and their effectiveness in preventing and detecting errors, as well as provides validity to the documents generated by the control system. Based on this knowledge, the auditor can determine whether additional evidence will be needed as follow-up to the preliminary estimate. For example, if an auditor determined that the previous low control risk attributed to the classification of purchases was unwarranted, then instead of analytical procedures as originally prescribed, vouching might be needed.

¶ 614 Applying Substantive Tests Prior to the Balance Sheet Date

Auditors can apply substantive tests to account balances prior to the balance sheet date to test significant matters early, making the audit less harried at year-end. However, in doing so there is an increased risk that misstatements at the balance sheet date may go undetected. The risk is proportional to the length of time between the interim substantive testing

---

[19] *Ibid.*

and the balance sheet date. The risk can be decreased, however, if the audit team makes substantive tests that extend from the interim date to the balance sheet date.

To apply interim substantive tests it is not necessary for the control risk to be less than maximum. However, if the effectiveness of the controls is such that the interim substantive tests will be impaired or cost ineffective, either for the interim period or the period between the interim period and balance sheet date, the auditor should consider substantive testing at the balance sheet date.

Additionally the timing of substantive tests may need to occur at or near the end of the reporting period to best address an identified risk of material misstatement due to fraud.[20]

¶615 Audit Programs

Auditing standards require an auditor to prepare a written audit program. The audit program represents the detailed audit procedures of obtaining evidence to accomplish the audit objectives.[21]

The auditor takes into account preliminary estimates of inherent and control risks and materiality. Then, based upon the acceptable detection risk related to the particular assertion, the auditor may decide that analytical procedures may be effective enough to achieve the audit objective. For another assertion and related detection risk the auditor may require a combination of tests of details and analytical procedures. However, as the audit progresses, unexpected conditions may require modifications to the audit program.

As the audit program steps are completed, audit team members should document who performed each procedure. Team members should initial or sign their name and the date completed as they complete each step. Not only does this indicate what has been completed, but also what still must be completed.

¶616 Audit Workpapers

In addition to the permanent file workpapers discussed in Chapter 5, workpapers should document evidence gathered for the current financial statement audit. They support the auditor's conclusions as well as serve as proof that the auditor conducted the audit in conformity with GAAS. The papers vary greatly in format and content because of various types of the audit engagements and audit firm standards and may be represented in paper form, electronic form, or other media.[22] Audit workpapers, in all

---

[20] *Ibid.*
[21] SAS No. 22, Planning and Supervision (AICPA, Professional Standards, vol. 1, AU sec. 311.05).

[22] SAS No. 96, Audit Documentation (AICPA, Professional Standards, vol. 1, AU sec. 339.05).

¶615

forms, should be retained for a reasonable period of time as well as for all statutory requirements.[23]

.01 Features

GAAS requires that the auditor plan the engagement.[24] The workpapers should indicate what was accomplished during the planning phase of the audit. For example, documentation of the planning phase (see Chapter 5) should include a workpaper such as a planning memorandum that encompasses numerous policies and procedures unique to the client's company.

SAS 99 requires that the auditor document consideration of fraud in the audit. This should include the initial planning meeting with audit team personnel to discuss the client's financial statement susceptibility to material misstatement due to fraud. This documentation should include who attended the meeting(s) and when. Additionally other documentation of fraud should include:[25]

1. Procedures that identified and assessed the risks of material misstatement due to fraud as well as the auditor's response to those risks.

2. The reasons supporting the auditor's conclusion, if no risk was identified for improper revenue recognition as a risk of material misstatement due to fraud.

3. The results of the procedures performed to assess the risk of management override of controls.

4. Documentation of any other fraud matter that required additional auditing procedures or auditor response.

5. How fraud matters were communicated to management, the audit committee, and others.

GAAS requires that assistants to the auditor be properly supervised.[26] The workpapers should document:

- Composition of the audit team including identification of reviewers[27]
- Audit staff performance is in accordance with generally accepted auditing standards
- Audit staff performance is in accordance with firm standards

---

[23] *Ibid.*
[24] SAS No. 1, Codification of Auditing Standards and Procedures (AICPA, Professional Standards, vol. 1, AU sec. 150.02, "Generally Accepted Auditing Standards").
[25] Statement on Auditing Standards No. 99, Consideration of Fraud in a Financial Statement Audit (AICPA, Professional Standards, vol. 1, AU sec. 316.83).
[26] SAS No. 1, Codification of Auditing Standards and Procedures (AICPA, Professional Standards, vol. 1, AU sec. 150.02, "Generally Accepted Auditing Standards").
[27] SAS No. 96, Audit Documentation (AICPA, Professional Standards, vol. 1, AU sec. 339.06).

¶ 616.01

- Evidence gathered by staff supporting the audit opinion has been adequately documented
- Documentation is sufficient to allow for review by other audit team members
- Understanding of the internal control structure be documented. Evidence of the understanding is contained in:
  - Internal control questionnaires
  - Descriptive memoranda
  - Flowcharts
- That the accounting records agree or are reconciled to the financial statements[28]

SAS 96 requires that the workpapers include:[29]

1. Abstracts or copies of significant contracts or agreements examined supporting significant transactions.
2. Documentation of the extent of internal control effectiveness.
3. A detail of all inspected documents or confirmations used in the substantive tests of details.
4. Documentation of significant audit findings, actions taken to address them, and resolution. This may include:
   a. Unusual transactions
   b. Complex transactions
   c. Estimates and uncertainties related to management assumptions
   d. Auditing procedures that indicate financial statements and/or disclosures are materially misstated
   e. Auditing procedures that were difficult to apply and reason for difficulty

If the control risk is less than maximum for some or all of the assertions, the internal control testing should be included in the workpapers.

Because of confidentiality issues, the auditor must be cognizant that there is no unauthorized access to the workpapers. Additionally, SAS 96 re-emphasizes that certain audit documentation may be provided to the client to assist them in certain bookkeeping processes such as reconciliations; however, the auditor's workpapers are not to serve as a substitute for the client accounting records.[30]

---

[28] *Ibid.*
[29] *Ibid.*
[30] *Ibid.*

¶ 616.01

.02 Individual Worksheets

Important characteristics of individual worksheets that appear in the workpapers are these:

1. The individual who prepared the worksheet should be indicated on it as well as the date prepared. If the client prepared the worksheet, that should be indicated also.

2. Each reviewer should be indicated on the worksheet as well as the date of the review.

3. Each page of the worksheet should indicate:

    a. The name of the client.

    b. The purpose of the worksheet.

    c. The financial statement.

    d. How the worksheet ties to the rest of the workpapers. Usually auditors use an index coding system.

    e. Repetitive auditing procedures are sometimes documented by using tickmarks. Whenever tickmarks are used in workpapers there should be a tickmark legend indicating what the tickmarks represent.

.03 Retention of Audit Evidence

The Sarbanes-Oxley Act of 2002 authorized the PCAOB to establish auditing standards that require registered public accounting firms to prepare and retain audit documentation for at least seven years "in sufficient detail to support the conclusions reached." The PCAOB has established PCAOB Auditing Standard No. 3, Audit Documentation and Amendment to Interim Auditing Standards.[31] Auditing Standard No. 3 establishes general requirements for documentation that registered auditors should prepare and retain in connection with audit engagements.

¶ 617 Evaluation of Evidential Matter

Having completed a thorough, objective accumulation of evidence, the auditor must consider whether the audit objectives have been achieved. If they have, evidence has been obtained that management assertions are appropriate or that there were misstatements to be corrected. However, the auditor cannot render an opinion on the financial statements if he or she harbors substantial doubt about any of the assertions. Additionally the auditor must look at the effects, both in an individual and aggregate manner, of the misstatements that have not been corrected by the client. The auditor should estimate the total misstatements in the account balances they have examined and assess if the financial statements taken as a

---

[31] PCAOB Release No. 2004-006, June 9, 2004. Available at *http://www.pcaobus.org*.

whole are materially misstated. If misstated, the client must revise the financial statements or the auditor cannot render an unqualified opinion.[32] Until the auditor has obtained sufficient competent evidence to eliminate this significant doubt, he or she may be required to express a qualified opinion or a disclaimer of opinion.

If the auditor identifies misstatements during the audit engagement, he or she should determine whether the misstatements were based upon fraudulent transactions. Even if the misstatements were immaterial, the auditor should evaluate the implications of management's involvement. Material misstatements due to fraud are discussed below.

¶ 618 Fraud Implications Arising During the Evaluation of Audit Results

During the planning stage of the audit engagement the auditor may become aware of certain fraud risk factors present with the client's operations. If, during the fieldwork, the auditor determines that misstatements have indeed occurred, the auditor should determine whether the misstatements are a result of fraud and are material to the financial statements.

Material misstatements could also be the result of unusual transactions that lack economic substance. Unusual transactions may be proper if they reflect an economic reality. However, for those lacking reality, unusual transactions could indicate a material misstatement due to fraud.

During the course of the audit, significant unusual transactions may come to light. These transactions may be revealed through the normal course of vouching or reviewing transactions in the general journal or during revenue cut-off testing. The auditor should evaluate any significant unusual transaction to determine that the transaction had a proper business rationale.

SAS 99 provides some considerations in understanding the business rationale behind an unusual transaction:[33]

1. Is the transaction unnecessarily complex, possibly involving multiple entities such as those involving special purpose entities?

2. Is the transaction visible to the audit committee and the board of directors? Has management discussed the transaction with the committee and board?

---

[32] SAS No. 98, Omnibus Statement on Auditing Standards, amending SAS No. 47, Audit Risk and Materiality in Conducting an Audit (AICPA, Professional Standards, vol. 1, AU secs. 312.34–312.41).

[33] Statement on Auditing Standards No. 99, Consideration of Fraud in a Financial Statement Audit (AICPA, Professional Standards, vol. 1, AU sec. 316.67).

3. Is the form of the accounting treatment more important to management than the treatment of the substance of the transaction?

4. Do the transactions involve previously unidentified related parties? And do those related parties have the substance or the financial strength to support the transaction without assistance from the entity under audit?

Failure to establish an economic basis for the recorded transaction could be an indication of fraud.

Sometimes fraud is not a single transaction but the accumulation of circumstances that management has established in such a way so as to create a material misstatement. Management bias in the valuation and quantification of accounting estimates is one such example. A bias in accruals, useful lives, and asset valuation could, in total, materially misstate the financial statements.

Auditors should, retrospectively, review the propriety of accounting estimates previously selected and reflected in prior year financial statements to determine if management judgment reflects a possible management bias. If a bias is found then the auditor should evaluate the circumstances to determine if they represent a risk of a material misstatement due to fraud.[34]

If any of the above types of misstatements is a result of fraud but not material, there may be still other detrimental implications regarding the matter. The auditor should determine what level of management was involved with the fraud. If key executives were involved, there may be a more pervasive problem throughout the organization. The auditor must understand the implications of such matters on the auditing procedures and reliability of evidence. Additionally, if the client is not taking the appropriate action regarding the fraud, the auditor may consider withdrawing from the engagement. Figure 6.3 summarizes actions in response to fraud.

Other AICPA auditing procedures[35] resulting from the detection of misstatements because of fraud are:

1. The matter should be brought to the appropriate level of management. This is the case even for matters considered immaterial to the financial statements.[36]

---

[34] *Ibid.*
[35] SAS No. 99, Consideration of Fraud in a Financial Statement Audit (AICPA, Professional Standards, vol. 1, AU sec. 316.77).
[36] Statement on Auditing Standards No. 99, Consideration of Fraud in a Financial Statement Audit (AICPA, Professional Standards, vol. 1, AU sec. 316.79).

2. The auditor should reach an understanding with the audit committee as to how to communicate about fraud committed by lower-level employees.[37]

3. The auditor should obtain evidence about the fraud's effect on the financial statements.

4. The auditor should suggest to the client that the executives consult with an attorney about the matter.

5. The auditor also should consider consulting with an attorney.

During the fieldwork phase any additional response to fraud should be documented. Also, all fraud, material or immaterial, should be communicated to the appropriate level of client management.

---

[37] Ibid.

¶ 618

Figure 6.3

Fraud Implications and the Evaluation of Audit Results

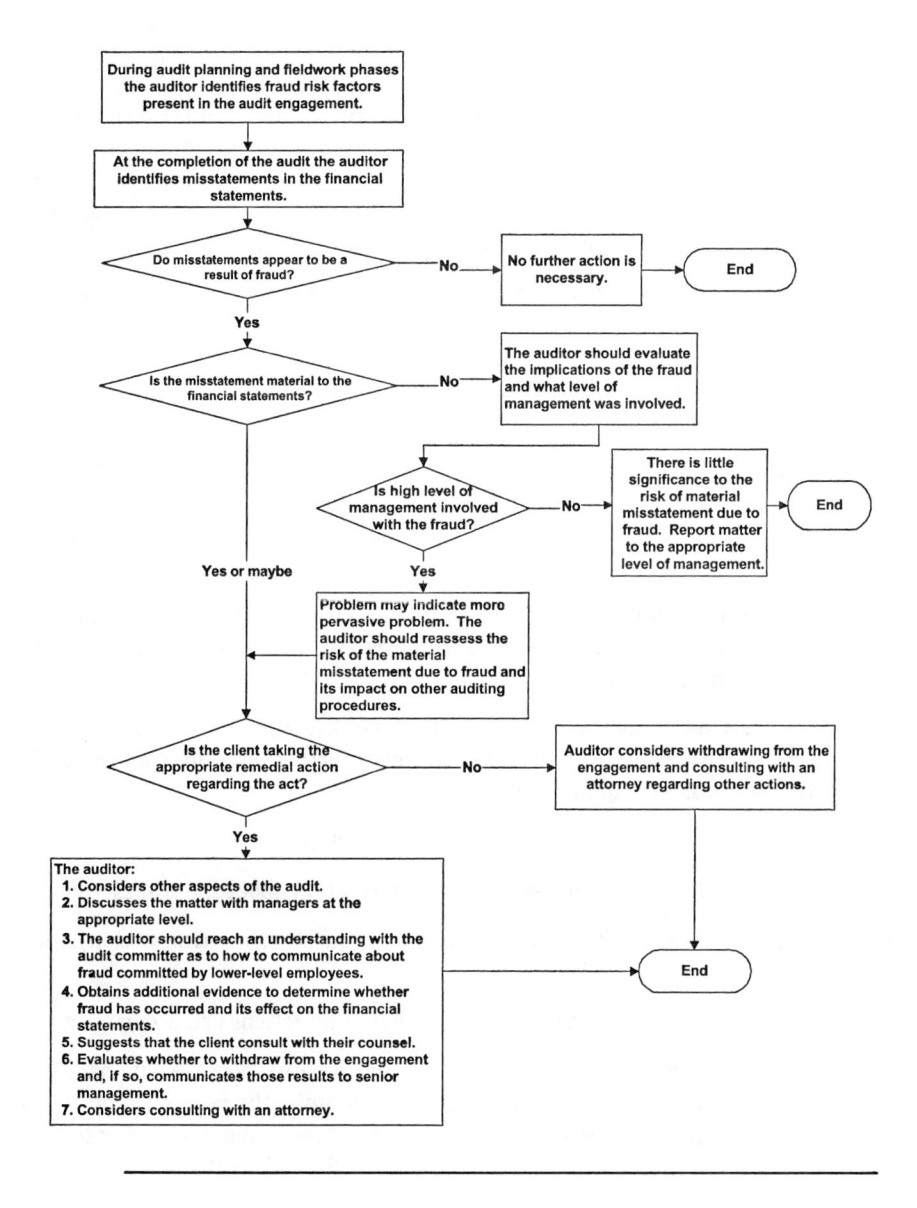

```
During audit planning and fieldwork phases the auditor identifies fraud risk factors present in the audit engagement.
        ↓
At the completion of the audit the auditor identifies misstatements in the financial statements.
        ↓
<Do misstatements appear to be a result of fraud?> ──No──> No further action is necessary. ──> End
        │Yes
        ↓
<Is the misstatement material to the financial statements?> ──No──> The auditor should evaluate the implications of the fraud and what level of management was involved.
        │                                                                            │
        ↓                                                                            ↓
<Is high level of management involved with the fraud?> ──No──> There is little significance to the risk of material misstatement due to fraud. Report matter to the appropriate level of management. ──> End
   Yes or maybe       │Yes
        │             ↓
        │       Problem may indicate more pervasive problem. The auditor should reassess the risk of the material misstatement due to fraud and its impact on other auditing procedures.
        ↓←──────────┘
<Is the client taking the appropriate remedial action regarding the act?> ──No──> Auditor considers withdrawing from the engagement and consulting with an attorney regarding other actions.
        │Yes                                                                         │
        ↓                                                                            ↓
The auditor:                                                                       End
1. Considers other aspects of the audit.
2. Discusses the matter with managers at the appropriate level.
3. The auditor should reach an understanding with the audit committer as to how to communicate about fraud committed by lower-level employees.
4. Obtains additional evidence to determine whether fraud has occurred and its effect on the financial statements.
5. Suggests that the client consult with their counsel.
6. Evaluates whether to withdraw from the engagement and, if so, communicates those results to senior management.
7. Considers consulting with an attorney.
```

¶ 618

¶ 619 Illegal Acts by Clients

Auditors do not hold themselves to be experts in the law. However, there are instances whereby an illegal act perpetrated by the client may have a direct effect on the amounts listed in the basic financial statements. Examples of the effects of these types of acts include tax accruals and revenue earned under certain government contracts. Auditing standards require that the auditor obtain sufficient evidence to provide reasonable assurance that the financial statements are free of material misstatements. Illegal acts that have a direct and material effect on the financial statements require reflection in the financial statement accounts affected. If the illegal act is material but does not directly affect the basic financial statements, disclosure of the matter is required.

If the auditor becomes aware of a possible illegal act, he or she should inquire of management not implicated in the matter whether the questionable act occurred. If management cannot verify satisfactorily that the questionable act did not occur, the auditor should further investigate the matter. The following evidence should be obtained to document:

- The nature of the questionable act
- The circumstances of the questionable act
- The effect on the financial statements[38]

Also, the auditor should obtain permission from the client to consult with the client's attorney or other specialists about the matter and its effect on the financial statements.

If the additional evidence obtained verifies that an illegal act may have been perpetrated, the auditor must further expand the steps of auditing procedures to include:

1. Vouching of any applicable transactions,
2. Confirming any significant information about the transactions,
3. Determining whether any of the questionable transactions had been authorized,
4. Considering whether any similar transactions had occurred, and
5. Considering the implications that the questionable acts have on other aspects of the audit. For example, the reliability of management representations made by those managers implicated in the questionable acts may need additional scrutiny.[39]

Once the additional substantiation is performed, the auditor should determine whether the client is taking appropriate action regarding the act.

---

[38] SAS No. 54, Illegal Acts by Clients (AICPA, Professional Standards, vol. 1, AU sec. 317.10).

[39] *Ibid.*, AU secs. 317.10 and 317.16.

If the client is not, the auditor may want to consider the implications the inaction has on the continuing relationship between the client and auditor. The auditor may consider withdrawing from the engagement. Figure 6.4 summarizes the auditor's procedures in situations of illegal acts.

Assuming that the auditor is satisfied with the management response to the questionable acts, the next question that must be resolved is the effect on the financial statements. If there is a material effect, the auditor must determine whether the act has a direct effect on the financial statements or an indirect effect, as just discussed.

Figure 6.4

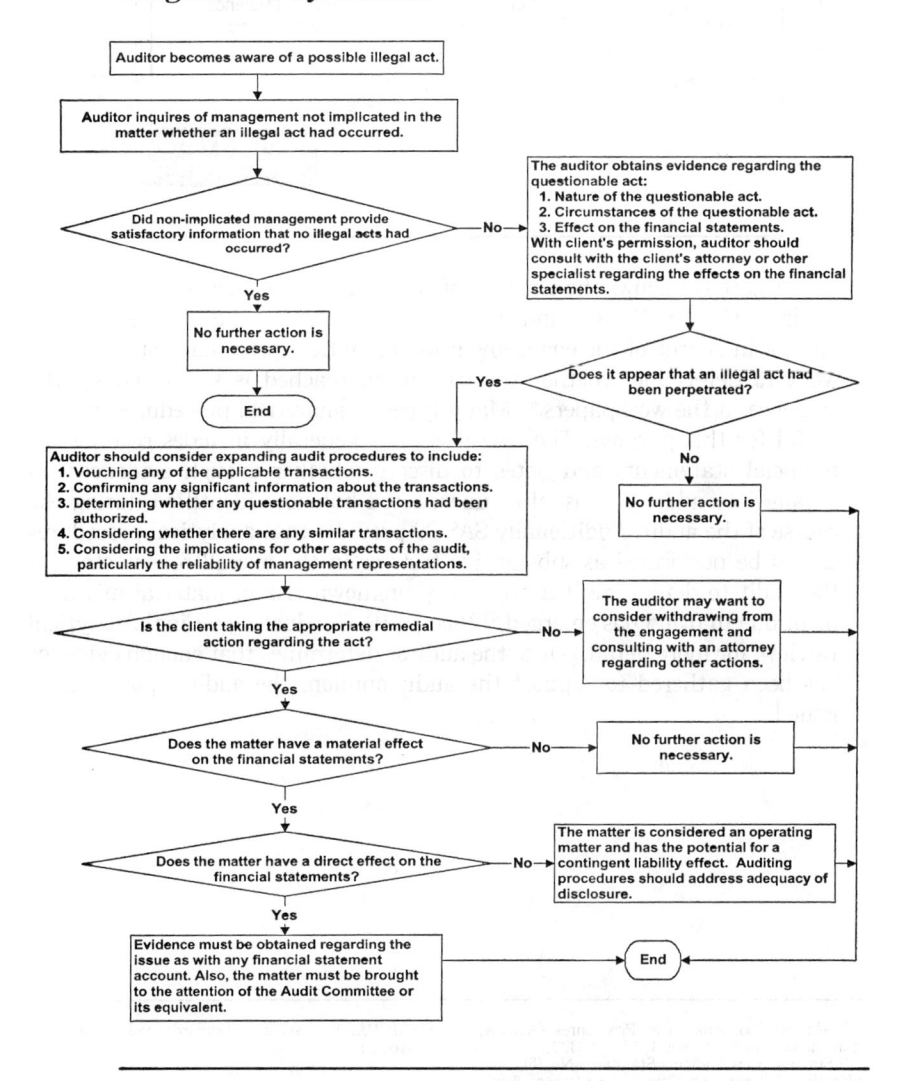

Illegal Acts by Clients

```
Auditor becomes aware of a possible illegal act.
        ↓
Auditor inquires of management not implicated in the
matter whether an illegal act had occurred.
        ↓
Did non-implicated management provide
satisfactory information that no illegal acts had  ——No→  The auditor obtains evidence regarding the
occurred?                                                 questionable act:
        Yes                                               1. Nature of the questionable act.
         ↓                                                2. Circumstances of the questionable act.
   No further action is                                   3. Effect on the financial statements.
      necessary.                                          With client's permission, auditor should
         ↓                                                consult with the client's attorney or other
        End                                               specialist regarding the effects on the financial
                                                          statements.
                                                                ↓
                                    ←——Yes——  Does it appear that an illegal act had
                                                  been perpetrated?
                                                        No
                                                         ↓
                                                  No further action is  ——→
                                                      necessary.
Auditor should consider expanding audit procedures to include:
1. Vouching any of the applicable transactions.
2. Confirming any significant information about the transactions.
3. Determining whether any questionable transactions had been
   authorized.
4. Considering whether there are any similar transactions.
5. Considering the implications for other aspects of the audit,
   particularly the reliability of management representations.
        ↓
Is the client taking the appropriate remedial   ——No→  The auditor may want to
     action regarding the act?                          consider withdrawing from
        Yes                                             the engagement and
         ↓                                              consulting with an attorney
                                                        regarding other actions.
Does the matter have a material effect  ——No→  No further action is  ——→
   on the financial statements?                      necessary.
        Yes
         ↓
Does the matter have a direct effect on the  ——No→  The matter is considered an operating
        financial statements?                         matter and has the potential for a
        Yes                                           contingent liability effect. Auditing
         ↓                                            procedures should address adequacy of
Evidence must be obtained regarding the               disclosure.
issue as with any financial statement
account. Also, the matter must be brought       ——→  End
to the attention of the Audit Committee or
its equivalent.
```

¶619

¶ 620 Final Review of Audit

Figure 6.5

Final Review Stages

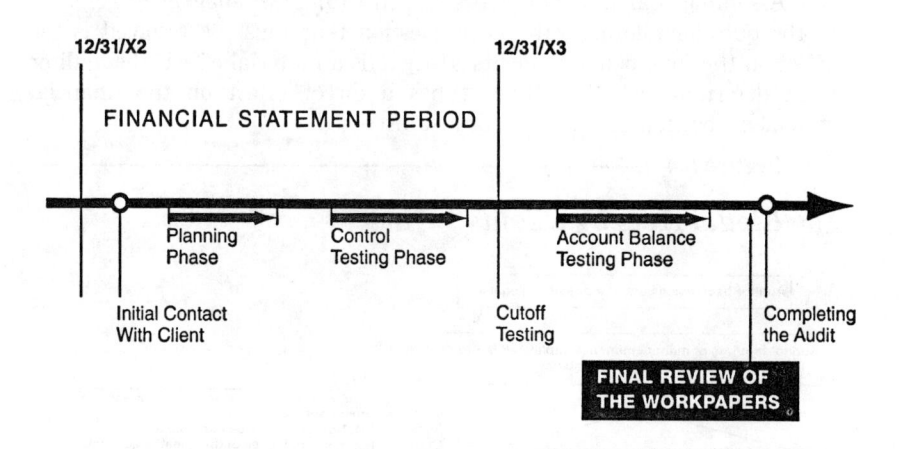

```
12/31/X2                    12/31/X3
│                           │
│  FINANCIAL STATEMENT PERIOD
│                           │
├──●────▶────▶────▶────▶────┼────▶────●────────▶
│   Planning   Control       Account Balance
│   Phase      Testing Phase  Testing Phase
│                           │                │
Initial Contact             Cutoff           Completing
With Client                 Testing          the Audit
                                             │
                                    FINAL REVIEW OF
                                    THE WORKPAPERS
```

Figure 6.5 shows the timeline of the final review stage of the financial audit. AICPA auditing standards require that during the final review, the auditor in charge of the engagement use analytical procedures on the audit work to determine whether the conclusion reached is supported by the evidence in the workpapers.[40] Many types of analytical procedures may be useful for this purpose. The overall review generally includes reading the financial statements and notes to discern whether enough evidence was obtained to address unusual or unexpected balances identified during the course of the audit. Additionally SAS 99 provides that analytical procedures should be performed as substantive tests or in the overall review stage of the audit to determine if a previously unknown risk of material misstatement due to fraud has emerged.[41] (See ¶ 710, Conducting a Final Analytical Review, for more detail.) Once the auditor determines that enough evidence has been gathered to support the audit opinion, the audit report can be issued.

---

[40] SAS No. 56, Analytical Procedures (AICPA, Professional Standards, vol. 1, AU sec. 329).
[41] Statement on Auditing Standards No. 99, Consideration of Fraud in a Financial Statement Audit (AICPA, Professional Standards, vol. 1, AU sec. 316.28).

¶ 621 The Sarbanes-Oxley Act of 2002 and the Auditor's Attestation of Internal Controls

The Sarbanes-Oxley Act of 2002 requires management to conclude on the effectiveness of the internal control over financial reporting. The Act further proposes that the PCAOB establish standards for auditor attestation of management's assessment of internal control effectiveness and that the auditor attestation be integrated into the financial statement audit.

The PCAOB adopted PCAOB Auditing Standard No. 2, An Audit of Internal Control Over Financial Reporting Performed in Conjunction with an Audit of Financial Statements, in March 2004.[42] PCAOB Auditing Standard No. 2 requires an integrated audit of the financial statements and internal control over financial reporting which addresses both audit of financial statements and audit of internal controls over financial reporting. Auditors are required to perform tests of controls to obtain sufficient and competent evidence about whether internal controls are adequate and effective. The gathered evidence should provide a basis to support an opinion regarding whether management's assessment of the effectiveness of internal control over financial reporting is fairly stated. Figure 6.5 compares and contrasts a registered auditor's consideration of internal controls pre- and post-Sarbanes-Oxley Act of 2002.

The objective of auditing the internal controls over financial reporting is to form an opinion about whether internal controls over financial reporting are effective. The audit of the internal controls includes these steps:

1. *Planning the internal control audit.* While many of the standard's procedures as proposed by the PCAOB are already encompassed in this chapter, the Sarbanes-Oxley Act of 2002 requires that management include a statement in the annual report about whether the internal controls over financial reporting are effective and that it is proposed that the auditor attest to management's assessment, as such, additional procedures are necessary. Planning the internal control audit includes evaluating the process management used to perform its assessment of internal control effectiveness as well as obtaining an understanding of the internal controls over financial reporting. The auditor needs to understand the internal controls over financial reporting both from the standpoints of design and operation. In order to gain this understanding the auditor should:

    a. Review management's assessment of the internal control effectiveness. For the auditor to conclude that they agree with management regarding the effectiveness of the internal controls, it is important that the auditor understand man-

---

[42] From the Public Company Accounting Oversight Board website *(http://www.pcaobus.org)*.

agement's process for determining if the internal controls are effective. To test management's assertion that the controls are effective, the process must be understood.

    b. Inquire of company personnel who are involved with the design of the internal controls.

    c. Review documents created and used in the internal control process.

    d. Establish that the designed controls are also functioning as designed. Therefore the auditor, during the planning phase, should determine which of the internal controls should be tested by management, the auditor, or others.

2. *Evaluating the effectiveness of both the design and operation of the internal controls.* During the internal control planning phase the auditor determined which of the controls should be tested to determine if the controls are functioning as designed. The auditor should obtain evidence to support an opinion about whether internal controls over financial reporting are effective. The evidence can be obtained by:

    a. Observing company personnel perform the controls.

    b. Inquiring of company personnel who perform the procedures that make up the internal controls.

    c. Performing a "walkthrough" of significant internal control processes, including tracing transactions through the accounting and information system to the financial reporting.

    d. Using the results of tests performed by management and others, such as internal auditors. The competency and objectivity of these individuals should be taken into consideration when determining to what extent their work can supplement that of the auditor. However their work cannot supplant that of the auditor who is still responsible for obtaining the principal evidence concerning the internal control effectiveness.

    e. Obtaining evidence about the operating effectiveness of internal control over financial reporting pertaining to all relevant assertions for all significant accounts or disclosures.

    f. Assessing the effectiveness of the client's corporate governance particularly the effectiveness of the audit committee's oversight.

3. *Forming an opinion about whether internal controls over financial reporting are effective.* If the auditor does not identify any significant internal control deficiency, the auditor can express

¶ 621

an unqualified opinion that management's assessment of the effectiveness of internal control over financial reporting is fairly stated in all material respects. If, however, internal control deficiencies are identified, the severity of the deficiency must be analyzed to form an opinion as to the probability of financial statement misstatement. Under certain circumstances the existence of a deficiency, if significant, may be strong evidence of the internal control ineffectiveness and an unqualified opinion cannot be rendered. Additional actions may also need to be taken such as communicating with the audit committee or even resigning from the audit engagement. PCAOB Auditing Standard No. 2 requires auditors to communicate in writing to the company's audit committee and management all discovered significant deficiencies and material weaknesses in internal controls over financial reporting. Appendix A of PCAOB Standard No. 2 presents seven different illustrative auditor reports on internal control over financial reporting. The illustrations will be further discussed in Chapter 10. The PCAOB suggests a combined auditor report expressing an opinion on financial statements and internal control when the auditors' opinion on financial statements, management's assessment of the effectiveness of internal control over financial reporting, and the auditor's opinion of the effectiveness of internal control over financial reporting are all unqualified.

¶ 622 Summary

The primary objective of the financial statement audit is for the auditor to express an opinion about the fair presentation of the financial statements. Auditors should obtain sufficient competent evidence in order to render an opinion. The auditor gathers sufficient and competent evidence during the two stages of fieldwork: the internal control testing phase and the year-end substantive account balance testing phase.

The financial statements are management's representations of the company's financial position and the results of operations, and management's assertions in the financial statements are audited by an external auditor. There are six management assertions: existence or occurrence, completeness, rights and obligations, valuation or allocation, presentation and disclosure, and compliance.

The purpose of understanding the internal controls of a client is to assist the auditor in identifying risks of misstatements as well as designing tests of controls and substantive tests. If the financial statements taken as a whole are misstated, the client must revise the financial statements or the auditor cannot render an unqualified opinion.

¶ 622

Chapter 7

Reaching Conclusions

¶ 701	Introduction
¶ 702	Auditing the Cash Account
¶ 703	Auditing Accounts Receivable
¶ 704	Auditing Accounts Payable
¶ 705	Other Procedures in the Financial Audit
¶ 706	Reviewing for Contingent Liabilities
¶ 707	Reviewing for Subsequent Events
¶ 708	Related Party Transactions
¶ 709	Reviewing the Company's Ability to Continue as a Going Concern
¶ 710	Final Fieldwork Assessment of the Risks of Material Misstatement Due to Fraud
¶ 711	Conducting a Final Analytical Review
¶ 712	Management Report on Internal Controls
¶ 713	Obtaining a Management Representation Letter
¶ 714	Summary

¶ 701 Introduction

This chapter describes the specific procedures surrounding the financial audit of selected accounts and related transactions as well as other procedures required by generally accepted auditing standards (GAAS) and PCAOB auditing standards. As described in Chapter 6, the amount and type of evidence gathered is risk-driven, based upon the audit, inherent, and control risks. When the control risk is judged preliminarily as less than maximum (i.e., "not weak") and the auditor wishes to be in a position to rely upon the controls effectuating the management assertions, those controls must be tested. In order to illustrate a broad audit coverage for the selected accounts in this chapter, many of the internal controls, tests of controls, substantive tests of transactions, detailed testing of account balance, and analytical procedures will be described and categorized by management assertion. Also, the assumption is made that there are no risks of material misstatement due to fraud.

First, this chapter gives a detailed description of the typical controls for a cash account, specifically, the general checking account and its related cash transactions that a company may institute to maintain accurate records for cash. The controls are categorized by management assertion. Along with each control the common test for that control is given, followed by the substantive test of transaction, and finally, the substantive year-end testing for the cash account. Summary tables contrast evidence gathered and the extent to which procedures are applied for two types of client companies: one with poor internal controls and the other with adequate controls.

In a similar format as for the cash account, the next two sections provide a detailed description of the internal controls, tests of controls, substantive tests of transactions, detailed testing of account balance, and analytical procedures for accounts receivable and accounts payable. The final section describes additional year-end auditing procedures necessary to finalize the financial audit engagement.

Chapter 7 objectives:

- To detail the specific procedures for auditing the cash account, accounts receivable, and accounts payable (see ¶ 701–704).

- To become familiar with other procedures required by generally accepted auditing standards (GAAS) and PCAOB auditing standards that do not pertain to account balances and transactions (see ¶ 705).

- To understand how to review for the possibility that contingent liabilities exist (see ¶ 706).

- To understand the auditing process for obtaining evidence regarding subsequent events (see ¶ 707).

- To be aware of the auditor's responsibility regarding related party transactions (see ¶ 708).

- To understand how to evaluate the client's ability to continue as a going concern (see ¶ 709).

- To become familiar with SAS 99's requirement of a final fieldwork assessment of the risks of material misstatement due to fraud (see ¶ 710).

- To define the objective of the final analytical review (see ¶ 711).

- To be aware of management's and auditors' responsibilities regarding the management report on internal controls (see ¶ 712).

- To list the purposes of obtaining a management representation letter (see ¶ 713).

¶ 701

¶ 702 Auditing the Cash Account

.01 Cash—General Checking

Categorized by each management assertion, the typical internal controls, tests of controls, substantive tests of transactions, detailed testing of account balances, and analytical procedures for the checking account are detailed here. One assumption used for this illustration is that parts of the client's bookkeeping system include manually prepared documents.

It is the nature of double-entry accounting that for all debit entries there are corresponding credit entries. As such, the controls governing the debit portion of the journal entry would be the same as those for the credit portion of the entry. For example, if an auditor reviewed and tested the internal controls surrounding $100 cash receipts, he or she would also be reviewing and testing the same controls governing the credit to the accounts receivable. To reduce redundancy of audit procedures, the auditor must be aware of this relationship in deciding the manner and content of the auditing procedures.

In addition, the same internal controls may address more than one management assertion. For example, the internal controls that were placed by management to give reasonable assurance that recorded cash receipts represent actual cash received (existence) may also be the same controls providing assurance that all cash receipts have been recorded (completeness).

.02 Cash Receipts—General Checking

An example will illustrate the internal controls for both cash receipts and disbursement as categorized by management assertion. Not all of the internal controls used as examples will be in force for every client. Conversely, some controls fulfill more than one control objective, creating some duplication of internal controls among the management assertions.

The assumptions used in this example are:

- The cash receipts journal is posted monthly to the general ledger, whereas the postings to the subsidiary accounts receivable occur continuously.

- The company receives its cash receipts via mail and through the use of cash registers.

Management assertion: existence. These internal controls are used to ensure that recorded cash receipts actually exist:

- Duties and functions are separated between the custody of cash receipts, recording of cash receipts, and the reconciliation of the checking account.

- Cash registers are used for cash sales.

¶ 702.02

- Employees who open the mail prepare a mail receipts log.
- Staff reconciles the mail receipts log and cash register tapes to the deposit slip and cash receipts journal daily.
- The bank reconciliation of the cash account is performed by an employee who does not have access to cash or recording of cash receipts.
- A company official reviews the bank reconciliation.

These tests of controls assess controls that the client has established to ensure that recorded cash receipts actually exist:

- The auditor inquires of management about the separation of duties and functions, specifically, the custody of cash receipts, recording of cash receipts, and the bank reconciliation.
- The auditor observes a separation of functions between the custody of cash receipts, recording of cash receipts, and the bank reconciliation.
- The auditor observes that a mail receipts log is being prepared.
- The auditor inspects documentation that the mail receipts log and cash register tapes are reconciled to the deposit slip and cash receipts journal.
- The auditor inspects the bank reconciliation of the checking account to determine that the person preparing the reconciliation does not have access to cash or recording of cash receipts.
- The auditor inspects the bank reconciliation for approval by a company official.

These substantive tests of transactions assess whether cash receipts actually exist:

- The cash receipts journal, general ledger, and accounts receivable subsidiary ledgers are checked for large and unusual amounts.
- Entries from the cash receipts journal are traced to deposits made on the bank statement.
- The auditor reconciles the cash deposits per the bank statement to the cash receipts journal.
- The auditor agrees the receipted deposits to the detailed support identifying source of cash receipt.

Management assertion: completeness. These internal controls are used to ensure that all cash receipts have been recorded in the general ledger:

¶ 702.02

- Duties and functions are separated between the custody of cash receipts, recording of cash receipts, and the reconciliation of the checking account.

- Cash registers are used for cash sales.

- Employees who open the mail prepare a mail receipts log.

- Staff reconciles the mail receipts log and cash register tapes to the deposit slip and cash receipts journal daily.

- The bank reconciliation of the cash account is performed by an employee who does not have access to cash or recording of cash receipts.

- A company official reviews the bank reconciliation.

- Accounting personnel who post cash receipts to customer accounts use customer-prepared remittance advices.

- Daily deposits of cash receipts are made intact; the full amount of receipts is deposited (none of the proceeds is withheld to pay other expenses).

- Customers receive monthly statements indicating that any disputes should be discussed with designated company personnel (e.g., customer assistance). The company personnel who deal with the disputes have no access to cash or the recording of cash transactions.

- Cash received by mail is reconciled daily to posting of cash receipts to customer accounts.

- All cash register tapes are retained as supporting documents for daily deposits.

- All cash receipts received in the mail are immediately stamped with a restrictive endorsement (i.e., "For deposit only" with the company's checking account number).

These tests of controls assess controls that the client has established to ensure that all cash receipts have been recorded:

- The auditor inquires of management about the separation of duties and functions, specifically, the custody of cash receipts, recording of cash receipts, and the bank reconciliation.

- The auditor observes a separation of functions between the custody of cash receipts, recording of cash receipts, and the bank reconciliation.

- The auditor observes that a mail receipts log is being prepared.

¶ 702.02

- The auditor inspects documentation that the mail receipts log and cash register tapes are reconciled to the deposit slip and cash receipts journal.

- The auditor inspects the bank reconciliation of the checking account to determine that the person preparing the reconciliation does not have access to cash or recording of cash receipts.

- The auditor inspects the bank reconciliation for approval by a company official.

- The client uses remittance advices to post to customer accounts.

- The auditor inspects documentation that cash received from mail and cash registers has been reconciled to the deposit slip.

- The auditor asks whether daily deposits of cash receipts are made intact, that the full amount of receipts is deposited (none of the proceeds is withheld to pay other expenses).

- The auditor observes that monthly statements are sent to customers and that customer disputes are directed to company personnel who have no access to cash or the recording of cash transactions.

- Documentation is checked to determine that cash received by mail is reconciled to the daily posting to customer accounts.

- The auditor determines that cash register tapes have been retained.

- The auditor observes that all cash receipts received in the mail are immediately stamped with a restrictive endorsement.

These substantive tests of transactions assess whether all cash receipts have been recorded:

- A sample of remittance advices is traced to details of receipted deposit slips.

- A sample of the mail receipts logs is traced to details of receipted deposit slips.

- The auditor reconciles the cash deposits per bank statement to the cash receipts journal.

Management assertion: posting to subsidiary ledgers. These internal controls are used to ensure that all cash receipts have been posted to the corresponding subsidiary ledgers (i.e., individual customer accounts):

- The detail of each deposit is adequately supported to identify the source of each cash receipt.

¶ 702.02

- Monthly statements are sent to customers and customer disputes are directed to company personnel who have no access to cash or the recording of cash transactions.

- At month's end the client verifies that the subsidiary accounts receivable subsidiary ledgers reconcile to the general ledger account.

These tests of controls assess controls that the client has established to ensure that all cash receipts have been posted to the corresponding subsidiary account:

- For a sample of deposit slips, the auditor inspects detailed support for adequacy.

- The auditor observes that monthly statements are sent to customers and that customer disputes are directed to company personnel who have no access to cash or the recording of cash transactions.

- The auditor determines whether the client verifies that the subsidiary accounts receivable subsidiary ledgers reconcile to the general ledger account.

These substantive tests of transactions assess whether cash receipts were posted to the corresponding subsidiary ledger account:

- Agree cash receipt journal entries to postings in the corresponding subsidiary ledger accounts.

- Agree cash receipt journal entries to the receipted deposit documentation.

- For a sample of days, the auditor recomputes the reconciliation of cash received from mail and cash registers to the deposit slip.

Management assertion: valuation. These internal controls are used to ensure that cash receipts were recorded at the correct value:

- Duties and functions are separated between the custody of cash receipts, recording of cash receipts, and the reconciliation of the checking account.

- Cash registers are used for cash sales.

- Employees who open the mail prepare a mail receipts log.

- Staff reconciles the mail receipts log and cash register tapes to the deposit slip and cash receipts journal daily.

- The bank reconciliation of the cash account is performed by an employee who does not have access to cash or recording of cash receipts.

¶ 702.02

- A company official reviews the bank reconciliation.

- Accounting personnel who post cash receipts to customer accounts use remittance advices.

- Daily deposits of cash receipts are made intact; the full amount of receipts is deposited (none of the proceeds is withheld to pay other expenses).

- Customers receive monthly statements indicating that any disputes should be discussed with designated company personnel (e.g., customer assistance). The company personnel who deal with the disputes have no access to cash or the recording of cash transactions.

- Cash received by mail is reconciled daily to posting of cash receipts to customer accounts.

- All cash register tapes are retained as supporting documents for daily deposits.

These tests of controls assess controls that the client has established to ensure that cash receipts were recorded at the correct value:

- The auditor inquires of management about the separation of duties and functions, specifically the custody of cash receipts, recording of cash receipts, and the bank reconciliation.

- The auditor observes a separation of functions between the custody of cash receipts, recording of cash receipts, and the bank reconciliation.

- The auditor observes that a mail receipts log is being prepared.

- The auditor inspects documentation that the mail receipts log and cash register tapes are reconciled to the deposit slip and cash receipts journal.

- The auditor inspects the bank reconciliation of the checking account to determine that the person preparing the reconciliation does not have access to cash or recording of cash receipts.

- The auditor inspects the bank reconciliation for approval by a company official.

- The client uses customer-prepared remittance advices to post to customer accounts.

- The auditor inspects documentation that cash received from mail and cash registers has been reconciled to the deposit slip.

¶ 702.02

- The auditor asks whether daily deposits of cash receipts are made intact, that the full amount of receipts is deposited (none of the proceeds is withheld to pay other expenses).

- The auditor observes that monthly statements are sent to customers and that customer disputes are directed to company personnel who have no access to cash or the recording of cash transactions.

- Documentation is reviewed to determine that cash received by mail is reconciled to the daily posting to customer accounts.

- The auditor determines that cash register tapes have been retained.

These substantive tests of transactions assess whether cash receipts were recorded at the correct value:

- The cash receipts journal is footed (totaled vertically) and the auditor agrees to the monthly total posted to the general ledger.

- The cash receipts journal, general ledger, and accounts receivable subsidiary ledgers are reviewed for any large and unusual amounts.

- Samples of entries from the cash receipts journal are traced to deposits made on the bank statement.

- The auditor reconciles representative cash deposits per the bank statement to the cash receipts journal.

- The auditor agrees representative receipted deposits to the detailed support identifying source of cash receipt.

Management assertion: classification. This internal control is used to ensure that cash receipts were recorded in the correct account:

- The company uses an adequate chart of accounts when recording cash receipts.

This test of controls assesses controls that the client has established to ensure that cash receipts were recorded in the correct account:

- The auditor reviews the chart of accounts to determine its adequacy.

This substantive test of transactions assesses whether cash receipts were recorded in the correct account:

- A sample of cash receipts from the cash receipts journal is reviewed as support for receipted deposits to determine proper account classification in the cash receipts journal.

¶ 702.02

Management assertion: timing. These internal controls are used to ensure that cash receipts were recorded for the proper period:

- Deposits are made on a daily basis.
- Staff reconciles the mail receipts log and cash register tapes to the deposit slip and cash receipts journal daily.
- Formal procedures clear credit suspense accounts to proper accounts as soon as possible.

These tests of controls assess controls that the client has established to ensure that cash receipts were recorded for the proper period:

- The auditor observes to determine whether there is unrecorded cash on hand at any point in time.
- The auditor examines documentation to determine there is a daily reconciliation of the mail receipts log and cash register tapes to the deposit slip and cash receipts journal.
- Inquiries are made about the procedures to clear credit suspense accounts to proper accounts as soon as possible.

These substantive tests of transactions assess whether cash receipts were recorded for the proper period:

- A sample of deposit slips has dates on deposit slips that agree with dates in the cash receipts journal, cash register tapes, and mail receipts log.
- The auditor reviews the credit suspense accounts for large and unusual amounts.

Table 7.1 summarizes how all management assertions about cash receipts would be audited for two types of clients: one with poor controls, the other with good controls.

¶ 702.02

Table 7.1

Summary of Auditing Procedures for Cash Receipts

Management Assertion: Existence

Tests of Controls—To test those controls that the client has established to ensure that recorded cash receipts actually exist.

	Client A (Poor Controls)	Client B (Good Controls)
a. Inquire about separation of duties and functions.	M*	G
b. Observe separation of functions.	S	G
c. Observe mail receipts log.	S	G
d. Mail receipts log, cash register tapes, deposit slip, and cash receipts journal reconciled.	S	G
e. Verify bank reconciliation by person with no access to cash or recording of cash receipts.	S	G
f. Inspect the bank reconciliation for approval.	S	G

Substantive Tests of Transactions—Cash receipts actually exist.

	Client A	Client B
a. Review cash receipts journal, general ledger, and accounts receivable subsidiary ledgers for large and unusual amounts.	G	M
b. Match cash receipts journal entries to deposits on the bank statement.	G	M
c. Reconcile deposits per bank statement to cash receipts journal.	G	M
d. Match receipted deposits to source of cash receipt.	G	M

Management Assertion: Completeness

Tests of Controls—To test those controls that the client has established to ensure that all cash receipts have been recorded.

	Client A	Client B
a. Inquire about separation of duties and functions.	M	G
b. Observe separation of functions.	S	G
c. Observe that a mail receipts log is being prepared.	S	G
d. Reconcile mail receipts log, cash register tapes, deposit slip, and cash receipts journal.	S	G
e. Bank reconciliation by person with no access to cash or recording of cash receipts.	S	G
f. Inspect the bank reconciliation for approval.	S	G
g. Observe remittance advices used for posting.	S	G
h. Cash received, cash registers reconciled to deposit slip.	S	G
i. Inquire that daily deposits of cash receipts are made intact.	M	G
j. Observe that monthly statements are sent.	S	G
k. Mail receipts are reconciled to account postings.	S	G
l. Determine cash register tapes are retained.	M	G
m. Observe mail receipts restrictively endorsed.	S	G

Substantive Tests of Transactions—All cash receipts have been recorded.

	Client A	Client B
a. Trace remittance advices to deposit slips.	G	M
b. Trace mail receipts log to deposit slips.	G	M
c. Reconcile bank deposits to cash receipts journal.	G	M

Management Assertion: Posting to Subsidiary Ledgers

Tests of Controls—To test those controls that client has established to ensure that all cash receipts have been posted to the corresponding subsidiary account.

	Client A	Client B
a. Inspect support for deposit slips.	S	G
b. Observe that monthly statements are sent.	S	G
c. Subsidiary accounts receivable are reconciled to general ledger control account.	S	G

¶ 702.02

	Client A (Poor Controls)	Client B (Good Controls)

Substantive Tests of Transactions—Cash receipts are posted to the corresponding subsidiary ledger account.

	Client A	Client B
a. Cash receipts journal entries agree with subsidiary ledgers and support the receipted deposit.	G	M
b. Mail receipts, cash registers agree with deposit slips.	G	M

Management Assertion: Valuation

Tests of Controls—To test those controls that the client has established to ensure that cash receipts were recorded at the correct value.

	Client A	Client B
a. Inquire about separation of functions.	M	G
b. Observe separation of functions.	S	G
c. Observe mail receipts log prepared.	S	G
d. Verify that mail receipts log, cash register tapes, deposit slip and cash receipts journal are reconciled.	S	G
e. Observe bank reconciliation by person with no access to cash or recording of cash receipts.	S	G
f. Inspect bank reconciliation for approval.	S	G
g. Observe remittance advices used for posting.	S	G
h. Verify that mail receipts, cash registers, deposit slip are reconciled.	S	G
i. Inquire that deposits are made intact.	M	G
j. Observe that monthly statements are sent.	S	G
k. Verify that mail receipts reconciled to customer accounts.	S	G
l. Observe that cash register tapes retained.	M	G

Substantive Tests of Transactions—Cash receipts were recorded at the correct value.

	Client A	Client B
a. Foot cash receipts journal, agree to general ledger.	G	M
b. Review cash receipts journal, general ledger, and accounts receivable subsidiary ledgers for large and unusual amounts.	G	M
c. Trace cash receipts journal to bank statement.	G	M
d. Reconcile bank deposits to cash receipts journal.	G	M
e. Agree deposits to source of cash receipt.	G	M

Management Assertion: Classification

Test of Controls—To test those controls that the client has established to ensure that cash receipts were recorded in the correct account.

	Client A	Client B
a. Review chart of accounts.	M	G

Substantive Test of Transactions—Cash receipts were recorded in the correct account.

	Client A	Client B
a. Determine proper account classification for deposits.	G	M

Management Assertion: Timing

Tests of Controls—To test those controls that the client has established to ensure that cash receipts were recorded for the proper period.

	Client A	Client B
a. Observe unrecorded cash on hand.	S	G
b. Verify that mail receipts log, cash register tapes, deposit slip, and cash receipts journal reconciled.	S	G
c. Inquire about suspense accounts.	M	M

Substantive Tests of Transactions—Cash receipts were recorded for the proper period.

	Client A	Client B
a. Observe dates of deposit slips, cash receipts journal, cash register tapes, and mail receipts log agree.	G	M
b. Review suspense accounts for large and unusual amounts.	G	M

* For procedures applied to both types of clients, G = great extent, M = moderate extent, and S = small extent (or not at all).

¶ 702.02

.03 Cash Disbursements—General Checking

The assumptions used in the cash disbursements example are:

- The client uses a cash disbursements journal that is posted monthly to the general ledger but posted to the subsidiary accounts payable continuously.

- Cash that is disbursed is paid by check.

Management assertion: occurrence. These internal controls are used to ensure that recorded cash disbursements actually occurred and were for legitimate business purposes:

- The functions of recording cash transactions, reconciling the bank account, and cash disbursement custody are separated.

- Blank checks are locked up when not in use.

- Checks are signed only after the supporting documentation is approved for payment by appropriate personnel, such as the accounts payable department.

- Check signers review the supporting documentation before signing the check.

- A company official reviews the bank reconciliation.

- All cash disbursements over a certain dollar limit require two signatures.

These tests of controls assess controls that the client has established to ensure that recorded cash disbursements actually occurred:

- The auditor inquires of management about the separation of duties and functions, specifically, the recording of cash disbursements, reconciling the bank account, and custody of cash disbursements (including check signing and mailing of checks).

- The auditor observes a separation of functions between the recording of cash disbursements, reconciliation of the bank account, and custody of cash disbursements (including check signing and mailing of checks).

- The auditor inspects the bank reconciliation of the checking account to determine that the person preparing the reconciliation does not have access to cash or recording of cash receipts.

- From a sample of cash disbursements, the auditor reviews supporting documentation to determine that cash disbursements approval was granted.

¶ 702.03

- For a sample of cash disbursements over a specific dollar amount (the limit as established by the client), the auditor determines that the checks contained two signatures.

These substantive tests of transactions assess whether cash disbursements actually occurred:

- The cash disbursements journal and general ledger cash, accounts payable, and accounts payable subsidiary ledgers are scanned for large or unusual entries.

- For a sample of cash disbursements, the auditor agrees the payee and amount to the original entry in the purchases journal.

- For a sample of cash disbursements, the auditor agrees the check number and amount from the cash disbursements journal to the entry in the bank statement for cancelled checks or the outstanding checklist.

- For a sample of cash disbursements, the auditor agrees information from supporting documentation to the check and entry in the cash disbursements journal for date, payee, and amount.

Management assertion: completeness. These internal controls are used to ensure that all cash disbursements have been recorded in the general ledger:

- All checks are prenumbered and the check sequence accounted for.

- A bank reconciliation is prepared monthly by an employee who is independent of cash custody (including check signing and the mailing of checks), cash transaction authorization, and recording.

These tests of controls assess controls that the client has established to ensure that all cash disbursements have been recorded:

- The auditor inspects checks to determine that they are prenumbered.

- The auditor inquires about the procedures to account for the sequence of checks.

- The bank reconciliation is inspected to determine that the preparer is independent of cash custody (including check signing and the mailing of checks), cash transaction authorization, and recording.

¶ 702.03

These substantive tests of transactions assess whether all cash disbursements have been recorded:

- The auditor reconciles or reviews the client-prepared reconciliation of the bank statement disbursements with the cash disbursements journal.
- The auditor reviews the bank statements for large and unusual disbursements, especially those disbursements that have no check number or have an unusual check number.

Management assertion: posting to subsidiary ledgers. These internal controls are used to ensure that all cash disbursements have been posted to the corresponding subsidiary ledgers (i.e., individual vendor accounts):

- Daily cash disbursements are reconciled by the amount debited in the accounts payable subsidiary ledgers.
- There is a monthly reconciliation of the accounts payable subsidiary ledger account and the control accounts payable account in the general ledger.
- For those vendors who send monthly customer statements to the client there is a monthly reconciliation of the accounts payable subsidiary ledger account to the vendor statement.

These tests of controls assess controls that the client has established to ensure that all cash disbursements have been posted to the corresponding subsidiary account:

- The auditor inspects the documentation that daily cash disbursements are reconciled to the total amount debited to the accounts payable subsidiary ledgers.
- The auditor inspects the documentation that indicates that the accounts payable subsidiary ledger account is reconciled monthly to the control accounts payable account in the general ledger.
- For a sample of accounts payable, the auditor inspects the monthly reconciliations of the vendor statements to the account balance for accuracy.

These substantive tests of transactions assess whether cash disbursements were posted to the corresponding subsidiary ledger:

- The mathematical accuracy of the cash disbursements journal is assessed.
- For selected months, the auditor agrees postings from the cash disbursement journal to the general ledger and accounts payable subsidiary ledgers.

¶ 702.03

Management assertion: valuation. These internal controls are used to ensure that cash disbursements are recorded at the correct value:

- The functions of recording cash transactions, reconciling the bank account, and cash disbursement custody are separated.

- Blank checks are locked up until they are ready to use.

- Checks are signed only after their supporting documentation is approved for payment by appropriate personnel, such as the accounts payable staff.

- Check signers review the supporting documentation before signing checks.

- A company official reviews the bank reconciliation.

- All cash disbursements over a certain dollar limit have two check signers.

These tests of controls assess controls that the client has established to ensure that cash disbursements were recorded at the correct value:

- The auditor inquires of management about the separation of duties and functions, specifically the recording of cash disbursements, reconciling the bank account, and custody of cash disbursements (including check signing and mailing of checks).

- The auditor observes a separation of functions between the recording of cash disbursements, reconciliation of the bank account, and custody of cash disbursements (including check signing and mailing of checks).

- The auditor inspects the bank reconciliation of the checking account to determine that the person preparing the reconciliation does not have access to cash or recording of cash disbursements.

- From a sample of cash disbursements, the auditor reviews supporting documentation to determine that cash disbursements approval was granted.

- For a sample of cash disbursements over a specific dollar amount (a limit established by the client as a control to ensure that at least two parties review the supporting material to the disbursement), the auditor determines that the checks contained two signatures.

¶702.03

These substantive tests of transactions assess whether cash disbursements were recorded at the correct value:

- For selected months, the auditor reconciles recorded cash disbursements appearing on the bank statement with the cash disbursements journal.
- For a sample of cash disbursements, the auditor agrees the entry in the cash disbursements journal to the amount of the cancelled check.
- For selected months, the auditor tests the mathematical accuracy of the cash disbursements journal.
- For selected months, the auditor agrees the monthly total from the cash disbursements journal to the posting in the general ledger.

Management assertion: classification. These internal controls are used to ensure that cash disbursements were properly classified:

- The company uses an adequate chart of accounts when recording cash disbursements.
- Checks are signed only after their supporting documentation is approved for payment by appropriate personnel, such as the accounts payable staff.
- Check signers review the supporting documentation before signing checks.

This test of controls assesses controls that the client has established to ensure that cash disbursements were properly classified:

- Review the chart of accounts to determine adequacy.

This substantive test of transactions assesses whether cash disbursements were properly classified:

- The auditor samples cash disbursements from the cash disbursements journal and reviews the propriety of the account classification in the cash disbursements journal, and, if applicable, their original entry in the purchases journal.

Management assertion: timing. These internal controls are used to ensure that cash disbursements were recorded for the proper period:

- Checks are signed as soon as possible after being cut.
- Checks are mailed as soon as possible after being signed.

These tests of controls assess controls that the client has established to ensure that cash disbursements were recorded for the proper period:

- The auditor inquires about checks held for signing.
- The auditor inquires about checks held for mailing.

¶ 702.03

- The auditor observes whether checks are held for a significant period before signing.
- The auditor observes whether checks are held for a significant period before mailing.

These substantive tests of transactions assess whether cash disbursements were recorded for the proper period:

- From any held checks (discussed above), the auditor determines whether any are unrecorded.
- Any unrecorded checks are traced.
- For a sample of cancelled checks, dates on the checks are compared with the cash disbursements journal.
- For a sample of cancelled checks, the auditor compares dates the checks were cancelled to the dates of the checks and inquires about significant date differences.

Table 7.2 summarizes how all management assertions about cash disbursements would be audited for two types of clients: one with poor controls, the other with good controls.

Table 7.2

Summary of Auditing Procedures for Cash Disbursements

Assumptions:
1. The client uses a cash disbursements journal that is posted monthly to the general ledger but posted to the subsidiary accounts payable continuously.
2. Cash is paid out using checks.

Management Assertion: Occurrence

Tests of Controls—To test those controls that the client has established to ensure that recorded cash disbursements actually occurred.

	Client A (Poor Controls)	Client B (Good Controls)
a. Inquire about separation of functions.	M*	G
b. Observe separation of functions.	S	G
c. Verify bank reconciliation by person with no access to cash or recording of cash disbursements.	S	G
d. Determine cash disbursements approval granted.	S	G
e. Where applicable, determine checks had two signatures.	S	G

Substantive Tests of Transactions—Cash disbursements actually occurred.

	Client A	Client B
a. Scan cash disbursements journal, general ledger cash, accounts payable, and accounts payable ledgers for large or unusual entries.	G	M
b. Agree payee and amount to the purchases journal.	G	M
c. Agree check number, amount to bank statement for cancellation or as an outstanding check.	G	M
d. Agree information from supporting documentation to check and cash disbursements journal.	G	M

¶ 702.03

Reaching Conclusions

	Client A (Poor Controls)	Client B (Good Controls)

Management Assertion: Completeness

Tests of Controls—To test those controls that the client has established to ensure that all cash disbursements have been recorded.

a. Determine checks are prenumbered.	M	G
b. Inquire about procedures to account for sequence of checks.	M	G
c. Verify bank reconciliation by person with no cash custody or cash transaction authorization and recording.	S	G

Substantive Tests of Transactions—All cash disbursements have been recorded.

a. Reconcile bank statement cash disbursements to cash disbursements journal.	G	M
b. Review the bank statements for large and unusual disbursements.	G	M

Management Assertion: Posting to Subsidiary Ledgers

Tests of Controls—To test those controls that the client has established to ensure that all cash disbursements have been posted to the corresponding subsidiary account.

a. Verify daily cash disbursements are reconciled to accounts payable subsidiary ledgers.	S	G
b. Verify accounts payable subsidiary ledgers are reconciled to general ledger.	S	G
c. Verify monthly vendor statements are reconciled to accounts payable balance.	S	G

Substantive Tests of Transactions—Cash disbursements were posted to the corresponding subsidiary ledger.

a. Mathematically test cash disbursements journal.	G	M
b. Check cash disbursement journal postings with general ledger and accounts payable subsidiary ledgers.	G	M

Management Assertion: Valuation

Tests of Controls—To test those controls that the client has established to ensure that cash disbursements were recorded at the correct value.

a. Inquire about separation of functions.	M	G
b. Observe separation of functions.	S	G
c. Verify bank reconciliation by person with no access to cash or recording of cash disbursements.	S	G
d. Determine cash disbursements approval granted.	S	G
e. Where applicable, determine checks contained two signatures.	S	G

Substantive Tests of Transactions—Cash disbursements were recorded at the correct value.

a. Agree bank statement disbursements to cash disbursements journal.	G	M
b. Agree cash disbursement journal entry to cancelled check.	G	M
c. Mathematically test cash disbursements journal.	G	M
d. Agree general ledger posting with cash disbursements journal.	G	M

Management Assertion: Classification

Test of Controls—To test those controls that the client has established to ensure that cash disbursements were properly classified.

a. Review chart of accounts.	M	G

Substantive Test of Transaction—Cash disbursements were properly classified.

a. Determine proper account classification in cash disbursements journal.	G	M

¶ 702.03

	Client A (Poor Controls)	Client B (Good Controls)

Management Assertion: Timing

Tests of Controls—To test those controls that the client has established to ensure that cash disbursements were recorded for the proper period.

a. Inquire about held checks for signing.	M	G
b. Inquire about held checks for mailing.	M	G
c. Observe whether checks are held before signing.	S	G
d. Observe whether checks are held before mailing.	S	G

Substantive Tests of Transactions—Cash disbursements were recorded for the proper period.

a. Observe whether held checks are unrecorded.	G	M
b. Compare cancelled check date with cash disbursements journal.	G	M
c. Compare cancellation date to check date.	G	M

* For procedures applied to both types of clients, G=great extent, M=moderate extent, and S=small extent (or not at all).

.04 Year-end Detailed Testing to Fulfill Audit Objectives for the Cash Balance—General Checking

As discussed in Chapter 6, the audit objectives for account balances are slightly different from those of transactions. The detailed testing at year-end verifies that cash as shown on the financial statements actually exists (existence or occurrence) as auditors:

- Obtain a bank cutoff statement for the first two weeks following year-end or subsequent to year-end bank statements from the client. (See the discussion entitled Bank Cutoff Statement in ¶ 702.05.)

- Prepare an interbank transfer schedule. (See the discussion entitled Interbank Transfer Schedule in ¶ 702.05.)

- Determine the propriety of all significant adjustments appearing in the cash account in the general ledger by reviewing supporting documentation.

Alternative 1. (See the discussion in ¶ 702.06 that compares audit procedures for high versus low combined inherent and control risks.) Using the client's year-end bank reconciliation, auditors:

1. Test the mathematical accuracy of the cash reconciliation.

2. Obtain a confirmation of the cash balance per bank as of year-end and agree balance per bank to the bank reconciliation. (See ¶ 702.05.)

3. Using the date listed on the bank cutoff statement or the subsequent bank statement, determine the reasonableness of the deposits per transit listed on the bank reconciliation.

4. Using the date of receipt on the deposit slips supporting the deposit in transit listed on the bank reconciliation, determine the propriety of the deposit in transit.

5. Trace checks cancelled with the bank cutoff statement or subsequent bank statement to the outstanding check list and cash disbursements journal.

Alternative 2. (See the discussion in ¶ 702.06 that compares audit procedures for high versus low combined inherent and control risks.) To prepare a proof of cash, auditors:

1. Agree the beginning bank reconciliation, column 1 of the proof of cash (last year's ending bank reconciliation) to the prior year's workpapers or the predecessor's workpapers.

2. Obtain a confirmation of the cash balance per bank as of year-end and agree balance per bank to the ending bank reconciliation, column 4. (See ¶ 702.05.)

3. Using the date listed on the bank cutoff statement or the subsequent bank statement, determine the reasonableness of the ending deposits per transit listed on the bank reconciliation.

4. Using the date of receipt on the deposit slips supporting the deposit in transit listed on the bank reconciliation, determine the propriety of the deposit in transit.

5. Trace checks cancelled with the bank cutoff statement or subsequent bank statement to the outstanding check list for the ending period, column 4 of the proof of cash.

To ascertain whether all cash transactions have been recorded (completeness), the alternative selected for the existence objective also fulfills the completeness, rights and obligations, and valuation and allocation objectives.

To decide whether cash as shown on the financial statements is presented properly and all necessary disclosures have been included in the notes to the financial statements (presentation and disclosure), auditors:

- Read the minutes of the board of directors and subcommittee minutes for discussions about any restrictions on the use of cash or compensating balances.

- Read loan agreements to determine whether there are any restrictions on the use of cash or compensating balances.

- Confirm with official of financial institutions to determine whether there are any restrictions on the use of cash or compensating balances. (See the discussion about cash confirmations appearing later in this chapter.)

¶ 702.04

- Read the notes to the financial statements to determine whether cash for restricted use and compensating balances are adequately disclosed.

Analytical procedures for substantive testing of cash. Auditors follow these steps:

1. Compare the current year's cash balances with those of the preceding year and investigate any significant variance with expected balances.

2. Calculate the quick and current ratios and investigate any significant variance with expected balances, previous history, and industry averages.

Table 7.3 summarizes how auditors apply year-end testing procedures to verify that cash in the account balance shown on the financial statements actually exists, has been recorded properly, is owned by the company, has been correctly valued, and has been presented and disclosed properly. The two types of clients are again compared to illustrate to what extent auditing procedures would be applied.

Table 7.3

Summary of Auditing Procedures for Year-End Testing of Cash Account Balance

Cash as shown on the financial statements actually exists. (Existence or Occurrence)

	Client A (Poor Controls)	Client B (Good Controls)
a. Obtain a bank cutoff statement, if applicable.	G*	S
b. Obtain subsequent-to-year-end bank statements.	G	M
c. Prepare an interbank transfer schedule.	G	M
d. Determine propriety of significant adjustments to cash.	G	M

General Checking

Alternative 1—Using the Client's Year-end Bank Reconciliation (typically for clients with moderate to good internal controls):

e. Test math accuracy of cash reconciliation.	S	M
f. Confirm cash balance per bank.	S	M
g. Determine reasonableness of deposits per transit on the bank reconciliation.	S	M
h. Determine whether date of receipted deposit slips supports deposit in transit.	S	M
i. Trace cancelled checks to the outstanding checklist and cash disbursements journal.	S	M

Alternative 2—Preparing a Proof of Cash (typically for those clients with poor internal controls for cash):

e. Prepare a proof of cash for the year's cash activity.	M	S
f. Agree beginning bank reconciliation to prior year's workpapers or predecessor's workpapers.	M	S
g. Confirm year-end cash balance.	M	S
h. Using bank statement information, determine reasonableness of deposits per transit.	M	S

¶ 702.04

	Client A (Poor Controls)	Client B (Good Controls)
i. Using the date of receipted deposit slips, determine propriety of deposit in transit.	M	S
j. Trace cancelled checks to the outstanding check list.	M	S

All cash transactions have been recorded. (Completeness)

Same alternative's procedures as for Existence.

Cash as shown on the financial statements is owned by the company. (Rights and Obligations)

Same alternative's procedures as for Existence.

Cash as shown on the financial statements is correctly valued. (Valuation and Allocation)

Same alternative's procedures as for Existence.

Cash is presented properly and all necessary disclosures have been included in the notes to the financial statements. (Presentation and Disclosure)

a. Read minutes of board of directors regarding cash.	M	M
b. Read loan agreements regarding cash.	M	M
c. Confirm restrictions on cash.	M	M
d. Read financial statement notes for adequate cash disclosure.	M	M

Analytical Procedures for Substantive Testing of Cash

1. Compare current and preceding year's cash for variance with expected balances.	M	G
2. Calculate quick and current ratios for significant variance with expected balances, previous history, and industry averages.	M	G

* For procedures applied to both types of clients, G=great extent, M=moderate extent, and S=small extent (or not at all).

.05 Other Issues Specific to Auditing the Cash Account

Confirming cash balances. It is a normal auditing procedure to confirm with the financial institutions the balance per bank used in the cash reconciliation. There is a standard form for this confirmation, appropriately entitled Standard Form to Confirm Account Balance Information with Financial Institutions. The American Institute of Certified Public Accountants, the American Bankers' Association, and the Bank Administration Institute have agreed upon the format for this confirmation. With this confirmation the auditor requests that the financial institutions confirm from their records the client's balance of cash as well as any loans that the client may have with the institution.

Any other information to be confirmed by the financial institution should be requested in a separate letter. For example, the auditor should explicitly request from an appropriate financial institution official in a separate communication any financing arrangements the institution has with the client or the institution's knowledge of guarantees made by the client on another party's indebtedness. Figure 7.1 is the Standard Form to Confirm Account Balance Information with Financial Institutions.

¶ 702.05

Figure 7.1

Standard Form to Confirm Account Balance Information with Financial Institutions

**STANDARD FORM TO CONFIRM ACCOUNT
BALANCE INFORMATION WITH FINANCIAL INSTITUTIONS**

CUSTOMER NAME

Financial Institution's Name and Address [   ]

We have provided to our accountants the following information as of the close of business on _____, 19____, regarding our deposit and loan balances. Please confirm the accuracy of the information, noting any exceptions to the information provided. If the balances have been left blank, please complete this form by furnishing the balance in the appropriate space below.* Although we do not request nor expect you to conduct a comprehensive, detailed search of your records, if during the process of completing this confirmation additional information about other deposit and loan accounts we may have with you comes to your attention, please include such information below. Please use the enclosed envelope to return the form directly to our accountants.

1. At the close of business on the date listed above, our records indicated the following deposit balance(s):

ACCOUNT NAME	ACCOUNT NO.	INTEREST RATE	BALANCE*

2. We were directly liable to the financial institution for loans at the close of business on the date listed above as follows:

ACCOUNT NO./ DESCRIPTION	BALANCE*	DATE DUE	INTEREST RATE	DATE THROUGH WHICH INTEREST IS PAID	DESCRIPTION OF COLLATERAL

_____ (Customer's Authorized Signature)   _____ (Date)

The information presented above by the customer is in agreement with our records. Although we have not conducted a comprehensive, detailed search of our records, no other deposit or loan accounts have come to our attention except as noted below.

_____ (Financial Institution Authorized Signature)   _____ (Date)

(Title)

EXCEPTIONS AND/OR COMMENTS

Please return this form directly to our accountants:
[   ]

* Ordinarily, balances are intentionally left blank if they are not available at the time the form is prepared.
[   ]

Approved 1990 by American Bankers Association, American Institute of Certified Public Accountants, and Bank Administration Institute. Additional forms available from: AICPA—Order Department, P.O. Box 1003, NY, NY 10108-1003

D 451 5951

Source: American Institute of Certified Public Accountants. Copyright 1990, 1999, 2001 by the American Instituted of Certified Public Accountants, Inc. Reprinted with permission.

¶ 702.05

Bank cutoff statement. The bank cutoff statement is a bank statement that is sent directly to the auditor by the bank. It represents a confirmation of the cash activity subsequent to year-end. The cutoff statement is usually a normal bank statement with cancelled checks enclosed, but it is for a stub period—possibly for the one to two weeks following year-end. The auditor needs the bank cutoff statement to obtain evidence about reconciling items on the bank reconciliation, such as deposits in transit and outstanding checks. Because it is a confirmation, the client does not have an opportunity to alter the statement or any of the cancelled checks accompanying it.

Interbank transfer schedule. *Kiting* is a method of defalcation using the cash accounts of a company to artificially inflate the value of cash. The method used in kiting is writing a check from one bank account to another. The net effect is zero. However, because the recognition of the disbursement is inappropriately excluded or deferred while the receipt is included, the account shows a net increase. The artificial cash balance can be used in a number of ways. This fraudulent method can be used at any point during the year, but the auditor must be cautious and address the possibility of kiting at year-end for financial statement purposes.

One method auditors use to uncover kiting is the interbank transfer schedule. This schedule shows all cash transfers between client bank accounts for a period of time prior to and subsequent to year-end, usually 7 to 10 days. A comparison of dates of the deposit and the corresponding disbursement should indicate that the debit to cash is recognized in the same period as the credit to cash. Table 7.4 is an example of an interbank transfer schedule.

Table 7.4

Section of an Interbank Transfer Schedule

Name of Disbursing Bank	Check Number	Amount	Date Disbursed per Books	Date Disbursed per Bank	Name of Receiving Bank	Date Deposited per Books	Date Deposited per Bank
Federal 21st...	2103	200,000.00	12/28/02	1/2/03	National 3rd	12/28/02	1/2/03
Federal 21st...	2190	250,000.00	12/30/02	1/5/03	National 3rd	12/30/02	1/4/03
Federal 21st...	2229	200,000.00	1/2/03	1/6/03	Bank of San Marin	1/2/03	1/5/03
Federal 21st...	2509	450,000.00	1/3/03	1/7/03	National 3rd	1/3/03	1/7/03
Federal 21st...	2617	200,000.00	1/4/03	1/8/03	Bank of San Marin	1/4/03	1/7/03

Proof of cash. The proof of cash is sometimes prepared by the auditor when the combined inherent and control risks are high. When the

¶ 702.05

risks are high, the books of the company provide little assurance to the auditor of their accuracy.

The format is divided into two major components: the top half, whereby the balance per bank activity is reconciled to actual activity; and the bottom half, in which the unadjusted balance per book activity is reconciled to actual activity. The first column represents the prior year's ending bank reconciliation. The second column reconciles the cash receipts—bank to actual and books to actual. The prior period's deposits in transit represent prior year's activity and should not be included in the current year's activity. It shows as a negative amount on the proof of cash. The current period's deposits in transit represent the current year's activity and are shown on the proof of cash as added values. The third column reconciles the cash disbursements—bank to actual and books to actual. Outstanding checks for the prior period and current period are indicated in a similar fashion to the deposits in transit. The final column is the current period's ending bank reconciliation.

If the cash receipts and disbursements can be reconciled between the bank and books, the auditor has gained some level of confidence about the amount of the cash receipts and disbursements activity.

The format for the proof of cash appears in Table 7.5.

¶ 702.05

Table 7.5

Proof of Cash

	Bank Balance 12/31/X2	Deposits per Bank for the year 20X3	Disbursements per Bank for the year 20X3	Bank Balance 12/31/X3
Balance	12,300.50 +	215,430.00	−216,790.00	10,940.50
Deposits in Transit 12/31/X2	2,100.00	−2,100.00		
Deposits in Transit 12/31/X3		4,313.00		4,313.00
Outstanding Checks 12/31/X2	−6,790.00		+6,790.00	
Outstanding Checks 12/31/X3			−8,790.00	−8,790.00
Adjusted Balance per Bank	7,610.50 +	217,643.00	−218,790.00	6,463.50

	Book Balance 12/31/02	Cash Receipts per Books 2003	Cash Disbursements per Books 2003	Book Balance 12/31/03
Unadjusted Balance	7,610.50 +	217,613.00	−219,077.00	6,146.50
Service Charges			66.00	66.00
NSF Checks		−415.00		−415.00
Check Printing Charges			52.00	52.00
Book Error - 2/3/X3 deposit		445.00		445.00
Book Error - check #3224			169.00	169.00
Adjusted Balance per Books	7,610.50 +	217,643.00	−218,790.00	6,463.50

.06 Comparison of Auditing Procedures for High Versus Low Combined Inherent and Control Risks

The tests of controls, substantive tests of transactions, tests of details of account balances, and analytical procedures as enumerated earlier for the general checking cash account will vary depending upon the assessment of the combined inherent and control risks. Table 7.6 compares two clients; the combined inherent and control risks are high for Client A and low for Client B. The amount of evidence and type of evidence that must be gathered by the auditor varies for each client. When the combined inherent and control risks are high, no testing of the internal controls will result and, generally, the auditor will test larger samples and gather more competent evidence.

The competence of evidence that is gathered for the cash account is illustrated with the auditing procedures necessary to review the existence of the cash accounts. Alternative 1 represents a high level of competent evidence obtained. Alternative 2 represents a lower level of competent

¶ 702.06

evidence because the controls surrounding the cash existence are strong and represent less risk to the auditor.

Table 7.6

Comparison of Clients with High Versus Low Combined Inherent and Control Risks

	Assessment Inherent Risk	Assessment of Control Risk	Acceptable Detection Risk	Amount of Evidence
Audit Client A ..	High	High	Low	A relatively large amount of competent evidence needed.
Audit Client B ..	Low	Low	High	A relatively small amount of competent evidence needed.

¶ 703 Auditing Accounts Receivable

Two major transactions affect accounts receivable: cash receipts and credit sales. The controls and audit testing surrounding cash receipts were described earlier for the cash account. Credit sales will be described here.

.01 Credit Sales

Management assertion: occurrence. These internal controls are used to ensure that recorded credit sales actually occurred:

- Recorded sales are supported by authorized shipping documents.

- Recorded sales are supported by approved customer orders.

- Shipments are made only after receiving an approved customer order.

- Sales invoices are prenumbered.

- Prenumbered sales invoices are properly accounted for.

- Only the credit department can add a customer to the customer master file.

- Only sales to customers listed in the customer master file are accepted when the sales are entered.

- Client customers receive monthly statements from the client.

- Customer disputes arising from the monthly statement are investigated by an employee who is an independent party of the recording function.

These tests of controls assess controls that the client has established to ensure that recorded credit sales actually occurred:

- The auditor examines a sample of sales invoices to determine that there are corresponding authorized shipping documents.
- The auditor examines a sample of sales invoices to determine that there are corresponding credit-approved customer orders.
- The auditor examines shipping documents to determine that credit was granted before the shipment took place.
- The auditor accounts for the numerical sequence of sales invoices.
- The auditor reviews error log to determine whether invalid customer numbers are accepted when they are entered.
- The auditor observes that monthly statements are sent to customers.
- The auditor determines that disputes with the monthly statement are sent to personnel who do not have a recording or cash custody function.

These substantive tests of transactions assess whether recorded credit sales actually occurred:

- The auditor scans the sales journal, general ledger, and accounts receivable subsidiary ledgers for large or unusual entries.
- A sample of sales invoices from the sales journal is compared for customer name, date, items purchased, and amount to the entry in the sales journal, accounts receivable subsidiary ledger, and copies of sales orders and shipping documents.
- For a sample of shipping documents, the auditor agrees inventory sales to entry of shipments in perpetual inventory records.

Management assertion: completeness. These internal controls are used to ensure that all credit sales have been recorded in the general ledger:

- Shipping documents are prenumbered.
- Prenumbered shipping documents are properly accounted for.
- Sales invoices are prenumbered.
- Prenumbered sales invoices are properly accounted for.

These tests of controls assess controls that the client has established to ensure that all credit sales have been recorded:

- The auditor should account for the numerical sequence of shipping documents.

¶ 703.01

- The auditor should account for the numerical sequence of sales invoices.

This substantive test of transactions assesses whether all credit sales have been recorded:

- The auditor should agree the detailed information for a sample of shipping documents to corresponding sales invoices, sales journal, and accounts receivable subsidiary ledgers.

Management assertion: posting to subsidiary ledgers. These internal controls are used to ensure that all credit sales have been posted to the corresponding subsidiary ledgers:

- Monthly statements are sent to customers.
- At the end of each month there is a check by personnel who do not have a recording or cash custody function that the subsidiary accounts receivable ledgers agree with the general ledger account.

These tests of controls assess controls that the client has established to ensure that all credit sales have been posted to the corresponding subsidiary account.

- The auditor observes that customer statements are mailed.
- The auditor determines whether the client verifies that the subsidiary accounts receivable ledgers reconcile to the general ledger account. If so, the auditor examines internal verification.
- The auditor should verify that the personnel who reconcile the subsidiary accounts receivable ledgers to the general ledger have no recording or cash custody function.

These substantive tests of transactions assess whether credit sales have been posted to the corresponding subsidiary account:

- The auditor tests the mathematical accuracy of the sales journal.
- The auditor agrees a sample of sales journal entries to postings to subsidiary accounts receivable accounts.

Management assertion: valuation. These internal controls are used to ensure that credit sales were recorded at the correct value:

- All terms of the sale are properly authorized.
- There is an independent check that all terms of sales are authorized.
- An approved price list is used for all sales.

¶ 703.01

Reaching Conclusions   249

These tests of controls assess controls that the client has established to ensure that credit sales were recorded at the correct value:

- The auditor inspects sales invoices for proper authorization.

- The auditor determines that there was an independent check on all the terms of the sales.

This substantive test of transactions assesses whether credit sales were recorded at the correct value:

- After selecting a sample of sales invoices from the sales journal, the auditor:
  - Recomputes information on the sales invoice
  - Agrees details of the sales invoice to the sales journal
  - Agrees details of the sales invoices to shipping documents, approved price lists, and customer orders

Management assertion: classification. This internal control is used to ensure that credit sales were properly classified:

- The company uses an adequate chart of accounts when recording credit sales.

This test of controls assesses controls that the client has established to ensure that credit sales were properly classified:

- The auditor reviews the chart of accounts to determine its adequacy.

This substantive test of transactions assesses whether credit sales were properly classified:

- A sample of sales invoices from the sales journal is examined for supporting documents and agreed to the sales transactions for proper account distribution.

Management assertion: timing. This internal control is used to ensure that credit sales were recorded for the proper period:

- Formal procedures ensure that the recording of sales occurs close to the point of sale.

This test of controls assesses the control that the client has established to ensure that credit sales were recorded for the proper period:

- The auditor reviews all unbilled shipments and unrecorded sales to determine whether there is any significant backlog and the reason it exists.

¶ 703.01

This substantive test of transactions assesses whether credit sales were recorded for the proper period:

- For a sample of sales invoices, the auditor reviews terms of sales (FOB destination/shipping point) and compares dates of recorded sales transactions with dates on shipping records.

.02 Year-end Detailed Testing to Fulfill Audit Objectives for Accounts Receivable Balance

At the end of the interim testing phase when the internal controls were tested and substantive tests of transactions performed, the auditor had to determine to what extent the account balances had to be tested and what audit objectives still needed to be met. Year-end detailed testing of the account balances results, in this case, for accounts receivable. As is discussed in Chapter 6, the audit objectives for account balances are slightly different from those of transactions.

The accounts receivable as shown on the financial statements actually exists.

- From a sample of accounts receivable, the auditor sends positive confirmation requests. (See ¶ 703.04 in this chapter for discussion of accounts receivable confirmations.)
- The auditor sends second requests to confirm the account balance for all customers who did not return the first request.
- The auditor performs alternative procedures for all confirmations not returned. (See the discussion at ¶ 703.04.)
- The auditor scans the detail of the accounts receivable for large or unusual balances.

All accounts receivable accounts have been recorded.

- Agree selected accounts from the accounts receivable subsidiary ledgers to the aged trial balance.

The accounts receivable as shown on the financial statements is owned by the company.

- The auditor reads the minutes of the board of directors and subcommittee meetings to determine whether accounts receivable has been assigned, pledged, or factored.
- Managers are asked whether any receivables have been assigned, pledged, or factored.

Accounts receivable as shown on the financial statements is correctly valued.

- From a sample of accounts receivable, the auditor sends positive confirmation requests. (See the discussion at ¶ 703.04 for accounts receivable confirmations.)

¶ 703.02

- The auditor sends second requests to confirm the account balance for all customers who did not return the first request.

- The auditor performs alternative procedures for all confirmations not returned. (See the discussion at ¶ 703.04.)

- The auditor scans the detail of the accounts receivable for large or unusual balances.

All accounts receivable included in the balance as shown on the financial statements have been recorded in the proper period.

- The auditor traces selected sales journal entries to shipping documents, noting the dates and shipping terms and determining whether they were recorded in the proper period.

- The auditor determines whether a significant number of sales returns occurred after the balance sheet date. He or she reviews the supporting documentation for the sales returns to determine whether they were recorded in the proper period.

Accounts receivable as shown on the financial statements has been recorded at net realizable value.

- From a sample of customer accounts on the aged accounts receivable, the auditor determines whether the customer account balance has been correctly aged based on the supporting documentation.

- The auditor recomputes the balance for each category in the aged accounts receivable detail.

- The auditor recomputes the total balance of the aged accounts receivable detail and agrees it to the general ledger.

- The credit manager is asked for the likelihood of collecting older accounts.

- The auditor examines subsequent cash receipts and assesses the reasonableness of the bad debt percentages for each category.

The accounts receivable as shown on the financial statements is presented properly and all necessary disclosures have been included in the notes to the financial statements.

- The minutes of the board of directors and subcommittee meetings are reviewed to determine whether the accounts receivable has been assigned, pledged, or factored.

- The auditor inquires of management whether any receivables have been assigned, pledged, or factored.

¶ 703.02

.03 Year-end Analytical Procedures for Accounts Receivable

For the year-end analytical procedures, the auditor employs these approaches:

- Calculates actual sales to client sales capacity for reasonableness. Significant fluctuations should be examined further.

- Compares sales growth to accounts receivable growth for reasonableness. Significant fluctuations should be examined further.

- Computes and compares accounts receivable turnover to industry average, prior years and expected amounts. Significant fluctuations should be examined further.

- Computes and compares any doubtful account expense as a percentage of credit sales and compares it to industry average, prior years and expected amounts. Significant fluctuations should be examined further.

.04 Other Issues Specific to Auditing Accounts Receivable

Confirmation of accounts receivable. As auditors confirm accounts receivables they are communicating directly with the customer. Auditors set about to confirm with the customer specific assertions about accounts receivable—typically existence and valuation. Although confirming accounts receivable is usually required by generally accepted auditing standards, it is not required when:

- Accounts receivable is immaterial.

- The use of confirmations would be ineffective—possibly when historically the auditor has had little success in confirming accounts receivable.

- The auditor's assessment of the inherent and control risks is low, and other procedures will provide sufficient evidence to reduce audit risk to an acceptable level.

Auditors use one of two types of accounts receivable confirmations. *Positive confirmations* (Figure 7.2) are sent to customers requesting that the customer review the balance due as of a date and return the letters directly to the auditor indicating whether they agree or disagree. Positive confirmations provide strong evidence for the existence and valuation assertions.

The second type of accounts receivable confirmation is the *negative confirmation* (Figure 7.3). When the auditor sends a negative confirmation to a customer, the customer is asked to review the account balance as of a specific date. However, he or she is requested to only respond to the auditor if the client disagrees with the balance indicated. The negative confirmation generally does not provide significant evidence about existence because a customer nonresponse is regarded as a correct balance. Negative confirmations should only be used when:

- There are a number of relatively small customer balances.
- The assessed level of control risk is low.
- The auditor believes that customers are likely to give proper attention to the request.

Figure 7.2

Positive Accounts Receivable Confirmation

Tamco Incorporated:

Our auditors, Wooden & Pushkin, LLP, are conducting an examination of the financial statements of Flair Apparel Inc. In connection with this audit, we request that you review the balance of your account as of December 31, 20X2 and confirm directly with our auditors whether the balance is correct and if not, please so state.

Flair's balance as of December 31, 20X2 for Tamco Incorporated is $76,650.00.

Please reply in the self addressed, stamped envelope. Your prompt reply is greatly appreciated. Thank you for your assistance.

John Thompson, Chief Accountant

Flair Apparel Inc.

Wooden & Pushkin, LLP

Oakland, California

The balance receivable from Tamco Incorporated of $76,650.00 as of December 31, 20X2 is correct except as noted below:

Date: _____

By _____

¶ 703.04

Figure 7.3

Negative Accounts Receivable Confirmation

Romano Batteries Inc.:

    Our auditors, Wooden & Pushkin, LLP, are conducting an examination of the financial statements of Flair Apparel Inc. In connection with this audit, we request that you review the balance of your account as of December 31, 20X2 and if it does not agree with your records, please report any exceptions directly to our auditors.

    Flair's balance as of December 31, 20X2 for Romano Batteries Inc. is $8,100.00.

    An addressed envelope is enclosed for your convenience in replying.

Wooden & Pushkin, LLP
Oakland, California

    The balance receivable from Romano Batteries Inc. of $8,100.00 as of December 31, 20X2 is not correct. My records indicate that the correct balance is: _____ Explanation: _____

Date: _____

By _____

Alternative procedures. When the auditor is not able to confirm a requested account balance, he or she should perform alternative procedures. The auditor should review the customer order, sales invoice, and shipping documents to determine who prepared the documents. The more individuals involved in their preparation, the less likely it is that the documents are fictitious. Then the corresponding cash receipt as seen in the accounts receivable subsidiary ledger should be agreed to a deposit slip detail and cash receipts journal. Similarly, a paid receivable is likely to be an actual receivable. For any accounts receivable remaining unpaid by the end of fieldwork, the auditor should review any correspondence the client had with the customer and discuss with the appropriate client personnel whether a write-off is warranted.

Sales cutoff test. The sales cutoff test is performed to determine whether sales were recorded in the proper period. If company accountants were to "hold their books open" so that January sales were actually recorded as December sales; accounts receivable, current and total assets, sales and operating income would be overstated. In order to detect whether the client had cut off the sales transactions properly, the auditor performs the sales cutoff test as of the balance sheet date. Sales invoices are selected from those recorded in the sales journal prior and subsequent to year-end, typically for five to 10 days. The auditor compares the terms of the sales invoices with those of the shipping documents to determine whether the sales had been recorded in the proper period.

¶ 703.04

Enron example. Enron created and capitalized four special purpose entities by issuing its own stock in exchange for about $1.2 billion of notes receivables (thereby increasing shareholder equity by $1.2 billion). GAAP requires such notes receivables to be presented as a reduction in shareholders' equity (and not an asset).[1] Should the external auditor find this material overstatement of shareholders' equity?

¶ 704 Auditing Accounts Payable

Two major types of transactions affect the accounts payable account: credit purchases (assuming all credit purchases, not just inventory) and cash disbursements. Cash disbursements have already been discussed with respect to the cash account. Following are the controls, tests of controls, substantive tests of transactions, detailed testing of account balances, and analytical review procedures for accounts payable and credit purchase transactions. An assumption used for the auditing procedures presented here is that purchases are for inventory as well as for noninventory items. Another assumption is that purchases are recorded when the invoices are received, not when the purchase orders are prepared.

.01 Credit Purchases

Management assertion: existence. These internal controls are used to ensure that recorded credit purchases actually occurred:

- The functions of purchasing, recording purchases, reconciling monthly vendor statements, and receiving the goods are separated.

- For each credit purchase there is complete documentation: purchase requisition, purchase order, receiving report, and a vendor's invoice.

- A supervisor approves the purchase order.

- The supporting documentation for the purchase is voided after payment is made.

- The invoices received from vendors are mathematically checked and quantities billed should agree with the receiving report.

- All goods are counted and inspected when received.

These tests of controls assess controls that the client has established to ensure that recorded credit purchases actually exist:

- The auditor observes that the same individuals are not purchasing, recording purchases, reconciling vendor statements, and receiving the goods.

---

[1] EITF Issue No. 85-1, *Classifying Notes Received for Capital Stock*, and SEC Staff Accounting Bulletin No. 40, Topic 4-E, *Receivables from Sale of Stock*.

¶ 704.01

- For a sample of purchases from the purchases journal, the auditor determines that there is complete documentation for each purchase: purchase requisition, purchase order, receiving report, and a vendor's invoice.

- The auditor reviews the purchase order for a supervisor's approval.

- The auditor reviews the supporting documentation for the purchase to determine that it has been voided.

- The auditor reviews the invoice to determine that it has been checked for mathematical accuracy and quantities received and billed.

- The auditor observes that all goods are counted and inspected when received.

These substantive tests of transactions assess whether credit purchases actually exist:

- The auditor scans the purchases journal, general ledger, and accounts payable subsidiary ledgers for large or unusual entries.

- For a sample of purchases, the auditor traces to the supporting documentation for amounts and prices.

- For a sample of applicable purchases, the auditor agrees amounts to subsidiary ledgers such as perpetual inventory records, equipment detail.

Management assertion: completeness. These internal controls are used to ensure that all credit purchases have been recorded in the general ledger.

- All purchase orders are prenumbered and the numbering sequence accounted for.

- All receiving reports are prenumbered and the numbering sequence accounted for.

- Goods received at the receiving dock are approved by the purchasing department.

These tests of controls assess controls that the client has established to ensure that all credit purchases have been recorded:

- The auditor inspects purchase orders to verify that they are prenumbered.

- The auditor inquires about the procedures to account for the sequence of purchase orders.

¶ 704.01

- The auditor inspects receiving reports to verify that they are prenumbered.

- The auditor inquires about the procedures to account for the sequence of receiving reports.

- Receiving dock personnel verify the authorization process for the receipt of goods.

This substantive test of transactions assesses whether all credit purchases have been recorded:

- The auditor agrees a sample of receiving report entries to the purchases journal.

Management assertion: posting to subsidiary ledgers. These internal controls are used to ensure that all credit purchases have been posted to the correct accounts payable subsidiary ledger (i.e., individual vendor accounts):

- Daily purchases are reconciled to the amount credited in the accounts payable subsidiary ledgers.

- There is a monthly reconciliation of the accounts payable subsidiary ledger account and the control accounts payable account in the general ledger.

- For those vendors who send monthly customer statements to the client there is a monthly reconciliation of the accounts payable subsidiary ledger account to the vendor statement.

These tests of controls assess controls that the client has established to ensure that all credit purchases have been posted to the correct accounts payable subsidiary ledger:

- The auditor inspects the documentation that daily purchases are reconciled to the total amount credited to the accounts payable subsidiary ledgers.

- The auditor inspects the documentation that indicates that the accounts payable subsidiary ledger account is reconciled monthly to the control accounts payable account in the general ledger.

- For a sample of accounts payable, the auditor inspects the monthly reconciliations of the vendor statements to the account balance for accuracy.

These substantive tests of transaction assess whether credit purchases were posted to the correct accounts payable subsidiary ledger:

- The mathematical accuracy of the purchases journal is assessed.

¶ 704.01

- For selected months, the auditor traces the purchases journal postings to the general ledger.

- The auditor agrees the supporting documentation for a sample of purchases in the purchases journal to postings in the accounts payable subsidiary ledgers.

Management assertion: valuation. These internal controls are used to ensure that credit purchases were recorded at the correct value:

- The functions of purchasing, recording purchases, reconciling monthly vendor statements, and receiving the goods are separated.

- For each credit purchase there is complete documentation: purchase requisition, purchase order, receiving report, and a vendor's invoice.

- A supervisor approves the purchase order.

- The supporting documentation for the purchase is voided after payment is made.

- The invoices are mathematically checked and quantities billed agree with the receiving report.

These tests of controls assess controls that the client has established to ensure that credit purchases were recorded at the correct value:

- The auditor observes that the same individuals are not purchasing, recording purchases, reconciling vendor statements, and receiving the goods.

- For a sample of purchases from the purchases journal, the auditor determines that there is complete documentation for each purchase: purchase requisition, purchase order, receiving report, and vendor's invoice.

- The auditor reviews purchase orders for a supervisor's approval.

- The auditor reviews the supporting documentation for purchases to verify that it has been voided.

- The auditor reviews the invoices to verify that they have been checked for mathematical accuracy and quantities received and billed.

These substantive tests of transactions assess whether credit purchases were recorded at the correct value:

- The auditor scans the purchases journal, general ledger, and accounts payable subsidiary ledgers for large or unusual entries.

¶ 704.01

- For a sample of purchases from the purchases journal, the auditor traces amounts to the supporting documentation for amounts and prices.

- For a sample of applicable purchases, the auditor agrees amounts to subsidiary ledgers such as perpetual inventory records and equipment detail.

Management assertion: classification. This internal control is used to ensure that credit purchases were properly classified:

- The company uses an adequate chart of accounts to record purchases.

This test of controls assesses controls that the client has established to ensure that credit purchases were properly classified:

- The auditor reviews the chart of accounts to determine adequacy.

This substantive test of transaction assesses whether credit purchases were properly classified.

- Sample purchases from the purchases journal are reviewed for supporting documentation to verify the proper account classifications in the purchases journal.

Management assertion: timing. These internal controls are used to ensure that credit purchases were recorded for the proper period:

- Formal procedures match incoming invoices with purchase orders and record the purchase as soon as possible.

- Formal procedures minimize backlogs of unmatched invoices and purchase orders (i.e., a daily inventory of backlogs of unmatched invoices is prepared and reported to supervisory personnel).

- All open purchase orders are periodically reviewed.

These tests of controls assess controls that the client has established to ensure that credit purchases were recorded for the proper period:

- The auditor reviews the procedures manual to determine whether there are formal procedures established to match incoming invoices with purchase orders and record the purchase as soon as possible.

- The auditor observes whether a significant backlog of unmatched vendors' invoices exists.

- The auditor inquires whether significant open purchase orders are periodically reviewed.

¶ 704.01

This substantive test of transactions assesses whether credit purchases were recorded for the proper period:

- Sample entries in the receiving reports are compared to vendor invoices and dates recorded in the purchases journal and any significant time delay is investigated.

.02 Year-end Detailed Testing to Fulfill Audit Objectives for Accounts Payable Balance

The accounts payable as shown on the financial statements actually exists:

- For a sample of individual vendor accounts payable, the auditor agrees the balances owed to supporting documentation to determine value and propriety of liability at year-end.

- The auditor reviews accounts payable subsidiary ledgers and sends confirmation requests for large balances, debit balances, zero balances, and any unusual or unexpected balance.

- For those vendors who did not reply to the confirmation request, the auditor reconciles the monthly vendor statement at year-end to the subsidiary ledger balance.

All accounts payable accounts have been recorded.

- Perform search for unrecorded liabilities. (See the discussion of this topic at ¶ 704.04.)

- If confirmation requests are sent to vendors, include some vendors that show a zero balance.

Accounts payable as shown on the financial statements represents an obligation to the company.

- The auditing procedures are the same as those for the existence assertion.

Accounts payable as shown on the financial statements is correctly valued.

- The auditing procedures are the same as those for the existence assertion.

Accounts payable as shown on the financial statements has been recorded in the proper period.

- Perform a purchases cutoff test. (See the discussion of this topic at ¶ 704.04.)

All accounts payable as shown on the financial statements is presented properly and all necessary disclosures have been included in the notes to the financial statements.

- The minutes of the board of directors and subcommittee minutes are reviewed for discussions about:
  - Refinancing accounts payable with long-term debt
  - Related-party transactions concerning accounts payable
  - Notes payable included in accounts payable
  - Due from officers included in accounts payable
- The financial statements are read to determine whether all of the above items, if material, are properly segregated in the financial statements or disclosed in the notes to the financial statements.

.03 Analytical Procedures for Substantive Testing of Accounts Payable

For the year-end analytical procedures, the auditor employs these approaches (see also Table 7.3):

- Computes and compares accounts payable turnover (credit purchases ÷ average accounts payable) to industry average, prior years, and expected amounts. Significant fluctuations should be examined further.
- Computes and compares purchases as a percentage of accounts payable to industry average, prior years, and expected amounts. Significant fluctuations should be examined further.
- Compares those expenses as shown in the purchases journal with prior years. Significant fluctuations should be examined further.

.04 Other Issues Specific to Auditing Accounts Payable

Search for unrecorded liabilities. The search for unrecorded liabilities is a test that is performed on cash disbursements subsequent to year-end. The supporting documentation for each significant disbursement beginning on the first day after year-end and continuing to the last day of fieldwork is reviewed to determine whether it is a disbursement for a transaction that occurred the previous year. If it is, it should be accrued and listed as an accounts payable. If it is not for the previous year, it should not appear in the accounts payable detail.

Also, as part of the search for unrecorded liabilities, on the last day of fieldwork the auditor should review all significant unpaid invoices to determine whether any should be accrued as of year-end. If so, these invoices should be included in the accounts payable detail.

Purchases cutoff test. For all significant purchases in the purchases journal for a period prior to and subsequent to year-end, the auditor should examine the supporting documentation to determine whether the purchase was recorded for the proper period.

¶ 704.04

Additionally, on the last day of the year-end the auditor should observe that the last receiving report is issued and review a sample of the supporting documents of prior and subsequent reports to verify that each purchase was recorded in the proper period.

¶ 705 Other Procedures in the Financial Audit

In addition to the specific audit areas that have been completed, there are other audit procedures that auditors employ to reach their conclusion. Because the financial statements do not contain only account balances and transactions, but also disclosures and overall financial statement presentation issues, additional auditing procedures are necessary. These are:

- Reviewing for contingent liabilities
- Reviewing for subsequent events
- Reviewing for related party transactions
- Reviewing the company's ability to continue as a going concern
- Evaluation of significant unusual transactions
- Retrospective review of significant accounting estimates
- Final fieldwork assessment of the risks of material misstatement due to fraud
- Final analytical review
- Obtaining a management representation letter

¶ 706 Reviewing for Contingent Liabilities

A contingent liability represents a currently existing potential loss to a third party that will be determined by a future event. Because the event has not taken place and may not even take place, the potential loss is considered contingent.

The probability of loss determines the financial statement effect. *Accounting for Contingencies*, Financial Accounting Standards Board (FASB) No. 5, describes three levels of likelihood of loss:

Probable—The future event or events will probably occur. If the amount can be reasonably estimated, the generally accepted accounting principle, conservatism, requires the loss to be accrued and indicated in the body of the financial statements as well as being disclosed in the notes to the statements. If the amount of a probable loss cannot be reasonably estimated, only disclosure is required.

Reasonably possible—If the chances that the future event or events will occur is more than remote but less than probable, disclosure in a footnote is required.

¶ 705

Remote—If the chance is great that the future event or events will not occur, neither financial statement recognition nor disclosure is required.

Examples of contingent liabilities are:

- Litigation whereby the client is a defendant.

- Income tax disputes where additional taxes may be assessed.

- Product warranties issued by the client.

- Guarantees of the obligations of third parties. The client may have guaranteed the obligation of a major supplier. The client is contingently obligated for the debt if the supplier defaults on the loan.

The auditor should investigate for the possibility that contingent liabilities exist.[2] Auditing procedures to obtain evidence regarding contingent liabilities include:

- Inquiries of management regarding contingent liabilities.

- Reviewing contracts, loan agreements, leases, and other documents for possible guarantees by the client.

- Obtaining bank confirmation about possible guarantees of third-party obligations.

- Reading the minutes of the board of directors and related subcommittees for circumstances that may create a contingent liability. For example, the board may discuss fines about to be imposed by a federal agency.

- A review of correspondence between the client and taxing authorities may indicate additional tax assessments are being imposed.

- Confirming with all attorneys performing legal services for the client that involve possible contingencies. An analysis of legal fees may assist the auditor in identifying attorneys assisting the client. Auditing standards, sec. 337, require inquiries of the client's legal representatives. The inquiries should concern any pending litigation or any other information involving legal counsel that is relevant to the financial statements. Information should be requested about existing material regarding:

    – Litigation involving the client

    – Claims against the client

---

[2] SAS No. 12, Inquiry of a Client's Lawyer Concerning Litigation, Claims, and Assessments (AICPA, Professional Standards, vol. 1, AU sec. 337.04).

¶ 706

- Probable unasserted claims (where an unfavorable outcome is reasonably possible)
- Assessments directed against the client

Figure 7.4 provides a sample inquiry letter directed to a client's attorney.

Figure 7.4

Inquiry of Attorney

Gentlemen:

Our auditors, Grayson & Farbe CPAs, are conducting an audit of our financial statements at December 31, 20X2, and for the year then ended. We have prepared, and furnished to Grayson & Farbe, a description and evaluation of certain contingencies, including those set forth below involving matters with respect to which you have been engaged and to which you have devoted substantive attention on behalf of the company in the form of legal consultation or representation. These contingencies are regarded by management of the company as material for this purpose. This request is limited to contingencies amounting to $50,000 individually or items involving lesser amounts that exceed $50,000 in the aggregate. Your response should include matters that existed at December 31, 20X2, and during the period from that date to the date of your response.

Please furnish to our auditors any explanation that you consider necessary to supplement the foregoing information, including an explanation of those matters as to which your views may differ from those stated and an identification of the omission of any pending or threatened litigation, claims, and assessments, or a statement that the list of such matters is complete.

We understand that whenever, in the course of performing legal services for us with respect to a matter recognized to involve an unasserted possible claim or assessment that may call for financial statement disclosure, if you have formed a professional conclusion that we should disclose or consider disclosure concerning such possible claim or assessment, as a matter of professional responsibility to us, you will so advise us and will consult with us concerning the question of such disclosure and the applicable requirements of Statement of Financial Accounting Standards No. 5. Please specifically confirm to our auditors that our understanding is correct.

Please specifically identify the nature of and reasons for any limitation on your response.

Sincerely,

Aimee Hardwicke, CEO
Carbolic Cleaning Company
March 4, 20X3

The attorney may refuse to respond to the auditor's inquiry due to lack of knowledge of matters involving contingent liabilities or a client confidentiality issue. If an attorney refuses to furnish information to the auditor because of lack of knowledge, there is no financial statement effect, and, it

¶ 706

will, therefore, not affect the evidence gathering. However, if the attorney refuses to provide information that affects the fair presentation of the financial statements, the auditor should modify the audit report due to a scope limitation. See Chapter 8, "Reporting Considerations," for issues in reporting when there are scope limitations.

¶ 707   Reviewing for Subsequent Events

Subsequent events are those events that occur between the balance sheet date and the date that the financial statements are issued. However, auditors are responsible for reviewing for subsequent events that occur between the balance sheet date and the last day of fieldwork (i.e., the date of the audit report). Figure 7.5 shows the timing of recognizing subsequent events.

Figure 7.5

Recognition of Subsequent Events

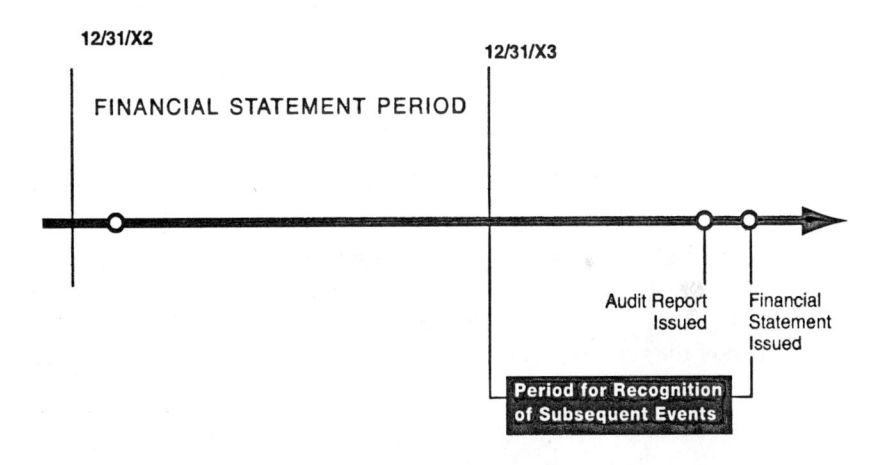

There are two types of subsequent events:

1. Those that provide additional information about a condition that existed as of the balance sheet date. These types of events, if material, require financial statement revision and disclosure in the notes to the financial statements. Examples of these types of subsequent events are:

    - Settlement of litigation accrued as of the balance sheet date

    - The write-off of a significant accounts receivable indicating that the allowance for doubtful accounts was understated as of the balance sheet date

2. Those events that occur that provide information about conditions that did not exist as of the balance sheet but are important information to the users of financial statements in order to make an informed judgment. These types of events require disclosure only. Examples of these types of events are:

- Loss of inventory due to fire
- Declaration of a cash or stock dividend
- Sale of a stock issue

The auditing process for obtaining evidence regarding subsequent events includes:

1. Inquiries of managers who have operating and financial responsibilities regarding subsequent events

2. Inquiries of attorneys about litigation, assessments, and claims

3. Reading the subsequent interim financial statements, noting any significant variances from forecasted amounts or from comparisons with the financial statements being audited

4. Reading the minutes of the board of directors and related subcommittees for discussions of significant events that occurred after the balance sheet date

5. Addressing subsequent events in the management representation letter

When an auditor becomes aware of a subsequent event that occurred between the last day of fieldwork and the audit report issue date, the auditor is obligated to obtain evidence about that event (Figure 7.6). For the dating of the audit report concerning such matters, see ¶ 804.

¶ 707

Figure 7.6

Time Frame for Subsequent Event Evidence Requirement

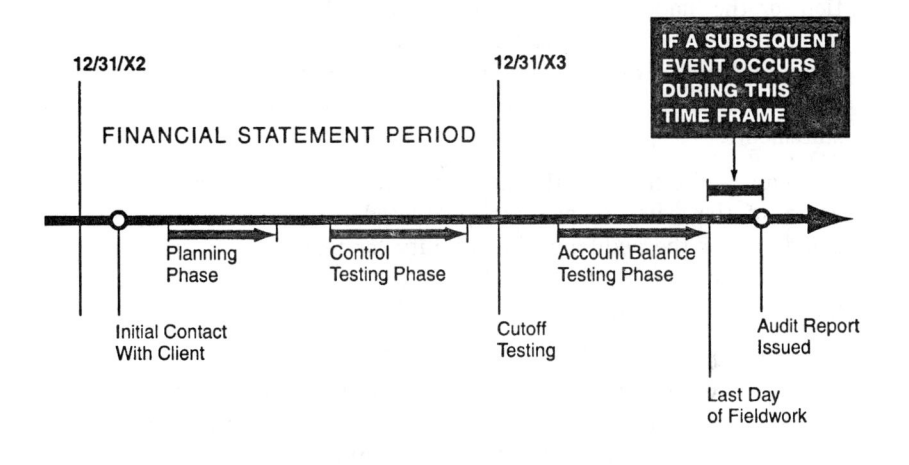

```
12/31/X2                          12/31/X3         IF A SUBSEQUENT
                                                   EVENT OCCURS
                                                   DURING THIS
          FINANCIAL STATEMENT PERIOD               TIME FRAME

       Planning        Control              Account Balance
       Phase           Testing Phase        Testing Phase

       Initial Contact      Cutoff                 Audit Report
       With Client          Testing                Issued

                                                   Last Day
                                                   of Fieldwork
```

¶ 708 Related Party Transactions

The term, "related party transactions", refers to those transactions where there is involvement of:

1. Common ownership between entities, either directly or through familial ties

2. Common management

3. Significant influence or control of one party over the other such that one of the parties may be hindered in pursuing its own separate interests

Related party transactions should be valued as if it were at "arm's length," that is, as if the parties were independent of one another. Arm's length transactions are conducted so that the value of the transactions approximates market value.

Material related party transactions should be disclosed in the notes to the financial statements. For this reason the auditor should obtain sufficient evidence so that he or she understands what the related party transaction actually represents, in other words, the economic substance of the transaction. Some related party transactions may not be disclosed and may be difficult for the auditor to discover.

There have been many instances of improper valuation of transactions involving related parties, especially those involving sales and exchanges of

¶ 708

property, loans, and stock transactions. In *United States V. Simon* [425 F 2d 796 (2d Cir. 1969)] also known as the Continental Vending case, inadequate disclosure by Continental Vending of certain related party transactions resulted in criminal liability for the CPAs involved in the audit. Currently, the auditors for Enron Corporation are under investigation for the inadequate disclosures of the off-balance sheet treatment of liabilities incurred by Special Purpose Entities (SPEs).[3] It appears that three of Enron's SPEs should have been consolidated in the financial statements and now require the restatement of Enron's financial statements.

During the course of the audit, it is incumbent upon the auditor to be aware of the existence of material related party transactions. Auditing standards for the auditor's responsibility for related party transactions is contained in Statements on Auditing Standards, No. 45, Omnibus Statement on Auditing Standards, AU sec. 334, *Related Parties*. The means of identifying related party transactions include:

1. Inquire as to what manner the company identifies transactions with related parties. For example, some companies require conflict of interest statements to be prepared by its management.

2. Inquire of management about company transactions with other entities owned directly or through familial ties, controlled, or influenced by:
   a. Company management
   b. Company directors
   c. Company stockholders

3. Review the minutes of the board of directors and subcommittees, such as the audit committee, to identify material transactions as well as related party transactions.

4. Review major transactions and accounting adjustment, especially those that are close to year end, to determine if they are related party transactions.

5. Compare those individuals involved, internal and external to the company, in major company transactions with the following:
   a. Filings with regulatory agencies indicating if company officers and directors also serve as managers and directors for other companies

---

[3] Testimony Concerning Recent Events Relating to Enron Corporation, Robert K. Herdman, Chief Accountant, U.S. Securities and Exchange Commission, Before the U.S. House of Representatives, Subcommittee on Capital Markets, Insurance and Government Sponsored Enterprises and the Subcommittee on Oversight and Investigation, Committee on Financial Services.

¶ 708

b. Names of managers and trustees for company-sponsored employee pension and trusts

c. Stockholders

d. Vendors/suppliers

e. Customer

f. Lenders

g. Borrowers

6. Review confirmation responses obtained from the following to determine if related party transactions transpired:

   a. Financial institutions when confirming cash and loan balances. There may be an indication that the company has guaranteed the loan of another entity.

   b. Confirmation responses of debtors.

   c. Confirmation responses of creditors.

Once related party transactions have been identified, the auditor must obtain an understanding of the transactions, i.e., the business reason for the transactions, the auditor should determine the transaction's effect on the financial statements. There are a number of audit procedures that could occur:

1. Determine if the board of directors approved the transactions.

2. Obtain appraisals of assets exchanged or sold in related party transactions.

3. Audit any intercompany account balances containing the related party transactions.

4. Review supporting documentation of the transactions.

¶ 709 Reviewing the Company's Ability to Continue as a Going Concern

Auditing standards require that auditors evaluate whether there is substantial doubt about a client's ability to continue as a going concern for at least one-year beyond the balance sheet date.[4] During the planning and fieldwork stages the auditor may identify conditions that raise doubts that the client will be able to continue as a going concern. For example, if the client is unable to meet its obligations when they become due without substantial disposition of its assets, this is an indication of possible financial difficulties. Other indications of a going concern problem are:

- Arrearages in dividends

---

[4] SAS No. 59, The Auditor's Consideration of an Entity's Ability to Continue as a Going Concern (AICPA, Professional Standards, vol. 1, AU sec. 341.02).

- Denial of ordinary trade credit by suppliers
- Negative cash flows from operating activities
- Restructuring of debt to meet obligations

A final going concern assessment should be made at the end of the audit because the auditor is in the best position to determine the client's financial condition. Much of the audit evidence already obtained can assist the auditor in the going concern determination. Analytical procedures, reviews of subsequent events, the minutes of the board of directors, and attorney inquiries can all provide the auditor with information about the client's ability to continue as a going concern.

If there is substantial doubt about the client's ability to continue as a going concern for the next year, the auditor should:

1. Obtain information about management's plans that are intended to mitigate the effect of the adverse conditions or events.
2. Assess the likelihood that such plans can be effectively implemented within a reasonable period of time.[5]

Auditing standards require that the auditor document the conditions that led them to believe the client has a going concern problem, as well as the auditing procedures performed, resolution, and auditor's judgment as to the effect on the financial statements and disclosures.[6]

If, upon review of management's plans, the auditor still concludes that there is substantial doubt about a going concern, he or she should consider the adequacy of disclosure about the entity's possible inability to continue as a going concern for a reasonable period of time.[7] If the disclosure is adequate, the auditor can issue an unqualified opinion with an explanatory paragraph expressing that there is substantial doubt about the company's ability to continue as a going concern. If the disclosure of the going concern problem is inadequate, the auditor should issue a qualified or adverse opinion. (For further discussion, see Chapter 8.)

¶ 710 Final Fieldwork Assessment of the Risks of Material Misstatement Due to Fraud

SAS 99 requires that at or near the completion of fieldwork, the auditor should evaluate whether the auditing procedures performed to date have addressed sufficiently the risks of material misstatement due to fraud made earlier in the audit. Additionally, the auditor with final responsibility for the audit is responsible to determine if there was sufficient and effective communication maintained throughout the audit engagement regarding information or conditions that highlight the risks of material misstatement

---

[5] *Ibid.*, AU sec. 341.03b.
[6] SAS No. 59, The Auditor's Consideration of an Entity's Ability to Continue as a Going Concern (AICPA, Professional Standards, vol. 1, AU sec. 341.03).
[7] *Ibid.*, AU sec. 341.03c.

due to fraud. The auditor also should consider if a meeting with members of the audit team is necessary to discuss these matters further.

¶ 711   Conducting a Final Analytical Review

Auditing standards[8] require that analytical procedures be applied at the final review stage of the audit. The objective of the final review is to determine that enough evidence has been gathered to support the audit conclusions reached on the financial statements. The final review is the last chance for the auditor to assess whether he or she has:

- Responded appropriately to unusual or unexpected balances identified in the planning or process of the audit
- Identified all material misstatements in the financial statements

The analytical procedures used in this review include reading the financial statements and notes and, together with an in-depth knowledge of the client's business, apply ratio analysis and other comparative techniques to evaluate the overall financial statement presentation. Additionally SAS 99 provides that analytical procedures should be performed as substantive tests or in the overall review stage of the audit to determine if a previously unknown risk of material misstatement due to fraud has emerged. The type of analytical procedures upon which the auditor should include, but not limited to, would address revenue valuation matters. The procedures are even stronger if revenue can be related to data that are difficult for management to alter. For instance, relating the reasonableness of revenue to production capacity, income, cost of goods sold, or cash flows are important comparisons. Relating revenue, income, and bad debt write-offs to industry trends also serve as independent corroboration of revenue reasonableness. If the auditor determines that not enough evidence has been obtained, additional evidence is sought in the areas identified in the final review.

¶ 712   Management Report on Internal Controls

As discussed in Chapter 6 (¶ 621), Act Sec. 404 of the Sarbanes-Oxley Act of 2002 requires (1) management to assess the effectiveness of the company's internal control over financial reporting, (2) management to include in the annual report its assessment of the effectiveness of internal control over financial reporting, and (3) registered auditors to attest to and report on management's assessment of internal control over financial reporting. PCAOB Auditing Standard No. 2 requires integrated audit of the financial statements and internal control over financial reporting. Thus, auditors should gather sufficient and competent evidence, thoroughly review obtained evidence, and use the evidence to support an opinion regard-

---

[8] SAS No. 56, Analytical Procedures (AICPA, Professional Standards, vol. 1, AU sec. 329).

ing whether management's assessment on the effectiveness of internal control over financial reporting is fairly stated.

¶713 Obtaining a Management Representation Letter

Management makes many representations to the auditor during the course of the audit. These representations are part of the audit evidence. Although the representations are considered audit evidence, they are not a substitute for other necessary auditing procedures that corroborate these representations. Auditing standards[9] require that auditors obtain a letter of representation from the client to document management's verbal representations made during the audit. The letter is prepared on the company's letterhead, addressed to the auditor, and signed by those individuals who have overall responsibility for operating and financial matters, usually the CEO and CFO. The letter should be dated no later than the auditor's report date.

The purposes of the letter are three-fold:

1. To remind managers that they are primarily responsible for the fair presentation of the financial statements. Management is responsible for the financial statement assertions. The management representation letter details many of the effects in the financial statements created because of the assertions. For example, the assertions reveal that related-party transactions and contingent liabilities have been disclosed to the auditors as well as being included in the notes to the financial statements.

2. To document management responses to auditor inquiries made during the audit process. The management representation letter confirms in writing many of the oral representations that management made to the auditor.

3. To reduce the possibility of misunderstanding concerning the matters contained in the representations. For example, managers may have represented to the auditor that it was their intention that an investment in stock be classified as available for sale. Their representation would serve as the support for treatment of the stock's classification on the balance sheet and the corresponding effects on the income statement. Making a written representation validates management's intention so that there is no future misunderstanding about the stock's classification.

Refusal by a client to prepare and sign the letter may require the auditor to issue a disclaimer of opinion or withdraw from the engagement.

---

[9] SAS No. 85, Management Representations (AICPA, Professional Standards, vol. 1, AU sec. 333).

There are, however, certain circumstances whereby an auditor could still render a qualified opinion upon a client's refusal to provide a representation letter. The situation depends on the nature of the representations not obtained. The auditor should evaluate any reliance that he or she has placed on other representations made by management during the course of the audit and consider whether the refusal may have additional effects on the audit report.

A number of items should be included in the management representation letter. However, it is necessary to tailor the letter to the particular circumstances of each client. Some of the more common items for inclusion and their general sequence of discussion are:

1. Management's acknowledgment of its responsibility:[10]
    a. For the fair presentation of the financial statements
    b. For the design and implementation of programs and controls to prevent and detect fraud
2. Confirmation that management made available to the auditors all:
    a. Financial records
    b. Related data
    c. Minutes of meeting of stockholders, directors, and committees of directors
3. Statement that the financial statements are error-free
4. Statement that there are no unrecorded transactions
5. Verification that the following items have been properly disclosed:
    a. Related-party transactions
    b. Noncompliance with aspects of contractual agreements
    c. Information concerning subsequent events
    d. Knowledge of fraud or suspected fraud affecting the entity involving:[11]
        i. Management,
        ii. Employees who have significant roles in internal control, or
        iii. Others where the fraud could have a material effect on the financial statements.

---

[10] SAS No. 99, Consideration of Fraud in a Financial Statement Audit (AICPA, Professional Standards, vol. 1, AU sec. 316.19).

[11] *Ibid.*

e. Knowledge of any allegations of fraud affecting the entity received in communications from employees, former employees, analysts, regulators, short sellers, or others[12]

f. Communications from regulatory agencies concerning matters that have a financial statement impact

g. Disclosure of arrangements involving restrictions on cash balances, such as a required compensating balance arrangement

h. Reduction of excess or obsolete inventories to net realizable value

i. Losses from sales commitments

j. Liens on assets, and assets pledged as collateral

k. Agreements to repurchase assets previously sold

l. Violations or possible violations of laws or regulations that should be disclosed in the financial statements

m. Unasserted claims or assessments that represent a probable assertion

n. Capital stock repurchase options on agreements or capital stock reserved for opinions, warrants, conversions, or other requirements

6. Statement that management is not aware of any additional subsequent events that would require recognition in the financial statements

An example of a management representation letter is shown in Figure 7.7.

[12] *Ibid.*

¶713

Figure 7.7

Management Representation Letter

Samuel & Samuel LLP:

We are providing this letter in connection with your audit of the financial statements of Flair Apparel Inc. as of December 31, 20X2, and the year then ended for the purpose of expressing an opinion about whether the financial statements present fairly, in all material respects, the financial position, results of operations, and cash flows of Flair Apparel Inc. in conformity with generally accepted accounting principles. We confirm that we are responsible for the fair presentation in the financial statements of financial position, results of operations, and cash flows in conformity with generally accepted accounting principles.

Certain representations in this letter are described as being limited to matters that are material. Items are considered material, regardless of size, if they involve an omission or misstatements of accounting information that, in the light of surrounding circumstances, makes it probable that the judgment of a reasonable person relying on the information would be changed or influenced by the omission or misstatement.

We confirm, to the best of our knowledge and belief, as of March 17, 20X3, the following representations were made to you during your audit.

1. The financial statements referred to above are fairly presented in conformity with generally accepted accounting principles.
2. We have made available to you all of the following:
   a. Financial records and related data
   b. Minutes of the meetings of stockholders, directors, and committees of directors, or summaries of actions of recent meetings for which minutes have not yet been prepared
3. There have been no communications from regulatory agencies concerning noncompliance with or deficiencies in financial reporting practices.
4. There are no material transactions that have not been properly recorded in the accounting records underlying the financial statements.
5. We believe that the effects of the uncorrected financial statement misstatements summarized in the accompanying schedule are immaterial, both individually and in the aggregate, to the financial statements taken as a whole.
6. We acknowledge our responsibility for the design and implementation of programs and controls to prevent fraud.
7. We have no knowledge of any fraud or suspected fraud affecting the entity involving:
   a. Management,
   b. Employees who have significant roles in internal control, or
   c. Others where the fraud could have a material effect on the financial statements.
8. We have no knowledge of any allegations of fraud or suspected fraud affecting the entity received in communications from employees, former employees, analysts, regulators, short sellers, or others.[13]

---

[13] *Ibid.*

¶713

9. The company has no plans or intentions that may materially affect the carrying value or classification of assets and liabilities.

10. The following have been recorded or disclosed in the financial statements:

    a. Related-party transactions, including sales, purchases, loans, transfers, leasing arrangements, and guarantees, and amounts receivable from or payable to related parties

    b. Guarantees, whether written or oral, under which the company is contingently liable

    c. Significant estimates and material concentrations known to management that are required to be disclosed in accordance with the AICPA's Statement of Position 94-6, *Disclosure of Certain Significant Risks and Uncertainties*

11. There are none of the following:

    a. Violations or possible violations of laws or regulations whose effects should be considered for disclosure in the financial statements or as a basis for recording a loss contingency

    b. Unasserted claims or assessments that our lawyer has advised us are probable of assertion and must be disclosed in accordance with Financial Accounting Standards Board (FASB) Statement No. 5, *Accounting for Contingencies*

    c. Other liabilities or gain or loss contingencies that are required to be accrued or disclosed by FASB Statement No. 5

12. The company has satisfactory title to all owned assets, and there are no liens or encumbrances on such assets nor has any asset been pledged as collateral.

13. The company has complied with all aspects of contractual agreements that would have material effect on the financial statements in the event of noncompliance.

   To the best of our knowledge and belief, no events have occurred subsequent to the balance sheet date and through the date of this letter that would require adjustment to or disclosure in the aforementioned financial statements.

Joseph Dore, Chief Executive Officer

Joan Gerth, Chief Financial Officer

Flair Apparel Inc.

March 17, 20X3

In addition to the previously illustrated representations, there may some less common items, such as:

- The client's recognition and use of a specialist's work in formulating financial statement balances

- The impairment of long-lived assets has been recognized

¶713

- Management's intention of refinancing short-term debt with long-term debt
- The post-retirement benefits have been eliminated

Based upon the results of the audit, the next decision the auditor makes would be which type of audit opinion is appropriate under the circumstances. Chapter 8 explores the types of opinions available.

¶714 Summary

An organization's financial statements reflect a set of management assertions. The auditor's responsibility is to determine whether the financial statements are fairly presented. To accomplish this, the auditor must design procedures to reach conclusions about management's assertions regarding the following: (1) existence or occurrence, (2) completeness, (3) rights and obligations, (4) valuation or allocation, and (5) presentation, disclosure, and (6) compliance.

First, the auditor follows specific procedures surrounding the financial audit of selected accounts and related transactions. Evidence that supports or refutes management assertions is gathered by performing tests of controls, substantive tests of transactions, detailed testing of account balances, and analytical procedures. To improve audit effectiveness and efficiency, the auditor must be aware of the relationships among assertions and their respective controls in deciding the manner and content of the auditing procedures.

The auditor must reach conclusions about the financial statements as a whole. Because the financial statements do not contain only account balances and transactions, but also disclosures and overall financial statement presentation issues, additional auditing procedures are necessary. These procedures require reviewing for contingent liabilities, reviewing for subsequent events, reviewing for related party transactions, reviewing the company's ability to continue as a going concern, evaluation of significant accounting estimates, final fieldwork assessment of the risks of material misstatement due to fraud, final analytical review, and obtaining a management representation letter.

Chapter 8

Reporting Considerations

¶ 801	Introduction
¶ 802	Auditing Standards
¶ 803	Categories of Audit Opinions
¶ 804	Special Reporting Considerations
¶ 805	Report of Independent Registered Public Accounting Firms
¶ 806	Summary

¶ 801 Introduction

Pursuant to the passage of the Sarbanes-Oxley Act of 2002, SEC implementation rules, and Public Company Accounting Oversight Board (PCAOB) auditing standards, registered auditors issue either two separate reports or a combined report on (1) annual financial statements of public companies and (2) internal control over financial reporting. The first section of this chapter focuses on audit report on financial statements, and the second section discusses an audit report on internal control over financial reporting.

Chapter 8 objectives:

- To recognize the value of an auditor's report and the methodology used to form the opinion contained within the report (see ¶ 801–802).
- To become familiar with the four major categories of opinions issued in audit reports (see ¶ 803).
- To explain the purpose and content of each of the three paragraphs in a standard unqualified audit report (see ¶ 803).
- To list the circumstances that might cause an auditor to modify his or her unqualified opinion (see ¶ 803).
- To understand when a qualified report is necessary (see ¶ 803).
- To explain the difference between a qualified and an adverse opinion (see ¶ 803).
- To recognize when it is appropriate to issue a disclaimer (see ¶ 803).

- To list other reporting considerations that affect the audit report (see ¶ 804).

- To understand new adjustments to the audit report as required by the PCAOB (see ¶ 805).

.01 Audit Reports

An auditor's report contains an audit opinion and is the highest level of assurance that an auditor can provide in an attestation of financial statements.[1] An auditor's opinion, issued at the completion of an audit (see Figure 8.1), states the degree to which financial statements conform to generally accepted accounting principles. The financial statements represent a presentation of financial data which communicates information about company resources, obligations, and operations. Financial statements include all of the following:

- **Balance sheet or statement of financial position** as of a point in time (or points of time if comparative balance sheets are presented)

- **Income statement** (or Statement of Revenue and Expenses) for a period of time (usually for the period of time between comparative balance sheets)

- **Statement of retained earnings** for the same period of time as the income statement

- **Statement of cash flow** for the same period of time as the income statement

- **Statement of Comprehensive Income**

- **Statement of Changes in Stockholder Equity** (or Changes in Owner's Equity)

- **Notes to the financial statements**

---

[1] Statements on Auditing Standards (SAS) No. 62, *Special Reports* (AICPA, Professional Standards, vol. 1, AU sec. 623.02).

¶ 801.01

Figure 8.1

Timeline for Issuing an Audit Report

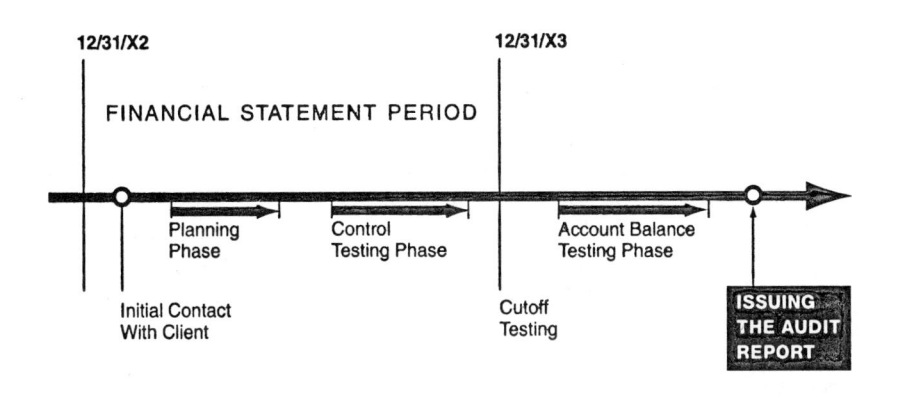

```
12/31/X2                          12/31/X3
|                                 |
|   FINANCIAL STATEMENT PERIOD    |
|                                 |
●────────────────────────────────●────────────●──────▶
    Planning      Control            Account Balance
    Phase         Testing Phase      Testing Phase

    Initial Contact    Cutoff           ISSUING
    With Client        Testing          THE AUDIT
                                        REPORT
```

¶ 802 Auditing Standards

To issue an opinion, an auditor must gather enough evidence to support his or her claim that financial statements do or do not conform with generally accepted accounting principles (GAAP). The methodology used to gather evidence is governed by generally accepted auditing standards (GAAS). The PCAOB has adopted and the SEC has approved PCAOB Auditing Standard No. 1, References in Auditor's Reports to the Standards of the Public Company Accounting Oversight Board.[2] PCAOB Auditing Standard No. 1 requires, as of May 24, 2004, that registered auditors' reports on financial statements audits and other engagements pertaining to public companies include a reference that the audit or other engagement was conducted in accordance with "the standards of the PCAOB (United States)." This standard replaces the previous references to "generally accepted auditing standards," "U.S. generally accepted standards," "auditing standards generally accepted in the United States of America," and "standards established by the AICPA." PCAOB Auditing Standard No. 1 also requires that registered auditors who reissue reports that were originally issued prior to May 24, 2004 or who issue reports that include comparative financial information on prior years state that the audit or review was conducted in accordance with "the standards of the Public Company Accounting Oversight Board (United States)." Furthermore, the title of the report should be "Report of Independent Registered Public Accounting Firm" and an auditor must include the city and state, or city and country in the case of non-U.S. auditors, from which the auditor's

---

[2] PCAOB Auditing Standard No. 1, References in Auditor's Reports to the Standards of the Public Company Accounting Oversight Board (May 14, 2004). Available at http://www.pcaobus.org.

report has been issued. It should be noted that financial statement audits of non-public companies are still conducted by auditors in accordance with GAAS. Thus, throughout this chapter we make reference to GAAS except for the audit of public companies. The standards require that an auditor be independent of the client, properly trained to perform the audit, and able to maintain professional care while conducting the audit. The standards also require audit planning plus an understanding of the organization's internal control structure for determining the extent of evidence to be gathered.

An auditor's objective is to obtain reasonable assurance that financial statements conform to GAAP and are free of material misstatements and fraud. Although an audit provides the highest level of assurance, an audit does not guarantee accuracy. Reasonable assurance implies that an auditor complied with GAAS and gathered evidence while maintaining an attitude of professional skepticism. Even when an auditor designs an audit that will detect material misstatements and fraud, he or she may not find fraud concealed through forgery or collusion. The skills needed to detect such fraud may be beyond those of an ordinary, reasonably competent auditor.

The value of an auditor's report is that it lends credibility to financial statements. Financial statements are more believable if an independent, competent individual has audited them and rendered an opinion as to their conformity with accounting principles.

Auditing standards require that when an auditor is associated with an organization whose financial statements are being used by third parties, the auditor must express in the audit report how much responsibility he or she is assuming for those financial statements.[3] If no responsibility is warranted, the auditor issues a disclaimer report. A disclaimer is used when an auditor renders no opinion on the financial statements and claims no responsibility for them. For these above reasons, each category of report contains special language addressing the auditor's responsibility.

¶ 803 Categories of Audit Opinions

The four major categories of opinions issued in audit reports are the following:

1. Unqualified opinion
2. Qualified opinion
3. Adverse opinion
4. Disclaimer of opinion

As illustrated in Figure 8.2, the unqualified opinion is the most positive report about financial statements, stating that the auditor has found them to conform to GAAP. The adverse opinion is the most unfavora-

---

[3] SAS No. 1, *Codification of Auditing Standards and Procedures* (AICPA, Professional Standards, vol. 1, AU sec. 150.02, "Generally Accepted Auditing Standards").

ble report, stating that the auditor has found the financial statements do not conform to GAAP. A qualified opinion is a report stating that the financial statements contain positive conformity to GAAP but that there is some noncomformity or there were difficulties gathering sufficient evidence to support some of the amounts and disclosures in the financial statements. A disclaimer of opinion represents no opinion, meaning that either not enough or no evidence was accumulated by the auditor to render an opinion on the financial statement's conformity to accounting principles, although the financial statements may or may not adhere to GAAP.

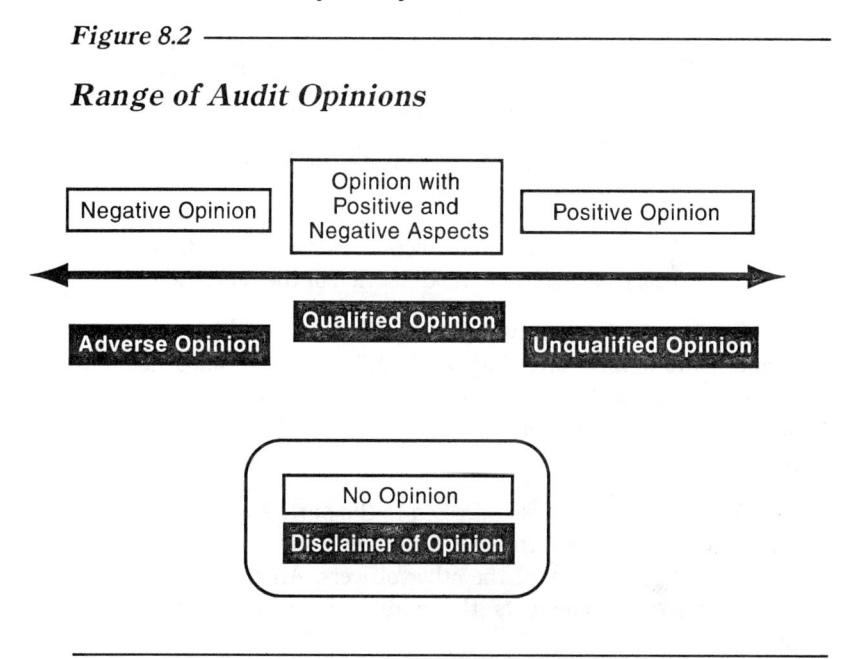

Figure 8.2

Range of Audit Opinions

```
        Negative Opinion    Opinion with          Positive Opinion
                            Positive and
                            Negative Aspects

        <--------------------------------------------------->

        Adverse Opinion    Qualified Opinion     Unqualified Opinion


                            No Opinion
                            Disclaimer of Opinion
```

.01 Unqualified Opinion Reports

A standard unqualified report is a clean opinion in the form of a positive assurance. It is the most positive statement an auditor can make on the compliance of financial statements to GAAP. An unqualified report means that the auditor found no exceptions with the financial statements' conformity to GAAP, and it asserts that he or she has no reservations with the financial statements. An unqualified opinion states that the financial statements fairly present, in all material respects, the financial position, results of operations, and cash flows of the entity in conformity with GAAP. It is given when an auditor was able to conduct an audit following GAAS and has found the financial statements to be fairly presented according to GAAP and applied consistently with prior years.

An unqualified opinion can only be expressed when an independent auditor has formed it based on an examination made according to GAAS in

¶ 803.01

which the financial statements conform to GAAP and contain all the informative disclosures needed to keep them from being misleading.

Standard unqualified reports can be issued when the following five conditions are met:

1. All four required statements are included.

2. The three general standards have been followed in all respects on the engagement.

3. Sufficient evidence has been accumulated and the auditor has conducted the engagement in a manner that enables the conclusion that the three standards of field work have been met.

4. The financial statements are presented in accordance with GAAP (including adequate disclosures.

5. There are no circumstances requiring the addition of an explanatory paragraph or modification of the report wording.

Contents of an unqualified opinion report.[4] The title of an audit should contain the word "independent," such as "Independent Auditor's Report." This statement is made to emphasize the independence the auditor maintains from management and that the financial statements are prepared by management.

An auditor's report is addressed to the parties who retained him or her, but never to management. That is, the addressee cannot be the chief executive officer or any of the other officers. An auditor is independent of management and conducts the audit on behalf of others. Addressees include:

- The board of directors
- The shareholders
- Audit Committee
- In the case of an acquisition, the potential acquiring company

A standard unqualified report consists of three paragraphs as shown (see Figure 8.3). The first paragraph clarifies the responsibilities of management and the auditor, and is referred to as the introductory paragraph. The second paragraph describes the nature of the audit and is called the scope paragraph. The final paragraph is the opinion paragraph, which is a concise statement of the auditor's opinion based on the audit.

---

[4] SAS No. 58, Reports on Audited Statements (AICPA, Professional Standards, vol. 1, AU sec. 508.08).

Figure 8.3

Paragraphs in an Unqualified Opinion Report

1. Introductory Paragraph
   ↓
2. Scope Paragraph
   ↓
3. Opinion Paragraph

The report should conclude with a signature and a date. The signature can be written by hand or printed, typically by the auditor in charge of the engagement.

The wording of a standard unqualified opinion is shown in Figure 8.4.

¶ 803.01

Figure 8.4

Language of an Unqualified Opinion Report [5]

Report of the Independent Auditor

We have audited the accompanying balance sheet of ABC Company as of December 31, 20X2, and the related statements of income, retained earnings, and cash flows for the year then ended. These financial statements are the responsibility of the company's management. Our responsibility is to express an opinion on these financial statements based on our audit.

We conducted our audit in accordance with auditing standards generally accepted in the United State of America. Those standards require that we plan and perform the audit to obtain reasonable assurance about whether the financial statements are free of material misstatement. An audit includes examining, on a test basis, evidence supporting the amounts and disclosures in the financial statements. An audit also includes assessing the accounting principles used and significant estimates made by management, as well as evaluating the overall financial statement presentation. We believe that our audit provides a reasonable basis for our opinion.

In our opinion, the financial statements referred to above present fairly, in all material respects, the financial position of ABC Company as of December 31, 20X2, and the results of its operations and its cash flows for the year then ended in conformity with accepted accounting principles generally accepted in the United States of America.

Mead & Co. LLP
March 21, 20X3

An auditor's report is dated to the last day of fieldwork. As illustrated in Figure 8.5 on the last day of fieldwork, the character of an audit changes with an auditor moving from "actively" auditing to "passively" auditing. Before the last day of fieldwork the auditor had full access to the books, records, and company personnel. After the last day of fieldwork, his or her access is limited. Dating the auditor's opinion as of the last day of fieldwork designates that transition and indicates the point at which he or she assumes no more responsibility to make inquiries or carry out any additional audit procedures.

---

[5] SAS No. 58, Reports on Audited Statements (AICPA, Professional Standards, vol. 1, AU sec. 508.08).

Figure 8.5

Dating an Audit Report as of the Last Day of Fieldwork

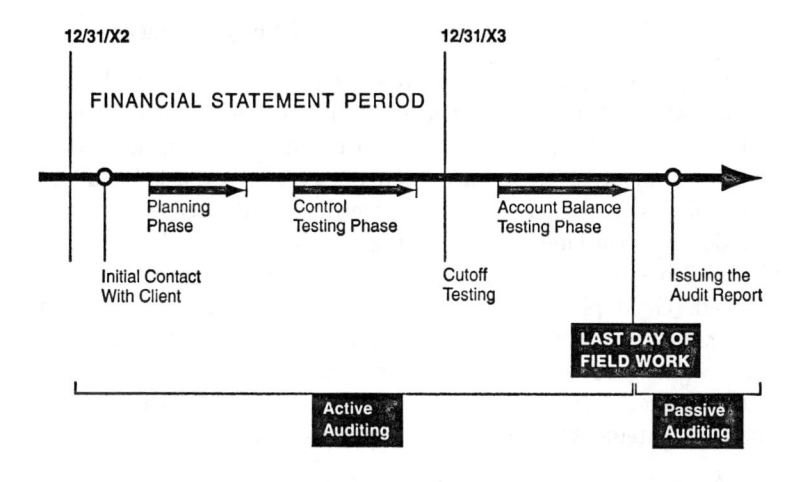

```
12/31/X2                         12/31/X3

         FINANCIAL STATEMENT PERIOD

    ○─────────────────────────────○──────────►
      Planning    Control          Account Balance     Issuing the
      Phase       Testing Phase    Testing Phase       Audit Report

      Initial Contact              Cutoff              
      With Client                  Testing             

                                         LAST DAY OF
                                         FIELD WORK

            Active                              Passive
            Auditing                            Auditing
```

Introductory paragraph in an unqualified opinion report. An introductory paragraph identifies the form of attestation engagement that an auditor conducted, that is, whether the financial statements were audited as opposed to a lesser form of attestation, such as a review. According to auditing standards a "report shall contain an expression of opinion regarding the financial statements, taken as a whole, . . ."[6] As such, the introductory paragraph also identifies the organization whose financial statements are being audited as well as the financial statements (income statement, statement of retained earnings, and statement of cash flow) for which periods and points in time (balance sheets or statements of financial position).

Contents of an introductory paragraph in an unqualified opinion report. An introductory paragraph emphasizes that management is primarily responsible for the company's financial statements and that the auditor is rendering an opinion on those financial statements. According to auditing standards, "in all cases where an auditor's name is associated with financial statements, the report should contain a clear-cut indication of the character of the auditor's work, if any, and the degree of responsibility the auditor is taking."[7]

All the following should be identified:

- Financial statements audited

---

[6] *Ibid.*, AU sec. 508.04.   [7] *Ibid.*, AU sec. 508.04.

¶ 803.01

- Organization audited
- Time frame or point in time of financial statements
- Management's responsibility for the financial statements
- Auditor's responsibility for the financial statements

Scope paragraph in an unqualified opinion report. A scope paragraph describes the nature of the audit and explains what the audit entails and that an audit is conducted in accordance with generally accepted auditing standards. The auditing standards reference also includes a jurisdictional designation. For example, wording in the scope paragraph may include "in accordance with auditing standards generally accepted in the United States of America." Auditing standards require that the audit be planned. Good planning assists an auditor in determining the nature, timing, and extent of the auditing procedures. In other words, an auditor plans what type of and how much evidence is needed, and when the evidence should be gathered to provide reasonable assurance that the financial statements are free of material misstatement.

All of the following should be specified in a scope paragraph:

- Generally accepted auditing standards (GAAS) were used
- The audit, conducted according to the standards is:
  - Planned
  - Performed for reasonable assurance that financial statements are materially correct
  - Uses sampling to support amounts and disclosures
  - Includes assessment of estimates used as well as overall presentation
- Auditor's belief that the audit evidence supports his or her opinion

A scope paragraph also addresses sampling, that is, evidence gathered on a test basis. Because of the volume of transactions that occur during an organization's normal operations, sampling is a necessary procedure in the audit process.

An auditor must also assess the estimates used by managers in their company's financial statements. Many estimates are used in accounting: depreciation is based upon useful lives and salvage values; bad debt expense and warranty cost are based upon historical experience; pension costs are based upon many actuarial calculations and estimated rates of return. An auditor should review such estimates to determine whether they are reasonable.

¶ 803.01

Finally, the scope paragraph concludes by stating that the evidence the auditor gathered supports his or her opinion.

Opinion paragraph in an unqualified opinion report. An opinion paragraph lets an auditor attest as to the fair presentation of the financial statements and that, in all material respects, they conform to GAAP, even though he or she cannot guarantee or certify that the statements are accurate. This is required by auditing standards that state, "The report shall state whether the financial statements are presented in accordance with generally accepted accounting principles."[8] In an opinion paragraph, an auditor expresses nothing more than his or her opinion as an independent, competent individual, duly trained as an auditor using reasonable judgment in the application of GAAS.

The opinion paragraph in an unqualified opinion report should specify that the financial statements:

- Are materially correct
- Conform to GAAP
- Inconsistent application of GAAP
- Omitted or inadequate disclosures

Explanatory paragraph added to an unqualified opinion report. Under certain circumstances an auditor may wish to modify an unqualified report by adding explanatory language to it in a separate paragraph. However, the opinion is still considered unqualified or "clean."

Circumstances that can result in a modification of the standard audit report:

1. The auditor's opinion is based in part on the report of another auditor.
2. The auditor wishes to emphasize a matter included in the financial statements.
3. The financial statements are affected by a departure from authoritative accounting principles.
4. Accounting principles have not been consistently applied.
5. The financial statements are affected by uncertainties concerning future events, the outcome of which cannot be estimated at the date of the auditor's report.

---

[8] SAS No.1, Generally Accepted Accounting Standards (AICPA, Professional Standards, vol. 1, AU sec. 150.02); the generally accepted accounting principles statement also includes a jurisdictional reference. For example, the wording may be "accounting principles generally accepted in the United States of America."

¶ 803.01

6. The scope of the auditor's audit is limited with respect to one or more audit procedures considered necessary in the circumstances.

7. The financial statements are affected by a departure from generally accepted accounting principles.

The circumstances may require the addition of an explanatory paragraph to an unqualified opinion or the issuance of an audit opinion other than the unqualified opinion (qualified, disclaimer, adverse). When circumstances call for such explanatory language, it is added *after* the opinion paragraph. Adding the additional language is not a qualification because it does not change the auditor's opinion or the financial statements. The auditor still considers that the financial statements fairly present GAAP. However modified language to an unqualified opinion indicates conditions explained below.

Accounting principle (or method) changed. When an organization changes from one accounting principle to another the comparative financial statements will be inconsistent in the application of accounting principles. If the change in accounting principle followed GAAP methodology, financial statements will still fairly present GAAP. The change, however, in such a case must be disclosed in the financial statements. An auditor should add an explanatory paragraph that briefly describes the change and then directs the reader's attention to the relevant footnote disclosure.

An event, transaction, or subsequent occurrence needs emphasis. An auditor may wish to emphasize a particular event, transaction, or subsequent occurrence that does not affect his or her unqualified opinion but may be important to the user of the financial statements. For example, if a material related-party transaction has occurred, such as the purchase of a building from a company that has common ownership with the audited organization, then the auditor may want to call attention to this transaction with an added explanatory paragraph.

Departure from GAAP made to not mislead. In rare situations, valuing an account or transaction using promulgated accounting principles may produce a misleading financial position or results of operations or cash flows. In such circumstances an auditor is required to depart from promulgated GAAP so that the financial statements are not misleading. The departure should be disclosed in the financial statements as well as the auditor's opinion. An explanatory paragraph added to the unqualified opinion should include a description of the departure and an explanation on why promulgated GAAP would be misleading.

Uncertainties such as litigation. The financial impact of some uncertainties are not estimable. For instance, if litigation will probably result in a material loss to the organization, then an amount should be accrued for the loss. However, if the loss cannot be estimated, there is no basis for the

¶ 803.01

accrual. Depending upon the final monetary settlement, the financial statement will show a material impact. If the organization has properly disclosed the uncertainty as required by GAAP, the financial statements are presented fairly per GAAP. Barring any other issues an unqualified opinion would be warranted. However, the litigation should be brought to the attention of the users of the financial statements through the use of an additional explanatory paragraph.

Concern about financial problems. An organization's financial health may prevent it from continuing to operate. If such a concern has been properly disclosed in the financial statements, the financial statements reflect GAAP, and the auditor can issue an unqualified opinion with an added explanatory paragraph describing the current concern or problem.

Consistency with other documents and financial information. When audited financial statements are contained in a larger document, such as an annual report, and that document contains other financial information such as the chairman of the board's letter to shareholders, that other financial information must be consistent with the financial statements. For example, if the letter to shareholders refers to a 20 percent sales growth but the financial statements only indicate a 5 percent growth, this inconsistency must be disclosed by the auditor in an explanatory paragraph in his or her report. Even though an explanatory paragraph is added, the report is still unqualified because the basic financial statements are still presented fairly per GAAP.

Comparative financial statements. When comparative financial statements are issued, explanatory language is required. For example, if a prior year's financial statements received a qualified or adverse opinion but have since been restated to properly reflect GAAP, an auditor should add an explanatory paragraph disclosing the following:

- Date of the auditor's previous report

- Type of opinion previously issued

- Circumstances that caused the auditor's restatement of opinion

- A statement that the restated opinion is different from the previous report

Omission of information. When specific information has been omitted from financial statements, an explanatory paragraph is required. Examples of the specific information are:

- Selected quarterly data required by Regulation S-K (Securities and Exchange Commission)

¶ 803.01

- Supplementary information required by GAAP but not considered part of the basic financial statements[9]

Other auditors involved. When a primary or principal auditor of a financial statement audit does not audit all of the financial statements but instead relies on the report of other auditors, the division of responsibility between the auditors should be stated.

Paragraph language in an unqualified report based on another auditor's report. When an auditor shares responsibility with another auditor, the wording of all three paragraphs of the standard report should be modified, but no explanatory paragraph is needed.[10]

1. **Introductory Paragraph**—Add language stating that another auditor audited a percentage of the total assets and revenues and that his or her report is being relied on.

2. **Scope Paragraph**—Add the following language: "We believe our audit and the report of other auditors provide a reasonable basis for our opinion."

3. **Opinion Paragraph**—Add the following language "In our opinion, based on our audits and the report of other auditors, the financial statements."

.02 Qualified Opinion Reports

When a qualified opinion is issued, the auditor has reservations about certain aspects of the financial statements, even though the overall presentation of the statements is fairly presented per GAAP. An auditor's reservations calling for a qualified report generally fall into two categories:

1. Scope limitation—The auditor's examination is unable to obtain sufficient evidence.

2. Departure from GAAP—Some nonpervasive area of the financial statements is deficient.

---

[9] SAS No. 58, Reports on Audited Statements (AICPA, Professional Standards, vol. 1, AU sec. 558.08, as amended by SAS No. 98).

[10] SAS No. 58, Reports on Audited Statements (AICPA, Professional Standards, vol. 1, AU sec. 508.12-13 and SAS No. 1, Part of Audit Performed by other Independent Auditors (AICPA, Professional Standards, vol.1, AU sec. 543.06).

¶ 803.02

Figure 8.6

Paragraphs in a Qualified Opinion Report

1. Introductory Paragraph
   ↓
2. Scope Paragraph
   ↓
3. Explanatory Paragraph
   ↓
4. Opinion Paragraph

As shown in Figure 8.6, qualified reports include a separate explanatory paragraph *before* the opinion paragraph, disclosing the reasons for the qualification or reservation. As previously discussed, a reservation arises from two circumstances.

Scope limitations. If an auditor cannot collect enough evidence on some matter contained in the financial statements he or she may issue a qualified report due to a scope limitation. If a scope limitation is imposed by a client, no opinion should be rendered. A disclaimer of opinion should be given. Whenever a scope limitation is not client-imposed and results from circumstances beyond anyone's control, a qualified opinion may be issued. For example, if current unresolved litigation may negatively affect the company, causing a solvency problem, there may likely be an adverse effect on the financial statements. An auditor who is not able to obtain sufficient evidence about the potential loss to the company could issue a qualified opinion because of the scope limitation. The component paragraphs in such a qualified opinion are:

> **Introductory Paragraph**—Language is the same as in an unqualified report.
>
> **Scope Paragraph**—Add the following language to the scope paragraph of the unqualified opinion: "Except as discussed in the following paragraph . . ."
>
> **Explanatory Paragraph**—The explanatory paragraph, which explains why evidence gathering was hampered, should include the following:

¶ 803.02

- Reasons for the auditor's conclusion for the explanatory paragraph.
- The effect of the departure on the financial position, operation results, and cash flows, if determinable. (If the effect is not determinable, then that must be stated.)
- Statement that the auditor was unable to obtain evidence regarding some issue in the financial statements.
- The dollar effect of the above issue (if the effect is not determinable, then that must be stated).

Opinion Paragraph—The opinion paragraph should include the following: "In our opinion, except for the effects of such adjustments, if any, as might have been determined to be necessary had we been able to examine evidence regarding the financial statements referred to ..."

Departure from GAAP. A qualified opinion should also be given when financial statements depart from GAAP. The departure could result from inadequate financial statement disclosure, inappropriate accounting principles used, unreasonable accounting estimates used, or the inconsistent application of accounting principles. In any event, the departure must be material in nature and affect the fair presentation of the financial position or operation results.

Inadequate financial statement disclosures. Auditing standards require that "informative disclosures in the financial statements are to be regarded as reasonably adequate unless otherwise stated in the report."[11] Without full financial statement disclosure as required by GAAP, the financial statements could be misleading. For example, if cumulative preferred stock dividends in arrears are not disclosed in the notes to the financial statements, a common stockholder may be misled regarding the proper dividend to which they are entitled.

Inappropriate accounting principles used or unreasonable accounting estimates used. A material departure from generally accepted accounting principles without mitigating circumstances misstates the financial position and/or the results of operations. Depending upon the gravity of the departure, either a qualified or adverse opinion should be issued. For example, if inventory is valued at cost instead of the lower of cost or market, and if market is less than cost, current assets and operating income would be overvalued.

Inconsistent use of accounting principles. According to auditing standards, "The report shall identify those circumstances in which such princi-

---

[11] SAS No. 1, Generally Accepted Auditing Standards (AICPA, Professional Standards, vol 1., AU sec. 150.02).

¶ 803.02

ples have not been consistently observed in the current period in relation to the preceding period."[12] Changes in accounting principles are permitted by GAAP if management can justify the change to an acceptable alternate method. For example, if the company's inventory is subject to inflation and the company uses the "first-in, first-out" inventory valuation methodology, management would be justified in changing to the "last-in, first-out" method. The latter method maximizes the value of cost of goods sold, thus reducing profits, but more importantly for some companies, minimizing income tax. However, if management changes to an unacceptable alternate accounting methodology or management cannot justify the change, and if the change is material, the auditor should consider either issuing a qualified or adverse opinion.

Figure 8.7 shows the wording of a qualified report with a departure from GAAP; the statement of cash flows was excluded from the basic financial statements. According to GAAP, whenever an income statement is presented, a statement of cash flows should accompany it.

The format of a qualified report with a departure from GAAP is as follows:

- The introductory and scope paragraphs remain the same as the unqualified opinion, except for cash flow.

- In the opinion paragraph it is stated, "In our opinion, except for the [reference to departure] as explained in the preceding paragraph, the financial statements referred to. . . "[13]

---

[12] *Ibid.*, AU sec. 150.02.
[13] SAS No. 58, Reports on Audited Financial Statements (AICPA, Professional Standards, AU sec. 508.39).

Figure 8.7

Language of a Qualified Opinion When the Statement of Cash Flows was Omitted [14]

Report of the Independent Auditor

We have audited the accompanying balance sheet of ABC Company as of December 31, 20X2, and the related statements of income and retained earnings for the year then ended. These financial statements are the responsibility of the company's management. Our responsibility is to express an opinion on these financial statements based on our audit.

We conducted our audit in accordance with auditing standards generally accepted in the United States of America. Those standards require that we plan and perform the audit to obtain reasonable assurance about whether the financial statements are free of material misstatement. An audit includes examining, on a test basis, evidence supporting the amounts and disclosures in the financial statements. An audit also includes assessing the accounting principles used and significant estimates made by management, as well as evaluating the overall financial statement presentation. We believe that our audit provides a reasonable basis for our opinion.

The company declined to present a statement of cash flows for the years ended December 31, 20X2. Presentation of this statement summarizing the company's operating, investing, and financing activities is required by generally accepted accounting principles.

In our opinion, except that the omission of a statement of cash flows results in an incomplete presentation as explained in the preceding paragraph, the financial statements referred to above present fairly, in all material respects, the financial position of ABC Company as of December 31, 20X2, and the results of its operations and for the year then ended in conformity with accounting principles generally accepted in the United States of America.

Mead & Co. LLP
March 21, 20X3

.03 Adverse Opinions

If, after the course of an audit, an auditor determines that financial statements are not fairly presented, an adverse opinion should be rendered. An adverse opinion is the strongest negative opinion an auditor can give. It is the opposite opinion of an unqualified report. With an adverse opinion an auditor is stating that the financial statements do not fairly present the financial position, operations results, and cash flows of the company in conformity with (GAAP). The difference between a qualified opinion, and an adverse opinion, however, is one of degree.

The materiality of the misstatement and its pervasiveness within the financial statements determine whether a qualified opinion or an adverse opinion is issued. Often the same types of auditor reservations about the

---

[14] *Ibid.*, AU sec. 508.44.

¶ 803.03

fairness of financial statement presentation that cause a qualified opinion to be rendered could also be so grave that an adverse opinion is appropriate. If the departure from GAAP causes a pervasive unfair presentation of the financial statements, a qualified opinion is not a strong enough warning to the financial statement's users. In such a case, an adverse opinion is appropriate.

Figure 8.8

Paragraphs in an Adverse Opinion Report

1. Introductory Paragraph

    ↓

2. Scope Paragraph

    ↓

3. Explanatory Paragraph

    ↓

4. Opinion Paragraph

The format of an adverse opinion is shown in Figure 8.8. An explanatory paragraph or paragraphs, depending on the facts, should precede the opinion paragraph. The separate explanatory paragraph should disclose the reasons for the adverse opinion and the principal effects on the financial statements of the matters causing the adverse opinion.[15]

The explanatory paragraph should include the following:

1. Reasons for the auditor's inconclusion of the explanatory paragraph.

2. The effect of the departure on the financial position, operation results, and cash flows, if determinable. (If the effect is not determinable, then that must be stated.)[16]

The wording of full adverse opinion is shown in Figure 8.9.

---

[15] *Ibid.*, AU sec. 508.59. [16] *Ibid.*, AU sec. 508.59.

Figure 8.9

Language of an Adverse Opinion [17]

Report of the Independent Auditor

We have audited the accompanying balance sheet of ABC Company as of December 31, 20X2, and the related statements of income, retained earnings, and cash flows for the year then ended. These financial statements are the responsibility of the Company's management. Our responsibility is to express an opinion on these financial statements based on our audit.

We conducted our audit in accordance with auditing standards generally accepted in the United States of America. Those standards require that we plan and perform the audit to obtain reasonable assurance about whether the financial statements are free of material misstatement. An audit includes examining, on a test basis, evidence supporting the amounts and disclosures in the financial statements. An audit also includes assessing the accounting principles used and significant estimates made by management, as well as evaluating the overall financial statement presentation. We believe that our audit provides a reasonable basis for our opinion.

As discussed in Note 15 to the financial statements, the company does not capitalize leases that meet criteria for capitalization. Generally accepted accounting principles require that leases that meet certain criteria be capitalized and a corresponding liability be accrued.

Because of the departure from generally accepted accounting principles identified above, as of December 31, 20X2, property, plant and equipment, net of accumulated depreciation, is understated by $12,345,000 and obligations under capital lease—current portion is understated by $3,810,000 and long-term portion by $13,045,000, and deferred income taxes of $1,400,000 has not been recorded. Additionally, current operating expenses are understated by $2,234,000, and retained earnings are overstated by $3,676,000.

In our opinion, because of the effects of the matters discussed in the preceding paragraphs, the financial statements referred to above do not present fairly, in conformity with accounting principles generally accepted in the United States of America, the financial position of ABC Company as of December 31, 20X2, or the results of its operations and its cash flows for the year then ended.

Mead & Co. LLP
March 21, 20X3

.04 Disclaimer of Opinion

When to issue a disclaimer of opinion. According to auditing standards, "A report shall contain an expression of opinion regarding the financial statements, taken as a whole, or an assertion to the effect that an opinion cannot be expressed. When an overall opinion cannot be expressed, the reasons therefore should be stated . . ." [18] A disclaimer of opinion states that the auditor does not express an opinion on the financial statements.

---

[17] *Ibid.*, AU sec. 508.60.

[18] SAS No. 1, Generally Accepted Auditing Standards (AICPA, Professional Standards, AU sec. 150.02).

The full text of a disclaimer of opinion is shown in Figure 8.10.

Figure 8.10

Language of a Disclaimer of Opinion

Report of the Independent Auditor

We did not audit the accompanying balance sheet of Tosne Corporation of December 31, 20X2 and the related statements of income, retained earnings, and cash flows for the year then ended. Accordingly, we do not express an opinion on them.

Mead & Co. LLP
March 21, 20X3

A disclaimer of opinion results from two situations:

1. **No audit conducted.** When an auditor does not audit the financial statements, he or she is in no position to assume any responsibility for them. The financial statements may be correct or incorrect, but the auditor does not know. A disclaimer of opinion gives no opinion and indicates that the auditor is assuming no responsibility. No introductory or scope paragraph is rendered.

2. **Unable to obtain sufficient evidence.** When an auditor is unable to obtain sufficient evidence to determine whether financial statements are presented fairly, he or she is precluded from complying with GAAS. An auditor cannot audit financial statements when not enough evidence is available or when a client imposes a scope limitation upon the auditor. Still, the financial statements may be correct or incorrect; however, especially in the case of a client imposed scope limitation, an auditor's professional skepticism should prevent the auditor from rendering an opinion. Following are examples of such circumstances:

   - *Uncertainties restrict scope of audit.* An uncertainty can arise about the operations of an organization due to circumstances beyond anyone's control. Such an uncertainty is a restriction on the scope of an audit and may require an auditor to qualify his or her opinion or disclaim an opinion. An auditor may issue a disclaimer of opinion when the magnitude of uncertainties about the client's ability to continue as a going concern is such that the auditor is uncomfortable issuing any opinion.

¶ 803.04

- *Client restricts scope of audit.* When a client imposes substantial restrictions on the scope of an audit, there is a significant risk that the client is trying to hide some important evidence, and an auditor should ordinarily disclaim an opinion. For example, when a client does not allow an auditor to read the minutes of the board of directors, any important information contained in the minutes that cannot be obtained elsewhere precludes the auditor from issuing an opinion. There is no scope paragraph, but there is an explanatory paragraph detailing the manner of scope limitation. The format of such a disclaimer is illustrated below.

  1. Modified Introductory Paragraph
  2. Explanatory Paragraph
  3. Disclaimer of Opinion Paragraph

The full text of a disclaimer of opinion with a client-imposed scope limitation is shown in Figure 8.11. Excluded are both the sentence in the introductory paragraph about the auditor's responsibility and the entire scope paragraph.

¶ 803.04

Figure 8.11

Language of a Disclaimer of Opinion Due to Client-Imposed Scope Limitation [19]

Report of the Independent Auditor

We were engaged to audit the accompanying balance sheet of Hygge Company as of December 31, 20X2, and the related statements of income, retained earnings, and cash flows for the year then ended. These financial statements are the responsibility of the company's management. [The sentence about the auditor's responsibility is omitted.]

[Scope paragraph omitted]

The company did not [allow us to confirm certain long-term notes receivable at year end. The notes amount to $12,000,000 and constitute 45 percent of the total notes receivable balance.] The Company's records do not permit the application of other auditing procedures to [the notes receivable balance.]

Because [we were not allowed to confirm certain notes receivable and were not able to apply other auditing procedures to satisfy ourselves as to the account balances,] the scope of our work was not sufficient to enable us to express, and we do not express, an opinion on these financial statements.

Mead & Co. LLP
February 23, 20X3

- *Opening balancies not audited.* It is possible for an opinion to be rendered on a company's balance sheet while the operational statements (income statement, retained earnings, and cash flows) receive a disclaimer of opinion. The above can occur when a company the was not audited the previous year. When not enough evidence can be gathered on the opening balances of the balance sheet accounts—even when the ending balances of the current year's operations appear to comply with generally accepted accounting principles—an auditor is limited to rendering an unqualified opinion only for the balance sheet. Because not enough evidence is available on the opening balances, the auditor must issue a disclaimer of opinion on the statements of operations, retained earnings and cash flows.

Additional issues in a disclaimer of opinion. A disclaimer of opinion cannot substitute for an audit opinion when there has been a material departure from GAAP. If there is sufficient evidence to afford an opinion on the financial statements taken as a whole and a material GAAP

---

[19] SAS No. 58, Reports on Audited Financial Statements (AICPA, Professional Standards, AU sec. 508.63).

¶ 803.04

departure exists, the auditor must determine whether a qualified or adverse opinion is appropriate. If there is a material departure from GAAP but insufficient evidence has been gathered to afford an opinion on the financial statements taken as a whole, a separate explanatory paragraph should be added to the disclaimer of opinion.

The format of a disclaimer of opinion report departing from GAAP is as follows:

1. Explanatory Paragraph

2. Disclaimer Paragraph

Contents of an explanatory paragraph in a disclaimer of opinion. The explanatory paragraph should include the following:

1. Reasons for the auditor's inconclusion of the explanatory paragraph.

2. The effect of the departure on the financial position, operations results and cash flows, if determinable. (If the effect is not determinable then that must be stated.)

If an auditor is not independent, a one paragraph disclaimer (see Figure 8.12) should be issued that specifically states his or her lack of independence; however, the reasons for the lack of independence should not be stated.

Figure 8.12

Language of a Disclaimer of Opinion Stating Lack of Independence

Report of the Independent Auditor

We are not independent with respect to Morke Corporation and the accompanying balance sheet as of December 31, 20X2, and the related statements of income, retained earnings, and cash flows for the year then ended were not audited by us and accordingly, we do not express an opinion on them.

Mead & Co. LLP
March 21, 20X3

¶ 804 Special Reporting Considerations

.01 Limited Reporting Engagement

The auditor can be engaged to render an opinion on one of the financial statements and not any of the others. For instance, the auditor may be engaged to issue an opinion on the balance sheet only. This can be

Reporting Considerations **303**

accomplished and is not considered a scope limitation as long as the information about the other financial statements is available to the auditor.

.02 Special Report Dating Issues

Under normal conditions the date of an auditor's report is the last day of fieldwork. However, if it comes to the attention of an auditor that a subsequent event occurred requiring financial statement adjustment or disclosure and the audit report has not been issued (as illustrated in Figure 8.13), the financial statements should be adjusted or the disclosure incorporated. If the adjustment or disclosure is not made by management, a qualified opinion should be issued.

Figure 8.13

Dating an Audit Report When a Subsequent Event Occurs

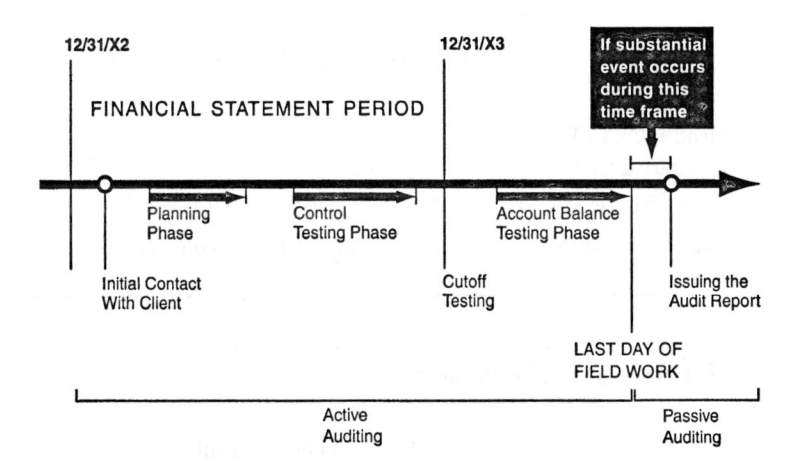

```
12/31/X2                              12/31/X3        If substantial
                                                      event occurs
         FINANCIAL STATEMENT PERIOD                   during this
                                                      time frame

         Planning        Control           Account Balance
         Phase           Testing Phase     Testing Phase

Initial Contact          Cutoff                       Issuing the
With Client              Testing                      Audit Report

                                          LAST DAY OF
                                          FIELD WORK

         Active                                       Passive
         Auditing                                     Auditing
```

If management properly reflects the subsequent event in the financial statements, the auditor must consider applying audit procedures to at least the subsequent event. The consequences of the additional audit procedures will result in two choices for dating the audit opinion:

1. **Dual date.** The auditor could obtain evidence on the subsequent event only and then "dual date" the auditor's report. The two dates will be the original "last day of fieldwork" and the date indicating closure on the work done on the subsequent event.

2. **New date.** The auditor could extend all of the account balance testing procedures to a later point after the original "last day of fieldwork" encompassing the work on the subsequent event and

¶ **804.02**

indicate a new "last day of fieldwork" as the audit report date. This alternative is more costly than the first because of all the additional time and effort involved to update all of the necessary fieldwork.

Figure 8.14 shows the options for dating a report when a subsequent event has occurred after fieldwork has been completed but before an audit report has been issued.

Figure 8.14

Language When Subsequent Events Change the Date of an Audit Report

Alternative 1— Dual Date

Report of the Independent Auditor

... in conformity with accounting principles generally accepted in the United States of America.

Mead & Co. LLP
February 23, 20X2,
 except for Note 16, as to which the date is March 12, 20X2

[Note 16 contains the information regarding the subsequent event.]

Alternative 2— New Date

Report of the Independent Auditor

... in conformity with accounting principles generally accepted in the United States of America.

Mead & Co. LLP
March 12, 20X2
[new last day of fieldwork]

.03 Reports on Comparative Statements

According to auditing standards, the "report shall contain an expression of opinion regarding the financial statements, taken as a whole."[20] When comparative financial statements are presented, that is, when more

---

[20] SAS No. 1, Generally Accepted Auditing Standards (AICPA, Professional Standards, AU sec. 150.02).

¶ 804.03

than one year is presented then an opinion on the financial statements "taken as a whole" includes all years presented. Figure 8.15 shows the wording of an unqualified opinion for comparative financial statements.

Figure 8.15

Language of an Unqualified Opinion for Comparative Financial Statements [21]

Report of the Independent Auditor

We have audited the accompanying balance sheets of ABC Company as of December 31, 20X1 and 20X2, and the related statements of income, retained earnings, and cash flows for the years then ended. These financial statements are the responsibility of the company's management. Our responsibility is to express an opinion on these financial statements based on our audit.

We conducted our audits in accordance with auditing standards generally accepted in the United States of America. Those standards require that we plan and perform the audit to obtain reasonable assurance about whether the financial statements are free of material misstatement. An audit includes examining, on a test basis, evidence supporting the amounts and disclosures in the financial statements. An audit also includes assessing the accounting principles used and significant estimates made by management, as well as evaluating the overall financial statement presentation. We believe that our audit provides a reasonable basis for our opinion.

In our opinion, the financial statements referred to above present fairly, in all material respects, the financial position of ABC Company as of December 31, 20X1 and 20X2, and the results of its operations and its cash flows for the year then ended in conformity with accounting principles generally accepted in the United States of America.

Mead & Co. LLP
March 17, 20X3

Because more than one year's financial statements are presented in comparative statements, it is possible to render different opinions for the different years presented. For example, if years ended December 31, 20X1 and 20X2 are presented, an unqualified opinion could be rendered on the year 20X1 and a qualified opinion on year 20X2 financial statements.

If comparative financial statements are presented and same auditor audited all the financial statements, the auditor should update the report on the financial statements for all prior years. Updating the report involves considering information that comes to the auditor's attention during the current year's audit, but that is related to any prior year's statements presented.

---

[21] SAS No. 58, Reports on Audited Financial Statements (AICPA, Professional Standards, AU sec. 508.08).

If an auditor has previously expressed a qualified or adverse opinion on the financial statements of a prior period because of a departure from GAAP, the prior-period financial statements should be restated in the current period to conform with GAAP. The auditor's updated report on the prior-period financial statements should express an unqualified opinion concerning the restated financial statements.

If the prior year's financial statements in the comparative financial statements were unaudited with the current year's audited financial statements, the prior year's statements should be clearly marked to indicate their status, and the report on the prior period should be reissued to accompany the current period report. Alternatively, the report on the current period should include as a separate paragraph a description of the responsibility assumed for the prior period's financial statements.

.04 Auditing Financial Statements for Use in Another Country

When financial statements of an international publicly held company are prepared for use in the United States, GAAP of the United States should be used. However, if the financial statements are prepared for use in another country using that country's auditing standards and accounting principles, the auditor should use the auditing standards of both the United States and the other country, with the former standards modified to accommodate the different accounting standards. For financial statements to be used both inside and outside the United States, the auditor may report on dual sets of statements for the client; one prepared in conformity with GAAP, and the other in conformity with the U.S. accounting standards of the other country. Figure 8.16 gives an example of the language employed for an unqualifed opinion.

Figure 8.16 ─────────────────────────

Phrasing of an Unqualified Opinion for Financial Statements Issued in Another Country [22]

Report of the Independent Auditor

We have audited the accompanying balance sheet of KJM Company as of December 31, 20X2, and the related statements of income, retained earnings, and cash flows for the years then ended which, as described in Note X, have been prepared on the basis of accounting principles accepted in [*name of country*]. These financial statements are the responsibility of the company's management. Our responsibility is to express an opinion on these financial statements based on our audit.

We conducted our audit in accordance with generally accepted auditing standards accepted in the United States (and in [name of country]). U.S. standards require that we plan and perform the audit to obtain reasonable assurance about whether the financial statements are free of material misstatement. An audit includes examining, on a test basis, evidence supporting the amounts and disclosures in the financial statements. An audit also includes assessing the accounting principles used and significant estimates made by management, as well as evaluating the overall financial statement presentation. We believe that our audit provides a reasonable basis for our opinion.

In our opinion, the financial statements referred to above present fairly, in all material respects, the financial position of KJM Company as of [at] December 31, 20X2, and the results of its operations and its cash flows for the year then ended in conformity with generally accepted accounting principles accepted in [*name of country*].

Mead & Co. LLP
March 21, 20X3

.05 Reports on Information Accompanying the Financial Statements in Other Documents

The basic financial statements are: the balance sheet, the income statement, the statement of cash flow, and the notes to the financial statements. When the basic financial statements have been prepared using GAAP, they present fairly the financial position and results of operations. However, in some circumstances management may wish to include additional information with the basic financial statements that are not required by GAAP.

Client-submitted document. If the document that includes the additional information has been prepared by the client and the auditor was not engaged to audit the information, the auditor should read the information to determine whether there are any material inconsistencies with the financial statements. An inconsistency may require the auditor to deter-

---

[22] SAS No. 51, Reporting on Financial Statements Prepared for use in Other Countries (AICPA, Professional Standards, AU sec. 534.10).

¶ 804.05

mine whether the financial statements and/or the auditor's report need revision. If neither the financial statements nor the report need revision, the additional information needs to be revised. If the additional information is not revised the auditor should consider one of the following actions:

- Withdraw from the engagement.
- Withhold the audit report.
- Issue the audit report with an explanatory paragraph describing the inconsistency. (If basic financial statements still fairly present GAAP despite the inconsistency, they should receive an unqualified report with an explanatory paragraph.) It is possible for the auditor to subject the additional information to auditing procedures. In that case, the auditor can express an opinion if the additional information is fairly stated in all material respects in relation to the financial statements. In doing so the auditor should give a clear indication of the degree of responsibility they are taking with respect to the additional information.

Auditor-submitted document. If the auditor submits a document that contains information in addition to GAAP requirements, the auditor must give a clear-cut indication as to how much responsibility the auditor is taking for the additional information. If the auditor decides to apply auditing procedures to the additional information, the level of materiality should be the same as used with the basic financial statements. Once the information has been subjected to auditing procedures and found to be consistent with the basic financial statements, the auditor can either issue a separate report on the information or add an opinion paragraph to the report on the basic financial statements. Figure 8.17 shows the wording for an unqualified opinion on additional information contained in auditor-submitted documents.

¶ 804.05

Figure 8.17 ───────────────────────────

Language for Additional Information Subjected to Auditing Procedures [23]

> Our audit was conducted for the purpose of forming an opinion on the basic financial statements taken as a whole. The [specific addtional component not required by accounting principles generally accepted in the United States of America, such as schedule of operating expense by departments] is presented for purposes of additional analysis and is not a required part of the basic financial statements. Such information has been subjected to the auditing procedures applied in the audit of the basic financial statements and, in our opinion, is fairly stated in all material respects in relation to the basic financial statements taken as a whole.

If the auditor decides not to apply any audit procedures to the additional information he or she must disclaim an opinion. Figure 8.18 shows the wording for a disclaimer of opinion on additional information contained in auditor-submitted documents.

Figure 8.18 ───────────────────────────

Language for Disclaimer on All of the Additional Information [24]

> Our audit was conducted in order to form an opinion about the basic financial statements as a whole. The [specific additional component not required by accounting principles generally accepted in the United States of America, such as schedule of operating expense by departments] is presented for purposes of additional analysis and is not required to be part of the basic financial statements. This information has not been subjected to the auditing procedures applied in the audit of the basic financial statements. Accordingly, we express no opinion about it.

If the auditor applies auditing procedures to the additional information and determines that the information is materially misstated in the basic financial statements, then he or she should recommend to the client to revise the information. If the client will not revise the information, the auditor must either modify the audit report on the additional information or include the information in the document.

.06 Condensed Financial Statements

Condensed financial statements are ones that do not present enough detail to fairly present the financial position or results of operations and,

---

[23] SAS No. 29, *Reporting on Information Accompanying the Basic Financial Statements in Auditor-Submitted Documents.* (AICPA, Professional Standards, AU sec. 551.12).

[24] *Ibid.*, AU sec. 551.13.

¶ 804.06

therefore, do not present fairly GAAP. Parties relying only upon condensed financial statements may be misled by the condensed presentation. Consequently, condensed financial statements should be read in conjunction with the most recent complete financial statements. Additionally, the condensed financial statements should be marked "condensed."

If the auditor were engaged to report on condensed financial statements that had been derived from audited financial statements, the report will be altered from that of the complete set of financial statements. Figure 8.19 shows the format of the unqualified opinion on condensed financial statements as derived from a complete set of audited financial statements.

Figure 8.19

Paragraphs in an Unqualified Opinion on Condensed Financial Statements

1. Introductory Paragraph (including reference to GAAS and report of audited financial statements)

   ↓

2. Opinion Paragraph (including fairness of condensed financial statements in relation to complete financial statements)

If a publicly held company (or company that is audited annually and whose financial statements are filed with a regulatory agency) prepares a document that contains both condensed financial statements and the audited financial statements from which the condensed ones were derived, an auditor has no further reporting responsibility for the document. However, if the auditor's name appears in the document and the audited financial statements are not included, then the auditor's name must be deleted or the auditor's report must be included in the document (see Figure 8.20).

The auditor's report should state the following:

- The auditor has audited and expressed an opinion on the complete financial statements following GAAS

- The date of the auditor's report on the complete financial statements

- The type of opinion expressed

- The auditor's opinion on whether the information in the condensed financial statements is fairly stated in all material respects in relation to the complete financial statements from which the condensed ones were derived[25]

Figure 8.20

Language of an Unqualified Opinion on Condensed Financial Statements [26]

Report of the Independent Auditor

We have audited, in accordance with auditing standards generally accepted in the United States of America, the consolidated balance sheet of BBB Company as of December 31, 20X2, and the related statements of income, retained earnings, and cash flows for the year then ended (not presented herein). In our report dated March 17, 20X3, we expressed an unqualified opinion on those financial statements.

In our opinion, the information set forth in the accompanying condensed financial statements is fairly stated, in all material respects, in relation to the financial statements from which that information has been derived.

Mead & Co. LLP
March 21, 20X3

If a nonpublicly traded company prepares a document that contains both condensed financial statements and the audited financial statements from which the condensed statements were derived, the auditor has no further reporting responsibility for the document. However, if the audited financial statements are not included in the document, then the auditor should issue an adverse opinion to be included in the document.

The format of the adverse opinion is shown in Figure 8.21 and the wording is shown in Figure 8.22. The flow chart in Figure 8.23 traces the auditor's steps in reporting on the condensed versions.

---

[25] SAS No. 42, Reporting on Condensed Financial Statements and Selected Financial Data (AICPA, Professional Standards, AU sec. 552.05).

[26] *Ibid.*, AU sec. 552.06.

¶ 804.06

Figure 8.21

Paragraphs in an Adverse Opinion on Condensed Financial Statements

1. Introductory Paragraph
   ↓
2. Scope Paragraph
   ↓
3. Explanatory Paragraph
   ↓
4. Opinion Paragraph

Figure 8.22

Language of an Adverse Opinion on Condensed Financial Statements [27]

Report of the Independent Auditor

We have audited the accompanying balance sheet of ABC Company as of December 31, 20X2, and the related statements of income, retained earnings, and cash flows for the year then ended (not presented herein). These financial statements are the responsibility of the company's management. Our responsibility is to express an opinion on these financial statements based on our audit.

We conducted our audit in accordance with auditing standards generally accepted in the United States of America. Those standards require that we plan and perform the audit to obtain reasonable assurance about whether the financial statements are free of material misstatement. An audit includes examining, on a test basis, evidence supporting the amounts and disclosures in the financial statements. An audit also includes assessing the accounting principles used and significant estimates made by management, as well as evaluating the overall financial statement presentation. We believe that our audit provides a reasonable basis for our opinion.

The condensed consolidated balance sheet as of December 31, 20X2, and the related condensed statements of income, retained earnings, and cash flows for the year then ended are presented as a summary and, therefore, do not include all of the disclosures required by accounting principles generally accepted in the United States of America.

In our opinion, because of the significance of the omission of the information referred to in the preceding paragraph, the condensed consolidated financial statements referred to above do not present fairly, in conformity with accounting principles generally accepted in the United States of America, the financial position of ABC Company as of December 31, 20X2, or the results of its operations or its cash flows for the year then ended.

Mead & Co. LLP
March 21, 20X3

---

[27] *Ibid.*, AU sec. 552.07 and Footnote 6.

Figure 8.23

An Auditor's Responsibility for Condensed Financial Statements

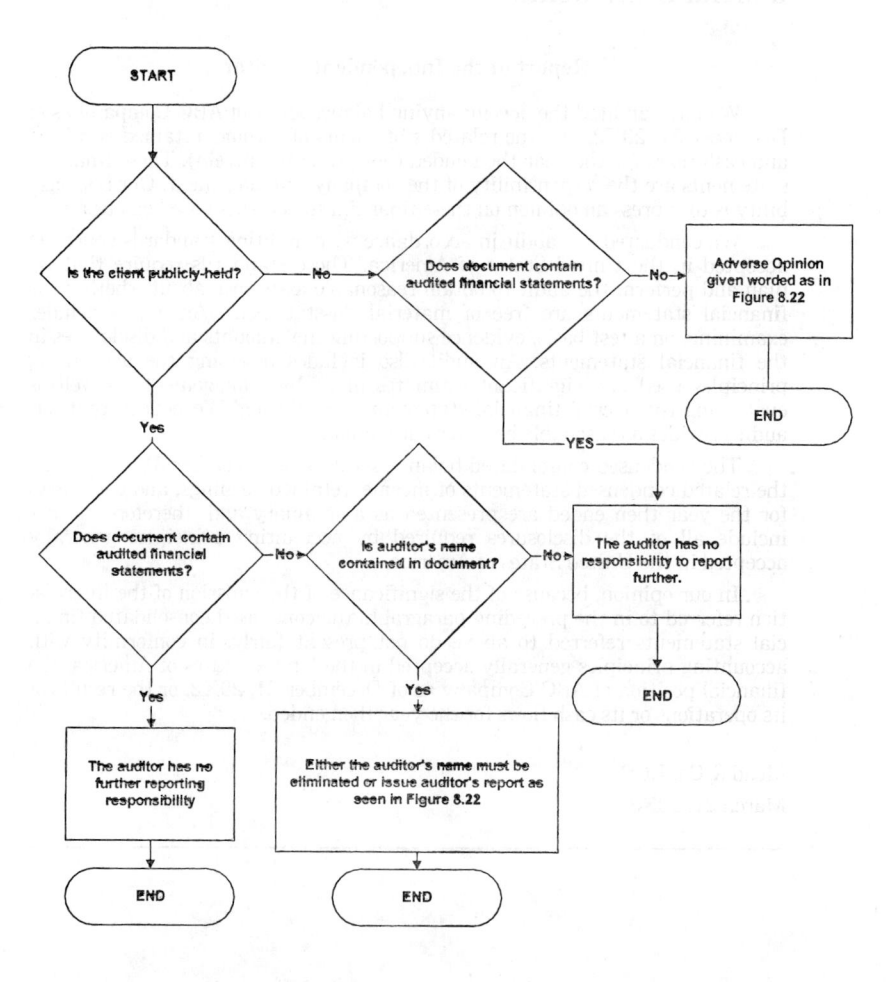

```
                          START
                            |
                            v
              Is the client publicly-held? --No--> Does document contain --No--> Adverse Opinion
                            |                     audited financial statements?    given worded as in
                           Yes                            |                            Figure 8.22
                            |                            YES                              |
                            v                             |                               v
              Does document contain --No--> Is auditor's name --No--> The auditor has no   END
              audited financial            contained in document?     responsibility to report
              statements?                        |                    further.
                    |                           Yes                         |
                   Yes                           |                          v
                    |                            v                         END
                    v                  Either the auditor's name must be
         The auditor has no            eliminated or issue auditor's report as
         further reporting              seen in Figure 8.22
         responsibility                           |
                    |                             v
                    v                            END
                   END
```

Source: Based on *Statements on Auditing Standards, No. 42 Reporting on Condensed Financial Statements and Selected Financial Data,* (AICPA, AU sec. 552), American Institute of Certified Public Accountants.

.07 Subsequent Discovery of Facts Existing at Date of Report

Auditing standards[28] require an auditor to follow certain procedures when he or she becomes aware of facts that may have existed as of the audit report date that may have affected the audit report had he or she known the facts at the time of the report issuance. The auditor must first determine if the newly-discovered facts are reliable and if they existed at the date of the audit report. The auditor should inquire of management and the board of directors about the facts. The auditor should advise the client to make appropriate disclosure of the facts and their impact upon the financial statements if:

1. It is determined that the facts are reliable and existed at the date of the audit report;
2. The audit report would have been affected if the information had been known at the date of the report; and
3. There are persons currently relying upon the financial statements who would attach importance to the information.

Disclosure will depend upon the circumstances. Prompt revision is desirable.

If the effect of the newly-discovered facts cannot be determined immediately without an investigation, the revised auditor's report and financial statements will be delayed. For example, presently Enron corporation's Board of Directors has formed a Special Committee to investigate certain related party transactions. Upon completion of the Special Committee's investigation Enron Corporation filed restated consolidated financial statements for the fiscal years ended December 31, 1997 through 2000 and for the first and second quarters of 2001.[29]

If the client refuses to cooperate, the auditor should notify each member of the board of directors of such refusal and of the fact that, in the absence of disclosure by the client, the CPA should notify each of the following that the CPA's report can no longer be relied upon:

1. The client
2. Regulatory agencies that have jurisdiction over the company
3. All persons relying on the financial statements

See Figure 8.24 to see the steps to be taken by an auditor who subsequently discovers facts that may have existed as of the audit report date that may have affected the audit report had the facts been known at the time of the report.

---

[28] SAS No. 1, Codification of Auditing Standards and Procedures (AICPA, Professional Standards, AU sec. 561.05).

[29] Enron Corporation, Quarterly Report (SEC form 10-Q), November 19, 2001.

¶ 804.07

Figure 8.24

Subsequent Discovery of Facts Existing at the Date of the CPA's Audit Report

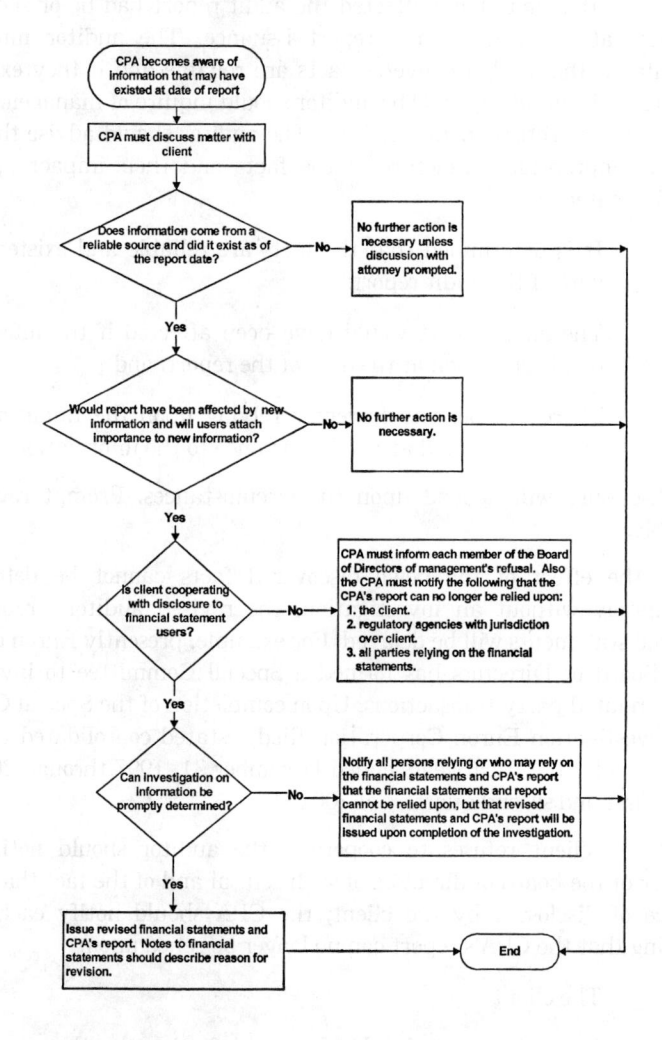

[Flowchart: CPA becomes aware of information that may have existed at date of report → CPA must discuss matter with client → Does information come from a reliable source and did it exist as of the report date? If No → No further action is necessary unless discussion with attorney prompted. If Yes → Would report have been affected by new information and will users attach importance to new information? If No → No further action is necessary. If Yes → Is client cooperating with disclosure to financial statement users? If No → CPA must inform each member of the Board of Directors of management's refusal. Also the CPA must notify the following that the CPA's report can no longer be relied upon: 1. the client. 2. regulatory agencies with jurisdiction over client. 3. all parties relying on the financial statements. If Yes → Can investigation on information be promptly determined? If No → Notify all persons relying or who may rely on the financial statements and CPA's report that the financial statements and report cannot be relied upon, but that revised financial statements and CPA's report will be issued upon completion of the investigation. If Yes → Issue revised financial statements and CPA's report. Notes to financial statements should describe reason for revision. → End]

¶ 805 Report of Independent Registered Public Accounting Firms

The Sarbanes-Oxley Act of 2002 authorized the PCAOB to issue auditing standards for registered public accounting firms. The PCAOB Release No. 2003-006, dated April 18, 2003, describes the establishment of "interim professional auditing standards" pertaining to auditing, attestation, quality control, and ethics to be used by registered public accounting firms.[30] These interim professional auditing standards were originally issued by the American Institute of Certified Public Accountants (AICPA) and were adopted by the PCAOB on a transitional basis to ensure continuity and certainty in the standards that govern audits of public companies. The PCAOB, on May 14, 2004, announced that its first auditing standard entitled "References in Auditors' Reports to the Standards of the Public Company Accounting Oversight Board" was approved by the SEC and is effective beginning May 24, 2004.

PCAOB Auditing Standard No. 1 marks the beginning of standards-setting responsibilities of the PCAOB and practically the end of standard-setting activities of the AICPA for registered public accounting firms.

PCAOB Auditing Standard No. 1 requires that:

1. A reference to generally accepted auditing standards in registered auditors' reports is no longer appropriate or necessary.

2. Registered auditors' reports on audits and other engagements relating to public companies include a reference that the audit or other engagement (review) was conducted in accordance with "the standards of the Public Company Accounting Oversight Board (United States)."

3. The title of the report states "Report of Independent Registered Public Accounting Firm."

4. The report includes the city and state, or the city and country in the case of non-U.S. auditors, from which the auditor's report has been issued.

5. The standard is effective for reports *issued* or reissued on or after May 24, 2004.

6. In circumstances where more than one auditing firm contributes to an audit of a consolidated entity, the entire audit must be performed in accordance with "the standards of the PCAOB (United States)."

Figure 8.25 presents an illustrative report on an audit of financial statements of public companies.

---

[30] PCAOB's rules on interim standards were adopted by the Board on April 16, 2003 and were approved by the SEC on April 25, 2003. SEC Release No. 33-8222. Available at *http://www.sec.gov*.

Figure 8.25 ─────────────────────────────

Report of Independent Registered Public Accounting Firm

We have audited the accompanying balance sheets of X Company as of December 31, 20X3 and 20X2, and the related statements of operations, stockholders' equity, and cash flows for each of the three years in the period ended December 31, 20X3. These financial statements are the responsibility of the Company's management. Our responsibility is to express an opinion on these financial statements based on our audits.

We conducted our audits in accordance with the standards of the Public Company Accounting Oversight Board (United States). Those standards require that we plan and perform the audit to obtain reasonable assurance about whether the financial statements are free of material misstatement. An audit includes examining, on a test basis, evidence supporting the amounts and disclosures in the financial statements. An audit also includes assessing the accounting principles used and significant estimates made by management, as well as evaluating the overall financial statement presentation. We believe that our audits provide a reasonable basis for our opinion.

In our opinion, the financial statements referred to above present fairly, in all material respects, the financial position of the Company as of [at] December 31, 20X3 and 20X2, and the results of its operations and its cash flows for each of the three years in the period ended December 31, 20X3, in conformity with U.S. generally accepted accounting principles.

[Signature]

[City and State or Country]

[Date]

───────────

Source: PCAOB Auditing Standard No. 1, References in Auditors' Reports to the Standards of the Public Company Accounting Oversight Board (PCAOB Bylaws and Rules, June 18, 2004), p. 126. Available at *http://www.pcaobus.org*.

¶ 806   Summary

An auditor follows established auditing standards (GAAS or PCAOB) to gather evidence to support his or her opinion that financial statements do or do not conform to generally accepted accounting principles. Auditing is a systematic process that is purposeful and structured and involves gathering and evaluating data on a sample basis, which is representative of the entire population. During this process, the focus of the auditor is on the fair presentation rather than the accuracy of financial statements.

Pursuant to the passage of the Sarbanes-Oxley Act of 2002, SEC implementation rules, and PCAOB auditing standards, registered auditors issue either two separate reports or a combined report on (1) annual financial statements of public companies and (2) internal control over financial reporting. The conclusion of an audit is the expression of an opinion in the audit report regarding the financial statements' adherence to GAAP. In the audit report, the auditor can communicate other matters about which financial statement users should also be aware. Depending on the circumstances, auditors can issue one of four opinions: unqualified opinion, qualified opinion, adverse opinion, and disclaimer of opinion. In addition, audit reports can be modified and expanded upon with explanatory paragraphs. By expressing an opinion on the financial statements, auditors lend credibility to financial statements by reducing the information risk for users of financial information.

Chapter 9

Reviews and Compilations

¶ 901	Introduction
¶ 902	Compilations, Reviews, and Audits
¶ 903	Compilations
¶ 904	Special Compilation Circumstances
¶ 905	Reviews
¶ 906	Additional Review Issues
¶ 907	Review Report According to PCAOB Standards
¶ 908	Summary

¶ 901 Introduction

The 1971 case of *1136 Tenants Corp. v. Max Rothenberg & Co.* had profound implications for CPAs. In this case the certified public accountant was found guilty for failing to uncover fraud with respect to the unaudited financial statements of a nonpublic company. The CPA claimed that the $600 per year engagement represented only "write-up" work (the preparation of financial statements only), which was based on information furnished by management. The CPA had even marked the financial statements as "unaudited," but the court found that because some auditing procedures had been performed, the CPA was guilty of performing a negligent audit.

Based on the increased risk attached to preparing "unaudited" financial statements, the American Institute of Certified Public Accountants (AICPA) decided to clarify and standardize procedures for unaudited financial statements. The Accounting and Review Services Committee of AICPA was formed to set forth guidelines for the preparation of unaudited financial statements for nonpublic companies.

The first pronouncement of the Accounting and Review Services Committee was issued in 1978. Statement on Standards for Accounting and Review Services No. 1 (SSARS 1) established the terms and standards for "compilations" and "reviews." These services are provided by CPAs for nonpublic company financial statements.

As a result of the standardization of the services CPAs provide for nonpublic company financial statements, the CPA's level of assurance regarding these financial statements has been clarified.

Since SSARS 1 was issued there have been seven more pronouncements regarding reviews and compilations as listed in Table 9.1.

Table 9.1

AICPA Statements on Standards for Accounting and Review Services

SSARS Number, Year and Title of Release

1 (1978)	Compilation and Review of Financial Statements
2 (1979)	Reporting on Comparative Financial Statements
3 (1981)	Compilation Reports on Financial Statements Included in Certain Prescribed Forms
4 (1981)	Communications Between Predecessor and Successor Accountants
5 (1982)	Reporting on Compiled Financial Statements
6 (1986)	Reporting on Personal Financial Statements Included in Written Personal Financial Plans
7 (1992)	Omnibus Statement on Standards for Accounting and Review Services — 1992
8 (2000)	Amendment to SSARS 1

The standards established by the Accounting and Review Services Committee apply only when CPAs provide services to nonpublic companies. CPA services offered for publicly-held company financial statements are governed by pronouncements of the Securities and Exchange Commission (SEC) and the Auditing Standards Board, which are codified in the Statements on Auditing Standards. SSARS No. 1 defines a nonpublic company as any entity other than one that meets either of these criteria:

- A company whose securities trade in a foreign or domestic public market, such as a stock exchange or over-the-counter market.
- A company that must file with a regulatory agency in preparation for the sale of any class of its securities in a public market.[1]

---

[1] Statement on Standards for Accounting and Review Services (SSARs) No. 1, *Compilations and Review of Financial Statements* (AICPA, Professional Standards, vol. 2, AR sec. 100.04).

Chapter 9 objectives:

- To clarify the CPA's level of assurance regarding unaudited financial statements (see ¶ 901–902).
- To understand when standards for compilation and review engagements should be applied (see ¶ 901–902).
- To become familiar with compilation procedures (see ¶ 903).
- To explain the purpose and content of each of the two paragraphs in a standard compilation report (see ¶ 903).
- To list the circumstances that might cause an auditor to modify his or her compilation report (see ¶ 904).
- To recognize the required procedures for a review engagement (see ¶ 905).
- To become familiar with the format of a review report and any possible modifications (see ¶ 905).
- To describe possible variations that might arise when reporting on comparative financial statements (see ¶ 906).
- To understand new adjustments to the review report as required by the PCAOB (see ¶ 907).

¶ 902 Compilations, Reviews, and Audits

.01 CPA Responsibility for Financial Statements Submitted

As shown in Figure 9.1 the CPA can accept different levels of responsibility with respect to nonpublic financial statements. The least responsibility the CPA takes for financial statements is that of the compilation. No procedures other than those delineated in ¶ 903 are performed on the compiled financial statements; therefore, the CPA accepts no responsibility for the statements.

Figure 9.1

A CPA's Responsibility for Financial Statements (Nonpublic Companies Only)

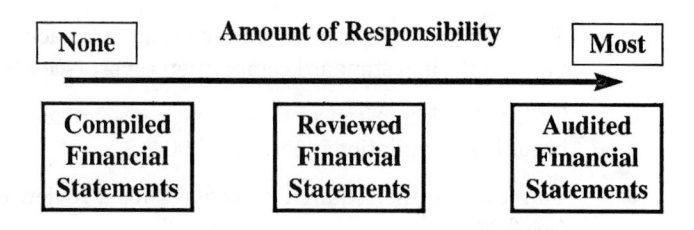

```
   None        Amount of Responsibility        Most
                ─────────────────────────▶

  Compiled            Reviewed              Audited
  Financial           Financial             Financial
  Statements          Statements            Statements
```

The next level of responsibility the CPA accepts on nonpublic companies' financial statements is that of a review. He or she uses some limited verification methodology for an SSARS review. Based upon the limited procedures employed by the CPAs they cannot state that, in their opinion, the financial statements present fairly generally accepted accounting principles (GAAP). That statement is too strong an opinion based on their limited procedures. The form of the review report is a weaker assurance—a negative assurance. The form of the review report is one whereby the CPA states that based upon these limited procedures, nothing came to his or her attention that indicates that the financial statements need modification in order for them to be in conformity with GAAP.

On August 1, 2002 the AICPA Accounting and Review Services Committee issued an Exposure Draft for a Proposed Statement on Standards for Accounting and Review Services. One of the issues addressed in the Exposure Draft is the wording of a disclaimer of opinion when a CPA is associated with the financial statements of a non-public company but has not performed any services with respect to the financial statements. Wording for the disclaimer should be as follows:

> The accompanying balance sheet of Mandig Incorporated as of June 30, 20X3, the related statements of income, and cash flows for the year then ended were not audited, reviewed, or compiled by us and, accordingly, we do not express an opinion or any other form of assurance on them.

.02 Financial Statement Submissions

Standards for compilation and review engagements apply when practitioners "submit" unaudited financial statements of nonpublic companies or are engaged to report on compiled financial statements.[2] The submission may only involve one of the financial statements such as the balance sheet or a complete set of financial statements.

According to the AICPA standards a "submission" is defined as a presentation to a client, or others, of financial statements that the practitioner has prepared either manually or through use of computer software.[3] If the service provided by the CPA is not considered a "submission of financial statements," the CPA need not comply with standards for a compilation or review engagement. The following are not considered "submissions of financial statements":

- The presentation of selected account balances
- The preparation or proposal of journal entries by the CPA
- Providing the client with a financial statement format without dollar amounts
- A "pro-forma" that the client can use to prepare financial statements
- Merely reading client-prepared financial statements
- Proposing correcting journal entries or disclosures

For example, if a client were to request that the CPA provide a presentation of cash and account receivable balances, the CPA would not be required to issue a compilation report. Presentations of elements, accounts, or items of a financial statement are exempt from SSARS applicability because presentations of these do not meet the criteria as financial statements.

.03 A Trial Balance vs. Financial Statements

Sometimes trial balances may, in substance, be a financial statement. If that is the case a CPA submitting such types of trial balances must conform to SSARS guidelines. Unlike financial statements, trial balances are not covered by standards for compilation and review engagements. The distinction, however, between a financial statement and a trial balance may not be obvious, regardless of how the financial presentation is labeled. As a result, some presentations labeled trial balances are, in substance, financial statements.

Attributes that would be considered in determining whether a financial presentation is more likely a financial statement or a trial balance are as follows:

1. Financial statements indicate subtotals of groups of accounts, typically in a balance sheet equation or profit format.

---

[2] *Ibid.*, AR sec. 100.06.   [3] *Ibid.*, AR sec. 100.04.

2. Financial statements net contra accounts against the related primary account, for instance: "Equipment, net of accumulated depreciation."

3. Trial balances list all of the general ledger accounts along with their corresponding debit and credit balance.

4. Financial statements have titles that identify their type of presentation. Examples are:

   a. Balance sheet
   b. Income statement
   c. Statement of cash flows
   d. Statement of revenue and expenses

The standards indicate that a "preponderance" of these attributes should be used in determining whether a labeled trial balance is actually a financial statement.[4]

.04 Other Comprehensive Basis of Accounting Other than GAAP (OCBOA)

The purpose of financial statements is to communicate financial information such as available business resources, obligations, and results of operations. GAAP require that financial statements be expressed by using the accrual basis of accounting. Those financial statements, along with the accompanying notes, constitute what are referred to as the balance sheet, income statement, statement of cash flows, and statement of retained earnings. Although other titles have been given to these statements (i.e., statement of financial position for the balance sheet and statement of revenues and expenses for the income statement), the above titles are reserved exclusively for financial statements using GAAP.

However, in some situations, rather then using GAAP, financial statements are prepared in accordance with other comprehensive basis of accounting (OCBOA). OCBOA financial statements can be compiled or reviewed. In instances of compilations and reviews, SSARS standards would apply.

A non-GAAP financial report uses another basis, such as:

- Cash basis, whereby revenues are recognized when cash is received and expenses are recognized when cash is paid

- Federal income tax basis, whereby the financial statements are prepared using the same methodology as the company's income tax returns

---

[4] Interpretation No. 15, "Differentiating a Financial Statement Presentation from a Trial Balance," of SSARs No.1, *Compilation and Review of Financial Statements* (AICPA, Professional Standard, vol. 2, AR sec. 9100.56-57).

¶ 902.04

- Regulatory basis, whereby the financial statements are prepared using the same basis that the company uses to comply with the regulatory requirements of a government agency within whose jurisdiction the company comes.[5]

A fourth basis is also described by auditing standards and represents a broad conceptual category whereby the criteria of the basis:

- Are definite and afford a consistent estimation or measurement by other competent financial statement preparers.

- Have substantial support, such as recognition by the AICPA's AcSEC or the Accounting Principles Board, whereas industry or trade publications on accounting are not generally recognized as being considered substantial support.

- Are applied to all material items appearing in financial statements. Limited application of the basis to supplementary information to the financial statements would not meet this requirement.

Financial statements prepared using the price-level basis of accounting meet these three criteria and would be considered as OCBOA financial statements.

Financial statements are prepared using an OCBOA basis for various reasons:

- OCBOA financial statements can be less complex and less costly to prepare because:
  - Some OCBOA financial statements employing the cash basis contain fewer accounts and line categories, such as accounts receivables and payables. In addition, if the cash basis is used a cash flow statement is unnecessary.
  - Some OCBOA financial statement information has been prepared, such as for companies that file to regulatory agencies.
  - The income tax returns may have already been prepared; therefore, financial statements prepared using the income tax basis would be easier to complete.

- OCBOA financial statement measurements may be more understandable to the financial statement user. For instance, a client may be more familiar with transaction measurements using income tax return methodology than GAAP.

---

[5] Statements on Auditing Standards (SAS) No. 62, Special Reports (AICPA, Professional Standards, vol. 1, AU sec. 623.04).

¶ 902.04

Titles of OCBOA financial statements cannot use GAAP terms such as balance sheet or income statement but must be descriptive in nature, such as "statement of assets and liabilities—income tax basis" or "statement of assets and liabilities arising from cash transactions." Notes to the financial statements should contain all informative disclosures that are appropriate for the accounting basis used. A summary of significant accounting policies should include a description of the OCBOA basis and how it differs from GAAP.

.05 **Subsequent Discovery of Facts Existing at the Date of the CPA's Compilation or Review Report**

Subsequent to the report date the CPA usually has no additional responsibility with respect to the issued financial statements. However, after the report date information could become known to the CPA that may have existed on the report date and that causes the financial statements to be incorrect. If the information is from a reliable source and would have affected the CPA report if the information were not reflected in the financial statements, SSARS standards suggest that the CPA may:

- Consider consulting with an attorney
- Apply procedures followed when financial statements are being audited, adapted for compilations and reviews[6]

Those auditing standards, adapted for compilations and reviews, recommend that the CPA follow these steps (see Figure 9.2):

1. Discuss the information with the client.
2. Determine whether the information is both reliable and existed at the date of the auditor's report.
3. Determine whether the information would have affected the report if it were known and had not been reflected in the financial statements.
4. Determine whether persons are relying or likely to rely on the financial statements who would attach importance to the information.
5. Advise the client to make appropriate disclosure of the newly discovered facts and their impact on the financial statements.
6. Assuming that the effect can be promptly determined, issue revised financial statements and auditor's report, disclosing the reasons for the changes to the CPA's report, and requesting that the client disclose the matter in the notes to the financial

---

[6] SAS No. 1, Codification of Auditing Standards and Procedures (AICPA, Professional Standards, vol. 1, AU sec. 561).

statements by describing the nature of the subsequently acquired information and of its effect on the financial statements.

7. Assuming that the effects on the financial statements cannot be determined without prolonged investigation, request that the client notify all persons relying on the financial statements and the related report that the statements and report should no longer be relied upon and that revised financial statements and CPA's report will be issued upon completion of an investigation.

If the client refuses to cooperate, the certified public accountant should notify each member of the board of directors of such refusal and of the fact that, in the absence of disclosure by the client, the CPA should notify each of the following that the CPA's report can no longer be relied upon:

- The client
- Regulatory agencies that have jurisdiction over the company
- All persons relying on the financial statements

Figure 9.2

Subsequent Discovery of Facts Existing at the Date of the CPA's Compilation or Review Report

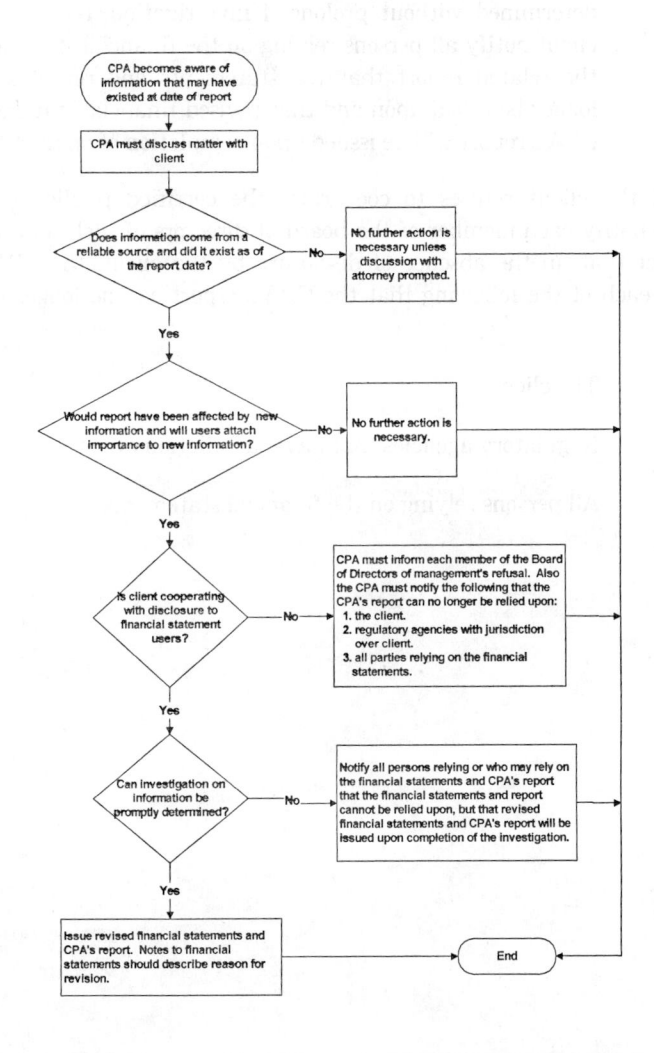

```
               CPA becomes aware of
               information that may have
               existed at date of report
                         │
                         ▼
               CPA must discuss matter with
                        client
                         │
                         ▼
            ╱ Does information come from a ╲          ┌─────────────────────────┐
           ╱  reliable source and did it    ╲──No───▶│ No further action is     │
           ╲  exist as of the report date?  ╱         │ necessary unless         │──┐
            ╲                              ╱          │ discussion with attorney │  │
                         │                            │ prompted.                │  │
                        Yes                           └─────────────────────────┘  │
                         ▼                                                          │
            ╱ Would report have been      ╲           ┌─────────────────────────┐  │
           ╱  affected by new information  ╲──No───▶│ No further action is     │──┤
           ╲  and will users attach         ╱         │ necessary.               │  │
            ╲ importance to new info?      ╱          └─────────────────────────┘  │
                         │                                                          │
                        Yes                                                         │
                         ▼                            ┌─────────────────────────┐  │
            ╱                              ╲          │ CPA must inform each    │  │
           ╱  Is client cooperating with    ╲         │ member of the Board of  │  │
           ╲  disclosure to financial        ╱──No──▶│ Directors of management's│  │
            ╲ statement users?              ╱         │ refusal. Also the CPA   │  │
                         │                            │ must notify the         │  │
                        Yes                           │ following that the CPA's│  │
                         ▼                            │ report can no longer be │  │
                                                      │ relied upon:            │  │
                                                      │ 1. the client.          │  │
                                                      │ 2. regulatory agencies  │  │
                                                      │    with jurisdiction    │  │
                                                      │    over client.         │  │
                                                      │ 3. all parties relying  │  │
                                                      │    on the financial     │  │
                                                      │    statements.          │  │
                                                      └─────────────────────────┘  │
                                                                                    │
            ╱                              ╲          ┌─────────────────────────┐  │
           ╱  Can investigation on          ╲         │ Notify all persons      │  │
           ╲  information be promptly        ╱──No──▶│ relying or who may rely │  │
            ╲ determined?                   ╱         │ on the financial        │  │
                         │                            │ statements and CPA's    │  │
                        Yes                           │ report that the         │  │
                         ▼                            │ financial statements    │  │
          ┌────────────────────────────┐              │ and report cannot be    │  │
          │ Issue revised financial    │              │ relied upon, but that   │  │
          │ statements and CPA's       │              │ revised financial       │  │
          │ report. Notes to financial │              │ statements and CPA's    │  │
          │ statements should describe │              │ report will be issued   │  │
          │ reason for revision.       │              │ upon completion of the  │  │
          └────────────────────────────┘              │ investigation.          │  │
                         │                            └─────────────────────────┘  │
                         └──────────────────▶(  End  )◀─────────────────────────────┘
```

¶ 903 Compilations

.01 Developing an Understanding with the Client

Because misunderstandings can occur it is important that the CPA and the client agree as to what services the CPA will provide. Although there is no requirement that the understanding be in writing, it is a good business practice to set the agreement as such. An engagement letter serves this purpose. It represents the details of formal agreement between the CPA and client. The engagement letter should identify such matters as:

- The nature of the services the CPA will provide and type of report expected
- Timing of the engagement
- A statement that the service cannot be relied upon to discover:
  - Errors in the financial statements
  - Fraud
  - Illegal acts of management
- That the CPA will disclose to the appropriate level of management if errors, fraud, or illegal acts are discovered
- Fees

Two copies of the engagement letter should be signed by the CPA as well as the client in the same manner as a contract. Each party should retain one file copy.

Figure 9.3 is an example of a Compilation Engagement Letter.

¶ 903.01

Figure 9.3

Engagement Letter—Compilation

To the Appropriate Addressee:

This letter is to confirm our understanding with you regarding the terms and objectives of our compilation engagement as well as the nature and limitations of the service we will provide to Doors and More Incorporated.

As agreed we will compile the company's financial statements for the year ended March 31, 20X3. The management of Doors and More Incorporated is responsible for the fair presentation of the financial statements. Our responsibility is to complete a compilation of Doors and More Incorporated's financial statements in accordance with the Statements on Standards established by the American Institute of Certified Public Accountants.

A compilation is limited to presenting, in the form of financial statements, information that is the representation of management. We will not audit or review the financial statements and, accordingly, will not express an opinion or any other form of assurance on them. However if we become aware of any errors, fraud, or illegal acts in the course of our engagement, we will bring it to the attention of appropriate Doors and More Incorporated management.

Our fees are based on the amount of time required for the services. In addition to the fees, you will be charged for all costs associated with the services rendered. We will notify you immediately of any circumstances we encounter which could significantly affect our initial estimate of total fees as follows:

Compilation of the financial statements of Doors and More
Inc. for the year ended March 31, 20X3 $2,800

If the foregoing correctly sets forth your understanding of the terms of our engagement, please so indicate by dating, signing, and returning the duplicate copy of this letter.

We appreciate this opportunity to serve you.

Perkins & Snyder P.C.
April 20, 20X3

Accepted: _____
by: Richard Farina, CEO

.02 Compilation Procedures

When management submits financial statements to third parties for their use, inherent in the statements are certain assertions that the statements present fairly the financial position and results of operations. A *compilation* is the process whereby the CPA takes management's financial data and prepares the financial statements. In other words, the CPA arranges the financial data into the form of financial statements. However, the financial statements are still considered the representation of management. The CPA does not perform any auditing procedures on the financial data and expresses no assurance about the financial statements.

When compiling financial statements using SSARS, the CPA must adhere to the following requirements. The CPA must:

- Have an understanding of GAAP applicable in the industry for which the company operates. This knowledge can be gleaned from AICPA Industry Guides, periodicals, formal education courses, and other individuals with industry experience.

- Understand the:
    - Company's operations
    - Company's record-keeping system
    - Company's accounting personnel qualifications
    - Accounting principles and practices to be used in the preparation of the financial statements

- Read the financial statements for obvious misstatements. Under normal circumstances the CPA is not required to extend the procedures beyond those listed here. However, in some instances the CPA may be required to inquire about matters contained in the financial statements.[7]

Inquiry is a process whereby the CPA communicates with the client's personnel about information important to the financial statements. Inquiry is a means of gathering evidence and is, therefore, necessary for the CPA rendering review and audit opinions. Because no opinion or any other form of assurance is expressed with a compilation report, inquiry is not required.

However, if, by reading the financial statements, the CPA notes an inconsistency or potential error in the financial statements, he or she should inquire about it.[8] If management's explanations are insufficient or if management refuses to provide explanations, the CPA should withdraw from the engagement.

.03 The Compilation Representation Letter

A representation letter is a letter from the client to the CPA that documents the verbal representations made by the client during the engagement. The letter serves as a reminder to management of their primary responsibility for the fair presentation of the financial statements. Although the client representation letter is required for SSARS reviews, they are not required for compilations.

Representation letters *may* be requested by the CPA because they confirm oral representations made to the CPA and reduce the possibility of misunderstanding about matters appearing in the financial statements. Management's refusal to provide a representation letter to the CPA consti-

---

[7] SSARs No. 1, *Compilations and Review of Financial Statements,* (AICPA, Professional Standards, vol. 2, AR sec. 100.10).

[8] *Ibid.,* AR sec. 100.09.

tutes a serious limitation to the CPA's compilation services and may be grounds for the CPA to disassociate him or herself from the client.

.04 The Form of the Compilation Report

The form of the standard compilation report comprises two paragraphs. The first identifies which financial statements have been compiled, for what company, for what time period, or for what time. Also stated in the first paragraph is that the compilation is in accordance with Statements on Standards for Accounting and Review Services issued by the American Institute of Certified Public Accounting.

The second paragraph, states that the financial statements are the representation of management and that the CPA has not audited or reviewed the statements and gives no assurance about them. Figure 9.4 below shows the two paragraphs of the compilation report.

Figure 9.4

Paragraphs in a Compilation Report

1. Introductory Paragraph

↓

2. Disclaimer of Opinion Paragraph

The contents of the introductory paragraph of the standard compilation report describe which financial statements were compiled, for what company, and for what time frame (for the income statement, retained earnings, and cash flows) or point in time (for the balance sheet.)

Contents of an introductory paragraph in a compilation report are as follows:

1. Financial statements compiled are identified:
   a. For what organization
   b. For which timeframe or point in time
2. Standards of the AICPA were used

Auditing standards require that the auditor's report include a reference to the country of origin for the accounting principles used in the financial statements. There is no such requirement for compiled financial statements; however, if it is appropriate to make such reference, then the CPA should do so.

The second paragraph detailing a compilation description and assurance disclaimer follows the introductory paragraph.

¶ 903.04

Reviews and Compilations 335

Contents of a description and disclaimer paragraph in a compilation report are as follows:

1. A compilation of financial statements:

   a. Is the representation of management

   b. Does not represent an audit or a review

2. The CPA does not render any assurance on the prospective financial statements.

Although it is common practice for the compilation report to be signed, either manually or electronically, it is not required by compilation standards. A standard to require a signature has been proposed in an exposure draft for revision to the Statement on Standards for Accounting and Review Services.

The date shown on the compilation report is the date on which the CPA completed the compilation. Also, each page of the financial statements should be marked, "See Accountant's Compilation Report."

Figure 9.5 shows the wording for a standard compilation report.

Figure 9.5

Language of a Compilation Report [9]

To the Appropriate Addressee:

We have compiled the accompanying balance sheet of Tosne Company as of December 31, 20X2, and the related statements of income, retained earnings, and cash flows for the year then ended, in accordance with Statements on Standards for Accounting and Review Services issued by the American Institute of Certified Public Accountants.

A compilation is limited to presenting in the form of financial statements information that is the representation of management. We have not audited or reviewed the accompanying financial statements and, accordingly, do not express an opinion or any other form of assurance on them.

Mead & Co. LLP
March 13, 20X3

If a Statement of Comprehensive Income is provided, the report should include it also in the introductory paragraph.

If the submitted financial statements are not expected to be used by third parties, the CPA could either issue the above-worded compilation report or document the understanding with the client through the engagement letter process, preferably signed by management and include that:[10]

---

[9] *Ibid.*, AR secs. 100.14 and 100.17. [10] *Ibid.*, AR sec. 100.21.

¶ 903.04

1. The financial statements are not intended for third party use
2. The nature and limitation of the services to be performed
3. The financial statements are the representation of management
4. The financial statements have not been audited or reviewed
5. No form of assurance will be provided on the financial statements
6. Management has knowledge of the accounting procedures applied as well as assumptions and estimates used in the preparation of the financial statements
7. The engagement cannot be relied upon to disclose errors, fraud or illegal acts

Additionally each page of the financial statements should be marked "Restricted for management's use only" or "Solely for the information and use by management of [name of entity] and not intended to be and should not be used by any other party."

A standard compilation report can also be issued for financial statements prepared using another basis of accounting other than generally accepted accounting principles. The standard report for OCBOA financial statements is structured as follows:

1. Introductory paragraph—financial statement titles modified for OCBOA basis
2. Disclaimer of opinion paragraph

The language of a standard compilation report for financial statements prepared using the cash basis of accounting is detailed in Figure 9.6.

¶ 903.04

Figure 9.6

Language of a Compilation Report for OCBOA Financial Statements (Cash Basis) [11]

To the Appropriate Addressee:

    We have compiled the accompanying statement of assets and liabilities arising from cash transactions of Hyggely Company as of December 31, 20X2, and the related statements of revenue collected and expenses paid for the year then ended, in accordance with Statements on Standards for Accounting and Review Services issued by the American Institute of Certified Public Accountants.

    A compilation is limited to presenting in the form of financial statements information that is the representation of management. We have not audited or reviewed the accompanying financial statements and, accordingly, do not express an opinion or any other form of assurance on them.

Mead & Co. LLP
March 13, 20X3

¶ 904 Special Compilation Circumstances

Normally, the standard compilation report is issued. However, circumstances arise that may require modifications or additions to the standard compilation report.

.01 Compilation with a Departure from GAAP or OCBOA

Departures from GAAP could mislead a financial statement user. Whenever CPAs become aware of such a departure, even in a document containing financial statements they did not compile, the CPAs should disassociate themselves from the document. However, when a CPA is compiling financial statements and becomes aware of a material departure, a financial statement adjustment and/or CPA disclosure is necessary.

Understanding the client's industry and record-keeping methodology enables the CPA to take a "common sense" look at the financial statements. In doing so, while reading the financial statements, or in another manner, the CPA may become aware of possible misstatements contained in the financial statements. The CPA first should obtain additional information about the matter to determine whether there is a departure from GAAP. An example of obtaining additional information is through inquiry of management. If it is determined that the financial statements contain a departure from GAAP, but are adjusted to correct the departure, the CPA can issue a standard compilation report.

---

[11] Interpretation No. 12, "Reporting on a Comprehensive Basis of Accounting other than Generally Accepted Accounting Principles," of SSARs No.1, *Compilation and Review of Financial Statements* (AICPA, Professional Standards, vol. 2, AR sec. 9100.45).

On the other hand, if the financial statements are not adjusted for the departure, the accountant is required to disclose the dollar effect of the GAAP departure on the financial statements. The dollar effect can be obtained from managers if they have determined the effect or from the results of the CPA's additional procedures. However, the accountant is not required to determine the effects of the departures if management has not done so. In those situations, the CPA is only required to add a statement to the report indicating that the effects of the departures have not been determined by management.

Figure 9.7 describes the CPA's decision-making process in reporting departures from GAAP.

¶ 904.01

Reviews and Compilations

Figure 9.7

Reporting GAAP Departures in Compiled Financial Statements

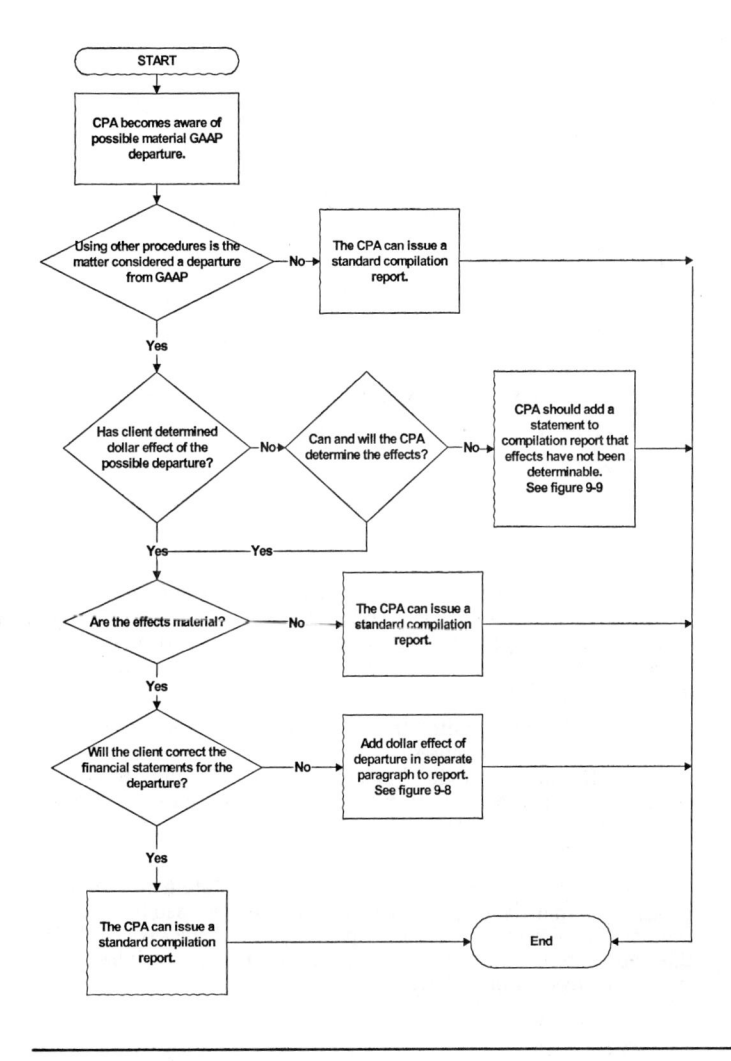

```
                    START
                      │
                      ▼
         ┌────────────────────────┐
         │ CPA becomes aware of   │
         │ possible material GAAP │
         │ departure.             │
         └────────────────────────┘
                      │
                      ▼
         ◇ Using other procedures is the ◇──No──▶ ┌─────────────────┐
           matter considered a departure          │ The CPA can issue a │
           from GAAP                              │ standard compilation│
                      │                           │ report.             │
                     Yes                          └─────────────────┘
                      ▼
         ◇ Has client determined ◇──No──▶ ◇ Can and will the CPA ◇──No──▶ ┌──────────────────────┐
           dollar effect of the            determine the effects?         │ CPA should add a     │
           possible departure?                      │                     │ statement to         │
                      │                            Yes                    │ compilation report   │
                     Yes────────────────────────────┘                     │ that effects have    │
                      ▼                                                   │ not been determinable│
         ◇ Are the effects material? ◇──No──▶ ┌─────────────────┐         │ See figure 9-9       │
                      │                       │ The CPA can issue a │     └──────────────────────┘
                     Yes                      │ standard compilation│
                      ▼                       │ report.             │
         ◇ Will the client correct the ◇──No─▶└─────────────────┘
           financial statements for the       ┌──────────────────────┐
           departure?                         │ Add dollar effect of │
                      │                       │ departure in separate│
                     Yes                      │ paragraph to report. │
                      ▼                       │ See figure 9-8       │
         ┌────────────────────────┐           └──────────────────────┘
         │ The CPA can issue a    │
         │ standard compilation   │──────────▶   End
         │ report.                │
         └────────────────────────┘
```

¶ 904.01

The format for the compilation report when there is a departure from GAAP is seen below. This format is used whether the dollar effects of the departure are known or unknown to the CPA.

Paragraphs in a compilation report with departure from GAAP are as follows:

1. Introductory paragraph
2. Modified disclaimer of opinion paragraph
3. Explanatory paragraph

Figure 9.8 is an example of a compilation report in which the effects of a departure from GAAP are not known.

Figure 9.8

Language of a Compilation Report in which Departure from GAAP and Effects of Departure Are Not Known [12]

To the Appropriate Addressee:

We have compiled the accompanying balance sheet of Snee Company as of December 31, 20X2, and the related statements of income, retained earnings, and cash flows for the year then ended, in accordance with Statements on Standards for Accounting and Review Services issued by the American Institute of Certified Public Accountants.

A compilation is limited to presenting in the form of financial statements information that is the representation of management. We have not audited or reviewed the accompanying financial statements and, accordingly, do not express an opinion or any other form of assurance on them. However, we did become aware of a departure from generally accepted accounting principles that is described in the following paragraph.

As disclosed in note 17 to the financial statements, management has informed us that the employees are entitled to a defined benefits pension plan, however, pension costs reflect a "pay-as-you-go" methodology. The effect of this departure from generally accepted accounting principles on the financial statements has not been determined.

Mead & Co. LLP
March 13, 20X3

Figure 9.9 is an example of a compilation report in which the effects of a departure from GAAP are known.

---

[12] SSARs No. 1, *Compilation and Review of Financial Statements* (AICPA, Professional Standards, vol. 2, AR sec. 100.41).

¶ 904.01

Figure 9.9

Language of a Compilation Report in which Departure from GAAP and Effects of Departure Are Known [13]

To the Appropriate Addressee:

We have compiled the accompanying balance sheet of Svinde Company as of December 31, 20X2, and the related statements of income, retained earnings, and cash flows for the year then ended, in accordance with Statements on Standards for Accounting and Review Services issued by the American Institute of Certified Public Accountants.

A compilation is limited to presenting in the form of financial statements information that is the representation of management. We have not audited or reviewed the accompanying financial statements and, accordingly, do not express an opinion or any other form of assurance on them. However, we did become aware of a departure from generally accepted accounting principles that is described in the following paragraph.

As disclosed in note 23 to the financial statements, generally accepted accounting principles require that inventory be valued at lower of cost or market. Management has informed us that inventory is valued at cost as calculated by the weighted-average method. The market value of inventory is less than cost. If generally accepted accounting principles had been followed, inventory, retained earnings, and operating income would be decreased by $38,000.

Mead & Co. LLP
March 13, 20X3

.02 Substantially All Disclosures Are Omitted

According to compilation standards,[14] a CPA can compile financial statements that omit footnote disclosures required by GAAP. This is permissible assuming that the omission is clearly disclosed in the report and there is no intent to mislead users. When footnote disclosures have been omitted, a third paragraph is added to the compilation report stating that management has elected to omit disclosures normally required by GAAP. This paragraph informs the user that if the financial statements contained that information, they might affect the user's conclusions.

Paragraphs in a compilation report when financial statements have all disclosures omitted are as follows:

1. Introductory paragraph
2. Disclaimer of opinion paragraph
3. Explanatory paragraph

---

[13] *Ibid.*, AR sec. 100.41.   [14] *Ibid.*, AR secs. 100.16 and 100.17.

An example of the compilation report whereby all of the notes to the financial statements have been excluded is shown in Figure 9.10. For compilation reports with omitted disclosures that were prepared on an OCBOA basis, the wording of the report is similar, except for the reference in the first and third paragraphs to the OCBOA basis of accounting.

Figure 9.10

Language of a Compilation Report Addressing Client-Omitted Disclosure [15]

To the Appropriate Addressee:

We have compiled the accompanying balance sheet of Rente Company as of December 31, 20X2, and the related statements of income, retained earnings, and cash flows for the year then ended, in accordance with Statements on Standards for Accounting and Review Services issued by the American Institute of Certified Public Accountants.

A compilation is limited to presenting in the form of financial statements information that is the representation of management. We have not audited or reviewed the accompanying financial statements and, accordingly, do not express an opinion or any other form of assurance on them.

Management has elected to omit substantially all of the disclosures required by generally accepted accounting principles. If the omitted disclosures were included in the financial statements, they might influence the user's conclusions about the financial position, results of operations, and cash flows. Accordingly, these financial statements are not designed for those who are not informed about such matters.

Mead & Co. LLP
March 13, 20X3

If it appears, through the omission of the notes to the financial statements, that the client's intent is to mislead users, the CPA should not comply with the request.

.03 The CPA Is Not Independent of the Client

Because the CPA is giving no assurance regarding compiled financial statements, there is no requirement for the CPA to be independent of the client whose financial statements are being compiled. In those cases where the CPA lacks independence with respect to the client, a separate paragraph should be added to the end of the compilation report stating that fact. No details as to why there is a lack of independence should be given.

Paragraphs in a compilation report with lack of CPA independence are as follows:

1. Introductory paragraph

---

[15] *Ibid.*, AR sec. 100.18.

Reviews and Compilations **343**

2. Disclaimer of opinion paragraph

3. Nonindependence paragraph

An example of the wording for a compilation report where the CPA lacks independence appears in Figure 9.11.

Figure 9.11

Language of a Compilation Report with Lack of CPA Independence [16]

To the Appropriate Addressee:

    We have compiled the accompanying balance sheet of Naese Company as of December 31, 20X2, and the related statements of income, retained earnings, and cash flows for the year then ended, in accordance with Statements on Standards for Accounting and Review Services issued by the American Institute of Certified Public Accountants.

    A compilation is limited to presenting in the form of financial statements information that is the representation of management. We have not audited or reviewed the accompanying financial statements and, accordingly, do not express an opinion or any other form of assurance on them.

    We are not independent with respect to Naese Company.

Mead & Co. LLP
March 13, 20X3

.04 Comparative Financial Statements

    When a CPA compiles financial statements for comparative purposes, the form of the report is identical to the standard compilation report except that the reference is made to the comparative years, as worded in Figure 9.12.

---

[16] *Ibid.*, AR sec. 100.19.

¶ 904.04

Figure 9.12 ─────────────────────────────

Language of a Compilation Report for Comparative Financial Statements [17]

To the Appropriate Addressee:

We have compiled the accompanying balance sheets of Naese Company as of December 31, 20X1 and 20X2, and the related statements of income, retained earnings, and cash flows for the years then ended, in accordance with Statements on Standards for Accounting and Review Services issued by the American Institute of Certified Public Accountants.

A compilation is limited to presenting in the form of financial statements information that is the representation of management. We have not audited or reviewed the accompanying financial statements and, accordingly, do not express an opinion or any other form of assurance on them.

Mead & Co. LLP

March 13, 20X3

───

However, if the financial statement disclosures for one of the comparative years has been omitted, the financial statements are not considered comparative, and no compilation report can be issued.

Additionally, the CPA must take certain precautions before client-prepared financial statements can appear with compiled financial statements for comparative purposes. As seen in Figure 9.13, before client-prepared financial statements can be shown in the same document as compiled financial statements the following must occur:

1. The compiled financial statements must appear on a separate page from those of the client-prepared financial statements. For instance, the compiled financial statement information cannot appear in columnar form next to client-prepared financial statements.

2. The report should indicate that the client-prepared financial statements have not been audited, reviewed, or compiled, and that the CPA does not assume any responsibility for them.

───

[17] SSARS No. 2, *Reporting on Comparative Statements* (AICPA, Professional Standards, vol. 2, AR sec. 200.09).

Figure 9.13

Client-Prepared Financial Statements Compared to Compiled Financial Statements [18]

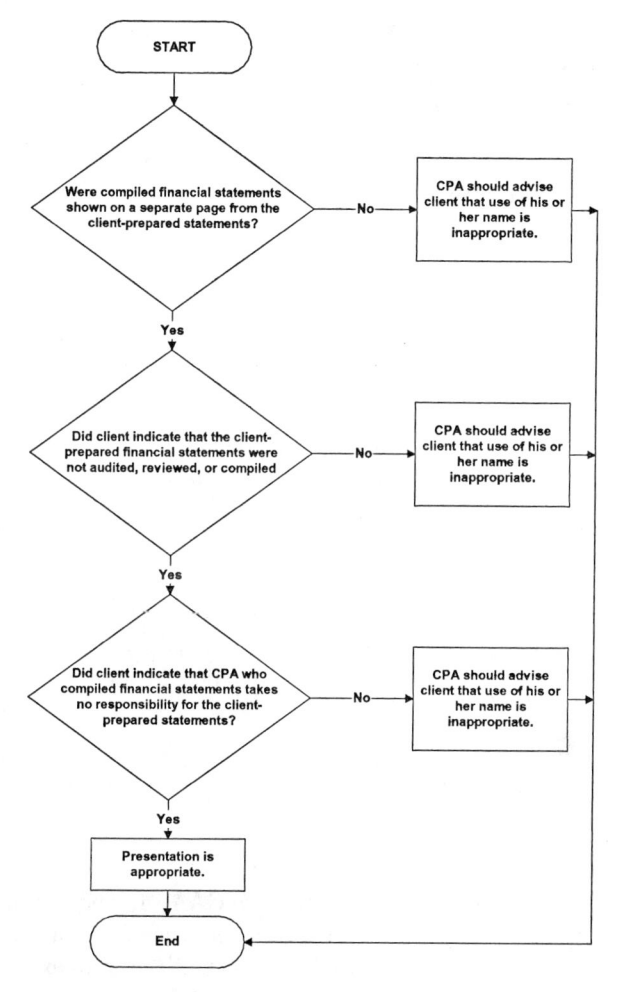

```
                        ┌─────────┐
                        │  START  │
                        └────┬────┘
                             │
                             ▼
              ╱─────────────────────────╲         ┌──────────────────┐
             ╱ Were compiled financial   ╲        │ CPA should advise│
            ╱  statements shown on a      ╲──No──▶│ client that use  │
            ╲  separate page from the     ╱       │ of his or her    │
             ╲ client-prepared statements?╱       │ name is          │
              ╲─────────────────────────╱         │ inappropriate.   │
                         │                        └────────┬─────────┘
                        Yes                                │
                         ▼                                 │
              ╱─────────────────────────╲                  │
             ╱ Did client indicate that   ╲       ┌──────────────────┐
            ╱  the client-prepared         ╲      │ CPA should advise│
            ╲  financial statements were   ╱──No─▶│ client that use  │
             ╲ not audited, reviewed,     ╱       │ of his or her    │
              ╲ or compiled               ╱       │ name is          │
               ╲─────────────────────────╱        │ inappropriate.   │
                         │                        └────────┬─────────┘
                        Yes                                │
                         ▼                                 │
              ╱─────────────────────────╲                  │
             ╱ Did client indicate that   ╲       ┌──────────────────┐
            ╱  CPA who compiled financial ╲       │ CPA should advise│
            ╱  statements takes no         ╲──No─▶│ client that use  │
            ╲  responsibility for the      ╱      │ of his or her    │
             ╲ client-prepared statements?╱       │ name is          │
              ╲─────────────────────────╱         │ inappropriate.   │
                         │                        └────────┬─────────┘
                        Yes                                │
                         ▼                                 │
                ┌─────────────────┐                        │
                │ Presentation is │                        │
                │ appropriate.    │                        │
                └────────┬────────┘                        │
                         │                                 │
                         ▼                                 │
                     ┌───────┐                             │
                     │  End  │◀────────────────────────────┘
                     └───────┘
```

When comparative financial statements are compiled and the previous year's financial statements had contained a departure from GAAP but have since been restated to conform with GAAP, the CPA should add an explanatory paragraph to the comparative compilation report.

Paragraphs in a comparative compilation report with the previous year restated to conform with GAAP are as follows:

---

[18] *Ibid.*, AR sec. 200.03.

¶ 904.04

1. Introductory paragraph
2. Disclaimer of opinion paragraph
3. Explanatory paragraph

Figure 9.14 below shows the wording for a comparative compilation report with the previous year restated.

Figure 9.14

Language of a Comparative Compilation Report with the Previous Year Restated to Conform with GAAP [19]

To the Appropriate Addressee:

We have compiled the accompanying balance sheets of Irsk Company as of December 31, 20X1 and 20X2, and the related statements of income, retained earnings, and cash flows for the years then ended, in accordance with Statements on Standards for Accounting and Review Services issued by the American Institute of Certified Public Accountants.

A compilation is limited to presenting in the form of financial statements information that is the representation of management. We have not audited or reviewed the accompanying financial statements and, accordingly, do not express an opinion or any other form of assurance on them.

In our previous compilation report dated March 7, 20X2, on the 20X1 financial statements, we referred to a departure from generally accepted accounting principles because the company did not carry its inventory at lower of cost or market. However, as disclosed in note 14, the company has restated its 20X1 financial statements to reflect its inventory in accordance with generally accepted accounting principles.

Mead & Co. LLP
March 13, 20X3

A client may engage a CPA to compile GAAP financial statements in one year because of some external requirement, such as for a bank loan. In the following year when the external requirement ceases to exist, the client may want the CPA to compile comparative cash-basis financial statements for the current and previous years. If such an engagement is performed, two different bases of accounting will be used for the same year's financial statements (GAAP and cash).

The standards do not prevent the CPA from compiling such financial statements and need not modify the compilation report for these circumstances. However, it is permissible for the CPA to add a paragraph to the compilation report indicating that another report has been issued on the entity's financial statements and that those financial statements had been

---

[19] *Ibid.*, AR sec. 200.15.

.05 Communication Between Successor and Predecessor CPAs

Although contact is not required before accepting a compilation engagement, a successor CPA may want to discuss the client's situation with the previous (predecessor) CPA who compiled the prior year's financial statements. Because of confidentiality issues, the successor CPA must obtain permission from the client to make inquiries of the predecessor CPA. Refusal by the client should be considered before the successor accepts the engagement.[20]

prepared in conformity with another basis of accounting than the stated financial statements.

If the successor is allowed to inquire of the predecessor, the following are suggested points of inquiry. Questions should address:[21]

- Integrity of management
- Disagreements the predecessor had with management
- Cooperation of management to accountant requests
- The predecessor's understanding of why there was a change in accountants

While the successor CPAs compile the financial statements they may become aware of information that affects previous financial statements reported upon by predecessor CPAs. The successor should request permission from the client to discuss the matter with the predecessor CPA. If the client refuses permission or the successor CPA is not satisfied with the predecessor's action on the matter, the successor should consult an attorney.

The August 2002 Exposure Draft for a Proposed Statement on Standards for Accounting and Review Services provides additional detail regarding communications between the predecessor accountant and successor accountant. As defined:[22]

> Successor Accountant—the accountant invited to make a proposal for an engagement to compile or review financial statements and is considering or has accepted the engagement.
>
> Predecessor Accountant—the accountant who (a) has reported on the most recent compiled or reviewed financial statements or was engaged to perform but did not complete a compilation or review of the financial statements, and (b) has resigned, declined to stand for reappointment, or been notified that his or her services have been, or may be, terminated.

According to the Exposure Draft there is still no requirement for the successor accountant to communicate with the predecessor but as stated in the current standards circumstances may warrant the successor CPA to discuss the client's situation with the predecessor CPA.

---

[20] SSARs No. 4, *Communications Between Predecessor and Successor Accounts* (AICPA, Professional Standards, vol. 2, AR sec. 400.04).

[21] *Ibid.*, AR sec. 400.05.

[22] Wording provided by the Exposure Draft of Proposed Statement on Standards for Accounting and Review Services, "Omnibus-2002" distributed August 1, 2002.

When the successor CPA communicates with the predecessor the inquiries should be specific regarding issues to assist the successor in determining to accept the engagement. Matters of fraud and illegal acts as well as the reason for the change of accountants are reasonable inquiry. Stricken from the current standards are inquiries by the successor regarding matters that would facilitate the conduct of the compilation or review services.

Unless unusual circumstances such as disciplinary proceedings or litigation prevent the predecessor CPA from responding, the predecessor should respond fully and on a timely basis including access to the prior engagement workpapers. The predecessor CPA may wish to document any understanding regarding the use of the workpapers. The Exposure Draft (Figure 9.15) provides an example of this understanding.

¶ 904.05

Figure 9.15 ───────────────────────────

Exposure Draft

[Date]

[Successor Accountant]

[Address]

We have previously [reviewed or compiled], in accordance with Statements on Standards for Accounting and Review Services the December 31, 20X1 financial statements of ABC Enterprises (ABC). In connection with your [review or compilation] of ABC's 20X2 financial statements, you have requested access to our workpapers prepared in connection with that engagement. ABC has authorized our firm to allow you to review those workpapers.

Our [review or compilation], and the workpapers prepared in connection therewith, of ABC's financial statements were not planned or conducted in contemplation of your [review or compilation]. Therefore, items of possible interest to you may not have been specifically addressed. Our use of professional judgment for the purpose of this engagement means that matters may have existed that would have been assessed differently by you. We make no representation about the sufficiency or appropriateness of the information in our workpapers for your purposes.

We understand that the purpose of your review is to obtain information about ABC and our 20X1 results to assist you in your 20X2 engagement of ABC. For that purpose only, we will provide you access to our workpapers that relate to that objective.

Upon request, we will provide copies of those workpapers that provide factual information about ABC. You agree to subject any such copies or information otherwise derived from our workpapers to your normal policy for retention of workpapers and protection of confidential client information. Furthermore, in the event of a third-party request for access to your workpapers prepared in connection with your (reviews or compilations) of ABC, you agree to obtain our permission before voluntarily allowing any such access to our workpapers or information otherwise derived from our workpapers, and to obtain on our behalf any releases that you obtain from such third party. You agree to advise us promptly and provide us a copy of any subpoena, summons, or other court order for access to your workpapers that include copies of our workpapers or information otherwise derived therefrom.

Please confirm your agreement with the foregoing by signing and dating a copy of this letter and returning it to us.

Very truly yours,

[Predecessor Accountant]

By: ──────────────

Accepted:

[Successor Accountant]

By: ────────────── Date: ──────────

¶ 904.05

.06 Supplemental Information

The basic financial statements are: the balance sheet, the income statement, and the statement of cash flow, and the notes to the financial statements. Sometimes, however, the client's managers wish to include additional information with the basic financial statements that are not required by GAAP. If a CPA submits a document that contains information in addition to GAAP requirements, he or she must give a clear-cut indication as to how much responsibility they are taking for the additional information.[23]

For compiled financial statements that include supplemental information, the CPA should also reference the supplemental information in the compilation report.

The August 2002 Exposure Draft for a Proposed Statement on Standards for Accounting and Review Services provides additional detail regarding supplemental information accompanying the basic financial statements. With respect to reporting on reviewed financial statements, an explanation regarding the additional information should be included in the review report, or a separate report on the other additional information should be presented. The report should indicate that the review has been performed for the purpose of expressing limited assurance that no financial statement revision is necessary for the financial statements to conform with generally accepted accounting principles, and either:[24]

- a. The other data accompanying the financial statements are presented only for supplementary analysis purposes and have been subjected to the inquiry and analytical procedures applied in the review of the basic financial statements, and the accountant did not become aware of any material modifications that should be made to such data, or
- b. The other data accompanying the financial statements are presented only for supplementary analysis purposes and have not been subjected to the inquiry and analytical procedures applied in the review of the basic financial statements, but were compiled from information that is the representation of management, without audit or review, and the accountant does not express an opinion or any other form of assurance on such data.

.07 Compilation Reports Included in Certain Prescribed Forms

A prescribed form is a preprinted template for companies to complete so that financial information can be gathered and used for various regulatory purposes, credit application submissions, and industry statistics.[25] Financial information included in these forms are for the use of the entity that requested it. Therefore, adequacy of the prescribed form can be assumed to be sufficient for the requesting entity.

---

[23] SSARs No. 1, *Compilation and Review of Financial Statements* (AICPA, Professional Standards, vol. 2, AR sec. 100.44).

[24] Wording provided by the Exposure Draft of Proposed Statement on Standards for Accounting and Review Services, "Omnibus-2002" distributed August 1, 2002.

[25] SSARS No. 3, *Compilation Reports on Financial Statements Included in Certain Prescribed Forms* (AICPA, Professional Standards, vol. 2, AR sec. 300.02).

When unaudited financial statement information of a nonpublic company is included in a prescribed form, the CPA should issue a modified compilation report, as shown in Figure 9.16.

Figure 9.16

Language of a Compilation Report for Certain Prescribed Forms [26]

To the Appropriate Addressee:

We have compiled the [identification of financial statements, including the period covered and name of company] included in the accompanying prescribed form in accordance with Statements on Standards for Accounting and Review Services issued by the American Institute of Certified Public Accountants.

A compilation is limited to presenting in the form prescribed by [name of requesting entity] information that is the representation of management. We have not audited or reviewed the accompanying financial statements and, accordingly, do not express an opinion or any other form of assurance on them.

These financial statements are presented in accordance with the requirements of [name of requesting entity], which differ from generally accepted accounting principles. Accordingly, these financial statements are not designed for those who are not informed about such differences.

Mead & Co. LLP
March 13, 20X3

.08 Specified Elements, Accounts, or Items of Financial Statements

As with auditing engagements, CPAs may be asked to compile specified elements, accounts, or items of financial statements (SE, A, or I). Examples of these types of items are:

- Current assets
- Schedule of accounts receivable
- Schedule of long-term notes payable
- Royalties
- Income tax expense

SSARS standards do not address compilations of these items.

.09 Graphs Accompanying Financial Statements

Graphs are used to depict quantitative trends and relationships among data in a straightforward, visual manner. Financial graphs include:

---

[26] *Ibid.*, AR sec. 300.03.

- Bar charts—comparisons of a company's gross margin over time
- Pie charts—the components of expenses
- Bar charts—comparisons of marketing costs to sales over time. Graphs such as these could be included with financial statements

Although SSARS standards are silent regarding accompanying graphs to financial statements, CPAs who compile the financial statements should treat graphs in the same manner as information accompanying the basic financial statements for supplementary analysis purposes.

.10 A Change from an Audit or Review to a Compilation

If the CPA originally was engaged to audit the financial statements or perform an SSARS review for a nonpublic company and then later was requested to compile the financial statements instead, the CPA should consider the justification for the change.[27]

If the circumstances are reasonable, the CPA could issue a compilation report. When considering the reasonableness of the request the CPA should determine the purpose of the change and how much additional work is needed to finish the audit or review. Reasonable justification for the change could be:

- A misunderstanding of the nature of the audit or review
- A change in circumstance for the client negating the need for the audit or review

The CPA must be alert to the financial statement effect as a result of the scope limitation resulting from the lesser compilation service. If the change to the compilation is the result of a client-imposed audit or review scope limitation, the CPA should consider not issuing a compilation report. For instance, if, as part of the audit or review, the CPA requested a client representation letter and the client refused to provide one and later requested the change to a compilation service, a compilation report should not be issued.

If justification for the change is reasonable, a compilation report can be issued. No reference to the change in service or the resulting scope limitation should be made in the report.

.11 Draft Financial Statements

Standards for Accounting and Review Services require that a CPA not consent to use his or her name in any document where unaudited financial statements are contained unless the CPA has indicated the amount of

---

[27] SSARs No. 1, *Compilation and Review of Financial Statements* (AICPA, Professional Standards, vol. 2, AR sec. 100.45).

¶ 904.10

responsibility that they are taking for them.[28] The CPA should either comply with the compilation and review standards and attach an appropriate report, or indicate that the unaudited financial statements were not compiled or reviewed and attach a disclaimer report to them.

However, CPAs can furnish draft financial statements to clients if the CPA performs each of the following:

- Marks the financial statements conspicuously as a "Draft," "Preliminary Draft," "Draft—Subject to Changes."

- Intends to submit those financial statements in final form accompanied by the appropriate compilation report.

If both of the above requirements are met, a CPA is not required to comply with the reporting provision of SSARS.

.12 Financial Statements Not to be Used by Third Parties

SSARS 8 amends SSARS 1 requirements for those financial statements that will be used by management only and not by third parties. In those circumstances when the CPA submits "for management use only" financial statements the following options are available to the CPA:

1. Use pre-SSARS 8 compilation standards.

2. Use SSARS 8 compilation standards whereby:

    a. No compilation report is required.

    b. Each page of the financial statement should suitably indicate that the financial statements are for management's use only.

    c. That an engagement letter be obtained that provides a representation that third parties are not expected to use the financial statements.

¶ 905 Reviews

The standards contained in the SSARS standards provide for an accounting service that offers limited assurance on nonpublic company financial statements. With an SSARS review the CPA performs inquiry and analytical procedures to provide a reasonable basis for expressing limited assurance. A limited assurance indicates that, based upon the inquiry and analytical procedures performed, nothing came to the attention of the CPA whereby material modifications needed to be made to the financial statements in order for them to be in conformity with GAAP.

---

[28] Interpretation No. 16, "Determining If the Accountant Has 'Submitted' Financial Statements Even When Not Engaged to Compile or Review Financial Statements," of SSARs No. 1, *Compilation and Review of Financial Statements* (AICPA, Professional Standards, vol. 2, AR sec. 9100.62).

A review of financial statements only provides limited assurance to the reader and, as a result, has fewer potential uses than audited statements. SSARS reviews do, however, have some definite advantages:

- The cost of a review can be substantially less than that of an audit.
- The limited assurance of reviewed statements may be all that is required by third parties and owners.
- There may be an advantage to having the CPA associated with the financial statements.

.01 Independence

Because the CPA is rendering a form of assurance when reporting on a review engagement the CPA must be independent of the client. Assurances from someone with an apparent conflict of interest are ineffective. If the CPA becomes aware that his or her independence has been impaired during a review engagement, a review report cannot be issued; instead, the engagement may be lowered to a compilation that would allow a report to be issued if the lack of independence is disclosed.

The same issues that impair CPA independence with respect to an audit client are applicable to CPAs' review services. The specific facts of any circumstance that appear to impair independence must be taken into consideration; however, the following represent situations described in AICPA's Code of Professional Conduct[29] that would typically impair CPA independence with respect to the client:

- The CPA's or CPA's spouse or CPA's dependent's ownership interest in a client.
- A CPA-client, debtor-creditor relationship. For instance, if a client still owes fees to the CPA for professional services rendered in prior years, the CPA is a creditor of the client, and is therefore not independent of the client. If the fees remain unpaid, the CPA may not issue a review report.
- The CPA's or CPA's spouse or CPA's dependent's employment by the client.
- The CPA provides other services to the review client that constitute client advocacy.
- The CPA's or CPA's spouse or CPA's dependent's bookkeeping services to a review client that calls for the CPA to initiate transaction classification and recording. The CPA reviewing the

---

[29] AICPA, Code of Professional Conduct Rule 101, *Independence* (AICPA, Professional Standards, vol. 2, ET sec. 101).

accounting records would appear to be reviewing his or her own work.

These items do not represent an exhaustive list of independence issues.

.02 Developing an Understanding with the Client

It is important, early in the engagement, to communicate with the client to minimize misunderstandings. An engagement letter serves as the contract between the CPA and client and clarifies what to expect from a review engagement. The engagement letter is beneficial to the client because it indicates what has been agreed upon and also provides clarification on such matters as management and CPA respective responsibilities, fees, type of report expected, and timing of the engagement.

As with auditing standards and compilation standards, there is no requirement that the understanding for the review services be in writing. However, the engagement letter is advisable to use, for the reasons just cited. It represents the details of formal agreement between the CPA and client and, as such, should identify such matters as:

- The nature of review services that the CPA will provide. The description should include:
    - Which financial statements will be reviewed
    - For what time frame
    - That the review services will be performed in accordance with Statements on Standards for Accounting and Review Services issued by the American Institute of Certified Public Accountants
    - That the review consists primarily of inquiries and analytical procedures
    - That a client representation from management will be required
    - That it will probably not be necessary to:
        - understand the company's internal controls
        - test the accounting records
        - obtain corroborating evidence based upon management response to inquiries
- Timing of the engagement
- A statement that the service cannot be relied upon to discover:
    - Errors in the financial statements
    - Fraud
    - Illegal acts of management

¶ 905.02

- Disclosure by the CPA to the appropriate level of management any errors, fraud, or illegal acts that are discovered
- Fees

Because the engagement letter serves as the details of an oral agreement, the CPA and the client should each sign the letter. Each party should retain one file copy.

Figure 9.17 is an example of an SSARS Review Engagement letter.

Figure 9.17 ─────────────────────────────

SSARS Review Engagement Letter

To the Appropriate Addressee:

This letter is to confirm our understanding with you regarding the terms and objectives of our review engagement as well as the nature and limitations of the services we will provide to Leather Coats Company.

We will review the balance sheet of Leather Coats Company as of December 31, 20X3, and the related statements of income, comprehensive income, and cash flows for the year then ended, in accordance with Statements on Standards for Accounting and Review Services issued by the American Institute of Certified Public Accountants. All information included in these financial statements is the representation of the management of Leather Coats Company.

A review consists principally of inquiries of company personnel and analytical procedures applied to financial data. It is substantially less in scope than an audit in accordance with generally accepted auditing standards, the objective of which is the expression of an opinion regarding the financial statements taken as a whole. Accordingly, we do not express such an opinion. In addition, a review cannot be relied upon to discover errors in record-keeping or those that appear in the financial statements, fraudulent transactions, fraudulent financial reporting, as well as illegal acts of company personnel. If, however, in the course of our review engagement we become aware of any errors, fraud, or illegal acts we will bring it to the attention of the appropriate Leather Coats Company management.

At the conclusion of our review, management must provide to us a representation letter confirming that:[30]

1. It is management's responsibility for the fair presentation of the financial position, results of operations, and cash flows in conformity with generally accepted accounting principles.
2. Management's belief that the financial statements are fairly presented in conformity with generally accepted accounting principles.
3. Management's full and truthful response to all inquiries.
4. Completeness of information.
5. Information concerning subsequent events.
6. [Any other pertinent information to be tailored to the situation.]

In addition it is not our current intention to:

1. Review the internal controls
2. Test accounting records beyond what has been discussed above
3. Obtain any corroborating evidence based upon management response to our inquiries

In addition to the review of the financial statements, we will prepare the federal and all state income tax returns for Leather Coats Company.

Our fees are based on the amount of time required for the services. In addition to the fees, you will be charged for all costs associated with the services rendered. We will notify you immediately of any circumstances we encounter which could significantly affect our initial estimate of total fees as follows:

---

[30] Wording provided by the Exposure Draft of Proposed Statement on Standards for Accounting and Review Services, "Omnibus-2002," distributed August 1, 2002.

¶ 905.02

Review of the financial statements of Leather Coats Company for the year ended March 31, 20X3	$18,800
Income tax return preparation for Federal and the States of California, Missouri, and Illinois	$15,000
Total	$33,800

If the foregoing correctly sets forth your understanding of the terms of our engagement, please so indicate by dating, signing, and returning the duplicate copy of this letter.

We appreciate this opportunity to serve you.

Plastron & Carapace P.C.

April 20, 20X3

Accepted: _____

by: Sydney Mellon, CEO

.03 Planning for the Review

SSARS requirements provide that the review is to be properly planned and any assistants be supervised. However because there is no specific guidance from SSARS standards on these matters, auditing standards, adapted for a review engagement, should be followed.

.04 Review Procedures

The CPA obtains a working knowledge of the industry in which the company operates, as well as important aspects of the company. Then the CPA applies analytical procedures designed to identify unusual items or trends in the financial statements that may need explanation. With a review, the CPA is attempting to determine whether the financial statements appear reasonable without applying audit-type tests. The limited testing results in a limited assurance from the CPA.

In order for CPAs to perform reviews they must acquire more information about the company and its operations beyond that necessary for compilations. The CPA must:

- Understand the GAAP applicable in the industry for which the company operates. This knowledge can be gleaned from AICPA Industry Guides, periodicals, formal education courses, and other individuals with industry experience.

- Understand the:
    - Company's organization
    - Company's operations, operating characteristics, production, and distribution
    - Company's record-keeping system

- Company's accounting personnel qualifications
- Accounting principles and practices to be used in the preparation of the financial statements
- Company's compensation methods
- Nature of the company's assets, liabilities, revenues, and expenses
- Types of products
- Operating locations
- Related party transactions

Additionally, unlike the compilation, some evidence is gathered supporting financial statement assertions. However, the amount of evidence is significantly less than that for an audit. The CPA is required to make inquiries and perform analytical procedures.

Inquiry is the process of interviewing client personnel regarding matters pertinent to the financial statements. The SSARS review inquiry procedures typically should include the following:

- The CPA should inquire of company personnel about:
  - The company's accounting principles and practices, including:
    - The record-keeping process of recording, classifying, and summarizing transactions
    - The manner in which the company accumulates financial statement disclosure items
    - Whether accounting principles used for the financial statements have been consistently applied
    - Events occurring subsequent to the balance sheet date but prior to the release of the financial statements of a financial manner
    - Any question that arises for the CPA regarding the financial statements emanating from any procedures the CPA applies, such as analytical procedures
  - Actions taken at meetings for:
    - Stockholders
    - Board of directors
    - Committees of the board of director
- For the application of analytical procedures, the CPA should determine what types of matters required accounting adjust-

¶ 905.04

ment in prior periods and apply analytical procedures accordingly.

Analytical procedures that the CPA employs in a review engagement help determine whether limited assurance can be given and no material modifications need be made to the financial statements. Analytical procedures comprise the process of evaluating financial information through the study of plausible relationships of data. Many accounts have a predictability quality and, as such, patterns of valuation can occur. Analytical procedures can be developed to take the predictability into account to determine the reasonableness of an financial statement balance.

For example, if in prior years the repairs and maintenance account contained costs that should have been capitalized but the account was adjusted accordingly, the current review should include analytical procedures that would direct attention to overcharging. A trend analysis of the repairs and maintenance account might highlight such issues.

Examples of analytical procedures are:

- Comparisons of current year financial data with that of the prior period data
- Comparisons of current year financial data with industry data
- Comparisons of client data with auditor-determined expected results
- Comparisons of client data with client-determined expected results

In order to make comparisons of data the CPA can use various techniques, such as:

- Ratio analysis
- Variance analysis
- Regression analysis

For SSARS reviews and evidence gathering methods the CPA is not required to extend the procedures beyond inquiries and analytical review. Excluded from SSARS review requirements are:

- Confirm account balances
- Observe inventory
- Test selected transactions by examining supporting documents
- Study and evaluate the client's internal controls

However, whenever the CPA believes information provided by the client is incorrect or incomplete, additional information should be sought.

¶ 905.04

Caution: If procedures are extended and if any of the four is performed, the engagement may appear to be an audit.

.05 The Review Representation Letter

The CPA is required to obtain a representation letter from the client for performing an SSARS review engagement. Review standards state that a CPA whose review client refuses to sign a client representation letter may not issue a review report.

The purpose of this letter is to document verbal representations made by the client to the CPA during the engagement and to reduce the possibility of misunderstanding about matters that have been represented to the CPA. The letter includes statements made by the client to the CPA stating:[31]

1. It is management's responsibility for the fair presentation of the financial position, results of operations, and cash flows in conformity with generally accepted accounting principles

2. Management's belief that the financial statements are fairly presented in conformity with generally accepted accounting principles

3. Management's full and truthful response to all inquiries

4. Completeness of information

5. Information concerning subsequent events

The representation letter is usually typed on client letterhead and signed by the client. The date of the letter is the same date as the CPA's review report—the date of completion of the CPA's inquiry and analytical procedures.

Figure 9.18 illustrates a representation letter.

---

[31] *Ibid.*

Figure 9.18

Language of a Representation Letter for a Review [32]

March 13, 20X3
[Date of Accountant's Report]

To Mead & Company LLP:
[The CPA]

In connection with your review of the balance sheet of Charles Corgi Industries, Inc. as of December 31, 20X2 and for the statements of income, retained earnings, and cash flows for the year then ended for the purpose of expressing limited assurance that there are no material modifications that should be made to the statements in order for them to be in conformity with generally accepted accounting principles, we confirm, to the best of our knowledge and belief, the following representations made to you during your review:

1. It is management's responsibility for the fair presentation of the company's financial position, results of operations, and cash flows in conformity with generally accepted accounting principles. In that connection, we confirm specifically that:

   a. The company's accounting principles, and the practices and methods followed in applying them, are as disclosed in our financial statements.

   b. There have been no changes during this review in our company's accounting principles and practices.

   c. We have no plans or intentions that may materially affect our carrying amounts or classification of assets and liabilities.

   d. There are no material transactions that have not been properly reflected in our financial statements.

   e. Our company has had no material losses (such as from obsolete inventory or purchase or sales commitments) that have not been properly accrued or disclosed in these financial statements.

   f. There are no violations or possible violations of laws or regulations whose effects should be considered for disclosure in our financial statements or as a basis for recording a loss contingency, and there are no other material liabilities or gain or loss contingencies that are required to be accrued or disclosed. Also, we have no unasserted claims or assessments that our attorney has advised us are probable of assertion that must be disclosed in accordance with Financial Accounting Standards Board Statement No. 5, Accounting for Contingencies.

   g. Charles Corgi Industries has satisfactory title to all of our owned assets, and there are no liens or encumbrances on such assets nor has any asset been pledged, except as disclosed in our financial statements.

   h. We have made no related-party transactions including sales, purchases, loans, transfers, leasing arrangements, and guarantees, and amounts receivable from or payable to related parties that have not been properly disclosed in the financial statements.

   i. Our company has complied with all aspects of contractual agreements that would have a material effect on our financial statements in the event of noncompliance.

---

[32] SSARs No. 1, *Compilation and Review of Financial Statements* (AICPA, Professional Standards, vol. 2, AR sec. 100.58).

¶ 905.05

j. To the best of our knowledge and belief, no events have occurred subsequent to the balance sheet date and through the date of this letter that would require adjustment to or disclosure in our financial statements.

k. We have no knowledge of concentrations existing at the date of the financial statements that make the entity vulnerable to the risk of a near-term severe impact that have not been properly disclosed in the financial statements. We understand that concentrations refer to volumes of business, revenues, available sources of supply, or markets or geographic areas for which events could occur that would significantly disrupt the company's normal finances within our next fiscal year.

l. Charles Corgi's company management has identified all significant estimates used in preparing the financial statements. The additional representations in items m through t may be appropriate in certain situations. This list of additional representations is not intended to be all-inclusive. In drafting a representation letter, you should consider the effects of other applicable pronouncements.

m. Our financial statements disclose all of the matters of which we are aware that are relevant to Charles Corgi's ability to continue as a going concern, including significant conditions and events, and our plans.

n. We have reviewed long-lived assets and certain identifiable intangibles to be held and used for impairment whenever events or changes in circumstances indicated that the carrying amount of those assets might not be recoverable and have appropriately recorded the adjustment.

o. Debt securities that have been classified as held-to-maturity have been so classified due to our intent to hold such securities to maturity and our ability to do so. All of our other debt securities have been classified as available-for-sale or trading.

p. We consider the decline in value of debt or equity securities classified as either available-for-sale or held-to-maturity to be temporary.

q. Accounts receivables reported in the financial statements represent valid claims against debtors for sales or other charges arising on or before the balance-sheet date and have been appropriately reduced to their estimated net realizable value.

r. We believe that the carrying amounts of all material assets will be recoverable.

s. We have properly disclosed all agreements to repurchase assets previously sold.

t. We have made provisions for losses to be sustained in the fulfillment of, or from the inability to fulfill, sales commitments.

2. We have advised you of all actions taken at meetings of stockholders, the board of directors, and committees of the board of directors (and our other similar bodies) that may affect the financial statements.

3. We have responded fully and truthfully to all inquiries made to us by you during your review.

Jack Oshman
Chief Executive Officer, Charles Corgi Industries Inc.

James Aries
Chief Financial Officer, Charles Corgi Industries Inc.

¶ 905.05

One revision to item f is likely if the client has not consulted with an attorney regarding legal issues. The representation might be worded as shown in Figure 9.19.

Figure 9.19

Revised Language for item F of a Representation Letter for a Review [33]

f. We are not aware of any pending or threatened litigation, claims, or assessments or unasserted claims or assessments that are required to be accrued or disclosed in our financial statements in accordance with Financial Accounting Standards Board Statement No. 5, Accounting for Contingencies, and we have not consulted our attorney concerning litigation, claims, or assessments.

.06 The Form of the Review Report

The form of the standard SSARS review report is contained in three paragraphs: introductory, scope, and opinion (Figure 9.20).

Figure 9.20

Paragraphs in a SSARS Review Report

1. Introductory Paragraph

↓

2. Scope Paragraph that Includes a Disclaimer of Audit Opinion

↓

3. Negative Assurance Paragraph

Contents of an introductory paragraph in an SSARS review report are as follows:

1. Types of financial statements reviewed
2. Name of organization
3. Timeframe or point in time

---

[33] *Ibid.*, AR sec. 100.58.

4. The fact that review of the financial statements was conducted according to SSARS

5. The fact that the financial statements are the representation of management

The introductory paragraph of an SSARS review report identifies the level of attestation that the auditor conducted, that is, a review the financial statements. The paragraph also identifies the organization whose financial statements are being reviewed, as well as the financial statements for which periods (income statement, statement of retained earnings, and statement of cash flow) and points in time (balance sheets or statements of financial position).

The introductory paragraph emphasizes that the financial statements are the representation of company's management and that the review was conducted according to Standards for Accounting and Review Services. No mention of the CPA's responsibility is made in the introductory paragraph.

The scope paragraph describes the nature of the review. The purpose of the scope paragraph is to explain what the review entails. The review standards require that the CPA conduct inquiries of company personnel as well as perform analytical procedures. However, details of what procedures were used should not be included in the scope paragraph.

Finally, the scope paragraph provides a disclaimer that a review is substantially smaller in scope than that of an audit and that the CPA is not rendering an audit opinion.

Contents of a scope paragraph in an SSARS review report are as follows:

1. Review standards require:

    a. Inquiry of company personnel

    b. Analytical procedures performed on the financial information

2. A review is smaller in scope than an audit

3. The CPA disclaims an audit opinion

The form of the opinion paragraph is that of a limited or negative assurance. That is, it makes clear that nothing came to the attention of the CPA's attention which would indicate that the financial statements need alteration. This is in contrast to the audit opinion, which is in the form of a positive assurance, that in the opinion of the CPA the financial statements are fairly presented.

Contents of an opinion paragraph in an SSARS review report are as follows:

¶ 905.06

1. Based upon the review, the CPA is not aware of any material modifications that need to be made to the financial statements.

The wording for the standard review report appears in Figure 9.21.

Figure 9.21 ─────────────────────────────────────

Language of a SSARS Review Report [34]

To the Appropriate Addressee:

We have reviewed the accompanying balance sheet of Glemsel Company as of December 31, 20X2, and the related statements of income, retained earnings, and cash flows for the year then ended, in accordance with Statements on Standards for Accounting and Review Services issued by the American Institute of Certified Public Accountants. All information included in these financial statements is the representation of the management of Glemsel Company.

A review consists principally of inquiries of company personnel and analytical procedures applied to financial data. It is substantially less in scope than an audit in accordance with generally accepted auditing standards, the objective of which is the expression of an opinion regarding the financial statements taken as a whole. Accordingly, we do not express such an opinion.

Based on our review, we are not aware of any material modifications that should be made to the accompanying financial statements in order for them to be in conformity with generally accepted accounting principles.

Mead & Co. LLP

March 13, 20X3

───

If a statement of Comprehensive Income has been provided and reviewed, the report wording should include it in the introductory paragraph.

The date shown on the review report is the date that the CPA completed the inquiry and analytical procedures. Also, each page of the financial statements should be marked, "See Accountant's Review Report."

A standard review report can also be issued for financial statements prepared using another basis of accounting other than generally accepted accounting principles. Figure 9.22 shows how the standard report for OCBOA financial statements is structured.

---

[34] *Ibid.*, AR sec. 100.36.

¶ 905.06

Figure 9.22

Paragraphs in a Review Report for Other Comprehensive Basis of Accounting (OCBOA) [35]

1. Introductory Paragraph—modified for OCBOA Basis

   ↓

2. Scope Paragraph that Includes a Disclaimer of Audit Opinion

   ↓

3. Negative Assurance Paragraph Modified for OCBOA Basis

An example of a standard review report for financial statements prepared using the cash basis of accounting is detailed in Figure 9.23. Note the reference to the OCBOA basis occurs in the introductory paragraph.

---

[35] Interpretation No. 12, "Reporting on a Comprehensive Basis of Accounting Other than Generally Accepted Accounting Principles," of SSARs No. 1, *Compilation and Review of Financial Statements* (AICPA, Professional Standards, vol. 2, AR sec. 9100.42).

¶ 905.06

Figure 9.23

Language of a Review Report on Income Tax Basis [36]

To the Appropriate Addressee:

We have reviewed the accompanying statement of assets, liabilities, and equity-income tax basis of Skidt Company as of December 31, 20X2, and the related statements of revenue and expenses—income tax basis for the year then ended, in accordance with Statements on Standards for Accounting and Review Services issued by the American Institute of Certified Public Accountants. All information included in these financial statements is the representation of the management of Skidt Company.

A review consists principally of inquiries of company personnel and analytical procedures applied to financial data. It is substantially less in scope than an audit in accordance with generally accepted auditing standards, the objective of which is the expression of an opinion regarding the financial statements taken as a whole. Accordingly, we do not express such an opinion.

Based on our review, we are not aware of any material modifications that should be made to the accompanying financial statements in order for them to be in conformity with the income tax basis of accounting, as described in note 19.

Mead & Co. LLP
March 13, 20X3

¶ 906 Additional Review Issues

.01 Reviews with a Departure from GAAP or OCBOA

Under most conditions the financial statements will be prepared using GAAP guidelines. GAAP establishes the rules for financial statement presentation, including the requirements for disclosures in the notes to the financial statements. However, financial statements prepared using a comprehensive basis of accounting other than GAAP (OCBOA) must also meet presentation and disclosure guidelines for that basis. Financial statements containing any material deviation from GAAP or OCBOA guidelines should be revised by the client in order for the financial statements to receive a standard review report. If, however, the deviation is not corrected in reviewed financial statements, the review report must be modified to disclose the conditions to the financial statement user.

The structure of the review report when there is a departure in the financial statements is seen in Figure 9.24. Note that there is an additional explanatory paragraph appearing after the opinion paragraph.

---

[36] *Ibid.*, AR sec. 9100.45.

¶ 906.01

Figure 9.24

Paragraphs in a SSARS Review Report with Departure from GAAP

1. Introductory Paragraph
   ↓
2. Scope Paragraph
   ↓
3. Opinion Paragraph
   ↓
4. Explanatory Paragraph

The wording of the opinion paragraph includes a reference to the departure from GAAP or OCBOA as described in the explanatory paragraph. Figure 9.25 illustrates a review report when there has been departure from GAAP.

¶ 906.01

Figure 9.25 ─────────────────────────

Language of a SSARS Review Report with Departure from GAAP [37]

To the Appropriate Addressee:

We have reviewed the accompanying balance sheet of Saldo Company as of December 31, 20X2, and the related statements of income, retained earnings, and cash flows for the year then ended, in accordance with Statements on Standards for Accounting and Review Services issued by the American Institute of Certified Public Accountants. All information included in these financial statements is the representation of the management of Saldo Company.

A review consists principally of inquiries of company personnel and analytical procedures applied to financial data. It is substantially less in scope than an audit in accordance with generally accepted auditing standards, the objective of which is the expression of an opinion regarding the financial statements taken as a whole. Accordingly, we do not express such an opinion.

Based on our review, with the exception of the matter described in the following paragraph, we are not aware of any material modifications that should be made to the accompanying financial statements in order for them to be in conformity with generally accepted accounting principles.

As disclosed in note 23 to the financial statements, generally accepted accounting principles require that inventory be valued at lower of cost or market. Management has informed us that inventory is valued at cost as calculated by the weighted-average method. The market value of inventory is less than cost. If generally accepted accounting principles had been followed, inventory, retained earnings, and operating income would be decreased by $38,000.

Mead & Co. LLP

March 13, 20X3

───────────────────────────────

.02 Comparative Financial Statements

For the CPA who has performed a review for each of the comparative financial statements, the review report reflects a limited assurance for each of the periods presented. The comparative review report represents the current period as well as an update for the prior period. Figure 9.26 is an illustration of such a report.

───────────────────────────────

[37] SSARs No. 1, *Compilation and Review of Financial Statements* (AICPA, Professional Standards, vol. 2, AR sec. 100.41).

¶ 906.02

Figure 9.26

Language of a Comparative Review Report [38]

To the Appropriate Addressee:

We have reviewed the accompanying balance sheets of Onde Company as of December 31, 20X1 and 20X2, and the related statements of income, retained earnings, and cash flows for the years then ended, in accordance with Statements on Standards for Accounting and Review Services issued by the American Institute of Certified Public Accountants. All information included in these financial statements is the representation of the management of Onde Company.

A review consists principally of inquiries of company personnel and analytical procedures applied to financial data. It is substantially less in scope than an audit in accordance with generally accepted auditing standards, the objective of which is the expression of an opinion regarding the financial statements taken as a whole. Accordingly, we do not express such an opinion.

Based on our reviews, we are not aware of any material modifications that should be made to the accompanying financial statements in order for them to be in conformity with generally accepted accounting principles.

Mead & Co. LLP
March 13, 20X3

When the comparative financial statements represent different levels of services performed by the same CPA, the comparative CPA report will reflect various structures, as detailed here.

Current period with compilation of prior period review. The CPA has two options as to the manner in which to report a current period compilation and a comparative prior period review:

1. Add a separate paragraph to current period's compilation report indicating:

    - The amount of responsibility the CPA is assuming for the prior period's financial statements
    - The original date of the CPA's review report
    - That no review procedures have been performed on the prior year's financial statements since the original report date

2. Reissue the prior period's review report along with the compilation report of the current period. These two reports can either be shown separately or in a combined manner.

---

[38] SSARs No. 2, *Reporting on Comparative Financial Statements* (AICPA, Professional Standards, vol. 2, AR sec. 200.09).

Paragraphs in a review of the current period with prior period compiled are as follows:

1. Introductory paragraph—compilation

2. Disclaimer of opinion paragraph—compilation

3. Explanatory paragraph with reference to review report

Figure 9.27 shows the language used to report a current year compilation and a comparable prior period review.

Figure 9.27

Language of a Compilation of the Current Period and Review of Prior Period Financial Statements [39]

To the Appropriate Addressee:

We have compiled the accompanying balance sheet of Lackluster Paints Inc. as of December 31, 20X2, and the related statements of income, retained earnings, and cash flows for the year then ended, in accordance with Statements on Standards for Accounting and Review Services issued by the American Institute of Certified Public Accountants.

A compilation is limited to presenting in the form of financial statements information that is the representation of management. We have not audited or reviewed the accompanying financial statements and, accordingly, do not express an opinion or any other form of assurance on them.

The accompanying 20X1 financial statements of Lackluster Paints Inc. were previously reviewed by us and our report dated March 19, 20X2, stated that we were not aware of any material modifications that should be made to those statements in order for them to be in conformity with generally accepted accounting principles. We have not performed any procedures in connection with that review engagement after the date of our report on the 20X1 financial statements.

Snyder & Co. LLP

February 11, 20X3

Current period with review of prior period compilation. If the current period is a review and the prior period is a compilation then the CPA updates the prior period compilation report with those of the current period.

---

[39] *Ibid.*, AR sec. 200.12.

¶ 906.02

Paragraphs in an SSARS review report for current period and compilation report for prior period for the same CPA are as follows:

1. Introductory paragraph—review report
2. Scope paragraph—review report
3. Opinion paragraph—review report
4. Compilation description and disclaimer—prior period

Figure 9.28 shows the language used to report a comparable review for the current period and compilation for the prior period.

Figure 9.28

Language of a Comparative Review Report for Current Period and Compilation Report for Prior Period [40]

To the Appropriate Addressee:

We have reviewed the accompanying balance sheet of Samuel Hardware Inc. as of December 31, 20X2, and the related statements of income, retained earnings, and cash flows for the year then ended, in accordance with Statements on Standards for Accounting and Review Services issued by the American Institute of Certified Public Accountants. All information included in these financial statements is the representation of the management of Samuel Hardware Inc.

A review consists principally of inquiries of company personnel and analytical procedures applied to financial data. It is substantially less in scope than an audit in accordance with generally accepted auditing standards, the objective of which is the expression of an opinion regarding the financial statements taken as a whole. Accordingly, we do not express such an opinion.

Based on our review, we are not aware of any material modifications that should be made to the accompanying financial statements in order for them to be in conformity with generally accepted accounting principles.

The accompanying 20X1 financial statements for Samuel Hardware Inc. were compiled by us. A compilation is limited to presenting in the form of financial statements information that is the representation of management. We have not audited or reviewed the 20X1 financial statements and, accordingly, do not express an opinion or any other form of assurance on them.

Angelo & Company LLP
March 13, 20X3

Current period with review of prior period audit. When the current period's financial statements have been reviewed, the CPA should issue a review report. However, if the prior period was audited, the CPA has two choices with respect to the audited financial statements:

[40] *Ibid.,* AR sec. 200.10.

1. Add a separate paragraph to current period's review report indicating:
   - The prior period's financial statements were audited.
   - The original date of the CPA's audit report.
   - The type of opinion expressed. If the type of opinion was not unqualified then the substantive reasons why the opinion was not unqualified should be described.
   - That there have been no auditing procedures performed since the audit report date.
2. Reissue the prior period's audit report along with the review report of the current period.

Paragraphs in a SSARS review report for current period and audit report for prior period for the same CPA are as follows:

1. Introductory paragraph—review report
2. Scope paragraph—review report
3. Opinion paragraph—review report
4. Explanatory paragraph referencing audit report

¶ 906.02

Figure 9.29 ──────────────────────────────

Language of a Review Report for Current Period and Separate Paragraph Referencing the Audit Report [41]

To the Appropriate Addressee:

We have reviewed the accompanying balance sheet of Gylle Company as of December 31, 20X2, and the related statements of income, retained earnings, and cash flows for the year then ended, in accordance with Statements on Standards for Accounting and Review Services issued by the American Institute of Certified Public Accountants. All information included in these financial statements is the representation of the management of Gylle Company.

A review consists principally of inquiries of company personnel and analytical procedures applied to financial data. It is substantially less in scope than an audit in accordance with generally accepted auditing standards, the objective of which is the expression of an opinion regarding the financial statements taken as a whole. Accordingly, we do not express such an opinion.

Based on our review, we are not aware of any material modifications that should be made to the accompanying financial statements in order for them to be in conformity with generally accepted accounting principles.

The financial statements for the year ended December 31, 20X1, were audited by us and we expressed an unqualified opinion on them in our report dated March 21, 20X2, but we have not performed any auditing procedures since that date.

Mead & Company LLP
March 13, 20X3

───

Current period with audit of prior period review. If the current period's financial statements are audited and the prior period is a review, the CPA should update the prior period review report by re-expressing the previous conclusion with that of the current period. The previous conclusion is contained in a separate paragraph after the audit opinion paragraph.

Figure 9.30 gives a sample of the audit opinion and seperate paragraph for the previous fiscal year's review report.

───

[41] *Ibid.*, AR sec. 200.29.

¶ 906.02

Figure 9.30

Language of an Unqualified Audit Opinion for the Current Year and a Separate Paragraph for the Prior Year's Review Report [42]

Report of the Independent Auditor

To the Board of Directors of ABC Company:

We have audited the accompanying balance sheet of Forny Company as of December 31, 20X2, and the related statements of income, retained earnings, and cash flows for the year then ended. These financial statements are the responsibility of the Company's management. Our responsibility is to express an opinion on these financial statements based on our audit.

We conducted our audit in accordance with auditing standards generally accepted in the United States of America. Those standards require that we plan and perform the audit to obtain reasonable assurance about whether the financial statements are free of material misstatement. An audit includes examining, on a test basis, evidence supporting the amounts and disclosures in the financial statements. An audit also includes assessing the accounting principles used and significant estimates made by management, as well as evaluating the overall financial statement presentation. We believe that our audit provides a reasonable basis for our opinion.

In our opinion, the financial statements referred to above present fairly, in all material respects, the financial position of Forny Company as of December 31, 20X2, and the results of its operations and its cash flows for the year then ended in conformity with accounting principles generally accepted in the United States of America.

The 20X1 financial statements were reviewed by us, and our report thereon, dated March 20, 20X2, stated we were not aware of any material modifications that should be made to those statements for them to be in conformity with generally accepted accounting principles. However, a review is substantially less in scope than an audit and does not provide a basis for the expression of an opinion on the financial statements taken as a whole.

Mead & Company LLP

March 21, 20X3

.03 Communication Between Successor and Predecessor CPAs

The Standards for Accounting and Review Services including the August 2002 Exposure Draft for Proposed Statement of Standards for Accounting and Review Services address the communication between the successor and predecessor CPAs. These standards are contained in ¶ 904.05.

---

[42] SAS No. 58, Reports on Audited Financial Statements (AICPA, Professional Standards, vol. 1, AU sec. 508.08), as amended, and Statement on Auditing Standards No. 26, Association with Financial Statements (AICPA, Professional Standards, vol. 1, AU sec. 504.17).

¶ 907 Review Report According to PCAOB Standards

PCAOB Auditing Standard No. 1 approved by the SEC in May 2004 requires registered public accounting firms to include a reference to the standards of the Public Company Accounting Oversight Board (United States) in both audit and review engagements. PCAOB Auditing Standard No. 1 is also applicable to other engagements such as review of interim financial information of public companies. Figure 9.31 presents an illustrative report on a review of interim financial statements. Several key points of this illustration review report are:

- The title is "Review Report of Independent Registered Public Accounting Firm."
- Type(s) of financial information (statements) reviewed should be stated in the introductory paragraph.
- A statement that the review was conducted in accordance with "the standards of the PCAOBUS" including a disclaimer of audit opinion should be in the scope paragraph.
- A negative assurance paragraph.
- City and state, or city and country, in which the review was conducted and reported.

Figure 9.31

Report of Independent Registered Public Accounting Firm

We have reviewed the accompanying [describe the interim financial information or statements reviewed] of X Company as of September 30, 20X3 and 20X2, and for the three-month and nine-month periods then ended. This (these) interim financial information (statements) is (are) the responsibility of the Company's management.

We conducted our review in accordance with the standards of the Public Company Accounting Oversight Board (United States). A review of interim financial information consists principally of applying analytical procedures and making inquiries of persons responsible for financial and accounting matters. It is substantially less in scope than an audit conducted in accordance with the standards of the Public Company Accounting Oversight Board, the objective of which is the expression of an opinion regarding the financial statements taken as a whole. Accordingly, we do not express such an opinion.

Based on our review, we are not aware of any material modifications that should be made to the accompanying interim financial (statements) for it (them) to be in conformity with U.S. generally accepted accounting principles.

[Signature]
[City and State or Country]
[Date]

Source: PCAOB Release No. 2003-025, Dec. 17, 2003. Available at *http://www.pcaobus.org*.

¶ 908 Summary

Auditors offer many forms of services in addition to audits of historical financial statements. Among these services is the preparation of "unaudited" financial statements for nonpublic companies. The Accounting and Review Services Committee of the AICPA is responsible for developing and issuing pronouncements of standards concerning the services and reports an accountant may render in connection with unaudited financial statements. These pronouncements are called Statements on Standards for Accounting and Review Services (SSARS). An auditor uses SSARS as a guideline when working on unaudited financial statements of nonpublic companies. In comparison, an auditor uses the Statements on Auditing Standards (SAS) as a guideline when working on all audited financial statements (both public and nonpublic companies) and when working on unaudited financial statements of public companies.

Unaudited financial statements of nonpublic companies require less work on the part of the auditor than do audited financial statements. In addition, accountants do not provide positive assurance for engagements other than audit. Compilation engagements are merely writing up financial statements and involve no auditing procedures; therefore, the CPA accepts no responsibility, and the report gives no assurance. Review engagements involve less work than an audit but more work than a compilation engagement. An auditor uses some limited verification methodology to review unaudited financial statements. As a result, the report gives a low level of negative assurance instead of an audit opinion.

In the case of audits, successor auditors are required to make certain inquiries of predecessor auditors when a new client is obtained. A management representation letter is also required. In compilation and review work, however, successor accountants are not required to communicate with predecessor accountants. Letters of representation are required for reviews but not for compilations. Still, SSARS strongly advises accountants to talk with the predecessor accountant and to obtain representation letters when conducting a compilation. Registered auditors should follow review standards adopted by the PCAOB when performing review and other related professional services for public companies.

¶ 908

Chapter 10

Special Reports and Other Selected Attestation Reports

¶ 1001   Introduction

¶ 1002   Reports Using Comprehensive Basis of Accounting Other than GAAP

¶ 1003   Audits of Specified Elements, Accounts, or Items of a Financial Statement

¶ 1004   Compliance with Aspects of Contractual Agreements or Regulatory Requirements

¶ 1005   Financial Presentations Prepared to Comply with Contractual Agreements or Regulatory Provisions

¶ 1006   Financial Information Presented in Prescribed Forms or Schedules that Require a Prescribed Form of Report

¶ 1007   Prospective Financial Statements

¶ 1008   Attestation of and Report on Internal Control (Public Companies)

¶ 1009   Summary

¶ 1001   Introduction

Auditing standards affecting Special Reports were revised in 1989 with Statements on Auditing Standards (SAS) No. 62, *Special Reports* and again in 1995 with SAS 77. These auditing standards, especially SAS 62, in addition to providing changes, also enable CPAs to provide new services not previously covered by the special report literature.

Auditing standards divides Special Reports into five categories:

1. Audits of financial statements prepared in conformity with a comprehensive basis of accounting other than generally accepted accounting principles (OCBOA)

2. Audits of specified elements, accounts, or items of a financial statement

3. Audits of compliance with aspects of contractual agreements or regulatory requirements related to audited financial statements

4. Audits of financial presentations prepared to comply with contractual agreements or regulatory provisions

5. Audits of financial information presented in prescribed forms or schedules that require a prescribed form of report

In addition to these Special Reports, this chapter includes other selected attestation reports as well as prospective financial statement reports. They illustrate the variety of reporting engagements that typify avenues of business for practitioners.

Chapter 10 objectives:

- To recognize how audit reports using Comprehensive Bases of Accounting Other than GAAP (OCBOA) differ from audit reports using GAAP (see ¶ 1001–1002).

- To understand how an audit of Specified Elements, Accounts, or Items (SEAI) of a financial statement relate to an audit of the complete financial statements (see ¶ 1003).

- To clarify the CPA's level of assurance regarding compliance with contractual agreements or regulatory requirements related to audited financial statements (see ¶ 1004).

- To list the two types of financial presentations prepared to comply with contractual agreements or regulatory provisions and be familiar with the unqualified reports for both (see ¶ 1005–1006).

- To be aware of how prospective financial statements are used and what services an auditor offers in regards to these statements (see ¶ 1007).

- To recognize the format of a report on internal controls (see ¶ 1008).

¶ 1002 Reports Using Comprehensive Basis of Accounting Other than GAAP[1]

The purpose of financial statements is to communicate financial information, such as available business resources, obligations, and results of operations. Generally accepted accounting principles (GAAP) require that financial statements be expressed by using the accrual basis of accounting. Revenues are generally recognized when earned and expenses recognized when incurred. However, in some situations, financial statements are prepared in accordance with a comprehensive basis of accounting other than

---

[1] Statements on Auditing Standards (SAS) No. 62, Special Reports (AICPA, Professional Standards, vol. 1, AU sec. 623).

GAAP. These are referred to in accounting literature as other comprehensive bases of accounting (OCBOA) statements, such as:

- **Cash basis,** whereby revenues are recognized when cash is received and expenses are recognized when cash is paid

- **Federal income tax basis,** whereby the financial statements are prepared using the same methodology as the company's income tax returns

- **Regulatory basis,** whereby the financial statements are prepared using the same basis that the company uses to comply with the regulatory requirements of a government agency under whose jurisdiction the company comes

A fourth basis is also described by auditing standards and represents a broad conceptual category where the criterion of the basis:

- Is definite and affords a consistent estimation or measurement by other competent preparers of financial statements

- Has substantial support, such as recognition by the AICPA's AcSEC or the Accounting Principles Board (industry or trade publications on accounting are not generally recognized as being considered substantial support)

- Is applied to all material items appearing in financial statements (limited application of the basis to supplementary information to the financial statements do not apply)

For example, financial statements prepared using the price-level basis of accounting meet these three criteria and would be considered as OCBOA financial statements.

GAAP financial statements, along with the accompanying notes, comprise the balance sheet, income statement, and statement of cash flows. Although other titles have been given to these statements (i.e., statement of financial position for the balance sheet and statement of revenues and expenses for the income statement), the aforementioned titles are reserved exclusively for financial statements using GAAP. OCBOA financial statements cannot contain GAAP titles. The auditor should be satisfied that the financial statement titles reflect the basis of accounting and do not use terminology typical to GAAP financial statements. For example, Balance Sheet—Cash Basis would be an improper title, whereas Statement of Assets and Liabilities Arising from Cash Transactions would be proper. If the auditor believes that the titles of the OCBOA financial statements are improper, an explanatory paragraph should be added to the auditor's report preceding the opinion paragraph describing the auditor's reservations about the titles. The explanatory paragraph should be followed by a qualified opinion.

¶ 1002

The contents of the unqualified report for financial statements prepared using OCBOA is similar to the standard audit opinion for GAAP financial statements except for:

- The title used for the OCBOA financial statements

- An explanatory paragraph briefly describing the comprehensive basis of accounting other than generally accepted accounting principles

Figure 10.1

Paragraphs in an Unqualified Opinion on Financial Statements Prepared Using OCBOA

1. Introductory Paragraph

↓

2. Scope Paragraph

↓

3. Description of OCBOA Basis

↓

4. Opinion Paragraph

As with a standard worded audit opinion rendered for GAAP financial statements, the title of the auditor's report should contain the word *independent*, such as "The Report of the Independent Auditor."

The contents of the unqualified report for OCBOA financial statements consists of four paragraphs as shown in Figure 10.1. The first paragraph (Figure 10.2) clarifies the responsibilities of management and the auditors, and is referred to as the introductory paragraph.

The paragraph identifies the type of attestation that the auditor has provided, that is, that the OCBOA financial statements have been audited. Next, the financial statements are identified. Finally, the introductory paragraph emphasizes the responsibilities of company's management and the auditor with respect to the identified financial statements.

¶ 1002

Figure 10.2 ─────────────────────────

Contents of an Introductory Paragraph

1. The audited financial statements prepared using a comprehensive basis of accounting other than GAAP are identified

2. Name of organization

3. Specific timeframe or point in time

4. Management's responsibility in connection with the OCBOA financial statements

5. Auditor's responsibility relating to the financial statements

─────────────────────────

The scope paragraph (Figure 10.3) describes the nature of the audit.

Figure 10.3 ─────────────────────────

Contents of a Scope Paragraph in OCBOA Financial Statements

1. GAAS was used

2. The standards require:

   a. Planning

   b. Auditing for reasonable assurance that financial statements are materially correct

   c. Sampling used to support amounts and disclosures

   d. Auditor assessment of estimates used as well as overall presentation

3. Belief that the audit evidence supports the opinion

─────────────────────────

The auditor situates an explanatory paragraph before the opinion paragraph describing the OCBOA basis to which the financial statements conform. Figure 10.4 describes the contents.

¶ 1002

Figure 10.4

Contents of a Description of OCBOA Basis in OCBOA Financial Statements

1. Financial statements have been prepared in conformity with an accounting basis other than GAAP.
2. Reference to the note whereby the financial statement user can obtain a more detailed description of the OCBOA basis.

The opinion paragraph (Figure 10.5) reflects the auditor's opinion that, in all material respects, the financial statements conform to the OCBOA accounting basis.

Figure 10.5

Contents of an Opinion Paragraph in OCBOA Financial Statements

1. The financial statements:
    a. Are materially fairly presented
    b. Conform to the OCBOA basis

The report should conclude with a manually or printed signature and the auditor's report should be dated as of the last day of fieldwork.

Figure 10.6 is an example of the standard wording of an unqualified opinion for financial statements that was prepared using the company's income tax basis. Note the title of the financial statements. The titles of balance sheet and income statement have been conspicuously eliminated.

Figure 10.6 ───────────────────────

Language of Financial Statements Prepared on the Entity's Income Tax Basis [2]

Report of the Independent Auditor

We have audited the accompanying statement of assets, liabilities, and capital—income tax basis of ABC Company as of December 31, 20X2, and the related statements of revenue and expenses—income tax basis and of changes in partners' capital accounts—income tax basis for the year then ended. These financial statements are the responsibility of the company's management. Our responsibility is to express an opinion about these financial statements based on our audit.

We conducted our audit in accordance with auditing standards generally accepted in the United States of America. Those standards require that we plan and perform the audit to obtain reasonable assurance about whether the financial statements are free of material misstatement. An audit includes examining, on a test basis, evidence supporting the amounts and disclosures in the financial statements. An audit also includes assessing the accounting principles used and significant estimates made by management, as well as evaluating the overall financial statement presentation. We believe that our audit provides a reasonable basis for our opinion.

As described in Note 20, these financial statements were prepared on the basis of accounting for income tax purposes, which is a comprehensive basis of accounting other than accounting principles generally accepted in the United States of America.

In our opinion, the financial statements referred to above present fairly, in all material respects, the assets, liabilities, and capital of ABC Company as of December 31, 20X2, and its revenue and expenses and changes in partners' capital accounts for the year then ended, on the basis of accounting described in Note 20.

Mead & Co. LLP
San Francisco, California
March 21, 20X3

───────────────────────

Another example of financial statements prepared using an OCBOA basis is shown in Figure 10.7. These financial statements were prepared using the cash basis of accounting.

---

[2] *Ibid.*, AU sec. 623.08.

¶ 1002

Figure 10.7

Language of Financial Statements Prepared Using the Cash Basis [3]

Report of the Independent Auditor

We have audited the accompanying statement of assets and liabilities arising from cash transactions of ABC Company as of December 31, 20X2, and the related statements of revenue collected and expenses paid the year then ended. These financial statements are the responsibility of the company's management. Our responsibility is to express an opinion about these financial statements based on our audit.

We conducted our audit in accordance with auditing standards generally accepted in the United States of America. Those standards require that we plan and perform the audit to obtain reasonable assurance about whether the financial statements are free of material misstatement. An audit includes examining, on a test basis, evidence supporting the amounts and disclosures in the financial statements. An audit also includes assessing the accounting principles used and significant estimates made by management, as well as evaluating the overall financial statement presentation. We believe that our audit provides a reasonable basis for our opinion.

As described in Note 19, these financial statements were prepared on the basis of cash receipts and disbursements, which is a comprehensive basis of accounting other than accounting principles generally accepted in the United States of America.

In our opinion, the financial statements referred to above present fairly, in all material respects, the assets and liabilities arising from cash transactions of ABC Company as of December 31, 20X2, and its revenue collected and expenses paid for the year then ended, on the basis of accounting described in Note 19.

Mead & Co. LLP
San Francisco, California
March 21, 20X3

When financial statements are audited that had been prepared using a basis as mandated by a regulatory agency, the auditor's unqualified report should contain an additional, fifth paragraph (Figure 10.8). The purpose of the paragraph (Figure 10.9) is to restrict use and dissemination of the auditor's report. The financial statements should be used within the company itself and by individuals representing the regulatory agency. This is applicable even if the financial statements filed with the regulatory agency will be available to the public.

---

[3] *Ibid.*, AU sec. 623.08.

¶ 1002

Figure 10.8

Paragraphs in a Report on Financial Statements Prepared Using Basis Prescribed by and for a Regulatory Agency

1. Introductory Paragraph
   ↓
2. Scope Paragraph
   ↓
3. Description of OCBOA Basis
   ↓
4. Opinion Paragraph
   ↓
5. Restricted Use of Report

Figure 10.9 ─────────────────

Language of Financial Statements Prepared Using a Basis Prescribed by a Regulatory Agency [4]

Report of the Independent Auditor

We have audited the accompanying statements of admitted assets, liabilities, and surplus—statutory basis of ABC Company as of December 31, 20X2, and the related statements of income and cash flows—statutory basis for the year then ended. These financial statements are the responsibility of the Company's management. Our responsibility is to express an opinion about these financial statements based on our audit.

We conducted our audit in accordance with auditing standards generally accepted in the United States of America. Those standards require that we plan and perform the audit to obtain reasonable assurance about whether the financial statements are free of material misstatement. An audit includes examining, on a test basis, evidence supporting the amounts and disclosures in the financial statements. An audit also includes assessing the accounting principles used and significant estimates made by management, as well as evaluating the overall financial statement presentation. We believe that our audit provides a reasonable basis for our opinion.

As described in Note 13, these financial statements were prepared in conformity with the accounting practices prescribed or permitted by the Insurance Department of [State], which is a comprehensive basis of accounting other than accounting principles generally accepted in the United States of America.

In our opinion, the financial statements referred to above present fairly, in all material respects, the admitted assets, liabilities, and surplus of ABC Company as of December 31, 20X2, and the results of its operations and cash flows for the year then ended, on the basis of accounting described in Note 13.

This report is intended solely for the information and use of the board of directors and management of ABC Company and [name of regulatory agency] and is not intended to be and should not be used by anyone other than these specified parties.

Mead & Co. LLP
San Francisco, California
March 21, 20X3

Required OCBOA financial statement disclosures are similar to those contained in GAAP financial statements. The auditor must assess the adequacy of the OCBOA financial statement disclosures in the same manner as GAAP ones. The auditor considers the adequacy of the summary of significant accounting policies as well as the disclosure of the basis used and how the OCBOA differs from GAAP. However, it is not necessary to quantify the effects of the differences between the OCBOA and GAAP presentations.

Additionally, it is not necessary to provide information that is not relevant to the OCBOA basis. For instance, the disclosure of the estimated

---

[4] *Ibid.*, AU sec. 623.08.

¶ 1002

useful lives for depreciable assets is not relevant for the cash basis financial statement.

If the auditor believes that the disclosures of the OCBOA financial statements are inadequate, an explanatory paragraph should be added to the auditor's report preceding the opinion paragraph. The explanatory paragraph should describe the auditor's reservations and should be followed by a qualified opinion.

¶ 1003 Audits of Specified Elements, Accounts, or Items of a Financial Statement

An auditor may be engaged to express an opinion on one or more specified elements, accounts, or items [SEAI] of the financial statements.[5] SEAI represent a part of, but significantly less than a complete financial statement. Examples of this type of engagement would be to audit one or more of the following:

- Current assets
- Accounts receivable
- Inventory
- Property and equipment
- Rentals
- Royalties
- Profit participation

The SEAI audit service may be performed either as a separate engagement or in conjunction with the audit of financial statements. However, to express an opinion on any SEAI that is based upon an entity's net income or stockholders' equity, the auditor must have audited the financial statements. For instance, if the auditor is engaged to render an opinion about a profit sharing account, it would be necessary to have audited the complete financial statements, specifically, net income.

In expressing an opinion on any SEAI, the auditor should use a level of materiality based not on the financial statements taken as a whole, but based on the individual element. Therefore, such an engagement is generally more extensive than if the SEAI were being considered in conjunction with an audit of the complete financial statements.

The content of an unqualified SEAI report when GAAP or OCBOA are used typically contains four paragraphs, as illustrated in Figure 10.10.

---

[5] *Ibid.*, AU sec. 623.11.

Figure 10.10 ─────────────────────────────

Paragraphs in a Report on One or More Specified Elements, Accounts, or Items (SEAI) in the Financial Statements

    1.   Introductory Paragraph

               ↓

    2.   Scope Paragraph

               ↓

    3.   Description of the Accounting Basis for the Presentation of the SEAI

               ↓

    4.   Opinion Paragraph

───

The SEAI report begins with the title of the report, which should contain the word, "independent," such as "Independent Auditor's Report." The first paragraph or introductory paragraph (Figure 10.11) describes which specific elements, accounts, or items in the financial statements were audited. If the complete financial statements were also audited, that should be stated in the introductory paragraph. Finally, this first paragraph clarifies the responsibilities of management and the auditors. As shown in Figure 10.11, the description of the accounting basis can be incorporated into the contents of the introductory paragraph.

If the SEAI report is made in conjunction with the audit of the financial statements, reference to the report and date of the auditor's report should be made in the introductory paragraph. If a departure in the financial statement audit report affects the SEAI matters, that should also be disclosed in the introductory paragraph.

Special Reports and Other Selected Attestation Reports **393**

Figure 10.11 ────────────────────────────────

Contents of an Introductory Paragraph in an SEAI Report

1. The audited specific elements, accounts, or items of the financial statements are identified.

2. Name of organization.

3. Specific time frame or point in time.

4. Management's responsibility in connection with the SEAI presentation.

5. Auditor's responsibility relating to the SEAI.

6. Optionally, describe the accounting basis of the SEAI presentation.

───────────────────────────

The scope paragraph (Figure 10.12) describes the nature of the SEAI audit.

Figure 10.12 ────────────────────────────────

Contents of a Scope Paragraph in an SEAI Report

1. GAAS used

2. The standards require:

    a. Planning

    b. Auditing for reasonable assurance that financial statements are materially correct

    c. Sampling used to support amounts and disclosures

    d. Auditor assessment of estimates used as well as overall presentation

3. Belief that the audit evidence supports the opinion

───────────────────────────

The explanatory paragraph is situated before the opinion paragraph and describes the basis for which the SEAI are presented. Figure 10.13 describes the content of the explanatory paragraph.

¶ **1003**

Figure 10.13

Contents of an Explanatory Paragraph About the Description of Accounting Basis in an SEAI Report

1. Description of the accounting basis for which the SEAI have been prepared
2. If necessary, a description of any source of interpretations made by management relating to the provisions of a relevant agreement

The opinion paragraph (Figure 10.14) reflects the auditor's opinion that the SEAI, in all material respects, conform to the basis of accounting described in the scope paragraph.

Figure 10.14

Contents of an Opinion Paragraph in an SEAI Report

1. That the specified elements, accounts or items in the financial statements:
   a. Are presented fairly (or not, or no opinion can be rendered)
   b. Are presented in all material respects
   c. Are presented in conformity with the basis of accounting described

The report should conclude with a handwritten or printed signature and the auditor's report should be dated as of the last day of fieldwork. Figure 10.15 is an example of an SEAI report when the complete financial statements were not audited, whereas Figure 10.16 is an SEAI report with the financial statements receiving an unqualified opinion.

¶ 1003

Figure 10.15 ─────────────────────────────

Language of an SEAI Report Relating to Inventory When Financial Statements Are Not Audited [6]

Report of the Independent Auditor

We have audited the accompanying schedule of inventory of ABC Company as of December 31, 20X2. This schedule is the responsibility of the Company's management. Our responsibility is to express an opinion about this schedule based on our audit.

We conducted our audit in accordance with auditing standards generally accepted in the United States of America. Those standards require that we plan and perform the audit to obtain reasonable assurance about whether the financial statements are free of material misstatement. An audit includes examining, on a test basis, evidence supporting the amounts and disclosures in the financial statements. An audit also includes assessing the accounting principles used and significant estimates made by management, as well as evaluating the overall financial statement presentation. We believe that our audit provides a reasonable basis for our opinion.

In our opinion, the schedule of inventory referred to above presents fairly, in all material respects, the inventory of ABC Company as of December 31, 20X2, in conformity with accounting principles generally accepted in the United States of America.

Mead & Co. LLP
San Francisco, California
March 21, 20X3

---

[6] *Ibid.*, AU sec. 623.18.

Figure 10.16

Language of an SEAI Report Relating to Inventory When Financial Statements Are Audited [7]

Report of the Independent Auditor

We have audited, in accordance with auditing standards generally accepted in the United States of America, the financial statements of ABC Company for the year ended December 31, 20X2, and have issued our report thereon dated March 13, 20X3. We have also audited the accompanying schedule of inventory of ABC Company as of December 31, 20X2. This schedule is the responsibility of the Company's management. Our responsibility is to express an opinion about this schedule based on our audit.

We conducted our audit of the inventory schedule in accordance with auditing standards generally accepted in the United States of America. Those standards require that we plan and perform the audit to obtain reasonable assurance about whether the financial statements are free of material misstatement. An audit includes examining, on a test basis, evidence supporting the amounts and disclosures in the financial statements. An audit also includes assessing the accounting principles used and significant estimates made by management, as well as evaluating the overall financial statement presentation. We believe that our audit provides a reasonable basis for our opinion.

In our opinion, the schedule of inventory referred to above presents fairly, in all material respects, the inventory of ABC Company as of December 31, 20X2, in conformity with generally accepted accounting principles.

Mead & Co. LLP
San Francisco, California
March 21, 20X3

If the auditor issued an adverse opinion or disclaimed an opinion about the complete financial statements, the auditor should consider whether reporting on the SEAI is essentially a piecemeal opinion. To determine whether the SEAI report would be considered a piecemeal opinion, he or she determines whether the SEAI would be considered a major portion of the financial statements. If the answer is positive, it would constitute a piecemeal opinion and the auditor should not render an SEAI report. However, if the auditor is satisfied that the report is not in effect a piecemeal opinion, an SEAI report can be issued, but must be presented separately from the report on the financial statements. The flowchart in Figure 10.17 represents this decision-making process.

---

[7] *Ibid.*, AU sec. 623.15.

¶ 1003

Special Reports and Other Selected Attestation Reports **397**

Figure 10.17

Reports About One or More Specified Elements, Accounts, or Items of a Financial Statement

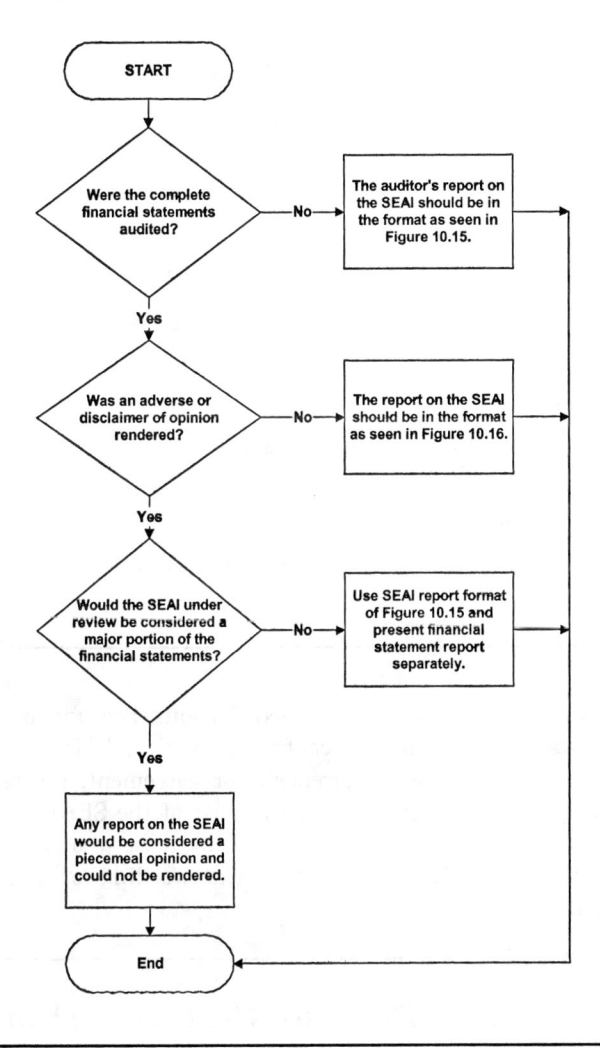

```
                    START
                      │
                      ▼
            ┌─────────────────┐
            │ Were the complete│        ┌──────────────────────┐
            │ financial       │──No───▶│ The auditor's report on│
            │ statements      │        │ the SEAI should be in  │
            │ audited?        │        │ the format as seen in  │
            └─────────────────┘        │ Figure 10.15.          │
                      │                └──────────────────────┘
                     Yes                          │
                      ▼                           │
            ┌─────────────────┐                   │
            │ Was an adverse or│       ┌──────────────────────┐
            │ disclaimer of   │──No───▶│ The report on the SEAI│
            │ opinion rendered?│       │ should be in the format│
            └─────────────────┘        │ as seen in Figure 10.16.│
                      │                └──────────────────────┘
                     Yes                          │
                      ▼                           │
            ┌─────────────────┐                   │
            │ Would the SEAI  │        ┌──────────────────────┐
            │ under review be │        │ Use SEAI report format│
            │ considered a    │──No───▶│ of Figure 10.15 and   │
            │ major portion of│        │ present financial     │
            │ the financial   │        │ statement report      │
            │ statements?     │        │ separately.           │
            └─────────────────┘        └──────────────────────┘
                      │                           │
                     Yes                          │
                      ▼                           │
            ┌─────────────────┐                   │
            │ Any report on   │                   │
            │ the SEAI would  │                   │
            │ be considered a │                   │
            │ piecemeal opinion│                  │
            │ and could not   │                   │
            │ be rendered.    │                   │
            └─────────────────┘                   │
                      │                           │
                      ▼                           │
                    ( End )◀──────────────────────┘
```

¶ 1003

Figure 10.18

Paragraphs in a Report on SEAI Prepared Using a Basis of Accounting Other Than GAAP or OCBOA

1. Introductory Paragraph
   ↓
2. Scope Paragraph
   ↓
3. Description of Accounting Basis
   ↓
4. Opinion Paragraph
   ↓
5. Restricted Use of Report

If the presentation of the specified elements, accounts or items in the financial statements is not in conformity with GAAP or OCBOA, but complies with some other requirements or agreement, the report should contain a final paragraph restricting the use of the SEAI (Figure 10.18). The report should be intended only for use by those who are parties to the agreement. Figure 10.19 illustrates the wording of the restrictive paragraph.

Figure 10.19

Language of a Restricted Use Paragraph in an SEAI Report [8]

This report is intended solely for the information and use of the board of directors and management of ABC Company and is not intended to be and should not be used by anyone other than these specified parties.

---

[8] *Ibid.*, AU sec. 623.20.

¶ 1004 Compliance with Aspects of Contractual Agreements or Regulatory Requirements

With another type of special report, the CPA is requested to report on a company's compliance with contractual agreements or regulatory agency compliance. This report may be in the form of a negative assurance based upon the audit of the financial statements and cannot be given unless the CPA has audited the financial statements to which the contractual agreements or regulatory compliance relates. Additionally, the report cannot be issued if the CPA has rendered an adverse opinion or disclaimed an opinion on the financial statements.

The report can be either a separate report or part of the audit report. If negative assurance is provided separately, the following information should be provided in the report:[9]

1. The title of the report must include the word *independent*
2. A paragraph stating that the financial statements:
    a. Were audited in accordance with GAAS
    b. Include the financial statement audit report date
    c. Indicate whether there were any departures from the standard audit report
3. A paragraph that:
    a. Refers to the applicable portion of the agreement or regulatory requirement
    b. Provides negative assurance
    c. States that the negative assurance is given in conjunction with the audited financial statements
    d. Specifies that the audit was not directed primarily at obtaining knowledge of compliance
4. A paragraph that provides a description and source of significant interpretations made by management
5. A paragraph that restricts the distribution of the report to those parties who are related to the company or the regulatory agency with which the report is being filed
6. The name of the CPA firm, either handwritten or printed
7. The date of completion of fieldwork

An example of a separate report on compliance with contractual provisions or regulatory requirements, respectively, can be seen in Figures 10.20 and 10.21.

---

[9] *Ibid.*, AU sec. 623.20.

Figure 10.20

Language of a Report on Compliance with Contractual Provisions Given in a Separate Report [10]

Report of the Independent Auditor

We have audited, in accordance with auditing standards generally accepted in the United States of America, the balance sheet of Brock Leisure Industries, Inc. as of December 31, 20X2, and the related statement of income, retained earnings, and cash flows for the year then ended, and have issued our report thereon dated March 17, 20X3.

In connection with our audit, nothing came to our attention that caused us to believe that the Company failed to comply with the terms, covenants, provisions, or conditions of sections XX to XX, inclusive, of the Indenture dated July 15, 20X2, with the XYZ Bank insofar as they relate to accounting matters. However, our audit was not directed primarily toward obtaining knowledge of such noncompliance.

This report is intended solely for the information and use of the boards of directors and management of Brock Leisure Industries, Inc. and XYZ Bank and is not intended to be and should not be used by anyone other than these specified parties.

Tompson & Comforte LLP
Oakland, California
March 22, 20X3

---

[10] *Ibid.*, AU sec. 623.21.

Figure 10.21 ─────────────────────────────

Language of a Report on Compliance with Regulatory Requirements Given in a Separate Report [11]

Report of the Independent Auditor

We have audited, in accordance with auditing standards generally accepted in the United States of America. The balance sheet of ABC Company as of December 31, 20X2, and the related statement of income, retained earnings, and cash flows for the year then ended, and have issued our report thereon dated March 17, 20X3.

In connection with our audit, nothing came to our attention that caused us to believe that the Company failed to comply with the accounting provisions in sections XX to XX, inclusive, of the [name of state regulatory agency]. However, our audit was not directed primarily toward obtaining knowledge of such noncompliance.

This report is intended solely for the information and use of the boards of directors and management of ABC Company and [name of state regulatory agency] and is not intended to be and should not be used by anyone other than these specified parties.

Tompson & Comforte LLP
Oakland, California
March 22, 20X3

If the negative assurance is being provided as an addition to the report on the financial statements, negative assurance should be provided after the opinion paragraph (see Figure 10.22).

---

[11] *Ibid.*, AU sec. 623.21.

Figure 10.22

Paragraphs in a Report About the Compliance with Contractual Agreements or Regulatory Provisions Added as a Separate Explanatory Paragraph to the Unqualified Opinion with Explanatory Paragraph

1. Introductory Paragraph

    ↓

2. Scope Paragraph

    ↓

3. Opinion Paragraph

    ↓

4. Negative Assurance About Compliance Paragraph

When the negative assurance about compliance with contractual agreements or regulatory provisions is added to the audited financial statement report (Figure 10.23), the additional paragraph(s) should:

- Refer to the applicable portion of the agreement or regulatory requirement

- Provide negative assurance

- State that the negative assurance is given in conjunction with the audited financial statements

- State that the audit was not directed primarily at obtaining knowledge of compliance

- Include a description and the source of significant interpretations made by management

- Include a statement that restricts the distribution of the report to those parties who are related to the company or the regulatory agency with which the report is being filed

¶ 1004

Figure 10.23

Language in a Report on Compliance with Regulatory Requirements Added in Paragraph Format to the Unqualified Financial Statement Auditor's Report [12]

Report of the Independent Auditor

Introductory Paragraph—same as the unqualified paragraph

Scope Paragraph—same as the unqualified paragraph

Financial Statement Opinion Paragraph—same as the unqualified paragraph

Additional Paragraphs Relating to Compliance with Regulatory Requirements:

In connection with our audit of the financial statements referred to above, nothing came to our attention that caused us to believe that the company failed to comply with the accounting provisions in sections XX to XX, inclusive, of the [name of state regulatory agency]. However, our audit was not directed primarily toward obtaining knowledge of such noncompliance.

This report is intended solely for the information and use of the boards of directors and management of ABC Company and [name of state regulatory agency] and is not intended to be and should not be used by anyone other than these specified parties.

Tompson & Comforte LLP
Oakland, California
March 22, 20X3

Figure 10.24 summarizes the process for delineating compliance issues concerning contractual agreements and regulatory requirements.

---

[12] *Ibid.*, AU sec. 623.21 (footnote 22).

Figure 10.24

Compliance with Contractual Agreements or Regulatory Requirements Related to Audited Financial Statements

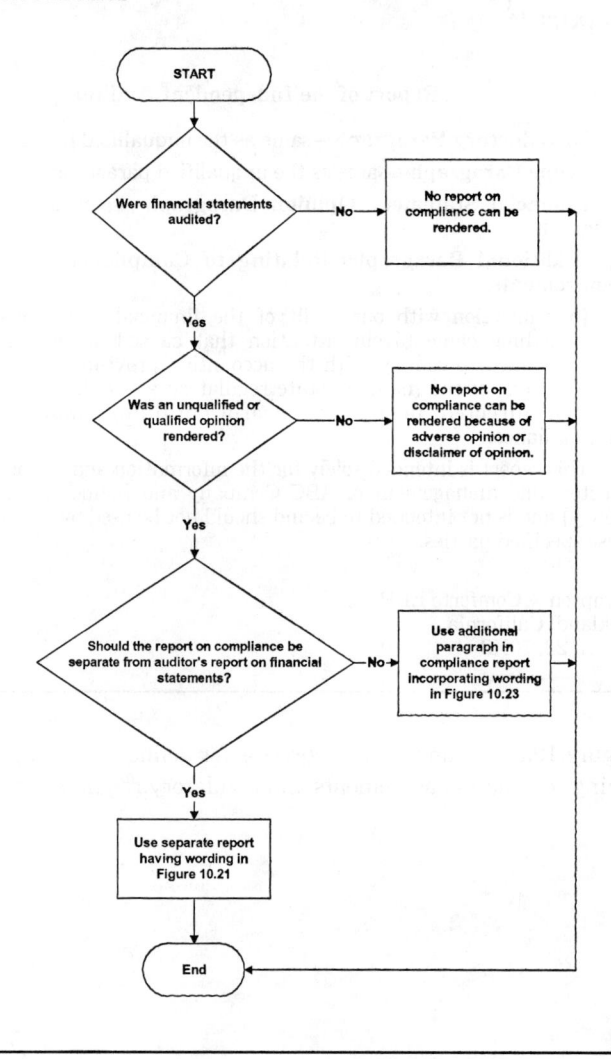

```
                    START
                      │
                      ▼
          ┌───────────────────────┐         ┌──────────────────┐
          │ Were financial        │── No ──▶│ No report on     │
          │ statements audited?   │         │ compliance can be│──┐
          └───────────────────────┘         │ rendered.        │  │
                      │ Yes                 └──────────────────┘  │
                      ▼                                           │
          ┌───────────────────────┐         ┌──────────────────┐  │
          │ Was an unqualified or │         │ No report on     │  │
          │ qualified opinion     │── No ──▶│ compliance can be│  │
          │ rendered?             │         │ rendered because │──┤
          └───────────────────────┘         │ of adverse opinion│ │
                      │ Yes                 │ or disclaimer of │  │
                      ▼                     │ opinion.         │  │
                                            └──────────────────┘  │
          ┌───────────────────────┐         ┌──────────────────┐  │
          │ Should the report on  │         │ Use additional   │  │
          │ compliance be separate│── No ──▶│ paragraph in     │  │
          │ from auditor's report │         │ compliance report│──┤
          │ on financial          │         │ incorporating    │  │
          │ statements?           │         │ wording in       │  │
          └───────────────────────┘         │ Figure 10.23     │  │
                      │ Yes                 └──────────────────┘  │
                      ▼                                           │
          ┌───────────────────────┐                               │
          │ Use separate report   │                               │
          │ having wording in     │                               │
          │ Figure 10.21          │                               │
          └───────────────────────┘                               │
                      │                                           │
                      ▼                                           │
                    End ◀──────────────────────────────────────────┘
```

¶ 1004

¶ 1005 Financial Presentations Prepared to Comply with Contractual Agreements or Regulatory Provisions

Two types of financial presentations have been prepared to comply with contractual agreements or regulatory provisions upon which an auditor can report:

1. Presentations prepared in compliance with a contractual agreement or regulatory provision that are not a complete set of financial statements or even a single financial statement. That is, not all of the assets, liabilities, revenues, or expenses are included in the detail of the presentation. However, what is presented conforms to GAAP or OCBOA.[13]

2. Presentations prepared on a basis of accounting prescribed in an agreement that do not conform to GAAP or OCBOA. The presentation does, however, represent a complete set of financial statements or at least a single financial statement.

On occasion an auditor is requested to audit only those assets and liabilities that will be included in a sale or transfer, instead of the entire company's assets and liabilities. However, although reports required by contractual agreements or regulation requirements may constitute an incomplete presentation, auditing standards specify that such a financial presentation should generally be regarded as a financial statement if the financial presentation is presented in accordance with GAAP or OCBOA.[14] This is a different scenario than an audit of specified elements, accounts, or items of a financial statement in as far as it more closely resembles the complete financial statements and represents an example of the first type of financial presentation above.

When reporting on these presentations, the auditor must be cognizant of the following matters:

- That the materiality level should be that of the presentation taken as a whole

- Adequate disclosure requirements should be met

- The presentation should be appropriately titled so that the special purpose of the presentation should be clear to the user

The unqualifed report for a financial presentation, which conforms with GAAP or OCBOA but is incomplete with respect to the company's financial statements, typically will contain five paragraphs, as illustrated in Figure 10.25.

---

[13] *Ibid.*, AU sec. 623.22. [14] *Ibid.*, AU sec. 623.25.

Figure 10.25

Paragraphs in a Report about a Financial Presentation Prepared to Comply with Contractual Agreements or Regulatory Provision [15]

(Conforms with GAAP or OCBOA but excludes certain aspects of the complete financial statements.)

1. Introductory Paragraph
   ↓
2. Scope Paragraph
   ↓
3. Description of Accounting Basis
   ↓
4. Opinion Paragraph
   ↓
5. Restricted Use of Report

The report for the financial presentation should begin with the title of the report which should contain the word, "independent," such as "Independent Auditor's Report." The introductory paragraph (Figure 10.26) describes which financial statements were audited as well as the delineation of management and auditor responsibilities.

---

[15] *Ibid.*, AU sec. 623.25.

¶ 1005

Figure 10.26

Contents of an Introductory Paragraph of a Financial Presentation

(Conforms with GAAP or OCBOA but excludes certain aspects of the complete financial statements.)

1. The audited financial presentation is identified
2. For what organization
3. For which timeframe or point in time
4. Management's responsibility with respect to the financial presentation
5. Auditor's responsibility with respect to the financial presentation

---

The scope paragraph, much like that of the standard audit opinion, describes the nature of the financial presentation audit.

Figure 10.27

Contents of a Scope Paragraph of a Financial Presentation

(Conforms with GAAP or OCBOA but excludes certain aspects of the complete financial statements.)

1. Generally accepted auditing standards were used
2. The standards require:
   a. Planning
   b. Auditing for reasonable assurance that financial statements are materially correct
   c. Sampling used to support amounts and disclosures
   d. Auditor assessment of estimates used as well as overall presentation
3. Belief that the audit evidence supports the opinion

The explanatory paragraph is situated before the opinion paragraph and describes the basis of the financial presentation. Figure 10.28 describes the contents of the explanatory paragraph.

¶ 1005

Figure 10.28 ─────────────────────────

Contents of an Explanatory Paragraph of a Financial Presentation

(Conforms with GAAP or OCBOA but excludes certain aspects of the complete financial statements.)

1. Description of the accounting basis for which the financial presentation has been prepared. If the basis is GAAP, a statement should be included that the presentation is not intended to represent the company's complete financial statements.
2. An explanation of what the financial presentation is intended to represent.

If the auditor's opinion is unqualified, the opinion paragraph (Figure 10.29) reflects the auditor's opinion that the financial presentation, in all material respects, conforms to GAAP or OCBOA.

Figure 10.29 ─────────────────────────

Contents of an Opinion Paragraph of a Financial Presentation

(Conforms with GAAP or OCBOA but excludes certain aspects of the complete financial statements.)

1. That the financial presentation:
    a. Is fair
    b. In all material respects
    c. In conformity with GAAP or OCBOA

Unless the report is being filed with the Securities and Exchange Commission, in which case no restrictive paragraph is included, the report should be intended only for use by those who are parties to the agreement. Figure 10.30 illustrates the wording of the restrictive paragraph, and Figure 10.31 shows the complete report.

¶ 1005

Figure 10.30 ─────────────────────────────

Contents of a Restrictive Paragraph of a Financial Presentation

(Conforms with GAAP or OCBOA but excludes certain aspects of the complete financial statements.)

    This report is intended solely for the information and use of the board of directors and management of ABC Company [or regulatory agency with which the report is being filed] and is not intended to be and should not be used by anyone other than these specified parties.

─────────────────────────────

The report should conclude with a handwritten or printed signature and the auditor's report should be dated as of the last day of fieldwork.

Figure 10.31

Language of an Unqualified Report on a Financial Presentation [16]

(Conforms with GAAP or OCBOA but excludes certain aspects of the complete financial statements.)

Report of the Independent Auditor

We have audited the statement of net assets sold of XYZ Company as of September 30, 20X2. This statement of net assets is the responsibility of XYZ Company's management. Our responsibility is to express an opinion on the statement of net assets sold based on our audit.

We conducted our audit in accordance with auditing standards generally accepted in the United States of America. Those standards require that we plan and perform the audit to obtain reasonable assurance about whether the financial statements are free of material misstatement. An audit includes examining, on a test basis, evidence supporting the amounts and disclosures in the financial statements. An audit also includes assessing the accounting principles used and significant estimates made by management, as well as evaluating the overall financial statement presentation. We believe that our audit provides a reasonable basis for our opinion.

The accompanying statement was prepared to present the net assets of XYZ Company pursuant to the purchase agreement described in Note 13, and is not intended to be a complete presentation of XYZ Company's assets and liabilities.

In our opinion, the accompanying statement of net assets sold presents fairly, in all material respects, the net assets of XYZ Company as of September 30, 20X2, in conformity with accounting principles generally accepted in the United States of America.

This report is intended solely for the information and use of the board of directors and management of XYZ Company [or regulatory agency with which the report is being filed] and is not intended to be and should not be used by anyone other than these specified parties.

Mead & Co. LLP
San Francisco, California
March 21, 20X3

These auditing standards also include those presentations of financial statements prepared on a basis of accounting prescribed in an agreement that does not conform to GAAP or OCBOA. The type of presentation does represent a complete set of financial statements or single financial statement.

The format of the auditor's report is similar to the unqualified report on a financial presentation that conforms to GAAP or OCBOA but excludes certain aspects of the complete financial statements. The title of the report

---

[16] *Ibid.*, AU sec. 623.26.

should contain the word, "independent," and is made up of five paragraphs (Figure 10.32).

Figure 10.32

Paragraphs in a Report on a Financial Statement Not Prepared Using GAAP or OCBOA [17]

1. Introductory Paragraph
   ↓
2. Scope Paragraph
   ↓
3. Description of Accounting Basis
   ↓
4. Opinion Paragraph
   ↓
5. Restricted Use of Report

The introductory paragraph should reference that the financial statements are for a special purpose and delineate management's and the auditor's responsibilities regarding the financial statements. The scope and restrictive paragraphs are identical to the preceding example. The contents of the explanatory paragraph should include:

- Description of the accounting basis for which the financial presentation has been prepared and a reference to notes in the financial statements that more fully describe the basis

- An explanation that the financial presentation is not intended to represent GAAP

The contents of the opinion paragraph should indicate that the financial presentation presents fairly, in all material respects, the described basis of accounting. A final paragraph restricting use of the financial presentation is also included. An example of the report is shown in Figure 10.33.

[17] *Ibid.*, AU sec. 623.27.

Figure 10.33

Language of a Report on Financial Statements Prepared Pursuant to a Loan Agreement that Results in a Presentation Not in Conformity with GAAP or OCBOA [18]

Report of the Independent Auditor

We have audited the accompanying statement of assets and liabilities of Grinshank Enterprises Inc. as of December 31, 20X2, and the related special purpose statements of revenues and expenses and cash flows for the year then ended. These financial statements are the responsibility of the Company's management. Our responsibility is to express an opinion on these financial statements based on our audit.

We conducted our audit in accordance with auditing standards generally accepted in the United States of America. Those standards require that we plan and perform the audit to obtain reasonable assurance about whether the financial statements are free of material misstatement. An audit includes examining, on a test basis, evidence supporting the amounts and disclosures in the financial statements. An audit also includes assessing the accounting principles used and significant estimates made by management, as well as evaluating the overall financial statement presentation. We believe that our audit provides a reasonable basis for our opinion.

The accompanying special-purpose financial statements were prepared for the purpose of complying with Section 6 of a loan agreement between Common Bank and the company as discussed in Note 13, and are not intended to be a presentation in conformity with accounting principles generally accepted in the United States of America.

In our opinion, the special purpose financial statements referred to above present fairly, in all material respects, the assets and liabilities of Grinshank Enterprises Inc. as of December 31, 20X2, and the revenues, expenses and cash flows for the year then ended, on the basis of accounting described in Note 13.

This report is intended solely for the information and use of the board of directors and management of Grinshank Enterprises Inc. and Common Bank and is not intended to be and should not be used by anyone other than these parties.

Cole & Bow LLP
St. Louis, Missouri
March 21, 20X3

¶ 1006 Financial Information Presented in Prescribed Forms or Schedules that Require a Prescribed Form of Report

In some situations the auditor is asked to issue a report that has prescribed wording. If the prescribed report is not consistent with the assurances that the auditor provides, the auditor has two options as to what to do:[19]

---

[18] *Ibid.*, AU sec. 623.30.   [19] *Ibid.*, AU secs. 623.32-.33.

1. If possible, the auditor should change the wording of the prescribed report to conform with auditing standards and submit it as is.

2. If changing the wording is not practical, a separate report with correct wording can be attached to the prescribed form.

¶ 1007 Prospective Financial Statements

Prospective financial statements are those that show predicted results for the financial position, income, and cash flows of a company.[20] Prospective financial statements are based on estimates and assumptions of future events applied to currently available information, the goal of which is to offer a possible look into the future. Lenders sometime require prospective financial statements as part of a loan application. Sometimes investors request prospective financial statements so as to determine the potential of a business venture. Managers use prospective financial statements in their decision-making process.

There are two types of prospective financial statements:

1. Forecasts
2. Projections

Forecasts present what the preparer believes will be the future financial position, results of operations, and cash flows. The forecast merges currently available information with reasonable assumptions regarding the company and the environment and predicts how the financial statements should appear. The format of the forecast may be expressed in a specific monetary amount or as a range of values. Because the forecast represents what the responsible parties, usually management, believe to be their best estimate of the future there can only be one forecast for a company. The forecast can be distributed for general use.

Financial projections present an expected financial position, results of operations, and cash flows given one or more hypothetical assumptions. However, unlike the forecast, there can be many projections depending upon the hypothetical assumptions used. For that reason, so as not to confuse the uninformed reader, projections are for restricted use only.

Pro-forma financial statements are not considered prospective financial statements because they reflect an historical presentation. Also, partial presentations are not considered prospective financial statements because of the inadequacy of presentation. Additionally, the standards for prospective financial statements do not apply when the prospective financial statements are to be used only for litigation services.

---

[20] Statement on Standards for Attestation Engagements, No. 10, Attestation Standards: Revision and Recodification (AICPA, Professional Standards, vol. 1, AT sec. 301).

.01 Minimum Requirements for a Prospective Financial Statement

According to auditing standards, the minimum elements of prospective financial statements are as follows:[21]

- Sales or gross revenue
- Gross profit or cost of goods sold
- Unusual or infrequently occurring items
- Provision for income taxes
- Discontinued operations or extraordinary items
- Income from continuing operations
- Net income
- Basic earnings per share and, if applicable, diluted earnings per share
- Significant changes in financial position
- A description of what management intends the prospective financial statements to present
- A statement that the assumptions are based on information about circumstances and conditions existing at the time the prospective information was prepared
- A warning that the prospective results may not be achieved—usually there are differences between the forecasted and actual results because assumptions can be wrong and unforeseen events can occur
- Summary of significant assumptions
- Summary of significant accounting policies

.02 Assumptions and Disclosures

In addition to the disclosure of important matters affecting the prospective financial statements, AICPA guidelines[22] require the disclosure of significant assumptions. Any assumptions that may vary having a significant effect on the prospective results should be disclosed. Those anticipated conditions used for the prospective financial statements that are expected to be significantly different also should be disclosed.

Assumptions made for projected financial statements that are considered hypothetical, especially those that management considers as having little probability of occurring, must be identified in the disclosures.

---

[21] *Ibid.*, AT sec. 301.68.   [22] *Ibid.*, AT sec. 301.06.

.03 Compilation of Prospective Financial Statements—Forecast

A CPA can either compile or examine prospective financial statements. To compile prospective financial statements the CPA should:[23]

- Possess adequate technical training to compile prospective financial statements. They should understand guidelines contained in the AICPA Audit and Accounting Guide, *Guide for Prospective Financial Information*.[24]

- Exercise due professional care in the performance of the compilation.

- Adequately supervise any assistants compiling the prospective financial statements.

- Understand the generally accepted accounting principles applicable in the industry for which the company operates.

- Understand:
  - Objectives of the engagement including client and practitioner responsibilities
  - Company's operations
  - Company's record-keeping system
  - Accounting principles and practices to be used in the preparation of the financial statements. (If historical financial statements are the basis for the prospective financial statements, the CPA should determine whether the same accounting principles had been used for both sets of financial statements)
  - Any proposed operation and key factors for performance success

- Assemble, to the extent necessary, the prospective financial statements based on the responsible parties assumptions.

- Perform the required compilation procedures, beginning by reading the prospective financial statements in light of the disclosed assumptions to determine whether:
  - Financial statements are presented in conformity with the guidelines of the AICPA
  - Assumptions and accounting policies used are obviously appropriate
  - There are any inconsistencies with the assumptions

---

[23] *Ibid.*, AT sec. 301. [24] *Ibid.*, AT sec. 301.69, Appendix B.

¶ 1007.03

- Establish an understanding about the compilation services a CPA will perform. The understanding should be documented in the workpapers which could include written communication with the client.

- Inquire about:
  - What accounting principles were used in preparing the prospective financial statements
  - How client identifies key factors for performance success
  - Results of operations for any expired prospective period
  - How the assumptions were developed

- Determine responsible party for all significant assumptions and consider if there are material omissions in assumptions when compared to key factors of successful performance.

- Determine whether all of the assumptions are sufficiently disclosed and consistent with one another.

- Test the mathematical accuracy of the application of the assumptions to the underlying data.

- Obtain a written and signed representation regarding the statements and assumptions.

- Issue a compilation report.

The format of the standard compilation report for a forecast (Figure 10.34) is contained in two paragraphs: the introductory and description paragraphs.

Figure 10.34

Paragraphs in a Standard Compilation Report on Forecasted Financial Statements

1. Introductory Paragraph

    ↓

2. Compilation Description and Disclaimer of Opinion and on Forecasted Results

The introductory paragraph (Figure 10.35) includes a description of the forecasted financial statements and that AICPA standards were used to compile the prospective financial statements.

¶ 1007.03

Figure 10.35 ───────────────────────────

Contents of an Introductory Paragraph for Forecasted Financial Statements [25]

1. Prospective financial statements compiled are identified

2. For what organization

3. For which time frame or point in time

4. Standards of the AICPA used

The second paragraph (Figure 10.36) describes what a compilation is and that the CPA is not rendering an audit opinion on the forecasted financial statements. Also, a disclaimer as to the ultimate results of the company's operations with respect to the prospective view is included.

Figure 10.36 ───────────────────────────

Contents of a Compilation Description and Disclaimer Paragraph for Forecasted Financial Statements

1. A compilation of forecasted financial statements:

    a. Is the representation of management

    b. Does not represent an audit

2. The CPA does not render any assurance on the prospective financial statements.

3. Disclaimer on results of forecast

4. The CPA has no responsibility to update report

An example of a complete compilation report for forecasted financial statements is shown in Figure 10.37.

---

[25] *Ibid.*, AT sec. 301.19.

Figure 10.37

Language of a Compilation Report on Forecasted Financial Statements [26]

To the Appropriate Addressee:

We have compiled the accompanying forecasted balance sheet, statements of income, retained earnings, and cash flows of ABC Company as of December 31, 20X4, and for the year then ending, in accordance with standards established by the American Institute of Certified Public Accountants.

A compilation is limited to presenting in the form of a forecast information that is the representation of management and does not include evaluation of the support for the assumptions underlying the forecast. We have not examined the forecast and, accordingly, do not express an opinion or any other form of assurance on the accompanying statements or assumptions. Furthermore, there will usually be differences between the forecasted and actual results, because events and circumstances frequently do not occur as expected, and those differences may be material. We have no responsibility to update this report for events and circumstances occurring after the date of this report.

Porter & Stout LLP
Golden, Colorado
February 11, 20X3

.04 Compilation of Prospective Financial Statements—Projection

The format of the projected financial statements is similar to the forecast except that the requirement that projected financial statements are for restricted use only is highlighted in a separate, third paragraph (Figure 10.38).

---

[26] *Ibid.*, AT sec. 301.19.

¶ 1007.04

Figure 10.38

Paragraphs in an Unqualified Opinion Report on Projected Financial Statements

1. Introductory Paragraph
   ↓
2. Compilation Description and Disclaimer of Opinion and on Projected Results
   ↓
3. Restricted Use Paragraph

An example of a report on a compiled set of projected financial statements appears in Figure 10.39.

Figure 10.39

Language of a Compilation Report on Projected Financial Statements [27]

To the Appropriate Addressee:

We have compiled the accompanying projected balance sheet, statements of income, retained earnings, and cash flows of ABC Company as of December 31, 20X4, and for the year then ending, in accordance with standards established by the American Institute of Certified Public Accountants. The accompanying projection was prepared for [state purpose of projection].

A compilation is limited to presenting in the form of a projection information that is the representation of management and does not include evaluation of the support for the assumptions underlying the projection. We have not examined the forecast and, accordingly, do not express an opinion or any other form of assurance on the accompanying statements or assumptions. Furthermore, even if [description of hypothetical assumption, e.g., "the loan is granted and the plant is built"], there will usually be differences between the forecasted and actual results, because events and circumstances frequently do not occur as expected, and those differences may be material. We have no responsibility to update this report for events and circumstances occurring after the date of this report.

The accompanying projections and this report were prepared for [state purpose, e.g., "negotiation to expand plant"] and are not intended to be and should not be used by anyone other than those specified parties.

Porter & Stout LLP
Golden, Colorado
February 11, 20X3

.05 Examinations of Prospective Financial Statements

As with historical financial statements, the client is responsible for the fair presentation of the prospective financial statement, whereas the CPA's responsibility lies with the work supporting the examination as well as the report itself. Forecasts quantify management's expectations. Projections quantify various management assumptions, but in either case the prospective financial statements do not represent the CPA's predictions. The CPA is rendering an opinion on the prospective financial statements as to their conformance with AICPA preparation guidelines, reasonableness of the assumptions, and adequacy of disclosure.

---

[27] *Ibid.*, AT sec. 301.20.

Special Reports and Other Selected Attestation Reports **421**

Figure 10.40

The Planning Phase for Examination of Prospective Financial Statements

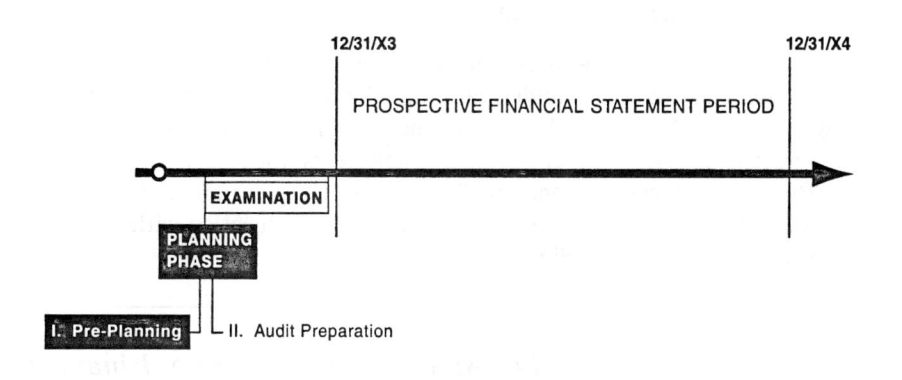

```
                    12/31/X3                              12/31/X4
                    PROSPECTIVE FINANCIAL STATEMENT PERIOD
         ┌──EXAMINATION──┐
       PLANNING
        PHASE
  I. Pre-Planning ── II. Audit Preparation
```

.06 Planning Phase—Preplanning Stage

The phase involves both preplanning (Figure 10.40) and preparation (Figure 10.41) stages. In preplanning, the auditor obtains information regarding the objectives of the engagement, the CPA's capabilities required for the engagement, and general information regarding the client. As with historical financial statement audits, the CPA should follow these steps:

1. Obtain an understanding of the engagement:
    a. The purpose for the examination of the prospective financial statements
    b. Who will be relying upon the audit report
    c. The overall strategy for expected scope
    d. Type of report
    e. Length of period covered by the prospective financial statements
2. Obtain background information regarding the prospective client's professional reputation
3. Determine to what extent the prospective client is willing and able to pay the examination fee
4. Review the auditor's own staffing capabilities
5. Determine the auditor's own as well as the staff's experience and knowledge with respect to:
    a. The prospective client's industry

¶ 1007.06

b. The prospective client's operation

c. Examinations of prospective financial statements

6. Determine that the auditing organization is independent with respect to the client

Once these above issues are satisfied the auditor can accept the engagement and the understanding should be documented in the workpapers. Documentation should include the understanding of the engagement, including the engagement's objectives, the responsibilities of the CPA and management, and the limitations of the examination. It is also recommended that there should be written communication with the client regarding the understanding.

Figure 10.41

Preparing for the Audit of Prospective Financial Statements

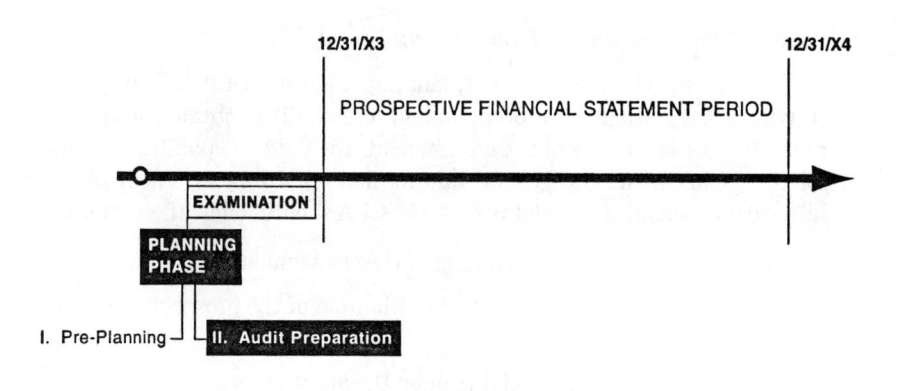

```
                    12/31/X3                              12/31/X4
                    PROSPECTIVE FINANCIAL STATEMENT PERIOD
           EXAMINATION
        PLANNING
        PHASE
I. Pre-Planning   II. Audit Preparation
```

.07 Planning Phase—Preparing for the Examination

The planning process is critical because it helps develop a stategy in conducting the engagement and ensure that examination resources are directed in an efficient, timely, and effective manner. In order to begin planning the engagement, knowledge about client matters, the external environment, and the industry in which the client operates must be understood. To assist the auditor in such matters, industry accounting and audit guides such as those prepared by the American Institute of Certified Public Accountants (AICPA) should be reviewed. Related planning phase activities may include:

- Becoming familiar with guidelines for the preparation and presentation of prospective financial statements.

¶ 1007.07

- Acquiring knowledge of the industry in which the client operates:[28]
  - Competitive conditions
  - Regulation
  - Technology
  - Accounting policies
- Acquiring information about the client's operations and accounting:
  - Accounting principles are used.
  - The level of the responsible party's experience in preparing prospective financial statements.
  - Information obtained while performing other services for the client; knowledge of events, transactions, practices obtained from other services could provide a significant insight on prospective financial statements.
  - Review patterns of past performance:
    - revenue and cost trends
    - turnover of assets
    - uses of physical facilities
    - management policies
  - What is the period covered by the prospective financial statements?

Consideration of other factors:

- The nature of the attestation report.
- Preliminary judgments of attestation risk, whereby the CPA may fail to modify the attestation report.[29]
- Assess the accuracy of underlying data.
- The materiality level of the client as a preliminary judgment, because materiality affects the application of examination procedures to prospective financial statements. Establishing a preliminary materiality level assists the CPA in designing examination procedures to detect material misstatements in the prospective financial statements. The preliminary level of materiality is based upon the auditor's judgment and is applied to the financial statements taken as a whole in the same manner as for historical financial statements.

---

[28] *Ibid.*, AT sec. 301.70, Appendix C.   [29] *Ibid.*, AT sec. 101.45.

¶ 1007.07

- Which items in prospective financial statements will likely require revision or adjustment.
- Determination of whether any of the conditions used as assumptions in the prospective financial statements may require the auditor to adjust or modify the examination procedures.
- Supervision of assistants are similar to those of audit engagements.

Figure 10.42

The Examination Phase of Prospective Financial Statements

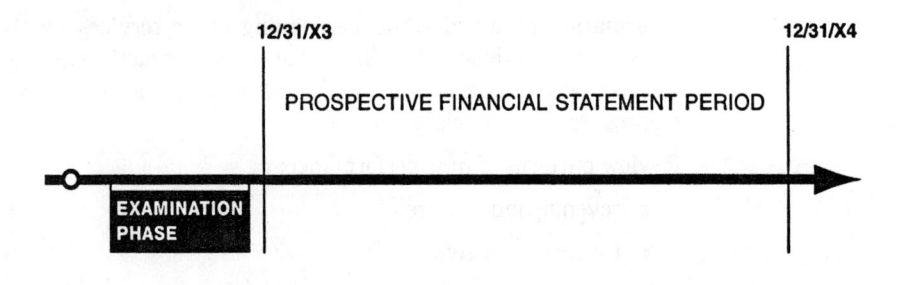

.08 Examination Phase

During the examination phase (Figure 10.42) the CPA's objective is to accumulate enough evidence to restrict attestation risk to an appropriate level and determine whether:[30]

- Prospective financial statements are in conformity with presentation guidelines of the AICPA
- Assumptions underlying the preparation of the prospective financial statements are reasonable

The prospective financial statement preparers must exercise judgment in selecting estimates and assumptions for the statements. Therefore, the CPA should select procedures to determine whether the assumptions used to prepare the prospective financial statements are reasonable. These procedures should include a review of whether:

- Sources come from both internal and external sources.
- Assumptions are consistent with the original source.
- The assumptions are consistent with one another.

---
[30] *Ibid.*, AT sec. 301.70.

Special Reports and Other Selected Attestation Reports **425**

- To what extent the underlying historical data is reliable and comparable to the prospective period. The reliability can be assessed using inquiry of management and analytical procedures.

Other procedures to be performed on the prospective financial statements include:

- Testing the mathematical accuracy of the financial statements.

- Determining whether the presentation:
  - Properly reflects the assumptions
  - Follows AICPA guidelines for prospective financial statements
  - Adequately discloses the assumptions
  - Uses accounting principles, in the case of a forecast, consistent with the underlying data and, in the case of a projection, consistent with the purpose of the presentation

- Sometimes the examination of prospective financial statements may include the work of a specialist.[31] Errors or misstatements made by specialists can cause misstatements in the prospective financial statements. However, the CPA is not responsible for reanalyzing the specialist's conclusions but does need to review the specialist's conclusions so as to determine if they appear reasonable.

- The CPA must read that information to see whether it either conflicts with the statements or contains a material misstatement of fact.

- Obtaining a representation letter from those parties responsible for the fair presentation of the prospective financial statements.

.09 The CPA's Report on Prospective Financial Statements

During the reporting phase of the examination (Figure 10.43) the CPA prepares the report on the prospective financial statements. The report emphasizes that the CPA is rendering an opinion on the conformity of the prospective financial statements with AICPA guidelines as well as the reasonableness of the underlying assumptions used to prepare the financial statements.

---

[31] *Ibid.*, AT sec. 201.16.

¶ **1007.09**

Figure 10.43

The Reporting Phase of Prospective Financial Statements

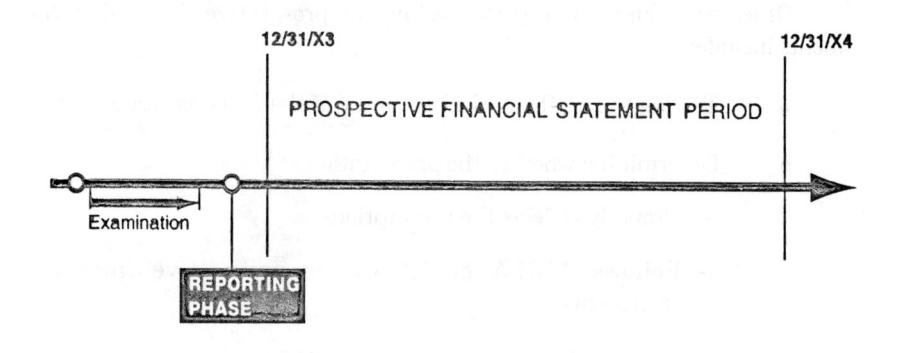

```
                    12/31/X3                                    12/31/X4
                       |                                           |
                       |  PROSPECTIVE FINANCIAL STATEMENT PERIOD   |
    ○──────────────○───|───────────────────────────────────────────▶
    Examination        |
                  ┌─────────┐
                  │REPORTING│
                  │ PHASE   │
                  └─────────┘
```

The format of the unqualified report on forecasted financial statements typically consists of the introductory, scope and opinion paragraphs (Figure 10.44).

Figure 10.44

Paragraphs in an Unqualified Report on Forecasted Financial Statements

1. Introductory Paragraph
   ↓
2. Scope Paragraph
   ↓
3. Opinion Paragraph with Disclaimer on Forecasted Results (Figure 10.46)

As is usual with introductory paragraphs, this one identifies the financial statements and assigns respective responsibilites to the management and CPA.

¶ 1007.09

Special Reports and Other Selected Attestation Reports **427**

Figure 10.45

Contents of an Introductory Paragraph in an Unqualified Report on Forecasted Financial Statements

1. Prospective financial statements examined are identified
2. For what organization
3. For which time frame or point in time
4. Responsibility of management
5. Responsibility of CPA

The scope paragraph identifies the attestation standards used by the CPA.

The opinion paragraph (Figure 10.46) states that the financial statements are presented using AICPA guidelines and that the assumptions are reasonable. Additionally, the CPA must disclaim an opinion on the results of the prospective financial statements as well as declaring that the auditing firm has no responsibility to update the report.

Figure 10.46

Contents of an Opinion Paragraph in an Unqualified Report on Forecasted Financial Statements

1. Financial statements:
    a. Are presented using AICPA guidelines
    b. Assumptions are reasonable
2. Disclaimer on results of forecast
3. CPA has no responsibility to update report

Figure 10.47 shows an example of the report on a forecasted financial statement.

¶ 1007.09

Figure 10.47

Language of a Report on the Examination of Forecasted Financial Statements [32]

Report of the Independent Auditor

We have examined the accompanying forecasted balance sheet, statements of income, retained earnings, and cash flows of TTT Pre-Owned Autos Inc. as of December 31, 20X4, and for the year then ending.

TTT Pre-Owned Auto Inc. Company's Management is responsible for the forecast. Our responsibility is to express an opinion on the forecast based on our examination. Our Examination was conducted in accordance with attestation standards for an examination of a forecast established by the American Institute of Certified Public Accountants and, accordingly, included such procedures as we considered necessary to evaluate both the assumptions used by management and the preperation and presentation of the forecast. We believe that our examination provides a reasonable basis for our opinion.

In our opinion, the accompanying forecast is presented in conformity with guidelines for presentation of a forecast established by the American Institute of Certified Public Accountants, and the underlying assumptions provide a reasonable basis for management's forecast. However, there will usually be differences between the forecasted and actual results, because events and circumstances frequently do not occur as expected, and those differences may be material. We have no responsibility to update this report for events and circumstances occurring after the date of this report.

Chee & Goode LLP
Seattle, Washington
July 7, 20X3

The report on projected financial statements is similar to the forecasted financial statement except that the statements are for restricted use. As such there is an additional paragraph (Figure 10.48) after the opinion paragraph.

---

[32] *Ibid.*, AT sec. 301.34.

Figure 10.48

Paragraphs in an Unqualified Report on Projected Financial Statements

1. Introductory Paragraph
   ↓
2. Scope Paragraph
   ↓
3. Opinion Paragraph with Disclaimer on Projected Results
   ↓
4. Restricted Use Paragraph

Figure 10.49 illustrates the report on a projected financial statement.

Figure 10.49

Language of an Unqualified Report on the Examination of Projected Financial Statements [33]

Report of the Independent Auditor

We have examined the accompanying projected balance sheet, statements of income, retained earnings, and cash flows of ABC Company as of December 31, 20X4, and for the year then ending.

ABC company's management is responsible for the projection which was prepared for [state special purpose]. Our responsibilty is to express an opinion on the projection based on our examination. Our examination was conducted in accordance with standards for an examination of a projection established by the American Institute of Certified Public Accountants and, accordingly, included such procedures as we considered necessary to evaluate both the assumptions used by management and the preparation and presentation of the projection. We believe that our examination provides a reasonable basis for our opinion.

In our opinion, the accompanying projection is presented in conformity with guidelines for presentation of a projection established by the American Institute of Certified Public Accountants, and the underlying assumptions provide a reasonable basis for management's projection [describe the hypothetical assumption.] However, even if [describe assumption] there will usually be differences between the forecasted and actual results, because events and circumstances frequently do not occur as expected, and those differences may be material. We have no responsibility to update this report for events and circumstances occurring after the date of this report.

The accompanying projections and this report were prepared for [identify specific parties] and should not be used by anyone other than these specified parties.

Chee & Goode LLP
Seattle, Washington
July 7, 20X3

.10 Updating the CPA's Report

In the opinion paragraph of the standard report on prospective financial statements states that they have no responsibility to update the report for events and circumstances occurring after the report date. As such the CPA has no responsibility to notify users of the report when actual results are different from the forecast.

The limitation on updating is different than revising the report when errors are discovered in the prospective financial statements. In those cases the CPA is required to consider notifying the financial statement users if a mistake was made at the time of the engagement.

---

[33] *Ibid.*, AT sec. 301.35.

.11 Modifications to the Accountant's Opinion

An examination of prospective financial statements could also result in a qualified, adverse, or disclaimed opinion. If, as a result of the examination, the prospective financial statement presentation contains a departure from AICPA guidelines, a qualified or adverse opinion should be rendered (Figure 10.50). The departure could come from two sources:

1. Misapplication of generally accepted accounting principles (GAAP) creating a measurement departure

2. Some aspect of the assumptions is unreasonable

Figure 10.50 ─────────────────────────────────

Paragraphs of a Qualified Report on Forecasted Financial Statements

1. Introductory Paragraph
   ↓
2. Scope Paragraph
   ↓
3. Explanatory Paragraph
   ↓
4. Qualified Opinion Paragraph
   with Disclaimer on Forecasted Results

───

The qualified and adverse reports should contain an additional paragraph(s) describing the departure and its effect on the prospective financial statements. The qualified opinion paragraph uses "except for" terminology, whereas the adverse report opinion paragraph states that the financial statements are not in conformity with guidelines established by the AICPA.

Figure 10.51 gives an example of an adverse opinion on forecasted financial statements.

¶ 1007.11

Figure 10.51

Language of an Adverse Report on the Examination of Forecasted Financial Statements [34]

Report of the Independent Auditor

We have examined the accompanying forecasted balance sheet, statements of income, retained earnings, and cash flows of ABC Company as of December 31, 20X4, and for the year then ending.

ABC Company's management is responsible for the forecast. Our responsibility is to express an opinion on the forecast based on our examination. Our examination was conducted in accordance with standards for an examination of a forecast established by the American Institute of Certified Public Accountants and, accordingly, included such procedures as we considered necessary to evaluate both the assumptions used by management and the preparation and presentation of the forecast. We believe that our examination provides a reasonable basis for our opinion.

As discussed under the caption "Sales" in the summary of significant forecast assumptions, the forecasted sales include, among other things, revenue from the company's federal defense contracts continuing at the current level. The new contracts have been signed and no negotiations are under way for new federal defense contracts. Furthermore, the federal government has entered into contracts with another company to supply the items being manufactured under the company's present contract.

In our opinion, the accompanying forecast is not presented in conformity with guidelines for presentation of a financial forecast established by the American Institute of Certified Public Accountants because management's assumptions, as discussed in the preceding paragraph, do not provide a reasonable basis for management's forecast. We have no responsibility to update this report for events or circumstances occurring after the date of this report.

Bedda & Bree LLP
Milwaukee, Wisconsin
July 7, 20X3

For those examination during which sufficient evidence was not available because of a scope limitation the CPA should disclaim an opinion. For example, if the CPA could not obtain sufficient evidence to evaluate the underlying assumptions or the presentation, a disclaimer of opinion should be rendered.

Figure 10.52 provides an example of a disclaimer report on forecasted financial statements.

---

[34] *Ibid.*, AT sec. 301.41.

¶ 1007.11

Figure 10.52

Language of a Disclaimer of Opinion on Forecasted Financial Statements [35]

To the Appropriate Addressee:

We were engaged to examine the accompanying forecasted balance sheet, statements of income, retained earnings, and cash flows of ABC Company as of December 31, 20X4, and for the year then ending. ABC Company's Management is responsible for the forecast.

As discussed under "Income from Investee" in the summary of significant forecast assumptions, this forecast includes income from an equity investee constituting 23 percent of forecasted net income, which is management's estimate of the company's share of the investee's income to be accrued for 20X4. The investee has not prepared a forecast for the year ending December 31, 20X4, and we were therefore unable to obtain suitable support for this assumption.

Because, as described above, we are unable to evaluate management's assumption regarding income from an equity investee and other assumptions that depend thereon, the scope of our work was not sufficient to express, and we do not express an opinion with respect to the presentation of or the assumptions underlying the accompanying forecast. We have no responsibility to update this report for events and circumstances occurring after the report date.

Ryan, Harville & Capitolo LLP
San Jose, California
August 25, 20X3

¶ 1008 Attestation of and Report on Internal Control (Public Companies)

There has been significant attention given to the internal control system of public companies during the past two decades. Lawmakers, regulators, and investors have also shown interest in management's report and auditors' attestation of internal control assertions. The AICPA has recommended that public companies issue management's assertion reports and auditors attest to management assertions on internal controls in its Statement on Standards for Attestation Engagements (SSAE) No. 2 in May 1993.[36] SSAE No. 2 provides guidance for the examination and the management assertion report about various aspects of a client's internal control structure (ICS), including design and operating effectiveness of the overall ICS, a segment of ICS, or based on criteria established by a regulatory agency.

---

[35] *Ibid.*, AT sec. 301.43.
[36] Statement on Standards for Attestation Engagements (SSAE) No. 2, Reporting on an Entity's Internal Control Structure over Financial Reporting (AICPA, May 1993).

The passage of the Sarbanes-Oxley Act of 2002 galvanizes more interest in management and auditor reporting on internal control. Act Sec. 404 requires (1) management to assess and report on the effectiveness of the company's internal control over financial reporting, (2) register public accounting firms to attest to and report on management's assessment of the client's internal control, and (3) the PCAOB to establish auditing standards providing guidance for registered auditors to attest to and report on management's assessment of the effectiveness of internal control. The PCAOB has adopted Auditing Standard No. 2, An Audit of Internal Control Over Financial Reporting Performed in Conjunction with an Audit of Financial Statements. This standard establishes an integrated audit of the financial statements and internal control over financial reporting. It addresses the audit of financial statements, the attestation of internal control over financial reporting, and the relationship between the audit of financial statements and attestation of internal control.

PCAOB Auditing Standard No. 2 requires practically three integrated reports on (1) financial statements audited by the registered public accounting firm, (2) management's assessment of the effectiveness of internal control over financial reporting, and (3) the effectiveness of internal control over financial reporting based on the auditor's attestation of internal control. To support these opinions, auditors gather sufficient and competent evidence about whether (1) financial statements are fairly presented in conformity with GAAP, (2) management's assessment on the effectiveness of internal control over financial reporting is fairly stated, and (3) internal control over financial reporting is effective. Appendix A of PCAOB Auditing Standard No. 2 provides guidance and direction on the auditor's report on internal controls and examples of how to apply the guidance in several different situations. Figure 10.53 presents the format and structure of a report expressing an unqualified opinion on management's assessment of the effectiveness of internal control over financial reporting and an unqualified opinion on the effectiveness of internal control over financial reporting. Figure 10.54 shows the example provided by the PCAOB, which illustrates guidance on the auditor's report on internal controls.

¶ 1008

Special Reports and Other Selected Attestation Reports **435**

Figure 10.53

Report of Independent Registered Public Accounting Firm

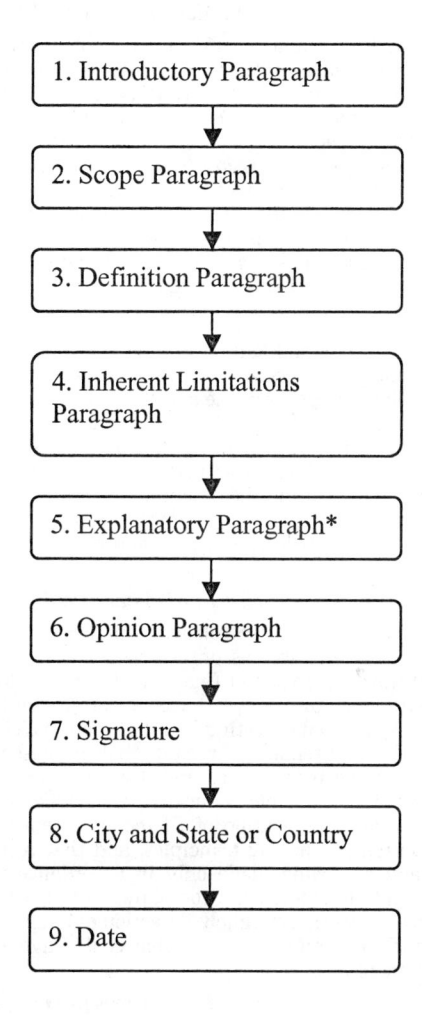

```
1. Introductory Paragraph
          ↓
2. Scope Paragraph
          ↓
3. Definition Paragraph
          ↓
4. Inherent Limitations Paragraph
          ↓
5. Explanatory Paragraph*
          ↓
6. Opinion Paragraph
          ↓
7. Signature
          ↓
8. City and State or Country
          ↓
9. Date
```

*The explanatory paragraph is required only when the auditor's opinion is other than unqualified. It may also be placed after the opinion paragraph when the auditor issues two separate reports on the audit of financial statements and internal controls and thus makes reference to opinion on the financial statement audit in the report on the internal control audit.

¶ 1008

Figure 10.54 ─────────────────────

Report of Independent Registered Public Accounting Firm

[Introductory paragraph]

We have audited management's assessment, included in the accompanying *[title of management's report]*, that W Company maintained effective internal control over financial reporting as of December 31, 20X3, based on *[Identify control criteria, for example, "criteria established in Internal Control—Integrated Framework issued by the Committee of Sponsoring Organizations of the Treadway Commission (COSO)."]*. W Company's management is responsible for maintaining effective internal control over financial reporting and for its assessment of the effectiveness of internal control over financial reporting. Our responsibility is to express an opinion on management's assessment and an opinion on the effectiveness of the company's internal control over financial reporting based on our audit.

[Scope paragraph]

We conducted our audit in accordance with the standards of the Public Company Accounting Oversight Board (United States). Those standards require that we plan and perform the audit to obtain reasonable assurance about whether effective internal control over financial reporting was maintained in all material respects. Our audit included obtaining an understanding of internal control over financial reporting, evaluating management's assessment, testing and evaluating the design and operating effectiveness of internal control, and performing such other procedures as we considered necessary in the circumstances. We believe that our audit provides a reasonable basis for our opinion.

[Definition paragraph]

A company's internal control over financial reporting is a process designed to provide reasonable assurance regarding the reliability of financial reporting and the preparation of financial statements for external purposes in accordance with generally accepted accounting principles. A company's internal control over financial reporting includes those policies and procedures that (1) pertain to the maintenance of records that, in reasonable detail, accurately and fairly reflect the transactions and dispositions of the assets of the company; (2) provide reasonable assurance that transactions are recorded as necessary to permit preparation of financial statements in accordance with generally accepted accounting principles, and that receipts and expenditures of the company are being made only in accordance with authorizations of management and directors of the company; and (3) provide reasonable assurance regarding prevention or timely detection of unauthorized acquisition, use, or disposition of the company's assets that could have a material effect on the financial statements.

[Inherent limitations paragraph]

Because of its inherent limitations, internal control over financial reporting may not prevent or detect misstatements. Also, projections of any evaluation of effectiveness to future periods are subject to the risk that controls may become inadequate because of changes in conditions, or that the degree of compliance with the policies or procedures may deteriorate.

[Opinion paragraph]

In our opinion, management's assessment that W Company maintained effective internal control over financial reporting as of December 31, 20X3, is fairly stated, in all material respects, based on *[Identify control criteria, for example, "criteria established in Internal Control—Integrated Framework issued by the Committee of Sponsoring Organizations of the Treadway Com-*

¶ 1008

Special Reports and Other Selected Attestation Reports **437**

mission (COSO)."]. Also in our opinion, W Company maintained, in all material respects, effective internal control over financial reporting as of December 31, 20X3, based on *[Identify control criteria, for example, "criteria established in Internal Control-Integrated Framework issued by the Committee of Sponsoring Organizations of the Treadway Commission (COSO)."].*

[Explanatory paragraph]

We have also audited, in accordance with the standards of the Public Company Accounting Oversight Board (United States), the *[identify financial statements]* of W Company and our report dated *[date of report, which should be the same as the date of the report on the effectiveness of internal control over financial reporting]* expressed *[include nature of opinion].*

[Signature]
[City and State or Country]
[Date]

Source: PCAOB Release No. 2004-001, March 9, 2004, pages 116-137, Appendix A—Illustrative Reports, Example A-1. Available at *http://pcaobus.org.*

¶ 1009 Summary

Auditors offer many forms of services in addition to audit reports of historical financial statements. Auditors lend credibility to reports viewed by third parties. In some circumstances, third parties, such as those involved with the company in a contract or regulatory bodies, may not be concerned with the complete set of financial statements. In other circumstances, financial statements are prepared in accordance with other comprehensive basis of accounting, referred to as OCBOA, because the complexity of GAAP may not always be relevant to examine the operations of a company.

Statements on Auditing Standards No. 62 and No. 77 apply to these special reports. The auditing standards divide special reports into five categories: audits of financial statements prepared in conformity with OCBOA, audits of SEAI, audits of compliance with aspects of contractual agreements or regulatory requirements related to audited financial statements, audits of financial presentations prepared to comply with contractual agreements or regulatory provisions, and audits of financial information presented in prescribed forms. Another reporting engagement open to CPAs is the compilation or examination of prospective financial statements.

The Sarbanes-Oxley Act of 2002 galvanizes more interest in management and auditor reporting on internal control. Act Sec. 404 requires management to design and maintain an adequate and effective disclosure and internal control system, and to report on the assessment of internal control over financial reporting. PCAOB Auditing Standard No. 2 requires registered auditors to express an opinion on (1) management's assessment of the effectiveness of internal control over financial reporting and (2) the effectiveness of internal control over financial reporting itself.

¶ 1009

Chapter 11

New or Proposed Assurance Services

¶ 1101 Introduction
¶ 1102 SSAE No. 10
¶ 1103 Risk Assessment
¶ 1104 Business Performance Measurements
¶ 1105 Information Systems Reliability
¶ 1106 Electronic Commerce (WebTrust)
¶ 1107 Health Care Providers
¶ 1108 Eldercare Assurance
¶ 1109 Seven Other Opportunities
¶ 1110 Trends in Internal Auditing
¶ 1111 Summary

¶ 1101 Introduction

Auditing revenue has not been growing and is actually declining. Consulting makes up about 45 percent of the big five's revenues (before the demise of Arthur Andersen). CPAs were shifting the mix of client services away from the traditional auditing and tax toward higher profit-margin consulting and assurance services. They expanded markets and services and focus on the needs of their clients. The Sarbanes-Oxley Act and Public Company Accounting Oversight Board (PCAOB) will stop the expanding role of nonaudit services.

The AICPA Special Committee on Assurance Services, known as the Elliot Committee, was established in response to this decline in the auditing revenue. The purpose of the committee was to identify new services in the assurance area,[1] and the committee issued a report in 1997. This report called for the development of additional services to serve the needs of clients (and to gain more revenue). The committee developed business plans for six assurance services with potential revenues of over $1 billion each:[2]

- Risk assessment
- Business performance measurement

---

[1] AICPA Online, "Assurance Services and Academia," 2001, http://www.aicpa.org/assurance/about/academia.htm.

[2] AICPA Online, "New Assurance Services," 2001, http://www.aicpa.org/assurance/about/newsvc/index.htm.

¶ 1101

- Information systems reliability (SysTrust)
- Electronic commerce (CPA WebTrust)
- Health care performance measurement
- Eldercare
- Seven other opportunities

The first four services developed were Eldercare, Performance View, Systrust, and Webtrust. These are discussed in detail later in this chapter.

Chapter 11 objectives:

- To understand how SSAE No. 10 defines assurance services (see ¶ 1101–1102).
- To define business risk and understand how to provide risk assessment services (see ¶ 1103).
- To identify business performance measurements (see ¶ 1104).
- To recognize the importance of IS reliability (see ¶ 1105).
- To learn about WebTrust and the services it provides (see ¶ 1106).
- To become familiar with healthcare providers and eldercare assurance (see ¶ 1107–1108).
- To be aware of trends in internal auditing (see ¶ 1109—1110).

¶ 1102 SSAE No. 10

Assurance services are defined by the Elliott Committee as "independent professional services that improve the quality of information or its context for decision makers." In order to expand the CPA's role into such services while maintaining rigid performance measures, fundamental changes were necessary.

Effective June 1, 2001, Statement on Standards for Attestation Engagements (SSAE) No. 10 was revised to allow CPAs to provide assurance on subject matters other than financial statements. An attest engagement is now defined as one in which an auditor is engaged to issue or does issue an examination, a review or an agreed-upon procedures report on a subject matter or assertion about a subject matter that is the responsibility of another party.[3] Also covered would be a report called for in the standard (e.g., examination, review, or agreed-upon procedure report).

This revised standard now allows a CPA to provide assurance as to the reliability of a system based upon criteria established by the AICPA (e.g.,

---

[3] Statement on Standards for Attestation Engagements No. 10, *Attestation Standards: Revision and Recodification* (AICPA, Professional Standards, Vol. 2, AT sec. 101.01).

SysTrust). Or a CPA can provide assurance as to whether systems and tools used in electronic commerce provide appropriate data integrity, security, privacy, and reliability (e.g., CPA WebTrust).

An attest engagement may be a part of a larger engagement (e.g., a feasibility study or business acquisition study). The SSAE No. 10 standards apply only to the attest portion of the engagement.[4] An attest engagement may take these forms:[5]

a. Historical or prospective performance or condition (for example, historical or prospective financial information, performance measurements, and backlog data)

b. Physical characteristics (for example, narrative descriptions, square footage of facilities)

c. Historical events (for example, the price of a market basket of goods on a certain date)

d. Analyses (for example, break-even analyses)

e. Systems and processes (for example, internal control)

f. Behavior (for example, corporate governance, compliance with laws and regulations, and human resource practices)

¶ 1103 Risk Assessment

An auditor can provide assurance that an organization's profile of business risks is comprehensive and that the entity has appropriate systems in place to effectively manage the risks. A business risk is a possibility that an action or event may adversely affect an entity's ability to achieve its business objectives and execute its strategies successfully. There are several types of business risks:

- Strategic environmental risk (e.g., from substitute products or changes in customer's preferences or capital availability)

- Operating environmental risk (e.g., from lost assets or market opportunities, damaged reputation, or ineffective or inefficient business processes)

- Information risk (e.g., from the use of poor quality information for operational, financial, or strategic decision making)[6]

Risk assessment services include:

- Identification and assessment of primary potential risks faced by a business or entity

---

[4] *Ibid*, 101.05.
[5] *Ibid*, 101.07.
[6] AICPA Online, "The Opportunity That Exists for the Profession," 2001, http://www.aicpa.org/assurance/about/opportun.htm.

- Independent assessment of risks identified by an entity
- Evaluation of an entity's systems for identifying and limiting risks

CPAs can provide context services to assist management, directors, and outside users in evaluating risk information. Context services relate to the overall decision-making environment with respect to business risk and might include consideration of the overall objectives and strategies as well as the environment of an entity. CPAs also can help smaller clients identify possible ways to mitigate excessive risk. Solutions include:

- Installation of risk-reduction systems and processes
- Transferring or sharing of the risk (through hedging, derivatives, insurance, contracting, pricing, or joint ventures and alliances)
- Avoidance of risk through prevention at the source (that is, "stay out of business")[7]

The AICPA believes that CPAs should provide risk-assessment services because of their reputation and skills. CPAs already have a reputation for providing risk assessments. Expertise of some CPAs would need to be enhanced and extended through studying business strategy, environment, objectives, and processes, and particular types of risks. Risk-assessment services by CPAs are a natural add-on to recurring auditing services. In fact, it will be important to distinguish risk-assessment services from services already included in an ordinary financial statement audit. Additional work is required, and the cost and value of these services is likely to be substantial, because senior personnel of the CPA firm are likely to conduct them.[8]

¶ 1104 Business Performance Measurements

Many organizations are using performance measures that cannot be determined by traditional financial accounting data, such as cash flow, sales, earnings per share, and return on investment. These accounting measurements are lagging indicators, whereas leading indicators are such things as customer satisfaction, product and service quality, process quality, and an innovative and motivated workforce.[9] Organizations use these operational and nonfinancial measures to define their strategic objectives and goals.

Because CPAs have historically provided assurance on financial accounting measures, they now have the opportunity and ability to provide assurance on these operational measures. The AICPA Special Committee on

---

[7] AICPA Online, "Assurance on Risk Assessment," 2001, http://www.aicpa.org/assurance/about/newsvc/risk.htm.
[8] Ibid.

[9] See R.S. Kaplan and D.P. Norton, *The Balanced Scorecard-Translating Strategy into Action* (Harvard Business School Press, 1996).

Assurance Services identified several potential performance measure services:[10]

For organizations that have performance measurement systems, services might include:

- Assessing the reliability of information being reported from the organization's performance measurement system

- Assessing the relevance of the performance measures (that is, how well they inform management about achievement of the performance objectives they have set)

For organizations that do not have performance measurement systems, services might include:

- Identifying relevant performance measures

- Helping design and implement a performance measurement system

For all organizations, services might include:

- Providing advice on how the organization can improve their performance measurement system and their actual results

Looking at the first assurance service mentioned above, namely "assessing the reliability of information being reported from an entity's performance measurement system," the following illustration describes what the organization currently measures and how the CPA might undertake this service:

> An organization might measure (1) the cost of its finance department, (2) the timelines of receiving information from the department, and (3) the quality of information received from that department, against internal goals and the results of other organizations that are comparable in size and operate in similar industries. For each performance measure used, the CPA can examine records at the organization to provide assurance on the reported results. The organization might use measures such as cost as a percentage of revenues or full-time-equivalent number of employees to evaluate the cost of its finance department. The CPA can provide assurance on these reported results by auditing them. The performance measurement system might also measure the quality of information received from the department by summarizing the results of surveying senior management, board of directors, investors, and creditors about the quality of information they received from the finance department. The CPA can provide assurance on the reported results by determining whether the survey sampled a sufficient number of individuals and determining that the performance measurement system properly summarized the results of the surveys. If the system compares the organization's results against the results of its competitors, the CPA can make inquiries as to the source of the competitors' results (e.g., appropriate and reliable databases), agree the reported results to the source, and assess the reliability of the source.[11]

---

[10] AICPA Online, "Assurance on Business Performance Measures," 2001, http://www.aicpa.org/assurance/about/newsvc/perf.htm.

[11] Ibid.

More basic than assessing the reliability of information being reported from a performance measurement system is the question of how to evaluate an organization's performance in the first place.

There is no magic formula or one right measurement for evaluating an organization's performance. One approach suggested by Richard L. Lynch and Kevin F. Cross suggests translating an entity's strategic objectives into operational terms for each core process (e.g., order fulfillment, new product introduction) and then into precise operational measures for each department or unit. Operational measures are then presented with financial measurements to evaluate the results of the activities performed.[12]

In the broadest of terms a performance measurement process should:

1. Identify important financial and nonfinancial factors
2. Measure these factors
3. Use the factors to develop and monitor strategic plans[13]

Individual performance measures must be understood in the context of the organization framework. One study grouped nonfinancial performance measures into five general categories. Based upon a questionnaire study of executives, the measures were ranked in order of importance under each category as follows:[14]

1. Customer service
   - Customer satisfaction
   - Delivery performance/customer service
   - Product/process quality
   - Service quality
2. Market Performance
   - Market effectiveness
   - Market growth
   - Market share
3. Goal achievement
   - Productivity
   - Environmental compliance
   - Strategic achievement
4. Innovation

---

[12] R.L. Lynch and K.F. Cross, *Measure Up! Yardsticks for Continuous Improvement* (Blackwell Publishers, 1995).
[13] B.P. Stivers, T.J. Couin, N.G. Hall, and S.W. Smalt, "How Nonfinancial Performance Measures are Used," http://college.hmco.com/accounting/readings/stivers.htm.
[14] Access this case development program at http://ftp.aicpa.org/public/download/members/div/career/edu/2000_01_lakeshore_bank.pdf.

¶ 1104

- New product development
- Manufacturing flexibility
- Technological capability
- R & D productivity
- Innovation

5. Employee involvement
    - Employee satisfaction
    - Employee turnover
    - Education/training
    - Core competencies
    - Internal recognition
    - Morale/corporate culture

Although executives view nonfinancial performance factors as important, they are not capturing data on these factors. Also, many companies are collecting data that are not being used by managers in the planning process.[15] CPAs can help capture this data and use the captured data to measure the performance of organizations.

One instructive study, the AICPA/Lawrence S. Maisel Survey, *Performance Measurement Practices,* set out to understand how performance measurement systems are used, why they are used, and what characteristics they must possess to be effective and beneficial. The survey found that companies view their performance measurement system more as tools to report business results and provide feedback on operations and individual performances rather than as tools to execute strategies and drive longer-term competitive advantage and sustainable shareholder values. Enterprises primarily use revenues/sales and net operating income as financial measures of business performance, and Customer Service/Satisfaction and Productivity as nonfinancial measures of business performance. Financial measures are given higher importance.[16]

The respondents said that the finance function is usually responsible for managing the company's performance measurement system. A decrease in profitability is the number one reason to revise performance measures. Companies use a variety of processes to revise the performance measurement system, including a top-down approach and a change in strategic direction.[17]

The survey found that only 35 percent of respondents rate their company's performance measurement system as effective or very effective,

---

[15] *Ibid.*
[16] L.S. Maisel, "Performance Measurement Practices Survey Results: Executive Summary," 2001, http://www.aicpa.org/cefm/perfmeas/index.htm, p.8.
[17] *Ibid.*

¶ 1104

43 percent as adequate, and 23 percent as poor or not effective. This is a strong indication of the need for performance measurement services in the marketplace.

Among the larger and largest companies there is a higher level of effectiveness than among small and medium enterprises. Companies with either a collaborative or entrepreneurial culture were more satisfied with the effectiveness of their performance measurement system than companies whose culture is command and control. The performance measurement system has an important impact on compensation and reward that is directly related to size; that is, the larger the company, the more the performance measurement system impacts compensation.[18]

Table 11.1 lists the percentages of use for each of the financial performance measures by the surveyed companies in the AICPA study.

Table 11.1
Comparative Use of Financial Performance Measures

Revenues/Sales	63%
Net Operating income	61%
Year-Over-Year Growth	55%
Gross Margin	52%
Earnings before interest and taxes (EBIT)	51%
Cash Flow	50%
ROA/ROI	32%
Earnings per Share	25%
EVA	12%

Source: AICPA/Maisel, "Performance Measurement Practices Survey Results," p. 13. Copyright 1990, 1999, 2001 by the American Institute of Certified Public Accountants, Inc. Reprinted with permission.

These same respondents used the nonfinancial performance measures shown in Table 11.2.

---

[18] *Ibid.*

¶ 1104

Table 11.2

Comparative Use of Nonfinancial Performance Measures

Customer Services/Satisfaction	70%
Productivity	47%
Market Share	42%
Quality and Process Related	40%
Employee Turnover	33%
Regulatory/ Compliance	29%
Time/ Speed/ Agility	23%
Innovation/ New product development	22%
Supplier	9%
Demographics	9%

Source: AICPA/Maisel, "Performance Measurement Practices Survey Results," p. 14. Copyright 1990, 1999, 2001 by the American Institute of Certified Public Accountants, Inc. Reprinted with permission.

¶ 1105 Information Systems Reliability

Information system assurance is the process of testing the integrity of an information system. An auditor can provide users with assurance that a system has been designed and operated to produce reliable data. Systems reliability comprises two general services:

1. *Management service:* assurance about the quality of systems that produce data for use by boards and management. This data set is broader than that used for financial reporting. Examples of specific data are information about customers, suppliers, employees, competitors, and market conditions.

2. *External services:* assurance about the quality of systems that produce financial reporting data that is used internally and externally. The future may bring continuous, real time assurance for both financial and nonfinancial data.[19] This involves some level of direct involvement in computer operations by the auditor.

.01 Existing CPA Services

Four well-established CPA services deal with the quality of information systems:

---

[19] AICPA Online, "Systems Reliability Assurance," 2001, *http://www.aicpa.org/assurance/about/newsvc/reliab.htm.*

1. Reports on the effectiveness of internal control over financial reporting measured against criteria (generally COSO) by a point in time (SSAE No. 2).

2. Communication of conditions identified during a financial statement audit that could adversely affect the reporting of data in the financial statements (SAS No. 60).

3. Reports intended for other auditors. These two types of reports are (1) a description of controls at a service organization at a point of time, and (2) selected tests of effectiveness to achieve specific control objectives over a period (generally six months) (SAS No. 70).

4. Consulting services that commonly involve systems design and implementation, but they do not provide explicit assurance.[20]

.02 SysTrust

A task force of the AICPA and the Canadian Institute of Chartered Accountants (CICA) developed the system reliability assurance service called SysTrust. Addressing a broad array of system activities, the task force developed four principles to use in evaluating whether a system is reliable:

1. *Availability:* The system is available for operation and use at times set forth in service-level statements or agreements.

2. *Security:* The system is protected against unauthorized physical and logical access.

3. *Integrity:* System processing is complete, accurate, timely, and authorized.

4. *Maintainability:* The system can be updated when required in a manner that continues to provide system availability, security, and integrity.[21]

Criteria have been established for each of the four principles against which a system can be evaluated. With these criteria an auditor can determine whether an organization's system meets these principles and criteria. Table 11.3 lists the SysTrust principles and criteria.

A SysTrust engagement provides users with assurance about whether an organization has maintained effective control over system reliability. A system here encompasses an infrastructure of hardware, software, people, procedures, and data that produces information. These components may be defined as follows:

---

[20] *Ibid.*
[21] Chartered Accountants of Canada, "CA SysTrust Service—A New Assurance Service on Systems Reliability," http://www.cica.ca/cica/cicawebsite.nsf/public/e__systrprincrit.

¶ 1105.02

New or Proposed Assurance Services 449

- *Infrastructure*. The physical and hardware components of a system, including facilities, mainframes, servers, and related components and networks.

- *Software*. The programs and operating software of a system, including operating systems, utilities, and business applications software such as enterprise resource planning (ERP) and financial systems.

- *Personnel*. The people involved in operating and using a system, including information technology (IT) personnel such as programmers and operators, system users, and management.

- *Procedures*. The programmed and manual procedures involved in operating a system, including IT procedures such as backup and maintenance, and user-based procedures, such as input.

- *Data*. The information used and supported by a system, including transaction streams, files, databases, and tables.[22]

Increasing reliance on information systems puts today's businesses at great risk. A number of disasters, such as the Code Red Worm, have caused costly system outages. Hackers shut down Yahoo! and eBay with denial-of-service attacks. Hershey missed candy deliveries worth $200 million in 1999 because of systems problems in a new computer system. Systems crashed at Amazon.com and ToyRUS.com. These system problems suggest that there is an important need for information systems reliability services, but at the same time suggests that CPAs may be subject to substantial liability risks themselves because of their reliance on SysTrust assurance reports. Consult Chapter 3 for information about legal liability.[23] These steps have been suggested once a practitioner decides to accept an assurance engagement:

1. Evaluate the integrity of the client's management
2. Identify special circumstances and unusual risks
3. Assess the firm's competencies to perform the SysTrust engagement
4. Evaluate independence
5. Determine the CPA's ability to use due care
6. Prepare an engagement letter

Practitioners should not use loss-limiting clauses and hold-harmless provisions to reduce litigation risks because the Securities and Exchange

---

[22] Efrim Boritz, Erin Mackler and Doug McPhie, "Reporting on Systems Reliability," *Journal of Accountancy* (November 1999): 79.

[23] Carl Pacini, S.E. Ludwig, W. Hillison, D. Sinason, and L. Higgins, "SysTrust and Third-Party Risk," *Journal of Accountancy* (August 2000): 73.

¶ 1105.02

Commission (SEC) considers such statements to be an impairment to an auditor's independence.[24]

Table 11.3 lists the four principles under SysTrust and the criteria under each principle. In order to earn an unqualified SysTrust report, a system must meet all of the four principles and 58 criteria. In the United States, a SysTrust engagement is performed under AICPA Statement on Standards for Attestation Engagements No. 1, *Attestation Standards*, and in Canada, the engagement is performed using standards found in the CICA Handbook.

---

[24] *Ibid.*, pp.77-78.

¶ 1105.02

Table 11.3

SysTrust Principles and Criteria

Availability: The system is available for operation and use at times set forth in service-level statements or agreements.

- **A1** **The entity has defined and communicated performance objectives, policies and standards for system availability.**
  - A1.1 The system availability requirements of authorized users—and system availability objectives, policies and standards—are identified and documented.
  - A1.2 The documented system availability objectives, policies and standards have been communicated to authorized users.
  - A1.3 The documented system availability objectives, policies and standards are consistent with the system availability requirements specified in contractual, legal and other service-level agreements and applicable laws and regulations.
  - A1.4 Responsibility and accountability for system availability have been assigned.
  - A1.5 Documented system availability of objectives, policies, and standards are communicated to entity personnel responsible for implementing them.
- **A2** **The entity utilizes procedures, people, software, data and infrastructure to achieve system availability objectives in accordance with established policies and procedures.**
  - A2.1 Acquisition, implementation, configuration and management of system components related to system availability are consistent with documented system availability objectives, policies and standards.
  - A2.2 There are procedures to protect the system against potential risks that might disrupt system operations and impair system availability.
  - A2.3 Continuity provisions address minor processing errors, minor destruction of records and major disruptions of system processing that might impair system availability.
  - A2.4 There are procedures to ensure that personnel responsible for the design, development, implementation and operation of system availability featured are qualified to fulfill their responsibilities.
- **A3** **The entity monitors the system and takes action to achieve compliance with system availability objectives, policies and standards.**
  - A3.1 System availability is periodically reviewed and compared with documented system availability objectives, policies and standards.
  - A3.2 There is a process to identify potential impairments to the system's ongoing ability to address the documented system availability objectives, policies and standards and to take appropriate action.
  - A3.3 Environmental and technological changes are monitored and their impact on system availability is assessed on a timely basis.

Security: The system is protected against unauthorized physical and logical access.

- **S1** **The entity has defined and communicated performance objectives, policies and standards for system security.**

¶ 1105.02

S1.1 The system security requirements of authorized users and the system security objectives, policies and standards are identified and documented.

S1.2 The documented system security objectives, policies and standards have been communicated to authorized users.

S1.3 Documented system security objectives, policies and standards are consistent with system security requirements defined in contractual, legal and other service-level agreements and applicable laws and regulations.

S1.4 Responsibility and accountability for system security have been assigned.

S1.5 Documented system security objectives, policies and standards are communicated to entity personnel responsible for implementing them.

S2 The entity utilizes procedures, people, software, data and infrastructure to achieve system security objectives in accordance with established policies and standards.

S2.1 Acquisition, implementation, configuration and management of system components related to system security are consistent with documented system security objectives, policies and standards.

S2.2 There are procedures to identify and authenticate all users authorized to access the system.

S2.3 There are procedures to grant system access privileges to users in accordance with the policies and standards for granting such privileges.

S2.4 There are procedures to restrict access to computer processing output to authorized users.

S2.5 There are procedures to restrict access to files on off-line storage media to authorized users.

S2.6 There are procedures to protect external access points against unauthorized logical access.

S2.7 There are procedures to protect the system against infection by computer viruses, malicious codes and unauthorized software.

S2.8 Threats of sabotage, terrorism, vandalism and other physical attacks have been considered when locating the system.

S2.9 There are procedures to segregate incompatible functions within the system through security authorizations.

S2.10 There are procedures to protect the system against unauthorized physical access.

S2.11 There are procedures to ensure that personnel responsible for the design, development, implementation and operation of system security are qualified to fulfill their responsibilities.

S3 The entity monitors the system and takes action to achieve compliance with system security objectives, policies and standards.

S3.1 System security performance is periodically reviewed and compared with documented system security requirements of authorized users and contractual, legal and other service-level agreements.

S3.2 There is a process to identify potential impairments to the system's ongoing ability to address the documented security objectives, policies and standards and to take appropriate action.

¶ 1105.02

S3.3 Environmental and technological changes are monitored and their impact on system security is periodically assessed on a timely basis.

Integrity: System processing is complete, accurate, timely and authorized.

I1) **The entity has defined and communicated performance objectives, policies and standards for system processing integrity.**

I1.1 The system processing integrity requirements of authorized users and the system processing integrity objectives, policies and standards are identified and documented.

I1.2 Documented system processing integrity objectives, policies and standards have been communicated to authorized users.

I1.3 Documented system processing integrity objectives, policies and standards are consistent with system processing integrity requirements defined in contractual, legal and other service-level agreements and applicable laws and regulations.

I1.4 Responsibility and accountability for system processing integrity have been assigned.

I1.5 Documented system processing integrity objectives, policies and standards are communicated to entity personnel responsible for implementing them.

I2 **The entity utilizes procedures, people, software, data and infrastructure to achieve system processing integrity objectives in accordance with established policies and standards.**

I2.1 Acquisition, implementation, configuration and management of system components related to system processing integrity are consistent with documented system processing integrity objectives, policies and standards.

I2.2 The information processing integrity procedures related to information inputs are consistent with the documented system processing integrity requirements.

I2.3 There are procedures to ensure that system processing is complete, accurate, timely and authorized.

I2.4 The information processing integrity procedures related to information outputs are consistent with the documented system processing integrity requirements.

I2.5 There are procedures to ensure that personnel responsible for the design, development, implementation and operation of the system are qualified to fulfill their responsibilities.

I2.6 There are procedures to enable tracing of information inputs from their source to their final disposition and vice versa.

I3 **The entity monitors the system and takes action to achieve compliance with system processing integrity objectives, policies and standards.**

I3.1 System processing integrity of performance is periodically reviewed and compared to the documented system processing integrity requirements of authorized users and contractual, legal and other service-level agreements.

I3.2 There is a process to identify potential impairments to the system's ongoing ability to address the documented processing integrity objectives, policies and standards and take appropriate action.

I3.3 Environmental and technological changes are monitored and their impact on system processing integrity is periodically assessed on a timely basis.

¶ 1105.02

Maintainability: The system can be updated when required in a manner that continues to provide for system availability, security and integrity.

M1 **The entity has defined and communicated performance objectives, policies and standards for system maintainability.**

M1.1 Documented system maintainability objectives, policies and standards address all areas affected by system changes.

M1.2 Documented system maintainability objectives, policies and standards are communicated to authorized users.

M1.3 Documented system maintainability objectives, policies and standards are consistent with the requirements defined in contractual, legal and other service-level agreements and applicable laws and regulations.

M1.4 Responsibility and accountability for system maintainability have been assigned.

M1.5 Documented system maintainability objectives, policies and standards are communicated to entity personnel responsible for implementing them.

M2 **The entity utilizes procedures, people, software, data and infrastructure to achieve system maintainability objectives in accordance with established policies and standards.**

M2.1 Resources available to maintain the system are consistent with the documented requirements of authorized users and documented objectives, policies and standards.

M2.2 Procedures to manage, schedule and document all planned changes to the system are applied to modifications of system components to maintain documented system availability, security and integrity consistent with documented objectives, policies and standards.

M2.3 There are procedures to ensure that only authorized, tested and documented changes are made to the system and related data.

M2.4 There are procedures to communicate planned and completed system changes to information systems management and to authorized users.

M2.5 There are procedures to allow for and to control emergency changes.

M3 **The entity monitors the system and takes action to achieve compliance with maintainability objectives, policies and standards.**

M3.1 System maintainability performance is periodically reviewed and compared with the documented system maintainability requirements of authorized users and contractual, legal and other service-level agreements.

M3.2 There is a process to identify potential impairments to the system's ongoing ability to address the documented system maintainability objectives, policies and standards and to take appropriate action.

M3.3 Environmental and technological changes are monitored and their impact on system maintainability is periodically assessed on a timely basis.

Source: Efrin Boritz, Erin Mackler and Doug McPhie, "Reporting on Systems Reliability," *Journal of Accountancy,* November 1999, pp. 75-79. Copyright 1999, 2001 from the *Journal of Accountancy* by the American Institute of Certified Public Accountants, Inc. Opinions of the authors are their own and do not necessarily reflect policies of the AICPA. Reprinted with permission.

¶ 1106 Electronic Commerce (WebTrust)

On August 1, 2001, the Code Red Worm infected almost 150,000 Internet-connected computers. The rate of infection doubled each hour early on that Wednesday. E-commerce privacy and security problems point out the downside of operating a commercial website.

The growth of electronic commerce has been hindered by a lack of confidence. For example, the best-known offline tax preparer (H&R Block) made nationwide headlines when severe privacy breakdowns on its website occurred. Customers called in saying they could view tax information about other taxpayers. Then on February 1, 2000, a surge in site visits shut down their website for three days.[25] CPAs through WebTrust can identify and help reduce e-commerce business risks and encourage online confidence and activity.

WebTrust engagements for entities that use Internet service providers (ISPs) should consider the risk and control environment of the ISP in addition to the entity itself. A WebTrust engagement performed by a CPA can:

- Identify risks, including possible privacy breaches, security gaps, and other systems affecting the customer interface

- Benchmark and encourage best practices

- Provide independent verification that the site complies with the international WebTrust Standards for e-commerce[26]

A comprehensive WebTrust review can provide a level of comfort to help mitigate the risks to e-commerce sites.

Many sites have passed a WebTrust examination. Some of the more notables include: Airmiles.ca, Alpine Bank, American Red Cross, Bell Canada, E*Trade Group, INC., Roger Clemens (Yankees pitcher), and Verisign.

Passed sites are periodically examined by a WebTrust licensed CPA to ensure compliance with the current WebTrust principles, which include: Online privacy, security, business practices and transaction integrity, availability, and WebTrust for Certification Authorities.[27]

---

[25] WebTrust, "H.D. Vest and WebTrust: A Case Study About Online Privacy Best Practices," 2001, http://www.cpawebtrust.org/onlncase.htm.

[26] WebTrust, "Overview of the WebTrust 3.0 Program," 2001, http://www.cpawebtrust.org/onlnover.htm.

[27] WebTrust, "Sites with WebTrust Seals," 2001, http://www.cpawebtrust.org/abtseals.htm.

A CPA can provide valuable e-commerce assurance services by addressing the risks and promoting the integrity and security of electronic transactions, electronic documents, and the supporting systems in the following areas:

- *Integrity services* provide assurance that (1) the elements of a transaction or document are as agreed among the parties, and (2) the systems that process and store transactions and documents do not alter those elements.

- *Security services* provide assurance that (1) the parties to transactions and documents are authentic and that such transactions and documents are protected from unauthorized disclosure, and (2) the systems that support transaction processing and storage provide appropriate authentication and protection.

- Consulting services can be directed toward assisting clients in (1) designing, developing, implementing, and monitoring electronic commerce systems and tools that provide high integrity and security, and (2) developing ways to use electronic commerce effectively to achieve business objectives.

- Electronic commerce service provider: A CPA can become a provider of electronic commerce services. Examples of these services include:

    1. Directly processing electronic transactions using high-integrity systems (that is, providing a value-added network service)

    2. Obtaining and storing complete copies of the electronic transactions and documents

    3. Developing and storing a digital signature of electronic transactions and documents that indicates their authenticity and detects alterations

    4. Providing authentic keys to be used for encryption, or digital signatures by operating the systems used to generate, process, and maintain such keys (that is, operating a "trusted key server")[28]

The degree of first amendment protection available to WebTrust service providers who are nonmedia parties is uncertain and controversial. Various procedural aspects of foreign law may render a foreign court more hospitable than a U.S. court to a CPA WebTrust service provider.[29]

---

[28] AICPA Online, "Electronic Commerce Assurance," 2001, http://www.aicpa.org/assurance/about/newsvc/elec.htm.

[29] Carl Pacini and David Sinason "The Law and CPA WebTrust," *Journal of Accountancy* (February 1999): 21 and 22.

¶ 1107 Health Care Providers

Another assurance service suggested by the AICPA is assurance on the effectiveness of health care providers. The health care industry has a total annual volume of over $1 trillion, or one-seventh of the U.S. economy. CPAs can assess and report on the quality of care delivered by health care providers. These services can be provided for hospitals, HMOs and similar operations, managed care firms, physician groups, and individual practitioners.[30]

¶ 1108 Eldercare Assurance

The U.S. Census Bureau estimates that the elderly population will double to 80 million in 2050. The Bureau indicates that 16.6 million people in the U.S. were 75 years or older in 2000, and that Americans age 65 or older control between $11 trillion to $13 trillion of the country's wealth.

CPAs can provide a combination of services in the areas of:[31]

- Consulting services: determine the community resources available to address an elderly person's needs.

- Assurance services: test service providers to make sure they meet agreed upon criteria.

- Direct services: pay bills, manage property, and submit insurance claims. Table 11.4 lists some of the potential services under the three categories.[32]

The AICPA Special Committee on Assurance Services Report defines Eldercare Services as follows:

> A service designed to provide assurance to family members that care goals are achieved for elderly family members no longer able to be totally independent. The service will rely on the expertise of other professionals, with the CPA serving as the coordinator and assurer of quality of services based on criteria and goals set by the client. The purpose of the service is to provide assurance in a professional, independent, and objective manner to third parties (children, family members or other concerned parties) that the needs of the elderly person to whom they are attached are being met.

CPAs are well-suited to help elderly Americans receive the right care and services.[33]

---

[30] AICPA Online, "Assurance on Performance Measures—Health Care Providers," 2001, http://www.aicpa.org/assurance/about/newsvc/health.htm.

[31] Karen Duggan, George Lewis, and Elizabeth Sammon, "Opportunity Knocks: CPA Elder Care Services," *Journal of Accountancy* (December 1999): 44.

[32] AICPA Online, "What are ElderCare Services and Why Should I Get Involved," 2001, http:// www.aicpa.org/assurance/eldercare/what.htm. Copyright 1990, 2001 by the American Institute of Certified Public Accountants, Inc. Reprinted with permission.

[33] Jon A. Meyer "Why One Firm Decided to Offer ElderCare Services and What They Did to Get Started," *The Practicing CPA* (November 1999).

Table 11.4

Potential Eldercare Assurance Services

Direct Services

1. Financial Services
   a) Receive, deposit, and account for client receipts.
   b) Ensure expected revenues are received.
   c) Make appropriate disbursements.
   d) Submit claims to insurance companies.
   e) Confirm accuracy of provider bills and appropriate reimbursements.
   f) Protect elderly from predators by controlling checkbook and other assets.
   g) Income tax planning and preparation.
   h) Gift tax return preparation.
   i) Preparation of employment tax returns for caregivers and household help.

2. Nonfinancial Services
   a) Help arrange for transportation, housekeeping, and other services.
   b) Manage real estate and other property.
   c) Visit and report on elderly on behalf of children in distant locations.

Assurance Services

1. Financial
   a) Review and report on financial transactions.
   b) Test for asserters' adherence to established criteria.
   c) Review investments and trust activity.
   d) Audit third party calculations, such as pension, insurance and annuity payments.
   e) Review reports from fiduciaries.

2. Nonfinancial
   a) Measure and report on care provider performance against established goals.
   b) Evaluate and report on the performance of other outside parties, such as contractors.

Consulting Services

1. Eldercare Planning
   a) Plan for housing and support service needs.
   b) Plan for declining competency.
   c) Plan for death or disability of one or both spouses.
   d) Evaluate alternative costs of retirement communities and other housing.

¶ 1108

New or Proposed Assurance Services

   e) Evaluate housing and care alternatives.
   f) Provide inventory of services available in the community.
   g) Estate planning.
2. Planning for Fiduciary Needs
   a) Financial power of attorney.
   b) Healthcare power of attorney.
   c) Guardianship.
   d) Trusteeship.
   e) Living wills.
   f) Advanced medical directives.
3. Evaluation of Financing Options
   a) Medicare and Medicaid.
   b) Long-term care insurance.
   c) Medigap insurance.
   d) HMOs.
   e) Annuities.
   f) Viatical insurance settlements.
   g) Reverse mortgages.
   h) Sale/leaseback of home.
   i) Flexible spending accounts.
4. Family Facilitation
   a) Mediate/arbitrate family disputes.
   b) Provide objectivity for highly emotional issues.
   c) Act as intermediary between parent and child.
5. Coordination of Support and Healthcare Services
   a) "Quarterback" team of healthcare, legal, and other professionals.
6. Other Consulting Services
   a) Help family monitor care.
   b) Establish standards of care expected.
   c) Communicate expectations to care providers.
   d) Establish performance measurement systems.

¶ 1109 Seven Other Opportunities

The AICPA provides seven other possible assurance opportunities:

1. Policy compliance
2. Outsourced internal availability
3. Trading partner accountability

¶ 1109

4. Mergers and acquisitions

5. ISO 9000 (see Chapter 4)

6. Association for investment management (AIMR) performance presentation standards compliance

7. World-Wide Web assertions

¶ 1110 Trends in Internal Auditing

Internal auditing professionals, like auditing professionals in public practice, face a rapidly changing environment. Like other auditors, they will need to adapt to industry trends in order to profit from change. Internal auditors work for organizations that are expanding into global operations. They face both threats and opportunities from outsourcing and now must market their services within the organization. New services also must be developed for internal organizational consumption. Internal auditors must be responsive to management needs and resource constraints. Offering their services within the organization today also will require a customer focus even when their customers are company personnel and not external clients.

.01 New Assurance Service Opportunities for Internal Auditing

The Institute of Internal Auditors Research Foundation published a study encouraging a proactive response within the internal auditing profession to expand value-added assurance services. Internal auditors "will best service their organizations by making sure that management understands the capabilities of internal auditing to offer a wide range of assurance services."[34]

This study suggests that internal auditors may be able to apply the WebTrust criteria or SysTrust criteria to their own organizations. They may be able to design new assurance services tailored to the unique needs of their organizations. Research indicates that internal auditors wish to be viewed as consultants or partners with management.

This study provides a table with external information flows that represent a potential set of assurance services:[35]

---

[34] G.L. Gray and M.J. Gray, "Assurance Services within the Auditing Profession," (Altmonte Springs, FL: The Institute of Internal Auditors Research Foundation, 2000), xii.

[35] Ibid., p.18.

¶ 1110.01

Table 11.5

Examples of External Information Flows

Source/Destination	Primary Flows	Examples
Equity Investors	Outbound	• Annual report • Other financial reports • Reports to analysts
Creditors	Outbound	• Financial statements • Other debt covenant information
Competitors	Inbound	• Business intelligence
Customers	Bi-directional	• Credit applications • Customer service • Returns and warranty statistics • Bid proposals
Regulators	Outbound	• SEC, EPA, EEOC, etc. reports
Employees	Bi-directional	• Job application forms • Benefit reports
Tax Authorities	Outbound	• Income tax returns • Sales tax returns • Property tax returns
Suppliers	Bi-directional	• Receiving reports • Quality control • Request for quotes

Chapter 13, the Internal Auditing Profession, discusses in detail current topics and trends in internal auditing.

¶ 1111 Summary

CPAs are shifting the mix of client services away from the traditional auditing and tax services toward higher profit-margin consulting and assurance services. CPAs have expanded markets and services and focused on the needs of their clients. The Sarbanes-Oxley Act and the PCAOB will stop the expanding role of nonaudit services.

Business risk is a possibility that an action or event may adversely affect an entity's ability to achieve its business objectives and execute its strategies successfully. The types of business risks are strategic environmental risk, operating environmental risk, and information risk.

Information system assurance is the process of testing the integrity of an information system. This has become very important. CPAs provide services such as SysTrust and WebTrust for website and information

¶ 1111

system assurance. A WebTrust engagement performed by a CPA can identify risks, including possible privacy breaches, security gaps, and other systems affecting the customer interface; benchmark and encourage best practices; and provide independent verification that the site complies with the international WebTrust Standards for e-commerce.

Chapter 12

Forensic Accounting Services

¶ 1201	Introduction
¶ 1202	Defining Forensic Accounting Services
¶ 1203	Some Early History
¶ 1204	Expert Witnessing Becomes Popular
¶ 1205	The Evidence Phase of Forensic Accounting
¶ 1206	The Term "Forensic Accounting" Is Born
¶ 1207	Judicial Procedure
¶ 1208	Evidence and Computer Technology
¶ 1209	Computer Forensics
¶ 1210	Forensic Accounting Practices
¶ 1211	Federal Rules of Evidence
¶ 1212	Courtroom Etiquette
¶ 1213	Measuring Damages
¶ 1214	AICPA's Consulting Guidelines
¶ 1215	Risk Management
¶ 1216	Forensic Accounting and Fraud Deterrence Certifications
¶ 1217	Future Trends in Forensic Accounting
¶ 1218	Summary

¶ 1201 Introduction

Reported corporate and accounting scandals of the early 2000s raised more interest in forensic accounting and fraud examination. With fraud a growing problem in almost all industries, and in companies of all sizes, the accounting profession is paying more attention to fraud prevention and detection. In the academic and business literature, the terms "forensic accounting" and "fraud examination" are often used interchangeably. However, forensic accounting practices are often classified into three areas: litigation support consulting, fraud examination, and expert witnessing. The auditor's responsibility for detecting and reporting financial statement fraud has been and will be of continued importance to the accounting profession in particular and to the investing public in general. A forensic accountant must be a due diligent auditor and effective investigator.

Chapter 12 objectives:

- To define forensic accounting services and be familiar with its early history (see ¶ 1201—1203).

- To recognize the increasing popularity of forensic accounting services and understand possible attacks against evidence gathered by an accountant (see ¶ 1204–1205).

- To identify how the term "forensic accounting" was born and the role of forensic accounting in judicial procedures (see ¶ 1206–1207).

- To understand how computer forensics works with forensic accounting and how to use computer technology as evidence (see ¶ 1208–1209).

- To become familiar with expert witnessing and federal rules of evidence (see ¶ 1210–1211).

- To be aware of the importance of courtroom etiquette (see ¶ 1212).

- To become familiar with how to measure damages and the AICPA's consulting guidelines (see ¶ 1213–1214).

- To understand risk management (see ¶ 1215).

- To be aware of certifications available to those interested in being forensic accountants (see ¶ 1216).

- To have an appreciation for future trends in forensic accounting (see ¶ 1217).

.01 History of Forensic Accounting

The scribes of ancient Egypt who inventoried the pharaohs' grain, gold, and other assets were the predecessors to today's accountant. Fraud prevention and detection were the accountant's main duty until the turn of the 20th century. Then, as accrual basis accounting became common, reporting issues became a top priority.[1] Over time there developed a need for a fraud auditor, and gradually the definition of forensic accounting changed from merely testifying in court to more of an investigative accountant: a financial detective with a suspicious mind. In the late 1980s and 1990s these dreaded gumshoes became more like bloodhounds and less like watchdogs (independent auditors) and seeing eye dogs (internal auditors).

---

[1] J. T. Wells, "So That's Why It's Called a Pyramid Scheme," *Journal of Accountancy*, Vol. 190 (October 2000): 91–93.

¶ 1201.01

The excitement aspects of the forensic accountant are illustrated by the following excerpt:

> If movie producers want to resurrect the detective genre, they should bring the crafty sleuths back as accountants. Playing up to today's big time demand to fight white-collar crime, these dashing auditors would expose financial fraud despite their adversaries' elaborate attempts at deception. A number of real-world Dick Tracys have already appeared; former FBI agents, federal prosecutors and other white-collar investigators have swelled the ranks of *forensic accounting* departments and hit the lecture circuits, bringing to accountants and auditors new opportunities for fraud-detection teamwork and training.[2]

Attorneys are increasingly turning to accounting specialists to uncover fiscal fraud.

Forensic accountants were engaged in tracing the money trail of the Al Qaeda terrorists after their attack of September 11, 2001. Ann E. Wilson said that following a financial trail is like eating a plate of spaghetti as the accountants and computer experts pored over banks records, credit card statements, brokerage transactions, and other financial records. "You start pulling on one piece and you don't know what you'll pull out and how far you'll have to go. It's a long and tedious process."[3] Of course, forensic accountants become involved in the more mundane tasks of the specialty: estate valuations, divorce settlements, fraud investigations, and mob money laundering.

Following the money trail and digging through financial records are only part of the forensic accountant's genre. The face of auditing is changing as audits become a loss leader.

In the early 1980s, there was a subtle shift in the way external auditors reviewed clients' records. Companies began to use computers to perform their record keeping, and intense competition caused the auditing fees to fall as much as 50 percent from the mid-1980s to the mid-1990s. Thus, auditors had to cut costs by reducing the labor-intensive process of reviewing hundreds of corporate accounts. They grew more reliant on internal controls and worked less with account balances and entries. Because top executives can circumvent internal controls, they could manipulate the records and cook the books. Eventually the results were the Enron, WorldCom, Xerox, Adelphia Communications, and the fall of Arthur Andersen in the early 2000s. Thus, the pendulum will swing back to more forensic techniques in audits and higher fees as a result of Sarbanes-Oxley and the Public Company Accounting Oversight Board (PCAOB).

Example: Much of the disputed line costs in the WorldCom debacle were initially expensed properly, but late entries were made to turn these costs into capitalized assets. Arthur Andersen was given limited access to

---

[2] Paul Demery, "Auditors' New Fraud Detection Role," *The Practical Accountant* (March 1997): 22–27.

[3] K. Kaplan, "Tracing the Money Trail of Terrorism," *Los Angeles Times* (Septemeber 24, 2001) at www.latimes.com/news/nationworld/nation/la-000076523sep24.story.

¶ 1201.01

the general ledger. The backup or support for the following $647 million entry was a yellow post-it note:

Property, Plant, and Equipment	$771,000,000
Operating Expenses	$771,000,000

¶ 1202 Defining Forensic Accounting Services

Forensic accounting is the action of identifying, recording, setting, extracting, sorting, reporting, and verifying past financial data or other accounting activities for setting current or prospective legal disputes or using such past financial data for projecting future financial data to settle legal disputes. For more details see *Forensic and Investigative Accounting*.[4]

A forensic accountant's credentials are like a three-layered wedding cake. The largest, bottom layer is a strong accounting background. A middle, smaller layer is a thorough knowledge of auditing, risk assessment and control, and fraud detection. The smallest, top layer of the cake is a basic understanding of the legal environment. The icing on the cake is a strong set of communication skills, both written and oral. In general, a forensic accountant is engaged in a combination of fraud detection and litigation support.

It should be noted that the auditing procedures for a fraud auditor may be quite different than procedures used by an external auditor. In general, an external auditor is responsible for finding only deliberate material misstatements of financial statements, so the forensic accountant must use additional investigative techniques.

Bologna and Lindquist give an excellent definition of *forensic accounting*:

> Forensic and investigative accounting is the application of financial skills and an investigative mentality to unresolved issues, conducted within the context of the rules of evidence. As a discipline, it encompasses financial expertise, fraud knowledge, and a strong knowledge and understanding of business reality and the working of the legal system. Its development has been primarily achieved through on-the-job training, as well as experience with investigating officers and legal counsel.[5]

A glamorous depiction of Lenny Cramer, a fictional accountant in the courtroom, appears in the novel *Accosting the Golden Spire*:

> Lenny liked the grueling task of preparing beforehand and participating in a courtroom battle over accounting principles. There was the challenge to react and respond to the many trick questions asked by the opposing attorney. Probably the stress was not worth the daily fees he received, but he loved it. He sometimes imagined the opposing attorney to be a black-clad medieval

---

[4] D.L Crumbley, L.E. Heitger, and G.S. Smith, *Forensic and Investigative Accounting* (Chicago: CCH INCORPORATED, 2003).
[5] G. Jack Bologna and Robert L. Lindquist, *Fraud Auditing and Forensic Accounting: New*

Tools and Techniques (New York: John Wiley and Sons, 1987), 47. See also W.T. Thornhill, *Forensic Accounting: How to Investigate Financial Fraud* (Burr Ridge, Ill.: Irwin, 1995), 10.

knight racing toward him on horseback with a long, sharp lance. Lenny always toppled the vicious knight in his daydreams.[6]

In writing about this fictional accountant, Lenny Cramer, a Dallas newspaper reporter, discussed this change in image for the accountant and auditor from the dull bean counter with no original ideas. "After all, everyone knows that bean counters are bespectacled, pale-skinned wretches who spend mind-numbing lives in dreary cubicles poring over faint computer printouts and dusty ledgers. Right?" Yet within recent years a bolder auditor has evolved with a suspicious mind. This forensic auditor looks behind the facade and does not accept records at their face value.[7]

In August 2000, *The Panel on Audit Effectiveness* recommended that forensic-type techniques should become an integral part of the external audit.[8]

Forensic accountants must appreciate the fact that financial statements may be wrong. Some companies use creative accounting techniques to disguise damaging information, to provide a distorted picture of the financial health of the business, to smooth out erratic earnings, or to boost anemic or lack of earnings. Forensic accountants should adopt a healthy skepticism in reading and evaluating financial reports. Businesses are often clever in hiding these accounting tricks and gimmicks, so auditors must be always alert to the signs of outright financial shenanigans. Forensic accountant Bruce Dubinsky says "It's not finding what you can see, but seeing what you can find."[9]

Forensic accountants note small errors and irregularities because they may point to the *modus operandi* of corrupt executives, employees, thieves, embezzlers, and defrauders. Because criminals may not be able to bury all of their tracks, forensic auditors look for the tip of the fraudulent iceberg. Basically, external auditors take a big picture, macro view of books, records, and controls, whereas the forensic accountant takes a micro view of a business.[10] Sophisticated software is used to sift through files, flagging relationships or patterns that normally do not occur.[11]

Fraud auditing and detection is covered in Chapter 19; this chapter concentrates on litigation support services. The focus is to familiarize forensic accountants with basic, general ideas and concepts about judicial proceedings and related rules of evidence. Reliance on just basic principles

---

[6] Iris Weil Collett and Jim Greenspan, *Accosting the Golden Spire* (Thomas Horton & Daughters, 26662 S. New Town Drive, Sun Lakes, AZ 85248: 1988), 62. *See also* I.W. Collett and Murphy Smith, *Trap Doors and Trogan Horses* (Sun Lakes, Az.: Thomas Horton & Daughters, 1991).

[7] Robert Dietz, "Accounting + Intrigue = Lenny Cramer," *Dallas Times Herald*, September 29, 1991, p. DI-I. *See also* "Sherlock Holmes and Forensic Accounting," http://acct.tamu.edu/kratchman/holmes.htm.

[8] *The Panel on Audit Effectiveness*, Public Oversight Board (August 31, 2000), p. 88.

[9] Luciana Lopex, "Forensic Accountant Uncovers Teachers Union Scandal," Fox news channel (April 28, 2003), http://www.foxnews.com/story/0, 2933,85360,00.htm.

[10] Paul Shaw and Jack Bologna, *Preventing Corporate Embezzlement* (Butterworth, 2000), 81.

[11] Luciana Lopez, "Forensic Accountant Uncovers Teachers Union Scandal," Fox news channel (April 28, 2003), http://www.foxnews.com/story/0, 2933,85360,00.htm.

¶ 1202

is not advised, however, so a forensic accountant should compare this material to the concepts and rules in the jurisdiction and court where the proceedings are pending and seek directions from counsel.

Appendix 6, "Forensic Accounting and Expert Witness Vocabulary," to this book provides definitions of important terms for forensic accounting and expert witnesses.

Two years later the AICPA released SAS No. 99, which did not even mention the word forensic. Why? SAS No. 99 did state that auditors should not assume that a client's management is honestly reporting results. SAS No. 99 calls for brainstorming before the actual audit, maintenance of a skeptical attitude, and the use of unpredictable audit tests. Some argue that SAS No. 99 watered down many of the forensic techniques offered by the Panel on Audit Effectiveness.

.01 AICPA Fraud Task Force Report

In 2003, the AICPA's Litigation and Dispute Resolution Services Subcommittee issued a report of its Fraud Task Force entitled "Incorporating Forensic Procedures in an Audit Environment." The task force paper provides guidance to practitioners in applying procedures in an audit environment in light of the Sarbanes-Oxley Act and the newly issued AICPA Statement on Auditing Standards (SAS) No. 99, Consideration of Financial Fraud in Financial Statement Audit.

The Fraud Task Force report covers the professional standards that apply when forensic procedures are employed in an audit and explains the various means of gathering evidence through the use of forensic procedures and investigation techniques.[12] As a traditional audit moves toward an investigation or an investigation moves toward an audit, the report covers the professional standards that apply to both an auditor and a forensic accountant.[13]

If forensic accountants are brought into an audit for purposes of complying with SAS No. 99, they are required to follow auditing standards. When forensic accountants are brought into an audit engagement for the purpose of conducting a separate investigation (and not an adjunct to an audit), because it is a litigation services engagement, consulting standards apply (rather than auditing standards).[14]

¶ 1203 Some Early History

Forensic accounting (or at least, accounting expert witnessing) can be traced as far back as 1817 to a court decision:

> *Meyer* v. *Sefton* was *inter alia*, an inquiry to determine the value of a bankrupt's estate. Here a witness who had examined the bankrupt's accounts

---

[12] R.L Durkins et. al, "Incorporating Forensic Procedures in an Audit Environment," *Litigation and Dispute Resolution Services Subcommittee Fraud Task Force* (New York: AICPA), 3.

[13] *Ibid.*, at 10.
[14] *Ibid.*

¶ 1202.01

was allowed to testify, since from the nature of the case such an inquiry could not be made in court.[15]

On March 12, 1824, a young accountant, by the name of James McClelland started his business in Glasgow, Scotland and issued a circular that advertised the various classes of work he was prepared to undertake. These classes included "the making up of Statements, Reports, and Memorials on Account Books, on disputed Accounts, and Claims for the purpose of laying before Arbiters, Courts, or Counsel."[16] In 1855, The Glasgow Institute was incorporated by Royal Charter. In its petition the following was noted: "Accountants are frequently employed by Courts of Law, both the Sheriff Courts and the Courts of Session, which is the Supreme Civil Tribunal in Scotland, to aid those Courts in their investigation of matters of accounting, which involves, to a greater or less extent, points of law of more or less difficulty."[17] The next year, 1856, corporate audits became required in England.

In the United States the accounting profession was taking form. The American Association of Public Accountants (eventually becoming the AICPA in 1957) was formed with 31 members in 1887. In 1896, New York State legislated the first CPA law, followed by the opening of a School of Commerce, Accounts, and Finance at New York University in 1900. Congress called for audit reports for large corporations in a 1902 Act.[18] In the first volume of the *Accountants' Index*, forensic-type articles are found under two categories: (1) Evidence and (2) Arbitration and Awards. Arbitration articles began as early as 1883,[19] and fraud-type articles began the next year.[20] Investigation-type articles started in 1889,[21] and the first expert witness article was by William H. Shawcross, entitled "How to Receive and Give Evidence" in 1898. This English barrister suggested the following:

> A further hint as to the giving of evidence is that *a witness should not show a testy disposition because he is questioned as to his professional qualifications.* In cases which involve difficult questions, which can only be adequately dealt with by experts, it is very material to know the qualifications they possess.[22]

---

[15] *Meyer v. Sefton*, 2 Stark. 274 (1817); see Clarence V. McArthur, "Evidence—Accountants as Experts," *Canadian Bar Review*, Vol. XXVI, No. 5 (May 1948): 873.

[16] Alex Moore, "The Accountant as an Expert Witness," *The Accountant* (June 29, 1907: 879 – 886. See also Leopold Frankel, "Court Testimony of Accountants," *Certified Public Accountant*, Vol. XIII, No. 5 (May 1933): 263.

[17] *Ibid.*, at 880.

[18] Anita Dennis, "Taking Account: Key Dates for the Profession," *Journal of Accountancy*, Vol. 190 (October 2000): 97–105.

[19] Astrup Cariss, "On Arbitration; and On Forms of Balance Sheets," *Accountant* (April 14, 1883); Joshua Slater, "Arbitration and Awards," *Accountant* (November 10, 17, 1883).

[20] Arnold T. Watson, "Falsified Accounts," *Accountant* (October 11, 18, 1884).

[21] Frank Creke, "Investigation of Public Companies' Accounts and Reports Thereof," *Accountant* (January 5, 1889): 7–11.

[22] William H. Shawcross, "How to Receive and Give Evidence," *Accountant*, Vol. XXIV, New Series, No. 1206 (January 15, 1898): 73. See also William N. Ashman, "Preparation of Accounts for the Court," *Business* (June 1895): 234–239.

¶ 1204 Expert Witnessing Becomes Popular

In the same year that *The Journal of Accountancy* was born (1905), a lawyer penned the article "The Accountant as an Expert Witness" in the first volume.[23] Cleveland Bacon stated that "judges all over the country recognize that experts are alone able to arrive at the true meaning of complicated accounts."[24] Further, an "accountant is frequently asked for pure opinion evidence, perhaps as to the meaning of certain figures and the inference to be drawn therefrom where the issue is the liability, negligence, or dishonesty of certain individuals." He asserted "that the certificate of certified public accountants is the most essential single element of" qualifying as an accounting expert witness. However, Bacon felt that real estate methods and values "are too far removed from the sciences to require any qualification except that derived from experience."

Two years later a Glasgow accountant, Alex Moore, stated that an accountant as an expert witness is required from time to time in criminal cases, "either to assist the Public Prosecutor in the preparation of the indictment, or to give evidence for the prosecution or for the defense." But "the widest sphere of work for the accountant as an expert witness is not, however, in criminal cases, but in civil cases and arbitrations."[25] He gave examples of disputes "affecting the correctness or otherwise of the application of figures in accounts, or the principle adopted in the application; questions as to the method of accounting under which the profit or loss arising from a business, adventure [sic], or other commercial transaction is ascertained; and questions with respect to valuation of goodwill or of shares in a limited company."[26] He saw no problem with accountants indicating their view on valuations, especially when valuing goodwill. Mr. Moore had the following to say about the qualification of an expert witness:

> An accountant may be thoroughly qualified to make all the investigations required, and to bring his results together in a satisfactory manner, such as will enable counsel to put a fair case before the court with confidence that it will be fully supported by the evidence. He may still, however, be wanting in some of the qualifications asked for in a good expert witness. He must be able to make a creditable appearance in the witness box, to put his evidence clearly before the Court, and to maintain his facts, arguments, and opinion under cross-examination, very often of a somewhat trying character.[27]

He also suggested that an accountant should not accept an expert witness job "unless he can honestly support the view which he is invited to sustain."[28] A thorough knowledge of the client's case, a complete grasp of his opponent's case, and refreshing one's memory immediately before taking the stand were recommended.

---

[23] Cleveland F. Bacon, "The Accountant as an Expert Witness," *Journal of Accountancy*, Vol. 1, No. 2 (December 1905): 99–105.

[24] *Ibid.*, at 100.

[25] Alex Moore, "The Accountant as an Expert Witness," *Accountant* (June 29, 1907): 880.

[26] *Ibid.*, at 882.

[27] *Ibid.*, at 885.

[28] *Ibid.*

¶ 1205 The Evidence Phase of Forensic Accounting

Arbitration was the driving force for accounting expert witnessing in England. In the United States the first federal income tax law was passed in 1913; the Federal Reserve Board and the Federal Trade Commission were created in 1913 and 1914, respectively. By 1921, all states had passed laws requiring examination for a CPA certificate. Numerous articles were published under the category of evidence, but by 1924 an editorial in the *Journal of Accountancy* published a reader's suggestion that the term *expert* should be omitted entirely from the pages of the *Journal*. The editorial stated that the word *expert* should suffer some kind of punishment. "It is becoming so sadly overworked and misused that the time is not far distant when the one who is accused of being an expert will have ground for action."[29]

From about 1925 to 1945, a steady stream of forensic-type articles were published in the United States (and other English-speaking countries) under the categories of evidence, fraud, and investigation. Albert S. Osborn described in 1926 fourteen possible attacks against evidence of an accountant on cross-examination (which were summarized by Max Lourie):

1. Insufficient preparation and experience to qualify as an expert witness
2. Inadequate examination of the issues presented
3. Improper presentation of the issues to the witness
4. Suspicion upon the testimony, based upon the witness's personal record and character
5. Use of misleading illustrations, selection of unfair examples, drawing of inferences not justified by facts, and improper emphasis or exaggeration
6. Impossibility of reaching a conclusion meriting serious consideration, on an issue not permitting adequate inquiry
7. Expression of an opinion unjustified by the reasons given
8. Basing the opinion upon vague and trivial facts insufficient to sustain any opinion, and arriving at a conclusion by guesswork
9. A biased and unfair attitude of the witness in the examination of the facts
10. The possibility that the problem is so difficult or unusual that even a competent and careful witness may be mistaken

---

[29] A.P. Richardson, "Casting Out 'Expert'," *Editorial Journal of Accountancy* (December 1924): 445; see also A.P. Richardson, "Arbitration: A New Field," *Editorial Journal of Accountancy* (October 1923): 286–287.

11. Influence of other things rather than technical findings on the opinion of the witness, and basing conclusions on reasons other than those given

12. Technical errors in the testimony of the expert witness

13. Serious errors made by the witness in other cases or at other times

14. Corruption or perjury of the witness, and his employment therefore [30]

¶ 1206 The Term "Forensic Accounting" Is Born

The first person to coin the description "forensic accounting" in print was probably Maurice E. Peloubet in 1946.[31] At that time Mr. Peloubet was a partner in the public accounting firm of Pogson, Peloubet & Co. in New York. He was a prolific writer, with the *Accountants Index* listing 23 articles under his name in the years 1944–1947.

After describing some early history of accounting (i.e., fourteenth-century Italian monastery brother and eighteenth-century Turkish merchant), Mr. Peloubet stated that "during the war both the public accountant and industrial accountant have been" and are now "engaged in the practice of forensic accounting."[32] Interestingly, he did not claim credit for coining the term.[33]

Mr. Peloubet suggested that until recently forensic accounting was only practiced in the courtroom, and that the preparation of financial statements includes some (but not all) of the characteristics of forensic accounting. As the number and power of administrative and regulatory agencies increase, the accountant finds himself "more involved in what is essentially a type of forensic practice." The preparation of data for and the appearance before such agencies "as a witness to facts, to accounting principles, or to the application of accounting principles is essentially forensic accounting practice rather than advocacy."[34]

Mr. Peloubet suggested that during the war, renegotiation, forward pricing, and contract termination were all exercises in forensic accounting. Dealings with the SEC are often of a forensic nature. The Robinson-Patman Act, public utility commissions, government lending agencies, and certain agricultural agencies provide ample fields for the exercise of forensic accounting.[35] The term forensic accounting "is the most fitting and inclusive" definition of "this great task we are called on to exercise the expository, the

---

[30] Albert S. Osborn, *The Problem of Proof*, 2nd ed. (Newark, N.J.: Essex Press, 1926), 394–395.

[31] Maurice E. Peloubet, "Forensic Accounting: Its Place in Today's Economy," *Journal of Accountancy*, Vol. 81, No. 6 (June 1946): 458–462.

[32] *Ibid.*, at 459.

[33] Two other people would later mistakenly in print claim credit for inventing the phrase: Max Lourie in 1953 and Robert Lindquist in 1986. Lindquist stated that he coined the phrase around 1976. Ann Shortell, "The New Crime Sleuths," *Maclean*, Vol. 99 (June 30, 1986): 26. Readers aware of an earlier use of the phrase, should please send evidence to the authors.

[34] Peloubet, "Forensic Accounting," at 460.

[35] *Ibid.*, at 461.

interpretative, and the arbitral functions"[36] as a result of the growth of government regulations.[37]

Wayne G. Bremser lists the modern role of forensic accountants:[38]

- Pretrial Support
  - Writing a report
  - Establishing causation
  - Gathering facts
  - Translating jargon
  - Organizing data
  - Formulating strategy
- Trial Support
- Expert Witnessing
- Settlement Support

When dealing with civil actions involving contract disputes, a forensic accountant generally must deal with three elements: proximate cause, reasonable certainty, and foreseeability. When dealing with fraud issues, the forensic accountant deals with four elements:

1. Misrepresentation of material fact
2. Made knowingly and with intent to defraud
3. Reliance on the misrepresentation by the victim
4. Resulting in damage from such reliance

Next the general concepts of judicial procedure and evidence applicable to forensic accounting are covered.

¶ 1207 Judicial Procedure

There are three branches of government: legislative laws (which takes precedence), executive (regulations), and judicial law (a referee). The Federal Rules of Civil Procedures (FRCP) govern U.S. district courts. In civil procedure, as in most other matters, legislative law takes precedence over case law, but case law controls in the absence of appropriate legislation. Courts usually apply their own procedural law but may apply the substantive law of another jurisdiction in order to determine the rights of the parties.

---

[36] *Ibid.*, at 462.
[37] *See* Alfred R. Roberts, ed., *The Story of A Fortunate Man: Reminiscences and Recollections of Fifty-Three Years of Professional Accounting* (London: Elsevier Science, 2001).
[38] W.G. Bremser, *Forensic Accounting and Financial Fraud* (Watertown, Mass.: American Management Association, 1995), 5–9.

Trial courts (often called "superior" or "district" courts) function primarily as triers of fact (e.g., U.S. Tax Court). Appellate courts review the law applicable to the facts, but they may not redetermine the facts (e.g., Fifth Circuit Court of Appeals). Expert witnesses testify in trial courts, where issues of facts are normally determined. An expert might help with a friend of the court filing (amicus curiae brief) for an appellate court. The Anglo-American legal system operates on the premise that the best way to get at the truth is through competing presentation of evidence (e.g., an adversarial system).

The court exercises a generally passive role, more or less as a referee, in contrast to some other systems, where the court takes the lead. Under the Anglo-American system the court will on occasion take a more active role, particularly to avoid a miscarriage of justice. Under some other systems, courts can base their fact findings solely on files compiled by judicial investigators and clerks. In general, the Anglo-American judicial system has an oral tradition for presentation of evidence (e.g., a testimonial tradition).

.01 Pleadings

There are basically two forms of pleadings: the complaint and the answer. The plaintiff files the complaint. The defendant's answer must admit or deny the allegations. The defendant also may raise affirmative defenses, which are deemed denied by the plaintiff. No reply is necessary. The court for good cause shown (including conforming to proof) often liberally permits amended and supplemental pleadings. If the defendant believes that the plaintiff has not followed some legal standard or stated a cause of action, the defendant may file a demurrer (e.g., a motion to dismiss).

The terms used to designate the parties may vary with the type of court and case. For example, consider the following citation of a Federal District Court decision: *Sharp v. United States*, 199 F. Supp. 743 (D. Del. 1961), aff'd 203 F.2d 783 (3rd Cir. 1962). Sharp is the plaintiff at the trial level, and the United States is the defendant. The appellate court, the United States Court of Appeal for the Third Circuit, reviewed the trial court decision and agreed with the lower court's decision. Sometimes a court will use the terms "petitioner" and "respondent." At the trial court level, "petitioner" is usually equivalent to "plaintiff," and "respondent" is equivalent to "defendant." On appeal, the moving party may be referred to as the "appellant" or the "petitioner," whereas the responding party may be referred to as the "appellee" or "respondent."

There are basically three types of evidence: testimony, writings, and objects. Evidence other than oral testimony is sometimes referred to as "real" evidence. This term represents mere terminology and does not express a superiority of tangible over oral evidence.

¶ 1207.01

Forensic Accounting Services

The burden of proof in civil cases is usually by a "preponderance of the evidence," meaning in substance "more likely than not," (more than 50 percent). Usually the party who has the burden of proof also had the burden of producing evidence. The party with the burden of proof has the obligation of making sure the ball is over the 50-yard line and in the opponent's territory. If the ball ends up on the 50-yard line, the party with the burden of proof loses. If the ball is in someone's end zone, that party loses by a directed verdict at the end of the trial.

.02 *Discovery Process*

After the pleadings, the discovery phase starts. The primary purposes of discovery are to enable parties to obtain information, narrow the issues, and, hopefully, promote settlement. Many state rules resemble or closely follow the Federal Rules of Civil Procedures (FRCP). However, the forensic practitioner needs to be familiar with the rules of the particular jurisdiction in which the case is pending.

Methods of discovery include:

- Interrogatories: Written questions propounded by one party, served on the other party (or witness), who must answer the questions under oath
- Requests for production of documents
- Depositions: One party takes oral testimony of the other party (or witness), under oath, outside of court and a transcript is made
- Subpoenas *duces tecum*: request for specified documents for inspection and copying (especially from people not parties to a lawsuit, e.g., expert witness)
- Physical examination
- Production of tangible things and entry upon land

An expert quite often will be deposed. B. P. Brinig has given the 10 commandments for depositions:

1. Always tell the truth, but answer only the question asked.
2. Think before answering.
3. Never answer a question you do not understand.
4. Do not guess or speculate.
5. Do not bring notes, diagrams, books, or other written material to the deposition unless a subpoena or your attorney requires you to do so.
6. Listen carefully to each objection made by your lawyer.

¶ 1207.02

7. Do not argue or become angry or hostile with the examining attorney.

8. Even if a question calls for a yes or no answer, ask to explain your response if you feel a qualification or explanation is required to complete your answer.

9. Be wary of questions which involve absolutes.

10. Do not memorize your answers before the deposition.[39]

Under Rule 26(a) of the FRCP, the parties must voluntarily disclose the identity of witnesses, relevant documents, computation of damages, and relevant insurance policies. Counsel is also required to meet and develop a proposed plan of discovery before formal discovery can occur. The FRCP contemplate that the court will actively oversee discovery from the beginning. In state courts, there is often not the same level of close supervision. The forensic accountant is advised to make special note of FRCP Rule 26(a)(2), which requires disclosure of the identity of experts, the opinions they will provide, and their qualifications, including a list of all of their publications in the last 10 years and all cases in which they have provided testimony in the last four years.

Discovery may not be made of certain privileged matters between the following:

- Attorney – client
- Husband – wife
- Physician – patient

The attorney's work product is also not subject to discovery. However, there is no privilege for litigation consultants.

.03 Motion for Summary Judgment

During the discovery phase or shortly before trial, one of the parties may bring a motion for summary judgment. Because of the decreasing importance of technical pleading, summary judgments have become very important as a means of avoiding the burden of unnecessary trials. The forensic accountant may play an important role in preparing supporting affidavits for summary judgment proceedings. The moving party submits one or more affidavits in support of its position. The opposing party may submit opposing affidavits. The court may grant summary judgment if it concludes that there is no triable issue of fact. The court must deny summary judgment if it concludes that a jury or trial judge could find against the party initiating the motion. In other words, the judge who rules on the motion for summary judgment does not "weigh the evidence,"

---

[39] B.P. Brinig, "The Art of Testifying," in *Handbook of Financial Planning for Divorce and Separation* (New York: John Wiley, 1990), 85–87.

¶ 1207.03

meaning to determine which party's evidence is most persuasive. In appropriate circumstances, the court will grant partial summary judgment in regard to specific issues.

.04 Evidence

The best evidence rule historically required that original documents be produced, rather than "secondary" evidence, including oral testimony. Today the rule is influenced by practicality and is often governed by statute. For example, usually a computer printout is admissible as an "original," provided it is authenticated, and a foundation of accuracy is laid. Frequently, the resolution depends on whether there really is a dispute over the document's admissibility. Then authenticity or hearsay is more likely to be an issue.

Embedded in forensic accounting is the concept of evidence. Forensic science is the application of science of law; it is the use of any scientific principle or technique that can be applied to identifying, recovering, reconstructing, or analyzing evidence during a civil or criminal investigation.[40]

Preparing for an investigation and securing and managing documentary evidence are important in determining the truth and building a criminal or civil case. Obviously, an important priority in document management is to maintain the integrity of all of the evidence. Because documents are often targets for destruction by theft or arson, any evidence should be stored off site.[41]

In the court of law, all relevant evidence is admissible, unless it is inadmissible due to another rule of evidence. Federal Rule of Civil Procedure 403 indicates that probative value is substantially outweighed by the danger of unfair prejudice, confusion of the issues, misleading the jury, or by considerations of undue delay, waste of time, or needless presentation of cumulative evidence. Hearsay evidence is not generally admissible, but there are many exceptions. Business records are a major exception, and a good lawyer can get most business records into a trial.

A forensic practitioner needs to gather, preserve, and present quality evidence. Two authors provide guidelines for measuring the persuasiveness of evidence:[42]

- The evidence must be *relevant* to the related conclusion.

- *Objective* evidence usually is more persuasive than subjective evidence (i.e., a physical count of inventory versus estimates; two auditors working independently getting the same result).

---

[40] Eoghan Casey, *Digital Evidence and Computer Crime* (London: Academic Press, 2001), 3.

[41] For more detail, see Helen Ehlers, "Fraud Investigations Need to Start with a Plan for Gathering and Handling the Evidence," *Internal Auditor* (October 1996): 38–43.

[42] R.L. Ratliff and I.R. Johnson, "Evidence," *Internal Auditor* (August 1998): 55–61.

- *Documented* evidence is typically more persuasive than undocumented evidence (i.e., 10 letters from customers praising a product).
- *Third-party* evidence is generally more persuasive than evidence from within the organization in question.
- *Large samples* generally are more persuasive than smaller samples.
- *Statistical samples* usually are more persuasive than nonstatistical samples.
- *Corroborated* evidence is usually more persuasive than uncorroborated evidence.
- *Timely* evidence is typically more persuasive than evidence produced after a delay.
- *Authoritative* evidence usually is more persuasive than nonauthoritative evidence.
- *Direct* evidence usually is more persuasive than indirect evidence (i.e., physical count of inventory is more persuasive than perpetual inventory records).
- Evidence from a *well-controlled* and reliable system usually is more persuasive than evidence from a poorly controlled or questionable system.

¶ 1208 Evidence and Computer Technology

Generally accepted auditing standards (GAAS) have always required external auditors to "Consider the methods the entity uses to process accounting information in planning the audit because such methods influence the design of the internal control."[43] The extent and complexity of computer processing influences the nature, timing, and extent of audit procedures. In completing this evaluation, the forensic auditor should consider the following:

- The extent to which the computer is used in each significant accounting application
- The complexity of the entity's computer operations, including the use of an outside service center
- The organizational structure of the computer processing activities
- The availability of data
- The use of computer-based audit techniques to increase the efficiency of performing audit procedures.[44]

---

[43] Statement on Auditing Standards (SAS) No. 48, *The Effects of Computer Processing on the Audit of Finacial Statements* (AICPA, Professional Standards, Vol. 1, AU sec. 311.09).

[44] *Ibid.*

Basically, external and forensic auditors must honestly and objectively evaluate their ability to audit certain technologies and obtain the necessary training or hire a specialist for areas they are not competent to audit.[45] In general, information technology influences audit procedures and evidential matter rather than specific audit objectives. Finally, information technology has greatly influenced the internal control structure of audit clients in two fundamental ways. First, the processing of transactions occurs faster and more complexly in computerized systems than in a manual system, causing increased inherent risk. Secondly, traditional internal controls such as segregation of duties and the existence of a paper trail are eliminated, causing control risk to rise.

Forensic electronic imaging is a process of scanning evidential and case-related documents into a magnetic medium (e.g., computer hard drive or an optical disk, such as CD-ROM). More and more private and governmental organizations are creating documents electronically rather than on paper. As imaging technology is advancing, forensic accountants must adopt and use this resource. A person can sort, analyze, and retrieve these documents without having to go through massive amounts of paper materials. There are often legal obligations to complete a civil or criminal case within a reasonable time frame that may force full disclosure of the materials collected. Evidential matters can be better preserved, and an investigation is better able to fulfill legal requirements for custody and control over vital evidence.[46]

For example, forensic accountants can use data mining to identify potentially fraudulent transactions for further investigation and follow-up. Vendor information can be analyzed and compared to employee records to identify payments made to a vendor with the same phone number or address as an employee. Additional applications analyze past transactions for variables present in fraudulent transactions and for use in flagging similar transactions before they are processed. Data mining enables an investigator to reveal valuable information and compile relationships that exist among large amounts of data.

¶ 1209 Computer Forensics

Electronic documents are now dealt with in investigations and the courtroom. SAS No. 80 states that substantive tests may not be sufficient for a system predominantly consisting of electronic evidence.[47] Thus, an auditor must perform tests of system control to determine that they are strong enough to mitigate the risks with electronic evidence. By combining system control tests with substantive evidence an auditor may issue an opinion. SAS No. 94 provides guidance to external auditors about the effect

---

[45] Ibid., sec. 311.10.
[46] Basil Orsini, "Electronic Imaging," *The White Paper* (July/August 1999): 24.
[47] Statement on Auditing Standards (SAS) No. 80, *Amendment to Statement on Auditing Standards* No. 31, Evidential Matter (AICPA, Professional Standards, vol. 1, AU sec. 326.14, "Use of Assertions in Developing Audit Objectives and Designing Substantive Tests").

of information technology on internal controls, and on the auditor's understanding of internal controls and assessment of control risk.

In both criminal and civil situations electronic evidence often will be collected. Reasonable workplace searches are legal under the Fourth Amendment to the U.S. Constitution, but there must be a reasonable purpose. The area to be searched must not be covered by an employee's expectation of privacy. Computer forensics may be defined as the procedures applied to computers and peripherals for gathering evidence that may be used in civil and criminal courts of law. For criminal investigations electronic evidence is sought with a warrant or possible subpoena. Electronic evidence for civil actions is sought through discovery requests such as interrogatories or depositions.

Computers and related equipment may be seized as evidence in a criminal matter, and such evidence must not be mishandled or accidentally destroyed. G. Stevenson Smith provides some tips:

1. Close phone line connections to the modem so data cannot be removed from a remote location.

2. Videotape and label all connections and cables so that equipment can be successfully reconnected at the lab and possibly returned without damage.

3. Do not turn on seized electronic equipment without advice from a forensic expert. Booby traps may erase data if correct passwords are not used.

4. Review all files in a bit-system or "read-only" mode to legally ensure that no alterations could have been made to the evidence.

5. A recorded chain of custody should be kept and signed by all parties, reviewing verified copies with the original copy sealed.[48]

Icove, Seger, and VanStorch[49] offer guidelines for forensic auditors examining computer evidence:

- Upon receipt of evidence, log evidence into appropriate evidence control system and assign it to an examiner.

---

[48] G. Stevenson Smith, "Collection and Control of Electronic Evidence," *Journal of Forensic Accounting*, Vol. 1 (2000): 285–286. *See also* Mark Bigler, "Computer Forensic," *Internal Auditor* (February 2000): 53–55.

[49] David Icove, Karl Seger, and William VanStorch, *Computer Crime, A Crimefighter's Handbook* (Sebastopol, Calif.: O'Reilly & Associates, 1995), 190–194.

- Use a unique numbering system to record the date and time received.

- Identify the examiner and prepare documentation for the chain of custody from evidence control to examiner.

- To transfer evidence to examiner, determine whether other expert analyses such as accounting, drug record analysis, etc., are necessary.

- Prepare chain of custody documentation for other experts as necessary for complete examination.

- Verify that all pieces of equipment listed as having been submitted are actually present.

- Mark and initial each piece of evidence as required by laboratory and prepare notes.

The forensic auditor should not use the software on the system being examined to boot the system for fear of destroying evidence. He or she should determine whether the submitted system is operational, then write-protect all diskettes and hard drives. After identifying the computer to be used for the examination, he or she can convert the directory/subdirectory listings, checking for hidden and deleted files using appropriate commercial or custom software. Then the auditor can display and print the files. The auditor should thoroughly document the examination, sending the printouts and report to the contributor or subject matter expert for any additional analysis. Finally, after the conclusions of the computer investigation, the auditor repacks the computer and all disks, then returns the evidence.

¶ 1210 Forensic Accounting Practices

Forensic accounting practices are often classified into three categories: litigation support consulting, fraud examination, and expert witnessing.[50] These three areas of forensic accounting practices can strengthen the quality of financial reporting by assisting in the prevention, detection, and correction of fraud-including occupational fraud, financial statement fraud, and investment fraud-and conducting risk and fraud vulnerability analysis.

.01 Litigation Support Consulting

This area of forensic accounting practice has increased significantly during the past two decades. Litigation consultants can assist attorneys to determine the relevancy, reliability, and usefulness of financial information presented for legal actions; to evaluate financial information presented to the court; and to help attorneys interpret the findings. The plaintiff and

---

[50] Zabihollah Rezaee. "Forensic Accounting Practices, Education, and Certifications." *Journal of Forensic Accounting* (2002, vol. III(2)): 207-224.

defense attorneys also utilize services provided by litigation consultants during the discovery and testimony process.

.02 Fraud Detection

The pervasiveness of reported corporate and accounting scandals along with increasing occupational fraud have created significant career opportunities for fraud auditors to prevent, detect, and correct occurrences of fraud. By issuing Statement on Auditing Standards (SAS) No. 99, the AICPA attempts to clarify the auditor's responsibility for detecting and reporting financial statement fraud. (SAS No. 99 and fraud detection are discussed in detail in Chapter 20.) The AICPA also promotes anti-fraud programs for corporations and anti-fraud education for colleges and universities. The AICPA has issued the following six leadership roles to assist organizations in preventing and detecting financial statement fraud:

1. Convene anti-fraud summits with corporate leaders, accountants, and market professionals

2. Partner with corporations to design and establish anti-fraud controls and programs

3. Establish enhanced attestation standards for CPAs to report on corporate anti-fraud programs

4. Establish an institute for fraud studies with the University of Texas and Association of Certified Fraud Examiners

5. Work with academia on anti-fraud curriculum and materials, and develop training programs to prevent fraud

6. Work with FASB and other standard-setting bodies on more timely and better quality financial reporting with different reporting needs for private vs. public companies (big GAAP vs. small GAAP)

Several professional organizations, including the AICPA, ACFE, IIA, IMA, Financial Executives International (FEI), Information Systems Audits and Controls Association (ISACA), National Association of Corporate Directors (NACD), and Society for Human Resource Management (SHRM), have jointly issued management and anti-fraud programs and controls (MAPCs) to assist companies to combat fraud.[51] MAPCs contain recommendations for (1) creating a culture of honesty and high ethics through setting the tone at the top, establishing a positive workplace environment, and providing ongoing monitoring processes, training, and discipline; (2) evaluating anti-fraud processes and controls by identifying and measuring fraud risks, mitigating fraud risks, and operating appropriate internal controls; and (3) developing a vigilant oversight process consist-

---

[51] American Institute of Certified Public Accountants (AICPA). Management Antifraud Programs and Controls. (2002) Available at http://www.aicpa.org.

ing of cooperation between the audit committee, senior executives, internal auditors, external auditors, and governing bodies such as the SEC and organized stock exchanges.

.03 Expert Witnessing

An accountant's testimony in court falls into one or both of two particular classes: direct testimony about facts at issue and expert opinion.[52] When testifying about his or her own bookkeeping entries or accounting procedures, an accountant is not an expert. However, Greeley states, "When an accountant testifies as to the effect of certain bookkeeping entries or accounting procedures, he gives his expert opinion and he is strictly an expert witness."[53] The author suggests that accountants must guard against giving answers that are not responsive and answers to questions not asked. He asserts that an expert witness should not take a fee contingent upon the result of the litigation: "A professional expert witness should not be a partisan, and his sphere is not that of an advocate for the side of the controversy by which he is employed."[54]

Generally, nonexpert witnesses are not permitted to give opinions, but expert witnesses may. Although experts are not required to testify from personal knowledge, they must be qualified. As a result there has been a series of precedent-setting U.S. Supreme Court cases, starting with a case entitled *Daubert v. Merrill Dow Pharmaceuticals, Inc.*[55] As a result of the *Daubert* decision, the court must in substance now make a preliminary finding regarding whether the reasoning and methodology the expert employs is scientifically valid and can be applied to the facts of the particular case. The trial court acts as a gatekeeper to ensure the scientific validity of the expert's testimony.

The *Kumho Tire Co. v. Carmichael*[56] decision extended the *Daubert* concept to all expert testimony, regardless of the subject matter; there is a thin line between scientific and other experts. In general, the expert witness will perhaps be asked a few more questions than previously would have been expected. These questions would generally extend to the methodology used, whether it is reliable, and why. Greater concern is warranted if the expert is relying on nontraditional methodologies or if the analysis is not well supported factually. Although the *Daubert* case and its progeny may not have substantive impact on forensic accounting methods and reasoning in general, these cases have probably resulted in heightened scrutiny in many instances of not only the methods used but the underlying factual support for the conclusions presented. A motion *in limine* may be used to exclude an expert witness report and/or testimony.

---

[52] Harold Dudley Greeley, "The Accountant as a Witness," *Journal of Accountancy*, Vol. 64, No. 1 (July 1937): 65–68; *See also* Arthur Collins, "Accountant in the Witness Box," *Accountant* (January 26, 1924): 129; A.E. Cutforth, "Accountant as Expert Witness," *Accountant* (November 21, 1931): 675–683.

[53] *Ibid.*, at 65.

[54] *Ibid.*, at 68.

[55] 509 U.S. 579 (1993).

[56] 143 L. Ed. 2d 238, 119 SCt 1167 (1999).

¶ 1210.03

The *Daubert* decision provided four factors for the trial judge to consider in this gatekeeper role, and the Ninth Circuit Court added a fifth to the list. These five factors are:

1. Whether the theory or technique used by the expert can be, and has been, tested

2. Whether the theory or technique has been subjected to peer review and publication

3. The known or potential rate of error of the method used; and

4. The degree of the method's or conclusion's acceptance within the relevant community

5. The theory that must exist before litigation begins

Courts will probably not exclude testimony on the basis of one factor alone. These five factors bear on Federal Rule of Evidence Rule 702 dealing with admission.

Not all states have accepted *Daubert* (about 10 have). Some states still follow the *Frye*[57] standard (about 14), and some states have their own tests (about 12). The following internet sites keep track of the states' standards: http://faculty.ncwc.edu/toconnor/daubert.htm, and http://www.effingham.net/michael/dbtp.html.

Recently a U.S. Tax Court judge explained that the court expects helpful and reliable testimony from an expert witness. A judge does not wish to be concerned with questions of reliability and helpfulness of expert testimony, but prefers to take helpfulness and reliability for granted. In this particular case the U.S. Tax Court appointed its own experts, and both Bank One Corporation and the IRS each had their own experts.[58]

Courts are rejecting expert witnesses using *Daubert* and *Frye*. A CPA's testimony about a defendant accused of insider trading was inadmissible because the methodology used for giving the opinion was no more than speculation.[59] An economist's testimony concerning loss figures for loss of guidance or counsel financial support was inadmissible, because it was not based on scientifically valid methodology.[60] The testimony by a former tax prosecutor that the government should not have filed the criminal tax case was inadmissible.[61]

Just saying that one is a CPA will not automatically qualify one as an expert. A CPA must carefully set out what the AICPA professional standards are (see Chapter 2), explain what CPA certification requires, and

---

[57] *Frye v. U.S.*, 293 F. 1013 (D.C. Cir. 1923).
[58] *Bank One Corp. v. Comm.*, Tax Ct. Dkt. Nos. 5759-95 and 5956-97; see Lee A. Sheppard, "Bank One: The Court's Experts Testify," *Tax Notes* (July 9, 2001): 163–169.
[59] *SEC v. Lipson*, 46 FSupp2d 758 (N.D. Ill. 1999).
[60] *Cochrane v. Schneider Natl. Carriers, Inc.*, 980 FSupp 374 (D. Kan. 1996).
[61] *U.S. v. Rice*, 52 F3d 843 (10th Cir. 1995), cert. denied, 116 SCt 2536 (1996).

¶ 1210.03

why he or she is entitled to be an expert in a particular situation. Judge Alex Kozinski says that attorneys must put this CPA evidence in every case, so that on an appeal the information is in the record.[62] If a trial judge says that the testimony of an expert is admissible, there is almost no way that the decision to admit evidence will be reversed on appeal.[63]

¶ 1211 Federal Rules of Evidence

Seven important Federal Rules of Evidence govern the testimony of expert witnesses: Rule 104(a), Rule 702, Rule 703, Rule 705, Rule 403, Rule 704, and Rule 706. A synopsis of each rule follows.

Rule 104(a): Preliminary Questions.

> Preliminary questions concerning the qualification of a witness, the existence of a privilege, or the admissibility of evidence shall be determined by the court. In making its determination [the court] is not bound by the rules of evidence except those with respect to privilege.

A challenge to expert testimony or the written report should be made prior to admission (e.g., motion *in limine*).

Rule 702: Testimony by Experts (after 2000).

> If scientific, technical, or other specialized knowledge will assist the trier of fact to understand the evidence or to determine a fact in issue, a witness qualified as an expert by knowledge, skill, experience, training, or education, may testify thereto in the form of an opinion or otherwise, if (1) the testimony is based upon sufficient facts or data, (2) the testimony is the product of reliable principles and methods, and (3) the witness has applied the principles and methods reliably to the facts of the case.

The *Daubert* decision adds five factors bearing on admission. See the earlier discussion of *Daubert*.

Rule 703: Bases of Opinion Testimony by Expert (after 2000).

> The facts or data in the particular case upon which an expert bases an opinion or inference may be those perceived by or made known to the expert at or before the hearing. If of a type reasonably relied upon by experts in the particular field in forming opinions or inferences upon the subject, the facts or data need not be admissible in evidence *in order for the opinion or inference to be admitted. Facts or data that are otherwise inadmissible shall not be disclosed to the jury by the proponent of the opinion or inference unless the court determines that their probative value in assisting the jury to evaluate the expert's opinion substantially outweighs their prejudicial effect.* [emphasis on original on website]

Rule 705: Disclosure of Facts or Data Underlying Expert Opinion.

> The expert may testify in terms of opinion or inference and give reasons therefore without first testifying to the underlying facts or data, unless the court requires otherwise. The expert may in any event be required to disclose the underlying facts or data on cross-examination.

---

[62] Alex Kozinski, "Expert Testimony After *Daubert*," *Journal of Accountancy* (July 2001): 59–60.

[63] *Ibid.*, at 60.

This rule allows an expert witness to present naked opinions, but if the testimony has an inadequate foundation the trial court can disallow the testimony.

Rule 403: Exclusion of Relevant Evidence on Grounds of Prejudice, Confusion, or Waste of Time.

> Although relevant, evidence may be excluded if its probative value is substantially outweighed by the danger of unfair prejudice, confusion of the issues, or misleading the jury, or by considerations of undue delay, waste of time, or needless presentation of cumulative evidence.

"Unfair prejudice" refers to an undue tendency to decide a decision on an improper basis, commonly, though not necessarily, an emotional one.

Rule 704: Opinion on Ultimate Issue.

> (a) Except as provided in subdivision (b), testimony in the form of an opinion or inference otherwise admissible is not objectionable because it embraces an ultimate issue to be decided by the trier of fact.
>
> (b) No expert witness testifying with respect to the mental state or condition of a defendant in a criminal case may state an opinion or inference as to whether the defendant did or did not have the mental state or condition constituting an element of the crime charged or of a defense thereto. Such ultimate issues are matters for the trier of fact alone.

"Otherwise admissible" means that the testimony must be admissible under Rules 702, 703, 705, and 403.

Rule 706: Court Appointed Experts.

> (a) **Appointment.**
>
> The court may on its own motion or on the motion of any party enter an order to show cause why expert witnesses should not be appointed, and may request the parties to submit nominations. The court may appoint any expert witnesses agreed upon by the parties, and may appoint expert witnesses of its own selection. An expert witness shall not be appointed by the court unless the witness consents to act. A witness so appointed shall be informed of the witness' duties by the court in writing, a copy of which shall be filed with the clerk, or at a conference in which the parties shall have opportunity to participate. A witness so appointed shall advise the parties of the witness' findings, if any; the witness' deposition may be taken by any party; and the witness may be called to testify by the court or any party. The witness shall be subject to cross-examination by each party, including a party calling the witness.
>
> (b) **Compensation.**
>
> Expert witnesses so appointed are entitled to reasonable compensation in whatever sum the court may allow. The compensation thus fixed is payable from funds which may be provided by law in criminal cases and civil actions and proceedings involving just compensation under the fifth amendment. In other civil actions and proceedings the compensation shall be paid by the parties in such proportion and at such time as the court directs, and thereafter charged in like manner as other costs.
>
> (c) **Disclosures of appointment.**
>
> In the exercise of its discretion, the court may authorize disclosure to the jury of the fact that the court appointed the expert witness.

¶ 1211

(d) **Parties' experts of own selection.**

Nothing in this rule limits the parties in calling expert witnesses of their own selection.[64]

¶ 1212 Courtroom Etiquette

Howard W. Wright[65] indicated that most court cases involving accounting arise because of some linguistic ambiguity in law, regulation, or contract. For the initial contact with the employing attorney, the forensic accountant must exhibit patience, and ask questions. Above all, he or she must not jump to any snap judgments about the merits of the case. Adverse comments about the merits of the case might discourage the attorney from continuing with the forensic aspect of the case. Such comments would be unfair if based on less than full knowledge.[66]

Wright gave other suggestions:

- Per diem rates are best for compensating an expert witness.

- Even a simple case requires about 10 days of involvement for the accountant.

- Success on the witness stand will be in direct proportion to the thoroughness of the research and fieldwork.

- Most effective witnesses do not use written notes in the witness box.

- On the stand the accountant should not be too erudite and should delve into theory only when absolutely necessary.

- Lawyers use hypothetical questions when the witness does not have firsthand knowledge in depth of all the facts involved.

- The best protection against extensive cross-examination is to be brief, absolutely accurate, and entirely calm.

- Although all witnesses and counsel may make up a team, the attorney is the captain.

- Not infrequently, judges like to know whether the witness really knows what he or she is talking about.

- The strong point of the opponent's case should be analyzed, because they probably are weak ones for the forensic accountant's client. The accountant should play "'devil's advocate" for the client by looking for issues the opposing side may present and preparing responses to them.

---

[64] From *Federal Rules of Evidence* as listed on http://www.law.cornell.edu/rules/fre.
[65] Howard W. Wright, "Some Suggestions for Expert Accounting Witnesses," *Journal of Accountancy* (March 1971): 63. See also H.W. Wright, "Forensic Accounting—It's Debatable," *Financial Executive* (February 1977): 16–22.
[66] *Ibid.*, at 63.

- The witness should not try to memorize his or her testimony, but develop the testimony in a logical sequence and then try to retain that sequence.

- The witness should be sure to get a good night's sleep before the day of testimony, avoiding use of alcohol for at least a day prior to testifying, and eating lightly on that day.

- The witness should never fence or argue with opposing counsel.

The first book that explored forensic accounting appeared in 1982, written by Francis C. Dykeman, a retired partner of Price Waterhouse. Both a CPA and attorney, Dykeman included an overview of the judicial process, trial attorney's cases, court systems, administrative agencies, working in an ambiguous environment, developing and managing information, preparing and presenting direct testimony, cross-examination, the trial, and other topics.[67]

In a chapter covering the behavior of an expert accounting witness, Dykeman provided 21 rules of conduct as a guide, including these:

1. Be punctual and make definite arrangements with the attorneys as to the time and place of testimony.

2. Make sure you understand a question before answering it.

3. Address the jury as much as possible, rather than the observers in the courtroom.

4. Use layman's language rather than accounting jargon.

5. Do not volunteer information beyond the required answer.

6. Avoid attempts at humor.

7. Be courteous to the opposing attorney.

8. Do not engage in personal exchanges with the opposing counsel, no matter what the apparent provocation.

9. Do not hesitate to pause before answering.[68]

In 1986, the AICPA issued Practice Aid 7, which contains six areas of litigation services:[69]

1. Damages
   - Lost Profits
   - Lost value

---

[67] Francis C. Dykeman, *Forensic Accounting: The Accountant as Expert Witness* (New York: John Wiley & Sons, 1982). *See also* Joseph Belogna, *Guidelines on Forensic Accounting* (Computer Systems, Inc., 1984).

[68] *Ibid.*, at 47–48.

[69] Management Advisory Services Practice Aids. Technical Consulting Practice Aid 7: *Litigation Services* (New York: AICPA, 1986).

¶ 1212

- Extra cost
- Lost cash flow
- Lost revenue
- Mitigation
- Personal injury
- Environmental

2. Antitrust Analyses
   - Price-fixing
   - Market share, market definition
   - Pricing below cost
   - Dumping and other price discrimination
   - Anti-competition actions
   - Monopolization

3. Accounting
   - CPA Malpractice
   - Bankruptcy and reorganization
   - Family law
   - Tracing
   - Contract cost and claims
   - Regulated industries
   - Frauds, civil and criminal
   - Historical analyses

4. Analyses
   - Tax bases
   - Cost allocations
   - Tax treatment of specific transactions

5. Valuation
   - Business and professional practices
   - Pension
   - Intangibles
   - Property

6. General Consulting
   - Arbitration
   - Mediation

- Statistical analyses
- Actuarial analyses
- Projections
- Industrial engineering
- Computer consulting
- Market analyses
- Industry practices
- Mergers and acquisitions
- Document management

The American Management Association offers a self-study course entitled *Forensic Accounting and Financial Fraud*. In it, Wayne Bremser suggests that forensic accountants can help in the following situations: antitrust, commercial contracts, patent infringement, trademark and copyright infringement, product liability, mergers and acquisitions, insurance claims, shareholder suits, reorganization and bankruptcy, taxation, malpractice, corporate fraud, arson, price fixing, and bid rigging.[70] In criminal cases the forensic accountant can help the prosecutor establish motive.[71] The course covers various fraudulent financial reporting schemes, methods of computing lost profits, damages, and damage calculations.[72]

The *Litigation Services Handbook*, third edition, lists 37 areas of civil litigation broken into damages techniques, civil litigation, intellectual property, antitrust/business combinations, mergers and acquisitions, bankruptcy, construction and environmental disputes, other civil litigation, family law, and criminal cases. Each of these areas can cover a chapter of a forensic accounting text by itself:

- Estimating lost profits and economic losses
- Calculating lost profits damages for new businesses
- Cost estimation
- Estimating cost of capital
- Interest as damages
- Business valuation
- Calculation of lost earnings
- Punitive damages
- Economic analyses of punitive damages

---

[70] Wayne G. Bremser, *Forensic Accounting and Financial Fraud* (Watertown, Mass.: American Management Association, 1995), 2.

[71] *Ibid.*, at 17–32.

[72] *Ibid.*

¶ 1212

- Tax treatment of damage awards
- Securities Acts Violations: damages
- Derivatives
- Materiality and magnitude
- Shareholder litigation
- Trademarks, trade secrets, and false advertising
- Copyright infringement matters
- Intellectual property rights
- Patent infringement damages
- Royalty audits
- Mergers, acquisitions, and divestitures
- Bankruptcy litigation
- Construction claims
- Environmental disputes
- Accountant's liability
- Business interruption claims
- U.S. Government contracts
- Federally insured banks
- International trade litigation
- Alter ego
- Employment discrimination litigation
- Division/valuation of marital property
- Child and spousal support awards
- Professional goodwill and related intangibles
- Tracing and apportionment of assets
- Marital dissolution: tax aspects
- Internal corporate investigations
- Tax fraud cases[73]

---

[73] R.L. Weil, M.J. Wagner, and P.B. Frank, *Litigation Services Handbook*, Third ed. (New York: John Wiley & Sons, 2001).

¶ 1213 Measuring Damages

A forensic accountant is often called upon to measure damages. In order to win a suit, the plaintiff must prove that (a) the defendant violated a legal right of the plaintiff, (b) this violation harmed the plaintiff, and (c) the harm caused the plaintiff to suffer damages. There are various approaches to calculating damages.

Two theories are used to determine damages; the one selected depends upon state laws. The theories are the out-of-pocket rule and the benefit-of-the-bargain rule. The out-of-pocket loss refers to the difference between the actual value received and the actual value conveyed. In other words, the damage award includes no opportunity costs in certain jurisdictions. The plaintiff can recover nothing beyond his or her investment.

Under the benefit-of-the-bargain theory, the damage includes not only the money invested but also other expenses, such as increased costs (i.e., interest expense), lost profits, and decreased value of the investment. There are three ways to calculate these lost profits: before-and-after method, yardstick approach, and hypothetical sales method. Each approach tries to determine the plaintiff's real gain.

- *Before-and-after method*: Take sales or sales growth before the act and compare to the comparable figures afterward.

- *Yardstick (or benchmark) approach*: Compare sales or sales growth of the company to other companies or to other industry averages.

- *Hypothetical (or direct) sales method*: Directly compute lost sales.

The before-and-after method is better for more mature businesses but fails to consider the possibility of increases in the future. Thus, the before-and-after method is not the best approach for a rapidly growing business.

The yardstick approach measures what a plaintiff would have done or accomplished without interference from the defendant. A yardstick may be the growth in sales by the industry as compared to the plaintiff's actual sales growth.

The hypothetical sales method is based upon a market model or sales projection created to compute lost profits. Often a computerized financial model is based upon a number of assumptions about revenues and expenses. An expert witness testifying about this method would require a strong background in computer modeling and statistics.[74]

---

[74] W.G. Bremser, *Forensic Accounting and Financial Fraud* (Watertown, Mass.: American Management Assoc., 1995), 65–66. *See also* R.C. Dunn and E.P. Harry, "Modeling and Discounting Future Damages," *Journal of Accountancy* (January 2000): 49–55.

Damages also may be calculated by lost asset value, lost personal earnings, and lost royalties or licensing fees.

¶ 1214 AICPA's Consulting Guidelines

Litigation services are considered to be a management consulting specialty,[75] and are defined as any professional assistance nonlawyers provide to attorneys in the litigation process.[76] A CPA offering such services should follow the AICPA Code of Professional Conduct, especially Article IV, which states that he or she should be impartial, intellectually honest and free of any conflicts of interest." See Chapter 2 for more about AICPA's Code.

The consultant should follow Rule 201 of the AICPA *Professional Standards*[77] Code as well as these additional general standards for consulting services:

Client Interest—Serve the client's interest by seeking to accomplish the objectives established by the understanding with the client while maintaining integrity and objectivity.

Understanding with Client—Establish with the client a written or oral understanding about the responsibilities of the parties and the nature, scope, and limitations of services to be performed, and modify the understanding if circumstances require a significant change during the engagement.

Communication with Client—Inform the client of (a) conflicts of interest that may occur pursuant to interpretations of Rule 102 of the Code of Professional Conduct, (b) significant reservations concerning the scope or benefits of the engagement, and (c) significant engagement findings or events.

Professional judgment should be used in applying Statements on Standards for Consulting Services in a specific instance, since any oral or written understanding with the client may establish constraints within which services are to be provided. For example, the understanding with the client may limit the practitioner's effort with regard to gathering relevant data. The CPA is not required to decline or withdraw from a consulting engagement when the agreed-upon scope of services includes such limitations.

CPAs and other experts may be hired strictly to advise about the facts and issues of the dispute and will not be called to testify about their work or opinions. This status generally provides a work product privilege, which

---

[75] Statement on Standards for Consulting Services No. 1, *Consulting Services: Definitions and Standards* (AICPA), Professional Standards, vol. 2, c. s. sec. 100).

[76] Consulting Services Practice Aid No. 93-4: *Providing Litigation Services* (New York: AICPA, 1993).

[77] Rule 201, *General Standards* (AICPA, *Professional Standards*, vol. 2, ET sec. 201.01).

protects all work performed for the attorney; that is, the efforts, opinions, advice, work product, and involvement of the CPA will not be disclosed to the opposing side. If the accountant is retained as an expert witness, there is no attorney–client privilege.

¶ 1215 Risk Management

An emerging trend is increasing the liability of the expert witness. The general courtroom rule is to extend immunity to a witness from civil liability from testimony and communication made in the course of litigation. However, there is no immunity for communications outside the context of the lawsuit.

In California there is no litigation privilege for a friendly expert witness. At the trial court level, Mattco Forge was awarded $42 million from Arthur Young & Company.[78] On appeal the higher court reversed the award damages and remanded the case for a new trial, stating that "like other defendants in negligence lawsuits, litigations support professionals are only responsible for the losses they cause."[79] However, the appeals court would not extend the litigation privilege to protect the expert witness.

There are exceptions to the immunity for expert witnesses where there are:

- Spoilation of evidence (losing or destroying evidence)
- Lying under oath
- Defamation lawsuits against opponent's witness
- Negligence (disappointed clients)

In a divorce case an expert witness (a court appointed accountant) was held liable for negligence. The husband brought suit against the accountant for negligence in the valuation of his business. The court rejected the accountant's argument that he was entitled to immunity.[80] Obviously, if an expert were to present false evidence, he or she could be subject to criminal procedures. A law firm was disqualified when the firm hired an expert shortly after opposing counsel had interviewed the expert.[81]

.01 Alternative Dispute Resolution (ADR)

Alternative dispute resolution (ADR) has gained increasing importance in recent years as a means to control cost and save time, when properly administered. Other advantages of using ADR include privacy, flexibility, and sometimes (but not always) minimum disruption of existing relationships between the parties. The latter advantage is one that is frequently overlooked. ADR comes in many forms. Only the most common

---

[78] *Mattco Forge v. Arthur Young & Co.*, 6 Cal. Rptr. 2d 781 (Cal. Ct. App. 1992).
[79] *Mattco Forge v. Arthur Young & Co.*, 6 Cal. Rptr. 2d 789 (Cal. Ct. App. 1997).
[80] *Levine v. Wiss & Co.*, 478 A2d 398 (N.J. 1984).
[81] *Shadow Traffic Network v. Superior Court*, 24 Cal. App. 4th 1067 (1994).

are mentioned here. A forensic accounting expert is advised to look into the practical opportunities of ADR.

Arbitration. The arbitration process is probably the oldest formal type of ADR and one with which most people are familiar. The process is an adversarial one, with both sides presenting their case and a neutral party or panel rendering a decision. An important aspect that usually distinguishes arbitration from judicial proceedings is the lack of any available judicial review. Usually, an arbitration decision cannot be set aside or revised by a court, even if it is unreasonable and not supported by the evidence. The limited exceptions are fraud and lack of jurisdiction. A party who is considering agreeing to arbitration of a claim should assume there will be no realistic opportunity for judicial review or redetermination of the claim.

Negotiation. Although it is often not recognized as such, negotiation is a form of ADR. It can resolve disputes and is an alternative to going to court. However, experience shows that parties often have a hard time coming to a result without the assistance of a "neutral." As a result, the concept of mediation has gained recent popularity.

Mediation. In certain respects, the process of mediation is a new psychological level of dispute resolution. The arbitration process is really just an extension of the trial, which itself is a procedural contest in which the party who is left standing at the end wins. The civil trial replaced its predecessors, trial by battle and trial by ordeal, with trial by due process procedures. That development was an improvement but required determination of the dispute by a third party: a court. Arbitration is not much different, except that it is perceived as less expensive or more convenient and may involve a more informed fact finder. Even those assumptions have been called into question in certain types of cases. With mediation, in contrast, the parties come to their own agreed-upon resolution with the aid of a skillful third party. However, a commitment by the parties to engage in and complete the process is an essential ingredient to mediation, because the process is voluntary. This commitment can arise out of a variety of practical needs, including the insight that it is the most practical and efficient means to resolve the matter.

The courts have recently developed a number of alternative devices to promote settlements. These include minitrials and summary jury trials. A number of private companies have been developed in which ADR services are provided, including a private trial by a "rent-a-judge." The "judges" are often former actual judges, many of whom have retired but want to continue working on a limited basis in their area of expertise. The parties may be able to elect mediation as a first option, with a shift to arbitration if mediation fails. In this manner, the uncertainty associated with a decision by someone else—the court or arbitrator—can serve as an incentive for the parties to reach a mutually agreed-upon result.

¶ 1215.01

¶ 1216 Forensic Accounting and Fraud Deterrence Certifications

Several organizations and associations are currently promoting forensic accounting practices and education, and sponsoring forensic accounting and fraud examination certifications. Recently, the American College of Forensic Examiners (ACFEi) has introduced a new designation of Certified Forensic Accountant (Cr.FA). The Cr.FA designation is recognized as a valuable credential for those who practice forensic accounting. Cr.FA candidates are expected to pass two comprehensive exams, meet the rigid qualifications and high standards of achievement, and be in compliance with the applicable laws and regulations governing their profession (e.g., State Boards of Accountancy requirements, federal regulations). To be eligible to take the Cr.FA exams, candidates should have a bachelor's degree in business or 10 years of accounting-related experience.

Candidates may take two exams. Examination 1 tests candidates' knowledge in financial and cost accounting, auditing, taxation, and governmental accounting. Examination 2 covers major areas of forensic accounting, including litigation consulting, expert witnessing, fraud investigation, loss and damage assessment, and valuation services. Exam 2 consists of five parts: introduction, the engagement, fraud investigations and fraudulent financial reporting, additional services of the forensic accountant, and valuation issues. Candidates are required to (1) submit photocopies of degrees, diplomas, certificates, and/or licenses; (2) provide three professional references; (3) have no record of disciplinary action during the past 10 years, and not currently be under investigation; (4) have no felony convictions within the past 10 years; and (5) agree to uphold the ACFEi principles of professional practice. Candidates with an accounting-related certificate (e.g., CPA, CMA, CIA, CVA) must pass exam 2 to obtain the certification (ACFEi, 2002).

The Certified Fraud Examiner (CFE) designation is another credential for fraud examiners to possess. The CFE is administered by the Association of Certified Fraud Examiners (ACFE; formerly the National Association of Certified Fraud Examiners). The association was established in 1988 (at least in part) to respond to the Treadway Commission Report, which made recommendations to reduce the incidence of fraud. The primary mission of the ACFE is to reduce the incidence of fraud and white-collar crime through prevention, detection, and education. To achieve this goal, the ACFE (1) provides bona fide qualification for CFEs through a uniform examination; (2) sets high standards of admission through demonstrated competence and continuing professional education; and (3) requires adherence to a strict code of ethics. Members consist of accountants, auditors, law enforcement personnel, investigators, students, academicians, attorneys, executives, managers, and loss prevention specialists. To be eligible to take the computerized Uniform CFE examination, the candidate should meet a set of educational and experience requirements based on a point system. A minimum score of 40 points is required to take the examination and 50 points to obtain certification by examination. A bachelor's degree counts for 60 points and two years of related experience for 10 points. Different combinations of points for education and experience can be determined in meeting the minimum requirements. The computerized Uniform CFE examination is currently offered in the United States and Canada, and residents of these countries must pass the examination to obtain CFE certification. Candidates in other countries can either sit for the U.S. or Canadian version of the examination or apply for an international waiver of examination. The CFE examination consists of 500 objective and true/false questions in four categories: (1) fraudulent financial transactions; (2) legal elements of fraud; (3) fraud investigation; and (4) criminology and ethics. Each section of the exam consists of 125 questions in a Windows format, on two computer disks, with a maximum completion time of 2.5 hours for each section, and it can be taken any time during the year. The applicant is allowed three attempts to pass all four parts of the exam before losing credit for previously completed sections. A score of 75 percent is required on each part to pass the exam.

The Forensic Accountants Society of North America (FASNA) is a member-driven and self-governed network of certified public accounting firms committed to the ongoing development of their members' knowledge, acquisition, and application in forensic accounting (FASNA, 2002). The FASNA serves as an active resource center designed to provide training, support, and business development to its member firms. Each new member firm is required to successfully complete two days of technical training in forensic accounting. Member firms also meet twice each year to discuss emerging developments and issues in forensic accounting.

The National Association of Certified Valuation Analysts (NACVA) has sponsored the Certified Forensic Financial Analyst (CFFA) since 2000. To obtain the CFFA designation, candidates should (1) have a college degree; (2) have work experiences in both business valuations (BV) and forensic accounting; (3) pass a 10-hour proctored exam; (4) successfully complete a 8-16 hour case study; (5) report 36 hours of continuing professional education every three years; and (6) adhere to BV standards (NACVA, 2002).

NACVA also has a newer Certified Fraud Deterrence (CFD) certificate that allows a practitioner to take a proactive role in fraud deterrence. An individual takes a five-day course, must pass an eight-hour written examination, and pass a 30-40 hour take-home case. A CFD can analyze a client or company system to expose weak points that would allow fraud to be committed against the company—internally or externally. Once the vulnerabilities have been identified, the practitioner will be able to recommend a cost-effective system of controls for the company.

¶ 1216

¶ 1217 Future Trends in Forensic Accounting

The knowledge, skills, and abilities of a forensic accounting sleuth will become more refined, and a well-developed body of knowledge will be created. Improvement in training and education will greatly enhance and standardize competences. With improved professionalism, demand for the forensic accountant will increase as corporations, audit committees, internal auditors, and management come to appreciate the special talents and objective approach such accountants can take. In some situations the forensic accountants will be brought in to investigate the minute any irregularities surface. In other situations, the independent auditors may measure risk factors and create policy that brings the sleuths in when certain scores are attained. In still other situations, the internal audit function may call for bringing in the forensic accountant at random times as a matter of routine. Although forensic accounting services have been used for many years, the specialty itself is in its infancy and will continue to evolve for many years to come. However, past events present clear evidence that external independent auditing, internal auditing, audit committee work, and management review will not eliminate financial reporting fraud. The cost of such fraud being what it is, such a state of affairs suggests a bright future for the forensic specialists regardless of who actually initiates the assignment.

A forensic accountant may or may not be a permanent member of an audit engagement. An in-house forensic accountant may be brought into an external audit for purposes of complying with SAS No. 99. A report by the AICPA Fraud Task Force[82] states that if the forensic indicia of fraud are clearly present, the audit may change to a forensic or fraud investigation. Thus, investigative techniques may be performed by the forensic accountant that are outside the scope of a traditional audit. Because litigation may be possible, such an investigator is required to follow both the Statement of Standards for Consulting Services[83] and Code of Professional Conduct.

If, instead, a forensic accountant is brought into an audit engagement to perform a separate investigation (and not as an adjunct to an audit), such an engagement is consulting, and consulting standards must be followed. Because litigation may occur in the future, the forensic investigator may eventually be an expert or lay witness.[84]

¶ 1218 Summary

Forensic accounting is the action of identifying, recording, setting, extracting, sorting, reporting, and verifying past financial data or other accounting activities for setting current or prospective legal disputes or using such past financial data for projecting future financial data to settle

---

[82] R.L Durkin et. al., "Incorporating Forensic Procedures in an Audit Environment" *Litigation and Dispute Resolution Services Committee* (New York: AICPA, 2003).

[83] AICPA Technical Consulting Special Report 03-01.

[84] AICPA Technical Consulting Special Report 03-01.

legal disputes. Although forensic accounting services have been used for many years, the specialty itself is in its infancy and will continue to evolve for many years to come. Forensic accounting practices are classified into three areas: litigation support consulting, fraud deterrence and detection, and expert witnessing.

Auditing procedures for a fraud auditor may be quite different than procedures used by an external auditor. Forensic accountants must use additional investigation techniques. According to Wayne G. Bremser, the modern role of forensic accountants involves pretrial support, trial support, expert witnessing, and settlement support. A forensic accountant may or may not be a permanent member of an audit engagement. An in-house forensic accountant may be brought into an external audit for purposes of complying with SAS No. 99, or a forensic accountant may be brought into an audit engagement to perform a separate investigation (and not as an adjunct to an audit). Because litigation may be possible, such an investigator is required to follow both the Statement of Standards for Consulting Services and the Code of Professional Conduct. The forensic investigator may eventually be an expert or lay witness.

Computer forensics has been the trend in forensic auditing during the last couple of years. In both criminal and civil court cases, electronic evidence is often collected. Computer forensics can be defined as the procedures applied to computers and peripherals for gathering evidence that may be used in civil and criminal courts of law.

¶ 1218

Chapter 13
IRS Auditing—Indirect Methods of Reconstructing Income

¶ 1301   Introduction
¶ 1302   Forensic Audit Approaches Used by IRS Agents
¶ 1303   Minimum Income Probes
¶ 1304   Lifestyle Probes
¶ 1305   IRS's Financial Status Audits
¶ 1306   Indirect Methods
¶ 1307   Tracing Assets
¶ 1308   Current State of Tax Compliance
¶ 1309   Summary

¶ 1301 Introduction

IRS auditing is considered one of the earliest and most effective methods of forensic accounting used to discover tax evasion. IRS auditors often use minimum income probes and lifestyle probes to identify red flags and clues to the possibility of unreported incomes or tax fraud. This chapter presents the four major indirect methods of restructuring income and thus to discover unreported taxable income. These methods are: Cash T, source and application of funds, net worth, and bank deposits. IRS auditors typically use these methods for auditing self-employed individuals.

Chapter 13 objectives:

- To become familiar with early techniques used by IRS agents and forensic audit approaches used by IRS agents (see ¶ 1301–1302).

- To understand how IRS agents employ minimum income probes and lifestyle probes (see ¶ 1303–1304).

- To recognize how the IRS's financial status audits are used to identify possible perpetrators (see ¶ 1305).

- To be aware of indirect methods used by the IRS (see ¶ 1306).

- To identify how to trace assets (see ¶ 1307).

- To understand the current state of tax compliance and fraud (see ¶ 1308).

.01 Overview of IRS Auditing

IRS agents were some of the earliest and most successful forensic accountants in the United States. Whereas other law enforcement agencies tried to pin a crime on 1930s gangster Al Capone and failed, a Criminal Investigation (CI) agent, an IRS forensic accountant penetrated the organized racketeering gangs resulting in the tax evasion conviction of Capone and other reigning gangsters. Al Capone failed to report large profits from gambling, bootlegging, and racketeering. Capone's defense that all the money came from illegal activities did not pass muster. Illegal income is taxable and must be reported.[1] According to former IRS Assistant Commissioner for Criminal Investigation Donald K. Vogel, "the Capone investigation was certainly not one of our biggest tax evasion investigations; however, it is a perfect example of what we do. When more conventional investigative techniques fail, we follow the money trail—the proceeds of crime eventually lead to the criminal."[2] Capone was convicted and sentenced to an 11-year prison term based on evidence from financial ledgers and bank statements.[3]

IRS agents use forensic techniques to catch taxpayers not paying their proper taxes. This chapter may be used by agents to develop their auditing techniques. In 2002, the IRS received $1.8 trillion in tax revenues, and annual non-compliance (the so-called tax gap or underground economy) is estimated by the IRS to be approximately 15 percent of revenue or $250 to $300 billion.[4]

Forensic accountants working in the private sector also can learn much from their public sector counterparts in the IRS. Some techniques used by IRS agents may be useful in the private sector. This chapter looks at some of the methods and means employed by the IRS to fight crime. For more than 80 years the IRS Criminal Investigation Division has been solving financial crimes and the stakes are huge. Relatively recent IRS estimates of the gross tax gap—the amount of tax imposed by law that is not paid voluntarily and timely—is roughly $275 billion for all 1998 income and employment taxes.[5]

Although private sector forensic accountants lack some of the access to tax return information and the authority to summons third-party records

---

[1] IRS Digital Daily, Criminal Investigation (CI) Special Agents are a Part of a "Bigger" Law Enforcement Team, http://www.irs.gov/irs/article/0,,id=107041,00.html.

[2] Statement of IRS Assistant Commissioner for Criminal Investigation Donald K. Vogel Before the House Subcommittee on Treasury, Postal Service and General Government, March 12, 1996.

[3] Thomas A. Buckhoff, "Forensic Accountants: Fraud Busters," *New Accountant*, High School ed. (2002): 9-10.

[4] IRS Oversight Board Testimony, April 2003.

[5] There is a wide range of estimates on the tax gap found in tax literature. This gap is no doubt a difficult number to estimate. The $275 billion figure comes from an IRS paper, The Impact of the IRS on Voluntary Tax Compliance, Alan H. Plumley, presented at the National Tax Association Conference, November 12-14, 2002.

¶ 1301.01

available to IRS agents, many of the techniques used by the IRS may be used by forensic accountants to indirectly calculate net income, expenditures, and net worth.

To prove unreported income and fraud, IRS agents use both direct and indirect methods. The direct methods (or transaction methods) involve probing missing income by pointing to specific items of income that do not appear on the tax return. A taxpayer may have omitted sales, a large real estate transaction, or stock sale from his or her tax return. In direct methods, the agents use conventional auditing techniques such as looking for canceled checks of customers, deed records of real estate transactions, public records, and other direct evidence of unreported income.[6]

When conventional direct methods prove unproductive and the IRS has a reasonable indication that there is a likelihood of unreported income, indirect methods may be employed. Indirect methods use economic reality and financial status techniques in which the taxpayer's finances are reconstructed through circumstantial evidence.

This chapter identifies the major indirect methods of proof used by the IRS, discusses the significance and application of these methods from the viewpoint of an IRS agent, and describes which method is appropriate for each type of business. Understanding the IRS practices helps a forensic accountant gain an understanding of the special tools and concepts involved in the indirect methods.

¶ 1302 Forensic Audit Approaches Used by IRS Agents

The IRS's use of indirect methods exemplifies the pros and cons of techniques that can prove fraud as well as invade taxpayers' privacy. In the plus column, indirect methods have been used in the successful prosecution of a significant number of criminal tax fraud cases. In the negative column are listed overzealous intrusions of privacy by agents, prompting congressional limits to be imposed.

In 1995, concerned about estimates of the amount of income escaping taxation, the IRS introduced Economic Reality (Lifestyle) Audits. These audits did not introduce any new techniques. The techniques were the same indirect techniques that had been successfully used for many years. What changed was the emphasis on the use of the techniques. The techniques were used regardless of whether they were necessary or lawful. In 1998, reacting to the overemphasis of these techniques, Congress enacted Code Sec. 7602(e) which limits the use of indirect methods by IRS agents.

---

[6] For a detailed discussion of IRS practices, see Robert E. Meldman and Richard J. Sideman, *Federal Taxation: Practice and Procedure*, 6th ed. (Chicago: CCH INCORPORATED, 2001).

¶ 1303 Minimum Income Probes

The IRS's authority to use an indirect method is contained in Code Sec. 446(b). The Code Section provides that "if no method of accounting has been regularly used by the taxpayer, or if the method of accounting does not clearly reflect income, the computation of taxable income shall be made under such method as, in the opinion of the Secretary, does clearly reflect income."[7]

The use of indirect methods to reconstruct income by the IRS is limited by Code Sec. 7602(e), which prohibits financial status or economic reality techniques to determine the existence of unreported income unless the agent has a reasonable indication that there is a likelihood of such unreported income.

The Internal Revenue Manual (IRM)[8] sets forth minimum income probes. For nonbusiness returns (having no Schedule C or F), an agent is to question the taxpayer or the representative about possible sources of income other than reported on the return. If there is no other information in the file indicating potential unreported income, such as a currency transaction report or an unreported Form 1099 report, the minimum income probe is met. However, for taxpayers who are self-employed and file a Schedule C or F, an analysis is made from tax return information to determine if reported income is sufficient to support the taxpayer's financial activities.

¶ 1304 Lifestyle Probes

Just like an IRS agent, a forensic accountant should be aware of the lifestyles of employees of companies as well. The lifestyle of a taxpayer or employee may give clues as to the possibilities of unreported income. Jack Bologna and Robert Lindquist[9] refer to this approach of looking at events, transactions, and environments in their covert aspects. They believe that fraud auditing is like an iceberg with many of the behavioral, covert aspects of the fraud below the water line, including:

- Attitudes
- Feelings (fear, anger, etc.)
- Values
- Norms
- Interactions
- Supportiveness
- Satisfaction

---

[7] Code Sec. 446(b).

[8] See IRM 4.10.4.

[9] G.J. Bologna and R.J. Lindquist, *Fraud Auditing and Forensic Accounting*, 2d ed. (New York: John Wiley, 1995), 36-37.

Of course, many of the structural, overt aspects are important, but the behavioral aspects below the surface can be extremely important. For example, a great deal of information about fraud can be found by listening, especially around the copy machine or break room (or wherever the employees congregate on breaks). Stakeouts and sifting through garbage may be off-beat ways to gather evidence. Interviewing peers, workers, and neighbors may be helpful. Further, in addition to examining financial documentation, a forensic accountant must focus on the individuals involved by interviewing witnesses and suspects.

Niamh Brennan and John Hennessy state that forensic accounting demands an awareness of motive. "Often a pattern of evidence only becomes apparent and understandable when the forensic accountant considers possible motive."[10] Robert J. Lindquist states: "You've got to have knowledge of fraud, what it looks like, how it works, how and why people steal. You're the bloodhound much more than the watchdog."[11] Sandi Smith says that often a suspect's lifestyle will give him or her away. "Forensic accountants can study computerized banking records, tax records, and the employee's human relations department records to create an individual profile."[12]

Certainly, obvious lifestyle changes may indicate fraud and unreported income:

- Lavish residence
- Expensive cars and boats
- Vacation home
- Private schools for children
- Exotic vacations

However, the investigator must keep in mind that a high living style may be obtained by going into debt or through "family money" such as gifts and inheritances.

¶ 1305 IRS's Financial Status Audits

In 1995 the IRS began a program known as Economic Reality Audits, which were also known as Lifestyle Audits. The emphasis of this program was to attempt to uncover unreported income by comparing the taxpayer's reported income with the taxpayer's lifestyle. These audits resulted in third-party contacts and searches of public records even when there was no indication of any wrongdoing. In 1998 Congress added Code Sec. 7602(e) to

---

[10] N. Brennan and J. Hennessy, *Forensic Accounting* (Dublin: Round Hall Sweet & Maxwell, 2002), 122-123.
[11] Terry Carter, "Accounting Gumshoes," *ABA Journal* (September 1997): 36.
[12] Sandi Smith, "Meet the Forensic Accountant: Sherlock Holmes of the Information Age," *IntuitAdvisor* (2002), www.intuitadvirsor.com.

limit these techniques to situations where there was a *reasonable* indication of unreported income.

In a memorandum dated August 6, 1998, the Assistant Commissioner (Examination) cautioned that due to privacy issues and the intrusiveness of inspecting a person's residence, such inspections should be limited to resolving specific issues such as the validity of deductions for an office or business located in the residence.

The IRS, in Chief Counsel Advice 200101030, concluded that a revenue agent may drive by a taxpayer's home and conduct a LEXIS search to determine whether a person purchased real estate during the year without violating the statutory prohibition against financial status audits.[13] Both of these activities are available to determine whether there is a reasonable likelihood of unreported income, which then allows the agent to use an indirect method.

The theory in the use of lifestyle audits is valid for both IRS agents and private sector forensic accountants. If someone is spending beyond his or her apparent means, there should be a concern. Making these concerns known to neighbors, business associates, financial institutions, and customers through third-party contacts based upon superficial information is prohibited for IRS agents and quite likely will result in legal action against forensic accountants.

If a forensic accountant suspects fraud or unreported income, a form of financial status audit may be appropriate that will enable the investigator to check the lifestyles of the possible perpetrators.

Consider one of the largest embezzlements in U.S. history. Between 1991 and 1997, Yasuyoshi Kato, the CFO at Day-Lee Foods, Inc., obtained off-book loans from U.S. affiliates of Japanese banks and issued checks to himself and his wife for about $62 million. The fraud was caught by the IRS, possibly as a result of an anonymous tip. Kato's opulent lifestyle gave him away: He owned two $10,000 macaws and a zoo-sized aquarium containing sharks and other exotic fish.

Kato forged daily accounting entries. He started stealing when he agreed to pay his wife and two daughters $50,000 a month for support in a divorce settlement although he earned only $150,000 a year in salary. He was sentenced to 63 months imprisonment and ordered to repay the embezzled funds at a rate of $500 per year.[14] The lesson for the agent or auditor here is that the lifestyle of an employee can be important in discovering fraud or finding unreported income.

---

[13] Chief Counsel Advice 200101030 (October 25, 2000), Financial Status Audits.

[14] "Steal a Million, Pay a Pittance," *Earth Island Journal* 13 (1) (Winter 1997-1998).

¶ 1305

¶ 1306 Indirect Methods

An indirect method should be used when the taxpayer has inadequate books and records, the books do not clearly reflect taxable income, or there is a reason to believe that the taxpayer has omitted taxable income. An indirect method also is appropriate when there is a significant increase in year-to-year net worth, when gross profit percentages change significantly for that particular business, or when the taxpayer's expenses (both business and personal) exceed reported income, and there is no obvious cause for the difference.

The four major indirect methods to spot unreported income are: cash T, source and application of funds, net worth, and bank deposits. Other methods used in specific industries are contained in the IRS's Market Segment Specialization Program (MSSP) Audit Technique Guides, which are available on the IRS website, *www.irs.gov*. A sample from the guides appears in Figure 13.1. Among these additional methods are Percentage of Markup, and Unit and Volume, which are used for businesses dealing primarily in cash and having a limited number of products and suppliers, such as, bars, restaurants, and gas stations.

.01 Market Segment Specialization Program

The Market Segment Specialization Program focuses on developing highly trained examiners for a particular market segment. A market segment may be an industry such as construction or entertainment, a profession like attorneys or real estate agents, or an issue like passive activity losses. An integral part of the approach used is the development and publication of Audit Technique Guides. These guides contain examination techniques, common and unique industry issues, business practices, industry terminology, and other information to assist examiners in performing examinations.

Audit Technique Guides are available on the IRS website in Adobe PDF format, and must be viewed with the *Acrobat Reader*. Several guides are now also available to view online in HTML.

Figure 13.1

Sample from MSSP Descriptions on IRS Website

A B C D E F G H I J K L M N O P Q R S T U V W X Y Z

Alaskan Commercial Fishing: Part 1—Catcher Vessels (7/95 229K)

    Specifically structured around the Alaskan industry but may be used as an outline for commercial fishing industry in other regions.

Alaskan Commercial Fishing: Part II—Processors & Brokers (7/95 280K)

    Concentrates on issues to be considered during audit of fish processing plants; larger, vertically integrated organizations; and fish brokers. Specifically capital assets and transactions and foreign related party transactions.

Alternative Minimum Tax For Individuals (12/99 304K)

    (View On-Line)

    Discusses brief history of Alternative Minimum Tax (AMT). Provides line-by-line instructions for computing AMT on Form 6251. Includes prior law (prior to 1993) and current law (1993 to 1998).

Investigators are cautioned that the extent to which an indirect method is used is to be determined on a case-by-case basis. There is no one indirect method applicable to each case.[15]

.02 Cash T

For a taxpayer who files a Schedule C or F, an agent may prepare a cash transaction account (cash T) to determine the understatement of income. A *cash T* is an analysis of all of the cash received by the taxpayer and all of the cash spent by the taxpayer over a period of time. The theory of the cash T is that if a taxpayer's expenditures during a given year exceed reported income, and the source of the funds for such expenditures is unexplained (e.g., taxpayer had no loans or nontaxable sources of income), such excess amount represents unreported income.

If the taxpayer spent more than he or she received, there is taxable income, unless the taxpayer can prove otherwise. The cash T in a simpler form is usually used in the preliminary stages of the audit. When an IRS agent is assigned a business tax return, the agent generally prepares a preliminary cash T using the information shown on the return. On the left (debit) side of the cash T, the agent would list all sources of income, and on the right (credit) side of the cash T the agent would list all applications of funds. In addition to the amount gathered from the tax return, an agent also would estimate personal living expenses using guidelines based on income and family size. If there is a preliminary understatement of income, this understatement would indicate to the agent to begin probing for

---

[15] IRM 4.10.4.6.2.

¶ 1306.02

evidence of the source of the preliminary understatement. An example of a preliminary cash T is shown in Table 13.1.

Table 13.1

Preliminary Cash-T[16]

Cash In		Cash Out	
Wages	XX	State/Fed. Withholding	XX
Interest Income		FICA Withholding	XX
Taxable	XX	Other Withholdings on Form W-2	XX
Non taxable	XX	Estimated Tax Payments	XX
Dividends	XX	Tax payments for Prior Years	XX
Tax Refunds/per Return	XX	—IDRS	
Tax Refunds/on IDRS	XX	Investment Interest	XX
Alimony Received	XX	Schedule C Purchases	XX
Schedule C Receipts	XX	Schedule C Expenses (Net of	XX
Schedule D Gross Sales	XX	Depreciation)	
Sale of Business Property–Form 4797	XX	Rental Expenses (Net of Depreciation)	XX
IRA/Pension/Annuity Distributions	XX	Schedule F Expenses (Net of Depreciation)	XX
Rental Income	XX	Assets/Invest. Purchases Form	XX
Schedule F Receipts	XX	Schedule D	
Unemployment Compensation	XX	Form 2119 Sale of Residence	XX
Social Security Benefits	XX	Form 4562 Depreciation	XX
Other Income	XX	Motor Vehicle Records (If	XX
Unreported IRP Amts.	XX	Available)	
Cash Distributions (If Available)		IRA/Pension/Annuity	XX
From S-Corps	XX	Contributions*	
From Partnerships	XX	Penalty—Early Savings	XX
From Fiduciaries	XX	Withdrawal	
Sale of Personal Residence (2119)	XX	Personal Living Expenses (PLE)**	XX
Advanced EITC	XX	Other "Cash Out" Items	XX
Other "Cash in" Items	XX		
Total	XXX	Total	XXX
Potential Understatement <Excess Funds Available>		XXXX	

---

* Contributions to retirement plans can be made after year end and still be deductible. This factor should be considered when inspecting prior and subsequent years.

** The entry for Personal Living Expenses (PLE) on the preliminary Cash-T is an estimate. Determine the personal living expenses (PLE) in the preliminary Cash-T by using information from the return and information in the case file. The resulting estimated PLE can be compared to Bureau of Labor Statistics to test for reasonableness.

---

[16] IRM 4.10.4.3.3.1.

¶ 1306.02

Form 4822. During the initial interview, an IRS agent is instructed to discuss potential understatements with the taxpayer or representative to attempt to reconcile the understatement. Two items not apparent in the preliminary cash T analysis that the agent needs to address at the initial meeting (if income understatement is indicated) are personal living expenses and the existence of a cash hoard. To arrive at living expenses, which is an application of funds, the agent, with the help of the taxpayer, completes IRS Form 4822, Statement of Annual Estimation of Personal and Family Expenses, shown in Figure 13.2.

¶ 1306.02

Figure 13.2

Form 4822 Used to Determine Living Expenses

Form **4822** (Rev. 6-83)	Department of the Treasury - Internal Revenue Service **STATEMENT OF ANNUAL ESTIMATED PERSONAL AND FAMILY EXPENSES**				
TAXPAYER'S NAME AND ADDRESS					TAX YEAR ENDED

		ITEM	BY CASH	BY CHECK	TOTAL	REMARKS
1. PERSONAL	EXPENSES	Groceries and outside meals				
		Clothing				
		Laundry and dry cleaning				
		Barber, beauty shop, and cosmetics				
		Education (tuition, room, board, books, etc.)				
		Recreation, entertainment, vacations				
		Dues (clubs, lodge, etc.)				
		Gifts and allowances				
		Life and accident insurance				
		Federal taxes (income, FICA, etc.)				
2. HOUSEHOLD	EXPENSES	Rent				
		Mortgage payments (including interest)				
		Utilities (electricity, gas, telephone, water, etc.)				
		Domestic help				
		Home insurance				
		Repairs and improvements				
		Child care				
3. AUTO	EXPENSES	Gasoline, oil, grease, wash				
		Tires, batteries, repairs, tags				
		Insurance				
		Auto payments (including interest)				
		Lease of auto				
4. DEDUCTIBLE ITEMS		Contributions				
	Medical Expenses	Insurance				
		Drugs				
		Doctors, hospitals, etc.				
	Taxes	Real estate (not included in 2. above)				
		Personal property				
		Income (State and local)				
		Interest (not included in 2. and 3. above)				
	Miscellaneous	Alimony				
		Union dues				
5. PERSONAL ASSETS, ETC		Stocks and bonds				
		Furniture, appliances, jewelry				
		Loans to others				
		Boat				
		TOTALS ▶				

Form 4822 (Rev. 6-83)

Searching for a Cash Hoard. An agent is instructed to question a taxpayer regarding beginning and ending cash-on-hand and to specifically inquire regarding the existence of a cash hoard. A *cash hoard* consists of money that is not in a bank account, or other readily verifiable location

¶ **1306.02**

that the taxpayer alleges should be in the beginning cash balance. The instructions to the agents regarding questioning for possible cash hoards can be found in the IRM.[17] The discussion here is summarized to illustrate how forensic accountants can uncover cash hoards using similar strategies to those of the agents.

Because cash on hand is an important aspect of all indirect methods, it is imperative that an investigator establish the amount and verify the taxpayer's statements of cash accumulations. Cash on hand information is a must in every indirect method. An adjustment for unreported income can be lost if this item is not determined at the beginning of the audit. If taxpayers are faced with an understatement, they will probably try to explain it away. The "cash in the mattress" defense cannot be used if the actual cash on hand has already been established.

In order to avoid any misunderstanding by the taxpayer, the meaning of cash on hand must be explained to him or her prior to answering any inquiry. Taxpayers must understand the term "cash on hand" in this context: any undeposited currency and coins they have for whatever purpose. Once this term is understood, the investigator should inquire about the existence of any cash on hand.

If a taxpayer attempts to avoid answering questions concerning cash, agents should try to pinpoint amounts by requesting an estimate such as "under a thousand dollars" and narrowing the range until the taxpayer agrees with a general amount.

A commitment should be sought concerning whether an individual had any large accumulations of cash during the period. Agents should pursue questions in this area until the taxpayer makes an affirmative statement regarding the existence or nonexistence of a cash hoard.

If taxpayers allege that they have what appears to be an inordinate amount of cash on hand (a cash hoard), the examiner should further inquire to establish:

- The amount of cash on hand at the end of each year under examination to the present (at the time of the interview).
- How it was accumulated
- Where it was kept and in what denominations
- Who had knowledge of it
- Who counted it
- When and where any of it was spent

---

[17] IRM 4.10.4.6.8.3.

¶ 1306.02

Information regarding cash hoards is necessary to establish the consistency and reliability of the taxpayer's statement. Usually no direct corroborating evidence is available, but statements made about the source and use of the funds can be verified. A forensic accountant may look for the following discrepancies, for example:

- The taxpayer may not have had sufficient taxable or nontaxable income in prior years to accumulate cash.

- Claims of a prior substantial cash hoard also might be rebutted by showing that the taxpayer lived frugally, borrowed money, made installment purchases, incurred large debts, was delinquent on accounts, had a poor credit rating, or filed for bankruptcy.

- Financial statements filed by the taxpayer at banks and other places can be reviewed to see whether the taxpayer disclosed the cash hoard on these statements.

A taxpayer's explanation for a cash hoard may change during an examination. The investigator should document the information *as it is received*. The documentation should include when and where the information was received, who was present, what was said, and when the documentation was prepared.

Preparing the Final Cash T. The sample in Table 13.2 is the format of an in-depth cash T, prepared with tax return information and information available in the case file prior to taxpayer/representative contact and then updated based upon information obtained during the examination process. The final cash T includes both internal and external sources of information.

Table 13.2

Final Cash T[18]

Cash In		Cash Out	
Wages		State/Fed Withholding	XX
Interest Income		FICA Withholding	XX
Taxable	XX	Other Withholdings	
Nontaxable	XX	on Form W-2	XX
Dividends	XX	Estimated Tax Payments	XX
Tax Refunds/Return	XX	Tax Payments for Prior	
Tax Refunds/IDRS	XX	Years—IDRS	XX
Alimony Received	XX	Investment Interest	XX
Sch C Receipts	XX	Sch C Purchases	XX
Sch D Gross Sales	XX	Sch C Expenses	XX
Sale of Business		(Net of Depreciation)	
Property—Form 4797	XX	Rental Expenses	XX

[18] IRM 4.10.4.5.3.7.

¶ 1306.02

IRA/Pension/Annuity		(Net of Depreciation)	
Distributions	XX	Sch F Expenses	XX
Rental Income	XX	(Net of Depreciation)	
Sch F Receipts	XX	Asset/Invest. Purchases	
Unemployment Comp.	XX	Form Schedule D	XX
Social Security		Purchase of	
Benefits	XX	Residence	XX
Other Income	XX	Form 4562	
Unreported IRP Amts.	XX	Depreciation	XX
Cash Distributions:		Motor Vehicle Records	
From S Corps.	XX	(If available)	XX
From Partnerships	XX	Contract Amounts	XX
From Fiduciaries	XX	Insurance Policies	XX
Sale of Personal		Cash on Hand—End of	
Residence (2119)	XX	Year*	XX
Advanced Earned		Ending Bank Balances**	XX
Income Credit	XX	IRA/Annuity/Pension	XX
Other "Cash In"		Contribution***	XX
Items	XX	Penalty—Early Savings	
Sale of Personal		Withdrawal	XX
Property	XX	Loan Repayments	XX
Cash on Hand—		Beginning Credit	
Beginning of Year*	XX	Card Balances	XX
Beginning Bank		Personal Capital	
Balance(s)**	XX	Acquisitions	XX
Ending Credit Card		Personal Living	
Balances	XX	Expenses (PLE)****	XX
Loan Proceeds	XX	Other "Cash Out"	
Child Support		Items	XX
Received	XX		
Nontaxable Amounts	XX		
(Inheritances, gifts, etc.)			
Accrual Bases T/Ps:		**Accrual Bases T/Ps:**	
Decrease-Accts/Rec	XX	Increase-Accts/Rec	XX
Increase-Accts/Pay	XX	Decrease-Accts/Pay	XX
Total	XX	Total	—
		Understatement	XXXX
		<Excess Funds Available>	

---

* Cash on hand represents the coins and currency that a taxpayer has on their person, in a safe deposit box or any other place outside the banking system.

** Cash in banks should be the reconciled balances at the beginning and end of the year; not the balances indicated on the bank statements.

*** Contributions to retirement plans can be made after year-end and still be deductible. This entry will be adjusted for the cash outlay(s) occurring in the year of examination.

**** The entry for Personal Living Expenses (PLE) on the final Cash-T is the actual expenses determined by the examination process.

¶ 1306.02

.03 Source and Application of Funds Method (Expenditure Approach)

The *source and application of funds method* (also referred to as the *expenditure method*) was approved for IRS use by the Supreme Court in 1942.[19] This technique is a variation of the net worth method (discussed later in this chapter) that shows increases and decreases in a taxpayer's accounts at the end of the year. Often the IRS agent uses the expenditure approach when a taxpayer is spending income lavishly rather than purchasing assets or investments. The expenditure approach is similar to the cash T, except that the data used is the increases and decreases in the taxpayer's accounts. As with the cash T, if the person's spending exceeds explainable total income, any difference may be unreported income (such as stolen funds or drug money). When dealing with taxpayers, the IRS often uses a cash expenditure approach because taxpayers can understand this approach. In the courtroom the IRS may use a net worth calculation to reconstruct income.[20]

The format of this method is to list the applications of funds first and then subtract the sources (see Figure 13.3). If the taxpayer's known cash sources exceed his or her known cash receipts (including cash on hand at the beginning of the year), any difference is unreported income. However, the IRS has the responsibility to perform reasonable net worth analysis, investigate all reasonable leads, and establish a likely source for the omitted income.

Figure 13.3

Source and Application of Funds Format[21]

Sample of Application of Funds Method Layout

1. Funds Applied:

Increase in cash on hand	$4,000
Increase in cash in banks	5,000
Increase in accounts receivable	21,400
Increase in loans receivable	13,000
Increase in inventory	19,000
Increase in stocks and bonds	12,500
Increase in furniture and fixtures	11,100
Increase in real estate	135,000
Increase in personal automobile	24,000
Decrease in accounts payable	11,500
Decrease in mortgage payable	23,000
Personal living expenses	29,700
Federal income tax paid	6,500
Nondeductible personal loss	3,500

---

[19] *W.R. Johnson*, SCt, 43-1 USTC ¶ 9470, 319 US 503, 63 SCt 1233.
[20] R.E. Meldman and R.J. Sideman, *Federal Taxation: Practice and Procedure*, 6th ed. (Chicago: CCH INCORPORATED, 2001), 764.
[21] IRM 4.10.4.6.4.7.

¶ 1306.03

Gifts made		10,000
Total Funds Applied		$329,200
2. Sources of Funds:		
Decrease in cash on hand		$3,100
Decrease in bank balance		2,000
Decrease in securities		13,500
Increase in accounts payable		11,800
Increase in notes payable		22,100
Increase in mortgage payable		121,500
Increase in accumulated depreciation		23,300
Tax exempt interest		1,700
Inheritance		42,000
Total Sources of Funds		$241,000
3. Understatement of Taxable Income:		
Total Application of Funds		$329,200
Total Sources of Funds		241,000
Adjusted gross income as corrected:		88,200
Less: Itemized deductions	31,600	
Personal exemptions (2)	5,000	(36,600)
Taxable income as corrected		51,600
Taxable income per return		23,700
Understatement of taxable income		$27,900

When the application of funds is greater than the source, a taxpayer is deemed to have an understatement of income. Both the cash T and the source and applications of funds methods are appropriate for taxpayers when a substantial amount of the income is not deposited in bank accounts and the expenditures on the tax return are not proportionate to the income reported.

.04 Net Worth Method

The net worth method is a common indirect balance sheet approach to estimating income. To use the net worth technique, an IRS agent must calculate the person's net worth (the known assets less known liabilities) at the beginning and ending of a period. The agent adds nondeductible living expenses to the increase in net worth. If there is a difference between the reported income and the increase in net worth during the year, the agent tries to account for the difference as (1) nontaxable income and (2) unidentified differences. Any unidentified difference may be an approximation of the amount of a theft, unreported income, or embezzlement amount (e.g., an inference of unreported income).

Revealing unreported income. This technique may be used when there is a year-to-year increase in net worth and the taxpayer does not have adequate records to determine taxable income or when fraud is strongly suspected. This indirect method was sanctioned by the Supreme Court in

¶ 1306.04

IRS Auditing—Indirect Methods of Reconstructing Income

1954 by *Holland v. U.S.*[22] The courts have established several safeguards to prevent the misuse of this method. An IRS agent must determine beginning net worth with reasonable accuracy, track down all leads given by the taxpayer to explain the source of the unreported income, and establish a reasonable source for the omitted income. If the person's net worth increase (as adjusted) exceeds the reported taxable income, there may be unreported income (or a previous cash hoard or large gift).

This technique may be appropriate for any taxpayer when two or more years of returns are being audited and the agent determines that there have been substantial changes in assets and liabilities from year to year.

Figure 13.4

Example of Net Worth Method

During 2003, John Connors sold his personal car for $2,500. He had purchased the car in 1999 for $6,000. In March 2003, he sold 500 shares of stock for $10,000. He had acquired the stock in December 1998 for $22,000. On January 11, 2003, he gave his nephew a truck that had been used solely in his business. The truck cost $9,000 in 2000. Depreciation totaling $6,500 had been previously deducted on the truck at the time of the gift. John paid the following personal expenses in 2003:

Food	$3,000
Real Estate Taxes on Home	2,500
Repairs to Home	300
Utilities	900
Personal Auto Expenses	1,800
Vacations	1,100
Department Store Purchases	1,700
Interest on Home Mortgage	2,000
Charitable Contributions	500
Life Insurance Premiums	1,500
Medical Bills	600
Entertainment	900
Other	300
Total	$17,100

For 2003, John reported adjusted gross income of $19,000. The balances in his bank accounts were $1,500 at the end of 2002 and $18,900 at the end of 2003. Assuming that John correctly reported his income for 2003, the net worth computation would appear as follows:

	12/31/00	12/31/03
Assets		
Cash in Banks	$1,500	$18,900
Personal Auto	6,000	-0-
Truck	9,000	-0-
Stock	22,000	-0-
Total Assets	$38,500	$18,900
Liabilities		
Reserve for Depreciation (Truck)	6,500	-0-
Net Worth	$32,000	$18,900

---

[22] *M.L. Holland*, SCt, 54-2 USTC ¶9714, 348 US 121, 75 SCt 127. *See also C.T. Conaway*, CA-5, 94-1 USTC ¶50,009, 11 F3d 40.

¶ 1306.04

Net Worth 12/31/03	$18,900
Net Worth 12/31/02	(32,000)
Net Worth Increase (Decrease)	($13,100)
Plus: Nondeductible Expenses and Losses	
Gift of Truck	2,500
Loss on Sale of Car	3,500
Loss on Stock in Excess of $3,000	9,000
Personal Living Expenses	17,100
Reconstructed Adjusted Gross Income	$19,000
Reported Adjusted Gross Income	$19,000
Understatement of Income	-0-[23]

Determining living expenses. The determination of nondeductible living expenses may not be easy. Kalman A. Barson made the following suggestions for determining expenses:

> For that you need to go into the checking and savings accounts of the individuals and, depending on the extent of the accuracy of the records involved, you may have to make certain assumptions. Interview the parties involved and reconstruct their standard of living, making some educated guesses as to what they spend on such mundane expenses as food, clothing, and various other elements of living that often leave little or no residual financial trail. Be as thorough as possible inasmuch as you are on less stable ground (even though the ultimate result may be a very supportable one) than if you had come up with proof in the form of actual cash deposits that were not reconcilable to reported income.[24]

The net worth analysis may be used when the forensic investigator is searching for hidden income in drug trafficking and insurance fraud situations. A person's lifestyle and spending habits may not match his or her reported income. Alternatively, in a divorce case a spouse may be showing a substantial *decrease* in income.

.05 Bank Deposit Method

Whereas the focus of the net worth method is on the year-end bank balances, as well as other assets and liabilities, the bank deposit method looks at the funds deposited during the year. This method attempts to reconstruct gross taxable receipts rather than adjusted. This bank deposit method was approved by the court almost 70 years ago in *L.M. Gleckman*.[25] An agent does not have to corroborate the unreported income by another method.[26]

The Fifth Circuit provided an excellent description of the bank deposit method in 1978 in the *Boulet* case:[27]

> In this case, the government used the bank deposit and cash expenditure methods. In order to use this method the government must establish a likely

---

[23] R.E. Meldman and R.J. Sideman, *Federal Taxation: Practice and Procedure*, 6th ed. (Chicago: CCH INCORPORATED, 2001), 781.
[24] K.A. Barson, *Investigative Accounting* (New York: Van Nostrand Reinhold Company, 1986), 98.
[25] CA-8, 35-2 USTC ¶ 9645, 80 F2d 394, cert. denied, 297 US 709, 56 SCt 501.
[26] *N. Stein*, CA-7, 71-1 USTC ¶ 9209, 437 F2d 775, cert. denied, 403 US 905, 91 SCt 2205.
[27] *R.M. Boulet*, CA-5, 78-2 USTC ¶ 9628, 577 F2d 1165, 1167, cert. denied, 439 US 1114, 99 SCt 1017.

¶ 1306.05

source of the income, that the taxpayer made deposits in a bank account and make a distinction between taxable and non-taxable income. The assumption is that the taxpayer's gross income is the total of the deposits minus loan proceeds, transfers and other non-taxable items. Nontaxable items include loans, gifts, transfers between accounts and cash the taxpayer had on hand at the beginning of the year. The doctor received fees in cash, which he gave his wife for groceries. This amount is added to the net bank deposits to arrive at gross receipts. The amount is compared with gross receipts on the tax return. If there is an excess amount, this will be unreported gross receipts.

The bank deposit method is appropriate when most of the income is deposited in banks and most of the expenses are paid by check. This technique may be used to audit income of physicians or dentists who normally receive payments from patients and insurance companies in the form of checks as mentioned in the Supreme Court decision above. A formula for computing gross income taken from the IRM is shown in Figure 13.5, and Figure 13.6 shows business gross receipts.[28]

Figure 13.5

Gross Receipts Formula

The formula for computing gross receipts is:

1.	Total bank deposits	$XXX
Less:		
2.	Nontaxable receipts deposited	(XXXX)
3.	Net deposits resulting from taxable receipts	$XXX
Add:		
4.	Business expenses paid by cash	$XXX
5.	Capital items paid by cash	XXX
6.	Personal expenses paid by cash	XXX
7.	Cash accumulated during the year from receipts	XXX
	Sub-Total	$XXX
8.	Less: Nontaxable cash used for (4) through (7)	(XXX)
	Gross receipts as corrected	$XXX

The following is a step-by-step explanation of the specific items used in the above computations of gross receipts.

Item 1—Total bank deposits means total deposits in all of the taxpayer's bank accounts. This amount includes the taxpayer's business and personal accounts, the spouse's accounts, and dependent children's accounts. (Note: This figure could vary if the spouse files a separate return.) The deposits should be reconciled, if possible, so that only the receipts during the current year are included. This is accomplished by totaling deposits as shown on the bank statements, and adding to this amount any current year's receipts, which were deposited in the subsequent year, and deducting any prior year's receipts, which were deposited in the current year.

EXAMPLE:

Deposits during 1995, per bank statements	$150,000
Add: 1995 Receipts deposited in 1996	13,000
Less: 1994 Receipts deposited in 1995	(11,500)
Reconciled Bank Deposits—	$151,500

---

[28] Internal Revenue Manual, Part 4, Chapter 10, Section 4 4.10.4.6.3.6 (5-14-1999).

Item 2—Nontaxable receipts deposited represent the duplicated and nontaxable items. Duplicated items include checks to cash where the proceeds are redeposited. An example is when the taxpayer writes a check payable to cash and obtains currency and/or coins from the bank in exchange for the check. This currency is then used to cash customers' checks which are deposited into the taxpayer's bank account; in effect, redepositing the funds withdrawn. This deposit must be eliminated in determining deposits from taxable receipts. Transfers between accounts are another example of nontaxable receipts. Transfers can occur between different checking accounts, different savings accounts, and between savings accounts and checking accounts (Note: All such transfers do not represent additional receipts since they are merely a shifting of funds from one account to another). Deposits from transfers must be eliminated in determining deposits from taxable receipts. Other common types of nontaxable receipts that are often deposited and must be eliminated in determining deposits from taxable receipts include loan proceeds, gifts, inheritances, Social Security benefits, nontaxable Veterans Administration benefits, etc.

EXAMPLE:

Reconciled Bank Deposits—1995		$151,000
Less: Nontaxable receipts deposited:		
Loan proceeds	$12,000	
Checks to cash redeposited	3,500	
Transfers between checking accounts	6,000	
Nontaxable Veterans Administration pension	14,000	($35,500)
Net deposits from taxable receipts		$116,000

Item 4—Business expenses paid by cash are computed in a negative manner by determining the business expenses paid by check and subtracting this amount from the total outlays reported on the return. Note: Total outlays on the return include only business expenses which require a cash outlay. Items such as depreciation, depletion and bad debts are not included in total outlays. This step is based on the assumption that outlays as disclosed on the return were actually made and could only have been paid for by either check or cash. The amount of business expenses paid by check can be negatively determined by subtracting the nonbusiness checks from the total checks written. This approach is used because an analysis of nonbusiness checks is necessary since the personal expenses and capital items paid for by check have to be known in order to determine the amounts of these items paid for by cash.

EXAMPLE:

Total outlays per return		
Computation of business checks for year:		
Balance @ 1-1-95	$10,000	
Add: Deposits	150,000	
Subtotal	$160,000	
Less: Balance @ 12-31-95	(8,000)	
Subtotal	$152,000	
Add: Checks written in 1995 but cleared in 1996	3,000	
Subtotal	$155,000	
Less: Checks written in 1994 but cleared in 1995	(6,000)	
Total checks written in 1995	$149,000	
Less: Nonbusiness checks:		
Checks to cash	$3,500	
Check transfers	6,000	
Personal expenses	34,500	
Capital items	15,700	($59,700)
Total business checks		$89,300
Total business expenses paid by cash		$50,700

Generally, the number of nonbusiness checks written is less than the number of business checks. Nonbusiness checks include checks for personal

¶ 1306.05

living expenses, capital purchases (personal and business), checks to cash redeposited, check transfers between accounts, and payments on liabilities. Checks for these items would be included even if the taxpayer deducted them on the return. Total checks written can be quickly computed by adding the total deposits to the beginning bank balance and subtracting the ending bank balance from that amount. The resulting figure must then be adjusted for checks written during the year, which have not cleared the bank and checks written in the prior year, which cleared during the current year. This is merely a reconciliation of the checks which insures that only the current year's checks are taken into account.

NOTE: The examiner should be satisfied that all checks have been presented. Should the taxpayer remove any portion of the nondeductible checks, the total, as computed, of deductible disbursements would be overstated. The result would invariably be distorted and reflect, although incorrectly, in favor of the taxpayer.

Item 5—Capital items paid by cash includes cash purchases of capital assets, cash deposited in savings accounts, and cash used to make payments on liabilities.

Item 6—Personal expenses paid by cash includes living expenses, income taxes, etc.

Item 7—Cash accumulated is the cash received by the taxpayer during the year which is on hand at the end of the year (it was neither expended nor deposited). It is the difference between the cash on hand at the beginning and end of the year.

Item 8—Nontaxable cash used for (4) through (7) is nontaxable cash used to pay expenses, purchase capital assets, deposit into savings accounts, make payments on liabilities, and to accumulate. Nontaxable cash includes: loans, withdrawals from savings accounts, gifts, inheritances, collection of loans receivable, non-taxable income, etc., not deposited.

Figure 13.6

Gross Business Receipts Formula[29]

The formula for computing gross business receipts is:

1.	Total bank deposits		$XXX
2.	Less; Nontaxable and nonbusiness receipts deposited		(XXX)
3.	Net deposits resulting from business receipts		$XXX
[...]	Add:		
[4.]	Business expenses paid by cash	$XXX	
[5.]	Capital items paid by cash	XXX	
[6.]	Personal expenses paid by cash	XXX	
[7.]	Cash accumulated during the year from receipts	XXX	
[...]	Sub-Total		$XXX
[8.]	Less: Non-taxable and nonbusiness cash used [...] for (4) through (7)		(XXX)
[...]	Gross business receipts as corrected		$XXX
[9.]	Adjustments for accrual basis taxpayers		$XXX

The following is a step-by-step explanation of the gross business receipts computation.

Item 1—Total bank deposits is the same as discussed in the gross receipts formula. [See IRM 4.10.4.6.3.6.1.]

---

[29] CCH has edited this table from the Internal Revenue Manual for explanation and clarity. Changes appear in brackets.

Item 2—Nontaxable and nonbusiness receipts deposited includes the same items as the gross receipts formula plus nonbusiness receipts deposited. In computing gross business receipts it is necessary to eliminate all nonbusiness deposits, whether taxable or not. Nonbusiness deposits include salaries, wages, dividends, rent, etc. In other words, deposits from any source but business receipts are eliminated.

Item 4—Is identical for both formulas. [See IRM 4.10.4.6.3 .6.1(2)c.]

Item 5—Is identical for both formulas. [See IRM 4.10.4.6.3.6.1(2)f.]

Item 6—Is identical for both formulas. [See IRM 4.10.4.6.3.6.1(2)g.]

Item 7—Is identical for both formulas. [See IRM 4.6.3.6.1(2)h.]

Item 8—Nontaxable and nonbusiness cash used for (4) through (7) includes the same items as the gross receipts formula [See IRM 4.10.4.6.3.6.1(2)i) plus nonbusiness cash used to pay expenses, purchase capital assets, deposit into savings accounts, make payments on liabilities, or accumulate. Nonbusiness cash is received from any source except business receipts.

Item [9]—[...See IRM 4.10.4.6.3.7 for explanation of adjustments for accrual basis taxpayers.]

¶ 1307 Tracing Assets

An example of asset tracing by a Special Agent involves Iraq's hidden financial assets. Special Agent Scott Schneider was sent to Baghdad to interview high-level detainees to obtain relevant documents for review. Agent Schneider uncovered and tagged for IRS inspection a room full of documents. Saddam Hussein and his two sons obtained about $2 billion of illegal funds from the U.N.'s Oil-for-Food program by exporting oil and being paid by cash or barter.

More than 10 years ago Kroll Associates, working for the Kuwait government, tried to trace Hussein's assets in order to seize them or have them frozen. Kroll felt that Hussein and his families had up to $10 billion in 1992, with $1 billion invested in Europe.

Agent Schneider found a nine-page handwritten letter by Saddam's half-brother, Barzan, explaining how Saddam could hide his wealth. *Tax Notes* printed a summary of this letter:[30]

- Discusses the feasibility of setting up companies abroad to obscure an unidentified (and presumably illicit) project. Decided not to pursue in part based on tax and interest issues and risk of discovery.

- Discusses payments to spies.

- Discusses difficulty of not arousing suspicion of individuals presumably used for this project or other intelligence functions.

- Identifies specified possible intelligence officers.

- Discusses an account in the name of a third party. Informs Saddam of the profitability of a gold transaction (buy low/sell higher) under that account.

---

[30] Amy Hamilton, "Armed Special Agent Scours Baghdad for Saddam Hussein's Loot," *Tax Notes* (August 23, 2003): 988-991.

- Discusses internal movement of funds from one individual to another.
- Discusses a proposal to avoid detection by authorities of a transaction (see quote).

Quote: "I would like to point out something which has caught my attention. In case there is a notion to withdraw the amount, I believe it should be transferred under a different name, and I suggest there should be a time limit to do so. The reasons are so the primary and secondary trustee will not be detected, as the transfer or withdrawal of the amount will attract the attention of the ... authorities, and disclose the subject matter. If there is enough suspicion the authorities can, according to law, seize the amount ...."

The IRS has sent so-called "jump teams" of two or three agents to European and Middle Eastern nations to follow up on Agent Schneider's leads. They have to trace layered transactions conducted with artificial entities to conceal the money.

¶ 1308 Current State of Tax Compliance

Tax compliance and fraud are growing problems for the IRS and the accounting profession. Unfortunately, not all taxpayers disclose all sources of income and are in full compliance with the tax laws, so there is a huge underground economy. Some people believe the Beatles' song, "Taxman," by George Harrison: "If you drive a truck, I'll tax the street; if you try to fix it, I'll tax your seat. If you get a cold, I'll tax the heat; if you take a walk, I'll tax your feet." But the possibility of being audited by the IRS has dropped as low as 1 in 200.

Over the years, through tax laws and court cases, the IRS has been provided with many tools to help foster tax compliance. The tax laws have been somewhat effective for individuals who are not self-employed. For example, the present tax laws require employers to report to the IRS the amount of wages paid to employees. However, for self-employed individuals, there are fewer methods of using a third party to determine taxable income. Therefore, in order to determine unreported income for a self-employed taxpayer, the IRS is allowed to use indirect methods. These methods are both time consuming and costly to the IRS (or to us as taxpayers) and place an undue burden on taxpayers who do comply with the tax laws.

Although Code Sec. 7602 limits the use of indirect methods, the Code does not prohibit or preclude its use. Until better methods of determining unreported income are provided, the IRS will probably continue to use the methods discussed in this chapter and sanctioned by tax law. The lack of better or less costly methods of determining taxable income for persons who are self-employed provides motivation for future research in this area. Likewise, forensic accountants may use these methods under appropriate circumstances. The lifestyles of taxpayers and employees may give clues to the possibility of unreported income or fraud.

¶ 1308

¶ 1309 Summary

IRS agents were some of the earliest and most successful forensic accountants in the United States. IRS agents' forensic techniques are used to catch taxpayers who are not paying their proper taxes.

IRS auditors use minimum income probes and lifestyles probes. The lifestyles of employees and taxpayers may give clues to the possibility of unreported income or fraud. A lavish residence, expensive cars and boats, a vacation home, private schools for children, and exotic vacations may indicate fraud and unreported income. The four major indirect methods to spot unreported income are: cash T, source and application of funds, net worth, and bank deposits.

These methods are both time consuming and costly to the IRS but are required for auditing self-employed individuals. Although the use of indirect methods has been limited by Code Sec. 7602, the Code does not prohibit or preclude their use. Forensic accountants may use these methods under appropriate circumstances as well.

Chapter 14

The Internal Auditing Profession

¶ 1401 Introduction
¶ 1402 The Modern Internal Auditing Function
¶ 1403 The Institute of Internal Auditors
¶ 1404 Future Trends in Internal Auditing
¶ 1405 Summary

¶ 1401 Introduction

Organizations look to their internal auditing function to provide value-added assurance and consulting services. The internal auditing staff regularly reports to a member of upper management and may have access to the audit committee of the board of directors. Internal auditors enjoy a special vantage point from which to view an entire organization. In addition, many internal auditing assignments are unique and challenging, requiring the highest quality technical, analytical, communication, and interpersonal skills. Many organizations use their internal auditing groups to develop future managers, with the result that positions as internal auditors are highly sought after as worthwhile places to begin careers. However, quite a few firms have outsourced the internal auditing function. Whether outsourced or performed in-house, the internal auditing function merits study by all practitioners.

Chapter 14 objectives:

- To define the modern internal auditing function (see ¶ 1401–1402).

- To become familiar with the Institute of Internal Auditors (IIA) and its activities (see ¶ 1403).

- To understand the research activity of the IIA (see ¶ 1403).

- To understand the professional standards activity of the IIA (see ¶ 1403).

- To understand the professional certifications and education and training activity of the IIA (see ¶ 1403).

- To become aware of future trends in internal auditing, including the Sarbanes-Oxley Act and PCAOB requirements for public companies to establish an independent internal audit function (see ¶ 1404).

¶ 1402 The Modern Internal Auditing Function

In June 1999, the Institute of Internal Auditors (IIA) adopted the following definition of internal auditing:

> Internal auditing is an independent, objective assurance and consulting activity designed to add value and improve an organization's operations. It helps an organization accomplish its objectives by bringing a systematic, disciplined approach to evaluate and improve the effectiveness of risk management, control, and governance processes.[1]

The definition contains important points that should be clarified. First, internal auditing is defined as an activity or process and not as a department. This distinction is important because the definition implies that internal auditors can either be directly employed by the organization or supplied by third-party contractors/outsourcers. Deciding between the two parties is the responsibility of upper management with the concurrence of the board of directors and based on sound business reasons.

Second, internal auditing is described as an independent, objective assurance and consulting activity. In the past, internal auditing was strictly an assurance activity that was expected to be independent of the activities it audited to prevent apparent conflicts of interest. Internal auditors were not allowed to make management decisions or perform management duties. However, many managers felt that internal auditors clung too tightly to independence and became aloof and out of touch with managers' needs. These managers wanted internal auditors to perform consulting activities for them in which objectivity was more important than independence.

Third, the IIA's definition implies that the purpose of the internal auditing function is to add value and improve an organization's operations by evaluating and improving the effectiveness of risk management, control, and governance processes. This represents a significant shift in the types of audits that internal auditors perform. In the past, internal auditing groups concentrated on performing financial and compliance (with company policies) audits. In many cases, organizations had this focus to lower the cost of the annual financial audit by the organization's external auditor. However, over time, many managers realized that internal auditing resources could be more economically spent performing other types of audits. In addition, most managers began to realize that the annual financial audit, although required, did not address the issues challenging leaders in running an organization. Managers, therefore, began requesting internal auditors to execute more operational and compliance audits, particularly those compli-

---

[1] *The Institute of Internal Auditors Professional Practices Framework,* copyright 1999 by the Institute of Internal Auditors, Inc., 247 Maitland Avenue, Altamonte Springs, Florida 32710-4201, U.S.A. Reprinted with permission.

ance audits focusing on the organization's compliance with laws and regulations (for example, environmental and safety laws) or outside vendors' adherence to contract terms. Thus, internal auditors performed fewer financial and compliance audits dealing with adherence to company policies.

The modern internal auditing function reports to upper management and may have exposure to the audit committee of the board of directors. It concentrates on operational audits and legal/contract compliance audits. The function may either be staffed by auditors directly employed by the firm or supplied by a vendor/outsourcer. The rest of this chapter explores the internal auditing profession and subsequent chapters deal with the management of an internal auditing function, the completion of an internal auditing assignment, and reporting and follow-up issues.

¶ 1403 The Institute of Internal Auditors

Individuals have been employed as internal auditors for thousands of years. However, it was not until 1941, when the IIA was established in New York, that a professional organization for internal auditors came into being. Since then, the IIA has grown steadily in membership and spread throughout the world to include approximately 80,000 members in more than 100 countries. The IIA's headquarters is located in Altamonte Springs, Florida near Orlando. Members most often interact with the IIA through one of 230 local chapters or National Institutes. In the United States, local chapters are grouped into districts within larger regions. The IIA has adopted the following mission statement:

> The IIA's mission is to be the primary international professional association, organized on a worldwide basis, dedicated to the promotion and development of the practice of internal auditing.
>
> The IIA is committed to:
>
> - Providing, on an international scale, comprehensive professional development activities, standards for the practice of internal auditing, and certification
>
> - Researching, disseminating, and promoting to its members and to the public throughout the world, knowledge and information concerning internal auditing, including internal control and related subjects
>
> - Establishing meetings worldwide in order to educate members and others as to the practice of internal auditing as it exists in various countries throughout the world
>
> - Bringing together internal auditors from all countries to share information and experiences in internal auditing and promoting education in the field of internal auditing

The IIA's activities fall into the following areas: (1) research, (2) professional standards, (3) professional certifications, and (4) education and training. Each is discussed here. Additional information can be obtained by contacting:

The Institute of Internal Auditors
247 Maitland Avenue
Altamonte Springs, Florida 32701-4201
Phone: (407) 830-7600
Fax: (407) 830-5171
Website: *www.theiia.org*

.01 Research

The IIA through the IIA Research Foundation (The Foundation) sponsors studies to develop and advance the practice of internal auditing. During its 1998 fiscal year, The Foundation invested more than $517,000 on research projects. The following recently completed research projects provide some insight into the types of studies supported:

- *Competency Framework for Internal Auditing* by William P. Birkett, Maria R. Barbera, Barry S. Leithead, Marian Lower, and Peter J. Roebuck (Altamonte, Fla.: IIA Research Foundation, 1999) examines the current practices within the internal auditing profession and evaluation of what internal auditing will be like in the future. This study draws data from more than 200 internal auditing experts in 21 countries.

- *Risk Management: Changing the Internal Auditor's Paradigm* by David McNamee and Georges M. Selim (Altamonte, Fla.: IIA Research Foundation, 1998) examines the entire business through the lens of risk. It identifies those practices that have allowed leading organizations to successfully identify and manage organizational risk and provides solutions that are valid not only today but also in the foreseeable future.

- *Using Neural Networks for Risk Assessment in Internal Auditing: A Feasibility Study* by Sridhar Ramamoorti and Richard O. Traver (Altamonte, Fla.: IIA Research Foundation, 1998) evaluates the potential for artificial intelligence applications in auditing, particularly, in the risk-assessment process.

- *Coordinating Total Audit Coverage: The Relationship Between Internal and External Auditors* by William L. Felix, Audrey A. Gramling, and Mario J. Maletta (Altamonte, Fla.: IIA Research Foundation, 1998) provides information about the interactions between internal auditors and their external auditors and the role internal auditing departments play in external financial statement audits.

- *An e-Risk Primer* by Xenia L. Parker (Altamonte, Fla.: IIA Research Foundation, 2001) describes the impact e-commerce has on business practices, identifies security risks associated

¶ 1403.01

with the digital world, proposes an e-commerce control strategy, develops a risk assessment program, and explores potential assurance services.

- *Independence and Objectivity: A Framework for Internal Auditors* by The Auditing Section Task Force of the American Accounting Association and sponsored by the The Institute of Internal Auditors Research Foundation (Altamonte, Fla.: IIA Research Foundation, 2001) discusses the importance of independence and objectivity, identifies potential threats to auditors' independence and objectivity, and proposes a framework for protecting auditors' independence and objectivity.

- *Internal Audit Reengineering: Survey, Model, and Best Practices* by P.P. Gupta (Altamonte, Fla.: IIA Research Foundation, 2001) argues that internal auditing functions must change or be eliminated, presents a methodology for reengineering internal auditing functions, and describes several examples of successful reengineering efforts.

Of the research studies cited, the first study, *Competency Framework for Internal Auditing* (CFIA), had one of the largest budgets ever funded and will probably have the greatest impact on the practice of internal auditing than any other study sponsored by The Foundation. It is well worthwhile, therefore, to examine it in more detail.

CFIA was the result of a global study of the internal auditing profession from 1996 to 1999 by a research team consisting of William P. Birkett (Australia), Maria R. Barbera (Australia), Barry S. Leithead (Australia), and Marion Lower (United Kingdom). The purpose of the CFIA study was to address the following four issues:

1. What will be the future role of internal auditing, and who are the primary customers?

2. How will the value proposition of internal auditing express itself in practice?

3. What will be the competencies required to provide value-added service, from the perspectives of both the internal auditing function and its role-takers?

4. How will these competencies be assessed?[2]

The CFIA study comprises six interrelated research projects:

1. *Competency Framework for Internal Auditing: An Overview* contains the executive summary of the CFIA study.

---

[2] Elaine R. McIntosh, *Competency Framework for Internal Auditing: An Overview*, copyright 1999 by the IIA Research Foundation, 247 Maitland Avenue, Altamonte Springs, Florida 32710-4201, U.S.A. Reprinted with permission.

¶ 1403.01

2. *Internal Auditing: The Global Landscape* documents the current status of internal auditing around the world. All national institutes, six U.S. chapters, and two Canadian chapters were surveyed for this study. The following topics were covered for each country's studies:

- The scope of internal auditing practice in that region
- The organization of internal auditing work
- The organization of its practitioners
- The major factors driving change
- Major problems or issues facing internal auditors
- The major points of difference in practice compared with practice internationally
- Any social or cultural issues peculiar to the region
- Issues involving the competence of internal auditors

3. *Competency: Best Practices and Competent Practitioners* explores the nature of internal auditing and the attributes of competent internal auditing functions and their practitioners. This study provides useful information for establishing or evaluating an internal auditing function. It also is a tool to assess the performance of individual auditors. This study is referenced often in the remainder of this chapter.

4. *Internal Auditing Knowledge: Global Perspectives* was the result of a literature review of authoritative references. This study addresses the following issues:

- What is to be understood by internal auditing in the future from a global perspective
- Attributes of a competent internal auditing function within organizations from the perspectives of global best practices
- Capabilities required of those taking key roles in a competent internal auditing function
- Suggestions for the best means of assessing competency

5. *The Future of Internal Auditing: A Delphi Study* presents the opinions of 136 internal auditing experts from 21 countries about the nature of internal auditing in the future, key tasks to be performed, drivers of change, skills and knowledge that will be required, and assessment criteria. Consensus seems to be that the scope of internal auditing will expand to provide assurance covering the full set of risk exposures faced by organizations against a background of constant change.

¶ 1403.01

6. *Assessing Competency in Internal Auditing: Structures and Methodologies* provides guidance on setting mechanisms for assessing competency both for departments and for all level of practitioners.[3]

Portions of the CFIA study findings are presented and discussed throughout this and succeeding chapters.

.02 Guidance Task Force

In 1997, the IIA established the Guidance Task Force to review the status of guidance provided to internal auditors and to recommend ways to improve guidance content and delivery. In 1999, the Guidance Task Force issued its final report, *A Vision for the Future,* in which the group proposed "The Framework for the Professional Practice of Internal Auditing" (see Figure 14.1).

---

[3] *Ibid.* pp. 5-6.

Figure 14.1

Proposed Professional Practices Framework

Internal Auditing Definition	Assurance Services	Implementation Standards	Code of Ethics	Implementation Standards	Consulting Services	Internal Auditing Definition
			Attribute Standards • Objectivity and Independence • Professional Proficiency • Demonstration of Compliance			
			Performance Standards • Managing Internal Auditing Processes • Assessing Risk, Control, Governance Processes • Planning the Engagement • Collecting and Analyzing Data • Evaluating Evidential Matter • Communicating Results of Work			
			Guidance — Practice Advisories			
			Guidance — Other			

Source: Adapted from IIA Guidance Taskforce, *A Vision for the Future: Professional Practices Framework for Internal Auditing,* copyright 1999 by the Institute of Internal Auditors, Inc., 247 Maitland Avenue, Altamonte Springs, Florida 32710-4201, U.S.A. Reprinted with permission.

.03 Professional Standards

The IIA controls the quality of services delivered by its members by issuing professional standards. It also protects the interests of parties (managers, board members, and the general public) affected by those services through its code of ethics. The purpose of the standards is to:

- Delineate basic principles that represent the practice of internal auditing as it should be

- Provide a framework for performing and promoting a broad range of value-added internal audit activities

¶ 1403.03

- Establish the basis for the measurement of internal audit performance
- Foster improved organizational processes and operations[4]

The IIA Board of Directors approved the proposed framework and definition of internal auditing on June 26, 1999. Existing standards are being revised and fit into the new guidance framework.

The key to understanding the new framework is to look upon the New Definition of Internal Auditing and the IIA Code of Ethics (IIA Code of Ethics are reproduced in Appendix A) as general guidance and the International Standards for the Professional Practice of Internal Auditing (IIA International Standards for the Professional Practice are reproduced in Appendix B) as specific guidance. The New Definition of Internal Auditing is an overall description of internal auditing; the Code of Ethics serves as a guide for the internal auditor's relationships with other internal auditors and their constituents; and the International Standards for the Professional Practice of Internal Auditing can be considered a guide for performing internal auditing services.

The New Definition of Internal Auditors was presented and discussed at the beginning of this chapter. The IIA Code of Ethics was drafted to address a dilemma faced by professional codes of conduct: Were the codes too general, they would give practitioners little or no practical guidance; were the codes too specific, practitioners would become obsessed with the letter rather than the spirit of the code. The IIA Code of Ethics addresses this dilemma by presenting fundamental principles that provide the spirit of the law and specific rules that provide the letter of the law.

The International Standards for the Professional Practice of Internal Auditing (ISPPIA) give more specific guidance concerning the actual practice of internal auditing. The ISPPIA are divided into attribute standards, performance standards, and implementation standards. The Attribute Standards address the characteristics of organizations and individuals performing internal audit activities. The Performance Standards describe the nature of internal audit activities and provide quality criteria against which the performance of these services can be measured. Implementation Standards exist for both assurance and consulting services. Implementation standards guide internal auditors on the correct means of meeting the Attribute and Performance standards.

The professional standards promulgated by the IIA appear to have been well thought out, organized, and clearly written (and therefore easily understood and adopted). Adherence to the professional standards remains strictly voluntary for IIA members. However, violators of the standards can

---

[4] *Standards for the Professional Practice of Internal Auditing,* copyright 2001 by the Institute of Internal Auditors, Inc., 247 Maitland Avenue, Altamonte Springs, Florida 32710-4201, U.S.A. Reprinted with permission.

¶ 1403.03

be reported to the IIA's Ethics Committee, which will conduct a thorough investigation following due process procedures. The IIA Board of Directors reviews and approves the recommendations of the Ethics Committee, which may include suspension or revocation of IIA membership if the member's violation is serious.

.04 Professional Certifications

The Certified Internal Auditor (CIA) certificate. The professional competence of internal auditors is usually demonstrated by obtaining professional certification. The first and chief professional certification maintained by the IIA remains the Certified Internal Auditor (CIA) designation established in 1974. The CIA designation is the only professional designation dealing with all aspects of the internal auditing profession, and in many respects it is the only truly global professional internal auditing designation.

To become a CIA, a candidate must meet requirements concerning education, character, work experience, and must pass the CIA exam. To meet the education requirements, a candidate must hold a bachelor's degree or its equivalent. Students in their senior year may sit for the CIA exam but will not be certified until they have earned their degree. Candidates must also submit a character reference from a responsible person, such as a supervisor, manager, educator, or CIA. Candidates may sit for the CIA exam before completing the experience requirement, but must attain 24 months of internal auditing (or equivalent) experience before becoming certified. Equivalent experience includes experience in audit/assessment disciplines such as external auditing, quality assurance, compliance, and internal control. Either a master's degree or work experience in related business professions (such as accounting, law, or finance) can be substituted for one year's experience.

The CIA exam is a truly global undertaking. The IIA, through its Board of Regents, offers the CIA exam in approximately 60 countries and in various languages, including French, Spanish, and Hebrew. The CIA exam is given on a Wednesday and Thursday in November and May. Candidates are notified of their scores by January for the November exam and by July for the May exam. The exam consists of four parts, with each part taking approximately 3.5 hours to complete. The following is an outline of the exam's content:

Part I—Internal Audit Process is comprised of Auditing (65–70%), Professionalism (10–20%), and Fraud (10–20%). It consists of 80 multiple-choice questions. The Auditing section covers different aspects of the auditing assignment, such as planning and administrating, identifying and prioritizing business objectives and risks, determining scope, evaluating internal controls, and procedures and management of the audit department. The test examines the application of these aspects of the auditing

¶ 1403.04

assignment to various types of internal audits, i.e., information technology, operations and programs, financial and compliance. Professionalism covers IIA Standards and the Code of Ethics—and starting in May 2002 the testing may include materials on the new Professional Practice Framework. In the Fraud section, prevention, detection, and investigation are covered as these activities apply to various types of fraud.

Part II—Internal Audit Skills is comprised of Problem Solving and Evaluating Evidence (45–60%), Data Gathering, Documentation, and Reporting (25–40%), and Sampling and Mathematics (10–20%). It consists of 80 multiple-choice questions. The Problem Solving section tests using logic and reasoning to solve problems and evaluate audit evidence to reach valid conclusions. The Data Gathering section tests the application of the appropriate tools and techniques for collecting and evaluating audit evidence. It also covers the application of workpaper and audit reporting guidelines, including the appropriate IIA standards. Sampling and Mathematics tests the application of sampling and mathematics to business situations. Probability distributions and theory are covered in this section as well.

Part III—Management Control and Information Technology is comprised of Management Control (30–40%), Operations Management (10–20%), and Information Technology (45–55%). It consists of 80 multiple-choice questions. The Management section covers internal control concepts, measures of performance, change facilitation, control self-assessment, and budget concepts. The Operations Management section examines management science, including such concepts as time series and regression analysis, queuing theory, sensitivity analysis, simulation models, critical-path method (CPM), and program evaluation and review technique (PERT). The Information Technology section tests on information systems strategies, policies, procedures, hardware, platforms, networks, telecommunications, data processing, systems development, security, contingency planning, and more.

Part IV—The Audit Environment is comprised of Financial Accounting (30–40%), Finance (20–30%), Managerial Accounting (20–30%), and Regulatory Environment (10–20%). It consists of 80 multiple-choice questions. The Financial Accounting section tests on the accounting cycle, cash controls, analyzing interrelationships among accounts, revenue recognition, inventory estimation methods, International Accounting Standards, and financial statement analysis. It also includes material on depreciation methods, long-term investments, asset retirements, bonds, prior-period adjustments, pensions, contingent liabilities, unearned revenues, differences in financial statement formats, differences between capital and operating leases, and intangible assets. Finance covers cost of capital, various types of debt, various types of equity, profit planning, implications of leveraging, valuation of a firm, interpreting and forecasting models, mergers and acquisitions, implications of bankruptcy, operation of financial markets,

¶ 1403.04

implications of dividend policies, sources of short-term financing, measures of performance, change facilitation, control self-assessment, and budget concepts. Managerial Accounting covers management of current assets, capital budgeting, interpreting budgeting models, cost-benefit analysis, cost allocation procedures, cost behavior patterns, activity-based costing, breakeven analysis, relevant costs, transfer pricing, and cost-volume-profit analysis. The Regulatory Environment looks at awareness of governments' monitoring of environmental issues, governments' impact on business, types of political structures, business practices of countries, import and export law, international trade methods, trade restrictions, and trade barriers. It also looks at the organization of governments, international laws, various forms of business organizations, types of taxes, and differences between tax reporting and financial reporting.

Beginning with the May 2004 exam, the CIA will be modified in the following manner:

- Parts I, II, and III of the new CIA exam will be defined at the "Core Global Syllabus" and cover material common to all internal auditors (corporate governance, risk management and control, and technology) and closely aligned to the IIA's Professional Practices Framework.

- Part IV will be changed to cover either a specialized audit-related area or knowledge of general business management. In addition, holders of many professional designations, such as the Certified Public Accountants or Chartered Accountants, will be given credit for Part IV through the IIA's Professional Recognition Credit program.

- The number of multiple choice questions will increase from 80 to 125 per part with no change in the allowable time of 3 1/2 hours per part. Essay questions will be shortened to allow for the increased number of multiple-choice questions.

Student members of the IIA are given a significant discount off the registration fee and part fees for the exam. Educators may take the exam for free. Further information concerning the CIA exam can be obtained by contacting the IIA at its website *http://www.theiia.org* and accessing the menu option entitled "Certification."

Other IIA professional designations. In the mid-1990s the IIA, in partnership with the Board of Environmental Auditing Roundtable, also established the Board of Environmental Auditor Certifications (BEAC). The BEAC subsequently began offering the Certified Professional Environmental Auditor (CPEA) designation (see Chapter 21 for additional information). In 1999, the IIA began offering the Certification in Control Self-Assessment (CCSA) designation, and in 2001, the Certified Government Auditor (CGAP) designation for governmental auditors. Both designations

¶ 1403.04

are further discussed here. Individuals interested in obtaining any of the IIA's professional certifications should visit the IIA's website at *http://www.theiia.org* for additional details and the most up-to-date information.

The CCSA was the IIA's first specialty designation and geared to those practitioners who wish to practice control self-assessment (discussed later in this chapter). Candidates must complete the following requirements to obtain a CCSA designation:

- **Education**—a bachelor's (four-year) or equivalent degree (a minimum of two years of post-secondary education with an accredited organization plus three years of general business experience may be substituted for a bachelor's degree)

- **Character reference**—a character reference signed by a CIA, CCSA, or the candidate's supervisor

- **Work experience**—one year of control-related business experience, such as Control Self Assessment, auditing, quality assurance, risk management, or environmental auditing verified by a CIA, CCSA, or the candidate's supervisor

- **Facilitation experience/training**—seven hours of acceptable facilitation experience or at least 14 hours of acceptable facilitation training

- **CCSA Exam**—earn a passing grade on the CCSA Exam[5]

CIA candidates are assumed to meet the education, character, and experience requirements. Candidates may also meet the experience requirements by attending certain specified IIA seminars.

The CCSA Exam is offered in the United States and Canada as a computer-based exam containing 125 multiple-choice (objective) questions and requiring approximately 2.5 hours to complete. The CCSA exam is also offered in paper and pencil format in conjunction with the CIA exam. Candidates are forbidden from disclosing current exam questions or answers. The exam content covers the following topics:

- **Domain 1—Control Self Assessment Fundamentals (5–10%)**
    A. Code of Ethics
    B. Ownership and accountability for control
    C. Reliance on operational expertise
    D. Comparison to traditional techniques of risk and control evaluation
    E. Control awareness and education
    F. Cooperation, participation, and partnership

- **Domain 2—Control Self-Assessment Program Integration (15%–25%)**
    A. Alternative approaches to CSA
    B. Supporting technology alternatives

---

[5] From the IIA web site, *www.theiia.org*. Reprinted with permission.

C. Cost/benefit analysis for implementation of the CSA process
D. Organizational theory and behavior
E. Strategic and operational planning processes
F. Change management and business process reengineering
G. Presentation techniques for successful integration
H. Organizational risk and control processes
I. Client feedback mechanisms (e.g., interviews, surveys)
J. Strategic CSA program planning methodologies or techniques, including resource allocation

- **Domain 3—Elements of the Control Self-Assessment Process (15%–25%)**
  A. Management's priorities and concerns
  B. Project and logistics management
  C. Business objectives, processes, challenges, and threats for the area under review
  D. Resource identification and allocation
  E. Culture of area under review
  F. Question development techniques
  G. Technology supporting the CSA process
  H. Facilitation techniques and tools
  I. Group dynamics
  J. Fraud awareness
  K. Evaluation/analytical tools and techniques (trend analysis, data synthesis, scenarios)
  L. Formulating recommendations or actions plans (practical, feasible, cost-effective)
  M. Nature of evidence (sufficiency, relevance, adequacy)
  N. Reporting techniques and considerations (types, audience, sensitive issues, access to information)
  O. Motivational techniques (creating support and commitment for recommendations)
  P. Monitoring, tracking, and follow-up techniques
  Q. Awareness of legal, regulatory, and ethical considerations
  R. Measuring CSA program effectiveness

- **Domain 4—Business Objectives and Organizational Performance (10%–15%)**
  A. Strategic and operational planning processes
  B. Objective setting, including alignment to the organization's mission and values
  C. Performance measures
  D. Performance management
  E. Data collection and validation techniques (e.g., benchmarking, auditing, consensus testing)

¶ 1403.04

- **Domain 5—Risk Identification and Assessment (15%–20%)**
    - A. Risk Theory
    - B. Risk models/frameworks
    - C. Understanding the risks inherent in common business processes
    - D. Application of risk identification and assessment techniques
    - E. Risk management techniques/cost-benefit analysis
- **Domain 6—Control Theory and Application (20%–25%)**
    - A. Corporate governance, control theory, and models
    - B. Techniques for determining control track record for the organization (e.g., reviews, audits, other assessments)
    - C. Relationship between informal and formal controls
    - D. Techniques for evaluating formal controls (manual or automated)
    - E. Techniques for evaluating informal controls/control environment
    - F. Control documentation techniques
    - G. Control design and application
    - H. Methods for judging and communicating about the overall effectiveness of the system of internal control[6]

Although it has only been in existence for a few years, the CCSA designation is fast becoming a recognized internal auditing specialty.

The newest specialty certification offered by the IIA is the Certified Financial Services Auditor (CFSA) for which the IIA assumed responsibility in June 2002 following a merger with the National Financial Services Auditors (NAFSA). The CFSA exam is a one-part computerized nondisclosed exam. The domains tested by the CFSA exam include: financial services auditing and banking, insurance, and securities.

To sit for the CFSA, a candidate must meet the following requirements:

- A bachelor's degree or two years of post-secondary education and three years of financial services experience.
- A character reference signed by a CIA, CCSA, CGAP, or CFSA.
- Two years of auditing experience in a financial services environment.

CIAs are assumed to have met the education and character requirements. CCSA and CGAP holders are assumed to have met the character reference requirement. Continuing updated information on this exam can be found on the IIA website under "Guidance" at *www.theiia.org*.

---

[6] *Ibid.*

¶ 1403.04

Other professional designations. Other certifications often held by internal auditors pertaining to tasks performed by internal auditors include:

- Certified Public Accountant (CPA) certificate or license issued by the various states in the United States

- Certified Information Systems Auditor (CISA) designation offered by the Information Systems Audit and Control Association (ISACA)

- Certified Fraud Examiner (CFE) designation offered by the Association of Certified Fraud Examiners

The CISA and CFE designations are discussed in the chapters dealing with information technology (Chapter 22) and fraud examinations (Chapter 19), respectively.

.05 Education and Training

Maintaining existing skills and obtaining new ones are the objectives of the IIA's education and training program, comprising seminars, conferences, books, publications, and other efforts. The IIA regularly holds seminars on specific internal auditing topics ranging in duration from one to five days. In addition, local chapters also sponsor educational programs. Conferences are held regularly at the international, regional, and district levels to bring internal auditors together and to present a broad mix of topics. Education and training is also accomplished by reading books or monographs, viewing educational videos, and completing self-study courses. The IIA provides all of these materials through its bookstore (1-407-830-7600 ext. 1 or the website, *theiia.org*). IIA publications include its flagship publication, *The Internal Auditor*, which is published six times annually and numerous newsletters and bulletins as well as the IIA website at *http://www.theiia.org*.

¶ 1404 Future Trends in Internal Auditing

The internal auditing profession, like most professions, is undergoing unprecedented change, to the extent that the profession will change more within the next decade than it has during its entire history. It is therefore important to introduce some of the more important trends affecting the profession so practitioners can understand and profit from these changes.

.01 Globalization

More and more organizations, regardless of their size, conduct business or otherwise interact with parties across international borders. Consequently, internal auditors are more frequently asked to conduct audits of entities located outside their home country. In order to succeed, internal auditors must learn to work with the other country's language, customs, and business practices, or at the very least to deal with a contracted auditor

¶ 1403.05

in the other country. In the 1990s, 60 percent of IIA members were from the United States and Canada. Today, 60 percent of IIA members are from outside the United States and Canada, and most new members are from outside the United States. As mentioned earlier, the CFIA study is a global study, and the CIA is a globally recognized professional designation. Another manifestation of globalization can be seen in the locations for recent and planned IIA international conferences—Montreal, New York, Buenos Aires, Washington, Las Vegas, and Sydney.

.02 Outsourcing

In the early 1990s, most internal auditing services were performed by employees of the organizations they audited. Today, independent contractors perform much of the internal auditing services by either staffing whole departments or supplying existing internal auditing departments with specialized services. Outsourcing overall has benefited the internal auditing profession by introducing competition into the market for internal auditing services. Today, a chief auditing executive must constantly ensure that his or her internal auditing staff are delivering value-added audit services efficiently, or the function will be outsourced. The Big-5 accounting firms have the resources and the economies of scale to hire specialists with skills that the average internal auditing group cannot hire or employ effectively. In addition, outsource firms perform internal auditing engagements for organizations that cannot afford a full-time audit group.

.03 Shift in Audit Services

Most internal auditing functions as late as the 1980s concentrated heavily on performing audits of internal controls, compliance with company policies, and contracts. Gradually, however, internal auditing functions shifted because of scarce in-house resources and competition from outsource firms. Internal auditing executives realized that they had to market their services more effectively. This meant becoming closer to management and the audit committee. It also meant actively soliciting the views of management and the audit committee on risk management and the scope of audit services. Internal auditing functions began to expand beyond simply determining whether a control existed to determining the best control possible, and from just determining when the spending and allocation of resources were properly recorded to determining whether the spending and allocation of resources were efficient and effective. Other changes quickly followed—from reviewing contractor compliance to assisting in the awarding of the contract, from reviewing controls functioning in an information technology system to participating on the design team to build necessary controls into the system.

The delivery of consulting services has caused the internal auditing profession to widen its scope from strictly auditing to providing assurance and consulting services, with a resultant emphasis on objectivity versus independence. The American Accounting Association (AAA) and the IIA co-

¶ 1404.03

sponsored a research project investigating the independence and objectivity of internal auditors.[7] The study identified professionalism (integrity, competence and the use of due care) and objectivity (uncompromising adherence to a code of moral values and the avoidance of deception, expediency, artificiality, or shallowness of any kind) as the two essential conditions for delivering value-added audit services. Maintaining objectivity or freedom from bias is more important than the appearance of independence. The study recommended that internal auditors proactively identify threats to objectivity and build controls into their work processes to prevent the threats from compromising their objectivity. Threats to objectivity identified by the study include: self-review, social pressure, economic interest, personal relationship, familiarity, cultural, racial and gender biases, and cognitive biases. Potential remedies to overcome threats to auditor objectivity include: organizational position and policies, strong corporate governance, incentives, use of teams, supervision/peer review, elapsed time/changed circumstances, limited audit scope, and internal consultations. Some proactive steps that auditors can take to protect their objectivity include: hiring practices, training, quality assurance reviews, rotation/reassignment, and outsourcing.

.04 The Paradigm Shift

Internal auditing is undergoing a shift from its traditional internal control paradigm to a risk-based paradigm. The implications for the profession of this shift are many and profound and are presented in Table 14.1. Internal auditors will have to get closer to managers and members of the audit committee by having regular face-to-face meetings as well as written and electronic communications, if they are to successfully implement the new paradigm. Internal auditors will thereby gain a deeper understanding of the processes driving their organizations. Objectivity becomes more important than independence or the appearance of objectivity under the risk-based paradigm. The time frame for audits will shift from the past to the future, and the emphasis from accounting or even information to operations. Organizations will employ auditors with the correct skill sets rather than the technical knowledge. The CFIA study forecasted this trend. Managers and members of the audit committee should view auditors as partners and problem solvers rather than problem generators.

---

[7] The Auditing Section Task Force of the AAA and the Institute of Internal Auditors Research Foundation, *Independence and Objectivity: A Framework for Internal Auditors* (Altamonte Springs, Fla.: The Institute of Internal Auditors Research Foundation, 2001).

Table 14.1

Changing the Internal Auditor's Paradigm

Characteristic	Old Paradigm	New Paradigm
Internal audit focus	Internal control	Business risk
Internal audit response	Reactive, after-the-fact, discontinuous, observers of strategic planning initiatives	Co-active, real-time, continuous monitoring, participants in strategic plans
Risk assessment	Risk factors	Scenario planning
Internal audit tests	Important controls	Important risks
Internal audit methods	Emphasis on the completeness of detail controls testing	Emphasis on the significance of broad business risks covered
Internal audit recommendations	Internal control: • Strengthened • Cost-benefit • Efficient/effective	Risk management: • Avoid/diversify risk • Share/transfer risk • Control/accept risk
Internal audit reports	Addressing the functional controls	Addressing the process risks
Internal audit role in the organization	Independent appraisal function	Integrated risk management and corporate governance

Source: Adapted from D. McNamee and G.M. Selim, *Risk Management: Changing the Internal Auditor's Paradigm,* copyright 1998 by the IIA Research Foundation, 247 Maitland Avenue, Altamonte Springs, Florida 32710-4201, U.S.A. Reprinted with permission.

.05 Future Internal Auditors?

What will future internal auditors look like? One indication can be found in the CFIA study that lists the knowledge, skills, and abilities (KSAs) that future auditors will need to perform internal auditing services. Table 14.2 lists these KSAs. Importantly, technical accounting knowledge is not stressed here. Indeed, technical knowledge of *any* type is not stressed, but skills and abilities are. The reader should also keep in mind that CFIA was a global study and represents the views of practitioners from around the world. Also noteworthy is that many of the skills relate to management, particularly risk and information management. Again, the current theme being stressed is that internal auditing has to go beyond the technical (accounting and information technology) to become partners with management if it is to survive and prosper.

¶ 1404.05

.06 Impact of the Recent Financial Scandals on the Internal Auditing Profession

Largely due to the work of the IIA, the internal auditing profession was well-positioned to respond to the recent wave of financial reporting scandals. The IIA leadership correctly positioned the internal auditing profession to assist policy makers in addressing such issues as corporate governance, risk identification/management, and internal control review and design. Consequently, many of the reforms enacted by the public and private sectors significantly raise the status of the internal auditing profession. For instance, the New York Stock Exchange issued new listing requirements that require all its listed companies to have internal auditing functions. The Sarbanes-Oxley Act prohibits a client's external auditor from performing any internal auditing work for the same client. It also strengthens audit committee membership and the interaction between it and the company's internal auditing function.

The Public Company Accounting Oversight Board created by the Sarbanes-Oxley Act requires publicly traded companies to adopt internal controls to prevent fraudulent financial fraud and for the company's external auditor test and issue an opinion concerning the adequacy of the company's controls. Most companies will rely on their internal auditors to comply with this provision resulting in more resources being given to the company's internal audit function. Lastly, the U.S. Securities and Exchange Commission in 2003 revised its regulations governing audit committee membership to require more financially qualified members. More audit committee members will know and understand the internal audit function's role in preventing fraudulent financial reporting.

Two sections of the Sarbanes-Oxley Act of 2002 address the role of internal auditing and internal controls in improving the quality and reliability of financial reports. First, Section 302 of the Act requires senior executives to certify that they have designed disclosure controls and procedures over financial reporting. Internal auditors can assist management to effectively discharge its certification responsibility under Section 302. Second, Section 404 of the Act requires public companies to include a report by management on internal control over financial reporting and an assessment of the effectiveness of these controls in their annual report. Internal auditors should assist management in the preparation of the internal control report in compliance with Section 404 of the Act. Furthermore, internal auditors should cooperate with independent registered auditors in gathering evidence for their attestation of and report on management assessment of internal control over financial reporting in accordance with PCAOB Auditing Standard No. 2. Indeed, PCAOB Auditing Standard No. 2 recommends registered auditors to cooperate with interim auditors and to utilize audit evidence gathered by internal auditors in the process of exposing an opinion on management assessment of the effectiveness of

¶ 1404.06

internal control over financial reporting and their own assessment of the effectiveness of internal control as an integrated part of an audit of financial statements.[8] While the Sarbanes-Oxley Act of 2002 does not explicitly require public companies to have an internal audit function, the NYSE requires that listed companies have an internal audit function.[9]

---

[8] PCAOB Auditing Standard No. 2, An Audit of Internal Control over Financial Reporting Performed in Conjunction with an Audit of Financial Statements (PCAOB Release No. 2004-001, March 9, 2004). Available at *http://www.pcaobus.org*.

[9] NYSE. "Final Recommendations of NYSE Corporate Accountability and Listing Standards Committee." (2002). Available at *http://www.nyse.com/press/1044027444976.html*.

Table 14.2

CFIA Assessing Competency in Internal Auditing: Assessment Criteria for Entering Internal Auditor

Panel A: Composite Role Performance Attributes

Responsibilities and authority	Takes responsibility for own learning Works under direction Assists in task performance
Learning/development	Develops an understanding of organization's risks and controls Works effectively, both individually and as part of a team Takes direction from other Accepts responsibility/accountability for own actions Knows when to ask questions Respects confidentiality of information Expresses ideas clearly and accurately Well organized in the workplace Engaged in further study and training
Task/operational	Develops working relationships within the organization Assists in identifying/analyzing potential risk areas Assists in the execution of internal auditing tasks and testing processes Assists in identifying noncompliance with control objectives Prepares portions of reports

Panel B: Knowledge and Understanding Composites

Organizational environments	Regulatory processes impacting organizations Competitive structures impacting organizations Industry structures Social expectations affecting organizations (e.g., in relation to ethical behavior, environmental management, equal opportunity/affirmative action)
Organizational functioning	The make up of organizations (e.g., structures, cultures, power, purpose) Governance mechanisms and issues Managerial roles Financing and resourcing
Risk and organizations	Sources/types of risks facing organizations The need for risk management
Control in organizations	The need for control in organizations Basic/best practice control models
Information technology and organizations	Data generation and information sources The need for information management Information management technologies
Internal auditing processes and technologies	The purpose/value of internal auditing Internal auditing tasks Internal auditing processes Competencies required for internal auditing work

Panel C: Cognitive and Behavioral Skills Composites

Cognitive Skills	Behavioral Skills
Technical skills	**Personal skills**
Communication	Morality
Expresses ideas clearly/accurately	Honesty
Literacy/report writing	Personal integrity
Presentational materials	Respects confidences
Numeracy	Reliable
Descriptive statistics	Directed
Sampling	Pursues self-development
Computer Literacy	Takes pride in achievements
Word processing/spreadsheets/	Enthusiastic
databases/presentation software	Self-starter/takes initiative
	Inquisitiveness
Analytical/constructive skills	Needs to know/learn
Research/reasoning	Curious
Investigation/fact finding	Questioning
Analysis/assessment of data/information	Flexibility
Evaluates impacts of alternative courses of action	Open to ideas
Documents reasoning/conclusions	Coping
Reaches sound conclusions	Accepts accountability for own actions
	Takes direction from others
	Well organized
	A time manager
	Intelligence
	Logical thinker
Appreciative/judgmental skills	Creative/lateral thinker
Discrimination	
Knows when to ask questions	**Interpersonal skills**
Value Orientations	Communications
Appreciates the value of further study/training	Listening/attentive
Appreciates the value of teamwork	Expresses ideas clearly
Judgment	People Skills
Appreciates the necessity for judgment	Empathy
	Responsive
	Recognizes and respects diversity in people
	Team Management
	Cooperative
	Consultative
	Develops relationships with others
	A team player

Source: Adapted from W.P. Birkett, M.R. Barbera, B.S. Leithhead, M. Lower, and P.J. Roebuck, *Risk Management: Competency Framework for Internal Auditing, Assessing Competency in Internal Auditing: Structures and Methodologies*, copyright 1999 by the IIA Research Foundation, 247 Maitland Avenue, Altamonte Springs, Florida 32710-4201, U.S.A. Reprinted with permission.

¶ 1405 Summary

The definition of internal auditing adopted by the Institute of Internal Auditors (IIA) in 1999 is "an independent, objective assurance and consulting activity designed to add value and improve an organization's operations. It helps an organization accomplish its objectives by bringing a systematic, disciplined approach to evaluate and improve the effectiveness of risk management, control, and governance processes."

The IIA's activities fall into the following areas: research, professional standards, professional certifications, and education and training. The purpose of the IIA's professional standards is to delineate basic principles that represent the practice of internal auditing to provide a framework for performing and promoting a broad range of value-added internal audit services, to establish the basis for the measurement of internal audit performance, and to foster improved organizational processes and operations. The professional competence of internal auditors is usually demonstrated by obtaining professional certification. This certification is called the CIA (certified internal auditor) certificate. The Sarbanes-Oxley Act of 2002 and the new PCAOB Auditing Standards recommend that internal auditors assist management in Section 404 internal control reporting compliance and cooperate with registered auditors to gather evidence for attestation of and reporting on internal control over financial reporting.

Chapter 15

Managing the Internal Auditing Function

¶ 1501   Introduction
¶ 1502   Authorizing and Organizing the Internal Auditing Function
¶ 1503   Coordinating the Internal Auditing Function with Organizational Policies
¶ 1504   Interactions with the Organization's External Auditor
¶ 1505   Quality Assurance
¶ 1506   Outsourcing
¶ 1507   The Audit Committee
¶ 1508   Summary

¶ 1501 Introduction

The chief auditing executive (CAE) manages the internal auditing function with the assistance and oversight of management and the audit committee. Traditionally, managers perform four tasks: organizing, planning, directing, and controlling. In the context of an internal auditing function, these four can be further broken down into the following six major responsibilities that a CAE bears (with their correspondence to the original four following in parentheses):

1. Authorizing and organizing the internal auditing function (organizing)
2. Performing risk assessment and scheduling audits (planning)
3. Coordinating internal auditing function and organization policies (directing)
4. Coordinating audit work with the organization's external auditors (planning)
5. Maintaining a quality control system (directing and controlling)
6. Preventing the outsourcing of the internal auditing function (organizing, planning, directing, and controlling)

All but the second step is discussed in this chapter. The second step is discussed in the next chapter.

¶ 1501

Chapter 15 objectives:

- To become familiar with the responsibilities and functions of a chief auditing executive (CAE) and the skills needed to become a CAE (see ¶ 1501).
- To understand how to authorize and organize the internal auditing function (see ¶ 1502).
- To understand the importance of coordinating the internal auditing function with organizational policies (see ¶ 1503).
- To learn about interacting with the organization's external auditor (see ¶ 1504).
- To understand the importance of quality assurance (see ¶ 1505).
- To become familiar with outsourcing (see ¶ 1506).
- To learn about the Audit Committee and its role (see ¶ 1507).

.01 Competency of Internal Auditors

What knowledge, skills, and abilities (KSAs) are necessary to be a successful CAE? Recall from Chapter 13 that the Institute of Internal Auditors (IIA) Research Foundation commissioned a global study of the internal auditing profession entitled, *Competency Framework for Internal Auditing* (CFIA). The CFIA study examined the KSAs required to be a successful CAE. In addition to the KSAs required of any auditing staff member, the CAE should possess the following cognitive skills:

- Strategies, networks, and cultures; systems design of risk management systems and improvement projects; and
- Recognizing the significance of organizational/environmental happenings, cultural and behavioral issues, nature/effects of diversity, questioning effectively to gather information, creating and effectively using resources, belief in the pursuit of best practice, and thriving on challenge.[1]

CAEs should also possess the following behavioral skills:

- Personal skills such as a determination to succeed, self-confidence, and visionary thinking.
- Organizational awareness such as an in-depth understanding of the business; using organizational networks, structures, power sources, and cultures to secure outcomes; and managing diversity creatively.

---

[1] Adapted from W.P. Birkett, M.R. Barbera, B.S. Leithhead, M. Lower, P.J. Roebuck, *Competency Framework for Internal Auditing, Assessing Competency in Internal Auditing: Structures and Methodologies* (Altamonte Springs, Fla.: The Institute of Internal Auditors Research Foundation, 1999), 65-69.

- Functional management skills such as developing: strategies for the internal auditing function; work structures, policies, and processes of the function; resources for the function; a vision of the function's organizational contribution/future; the culture of the function; a developmental path for the function; and staff as a value-adding organizational team.

- Organizational management skills such as: building effective communications about the progress/outcomes of internal auditing work; contributing to the development of an organization's goals and strategies, with respect to risk and control; promoting understanding of an organization's goals and strategies, by reference to risk/control issues; and managing organizational/situational complexity.

Actually, few successful CAEs excel or even possess all of these skills. However, a CAE or prospective CAE should use the KSA list to determine his or her strengths and weaknesses and to construct a development program to acquire as many of the KSAs as possible.

¶ 1502 Authorizing and Organizing the Internal Auditing Function

A newly appointed CAE must first reach an understanding with management and the board of directors (or audit committee of the board of directors) concerning the internal auditing function's role within the organization. The CAE should document the understanding reached concerning these issues in the form of a written *charter*. The charter is a contract and, therefore, should be in writing to prevent future misunderstandings. Some internal auditing groups print their charters on bonded paper and frame them. Others place them in their organization's policy and procedures manual. Either location is acceptable as long as the charter is written down. The charter should be distributed to every member of the internal auditing function, members of the audit committee, and key members of management. This educates key members of the organization about the functions of internal auditing. External providers of internal auditing services should use an engagement letter in lieu of a charter to document their relationship with management.

Regardless of what written form the charter takes, it should encompass the following issues:

1. Purpose of the charter
2. Nature of internal auditing
3. Objective of internal auditing
4. Scope of internal auditing
5. Responsibility and authority of internal auditing

6. Responsibility for detecting fraud
7. Performance standards
8. Approval by CEO or official with equivalent authority

The sample internal auditing charter shown in Figure 15.1 covers each of these points.

Figure 15.1

Sample Internal Auditing Function Charter

Introduction

The purpose of this charter is to establish the internal auditing function's position within this organization; authorize its access to records, personnel, and physical properties relevant to the performance of audits; and define the scope of internal auditing activities.

Nature of Internal Auditing

Internal auditing is an independent, objective assurance and consulting activity designed to add value and improve an organization's operations. It helps an organization accomplish its objectives by bringing a systematic, disciplined approach to evaluate and improve the effectiveness of risk management, control, and governance processes.

Objective of Internal Auditing

The objective of internal auditing is to assist members of the organization in the effective discharge of their responsibilities. To this end, internal auditing furnishes the members with analyses, appraisals, recommendations, counsel, and information concerning the activities reviewed. The auditing objective includes promoting effective control at reasonable cost.

Scope of Internal Auditing

The scope of internal auditing encompasses the examination and evaluation of the adequacy and effectiveness of the organization's system of internal control and the quality of performance in carrying out assigned responsibilities. The scope of internal auditing includes:

- Reviewing the reliability and integrity of financial and operating information and the means used to identify, measure, classify, and report such information.
- Reviewing the systems established to ensure compliance with those policies, plans, procedures, laws, and regulations that could have a significant impact on operations and reports, and determining whether the organization is in compliance.
- Reviewing the means of safeguarding assets from various types of losses, such as those resulting from theft, fire, improper or illegal activities, and exposure to the elements and, as appropriate, verifying the existence of such assets.
- Appraising the economy and efficiency with which resources are employed.
- Reviewing operations or programs to ascertain whether results are consistent with established objectives and goals and whether the operations or programs are being carried out as planned.
- Consulting engagements as identified by management and approved by the audit committee, provided the internal auditing function has the competency and the resources to complete the consulting engagement without significantly impacting the organization's auditing plan.

Responsibilities and Authority of Internal Auditing

The Chief Audit Executive (CAE) is responsible for carrying out an internal auditing program as previously described. This responsibility includes coordinating internal auditing activities with the organization's external auditors and others to best achieve the auditing objectives and those of the organization.

¶ 1502

In carrying out this mission, the CAE is given access to all records, personnel, and physical properties relevant to the performance of audits. Any instances in which records, personnel, or physical properties relevant to an audit are not made available to the CAE upon his or her request will be reported to the CEO and the board of directors (or designated subcommittee).

The CAE reports directly to the CEO with direct access to the board of directors or designated subcommittee (audit committee). The CAE will submit annually to the CEO for approval and to the board of directors (or its designated subcommittee) for its information a summary of the department's audit work schedule, staffing plan, and financial budget.

The CAE, upon the completion of an audit, will discuss the audit findings with the member of management responsible for the area audited. A written report of the audit findings and the manager's response will be sent to the CEO within 30 days of the audit's completion (with a copy to the chair of the audit committee). Follow-up procedures will vary depending on the severity of the audit findings, but will occur within one year at the latest.

Fraud

Deterrence of fraud is the responsibility of management. The internal auditing function is responsible for examining and evaluating the adequacy and the effectiveness of management's actions to fulfill this obligation.

Internal auditors should have sufficient knowledge of fraud to be able to identify indicators that fraud might have occurred. If significant control weaknesses are detected, additional tests conducted by internal auditors should include ones directed toward the identification of other indicators of fraud.

Internal auditors are not expected to have knowledge equivalent to that of a person whose primary responsibility is to detect and investigate fraud. Also, auditing procedures alone, even when carried out with due professional care, do not guarantee that fraud will be detected. The internal auditing function will assist in the investigation of fraud in order to:

- Determine whether controls need to be implemented or strengthened
- Design audit tests to help disclose the existence of similar frauds in the future
- Help meet the internal auditor's responsibility to maintain sufficient knowledge of fraud

A written report issued at the conclusion of the investigation will include all findings, conclusions, recommendations, and corrective action taken.

Performance Standards

Internal audits will be performed according to organizational policy, the Standards as issued by the IIA, and good business sense.

Signature _____   Date _____

  Chief Executive Officer,

  Sample Company, Inc.

Signature _____   Date _____

  Chairman of Audit Committee

  Sample Company, Inc.

¶ 1502

First in importance is that the internal auditing function should report to an official within the organization who can implement its findings. Ideally, this usually means reporting functionally to the CEO and administratively to a vice-presidential level official, and having access to the audit committee or board of directors. The internal auditing function should not report to the chief financial officer because many of the audits are performed in areas under this official's responsibility. In addition, the internal auditors may be perceived as accounting or finance types and lack credibility with operational personnel in the organization.

Another key issue is the scope or types of audits that the internal auditing function will perform. Ideally, the CAE should determine the types of audit to be performed—operational, compliance and financial audits or any combination of the three—based on his or her professional judgment. However, some boards and management teams do not believe that their internal auditing function have the expertise to perform some of these types of audits. These leaders may limit the types of audits to be performed. Such limitations are fine as long as they are so stated in the internal auditing function's charter. In addition, the CAE may over time succeed in convincing management to remove such limitations.

The last issue needing clarification concerns the internal auditing function's responsibility for fraud. Numerous studies have documented the inability of internal audits to uncover fraud. There are numerous, well-justified reasons for this. Therefore, the charter should contain language stating that internal auditors cannot be expected to uncover all instances of fraud, but that when fraud is uncovered the internal auditing function will conduct a full investigation to aid in the recovery of lost assets, the prosecution of perpetrators, and also to design controls to prevent similar instances of fraud in the future. The charter should be approved by senior management and submitted to the board for its acceptance. The CAE should review the charter at least annually to ensure that it still reflects the current conditions.

¶ 1503 Coordinating the Internal Auditing Function with Organizational Policies

The organization's policies and procedures will cover most organizational issues pertaining to the internal auditing function. However, there are some issues peculiar to an internal auditing function that the CAE will need to address. First, he or she needs to ensure that appropriate job descriptions for all levels of internal auditor (e.g., staff, in-charge, and management levels) are kept current. The CAE should pay particular attention to matching job requirements to qualifications concerning education and professional certification, as shown in Table 15.1.

Table 15.1

Job Requirements and Qualifications for Various Levels of Internal Auditors

Level	Requirements	Qualifications
Staff	Conduct audit tests	Bachelor's degree
		1–3 years audit experience
In-charge	Supervise Audits	Bachelor's degree
		Professional certification
		3-5 years audit experience
Manager	Manage several audits concurrently	Masters degree
		Professional certification
		5–10 years audit experience
Chief auditing executive	Manage the internal auditing function	Masters degree
		Professional certification
		11+ years audit experience

The CAE's second key action should be to ensure that professional staff receives an adequate amount of continuing education to enable it to perform scheduled audits and stay current with developments in the profession. Third, the CAE should support professional activities such as certification (CIA, CISA, CFE, etc.), and membership in professional societies (IIA, ISACA, ACFE, etc.). Fourth, the CAE should implement fair policies concerning business travel and overtime. Fifth, the professional staff should gain and maintain an awareness of ethics; the internal auditing function should have a procedure for resolving ethical challenges. Finally, and probably most importantly, the CAE should develop professional staff through a system of fair performance evaluation and mentoring.

¶ 1504 Interactions with the Organization's External Auditor

Internal audit functions can interact in any number of ways with the company's external auditors. At the lowest level, the internal auditing function can "loan" auditors to the external auditors. However, this is a less than perfect solution. The chief problem with this arrangement lies in the opportunity cost of not identifying cost savings because internal auditors were completing the financial audit. Furthermore, internal auditors tend to have more years of audit experience and education than their public accounting counterparts, and this can lead to friction. For example, many in-charges with an organization's external audit firm will be in their twenties and possess only a few years of auditing experience. Often these external auditors have difficulty supervising internal auditing staff members who are much older and better educated, with more experience. Many external auditors look down on internal auditors while many internal auditors don't place much value on the work performed by external auditors.

To promote a somewhat higher degree of cooperation, the CAE and the external audit partner can meet and agree to audit different locations within the organization. For instance, suppose an organization was composed of relatively independent districts or franchises. Then the external audit partner and CAE would divide up the district headquarters that each would audit. Although better than the first approach, this arrangement is less than perfect because it doesn't maximize the contribution that internal auditing can offer to the organization.

A preferable arrangement is shown Figure 15.2. It fully uses the contributions of both the internal and external auditors. In this arrangement the internal auditing function is responsible for operational and compliance audits, whereas the external auditor is responsible for the financial audit. Both groups share responsibility for risk assessment and the review of the organization's internal control structure. Internal auditors and external auditors need to foster mutual respect for the other's contributions and fully cooperate in serving the needs of the organization. Some activities that can foster an atmosphere of coordination and cooperation include:

- Holding joint planning meetings
- Sharing findings
- Reviewing each other's workpapers
- Attending audit committee meetings together

Finally, many company officials argue that their organization realizes substantial savings in external audit fees from using internal auditors to perform the annual financial audit. However, any cash savings thus realized must be weighed against opportunity costs of the operational audits not performed, the greater losses incurred by being in noncompliance with laws and regulations, or the failure to reveal fraud.

¶ 1504

Figure 15.2

Coordinated Audit Coverage Between Internal and External Auditors

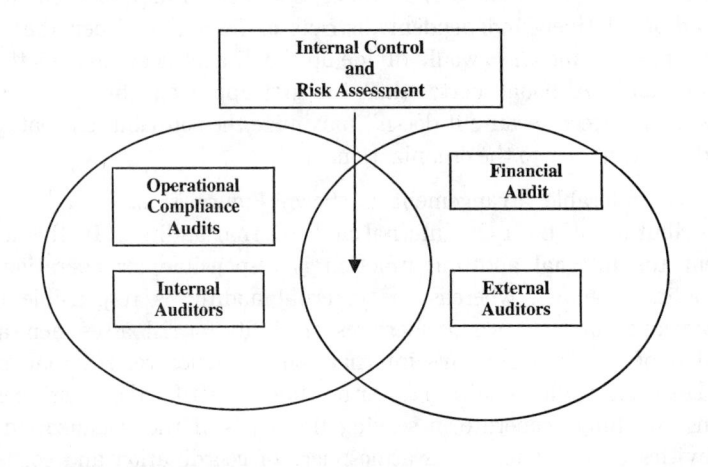

¶ 1505 Quality Assurance

For the internal auditing function to be successful, the CAE must establish a system to control the quality of the services that internal auditors perform. The traditional approach to quality control stressed supervision, internal review, and external review. Supervision meant explaining to subordinates the task to be performed, evaluating their progress, and giving them appropriate feedback as the task was performed. Periodically internal and external reviews were conducted to ensure that the internal auditing function complied with professional standards and that individual audits were performed correctly. The trouble with this system—and especially with the internal and external reviews—was that they took place after the delivery of services and their results could only affect future audits. Consequently, many internal auditing functions adopted a Total Quality Management (TQM) approach to controlling audit quality.

Under TQM, audit quality is assessed in terms of customer satisfaction, and performance measures are identified to measure customer satisfaction. Progress is tracked by observing steady improvement in the performance measures over time. Most internal auditing functions today track some performance measures. The CAE should adopt measures for each major internal auditing function: input, process, output, and overall management, as shown in Figure 15.3.

Figure 15.3

Internal Auditing TQM Process Model

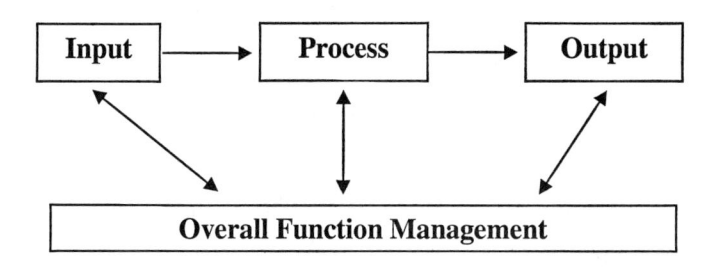

```
┌───────┐     ┌─────────┐     ┌────────┐
│ Input │ ──► │ Process │ ──► │ Output │
└───────┘     └─────────┘     └────────┘
     ▲            ▲              ▲
      ╲           │             ╱
       ╲          │            ╱
        ▼         ▼           ▼
      ┌──────────────────────────┐
      │ Overall Function Management │
      └──────────────────────────┘
```

Under a TQM system, the CAE adopts one or more performance measures for each of the four areas. To measure input, the CAE could choose average years of auditing experience for the audit staff or educational levels or certifications. Process could be measured using auditee satisfaction survey results. Output could be measured in terms of significant findings or the time required to release the report. Audit committee and management surveys could be used to measure overall audit function management.

CAEs should keep the following points in mind when adopting performance measures:

- Performance measures should not be selected and evaluated individually; they should be tied to the internal auditing function's mission and goals.

- Internal auditing function performance should be evaluated based on the four functions—input, process, output, and overall function management.

- Internal auditing function missions and goals should be stated as an integrated set of objectives and measures that describe long-term drivers of success.

- Key parties both outside and inside the internal auditing function (audit committee and management) should participate in the process of selecting performance measures.

CAEs should note that failure to adopt performance measures voluntarily may lead others to impose them on the internal auditing function.

The IIA recognized the importance of benchmarking when it launched the Global Auditing Information Network (GAIN) program to gather and distribute information to participating internal auditing functions on nu-

¶ 1505

merous benchmarking measures. In 1998, the IIA conducted a study[2] to determine which performance measures were preferred by CAEs. The CAEs participating in the study preferred the following measures:

- Auditee satisfaction survey results
- Percent of audit recommendations implemented
- Audit committee satisfaction survey results
- Audit committee importance of audit issue
- Management expectation of internal auditing
- Staff experience
- Training hours per internal auditor

Other measures receiving positive ratings included:

- Auditing viewed by the audit committee
- Auditor education levels
- CAE reporting relationships—functional
- Number of management requests
- Completed versus planned audits
- Number of process improvements

The 1998 study also broke down the internal auditing functions (input, processing, output, and management) into 16 performance areas that CAEs were asked to rank. The following performance areas received the highest rankings:

- Auditor quality
- Quality of findings
- Accuracy of reports
- Management satisfaction
- Standing with audit committee
- Auditee relations
- Audit committee effectiveness
- Timeliness of reports

---

[2] D.E. Ziegenfuss, *Using GAIN Performance Measures to Develop a Performance Index for Internal Auditing Organizations* (The Tidewater and New York Chapters, Institute of Internal Auditors, 1998). Reprinted with permission.

¶ 1505

The CAEs in the study consistently gave very low rankings to the following performance areas:

- Audit mix
- Compliance with audit plans
- Auditor quantity
- Quantity of findings

These results are intended to provide some guidance to CAEs in selecting performance measures or performance areas to use in evaluating their auditing functions.

¶ 1506 Outsourcing

Outsourcing in the context of an internal auditing staff is an arrangement for performance of internal auditing services by a party external to the organization. In the past, outsourcers performed audits that were beyond the ability of the internal auditing staff to perform. These included audits that required specialized skills or additional resources to complement the internal auditing function. Examples of specialized skills include inventory valuation experts, actuaries who could determine the reasonableness of pension expenses, financial experts who examined investment portfolios, and many more. Likewise, an internal auditing function might need outside assistance in coordinating a lengthy fraud investigation.

.01 Paradigm Shift from Internal Staff to Outsourcers

In general, these situations happened rarely or infrequently. However, during the 1990s, outsourcers took over entire internal auditing functions to the point that the threat of outsourcing entire auditing duties must be recognized and met by CAEs. Usually the best response involves meeting the needs of management and the audit committee by performing value-added audits and consulting engagements. On the other hand, many public accounting firms may find the performance of internal auditing services to be a lucrative addition to their repertoire of services for clients. Public accounting firms should be sensitive to potential independence problems in performing internal auditing for those clients for which the firm also performs the annual financial audit.

.02 Marketing Internal Auditing Services

Individuals wishing to perform internal auditing services should develop a marketing plan to identify potential clients and internal auditing services that could be performed. Clients that lack an internal auditing function would probably make the best initial contacts. All types of organizations (not-for-profit and government entities) should be included. The outsourcer should then contact key individuals such as the CEO or board members to conduct formal sales presentations.

¶ 1506.02

Once a steady practice has been developed, the outsourcer can then expand to handle large existing internal auditing functions. All outsourcing engagements should be documented with an executed engagement letter or contract.

¶ 1507 The Audit Committee

No discussion of managing internal auditing functions would be complete without covering the role of the audit committee in organizational governance. The audit committee is the subcommittee of an organization's board of directors charged with overseeing the organization's financial reporting and internal control processes. To be effective, the audit committee should be composed of outside directors (not employed by the organization). Several studies conducted during the 1980s and 1990s found that effective audit committees are the key ingredient in establishing the overall "tone at the top" or attitude toward internal controls. Audit committees govern management, the external auditors, and internal auditors.

In 1998, The U.S. Securities and Exchange Commission (SEC) with the New York Stock Exchange and NASDAQ exchanges sponsored "The Blue Ribbon Committee on Improving the Effectiveness of Corporate Audit Committees." Figure 15.4 lists the Blue Ribbon Committee's recommendations. In addition, Figure 15.5 presents a sample audit committee charter, and Figure 15.6, the current SEC regulations pertaining to audit committees.

In response to the financial reporting scandals, Congress passed the Sarbanes-Oxley Act of 2002. Section 301 of the Act requires the SEC to issue additional rules governing audit committees. These additional rules are presented in Figure 15.7.

CAEs should establish excellent working relationships with their organization's audit committee to ensure its support of the internal auditing function. The CAE should begin by evaluating the effectiveness of the audit committee by determining the extent to which it complies with the provisions of the Blue Ribbon Commission's recommendations and SEC regulations. Even though they apply only to publicly traded companies, many organizations recognize their merit and are voluntarily adopting their provisions. The CAE could possibly work with the audit committee chair, management, and the organization's external auditor to improve the committee's functioning. A good working relationship is particularly important if the organization is to properly address major fraud or illegal acts in the organization. For most organizations, it isn't a matter of *if* but *when* irregularities will occur; therefore, the organization must be prepared to properly address these issues *before* they occur.

¶ 1507

Figure 15.4

1999 Blue Ribbon Committee on Improving the Effectiveness of Corporate Audit Committees

Five Guiding Principles for Audit Committee Best Practices

Principle 1. The Audit Committee's Key Role in Monitoring the Other Component Parts of the Audit Process.

Principle 2. Independent Communication and Information Flow between the Audit Committee and the Internal Auditor.

Principle 3. Independent Communication and Information Flow between the Audit Committee and the Outside Auditors.

Principle 4. Candid Discussions with Management, the Internal Auditor, and Outside Auditors Regarding Issues Implicating Judgment and Impacting Quality.

Principle 5. Diligent and Knowledgeable Audit Committee Membership.

Recommendation 1

Both the New York Stock Exchange (NYSE) and the National Association of Securities Dealers (NASD) adopt the following definition of independence for purposes of service on the audit committee:

> Members of the audit committee shall be considered independent if they have no relationship to the corporation that may interfere with the exercise of their independence from management and the corporation.

Recommendation 2

The Audit Committee should be composed solely of independent directors.

Recommendation 3

At least three members of the audit committee should be financially literate.

Recommendation 4

The audit committee should adopt a formal written charter that has been approved by the full board and reviewed annually. This charter should specify the audit committee's responsibilities, including structure, processes, and membership requirements.

Recommendation 5

The SEC should adopt rules requiring the audit committee to disclose in its company's proxy statement whether a formal charter has been adopted and whether the audit committee met the charter's provisions. The charter should be disclosed in the proxy statement or the annual report at least once every three years or immediately following any significant amendment.

Recommendation 6

Specifically state in the Audit Committee Charter the following:

> The outside auditor is ultimately accountable to the board of directors and the audit committee as the representatives of shareholders, has the authority and responsibility to select, evaluate, and replace the outside auditor.

Recommendation 7

The audit committee charter should specify that the audit committee receive from the outside auditors a formal written statement delineating all relationships between the auditor and the company, and the audit committee is also responsible for actively engaging in a dialogue with the auditor with respect to any disclosed relationships or services that may impact their objectivity and independence.

Recommendation 8

GAAS be changed to require the outside auditor to discuss with the audit committee:

- The clarity of the company's financial disclosures

- Degree of aggressiveness or conservatism of the company's accounting principles and accounting estimates

- Other significant decisions made by management in preparing the financial disclosure and reviewed by the outside auditors

Recommendation 9

SEC should require companies to include a letter from the audit committee in the company's annual report and Form 10-K Annual Report disclosing whether or not, with respect to the prior fiscal year:

- Management has reviewed the audited financial statements with the audit committee and the outside auditors have discussed with the audit committee and the outside auditor's judgment of the quality of those principles

- The members of the audit committee have discussed among themselves the quality of those principles

- The audit committee believes the company's financial statements are fairly presented in conformity to GAAP.

Recommendation 10

The SEC requires a reporting company's outside auditor conduct a SAS 71 Interim Financial Review prior to the company filing its Form 10-Q. SAS 71 be amended to require the outside auditor discuss with the audit committee the matters discussed in AU Section 380, Communication with the Audit Committee prior to filing of the Form 10-Q:

- Significant Adjustments

- Management Judgments

- Accounting Estimates

- Significant New Accounting Policies

- Disagreements with Management

Source: Excerpted from the *Report and Recommendations of the Blue Ribbon Committee on Improving the Effectiveness of Corporate Audit Committees.* Copies of the entire report can be obtained form the public affairs offices of the NYSE of the NASD, or online at *www.nyse.com* or *www.nasd.com.*

¶ 1507

Figure 15.5

Sample Audit Committee Charter

The audit committee is a committee of the board of directors. Its primary function is to assist the board in fulfilling its oversight responsibilities by reviewing the financial information that will be provided to the shareholders and others, the systems of internal controls which management and the board of directors have established, and the audit process.

In meeting its responsibilities, the audit committee is expected to:

1. Provide an open avenue of communication between the internal auditors, the independent accountant, and the board of directors
2. Review and update the committee's charter annually
3. Recommend to the board of directors the independent accountants to be nominated, approve the compensation of the independent accountants, and review and approve the discharge of the independent accountants
4. Review and concur in the appointment, replacement, reassignment, or dismissal of the director of internal auditing
5. Confirm and assure the independence of the internal auditor and the independent accountant, including a review of management consulting services and related fees provided by the independent accountant
6. Inquire of management, the director of internal auditing, and the independent accountant about significant risks or exposures and assess the steps management has taken to minimize such risk to the company
7. Consider, in consultation with the independent accountant and the director of internal auditing, the audit scope and plan of the internal auditors and the independent accountant
8. Consider with management and the independent accountant the rationale for employing audit firms other than the principal independent accountant
9. Review with the director of internal auditing and the independent accountant the coordination of audit effort to assure completeness of coverage, reduction of redundant efforts, and the effective use of audit resources
10. Consider and review with the independent accountant and the director of internal auditing:
    (a) The adequacy of the company's internal controls including computerized information system controls and security
    (b) Any related significant findings and recommendations of the independent accountant and internal auditing together with management's responses thereto
11. Review with management and the independent accountant at the completion of the annual examination:
    (a) The company's annual financial statements and related footnotes
    (b) The independent accountant's audit of the financial statements and his or her report thereon
    (c) Any significant changes required in the independent accountant's audit plan

¶1507

(d) Any serious difficulties or disputes with management encountered during the course of the audit

(e) Other matters related to the conduct of the audit which are to be communicated to the committee under generally accepted auditing standards

12. Consider and review with management and the director of internal auditing:

    (a) Significant findings during the year and management's responses thereto

    (b) Any difficulties encountered in the course of their audits, including any restrictions on the scope of their work or access to required information

    (c) Any changes required in the planned scope of their audit plan

    (d) The internal auditing department budget and staffing

    (e) The internal auditing department charter

    (f) Internal auditing's compliance with The IIA's *Standards for the Professional Practice of Internal Auditing* (Standards)

13. Review filings with the SEC and other published documents containing the company's financial statements and consider whether the information contained in these documents is consistent with the information contained in the financial statements

14. Review with management, the independent accountant, and the director of internal auditing the interim financial report before it is filed with the SEC or other regulators

15. Review policies and procedures with respect to officers' expense accounts and perquisites, including their use of corporate assets, and consider the results of any review of these areas by the internal auditor or the independent accountant

16. Review with the director of internal auditing and the independent accountant the results of their review of the company's monitoring compliance with the company's code of conduct

17. Review legal and regulatory matters that may have a material impact on the financial statements, related company compliance policies, and programs and reports received from regulators

18. Meet with the director of internal auditing, the independent accountant, and management in separate executive sessions to discuss any matters that the committee or these groups believe should be discussed privately with the audit committee

19. Report committee actions to the board of directors with such recommendations as the committee may deem appropriate.

20. Prepare a letter for inclusion in the annual report that describes the committee's composition and responsibilities, and how they were discharged

21. The audit committee shall have the power to conduct or authorize investigations into any matters within the committee's scope of responsibilities. The committee shall be empowered to retain independent counsel, accountants, or others to assist it in the conduct of any investigation.

22. The committee shall meet at least four times per year or more frequently as circumstances require. The committee may ask members or management or others to attend the meeting and provide pertinent information as necessary.

¶ 1507

23. The committee will perform such other functions as assigned by law, the company's charter or bylaws, or the board of directors.
24. The membership of the audit committee shall consist of at least five independent members of the board of directors who shall serve at the pleasure of the board of directors. Audit committee members and the committee chair shall be designated by the full board of directors upon the recommendation of the nominating committee.
25. The duties and responsibilities of a member of the audit committee are in addition to those duties set out for a member of the board of directors.

Source: Price Waterhouse, *Improving Audit Committee Performance: What Works Best* (Altamonte Springs, Fla.: The Institute of Internal Auditors, 1993). Reprinted with permission.

Figure 15.6

SEC Rules for Audit Committees (Summary)

The new rules require the following:

- Companies' independent auditors review the financial information included in the companies' Quarterly Reports on Form 10-Q or 10-QSB prior to the companies filing such reports with the Commission;
- Extend the requirements of Item 302(a) of Regulation S-K (requiring at fiscal year end appropriate reconciliations and descriptions of any adjustments to the quarterly information previously reported in a Form 10-Q for any quarter) 12 to a wider range of companies;
- Require that companies include reports of their audit committees in their proxy statements; in the report, the audit committee must state whether the audit committee has:
    (i) reviewed and discussed the audited financial statements with management;
    (ii) discussed with the independent auditors the matters required to be discussed by Statement on Auditing Standards No. 61,14 as may be modified or supplemented; and
    (iii) received from the auditors disclosures regarding the auditors' independence required by Independence Standards Board Standard No. 1,15 as may be modified or supplemented, and discussed with the auditors the auditors' independence;
- Require that the report of the audit committee also include a statement by the audit committee whether, based on the review and discussions noted above, the audit committee recommended to the Board of Directors that the audited financial statements be included in the company's Annual Report on Form 10-K or 10-KSB (as applicable) for the last fiscal year for filing with the Commission;
- Require that companies disclose in their proxy statements whether their Board of Directors has adopted a written charter for the audit committee, and if so, include a copy of the charter as an appendix to the company's proxy statements at least once every three years;
- Require that companies, including small business issuers,16 whose securities are quoted on NASDAQ or listed on the American Stock Exchange ("AMEX") or New York Stock Exchange ("NYSE"), disclose in their proxy statements whether the audit committee members are "independent" as defined in the applicable listing standards,17 and disclose certain information regarding any director on the audit committee who is not "independent" (see Section III.D below);
- Require that companies, including small business issuers, whose securities are not quoted on NASDAQ or listed on the AMEX or NYSE disclose in their proxy statements whether, if they have an audit committee, the members are "independent," as defined in the NASD's, AMEX's or NYSE's listing standards, and which definition was used; and
- Provide "safe harbors" for the new proxy statement disclosures to protect companies and their directors from certain liabilities under the federal securities laws.

Source: U.S. Securities and Exchange Commission, Release No. 34-42266; File No. S7-22-99, RIN 3235-AA83, 17 CFR Parts 210, 228, 229, and 240.

Figure 15.7

Amendments to SEC Rules for Audit Committees Required by Sarbanes-Oxley Act of 2002 (Summary)

Audit Committees of publicly traded companies in the United States must comply with the following measures:

- Each member of the audit committee of the issuer must be independent as defined by SEC regulation, namely audit committee members cannot accept any payment for advising, consulting, or other work other than for being an audit committee member;

- The audit committee must be directly responsible for the appointment, compensation, retention, and oversight of the work of the public accounting firm engaged for the purpose of preparing or issuing an audit report or performing other audit, review, or attest services for the company, and each such public accounting firm must report directly to the audit committee;

- Each audit committee must establish procedures for the receipt, retention, and treatment of complaints regarding accounting, internal accounting controls, or auditing matters, including procedures for the confidential, anonymous submission by employees of concerns regarding questionable accounting or auditing matters;

- Each audit committee must have the authority to engage independent counsel and other advisors, as it determines necessary to carry out its duties; and

- Each issuer must provide appropriate funding for the audit committee.

Source: U.S. Securities and Exchange Commission, Release No. 33-8220 and 34-47654; File No. S7-02-03, RIN 3235-A175, 17 CFR Parts 228, 229, 240, 249 and 274.

¶1508 Summary

The chief auditing executive (CAE) manages the internal auditing function with the assistance and oversight of management and the audit committee. The six major responsibilities of a CAE are authorizing and organizing the internal audit function, performing risk assessment and scheduling audits, coordinating audit work with the organization's external auditors, coordinating internal auditing functions and organization policies, maintaining a quality control system, and preventing the outsourcing of the internal auditing function.

The internal auditors and external auditors interact in a number of ways, such as holding joint planning meetings, sharing findings, reviewing each other's workpapers, and attending audit committee meetings together. These activities can foster an atmosphere of coordination and cooperation between internal and external auditors.

The Total Quality Management approach for quality assurance has replaced the traditional approach to quality control. Quality is now assessed in terms of customer satisfaction, and performance measures are identified to measure customer satisfaction.

¶ 1508

Chapter 16

Scheduling and Performing the Internal Auditing Engagement

¶ 1601   Introduction
¶ 1602   Traditional Risk Assessment and Audit Scheduling
¶ 1603   Risk-Based Audit Planning
¶ 1604   The Individual Audit Assignment
¶ 1605   Fact-Finding Interviews
¶ 1606   Summary

¶ 1601 Introduction

Audits do not operate in a vacuum. They must be tied into the management of the internal auditing function. This chapter combines risk assessment and audit scheduling with the individual auditing engagement to emphasize the importance of linking these two topics. Internal auditors must understand the importance of this link to understand why a particular audit is being conducted. Outside auditors should also perform an organization-wide risk assessment to determine the audit needs of the client. One way of integrating macro and micro views of risk is for the internal auditing function to adopt a risk management perspective. The chapter presents the risk management approach after the traditional risk assessment approach.

Chapter 16 objectives:

- To identify how to do a traditional risk assessment and audit scheduling for an internal audit engagement (see ¶ 1601–1602).
- To understand risk-based audit planning (see ¶ 1603).
- To detail the four steps involved in the individual audit assignment (see ¶ 1604).
- To become familiar with the fact finding interviews (see ¶ 1605).

¶ 1602 Traditional Risk Assessment and Audit Scheduling

All managers establish goals and objectives, and then allocate scarce resources to meet those goals and objectives. In the context of an internal auditing function, this task of setting objectives begins with risk assessment

¶ 1602

and the development of an audit plan or schedule of audits. The chief auditing executive (CAE) should divide the organization into audit units. These may be organizational units (such as departments), functions, systems, policies and procedures, contracts, or accounts. Two key points need to be made: first, the universe of audit units must cover every aspect of the organization; and second, the audit units should be identified in such a manner to allow for efficient and effective audits. When audit units are not appropriately defined, the audit may require too many resources to be effectively managed or it may take too long to complete.

The next step for the CAE is to rank the audit units in terms of risk—the likelihood that an event or action may adversely affect the organization. Risk in the internal auditing context includes operational, compliance, and financial reporting risks. It is broader than the traditional definition of audit risk in terms of errors in the financial statements. Directly measuring risk is nearly impossible. Instead, CAEs rely on risk factors. Many risk factors are currently being used by CAEs, including:

- Ethical climate (compliance audits)
- Pressure on management to meet objectives (compliance, operational, financial audits)
- Competence of personnel (compliance, operational, financial audits)
- Adequacy of personnel (compliance, operational, financial audits)
- Integrity of personnel (compliance, operational, financial audits)
- Asset size (financial audits)
- Liquidity (financial audits)
- Transaction volume (financial audits)
- Financial and economic conditions (compliance, operational, financial audits)
- Complexity or volatility of activities (compliance, operational, financial audits)
- Impact of customers (operational audits)
- Impact of suppliers (operational audits)
- Impact of government regulations (compliance audits)
- Degree of computerized information systems (operational audits)

¶ 1602

- Geographical dispersion of operations (operational audits)
- Adequacy and effectiveness of the internal control system (compliance, operational, financial audits)
- Organizational change (operational audits)
- Operational change (operational audits)
- Technological change (operational audits)
- Economic changes (operational audits)
- Management judgments concerning accounting estimates (financial audits)
- Acceptance of audit findings and corrective action taken (compliance, operational, financial audits).[1]

The CAE should use extreme caution in choosing among risk factors to evaluate. First, a risk factor must be capable of being measured while the auditor executes the risk assessment. Some risk factors—adequacy of internal controls being one—can only be determined after the audit is completed. Second, values for the risk factor should be easy to gather or assess. For instance, determining the adequacy of personnel may be accomplished by reviewing personnel files, but this is an extremely time-consuming process. Third, the risk factor should differ among the auditable units. External factors such as economic conditions may affect the entire organization equally and would not be much help in ranking auditable units. Lastly, the risk factor should not cause embarrassment to the auditing function or potential auditees. Auditors may wish to avoid risk factors such as ethical climate or integrity of personnel, which may cause the CAE and potential auditees embarrassment when the CAE's risk assessment is discussed with upper management and the audit committee. Alternatively, the auditor may wish to focus on potentially less embarrassing factors that measure risk while showing the plant in a favorable light, such as competency of operations.

There is no established wisdom that identifies the appropriate number of risk factors to use. In general, the number of risk factors should not be too large or the risk assessment may become too cumbersome. On the other hand, too few risk factors may not totally measure risk. The risk factors chosen should also agree with the types of audits to be performed as shown in Figure 16.1. In other words, some risk factors (size of assets or amount of revenue) are acceptable for financial audits but not for operational audits or compliance audits, and vice versa.

---

[1] *Standards for the Professional Practice of Internal Auditing,* sec. 520.03.05, copyright 2001 by the Institute of Internal Auditors, Inc., 247 Maitland Avenue, Altamonte Springs, Florida 32710-4201 U.S.A. Reprinted with permission.

Figure 16.1

Internal Auditing Risk Assessment Model

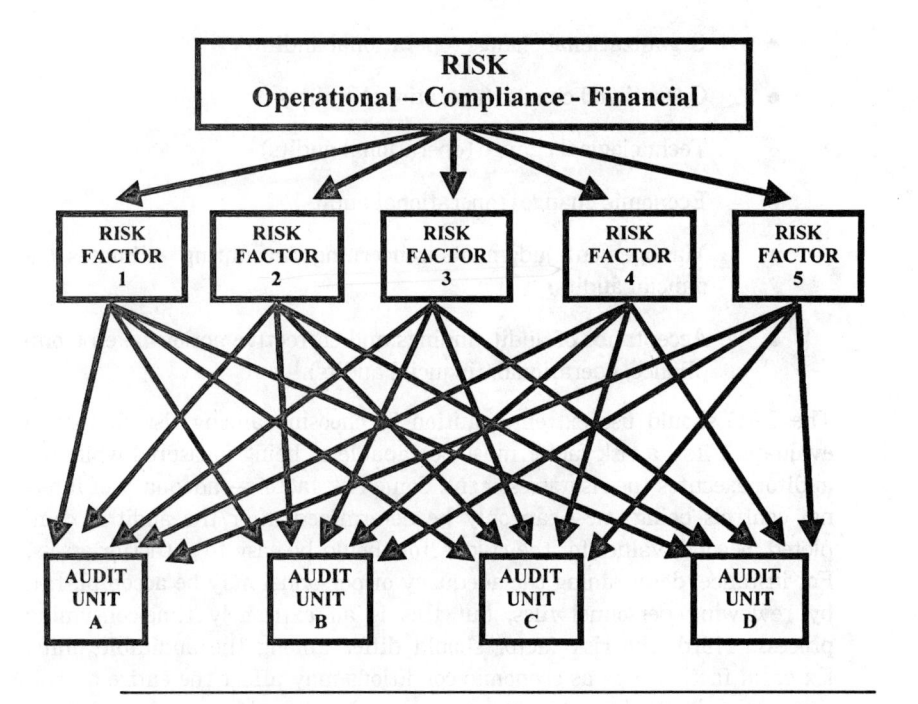

```
                    RISK
         Operational – Compliance - Financial

   RISK      RISK      RISK      RISK      RISK
  FACTOR    FACTOR    FACTOR    FACTOR    FACTOR
     1         2         3         4         5


   AUDIT     AUDIT     AUDIT     AUDIT
   UNIT      UNIT      UNIT      UNIT
     A         B         C         D
```

The CAE should also consider the relative importance of the risk factors. Some CAEs place differing weights on the risk factors they choose. Consider this scenario:

> A CAE uses five risk factors: organizational change, impact on customer, amount of transaction flow, degree of computerization, and time since last audit. The CAE then assigns 30 percent of the audit units' risk to the first risk factor, 30 percent to the second risk factor, but only 15 percent to each of the next two and 10 percent to the final risk factor.

Once the CAE has chosen the risk factors and determined their relative weights, the CAE should use them to rank the auditable units. The CAE does this by ranking the auditable units using the first risk factor, then the second risk factor and so on, until all the auditable units have been ranked according to all the risk factors.

Once the audible units are ranked, the CAE should estimate the resources (time and expenses) to complete the audit of each unit. The CAE should then establish a cutoff point that is a cumulative measure of risk factors used as a decision tool to determine which audit units should be

¶ 1602

examined. This cutoff point should take into consideration the total amount of resources available to the internal auditing department. Audits should be performed for those units ranked above the cutoff. The CAE should then prepare an audit plan scheduling those audits above the cutoff. The plan should be scheduled to reduce the impact on the auditee's operations. In other words, audits of operational units should be done during slack times rather than busy times. The CAE should present the annual audit plan to the official responsible for the internal auditing function for the official's approval and submit it to the audit committee or board of directors. On a periodic basis, the CAE should provide management and the audit committee with activity reports detailing the internal auditing function's progress in completing the annual audit plan and any deviations from it.

Figure 16.2 presents an example of an internal auditing function annual plan for a typical service organization. The following five risk factors and their relative weights were used to perform the risk assessment:

1. Customer impact (35%)
2. Complexity of operations (30%)
3. Organizational changes (15%)
4. Degree of computerization (10%)
5. Time since last audit (10%)

For simplicity, it was assumed that this auditing function operated with no expenses and that only one auditor year of labor was available.

Figure 16.2

Sample Internal Auditing Department Audit Plan

Panel One: Cover and Approval Sheet
20XX Annual Audit Plan
　　Submitted by:
　　Date:
　　Approved by:
　　Date:

Panel Two: Risk Analysis

Audit Unit	Customer Impact RF1 35%	Complexity of Operations RF2 30%	Organizational Changes 3 RF3 15%	Degree of Computerization RF4 10%	Time Since Last Audit RF5 10%	Total Risk Cols 1-5 100%	Budgeted Hours	Cumulative Hours
District Audits	5	3	5	5	1	4.00	240	240
Accounts Receivable	5	2	3	3	5	3.60	120	360
Billing	5	2	3	3	5	3.60	120	480
Purchasing	4	2	3	5	5	3.45	120	600
Information Technology	2	5	3	5	3	3.45	200	800
Cashiering	5	2	3	3	3	3.40	80	880
Physical Inventory	5	2	3	3	3	3.40	80	960
Safety	5	3	1	3	3	3.20	60	1020
Human Resources	3	3	5	3	1	3.10	120	1140
Contractor Audits	3	3	3	1	5	3.00	160	1300
Fleet Maintenance	5	2	1	3	1	2.90	60	1360
Personal Computer Security	2	3	3	5	3	2.85	160	1520
General Ledger	2	2	3	3	5	2.55	120	1640
Accounts Payable	2	2	3	3	5	2.55	200	1840
Check Processing	2	2	3	5	3	2.55	80	1920
Building Maintenance	3	2	1	3	1	2.20	60	1980
Executive Compensation	1	1	5	1	5	2.00	40	2020
Conflict of Interest Policy	1	1	5	1	5	2.00	40	2060
Officers' Expense Reports	1	1	5	1	5	2.00	40	2100

¶ 1602

Scheduling and Performing the Internal Auditing Engagement   **577**

Panel Three: Time Analysis

		Hours:	Percent:
Total Hours:	260 × 8 =	2080	100%
Administrative:			
Holidays	11 × 8 =	88	
Vacation	15 × 8 =	120	
Training		40	
Audit Committee Meetings		40	
Administrative		65	
Subtotal		353	17%
Audit Hours (See Audit Schedule):		1436	69%
Special Projects:		291	14%
Total Hours:		2080	100%

Panel Four: Audit Schedule

Quarter:	Audit:	Hours:
I.	District Audits	240
	Accounts Receivable	120
	Subtotal	360
II.	Billing	120
	Purchasing	120
	Information Technology (Start)	120
	Subtotal	360
III.	Information Technology (Finish)	80
	Cashiering	80
	Physical Inventory	80
	Safety	60
	Subtotal	300
IV.	Human Resources	120
	Contractor Audits	160
	Fleet Maintenance	60
	Subtotal	340
	Total	1360

¶ 1603 Risk-Based Audit Planning

The traditional risk assessment method suffers because it causes CAEs and their staffs to focus on the risk factors rather than the underlying risks resulting in the risk assessment not staying in tune with changes in the risks. Second, traditional risk assessment only focuses on risk during the organizational planning phase and does not filter down to the individual audit assignments where the emphasis becomes controls. For these reasons, many internal auditing functions adopted risk-based planning and audits. Figure 16.3 shows the steps in a risk based planning model: (1) risk identification, (2) risk assessment, (3) risk management strategies, and (4) risk communication. Note that each step is focused on the organization.[2]

Figure 16.3

Risk Management Based Audit Planning Cycle

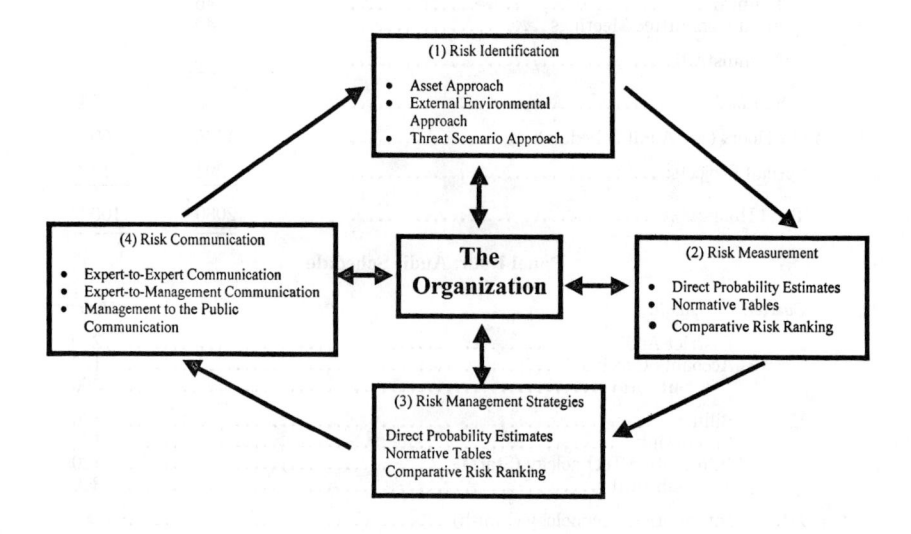

```
                    ┌─────────────────────────────┐
                    │  (1) Risk Identification    │
                    │  • Asset Approach           │
                    │  • External Environmental   │
                    │    Approach                 │
                    │  • Threat Scenario Approach │
                    └─────────────────────────────┘
                                 ↕
┌──────────────────────────┐  ┌──────────────┐  ┌──────────────────────────────┐
│ (4) Risk Communication   │  │     The      │  │ (2) Risk Measurement         │
│ • Expert-to-Expert       │↔ │ Organization │ ↔│ • Direct Probability Estimates│
│   Communication          │  │              │  │ • Normative Tables           │
│ • Expert-to-Management   │  └──────────────┘  │ • Comparative Risk Ranking   │
│   Communication          │         ↕          └──────────────────────────────┘
│ • Management to the      │
│   Public Communication   │
└──────────────────────────┘
                    ┌─────────────────────────────┐
                    │ (3) Risk Management Strategies│
                    │ Direct Probability Estimates │
                    │ Normative Tables             │
                    │ Comparative Risk Ranking     │
                    └─────────────────────────────┘
```

Source: Adapted from D. McNamee and G.M. Selim, *Risk Management: Changing the Internal Auditor's Paradigm,* copyright 1998 by the IIA Research Foundation, 247 Maitland, Altamonte Springs, Florida 32710-4201. Used with permission.

Internal auditors principally rely on three approaches to risk-based audit planning: the asset approach, the external environment approach, and the threat scenario approach. In using the asset approach, the internal auditor identifies each of the organization's assets and then determines what could cause the asset to be lost or materially impaired. The external environment approach examines the risk that economic, financial, physical, government regulation, technology, markets, customers/constituents, suppliers, and other similar forces may pose to the organization's ability to reach its objectives. The threat scenario approach relies on the internal auditor to develop narrative of likely scenarios for specific threats, such as natural disasters or illegal acts. Threat scenarios may be particularly beneficial in evaluating the risk posed by events that are infrequent but

---

[2] Adapted from D. McNamee and G.M. Selim, *Risk Management: Changing the Internal Auditor's Paradigm,* copyright 1998 by the IIA Research Foundation, 247 Maitland, Altamonte Springs, Florida 32710-4201.

¶ 1603

catastrophic. Any or all of these approaches can and should be adapted and integrated into the traditional risk assessment procedures.

Additional tools for measuring risks include direct probability estimates, normative tables, and comparative risk ranking. Direct probability estimates measure risks by assigning probabilities to an event's likelihood and consequences similar to the manner in which insurance underwriters assess risk. This method requires historical data that often are inaccurate predictors of future events. Normative tables measure and classify risk into categories using existing conditions as norms to judge the likelihood of predicted conditions or events. Comparative risk ranking achieves the same result as normative tables, but in a more direct manner by actually comparing risks directly against each other.

Once risks are identified, strategies should be employed to mitigate their effects. These strategies include controls (policies and procedures), sharing or transferring the risk (insurance), and diversifying and/or avoiding risk (changing operations such as reducing toxic waste produced). Auditors should choose the mix of strategies that are the most cost effective. Auditors should work with appropriate members of management and members of the audit committee throughout the entire process. Auditors should fully explore all the communication options, such as expert-to-expert, expert-to-management, and management-to-public communications in opening as many communication channels as possible within the organization.

In July 2003, the Committee of Sponsoring Organizations of the Treadway Commission (COSO) issued an exposure draft entitled, "Enterprise Risk Management Framework (ERMF)."[3] The ERMF basically applies the risk based auditing concepts described above to the COSO's Internal Control Framework. Both frameworks provide a good basis for audit planning and are further discussed in the Chapter 18 "Compliance Audits."

At least the CAE should position the internal auditing function as a key player in implementing the organization's enterprise risk management process and use its results to plan and schedule audit engagements. Next, the auditing function should ensure that individual business units have completed their portions of the organization's enterprise risk management process. If it has implemented enterprise risk management, then the auditing function should rely on the business unit's results to conduct the audit. If the business unit hasn't implemented enterprise risk management then the internal auditing function should assist it in implementing enterprise risk management.

---

[3] Committee of Sponsoring Organizations of the Treadway Commission, *Enterprise Risk Management Framework (Exposure Draft)*, July 2003.

¶ 1604 The Individual Audit Assignment

Numerous issues arise in executing a typical internal auditing engagement. The individual audit begins when the CAE assigns an in-charge auditor and ends with follow-up procedures. The in-charge auditor usually completes the following steps:

1. Set objectives for the audit
2. Conduct a preliminary survey
3. Assess risk and identify controls
4. Develop an audit program and budget
5. Perform the steps in the audit program
6. Review and assess audit results
7. Communicate audit results to appropriate parties
8. Conduct follow-up procedures after an appropriate period of time

The first four steps constitute the planning phase of the audit. Steps 5 and 6 are the fieldwork phase and the last two steps comprise the reporting and follow-up phases. Hence, the typical internal auditing assignment has four phases: (1) planning, (2) fieldwork, (3) reporting, and (4) follow-up. Of these, the planning phase is by far the most important. The other phases build on it, and if planning is not done properly the audit will be misdirected.

.01 Step 1: Setting Objectives for the Audit

The audit assignment begins when the CAE assigns the auditable unit to an in-charge auditor. At this time it is appropriate for the CAE and the in-charge auditor to discuss and reach agreement on the purpose and scope of the audit. Audit objectives depend on the type of audit being conducted. For a financial audit, the audit objective will be determining the fairness of accounting records of the auditable unit being audited. For a compliance audit, the audit objective will be determining that the auditable unit is in compliance with laws and regulations, or company procedures, or with contractual terms. For an operational audit, the audit objective will be determining that the auditable unit's operations are managed as effectively and efficiently as possible. Finally, many organizations will integrate all three types of audit into an audit assignment; thus, the overall audit objectives will include all of these. The CAE and in-charge auditor should also reach agreement on other issues concerning the overall direction of the audit, such as:

- The relationship of the auditable unit to the overall organization

- Key auditee personnel
- Impressions on how the auditable unit is performing
- The risk ranking for the auditable unit from the auditing department's annual risk assessment
- Recent changes affecting the auditable unit both from without and within
- Special areas of concern by management
- Sources of information on the auditee's operations
- The distribution of the audit report

Continued communication should be maintained between the CAE and the in-charge auditor throughout the audit. Therefore, it is important that an extremely good working relationship exist and that the in-charge auditor and the CAE are comfortable with each other's professional judgment. The in-charge auditor needs to know when to ask for assistance and when to make a decision without consulting the CAE. The CAE, on the other hand, needs to trust the judgment of the in-charge auditor.

.02 Step 2: Conduct a Preliminary Survey

Purpose. The purpose of the preliminary survey is to gain the information necessary to plan the audit. However simply stated, this can be a complex and exhausting process. The auditor must use professional judgment to identify and process information relevant to the audit from the large amount of information available. One way the in-charge auditor can manage this tremendous flow of information is to develop more specific audit objectives. Another approach is to limit or increase the scope of the audit if the auditable unit proves to be too big or too small.

The first meeting. The in-charge auditor should meet with auditee management shortly after the in-charge is assigned to the audit. This meeting is crucial not only because it functions as an icebreaker but also because first impressions will help to set the overall tone of the auditor-auditee relationship. Therefore, it is important that this meeting be professionally conducted. It should be conducted at the auditee location and be held mid-morning or mid-afternoon and never on the day preceding or following a holiday or weekend. There should be an equal number of auditee and auditor attendees, but the maximum number of attendees should not exceed 10. The meeting should begin with introductions. Small talk may be used to begin the meeting but guarded against subsequently; both parties should avoid potentially controversial topics. Likewise, the shift from small talk to business should be smooth and not abrupt. Auditee personnel are introduced first, followed by the auditor attendees. The in-charge auditor then explains the purpose of the audit and gives a brief description of how the audit will be conducted. This is done to allay any fears the auditee may

¶ 1604.02

have that this is other than a routine procedure or that fraud is suspected. Afterward, the in charge auditor may want to ask the auditee some general questions concerning the auditable unit's performance, recent changes, and areas of high risk. The meeting should not be allowed to last too long— an hour at the longest. A productive conclusion is to have the in-charge auditor obtain a list of auditee personnel who can be contacted for further information. Preparing a list of documents or information needed before the meeting is a good strategy. The meeting should be concluded in a businesslike but friendly manner.

Sources of information. In conducting the interview the auditor is limited only by his or her imagination in terms of potential sources of information for the preliminary survey. The internal auditing charter should authorize the auditor to gain unlimited access to all records and personnel maintained by the client. Having the authority to access records and personnel is one thing; actually doing so more often depends on the auditor's interpersonal skills. Most information will be obtained by reviewing documents, conducting interviews, or observing actual operations. The degree to which each source is relied on varies by audit type. For instance, an auditor will normally review more documents during a compliance audit than during an operational audit. Likewise, during an operational audit, the auditor generally relies more on interviewing and observation than during a compliance audit. Specific sources of information may include the following:

- Company policy and procedures manual
- Auditee policy and procedures manual
- Financial records and reports
- Prior audit workpapers if relevant
- Operational reports
- Plant tours
- Contracts
- Applicable laws and regulations
- Correspondence files
- Organizational newsletters
- Completed forms
- Websites

Specific questions to be answered. Specific questions to be answered during the preliminary survey include those pertaining to all types of audits and those pertaining to a financial, compliance, or operational audit. Questions pertaining to all types of audits include:

¶ 1604.02

Scheduling and Performing the Internal Auditing Engagement

- What function does this auditable unit perform?
- How well is it performing this function?
- How crucial is this function to the overall success of the organization?
- How risky is this auditable unit as determined by the auditing department's annual risk assessment?
- What is upper management's view of this auditable unit?
- What is the management style of this auditable unit?
- What are the auditable unit's strengths and weaknesses?
- What are the auditable unit's challenges and opportunities?
- What changes have occurred or will occur to this auditable unit?
- How positive is employee morale?
- What is employee turnover?
- What is the background and experience of the auditable unit's management?
- How does the auditable unit process information?
- How sophisticated is its use of technology?

Questions pertaining exclusively to financial audits include:

- How big is this auditable unit in terms of sales, assets, or overall budget?
- What is the nature of the transactions handled by the financial reporting system?
- What are the major financial reporting risks?
- What controls exist to address these risks?
- Do any factors that would increase the probability of fraud exist?
- How are transactions recorded and processed into financial statements?
- What is the degree of computerization in this process?

Questions pertaining exclusively to compliance audits include:

- What are the major legal exposures faced by the auditable unit?
- What policies and procedures exist to address these exposures?

¶ 1604.02

- Do major contracts exist with outside vendors to deliver goods or services for the auditable unit?

- Does the auditable unit possess a copy of the written contract for these services?

- Did the appropriate organizational officials review the contract before it was signed?

- How does the auditable unit control adherence to the terms and conditions of the contract by the vendor?

- What is the vendor's track record in completing the terms and conditions of the contract?

Questions pertaining exclusively to operational audits include:

- What is the auditable unit's mission?

- How has this mission been translated into goals and objectives?

- Do all employees understand the auditable unit's goals and objectives?

- How is the performance of the auditable unit measured and evaluated?

- Do controls exist to address the major threats to the auditable unit meeting its goals and objectives?

Documenting the results of the preliminary review. The audit team should organize the vast amount of information gathered during the preliminary interview into a through knowledge of the auditable unit. The audit team should document this understanding in their workpapers. The documentation may take the form of narratives, flowcharts, photographs, company records, and even videos. The audit team should use the form or forms of documentation that is most suitable for the information being documented. For example, narratives are quick and easy to write and are suitable for relatively simple and straightforward operations. However, flowcharts are more appropriate for more complex and involved operations, particularly when many parties handle a transaction or operation. Videos are appropriate in documenting operations or actual conditions such as unsafe or dirty work areas.

.03 Step 3: Assessing Risk and Identifying Controls

The preliminary survey should result in a clear and complete understanding of the auditable unit. The in-charge auditor should use the results of the preliminary survey to identify major risks or threats that could prevent the auditable unit from meeting its goals and objectives. This risk assessment is similar to the one performed by the CAE for the entire organization except that this one is focused within the auditable unit and is

¶ 1604.03

a little more informal because risk factors are not developed and the relative riskiness of the threats is not determined. Rather, the in-charge usually ensures that adequate controls exist to address each threat. The in-charge should develop audit findings for unaddressed threats and design tests for the controls addressing significant risks.

.04 Step 4: Developing an Audit Program and Budget

The in-charge auditor should document the results of the risk assessment by developing a list of audit findings, an audit program, and a budget. The list of audit findings will be discussed in Chapter 16 because it is part of the reporting process. The audit program is a step-by-step description of the audit procedures to be performed during the fieldwork (evidence gathering) portion of the audit. It is necessary because it provides documentation of the audit work performed and direction to assist auditors. The audit program should be organized by audit objective. The proper way to develop an audit program is to first develop audit objectives, then to identify the type and amount of audit evidence needed to meet the audit objectives, and finally to determine the appropriate audit procedures that will gather the type and amount of audit evidence needed.

The in-charge auditor should use the audit program to produce a budget or estimate of the resources needed to complete the audit. Most of the resources will consist of time spent by the audit team in completing the audit program and can prove extremely difficult to estimate given the unique nature of most internal audit assignments. Past experience may not be much help either. The best method of producing a good estimate is to use the audit program, estimating the time needed to complete each of its steps, and then summing the time needed for all the steps. Other costs that may have to be estimated include travel costs to distant locations, computer processing costs, specialists' costs, and special materials costs. The resulting audit program and budget should be discussed and approved by the CAE before the commencement of the fieldwork.

The relationships among operating objectives, operating procedures, audit objectives, audit procedures, and audit evidence are shown graphically in Figure 16.4 and discussed here.

Figure 16.4

Audit Program Development

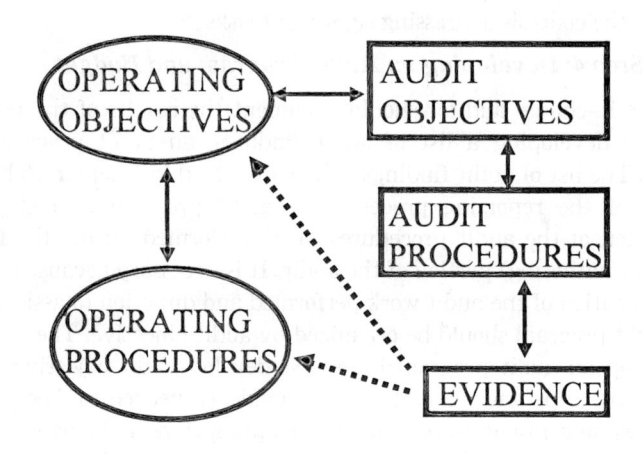

```
    OPERATING  ←——→  AUDIT
    OBJECTIVES        OBJECTIVES
        ↕                 ↕
        │             AUDIT
        │             PROCEDURES
        ↓                 ↕
    OPERATING  ←·····  EVIDENCE
    PROCEDURES
```

Operating objectives. Operating objectives are the results sought by operating managers. For example, a personnel manager may have the operating objective to fill personnel vacancies in the organization within 60 days of being notified of a vacancy by a line manager. Operating objectives should agree and support the auditee's mission and ultimately the organization's mission. In addition, operating objectives should be clearly written and measurable.

Operating procedures. Operating procedures ensure that the operating objectives are met. A personnel function serves as an example: All personnel positions will have job descriptions and all advertised openings will agree with their positions' job descriptions.

Audit objectives. Audit objectives translate the overall purpose of the audit into specific measurable outcomes. Audit objectives should relate to each operating objective of the auditee. Auditors use audit objectives to determine whether the auditee's operating objectives are being met. Audit objectives are the issues that the audit seeks to address. For example, advertising openings using the same personnel function: Ensure that a job description exists for every position. Ensure that all agree with their positions' descriptions.

Audit procedures. Audit procedures are the means of obtaining the evidence required to meet the audit objectives. Audit procedures are phrases using action verbs because they describe activities auditors perform. Common audit procedures include:

¶ 1604.04

- Observing— actively seeing auditee personnel perform their duties while relating what is being seen to other aspects of audit
- Questioning— verbal or written inquiry
- Analyzing— relating two or more kinds of audit evidence
- Verifying— comparing audit evidence from two sources
- Investigating— following up on unusual phenomena that come to the auditor's attention
- Evaluating— relating audit evidence to auditor selected criterion.

Using the personnel function again, an appropriate audit procedure to use to gather evidence for the two audit objectives would include verifying that the content of personnel ads agrees with job descriptions.

Audit evidence. Audit evidence is the information auditors use to address audit objectives and, indirectly, operating procedures. Audit evidence must be sufficient (a quantity sufficient to persuade the auditor) and competent (appropriate quality, free from bias, objective, and free from bias). The auditor's professional judgment, knowledge of similar audits, and common sense determine the amount and type of audit evidence to be obtained during the audit. Types of audit evidence include:

- **Physical evidence,** gathered by one of the five senses: sight, touch, taste, hearing, and smell
- **Testimonial evidence,** gathered from statements made by auditees or third parties
- **Documentary evidence,** from records whether in paper or electronic format
- **Analytical evidence,** gathered by comparing two or more measures or amounts

Auditors are becoming increasingly skeptical of documentary evidence because of the proliferation and quality of document scanning and altering software that can make counterfeit copies of virtually any document. Auditors are coming to relying on analytical evidence to give them an indication whether a particular transaction or activity makes common sense. Using the personnel function example one last time: An auditor would most likely rely on documentary evidence such as copies of the printed personnel ads and the job descriptions maintained by the personnel department to verify that the content of personnel ads agrees with job descriptions.

¶ 1604.04

.05 Step 5: Performing the Steps in the Audit Program

The audit fieldwork or evidence gathering phase of the audit should begin immediately after the audit program and budget are approved by the CAE. The in-charge auditor should ensure that all steps in the audit program are completed in a businesslike manner. The focus of this phase is the reaction of the audit team to evidence that appears to contradict the understanding gathered during the planning phase. Examples include a control that is not functioning, discrepancies in an account balance, or an overpayment to a vendor. Each contradiction or discrepancy must be fully investigated to determine its cause. The in-charge should always be alert to the possibility of fraud and, hence, should not be too quick to dismiss any discrepancy, no matter how insignificant it may appear. Likewise, budget overruns should be discussed and evaluated with the auditors responsible to determine the cause or causes of the overrun. The discussion should be centered on improving future audits and not on placing blame and punishing the "guilty." Such an unconstructive attitude only causes audit assistants to hide or not investigate potentially significant findings. The in-charge and CAE can also prevent most budget overruns by constantly evaluating assistants' progress in completing the audit. This evaluation may involve daily progress reports to keep the audit work flowing.

.06 Step 6: Reviewing and Assessing Audit Results

The in-charge auditor should review and assess results as the audit team uncovers discrepancies and completes the audit program. The in-charge should determine whether more work is necessary to fully understand the discrepancy's cause. The audit team should discuss its progress periodically in private away from auditee personnel. This can be accomplished during lunch or back in the audit department offices. Precautions against eavesdropping should be taken if the discussion occurs in a restaurant. It should be kept in mind that the purpose of this discussion is to determine the appropriate response to the discrepancy and may involve a suspicion of fraud. In other circumstances the audit team's initial findings may prove foolish or unwarranted. In both cases, the audit team's image or effectiveness may be seriously compromised if the contents of the discussion are shared with the auditee. Discrepancies are best discussed with lower level personnel to gather understanding of their causes. Additional discussions should occur with less conflict with higher-ranking personnel.

Periodically, the in-charge auditor should report the results of the audit to the CAE. This will allow him or her to suggest alternative procedures to the in-charge but also to remain in contact with the audit team. At the completion of the fieldwork, the in-charge auditor should perform one final review of the audit findings and reach an overall conclusion concerning the auditable unit. The CAE should concur with the in-charge's overall conclusion or know the reasons for any difference of opinion.

¶ 1604.05

.07 Step 7: Communicating Audit Results to Appropriate Parties

This step is covered in the next chapter.

.08 Step 8: Conducting Follow-up Procedures after Appropriate Period of Time

The CAE should schedule a follow-up audit after the auditee management has had an appropriate time period to address the issues in the audit report. This may be anywhere from six months for audits that did not identify many issues to a year or two years for audits that identified many or difficult issues. Regardless of the interval until such follow-up is performed, its purpose is to determine the extent to which the auditee has addressed the issues in the audit report. It is therefore vital that the auditee's response to listed remedies actually addresses the cause of the issue in the audit report and not the symptom. The in-charge and the CAE must ensure handling of the root cause when the auditee response to the audit report is received; failure to ensure this compromises the effectiveness of follow-up procedures. The in-charge performs steps 1 through 8, except that the audit objective for the follow-up audit becomes determining the implementation of the actions that the auditee proposed in addressing the audit issues.

¶ 1605 Fact-Finding Interviews

Internal auditors conduct multiple fact-finding interviews during the course of a typical audit assignment. The success of the audit often depends on the ability of the auditor to successfully carry out fact-finding interviews. In addition, the overall reputation of the internal auditing function in the organization is determined by the give and take between an auditor and auditee during fact-finding interviews. Therefore, it is important to discuss fact-finding interviews at this point in the chapter.

The auditor should exercise caution in scheduling the interview, calling the interviewee well in advance. If immediate contact isn't made, the auditor should persevere, stating the purpose of the interview when the interviewee is finally contacted. The interviewee should be told what records are needed. The time for the interview should be mutually convenient. The auditors should aim for one-to-one interviews, in the interviewee's office. Again, the parties should avoid the hours right before and after lunch and on the last hour of Friday or the day before a holiday or vacation.

In preparing for the interview, the auditor should keep these tips in mind:

- Do your homework!
- Know whom you are interviewing.

- Be aware of recent or proposed changes affecting the interviewee's operation.
- Determine the objectives of the interview.
- Prepare an informal agenda.
- Do a walk-around if possible.

Auditors often have difficulty in opening an interview or "breaking the ice." Some "ice breaking " tips include the following:

- Meet the interviewee before the interview.
- Always arrive on time.
- Start the interview in a friendly manner.
- Recognize the interviewee's feelings.
- State the purpose of the interview.
- Minimize the small talk.
- Make the transition into interview as smooth as possible.

In conducting the interview, an auditor should pose different types of questions. Open-ended questions allow the interviewee to think before answering and provide the auditor with an opportunity to evaluate the interviewee. An example of an open ended question is, "Can you tell me how your department meets its mission?" The auditor should then follow-up the open-ended question with a close-ended question (a question requiring a yes or no answer).

The auditor should use contrasting tones in his or her voice when asking questions and stay relaxed, thinking through questions before asking them. Simple and familiar works best. The auditor shouldn't stare, but maintain eye contact and give the interviewee time to respond. The auditor should be alert to negative reactions but maintain control even if the interviewee becomes abusive. The interviewee should not be interrupted nor should his or her body language be misinterpreted.

Distractions are nearly always present during an interview, and auditors cannot allow them to ruin it. Common distractions include:

- The other person's appearance, mannerisms, speech, or body odor
- External factors such as noise, temperature, light, and moisture
- The other person's speech pattern
- Letting other subjects crowd your mind
- Becoming angry or upset
- Thinking of the next question

¶ 1605

Distractions can be mitigated by looking at the person speaking, sitting up and being alert, hearing the other person out, listening to what is being said, and giving normal feedback to the other person.

The auditor should occasionally reflect on and restate the key points covered during the interview. The auditor should have the interviewee repeat an answer if he or she doesn't understand the response, asking for concrete examples and trying to distinguish between opinion and fact. The auditor should ask the interviewee to define unclear terms such as "important," and be wary of answers that contain sweeping generalizations, are too pat and smoothly stated, and contain many unfamiliar or complex terms that the auditor barely understands.

Note taking should be minimal during the interview, with the subject granting the auditor permission to take notes. Recording only the essence—not verbatim testimony—is preferable, and the auditor should not use a formal looking document. The auditor's second role during note taking is to keep the conversation going, by keeping a relaxed and interested posture while reading back factual notes periodically. The interviewer should be careful in recording comments because some people can read upside down. Finally, a good practice is to review all notes, in a secure location, immediately after the interview ends.

Auditors should close fact-finding interviews cordially, making future inquiries possible and starting a good working relationship with the auditee and staff. Some tips for closing the interview include:

- Briefly summarize the understanding of what the interviewee said.
- Ask the interviewee whether there is any additional information to offer.
- If time has elapsed since an initial session, schedule another interview.
- Leave an opening for additional interviews or questions.

The auditor should rerecord and supplement descriptions of the key points covered during the interview as soon after the interview closes as possible. A formal document can be generated while the auditor looks for inconsistencies within notes. This file document should use clear and precise language and not cite the interviewee out of context. An ideal interview summary concentrates on the facts.

¶ 1605

¶ 1606 Summary

This chapter combines risk assessment and audit scheduling with the internal audit engagement to emphasize the importance of linking these two topics. The CAE should use extreme caution in choosing among risk factors to evaluate. The risk factor must be capable of being measured while the auditor executes the risk assessment. Values for the risk factor should be easy to gather or access. The risk factor should differ among the auditable units. Lastly, the risk factor should not cause embarrassment to the auditing function or potential auditees.

The internal audit begins when the CAE assigns an in-charge auditor and ends with follow-up procedures. The in-charge auditor usually completes the following steps: setting up objectives for the audit, conducting a preliminary survey, assessing and identifying controls, developing an audit program and budget, performing the steps in the audit program, reviewing and assessing the audit results, communicating audit results to appropriate parties, and conducting follow-up procedures after an appropriate period of time.

Some tips for closing a fact finding interview are briefly summarizing the understanding of what the interviewee said, asking the interviewee whether there is any additional information to offer, scheduling another interview if time has elapsed since an initial session, and leaving an opening for additional interviews or questions.

Chapter 17

Reporting Internal Audit Assignment Results

¶ 1701   Introduction
¶ 1702   The Reporting Process
¶ 1703   The Report Format
¶ 1704   Individual Audit Findings
¶ 1705   Editing and Proofreading the Report
¶ 1706   Sample Report
¶ 1707   Summary

¶ 1701 Introduction

How does an internal auditor know whether he or she effectively communicates the results of an audit assignment? The auditee enthusiastically implements the findings and may even compliment the auditor. On the other hand, an auditor can tell that he or she was ineffective if the auditee does not implement the findings or implements them in a half-hearted manner and begins a hate campaign against the internal auditor.

The audit report is the principal product of the audit assignment and, as such, is the one element of the audit that will face the most scrutiny—hence, the importance of producing well crafted audit reports that are well received by auditees, upper management, and the audit committee. After all, the essence of the internal auditor's job is to initiate change with as little organizational ill will as possible.

An auditor never knows who will be reading an audit report. An audit report that is quickly written to meet a deadline may look extremely unprofessional to a reader years later who is unaware of the circumstances surrounding its drafting. This experience can be similar to going back and reading one's college or high school research reports. The point here is that audit reports must stand the passage of time.

Each internal auditing engagement has unique findings; therefore, each internal auditing report must be written to fit the particular engagement. This fit is much more difficult to achieve than the task faced by external auditors in placing a standard opinion on a set of financial statements. Standard language can only be used sparingly if the audit report is objective, clear, concise, constructive, and timely.

¶ 1701

This chapter provides some guidance for effectively communicating internal audit results. First, the reporting process is described. Next, the chapter examines the actual audit report itself and the content and organization of individual audit findings. The chapter concludes with editing and proofreading tips.

Chapter 17 objectives:

- To describe the internal audit reporting process (see ¶ 1701–1702).

- To become familiar with the internal audit report format (see ¶ 1703).

- To understand the content and organization of individual audit findings (see ¶ 1704).

- To recognize the importance of editing and proofreading the report (see ¶ 1705).

¶ 1702 The Reporting Process

Audit reports are a product of the internal auditing function. The chief auditing executive (CAE) should constantly evaluate the impact that the entire internal auditing process has on the reports produced by the department. For instance, the internal auditing charter should list the types of audits the internal auditing organization is permitted to perform. The results of an operational audit should be reported differently than the results of a financial or compliance audit. The internal auditing charter should also specify the distribution list for internal audit reports. Internal auditors should write reports to match readers'/officials' preferences concerning organization, format, and style.

In performing the annual risk assessment and establishing the audit schedule, the CAE influences the subsequently written audit reports in terms of audience (auditee management), size (auditee size), and timing (schedule). Finally, the audit team in performing the individual audit assignment influences the audit reports in terms of content (audit findings), style (initial draft), and initial reception by the auditee. The CAE should regularly ask auditees, upper management, and audit committee members for their comments and suggestions for improving the reporting process. The CAE should design a process that is fair to the auditee but produces timely reports for upper management and the audit committee. The CAE should ensure that due process is followed, allowing auditees several opportunities to voice their views of audit findings before the final report is issued.

The reporting process begins when the initial finding is uncovered. The auditor uncovering the finding should draft a complete description of the finding both in the area of the workpapers pertaining to the area being audited and in the part of the workpapers controlling all the comments from the audit. The auditor should discuss the finding with the in-charge auditor and other members of the audit team if appropriate. Following this discussion, the audit finding will be either accepted as is, dropped because it is weak and unsupportable, revised, or investigated further. The finding should also be discussed with the auditee on an informal basis. The resulting discussion will give the audit team the auditee's initial feelings concerning the finding. This is the best time for the auditor and auditee to discuss an audit finding and to revise or drop audit findings with a minimum of conflict and embarrassment.

At the completion of fieldwork, the in-charge should review all the audit findings produced during the audit process and write a final report draft. The CAE should then review the final report. The in-charge should formally present the final report draft to the auditee in an exit interview. The in-charge should send the final report draft to the auditee several days before the exit meeting to allow him or her time enough to prepare a response.

At the exit meeting, the in-charge should present the findings in a professional manner using a conversational tone. The in-charge should constantly record and monitor the auditee's response to individual audit findings and the overall report format. If the report is written and presented properly, the auditee will undoubtedly agree to most of the findings without significant modifications. However, valid disagreements may and probably will arise. The auditor must handle the situation in the best manner possible by agreeing to disagree. The in-charge must remain in control of the exit interview even if the auditee becomes upset and insulting. The in-charge must exercise the utmost self-control and tact in dealing with an upset auditee.

Once the exit interview is completed, the in-charge auditors should revise the report one last time and submit it to the CAE, who then formally issues the final report to the appropriate officials within the organization. The auditee should be given a reasonable amount of time to reply to the final report. The CAE and in-charge should review the response by the auditee for reasonableness. The CAE and in-charge may have to rebut the auditee response to upper management or the audit committee. Hopefully, those instances will be rare because of the potential for disaster to both sides. Needless to say, only the most significant findings should be allowed to be aired at this level of the organization. Regardless of whose view ultimately prevails, both sides lose. Upper management will conclude that the internal auditor lacks the power of persuasion and proper judgment to resolve the issue. Upper management will view the auditee as trying to get away with something by abusing the auditor or lacking the business skills to see the merit of the auditor's proposals.

¶ 1702

¶ 1703 The Report Format

The CAE determines the overall appearance and organization for internal audit reports issued. The CAE should not determine this in isolation but should rely on the comments and suggestions of the audit staff, upper management, and the audit committee members. The report must look as professional as possible for obvious reasons. It is the only product produced by the internal auditing function that is seen. It also competes in appearance with the organization's external auditor's written communications that are highly professional. The CAE should seriously consider hiring a professional writer(s) and/or graphic artist(s) to enhance the report's quality. The CAE can also improve the quality of the reports by seeking comments from upper management and the audit committee.

The CAE should use the best means of communicating the audit results. This may mean preparing a comprehensive written report for the auditee, management, audit committee, and external auditor. It might involve a PowerPoint presentation for the exit meeting; and a summary for upper management and the audit committee. The summary could be distributed by e-mail and posted on the organization's web page for key members of upper management and audit committee members. The purpose of doing this is not to punish or embarrass any auditee but to educate the entire organization of an internal control weakness or potential cost savings.

The report can take many forms but, in general, should begin with an executive summary, followed by a more detailed presentation of the audit findings, and concluding with supporting material such as appendices, tables, and graphs. Figure 17.1 presents this scheme. This enables the reader to understand the issues quickly and to decide whether more detail is needed. Thus, the reader is spared much time examining unwanted or unneeded detail.

Figure 17.1

Internal Audit Report Format

Organization

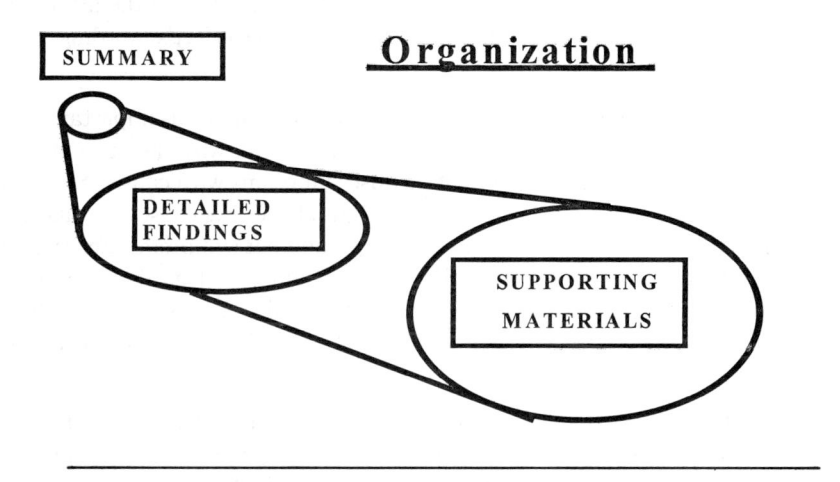

[Diagram showing SUMMARY, DETAILED FINDINGS, and SUPPORTING MATERIALS as overlapping/nested ellipses]

The executive summary should be no more than one page in length and should be able to be read within 30 minutes. Some auditing functions have even begun to rely on graphic displays to summarize audit results. For example, audit findings could be drawn as circles, with the size of the circle representing the seriousness of the findings. This is particularly useful when the report is presented on the Internet and the reader can click on each circle for more text and supporting detail.

¶ 1704 Individual Audit Findings

.01 Components

Audit findings generally have five components: criterion, condition, effect, cause, and recommendations. *Criterion* represent the standards used in evaluating the auditee. This is fairly straightforward for financial audits in that generally accepted auditing standards (GAAS) have been developed. The criterion is also relatively straightforward for compliance audits in that company policy, contracts, and laws/regulations are present. However, such is not the case with operational auditing, for which general unpublished principles of good business common sense are often relied upon.

The *condition* component should present the auditee's current state of affairs as found by the auditor. The condition should be written as objectively as possible. The auditor should avoid placing blame and restrict the use of inflammatory language. This usually means sticking to the facts and avoiding ambiguous or relative modifiers.

The *effect* is the result or possible result of the current condition. It provides the justification for the audit finding. Unless the effect is signifi-

¶ 1704.01

cant, the audit finding probably should not be made. However, the auditor should not inflate or magnify the significance of the audit finding to avoid losing credibility. On the other hand, the effect's seriousness should not be downplayed, or the auditee may not give the audit finding the attention it deserves. Rather, the auditor should match the effect's wording to the significance of the condition.

The *cause* component of the audit finding is almost as important as the effect. The cause component represents the reason why the current condition exists. The auditor must not confuse symptoms with causes. Symptoms are only the manifestation or outward signs of the true cause. The auditor is only effective if he or she addresses causes and not symptoms. For example, suppose the auditor observes that a large number of goods are routinely returned to vendors. This is a symptom. The real cause, as uncovered by the auditor upon further investigation, was the lack of clear specifications in purchase orders.

The *recommendation(s)* address the cause(s) and represents the auditor's prescribed actions for the auditee. The auditor can often rely on the auditee's expertise to develop recommendations. However developed, the auditor must ensure that the recommendations are clearly stated and address the cause and not symptoms. In addition, the recommendations must make common sense and be cost effective. The auditor should be careful in making recommendations because the auditee may take the auditor at his or her word. The old Chinese proverb, "Beware of what you wish because you may get it," can be rephrased, "Beware of what you recommend because the auditee may implement it." For example, suppose an auditor notices that the auditee has too many photocopying machines and recommends the auditee reduce their number. The auditee complies by eliminating all copiers except for two and requiring requisition forms for all copying. The resulting logjam is a nightmare and far offsets any cost savings realized from reducing the number of copiers.

.02 Order of Compenents in the Report

The order in which the five audit finding components are arranged in the report depends on the type of finding. Compliance audit findings usually begin with the criterion, then present the condition, and finally the recommendation, without cause and effect components.

Compliance Audit Finding Example

Company policy requires two bonded employees to open the mail and prepare the daily bank deposit [criterion]. On all four occasions when we observed the mail-opening procedures, only one unbonded employee opened the mail and prepared the bank deposit [condition]. We recommend that two bonded employees open the mail and prepare the daily bank deposit [recommendation].

Financial audit findings start with the effect and condition, then present the cause, criterion, and recommendation.

¶ 1704.02

Financial Audit Finding Example

Customer checks could be misplaced and not posted to customer accounts, resulting in angry customers [effect]. During our audit we observed that one employee opened the mail and prepared the daily bank deposit [condition]. Further inquiry revealed that all other employees were busy with other duties and were not free to open mail and prepare the daily bank deposit [cause]. However, good business practices require at least two employees open the mail and prepare the bank deposit [criterion]. We recommend that the department hire additional staff to enable two bonded employees to open the mail and prepare the daily bank deposit [recommendation].

Operational audit findings start with the recommendation, then present the criterion and condition, and finish with the effect and cause.

Operational Audit Finding Example

We recommend that cash receipts be deposited daily [recommendation]. Good business practices specify that cash receipts be deposited daily to improve liquid asset management [criterion]. During our audit we observed on several occasions that cash receipts were not deposited daily [condition]. Failure to deposit cash receipts daily delays the use of those funds and decreases the effectiveness of liquid asset management [effect]. Further inquiry revealed that the office manager did not feel it was important to daily deposit cash [cause].

¶ 1705 Editing and Proofreading the Report

Typographical errors, poor writing, or other mishaps can kill a report's effectiveness. Therefore, the CAE must establish the most stringent quality assurance process possible to prevent such problems. This process starts when the audit finding is initially drafted and continues until the final report is issued. The CAE should periodically assess the overall effectiveness of the audit reporting process.

Some tips to avoid reporting mishaps:

- Actually proofread the report against the text of previous drafts.
- Don't rely on spellcheckers.
- Watch for trick words.
- Edit three ways—for content, for spelling/grammar, and for mechanics/grammar.

Overall writing tips include the following:

- Organization and appearance are everything.
- Use one thought per sentence.
- Write short paragraphs.
- Insert headings and subheadings to break up long paragraphs.
- Use the active voice.
- Substitute shorter words for longer words.

¶ 1705

- Avoid the use of imprecise modifiers. Be specific.
- Do not use verbs as nouns and nouns as verbs.

¶ 1706 Sample Report

Internal auditors should be experts at communicating the results of their audits. This chapter suggested integrating report writing with the other aspects of the internal auditing function. The remainder of this chapter presents a sample report based on U.S. Government Accounting Office (GAO) report available on the Internet at *http://www.gao.gov*. It offers a representative example of an operational audit: The auditors go beyond the actual parts shortages (compliance issues) to examine the causes and implications of the parts shortages. Note that the organization of the sample report follows the scheme shown in Figure 17.1. Short explanatory comments appear bracketed in italics at the beginning of the report's sections.

[Title page]
Report to Congressional Committees
United States General Accounting Office
June 2001
AIR FORCE INVENTORY
Parts Shortages Are Impacting Operations
and
Maintenance Effectiveness
GAO-01-587

[Table of contents reveals the overall organization of report]

Contents

Transmittal Letter

Results in Brief

Background

Spare Parts Shortages Adversely Affect Mission Performance, Economy and Efficiency of Operations, and Retention of Military Personnel

Shortages of Specific Spare Parts Occurred for Multiple Reasons

Overall Initiatives Exist to Address Problems

Agency Comments

Scope and Methodology

Appendix I: Management Weaknesses Have Contributed to Spare Parts Shortages (Not Shown)

Appendix II: E-3, C-5, and F-100-220 Engine Parts and Part Function (Not Shown)

Appendix III: Spare Parts Reviewed and Reasons for Shortage (Not Shown)

Appendix IV: Air Force Deputy Chief of Staff, Installations and Logistics, Directorate of Supply, Spare Parts Initiatives (Not Shown)

Appendix V: Comments From the Department of Defense (Not Shown)

Related GAO Products (Not Shown)

Tables

Table 1 Reported Rates for Aircraft That Were Mission Capable and Not Mission Capable Due to Supply Problems

Table 2 Reported Mission-Capable Goals and Rates for the E-3

Table 3 Reported Goals and Rates at Which E-3 Aircraft Were Not Mission Capable Due to Supply Problems

Table 4 Reported Mission-Capable Goals and Rates for the C-5 Aircraft

Table 5 Goals and Rates at Which the C-5 Aircraft Were Reported Not Mission Capable Due to Supply Problems

Table 6 F-100-220 War Readiness Engine Goal and Reported Usable Engines Available, by Quarter

Table 7 Reasons for Shortages of 75 Spare Parts for Selected Engine and Aircraft

Figures

Figure 1 E-3, C-5, F-15, and F-16 Aircraft

¶ 1706

[Executive summary]

Transmittal Letter

June 27, 2001

Congressional Committees

Having spare parts available when needed to perform required maintenance is critical to the Department of Defense's accomplishment of its missions. Shortages of spare parts are a key indicator of whether the billions of dollars annually spent on these parts are being used in an effective, efficient, and economical manner. Since 1990, we have designated the Department's management of its inventory, including spare parts, as high risk because its inventory is vulnerable to fraud, waste, and abuse.

The National Defense Authorization Act for Fiscal Year 2000 requires us to evaluate various aspects of the military services' logistics support capability, including the provision of spare parts.[1] Also, the Chairman, House Committee on Appropriations, and the Chairman, Subcommittee on Defense, House Committee on Appropriations, requested that we review issues related to the quality and availability of spare parts for aircraft, ships, vehicles, and weapon systems. In response to these requests, we reviewed known spare parts shortages within the services. For this report, our objectives were to determine (1) the impact of spare parts shortages on three selected Air Force systems and (2) the reasons for the shortages. Additionally, we identified the overall initiatives that the Air Force and the Defense Logistics Agency have in place or planned to address the shortages.

To address our objectives, we reviewed the Air Force's E-3 early airborne warning and control system aircraft; the C-5 transport aircraft; and the F-100-220 engine, which is used in some F-15 and F-16 fighter aircraft; we also reviewed 75 parts that were in short supply for these systems. We selected these systems because they are key to fulfilling Air Force missions. The Air Force sets goals to have a certain number of each aircraft available and capable of performing its missions at any given time. It measures the impact of parts shortages on aircraft availability by determining the percentage of aircraft that cannot meet mission requirements because parts needed for repairs are unavailable. The Air Force and the Defense Logistics Agency are responsible for managing and providing spare parts for the Air Force's aircraft. *[More detail is given after the executive summary]*

Results in Brief

Spare parts shortages on the three systems we reviewed have adversely affected the performance of assigned missions and the economy and efficiency of maintenance activities. Specifically, the Air Force did not meet its mission-capable goals for the E-3 or C-5 during fiscal years 1996–2000, nor

---

[1] P.L. 106-65. sec 364.

¶ 1706

did it meet its goal to have enough F-100-220 engines to meet peacetime and wartime goals during that period. For example, in fiscal year 2000 the E-3s were not mission capable for supply reasons 11.3 percent of the time. In other words, 3 or 4 of the total of 32 E-3 aircraft were not available during the year. In fiscal year 2000, the C-5s were not mission capable for supply reasons 18.1 percent of the time, or almost 23 of 126 C-5s were not mission capable. Also, maintenance personnel have been required to use the inefficient practice of removing parts from one aircraft for use on another. Maintenance personnel report that this practice can require double the work since they also have to fix the aircraft that parts are removed from. Lastly, the shortages may affect personnel retention. We recently reported that one of the six factors cited by military personnel as sources of dissatisfaction and reasons to leave the military related to work circumstances such as the lack of parts and materials to successfully complete daily job requirements.

The majority of reasons cited by item managers at the maintenance facilities for spare parts shortages were most often related to more spares being required than were anticipated by the inventory management system and delays in the Air Force's repair process as a result of the consolidation of repair facilities. Other reasons included (1) difficulties with producing or repairing parts, (2) reliability of spare parts, and (3) contracting issues. For example, the anticipated quarterly demand for a machine bolt for the F-100-220 engine was 828, but actual demand turned out to be over 12,000. As a result, some F-100-220 engines were not mission capable because they were waiting for more bolts to be obtained. In another case, a contractor produced sufficient quantities of a visor seal assembly for the C-5, but the parts failed to meet design tolerances. As a result of this production problem, demands for this part could not be met.

The Air Force and the Defense Logistics Agency have numerous overall initiatives under way or planned that may alleviate shortages of the spare parts for the three aircraft systems we reviewed. The initiatives generally address the reasons we identified for the shortages. For example, the Air Force Materiel Command is developing a model to better forecast the repair facilities' demands for parts needed in the repair process. In another Results in Brief overall initiative, the Command is developing a pilot program to have contractors bypass the supply system and fill the supply bins for maintenance personnel directly. This is an attempt to expedite the delivery of repair parts. To ensure that the initiatives are achieving the goals of increasing efficiencies in the supply system, the Air Force has developed a Supply Strategic Plan that contains specific goals and outcome-oriented measures for the initiatives. While the initiatives are intended to improve processes for providing spare parts, they would likely result in increased costs and larger inventories of needed spare parts.

¶ 1706

The Air Force's plan is in keeping with our previous recommendations to improve overall logistics planning. We are, therefore, not making recommendations at this time. We will separately review the overall approach and initiatives, once they are more fully developed, to determine whether there are opportunities to enhance these efforts. The Department of Defense generally concurred with this report.

[More detail follows here]

Background

In January 2001, we reported on Department of Defense management challenges and noted that the Department has had serious weaknesses in its management of logistics functions and, in particular, inventory management.[2] We have identified inventory management as a high-risk area since 1990.[3] In 1999, we reported on the Air Force's specific problems in managing spare parts and noted an increase in the percentage of some of its aircraft that were not mission capable due to supply problems.[4] (See Appendix I for examples from our reports on management weaknesses related to the Air Force.) Also, the Secretary of the Air Force reported that the readiness of the Air Force has declined since 1996 and attributed this overall decline, in part, to spare parts shortages.[5] Table 1 shows the percentage of all aviation systems that were mission capable and the percentage of aircraft that were not mission capable due to supply problems from fiscal year 1996 through the first quarter of fiscal 2001.

Table 1: Reported Rates for Aircraft That Were Mission Capable and Not Mission Capable Due to Supply Problems

Fiscal year	Aircraft reported as mission capable (%)	Aircraft reported as not mission capable due to supply problems (%)
1996	78.5	11.0
1997	76.6	12.6
1998	74.3	13.9
1999	73.5	14.0
2000	72.9	14.3
2001 (1st quarter)	72.9	14.0

Source: The Air Force's Multi-Echelon Requirements and Logistics Information Network.

As Table 1 shows, the percentage of all Air Force systems reported as not mission capable due to supply problems steadily increased from fiscal year 1996 through fiscal year 2000. The Air Force requested additional funding to address concerns with spare parts shortages. The Air Force states in the

---

[2] Major Management Challenges and Program Risks: Department of Defense (GAO-01-244, January 2001).

[3] High Risk Series: An Update (GAO-01-263, January 2001).

[4] Air Force Supply: Management Actions Create Spare Parts Shortages and Operational Problems (GAO/NSIAD/AIMD-99-77, April 29, 1999).

[5] Annual Report to the President and the Congress, part VI: Statutory Reports, Secretary of the Air Force.

¶ 1706

Department of Defense Quarterly Readiness Report to the Congress[6] for July through September 2000 that funding Congress provided in earlier years has begun to improve the availability of spares, citing a 58 percent reduction in parts that have been ordered but not received since December 1998. The Secretary also expressed cautious optimism that recent congressional funding would improve the availability of spare parts and aircraft mission-capable rates. In the most recent quarterly readiness report (October through December 2000), the Air Force cautions that although as of early December 2000 overall mission-capable rates had improved from average fiscal year 2000 rates, this improvement had come at the cost of the increased use of the practice of removing parts from one aircraft for use on another, that is, cannibalization.[7]

Because of concerns that spare parts shortages were causing readiness problems, the Air Force received in fiscal 1999 an additional $904 million in obligation authority from the Department of Defense to buy more spare parts. This amount consisted of $387 million to buy spare parts attributable to the Kosovo operation, $135 million to buy engine-related spare parts for the Oklahoma City Air Logistics Center, and $382 million to overcome the accumulated shortfall of spare parts inventories. Also in 1999, the Department of Defense announced plans to provide $500 million to the Defense Logistics Agency to purchase spare parts for all the services over fiscal years 2001–2004. Of that $500 million, $213.8 million is to be for parts to be used on Air Force aircraft. According to a Department of Defense official, the Air Force was provided the first $50 million in fiscal 2001 to pass on to the Defense Logistics Agency to pay for Air Force parts ordered in fiscal year 2000. The Air Force and the other military services received additional funds in fiscal year 1999 that, unlike the funds cited above, were placed largely in operations and maintenance accounts. In a separate report issued earlier this year, we indicated current financial information did not show the extent to which these funds were used for spare parts.[8] However, the Department plans to annually develop detailed financial management information on spare parts funding uses but does not plan to provide it to Congress. We, therefore, recommended to the Secretary of Defense that the information to be developed annually by the Department and the services on the quantity and funding of spare parts be routinely provided to Congress as an integral part of the Department's annual budget justification; the Department agreed to do so.

The aviation systems that we reviewed are vital to the Air Force achieving its missions. The E-3 provides surveillance of the airspace and manages the

---

[6] Department of Defense Quarterly Readiness Report to the Congress is a review of individual service and joint readiness on a quarterly basis and is submitted to Congress by the Secretary of Defense no later than 45 days after the end of each quarter.

[7] We are separately reviewing this issue and will report the results later this year to the Chairman, Subcommittee on National Security, Veterans Affairs, and International Relations, House Committee on Government Reform.

[8] Defense Inventory: Information on the Use of Spare Parts Funding Should Be Provided to Congress (GAO-01-472, April 2001).

¶ 1706

flight of all aircraft in an assigned battlefield area. The Air Force first received E-3s in 1977, and an Air Force official told us that it is the oldest aircraft in the Air Force in terms of operational hours flown. The C-5 is the Air Force's largest cargo aircraft, carrying cargo such as Army tanks, and is one of the largest aircraft in the world. About 70 percent of the oversized cargo required in the critical first 30 days of one major war scenario would be the type of cargo the C-5 carries. The Air Force first received operational C-5 aircraft in 1970, and according to Air Force officials, one of the reasons for the lower than expected mission-capable rates in recent years for the C-5 aircraft is its age. The F-100-220 engine powers many of the Air Force's F-15 and F-16 fighter aircraft and, according to an Air Force official, will become increasingly critical to operations as some older engines are replaced with the F-100-220. For each of these systems, we judgmentally selected for review 25 parts, a total of 75, with the highest number of hours or incidents of unavailability for given time periods.

Figure 1: E-3, C-5, F-15, and F-16 Aircraft

C-5 aircraft

F-15 with F-100-220 engine

E-3 aircraft

F-16 with F-100-220 engine

Air Force spare parts are classified as either consumables or reparables. Consumable items, which are mostly managed by the Defense Logistics Agency, are those items that are discarded when they fail because they cannot be cost-effectively repaired. Reparable items, managed by the Air Force Materiel Command, are items that can be cost-effectively repaired. The Command's mission is to research, develop, test, acquire, deliver, and logistically support Air Force weapon systems.

¶ 1706

[Effect statements follow]

Spare Parts Shortages Adversely Affect Mission Performance, Economy and Efficiency of Operations, and Retention of Military Personnel

The shortages of spare parts for the three aircraft systems we reviewed have not only affected readiness but also have created inefficiencies in maintenance processes and procedures and may adversely affect the retention of military personnel. Two aircraft we reviewed, the E-3 and C-5, did not meet their mission-capable goals in fiscal years 1996–2000 and were not mission capable due to supply problems from 7.3 percent to 18.1 percent during the same period. The number of usable spare F-100-220 engines that the Air Force had on hand fell short of its goal by as few as 6 and as many as 104 engines during the same period.

Spare Parts Shortages Contributed to Three Systems' Failure to Meet Mission Performance Goals

The Air Force did not achieve its mission-capable goals during fiscal years 1996–2000 for any of the three Air Force aircraft systems we reviewed, in part, due to spare parts shortages. Table 2 shows the mission-capable goals and actual rates for the E-3 aircraft for fiscal years 1996-2000, and Table 3 shows the rates at which the E-3 was not mission capable due to supply problems during the same period.

Table 2: Reported Mission-Capable Goals and Rates for the E-3

Fiscal year	Mission-Capable goal	Reported mission-capable rate (%)	Difference (%)
1996	85	82.5	(2.5)
1997	85	79.2	(5.8)
1998	85	71.9	(13.1)
1999	85	73.5	(11.5)
2000	73	72.8	(0.2)

Source: The Air Force's Multi-Echelon Requirements and Logistics Information Network.

The goal for the E-3 was lowered to 73 percent from March through September 2000 based on an Air Force assessment of its ability to achieve its mission-capable goal. The Air Force recognized that it had failed to achieve historical performance levels to the point that falling short of the standard had become the norm. Citing constraints regarding spare parts, maintenance personnel, and repair equipment, the Air Force lowered mission-capable goals for the E-3 and other aircraft with the intent of providing maintenance personnel with more achievable targets. The mission-capable goal for the E-3 aircraft rose to 81 percent in fiscal year 2001, and it is planned to return to 85 percent in fiscal year 2002.

¶ 1706

Table 3: Reported Goals and Rates at Which E-3 Aircraft Were Not Mission Capable Due to Supply Problems

	Total not mission capable due to supply problems		
Fiscal year	Goal	Reported rate (%)	Difference (%)
1996	6 or less	7.3	(1.3)
1997	6 or less	9.4	(3.4)
1998	6 or less	12.9	(6.9)
1999	6 or less	11.9	(5.9)
2000	12 or less	11.3	0.7

Source: The Air Force's Multi-Echelon Requirements and Logistics Information Network.

The goal was 12 percent or less from March through September 2000 and was raised based on an Air Force assessment of the aircraft's ability to achieve the not mission capable due to supply problems goal for the E-3 and other aircraft. The Air Force recognized that it had failed to achieve historical performance levels to the point that falling short of the standard had become the norm. Citing constraints regarding spare parts, maintenance personnel, and repair equipment, the Air Force raised its goal for not mission capable due to supply problems for the E-3 and other aircraft with the intent of providing maintenance personnel with more achievable targets. The not mission capable due to supply problems goal changed to 8 percent in fiscal year 2001, and it is planned to return to 6 percent in fiscal year 2002.

The reported rate for total not mission capable due to supply problems in fiscal year 2000, 11.3 percent, equated to about 3 or 4 E-3s of the total of 32 aircraft being not mission capable due to supply problems.

The C-5 also did not achieve its goals during fiscal years 1996-2000. Table 4 shows the C-5's mission-capable goals and actual mission-capable rates for those years, and Table 5 shows the rates at which the C-5 was not mission capable due to supply problems as well as its goals during the same period.

Table 4: Reported Mission-Capable Goals and Rates for the C-5 Aircraft

	Mission capable rates		
Fiscal year	Goal	Reported rate (%)	Difference (%)
1996	75	64.2	(10.8)
1997	75	62.7	(12.3)
1998	75	61.2	(13.8)
1999	75	59.5	(15.5)
2000	75	60.8	(14.2)

Source: The Air Force's Multi-Echelon Requirements and Logistics Information Network.

¶ 1706

Table 5: Goals and Rates at Which the C-5 Aircraft Were Reported Not Mission Capable Due to Supply Problems

	Total not mission capable due to supply problems		
Fiscal year	Goal	Reported rate (%)	Difference (%)
1996	9 or less	15.6	(6.6)
1997	8.5 or less	15.2	(6.7)
1998	8.5 or less	16.8	(8.3)
1999	8.5 or less	17.3	(8.8)
2000	8.5 or less	18.1	(9.6)

Source: The Air Force's Multi-Echelon Requirements and Logistics Information Network.

The reported rate for total not mission capable due to supply problems in fiscal year 2000, 18.1 percent, equated to almost 23 C-5s of the fleet of 126 aircraft being not mission capable, at least in part, due to supply problems.

With regard to the F-100-220 engine, the Air Force never met its goal, called the war readiness engine goal, during fiscal years 1996–2000 (see Table 6). The goal can change each fiscal year for the number of usable—ready to be installed in an aircraft—spare engines the Air Force would like to have on hand to meet wartime needs. In some cases, it has had F-15s or F-16s grounded due to the lack of the engine. When the number of usable spare engines is shown as a negative number, there are not enough engines for all the aircraft required for peacetime operations; in other words, aircraft that would otherwise be available to fly are grounded because they lack engines. During fiscal years 1996 through 2000, this occurred in five different quarters.

Table 6: F-100-220 War Readiness Engine Goal and Reported Usable Engines Available, by Quarter

Fiscal year	War readiness engine goal	Usable spare engines	Difference
1996-1	54	10	(44)
1996-2	54	22	(32)
1996-3	54	48	(6)
1996-4	54	42	(12)
1997-1	68	-5	(73)
1997-2	68	11	(57)
1997-3	68	17	(51)
1997-4	68	14	(54)
1998-1	90	-1	(91)
1998-2	90	-13	(103)
1998-3	90	3	(87)
1998-4	90	17	(83)
1999-1	90	40	(50)
1999-2	90	41	(49)
1999-3	90	-14	(104)
1999-4	90	0	(90)
2000-1	84	-6	(90)
2000-2	84	16	(68)
2000-3	84	38	(46)
2000-4	84	44	(40)

Source: Oklahoma City Air Logistics Center, Department of the Air Force.

¶ 1706

Spare Parts Shortages Can Cause Inefficient Maintenance Practices and May Hamper Efforts to Retain Maintenance Personnel

To compensate for a lack of spare parts, maintenance personnel sometimes remove usable parts from aircraft for which spare parts are unavailable to replace broken parts on others. Maintenance personnel at Seymour-Johnson Air Force Base said that this practice is necessary to attempt to maintain mission-capable rates when spare parts are not available. As we have previously reported, the result of this practice is that maintenance personnel spend a large amount of time cannibalizing parts and performing double work.[9] According to a Naval Postgraduate School thesis, there is also the potential for breaking the needed part or causing collateral damage while removing the part. Additionally, a part removed from another aircraft will likely not last as long as a part from the supply system and will require maintenance sooner.

Additionally, our past work shows that spare parts shortages may affect retention. In August 1999, we reported on the results of our December 1998 through March 1999 survey of about 1,000 Army, Navy, Air Force, and Marine Corps active duty personnel that were selected based on their work in jobs in which the Department of Defense believed were experiencing retention problems. More than half of the respondents stated that they were dissatisfied and intended to leave the military. The majority of factors were associated with work circumstances such as the lack of parts and materials needed to successfully complete daily job requirements. Both officers and enlisted personnel ranked the availability of needed equipment, parts, and materials among the top 2 of 44 quality-of-life factors that caused their dissatisfaction.[10]

[Causes are presented]

Shortages of Specific Spare Parts Occurred for Multiple Reasons

Spare parts shortages on the three systems we reviewed occurred for various reasons. In addition, an internal Department of Defense study found similar reasons for spare parts shortages.

---

[9] GAO/NSIAD/AIMD-99-77, April 29, 1999.
[10] Military Personnel: Perspectives of Surveyed Service Members in Critical Specialties (GAO/NSIAD-99-197BR, August 16, 1999).

¶ 1706

Selected Systems Have Experienced Parts Shortages for Multiple Reasons

The 75 parts (25 for each system) we selected for review were recorded as being the cause for the most hours of the systems being not mission capable due to supply problems for a given time period. Specific parts were in short supply for numerous and varied reasons. Because of the interrelated nature of the supply system, some of the parts were unavailable for more than one reason. Table 7 provides a summary of the reasons for the shortages of the top 25 problem parts for each system for a given month. (See Appendix II for a more detailed list of the parts discussed in this report).

Table 7: Reasons for Shortages of 75 Spare Parts for Selected Engine and Aircraft

Reason	F-100-220[a]	E-3[b]	C-5[c]	Total
Demands were not anticipated	10	11	5	26
Changes in location of repairs	7	7	8	22
Parts production problems	3	5	10	18
Component reliability	5	2	9	16
Contracting issues	4	3	3	10
Other	3	9	0	12
Total	**32**	**37**	**35**	**104**

Note: The totals exceed 25 because some parts were unavailable for multiple reasons.

[a] The time period for the shortages was April 2000.
[b] The time period for the shortages was March 2000.
[c] The time period for the shortages was July 2000.

Source: Our analysis of Air Force Materiel Command data.

Actual Demands Were Greater Than Anticipated

Greater demand than anticipated by repair activities for the spares we reviewed was one of the most frequent reasons parts were not available. According to agency officials, the Air Force and the Defense Logistics Agency forecast the demand for parts using past data on usage of parts.[11] According to current policy, if a part had no demands over the specified period and no anticipated future demands, it may not be purchased for stock. Twenty-six (about 35 percent) of the 75 parts we reviewed were unavailable because of unanticipated demands for spare parts. For example, there had been no demand for a tension regulator for the C-5 since 1993, and it was therefore not on hand when needed through the end of July 2000. As of July 2000, C-5 aircraft had not been mission capable for a total of 155 operational days (24-hour days) due to the lack of this part. In another case, the demand calculated from past experience for a machine bolt for the F-100-220 engine was far less than the demand by the end of April 2000. In that case, the average quarterly demand for the bolt was 828

---

[11] When establishing initial spares for new weapon systems, the Air Force uses, in part, engineering estimates to determine the quantities of spare parts to purchase.

¶ 1706

but increased to over 12,000 in one quarter. The item manager did not know the specific reasons for this increase in demand. At the end of April 2000, in 96 cases the lack of this bolt rendered F-100-220 engines not mission capable. Also, in the case of a metallic seal for the engine, demand increased after responsibility for the repair of the seal was transferred from a closing repair facility. Parts managers speculated that workers at the new repair facility were replacing this item more often than at the previous repair facility as a part of their routine maintenance efforts. As a result of the lack of this seal, F-100-220 engines were not mission capable in 11 cases by the end of April 2000.

Changes in Location of Repairs

Twenty-two (about 29 percent) of the parts reviewed were on back orders because of difficulties related to the transfer of workload from two maintenance facilities that were closing. As a result of the Base Realignment and Closure Commission's 1995 recommendations, the Air Force consolidated its air logistics centers, or maintenance repair facilities, from five to three locations and increased its use of contractor repair capability. Air Force data indicated that back orders for critical parts affected by the consolidation peaked at about 615,000 in December 1998 before falling to 374,000 by the end of fiscal 1999 and to just over 258,000 by December 2000, a 58 percent reduction. The Department of Defense cited underestimated workloads in several key shops at the remaining three air logistics centers as the primary reason for the increase in back orders.

For one part we reviewed, a blade lock retainer for an F-100-220 engine, a closing air logistics center had repaired the part on a special, as-needed basis and did not record demands for repair. When responsibility for repair of the part was transferred to the Oklahoma City Air Logistics Center, the Center had no demand data for the part and had not ordered replacement retainers, and no retainers were on hand to install on engines as needed. As a result of the lack of this blade lock retainer, F-100-220 engines were not mission capable in 22 instances by the end of April 2000. Also, the receiving air logistic centers did not have some of their repair shops ready as planned when items were to be transferred. For example, a hydraulic valve for the E-3 was unavailable because the receiving air logistics center did not have a required test stand repaired and certified in time to prevent this part from being unavailable when needed. Because of the lack of this part, by the end of March 2000, E-3 aircraft had accumulated a total of about 8 operational days of time not mission capable.

Parts Production Problems

Production problems were at least partially the cause of the unavailability of 18 (24 percent) of the spare parts reviewed. Several examples follow.

- The sole-source contractor for a C-5 part could not deliver as many aircraft turbines as the Air Force needed in the time

¶ 1706

specified in the contract. As of July 2000, due to the lack of the turbine, C-5s had accumulated about 335 days of not mission capable time.

- Although a contractor produced sufficient quantities of the visor seal assembly for the C-5, the parts failed to meet design tolerances. As a result, C-5s had accumulated the equivalent of 186 operational days of not mission capable status by the end of July 2000.

- Most of the dual ignition exciters for the F-100-220 engine that a contractor produced failed quality inspections, and the contractor therefore could not provide a quantity sufficient to satisfy Air Force demands. By the end of April 2000, the lack of dual ignition exciters had caused F-100-220 engines to be not mission capable in 104 cases.

- A contractor agreed to increase production of an augmentor nozzle for the F-100-220 engine to meet the demand created by the Kosovo air campaign. The contractor scaled back production after the campaign was over. According to an Air Force official, this was within the terms of the contract, which called for an average number of parts per month. However, overall demand for this part exceeded supply. By the end of April 2000, the lack of the nozzle had caused F-100-220 engines to be not mission capable in 63 cases.

- At an Air Force repair facility, spares of an augmentor fuel control for the F-100-220 engine were mistakenly disposed of instead of being turned in for repair, and the controls had to be bought on an emergency basis to make repairs. Through April 2000, having to purchase this item on an emergency buy resulted in 30 incidents of F-100-220 engines being classified not mission capable.

Component Reliability

Sixteen (about 21 percent) of the parts that we reviewed were unavailable because the life of parts was shorter than the Air Force had predicted. Thus, the parts in stock were exhausted before the Air Force could replace them. For example, a skid detector for the C-5 aircraft experienced a 50 percent increase in failures, and all the spare parts were used before the item could be ordered and restocked. Through July 2000, C-5 aircraft were not mission capable for over 368 operational days due to the lack of this part. Some reliability problems raised safety concerns and created new, and higher, requirements for the part. For example, when a nozzle in the augmentor duct on some F-100-220 engines began to fall off due to cracks at the rivet head, the Air Force began to replace the duct routinely as each aircraft came in for maintenance. By the end of April 2000, the lack of this part had resulted in F-100-220 engines not being mission capable in 34 cases.

¶ 1706

Contracting Issues

Both the Air Force and the Defense Logistics Agency have encountered a variety of problems in contracting for spare parts needed for repairs. Ten (about 13 percent) of the parts we reviewed were unavailable, at least in part, because of contracting issues. These issues included lengthy price negotiations, a contract requirement to have a minimum number of units before beginning repairs, failure of a contractor to meet the delivery date, and termination of a contract. For example, the Defense Logistics Agency did not have a straight pin for the F-100-220 engine in stock because the sole-source company wanted a price that the Agency was unwilling to pay. This resulted in extended negotiations with the company before an award could be made. By the end of April 2000, the lack of this part had caused F-100-220 engines to be not mission capable in nine cases. In another case, to obtain an acceptable price for a contract for the repair of a temperature indicator for the E-3 aircraft, the Air Force was required to provide a minimum of 10 regulators for repair. By the time 10 units were accumulated and shipped, the demand for the part had exceeded the supply. Through March 2000, E-3 aircraft were not mission capable over 19 operational days due to the lack of this part. Also, a contract for an axle beam fitting for the C-5 aircraft had to be terminated because the contractor requested too many delivery schedule extensions. As of July 2000, the equivalent of one C-5 aircraft was not mission capable for 124 operational days.

Other Reasons

Twelve (16 percent) of the parts we reviewed were unavailable for reasons other than those we have already cited. In one case, the Air Force used an incorrect replacement rate for an engine core, and as a result, the repair of parts was not timely. Through April 2000, F-100-220 engines were not mission capable due to the lack of this part in 33 cases. Also, the limited repair facility capacity for certain spare parts, such as electric generators, created shortages of the parts. By the end of March 2000, E-3 aircraft had been not mission capable for almost 10 operational days due to the lack of this part. In another case, because maintenance facilities prioritize repairs based on current Air Force requirements, a receiver transmitter was not repaired in time to avoid a shortage because higher priority items had to be repaired first. As a result, over 15 operational days of not mission capable time had been accumulated on E-3s by the end of March 2000. In another case, the required part, a vaneaxial fan, was on hand, but E-3 aircraft had accumulated over 15 operational days of not mission capable time by the end of March 2000 because of the time it took to ship the part overseas. In some cases, no spare parts had been purchased when an aircraft was being modified or the technical data for the modification was incomplete. At the end of March 2000, over 10 operational days of not mission capable time

¶ 1706

had accumulated for E-3 aircraft due to the lack of a control indicator that fell into this category.

[Corroborating evidence]

Department of Defense Internal Study Found Similar Reasons for Shortages

An internal study conducted by the Department of Defense found similar reasons for Air Force reparable spare parts shortages.[12] The study examined parts causing aircraft to be not mission capable and found that there were two reasons for the shortages. The first reason was an insufficient inventory of certain reparable parts. The second was that although there were enough parts in the system, other constraints prevented a repair facility from repairing the parts in a timely manner. The study states that this may have happened for several reasons. The parts may not have been returned from units to the repair facility, a repair facility may have lacked capacity in certain key areas such as manpower or testing equipment, the consumable parts required to fix the reparable item may not have been available, or the item managers may not have requested the repair facility to repair a part because of a lack of funding.[13] The study contained a recommendation that the Air Force provide $609 million for fiscal years 2002 to 2007 to improve the availability of reparable spare parts. According to a Department of Defense official, the Air Force plans to provide the funds.

[mitigating factors]

Overall Initiatives Exist to Address Problems

The Air Force and the Defense Logistics Agency have overall initiatives under way or planned to improve the availability of spare parts. The initiatives are intended to improve the efficiency of the supply system and increase the requirements for spare parts. The initiatives generally address the specific reasons for shortages identified by our review, with the exception of changes in the location of repairs that is not a recurring problem. The Air Force has developed a Supply Strategic Plan that includes a management framework and specific goals and outcome-oriented measures for its initiatives. We have made various recommendations to address this issue. The Air Force has actions under way to respond to address these recommendations; therefore, we are not making any additional recommendations at this time. We will be reviewing the strategic plan's initiatives, once they are more developed, to evaluate their likely effectiveness and to assess whether additional initiatives are needed.

---

[12] Office of the Secretary of Defense, Program Analysis and Evaluation, Aviation Spare Parts Inventory Funding for Readiness, February 2001.

[13] We also found in our 1997 study that even though military units had funds to purchase spare parts, the supply group did not always have sufficient funds to buy new parts or pay for the repair of broken parts that customers needed. See Air Force Supply: Management Actions Create Spare Parts Shortages and Operational Problems (GAO/NSIAD/AIMD-99-77, April 29, 1999).

¶ 1706

Air Force Supply Strategic Plan

The Air Force is regularly monitoring which spare parts are unavailable for the longest period of time and undertakes ad hoc actions to resolve the problems causing the shortage. In 1999, the Air Force developed the Supply Strategic Plan to help create an integrated process for supply planning, to facilitate the exchange of information throughout the supply system, and to improve measures of effectiveness for the supply system. The plan, which was updated in January 2001, establishes five goals for the Air Force supply community to achieve by 2010.

Supply Strategic Plan Goals

- Manage assets effectively
- Organize, train, and equip supply personnel
- Support Department of Defense operations
- Establish and implement fuel policy
- Implement effective financial management

Each goal has associated objectives to be achieved in the next 4 to 7 years and tasks to be completed in the next 1 to 4 years.

Objectives to Support Supply Strategic Plan

In support of the Supply Strategic Plan, the Air Force Deputy Chief of Staff, Installations and Logistics, Directorate of Supply,[14] established in 1999 the Supply Foundation Project, which includes 10 objectives with associated initiatives for each. The Directorate views the project as a comprehensive means of improving the supply system. The first objective is to improve spare parts management. The intent is to determine the baseline for formulating a spare parts policy; to determine the overall trend for spare parts, that is, are shortages increasing or decreasing; and to develop and implement initiatives to reduce the shortages of spare parts.

Within the objective of improving spare parts management, the Directorate has initiatives within the goal of managing assets under way or under study.

Initiatives for Managing Assets

- Improve the progress for determining requirements for spare parts
- Improve the process for funding the parts
- Increase the stock of certain parts

---

[14] The Air Force Directorate of Supply establishes and implements Air Force supply and fuel policy. The Directorate also prepares, executes, and manages budget programs totaling over $17 billion annually for Air Force aircraft, missiles, munitions, communications, and vehicles.

¶ 1706

- Increase the parts contained in readiness spares packages (deployment kits for maintaining aircraft)
- Coordinate with the defense logistics agency to ensure that it buys the most critically needed parts from the Air Force portion of the $500 million provided by the Department of Defense for fiscal years 2001 to 2004
- Reduce the time that customers wait for parts

For each of these initiatives, the Air Force has established short-term and long-term milestones and accountability for implementation by assigning program responsibility to specific offices and individuals. The measures for success include achieving goals such as (1) increasing the issuance of parts when requested, (2) increasing the stock of certain parts, (3) improving total rates for aircraft not mission capable for supply reasons, and (4) lowering cannibalization rates. (See Appendix IV for a complete listing of these Air Force initiatives.)

Air Force Materiel Command Initiatives

In addition to the initiatives contained in the Air Force Supply Strategic Plan, the Air Force Materiel Command also has actions under way and planned to separately address more specific aspects of spare parts management and policies. According to Air Force officials, these actions are being coordinated with the Air Force Deputy Chief of Staff, Installations and Logistics, Directorate of Supply. As part of its Constraints Analysis Program, the Air Force Materiel Command identified six major problems that had prevented it from providing timely support to the warfighter. These problems were unavailability of consumable parts; unreliability of parts; poor management of the suppliers of parts; inadequate workload planning; ineffective inventory management; and inefficient policies regarding which parts are repaired and, if repair is needed, where the repairs should be made. The Command focused its initial efforts on studying ways to resolve the problems with supplier management, parts reliability, and unavailability of consumable parts. Implementation plans are being developed for actions for each of these problems while the remaining problems are being studied. The Command is also developing (1) a model to forecast the repair facilities' demands for consumable spare parts and electronically transmit this data to the Defense Logistics Agency and (2) a pilot program to have contractors bypass the supply system and fill the supply bins for maintenance personnel directly.

Defense Logistics Agency Initiatives

Among the efforts the Defense Logistics Agency has under way to improve the availability of spare parts are its Aviation Investment Strategy and Aging Aircraft Program.

¶ 1706

Aviation Investment Strategy

The Defense Logistics Agency's major initiative to resolve aircraft spare parts shortages is its Aviation Investment Strategy. This fiscal year 2000 initiative focuses on replenishing consumable aviation repair parts with identified availability problems that affect readiness. Of the $500 million that the Defense Department budgeted for this purpose, $213.8 million was the Air Force portion. As of December 2000, $95.3 million had been targeted for Air Force spare parts and $22.3 million worth of parts had been delivered.

Aging Aircraft Program

The goal of the Defense Logistics Agency's Aging Aircraft Program is to consistently meet the goals for spare parts availability for the Army, Navy, and Air Force aviation weapon systems. The program's focus will be to (1) provide inventory control point personnel with complete, timely, and accurate information on current and projected parts requirements; (2) reduce customers' wait times for parts for which sources or production capabilities no longer exist; and (3) create an efficient and effective program management structure and processes that will achieve the stated program goals. The Agency plans to spend about $20 million during fiscal years 2001–2007 on this program.

Air Force Has Responded to Our Recommendations for Better Planning

We recommended in November 1999 that the Secretary of the Air Force develop a management framework for implementing best practice initiatives based on the principles embodied in the Government Performance and Results Act. The Department of Defense concurred with our recommendation and stated that the Air Force is revising its Logistics Support Plan to more clearly articulate the relationships, goals, objectives, and metrics of logistics initiatives.[15] As a part of the Supply Strategic Plan, the Air Force included initiatives intended to improve the availability of spare parts.

We also recommended in January 2001 that the Department develop an overarching plan that integrates the individual service and defense agency logistics reengineering plans to include an investment strategy for funding reengineering initiatives and details on how the Department plans to achieve its final logistics system end state.[16]

Since the Air Force and the Department of Defense are taking actions on our previous recommendations to improve overall logistics planning, we are not making new recommendations at this time.

---

[15] Defense Inventory: Improved Management Framework Needed to Guide Air Force Best Practice Initiatives (GAO/NSIAD-00-2, November 18, 1999).

[16] GAO-01-244, January 2001 and GAO-01-263, January 2001.

¶ 1706

[The auditee's response is included]
Agency Comments

The Acting Deputy Under Secretary of Defense for Logistics and Materiel Readiness, in commenting on a draft of this report, indicated that the Department of Defense generally concurred with the report. The Department's comments are reprinted in their entirety in Appendix V (not shown due to space limitation).

[A description of the audit steps performed]
Scope and Methodology

To determine the impact of the shortages of spare parts, we reviewed data on the Air Force's mission-capable goals and actual rates and goals and actual rates for aircraft not mission capable due to supply problems for selected months from the Office of the Secretary of the Air Force, Installations and Logistics Directorate. We did not independently verify these data. From these data, we selected three systems for review that had experienced difficulties in achieving mission-capable goals or in the case of the F-100-220 engine readiness goals for the number of usable engines on hand. We also reviewed data on cannibalizations provided by the Air Combat Command, Hampton, Virginia; the Office of the Secretary of the Air Force, Installations and Logistics Directorate, Washington, D.C.; and Seymour-Johnson Air Force Base, Goldsboro, North Carolina. Using the data, we discussed with maintenance personnel the impact of cannibalizations on spare parts shortages. We also used data from studies conducted by the Department of Defense regarding spare parts shortages and their impacts. Lastly, we drew relevant information from our recently issued reports.

To determine the reasons for these part shortages, we visited the air logistics centers at Tinker Air Force Base (E-3), Oklahoma City, Oklahoma; Warner-Robins Air Force Base (C-5), Robins, Georgia; Kelly Air Force Base (F-100-220 aircraft engine), San Antonio, Texas; and the Defense Supply Center Richmond, Richmond, Virginia. To identify specific reasons, we discussed the specific parts shortages with those who manage these items at these locations. We also reviewed our related work on Air Force and Department of Defense inventory management practices to identify systemic management problems that are contributing to spare parts shortage.

To determine what overall actions are planned or under way to address overall spare parts shortages for Air Force aircraft and the management framework for implementing the overall initiatives, we visited the Air Force headquarters, the Joint Chiefs of Staff Logistics Directorate, and the Office of the Secretary of Defense, located in the Washington, D.C. area; the Defense Logistics Agency located at Fort Belvoir, Virginia, and the Defense Supply Center located in Richmond, Virginia; the Air Force Materiel Command, Dayton, Ohio; and the air logistics centers at Tinker Air Force

¶ 1706

Base, Oklahoma (E-3), Warner-Robins Air Force Base, Georgia (C-5), and Kelly Air Force Base, Texas (F-100-220). We discussed with officials at each of these locations Air Force initiatives regarding spare parts, their progress and results to date, the planned completion dates for some initiatives, and additional steps needed to address spare parts shortages. We also compared the reasons for the shortages we found with Scope and Methodology the overall initiatives under way or planned to determine if there were any areas that were not being addressed. We did not review these plans or the specific initiatives.

Our review was performed from February 2000 to April 2001 in accordance with generally accepted government auditing standards.

We are sending copies of this report to the Secretary of Defense; the Secretary of the Air Force; the Director, Office of Management and Budget; and the Director, Defense Logistics Agency. We will also make copies available to others upon request.

Please contact me at (202) 512-8412 if you or your staff have any questions regarding this report. Key contributors to this report were Lawson Gist Jr., John Beauchamp, Willie Cheely Jr., and Nancy Ragsdale.

[Issuing authority]

David R. Warren
Director
Defense Capabilities and Management

[Distribution]

The Honorable Carl Levin, Chairman, Committee on Armed Services, United States Senate

The Honorable John Warner, Ranking Minority Member, Committee on Armed Services, United States Senate

The Honorable Daniel Inouye, Chairman, Subcommittee on Defense, Committee on Appropriations, United States Senate

The Honorable Ted Stevens, Ranking Minority Member, Subcommittee on Defense, Committee on Appropriations, United States Senate

The Honorable Bill Young, Chairman, Committee on Appropriations, United States House of Representatives

The Honorable Bob Stump, Chairman, Committee on Armed Services, United States House of Representatives

The Honorable Ike Skelton, Ranking Minority Member, Committee on Armed Services, United States House of Representatives

The Honorable Jerry Lewis, Chairman, Subcommittee on Defense, Committee on Appropriations, United States House of Representatives

¶ 1706

The Honorable John Murtha, Ranking Minority Member, Subcommittee on Defense, Committee on Appropriations, United States House of Representatives

¶ 1707 Summary

The audit report is the principal product of the audit assignment and as such is the one element of the audit that will face the most scrutiny—hence, the importance of producing well-crafted audit reports that are well-received by auditees, upper management, and the audit committee. In order to initiate change with as little organizational ill will as possible, the chief auditing executive should regularly ask auditees, upper management, and audit committee members for their comments and suggestions for improving the reporting process. The CAE should ensure that due process is followed, allowing auditees several opportunities to voice their views of audit findings before the final report is issued.

Each internal auditing engagement has unique findings; therefore, each internal auditing report must be written to fit the particular engagement. Internal auditors should write reports to match readers'/officials' preferences concerning organization, format, and style. The CAE determines the overall appearance and organization for internal audit reports issued. The CAE, however, does not determine this in total isolation; the CAE relies on the comments and suggestions of the audit staff, upper management, and the audit committee members.

Chapter 20
Fraud Auditing

¶ 2001 Introduction
¶ 2002 Some History of Fraud Detection
¶ 2003 The Fraud Investigation Process
¶ 2004 External Auditor's Responsibilities
¶ 2005 Fraudulent Financial Reporting
¶ 2006 Detecting Cooked Books
¶ 2007 Financial Statement Fraud Risk Factors
¶ 2008 Horizontal and Vertical Analysis
¶ 2009 Other Forensic-Type Audit Procedures
¶ 2010 Ratio Analysis
¶ 2011 Misappropriation of Assets Fraud Risk Factors
¶ 2012 Some Asset Misappropriation Schemes
¶ 2013 Selected Indicia of Fraud
¶ 2014 Corporate Fraud Task Force
¶ 2015 Summary

¶ 2001 Introduction

Globalization, technological advances, and the complexity of business make organizations more vulnerable to abuse. Reported corporate and accounting scandals of the early 2000s have raised serious concerns about the effectiveness of the corporate governance structure, internal control system, and audit functions to prevent and detect employee and management fraud. The reported financial scandals caused by alleged financial statement fraud have cost investors and pensioners more than $100 billion in the early 2000s, and have eroded investor confidence and public trust in published audited financial statements. The Sarbanes-Oxley Act of 2002 was passed in response to these high-profile scandals and subsequent erosion in investor confidence. This chapter describes the nature and type of fraud as well as methods and procedures for preventing, detecting, and correcting fraud.

Chapter 20 objectives:

- To list the three categories of fraud found in the business environment and the three categories of occupational fraud (see ¶ 2001).

- To be aware of the gap that exists between the expectations of the financial statement users and the responsibility of auditors to detect fraud (see ¶ 2002 and ¶ 2014).

- To understand internal and external auditors' responsibilities with respect to detecting and reporting errors, frauds, and illegal acts (see ¶ 2002 and ¶ 2004).

- To detail the requirements required by SAS No. 99 that an auditor needs to perform in order to fulfill external auditors' responsibilities regarding the detection of fraud (see ¶ 2002, ¶ 2007, and ¶ 2011).

- To become familiar with the factors that contribute to fraud (see ¶ 2003 and ¶ 2013).

- To be aware of the two kinds of fraud that may cause material misstatements in financial statements (see ¶ 2004).

- To identify the five types of financial statement frauds and some procedures an auditor uses to detect financial statement fraud (see ¶ 2005–2010).

- To recognize the categories of misappropriation schemes and the red flags for identifying misappropriation of assets fraud (see ¶ 2011–2012).

.01 Nature and Types of Fraud

SEC Chairman William Donaldson responded to the question of why there is "such appalling fraud" in business in the following manner. "There are 15,000 companies out there," and "the majority of those companies are run by honest, dedicated people." But he admitted that "there has been in my view, a gradual erosion, not venal, but gradual erosion of corporate ethics over the bull market of the last decade, and particularly the last five years."[1]

Black's Law Dictionary defines fraud as any multifarious means people can devise, and which are resorted to by one individual to obtain an advantage over another by false suggestions or suppression of the truth. The term includes all surprises, tricks, cunning, or dissembling, and any unfair way another is cheated.[2]

---

[1] Bobby Eberle, "Justice Department Celebrates One Year of Corporate Fraud Task Force," *Talon News*, July 23, 2003, www.gopusa.com/news/2003/july/0723corporatefraud.shtml.

[2] H.C. Black, *Black's Law Dictionary*, 5th ed. (St. Paul: West Publishing Co., 1979), 468.

Fraud can be broken into various categories. Joseph T. Wells indicates that occupational fraud includes asset misappropriation, corruption, and fraudulent statements.[3] Three broad categories exist for Robertson: employee fraud, management fraud, and external fraud involving theft and other improper action by non-employees.[4] *Employee fraud* involves people taking money or property from their employers. Kiting, embezzlement, theft, and kickbacks are examples of employee fraud. *Management fraud* is the actions of employees and officers to inflate reported earnings and assets or deflate expenses and liabilities in order to deceive parties outside the organization. Cendant, Rite Aid, Phar-Mor, Rent-Way, ZZZZ Best, Sunbeam, and Equity Funding are examples of financial statement fraud.

Albrecht, Wernz, and Williams classify fraud using six groups:

1. Employee embezzlement (the taking of organizational assets)
2. Management fraud (false financial reporting)
3. Investment scam (the selling of worthless or near-worthless investments)
4. Vendor fraud (charging for goods or services not provided, overcharging for goods or services, or providing inferior goods)
5. Customer fraud (customers not paying for goods, obtaining a good, or obtaining a good not due to the customer)
6. Miscellaneous fraud (a deception not included in any of the above categories)[5]

Howard R. Davia divides fraud auditing into two types: reactive and proactive. In *reactive fraud auditing* the investigator begins with evidence that a fraud has probably occurred and then attempts to find, confirm, and document it. In *proactive fraud auditing* the investigator has few clues that fraud has occurred, so audit procedures are different from those used to practice reactive fraud auditing.[6]

External and internal auditors, in general, do not audit proactively; instead, they look for fraud that will result in material misstatements in the financial statements. There are, however, fraud specialists, such as certified fraud examiners and certified forensic accountants, and certified fraud deterrence analysts. Fraud auditors are, in general, traditional auditors by education and experience, but they have training in investigative skills and rules of evidence.

---

[3] J.T. Wells, *Occupational Fraud and Abuse* (Austin: Obsidian Publishing Co., 1997), preface.
[4] J.C. Robertson, *Fraud Examination for Managers and Auditors* (Austin: Viesca Books, 2000), ii.
[5] W.S. Albrecht, G.W. Wernz, and T.L. Williams, *Fraud: Bring Light to the Dark Side of Business* (New York: McGraw-Hill, 1995).
[6] H.R. Davia, *Fraud 101* (New York: John Wiley & Sons, 2000), 34–39.

¶ 2001.01

As Joseph W. Koletar states in his book, *Fraud Exposed*:[7] "Let's face it, we in the forensic profession labor in an obscure corner of the vineyard. We are the carefully selected, trusted, highly trained guardians of one of the last great secrets remaining on the face of the earth—the $600 billion, more or less annual problem nobody knows about." Fraud is truly an annual $600 billion gorilla.

¶ 2002 Some History of Fraud Detection

Fraud detection was the job of external auditors until the start of the 1900s. Independent auditors began to depart from the primary mission of detecting fraud and moved to the verification of financial statement balances. Soon an expectation gap developed: The public expects independent accountants to detect fraud, but auditors state that they are only responsible for detecting material financial statement fraud.

As a result of a number of high-profile financial statement frauds (i.e., McKesson & Robbins), the independent Cohen Commission was established by the AICPA in 1974. The Cohen Commission's report was published in 1978; it recognized this expectation gap and provided a section dealing with the responsibility for the detection of fraud. In 1985, this commission became known as the Treadway Commission (Committee of Sponsoring Organizations of the Treadway Commission (COSO)), and in 1992 it issued a report entitled *Internal Controls—Integrated Framework*, which stressed the need for enhancing internal controls. Then again in March 1999, COSO issued *Fraudulent Financial Reporting: 1987–1997: An Analysis of U.S. Public Companies*. The commission stated that many frauds are initiated in quarterly Form 10-Q, with the first manipulation sometimes involving relatively small amounts. Once the initial fraud remains undetected, the fraud scheme is repeated in subsequently issued financial statements, with the fraud amount increasing over time.[8]

In 1993, the Association of Certified Fraud Examiners published the results of a survey of 2,608 certified fraud examiners (CFEs). The most common type of fraud schemes noted in the survey were asset misappropriation (86 percent), corruption (11 percent), and fraudulent financial statements (two percent). Although fraudulent statements were the most costly scheme per case, asset misappropriation represented the total largest loss ($271 million versus $12 million for fraudulent statements). This same study said that fraud and abuse cost U.S. organizations an estimated $400 billion annually ($9 per day per employee).[9]

The accounting profession finally expanded the auditor's responsibility in detecting fraud and illegal acts with SAS No. 82 in 1997 (superseded by

---

[7] J.W. Koletar, *Fraud Exposed* (Hobeken: John Wiley, 2003).
[8] *COSO—Committee of Sponsoring Organizations of the Treadway Commission Report*, 1999, p. 34.
[9] *Report to the Nation on Occupational Fraud and Abuse* (Austin: ACFE, 1993). Abuse is the practice of an employee that costs an organization money, but there may be no law broken (i.e., one employee getting paid for more hours than he or she works, or takes a longer lunch break).

SAS No. 99) by clearly stating that the detection of material *misstatement in financial statements* is central to an audit. Yet paragraph 10 states the difficulties of detecting fraud when collusion and/or falsifying documents are present:

> An auditor cannot obtain absolute assurance that material misstatements in the financial statements will be detected. Because of (a) the concealment aspects of fraudulent activity, including the fact that fraud often involves collusion or falsified documentation, and (b) the need to apply professional judgment in the identification and evaluation of fraud risk factors and other conditions, even a properly planned and performed audit may not detect a material misstatement resulting from fraud. Accordingly because of the above characteristics of fraud and the nature of fraud evidence . . . the auditor is able to obtain only reasonable assurance that material misstatements in the financial statements, including misstatements resulting from fraud, are detected.[10]

The standard clearly states that the detection of material misstatement in financial statements is central to an audit. Although auditors have previously had the responsibility to detect material misstatement caused by fraud, SAS No. 82 details much more specifically what is required to fulfill those responsibilities. Now, auditors must specifically assess and respond to the risk of material misstatement due to fraud and must assess that risk from the perspective of the broad categories listed in the SAS. In addition, the external auditor has to satisfy new documentation and communication requirements.

Basically, GAAP audit standards are not designed to catch fraud other than financial statement fraud. Independent auditors are not charged professionally with finding asset fraud, but rather merely material misstatement of financial statements. Clearly, there is a gap between user expectations and the product that independent auditors deliver. The typical audit client is probably unwilling to pay for an audit that would catch most fraud, so this expectation gap will not disappear. However, the typical juror probably believes that the purpose of an external or internal audit is to uncover *most* types of fraud or wrongdoing.

Consider one of the largest embezzlements in U.S. history. Between 1990 and 1997, Yasuyoshi Kato, the CFO at Day-Lee, Inc., obtained off-book loans from U.S. affiliates of Japanese banks and issued checks to himself and his wife for about $63 million. This fraud was caught by the IRS, possibly as a result of an anonymous tip. Kato's opulent lifestyle gave him away: he owned two $10,000 macaws, and a zoo size aquarium containing sharks and other exotic fish.

Kato forged daily accounting entries. He started stealing when he agreed to pay his wife and two daughters $50,000 a month for support in a divorce settlement, although he earned only $150,000 a year in salary. He was sentenced to 63 months imprisonment and ordered to repay the

---

[10] SAS No. 82, *Consideration of Fraud in a Financial Statement Audit* (AICPA, *Professional Standards,* vol. 1, AU secs. 110, 230, 312, and 316).

embezzled funds at a rate of $100 per year. The lesson for auditors here is that the lifestyle of an employee can be important in catching fraud.

Possibly because of publicity from so many high-profile fraud cases (e.g., Waste Management, Cendant, Rent-Way), the Public Oversight Board appointed a panel that issued the *Panel on Audit Effectiveness* on August 31, 2000, which stated that "auditors should perform some 'forensic-type' procedures on every audit to enhance the prospect of detecting material financial statement fraud." But the panel members stated that complying with GAAS cannot and will not guarantee that auditors will detect all material fraud.

Chaired by Shaun F. O'Malley, this panel suggested that the forensic fieldwork phase does not mean converting a GAAS audit to a fraud audit. Panel members suggested an attitudinal shift in the auditor's degree of skepticism to "presume the possibility of dishonesty at various levels of management, including collusion override of internal control and falsification of documents."[11]

An auditor should perform either tests of details or precise substantive procedures, but not merely tests of controls. Because management can override controls, tests of controls may not be effective in detecting fraud. Because of the public's attitudinal shift toward professional skepticism, the external auditor should not use the work of the internal auditors in performing the tests for searching for fraud. External auditors may take into consideration, however, the results of internal auditors test results designed to detect fraud in deciding which of their own tests to employ.[12]

Surprise or unpredictable elements should be incorporated into the audit tests, including:

- Recounts of inventory items and unannounced visits to locations
- Interviews of financial and nonfinancial client personnel in different locations
- Requests for written confirmations from client employees regarding matters about which they have made representations to the auditors
- Counting the cash twice in one day
- Requests for written confirmations from customers and vendors that otherwise would not be made (e.g., looking for companies set up by insiders)
- Tests of accounts not normally performed annually

---

[11] *Panel on Audit Effectiveness: Report and Recommendations* (Public Oversight Board, 2000), p. 89. See www.pobauditpanel.org.

[12] *Ibid.*, p. 91.

¶ 2002

- Tests of accounts that are deemed low risk
- Use of technologically advanced audit tools (e.g., ACL, query tools, Benford's Law)
- Placing marked money at locations where cash collections are gathered and turned over for deposit
- Match-up of payroll with life and medical insurance deductions because ghost employees seldom elect these insurance coverages, as well as looking for multiple employees having the same address
- Covert surveillance if appropriate (e.g., watching employees clocking onto a work site to make sure they use only one card)

In response to the research and recommendations made by the Public Oversight Board's Panel on Audit Effectiveness in 2000, the AICPA issued Statement on Auditing Standards (SAS) No. 99, Consideration of Fraud in a Financial Statement Audit. The main points of the standard are as follows:

- *Increased emphasis on professional skepticism*—Members of the audit team must exchange ideas or brainstorm how fraud could occur so that they might design audit tests responsive to the risks of fraud.
- *Discussions with management*—Auditors must ask the client's management and other employees about the risk of fraud, and whether they know of its existence in the organization.
- *Unpredictable audit tests*—Auditors should design tests that would be unpredictable and unexpected and should test areas, locations, and accounts that otherwise might not be tested.
- *Responding to management override of controls*—The engagement team must test for management override of controls.

For example, in September 2003, American International Group, Inc. agreed to pay a $10 million fine in settlement of civil charges from the SEC with regards to a financial product AIG sold to Brightpoint, Inc. Allegedly AIG sold Brightpoint a retroactive insurance policy in 1999 to help Brightpoint falsify their earnings. The SEC accused Brightpoint of fraud and book and record keeping violations.[13] Here two external auditors and two internal auditing groups missed the fraud.

COSO (sponsored by American Institute of Certified Public Accountants, American Accounting Association, Financial Executives International, The Institute of Internal Auditors, and the Institute of Management

---

[13] Randall Smith and Theo Francis, "AIG Is Charged By SEC With Fraud," *Wall Street Journal*, September 12, 2003, pp. A-3 and A-8.

Accountants) sees itself as an organization that creates frameworks from which the standard setting bodies and other authorities might develop their materials. They released a new draft for an Enterprise Risk Management Framework that is in the comment phase until mid-October 2003. It is discussed and a copy is available at *http://www.coso.org*. The document itself carries little real authority, but like the previous framework, it may be acted upon by organizations. The long term question is whether the SEC and the Public Company Accounting Oversight Board (PCAOB) are going to pay much attention to such a framework, because they may not have much use for at least some of the sponsoring member organizations. Or does the framework in some way reflect the direction of the SEC and the PCAOB? Will the SEC be more inclined to view this report as another attempt at self-regulation too late to be of any use? One has to wonder how much of an appetite the SEC has for any of this material since it took a long time for the previous COSO framework to impact auditing authority.

.01 The Role of Internal Auditors

There are other combatants of fraud besides the external, independent auditor. The internal auditor (a Certified Internal Auditor, or CIA) should be in a position to uncover fraud, yet the internal auditing profession does not wish to accept the responsibility of finding fraud on the job. The professional CIA standards defines fraud as follows:

> Any illegal acts characterized by deceit, concealment, or violation of trust. These acts are not dependent upon the application of threat of violence or physical force. Frauds are perpetrated by individuals and organizations to obtain money, property or services; to avoid payment or loss of service; or to secure personal or business advantage.[14]

The Institute of Internal Auditors (IIA) Due Professional Care Standard (Section 280) assigns the internal auditor the task of assisting in fraud control by examining and evaluating the adequacy and effectiveness of the internal control system. However, the primary responsibility for deterrence of fraud is placed on management, which is responsible for establishing and maintaining the control systems. In general, the internal auditor is more concerned with employee fraud than with management and other external fraud.[15] Yet the 1999 COSO study said that in three-quarters of the fraud cases the chief executive officer is directly involved. So, not surprisingly, the majority of fraud is uncovered from tips and complaints from other employees.[16]

The IIA standards state that the auditor must consider the possibility of material irregularities or noncompliance during an internal audit. The internal auditor's responsibility for detecting fraud includes having suffi-

---

[14] Institute of Internal Auditors, *Standards for the Professional Practice of Internal Auditing* (Altamonte Springs, Fla.: The Institute of Internal Auditors, 2001).

[15] Institute of Management and Administration, Press Release, "Employee Fraud #1: Concern of Internal Auditors" (New York: Institute of Management and Administration, September 13, 1999).

[16] Association of Certified Fraud Examiners, *Report to the Nation on Occupational Fraud Abuse*, www.cfenet.com.

¶ 2002.01

cient knowledge of fraud to identify indicators that fraud has been committed. He or she should be alert to opportunities that could allow fraud, and if found, the auditor should notify the appropriate authorities in the organization if there are sufficient indicators to recommend an investigation. If the internal auditor recommends an investigation, he or she must follow up to determine that the internal auditing department has fulfilled its responsibilities.[17]

But as stated earlier, often management itself is involved with the fraud. The 1999 COSO report stated that in 72 percent of the cases reviewed, the CEO was named in the SEC's complaint, and in 43 percent, the CFO. What is the internal auditor's responsibility in these cases? For example, in October, 2000, Rent-Way, Inc., announced the possibility of accounting improprieties involving wholesale reduction in expenses. These improprieties were uncovered when the CFO went on vacation. Thus, auditors should beware of employees who do not take vacations! A later audit by PricewaterhouseCoopers found $129 million in Rent-Way's accounting improprieties and year-end adjustments covering a period of three years. Rent-Way's controller and chief accounting officer was fired, and the company's president and chief operating officer was asked to resign. Where were the company's internal auditors? What does the internal auditor do when there is massive fraud at the highest levels? In the case of an *external* auditor, if the perpetrator controls the audit committee and/or the board of directors, the independent auditor should go directly to the client's legal counsel.

SIAS No. 2, *Communicating Results* gives guidance for actions of internal auditors when internal audit reports are issued as a result of a fraud investigation. Internal auditors should:

- Notify management or the board when the incidence of significant fraud has been established to a reasonable certainty.

- If the results of a fraud investigation indicate that previously undiscovered fraud materially adversely affected previous financial statements, for one or more years, inform appropriate management and the audit committee of the Board of Directors of the discovery.

- Include in a written report all findings, conclusions, recommendations, and corrective actions taken.

- Submit a draft of the written report to legal counsel for review, especially when the internal auditor chooses to invoke client privilege.

---

[17] Institute of Internal Auditors, *Statement on Internal Auditing Standards* (SIAS) No. 3, 1985.

.02 The Role of Fraud Specialists

The certified fraud examiner (CFE) is another professional specialty that has an interest in fraud detection. A CFE often holds another professional certificate (i.e., CPA or CIA) and is normally not responsible for initially detecting fraud. Instead, a CFE becomes involved with a situation when an allegation of fraud is made. There are approximately 25,000 CFEs and associate members in 70 countries. The Association of Certified Fraud Examiners, headquartered in Austin, Texas, is dedicated to reducing the incidence of fraud and white-collar crime through prevention and education. A CFE is a gatherer of facts and may not express an opinion as to the guilt or innocence of any person or party (i.e., the courts should assign blame).

A younger professional group is the Diplomate American Board of Forensic Accountants (DABFA), which is a branch of the American College of Forensic Examiners. In 2001, this multidisciplinary group (15,000 members) developed a new certified forensic accountant (CrFA) certificate.[18]

The Association of Certified Fraud Specialists is an educational, nonprofit corporation headquartered in Sacramento California. They offer a certified fraud specialist certification (CFS).

The National Association of Certified Valuation Analysts (NACVA) offers both a Certified Forensic Financial Analyst (CFFA) certificate and a newer Certified Fraud Deterrence (CFD) certificate.[19]

The certified protection professional (CPP) is a certificate issued by the American Society of Industrial Security. With more than 8,000 members, the organization describes certificate holders as professionals who "demonstrate their competency in the areas of security solutions and best-business practices."

¶ 2003 The Fraud Investigation Process

Both external and internal auditors are being, and will be, forced to develop fraud awareness audit techniques. Jack Robertson states that "auditors need to understand fraud and potential fraud situations, and they need to know how to ask the right kind of questions during an audit."[20] The Panel on Audit Effectiveness recommended in its report that auditors perform some forensic-type procedures on every audit to enhance the prospects of detecting material financial statement fraud. This forensic phase "should become an integral part of the audit, with careful thought given to how and when it is to be carried out."[21]

---

[18] For information, contact American College of Forensic Examiners, 2750 E. Sunshine, Springfield, MO 65804, 800-423-9737.

[19] NACVA, 1245 East Brickyard Road, Suite 110, Salt Lake City, Utah 84106, 801-486-0600.

[20] J.C. Robertson, *Fraud Examination for Managers* (Austin: Viesca Books, 2000), 187.

[21] *Panel on Audit Effectiveness*, p. 88.

¶ 2002.02

There are three major factors in fraud: motive, opportunity, and lack of integrity (or rationalization). SAS No. 99 uses similar pressures/incentives, opportunity, and attitudes/rationalizations. If the three factors are present in members of an organization, fraud will probably occur. An economic *motive* may be the simple need for money to pay hospital bills, to buy drugs, to pay off gambling debts, or to make alimony payments. The absence or lapse of internal controls in an organization is a tempting, open door or *opportunity* for fraud. Finally, the *lack of integrity* or *ability to rationalize* criminal behavior completes the pyramid and enables an individual to engage in fraudulent activities without admitting to being a criminal.

Fraud auditing is not easy, and such an audit is often conducted after fraudulent activity has been suspected or detected. The Panel on Audit Effectiveness states that many fraud auditing techniques are not practical, or are impossible to apply in a GAAS audit. As an example, in a fraud audit company employees may be interviewed with their own attorney present or under grants of immunity.[22]

Fraud, by its nature, is concealed by falsified documents, including forgery, and external auditors are not trained in document authentication. The structural behavioral considerations of fraud are like an iceberg: many of the behavioral considerations lurk beneath the surface, endangering the unsuspecting auditor.[23] Collusion among management and other parties hides fraud, and auditors do not have the investigative powers to obtain evidence under oath. A GAAS audit is not a detailed forensic examination of evidence, because a forensic audit is often performed on a limited number of accounts. Thus, a GAAS audit is designed to find only material misstatements.[24]

Barbara Apostolou compared the differences between a fraud audit and the typical financial audit, as summarized in Table 20.1.[25]

---

[22] *Ibid.*, p. 89, note 32.
[23] G.J. Bologna and R.J. Lindquist, *Fraud Auditing and Forensic Accounting*, 2d ed. (New York: John Wiley & Sons, 1995), 47.
[24] *Panel of Audit Effectiveness*, pp. 75-76.
[25] Adapted from B. Apostolou, *"Course 992003:* Fundamentals of Fraud Detection and Prevention," www.education.smartpros.com.

Table 20.1

Comparison of Auditing and Fraud Examination

Issue	Financial Audits	Fraud Examinations
Timing	Recurring: conducted on a regular basis	Nonrecurring: conducted only with sufficient predication
Scope	General: collection of sufficient, competent data to support the opinion rendered	Specific: conducted to resolve specific allegations
Objective	Opinion: expressed on financial statements	Affix blame: determine whether fraud occurred and who is responsible—adversarial in nature
Methodology	Audit techniques applied primarily to financial data	Fraud examination techniques applied as document examination, public record searches, and interviews
Presumption	Professional skepticism.	Proof to support or refute an allegation of fraud

Subsequent discussion in this chapter divides fraud into two categories:

1. Financial statement fraud and fraudulent financial reporting
2. Misappropriation of assets or asset-theft fraud (defalcation)

The external auditor has a responsibility to plan and perform the audit to obtain reasonable assurance about whether the financial statements are free of material misstatements, whether caused by error or fraud.[26] In general, financial statement fraud does not involve the theft of assets, and the external auditor tends to look for financial statement fraud.

¶ 2004 External Auditor's Responsibilities

Financial statement fraud has been and continues to be the focus of the auditing profession. During the 1890s, external auditors viewed the detection of fraud in general, and financial statement fraud in particular, as the primary purpose of the financial audit. The auditing profession had moved from the acceptance of fraud detection as a primary purpose to the expression of an opinion on fair representation of financial statements during the twentieth century. The accounting profession has initially addressed the external auditor's responsibility for financial statement fraud

---

[26] SAS No. 82, *Consideration of Fraud in a Financial Statement Audit*, (AICPA, Professional Standards, vol. 1, AU sec. 316).

detection in SAS No. 82 and recently in SAS No. 99, titled *Consideration of Fraud in a Financial Statement Audit*.[27] SAS No. 82, which is superceded by SAS No. 99, required the independent auditor to consider a broad range of fraud risk factors in assessing the risk of occurrences of financial statement fraud and to use this assessment in audit planning to detect fraud.

Independent auditors assess the risk of *material* misstatements of the financial statements due to fraud, and they must consider that assessment in designing the audit procedures they perform. SAS No. 82 describes risk factors that the auditor should consider and notes that the auditor must have a questioning mind and apply critical judgment to the audit evidence.

The risk assessment tells the auditor how to respond. Existing audit procedures may be sufficient to obtain reasonable assurance that the financial statements are free of *material* misstatement due to fraud. Even though the amounts are not material, if the items involve higher management the auditor may need to reevaluate the risk of material misstatement due to fraud and the impact on the audit (i.e., there may be a pervasive problem).

If there is a significant risk of fraud, the auditor should consider withdrawing from the engagement and communicating the reasons to the audit committee (or equivalent authority). The disclosure of fraud to parties other than senior management and/or the audit committee is not the auditor's responsibility.

The auditor should document in his or her workpapers evidence of the performance of the risk assessment. Documentation should include any risk factors identified and the auditor's responses to them.

The risk factors listed in SAS No. 82 are broken into fraudulent financial reporting and misstatements arising from misappropriation of assets. These factors are difficult to assess, and they may exist when there is no fraud. If the risk factors are present, the standard does not suggest a response.

The Auditing Standards Board (ASB) of the AICPA, by issuing SAS No. 99, attempts to clarify, but not to expand, the auditor's responsibility to detect and report financial statement fraud. SAS No. 99 states, "The auditor has a responsibility to plan and perform the audit to obtain *reasonable assurance* about whether the financial statements are *free of material misstatement*, whether caused by *error or fraud* (emphasis added)." SAS No. 99 makes it clear that the auditor's responsibility for detecting fraud is framed by the concepts of reasonable, but not absolute, assurance and materiality and is subject to cost/benefit decisions inherent

---

[27] SAS No. 99, *Consideration of Fraud in a Financial Statement Audit*, (AICPA, Professional Standards, vol. 1, AU sec. 316).

in the audit process. However, while auditors are not expected to detect all employees' frauds, the public expects auditors to detect material financial statement fraud perpetrated by management with the purpose of misleading investors and creditors. Independent auditors provide reasonable assurance that financial statements are not materially misstated and therefore, they are free of material errors, irregularities, and fraud. This level of assurance is given in an audit report based on the audit of financial statements. While SAS No. 99 is not suggesting any changes to the auditor's current responsibilities for detecting fraud in a financial statement, it provides new guidelines, concepts and requirements to aid auditors in fulfilling those responsibilities. These guidelines:

1. Describe fraud and its characteristics;

2. Discuss the need for auditors to exercise professional skepticism in conducting financial audits;

3. Require auditors to discuss among the audit team members regarding the risks of material misstatement due to fraud;

4. Require auditors to obtain competent and sufficient evidence to identify risks of material misstatement due to fraud through inquiring of management, performing analytical procedures, and considering fraud risk factors;

5. Identify fraud risk factors and assess these risk factors by considering the client's programs and controls;

6. Require auditors to respond to the results of the risk assessment by (a) determining its overall effect on how the audit is conducted; (b) considering its impact on the nature, timing, and extent of the auditing procedures to be performed; and (c) performing certain procedures (e.g., examining journal entries and other adjustments, reviewing accounting estimates and unusual transactions) to further address the likelihood of occurrence of fraud involving management override of controls;

7. Require auditors to evaluate audit evidence indicating the likelihood of financial misstatements due to fraud and their implications for fair presentation of financial statements;

8. Provide guidance regarding auditors' communications about fraud to management, the audit committee, and others;

9. Describe appropriate documentations of auditors' consideration of fraud.

SAS No. 99 is effective for audits of financial statements for periods beginning on or after December 15, 2002, while early application of its provisions is permissible. SAS No. 99 adopts the fraud triangle presented in

¶ 2004

Figure 20.1 to address the three most common factors pertaining to the commission of fraud.

Figure 20.1

SAS No. 99: The Fraud Triangle

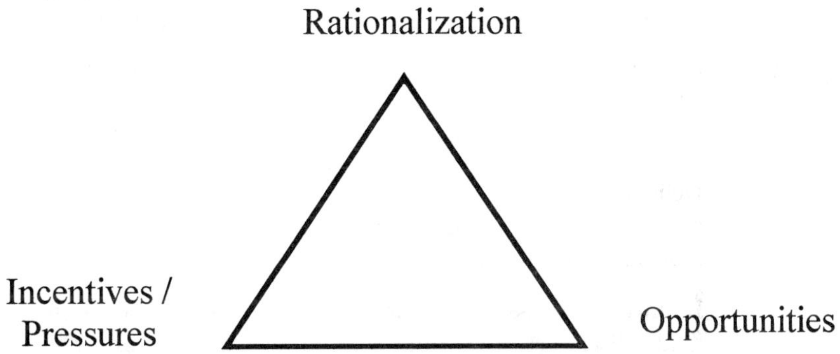

```
            Rationalization
                 /\
                /  \
               /    \
              /      \
Incentives / /_____\ Opportunities
Pressures
```

1. Incentives/pressures are motivations and pressures that cause fraud perpetrators to engage in fraud, such as financial incentives of desire to maintain a particular lifestyle and medical programs.

2. Opportunities for engaging in fraud are provided through lack of vigilant corporate governance and ineffective internal controls.

3. Rationalization is justification and reconciliation to rationalize a wrongful act (e.g., "I was only borrowing it").

¶ 2005 Fraudulent Financial Reporting

Financial statement fraud has become daily press with reports challenging the corporate responsibility and integrity of major companies such as Lucent, Xerox, Rite Aid, Waste Management, MicroStrategy, KnowledgeWare, Raytheon, Sunbeam, Enron, WorldCom, Global Crossing, Adelphia, Qwest, and Tyco that were recently alleged by the SEC for committing fraud. Top management teams including chief executive officers (CEOs) and chief financial officers (CFOs) of these companies are being accused of cooking the books. Occurrences of financial statement fraud by high-profile companies have raised concerns about the integrity, transparency, and reliability of the financial reporting process and have challenged the role of corporate governance in preventing and detecting financial statement fraud.

The definition of financial statement fraud can be found in a number of authoritative reports (e.g., SAS No. 99). Financial statement fraud is defined as deliberate misstatements or omissions of amounts or disclosures of financial statements to deceive financial statement users, particularly investors and creditors. Financial statement fraud may involve the following schemes:

1. Falsification, alteration, or manipulation of material financial records, supporting documents, or business transactions.

2. Material intentional omissions or misrepresentations of events, transactions, accounts, or other significant information from which financial statements are prepared.

3. Deliberate misapplication of accounting principles, policies, and procedures used to measure, recognize, report, and disclose economic events and business transactions.

4. Intentional omissions of disclosures or presentation of inadequate disclosures regarding accounting principles and policies and related financial amounts.[28]

The above definition focuses on the deliberate wrongful act committed by public traded companies that harms users through materially misleading financial statements. The recent SAS No. 99, titled *Consideration of Fraud in a Financial Statement Audit* and issued by the Auditing Standards Board (ASB) of the American Institute of Certified Public Accountants (AICPA) in November 2002, defines two types of misstatements relevant to an audit of financial statements and auditors' consideration of fraud. The first type is misstatements arising from fraudulent financial reporting which are defined as "intentional misstatements or omissions of amounts or disclosures in financial statements designed to deceive financial statement users." The second type is misstatements arising from misappropriation of assets, which are commonly referred to as theft or defalcation. Fraudulent financial statements can be used to unjustifiably sell stock, obtain loans or trade credit, and/or improve managerial compensation and bonuses.

Loss of public confidence in quality and reliability of financial statements caused by the alleged fraudulent activities is the most damaging and costly effect of fraud. Financial statement fraud is harmful in many ways because it:

1. Undermines the reliability, quality, transparency, and integrity of the financial reporting process. An increasing number of financial restatements and recent enforcement acts by the SEC

---

[28] Zabihollah Rezaee. *Financial Statement Fraud: Prevention and Detection.* New York: John Wiley and Sons, Inc., 2002.

¶ 2005

against big corporations (e.g., Enron, WorldCom, Xerox, ImClone, Global Crossing, Qwest, Halliburton, Bristol-Myers, Tyco, Dynegy, Adelphia Communications, and Computer Associates) for alleged financial statement fraud have severely undermined the public confidence in the veracity of financial reports.

2. Jeopardizes the integrity and objectivity of the auditing profession, especially auditors and auditing firms. The jury's guilty verdict of obstruction of justice ended Andersen's audit practice in 2003. Arthur Andersen was one of the Big Five international public accounting firms.

3. Diminishes the confidence of the capital markets, as well as market participants, in the reliability of financial information. The capital market and market participants, including investors, creditors, employees, and pensioners, are affected by the quality and transparency of financial information they use in making investment decisions.

4. Makes the capital market less efficient. Auditors reduce the information risk that may be associated with the published financial statements and thus make them more transparent. The information risk is the likelihood that financial statements are inaccurate, false, misleading, biased, and deceptive. By applying the same financial standards to diverse businesses and by reducing the information risk, accountants contribute to the efficiency of our capital markets.

5. Adversely affects the nation's economic growth and prosperity. Accountants are expected to make financial statements among corporations more comparable by applying the same set of accounting standards to diverse businesses. This enhanced comparability makes business more transparent, the capital markets more efficient, the free enterprise system possible, and the economy more vibrant and prosperous. The efficiency of our capital markets depends on receiving objective, reliable, and transparent financial information. Thus, the accounting profession, especially practicing auditors, plays an important role in our free enterprise system and capital markets. However, Enron, WorldCom, and Global Crossing debacles cast some doubt that the role of accountants can be compromised.

6. Results in huge litigation costs. Corporations and their auditors are being sued for alleged financial statement fraud and related audit failures by a diverse group of litigants including class action suits by small investors and suits by the U.S. Justice Department. Investors also are given the right to sue and

¶ 2005

recover damages from those who aided and abetted securities fraud.

7. Destroys careers of individuals involved in financial statement fraud such as top executives being barred from serving on the board of directors of any public companies or auditors being barred from practice of public accounting. Several senior executives of Adelphia Communications were arrested on July 24, 2002, for allegedly committing fraud by stealing hundreds of millions of dollars from the battered cable company and engaging in financial shenanigans.

8. Causes bankruptcy or loss of substantial economic losses by the company engaged in financial statement fraud. WorldCom, with $107 billion in assets and $41 billion in debt, finally filed for Chapter 11 bankruptcy protection on July 21, 2002. WorldCom's bankruptcy is the largest U.S. bankruptcy ever, almost twice the size of Enron.

9. Encourages regulatory intervention. Regulatory agencies (e.g., the SEC) considerably influence the financial reporting process and related audit functions. The current perceived crisis in the financial reporting process and audit functions has encouraged lawmakers to establish accounting reform legislation (i.e., Sarbanes-Oxley Act of 2002). This Act will drastically change the self-regulating environment of the accounting profession to a regulatory framework under the SEC oversight function.

10. Causes destruction in the normal operations and performance of alleged companies. Alleged financial statement fraud of Enron, WorldCom, Global Crossing, and Adelphia has caused these high profile companies to file bankruptcy and their top executives have been fined and, in some cases, indicted for violation of Securities Acts.

11. Raises serious doubt about the efficacy of financial statement audits. The financial community is demanding high-quality audits, and auditors should improve their audit effectiveness and efficacy to produce the needed assurance.

12. Erodes public confidence and trust in the accounting and auditing profession. One message that comes through loud and clear these days in response to the increasing number of financial restatements and alleged financial statement fraud is that the public confidence in the financial reporting process and related audit functions is substantially eroded.[29]

---

[29] Ibid.

Rezaee presents a 3Cs model of financial statement fraud as depicted in Figure 20.2. The 3Cs model consists of conditions, corporate structure, and choices.[30]

Figure 20.2

3Cs Model of Financial Statement Fraud

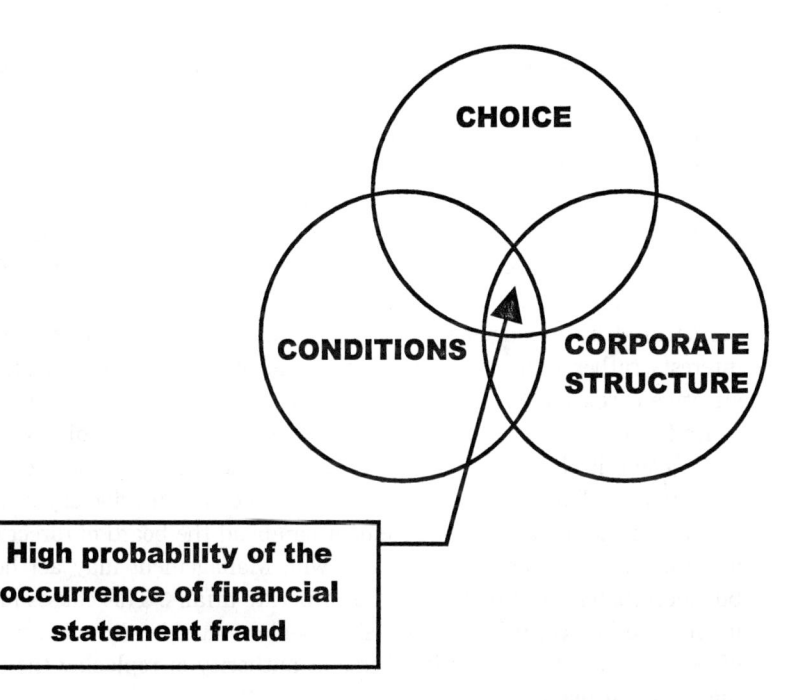

[Venn diagram of three overlapping circles labeled CHOICE, CONDITIONS, and CORPORATE STRUCTURE, with the intersection pointing to a box labeled "**High probability of the occurrence of financial statement fraud**"]

- Conditions are the motivations and pressures to engage in financial statement fraud.

- Corporate structure is the organization of corporate governance which may create an environment that increases the likelihood of fraud (aggressiveness, arrogance, cohesiveness, loyalty, blind trust, control ineffectiveness, lack of vigilant oversight, gamesmanship).

- Choice is the decision made by management to engage in financial statement fraud.

Source: Zabihollah Rezaee. "The Three Cs of Fraudulent Financial Reporting," *Internal Auditor.* October 2003, 56-61.

---

[30] Zabihollah Rezaee. "The Three Cs of Fraudulent Financial Reporting," *Internal Auditor.* October 2003, 56-61.

Prevention and detection of financial statement fraud is the responsibility of all corporate governance participants and those involved with the financial statements' supply chain. These individuals are members of the board of directors including the audit committee, management, internal auditors, external auditors, the SEC, and users of financial reports. Figure 20.3 presents financial statement fraud, occurrence, prevention, detection, and correction.

The existence of responsible and effective corporate governance (consisting of a vigilant and active board of directors, an effective audit committee, and an adequate and effective internal audit function) discovers the intended financial statement fraud and prevents its occurrence. When financial statement fraud is prevented at this stage, the financial information will not be misleading. However, ineffective and irresponsible corporate governance, along with the gamesmanship attitude of corporate governance, would fail to prevent the deliberate financial statement fraud perpetrated by management. Management may operate in its own self-interests rather than the interests of stakeholders. Lack of adequate and effective corporate governance (e.g., internal control) may create opportunities for management to appoint the board of directors, auditors, and the audit committee and offer the monetary incentive of their continued employment. This potential for moral hazard causes a fiduciary conflict of interest in the sense that management can bend the board of directors, the audit committee, and auditors to its will. Management may act honestly but incompetently in managing the corporate affairs. This causes management to be ineffective in creating shareholder value. In this case, the board of directors should exercise its oversight authority of replacing the current management team.

The board of directors and its representative audit committee should oversee (1) the integrity, quality, transparency, and reliability of the financial reporting process; (2) the adequacy and effectiveness of internal control structure in preventing, detecting, and correcting material misstatements in the financial statements; and (3) the effectiveness, efficacy, and objectivity of audit functions. Enron, WorldCom, and Global Crossing debacles indicate that many boards of directors are not good caretakers. Boards are theoretically elected to act as the shareholders' eyes and ears to ensure creation of shareholder value. Boards are elected to hire executives (e.g., top management team) and drive their performance through the carrot (higher executive compensation) and the stick (compensation cuts and termination). However, lack of due diligence by the board of directors creates opportunities for management to engage in financial statement fraud. The board of directors and audit committee of Enron came under sharp criticism for allowing the use of special purpose entities to overstate earnings and understate liabilities. Some directors and audit committee members were even being accused of "insider trading" for making misleading statements about the company's prospects and selling more than $1 billion worth of stock during the last three years before the Enron crisis.

Four recent fraud studies, conducted by Ernst & Young, 2002; the Committee of Sponsoring Organizations of the Treadway Commission (COSO), 1999; the Institute of Management and Administration (IOMA) and the Institute of Internal Auditors (IIA), 1999; and KPMG, 2003, provide insights into the better understanding of fraud incidents, causes and effects of frauds, and ways to prevent and detect their occurrences. These studies indicate that financial statement fraud is typically perpetrated by top management teams including presidents, CEOs, CFOs, controllers, and other top executives. Thus, vigilant oversight function of the board of directors and its representative audit committee in (1) setting a "tone at the top" demonstrating commitment to high quality financial reports; (2) discouraging and punishing fraudulent financial activity; and (3) monitoring managerial decisions and actions as related to the financial reporting process can substantially reduce instances of financial statement fraud. Fraud studies underscore the need for the involvement of all corporate governance participants, including the board of directors, the audit committee, management, internal auditors, external auditors, and governing bodies, as part of a broad effort to prevent and detect financial statement fraud and, thus, improve quality, integrity, transparency, and reliability of financial statements. The majority of the recent disclosed alleged financial statement frauds have been in revenue reporting (e.g., Enron, WorldCom). Enron created private partnerships known as special purpose entities (SPEs) to overstate earnings and hide liabilities. WorldCom improperly reported $11 billion of expenses as capital expenditures to overstate earnings and net cash flows from operating activities. Adelphia Communications allowed its founder and controlling owner to borrow under a credit facility shared with and guaranteed by the company and then to use the proceeds to buy shares of the company. Global Crossing and Qwest engaged in back-to-back swaps for fiber-optic capacity with no business purpose except to manipulate earnings.

Several strategies can be established to prevent, detect, and correct financial statement fraud. Examples of these strategies are (1) establishment of responsible corporate governance, a vigilant board of directors and audit committee, diligent management, and adequate and effective internal audit functions; (2) utilization of an alert, skeptical external audit function, responsible legal counsel, adequate and effective internal control structure, and external regulatory procedures; and (3) implementation of appropriate corporate strategies for correction of the committed financial statement fraud, elimination of the probability of its future occurrences, and restoration of confidence in the financial reporting process. Financial statement fraud occurs when one or a combination of these strategies is relaxed due to self-interest, lack of due diligence, pressure, over-reliance, or

¶ 2005

lack of dedication. The opportunity of occurrence of financial statement fraud is significantly increased when these strategies are inadequate and ineffective.

The pervasiveness of corporate and accounting scandals of the early 2000s encouraged several organizations to establish "financial scandal sheets" online to keep track of these scandals. Table 20.3 presents these scandals, their allegations, and the reported dates in alphabetical order.

Fraud Auditing 691

Figure 20.3

Financial Statement Fraud Occurrence, Prevention, Detection and Correction

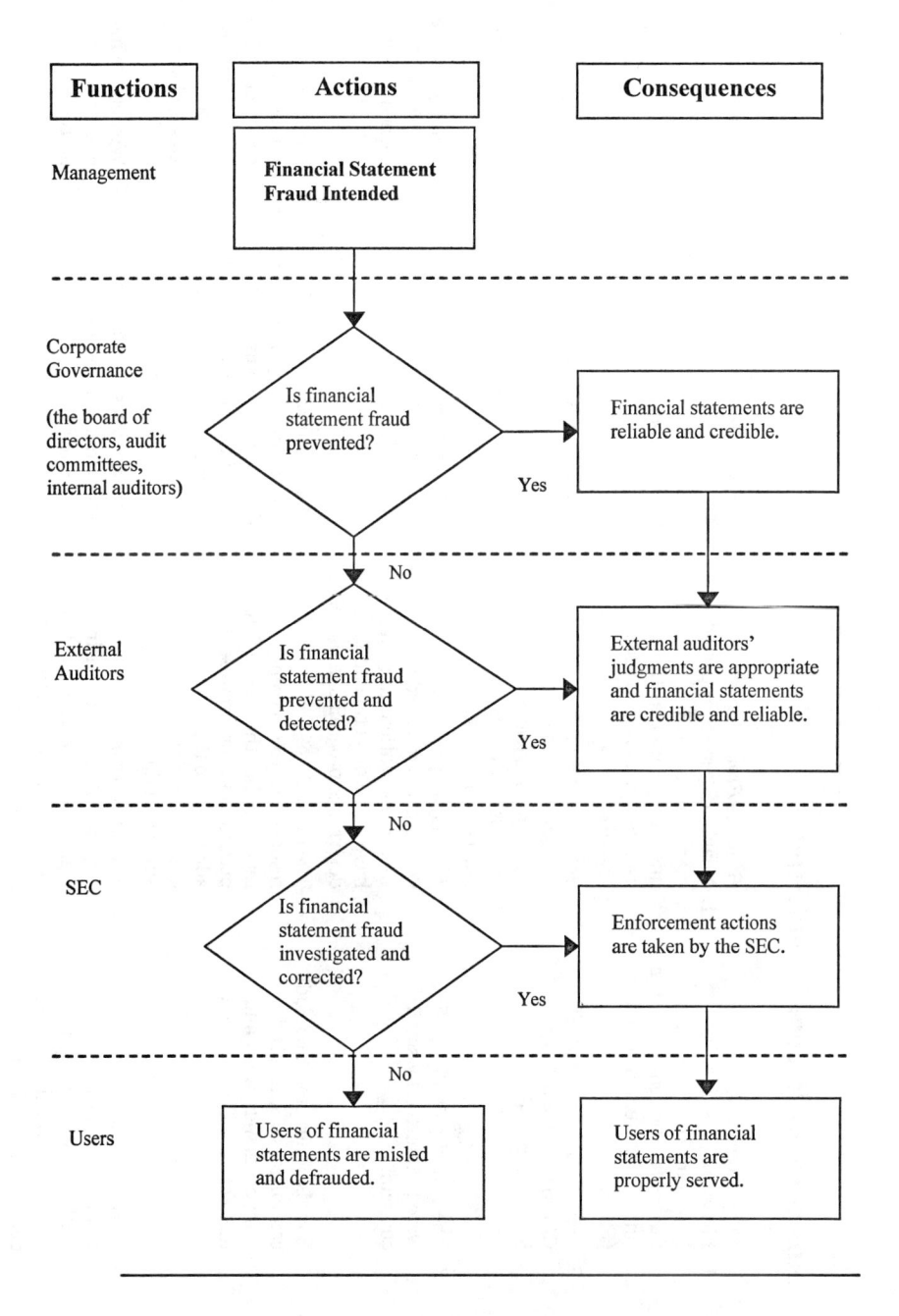

Functions	Actions	Consequences
Management	Financial Statement Fraud Intended	
Corporate Governance (the board of directors, audit committees, internal auditors)	Is financial statement fraud prevented? → Yes	Financial statements are reliable and credible.
External Auditors	↓ No Is financial statement fraud prevented and detected? → Yes	External auditors' judgments are appropriate and financial statements are credible and reliable.
SEC	↓ No Is financial statement fraud investigated and corrected? → Yes	Enforcement actions are taken by the SEC.
Users	↓ No Users of financial statements are misled and defrauded.	Users of financial statements are properly served.

¶ 2005

Table 20.2
Summary of Recent Fraud Studies

COSO Report[1]

1. Financial pressures were important contributory factors for the commitment of financial statement fraud (FSF).

2. Top executives (e.g., CEOs, CFOs) were commonly involved in FSF.

3. The majority of alleged FSF were committed by small companies.

4. Boards of directors and audit committees of the fraud companies were weak and ineffective.

5. Adverse consequences for fraud companies were bankruptcy, significant changes in ownership, and delisting by national stock exchanges.

Business Fraud Survey[2]

1. Nearly 15 percent reported management misappropriation as the greatest fraud risk to their organization.

2. Sixty percent of the respondents reported their department's fraud risk analysis process as being reactive in nature.

3. The majority of respondents (72 percent) reported that their organizations did not have fraud detection and deterrence programs in place.

4. The majority of the respondents (68 percent) reported that they never felt pressured to compromise the adherence to their organization's standards of ethical conduct.

5. The majority of the respondents reported their organization's external auditors as being ineffective in preventing and detecting fraud.

KPMG Survey[3]

1. More companies report incidents of fraud compared to five years ago.

2. Medical insurance claims fraud had the greatest average cost per incident followed by financial statement fraud (FSF).

3. FSF resulted in an average loss of more than $1 million per incident.

4. More than 75 percent of responsible companies report they will launch new anti-fraud initiatives in response to the Sarbanes-Oxley Act.

5. Various types of collusion were cited as important causes of fraud.

Ernst & Young Survey[4]

1. More than 20 percent of the respondents were aware of fraud in their workplace.

2. Nearly 80 percent would be willing to turn in a colleague thought to be committing a fraudulent act.

3. Employees lose a staggering 20 percent of every dollar earned to some type of workplace fraud.

4. Most frequently committed frauds are theft of office items, claiming extra hours worked, inflating expense accounts, and taking kickbacks from suppliers.

5. Women are more likely than men to report fraudulent activities.

¶ 2005

Fraud Auditing

6. Cumulative amounts of FSF were relatively significant and large.

7. More than half of the alleged FSF involved overstatement of revenues.

8. Most FSF were not isolated to a single fiscal period.

9. Fifty-five percent of the audit reports issued in the last year of the fraud period contained unqualified opinions.

10. The majority of the sample fraud companies (56 percent) were audited by a Big Eight/Big Five auditing firm.

6. The majority of the respondents believed that more budgets should be devoted to fraud-related activities and training in their internal audit department.

6. Personal financial pressures were considered as important red flags signaling the possibility of fraud occurrence.

7. Suggested fraud prevention and detection strategies are: effective internal controls, the tone at the top, training courses in fraud prevention and detection, a corporate code of conduct, and ethics training.

6. Older employees were more likely to be willing to report fraudulent activities than younger employees.

Sources:

[1] Committee of Sponsoring Organizations of the Treadway Commission (COSO). "Fraudulent Financial Reporting: 1987-1997, An Analysis of U.S. Public Companies." (1999).

[2] The Institute of Management and Administration (IOMA) and the Institute of Internal Auditors (IIA). "Business Fraud Survey." (1999). Available at *http://www.theiia.org*.

[3] KPMG. "2003 Fraud Survey." (2003). Available at *http://www.kpmg.com*.

[4] Ernst & Young. "American Works: Employers Lose 20 Percent of Every Dollar to Work Place Fraud." (2002). Available at *http://www.ey.com/global/Content.nsf/US/Media_-_Release_-_08-05-02DC*.

¶ 2005

Table 20.3

Reported Financial Scandals

Company	Allegations	Reported Date
Adelphia Communications	Granted $3.1 billion in off-balance-sheet loans to its founder; overstated results by inflating capital expenses and hiding debt; used billions of dollars of company money for personal use.	April 2002
AES/Dennis W. Bakke	Used secured equity-linked loans to inflate revenues and bolster stock prices.	June 2002
AOL Time Warner	Inflated advertisement revenue to increase stock prices. Inflated sales by booking barter deals and ads it sold on behalf of others as revenue to keep its growth rate up and seal the deal.	July 2002
Anicom Inc.	A variety of accounting fraud charges including bank fraud, lying to the SEC, and making false statements.	October 23, 2003
Arthur Andersen	Shredded documents related to audit client Enron after the SEC launched an inquiry into Enron.	November 2001
Bristol-Myers Squibb	Inflated sales by offering incentives to wholesalers. Inflated its 2001 revenue by $1.5 billion by "channel stuffing," or forcing wholesalers to accept more inventory than they can sell to get it off the manufacturer's books.	July 2002
Citigroup	Assisted Enron Corp. and others to set up sham transactions to alter their finances.	October 2001
CMS Energy	Overstated revenues by about $4.4 billion in 2000 and in 2001 by using "round-trip" trades to artificially boost energy trading volume.	May 2002
Cutter & Buck, Inc.	A variety of criminal and civil charges pertaining to financial reporting fraud.	August 8, 2003
Duke Energy	Engaged in 23 "round-trip" trades to boost trading volumes and revenue.	July 2002
Dynegy	Inflated revenue and volume by executing "round-trip" trades to artificially boost energy trading volume and cash flow.	May 2002
El Paso	Used 125 "round-trip" trades to artificially boost energy trading volume.	May 2002
Enron	Boosted profits and hid debts totaling over $1 billion by improperly using off-the-books partnerships; manipulated the Texas power market; bribed foreign governments to win contracts abroad; manipulated California energy market.	October 2001

¶ 2005

Global Crossing	Engaged in network capacity "swaps" with other carriers to inflate revenue; shredded documents related to accounting practices.	February 2002
Halliburton	Improperly booked $100 million in annual construction cost overruns before customers agreed to pay for them.	May 2002
HPL Technology	Inflated stock prices by allowing executives following IPO to sell 85,500 shares at inflated prices.	October 2002
Homestore.com	Inflated sales by booking barter transactions as revenue.	January 2002
IMClone Systems	Charged with insider trading.	August 2002
JP Morgan Chase	Assisted Enron Corp. and others to set up sham transactions to change their financing.	October 2001
Kmart	Used accounting practices intended to mislead investors about its financial health by improperly accounting for vendor allowances.	January 2002
Merck	Recorded $12.4 billion in consumer-to-pharmacy co-payments that Merck never collected.	July 2002
Mirant	Overstated various assets and liabilities.	July 2002
Network Associates	Overstated revenues and understated expenses from 1998 to 2000.	July 2001
Nicor Energy, LLC, a joint venture between Nicor and Dynegy	Independent audit uncovered accounting problems that boosted revenue and underestimated expenses.	July 2002
Parmalat	Falsified bank statements by improperly claiming that it had $5 billion cash in a Bank of America account.	December 2003
Peregrine Systems	Overstated $100 million in sales by improperly recognizing revenue from third-party resellers.	May 2002
Qwest Communications International	Inflated revenue using network capacity "swaps" and improper accounting for long-term deals.	February 2002
Reliant Energy	Engaged in "round-trip" trades to boost trading volumes and revenue.	May 2002
Rite Aid	Inflated revenues by $1.6 billion from 1997-1999.	August 2002

¶ 2005

Tyco	Ex-CEO L. Dennis Kozlowski indicted for tax evasion. SEC investigating whether the company was aware of his actions, possible improper use of company funds and related-party transactions, as well as improper merger accounting practices by improperly creating cookie jar revenues.	May 2002
WorldCom	Overstated cash flow by booking $3.8 billion in operating expenses as capital expenses; gave founder Bernard Ebbers $400 million in off-the-books loans.	March 2002
Xerox	Falsified financial results for five years, boosting income by $1.5 billion.	June 2000

Sources:

CBS MarketWatch Scandal Sheet. Available at *http://cbs.marketwatch.com/news/features/scandal_sheet.asp*.

Citizen Works—Corporate Scandal Fact Sheet. Available at *http://www.citizanworks.org/enron/corp-scandal.php*.

Forbes. The Corporate Scandal Sheet (as of August 26, 2002). Available at *http://www.forbes.com/home/2002/07/25/accountingtracker-print.html*.

There is a fine line between legitimate and illegitimate earnings management—somewhat like the difference between lightning and a lightning bug. Michael R. Young suggests two types of managed earnings: "One type is simply conducting the business of the enterprise in order to attain controlled, disciplined growth. The other type involves deliberate manipulation of the accounting in order to create the *appearance* of controlled, disciplined growth—when, in fact, all that is happening is that accounting entries are being manipulated."[31] *The Panel on Audit Effectiveness* refused to define it,[32] and the definition of illegitimate earnings management is a constantly changing, larger category—what is legitimate today may be illegitimate tomorrow. The panel did not believe the GAAS audit should become a fraud audit, however, and the primary responsibility for the prevention and detection of fraud rests with management, the board of directors, and the audit committee. But in all audits the degree of audit effort in forensic-type steps should be more than inconsequential.[33]

.01 SEC Efforts

The Securities and Exchange Commission (SEC) is working closely with criminal prosecutors to attack financial statement fraud. Richard Walker, the SEC's director of enforcement, stated in a speech to the AICPA

---

[31] M.R. Young, *Accounting Irregularities and Financial Fraud: A Corporate Governance Guide* (2000), 13. But the difference between the two is like the difference between tax avoidance and tax evasion: free room and board in Leavenworth.

[32] *Panel on Audit Effectiveness*, p. 77.
[33] *Ibid.*, p. 24.

¶ 2005.01

in Washington in 1999 that the agency continues "to see an unacceptably higher number of busted audits." The SEC plans to increase its attacks on companies' weak internal controls and the individuals at companies "responsible for doctoring the books." In essence, the message is: Cook the books and you will go directly to jail without passing go.[34]

According to Richard Walker, the SEC plans to bring more enforcement cases against "weak-kneed auditors" and consulting auditors for corporate audit clients who have become soft on the companies' books.[35] Generally, the SEC starts an informal probe of a company if the commission believes there is information that the firm should be investigated. An informal inquiry may be expanded to a formal investigation, which may lead to the filing of civil or criminal charges. (See Chapter 3, "Legal Liability.")

.02 Milestone Cases

Many auditors are aware of the landmark fraudulent financial statement cases. McKesson-Robbins, Inc., was caught overstating physical inventory and sales by $19 million. Another case was Nick Leeson, a Singapore trader, who single-handedly bankrupted Baring PLC with his derivatives trading in 1995. The Great Salad Oil Swindle by Anthony DeAngelis in the late 1950s, Equity Funding in the late 1960s, and ZZZZ Best Carpet cleaning service all remind auditing practitioners of the dangers of fraud. More current situations include those at Tyco International, Rite Aid, Plains All-American Pipeline, Comptronix Corp., Sequoia Systems, Phar-Mor, L.A. Gear, Digital Equipment Corporation, Enron, Xerox, World Com, and Heath South.

The troubled Canadian theater company, Livent, Inc., illustrates how difficult it is for auditors to detect fraud when collusion exists among executives and records are falsified. The Livent saga hit the spotlight in August 1998 when Livent founder and CEO, Garth Drabinsky, and Livent President, Myron Gottlieb, were suspended after an investigation by Livent's new managers led to allegations of financial irregularities. The company also filed for bankruptcy protection in a U.S. bankruptcy court.

On January 13, 1999, the SEC sued Livent and nine former senior officers, directors, and members of the accounting staff for engaging in a "multifaceted and pervasive accounting fraud" spanning eight years from 1990 to 1998. Five individuals were also charged with insider trading. According to the SEC, Drabinsky and Gottlieb manipulated income and operating cash flows with the active participation of several longtime associates as well as several individuals in the company's accounting department. Livent's former chief financial officer and the former Deloitte

---

[34] Statement by Richard H. Walker, SEC's Director of Enforcement, December 7, 1999.
[35] Elizabeth MacDonald, "SEC to Boost Accounting-Fraud Attack, Work More with Criminal Prosecutors," *The Wall Street Journal*, December 8, 1999, p. A-4.

and Touche engagement partner for Livent's 1995 audit also participated in the scheme. Drabinsky and Gottlieb also obtained the support and assistance of numerous Livent personnel in this widespread fraud.

The SEC alleges that Drabinsky and Gottlieb conducted the fraudulent scheme using several approaches, all of which violated GAAP. From 1990 through 1994, Drabinsky and Gottlieb operated a kickback scheme with two Livent vendors who siphoned approximately $7 million (in Canadian dollars) from the company for their personal benefit. Drabinsky and Gottlieb allegedly directed the vendors to artificially inflate invoices. Livent then paid the invoices, and the vendors returned most of the money directly to Drabinsky and Gottlieb.

In addition, the SEC alleges that beginning in 1994 and continuing through the first quarter of 1998, Drabinsky and Gottlieb used three techniques to pump up Livent's financial results. First, Livent pushed preproduction costs for shows to fixed assets such as the construction of theaters. Next, Livent simply eliminated certain expenses from ongoing productions and reentered them as preproduction costs for other shows. Finally, Livent erased operating expenses from ongoing productions and reentered them as preproduction costs for other shows.

According to the SEC, for each reporting period, Drabinsky generally directed the extent of manipulations required to achieve the desired results. Further, two senior Livent controllers wrote a computer program enabling the accountants to make wholesale adjustments to millions of dollars of invoices. Finally, the manipulations were so involved that the senior controller maintained two sets of books to keep track of the manipulations and to monitor Livent's true financial condition. All of these manipulations were designed to understate expenses, inflate earnings, disguise unsuccessful theatrical productions as profitable, and to meet quarterly and annual expectations of Wall Street.

This alleged fraud was massive, widespread, pervasive, and involving numerous Livent personnel in its execution. Why was it not detected? Deloitte claims it observed GAAS. One lesson readily derived from analyzing this situation is how difficult it is to detect fraud when collusion among managers occurs and when records are falsified. At Livent, the collusion allegedly occurred among the top officials as well as deep within the organization. The widespread cooperation within the management ranks combined with a systematic and sophisticated falsification of the records was successful in deceiving the outside auditors, enabling Livent to raise more than $179 million in public equity and in the debt markets.

¶ 2006 Detecting Cooked Books

Lee Seidler maintains that external auditors have a poor record of uncovering fraud, stating, "No major fraud has ever been discovered by auditors." He believes that auditors will continue to miss fraud because much of their work is predicated on the assumption that separation of duties prevents fraud. His analysis of the Equity Funding decision concludes that the decision "shakes the foundation of auditing, in that so much is based on the assumption that people don't collude, or they wouldn't collude very long."[36] However, in Equity Funding they colluded for nine years. The *Panel on Audit Effectiveness* states that "GAAS dismiss collusion as impossible or too difficult to detect and pointly explain the lack of expertise of auditors with respect to determining the authenticity of documents. Yet all or most financial reporting frauds involve collusion, and many involve falsified documentation."[37]

Auditors must appreciate the fact that financial statements may be wrong. Some companies use creative accounting techniques to disguise damaging information, to provide a distorted picture of the financial health of the business, to smooth out erratic earnings, or to boost the perception of anemic or lack of earnings. Forensic auditors should adopt a healthy skepticism when reading and evaluating financial reports. Businesses are often clever in hiding these accounting tricks and gimmicks, so users must be ever alert to the signs of outright financial shenanigans. The fraud auditor must attack financial statement and company information the way the fictional Sherlock Holmes approached murder cases.

According to Howard M. Schilit, "financial shenanigans are acts or omissions intended to hide or distort the real financial performance or financial condition of an entity."[38] Schilit provides seven shenanigans; the first five boost current year earnings, and the last two shift current-year earnings to the future:

1. Recording revenue before it is earned (sales on consignment, e.g., Cendant and Sunbeam)

2. Creating fictitious revenue (false journal entries; almost 40 percent of earnings misstatements from 1995 to 1999 involved revenue recognition, and half of these involved complete fabrication, e.g., Kroger)

3. Boosting profits with nonrecurring transactions (selling stock for a gain)

4. Shifting current expenses to a later period (debiting an asset account rather than expensing, e.g., Waste Management)

5. Failing to record or disclose liabilities

6. Shifting current income to a later period (recognizing current revenues as deferred revenue)

7. Shifting future expenses to an earlier period (expensing items that should be debited to an asset account, e.g., software costs)

---

[36] George Mannes, "Cracking the Books II: Reliving Equity Funding, Part 2," TheStreet.com, 10/22/99.

[37] *Panel on Audit Effectiveness*, p. 86.

[38] H.M. Schilit, *Financial Shenanigans* (New York: McGraw-Hill, Inc., 1993).

¶ 2006

Auditors often forget to use financial statement analysis to detect false and misleading statements. Accountants may get bogged down in details and forget to look at the overall picture. On August 4, 1994, California Micro Services Corporation, a high-flying computer chip maker, disclosed that it was writing off half of its accounts receivables, primarily because of product returns. Its stock plunged 40 percent after the announcement, and shareholders filed suit alleging financial shenanigans. Despite these events, the company's external auditors, Coopers and Lybrand, gave the company's books a clean bill of health the following month. Shortly thereafter, it became clear that Coopers and Lybrand had failed to detect an accounting scam. An internal Cal Micro investigation uncovered "preposterous" revenue numbers "almost immediately," says Wade Meyercord, Cal Micro's current chairman.[39]

Five years later, severe penalties were imposed upon the auditing team representing Coopers and Lybrand. The SEC took action to bar the engagement partner and the engagement manager from signing off on public company audits. They were accused of "conducting the audit in a vacuum" and "recklessly ignoring unmistakable red flags." A hearing on the allegation was conducted by an SEC administrative law judge.

Cendant is a marketing and franchising firm that owns franchising rights to such brands as Days Inn and Ramada hotels, Century 21 real estate brokerage, and Avis car rental. Cendant is also the parent company of Sierra On-line, Blizzard Entertainment, and Berkeley Systems. However, the irregularities occurred in the company's membership division, which encompasses travel, dining, entertainment, and shopping club memberships. Disclosure of Cendant's accounting irregularities in April of 1998 caused the collapse of the stock by 46.5 percent in a single day. This decline represented a decrease in Cendant's market capitalization (price per share times the number of shares outstanding) of approximately $14 billion.

In December 1999, Ernst & Young agreed to pay $335 million to the shareholders of Cendant, settling one of the two lawsuits that accuse the auditing firm of failing to detect an accounting fraud at CVC International, a company that Cendant later acquired. Ernst was the outside auditor of CVC, which is alleged to have recorded about $500 million in fake recovery during a period of three years.

This settlement, however, did not end the difficulties faced by Ernst & Young concerning the Cendant issues, because Cendant sued Ernst for negligence in federal court. Meanwhile, Ernst countersued Cendant, accusing both former managers of CVC International and some current Cendant executives of "collusive fraud."[40]

---

[39] Elizabeth MacDonald, "Auditors Miss a Fraud and SEC Tries to Put Them Out of Business," *The Wall Street Journal*, January 6, 2000, p. 1.
[40] Michelle Pacelle and Elizabeth MacDonald, "Ernst & Young Settles One Suit in Cendant Scandal," *The Wall Street Journal*, December 24, 1999, p. B-9.

The government expressed concern about the ties between CVC and its auditors. At least four of CVC's financial mangers were formerly Ernst & Young employees. Ernst denied any implication that these ties affected the firm's independence. The SEC cites the Cendant case, along with accounting failures such as Sunbeam and Waste Management, as the reasons for tighter security of auditing firms. (Also see Chapter 2, "The Code of Professional Conduct.")

The issue of independence was highlighted when the SEC accused PricewaterhouseCoopers, the world's largest accounting firm, of violating rules requiring the firm not to have investments in companies it audited. The report, prepared by a law firm, documented a system in which violations were routine, with many partners unfamiliar with the details of the rules and little effort by many in the firm to enforce them.[41]

The SEC asserted that 31 of the 43 top partners of the firm had committed at least one violation of independence. Six of the 11 partners responsible for enforcing the rule prohibiting a stake in the company being audited had violated that rule at least once. The investigation found a total of 8,064 violations by partners and employees of PricewaterhouseCoopers.

Lynn Turner called the report "a sobering reminder that accounting professionals need to renew their commitment to the fundamental principle of auditor independence."[42] He said that a new study would review the performance of other major accounting firms, adding that "I am concerned about whether the new study will find any differences between the firms."[43]

J.T. Wells divides financial statement frauds into five types: fictitious revenues (dummy sales), fraudulent asset valuations (overvaluing inventory), timing differences (holding books open, recording revenue when services are still due, or shipping goods before sale is final), concealed liabilities and expenses (stashing unpaid bills in desk), and improper disclosures. One scam, the Crazy Eddie $120 million ripoff, used all five methods.[44]

The 1999 COSO study said that the fictitious revenues method was the most popular, accounting for more than half of the schemes in its analysis. Fictitious sales can occur from false journal entries, false sales to existing customers, and false sales to ghost customers. Management fraud can often be detected by interviewing senior staff members and recently departed employees. Auditors should ask the simple question: "Do you suspect

---

[41] Floyd Norris, "Accounting Firm Is Said to Violate Rules Routinely," *The New York Times*, January 7, 2000, p.1.

[42] *Ibid.*

[43] *Ibid.*

[44] Joseph T. Wells, "So That's Why It's Called a Pyramid Scheme," *Journal of Accountancy* (October 2000): 93-94.

anyone in management might be committing fraud or secretly stealing from the company?"

Certain clues or red flags may suggest that a company is engaging in financial shenanigans:

- **Earnings problem.** One of the most significant red flags is a downward trend in earnings. Companies are required to disclose earnings for the last three years in the income statement, so do not look just at the "bottom line." The trend in operating income is just as important as the trend in earnings.

- **Reduced cash flow.** To a certain extent, management can exploit GAAP to produce the appearance of increased earnings. Some popular shenanigans include booking sales on long-term contracts before the customer has paid up, delaying the recording of expenses (e.g., in 1998, 1999, and 2000 Xerox improperly used a $100 million reserve to offset related expenses), failing to recognize the obsolescence of inventory as an expense, and reducing advertising and research and development expenditures. *You can use the cash flow statement to check the reliability of earnings.* If net income is moving up while cash flow from operations is drifting downward, something may be wrong. (Cash from operations should not increase or decrease at a different rate than net income.)

- **Excessive debt.** Crucial to determining whether a company can weather difficult times is the debt factor. Companies burdened by too much debt lack the financial flexibility to respond to crises and to take advantage of opportunities. Small companies with heavy debt are particularly vulnerable in economic downturns. Auditors should pay special attention to a company's debt-to-equity ratio, the total debt to stockholders' or owners' equity, especially when worried about going concern problems. While the optimum ratio varies from industry to industry, the amount of stockholders' or owners' equity should significantly exceed the amount of debt. This information is available on the balance sheet.

For example, in June 2001, PricewaterhouseCoopers said in a Securities Exchange Commission filing that because of Rent-Way's violation of several debt covenants, the auditing firm had substantial doubt about the company's ability to continue as a "going concern."

- **Overstated inventories (California Micro) and receivables (BDO Seidman).** Look at the ratio of accounts receivables to sales and the ratio of inventory to cost of goods sold. If accounts receivables exceeds 15 percent of annual sales and inventory exceeds 25 percent of cost of goods sold, be careful. If customers are not paying their bills and/or the company is saddled with aging merchandise, problems will eventually arise. Overstated inventories and receivables are often at the heart of corporate fraud, resulting in future declines in profits. As significant as the ratios are, trends over time are also important. Although there may be good reasons for a company to have bloated or increasing inventory or receivables, it is important to determine if the condition is a symptom of financial difficulty.

- **Inventory plugging.** Inventory fraud is an easy way to produce instant earnings and improve the balance sheet. Crazy Eddie, an electronic equipment retailer, allegedly recorded sales to other chains as if they were retail sales (rather than wholesale sales).

- **Balancing act.** Inventory, sales, and receivables usually move in tandem, because customers do not pay up front if they can avoid it. Neither inventory nor accounts receivable should grow faster than sales. [For example, in 2000, Purchase Pro's accounts receivable soared $13.2 million to $23.4 million, while its revenue during the same period was only $17.3 million.] Furthermore, inventory normally moves in tandem with accounts payable, since a healthy company does not often pay cash at the delivery dock as purchases are received.

- **CPA switching.** Auditor switching and the financial condition of a company are correlated to a certain extent. Firms in the midst of financial distress switch auditors more frequently than healthy companies.

- **Hyped sales.** According to court documents, CEO Emanuel Pinez at Centennial used a form of trickery rarely seen: He hyped sales by using his ample personal fortune to fund purchases. "Any auditor would have had a hard time catching that," says William Coyne, an accounting professor at Babson College. Centennial Director John J. Shields, a former CEO of Computervision Corp., says in an affidavit that Pinez admitted to him that he altered inventory tags and recorded sales on products that were never shipped. Pinez's lawyer said he was innocent.

- **Reducing expenses.** In 2000, Rent-Way disclosed that their CAO had artificially reduced the company's expenses—a reduction of $129 million. There was no one big item, but there were a dozen smaller instances of hiding or understating expenses,

¶ 2006

from automobile maintenance to insurance payments. The stock plummeted 72 percent, from $23.44 to $6.50.[45]

¶ 2007 Financial Statement Fraud Risk Factors

SAS 82 provides three lists of fraud risk factors for financial statements fraud based upon financial reporting, industry conditions, and operating characteristics:

    A. **Management Characteristics and Influence Over the Control Environment**

        a. A motivation by management to engage in fraudulent financial reporting. Specific indicators might indicate:

            i. A significant portion of management's compensation represented by bonuses, stock options, or other incentives, the value of which is contingent upon the entity achieving unduly aggressive targets for operating results, financial position or cash flow

            ii. An excessive interest by management in maintaining or increasing the entity's stock price or earnings trend through the use of unusually aggressive accounting practices

            iii. A practice by management of committing to analysts, creditors, and other third parties to achieve what appear to be unduly aggressive or clearly unrealistic forecasts

            iv. An interest by management in pursuing inappropriate means to minimize reported earnings for tax motivated reasons

        b. A failure by management to display and communicate an appropriate attitude regarding internal control and the financial reporting process such as:

            i. An effective means of communicating and supporting the entity's values or ethics, or communication of inappropriate values or ethics

            ii. Domination of management by a single person or small group without compensating controls such as effective oversight by the board of directors or audit committees

            iii. Inadequate monitoring of significant controls

---

[45] Q.S. Kim, "Rent-Way Details Improper Bookkeeping," *The Wall Street Journal*, June 8, 2001, p. C-1. Q.S. Kim, "Debt Violations Cloud the Future of Rent-Way, Inc.," *The Wall Street Journal*, July 3, 2001, p. B-3. Copyright 2000, 2001, Dow Jones and Company, Inc. Republished with permission of Dow Jones and Company, Inc. via Copyright Clearance Center.

Fraud Auditing

      iv. Management failing to correct known reportable conditions on a timely basis

      v. Management setting unduly aggressive financial targets and expectations for operating personnel

      vi. Management displaying a significant disregard for regulatory authorities

      vii. Management continuing to employ an ineffective accounting, information technology, or internal auditing staff

  c. Nonfinancial management's excessive participation in, or preoccupation with, the selection of accounting principles or the determination of significant estimates

  d. High turnover of senior management, counsel, or board members

  e. Strained relationships between management and the current or predecessor auditor. Including the following specific examples:

      i. Frequent disputes with the current or predecessor auditor on accounting, auditing, or reporting matters

      ii. Unreasonable demands on the auditor, including unreasonable time constraints regarding the completion of the audit or the issuance of the auditor's reports

      iii. Formal or informal restrictions on the auditor that inappropriately limit his or her ability to communicate effectively with the board of directors or the audit committee

      iv. Domineering management behavior in dealing with the auditor, especially involving attempts to influence the scope of the auditor's work

  f. Knowledge of history of securities law violations or claims against the entity or its senior management alleging fraud or violations of securities laws

B. Industry Conditions

  a. New accounting, statutory, or regulatory requirements that could impair the financial stability or profitability of the entity

  b. High degree of competition or market saturation, accompanied by declining margins

¶ 2007

c. Declining industry with increasing business failures and significant declines in customer demand

d. Rapid changes in the industry, such as high vulnerability to rapidly changing technology or rapid product obsolescence

C. **Operating Characteristics**

a. Inability to generate cash flows from operations while reporting earnings and earnings growth

b. Significant pressure to obtain additional capital necessary to stay competitive considering the financial position of the entity

c. Assets, liabilities, revenues, or expenses based on significant estimates that involve unusually subjective judgments or uncertainties, or that are subject to potential significant change in the near term in a manner that may have a financially disruptive effect on the entity—such as ultimate collectibility of receivables, timing of revenue recognition, realizability of financial instruments based on the highly subjective valuation of collateral or difficult to access repayment sources, or significant deferral of costs

d. Significant related-party transactions not in the ordinary course of business or with related entities not audited or audited by another firm

e. Significant, unusual, or highly complex transactions, especially those close to year-end, that pose difficult "substance over form" questions

f. Significant bank accounts or subsidiary or branch operations in tax haven jurisdictions for which there appears to be no clear business jurisdiction

g. Overly complex organizational structure involving numerous or unusual legal entities, managerial lines of authority, or contractual arrangements without apparent business purpose

h. Difficulty in determining the organization or individual(s) that control(s) the entity

i. Unusual rapid growth, especially compared to other similar not-for-profit organizations

j. Especially high vulnerability to changes in interest rates

k. Unusual high dependence on debt or marginal ability to meet debt repayment requirements; debt covenants that are difficult to maintain

l. Unrealistically aggressive sales or profitability incentive programs

m. Threat of imminent bankruptcy or foreclosure

n. Adverse consequences or significant pending transactions, such as a contract award, if poor financial results are reported

o. Poor or deteriorating financial position when management has personally guaranteed significant debts of the entity[46]

¶ 2008 Horizontal and Vertical Analysis

Many red flags for fraud are detected by percentage analysis (both horizontal and vertical) and by ratio analysis. Many auditors forget how these simple techniques could enable audit teams to spot dangerous financial situations. *Horizontal analysis (or trend analysis)* assists in the search for inequalities by using the financial statements of some prior year as the base and expressing the components of a future year as percentages of each component in base year. This technique may be used for balance sheet and income statement comparisons, but it is used less frequently in the analysis of the statement of cash flow because of the lack of regularity with which items recur in this statement. Typically, horizontal analysis starts with a base year, and each successive year is compared with the base year. The significant changes in account balances (in dollars and percentages) from period to period should be investigated to determine the reason for the change. The changes could signify financial improvement or decline in the specific company or its industry. Regression analysis is a more sophisticated version of trend analysis.

For example, suppose advertising in the base year was $100,000 and in the next three years was $120,000, $140,000, and $180,000, respectively. A horizontal comparison expressed as a percentage of the base year amount of $100,000 would appear as follows:

	Year 4	Year 3	Year 2	Year 1
Dollar amount	$180,000	$140,000	$120,000	$100,000
Horizontal Comparison	180%	140%	120%	100%

Here are some red flags revealed by horizontal analysis:

- When deferred revenues (on the balance sheet) rise sharply, a company may be having trouble delivering its products as promised.

- If either accounts receivable or inventory is rising faster than revenue, the company may not be selling its goods as fast as

---

[46] SAS No. 82, Consideration of Fraud (AICPA, *Professional Standards*, vol. 1, AU sec. 316.17). Reprinted with permission.

necessary for healthy returns or is having trouble collecting money from customers. For example, in 1997 Sunbeam's revenue grew less than one percent, but accounts receivable jumped 23 percent and inventory grew by 40 percent. Six months later in 1998 the company shocked investors by reporting a $43 million loss.

- If cash from operations is increasing or decreasing at a different rate than net income, the company may be being manipulated.

- Falling reserves for bad debts in relation to account receivables falsely boost revenue.

Vertical analysis (often referred to as commonsize statements) presents every item in a statement as a percentage of the largest item in the statement. When vertical analysis is used to compare financial statements from several periods, changes in the relationships among items can be easily determined.

Vertical analysis can be used for all the basic financial statements. In using the income statement, net sales are usually expressed as 100 percent, and all other items are compared with net sales. The largest item on the balance sheet is total assets, which is expressed as 100 percent, and the statement of cash flows usually uses the change in cash as base. A simple vertical analysis is shown in Table 20.4.

Table 20.4

Simple Vertical Analysis

Income Statement

	Dollar Amounts	Percent
Sales	$400,000	100%
Cost of Goods Sold	160,000	40%
Gross Profit	240,000	60%
Selling Expenses	40,000	10%
Administrative Expenses	60,000	15%
Operating Profit	140,000	35%
Income Taxes	28,000	7%
Net Income	$112,000	28%

Several websites can assist auditors/investors in avoiding scams and dubious investments. StockDetective.com alerts users to Wall Street "no gooders" who are targets of SEC actions. It also presents "stinky stocks," targeting companies with stocks of questionable value. Another useful site is *www.nasdr.com*, which contains disclosure information about licensed brokers and member firms, including records of disciplinary and enforce-

Fraud Auditing

ment actions. Finally, the NASAA operates a website, *www.nasaa.org*, that provides educational investor protection material along with links to various regulatory agencies, as well as investor protection groups.

¶ 2009 Other Forensic-Type Audit Procedures

Other forensic-type audit procedures can include extended procedures or analytics. Analytics will tell where to go to audit and for what to search. Analytical procedures are often less expensive than tests of details. Analytics can lie, however, and people do not understand them. For example, Lyndon B. Johnson once said that he wanted everyone to have above average housing. Auditing analytical procedures are performed by studying and comparing relationships among both financial and nonfinancial information. SAS No. 56 indicates that the "expected effectiveness and efficiency of an analytical procedure in identifying potential misstatements depends on, among other things (a) the nature of the assertion, (b) the plausibility and predictability of the relationship, (c) the availability and reliability of the data used to develop the expectation, and (d) the precision of the expectation."[47]

SIAS No. 8 indicates that the application of analytical auditing procedures is based on the proposition that, in the absence of known conditions to the contrary, relationships among information may reasonably be expected to exist and continue into the future. Some examples of contrary conditions include unusual or nonrecurring transactions or events; accounting, organizational, operational, environmental and technological changes; inefficiencies; ineffectiveness; errors; irregularities; and illegal acts.

SIAS No. 8 suggests these analytical techniques:

- Comparison of current period information with similar information for prior periods
- Comparison of current period information with budgets or forecasts
- Study of relationships of financial information with the appropriate nonfinancial information (for example, recorded payroll expense compared to changes in average number of employees)
- Study of relationships among elements of information (for example, fluctuation in recorded interest expense compared to changes in related debt balances)
- Comparison of information with similar information for other organizational units
- Comparison of information with similar information for the industry in which the organization operates[48]

---

[47] SAS No. 56, *Analytical Procedures* (AICPA, *Professional Standards*, vol. 1, AU sec. 329.11).

[48] IIA, SIAS No. 8.

¶ 2010 Ratio Analysis

Ratio analysis is a subset of trend analysis that can be used to compare relationships among financial statement accounts over time. A number of useful ratios may be used to spot red flags, especially by comparing ratios over time:

$$\text{Current ratio} = \frac{\text{Current assets (cash and equivalents, receivables and inventories)}}{\text{Current liabilities (payables, accruals, taxes, and debt due in 1 year)}}$$

$$\text{Quick ratio (Acid-test)} = \frac{\text{Cash and equivalents plus receivables}}{\text{Current liabilities}}$$

Working capital = Current assets — Current liabilities

$$\text{Inventory turnover} = \frac{\text{Cost of goods sold}}{\text{Average inventory}}$$

The number of days inventory is on hand can be calculated as $\dfrac{365}{\text{Inventory turnover}}$

$$\text{Receivables turnover} = \frac{\text{Net credit sales}}{\text{Average receivables}}$$

$$\text{Gross Margin} = 1 - \frac{\text{Cost of goods sold}}{\text{Sales}}$$

$$\text{Expense ratio} = \frac{\text{Selling general and administrative expenses}}{\text{Sales}}$$

$$\text{Operating margin} = \frac{\text{Operating income}}{\text{Sales}}$$

$$\text{Profit margin} = \frac{\text{Net income before extraordinary items}}{\text{Sales}}$$

$$\text{Interest coverage ratio} = \frac{\text{Income before interest and taxes}}{\text{Fixed charges}}$$

$$\text{Margin of safety} = \frac{\text{Income after fixed charges before income taxes}}{\text{Sales}}$$

$$\text{Debt-to-equity ratio} = \frac{\text{Total current and long-term} + \text{capitalized leases}}{\text{Total stockholder's equity}}$$

$$\text{Return on assets (ROA)} = \frac{\text{Net income}}{\text{Average total assets}}$$

$$\text{Return on equity (ROE)} = \frac{\text{Net income}}{\text{Average common equity}}$$

$$\text{Return on invested capital} = \frac{\text{Earnings before interest and taxes}}{\text{Average invested capital}}$$

$$\text{Number of years to pay off debt by application of internally generated cash flows} = \frac{\text{Total fixed obligations}}{\text{Operating cash flows}}$$

$$\text{Ratio of senior debt to capital} = \frac{\text{Total senior debt}}{\text{(Subordinated debt} + \text{net worth)}}$$

.01 Benford's Law

Some techniques can be used for both financial statement fraud and asset theft fraud. In the 1930's, Frank Benford discovered that the distribution of initial digits in natural numbers is not random, but instead follows a predictable pattern based upon a formula subsequently given his name.[49] For example, there is an approximately 30.1 percent chance that the first digit in a number will be 1, and only a 4.6 percent chance that the first digit will be a 9. With computers, Benford's Law may be used to detect anomalies in financial, tax, and economic data. It is possible to detect fraudulent numbers and errors in bookkeeping or accounting by comparing the frequency of the appearance of initial digits in a list of numbers.[50]

David G. Banks developed a five-step Benford's Law analysis run under Microsoft Excel. First, the auditor selects a population for analysis. Second, he or she assembles the raw data in a format acceptable to Excel. Third, the auditor cleans nonnumeric leading characters (such as letters or dollar signs) and decimal points. Fourth, he or she extracts leading digits and stores them for analysis. Finally, the auditor executes the final analysis. Although these steps can be executed manually in Excel, the task is shortened by running macros.[51]

---

[49] Probability (x is the first digit)=Log 10 (x + 1) − Log 10(x)
[50] David G. Banks, "Benford's Law Made Easy," *The White Paper* (September/October, 1999): 20.
[51] *Ibid.*, at 21.

Richard Lanza believes that Benford's Law can be used to identify fraud in large data sets by detecting potentially invented numbers in the following situations:

- Investment sales/purchases
- Check register
- Sales history/price history
- 401(k) contributions
- Inventory unit costs
- Expense accounts
- Wire transfer information
- Life insurance policy values
- Asset/liability accounts
- Bad debt expenses[52]

This powerful tool is easy to use, requiring no programming experience. It uses menus to guide the user through the audit and requires minimal setup time.[53]

.02 DATAS

Another analytical tool, Digital Analysis Tests and Statistics (DATAS), can help forensic auditors be more effective and efficient by presenting various high-level analyses along with the ability to drill down deeper as needed.[54] This tool identifies process inefficiencies, errors, and fraud by searching for abnormal digit and number patterns, round number occurrences, and duplications of numbers.[55]

¶ 2011 Misappropriation of Assets Fraud Risk Factors

Nonspecialist external or internal auditors do not profess to discover asset-theft fraud as a fraud auditor would do. Fraud auditors or proactive fraud auditors do search for fraud in financial statement balances. But even SAS 82 provides an outline of risk factors (red flags) for identifying misappropriation of assets fraud:

A. **Susceptibility of Assets to Misappropriation**

a. Large amounts of cash on hand or processed

b. Inventory characteristics, such as small size, high value, or high demand

---

[52] Richard B. Lanza, "Using Digital Analysis to Detect Fraud," *Journal of Forensic Accounting: Auditing, Fraud & Taxation*, Vol. 1 (2000): 293.

[53] *Ibid.*, at 295.

[54] www.digitalanalysisonline.com.

[55] Richard B. Lanza, "Using Digital Analysis to Detect Fraud," *Journal of Forensic Accounting: Auditing, Fraud & Taxation*, Vol. 1 (2000): 291.

¶ 2010.02

c. Easily convertible assets, such as bearer bonds, diamonds, or computer chips

   d. Fixed asset characteristics, such as small size, marketability (computers)

B. **Control**

   a. Lack of appropriate management oversight

   b. Lack of job applicant screening procedures relating to employees with access to assets susceptible to misappropriation

   c. Inadequate record keeping with respect to assets susceptible to misappropriation

   d. Lack of appropriate segregation of duties or independent checks

   e. Lack of appropriate system of authorization and approval of transactions

   f. Poor physical safeguards over cash, investments, inventory, or fixed assets

   g. Lack of timely and appropriate documentation of transactions

   h. Lack of mandatory vacations for employees performing key control functions[56]

C. **Other Risk Factors**

   a. Anticipated future employee layoffs that are known to the workforce

   b. Employees with access to assets susceptible to misappropriation who are known to be dissatisfied

   c. Known unusual changes in behavior or lifestyle of employees with access to assets susceptible to misappropriation

   d. Known personal financial pressures affecting employees with access to assets susceptible to misappropriation[57]

The *Panel on Audit Effectiveness* indicates that "SAS No. 82 falls short in effectively deterring fraud or significantly increasing the likelihood that the auditor will detect material fraud, largely because it fails to direct auditing procedures specifically toward fraud detection."[58] Further, "auditors do not appear to place any special emphasis on the areas where the risk of misappropriation of assets is considered significant."[59] The panel recommends new requirements over and above those currently applied in GAAS audits.

---

[56] SAS No. 82, Consideration of Fraud (AICPA, Professional Standards, vol. 1, AU sec. 316.19).
[57] *Ibid.*, sec. 316.20.
[58] *The Panel on Audit Effectiveness*, p. 86.
[59] *Ibid.*, p. 87.

The panel members suggest that auditors should perform substantive tests directed at the possibility of fraud, including tests to detect the overriding of controls by management. These tests should be conducted approximately at the balance sheet date for high-risk balance sheet accounts and throughout the year for income statement accounts. Substantive tests emphasize the verification of transactions recorded in the journals and then posted to the general ledger.

High-risk areas to audit "include balance sheet or income statement accounts affected by revenue recognition policies, deferred costs, asset additions resulting from complex transactions such as business combinations accounted for as purchases, reserves that are highly dependent on management's intentions or representations, accounts (or elements of them) not subject to systems-driven controls, and related party transactions."[60]

Fraud auditors and nonspecialists alike should test material balance sheet accounts that generally turn over several times during the year, such as trade receivables, inventory, payables, cash, and securities. Nonstandard entries requiring management's approval or involvement (including computer record entries) should be tested. Sometimes called "top-side" or "post-closing" entries, they are usually initiated by management-level personnel and are not routine or associated with the normal processing of transactions.[61]

¶ 2012 Some Asset Misappropriation Schemes

An auditor should be aware of the various fraudulent schemes used to misappropriate assets. Fraud by its nature is elusive, but misappropriation schemes may be broken into these broad categories:

- Cash
- Accounts receivable
- Fictitious disbursements
- Ghost inventory
- Other assets (securities, fixed assets, etc.).

Cash schemes are probably the most numerous of the misappropriation schemes in occurrence, but ghost inventory schemes tend to be more costly.

Misappropriated assets may be concealed on the books as either a false debit or an omitted credit. Or they may not be concealed, resulting in the books being out-of-balance. However, because tangible assets are rarely entirely counted, the out-of-balance tally is not necessarily discovered.

.01 Cash Schemes

Fraudulent activities involving cash or checks include:

---

[60] *Ibid.*   [61] *Ibid.*, p. 83, note 83, and pp. 89-90.

¶ 2012.01

- Embezzlement or skimming, which involves converting business receipts to one's personal use and benefit, employing such techniques as cash register thefts, understated/unrecorded sales, theft of incoming checks, swapping checks for cash, or short-term skimming by putting diverted cash into an interest-bearing account. Both skimming and money laundering may be revealed using the gross profit analysis. Vertical and horizontal analysis can catch skimming on a grand scale. Other detection procedures include ratio analysis, comparisons of receipts with deposits, surprise cash counts, and investigation of customers' complaints. Fraud auditors look for irregular entries to the cash account.

- Kiting or building up balances in bank accounts by floating checks drawn against similar accounts in other banks. Auditors look for frequent deposits and checks in the same amount, large deposits on Fridays, and short time lags between deposits and withdrawals. A bank reconciliation audit is important in revealing kiting.

- Theft of checks, often from the bottom or middle of the check stack or from an inactive account. Checks also may be intercepted and the payee altered.

- Intercepted checks, forged endorsements, and altered checks.

Some situations raising red flags of converted checks include the following:

- A bank or check cashing institution employee questions the validity of the check.

- A dual endorsement is not allowed or causes check verification at the cashing institution.

- Canceled checks with dual endorsements are scrutinized.

- A forged endorsement is discovered.

- An employee opens a bank account with a name similar to the victim company.

- An alteration of the check payee or endorsement is discovered.[62]

.02 Accounts Receivable Fraud

Accounts receivable schemes have the advantage of not involving inventory. ZZZZ Best's Barry Minkow said that "accounts receivables are a wonderful thing for a fraudster like me. They immediately increase

---

[62] J.T. Wells, *Occupational Fraud and Abuse* (Austin: Obsidian Publishing, 1997), 121. Reprinted with permission.

profits. But they also do something else—they explain why my company doesn't have any cash; it's all tied up in accounts receivables."[63]

Here are three main types of fraud involving receivables:

1. Lapping or recording payments on a customer's account sometime after the receipt of the payment. Here the perpetrator takes cash and covers the loss with the receipt from another customer. The process repeats over and over, as the employee continues covering each account with a subsequent payment

2. Fictitious receivables, or covering a fictitious sale with a fictitious receivable, which may eventually be written off (e.g., Sunbeam)

3. Borrowing against accounts receivable, in which the receivables are offered as collateral

Auditing steps to reveal receivables fraud focus on independently verifying customers who have not paid, reviewing writeoffs, and reviewing customer complaints. Cendant improperly accrued reserves related to membership cancellations. Lernout and Hausple Speech Products fabricated about 45 percent of its sales ($373 million).

Joseph T. Wells suggests these questions auditors may raise to suggest fictitious receivables and sales:

- Is the business negotiating financing based upon receivables?
- Have receivables increased faster than sales?
- Have receivables grown significantly?
- Is the ratio of credit sales to cash sales growing?
- Compared with sales and receivables, is cash dropping?
- Has the cost of sales fallen, compared to sales?
- Compared to sales, have shipping costs decreased?
- Has accounts receivable turnover slowed?
- Toward the end of the period, are there unusually large sales?
- Has there been substantial reversal in the first period after the increase?[64]

.03 Fictitious Disbursements

Clever payroll employees attempt fraud using means like these:

- Multiple payments to same payee

---

[63] J.T. Wells, "Follow Fraud to the Likely Perp," *Journal of Accountancy*, (March 2001): 92.

[64] *Ibid.*

¶ 2012.03

- Multiple payees for the same product or service
- Ghosts on the payroll
- Shell companies and/or fictitious persons
- Bogus claims
- Overstatements of refunds or bogus refunds at cash register
- Many fictitious expense schemes (i.e., meals, mileage, sharing taxi, claiming business expenses never taken)
- Duplicate reimbursements
- Overpayment of wages

.04 Inventory Fraud

The 1999 Treadway Commission study said that misstated asset valuation accounted for almost half of the cases of fraudulent financial statements, and inventory overstatement made up a majority of these valuations. Phar-Mor, ZZZZ Best, Equity Funding, the Salad Oil Swindle, and McKesson and Robbins cases are inventory fraud examples.

Kickbacks often involve a vendor/supplier and an employee, and involve the sale of unreported inventory or payment of an inflated price. Auditors check for many uses of the same vendor, prices higher than those of other vendors, a purchasing agent who does not take a vacation, or invoices for which only photocopies are available. See the earlier example of the Livent, Inc. kickback scheme.

The fraudsters try fictitious inventory, manipulation of inventory count, nonrecording of purchases, and fraudulent inventory capitalization. Fraud by short (partial) shipments of inventory but payment for a full shipment, is a common scheme. Unsupported journal entries, inflated inventory count sheets, bogus shipping and receiving reports, and fake purchase orders are used to inflate the inventory figures.

Some inventory questions that arouse warning signs include the following:

- Is inventory turnover falling?
- Is the percentage of inventory to total assets increasing over time?
- Is inventory increasing faster than sales?
- Have shipping costs decreased as a percentage of inventory?
- Has the cost of sales fallen with respect to sales?
- Are there significant adjusting entries that increase inventory?

The data warehousing method of detection can be used by auditors. This technique is a process, not a product, for assembling and managing data from various sources for the purpose of gaining a single, detailed view of part or all of a business. For example, an auditor could use data mining to identify potentially fraudulent transactions for further investigation and follow-up. Fraud often occurs with vendors, so vendor information could be analyzed and compared to employee records to identify payments made to a vendor with the same phone number or address as an employee. Additional applications of data warehousing include analyzing past transactions for variables present in fraudulent transactions and for flagging similar transactions before they are processed.

¶ 2013 Selected Indicia of Fraud

The following list of selected indicia of fraud was collected from a review of accounting literature on the topic. It is presented for illustrative purposes only and is not exhaustive. The conditions listed as indicia here do not necessarily indicate the existence of fraud; rather, each is an indication that fraud may be present. Many times legitimate activity or other reasons may explain these indicia of fraud. For example, an employee enjoying a lifestyle not readily explained by his or her current earnings may have previously inherited a substantial sum of money. As a result, the auditor should exercise appropriate caution in forming opinions before an adequate investigation is completed. Even then, the auditor should avoid offering opinions about guilt or innocence because the ultimate conclusion of law is a matter for the trier of fact:

- Lack of written corporate policies and standard operating procedures
- Lack of interest in or compliance with internal control policies, especially division of duties
- Disorganized operations in such areas as bookkeeping, purchasing, receiving, and warehousing
- Unrecorded transactions or missing records
- Bank accounts not reconciled on a timely basis
- Continuous out of balance subsidiary ledgers
- Continuous unexplained differences between physical inventory counts and perpetual inventory records
- Bank checks written to cash in large amounts
- Handwritten checks in a computer environment
- Continual or unusual fund transfers among company bank accounts

- Fund transfers to offshore banks
- Transactions not consistent with the entity's business
- Deficient screening procedures for new employees
- Reluctance by management to report criminal wrongdoing
- Unusual transfers of personal assets
- Heavy selling of Stock by insiders
- Employees living beyond their means
- Sudden resignation of company officers
- Recurring nonrecurring charges
- Vacations not taken
- Large Loans to executives
- Negative cash flow from operations
- Frequent or unusual related-party transactions
- Employees in close association with suppliers
- Expense account abuse
- Business assets dissipating without explanation
- Inadequate explanations to investors about losses[65]

Indicators of fraud need to be investigated and auditors need to have suspicious minds. According to reports coming from the mass amount of data written on Enron, some of these indicators were present in that company's operations. There was heavy selling of stock by Enron insiders. There were fund transfers to offshore banks—Enron had more than 850 offshore accounts. There were frequent related-party transactions involving Enron special purpose entities and at least one sudden resignation of a company officer. The Enron stakes are so high that everything about the situation will become part and parcel of accounting and legal literature for some time to come. For auditors, it will serve as a constant reminder to be more watchful in each and every engagement. For the accounting community, regulators, and those in government charged with protecting investors, it has already become a rallying cry for increased regulation and change.

---

[65] AICPA online, Practice Area Survey—Fraud Investigation, *http://aicpa.org/members/div/mcs/fraudin.htm.*

¶ 2013

¶ 2014 Corporate Fraud Task Force

By executive order on July 9, 2002, George Bush created the interagency Corporate Fraud Task Force to coordinate investigations into alleged misconduct at major corporations (e.g., Adelphia Communications and Quest Communications). Another goal is to equip local staffs with the expertise and resources to obtain indictments.

The 17 agency task force is led by the Deputy Attorney General. In the past, accounting fraud has been difficult to prosecute, but lawyers now believe many common accounting restatements can put corporate executives at risk for jail time.

According to John K. Markey, "With the new Sarbanes-Oxley requirement to have strong internal controls and officer certification of financial statements, the bar has been lowered on the 'knew or should have known' standard. The presumption will be that the CFO must have known if something has gone wrong." The Department of Justice is now encouraging prosecutors to "flip" lower level participants to get the "big guys." The FBI has an agency-staffed hotline that should "generate four or five new corporate fraud cases each month."[66]

On its one-year anniversary date, Deputy Attorney General Larry Thompson said that the task force has overseen a "string of successful and complex investigations and prosecutions." Thompson said that "the task force has obtained over 250 corporate fraud convictions or guilty pleas, including guilty pleas or convictions of at least 25 former CEOs." Thompson continued, "The task force has, through its work and investigations and prosecutions, charged 354 defendants with some type of corporate fraud in connection with 169 cases. We have over 320 investigations pending, involving in excess of 500 individuals and companies as subjects of these investigations."[67]

SEC Chairman William Donaldson said that from October 2002 to the end of June 2003, "the SEC has filed 443 enforcement actions, 137 of which involved financial fraud on reporting, eleven companies have been suspended from trading, and the assets of 30 companies have been frozen."[68] For the year ending June 30, 2003, there were 354 financial restatements, an increase of 53 percent since 1999. That is more restatements than in the history of the world up to now.

"The SEC filed almost 50 percent more financial fraud and reporting cases than in the previous fiscal year," Donaldson stated, "During the same time, the SEC more than doubled the number of offending officers and directors that it sought to bar from future service in public companies."[69]

---

[66] Alix Nyberg, "Fraud Squad," *CFO* (April 2003): 36-44.
[67] Bobby Eberle, "Justice Department Celebrates One Year of Corporate Fraud Task Force," *Talon News*, July 23, 2003, http://www.gopusa.com/news/2003/july/0723corporatefraud.shtml.
[68] *Ibid.*
[69] *Ibid.*

¶ 2015 Summary

Due to recent highly publicized cases and the resulting heightened awareness of fraudulent financial reporting, an expectation gap now exists between what users of financial statements expect (an elimination of information risk with auditors detecting fraud and reporting illegal incidents publicly) and what auditors are responsible to provide (a reduction in information risk with auditors providing reasonable assurance that financial statements are free of material misstatements due to error or fraud). As a result, CPAs are increasingly under pressure to perform proactive and reactive fraud-related services.

External and internal auditors do not audit proactively; instead, they look for fraud that will result in material misstatements in the financial statements. The AICPA responded to the rise of white-collar crime by issuing SAS No. 99, which gives independent, external auditors guidance regarding the detection of financial-statement fraud and clarifies an auditor's responsibilities to detect fraud.

In addition, CPAs are providing specific services to fight white-collar crime and fraud. Fraud accountants find, analyze, and provide evidence of fraud for their clients and present that evidence before a court of law. Fraud auditors are traditional accountants by education and experience, but they have training in investigative skills and rules of evidence.

Chapter 21

Environmental and Quality Audits

¶ 2101   Introduction
¶ 2102   U.S. Environmental Statutes
¶ 2103   The Environmental Protection Agency (EPA)
¶ 2104   Accounting Guidelines
¶ 2105   Principles and Framework
¶ 2106   ISO 14000
¶ 2107   Certifications
¶ 2108   The Role of the Environmental Auditor
¶ 2109   New Approach Systems
¶ 2110   Information Needs
¶ 2111   Organizational Responsibilities for Environmental Auditing
¶ 2112   ISO 14000 Guidelines
¶ 2113   Summary

¶ 2101   Introduction

Environmental auditing probably originated in the United States in the early 1970s to determine whether a company or industry was in compliance with the current regulatory rules and internal policies and standards. Originally, environmental audits were compliance audits, but today operational, systems, preventative, and audits of specific transactions are common.

According to the International Chamber of Commerce, an environmental audit is:

> the systematic examination of the interactions between any business operation and its surroundings. This includes all emissions to air, land, and water; legal constraints; the effects on the neighboring community, landscape and ecology; and the public's perception of the operating company in the local area. Environmental audit does not stop at compliance with legislation. Nor is it a 'greenwashing' public relations exercise. Rather it is a total strategic approach to the organization's activities.[1]

---

[1] The International Chamber of Commerce website can be accessed at *www.iccwbo.org*.

Thus, environmental auditors have gone from asking, "Do we comply?" to "How is the best way we can protect the environment and comply with environmental laws?"

Chapter 21 objectives:

- To understand how recent changes in government policy affected the audit objective (see ¶ 2101–2104).

- To identify the controls that an organization should implement to mitigate its legal exposure from environmental regulation (see ¶ 2105–2112).

- To define the role of the environmental auditor (see ¶ 2105–2112).

¶ 2102 U.S. Environmental Statutes

The environmental liabilities in the United States have been estimated to be between two percent to five percent of the gross domestic products.[2] The U.S. International Trade Commission (USITC) estimated expenditures by U.S. steel producers to meet the requirements of the 1990 amendments to the Clean Air Act could add $17 per ton to raw steel prices, or more than five percent of the cost of production.[3] Further, an accounting system identifies separately only a small portion of the costs of regulatory compliance. "A $1 increase in the visible costs of regulation is associated with a $9.23 increase in total cost (at the margin) for the integrated-mill sector and $10.68 for the mini-mill sector."[4] Basically, these costs are hidden in other accounts. In 1988, *The Wall Street Journal* estimated the total collective cost of compliance with federal statutes could be as high as $100 billion.[5] The EPA levied $75 billion in criminal fines in 1996.[6]

Environmental laws can be classified as preventive or remedial. Prevention laws, starting with the 1948 Clean Water Act, are intended to protect the air, land, and water from hazardous materials. Table 21.1 is a chronology and summary of the major U.S. laws aimed at the prevention of environmental damages. Remediation environmental laws are for identifying, seeking compensation from, and fining all potentially responsible parties (PRPs). For example, the Comprehensive Environmental Response, Compensation, and Liability Act (CERCLA, also known as "Superfund") of 1980, and the Superfund Amendments and Reauthorization Act (SARA) of 1986 made companies potentially liable for cleanup of existing and future

---

[2] S.D. Beets and C.C. Souther, "Corporate Environmental Reports: The Need for Standards and an Environmental Assurance Service," *Accounting Horizon*, Vol. 13, No. 2 (1999): 129-145.

[3] U.S. International Trade Commission (USITC), *Steel Industry Annual Report on Competitive Conditions in the Steel Industry and Industry Efforts to Adjust and Modernize*, Report to the President, Investigation No. 332-289, Washington, D.C. : Government Printing Office.

[4] Satish Joshi, Ranjani Krishnan, and Lester Lave, "Estimating the Hidden Costs of Environmental Regulation," *The Accounting Review*, Vol. 76, No. 2 (April 2001): 195.

[5] A.K. Naj, "See No Evil, Can $100 Billion Have No 'Material Effect' on Balance Sheets," *The Wall Street Journal* (May 11, 1998), pp. 1 and 12.

[6] Environment Protection Agency, *Enforcement and Compliance Assurance Accomplishments Report FY 1996*, Washington, D.C., EPA, 1997.

damage to the environment, even when existing damage might have been caused by a prior owner.

Fines and penalties under CERCLA can be civil and criminal, or both. Liability can be joint and several, aimed at both the corporation and individuals. For example, the EPA has collected more than $14 billion of Superfund commitments from PRPs, with commitment in 1996 alone exceeding $1.3 billion.[7] The EPA levied more than $75 billion in criminal fines in 1996.[8] Table 21.2 is a chronology and summary of those U.S. laws aimed at determining liability for environmental remediation.

Table 21.1

Major U.S. Legislation Relating to Environment Prevention

Legislation	Year Enacted	Highlights
Clean Water Act (CWA)	1948	Established to maintain the biological and physical integrity of U.S. waterways. Mandates comprehensive federal regulation of all potential source of water pollution. Amended in 1972 and 1977.
Clean Air Act (CAA)	1963	Mandated comprehensive federal regulation of all potential sources of air pollution. Amended in 1970, 1977, and 1990.
Solid Waste Disposal Act	1965	Addressed issues related to disposal of hazardous wastes, management of solid wastes, and illegal dumping. Amended in 1980 to allow greater enforcement power by EPA. Also amended in 1984.
National Environmental Policy Act	1969	Established a national policy for the environment and created the Council on Environmental Quality.
Occupational Safety and Health Act (OSHA)	1970	Requires extensive training and reporting of health-related issues for employees.
Marine Protection, Research, and Sanctuaries Act	1972	Regulates the disposal of chemicals and other materials into oceans and waterways.
Federal Insecticide, Fungicide, and Rodenticide Act	1972	Granted EPA authority to study, control, and require users to register when purchasing pesticides.
Endangered Species Act	1973	Established a program for the identification, protection, and monitoring of endangered plants and animals.
Safe Drinking Water Act (SDWA)	1974	Established standards for injection wells and drinking water.

---

[7] *Ibid.*   [8] *Ibid.*

Legislation	Year Enacted	Highlights
Resource Conservation and Recovery Act (RCRA)	1976	Required the "cradle to grave" regulation of wastes. Imposed restrictions on companies associated with both hazardous and nonhazardous wastes. Prohibited open dump sites.
Toxic Substances Control Act (TSCA)	1976	Regulated the manufacturing, processing, and distribution of chemical substances capable of adversely affecting the health or environment.
Surface Mining Control and Reclamation Act	1977	Instituted a program to protect the environment from the effects of surface coal mining. Established reclamation guidelines for areas affected by surface coal mining.
Hazardous and Solid Waste Amendments	1984	Established regulations for the manufacturing, distribution, use, and monitoring of underground storage tanks, including biannual inspection.
Pollution Prevention Act	1990	Established guidelines for the modification of equipment and processes, the redesign of products, and improvement of managerial techniques related to pollution prevention. Increased the number of criminal enforcement agents.
Land Disposal Program and Flexibility Act	1996	Exempted hazardous waste from RCRA regulation if it was treated to a point where it no longer exhibited the characteristic that made it hazardous and was subsequently disposed of in a facility regulated under the Clean Water Act or the Safe Drinking Water Act.
Chemical Safety Information, Site Security and Fuels Regulatory Relief	1999	Removed flammable fuels from the list of substances to be reported

Source: M. Abdol Mohammadi, P. Burnaby, and J. Thibodeau, "Environmental Accounting in the U.S.: From Control and Prevention to Remediation," *Asia Pacific Journal of Accounting* (December 1997), pp. 199–217. Used with permission. The *Asia-Pacific Journal of Accounting* (APJA) has become the *Asia-Pacific Journal of Accounting and Economics* (APJAE).

Table 21.2

Major U.S. Legislation Relating to Environmental Remediation Liability

Legislation	Year Enacted	Highlights
Resource Conservation and Recovery Act (RCRA)	1976	Established standards for the management of hazardous wastes. Authorized EPA to conduct removal activities, seek injunctive relief, and initiate cost recovery actions.
Comprehensive Environmental Response, Compensation, and Liability Act (CERCLA or Superfund)	1980	Established a program to identify hazardous sites; identify responsible parties; seek remediation by responsible parties or the government; to compensate local, state and federal governments for damages to natural resources; and to provide remedies against PRPs. Established a $1.6 billion trust fund to cover the cost to remediate abandoned sites. Provided for all "potential polluters" to pay into fund.
Hazardous and Solid Waste Amendments	1984	Amended RCRA. Expanded the liability associated with hazardous waste storage, treatment, and disposal facilities.
Superfund Amendments and Reauthorization (SARA)	1986	Extended CERCLA. Increased fund to $8.5 billion. Provided detailed standards of remediation and settlement. Broadened criminal sanctions.
The Oil Pollution Act (OPA)	1990	Imposed strict joint and several liability for damages from an oil spill in the waters from vessels and facilities. Responsible parties became liable for removal costs and compensatory damages.
Pollution Prosecution Act (PPA)	1990	Contained numerous enhancements to the EPA's criminal enforcement program.

Source: M. Abdol Mohammadi, P. Burnaby, and J. Thibodeau, "Environmental Accounting in the U.S.: From Control and Prevention to Remediation," *Asia-Pacific Journal of Accounting* (December 1997), pp. 199-217. Used with permission. The *Asia-Pacific Journal of Accounting* (APJA) has become the *Asia-Pacific Journal of Accounting and Economics* (APJAE).

¶ 2103 The Environmental Protection Agency (EPA)

The EPA was established in 1970 to consolidate into one agency the various federal research, monitoring, standard-setting, and enforcement activities to ensure environmental protection. The EPA's mission is to protect human health and to safeguard the natural environment—air, water, and land—upon which life depends.

According to President Richard Nixon, the principal roles and functions of the EPA would be:

- The establishment and enforcement of environmental protection standards consistent with national environmental goals.

- Conducting research on the adverse effects of pollution and on methods and equipment for controlling it, the gathering of information on pollution, and the use of this information in strengthening environmental protection programs and recommending policy changes.

- Assisting others, through grants, technical assistance and other means in arresting pollutors of the environment.

- Assisting the Council on Environmental Quality in developing and recommending to the president new policies for the protection of the environment.[9]

The primary means of civil and criminal enforcement authority are:

1. Imposing penalties for breaking environmental laws

2. Seeking injunctive relief when parties are acting in noncompliance

3. Seeking injunctive relief requiring parties to correct or restore environmental damage

4. "Extra" actions or Supplemental Environmental Projects (SEPs) that must be undertaken by violators[10]

The government's "command and control" philosophy during this early history caused environmental audits to first focus on compliance. A number of problems arose, however. Environmental audits were exclusively concerned with whether organizations were legally complying with these complex technical laws and regulations that almost no one had the skills to decipher. Consequently, the legal, engineering, and internal audit departments were uncomfortable with the audit responsibility.[11] Also, most agencies adopted a "zero tolerance" policy for violations. Penalties included crippling fines of up to $25,000 per day of violation, and criminal penalties were imposed as well. Not surprisingly, few people volunteered to be auditors.

In this climate, environmental audits were undertaken on an ad hoc basis. Auditors were not responsible for taking a holistic look at the organizations' approach to environment management, nor were they responsible for helping management devise better processes that would reduce the impact on the environment. One of the most common findings of

---

[9] http://www.epa.gov/history/org/origins/reorg.htm.
[10] The EPA issues an *Annual Report on Enforcement and Compliance Assurance Accomplishments* that describes and measures enforcement activities. See www.epa.gov for more information.

[11] Ron Black, "A New Leaf in Environmental Auditing," *Internal Auditor*, Vol. 55 (June 1998): 24.

¶ 2103

these outside consultants was that the environmental auditing function was situated incorrectly, often reporting to managers of the very areas they audited. Objectivity and independence were impaired as a result.[12]

The EPA's early policies actually discouraged performance of audits in two important aspects. First, the EPA would not ensure confidentiality of the reports. Second, the EPA retained discretion as to whether it would pursue enforcement against companies that voluntarily disclosed violations identified during an audit.[13] Many organizations debated the wisdom of undertaking self-audit at all. Such audits had to be carefully planned, because inadvertently providing evidence of a violation could result in unexpected liabilities. Management had to be committed to correct any problems as soon as they were discovered in order to minimize any potential fines and penalties.[14]

Most organizations ultimately accepted the fact that although problems may arise during an environmental audit, the risk of noncompliance is still better managed by conducting the audit, if only because *not* having proper procedures in place can increase the risk of criminal enforcement action.[15] Experience indicated that prosecutors considered good-faith efforts to manage environmental problems in deciding whether to pursue punitive criminal action rather than civil penalties.[16] The major purpose of the environmental audit eventually became keeping track of compliance with regulatory requirements, and spotting and correcting problems before the enforcement agencies learned what had transpired.

During the 1990s, the EPA became more flexible in overseeing the way in which corporations managed environmental risks as long as the goals were achieved. This more collaborative approach provides management with an incentive to design *environmental management systems*, which are cost effective, emphasize prevention, and continuously improve.[17]

The EPA's milder approach is summarized by Tucker and Kasper as follows:

- A broader mission for enforcement with a focus on environmental results rather than the number of enforcement actions taken

- Changing the relationship between government and industry from an adversarial approach to one in which both groups cooperate in solving problems

---

[12] *Ibid.*

[13] Robert R. Tucker and Janet Kasper, "Pressures for Change in Environmental Auditing and in the Role of the Internal Auditor," *Journal of Managerial Issues*, Vol. 10, No. 3 (Fall 1998): 340.

[14] Ned Abelson and John Balco, "Keeping the CEO Out of Jail: The Risks of an Environmental Audit," *Risk Management*, Vol. 39 (February 1992): 14.

[15] Ned Abelson and John Balco, "Keeping the CEO Out of Jail," p. 14; Michael S. McMahon, "The Growing Role of Accountants in Environmental Compliance," *The Ohio CPA*, Vol. 54 (April 1995): 21.

[16] Ned Abelson and John Balco, *ibid.*

[17] Robert R. Tucker and Janet Kasper, "Pressures for Change," p. 340.

- Changing the approach from one of enforcing all laws equally to one of setting priorities and recognizing limited resources

- Realizing that one method of correcting a problem is not useful in all situations

- Moving toward multimedia, multipollutant deterrence programs

- Empowering the public with information by increasing public awareness, the EPA is able to form partnerships and improve data quality and data access[18]

¶ 2104 Accounting Guidelines

Once environmental risks are identified, an auditor must be aware of numerous accounting standards applicable to environmental problems. Some of these accounting pronouncements are summarized here.

FASB Emerging Issues Task Force (EITF) Issue No. 89-13, *Accounting for the Cost of Asbestos Removal:* Costs incurred to treat asbestos within a reasonable time period after an asset with a known asbestos problem is acquired should be capitalized as part of the cost of the acquired asset subject to an impairment test for the asset. Also, when costs are incurred in anticipation of a sale of an asset, these costs should be deferred and recognized in the period of the sale to the extent that these costs can be covered from the estimated sales price.

EITF Issue No. 90-8, *Capitalization of Costs to Treat Environmental Contamination:* Affirmed EITF No. 89-13, but did not take a position as to the disposition of environmental containment costs incurred on existing assets. These costs should be expensed unless they extend the life or capacity of the asset, they prevent environmental contamination that has not yet occurred, or these costs were incurred to prepare the asset for sale.

EITF Issue No. 93-5, *Accounting for Environmental Liabilities*: A two-event approach should be used to separate an environmental liability from any potential claims for recovery. Any loss from the recognition of an environmental liability should be decreased only where the realization of a claim for recovery is probable.

Statement of Financial Accounting Standards (SFAS) No. 5, *Accounting for Contingencies:* A liability should be recognized in the financial statements only if the loss is probable and the amount can be estimated. Then the loss is charged against income and a liability is recorded. Otherwise, the contingency should be described in the footnotes of the financial statements.

---

[18] *Ibid.*

Financial Accounting Standards Board (FASB) Interpretation No. 14 (1976), *Reasonable Estimation of the Amount of the Loss:* Do not delay the recognition or disclosure of a loss; estimate it within a range.

Statement of Financial Accounting Standards (SFAS) No. 19, *Financial Accounting and Reporting by Oil and Gas Producing Companies*: For companies using the successful efforts method, future dismantlement, restoration, and environmental reclamation costs are expenses that would be recognized in the period(s) during which the related oil and gas reserves are produced (not at the time the activities are actually undertaken).

AICPA Statement of Position (SOP) 96-1, *Environmental Remediation Liabilities:* Environmental remediation liabilities are to be accrued when the criteria of SFAS No. 5 are met, and benchmarks are included to aid in determining when the liabilities are to be recognized.

Staff Accounting Bulletin (SAB) No. 92, *Accounting and Disclosures Relating to Loss Contingencies:* Do not delay recognition of a liability until only a single estimate can be determined.

FASB Exposure Draft 158-B, *Accounting for Liabilities Related to Closure or Removal of Long-Lived Assets:* Costs of nuclear power plant decommissioning (which meet the established definition of a liability) are to be recognized immediately.

¶ 2105 Principles and Framework

Now that the legal exposure posed by environmental regulation has been presented, it is imperative to identify the controls that an organization should implement to mitigate its legal exposure. Usually these internal controls will take the form of an environmental management system (EMS).

An EMS is a part of an organization's system of internal controls that allows the organization to protect the environment and manage environmental issues. In some organizations there is an internal auditing department and a separate environmental auditing department. Environmental auditing does require a number of skills and expertise—those of an auditor, engineer, scientist, and regulatory specialist. Some argue that an internal auditor can provide vital services in the environmental areas.

R.S. Greenberg gives the following definition of environmental management:

> Internal control of environmental management is the process by which an entity's board of directors, management and other personnel seek to obtain reasonable assurance regarding the achievement of objectives in one or more categories:
>
> - Effectiveness and efficiency of environmental operations
> - Reliability of financial information relating to environmental activities
> - Compliance with applicable environmental laws and regulations[19]

---

[19] R.S. Greenberg, "Applying Internal Control to Environmental Management," *Environmental Finance* (Spring 1992): 13-21.

Principles of an EMS have been developed, and standards for evaluating compliance have been produced. A key concept in these principles and standards is *sustainable development*. Sustainable development relates to achieving an equilibrium in the use of renewable natural resources, preservation of wildlife habitat and diversity, plus conservation of nonrenewable natural resources through efficient use and planning.[20] Various groups have attempted to translate sustainability principles into operational terms, intended to be integrated into business management. Some of the better known groups include:

- The Responsible Care Program of the Chemical Manufacturers' Association

- The Business Charter for Sustainable Development published by the International Chamber of Commerce

- The "Valdez Principles," developed in 1989 by the Coalition for Environmentally Responsible Economies (CERES) as a comprehensive environmental policy for corporations

In addition to these principles, three voluntary standards have already emerged:

- British standard 7750 (1992)
- Audit Scheme or "Eco-Audit" (1992)
- ISO 14000 (1996)

Because ISO 14000 is most likely to affect U.S. companies, a detailed discussion is warranted.

¶ 2106 ISO 14000

The International Standards Organization (ISO) developed ISO 9000 as a management system standard (see Chapter 4), and ISO 14000 is an EMS. Adequate and uniform environmental standards did not exist prior to ISO 14000. Many organizations now look to the ISO to provide a uniform framework to manage their environmental impacts. ISO 14000 is a comprehensive environmental quality standard that provides a basis for society to compare a firm's sensitivity to environmental issues. It provides flexible guidelines for maintaining a management system that will ensure external compliance while promoting continuous improvement in performance. To obtain ISO 14000 certification, organizations must maintain an environ-

---

[20] Robert R. Picard, "Environmental Management: What's Auditing Got to Do with It?," *Internal Auditor*, Vol. 55 (June 1998): 32.

mental management system and monitor this system with environmental auditing.[21]

ISO 14000 is a voluntary *management system* series of standards, requiring conformity with an organization's policies and systems.[22] Auditors should find the standards useful because they provide guidelines in assessing the sufficiency and effectiveness of the EMS, and ascertaining and guaranteeing compliance with pertinent environmental laws and regulations. In addition, ISO 14000 also provides guidance in attesting information contained in environmental reports and ensuring efficiency, effectiveness, and economy of environmental operations and performance. These standards provide specific, voluntary benchmarks that should assist auditors in:

- Assessing the adequacy and effectiveness of the environmental management system
- Determining and ensuring compliance with applicable laws and regulations
- Attesting to the information presented in reports
- Ensuring efficiency, effectiveness, and economy of operations and performance[23]

These benchmarks are divided into six categories:

1. Environmental management system: Establishing organization goals, principles, systems, and techniques (ISO 14001, 14002, 14004).

2. Environmental auditing: Designing audit procedures to examine compliance with applicable legislation, regulation, and standards (ISO 14010, 14011, 14012, 14013, 14014).

3. Environmental labeling: Using labeling and claims as a marketing tool; preventing unwarranted claims by reducing trade barriers (ISO 14015, 14020, 14021, 14024, 14025).

4. Environmental performance evaluation: Evaluating environmental performance of management systems and ensuring that environmental requirements, including ISO 14000 standards, are being met (ISO 14031, 14032).

5. Life-cycle assessment: Creation of support documents to provide guidance about life-cycle assessment, including inventory analysis and production process (ISO 14040, 14042, 14043, 14047, 14048, and 14049).

---

[21] Tucker and Kasper, "Pressures for Change," p. 340.
[22] Picard, "Environmental Management," p. 32.
[23] Zabihollah Rezaee, "ISO 14000," *Internal Auditor*, Vol. 53 (October 1996): 56.

6. Examining the potential effects of products on the environment and setting standards for reducing environmental effects (ISO 14064).[24]

ISO does not itself issue certificates. Instead, independent bodies worldwide conduct and issue certificates. A database of accredited registrars can be found at the ISO website, *www.iso14000.net*. To be approved for an ISO 14000 series certificate, an organization must meet ISO 14001 standards, which are the series' EMS standards. Once approved, an organization will receive a certification to ISO 14001 and be listed in a register or directory. CPAs can help organizations establish an EMS and receive a certification to ISO 14001. Legal questions about the ISO 14000 series can be found at *www.lawinfo.com*.

Similar to ISO 9000 quality management standards, these ISO 14000 standards will probably become a necessity for doing business and competing in the international market. These standards provide invaluable environmental benchmarkings that should be of value as organizations address their important environmental risks and issues.[25] By the end of 2000, total worldwide certificates awarded exceeded 22,897, with 1,042 U.S. registrants.

¶ 2107 Certifications

Principles for an EMS have been introduced (e.g., ISO 9000 and ISO 14000), and standards for evaluating compliance are emerging. There is also an increased interest in certification. The IIA and the Environmental Auditing Roundtable (EAR) introduced the Board of Environmental, Health & Safety Auditor Certifications' (BEAC) 14000 Plus certification program in August 1997. The newest BEAC certification program recognizes environmental professionals and promotes high standards of ethical practice and professional competence and is distinguished by the professional designation of certified professional environmental auditor (CPEA). The CPEA designation demonstrates competence and represents the exceptional knowledge, skill, and understanding of highly effective and fully qualified environmental professionals.[26]

The oldest accounting-type environment organization is the Auditing Roundtable. The Roundtable is the original professional organization dedicated to furthering the development and professional practice of Environmental, Health, and Safety (EHS) auditing. The Roundtable was founded in January 1982, when managers of 10 corporate environmental audit programs met to discuss their auditing programs and practices. The Round-

---

[24] Z. Rezaee, "Help Keep the World Green," *Journal of Accountancy* (November 2000): 58-59.

[25] See *www.iso.org* for additional information on the International Organization for Standardization and ISO 14000.

[26] For more information on the BEAC, see *www.beac.org* or contact the Board of Environmental Auditor Certifications at 249 Maitland Avenue, Altamonte Springs, Florida 32701.

table has held regular meetings since that time and has undergone many important changes.

This group represents the voice of the profession, with more than 800 members, all of whom have agreed to abide by the Roundtable's Code of Ethics. Its mission is to enhance the practice of EHS auditing by creating a national forum and organization to advance ideas, procedures, and member interaction.[27]

¶ 2108 The Role of the Environmental Auditor

A CPA can develop an auditing niche in certifying and auditing EMSs under ISO 14000. However, an auditor's role in environmental management includes a number of functions besides compliance considerations and often involves forensic or litigation issues (see Chapter 12):

- Economic benefit analysis: Calculation of a penalty equal to the benefit accruing as a result of a purported violation requires careful accounting analysis.

- Inability to pay: Regulatory policy permits a business to receive a reduction in any penalty, commensurate with the business's inability to pay. Tax returns and audited financial statements may be used to demonstrate this inability to pay. The defense should have a clear understanding of these important documents.

- Cost recovery: Private cost recovery actions under CERCLA (Superfund) must include careful evaluation of these costs and documentation showing that reported spending actually occurred.

- Settlement mechanisms: Code Sec. 468B provides for deductibility of qualified settlement funds immediately, rather than waiting until the funds are actually spent on remediation. An organization needs a competent accountant to deal successfully with some obscure IRS provisions.

Other operating areas of accounting/environmental interface include the following:

- Financial assurance: Multiple hazardous materials regulations, most notably those for underground storage tanks, require owners and operators to demonstrate financial assurance for closure costs. This task is appropriately delegated to the accountants.

- Deductibility of expenses: Code Sec. 198 permits the immediate deduction of certain environmental remediation expenditures.

---

[27] The Auditing Roundtable, 15111 N. Hayden Road, Suite #160355, Scottsdale, AZ 85260-2555, 480-659-3738.

But as one author stated, this is an area of indefinite guidelines.[28]

- Capital budgeting for environmental control equipment: Although businesses must provide required controls whether they like it or not, the capital expenditure can be made more palatable by applying appropriate managerial accounting and capital budgeting techniques.

- Pollution prevention: Materials released to the environment represent waste and loss as well as pollution. Significant cost savings have been achieved by reducing emission and waste volume.

¶ 2109 New Approach Systems

Companies have found that regulatory compliance in itself does not necessarily mitigate environmental risk. Risks not covered by legislation include public perception and the sustainability of raw materials. The primary role of an auditor is to assess how effectively organization systems:

- Identify the process points that impact the environment
- Measure the potential for damage
- Mitigate the risks represented by such potentials[29]

Compliance assessment remains an important part of environmental auditing. However, compliance audits verify external compliance at the time the audit was performed, whereas an EMS audit considers whether the management system is in place to ensure compliance continuously.[30]

Compliance assessment is increasingly performed by line personnel using automated self-assessment tools.[31] This shifting of duties enables the auditor to remain in his or her office studying reports generated by the compliance self-assessment software and determining whether problems were addressed in a timely manner, whereas line personnel struggle with new software, production schedules, machine breakdowns, unexpected absences, arrogant staff, useless management, drug problems, and late deliveries.

The auditor's broad investigative skills provide other essential support to an EMS, as the focus of many corporate programs has shifted from compliance to the ongoing reduction of the overall environmental impact. Environmental auditing is now more properly described as a risk-management tool for taking a systematic and objective inventory of a company's

---

[28] L.M. Nichols, "Tax and Financial Accounting Treatment of Environmental Remediation Costs: An Area of Indefinite Guidelines," *Oil, Gas, & Energy Quarterly* (December 1998): 279-284.

[29] Ron Black, "A New Leaf in Environmental Auditing," *Internal Auditor*, Vol. 55 (June 1998): 24.

[30] Tucker and Kasper, "Pressures for Change," p. 340.

[31] Ron Black, "A New Leaf," p. 24.

environmental assets and liabilities. By monitoring the adequacy and effectiveness of a management control system, auditing has been shown to be an effective technique to reduce overall exposure to environmental risks.[32] Successful companies extend the systems management concept beyond plant operations to consideration of the entire product life cycle, from raw material supplies to product packaging and ultimate disposal by the end user.[33]

¶ 2110 Information Needs

The traditional role of auditors includes providing services such as attestation, assurance, and internal compliance audits. These services lend credibility to information. Evidence of current environmental information needs includes:

- The public is now voicing needs for information about environmental risks and assessments.[34]

- Investors and lenders seek assurance through environmental audits so that a company can maintain its profitability through sustainability of operations.[35]

- Mounting environmental liabilities impact shareholder value. Auditors play a role in the valuation of environmental liabilities.[36]

- Managers indicate their need to clearly understand cost implications as well as potential benefits from company interactions with the environment.[37]

- Eco-labeling, a competitive marketing tool, requires substantiation by an internal auditing process.[38] (*Eco-labeling* refers to some form of certification program or seal of approval that a service or product is environmentally responsible.)

Internal or external auditors may wish to perform these services either as stand-alone engagements or as part of an operational or financial audit. Some statistics illustrate the extent of environmental reporting:

- 44 percent of Fortune 250 companies in the nonfinancial sector produce an annual report of environmental performance, including descriptions of environmental initiative and product development, quantification of emission and waste reductions and resource-use efficiency improvement.

---

[32] Halley I. Moriyama, "The Environmental Audit," *Directors & Boards*, Vol. 15 (Summer 1991): 21.
[33] *Ibid.*
[34] Mary Ann Reynolds, "Greener CPA: An Alternative Vision," *The Ohio CPA Journal*, Vol. 60 (January–March 2001): 61.
[35] Tucker and Kasper, "Pressures for Change," p. 340.
[36] Moriyama, "The Environmental Audit," p. 21.
[37] Reynolds, "Greener CPA," p. 61.
[38] *Ibid.*

- Additionally, 15 percent of banks, insurance and securities companies issue environmental annual reports.
- 19 percent of the environmental reports had been verified by an independent party.
- AT&T has issued "triple bottom line" reports, comprising economic, environmental, and social performance.[39]

¶ 2111 Organizational Responsibilities for Environmental Auditing

In a research paper survey[40] of environmental auditing, responding directors of internal auditing departments reported the following levels with their primary responsibility for environmental auditing:

```
Corporate level ........................... 75.1%
Division level ............................ 12.7%
Operating facility level .................. 20.4%
```

The same respondents reported these five groups had responsibility for environmental auditing:[41]

```
Environmental affairs ...................... 47%
Health and safety .......................... 22.2%
Environmental engineering .................. 21.1%
Legal ...................................... 19.5%
Internal auditing .......................... 9.7%
```

In the same survey more than 55 percent of the respondents reported that the internal auditing function has some involvement in environmental auditing in their companies. They indicated that the overall involvement was slight, providing support in a few areas of environmental auditing. Table 21.3 shows the involvement of internal auditors in specific environment areas.[42]

---

[39] Ibid.
[40] J.R. Byington and S.N. Campbell, "Internal Environmental Auditing," *Oil, Gas & Energy Quarterly* (September 1997): 957-969.
[41] Ibid.
[42] Ibid., p. 968.

¶ 2111

Table 21.3

Involvement of Internal Auditing Function in Specific Areas of Environmental Auditing

Extent of Internal Auditing Function's Current Involvement in Each Area of Environmental Auditing	Cases	Mean
Financial accounting for environmental liabilities	105	3.56
Compliance with company environmental policies	103	3.12
Compliance with environmental regulations	104	3.04
Acquisition candidates' environmental performance	104	2.45
Environmental liabilities and risks of property transfers	105	2.42
Programs and facilities for the TSD of hazardous wastes	104	2.41
Environmental management systems	100	2.31
Pollution prevention and waste minimization programs	103	2.13
Contractors' programs and facilities for the TSD of hazardous wastes	101	1.67
Suppliers' environmental performance	100	1.46

Scale: 1=None 2=Slight 3=Small 4=Moderate 5=Considerable 6=Great 7=Maximum

Environmental audits traditionally have been concerned with whether an organization is legally complying with complex, technical regulations, but as stated earlier, the legal, engineering, and internal audit departments are uncomfortable with the idea of internal auditing taking on that role. Now that the focus has shifted to EMSs, functional rather than legal responsibilities are the central issue. This change in emphasis makes it much easier for internal auditing to accept responsibility for environmental audits.[43]

Internal auditing is well established, and the profession has developed structured processes and standards for measuring the effectiveness of systems. Internal auditors often have an independent reporting hierarchy. But internal auditors may not possess the technical knowledge necessary to handle environmental systems audits. An environmental engineer who is thoroughly familiar with regulatory requirements, supported by a specialist in environmental law, can best assess an area's compliance with government regulations. An internal auditor, on the other hand, is particularly well suited to evaluate conformance to the company's EMS specifications.[44]

---

[43] Ron Black, "A New Leaf," p. 24
[44] Robert Picard, "Environmental Management," p. 32.

The team needs to be proficient in compliance, liability, waste management, risk assessment, and review and management of audits.

Reporting and certification allow the professional to use developed audit skills in auditing environmental processes, tracking the chain of custody documentation, performing environmental process compliance audits, and monitoring continuous improvements. The AICPA Statements on Standards for Attestation Engagements (SSAE) Nos. 3 and 4 are highly relevant to this work, and the independent accounting profession is uniquely qualified to take a positive position in the emerging environmental management marketplace.[45] SSAE No. 3 applies to compliance attestations in relation to reporting on an organization's compliance with requirements of specific laws, regulations, and rules. SSAE No. 4 applies to agreed-upon procedures when a CPA is engaged to issue a report of findings based on specific procedures performed on the subject matter of an assertion.

The internal auditing approach to environmental management, like its approach to other business processes, emphasizes internal control. *Internal control* is defined as a process designed to provide reasonable assurance regarding the achievement of objectives relating to:

- Effectiveness and efficiency of operations
- Reliability of financial reporting
- Compliance with laws and regulations[46]

The components of a successful EMS are similar to components of an internal control system. Tucker and Kasper summarize these requirements as follows:

1. An adequate and effective environmental management system (EMS) requires the committed involvement of top level management and the support of the internal audit function.

2. The EMS also should define goals to encourage awareness and promote management commitment to addressing environmental matters.

3. Further, an EMS should establish policies and procedures to achieve goals and institute an audit function to monitor progress toward those goals and adherence to policies, procedures, laws, and regulations.

4. In addition, an EMS involves the development of strategic plans to study new initiatives, trends, and regulations.

---

[45] Mary Ann Reynolds, "Greener CPA," p. 61.
[46] Tucker and Kasper, "Pressures for Change," p. 340.

¶ 2111

5. Environmental risk assessment programs and plans for dealing with these risk exposures also are components of an EMS.

6. Finally, the EMS should provide adequate financial information to properly recognize and disclose the corporation's environmental costs and obligations.[47]

¶ 2112 ISO 14000 Guidelines

ISO 14000 provides guidelines for education, work experience, auditor training, personal attributes and skills. Internal auditors may already possess the essential attributes, as well as have deficient areas in which "tooling up" may be necessary. Guidelines include the following knowledge, skills, and abilities and personal attributes:

Knowledge, skills, and abilities:

1. High school diploma or equivalent

2. Work experience and understanding in:

   a. Environmental science and technology

   b. Technical and environmental aspects of facility operations

   c. Relevant requirements of environmental laws, regulations, and related documents

   d. Environmental management systems and standards

   e. Audit procedures, processes, and techniques

Personal attributes and skills:

1. Competence

2. Interpersonal skills

3. Independence and objectivity

4. Personal organization skills

5. Ability to reach sound judgments

6. The ability to react with sensitivity to the conventions and culture of the country or religion in which the audit is performed.[48]

Other helpful advice for managing an environmental auditing department is provided by Tucker and Kasper:

1. Train auditors with accounting backgrounds in the basics of environmental auditing and the environmental laws

---

[47] *Ibid.*
[48] Robert R. Picard, "Environmental Management," p. 32.

2. Foster academic programs and environmental curricula that will provide the necessary common knowledge of environmental auditing practice

3. Encourage environmental auditor certification within the audit staff

4. Develop joint audits with environmental and internal auditors to permit sharing of ideas and knowledge

5. Provide input in structuring the environmental and internal auditors to permit and design audit programs to monitor and continuously improve this system[49]

The proper composition of an environmental auditing department is unclear. The environmental auditing department, like other internal auditing departments, must rely on personnel who possess a mix of skills. Appropriate staffing depends on the nature of the specific assignment. To assess technical performance, a technical team of engineers and attorneys should be formed. To verify records and find that policies and procedures are being followed, people with experience in auditing (and not necessarily as much expertise in environmental control) are good team members. The following quotes by managers involved with EMS are informative:

> A quality management systems auditor, no matter how experienced, lacks the specialization to be an effective environmental management system auditor. In our organization, the environmental management system auditor performs a systems audit to determine whether the environmental management system has been implemented and maintained, and if it conforms with the ISO 14001 standard. A team of environmental engineers who have been trained as internal auditors performs a more tactical audit.

> Some managements believe that internal auditors possess strengths not easily developed by technical engineers. Good internal auditors are skilled investigators familiar with their organizations' operations. As a result they are more likely to uncover substantive issues, even from a compliance standpoint.

> I prefer in-depth involvement from our internal audit staff as we review our environmental management system. A good internal auditor is skilled at following a line of questioning that gets us to the root cause of our problems and isn't satisfied with a superficial inquiry. A balance of auditor skills and subject matter skills is critical. Good auditors can acquire subject matter skills. However, assertiveness, a probing nature, and the ability to remain focused while sorting through mounds of data are absolutely necessary traits that are a natural part of a person's psyche and are not easily learned.[50]

¶ 2113 Summary

The role of auditors in environmental issues is changing rapidly. Recent shifts in social outlook and government policy have changed the audit objective from compliance to a management systems focus with an emphasis on internal control.

---

[49] Tucker and Kasper, "Pressures for Change," p. 346.

[50] Robert R. Picard, "Environmental Management," p. 32.

A comprehensive management standard, ISO 14000, has been promulgated to assist organizations in managing their environmental requirements and in ensuring that their environmental policies and practices conform with their missions and goals. The ISO 14000 standard also is useful to internal auditors because it provides a basis for assessing organizational compliance.

Internal auditors may not possess the technical knowledge necessary to assess a company's compliance with government regulations. These assessments are best left to an environmental engineer who is thoroughly familiar with regulatory requirements, supported by a specialist in environmental law. An internal auditor, however, is well suited to verify records and find that policies and procedures are being followed, to evaluate conformance with ISO 14000. An internal auditor focusing in environmental requirements should obtain the designation of certified professional environmental auditor (CPEA). The CPEA designation demonstrates competence and represents the exceptional knowledge, skill, and understanding of highly effective and fully qualified environmental professionals.

Chapter 22

Integrating Analytical Procedures and Sampling into Audit Tests

¶ 2201   Introduction
¶ 2202   Analytical Procedures
¶ 2203   Basic Sampling Concepts
¶ 2204   Risks of Sampling
¶ 2205   Audit Testing Decisions
¶ 2206   Conducting an Attribute Sampling Test
¶ 2207   Conducting a Variable Sampling Test
¶ 2208   Tips for Accurate Sampling
¶ 2209   Summary

¶ 2201 Introduction

This chapter describes how auditors can use analytical procedures and sampling to efficiently conduct audits by integrating sampling into the other audit tests. The chapter begins with a general overview and discussion of analytical procedures. Specific types of analytic procedures are then presented and discussed. The chapter gives a general overview of sampling. Specific types of sampling are then presented. Some important considerations are listed and discussed. The presentation in this chapter should be applicable to the vast majority of engagements. However, when confronted by a situation not covered by this chapter, the auditor should consult specialized audit sampling books.

Chapter 22 objectives:

- To list the five types of analytical procedures (see ¶ 2202).

- To understand when to use analytical procedures during the audit (see ¶ 2202).

- To understand how to assure analytical procedure precision (see ¶ 2202).

- To specify when an application of audit procedures is considered audit sampling (see ¶ 2203).

- To describe the methods used to select a sample (see ¶ 2203).

- To comprehend the risks of sampling (see ¶ 2204 and ¶ 2208).
- To define attribute sampling and how to conduct an attribute sampling test (see ¶ 2205–2207).
- To define variable sampling and how to conduct a variable sampling test (see ¶ 2205–2207).

.01 Application of Analytical Procedures and Sampling

Auditors use analytical procedures and sampling because these approaches are efficient. Analytical procedures are simple to calculate and provide a reasonableness or reality check on audit results. Sampling allows the auditor to reach a conclusion about a population without having to test each item in the population. For example, presidential polls concerning the voting preferences of nearly 100 million voters are based on samples of a few thousand voters. The auditing profession became obsessed with sampling during the late 1970s and early 1980s. Statisticians from academia were employed to come with the most complex and esoteric sampling techniques possible. Many firms bragged about their use of statistical sampling. Seminars, many lasting as long as a week, were conducted to educate auditors in statistical sampling methods. However, this craze has passed, largely due to the fact that auditors do not have the time to learn and apply these complex sampling techniques. Auditors also came to realize that the precision of their "quick and dirty" sampling techniques was acceptable for their purposes. The additional benefit in the form of increased precision was not worth the additional expenditure of time.

Auditors should always keep in mind that the reason they use analytics and sampling is to identify "unusual" transactions for subsequent follow-up. Auditors often initially discover fraudulent transactions through analytics but fail to realize it because they do not adequately investigate unusual analytical relationships or sampling exceptions. Consider the following two examples.

Example: Suppose that a client claims to specialize in the construction of church sanctuaries. The auditor establishes that during the previous year, the client completed ten projects with an average value of $10 million. However, the auditor investigates further and finds out that the average new church sanctuary costs averages only $2 to $3 million to build. The auditor then examines the client's construction project and finds that they are either bogus or the revenue has been inflated.

Example: An auditor using sampling to test the accuracy of inventory records only finds one instance in which the inventory records differed from the actual inventory (an exception). Although an acceptable error rate, the auditor decides to vigorously investigate the exception by taking additional counts and physically investigating the contents of boxes. The auditor is rewarded for being persistent by uncovering a

¶ 2201.01

massive inventory fraud. Many of the boxes in hard to get to locations in the warehouse contained bricks or other heavy items and not merchandise.

¶ 2202 Analytical Procedures

Analytical procedures are the study or comparison of the relationship between two or more measures for the purpose of establishing the reasonableness of each one compared. They are based on the assumption that in the absence of known conditions to the contrary, relationships among information may be expected to exist and continue. Analytical procedures help auditors identify unexpected differences, the absence of expected differences, possible errors or fraud, and other unusual or rarely occurring events. It cannot be overstated enough that auditors must fully investigate all unusual trends or relationships uncovered by analytical procedures because this may be the only sign that fraud has occurred.

.01 Types

There are five types of analytical procedures:[1]

1. Comparison with prior periods—for example, examining the trend for sales over a 10-year period, or comparing the balance sheet accounts from one period to another (also referred to as horizontal analysis). The auditor should examine the gross amount and percentage changes for proper analysis.

    Generally, current assets and liabilities can be expected to change in proportion to sales. Auditors should investigate current assets such as accounts receivable and inventory that do not change in proportion to sales. Accounts receivable that grow at a greater rate than sales may indicate bogus sales or delivery of goods to a fraudster who doesn't intend on paying for the goods. Inventories that do not grow in proportion to sales could indicate bogus sales. On the other hand, inventories that grow slower than sales could indicate obsolete or slow moving inventory that should be written off. Auditors should also pay strict attention to the Allowance for Doubtful Accounts as it relates to increases or decreases in sales to ensure that it is adequate to cover future write-offs. Controls over the granting of credit and the write-offs of accounts receivable should be evaluated, and individual accounts written-off should be investigated. Changes in current liabilities should also correspond to changes in sales. Accounts payable that change faster than sales could indicate a client having cash flow problems. On the other hand, accounts payable that change slower than sales could indicate unrecorded liabilities.

---

[1] SAS No. 56, Analytical Procedures (AICPA, Professional Standards, vol.1, AU sec. 329.05).

2. Comparison within period—for example, presenting each account in the balance sheet as a percentage of total assets and then comparing the percentages for two or more periods to determine the relative changes in accounts (whole dollar financials or vertical analysis). This analysis will show individual accounts with abnormal changes relative to the other accounts that could indicate fraud or mismanagement.

   Vertical analysis is useful for analyzing the income statement and an organization's various margins. Generally, gross and profit margins should remain stable, and significant changes should be investigated. Increasing margins could indicate bogus sales or unrecorded costs, while decreasing margins could indicate increased competition or financial distress.

3. Comparison with expectations—for example, variance analysis.

   This analytic can provide insight into a client management's knowledge of their business. Wide variations in actual results from budgeted or anticipated results generally indicate that a client's management lacks a basic knowledge of their business. Auditors in such situations should fully investigate and verify the accuracy of all estimates made by management, particularly: the allowance for doubtful accounts, collectibility of past due accounts receivable, obsolescence of inventory, warranty expenses, and especially accruals. For instance, waste management companies are required to estimate the cost of closing and monitoring landfills. This is usually a large amount that will take place many years in the future and can have a significant impact on net income if not done properly. For these clients, auditors should first determine that their client could perform short-term forecasts and budgets accurately by reviewing the number and amount of variances. Only then can the auditor evaluate the ability of the client to prepare long-term estimates. For all accruals, auditors should track the amount accrued to the amount eventually paid out. Again, large discrepancies may indicate that management lacks basic knowledge of their business or is trying to purposely misstate the financial statements.

4. Comparison with industry averages—for example, ratio analysis or benchmarking.

   Benchmarking to industry standards provides a reality check for a client's financial statements. The construction company example presented above is a classic use of this analytical technique. Auditors should calculate basic financial ratios for their clients and compare them to industry averages. In addition, auditors should track ratios over at least five years to

¶ 2202.01

determine significant trends. Ratios that differ significantly from industry averages may be due to poor management or fraud. Auditors should fully investigate to determine which is the case. Finally, auditors should always consider the possibility that their clients may not remain in business if significant ratios such as the quick ratio, accounts receivable and inventory turnover ratios, and debt coverage ratios significantly deteriorate over time. These situations are known as "Going-Concerns" and the auditors' responsibilities for clients with "Going-Concern" issues are explained in ¶ 709 of this *Guide*. Many times, the auditors are the first ones to alert management to the danger facing the organization.

5. Comparison with other operating information—for example, comparing the amount of revenue recorded to the amount of gas used by the organization's delivery fleet.

This analytical technique requires the greatest amount of creativity to effectively implement particularly in determining the operating information to use. However, this technique can provide the most insight into financial statement accounts and is often the only manner in which to uncover massive financial statement fraud. For instance, during the 1970s, Equity Funding was the fastest growing insurance company in the United States. Unfortunately, most of its insurance policies were bogus. Auditors could have detected this fraud earlier had they simply calculated the percentage of the U.S. population that Equity Funding would have had to insure to realize its rapid growth. The unusually high percentage should have caused the auditors to investigate the number of policies being issued. In general, the number of items shipped by a company should relate to its amount of sales and cost of goods recorded. The number of hours billed for services should closely approximate the hours paid. Many more examples exist for practically any business or industry. Auditors should develop some for each of their clients.

.02 When to Use Analytical Procedures

Analytics can be used anytime during the audit. During the planning phase, analytics can be used to identify abnormal trends for follow-up during the audit. They can also be used during the internal auditing function's annual risk assessment to identify high risk auditable units. Analytics can be used during fieldwork as corroboration of other audit tests. For instance, an auditor working for a cable company may test revenue by multiplying the average number of customers by published rates. Finally, auditors can use analytics as a quality assurance procedure in wrapping up an audit. For example, an audit supervisor may compare the time required by various auditors to complete the same audit test.

¶ 2202.02

.03 Steps in Applying Analytical Procedures

Statement on Auditing Standards (SAS) No. 56 of the AICPA requires application of analytical procedures during the planning and final review phases of an audit engagement.[2] Analytical procedures should assist auditors in planning the nature, timing, and extent of other audit procedures. Analytical procedures can also be used during the evidence-gathering phase of an audit engagement as a substantive test of management's assertions. Analytical procedures should be used in the final review phase of an audit engagement to determine the overall reasonableness of financial statements. Steps involved in applying analytical procedures are:

- Identify the calculations/comparisons to be made
  - Absolute data comparisons
  - Common-size financial statements
  - Ratio analysis
  - Trend analysis
- Develop expectations (estimated probable outcomes)
  - Client financial information for comparable prior period(s) giving consideration to known changes
  - Anticipated results based on formal budgets or forecasts
  - Relationships among elements of financial information within the period
  - Industry data
  - Relationships of financial information with relevant nonfinancial information
- Perform the calculations/comparisons
- Analyze data and identify significant differences
- Investigate significant unexpected differences
- Determine effects on audit planning, evidence-gathering procedures, and review phase of the audit engagement

.04 Controlling Data Quality of Input

Analytical procedures are only as good as the information used to calculate them. An analytical procedure precision depends upon the time periods being compared. For example, comparing daily totals is more precise than comparing monthly or yearly totals. This is because small trends average out over a period of time. The precision of an analytical procedure is directly related to the reliability of the information used to

---

[2] SAS No. 56, Analytical Procedures (AICPA, Professional Standards, vol.1, AU sec. 329.05).

calculate it. Third-party evidence is generally preferred to auditee-maintained evidence.

.05 Applying Analytical Procedures

In summary, analytical procedures are becoming more important as documentary evidence loses credibility due to information technology. Second, analytics are only as good as the information used to calculate them. Third, analytics must be backed up with detailed testing.

Finally, often with analytical procedures, something *not* happening is the important trend—much like the Sherlock Holmes story involving the dog that didn't bark, thus alerting Holmes that the perpetrator was someone the dog knew. For example, inventory levels are not increasing at the same rate as sales and accounts receivable, indicating that fictitious sales are being recorded and inventory levels are not rising because actual products are not needed to support fictitious revenue. In this case the auditor would further investigate the veracity of accounts receivable, paying particular attention to the actual existence of customers whose accounts are past due. Fake customers usually do not keep their accounts current for long.

¶ 2203 Basic Sampling Concepts

Sampling is the application of an audit test to less than 100 percent of an account balance or class of transactions (sample) for the purposes of reaching a conclusion about the entire account balance or class of transactions. The process of reaching a conclusion about an entire population based on a sample is called *extrapolation*. For extrapolation to be successful two conditions must be met: (1) the sample must be representative of the population, and (2) the results must be quantitatively evaluated. Auditors generally do not consider the following four activities as sampling: (1) testing every item in a population (100 percent testing), (2) testing no items in a population (zero testing), (3) analytical procedures, and (4) inquiry and observation (I&O).

Statistical sampling occurs when every item in a population has an equal chance of being selected and the sample is randomly chosen. Conclusions from statistical sampling can be stated with mathematical precision according to the laws of chance. Hence, statistical sampling usually meets both criteria for effective extrapolation. However, statistical sampling requires additional time and effort to apply, and many populations are not large enough (greater than 100 items) for it to be used. Nonstatistical samples, on the other hand, are relative easy to apply, but the interpretation of their results leaves much to be desired. Auditors can legitimately use nonstatistical sampling to evaluate the items as being processed correctly or incorrectly, but never to reach overall conclusions concerning the population. It should also be pointed out that the auditor is always free to use analytical procedures to identify items for evaluation, and this is not considered sampling. At any rate, it should be clear from this discussion that auditors should mix analytical procedures with statistical and nonstatistical sampling techniques in selecting items for evaluation during an audit.

Consecutively numbered items such as checks can be selected randomly by using either a random number table or a computer routine such as @random on most spreadsheet programs. Selecting items in this manner generally results in a representative sample. However, many populations are not consecutively numbered; in those instances an auditor can choose a random starting point and then select every nth item until the required number of items are selected. For example, suppose an auditor is examining an inventory consisting of 1,000 items from which the auditor wishes to select 10 items. The sampling interval would be 100 or 1000 items in the population divided by 10 items in the sample. The auditor would then randomly choose a number from 1 to 100, say 38, and then select every 100th item after that, or 138, 238, 338 until 938. This technique is called *systematic* or *interval sampling*, and generally results in a representative sample unless the selection hits an underlying pattern in the population, in which case the sample will be biased. Finally, there is *block* or *cluster sampling*, in which items are grouped together (locations or file cabinet drawers) and selected on the basis of the grouping. Each selected group is then audited thoroughly. For example, suppose an auditor is testing a client with 10 branch locations. The auditor randomly chooses two branch locations and then performs 100 percent testing of transactions only at the selected locations. This is not statistical sampling and rarely results in a representative sample.

¶ 2204 Risks of Sampling

The ultimate risk for auditors in sampling is drawing an invalid conclusion. Invalid conclusions can arise from the sample itself (sampling risk) or from without the sample (nonsampling risk). Examples of nonsampling risk include the following: (1) a poorly designed or irrelevant audit test, (2) an incorrectly applied audit test, or (3) an incorrectly drawn conclusion. Nonsampling risk can be controlled through effective planning and supervision. Sampling risks can be classified according to incorrect positive and incorrect negative conclusions. In attribute or control testing, auditors use the term "incorrect positive" to describe the risk of overreliance and an "incorrect negative" to describe the risk of underreliance. Overreliance, or concluding that a control is functioning when it is not, is very serious because the auditor has assessed control risk too low; consequently, detection risk becomes too high, resulting in the performance of less auditing testing than warranted if given the auditee's actual risk level. Underreliance, on the other hand, results in more audit testing than would have been done if the control risk were correctly assessed.

¶ 2204

The two types of sampling risk are each significant when account balance testing is concerned. A false positive occurs when the auditor concludes that an account balance is fairly stated when it is not. The result is that the financial statements contain a material error. Likewise, an auditor is likely to change a correct account balance to an incorrect one if the auditor incorrectly believes the account balance to be wrongly stated (false negative). Both mistakes result in an incorrectly stated account balance and auditors must take them into account in designing sampling plans.

¶ 2205 Audit Testing Decisions

An auditor makes certain decisions in designing audit tests that are presented in the decision tree presented by Figure 22.1. The first decision is whether to sample. The auditor will choose not to sample in the overwhelming majority of instances, remembering that there are four activities not considered audit sampling: (1) 100 percent testing, (2) no testing, (3) analytical procedures, and (4) inquiry and observation. Generally, auditors will sample in those instances when the account balance is composed of a high volume of low dollar amount transactions. These include the balance sheet accounts representing accounts receivable, inventory, accounts payable, and (in certain instances) fixed assets. Income statement accounts that meet this criterion include revenue or sales, purchases, and payroll. In addition to these accounts, auditors sample when testing controls over individual revenue, purchases, and payroll transactions.

Figure 22.1

Sampling Decision Tree

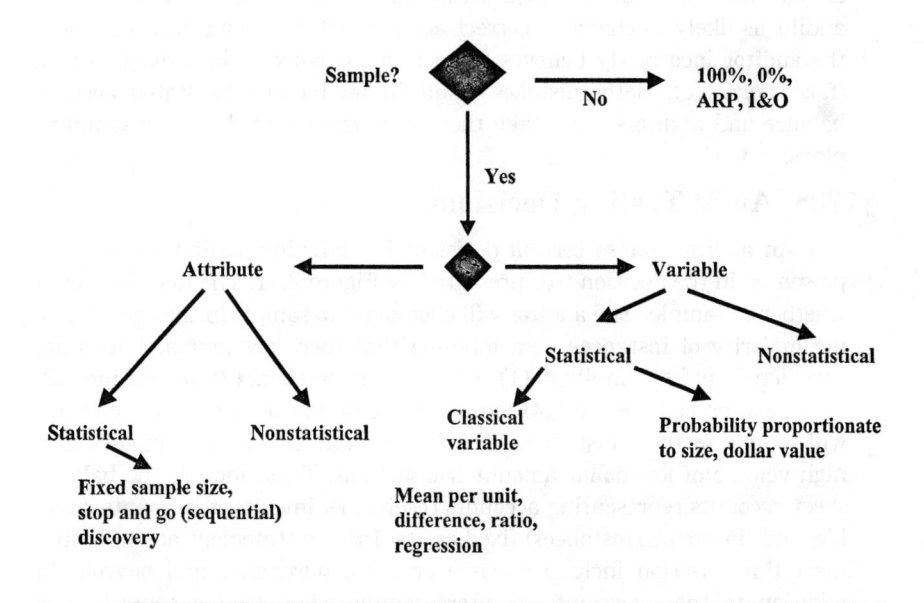

```
                    Sample? ──No──► 100%, 0%,
                      │              ARP, I&O
                     Yes
                      │
            ┌─────────┴─────────┐
         Attribute            Variable
            │                    │
                        ┌────────┴────────┐
                    Statistical      Nonstatistical
     ┌──────┴──────┐       │                │
 Statistical  Nonstatistical  Classical    Probability proportionate
     │                        variable     to size, dollar value
 Fixed sample size,
 stop and go (sequential)   Mean per unit,
 discovery                  difference, ratio,
                            regression
```

Once the decision to sample is made, the auditor will choose an attribute test for cases of control testing and variable sampling for account balance testing. Next, the auditor must determine whether statistical or nonstatistical sampling is appropriate. Finally, statistical sampling involves some additional choices. Attribute statistical sampling can take the form of fixed sample size sampling, stop-and-go (sequential) sampling, or discovery sampling. Of the three sampling techniques, stop-and-go is overwhelmingly preferred to the other two and will be discussed in detail. The reader should consult the auditing sampling books listed in the footnotes to this chapter.

Variable sampling plans can take one of two forms: classical variable and probability proportional to size (PPS) or dollar-unit sampling. The classical variable approach is based on the normal distribution curve and treats each item in a population as a sampling unit. For example, imagine the following accounts receivable balances:

Account Number	Amount	Cumulative Dollar Amount
1000	$100	1–100
2000	$200	101–300
3000	$300	301–600
4000	$400	601–1,000

¶ 2205

Classical variable sampling treats each item as a separate sampling unit. Each, therefore, has a one in four or even probability of being selected. PPS sampling relies on the Poisson distribution and treats each dollar of an item's value as a sampling unit. For instance, using the accounts receivable listed above, Account 1000 would have sampling units 1 through 100, Account 2000 would have sampling units 101–300, etc. Account 1000 would have a probability of being selected of 100 out of 1,000 or 1 in 10, whereas Account 4000 would have 400 out of 1,000 or 40 percent. PPS, therefore, gives added weight to larger dollar items, which seems reasonable to most auditors. Under a classical variable plan there are four sampling techniques: mean per unit, difference, ratio, and regression. All four techniques rely on the same formula to determine sample size, but each then calculates a different test statistic for the sample to use in extrapolating a value for the population. For instance, in a mean per unit sampling, a sample is drawn and then the average value of the units in the sample is calculated and multiplied by the number of items in the population to arrive at an estimate of the account balance. Using a difference technique, the test statistic is the observed difference between an item's recorded value and its value as determined by the auditors. An average difference is calculated for the sample and multiplied by the total number of items in the population to arrive at an estimate of total error for the account being tested. Ratio sampling is by far the easiest and most frequently used classical variable sampling technique and is the one illustrated later in this chapter. Regression involves plotting a least squares equation after plotting each sample item's recorded value and observed value as coordinates. The total book value of the inventory is then inserted into the equation to arrive at an estimated audit value.

Classical variable and PPS are appropriate under different circumstances. Generally, PPS is simpler and quicker to use. It is generally applied in conjunction with systematic sampling. As stated above, PPS does not rely on the normal distribution curve and, consequently, does not require an estimate of the population's standard deviation to be performed as does classical variable. The use of PPS results in smaller sample sizes than classical variable employs. However, classical variable is more appropriate if numerous errors are anticipated. Also, the classical variable technique is also appropriate for accounts that could be understated, such as liabilities and expenses.

¶ 2206 Conducting an Attribute Sampling Test

Recall that attribute sampling is associated with control testing, in which the auditor seeks to determine a control's occurrence rate. The auditor is therefore seeking the presence of the attribute; the control is functioning or it is not functioning. Actually, the auditor is estimating the frequency rate for when the control is not functioning and then evaluating whether that is low enough to conclude that the control is effectively functioning. As stated above, there are three types of attribute testing techniques—stop-and-go (sequential), fixed sample size, or discovery. Stop-and-go will be presented now; for the others, the reader can refer to one of the statistical sampling books cited in the footnotes to this chapter. For purposes of the current discussion, check signing will be used as an example because controls over check signing are important for all organizations.

.01 Stating Test Objectives

The first step in conducting any audit test is to determine the test's objectives. Using check signing as an example, an auditor would state the test's objectives thusly: "Ensure that checks are properly signed as evidence that the check was compared to proper supporting documentation."

.02 Conditions for Failure

The second step entails determining what conditions would have to exist for the auditor to conclude that the checks were not properly signed. In the current example, the auditor would conclude that the checks were not properly signed under any of the following conditions:

- A check was not signed.
- A check was not signed by the proper official(s).
- The signature was a forgery. Obviously, the last condition would require additional investigation due to direct evidence of fraud, but the other two conditions also could involve fraud as well.

.03 Sampling Unit and Population

The third step of an audit test involves identifying the sampling unit and population. In the current instance, the sampling unit will be each individual check. Identifying the population involves determining the audit period. For external auditors this is usually the year covered by the income statement being audited. Internal auditors, on the other hand, are not covered by such time constraints; the audit period may be anything from three months to several years. Once the audit period is specified, the auditor needs to ensure that every item in the population has an equal chance of being selected. This is usually easily done for checks because they are prenumbered and the auditor merely has to consult the check log for the range of check numbers used during the audit period. Any missing checks should be treated as exceptions and should be further investigated.

.04 Setting Sample Size

The fourth step of the audit test deals with determining the sample size, and here is where stop-and-go sampling is really useful. Under this technique the auditor will select a relatively small initial sample to test. If no exceptions are found, the auditor concludes that the control is functioning. If one or more exceptions are found, the auditor can either select more items to test or conclude the control is not functioning. Usually the auditor

¶ 2206.01

will pull a maximum of three samples before concluding the control is not functioning. A typical stop-and-go sampling table will look like Table 22.1.

Table 22.1

Example of Stop-and-Go Sampling Table

Step	Cumulative Sample Size to Use	Stop If Cumulative Deviations To	Sample More If Deviations Are	Go to Step 4 If Deviations Are at Least
1	37	0	1-2	3
2	56	1	2	3
3	73	2		3
4	Conclude that control is not functioning.			

Some important points about some basic statistical concepts must be pointed out. The example illustrated in the table was computed at the 97.5 percent reliability level—in other words, the auditor can be 97.5 percent certain of the results or, conversely, the auditor faces an overreliance risk of 2.5 percent. In addition, the computation assumed a tolerable rate of 10 percent. Lower tolerable rates will result in greater sampling sizes. The following equation[3] was used to calculate the values in Table 22.1:

$$n = \frac{rf}{tr}$$

Where:

n = initial sample size

rf = risk factor from Table 22.2 for level of risk of over reliance selected

tr = tolerable rate

---

[3] D.M. Guy, D.R. Carmichael, and O.R. Whittington, *Audit Sampling: An Introduction* (New York: John Wiley & Sons, 1998), 64.

¶ 2206.04

Table 22.2

Determining Sample Size for Stop-and-Go (Sequential) Sampling

	Risk Factors for Risk of Overreliance		
Number of Deviations	10%	5%	2.5%
0	2.4	3.0	3.7
1	3.9	4.8	5.6
2	5.4	6.3	7.3
3	6.7	7.8	8.8
4	8.0	9.2	10.3
5	9.3	10.6	11.7

Source: D.M. Guy, D.R. Carmichael, and O.R. Whittington, *Audit Sampling: An Introduction* (New York: John Wiley & Sons, 1998), p. 61.

Additional details concerning stop-and-go testing can be obtained from the statistical sampling books in the footnotes to this chapter.

.05 Selecting and Testing Sample

The fifth step of an audit test using attribute sampling involves the selection of the sample and the performance of the audit tests on the items selected. Because checks are prenumbered, random sampling can be used to select the number of items specified in the fourth step.

.06 Evaluating and Documenting Results

The sixth step involves evaluating the results of the test. Suppose in the current example that only two exceptions are discovered of the 73 items tested. The auditor can conclude that the exception rate is low enough to conclude the control is functioning. However, even though the overall exception rate is low, the auditor must investigate both exceptions to determine whether they are unintentional errors or intentional fraud. This point cannot be stressed enough. Too often auditors stop with an overall occurrence rate and do not investigate individual exceptions indicating the presence of fraud. Every exception must be investigated. Finally, the auditor should fully document the above in the workpapers. Of particular importance to workpaper reviewers are the definition of exceptions, the factors used in calculating sample size, and the further investigation and disposition of exceptions.

¶ 2206.05

¶ 2207 Conducting a Variable Sampling Test

Variable sampling is associated with account balance testing, in which the auditor seeks to determine whether an account is properly stated. As noted earlier, there are two forms of variable sampling—classical variable sampling (CVS) and probability proportional to size (PPS) or dollar-unit sampling. Within CVS there are mean per unit, difference, ratio, and regression techniques. PPS will be illustrated because it is generally easier to apply than CVS, but ratio sampling is also presented because it is the most widely used and easiest version of CVS to apply. For purposes of the current discussion, accounts receivable will be used as an example because nearly all organizations grant credit to their customers and, therefore, have accounts receivable.

.01 Stating Test Objectives

The steps involved in completing a variable sampling test are similar to those for attribute sampling. Likewise, both PPS and CVS have similar steps. The first step is to determine the test's objectives. Using accounts receivable as an example, the objective can be stated as, "Estimate the value of accounts receivable."

.02 Defining the Population

The second step entails defining the population in terms of sampling unit, completeness of the population, and individual significant items. In terms of accounts receivable, the population will include all accounts receivable as of the balance sheet date, say December 31, 20X0. Each individual accounts receivable will constitute a sampling unit under CVS, whereas a unit's cumulative dollar amount will be its sampling unit under PPS. An auditor can ensure the completeness of accounts receivable by footing the accounts receivable subsidiary ledger and comparing the balance to the general ledger control account. The auditor should review the subsidiary ledger to identify potentially significant or strange accounts, such as those with credit balances.

.03 Setting Sample Size and Selecting the Sample

Once the population is defined, the auditor should determine the sample size, and here is where PPS and CVS sampling differ significantly. The following formula [4] is used for PPS to determine the sample size:

$$n = \frac{BV \times RF}{M}$$

Where:

n = sample size

---

[4] L.B. Sawyer and M.A. Dittenhofer, *Sawyer's Internal Auditing: The Practice of Modern Internal Auditing*, 4th Edition (Altamonte Springs, Fla.: The Institute of Internal Auditors, 1996), 482.

BV=book value of population

RF=risk factor based on Poisson distribution where the corresponding reliability levels and risk factors are as follows:

Reliability Level	Risk Factor
99%	4.605
95%	2.996
90%	2.300

M=maximum tolerable error

In addition, recall that PPS is usually associated with systematic sampling in which the auditor will choose a random starting point and take every nth item. The every nth item represents the sampling interval and is calculated according to the following formula:

$$I = \frac{BV}{n}$$

Where:

I=sampling unit

BV=book value

n=sample size

Suppose for an example that a client has accounts receivable totaling $1,000,000, that the auditor desires a reliability level of 95 percent, and the auditor is willing to accept an error of $25,000. The sample size will equal ($1,000,000× 2.996)÷$25,000=120.

The following formula is used for CVS:

$$n = ((Z \times SD \times N) \div A)^2$$

Where:

n=first estimate of sample size

SD=standard deviation of the sample

A=precision (tolerable error)

N=number of items in the total population

Z=standard deviation factors with corresponding reliability levels and risk factors from the normal distribution:

Reliability Level	Risk Factor
99%	2.2758
95%	1.9600
90%	1.6449

In addition, there is a population adjustment formula:

$$n' = n \div (1 + (n \div N))$$

¶ 2207.03

Where:

n' = adjusted sample size

N = number of items in population[5]

Notice that an estimate of population standard deviation must be computed under this method. This can be estimated by taking a preliminary sample. Assume that an auditor took an initial sample of 50 items and calculated the sample's standard deviation of $15. Further assume that the number of items in the population total 10,000, the auditor desires a 95 percent reliability level, and he or she is willing to tolerate a $25,000 error. The resulting sample size would equal:

$$((1.96 \times 15 \times 10{,}000) \div 25{,}000)^2 = 11.76^2$$

This result yields 138 unadjusted and 136 when adjusted for population. Because 50 items were already selected, the auditor need only select 86 additional items. Usually, CVS sampling relies on random sampling.

Once the sample size has been determined, the auditor can pull the sample items or give the auditee a list of items to be pulled.

.04 Testing Sample

Once the sample is selected, the auditor should perform the audit test on each item in the population. For example, in this case he or she would send out confirmations for the selected accounts receivable. Once the confirmations are received, the auditor can evaluate the sample items to estimate the population value. The estimated value of the population for a PPS sample will equal the book or recorded value if no exceptions are noted. If some exceptions are noted, some rather complex formulas come into play that are beyond the scope of this work to present. For CVS ratio sampling, the following formula is used to estimate population value:

$$R = \frac{\Sigma av}{\Sigma bv} \text{ and } EV = R * BV$$

Where:

R = ratio of the sample book value or recorded value to audit value.

bv = book or recorded value for a particular item in the sample

av = audited value for a particular item in the sample

EV = estimated total value of the population

BV = total book or recorded value of the population[6]

---

[5] *Supra* note 1, pp. 97–99.   [6] *Ibid.*, p. 110.

Notice that an R value greater than 1 means the population is overstated, an R equal to 1 means the population is correctly stated, and an R less than 1 means a population is understated. In this example, suppose that the $R=0.996$; estimated accounts receivable would be 996,000, well within the tolerable error of $25,000. However, auditors are again cautioned to investigate all discrepancies, regardless of their monetary amount or apparent insignificance.

.05 Documenting Results

Finally, the auditor should fully document this test, especially the test's objectives, population attributes, calculation of sampling size, evaluation of sample items, and disposition of discrepancies.

¶ 2208 Tips for Accurate Sampling

Some important points should be kept in mind concerning sampling. First, the auditor should know and manage the risks associated with sampling. Second, the auditor must remain objective and professionally skeptical in planning and conducting the audit test, particularly when evaluating the sample results. Next, the auditor should know as much as possible about the data being examined. The auditor should be sensitive to the presence of underlying patterns that could bias sample results. Large or significant items should be analyzed and separately examined. Finally, the auditor *must* fully investigate all exceptions, even if the overall exception rate is acceptable, because the one exception found could uncover a major fraud and might be the only chance the auditor gets.

¶ 2209 Summary

Auditors use analytical procedures and sampling to identify "unusual" transactions for subsequent follow-up. Because these techniques quickly alert auditors to items that need further investigation and help them focus their efforts, analytical procedures and sampling help auditors conduct more efficient audits.

Using analytical procedures, auditors compare two sets of data and assess the reasonableness of each set in relation to the other. Analytical procedures help auditors identify unexpected differences, the absence of expected differences, possible errors or fraud, and other unusual or rarely occurring events. Once the auditor identifies these abnormalities, he or she must fully investigate all unusual trends or relationships uncovered by the analytical procedures.

Auditors may not wish to test all of a company's transactions and events because transactions may be too numerous for the auditors to verify each one separately in a timely manner. As a result, the auditors will use audit sampling to test the transactions. Even when facing time or budget constraints, auditors do not test these transactions haphazardly. Instead, auditors follow established methods to choose the sample and ensure that the selected sample is representative of the entire population. These samples can then be used to make two kinds of decisions—an assessment of control risk and an evaluation of whether financial statement assertions in an account balance are fairly presented.

Chapter 23
IT and the Auditor

¶ 2301 Introduction
¶ 2302 Historical Background
¶ 2303 IT Controls
¶ 2304 IT Control Frameworks
¶ 2305 Variety of IT Systems
¶ 2306 The Computer and the Auditor
¶ 2307 IT Auditing Organizations
¶ 2308 Academic Preparation for Becoming an IT Auditor
¶ 2309 Summary

¶ 2301 Introduction

This chapter presents several aspects of information technology and their implications in auditing. First, the chapter presents some of the controls that an auditor would expect to find in reviewing an organization's information technology system. Various types of information technology and their impact on controls are then presented and discussed. Second, the chapter presents and discusses the various approaches that auditors can use in interfacing with information technology. Finally, the chapter discusses professional organizations, certifications, and skill sets that apply to IT auditing.

Chapter 23 objectives:

- To understand the implications of new technology advances on the auditing profession (see ¶ 2301).

- To determine the auditor's role in auditing the information system of a company (see ¶ 2302).

- To recognize the controls that an auditor would expect to find in reviewing an organization's information technology (IT) system (see ¶ 2303).

- To identify two IT control frameworks to help auditors in evaluating information systems (see ¶ 2304).

- To recognize various types of information technology and their impact on controls (see ¶ 2305).

- To explain approaches that auditors can use in interfacing with information technology (see ¶ 2306).

- To recognize professional organizations, certifications, and skill sets that apply to IT auditing (see ¶ 2307–2308).

.01 Emerging ITs

The American Institute of Certified Public Accountants (AICPA) annually compiles lists of the "Top Ten" information technology (IT) issues, applications, and technologies, together with a list of emerging technologies (see Table 23.1 for the 2001–2003 lists). The lists provide a snapshot concerning the state of the art in IT during that period. Significant changes have occurred within the items on the lists. For example, only three issues from the 2001 lists made all three lists (security technologies, wireless technologies, and remote connectivity tools); one issue made two lists (communications technologies-bandwidth), and six issues only made the 2001 list. Changes to IT will continue to occur rapidly and dramatically. The tremendous pace of technological change has many implications for auditors. First and foremost, despite change, certain "low-tech" concepts remain constant. Second, the technical knowledge needed to understand systems fully is changing as fast as the technology is changing. Auditors who attempt to keep up with this change will surely fail. Therefore, auditors must learn to leverage the technical knowledge of technicians to successfully complete audit assignments. Third, there is such a wide range of technologies in use that no one auditor will be able to master all of them. Therefore, auditors will have to work together in teams, with each member developing specialties. Fourth, successful information technology auditors will have to improvise, become creative, and commit to life-long learning to succeed.

¶ 2301.01

Table 23.1

Top Technologies Lists for Information Technology 2001–2003

Rank	2001	2002	2003
1	Security Technologies	Business and Financial Reporting Applications	Information Security
2	XML (Extensible Markup Language)	Training & Technology Competency	Business Information Management
3	Communications technologies-bandwidth	Information Security and Controls	Application Integration
4	Mobile Technologies	Quality of Service	Web Services
5	Wireless Technologies	Disaster Recovery	Disaster Recovery Planning
6	Electronic authorization	Communications Technologies—Bandwidth	Wireless Technologies
7	Encryption	Remote Connectivity Tools	Intrusion Protection
8	Electronic authentication	Web-based and web-enabled applications	Remote Connectivity
9	Remote connectivity tools	Qualified IT Personnel	Customer Relationship Management
10	Database Technologies	Messaging Applications	Privacy

Source: AICPA Top Technologies Task Force website; *www.toptentechs.com.*

¶ 2302 Historical Background

Most organizations began to automate at least some of their functions during the 1960s and 1970s. These efforts were generally centered around identifying manual processes that could be automated, and these automation efforts were labeled "electronic data processing" (EDP). The computers facilitating this automation were chiefly large mainframe computers located in centrally located and controlled data centers. Raw data was converted into a machine-readable medium (punch cards), processed, and output in a user-readable medium (usually a printed report). During this period, EDP was centralized, not very user friendly, but well controlled.

During the 1970s, EDP personnel started to integrate automated functions by having applications and even different computers communicate directly with one another. EDP suddenly became information systems (IS) or management information systems (MIS). Airline reservation systems and similar applications were able to directly support upper management decision making. Many organizations experimented with decentralizing their computer operations by placing minicomputers throughout their organizations. A decentralized IS was generally responsive to user department needs but was extremely costly in terms of redundant and underused resources. Security also suffered in decentralized IS because user departments were not familiar enough with control issues to competently design and maintain them. Most organizations subsequently went with distributive IS, in which a centralized IS department existed to coordinate purchases of compatible equipment and train user departments in maintaining proper security.

The rapid development and widespread distribution of personal computers (PCs) during the early to mid-1980s, the further integration of PCs into networks, and, finally, the development of the Internet, have caused practitioners to change the IS nomenclature to information technology (IT). PCs replaced mainframes and minicomputers because PCs were less expensive, yet possessed sufficient computing power required for user applications. PCs produced in the 1980s had processing speeds of 12 megahertz per second and hard drives with 20 megabytes or so of memory. PCs built in 2001, by contrast, possess processing speeds in excess of 1 gigahertz per second and hard drives capable of storing several hundred gigabytes of data. Connecting PCs into local area networks (LANs), wide area networks (WANs), and the Internet have further improved information processing, internal communication, and (hopefully) decision making. The Internet has had the same impact between organizations and individuals.

Despite the rapid and far-reaching changes in IT, the auditor's role remains the same: to ensure that the organization has adequate controls in place to mitigate risks that could prevent the organization from fulfilling its objectives. In an IT context, this means that the auditor must first understand the organization's IT system well enough (1) to identify the risks significant enough to impact the organization's ability to fulfill its objectives, and (2) to design tests that help ensure controls function to mitigate those risks. The remainder of this chapter covers both topics. The first part of the chapter lists and discusses some risks and controls common to all IT systems. The second part discusses approaches that auditors can take in ensuring that necessary controls are functioning.

¶ 2303 IT Controls

IT controls have traditionally been classified as either general (system-wide) or application (specific) controls. This classification was clear and straightforward when most organizations operated only one mainframe computer system. The auditor would review and examine the general controls operating over the mainframe and then review and examine controls for a sample of applications. Although the typical IT system has more hardware and components today, the basic classification of controls remains valid. If anything, the current IT environment causes auditors to focus almost exclusively on the system-wide issues. The auditor's review of

¶ 2303

an IT system can provide valuable information to upper management concerning unforeseen risks if the auditor can objectively evaluate the organization's IT system from a strategic perspective in terms of the organization's objectives.

.01 General (System-wide) Controls

General or system-wide controls should address the organization's strategic risks. These include: overall system vision and governance, use of resources, personnel issues, business continuation, and security. This section briefly explores each of these issues.

Overall system vision and governance. The organization's information technology vision should be in line with the organization's vision. The organization should appoint a chief information officer (CIO) official with enough authority, visibility, and prestige to ensure that these two visions are aligned. The CIO should establish a strategic planning process with input from key user constituents, such as an IT steering committee. The IT steering committee should have a charter, envelop a broad representation of IT users, and hold regular and business-like meetings. The IT steering committee's mission is to recommend strategy and policy for the IT system. The committee should also make recommendations concerning major changes to the system using acceptable capital budgeting techniques. The CIO should adopt procedures to ensure that changes to the structures proceed in a business-like manner and do not compromise the IT system's integrity. Many organizations employ the life-cycle approach, in which changes to the system go through the following clearly defined steps: problem identification, feasibility study, design, implementation, and post-implementation review. Auditors should review the overall strategic planning efforts, and the functioning of the IT steering committee to ensure that the IT system vision is in line with the organization's vision, and that changes to the system make good business sense and are in line with the IT system vision. Auditors should become involved as consultants early in the development life cycle to ensure that key internal controls are designed into the IT system. Auditors should evaluate whether the managers of the organization's IT system are able to learn from past mistakes. In addition, most changes to an IT system will take the form of packages developed by outside vendors. Hence, auditors should spend a good deal of resources reviewing the compliance of these outside vendors with the terms and conditions of their contracts.

Evaluating an IT system's performance is a key management issue. The U.S. General Accounting Office (GAO) produced a report entitled *Measuring Performance and Demonstrating Results of Information Technology Investments*, which recommends that organizations complete the following steps in developing successful IT performance measures:

- Follow an IT "results chain."

¶ 2303.01

- Follow a balanced scorecard approach.
- Target measures, results, and accountability at different decision-making tiers.
- Build a comprehensive measure, data collection, and analysis capability.
- Improve performance of IT business processes to better support mission goals.[1]

The GAO study recommends starting out with the basics and then becoming more sophisticated over time. For instance, an organization could initially focus on:

- Delivery of reliable, cost-effective, high-quality IT products and services
- Adherence to industry standards for systems design, cost estimation, development, and implementation
- Internal customer satisfaction
- Staff productivity
- Technical skills and capability

Organizations that fail to evaluate the performance of their IT systems could be wasting numerous resources. The IT system should not be any different than other assets in that their performance should be evaluated to allow improvements to be identified and implemented.

Use of resources. Organizations should effectively and efficiently use their IT resources. This is especially challenging given the current circumstances, in which most personal computers are obsolete after two years and program changes may occur monthly. Unfortunately, there are no easy solutions to these circumstances. Some organizations lease their equipment. Others have totally outsourced their IT system. Scheduling the use of IT resources continues to be a key concern, regardless of how the IT resources are obtained. Ideally, the use of IT resources should be flat and exactly match the IT systems capacity. Unfortunately, most organizations experience twin peaks of IT usage—morning and afternoon—followed by evening fall-off in demand. Faced with frequent hardware obsolescences, continual software revisions, and uneven system usage, an organization is forced to build a larger IT system than it needs. Many organizations shift large data processing and record-updating projects to off-peak evening hours, thus freeing up critical peak capacity for inquiry and decision support data processing when staff is present during business hours. Finally, organiza-

---

[1] United States Government Accounting Office, *Measuring Performance and Demonstrating Results of Information Technology Investments* (Washington, D.C.:U.S. Government Printing Office, Document GAO/AIMD-98-89, 1998).

¶ 2303.01

tions should ensure that employees use the IT system solely for organization-related tasks. Clear and explicit policies should be promulgated and released stating that personal use of the organization's IT system is prohibited, and that employees that abuse the policies will be properly disciplined.

Personnel issues. IT organizations face several important human resource challenges. Foremost among these is obtaining and keeping staff that possess the knowledge, skills, and abilities to run the IT system. Turnover can occur naturally due to employee aging, accidents, and illnesses, but is aggravated by the tremendous demand exceeding supply worldwide for trained IT personnel. Many CIOs are reluctant to subsidize their IT personnel for fear that once trained, the IT personnel will leave the organization for better-paying positions elsewhere. This strategy seldom works in the long run because the organizations acquire a bad reputation and are forced to pay premiums to attract qualified employees. The real solution lies in paying competitive wages, plus developing and nurturing IT personnel to succeed and stay with the company. Documentation and task sharing can also help to mitigate the loss through key personnel turnover. The auditor should be wary of an above-normal turnover rate among IT personnel; this could be a sign of additional management problems.

Ergonomics, the study of the effects of human beings' interactions with machines, has recently become a serious issue in most organizations. Human beings are beginning to understand that prolonged interaction with one specific machine, the computer, can lead to subtle long-term, often serious health consequences. Interaction with computers has been recently cited as being a leading cause of carpal tunnel syndrome and other repetitive motion illnesses, as well as cancer, blood clots, back problems, and other ailments. The Clinton Administration in the United States proposed some fairly stringent safety requirements meant to safeguard workers' safety. Although the regulations were not formally enacted, the safety issues they were designed to address remain. Auditors should be concerned because computer-related injuries, like other workplace injuries, cost organizations much in terms of lost productivity and health care claims.

Auditors should ensure that the CIO has implemented sensible policies and procedures to safeguard workers from the safety hazards of interacting with computers, such as:

- Ensuring that desks and chairs are ergonomically designed and of the proper size for personnel using them

- Ergonomic keyboards or voice-activated software are used if possible to reduce the impact of typing

- Training employees to take stretch breaks and periodically grab objects like tennis balls or sand filled balloons to increase blood circulation and delay the onset of carpal tunnel syndrome

¶ **2303.01**

- Properly lighted, clean, ventilated offices
- Properly maintained, current computer equipment and software
- Clean computer equipment and offices to prevent the proliferation of vermin
- Required annual physicals and regular counseling for employees concerning healthy living practices (particularly stress reduction techniques)
- Required annual employee vacations
- Reviews of work schedules of employees working overtime on a regular basis to find ways of reducing the amount of overtime (e.g., having the worker perform his or her duties more efficiently, hiring additional employees, or shifting job responsibilities to underused employees)

The list is not exhaustive because health officials are constantly conducting new studies concerning the health consequences of human beings interacting with computers.

Business continuation. Organizations need to ensure that they can survive when their IT systems fail. A classic example in business continuation planning occurred in the wake of the Federal Building bombing in Oklahoma City. The credit union was fully functioning within several days of the bombing despite the absence of two-thirds of its staff, who were killed in the explosion. Most business continuation plans take into account software needs through offsite backup procedures. Most business continuation plans take into account hardware needs, either through agreements with other users, manufacturers, or by maintaining secure sites. However, few business continuation plans take into account missing personnel. For instance, an organization located on the East Coast of the United States needs to plan for hurricanes (other parts of the country should plan for other natural disasters, such as floods or tornadoes). Key personnel may be more concerned with the safety of their families and themselves than the organization's IT system. In such an event, key personnel may also be injured, killed, or otherwise prevented from coming to their normal or alternative work location. Lastly, business continuation plans probably will not be effective unless they are periodically tested in conditions that closely resemble an actual emergency. Numerous business and military examples show that when disaster struck, organizations relied on plans that had not been properly tested or evaluated before their implementation. In most of these situations, the organizations did not survive. Business continuation plans must be tested at least annually, and the CIO should ensure that the organization addresses any shortcomings.

¶ 2303.01

Auditors used to stress the routine backup of data and programs. Although this is still a crucial issue, most auditors evaluate the adequacy of an organization's backup procedures as part of business continuation planning. Also, computer networks (WANs, and LANs), especially those linked to the Internet, allow organizations to easily backup information and programs throughout the network.

Security. Organizations must ensure that employees are given access to the IT system based on the information required to perform their job-related duties. The protection of privacy has become an important issue in the United States. Congress recently passed a stricter privacy law affecting banks and other financial institutions. In addition, consumers have expressed displeasure with the unauthorized release of their personal information. Unsolicited telemarketing phone calls interrupting families at home, e-mail and fax spam clogging up telecommunications resources, and individuals impersonating unsuspecting victims (impersonation fraud) racking up large credit card balances are all manifestations of this problem.

Organizations should first ensure that individuals outside the organization cannot access their IT system. Common safeguards include:

- Physically denying access to facilities through the use of locks, fences, and staffed checkpoints
- Proper use of user names and passwords
- Installation of boundary protection, allowing individuals access to only those parts of the IT system required to perform their job responsibilities
- The use of logs that record IT system usage
- Installation of communication controls, such as encryption algorithms for messages containing sensitive data

The CIO should ensure that the organization has a proactive privacy policy that protects employees', customers', and vendors' personal information and the trade secrets of the organization.

.02 Application Controls

Application controls address the risks implicit in running individual routines or applications such as payroll, general accounting, marketing, and billing. Increasingly, these applications are integrated in large applications called enterprise resource planning, or ERP systems. SAP and Peoplesoft are examples of ERP vendors. Another current trend is for organizations to delegate responsibility for running applications to end-user departments. Auditors should be concerned with "end-user environments" because often the end-user is totally unaware of control considerations. Regardless of the number of applications in an IT system, each application must have adequate controls functioning across every application, because it only takes one vulnerable application to compromise the entire IT system. Application controls can be classified into input controls (controls over the translation of data into machine-readable format), processing controls (controls over the manipulation of data into information), and output controls (controls over the translation of information into reader-usable format).

Data input into computers has come a long way from the era of keying data onto punch cards and using a card reader to translate the data into machine-readable format. Now most data is entered directly from electronic format through bar codes or from other computers; thus, input errors are becoming relatively rare. However, humans do occasionally enter data directly using keyboards; this can be controlled through the use of traditional means such as record counts, batch totals, hash totals, manual comparison of edit listings with source documents, specialized input screen formats, and reasonable checks.

Likewise, computers accurately process data into machine-readable format. However, when things go wrong with computer programs, they can go very wrong due to the speed with which computers operate. Reasonableness checks and manual recalculation of processing results are often sufficient to ensure that computer programs are running as intended.

The biggest exposure relative to an application's output lies with ensuring that its distribution is strictly limited to those individuals with a job-related need for the output. Few errors occur in the translation of machine-readable information into a user-friendly format that reasonableness checks and manual recalculations cannot adequately control. A more important issue confronting organizations lies in ensuring that the right information is produced to support the organization's mission.

¶ 2304 IT Control Frameworks

The previous discussion was presented in a general/informal manner due to space limitations. There are numerous detailed IT control frameworks that the reader should consult for additional, detailed guidance. The COBIT® control framework, developed by the IT Governance Institute and the Information Systems Audit and Control Foundation (ISACF™), and the SysTrust℠ control framework, developed by the American Institute of Certified Public Accountants (AICPA), are two of the more recognized control frameworks and will be discussed here.

In 1992, Information Systems Control Association (ISACA), which is affiliated with ISACF, published its initial collection of IT controls, "Control Objectives: Controls in an Information Systems Environment: Controls Guidelines and Audit Procedures."[2] The Control Objectives, lead to the creation of a comprehensive control framework entitled, "COBIT: Control

---

[2] Information Systems Audit and Control Foundation, *Control Objectives: Controls in an Information Systems Environment: Controls Guidelines and Audit Procedures* (Carol Stream, Illinois: The EDP Auditors Foundation, Inc., 1992).

Objectives for Information and related Technology." The third edition of COBIT, issued in 2000, consists of six volumes:

1. Executive Summary
2. Framework
3. Control Objectives
4. Management Guidelines
5. Audit Guidelines
6. Implementation Tool Set[3]

.01 COBIT Framework

The COBIT framework is presented in Figure 23.1. COBIT stresses the importance of aligning IT governance with the organization's governance through strategic planning. Once this is done, the organization can identify the information necessary to accomplish its mission and the IT resources required to produce that information.

---

[3] The IT Governance Institute and the COBIT Steering Committee, *COBIT: Control Objectives for Information and related Technology*, 3d ed., (Rolling Meadows, Illinois: Information Systems Audit and Control Foundation and IT Governance Institute, 2000).

Figure 23.1

COBIT Model

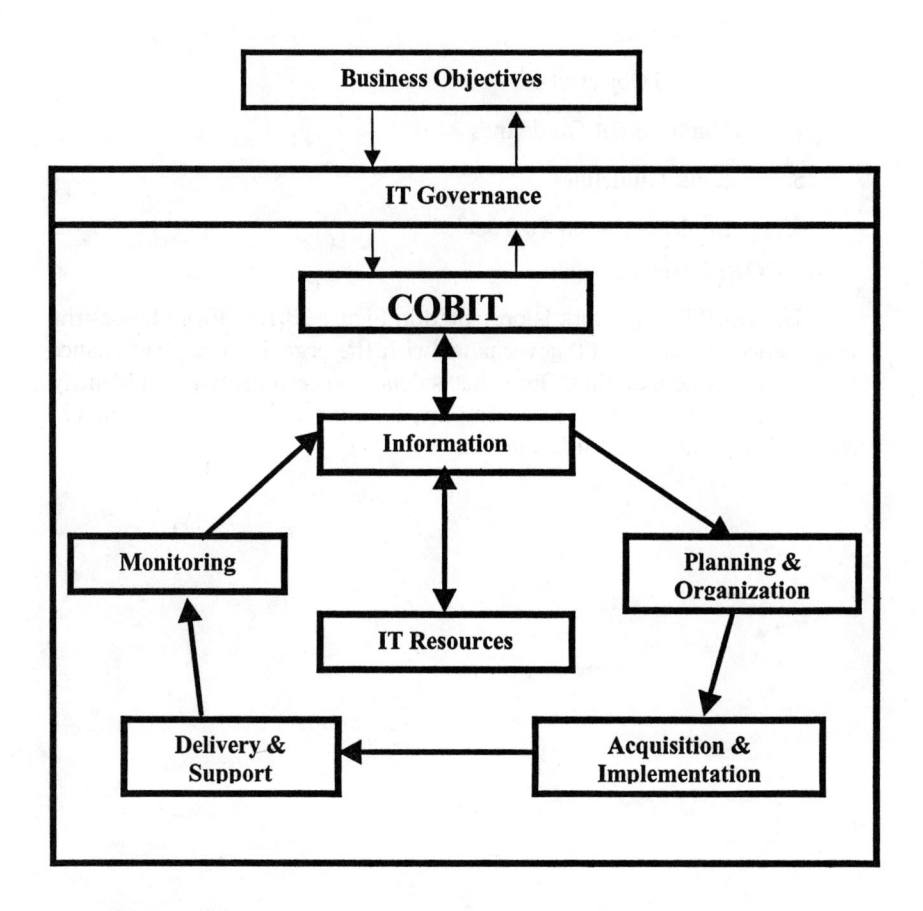

[Diagram: Business Objectives ↔ IT Governance ↔ COBIT ↔ Information, with IT Resources in center, surrounded by four domains: Monitoring, Planning & Organization, Acquisition & Implementation, and Delivery & Support, arranged in a cycle.]

Source: The COBIT Steering Committee and the IT Governance Institute, COBIT 3rd Edition Control Objectives (Rolling Meadows, Ill.: Information Systems Audit and Control Foundation, 2000), p. 7. Reprinted with permission.

After identifying IT resources that provide mission-critical information, the organization evaluates its information and IT resources using four domains from the COBIT model: planning and organization, acquisition and implementation, delivery and support, and monitoring. Each domain consists of processes that satisfy business requirements that are in turn enabled by control statements after considering specific control practices. Table 23.2 presents the COBIT framework detail.

¶ 2304.01

Table 23.2

COBIT Framework Detail

Information Principles	**Effectiveness**—deals with information being relevant and pertinent to the business process as well as being delivered in a timely, correct, consistent, and usable manner. **Efficiency**—concerns the provision of information through the optimal (most productive and economical) use of resources. **Confidentiality**—concerns the protection of sensitive information from unauthorized disclosure. **Integrity**—relates to the accuracy and completeness of information as well as to its validity in accordance with business values and expectations. **Availability**—relates to information being available when required by the business process now and in the future. It also concerns the safeguarding of necessary resources and associated capabilities. **Compliance**—deals with complying with those laws, regulations, and contractual arrangements to which the business process is subject, i.e., externally imposed business criteria. **Reliability of Information**—relates to the provision of appropriate information for management to operate the entity and for management to exercise its financial and compliance reporting responsibilities.
IT Resources	**Data**—are objects in their widest sense (i.e., external and internal), structured and nonstructured, graphics, sound, etc. **Application Systems**—are understood to be the sum of manual and programmed procedures. **Technology**—covers hardware, operating systems, database management systems, networking, multimedia, etc. **Facilities**—are all the resources to house and support information systems. **People**—include staff skills, awareness and productivity to plan, organize, acquire, deliver, support, and monitor information systems and services.
Domains and Processes	**Planning and Organization**—covers strategy and tactics, and concerns the identification of the way IT can best contribute to the achievement of the business objectives. Furthermore, the realization of the strategic vision needs to be planned, communicated, and managed for different perspectives. Finally, a proper organization as well as technological infrastructure must be put in place. Processes related to this domain include: 1.0 Define a strategic IT plan 2.0 Define the information architecture 3.0 Determine technological direction 4.0 Define the IT organization and relationships 5.0 Manage the IT investment 6.0 Communicate management aims and direction 7.0 Manage human resources 8.0 Ensure compliance with external requirements 9.0 Assess risks 10.0 Manage projects 11.0 Manage quality

¶ 2304.01

Acquisition & Implementation—to realize the IT strategy, IT solutions need to be identified, developed, or acquired, as well as implemented and integrated into the business process. Changes in and maintenance of existing systems are covered by this domain to make sure that the life cycle is continued for these systems. Processes related to this domain include:

1.0	Identify automated solutions
2.0	Acquire and maintain application software
3.0	Acquire and maintain technology infrastructure
4.0	Develop and maintain procedures
5.0	Install and accredit systems
6.0	Manage changes

Delivery & Support—is concerned with the actual delivery of required services, which range from traditional operations over security and continuity aspects to training. In order to deliver services, the necessary support processes must be set up. Processes related to this domain include:

1.0	Define and manage service levels
2.0	Manage third-party services
3.0	Manage performance and capacity
4.0	Ensure continuous service
5.0	Ensure systems security
6.0	Identify and allocate costs
7.0	Educate and train users
8.0	Assist and advise customers
9.0	Manage the configuration
10.0	Manage problems and incidents
11.0	Manage data
12.0	Manage facilities
13.0	Manage operations

Monitoring—All IT processes need to be regularly assessed over time for their quality and compliance with control requirements. This domain thus addresses management's oversight of the organization's control process and independence assurance provided by internal and external audit or obtained from alternative sources. Processes related to this domain include:

1.0	Monitor the processes
2.0	Assess internal control adequacy
3.0	Obtain independent assurance
4.0	Provide for independent audit

New Management Guidelines have been added to COBIT. These Management Guidelines present maturity models, critical success factors, key goal indicators, and key performance indicators, in response to management's need for control and measurability of IT. COBIT also presents a detailed framework for conducting an IT audit.

.02 SysTrust Control Framework

The AICPA, in conjunction with the Canadian Institute of Chartered Accountants (CICA), developed SysTrust services to provide assurance that IT systems were reliable. Table 23.3 presents the SysTrust control framework that is based on the study results.

¶ 2304.02

Table 23.3

SysTrust Principles and Criteria

Availability: The system is available for operation and use at times set forth in service level statements or agreements.	Criteria A1 The entity has defined and communicated performance objectives, policies, and standards for system availability. A2 The entity uses procedures, people, software, data, and infrastructure to achieve system availability objectives in accordance with established policies and standards. A3 The entity monitors the system and takes action to achieve compliance with system availability objectives, policies, and standards.
Security: The system is protected against unauthorized physical and logical access.	Criteria S1 The entity has defined and communicated performance objectives, policies, and standards for system security. S2 The entity uses procedures, people, software, data, and infrastructure to achieve system security objectives in accordance with established policies and standards. S3 The entity monitors the system and takes action to achieve compliance with system security objectives, policies, and standards.
Integrity: System processing is complete, accurate, timely and authorized.	Criteria I1 The entity has defined and communicated performance objectives, policies, and standards for system processing integrity. I2 The entity utilizes procedures, people, software, data, and infrastructure to achieve system processing integrity objectives in accordance with established policies and standards. I3 The entity monitors the system and takes action to achieve compliance with system processing integrity objectives, policies, and standards.
Maintainability: The system can be updated when required in a manner that continues to provide for system availability, security, and integrity.	Criteria M1 The entity has defined and communicated performance objectives, policies, and standards for system maintainability. M3 The entity monitors the system and takes action to achieve compliance with maintainability objectives, policies, and standards.

Source: American Institute of Certified Public Accountants website, *http://www.aicpa.org/assurance/systrust/princip.htm,* July 26, 2001. Used with permission.

The SysTrust control framework is built on four principles: availability, security, integrity, and maintainability. Criteria and subcriteria (not shown in the table) pertain to each principle. The SysTrust framework resembles the COBIT model. CPAs can perform any of the following types of SysTrust engagements as long as applicable professional standards and licensing agreements are followed:

- SysTrust examination to determine whether the internal controls functioning over a client's systems meet the SysTrust principles and criteria during a specific period of time
- Reporting on selected SysTrust principles
- Engagements for systems in the preimplementation phase
- Agreed-upon procedures engagements
- Consulting engagements

Additional information concerning SysTrust services is available from the following AICPA website: *www.aicpa.org/assurance/systrust/index.htm.*

¶ 2305 Variety of IT Systems

This discussion examines the control issues peculiar to various IT systems. However, the reader should keep in mind that unless otherwise stated, the concepts discussed earlier apply to all of the systems covered here.

.01 Batch Systems

The earliest computer systems processed raw records in groups called *batches* (e.g., employee time cards). The input, processing, and output of the batch was controlled by keeping track of the number of records (record count), a field's sum that made mathematical sense (control total), such as hours worked, or a field's sum that did not make mathematical sense (hash total), such as social security numbers. In addition, the time cards could be manually checked with edit listings. The computer could also perform numerous edit checks, such as comparing employee names and social security numbers listed on the time cards with employee names and social security numbers listed in the employee master file. The batch process was strictly controlled and relatively inexpensive. However, batch systems were also slow and unresponsive to user inquiry.

.02 Online Systems

Organizations then began constructing systems that processed transactions fast enough to influence decisions. These so-called online-real-time systems include airline and hotel reservation systems. The chief risks with online systems lie in access security and backup. Employees must practice effective login procedures to prevent unauthorized entry to and use of the system. In addition, the system must be continuously backed up to enable the reconstruction of information should the system inadvertently go down.

.03 Database Systems

The next step organizations took was creating large databases to support management decision making. This is similar to putting all of a company's eggs in one basket. Needless to say, the chief concern lies in maintaining the integrity of the database through access controls and boundary protection within the database. Backup of the database records is crucial, because all the company's data is in one system.

.04 Data Warehousing

Organizations take the database system one step further when they analyze the data within their database for meaningful relationships. This procedure, known as data warehousing, can enable an organization to maximize use of data acquired in the normal course of business. *Data warehousing* is the assembling and managing of data from various sources for developing a single detailed view of part or all of a business. For instance, information gathered from customers as sales occur can be used to identify future customers more likely to purchase the organization's products in the future. Marketing efforts can then be targeted to those customers, thus husbanding precious marketing resources.

.05 Networks

Organizations began connecting their computers into networks as they were constructing databases to support management decision making. Most security functions within a network are controlled by a network administrator, and auditors should closely scrutinize his or her activities. Access control is also critical, as is the integrity of any network telecommunications.

.06 Personal Computers

Personal computers—whether part of a network or standing alone—pose unique risks to organizations. First, physical access to most PCs is not guarded, and most stand-alone PCs can be powered up and operated by anyone. Second, backup procedures are usually not performed on hard disks of stand-alone PCs. Third, the acquisition of PCs is often based on political clout and an individual's job responsibilities. Fourth, employees often physically abuse the PCs assigned to them by eating, drinking, or smoking while using the PCs. Lastly, employees can easily conceal the theft of valuable data stored on a portable medium.

.07 Service Bureaus

Some organizations still rely on service bureaus for much of their data processing needs. In some circumstances, several organizations pool their resources to construct a shared IT system. Still other organizations outsource their entire IT systems. The user organizations must nevertheless

¶ 2305.07

ensure that the service bureau maintains adequate control over the users' data. Auditors may either personally review and test the service bureau controls or rely on the work of an independent auditor hired by the service center.

.08 End-User Systems

End-user systems are systems in which nearly all the responsibility for critical applications has been placed with the user-department management. Auditors for such functions should be concerned with the technical competence of end-user personnel, particularly as it relates to the design and operation of controls. Auditors may have to educate end-user personnel concerning proper control procedures. The use of control self-assessment techniques is particularly appropriate for end-user systems.

.09 E-Commerce

Electronic commerce (e-commerce) is "the exchange of goods and services using an electronic infrastructure."[4] Although most people think of e-commerce as dealing exclusively with the Internet, the concept is much broader, and may include transactions over regular phone lines. The chief control concern centers on whether the organization has thought out its overall business strategy concerning e-commerce. Numerous companies based on the Internet, so-called dot.com companies, went out of business during 2000 and 2001 because of poorly thought out business plans. The remaining companies that do business on the Internet are traditional companies that established a presence on the web, but did not stake their whole business existence on e-commerce.

The Internet was designed to withstand a nuclear war and not to conduct business, with the result that many basic business controls are missing. The Internet functions like a gigantic postal system, with most information being sent in packets like postcards. Virtually anyone who processes the packets is able to read their content. It is not surprising that e-commerce control issues center on the privacy and security of the transmitted information. Other control issues deal with business practices, transaction integrity, and availability of service.

Organizations use programs called "cookies" that are placed on a customer's computer when the customer accesses the organization's website. The cookie then tracks the customer's Internet usage and transmits this information back to the organization. In addition, many organizations obtain customer information directly when they log onto websites such as hotel reservation systems. Much controversy surrounds the sharing of this customer information with third parties, and an organization is ethically (if not legally) required to notify customers that any information supplied will

---

[4] X.L. Parker, *An e-Risk Primer* (Altamonte Springs, Fla.: The Institute of Internal Auditors Research Foundation, 2001), 1.

be shared with third parties. Organizations typically deal with the other control issues by using data encryption or by setting up secure two-party Internet portals. The downloading of destructive programs (viruses or worms) is a constant threat to any computer linked to the Internet. Most organizations have established so-called firewalls that filter incoming messages for viruses. Still another concern is that hackers will break into a website and deface it or launch a denial of service attack in which they bombard the website with a huge number of hits in a very short time to prevent legitimate customers from accessing the site.

The AICPA responded to the public's concern with doing business over the Internet by developing its WebTrust services. WebTrust is described by the AICPA as an attest-level engagement provided by specially licensed public accounting firms. WebTrust practitioners "audit" online businesses to verify compliance with WebTrust principles and criteria dealing with privacy, security, availability, confidentiality, consumer redress for complaints, and business practices. The WebTrust practitioner affixes a WebTrust seal to the website of businesses that comply with the WebTrust principles and objectives. More information concerning the WebTrust program can be obtained by visiting the following website: *www.aicpa.org/assurance/webtrust/index.htm.*

¶ 2306 The Computer and the Auditor

Auditors can generally interact with the computer to (1) ensure controls are adequate, (2) verify that account balances are fairly stated, and (3) check whether programs are running as designed and intended. Auditor interaction can take one of three forms: around (without) the computer, through (with) the computer, or continuous (electronic) auditing. Many auditors lump the last two forms together into the widely used term "computer-assisted auditing techniques." However, this name blurs important distinctions between the two forms of interaction.

.01 Auditing Around (Without) the Computer

Auditing around the computer is the oldest form of auditor interaction with computers. The auditor basically treats the computer as a black box and manually recomputes the system's output from input documentation (for example, manually recomputing individual entries on a payroll register from time cards, personnel records, and withholding forms). This approach is appropriate where the following conditions exist: (1) processing steps are relatively simple, (2) transactions are not too numerous, and (3) an adequate audit trail exists or can be easily recreated. Fewer and fewer systems exhibit any of the three conditions. Under this approach, auditors gather sufficient and competent audit evidence by taking a sample of computer outputs and tracing them back manually to source documents or computer inputs.

.02 Auditing Through (With) the Computer

Auditors were therefore forced to interact differently with computers. Auditing through the computer involves using the auditee's IT system to audit itself. A simple form of this approach is to introduce test data into the auditee's IT system and compare the results to those the auditor arrived at using the test data but an IT system under the auditor's control. Although simple, this technique may result in the contamination of the auditee's data. Another technique is to obtain the auditee's actual data and use an auditor-controlled IT system to process it. The two sets of results can then be compared. A third technique is for the auditor to manually check the code of critical programs. This is a time-consuming and laborious process and of dubious value for large programs. Finally the most sophisticated technique is the so-called integrated test facility, which is nothing more complicated than a set of programs that the auditor places on an auditee's IT system to which the auditor maintains strict access, and that routinely gathers information and performs tests as the auditee's IT system functions.

.03 Continuous (Electronic) Auditing

The use of the Internet and electronic commerce has significantly changed the way business is conducted and financial information is prepared and disseminated. A rapidly growing number of organizations are using the Internet and doing business on the World Wide Web. In this ever-advancing technological environment, business transactions are conducted entirely in an electronic form, and financial reports are prepared online and in real-time. Under the online and real-time financial reporting process, a significant portion of financial information and related audit evidence is available only in an electronic form. The development of eXtensible Markup Language (XML) and its financial version, eXtensible Business Reporting Language (XBRL), has enabled businesses to move toward electronic financial reporting.

XBRL allows organizations to (1) describe the financial information and establish "tags" for financial items in structured documents; and (2) prepare one set of financial statements in a format that will be viewable and usable within many applications.[5] A rapid growth of the use of electronic financial reporting under the XBRL platform is likely to require auditors to employ on-line, electronic, and continuous auditing techniques. Continuous auditing is defined by Rezaee et al as "a comprehensive electronic audit process that enables auditors to provide some degree of assurance on continuous information simultaneously with, or shortly after, the disclosure of that information."[6] The joint study of the North American

---

[5] See Z. Rezaee, A. Sharbatoghlie, R. Elam, and P. McMickle. "Continuous Auditing: Building Automated Auditing Capabilities." *Auditing: A Journal of Practice and Theory*. (2002) Vol. 21(1): 147-163, for in-depth discussion of the use of XBRL and continuous auditing in the financial reporting process.
[6] *Ibid*, p. 150.

accounting organizations (the Canadian Institute of Chartered Accountants-the CICA, and the American Institute of Certified Public Accountants-the AICPA), in 1999, issued a research report on continuous auditing. This report defines continuous auditing as "a methodology that enables independent auditors to provide written assurance on a subject matter using a series of auditors' reports issued simultaneously with, or a short period of time after, the occurrence of events underlying the subject matter."[7] Continuous auditing allows auditors to (1) focus on system and operational audits, and (2) utilize computer-assisted audit tools and techniques (CATTs) such as automated software, embedded audit modules, integrated test facilities, data warehouses, data mining, and audit-specific data marts to evaluate the effectiveness of internal control over financial reporting (under Section 404 of the Act) and conduct financial statement audits electronically.

The final form of interaction, (continuous auditing), involves the automation of manual audit functions. Several studies have indicated that auditors most commonly rely on computers for the following five functions: reading and analyzing electronic files, word processing, spreadsheets, presentations, and workpaper/audit administration. ACL and Idea are two examples of software designed specifically for reading and analyzing files. However, many auditors rely on traditional statistical packages such as SAS and SPSS. Still other auditors rely on the query function in widely available programs such as Microsoft Access. Most auditors rely on the commonly available office suites such as those developed by Microsoft, Corel, and Lotus for word processing, spreadsheets, and presentations software. Finally, there are some specific workpaper/audit administration software packages available, and some audit departments develop their own forms using the commonly available office suites.

Auditors have downloaded and manipulated electronic data since computers were first used in business. At first, this involved downloading accounts receivable, inventory, and accounts payable subsidiary records and proving their mathematical accuracy by footing and cross-footing them. Next, auditors selected samples of items for confirmations, test counts, or further investigation. Recently, many auditors have taken reading and analyzing data to a higher level called "data mining." *Data mining* is the process used to reveal information and compile relationships that exist in large amounts of data. Data mining involves: selecting data; exploring the data through statistics or visually; modifying the data; modeling the data using regression, neural networks, and/or rule induction; and finally, assessing the data.

---

[7] Study Group. Research Report: Continuous Auditing. The Canadian Institute of Chartered Accountants and the American Institute of Certified Public Accountants. Toronto, Canada and New York, NY (1999).

¶ 2306.03

¶ 2307 IT Auditing Organizations

The Information Systems Audit and Control Association (ISACA) remains the principal professional organization dedicated to IT auditing. ISACA is global professional organization headquartered in Rolling Meadows, Illinois near Chicago. ISACA provides a range of services similar to other professional accounting bodies. ISACA develops and administers the Certified Information Systems Auditor (CISA®) designation. The CISA designation is well recognized and worth pursuing for individuals interested in a career as an IT auditor. To become a CISA, an individual must meet the following requirements:

- Successfully complete the CISA exam
- Complete five years experience as an information systems auditor or the equivalent
- Agree to abide by the ISACA Code of Professional Ethics
- Complete a minimum of 20 contact hours of continuing professional education annually or a minimum of 120 contact hours during a fixed three-year period

The CISA exam is given once annually in June and consists exclusively of multiple choice (objective) questions. ISACA designs the CISA exam to be completed in four hours, and it covers the following process and content areas:

- The IS Audit Process (10 percent)
- Management, Planning, and Organization of IS (11 percent)
- Technical Infrastructure and Operational Practices (13 percent)
- Protection of Information Assets (25 percent)
- Disaster Recovery and Business Continuity (10 percent)
- Business Application System Development, Acquisition, Implementation, and Maintenance (16 percent)
- Business Process Evaluation and Risk Management (15 percent)[8]

The CISA exam content is based on an ISACA analysis of current IT audit practice. Additional information about ISACA can be obtained by contacting the organization at:

---

[8] From ISACA website, *www.isaca.org/cisacont.htm*.

Information Systems Audit and Control Association
IT Governance Institute
3701 Algonquin Road, Suite 1010
Rolling Meadows, Illinois 60008 USA
Phone: 847-253-1545
Fax: 847-253-1443
E-mail: *research@isaca.org*
Websites: *www.ITgovernance.org* and *www.isaca.org*

The AICPA recently inaugurated two new IT-related services (WebTrust and SysTrust) and an IT certification, Certified Information Technology Professional (CITP). To qualify for the CITP designation an individual must:

- Be a member in good standing of the AICPA
- Hold a valid and unrevoked CPA certificate issued by a legally constituted state authority
- Agree to comply with all the requirements for reaccredidation
- Complete the online CITP assessment tool and accumulate at least 100 points
- Pass the CITP examination (if required)
- Submit three references to substantiate business experience in technology-related services

The CITP assessment tool assigns points in the following categories:

1. Business Experience Requirement—consisting of teaching, evaluating, designing, facilitating, selecting, leading, developing, maintaining, participating, operating, managing, or selling in the following areas:
   - Information Technology Strategic Planning
   - Information Systems Management
   - Systems Architecture
   - Business Applications and Electronic Business
   - Security, Privacy, and Contingency Planning
   - System Development, Acquisition and Project Management
   - Systems Auditing and Internal Control
   - Databases and Database Management
2. Life-Long Learning in the following categories:
   - Continuing education, approved courses at an accredited university or college, other continuing education courses,

¶ 2307

trade association conferences, and nontraditional learning methods

- Presenting

- Other certifications

- Authoring

3. Completing the CITP exam (if required) with a minimum score of 75. The CITP examination content covers the following topics:

- Information Technology Strategic Planning (18 percent)

- Information Systems Management (15 percent)

- Systems Architecture (11 percent)

- Business Applications and Electronic Business (16 percent)

- Security, Privacy and Contingency Planning (11 percent)

- System Development, Acquisition and Project Management (13 percent)

- Systems Auditing and Internal Control (8 percent)

- Databases and Data Base Management (8 percent)[9]

Additional information concerning the CITP may be obtained by accessing the website citp.aicpa.org.

The Institute of Internal Auditors (IIA) is developing an IT auditing designation. In addition, the IIA maintains probably the most comprehensive website dealing with IT auditing: *www.itaudit.org*. The website contains hundreds of articles and links to other websites for IT auditing.

¶ 2308 Academic Preparation for Becoming an IT Auditor

IT auditing is one of the most highly paid and exciting occupations. How does one become an IT auditor? The first step is to acquire the knowledge, skills, and abilities (KSAs) required of an IT auditor. A good starting point is to examine Table 23.4, which presents the SysTrust competency model.

---

[9] From CITP website, *citp.aicpa.org/bok.htm*. Reprinted with permission.

Table 23.4

SysTrust Competency Model

Personal Attributes	Insight and judgment
	Integrity and ethics
	Continuous personal improvement
	Commitment and performance stability
	Interpersonal orientation
	Project management skills
	Innovative/creative thinking
	Presenting/speaking
	Effective business writing
	Professional demeanor
Leadership Qualities	Strategic thinking and planning
	Facilitating
	Negotiating and persuading
	Teamwork
	Coaching and empowerment
	Problem solving
	Decision making
	Crossfunctional perspective
Broad Business Perspective	Firm readiness
	Risk management
	Marketing
Functional Expertise	Engagement management
	System reliability—availability
	System reliability—security
	System reliability—integrity
	System reliability—maintainability
	Technology

Source: American Institute of Certified Public Accountants, SysTrust Competency Model website, *http://www.aicpa.org/assurance/systrust/comp.htm*, July 26, 2001.

Those interested in IT auditing should also review the content outlines for the CISA and CITP exams. The Information Systems Audit and Control Foundation (ISACF), which is an organization affiliated with ISACA, issued a model curriculum for undergraduate and graduate information systems auditing programs. In the model curriculum, ISACF recommends students study the following topics:

- Information technology and use
- Systems analysis, design, development, purchase and implementation
- Internal control and documentation of IS
- Data structures and data base concepts and management
- Information systems applications and processing cycles

¶ 2308

- Management and monitoring of IS
- Computer programming languages and procedures
- Communications and networks
- Model based systems (decision support and expert systems)
- Systems security and disaster recovery planning
- Auditing of IS and its role in business.[10]

Post-baccalaureate studies should focus on the following skills:

- Proficiency as an auditor
- Ability to review and evaluate IS internal control, management of IS project management, and recommendation of the extent of audit procedures required
- Understanding of IS system design and operations
- Knowledge of programming languages and techniques and the ability to apply computer-assisted audit techniques and assess their results
- General familiarity with computer operating systems and software
- Ability to identify and reconcile problems with client data file format and structure
- Ability to bridge the communications gap between the auditor and the IS professional, providing support and advice to management
- Knowledge of when to seek the assistance of an IS professional.[11]

Currently, there is a big demand for IT auditors, and employers generally pay a premium of $5,000 to $20,000 in annual salary over the annual salary of non-IT auditors. However, this heavy demand is no doubt due to the fast-changing nature of IT auditing and the difficulty of staying current and not becoming burnt out with the field. It is a commonly held belief that IT auditors are obsolete in one to two years if they do not learn new skills. A non-IT auditor, on the other hand may be able to postpone obsolescence longer, perhaps two to five years. The important point to remember is that IT is changing; therefore, IT auditing is also changing and there is no time like the present to be an IT auditor.

---

[10] ISACF Task Force for Development of Model Curricula in Information Systems Auditing at the Undergraduate and Graduate Levels, Academic Relations Committee and the Research Board, Model Curricula for Information Systems Auditing at the Undergraduate and Graduate Levels (Rolling Meadows, Ill.: The Information System Audit and Control Foundation, 1998), 12.

[11] Ibid., pp. 12-13.

¶ 2309 Summary

Changes to IT continue to occur rapidly and dramatically. The auditing profession must keep pace with these changes. Auditors need to audit internal control systems that involve technologically advanced information systems. However, auditors can also use technological advances to help perform tests and identify evidence.

Despite the rapid and far-reaching changes in IT, the auditor's role remains the same: to ensure that the organization has adequate controls in place to mitigate risks that could prevent the organization from fulfilling its objectives. The auditor must evaluate the IT system to find risks and ensure that controls are in place to mitigate these risks. The COBIT and SysTrust IT control models are two valuable tools with which to evaluate information systems.

The use of the Internet and electronic commerce has significantly changed the way business is conducted and financial information is prepared and disseminated. Organizations worldwide are moving toward the use of electronic financial reporting under the XBRL platform. Auditors should employ continuous auditing methodology when their clients use electronic financial reporting in preparing and disclosing financial information. A variety of computer-assisted audit tools and techniques (CATTs) are available to auditors as discussed in this chapter in conducting continuous auditing.

Chapter 24
International Auditing Standards

¶ 2401 Introduction
¶ 2402 International Auditing Standards and Audit Planning (ISA 300)
¶ 2403 International Auditing Standards and Performing Fieldwork
¶ 2404 International Auditing Standards and Audit Reports
¶ 2405 Global Convergence of Auditing Standards
¶ 2406 Summary

¶ 2401 Introduction

Globalization is one of the most profound challenges facing corporations in the United States and abroad. Cross-border business and related free trade agreements (e.g., NAFTA, GAAT) and European Unification (EU) have promoted convergence in international accounting and auditing standards. This chapter describes: (1) various aspects of international auditing standards including audit planning, performing fieldwork, and preparing audit reports; and (2) global convergence of auditing standards.

Chapter 24 objectives:

- To understand the reasons for and the components of the overall audit plan as required by ISAs (see ¶ 2401–2402).
- To recognize ISA requirements for audit evidence and performing fieldwork (see ¶ 2403).
- To become familiar with the categories of opinions issued in audit reports (see ¶ 2404).
- To explain the purpose and content of each of the three paragraphs in a standard unqualified audit report (see ¶ 2404).
- To understand the international convergence and coordination in the auditing standards-setting process (see ¶ 2405).

.01 Development of International Auditing Standards

Multinational enterprises (MNEs) develop, manufacture, and provide goods and services in multiple countries. The capital investment in these corporations typically extends beyond national borders as does their income flow. One reason for the MNEs' success is that they can take advantage of economical sources of labor, energy, and raw materials in the various geographical locations in which they operate.

As MNEs began to proliferate after World War II, a growing number of countries became the headquarters for MNEs' parent companies. The parent company's stock would be typically listed on the stock exchange of the country where the headquarters resided. Nonetheless, whatever country's capital market is involved, the need for investor confidence in the market is a crucial element to sustain the economic growth of that country. Investor confidence is enhanced when the corporate financial reporting is verified by independent audits.

Accounting and the related statutory audit process should provide investors with information that is comparable, transparent, and reliable. However, the various accounting and auditing standards used throughout the world may not meet all of these objectives. Various national governments require companies headquartered within their borders to submit financial statements prepared using indigenous accounting standards. Likewise, the company's auditors are required to use local auditing standards. As the requirements for auditing extended over many national borders, it became apparent that the various sets of accounting principles in use and the equally numerous auditing standards all may not be equally effective.

¶ 2401.01

Figure 23.1

Sample of 2002 European Company Financial Statements[1]

Company	Accounting Principles Used	Audit Standards Referenced
Carlsberg A/S	Danish Financial Statements Act	Danish Auditing Standards
	Danish Accounting Standards	International Auditing Standards
	Copenhagen Stock Exchange	
Unilever N.V.	Netherlands	Netherlands Auditing Standards
	United Kingdom	United Kingdom Auditing Standards
		United States Auditing Standards
Associated British Foods plc	[British] Companies Act of 1985	United Kingdom Auditing Standards
Bayer Group	International Accounting Standards	German Institute of Certified Public Accountants
		International Auditing Standards
Compagnie Generale des Etablissements Michelin	French Generally Accepted Accounting Principles	French Auditing Standards

Even today, accounting principles and auditing standards vary greatly. Figure 24.1 shows a sample of European companies and the accounting and auditing standards used, typically by government mandate, for their 2002 financial statements.

Recognizing the growing need for accounting and auditing consistency among the many countries, the International Federation of Accountants (IFAC) was created in 1977. It was formed as the result of an agreement signed by 63 accountancy bodies representing 49 countries. IFAC's purpose is to develop and promote uniformity of the many standards applicable to

---

[1] Source of financial statement information—annual reports.

¶ 2401.01

accountants: accounting, auditing and assurance services, educational, and quality assurance. Today IFAC is comprised of 155 professional accounting bodies, representing 2.5 million accountants.

One of the organizations formed by IFAC is the International Auditing and Assurance Standards Board (IAASB). Formerly known as the International Auditing Practices Committee (IAPC), the IAASB is an independent audit standard-setting entity. This organization is authorized to issue international auditing standards known as International Standards on Auditing (ISAs). These standards contain the basic principles and essential procedures as well as the guidance for their application.

In addition to the standards, the International Auditing and Assurance Standards Board (IAASB) has issued International Auditing Practice Statements (IAPS). These statements provide practical assistance to auditors in implementing the standards or on related subjects and promote good practice.

Financial statements are usually presented, at least, annually and are prepared to meet the needs of a wide range of individuals. For many of these financial statement users, the statements are their primary source of corporate information. It is important that the accounting and auditing bases are effective. International accounting and auditing standards as promulgated by International Accounting Standards Board (IASB) and the IAASB have been designed for such use. Various organizations and individuals support the effectiveness of the international standards. Robert Tie writes in the AICPA's JOURNAL OF ACCOUNTANCY that IFAC "will help the world's nations increase the transparency, reliability and consistency of their financial statements."[2] The World Bank and other regional development banks have expressed support for an initiative to establish one set of auditing and assurance standards for both private and public sector entities.[3]

The International Organization of Securities Commissions (IOSCO) is the world's largest international group of securities market regulators numbering 91 countries. IOSCO has endorsed international statements on auditing issued by IFAC's international auditing practices committee. In IOSCO's opinion, the international auditing standards are comprehensive and audits conducted in accordance with them can be relied upon by securities regulatory authorities for multinational reporting purposes. In 1992, IOSCO passed a resolution recommending that "its members take all steps necessary and appropriate in their respective jurisdictions to accept audits conducted in accordance with the statements for cross-border offerings and continuous reporting by foreign issuers."[4]

---

[2] Robert Tie, "IFAC, Firms to Apply International Standards Consistently," *Journal of Accountancy* (April 2000): 20.
[3] IAASB Action Plan 2003–2004.
[4] A Resolution Concerning International Standards on Auditing—Passed by the Presidents' Committee, October 1992.

¶ 2401.01

One of the members of IOSCO, the Securities and Exchange Commission (SEC) of the United States, is involved in the development of a globally accepted, high quality financial reporting framework. The SEC is also involved with international standard-setting.

> Currently, issuers wishing to access capital markets in different jurisdictions must comply with the requirements of each jurisdiction, which differ in many respects. We recognize that different listing and reporting requirements may increase the costs of accessing multiple capital markets and create inefficiencies in cross-border capital flows. Therefore, we are working with other securities regulators around the world to reduce these differences. To encourage the development of accounting standards to be considered for use in cross-border filings, we have been working primarily through IOSCO, and focusing on the work of the International Accounting Standards Committee (IASC). Throughout this effort, we have been steadfast in advocating that capital markets operate most efficiently when investors have access to high quality financial information.[5]

The European Union (EU) was set up after World War II. Today, there are 15 countries that belong to the EU, and that number will grow as the EU is preparing for the addition of several more countries from eastern and southern Europe. One of the principal objectives of the EU is to promote economic progress among the members. This is to be accomplished by opening up borders to allow more freedom for individuals traveling between EU countries as well as the free flow of goods and services. Additionally, solidarity among the members would be enhanced by common policies and financial instruments.

The EU provides a structure for instituting common policies on accounting and auditing. The Committee on Auditing was established in May 1998. The Committee meets twice per year and represents a platform whereby the audit regulators from the membership meet with other audit professionals. The overall objective of the Committee is to develop a common view on a statutory audit for the EU members. Enacted on May 21, 2003, the Commission of the European Communities requires auditors of financial statements to comply with International Standards on Auditing in the performance of their audits by 2005.[6] This follows on the heels of the June 2002 adoption of International Accounting Standards as promulgated by the International Accounting Standards Board.[7]

This chapter reviews many of the International Standards on Auditing (ISAs) as promulgated by the IAASB and highlights the differences to generally accepted auditing standards of the United States. As indicated in Figure 24.2, the international standards are categorized into section numbers much like that of its U.S. counterpart. The IAASB provides the

---

[5] SEC Concept Release: International Accounting Standards, Securities and Exchange Commission, 17 CFR Parts 230 and 240 [Release Nos. 33-7801, 34-42430; International Series No. 1215], File No. S7-04-00 [RIN: 3235-AH65].

[6] "Communication from the Commission to the Council and the European Parliament—Reinforcing the Statutory Audit in the EU" Brussels, May 21, 2003, http://europa.eu.int/eur-lex/pri/en/dpi/cnc/doc/2003/com2003_0286en01.doc.

[7] http://europa.eu.int/rapid/start/cgi/guesten.ksh?p_action.gettxt=gt&doc=IP/02/1967/0/RAPID&lg=EN (June 2002, see IP/02/827).

¶ 2401.01

international standards to the public with online access. (See *http://www.ifac.org/IAASB*.)

Figure 24.2

Handbook of International Auditing, Assurance, and Ethics Pronouncements 2003 Edition[8]

100-199 Introductory Matters
- 100 Assurance Engagements
- 120 Framework of International Standards on Auditing

200-299 Responsibilities
- 200 Objective and General Principles Governing an Audit of Financial Statements
- 210 Terms of Audit Engagements
- 220 Quality Control for Audit Work
- 230 Documentation
- 240 The Auditor's Responsibility to Consider Fraud and Error in an Audit of Financial Statements
- 250 Consideration of Laws and Regulations in an Audit of Financial Statements
- 260 Communications of Audit Matters with Those Charged with Governance

300-399 Planning
- 300 Planning
- 310 Knowledge of the Business
- 320 Audit Materiality

400-499 Internal Control
- 400 Risk Assessments and Internal Control
- 401 Auditing in a Computer Information Systems Environment
- 402 Audit Considerations Relating to Entities Using Service Organizations

500-599 Audit Evidence
- 500 Audit Evidence
- 501 Audit Evidence—Additional Considerations for Specific Items
- 505 External Confirmations
- 510 Initial Engagements-Opening Balances
- 520 Analytical Procedures
- 530 Audit Sampling and Other Selective Testing Procedures
- 540 Audit of Accounting Estimates
- 545 Auditing Fair Value Measurements and Disclosures
- 550 Related Parties

---

[8] International Federation of Accountants, *Handbook of International Auditing, Assurance, and Ethics Pronouncements*, 2003 ed. (New York: International Federation of Accountants), 159.

560 Subsequent Events
570 Going Concern
580 Management Representations

600-699 Using Work of Others
600 Using the Work of Another Auditor
610 Considering the Work of Internal Auditing
620 Using the Work of an Expert

700-799 Audit Conclusions and Reporting
700 The Auditor's Report on Financial Statements
710 Comparatives
720 Other Information in Documents Containing Audited Financial Statements

800-899 Specialized Areas
800 The Auditor's Report on Special Purpose Audit Engagements
810 The Examination of Prospective Financial Information

900-999 Related Services
910 Engagements to Review Financial Statements
920 Engagements to Perform Agreed-Upon Procedures Regarding Financial Information
930 Engagements to Compile Financial Information

¶ 2402 International Auditing Standards and Audit Planning (ISA 300)

International auditing standards for planning the financial statement audit of financial statements include many of the same procedures as the U.S. auditing standards. The purpose of audit planning is to develop an overall audit strategy as well as to determine the expected nature, timing, and extent of the audit. Adequate planning assists in:

1. Assigning work to personnel
2. Coordinating auditors with experts
3. Identifying potential problems in the audit

To assist in the planning process, the auditor may wish to discuss certain aspects of the overall audit strategy as well as audit procedures with the audit committee and company management in order to improve efficiency and the effectiveness of the audit. In addition, the overall audit plan should include the following:

1. Knowledge of the business
2. Understanding of the accounting and internal control systems
3. Risk and materiality

¶ 2402

4. Nature, timing, and extent of procedures

5. Coordination, direction, supervision, and review

6. Other matters

This plan will assist the auditor in developing the audit program which represents the expected and specific nature, timing, and extent of the audit procedures needed to fulfill the overall audit strategy.

.01 Planning and Obtaining Knowledge of the Business (ISA 310)

The purpose of having a knowledge of the business is to assist the auditor in determining those events, transactions, and practices that have an effect on the financial statements. In addition to the operations of the company, the auditor needs to understand the economy and industry in which the company operates. In obtaining knowledge of the business, the auditor is in a better position to assess risks and identify problems. Obtaining knowledge of the business begins in the pre-planning stage, before acceptance of the engagement and continues throughout. The auditor obtains the knowledge by:

1. Prior year's working papers
2. Discussions with:
   a. Internal audit personnel
   b. Legal advisors
   c. Outside experts of the industry
3. Reviewing publications related to the industry
4. Reviewing legislation and regulations affecting the entity
5. Visiting the premises
6. Reviewing internal documents such as:
   a. Budgets
   b. Minutes of meetings
   c. Interim financial statements
   d. Management policy manuals
   e. Job descriptions
   f. Promotional literature

Assistants in the audit team should have enough knowledge of the business to be able to carry out the work assigned to them.

The appendix of ISA 310 has an extensive checklist of matters to consider in obtaining knowledge of the business.

¶ 2402.01

.02 The Relationship between Materiality and Audit Risk (ISA 320)

According to international auditing standards, audit risk is the "risk that the auditor gives an inappropriate audit opinion when the financial statements are materially misstated."[9] Something is considered material if its omission or misstatement could influence the economic decisions of users taken on the basis of the financial statements.[10] The planning process should include an assessment of the materiality related to specific accounts or classes of transactions. The purpose of this assessment is to provide a baseline on what would make the financial statements materially misstated.

There is an inverse relationship between audit risk and the level of what is considered material. If the materiality level is high, then the audit risk is low. This relationship is used by the auditor to determine the nature, timing, and extent of the auditing procedures necessary to reduce the audit risk to an acceptable level. This is similar to the theory suggested by U.S. auditing standards.

.03 Planning and Material Misstatement Due to Fraud

When planning for a financial statement audit, the auditor should consider the risk of material misstatements in the financial statements resulting from not only errors but also fraud.[11] International auditing standards define fraud as an intentional act by one or more individuals among management, those charged with governance, employees, or third parties involving the use of deception to obtain an unjust or illegal advantage. There are some similarities between international standards and U.S. auditing standards SAS 99, Consideration of Fraud in a Financial Statement Audit, in this regard.

Fraud is distinguished from errors which are unintentional. For a fraud to occur, typically there must be the motivation to commit fraud as well as a perceived opportunity to commit the fraud. (For more discussion, see Chapter 20). Unlike error, fraud is intentional and quite often involves a deliberate cover-up. The misstatements due to fraud are categorized as follows:

1. Fraudulent financial reporting
2. Misappropriation of assets

Management is primarily responsible for the prevention and detection of fraud and errors in the financial statements. It is management who must establish the control environment and maintain the policies and procedures necessary for the company's operations. The auditor's responsibility is to

---

[9] International Standards on Auditing (ISA) 400.
[10] International Accounting Standards Committee's "Framework for the Preparation and Presentation of Financial Statements."
[11] ISA 240.

conduct an audit sufficiently as to be in a position to express an opinion whether the financial statements have been prepared, in all material respects, in accordance with an identified financial reporting framework. If the auditor uses international auditing standards in conducting their audit, then there is reasonable assurance that the financial statements, taken as a whole, are free from material misstatement. However, reasonable assurance does not mean absolute assurance. There is a risk that material misstatements may not be detected and that risk is higher with fraud than errors due to the probability of concealment, collusion, and management overriding controls. Auditing procedures that are effective in detecting misstatements due to error may not be effective in detecting fraud.

During the planning phase of the audit, the audit team should discuss amongst themselves the susceptibility of the entity to material misstatements in the financial statements resulting from fraud or error. The team should discuss where they think error and fraud might occur, which procedures might uncover the misstatements, who should carry out the procedures, and how they can communicate the results among themselves.

Proper planning should include inquiries of management as to how and how often management assessed the risk of misstatement and which internal controls they put in place to address the risks. Inquiries should also determine if management is aware of any frauds, suspected frauds, or material errors. These inquiries will not only provide useful answers to the above questions but also provide insight as to how management has discharged their responsibilities. Answers to these queries should be in writing and are typically included in the management representation letter (see ISA 580) if the auditor is using this process.

Additional inquiries could be directed to others involved in corporate governance, such as the audit committee. Answers to these questions corroborate management's answers as well as provide an opportunity to discuss matters involving management, such as management's failure to respond to an identified material weakness.

.04 Risk Assessment and Internal Controls (ISA 400)

For the auditor to properly understand audit risk and thus reduce it to an acceptable level, they must first understand the components of audit risk:

1. Inherent risk—the susceptibility of an account balance or class of transactions to misstatement that could be material, individually or when aggregated with misstatements in other balances or classes, assuming that there were no related internal controls.

2. Control risk—risk that a misstatement, that could occur in an account balance or class of transactions and that could be material individually or when aggregated with misstatements

in other balances or classes, will not be prevented or detected, and corrected on a timely basis by the accounting and internal control systems.

3. Detection risk—risk that an auditor's substantive procedures will not detect a misstatement that exists in an account balance or class of transactions that could be material, individually or when aggregated with misstatements in other balances or classes.

To properly develop an overall audit plan, the auditor must assess the inherent risk both at the financial statement level and at the account balance and class of transactions level. At the financial statement level, the auditor looks at broader issues such as management integrity and experience, the economy, competitive forces, and related parties. At the account balance level, the auditor should assess which accounts are likely to be misstated.

Next, the auditor must understand the internal control system so as to properly plan the audit and develop an effective audit strategy. As such, the auditor is only concerned with aspects of the internal controls that affect the financial statements, that is, those policies and procedures within the accounting and internal control systems that are relevant to the financial statement assertions. (This is a more limited approach than is prescribed by U.S. auditing standards. See Chapter 19 for a discussion of U.S. Auditing Standards regarding internal controls.) To understand the internal control system the auditor may:

1. Perform a "walk-through" test which consists of tracing various transactions through the accounting system. This particular test may be performed in the planning stage to understand the internal control system but may also be considered a test of control, depending upon the nature and extent of the test.

2. Make inquiries of management and other personnel regarding the internal controls.

3. Observe internal control system activities.

4. Inspect documents used and produced by the internal control system.

Once the auditor obtains an understanding of the accounting and internal control systems, they should make a preliminary assessment of the control risk for each material account balance or class of transaction. The control risk is high if the internal controls are not effective or it is not efficient to evaluate the internal control systems. If the control risk is not considered high, the auditor should identify the internal controls likely to prevent or detect a material misstatement. Next, the auditor must test those controls to substantiate that the controls are effective and have been

¶ 2402.04

used throughout the period. The lower the assessment, the more support the auditor needs to obtain. (Assessing the control risk at high is slightly different terminology from that of U.S. standards which uses the phrase "assessing the control risk at the maximum level.")

As the auditor assesses both the inherent and control risks, the auditor can:

1. Identify potential material misstatements.

2. Better understand the factors that affect the risk of material misstatements.

3. Develop appropriate audit procedures based upon the necessary nature, timing, and extent of evidence needed to reduce detection risk and, thus, audit risk.

Unlike SAS 99, which is integrated into the existing U.S. auditing standards, ISA 240 is a separate section in the International auditing standards devoted to material misstatements due to fraud and errors. This section addresses the assessment of inherent and control risks in this context. The auditor should be cognizant of how financial statements might be materially misstated as a result of fraud and errors, with an emphasis on fraud detection. This can be done by taking into account whether fraud risk factors are present, indicating that there may be fraudulent financial reporting or misappropriation of assets. (See Chapter 20 for a more detailed list of fraud risk factors.) The presence of the fraud risk factors affect the auditor's assessment of the inherent and control risks. Identifying fraud risk factors direct the auditor to those events or conditions that provide opportunity, motive, or means to commit fraud, or may be an indication that fraud has already occurred. As such, it is important that the auditor use professional judgment in considering the fraud risk factors, individually or in combination, and whether there are specific controls mitigating the risk.

The fact that fraud risk factors are present may mean that the auditor should assess the inherent and control risks at a level higher than would have been the case without the factors. However, if there are controls that possibly mitigate the risk, then testing those controls may allow for a final assessment of control risk to be less than high.

In any event, with or without the presence of fraud risk factors, for an auditor to give a control risk final assessment as less than high, the controls must be tested. Then, based upon the tests of controls, the auditor can make a final assessment of the control risk. Those tests of controls usually are categorized as:

1. Inspection

2. Inquiry

3. Reperformance

¶ 2402.04

The auditor should document their understanding and assessment of the internal control systems. Documentation is usually in the form of flowcharts, questionnaires, checklists, or descriptive narratives.

As with U.S. auditing standards, there is an inverse relationship between detection risk and the combined level of inherent and control risks. See Chapter 6 for a detailed explanation of this relationship. In any event and regardless of the assessed levels of inherent and control risks, some substantive procedures for material account balances and classes of transactions must still be performed. These tests are designed to detect material misstatements in account balances. The higher the inherent and control risk assessment, the more substantive procedures must be performed. In designing the substantive procedures, the auditor should address the fraud risk factors that the auditor has identified as being present. The auditor's response to those factors is influenced by their nature and significance. Even though fraud risk factors have been identified as being present, the auditor's judgment may be that the audit procedures, including both tests of control, and substantive procedures, already planned, are sufficient to respond to the fraud risk factors.

If an auditor cannot reduce detection risk to an acceptable level regarding a financial statement assertion, the auditor should express a qualified opinion or a disclaimer of opinion.

Whenever the auditor becomes aware of a weakness in the internal control system, this information should be communicated to the most appropriate level management as soon as it is practical. Written communication is typical but oral communication is allowed. However, if weaknesses are orally communicated then the communication should be documented in the working papers. Additionally, it is important that the auditor communicates to management that the weakness came to light as a result of the financial statement audit and not to determine the adequacy of the internal control system for management purposes.

The overall audit plan describing scope and conduct needs to be documented in the working papers. A description of the overall audit plan should contain at least the following:

1. The auditor's understanding of the business—operational, accounting, and control systems

2. Expected assessment of inherent and control risks

3. Expected level of materiality

4. Description of any possible material misstatements

5. Any complex accounting areas

6. Effect of technology

¶ 2402.04

7. Work of the internal auditor
8. Involvement of experts
9. Staffing requirements
10. Description of any going concern issues
11. Any area requiring special attention
12. Terms of the engagement

.05 Materiality (ISA 320)

The auditor should consider materiality and its relationship to audit risk. Materiality is a matter of professional judgment and is defined by "the International Accounting Standards Committee's Framework for the Preparation and Presentation of Financial Statements" in the following terms:

> "Information is material if its omission or misstatement could influence the economic decisions of users taken on the basis of the financial statements. Materiality depends on the size of the item or error judged in the particular circumstances of its omission or misstatement. Thus, materiality provides a threshold or cut-off point rather than being a primary qualitative characteristic which information must have if it is to be useful."

In order to properly design an audit plan, the auditor must quantify material misstatements and to do so must establish an acceptable materiality level. However, in determining materiality both quantitative and qualitative factors must be considered.

Materiality must be considered both at the individual account level as well as the overall financial statement level. The auditor must consider that misstatement might be such that, as individuals, they do not represent a material amount, but cumulatively they may constitute a material misstatement.

"The auditor should develop and document an audit program setting out the nature, timing, and extent of planned audit procedures required to implement the overall audit plan." Depending upon the circumstances, the overall audit strategy as well as the audit program may need revision should circumstances warrant such.

¶ 2403 International Auditing Standards and Performing Fieldwork

.01 Audit Evidence (ISA 500)

As with U.S. auditing standards, international auditing standards require that the auditor obtain sufficient and appropriate evidence to be able to draw reasonable conclusions on which to base their audit opinion. The term "appropriate" relates to the U.S. equivalent term "competent." The standards define audit evidence as "information obtained by the auditor in arriving at the conclusions on which the audit opinion is based."

¶ 2402.05

Sufficiency of evidence is the term referring to quantity of evidence and is based upon the auditor's judgment. Methods of obtaining evidence are usually based upon sampling methods such as judgmental or statistical. When making their judgment, the auditor should take into consideration the inherent risk, effectiveness of the internal control system, the related control risk, and materiality. Evidence appropriateness is similar to the concept of competency as is discussed in Chapter 6. Appropriateness is based upon the evidence quality and relevance to the financial statement assertion as well as the reliability of the evidence. The latter characteristic addresses persuasiveness of the evidence. Externally-generated evidence is generally considered more believable or persuasive than internally-generated evidence. If sufficient appropriate evidence cannot be obtained, the auditor should issue a qualified or disclaimer of opinion due to a scope limitation.

Regarding the sources of evidence, international auditing standards refer to sources in a similar manner as the U.S. standards. Audit evidence is derived during the audit process while in the planning stage, control testing phase, and the substantive tests for material misstatements; the latter includes tests with details of transactions and balances and analytical procedures.

International and U.S. auditing standards terminology used to describe the financial statement assertions are similar:

1. Existence: an asset or a liability exists at a given date.
2. Rights and obligations: an asset or a liability pertains to the entity at a given date.
3. Occurrence: a transaction or event took place which pertains to the entity during the period.
4. Completeness: there are no unrecorded assets, liabilities, transactions or events, or undisclosed items.
5. Valuation: an asset or liability is recorded at an appropriate carrying value.
6. Measurement: a transaction or event is recorded at the proper amount and revenue or expense is allocated to the proper period. (U.S. standards refer to this latter description as "allocation.")
7. Presentation and disclosure: an item is disclosed, classified, and described in accordance with the applicable financial reporting framework.

Enough audit evidence should be obtained to address each applicable assertion for each material account. The types of procedures used to obtain evidence are categorized in one of the following:

¶ 2403.01

1. Inspection of documentary evidence or tangible assets.

2. Observation of processes or procedures.

3. Inquiry and confirmation— Inquiry is a request for information from knowledgeable individuals, internal or external to the audit client. (U.S. standards attach a slightly different meaning to inquiry. Those standards typically consider inquiry as made of client personnel and not outsiders.) With the confirmation process, there is a request by the auditor to an outside party for corroborating information with the accounting records.

4. Computation is checking the mathematical accuracy of documents and accounting records.

5. Analytical procedures "consist of analysis of significant ratios and trends including the resulting investigation of fluctuations and relationships that are inconsistent with other relevant information or deviate from predicted amounts."

Some audit procedures can address more than one assertion.

.02 Audit Evidence—Additional Considerations (ISA 501)

International auditing standards also address more specific methods of obtaining audit evidence. ISA 501 lists a number of these methods.

Attendance at physical inventory counting. (U.S. terminology—"observation of inventories").[12] The requirements for inventory observation are similar to U.S. standards. The auditor must observe the physical inventory count for inventories that are material to the financial statements. When it is not possible to do so, alternative procedures are to be employed.

In planning for the inventory observation, the auditor should consider:

1. The nature of the accounting and internal control systems used regarding inventory.

2. Inherent, control and detection risks, and materiality related to inventory.

3. Whether adequate procedures are expected to be established and proper instructions issued for physical inventory counting.

4. The timing of the count.

5. The locations at which inventory is held.

6. Whether an expert's assistance is needed.

---

[12] ISA 501; AICPA, International Standards on Auditing, *Audit Evidence* (AICPA, Professional Standards, vol. 2, AU sec. 8501.08).

Additionally, the auditor should review management's instructions concerning the inventory count. Of specific importance is management's control over shipping and receipt of inventory before and after the cutoff date, unused stock count sheets, consigned inventory, management's identification of work-in-process stage of completion, as well as obsolete and damaged inventory.

During the observation, the auditor should take test counts from the floor to the count sheets and from the count sheets to the floor to determine the accuracy of the count sheets.

Later, during the fieldwork testing phase of the audit, the auditor should test the final inventory listing to determine if they accurately reflect actual inventory counts.

The auditor can confirm inventory held by third parties.

Inquiry regarding litigation and claims. Contingent liabilities can have a material effect on the financial statements. Litigation and claims represent a category of contingent liability. As with U.S. auditing standards, international standards require the auditor to perform procedures to identify litigation and claims. (U.S. standards use the term "litigation, claims, and assessments.") These procedures should include:

1. Inquire of management about litigation and claims.

2. Obtain representations from management that they have disclosed all information to the auditor regarding litigation and claims.

3. Review board minutes and correspondence with the client's attorneys.

4. Analyze the legal expense accounts to determine which attorneys have worked for the client.

5. Use any information obtained regarding the entity's business including information obtained from discussions with any in-house legal department.

Upon discovery of litigation and claims, the auditor must communicate with the client's attorney. The purpose of the communication is to determine whether the litigation and claims are material to the financial statements as well as directing the auditor in obtaining additional evidence. If management refuses to allow the auditor to communicate with the attorney, then this should be considered a scope limitation that could lead to a qualified or disclaimer of opinion. (This audit standard is similar to U.S. standards.)

¶ 2403.02

Communication with the attorney should be in writing. A letter should be prepared by the client but sent by the auditor. The letter should include the following items:

1. A list of litigation and claims.

2. Management's assessment of the outcome of the litigation or claim and its estimate of the financial implications, including costs involved.

3. A request that the lawyer confirm the reasonableness of management's assessments and provide the auditor with further information if the list is considered by the lawyer to be incomplete or incorrect.

If the attorney refuses to communicate with the auditor, then the auditor should attempt to determine if alternative procedures are available. If not, then this should be considered a scope limitation that could lead to a qualified or disclaimer of opinion.

.03 External Confirmations (ISA 505)

The term "external confirmation" is the same as the U.S. term "confirmation." The definition as provided by international standards for an external confirmation is the "process of obtaining and evaluating audit evidence through a direct communication from a third party in response to a request for information about a particular item affecting assertions made by management in the financial statements." The concept of a positive versus negative confirmation is the same as U.S. auditing standards as well. The positive confirmation requests an answer from the recipient if they agree with the assertion or disagree with the assertion, whereas the negative only requests a response when there is disagreement.

One distinction in the confirmation process, however, between international and U.S. standards lies with international standards allowing for a more flexible approach to management requests for certain balances and information not to be confirmed. If the auditor accepts management's request, the auditor could use alternative procedures to obtain sufficient appropriate evidence.

.04 Analytical Procedures (ISA 520)

Analytical procedures are defined as "the analysis of significant ratios and trends including the resulting investigation of fluctuations and relationships that are inconsistent with other relevant information or deviate from predicted amounts."

As with U.S. standards, the international standards require the auditor to apply analytical procedures at the planning phase of the audit as well as at the overall review stage of the audit. Auditors are permitted to use

¶ 2403.03

analytical procedures at other stages as well, for example, as a substantive procedure in tests of details in account balance testing.

Issues for the auditor to consider when using analytical procedures in substantive audit testing:

1. Objectives of the analytical procedures.
2. The extent to which the analytics are reliable.
3. Nature of the entity and the degree to which information can be disaggregated so that analytical procedures can be applied.
4. To what extent information is available, both financial as well as nonfinancial.
5. Reliability, including the independence of the sources, of the information to be used for the analytical testing.
6. Relevance of the information available.
7. Comparability of the available information (e.g., industry averages) to client information.
8. Knowledge gained during previous audits.
9. Knowledge of the effectiveness of the client's internal control systems.

International auditing standards emphasize that caution should be applied when using analytical procedures. The auditor's assessment of risk will affect how much reliance the auditor can place on the results of analytical procedures.

Further investigation is warranted when analytical procedures identify unusual items, beginning with inquiries of management and possibly obtaining additional evidence. (See Chapters 6 and 22 for further discussions.)

.05 Audit Sampling and Other Selective Testing Procedures (ISA 530)

ISA 530 provides guidance for sampling. The material in this section is equivalent to that discussed in this text. (See Chapters 6 and 22.)

.06 Related Parties (ISA 550)

According to International Accounting Standard 24, related parties exist if "one party has the ability to control the other party or exercise significant influence over the other party in making financial and operating decisions." A related party transaction is one whereby resources or obligations are transferred between related parties, regardless of whether a price is charged.

Related party transactions can affect the financial statements and its disclosure. As such, the auditor should obtain sufficient appropriate (United States uses "competent") audit evidence in order to identify related party transactions and evaluate their effects on the financial statements and disclosures.

Management is responsible for the adequacy of the internal control systems that identify and account for related party transactions. The auditor must obtain a sufficient knowledge of the client's business and industry in order to identify related party transactions.

The purpose of knowledge of related party transactions is for the auditor to estimate:

1. Its effect on the financial statements as required by a financial reporting framework, such as international accounting standards.

2. Its possible effect on the client's tax liability, depending upon local jurisdiction.

3. The knowledge of the source of audit evidence. Its independence from the client helps to differentiate and determine the degree of reliance that may be placed on evidence from unrelated third party sources.

4. Whether related party transactions have been the subject of fraudulent schemes.

International auditing standard procedures to identify related parties and their transactions are similar to their U.S. counterpart. ISA 550 provides a detailed list of common procedures.

.07 Subsequent Events (ISA 560)

International auditing standards regarding subsequent events are similar to U.S. standards provided in Chapter 7.

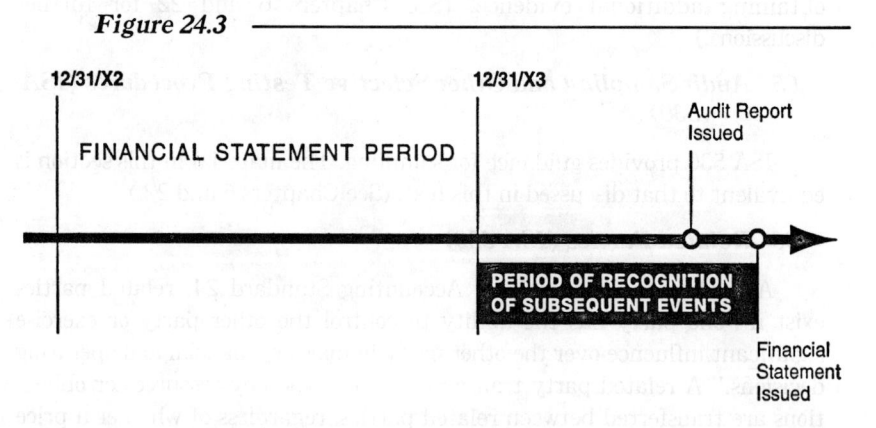

Figure 24.3

12/31/X2

FINANCIAL STATEMENT PERIOD

12/31/X3

Audit Report Issued

PERIOD OF RECOGNITION OF SUBSEQUENT EVENTS

Financial Statement Issued

¶ 2403.07

There are two types of subsequent events established by international accounting standards—International Accounting Standard 10, "Contingencies and Events Occurring After the Balance Sheet Date." These two types are:

1. Those events that provide further evidence of conditions that existed at period end.

2. Those events that are indicative of conditions that arose subsequent to period end.

Because of the nature of subsequent events, it is most practical to perform audit procedures to identify subsequent events as close as possible to the date of the auditor's report. These procedures usually include:

1. Reviewing procedures management has established to ensure that subsequent events are identified.

2. Reading minutes of the meetings of shareholders, the board of directors, and audit and executive committees held after period end and inquiring about matters discussed at meetings for which minutes are not yet available.

3. Reading the entity's latest available interim financial statements and, as considered necessary and appropriate, budgets, cash flow forecasts, and other related management reports.

4. Inquiries, or extending previous oral or written inquiries, of the entity's lawyers concerning litigation and claims.

5. Inquiries of management as to whether any subsequent events have occurred which might affect the financial statements.

.08 Facts Discovered After the Date of the Auditor's Report but Before the Financial Statements are Issued

The auditor does not have any responsibility to perform auditing procedures after the date of the auditor's report. Subsequent to the auditor report date but prior to the issuance of the financial statements, it is management's responsibility to inform the auditor of events that occur that may have financial statement impact. If the auditor becomes aware of such events, the auditor should consider if the financial statements need adjustment. This matter must first be discussed with management. If it is determined that the financial statements need adjustment and management adjusts the financial statements, the auditor would obtain the additional evidence necessary in the circumstances and would provide management with a new report on the amended financial statements. The revised auditor's report should be dated no earlier than the date that the revised financial statements are signed or approved by the Board of

Directors or equivalent. Audit procedures should be extended to the date of the new auditor's report.

Figure 24.4

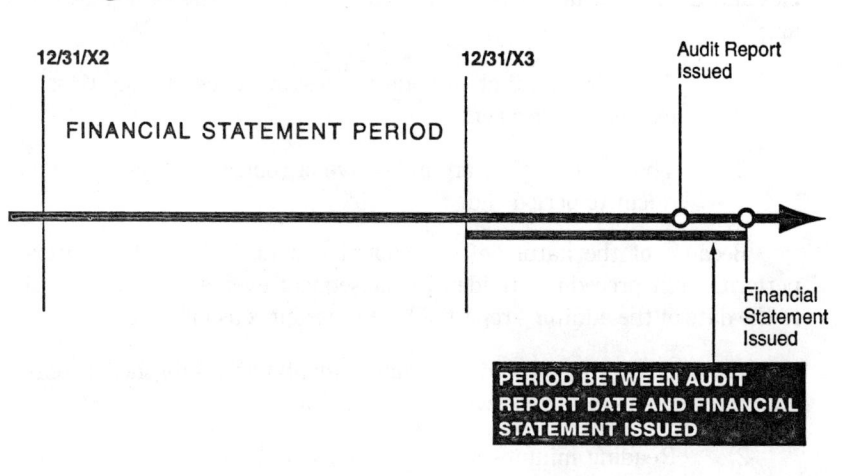

```
12/31/X2                    12/31/X3         Audit Report
                                             Issued
        FINANCIAL STATEMENT PERIOD

                                                  Financial
                                                  Statement
                                                  Issued

                              PERIOD BETWEEN AUDIT
                              REPORT DATE AND FINANCIAL
                              STATEMENT ISSUED
```

If the auditor determines that the financial statements need to reflect the event and management refuses to do so, then the auditor must issue a qualified opinion or an adverse opinion. In those situations where the auditor's report has already been issued, the auditor must "notify those persons ultimately responsible for the overall direction of the entity not to issue financial statements and the auditor's report thereon to third parties." If, however, the financial statements are subsequently released, the auditor needs to obtain legal counsel.

Figure 24.5

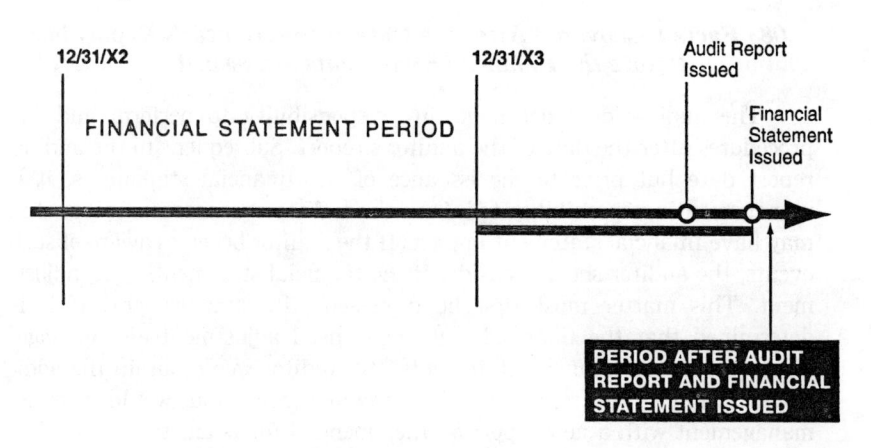

```
12/31/X2                    12/31/X3         Audit Report
                                             Issued
        FINANCIAL STATEMENT PERIOD                Financial
                                                  Statement
                                                  Issued


                                             PERIOD AFTER AUDIT
                                             REPORT AND FINANCIAL
                                             STATEMENT ISSUED
```

¶ 2403.08

U.S. standards refer to "subsequent discovery of facts that existed at the balance sheet date." International standards address the same issue but do not use the same title. If, after the financial statements have been issued, the auditor becomes aware of a fact which existed at the date of the auditor's report (see Figure 24.5) and which, if known at that date, may have caused the auditor to modify the auditor's report, the auditor should consider whether the financial statements need revision, should discuss the matter with management, and take appropriate action.

If it is deemed necessary to revise the financial statements and management does so, the auditor would obtain the appropriate evidence necessary in the circumstances. This includes:

1. Review the steps taken by management to ensure that anyone in receipt of the previously issued financial statements, together with the auditor's report, is informed of the situation.

2. Issue a new report on the revised financial statements.

The revised auditor's report should include an "emphasis of a matter" paragraph referring to the note in the financial statements that discusses the revision and to the earlier report issued by the auditor. The date of the revised auditor's report would be when the revised financial statements are approved, which coincides with the evidence obtained by the auditor necessary to extend the auditor's report. International standards refer to local regulations of some countries which permit the auditor to restrict the audit procedures regarding the revised financial statements to the event only, and the revised auditor's report would contain a statement to that effect. This latter reference is applicable to U.S. standards and is termed, "dual dating" the auditor's report. (See Chapter 8 for more discussion.)

.09 Going Concern (ISA 570)

The going concern principle is an assumption that a company will continue to operate with neither the intent nor necessity to liquidate. When a business is not considered a going concern, then there is an effect on the valuation and disclosure in the financial statements. It is required, in some financial reporting frameworks, that management make an explicit assessment of the company's ability to continue as a going concern. This is true with international accounting standards (as with U.S. accounting standards.) The auditor must consider, both in the planning of the audit and the performance of audit procedures, the appropriateness of management's use of the going concern principle in the preparation of the financial statements and if any related disclosure is necessary for the financial statements.

While planning the audit, the auditor should consider whether there are any conditions that cast significant doubt on the entity's ability to continue as a going concern. Management may have made an assessment of the going concern of the company already. For audit purposes, the assess-

¶ 2403.09

ment should be for a period of at least 12 months from the balance sheet date. As such, the auditor should inquire of management their assessment of the company's going concern.

During the audit, the auditor should remain alert for information that casts doubt on the entity's ability to continue as a going concern. The auditor may become aware of such information during the planning and fieldwork stages of the audit, including subsequent events procedures. Other than inquiry of management, the auditor does not have a responsibility to specifically design procedures to test for indications of events or conditions which cast significant doubt on the entity's ability to continue as a going concern.

If there is a problem concerning a client's ability to continue as a going concern, additional evidence should be obtained:

1. Review management's plans for future actions based on its going concern assessment.

2. Obtain sufficient appropriate audit evidence to confirm or dispel whether material uncertainties exist, including considering the effect of any plans of management to address the going concern issue.

3. Seek written representations from management regarding its plans for future action.

In considering if management's plan for the company's continued operation are feasible, procedures suggested by international auditing standards relevant in this regard are:

1. Analyzing and discussing cash flow, profit, and other relevant forecasts with management.

2. Analyzing and discussing the entity's latest available interim financial statements.

3. Reviewing the terms of debentures and loan agreements and determining whether any have been breached.

4. Reading minutes of the meetings of shareholders, the board of directors, and important committees for reference to financing difficulties.

5. Inquiring of the entity's lawyer regarding the existence of litigation and claims and the reasonableness of management's assessments of their outcome and the estimate of their financial implications.

6. Confirming the existence, legality and enforceability of arrangements to provide or maintain financial support with related and

third parties and assessing the financial ability of such parties to provide additional funds.

7. Considering the entity's plans to deal with unfilled customer orders.

8. Reviewing events after period end to identify those that either mitigate or otherwise affect the entity's ability to continue as a going concern.

If, after having obtained evidence, the auditor determines that a material uncertainty exists casting significant doubt on the entity's ability to continue as a going concern, then financial statement disclosure is required. If properly disclosed in the financial statements, this could result in an unqualified opinion with an emphasis relating to the going concern issue. If management does not properly disclose the matter, then a qualified or adverse opinion should be rendered.

.10 Management Representations (ISA 580)

Included in the evidence-gathering process is management's acknowledgement of the fair presentation for the financial statements in accordance with a relevant financial reporting framework as well as approving the financial statements. The auditor can obtain management's acknowledgement for the fair presentation through:

1. The minutes of the board of directors or similar body

2. A signed copy of the financial statements

3. A letter from the auditor outlining the auditor's understanding of management's representations, duly acknowledged and confirmed by management

4. Obtaining a written representation from management

(The last method is the only approved method for U.S. auditing standards.)

Management inquiry is a form of evidence and should be corroborated whenever possible. Sometimes representations by management are the only feasible evidence that the auditor can obtain. These representations could be in the form of summarized oral discussions, but written representations are recommended.

ISA 240 does, however, require certain representations from management be in writing. Management must state that they:

1. Acknowledge their responsibility for the implementation and operations of accounting and internal control systems that are designed to prevent and detect fraud and error.

¶ 2403.10

2. Believe that the effects of those uncorrected financial statement misstatements aggregated by the auditor during the audit are immaterial, both individually and in the aggregate, to the financial statements taken as a whole. A summary of such items should be included in or attached to the written representation.

3. Have disclosed to the auditor all significant facts relating to any frauds or suspected frauds known to management that may have affected the entity.

4. Have disclosed to the auditor the results of its assessment of the risk that the financial statements may be materially misstated as a result of fraud.

When the auditor decides or is required to obtain a Management Representation Letter, its content will vary with each client. An example of a Management Representation Letter appears in Figure 24.6. The letter should be addressed to the auditor and signed by those parties who are responsible for the financial statements, such as the chief executive and chief financial officers. The letter is ordinarily dated the same date as the auditor's report.

Because of the nature of fraud and the problems that could result, it is important that the Management Representation Letter also address fraud issues. ISA 240 provides guidance on these inclusions and has been incorporated into the example.

¶ 2403.10

Figure 24.6————————————————————————————

Management Representation Letter

To Ekstase LLP:

This representation letter is provided in connection with your audit of the financial statements of Plyndre A/S for the year ended 31 December 20X2 for the purpose of expressing an opinion as to whether the financial statements give a true and fair view of the financial position of Plyndre A/S as of 31 December 20X2 and of the results of its operations and its cash flows for the year then ended in accordance with international accounting standards. [indication of relevant financial reporting framework]

We acknowledge our responsibility for the fair presentation of the financial statements in accordance with international accounting standards. [indication of relevant financial reporting framework]

We acknowledge our responsibility for the implementation and operations of accounting and internal control systems that are designed to prevent and detect fraud and error.

We believe the effects of those uncorrected financial statement misstatements aggregated by the auditor during the audit are immaterial, both individually and in the aggregate, to the financial statements taken as a whole. [A summary of such items is attached.]

We confirm, to the best of our knowledge and belief, the following representations:

- That we have disclosed to you all significant facts relating to any frauds or suspected frauds known to management that may have affected the entity.
- That we have disclosed to you the results of our assessment of the risk that the financial statements may be materially misstated as a result of fraud.
- There have been no irregularities involving management or employees who have a significant role in the accounting and internal control systems or that could have a material effect on the financial statements.
- We have made available to you all books of accounts and supporting documentation and all minutes of meetings of shareholders and the board of directors (namely those held on 15 March and 30 September 20X2, respectively).
- We confirm the completeness of the information provided regarding the identification of related parties.
- The financial statements are free of material misstatements, including omissions.
- Plyndre A/S has complied with all aspects of contractual agreements that could have a material effect on the financial statements in the event of noncompliance.

There has been no noncompliance with requirements of regulatory authorities that could have a material effect on the financial statements in the event of noncompliance.

The following have been properly recorded and when appropriate, adequately disclosed in the financial statements:

(a) The identity of, and balances and transactions with, related parties.

(b) Losses arising from sale and purchase commitments.

(c) Agreements and options to buy back assets previously sold.
(d) Assets pledged as collateral.

- We have no plans or intentions that may materially alter the carrying value or classification of assets and liabilities reflected in the financial statements.

- We have no plans to abandon lines of product or other plans or intentions that will result in any excess or obsolete inventory, and no inventory is stated at an amount in excess of net realizable value.

- Plyndre A/S has satisfactory title to all assets and there are no liens or encumbrances on the company's assets, except for those that are disclosed in Note 15 to the financial statements.

- We have recorded or disclosed, as appropriate, all liabilities, both actual and contingent, and have disclosed in Note 9 to the financial statements all guarantees that we have given to third parties. There have been no events subsequent to 31 December 20X2 which require adjustment of or disclosure in the financial statements or Notes thereto.

- No claims in connection with litigation have been or are expected to be received.

- There are no formal or informal compensating balance arrangements with any of our cash and investment accounts. Except as disclosed in Note 3 to the financial statements, we have no other line of credit arrangements.

- We have properly recorded or disclosed in the financial statements the capital stock repurchase options and agreement and capital stock reserved for options, warrants, conversions, and other requirements.

Plynder Apparell A/S
17 March 20X3

If management refused to provide the auditor with a management representation letter, then the auditor would issue a qualified or disclaimer opinion due to a scope limitation.

.11 Considering the Work of Internal Audit (ISA 610)

The external auditor should consider the work performed by the internal auditor in conducting the external audit. The definition of "internal auditing" is an appraisal activity established within an entity as a service to the entity. Its functions include, among other things, examining, evaluating, and monitoring the adequacy and effectiveness of the accounting and internal control systems.

It is the external auditor's responsibility to render a financial statement audit opinion as well as to determine the nature, timing, and extent of external audit procedures; however, certain portions of the internal auditor's work may be useful to the external auditor.

Usually the internal auditor reviews the internal control system as it relates to:

¶ 2403.11

1. Financial and operating information.
2. The economy, efficiency, and effectiveness of operations including nonfinancial controls of an entity.
3. Compliance with laws, regulations, and other external requirements and with management policies and directives and other internal requirements.

Some of these aspects of internal auditing may be useful for the external auditor in determining the nature, timing, and extent of external audit procedures. As such, an effective internal auditing department may reduce the amount of procedures needed by the external auditor. In order to determine the usefulness of the internal auditor's work, the external auditor should first obtain an understanding of the internal audit function. This would occur during the planning phase of the external audit.

To understand and make a preliminary assessment of the internal audit function, the external auditor should understand and obtain evidence for each of the following regarding the internal auditor:

1. Organizational status of the internal auditing function and its ability to be objective.
2. The nature and extent of internal auditing assignments.
3. The technical competence of the internal auditors.
4. Due professional care used by the internal auditors in their work.

Once it has been determined that the internal auditor's work may assist the external auditor, there needs to be a discussion between the auditors to coordinate work schedules. This discussion should occur as early as possible in the audit process and should continue periodically in order to keep each other informed of relevant matters.

For any of the internal auditor's work to be used to assist the external auditor, it should be tested for adequacy. The evaluation should consider the scope of the internal auditor's work and whether the preliminary assessment of the internal audit function remains appropriate. Additionally, when considering the work of the internal auditor, the external auditor should determine if:

1. The work is performed by persons having adequate technical training and proficiency as internal auditors
2. The work of assistants is properly supervised, reviewed, and documented
3. Sufficient appropriate audit evidence is obtained to afford a reasonable basis for the conclusions reached

¶ 2403.11

4. Conclusions reached are appropriate in the circumstances and any reports prepared are consistent with the results of the work performed

5. Any exceptions or unusual matters disclosed by internal auditing are properly resolved

Finally, the external auditor should document the internal auditor's conclusions regarding any of the specific internal auditing work that has been evaluated and tested.

.12 The Auditor's Responsibility to Consider Fraud and Errors—Fieldwork Issues (ISA 240)

International auditing standards treat the topic of fraud and financial statement error in a separate section of the standards, ISA 240, "The Auditor's Responsibility to Consider Fraud and Error in an Audit of Financial Statements." (That portion of section 240 dealing with the planning phase is discussed at ¶ 2402.03.)

Management is primarily responsible for the prevention and detection of fraud and error. The auditor is responsible, after having applied international auditing standards, to opine whether the financial statements are prepared, in all material respects, in accordance with an identified financial reporting framework. If the auditor conducts an audit in accordance with those standards, they can be reasonably assured that the financial statements contain no material misstatements. However, reasonable assurance is not absolute and therefore cannot guarantee that the financial statements are free from material misstatement.

Material misstatements due to fraud are more difficult to detect than those due to errors because fraud almost always involves an active cover-up. Those audit procedures that are effective for detecting an error may not be effective in detecting fraud. With this in mind, it is important that the auditor performs an audit with an attitude of professional skepticism as is discussed in ISA 200, "Objective and General Principles Governing an Audit of Financial Statements."

As is discussed in the planning phase, the auditor should document fraud risk factors identified as being present during the auditor's assessment process as well as their response to such factors. During subsequent testing, if additional fraud risk factors are identified that require additional audit procedures, that also should be documented.

If, during the audit, the auditor encounters a potential material misstatement in the financial statements due to fraud or error, the auditor should alter the nature, timing, and extent of their auditing procedures to determine whether the financial statements are, in fact, materially misstated. If the misstatement is the result of fraud, the auditor should

¶ 2403.12

consider the implications of the misstatement in relation to other aspects of the audit, particularly the reliability of management representations.

.13 Communication

When the auditor identifies a misstatement due to fraud, or a suspected fraud, or error, the auditor should consider the auditor's responsibility to communicate that information to management on a timely basis so that management can take action on the matter. Additionally, those charged with governance should also be apprised of the matter and, in some circumstances and jurisdictions, to regulatory and enforcement authorities as well.

As it is with misstatement due to fraud, the auditor should communicate identified material misstatement resulting from error. The communication should be on a timely basis and to the appropriate level of management. Also, the auditor should consider the need to report to those charged with governance those uncorrected misstatements aggregated by the auditor during the audit that were determined by management to be immaterial, both individually and in the aggregate, to the financial statements taken as a whole.

With respect to communications to regulatory and enforcement authorities, the auditor has a professional duty of confidentiality with respect to the client. However, depending upon the various jurisdictions, the auditor may have legal requirements concerning the communication of fraud and material errors to such authorities. In such matters, the auditor should consider seeking legal counsel.

¶ 2404 International Auditing Standards and Audit Reports

The product of the audit is the report. It lends credibility to the financial statements and in the case of publicly-held companies, the audit reporting system enhances investor confidence in the capital markets. The IAASB, through the International Standards on Auditing (ISA), has established standards on the form and content of the auditor's report. ISA 700 on reporting is similar to U.S. auditing standards and are issued after the auditor has assessed the conclusions drawn from the audit evidence obtained. An auditor is associated with financial information when the auditor attaches a report to that information or consents to the use of the auditor's name in a professional connection. If the auditor is not associated in this manner, third parties can assume no responsibility of the auditor.

The auditor's opinion enhances the credibility of financial statements by providing a high, but not absolute, level of assurance. Absolute assurance in auditing is not attainable as a result of such factors as the need for judgment, the use of testing, the inherent limitations of any accounting and internal control systems, and the fact that most of the evidence available to the auditor is persuasive, rather than conclusive, in nature. The auditor's report should contain a clear written expression of opinion on the financial statements taken as a whole. Whenever the auditor expresses an opinion that is other than unqualified, a clear description of all the substantive reasons should be included in the report and, unless impracticable, a quantification of the possible effect(s) on the financial statements.

The following represent the basic types of audit reports:

1. Unqualified report—is issued when the auditor has conducted an examination of the financial statements in accordance with applicable auditing standards and has found that the financial statements present fairly the financial position of the company.

2. Qualified report—is issued when the auditor concludes that an unqualified opinion cannot be expressed because of the effect of a disagreement with management regarding financial statement presentation or disclosure, or there has been a limitation on the audit scope. However, the disagreement or limitation is not so material and pervasive as to require an adverse opinion or a disclaimer of opinion. A qualified opinion should be expressed as being except for the effects of the matter to which the qualification relates.

3. Adverse report—is issued when the effect of a disagreement is so material and pervasive to the financial statements that the auditor concludes that a qualification of the report is not adequate to disclose the misleading or incomplete nature of the financial statements.

4. Disclaimer of opinion— is issued when the possible effect of a limitation on scope is so material and pervasive that the auditor has not been able to obtain sufficient appropriate audit evidence and accordingly is unable to express an opinion on the financial statements.

The format of the unqualified auditor's report should be:

1. The auditor's report title—The title should specify who is issuing the report. The title "Independent Auditor" is an example of an appropriate title.

2. The address—The report is usually addressed to the shareholders or the board of directors of the audit client.

3. Introductory (also referred to as Opening) paragraph—The introductory paragraph should identify:

    a. The name of the company

    b. The financial statements that have been audited

    c. The date of and period covered by the financial statements

d. A statement that the financial statements are the responsibility of the company's management; however, the level of management responsible for the financial statements will vary according to the legal situation in each country and as such it also may be necessary to refer to a particular jurisdiction within the country of origin to identify clearly the financial reporting framework used.

e. A statement that the responsibility of the auditor is to express an opinion on the financial statements based on the audit.

The following is an introductory paragraph as suggested by ISA standards:

> We have audited the accompanying balance sheet of the ABC Company as of December 31, 20X2, and the related statements of income, and cash flows for the year then ended. These financial statements are the responsibility of the Company's management. Our responsibility is to express an opinion on these financial statements based on our audit.

4. Scope paragraph— The scope paragraph should identify:

   a. The audit was conducted in accordance with ISAs or in accordance with relevant national standards or practices as appropriate. If not stated, it is assumed that the audit has been carried out in accordance with established standards or practices of the country indicated by the auditor's address.

   b. A statement that the audit was planned and performed to obtain reasonable assurance about whether the financial statements are free of material misstatement.

   c. Evidence is examined to support:

      (1) The financial statement amounts and disclosures

      (2) Assessing the accounting principles used in the preparation of the financial statements

      (3) Assessing the significant estimates made by management in the preparation of the financial statements

      (4) Evaluating the overall financial statement preparation

   d. Some evidence may be gathered on a test basis (a sample drawn).

   e. A statement that the audit provides a reasonable basis for the opinion.

The following is a scope paragraph as suggested by ISA standards:

¶ 2404

We conducted our audit in accordance with International Standards on Auditing (and, if applicable, refer to relevant national standards). Those Standards require that we plan and perform the audit to obtain reasonable assurance about whether the financial statements are free of material misstatement. An audit includes examining, on a test basis, evidence supporting the amounts and disclosures in the financial statements. An audit also includes assessing the accounting principles used and significant estimates made by management, as well as evaluating the overall financial statement presentation. We believe that our audit provides a reasonable basis for our opinion.

5. Opinion paragraph— The opinion paragraph should identify:

   a. The financial reporting framework used to prepare the financial statements. When International Accounting Standards are not used, the country of origin should be identified.

   b. A statement that the financial statements are presented fairly, in all material respect in accordance with the financial reporting framework. International auditing standards also allow the phrase "a true and fair view" to be substituted for "presented fairly, in all material respects."

   c. Where applicable, a statement should be made if the financial statements comply with a statutory requirement.

The following is a scope paragraph as suggested by ISA standards:

In our opinion, the financial statements give a true and fair view of (or "present fairly, in all material respects,") the financial position of the Company as of December 31, 20X2, and of the results of its operations and its cash flows for the year then ended in accordance with International Accounting Standards (or [title of financial reporting framework with reference to the country of origin]) (and comply with applicable statutory requirements).

The date of the auditor's report should be as of the completion date of the audit, which is slightly different than U.S. standards which is the last day of fieldwork. The completion date represents that point whereby the effects of transactions, and events upon the financial statements up to that point, have been considered by the auditor. The completion date should not be any earlier than the date that the financial statements have been signed and approved by management or the Board of Directors or equivalent. The city whereby the auditor is based should be indicated, followed by the auditor's signature. The signature should be manual and signed on behalf of the firm or the auditor's personal signature, depending upon jurisdiction.

However, because of the many international jurisdictions, international auditing standards allow for flexibility in the format. Figure 24.7 is an example of the standard worded unqualified opinion for a medium-sized, nonpublicly-traded company using current Danish and ISA auditing standards (as incorporated for Danish use in "Revisionspaategninger MV. Paa

AArsrapporter," December 2002 by the Foreningen af Statsautoriserede Revisorer (*www.fsr.dk*)).

Figure 24.7

An Example of a Standard Unqualified Opinion—Danish and ISA Auditing Standards

To the Shareholders of Billig A/S:

We have audited the accompanying annual report of the Billig Group and the Parent Company for the financial year 1 January—31 December 20X2.

The Annual Report is the responsibility of the Company's Board of Directors and Board of Executives. Our responsibility is to express an opinion on the annual report based on our audit.

Basis of Opinion

We conducted our audit in accordance with Danish and International Standards on Auditing (ISA). Those standards require that we plan and perform the audit to obtain reasonable assurance about whether the financial statements are free of material misstatement. An audit includes examining, on a test basis, evidence supporting the amounts and disclosures in the annual report. An audit also includes assessing the accounting principles used and significant estimates made by management, as well as evaluating the overall annual report presentation. We believe that our audit provides a reasonable basis for our opinion.

Our audit has not resulted in any qualification.

Opinion

In our opinion, the annual report gives a true and fair view of the financial position of the Group and the Parent Company as of 31 December 20X2, and of the results of its operations for the financial year 1 January— 31 December 20X2 in accordance with the Danish Financial Statement Act.

Mead & Co. LLP
Copenhagen, 21 March 20X3

Under Danish law, the term "annual report" is used instead of "financial statements," also an additional statement is added following the scope paragraph noting that the audit resulted in no qualifications, and the auditor must sign their own name to the report.

An unqualified opinion is appropriate whenever the auditor, based upon their testing, determines that the financial statements are presented fairly, in all material respects, in accordance with the identified financial reporting framework. Occasionally the auditor feels that the unqualified opinion is appropriate but wants to point out some important issue with the financial statements to the user. International standards provide for modified unqualified reports to emphasize a matter. Formats of the modified opinion are similar to the standard unqualified but include a final paragraph after the opinion paragraph. Examples of the types of matters which the auditor may wish to emphasize are:

¶ 2404

1. A going concern issue not requiring qualification or disclaimer
2. A significant uncertainty
3. Other matters not affecting the financial statements, e.g., an erroneous statement in the annual report not corrected by the client

Figure 24.8 describes the format of the unqualified opinion with an explanatory paragraph.

Figure 24.8

Unqualified Opinion with Explanatory Paragraph

Introductory Paragraph
↓
Scope Paragraph
↓
Opinion Paragraph
↓
Explanatory Paragraph

Unqualified opinions are not appropriate when there has been a limitation on the scope of the auditor's work or there is a disagreement with management regarding the acceptability of the accounting policies selected, the method of their application, or the adequacy of financial statement disclosures. However, in either of the cases above, the effect of the disagreement or limitation cannot be so material as to require an adverse or disclaimer of opinion. Any opinion other than unqualified must include the reason for the departure, as well as a quantification of the financial statement effect and set off in a separate paragraph.

If the auditor is unable to carry out an audit procedure that they consider necessary, then it may be appropriate to issue a qualified opinion due to a scope limitation. The circumstances may include inadequate recordkeeping, timing problems such as inventory observation, or an unknown result such as litigation. The term "client-imposed" scope limitation, as is discussed in U.S. auditing standards and requires a disclaimer of opinion, does not appear in the international auditing standards. When to

¶ 2404

use a qualified opinion or a disclaimer of opinion for scope limitations is determined by auditor judgment.

Figure 24.9

Qualified Opinion—Scope Limitation

Introductory Paragraph
↓
Scope Paragraph
↓
Explanatory Paragraph
↓
Opinion Paragraph

Figure 24.10

Qualified Report Due to a Limitation on the Audit Scope

Introductory Paragraph—wording is the same as in the Unqualified Opinion.

Scope Paragraph:

Except as discussed in the following paragraph, we conducted ... [the rest of the paragraph is worded the same as the unqualified opinion.]

Explanatory Paragraph:

We were not able to confirm the notes receivable of 190.000 EUR and were not able to satisfy ourselves as the net realizable value of the notes by other audit procedures.

Opinion Paragraph:

In our opinion, except for the effects of such adjustments, if any, as might have been determined to be necessary had we been able to satisfy ourselves as to the net realizable value of the notes, the 20X2 financial statements referred to above give a true and fair view of the financial position of Decanter A/S as of December 31, 20X2, and of the results of its operations and its cash flows for the year then ended in accordance with international accounting standards.

If it is deemed appropriate to issue a qualified opinion due to a disagreement with management regarding the acceptability of the account-

¶ 2404

ing policies selected, the method of their application, or the adequacy of financial statement disclosures, then the opinion should use the form as seen in Figure 24.11. The explanatory paragraph comes before the opinion paragraph. The opinion paragraph should be expressed as being "except for" the effects of the matter to which the qualification relates.

Figure 24.11

Qualified Opinion—Accounting Disagreement

Introductory Paragraph
↓
Scope Paragraph
↓
Explanatory Paragraph
↓
Opinion Paragraph

Figure 24.12

Qualified Report Due to a Disagreement with Management Regarding Accounting Issue

Introductory and Scope Paragraphs—are the same as in the Unqualified Opinion

Explanatory Paragraph:

As discussed in Note 12 to the financial statements, certain leases have not been appropriately capitalized in the financial statements which, in our opinion, is not in accordance with International Accounting Standards. Accordingly, the fixed assets should be increased by 170 mEUR and accumulated depreciation by 32 mEUR and the income for the year and retained earnings should be increased by 22 mEUR.

Opinion Paragraph:

In our opinion, except for the effect on the financial statements of the matter referred to in the preceding paragraph, the 20X2 financial statements referred to above give a true and fair view of the financial position of Decanter A/S as of December 31, 20X2, and of the results of its operations and its cash flows for the year then ended in accordance with international accounting standards.

¶ 2404

A disclaimer of opinion should be issued whenever the limitation on audit scope is so material and pervasive that the auditor has not been able to obtain sufficient audit evidence and accordingly is unable to express an opinion on the financial statements. Figure 24.13 is an example of the wording of the disclaimer of opinion.

Figure 24.13

Disclaimer of Opinion

We were engaged to audit the accompanying balance sheet of the ABC Company as of December 31, 20X2, and the related statements of income, and cash flows for the year then ended. These financial statements are the responsibility of the Company's management.

We were not able to observe all physical inventories due to limitations placed on the scope of our work by the Company.

Because of the significance of the matters discussed in the preceding paragraph, we do not express an opinion on the financial statements.

The adverse opinion is issued when there is disagreement with management regarding an accounting treatment in the financial statements and the effect is so material and pervasive to the financial statements that, in the auditor's judgment, a qualified opinion is not adequate to disclose the misleading or incomplete nature of the financial statements.

Figure 24.14

Adverse Opinion

Introductory Paragraph

↓

Scope Paragraph

↓

Explanatory Paragraph

↓

Opinion Paragraph

¶ 2404

Figure 24.15 ─────────────────────────────

Adverse Opinion

Introductory and Scope paragraphs—wording is the same as in the Unqualified Opinion

Explanatory Paragraph:

The Company capitalizes certain maintenance costs incurred which, in our opinion, is not in accordance with International Accounting Standards. Accordingly, the fixed assets, income and retained earnings should be decreased by 1.020 mEUR.

Opinion Paragraph:

In our opinion, because of the effects of the matters discussed in the preceding paragraph, the 20X2 financial statements do not give a true and fair view of the financial position of the Company as of December 31, 20X2, and of the results of its operations and its cash flows for the year then ended in accordance with international accounting standards.

Comparatives financial statements produce many derivative effects. The comparative financial statements could differ for a variety of reasons. There could be different auditors, applications of auditing, and/or accounting standards.

When the comparative financial statements have been audited by the same auditor using the same accounting framework, and an unqualified opinion has been determined as appropriate for each, then a combined unqualified audit opinion for the comparative financial statements is appropriate. The combined opinion makes reference to the financial statements and time frames involved.

The term "corresponding figures" represents those financial statements presented and compared to the current set of financial statements being audited. The corresponding figures could have been audited by other auditors or not audited at all and may have been prepared using different accounting principles than the current financial statements. International auditing standards require that the auditor obtain sufficient appropriate audit evidence and that the corresponding figures meet the requirements of the relevant financial reporting framework. In order to fulfill this requirement, the auditor must determine that the corresponding figures are consistent with the current period or whether appropriate adjustments and/or disclosures have been made.

If the prior period financial statements had been audited by another auditor, the incoming (U.S. standards use the term, "successor") auditor should determine if the corresponding figures meet the above criteria. Unlike U.S. auditing standards, no specific procedures are required as to methodology of meeting the above criteria. When the prior year's financial

¶ 2404

statements have not been audited, the incoming auditor should state that in the current year's audit report.

Also, in some jurisdictions, such as the United States, the incoming auditor is allowed to refer to the predecessor's audit report when comparative financial statements are involved. In those situations, the international standards require the incoming auditor to include in their report:

1. That the financial statements of the prior period were audited by another auditor
2. The type of report issued by the predecessor and if modified, why it was modified
3. The date of that report

If the incoming auditor, during the course of this year's audit, determines that the prior year's financial statements contained material misstatements, the incoming auditor should obtain approval by management to contact the previous auditor for resolution.

In those situations whereby the current auditor had also audited the prior period financial statements and the comparative figures contain unresolved matters that had led to a qualified, adverse, or disclaimer report, the current year's audit opinion should be modified for the corresponding figures, whether they affect the current year's amounts or not. Of course, if the matter has been corrected, this year's report needs no modification; possibly an unqualified opinion that emphasizes the matter would be appropriate depending upon the amount of the modification.

¶ 2405 Global Convergence of Auditing Standards

There is a recent move toward global convergence of auditing standards as the European Commission (EC) and the Public Company Accounting Oversight Board (PCAOB) work closely to resolve their differences and establish uniform and globally accepted auditing standards. The EC is currently working on establishing (1) a new auditing framework to strengthen controls over the audit profession; (2) requirements for mandatory independent audit committees for listed companies; (3) a mechanism for stricter auditor rotation requirements and strengthened sanctions; and (4) procedures for directors' responsibility for financial reports and accounts of public companies.[13] These initiatives by the EC will bring European auditing standards more in line with auditing provisions of the Sarbanes-Oxley Act and create opportunities for the global convergence of auditing standards. The International Federation of Accountants has made the following recommendations for improving the availability of financial reports and the credibility of audit functions:[14]

---

[13] Available at *http://www.ifac.org*. [14] *Ibid.*

1. Effective corporate ethics codes need to be in place and actively monitored.

2. Corporate management must place greater emphasis on the effectiveness of financial management and controls.

3. Incentives to misstate financial information need to be reduced.

4. Boards of directors need to improve their oversight of management.

5. Threats to auditor independence need to receive greater attention in corporate governance processes and by auditors themselves.

6. Audit effectiveness needs to be raised primarily through greater attention to audit quality control processes.

7. Codes of conduct need to be put in place for other participants in the financial reporting process, and their compliance should be monitored.

8. Audit standards and regulation need to be strengthened.

9. Accounting and reporting practices need to be strengthened.

10. The standard of regulation of issuers needs to be raised.

The International Auditing and Assurance Standards Board (IAASB), in February 2004, approved its International Standard on Auditing (ISA) 220, Quality Control for Audit of Historical Financial Information.[15] ISA 220 requires that:

- The engagement team implements quality control procedures that are applicable to the individual audit engagement.

- The engagement partner takes responsibility for the overall quality on each audit engagement.

- The engagement partner ensures that members of the engagement team have complied with ethical requirements.

- The engagement partner ensures compliance with independence requirements.

- The engagement partner ensures compliance with established policies and procedures regarding the acceptance and continuance of clients.

---

[15] James Hamilton. "European Commission Pledges to work with PCAOB on Sarbanes-Oxley," PCAOB Reporter, CCH Washington Service Bureau. Available at *http://www.wsb.com* (March 15, 2004).

International Auditing Standards

- The engagement partner ensures that the engagement team collectively has appropriate capabilities, competence, and time to perform that audit engagement.

- The engagement partner is responsible for the direction, supervision, and performance of the audit engagement and the auditor's report.

The International Standard on Quality Control (ISQC) No. 1 of the IAASB defines elements of a system of quality control as follows:[16]

- Leadership responsibilities for quality within the firm
- Ethical requirements
- Acceptance and continuance of client relationships and specific engagements
- Human resources
- Engagement performance
- Monitoring

It appears the greatest incentive to implement international auditing standards lies with the European Union. The EU's desire for a single, capital market, representing over 7,000 companies, requires that the individual member-state auditing standards be subjected to a single set of standards. Additionally, U.S. pressure to register EU audit firms with the PCAOB and the EU reaction has further exasperated the drive for a single set of European auditing standards. As stated by the EU's Internal Market Commissioner, Frits Bolkestein, "The integration of European capital markets requires the quality of auditing in the EU to be reinforced further... I do not accept the imposition of U.S. standards on our firms and that is why the European Union strongly opposes registration of EU audit firms with the United States' Public Company Accounting Oversight Board. The EU will regulate its own businesses."[17]

However, Section 106(a) of the Sarbanes-Oxley Act states that any non-U.S. public accounting firm that prepares or furnishes an audit report pertaining to U.S. public companies is subject to the Act's provisions, the SEC's rules, and the PCAOB's professional standards. The PCAOB has voted to adopt rules pertaining to the oversight of non-U.S. public accounting firms. The PCAOB has proposed a framework under which it may partially rely on a non-U.S. system to reestablish compliance rules with the provisions of the Act.

---

[16] International Federation of Accountants.
[17] Press Release, ref:PR32 Federation des Experts Comptables Europeens, 21 May 2003.

¶ 2405

On May 21, 2003, the European Federation of Accountants, representing 500,000 accountants throughout Europe, called on the European Commission to adopt international auditing standards in the European Union by 2005.[18] This is in support of what had already been proposed by the European Commission and planned by the IAASB setting out the same deadline.[19]

However, adopting international auditing standards is not a panacea for the EU. Unlike the United States, many European countries require that their nonpublicly held companies be annually audited as well. This includes many small, privately-held companies not registered on any stock exchange. International auditing standards and the increased audit scope it brings, applied to these small companies, may prove too costly for general implementation. Another problem that must be taken into consideration is the country-specific audit procedures that would be required, in addition to the international auditing standards. This further exasperates the aforementioned cost of the small, privately-held company audit. Currently these matters are under debate.

¶ 2406 Summary

Accounting and the related statutory audit process should provide investors with information that is comparable, transparent, and reliable; however, the accounting principles and auditing standards in use throughout the world vary greatly. In order to provide greater accounting and auditing consistency among the countries, 63 accountancy bodies representing 49 countries formed the International Federation of Accountants (IFAC) to develop and promote uniform standards. The International Auditing and Assurance Standards Board (IAASB), an arm of IFAC, issues the international auditing standards known as International Standards on Auditing (ISAs).

The international auditing standards for planning the financial statement audit of financial statements, for fieldwork, and for the form and content of the audit report include many of the same procedures as the U.S. auditing standards. There is a move toward global convergence on auditing standards as the IAASB is closely working with the PCAOB to establish uniform and globally accepted auditing standards.

---

[18] *Ibid.*

[19] IAASB Action Plan 2003-2004.

Chapter 25
Government Auditing

¶ 2501   Introduction
¶ 2502   Professional Organizations
¶ 2503   Professional Certifications
¶ 2504   Professional Standards
¶ 2505   Summary

¶ 2501 Introduction

Government entities are an important part of the economy. Constituents pay taxes and other fees to government entities in return for services. In contrast to the private sector, resource allocations in the government sector typically are the result of political decisions. The major reason for this is that government entities lack a standardized performance measure that for-profit companies have in "Net Income" or "EPS." Nevertheless, constituents demand accountability from their government officials. Specifically, legislators, other government officials, and the public want to know whether government resources are properly managed and used in compliance with laws and regulations, government programs are achieving their objectives and desired outcomes, and government programs are being provided efficiently, economically, and effectively.[1] Government officials for their part rely on auditors to assist them in the discharge of their stewardship responsibility. Government auditors can either be employees or third party contractors and may function at the federal, state, and local levels. The scope of government audits run the full range of audits: financial, operational, and compliance.

Chapter 25 objectives:

- To recognize the professional accounting organizations that specifically represent the interests of government accountants or auditors (see ¶ 2501–2502).

- To identify certifications and skill sets that apply to government auditing (see ¶ 2503).

- To understand when to apply U.S. Generally Accepted Government Auditing Standards (GAGAS) (see ¶ 2504).

---

[1] Comptroller General of the United States, *Government Auditing Standards*, 2003 Revision, paragraph 1.11.

- To list the four GAGAS general standards (see ¶ 2504).
- To detail the topics of GAGAS standards for financial audits (see ¶ 2504).
- To list the topics covered by GAGAS for attestation engagements (see ¶ 2504).
- To detail the GAGAS performance audit fieldwork standard topics (see ¶ 2504).
- To explain the purpose of the Single Audit Act (see ¶ 2504).

¶ 2502 Professional Organizations

Each of the major professional accounting organizations, such as the American Institute of Certified Public Accountants (AICPA), the various state CPA societies, and the Institute of Internal Auditors (IIA), have sections or divisions devoted to government auditors. However, only the Association of Government Accountants (AGA) and the National Association of Local Government Auditors (NALGA) specifically represent the interests of government accountants or auditors. Federal accountants and auditors tend to dominate AGA while state and local government accountants and auditors tend to dominate NALGA. The contact information for AGA is:

Association of Government Accountants
2208 Mount Vernon Avenue
Alexandria, VA 22301-1314
Toll Free Phone: 800-AGA-7211
Main Phone: 703-684-6931
FAX: 703-548-9367
Website: www.agacgfm.org

The contact information for NALGA is:

NALGA
2401 Regency Road, Suite 302
Lexington, KY 40503
Toll Free Phone: 859-276-0686
Website: www.nalga.org

In addition to education programs, NALGA also administers a comprehensive peer review program for local government audit functions.

¶ 2503 Professional Certifications

The AGA maintains the Certified Government Financial Manager (CGFM). Although not an auditing designation, many federal government auditors hold the CGFM designation. To become a CGFM an applicant must have a baccalaureate degree with 24 hours in financial management topics (accounting, financial, management, etc.), pass the CGFM exam,

¶ 2502

and complete two years of work experience in professional level government financial management positions. The CGFM exam actually consists of three exams. Exam one covers the government environment; exam two covers government accounting, financial reporting, and budgeting; and exam three covers government financial management and control. The three CGFM examinations are administered year-round in a multiple-choice, computerized format on behalf of AGA by NetCertification, Inc. via the Prometric Technology Centers. More information may be obtained about this exam by going to the CGFM website at *www.agacgfm.org/cgfm/cgfmdefault.aspx*.

The IIA actually maintains the only truly professional government auditing designation—the Certified Government Auditing Professional (CGAP). Candidates must meet the following requirements to obtain the CGAP designation:[2]

- Education—A baccalaureate degree or an associates degree plus five years of work experience in a government environment.

- Character reference—A character reference submitted by a CGAP, Certified Internal Auditor (CIA), a Certificate in Control Self Assessment (CCSA), a Certified Financial Services Auditor (CFSA), or the candidate's supervisor.

- Work experience—Two years of auditing experience in a government environment verified by a CGAP, CIA, CCSA, CFSA, or the candidate's supervisor.

- Special considerations—CIAs are assumed to meet the education and character requirements; holders of the CCSA and CFSA designations meet the character requirement.

The content of the CGAP exam consists of four domains: Standards and Control/Risk Models, Government Auditing Practice; Government Auditing Methodologies and Skills; and Government Auditing Environment.

- **Domain 1—Standards and Control/Risk Models (5%–10%)**
  A. Role of a comprehensive set of auditing/evaluation standards
  B. Application of appropriate standards in all assignments
  C. Professional standards
  D. Comprehensive internal control/risk models
  E. IIA Code of Ethics

- **Domain 2—Government Auditing Practice (35%–45%)**
  A. Management of the audit function
  B. Types of audit services
  C. Processes for delivery of audit services

---

[2] From the IIA website, *www.theiia.org*. Reprinted with permission.

- **Domain 3—Government Auditing Methodologies and Skills (20%–25%)**
    A. Management concepts and techniques
    B. Performance measurement
    C. Program evaluation
    D. Quantitative methods
    E. Qualitative methods
    F. Methods for the identification and investigation of integrity violations
    G. Research/data collection techniques
    H. Analytical skills
- **Domain 4—Government Auditing Environment (25%–35%)**
    A. Basic structure of government
    B. Financial management
    C. Implications of various service delivery methods
    D. Implications of delivering services to citizens
    E. Impact of public scrutiny
    F. Unique purchasing and procurement requirements
    G. Unique characteristics of human resources management
    H. Performance management[3]

The CGAP exam contains 125 multiple-choice questions and is given twice a year on the same dates and sites as the CIA exam in the United States and Canada. More information concerning the CGAP designation can be obtained from the following website: *www.theiia.org/iia/index.cfm?doc_id=926.*

¶ 2504 Professional Standards

.01 U.S. Generally Accepted Government Auditing Standards (GAGAS)

The government entity that uses the auditor's report specifies the performance standards that the audit must meet. In the United States, most government entities are audited according to Generally Accepted Government Auditing Standards (GAGAS) published by the U.S. General Accounting Office (GAO). These standards are also referred to as "The Yellow Book" because the early bound editions had a yellow cover. The latest revision of GAGAS were issued in June 2003 and can be obtained from the GAO website: *www.gao.gov.* The Yellow Book is organized into the following sections: applicability, types of government audits and attestation engagements, general standards, standards for financial audits, standards for attestation engagements, and standards for performance audits.

---
[3] *Ibid.*

.02 Applicability

GAGAS apply to audits and attestation engagements of government entities, programs, activities, and functions, and of government assistance administered by contractors, nonprofit entities, and other nongovernmental entities. Some laws that mandate the use of GAGAS include:

* The Inspector General Act of 1978 as amended in 2000,
* The Chief Financial Officers Act of 1990, and
* The Single Audit Act Amendments of 1996.

Even if not mandated by law, the use of GAGAS is highly recommended in performing audit or attestation services for a government entity. GAGAS incorporate the fieldwork and reporting standards of Generally Accepted Auditing Standards (GAAS) while adding additional requirements to the GAAS general standards. Likewise, GAGAS may be used in conjunction with other standards issued by professional organizations such as the Standards for the Professional Practice of Internal Auditing (SPPIA) issued by the Institute of Internal Auditors (IIA). The relationship of the AICPA standards and the IIA Standards to GAGAS and the Single Audit Act is shown in Figure 25.1. Officials of the audited entity are responsible for:

- Applying those resources efficiently, economically, effectively, and legally to achieve the purposes for which the resources were furnished or the program was established;
- Complying with applicable laws and regulations;
- Establishing and maintaining effective internal control;
- Providing appropriate reports to those who oversee their actions;
- Addressing the findings and recommendations of auditors; and
- Following sound procurement practices when contracting for audits and attestation engagements, including ensuring that procedures are in place for monitoring contract performance.[4]

Auditors for their part need to observe the principles of serving the public interest and maintaining the highest degree of integrity, objectivity, and independence. Audit organizations have the responsibility to ensure (1) independence and objectivity are maintained in all phases of the assignment, (2) professional judgment is used in planning and performing the work and in reporting the results, (3) the work is performed by personnel who are professionally competent and collectively have the necessary skills

---

[4] Comptroller General of the United States, *Government Auditing Standards*, 2003 Revision, paragraph 1.18.

and knowledge, and (4) an independent peer review is periodically performed resulting in an opinion issued as to whether an audit organization's systems of quality control is designed and being complied with to provide reasonable assurance of conforming with professional standards.[5]

Figure 25.1

Relationship of AICPA Standards and IIA Standards to GAGAS and Single Audit Act

Generally Accepted Auditing Standards (AICPA) All External Audits	Standards for the Professional Practice of Internal Auditing (IIA) All Internal Audits

GAGAS GENERAL STANDARDS All GAGAS Audits

GAGAS Financial Audit - Fieldwork and Reporting Standards	GAGAS Performance Audit Fieldwork And Reporting Standards	GAGAS Attestation Engagements Fieldwork and Reporting Standards

The Single Audit Act Requirements

.03 Types of Government Audits and Attestation Engagements

Types of government audits and attestation engagements include financial audits, attestation engagements, performance audits, and nonaudit services provided by audit organizations. Financial audits are concerned with providing reasonable assurance that financial statements are presented fairly in all material respects in conformity with Generally

---

[5] *Ibid.*, paragraph 1.27.

Accepted Accounting Principles (GAAP) or with a comprehensive basis of accounting other than GAAP. Additional objectives of a financial audit include:

- Providing special reports for specified elements, accounts, or items of a financial statement;
- Reviewing interim financial information;
- Issuing letters for underwriters and certain other requesting parties;
- Reporting on the processing of transactions by service organizations; and
- Auditing compliance with regulations relating to federal award expenditures and other governmental financial assistance in conjunction with or as a by-product of a financial statement audit.[6]

Attestation engagements concern examining, reviewing, or performing agreed-upon procedures on a subject matter or an assertion about a subject matter and reporting on the results. Possible subjects of attestation engagements could include the following:

- An entity's internal control over financial reporting;
- An entity's compliance with requirements of specified laws, regulations, rules, contracts, or grants;
- The effectiveness of an entity's internal control over compliance with specified requirements, such as those governing the bidding for, accounting for, and reporting on grants and contracts;
- Management's discussion and analysis (MD&A);
- Prospective financial statements or pro-forma financial information;
- The reliability of performance measures;
- Final contract cost;
- Allowability and reasonableness of proposed contract amounts; and
- Specific procedures performed on a subject matter.[7]

Performance audits entail an objective and systematic examination of evidence to provide an independent assessment of the performance and management of a program against objective criteria as well as assessments that provide a prospective focus or that synthesize information on best

---

[6] *Ibid.*, paragraph 205.   [7] *Ibid.*, paragraph 2.07.

practices or cross-cutting issues.[8] Performance audits encompass a wide variety of objectives including:

- Assessing program effectiveness and results;
- Economy and efficiency;
- Internal control;
- Compliance with legal and other requirements; and
- Objectives related to providing prospective analyses, guidance, or summary information.[9]

Audit organizations may also perform nonaudit services that do not impair the audit organization's independence as defined by the general standards of GAGAS. Nonaudit services differ from financial audits, attestation engagements, and performance audits in that auditors perform tasks requested by management that directly support the entity's operation, or provide information or data to a requesting party without providing verification, analysis, or evaluation of the information or data, and therefore, the work does not usually provide a basis for conclusions, recommendations, or opinions on the information or data. Nonaudit services may or may not result in a report and are synonymous with consulting services. GAGAS does not cover nonaudit services and auditors should not report that these services were conducted according to GAGAS.[10]

.04 GAGAS General Standards

GAGAS general standards cover the independence of the audit organization and its individual auditors, the exercise of professional judgment in the performance of work, and the preparation of related reports; the competence of audit staff; and the existence of quality control systems and external peer reviews. The general standards provide the underlying framework for effectively applying the fieldwork and general standards.[11]

The GAGAS general standard relating to independence reads:

> In all matters relating to the audit work, the audit organization and the individual auditor, whether government or public, should be free both in fact and appearance from personal, external, and organizational impairments to independence.[12]

Personal impairments to independence result from relationships and beliefs that might cause auditors to limit the extent of the inquiry, limit disclosure, or weaken or slant audit findings in any way.[13] Personal impairments of individual auditors include but are not limited to the following:

1. Immediate family (spouse, spouse equivalent, or dependent) or close family member (parent, sibling, or nondependent child)

---

[8] *Ibid.*, paragraph 2.09.
[9] *Ibid.*, paragraph 2.09.
[10] *Ibid.*, paragraphs 2.14–2.15.
[11] *Ibid.*, paragraph 3.02.
[12] *Ibid.*, paragraph 3.03.
[13] *Ibid.*, paragraph 3.07.

¶ 2504.04

who is a director or officer of the audited entity, or as an employee of the audited entity is in a position to exert direct and significant influence over the entity or the program under audit;

2. Financial interest that is direct, or is significant/material though indirect, in the audited entity or program;

3. Responsibility for managing an entity or decision making that could affect operations of the entity or program being audited; for example as a director, officer, or other senior position of the entity, activity, or program being audited, or as a member of management in any decision making, supervisory, or ongoing monitoring function for the entity, activity, or program under audit (Auditors are not precluded from auditing pension plans that they participate in if (1) the auditor has no control over the investment strategy, benefits, or other management issues associated with the pension plan and (2) the auditor belongs to such pension plan as part of his/her employment with the audit organization, provided that the plan is normally offered to all employees in equivalent employment positions);

4. Concurrent or subsequent performance of an audit by the same individual who maintained the official accounting records when such services involved preparing source documents or originating data, in electronic or other form; posting transactions (whether coded by management or not coded); authorizing, executing, or consummating transactions (for example, approving invoices, payrolls, claims, or other payments of the entity or program being audited); maintaining an entity's bank account or otherwise having custody of the audited entity's funds; or otherwise exercising authority on behalf of the entity, or having authority to do so;

5. Preconceived ideas toward individuals, groups, organizations, or objectives of a particular program that could bias the audit;

6. Biases, including those induced by political, ideological, or social convictions, that result from employment in, or loyalty to, a particular type of policy, group, organization, or level of government; and

7. Seeking employment with an audited organization during the conduct of the audit.[14]

Because it is impossible to identify every situation that could result in a personal impairment, audit organizations should establish requirements

---

[14] *Ibid.*, paragraph 3.07.

¶ 2504.04

to identify personal impairments and assure compliance with GAGAS independence standards that:

1. Will enable the identification of personal impairments to independence, including whether performing nonaudit services affects the subject matter of audits and applying safeguards to appropriately reduce that risk;

2. Communicate the audit organization's policies and procedures to all auditors in the organization and assure understanding of requirements through training or other means such as auditors periodically acknowledging their understanding;

3. Establish internal policies and procedures to monitor compliance with the audit organization's policies and procedures;

4. Establish a disciplinary mechanism to promote compliance with the audit organization's policies and procedures; and

5. Stress the importance of independence and the expectation that auditors will always act in the public interest.[15]

Audit organizations should comply with the following safeguards concerning nonaudit services:

1. The audit organization should document its consideration of the nonaudit services as discussed in GAGAS, paragraph 3.13, including documentation for its rationale that providing the nonaudit services does not violate the two overarching principles.

2. Before performing nonaudit services, the audit organization should establish and document an understanding with the audited entity regarding the objectives, scope of work, and product or deliverables of the nonaudit service. The audit organization should also establish and document an understanding with management that (1) management is responsible for the substantive outcomes of the work and, therefore, has a responsibility to be in a position in fact and appearance to make an informed judgment on the results of the nonaudit service and (2) the audited entity complies with the following:

    a. Designates a management-level individual to be responsible and accountable for overseeing the nonaudit service,

    b. Establishes and monitors the performance of the nonaudit service to ensure that it meets management's objectives,

---

[15] *Ibid.*, paragraph 3.08.

¶ 2504.04

> c. Makes any decisions that involve management functions related to the nonaudit service and accepts full responsibility for such decisions, and
>
> d. Evaluates the adequacy of the services performed and any findings that result.

3. The audit organization should preclude personnel who provided the nonaudit services from planning, conducting, or reviewing audit work of subject matter involving the nonaudit service under the overarching principle that auditors cannot audit their own work.

4. The audit organization is precluded from reducing the scope and extent of the audit work below the level that would be appropriate if an unrelated party performed the nonaudit work.

5. The audit organization's quality control systems for compliance with independence requirements should include: (1) policies and procedures to assure consideration of the effect on the ongoing, planned, and future audits when deciding whether to provide nonaudit services, and (2) a requirement to have the understanding with management of the audited entity documented.

6. By their nature, certain nonaudit services impair the audit organization's ability to not to audit its own work or make management decisions. In these cases, the audit organization should communicate to management of the audited entity that the audit organization will not be able to perform subsequent audit work related to the subject matter of the nonaudit service.

7. For individual audits selected for inspection during a peer review, all related nonaudit services should be disclosed to the audit organization's peer reviewer, and the audit documentation required by the independence standards should be made available for inclusion in the audit organization's peer review.[16]

The following are some nonaudit services that would not create an impairment to the audit organization's independence as long as (1) auditors avoid situations that would conflict with the overarching principles of providing management functions and auditing their own work and (2) provide safeguards as identified above:

1. Providing basic accounting assistance limited to services such as preparing draft financial statements that are based on management's chart of accounts and trial balance and any adjusting, correcting, and closing entries that have been approved by management; preparing draft notes to the financial statements

---
[16] *Ibid.,* paragraph 3.17.

based on information determined and approved by management; preparing a trial balance based on management's chart of accounts; maintaining depreciation schedules for which management has determined the method of depreciation, rate of depreciation, and salvage value of the asset. The audit organization, however, cannot maintain or prepare the audited entity's basic accounting records or maintain or take responsibility for basic financial or other records that the audit organization will audit. As part of this prohibition, auditors should not post transactions (whether coded or not coded) to the entity's financial records or to other records that subsequently provide data to the entity's financial records.

2. Providing payroll services limited to services such as computing pay amounts for the entity's employees based on entity-maintained and approved time records, salaries or pay rates, and deductions from pay; generating unsigned payroll checks; transmitting client approved payroll data to a financial institution provided management has approved the transmission and limited the financial institution to making payments only to previously approved individuals. In cases in which the audit organization was processing the entity's entire payroll and payroll was a material amount to the subject matter of the audit, this would be a violation of one of the overarching principles of independence and the auditors would not be deemed independent under GAGAS.

3. Providing appraisal or valuation services limited to services such as reviewing the work of the entity or a specialist employed by the entity where the entity or specialist provides the primary evidence for the balances recorded in financial statements or other information that will be audited; valuing an entity's pension, other post-employment benefit, or similar liabilities provided management has determined and taken responsibility for all significant assumptions and data.

4. Preparing an entity's indirect cost proposal or cost allocation plans provided management assumes responsibility for all significant assumptions and data.

5. Providing advisory services on information technology limited to services such as advising on system design, system installation, and system security if management, in addition to the safeguards listed above, acknowledges responsibility for the design, installation, and internal control over the entity's system and does not rely on the auditors' work as the primary basis for determining (1) whether to implement a new system, (2) the

¶ 2504.04

adequacy of the new system design, (3) the adequacy of major design changes to an existing system, and (4) the adequacy of the system to comply with regulatory or other requirements. However, the audit organization should not operate or supervise the operation of the entity's information technology system.

6. Providing human resource services to assist management in its evaluation of potential candidates when the services are limited to activities such as serving on an evaluation panel to review applications or interviewing candidates to provide input to management in arriving at a listing of best qualified applicants to be provided to management. The auditors should not recommend a single individual for a specific position, nor should the auditors conduct an executive search or a recruiting program for the audited entity.

7. Preparing routine tax filings in accordance with federal tax laws, rules, and regulations of the IRS, and state and local tax authorities, and any other applicable laws.

8. Gathering and reporting on unverified external or third-party data to aid legislative and administrative decision making.

9. Advising an entity regarding its performance of internal control self-assessments.

10. Assisting a legislative body by developing questions for use at a hearing.[17]

External impairments involve factors external to the audit organization that may restrict its independence. External impairments to independence occur when auditors are deterred from acting objectively and exercising professional skepticism by pressures, actual or perceived, from management and employees of the audited entity or oversight organizations. Examples include:

1. External interference or influence that could improperly or imprudently limit or modify the scope of an audit or threaten to do so, including pressure to reduce inappropriately the extent of work performed in order to reduce costs or fees;

2. External interference with the selection or application of audit procedures or in the selection of transactions to be examined;

3. Unreasonable restrictions on the time allowed to complete an audit or issue the report;

4. Interference external to the audit organization in the assignment, appointment, and promotion of audit personnel;

---

[17] *Ibid.*, paragraph 3.18.

¶ 2504.04

5. Restrictions on funds or other resources provided to the audit organization that adversely affect the audit organization's ability to carry out its responsibilities;

6. Authority to overrule or to inappropriately influence the auditors' judgment as to the appropriate content of the report;

7. Threat of replacement over a disagreement with the contents of an audit report, the auditors' conclusions, or the application of an accounting principle or other criteria; and

8. Influences that jeopardize the auditors' continued employment for reasons other than incompetence, misconduct, or the need for audit services.[18]

A government audit organization's independence may be impaired by its place within government and the structure of the government entity that the audit organization is assigned to audit. In general, a government audit organization is independent of a third party if the entity that employs it is independent of the third party. The status of the audit organization within the entity itself must be evaluated using the following factors:

1. First, a government audit organization may be presumed to be free from organizational impairments to independence from the audited entity to report externally if the audit organization is:

    - Assigned to a level of government other than the one to which the audited entity is assigned (federal, state, or local), for example, a federal auditor auditing a state government program, or

    - Assigned to a different branch of government within the same level of government as the audited entity, for example, a legislative auditor auditing an executive branch program.

2. Second, a government audit organization may also be presumed to be free from organizational impairments for external reporting if the audit organization's head meets any of the following criteria:

    - Directly elected by voters of the jurisdiction being audited;

    - Elected or appointed by a legislative body subject to removal by a legislative body and reports the results of audits to and is accountable to a legislative body;

    - Appointed by someone other than a legislative body, so long as the appointment is confirmed by a legislative body and removal from the position is subject to oversight or approval

---

[18] *Ibid.*, paragraph 3.19.

¶ 2504.04

by a legislative body, and reports the results of audits to and is accountable to a legislative body; or

- Appointed by, accountable to, reports to, and can only be removed by a statutorily created governing body, the majority of whose members are independently elected or appointed and come from outside the organization being audited.[19]

In addition, the government auditing organization should install the following safeguards to prevent organizational impairments:

1. Statutory protections that prevent the abolishment of the audit organization by the audited entity;

2. Statutory protections that require that if the head of the audit organization is removed from office, the head of the agency should report this fact and the reasons for the removal to the legislative body;

3. Statutory protections that prevent the audited entity from interfering with the initiation, scope, timing, and completion of any audit;

4. Statutory protections that prevent the audited entity from interfering with the reporting on any audit, including the findings, conclusions, and recommendations, or the manner, means, or timing of the audit organization's reports;

5. Statutory protections that require the audit organization to report to a legislative body or other independent governing body on a recurring basis;

6. Statutory protections that give the audit organization sole authority over the selection, retention, advancement, and dismissal of its staff; and

7. Statutory access to records and documents that relate to the agency, program, or function being audited.[20]

A head of a government internal audit organization should be accountable to the head or deputy head of the government entity, required to report the results of the audit organization's work to the head or deputy head of the government entity, and located organizationally outside the staff or line management function of the unit under attack.[21]

The general standard relating to professional judgment reads:
Professional judgment should be used in planning and performing audits and attestation engagements and in reporting the results.[22]

---

[19] *Ibid.*, paragraph 3.24.
[20] *Ibid.*, paragraph 3.25.
[21] *Ibid.*, paragraph 3.27.
[22] *Ibid.*, paragraph 3.39.

¶ 2504.04

This standard requires auditors to exercise reasonable care and diligence and to observe the principles of serving the public interest and maintaining the highest degree of integrity, objectivity, and independence in applying professional judgment to all aspects of their work. This standard also imposes a responsibility upon each auditor performing work under GAGAS to observe GAGAS. If auditors state they are performing their work in accordance with GAGAS, they should justify any departures from GAGAS. Auditors should use professional judgment in all aspects of an engagement.

Professional judgment requires auditors to exercise professional skepticism, which is an attitude that includes a questioning mind and a critical assessment of evidence. Auditors neither assume that management is dishonest nor assume unquestioned honesty. Absolute assurance is not attainable because of the nature of evidence and the characteristics of fraud. Therefore, an audit or attestation engagement conducted in accordance with GAGAS may not detect a material misstatement or significant inaccuracy, whether from error or fraud, illegal acts, or violations of provisions of contracts or grant agreements. Accordingly, while this standard places responsibility on each auditor and audit organization to exercise professional judgment in planning and performing an assignment, it does not imply unlimited responsibility, nor does it imply infallibility on the part of either the individual auditor or the audit organization.[23]

The general standard relating to competence reads:

The staff assigned to perform the audit or attestation engagement should collectively possess adequate professional competence for the tasks required.

This standard places responsibility on the audit organization to ensure that each audit or attestation engagement is performed by staff that collectively have the knowledge, skills, and experience necessary for that assignment. Audit organizations should have a process for recruitment, hiring, continuous development, and evaluation of staff to assist the organization in maintaining a workforce that has adequate competence. Specific technical knowledge and competence required of government auditors include the following:

1. Knowledge of GAGAS applicable to the type of work they are assigned and the education, skills, and experience to apply such knowledge to the work being performed;

2. General knowledge of the environment in which the audited entity operates and the subject matter under review;

3. Skills to communicate clearly and effectively, both orally and in writing; and

4. Skills appropriate for the work being performed. For example:

---

[23] *Ibid.*, paragraphs 3.34–3.38.

¶ 2504.04

- If the work requires use of statistical sampling, the staff or specialists should include persons with statistical sampling skills;
- If the work requires extensive review of information systems, the staff or specialists should include persons with information technology skills;
- If the work involves review of complex engineering data, the staff or specialists should include persons with engineering skills; or
- If the work involves the use of specialized audit methodologies or analytical techniques, such as the use of complex survey instruments, actuarial-based estimates, or statistical analysis tests, the staff or specialists should include persons with skills in those methodologies or techniques.[24]

In addition, auditors that perform financial audits should be knowledgeable in GAAP and GAAS and should be licensed CPAs. In addition, auditors performing attestation functions should be familiar with the AICPA's Statement on Standards for Attestation Engagements (SSAE). Auditors performing work under GAGAS should complete, every two years, at least 80 hours of Continuing Professional Education (CPE) that directly enhances the auditor's professional proficiency with at least 24 hours being in subjects directly related to government auditing, the government environment, or the specific or unique environment in which the audited entity operates. At least 20 hours of the 80 should be completed in any one year of the two-year period.[25]

> The general standard relating to quality control and assurance reads:
> Each audit organization performing audits and/or attestation engagements in accordance with GAGAS should have an appropriate internal quality control system in place and should undergo an external peer review.

An audit organization's system of quality control includes the audit organization's policies and procedures adopted to ensure that the organization complies with applicable standards governing audits and attestation engagements. An audit organization's internal quality control system should include procedures for monitoring, on an ongoing basis, whether the policies and procedures related to the standards are suitably designed and are being effectively applied. The nature and extent of an audit organization's internal quality control system depends on a number of factors, such as its size, the degree of operating autonomy allowed its personnel and its audit offices, the nature of its work, its organizational structure, and appropriate cost-benefit considerations.

Audit organizations performing audits and attestation engagements in accordance with GAGAS should have an external peer review of their

---

[24] *Ibid.*, paragraphs 3.40–3.42.   [25] *Ibid.*, paragraph 3.45.

¶ 2504.04

auditing and attestation engagement practices at least once every three years by reviewers independent of the audit organization being reviewed. The external peer review should determine whether, during the period under review, the reviewed audit organization's internal quality control system was adequate and whether quality control policies and procedures were being complied with to provide the audit organization with reasonable assurance of conforming with applicable professional standards. Members of the external peer review team should meet the following requirements:

1. Each review team member should have current knowledge of GAGAS and of the government environment relative to the work being reviewed.

2. Each review team member should be independent (as defined in GAGAS) of the audit organization being reviewed, its staff, and the audits and attestation engagements selected for the external peer review.

3. Each review team member should have knowledge on how to perform a peer review.[26]

The peer review engagement should meet the following requirements:

1. The peer review should include a review of the audit organization's internal quality control policies and procedures, including related monitoring procedures, audit and attestation engagement reports, audit and attest documentation, and other necessary documents. The review should also include interviews with various levels of the reviewed audit organization's professional staff to assess their understanding of and compliance with relevant quality control policies and procedures.

2. The review team should use one of the following approaches to selecting audits and attestation engagements for review: (1) select audits and attestation engagements that provide a reasonable cross section of the assignments performed by the reviewed audit organization in accordance with GAGAS or (2) select audits and attestation engagements that provide a reasonable cross section of the reviewed audit organization's work subject to quality control requirements, including one or more assignments performed in accordance with GAGAS.

3. The peer review should be sufficiently comprehensive to provide a reasonable basis for concluding whether the reviewed audit organization's system of quality control was complied with to provide the organization with reasonable assurance of conforming to professional standards in the conduct of its work.

---

[26] *Ibid.*, paragraph 3.53.

¶ 2504.04

4. The review team should prepare a written report(s) communicating the results of the external peer review. The report should indicate the scope of the review, including any limitations thereon, and should express an opinion on whether the system of quality control of the reviewed audit organization's audit and/or attestation engagement practices was adequate and was being complied with during the year reviewed to provide the audit organization with reasonable assurance of conforming with professional standards for audits and attestation engagements. The report should state the professional standards to which the reviewed audit organization is being held. The report should also describe the reasons for any modification of the opinion. When there are matters that resulted in a modification to the opinion, reviewers should report a detailed description of the findings and recommendations, either in the peer review report or in a separate letter of comment or management letter, to enable the reviewed audit organization to take appropriate actions. The written report should refer to the letter of comment or management letter if such a letter is issued along with a modified report.[27]

Audit organizations should ensure that copies of their most recent peer review report are sent to prospective clients, other auditors relying on their audits, and oversight boards.

.05 GAGAS Standards for Financial Audits

GAGAS standards for financial audits include fieldwork standards and reporting standards (in addition to the GAAS fieldwork and reporting standards. The financial audit fieldwork standards include auditor communication; considering previous results of audits and attestation engagements; detecting material misstatements from violations of contract or grant provisions; pursuing indications of fraud, illegal acts, violations of contract or grant provisions; developing elements of a finding for a financial audit; and audit documentation.

The financial audit fieldwork standard related to auditor communication in a financial audit reads:

> Auditors should communicate information regarding the nature, timing, and extent of planned testing and reporting and the level of assurance provided to officials of the audited entity and to the individuals contracting for or requesting the audit.[28]

GAGAS broadens the parties with whom auditors must communicate by requiring auditors to communicate specific information during the planning stages of a financial audit, including any potential restriction of the auditors' reports, to reduce the risk that the needs or expectations of the parties involved may be misinterpreted. Auditors should use their profes-

---

[27] Ibid., paragraph 3.54.   [28] Ibid., paragraph 4.06.

sional judgment to determine the form, content, and frequency of the communication; although, written communication is preferred.[29]

Auditors should communicate their responsibilities for the engagement to the appropriate officials of the audited entity, including: the head of the audited entity, the audit committee or board of directors or other equivalent oversight body in the absence of an audit committee, and the individual who possesses a sufficient level of authority and responsibility for the financial reporting process, such as the chief financial officer. In situations in which auditors are performing the audit under a contract with a party other than the officials of the audited entity, or pursuant to a third party request, auditors should also communicate with the individuals contracting for or requesting the audit, such as contracting officials or members or staff of legislative committees. When auditors are performing the audit pursuant to a law or regulation, auditors should communicate with the members or staff of legislative committees who have oversight of the entity being audited.[30]

Auditors should coordinate communications with the responsible government audit organization and/or management of the audited entity and may use the engagement letter to keep interested parties informed. If an audit is terminated before it is completed, auditors should write a memorandum for the record that summarizes the results of the work, and this requirement applies only to situations where the law or regulation specifically identifies the entity to be audited.

In communicating the nature of services and level of assurance provided, auditors should specifically address their planned work and reporting related to testing internal control over financial reporting and compliance with laws, regulations, and provisions of contracts or grant agreements. During the planning stages of an audit, auditors should communicate their responsibilities for testing and reporting on internal control over financial reporting and compliance with laws, regulations, and provisions of contracts or grant agreements. Such communication should include the nature of any additional testing of internal control and compliance required by laws, regulations, and provisions of contracts or grant agreements, or otherwise requested, and whether the auditors are planning on providing opinions on internal control over financial reporting and compliance with laws, regulations, and provisions of contracts or grant agreements.[31]

The financial audit fieldwork standard related to considering the results of previous audits and attestation engagements for financial audits performed in accordance with GAGAS reads as follows:

> Auditors should consider the results of previous audits and attestation engagements and follow up on known significant findings and recommendations that directly relate to the objectives of the audit being undertaken.[32]

---

[29] Ibid., paragraph 4.07.
[30] Ibid., paragraphs 4.08–4.09.
[31] Ibid., paragraph 4.10.
[32] Ibid., paragraph, 4.14.

¶ 2504.05

Auditors need to exercise professional judgment in determining the prior periods, the level of work to follow up on significant findings, and the effect of risk assessment and audit procedures in planning the current audit.

The financial audit fieldwork standards concerning detecting material misstatements resulting from violations of contract or grant provisions reads as follows:

> Auditors should design the audit to provide reasonable assurance of detecting material misstatements resulting from violations of provisions of contracts or grant agreements that have a direct and material effect on the determination of financial statement amounts or other financial data significant to the audit objectives. If specific information comes to the auditors' attention that provides evidence concerning the existence of possible violations of provisions of contracts or grant agreements that could have a material indirect effect on the determination of financial statement amounts or other financial data significant to the audit objectives, auditors should apply audit procedures specifically directed to ascertain whether violations of provisions of contracts or grant agreements have occurred or are likely to have occurred.
>
> Auditors should be alert to situations or transactions that could be indicative of abuse, and if indications of abuse exist that could significantly affect the financial statement amounts or other financial data, auditors should apply audit procedures specifically directed to ascertain whether abuse has occurred and the effect on the financial statement amounts or other financial data.[33]

Basically this standard requires the auditor to specifically find material misstatements due to noncompliance with contracts or grants. This means planning the audit and evaluating evidence for the existence of material noncompliance with contracts or grants. When an auditor uncovers deficiencies in internal control, fraud, illegal acts, violations of contracts or grants, and abuse, then the auditor is required by GAGAS to perform additional audit procedures to develop the finding until the relevant audit objectives are met.

The financial audit fieldwork standard concerning audit documentation reads as follows:

> Audit documentation related to planning, conducting, and reporting on the audit should contain sufficient information to enable an experienced auditor who has had no previous connection with the audit to ascertain from the audit documentation the evidence that supports the auditors' significant judgments and conclusions. Audit documentation should contain support for findings, conclusions, and recommendations before auditors issue their report.[34]

The auditor should design the form and content of audit documentation to meet the circumstances of the particular audit. Likewise the auditor should use the professional judgment to determine the quantity, type, and content of audit documentation. Audit documentation should be prepared to provide a clear understanding of its purpose and source and the conclusions the auditors reached, and it should be appropriately organized to provide a clear link to the findings, conclusions, and recommendations

---

[33] *Ibid.*, paragraph 4.17. [34] *Ibid.*, paragraph 4.22.

contained in the audit report. Audit documentation should also contain the following items:

1. The objectives, scope, and methodology of the audit;

2. The auditors' determination that certain additional government auditing standards do not apply or that an applicable standard was not followed, the reasons therefore, and the known effect that not following the applicable standard had, or could have had, on the audit;

3. The auditors' consideration that the planned audit procedures are designed to achieve audit objectives when evidential matter obtained is highly dependent on computerized information systems and is material to the objective of the audit and that the auditors are not relying on the effectiveness of internal control over those computerized systems that produced the information. The audit documentation should specifically address:

  - The rationale for determining the nature, timing, and extent of planned audit procedures;

  - The kinds and competence of available evidential matter produced outside a computerized information system and/or plans for direct testing of data produced from a computerized information system; and

  - The effect on the audit report if evidential matter to be gathered does not afford a reasonable basis for achieving the objectives of the audit.

4. Evidence of supervisory review, before the audit report is issued, of the work performed that supports findings, conclusions, and recommendations contained in the audit report.[35]

Audit organizations need to adequately safeguard the audit documentation associated with any particular engagement. Audit organizations should develop clearly defined policies and criteria to deal with situations where requests are made by outside parties to obtain access to audit documentation, especially in connection with situations where an outside party attempts to obtain indirectly through the auditor information that it is unable to obtain directly from the audited entity. In developing such policies, audit organizations need to consider applicable laws and regulations that apply to the audit organizations or the audited entity.[36]

Reporting standards for GAGAS financial audits cover the following topics: reporting auditors' compliance with GAGAS; reporting on internal controls and compliance with laws, regulations, contracts and grants; reporting deficiencies in internal control, fraud, illegal acts, violations of

---

[35] *Ibid.*, paragraph 4.24.   [36] *Ibid.*, paragraphs 4.25–4.26.

¶ 2504.05

contracts or grant agreements, and abuse; reporting views of responsible officials; reporting privileged and confidential information; and report issuance and distribution. GAGAS requires auditors to state in their reports that the audit was performed in accordance with GAGAS or if GAGAS was not followed then the specific GAGAS requirement(s) not being followed, the reason it is not being followed, and the audit impact of not following the standards. In addition, auditors may include in the results of other financial audits in addition to the GAGAS financial report.[37]

The financial audit reporting standard concerning internal control reads:

> When providing an opinion or a disclaimer on financial statements, auditors should include in their report on the financial statements either a (1) description of the scope of the auditors' testing of internal control over financial reporting and compliance with laws, regulations, and provisions of contracts or grant agreements and the results of those tests or an opinion, if sufficient work was performed, or (2) reference to the separate report(s) containing that information. If auditors report separately, the opinion or disclaimer should contain a reference to the separate report containing this information and state that the separate report is an integral part of the audit and should be considered in assessing the results of the audit.[38]

Auditors may report on these matters in a separate report or reports. When auditors report on these matters as part of the opinion or disclaimer on the financial statements, they should include an introduction summarizing key findings in the audit of the financial statements and the related internal control and compliance work. Auditors should not issue this introduction as a stand-alone report. When auditors report these matters separately (including separate reports bound in the same document), the opinion or disclaimer on the financial statements should state that the auditors are issuing those additional reports. The opinion or disclaimer on the financial statements should also state that the reports on internal control over financial reporting and compliance with laws and regulations and provisions of contracts or grant agreements are an integral part of a GAGAS audit and should be considered in assessing the results of the audit.[39]

The financial audit reporting standard dealing with reporting deficiencies in internal control, fraud, illegal acts, violations of contracts or grants, and abuse is stated thusly:

> For financial audits, including audits of financial statements in which the auditor provides an opinion or disclaimer, auditors should report, as applicable to the objectives of the audit, (1) deficiencies in internal control considered to be reportable conditions as defined in AICPA standards, (2) all instances of fraud and illegal acts unless clearly inconsequential, and (3) significant violations of provisions of contracts or grant agreements and abuse. In some circumstances, auditors should report fraud, illegal acts, violations of provisions of contracts or grant agreements, and abuse directly to parties external to the audited entity.[40]

---

[37] *Ibid.*, paragraphs, 5.06–5.07.
[38] *Ibid.*, paragraph 5.05.
[39] *Ibid.*, paragraphs 5.09–5.10.
[40] *Ibid.*, paragraph 5.12.

Auditors should report deficiencies in internal control as defined in the AICPA standards and discussed in ¶ 303.01 of this audit guide. The auditor should identify those reportable conditions that individually or in the aggregate constitute material weaknesses. Auditors should place their findings in proper perspective by providing a description of the work performed that resulted in the finding. To give the reader a basis for judging the prevalence and consequences of these findings, the instances identified should be related to the population or the number of cases examined and is quantified in terms of dollar value, if appropriate.

To the extent possible, in presenting audit findings such as deficiencies in internal control, auditors should develop the elements of criteria, condition, cause, and effect to assist management or oversight officials of the audited entity in understanding the need for taking corrective action. In addition, if auditors are able to sufficiently develop the findings, they should provide recommendations for corrective action. The following is a description of the elements of a finding:

1. Criteria: The required or desired state or what is expected from the program or operation.

2. Condition: What the auditors found regarding the actual situation. Reporting the scope or extent of the condition allows the report user to gain an accurate perspective.

3. Cause: The factor or factors responsible for the difference between condition and criteria. In reporting the cause, auditors may consider whether the evidence provides a reasonable and convincing argument for why the stated cause is the key factor or factors contributing to the difference as opposed to other possible causes. The auditors also may consider whether the identified cause could serve as a basis for the recommendations.

4. Effect: The difference between what the auditors found (condition) and what should be (criteria). Effect is easier to understand when it is stated clearly, concisely, and, if possible, in quantifiable terms. The significance of the reported effect can be demonstrated through credible evidence.[41]

Auditors should separately report deficiencies in internal control that are not reportable conditions in a management letter to officials of the audited entity unless the deficiencies are clearly inconsequential considering both quantitative and qualitative factors. Auditors should refer to the separate management letter in the report on internal control. Auditors should include in their audit documentation descriptions of all communications to officials of the audited entity about deficiencies in internal control found during the audit.[42]

---

[41] *Ibid.*, paragraph 5.15.   [42] *Ibid.*, paragraph 5.16.

¶ 2504.05

GAGAS further requires auditors to report fraud and illegal acts in writing and also include reporting on significant violations of provisions of contracts or grant agreements and significant abuse. To give the reader a basis for judging the prevalence and consequences of these findings, the instances identified should be related to the population or the number of cases examined and is quantified in terms of dollar value, if appropriate. If the results cannot be projected, auditors should limit their conclusion to the items tested. To the extent possible, auditors should develop in their report the elements of criteria, condition, cause, and effect when fraud, illegal acts, violations of provisions of contracts or grant agreements, or abuse is found. Auditors should develop their findings following the guidance for reporting deficiencies in internal control as described above.[43]

When auditors detect immaterial violations of provisions of contracts or grant agreements or abuse, they should communicate those findings in a management letter to officials of the audited entity unless the findings are clearly inconsequential considering both qualitative and quantitative factors. Auditors should refer to that management letter in their audit report on compliance. Auditors should include in their audit documentation evidence of all communications to officials of the audited entity about fraud, illegal acts, violations of provisions of contracts or grant agreements, and abuse.[44]

GAGAS require auditors to report fraud, illegal acts, violations of provisions of contracts or grant agreements, and abuse directly to parties outside the audited entity in when the audited entity is required by law or regulation to report such matters, and management fails to take appropriate action to remedy the fraud, noncompliance, or abuse. These requirements are in addition to any direct reporting legal requirements. Auditors should meet these requirements even if they have resigned or been dismissed from the audit prior to its completion. Auditors should limit their public reporting to matters that would not compromise those proceedings, such as information that is already a part of the public record.[45] If the auditors' report discloses deficiencies in internal control, fraud, illegal acts, violations of contracts or grants, or abuse, auditors should report the views of responsible officials concerning the findings, conclusions, recommendations, and planned corrective actions. If certain pertinent information is prohibited from general disclosure, then the audit report should state the nature of the information omitted and the requirement that makes the omission necessary. Government auditors should submit audit reports to the appropriate officials of the audited entity and to appropriate officials of the organizations requiring or arranging for the audits, unless legal restrictions prevent it. Auditors should also send copies of the reports to other officials who have legal oversight authority or who may be responsible for acting on

---

[43] *Ibid.*, paragraphs 5.17–5.19.
[44] *Ibid.*, paragraph 5.20.
[45] *Ibid.*, paragraphs 5.21–5.25.

audit findings and recommendations and to others authorized to receive such reports. Unless the report is restricted by law or regulation, or contains privileged and confidential information, auditors should clarify that copies are made available for public inspection. Nongovernmental auditors should clarify report distribution responsibilities with the party contracting for the audit and follow the agreements reached.[46]

.06 GAGAS for Attestation Engagements

GAGAS for attestation engagements in addition to AICPA Statements on Standards for Attestation Engagements (SSAE) cover auditor communication, considering the results of previous audits and attestation engagements, internal control, detecting fraud and illegal acts, developing elements of findings for attestation engagements and attest documentation. In performing an attestation engagement, auditors issue an examination, a review, or an agreed-upon procedures report on a subject matter, or an assertion about a subject matter that is the responsibility of another party. An examination occurs when the auditor performs sufficient testing to express an opinion on whether the subject matter is based on the criteria in all material respects based on the criteria. In a review engagement, the auditor performs sufficient testing to express a conclusion about whether any information came to the auditors' attention that indicates the subject matter is not based on the criteria. Finally during an agreed upon procedures engagement, the auditor performs testing to issue a report of findings based on specific procedures performed on subject matter.[47]

Auditor communication should include information regarding the nature, timing, and extent of planned testing and reporting on the subject matter or assertion about the subject matter, including the level of assurance provided, to officials of the audited entity and to the individuals contracting for or requesting the attestation engagement. GAGAS does not require this communication to be in writing and the communication may be part of the communication for a larger audit if the attestation is a part of the audit. The parties the auditor should include in the communication include the head of the audited entity, the audit committee or board of directors, the individual who possesses a sufficient level of authority and responsibility for the subject matter, and any third parties who requested the attestation engagement.

Auditors should consider the results of previous audits and attestation engagements and follow up on known significant findings and recommendations that relate directly to the subject matter of the attestation engagement being performed. Auditors need to inquire of the audited entity's officials to identify previous engagements. Significant findings and recommendations are those that, if not corrected, could affect the results of the current engagement. Auditors should use their professional judgment in

---

[46] Ibid., paragraphs 5.26–5.38. [47] Ibid., paragraphs 6.01–6.03.

determining prior periods to be considered, and the level of work necessary to follow up on significant findings and the effect on the risk assessment and attestation procedures in planning the current attestation engagement.[48]

In planning an attestation engagement, the auditor is required by GAGAS to "Obtain a sufficient understanding of internal control that is material to the subject matter or assertion to plan the engagement and design procedures to achieve the objectives of the attestation engagement."[49] Likewise, auditors should plan examination-level attestation engagements to provide reasonable assurance of detecting fraud, illegal acts, violations of provisions of contracts, or grants and abuse that could have a material effect on the subject matter of the attestation engagement. Auditors should be alert to situations or transactions that could be indicative of fraud, illegal acts, and violations of contracts, or abuse when planning the engagement. When the auditor identifies such risk factors, the auditor should document the risk factors identified and the auditor's response to those risk factors. The auditor also has the responsibility to determine if fraud, etc. has occurred and its affect on the current engagement. The auditor should comply with all legal and professional responsibilities in reporting instances of fraud, illegal acts, and etc. to the entity being audited and third parties.[50]

Auditors should ensure that engagement objectives are met in developing elements of findings. Likewise, attestation documentation should "contain sufficient information to enable an experienced auditor who has had not previous connection with the attestation engagement to ascertain from the attest documentation the evidence that supports the auditors' significant judgments and conclusions."[51] In addition to the attest documentation required by the AICPA standards, GAGAS required attest documentation for the following issues:

- The objectives, scope, and methodology of the attestation engagement, including any sampling and other selection criteria used;

- The auditor's determination that certain additional government auditing standards do not apply or that an applicable standard was not followed, the reasons therefore, and the known effect that not following the applicable standard had, or could have had, on the attestation engagement;

- The work performed to support significant judgments and conclusions, including descriptions of transactions and records examined;

---

[48] *Ibid.*, paragraphs, 6.10–6.12.
[49] *Ibid.*, paragraph 6.13.
[50] *Ibid.*, paragraphs 6.15–6.20.
[51] *Ibid.*, paragraph 6.22.

- The auditors' consideration that the planned attestation procedures are designed to achieve objectives of the attestation engagement when evidential matter obtained is highly dependent on computerized information systems and is material to the objective of the engagement, and the auditors are not relying on the effectiveness of internal control over those computerized systems that produced the information. The attest documentation should specifically address:

    a. The rationale for determining the nature, timing, and extent of planned audit procedures;

    b. The kinds and competence of available evidential matter produced outside a computerized information system, and/or plans for direct testing of data produced from a computerized information system; and

    c. The effect on the attestation engagement report if evidential matter to be gathered does not afford a reasonable basis for achieving the objectives of the engagement; and

    d. Evidence of supervisory reviews, before the report on the attestation engagement is issued, of the work performed that supports findings, conclusions, and recommendations contained in the report.[52]

Auditors should make arrangements to make attestation engagement documentation available, upon request, in a timely manner to other auditors. Contractual arrangements should provide for full and timely access to documentation to facilitate reliance by others on the auditors' work.[53] Additional GAGAS attest reporting standards include:

- The report should contain a statement that the engagement was performed according to GAGAS;

- Deficiencies in internal control, fraud, illegal acts, violations of provisions of contracts or grants, and abuse should be reported to the entity being audited and to third parties as required by professional standards and legal requirements;

- The report should include the views of responsible officials;

- Auditors should describe sensitive information omitted from the generally distributed report and the legal basis for restricting the distribution of that information; and

- Auditors should distribute the attestation engagement reports to officials having legal oversight authority for the entity being audited and to others authorized to receive such reports.[54]

---

[52] Ibid., paragraph 6.24.
[53] Ibid., paragraphs 6.25–6.26.
[54] Ibid., paragraphs 6.28–6.54.

These requirements follow the reporting requirements for financial audits described above.

.07 GAGAS for Performance Audits

GAGAS for performance audits include fieldwork and reporting standards. This chapter adds details to the general discussion of performance audits contained in ¶ 1806 and ¶ 1808, Chapter 18, "Operational Auditing." The GAGAS fieldwork standards deal with the following issues: planning the audit; supervising staff; obtaining sufficient, competent, and relevant evidence; and preparing audit documentation.

GAGAS requires auditors to adequately plan their work. Auditors should define audit objectives, and the scope and methodology to achieve those objectives. Planning is a continuous process throughout the audit and auditors should make adjustments as circumstances warrant. Planning should be documented and address the following issues:

- Considering the significance of various programs and the needs of potential users of the audit report;
- Obtaining an understanding of the program to be audited;
- Obtaining an understanding of internal control as it relates to the specific objectives and scope of the audit;
- Designing methodology and procedures to detect significant violations of legal and regulatory requirements, contract provisions, or grant agreements;
- Identifying the criteria needed to evaluate matters subject to audit (see paragraph 7.28);
- Considering the results of previous audits and attestation engagements that could affect the current audit objectives;
- Identifying potential sources of data that could be used as audit evidence;
- Considering whether the work of other auditors and experts may be used to satisfy some of the audit objectives;
- Providing appropriate and sufficient staff and other resources to perform the audit;
- Communicating general information concerning the planning and performance of the audit to management officials responsible for the program being audited and others as applicable; and
- Preparing an audit plan.[55]

---

[55] *Ibid.*, paragraphs 7.02–7.07.

In carrying out their audit plans, auditors should ensure that staff working on the engagement are properly supervised. Proper supervision involves: giving sufficient guidance to staff to complete their assignments, staying informed about significant problems encountered by staff assigned to them, reviewing the staff's work, and providing effective on-the-job training.[56] Auditors should obtain sufficient, competent, and relevant evidence to provide a reasonable basis for the auditor's findings and conclusions. Sufficiency of evidence refers to the amount of evidence required to persuade a knowledgeable person of the validity of the findings. Evidence is competent when it is valid, reliable, and consistent with fact, in other words, is the evidence accurate, authoritative, timely, and authentic. Finally, evidence is relevant when it has a logical relationship with the issue being addressed. The following factors are useful in judging the competence of evidence:

- Evidence obtained when internal controls are effective is more competent than evidence obtained when controls are weak or nonexistent. Auditors should be particularly careful in cases where controls are weak or nonexistent and should, therefore, plan alternative audit procedures to corroborate such evidence.

- Evidence obtained through the auditors' direct physical examination, observation, computation, and inspection is more competent than evidence obtained indirectly.

- Examination of original documents provides more competent evidence than do copies.

- Testimonial evidence obtained under conditions where persons may speak freely is more competent than testimonial evidence obtained under compromising conditions (for example, where the persons may be intimidated).

- Testimonial evidence obtained from an individual who is not biased or has complete knowledge about the area is more competent than testimonial evidence obtained from an individual who is biased or has only partial knowledge about the area.

- Evidence obtained from a credible third party may in some cases be more competent than that secured from management or other officials of the audited entity.[57]

Finally audit documentation standards are similar to those for financial, compliance, and attestation standards presented earlier in this chapter and do not need to be further presented.

GAGAS reporting standards for performance audit reports require that they include the objectives, scope, and methodology; the audit results,

---

[56] *Ibid.*, paragraphs 7.44–7.47. [57] *Ibid.*, paragraphs 7.52–7.53.

¶ 2504.07

including findings, conclusions, and recommendations, as appropriate; a reference to compliance with GAGAS; the views of responsible officials; and if applicable, the nature of any privileged and confidential information omitted.[58] GAGAS also requires the report to be timely, complete, accurate, objective, convincing, clear, and as concise as the subject permits.[59] Government auditors should submit performance audit reports to the appropriate officials of the audited entity and to the appropriate officials of the organizations requiring or arranging the audits unless legal restrictions prevent it. Auditors should also send copies of their report to other officials who have legal oversight authority or who may act on audit findings and to others authorized to receive such reports. Auditors should clarify whether copies are available for public inspection. Finally, nongovernmental auditors should arrange report distribution responsibilities with the party contracting for the audit and follow the agreements reached.[60]

.08 The Single Audit Act

Entities receiving over $300,000 in funds from the U.S. federal government must comply with GAGAS and the Single Audit Act. An organization should monitor the amount of aid it receives from the U.S. federal government especially if the amount is close to the $300,000 Single Audit Act threshold. This section describes the requirements of AICPA Statement of Position 98-3, *Audits of States, Local Governments, and Not-for-Profit Organizations Receiving Federal Awards* that contains guidance concerning the Single Audit Act and the Yellow Book.

Organizations that receive more than $300,000 in financial assistance from the U.S. federal government are required to comply with the provisions of the Single Audit Act and Generally Accepted Government Auditing Standards, also referred to as GAGAS or the Yellow Book. In addition, some U.S. federal agencies and state agencies may require the audit of the organization to comply with GAGAS. Additional requirements pertaining to the Single Audit Act are contained in OMB Circular A-133, OMB A-133 Compliance Supplement, and the Catalog of Federal Domestic Assistance (CFDA). SOP 98-3 then incorporates these requirements into the AICPA auditing standards.

The Single Audit Act was adopted to eliminate the need for multiple audits of recipients of U.S. federal government aid. The purpose of the single audit act is to give assurance to the granting agencies that the recipient entity complies with the provisions of their grants. The Single Audit Act was significantly revised in 1996. This revision raised the threshold for being subject to the Single Audit Act from $25,000 to $300,000 and changed the manner in which the auditor selects programs to be tested.

---

[58] *Ibid.*, paragraph, 8.07.
[59] *Ibid.*, paragraph, 8.38.
[60] *Ibid.*, paragraph, 8.54.

In completing an audit under the Single Audit Act, the organization may choose between a program specific audit and a single audit, depending on the type of aid received. If the organization receives funds under one grant, and the grant does not require a financial statement audit, then the organization may elect to have a program-specific audit. The auditor performing the program-specific audit will test the organization's controls that ensure compliance with the grants provisions and applicable laws and regulations, and the organization's actual compliance with the specific terms of the grant and the terms of laws and regulations affecting all recipients of U.S. Federal government aid. The auditor then must issue opinions concerning the internal control system and compliance with the terms of the grant and applicable laws and regulations.

Single audits are much more complex. First, the auditor must test whether the schedule of financial aid is presented fairly. This schedule lists the amounts and sources of aid from the U.S. federal government. The auditor must then identify major programs. Similar programs may be combined into a "cluster of programs" and treated as a single program if they have the same CFDA number, are awarded by the same agency for the same purpose, or are specified as clusters by OMB Circular A-133.

The auditor must first identify "Type A" and "Type B" programs. A Type A program is generally any program with Federal awards expended of the larger of $300,000 or three percent of total federal awards expended. All other programs are considered Type B programs. The next step is for the auditor to identify "low risk" Type A programs by determining if the program meets the following conditions:

- The program was audited as a major program in at least one of the two most recent audit periods,

- No audit findings were identified nor was the program was identified as high risk, and

- The program does not meet the risk criterion contained in OMB Circular A-133.

After the Type A programs are evaluated, the auditor must identify high-risk Type B programs in much the same manner. Major programs are basically all Type A programs except those classified as low risk and all high-risk Type B programs subject to two options. The auditor may either select one-half the high risk Type B programs up to the number of low risk Type A programs or one high risk Type B program for each low risk Type A program. In general, the number of major programs audited must equal at least 50 percent of the total amount of U.S. federal government aid expended. All Type A programs must be audited as major programs at least once every three years. However, auditees that meet the following criterion may be considered low risk:

¶ 2504.08

- Single audits were performed on an annual basis,
- The auditor's opinions on the financial statements and the schedule of expenditures of federal awards were unqualified,
- No material weaknesses in internal control were identified,
- None of the federal programs has audit findings from any of the following in either of the preceding two years in which they were classified as Type A programs:
  - Material weaknesses in internal controls,
  - Noncompliance with the provisions of laws, regulations, contracts, or grant agreements that had a material effect on the Type A programs, and
  - Known or likely questioned costs that exceed five percent of the total federal awards expended for a Type A program during the year.

The auditor of a "low risk" auditee need only audit major programs equal to 25 percent of the total amount of U.S. federal government aid expended.

The auditor is required by OMB A-133 to issue the following reports for a single audit:

- Report on the supplementary schedule of expenditures of federal awards,
- Report on internal control over major programs,
- An opinion as to whether the auditee complies with laws, regulations, and the provisions of contracts or grant agreements which have a direct and material effect on each major program,
- Schedule of findings and questioned costs that include a summary of the auditor's results.

In addition, GAGAS requires the auditor to issue the following reports:

- Opinion on the financial statements,
- Report on the internal control system, and
- Report on compliance with laws and regulations that may have a direct and material effect on the financial statements.

It is generally a good idea for the organization to have the same audit firm perform both the normal financial audit and the single audit. This permits the audit firm to work efficiently by using the same tests for both engagements. Internal auditors can perform much of the additional compliance testing required by GAGAS and the Single Audit Act.

¶ 2504.08

¶ 2505 Summary

Management is responsible for operating an organization in an effective and efficient manner. In the profit-oriented sector, this usually means creating shareholder value. However, organizations in the not-for-profit sector do not have a measure such as net income or profit to guide the allocation of resources. Still constituents pay taxes and other fees to government entities in return for services and demand accountability from their government officials as a result.

The government entity that uses the auditor's report specifies the performance standards that audit must meet. In the U.S., most government entities are audited according to Generally Accepted Government Auditing Standards (GAGAS) published by the U.S. General Accounting Office (GAO). GAGAS incorporate the fieldwork and reporting standards of Generally Accepted Auditing Standards (GAAS). Likewise, GAGAS may be used in conjunction with other standards.

Auditors need to observe the principles of serving the public interest and maintaining the highest degree of integrity, objectivity, and independence. Auditors assist government officials in the discharge of their stewardship responsibility.

Chapter 26
Ethics and Corporate Governance

¶ 2601 Introduction
¶ 2602 Ethical Considerations
¶ 2603 Ethics and Corporate Governance Education
¶ 2604 Corporate Governance
¶ 2605 Causes and Effects of Financial Scandals
¶ 2606 Corporate Governance After the Sarbanes-Oxley Act
¶ 2607 Future of the Accounting Profession
¶ 2608 Summary

¶ 2601 Introduction

Reported corporate and accounting scandals (e.g., Enron, Worldcom, Global Crossing, Qwest, Tyco, Adelphia, Parmalat, and Andersen) have reinvigorated substantial interest and discussion on corporate ethical conduct, corporate governance, and accountability. Unethical corporate conduct, lack of vigilant corporate governance, unreliable financial reports, and ineffective audits are widely cited as reason for the loss of investor confidence and public trust in public financial information. Lawmakers (Congress), regulators (the SEC), and national stock exchanges (NYSE, NASDAQ, AMEX) have responded by taking initiatives such as the Sarbanes-Oxley Act of 2002, SEC rules to implement provisions of the Act, and corporate governance guiding principles to restore eroded investor confidence and public trust in the financial reporting process. This chapter discusses ethical considerations and corporate governance characteristics that assist organizations' efforts toward restoration of investor confidence and public trust.

Chapter 26 objectives:

- To be aware of the purpose and content of corporate codes of conduct (see ¶ 2602).

- To understand the importance of teaching ethics in business schools (see ¶ 2603).

- To recognize corporate governance's role in financial reporting and the participants in corporate governance (see ¶ 2604).

- To detail the causes and effects of financial scandals and the roles of the participants in corporate governance in preventing future financial scandals (see ¶ 2605–2606).

- To become familiar with the current state of the accounting profession and the need to restore public trust in the profession (see ¶ 2607).

¶ 2602 Ethical Considerations

Improved ethical conduct for all organizations, particularly public companies, appears to be a national trend. Society is holding corporations responsible and accountable for their ethical behavior, business activities, and financial reports. The public, legislators, and regulators are also taking a closer look at corporations' codes of conduct. Traditionally, corporations have established codes of conduct to promote ethical behavior and resolve conflicts of interest. However, corporate codes of conduct have received more attention after the recent wave of financial scandals and Congressional responses to the scandals. Section 406 of the Sarbanes-Oxley Act directed the SEC to issue rules requiring public companies to establish and disclose their corporate codes of conduct. A reporting company in the SEC jurisdiction should disclose whether or not it has a code of conduct for its principle financial officer, controller, principle accounting officer, or persons performing financial functions. The SEC has issued its final rule 33-8177, "Disclosure Required by Sections 406 and 407 of the Sarbanes-Oxley Act of 2002," which requires public companies to disclose whether they have adopted a code of ethics for their senior executives, CFO, and controllers, and if not, disclose why they have not done so. Corporate codes of conduct should (1) foster corporate moral principles and values, (2) set a tone for employees in encouraging ethical behavior, (3) communicate and monitor ethical expectations to employees, (4) resolve ethical conflicts of interest, (5) demonstrate corporate commitment to ethical values, and (6) restore investor confidence and public trust in corporate America.

During the past several decades, the accounting profession has argued that self-regulation is the most effective approach to promote ethical behavior and the compliance with the AICPA's rules of conduct (see Chapter 2) which should result in a more ethical decision-making process for practicing CPAs. However, the wave of financial scandals in 2001 and 2002 prove that self-imposed regulations and rules of conduct were not immune from conflicts of interest, and have become the target of highly visible and negative publicity in the wake of audit failures (e.g., Andersen) and resulting lawsuits against public accounting firms. Table 26.1 shows a sample of recent lawsuits against public accounting firms for the perceived audit failures and related costs of settlement.

Table 26.1

Audit Failures and Related Settlements

Client	Auditor	Settlement
Sunbeam	Andersen	$251 million
Waste Management	Andersen	$220 million
Baptists Fdtn	Andersen	$215 million
Cendant	Enrst & Young	$335 million
Enron	Andersen	$375 million
Lincoln Savings	Arthur Young	$400 million
RiteAid	KPMG	$125 million

Client	Auditor	Amount of Lawsuit Pending
Barings Bank	Coopers & Lybrand	$1.4 billion
Superior Bank	Ernst & Young	$2.2 billion
First Nat'l Bank of Keystone	Grant Thornton	$169 million

The creation of the Public Company Accounting Oversight Board (PCAOB) by the passage of the Sarbanes-Oxley Act of 2002 practically ended the era of self-regulation and peer reviews for registered public accounting firms. The Act authorized the PCAOB to (1) register and monitor public accounting firms that audit public companies; (2) establish auditing, quality control, and ethical standards for registered public accounting firms; (3) inspect registered public accounting firms' compliance with applicable laws, rules, and regulations, including the Act; and (4) investigate financial irregularities.

- In the first week of October 2003, the PCAOB adopted its final rules for inspection of registered accounting firms:
  — Annual inspections for firms that do the largest volume of audit work (more than 100 public clients).
  — Triennial inspections for firms that do some volume of audit work (less than 100 public clients).
  — Special inspections are not subject to a schedule and would be conducted as necessary.
- The PCAOB is authorized to:
  — Report information indicating possible violations of law or professional standards to the SEC, other regulators, or law enforcement authorities, and appropriate state regulatory authorities.
  — Commence its own investigation or disciplinary proceeding based on relevant information.

¶ 2602

- Registered inspected accounting firms may submit written comments on a draft inspection report before the PCAOB issues a final report.

- Make portions of a final inspection report that deal with criticisms or potential defects in a firm's quality control systems, if the firm fails to address those issues to the PCAOB's satisfaction within 12 months after the issuance of the final inspection report.

Corporate codes of ethical conduct including compliance with applicable laws and regulations are essential to the long-term success of corporations, reliability of their financial reports, and integrity of the capital markets. Public companies should establish codes of ethical conduct that:

1. Comply with the provisions of the Act (Section 406) and requirements of SEC rules for the establishment and disclosure of codes of ethics for their executives (CEOs, CFOs, and controllers).

2. Emphasize the importance of ethical behavior to the corporation and its business.

3. Address the audit committee working relationships and professional interactions with registered auditors.

4. Encourage compliance with the corporation's applicable laws, rules, and regulations.

5. Communicate corporate codes of ethics to all employees, and require compliance with such codes and monitor employees' work-related behavior.

6. Disclose requirements of codes of ethics along with practices, policies, and procedures adopted and enforced to promote ethical behavior.

¶ 2603 Ethics and Corporate Governance Education

Reported ethical debacles in corporations encourage business schools to review and revitalize their commitment to provide ethics education in preparing business students to become ethical business leaders. Business schools worldwide are offering ethics education to advance students' ethical awareness, ethical reassessing skills, and ethical principles. The Ethics Education Task Force of AACSB International issued its report, "Ethics Education in Business Schools," in January 2004, which requires that ethics be taught in business schools.[1] This report addresses the four broad themes of ethics education as: the responsibility of business in society; ethical

---

[1] AACSB International. Ethics Education in Business Schools. Ethics Education Task Force of AACSB International (January 15, 2004). Available at http://www.aacsb.edu.

decision-making; ethical leadership; and corporate governance. These four themes should constitute a framework for teaching ethics and corporate governance in business schools.

.01 Responsibility of Business in Society

Traditionally, profit maximization has been viewed as the primary purpose of corporations. The creation and enhancement of shareholder value has also received some attention and support as shareholders require a desired return on their investment. However, the creation of stakeholder value has gained considerable support in the wake of recent corporate and accounting scandals. The AACSB's report underscores the importance of goals other than creating shareholder value such as compliance with applicable laws and regulations, paying taxes, producing safe products services, developing new technologies, awareness of social and environmental impacts, and creating jobs and investments. The reports suggests that business students should be taught about the creation of stakeholder value whereas society depends on business for wealth creation and business relies on society to provide opportunities and an environment to create wealth.

.02 Ethical Decision-Making

The report suggests that business schools adopt a variety of ethical decision-making approaches such as consequentialist, deontology, and virtue ethics in teaching ethics education. The consequentialist approach trains students to evaluate the consequences of their decisions in terms of harms and benefits to those affected by the decision (multiple stakeholders) and to make the decision that results in the greatest good for the greatest number. A deontological approach requires students to use relevant and existent ethical codes of conduct, standards, rules, and moral principles as a guide to make the best ethical decision. The virtue ethics approach highlights the importance of the character or the integrity of the moral mentor, actor, or professional community in guiding ethical decision-making. Any of these approaches or a combination of them can be used and applied to a hypothetical ethical decision-making dilemma or actual ethical case to teach ethics education and advance students' ethical decision process. Business schools should use multiple frameworks to improve students' ethical decision-making skills consisting of the following steps:

1. Examine and clarify the alternative actions. Ask what the relevant possibilities for action in the circumstances are. Search for all the action alternatives available.

2. Think through the consequences of each possible action. Try to predict a hypothetical future state of affairs that would follow action on each alternative.

¶ 2603.02

3. Use imagination to project oneself into these hypothetical future states of affairs. Think about what it will be like to live with the decision.

4. Identify oneself with the points of view of other people who will be affected by the decision. Put oneself in their shoes in these hypothetical futures.

.03 Ethical Leadership

The AACSB's report suggests business schools develop students' ethical leadership skills to become effective and successful executives. Executives must be both "moral persons" and "moral managers." Individuals become moral persons by adhering to moral principles and ethical standards and by applying their own ethical decision-making skills to organizational decisions. Individuals become moral managers by setting a "tone at the top" of promoting ethical behavior and monitoring and enforcing ethical conduct throughout the organization. Business schools in general and accounting programs in particular should prepare students to become executives who are facing the ethical expectations of real business. Business schools, by offering a course in ethics and the social responsibility of business schools, should bring to the classroom hypothetical or actual ethical dilemma situations and teach students about the cognitive and managerial/leadership skills in an organizational setting.

.04 Corporate Governance Education

The AACSB's report suggests that business schools provide both ethics education and a solid background in corporate governance because responsible corporate governance can be an important deterrent to unethical conduct. Corporate governance structure, mechanisms, and functions are discussed in ¶ 2604. However, the report suggests the following topics be included in corporate governance education throughout the business curriculum:

- Characteristics of effective corporate governance.
- The role and responsibilities of the board of directors.
- Functions and responsibilities of the audit committee.
- The role and responsibilities of top management team (executives).
- Corporate governance mechanisms including internal controls.
- The role and responsibilities of auditors, both internal and external.
- A compliance program to ensure compliance with applicable laws and regulations, including the Sarbanes-Oxley Act.

- The role and responsibilities of regulatory bodies including the SEC and financial and auditing standard-setting bodies (FASB, PCAOB).

- The role and responsibilities of legal counsel, financial analysts, and those who are associated with the reporting process.

¶ 2604 Corporate Governance

Corporate governance is defined as a "mechanism by which a corporation is managed and monitored."[2] Standard and Poor's (S&P) defines corporate governance as "encompassing the interactions between a company's management, its board of directors, and its financial stockholders (e.g., shareholders and creditors).[3] The role of corporate governance in financial reporting is to provide high-quality financial information that is useful, relevant, transparent, and reliable. Figure 26.1 shows that high-quality financial information can be achieved when all corporate governance participants work diligently and are held accountable for their actions. Corporate governance participants are the board of directors, audit committee, top management team, internal auditors, external auditors, and governance bodies. These corporate governance participants make up the six legs of the six-legged stool of the financial reporting problem depicted in Figure 26.1 and constitute the financial reporting supply chain as shown in Figure 26.2. Figures 26.1 and 26.2 underscore the importance of interactions among all corporate governance participants and their working relations in producing high-quality financial reports. Traditionally, management was held primarily responsible for quality, reliability and transparency of financial reports, and auditors only expressed their opinion on financial reports. Nevertheless, with current initiatives in corporate governance, Congressional responses (e.g., the Sarbanes-Oxley Act), and regulations (e.g., SEC rules), all corporate governance participants assume some degree of responsibility for the preparation and dissemination of financial reports of public companies.

Financial reports play an important role in preserving integrity and efficiency in capital markets and the general economy. Financial disclosures under SEC regulations are necessary to provide investors and other stakeholders with reliable information to make sound economic decisions. Figure 26.3 shows that high-quality financial information is more accurate, more complete, and more reliable and transparent than low quality financial information. High-quality financial information contains lower risk—the risk that financial information is misleading—and thus is more trustworthy than low-quality information. More trustworthy financial information is more value relevant, which may lead to more rational decision-

---

[2] Zabihollah Rezaee. Corporate Governance Role in Financial Reporting. Research in accounting regulations. Forthcoming (2004). Vol. 17.

[3] Standard and Poor's. Corporate governance scores—criteria, methodology, and definitions (2002). Available at http://www.governance.standardandpoors.com.

making by investors and in turn improves the efficiency and integrity of the capital markets. More efficient capital markets generate high stock prices, which may result in more economic growth and prosperity for the nation.

Figure 26.1

Six-Legged Stool of the Financial Reporting Process

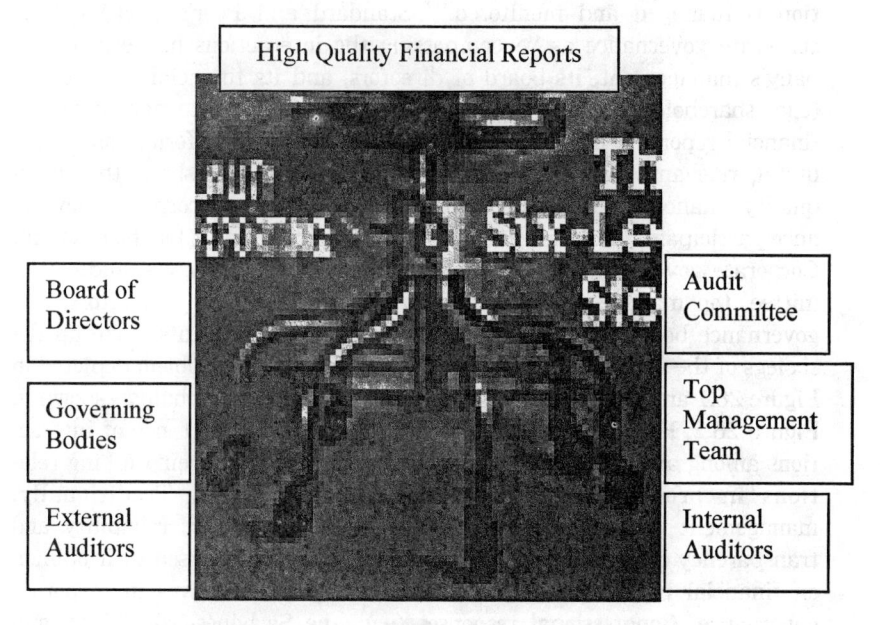

- High Quality Financial Reports
- Board of Directors
- Governing Bodies
- External Auditors
- Audit Committee
- Top Management Team
- Internal Auditors

Source: Zabihollah Rezaee. "High Quality Financial Reporting: The Six-Legged Stool." *Strategic Finance* (February 2003): 26-30.

Figure 26.2

Financial Reporting Supply Chain

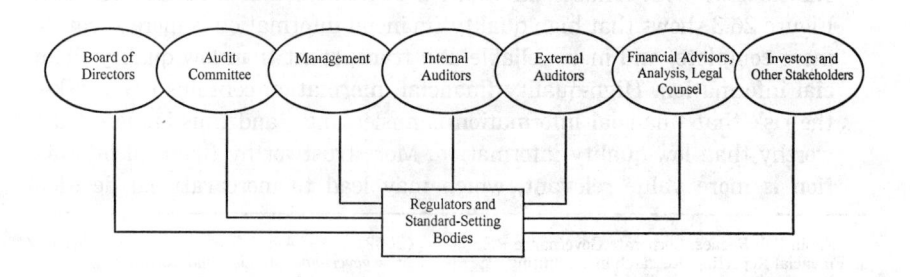

Board of Directors → Audit Committee → Management → Internal Auditors → External Auditors → Financial Advisors, Analysis, Legal Counsel → Investors and Other Stakeholders

Regulators and Standard-Setting Bodies

¶ 2604

Figure 26.3

The Role of Financial Reporting

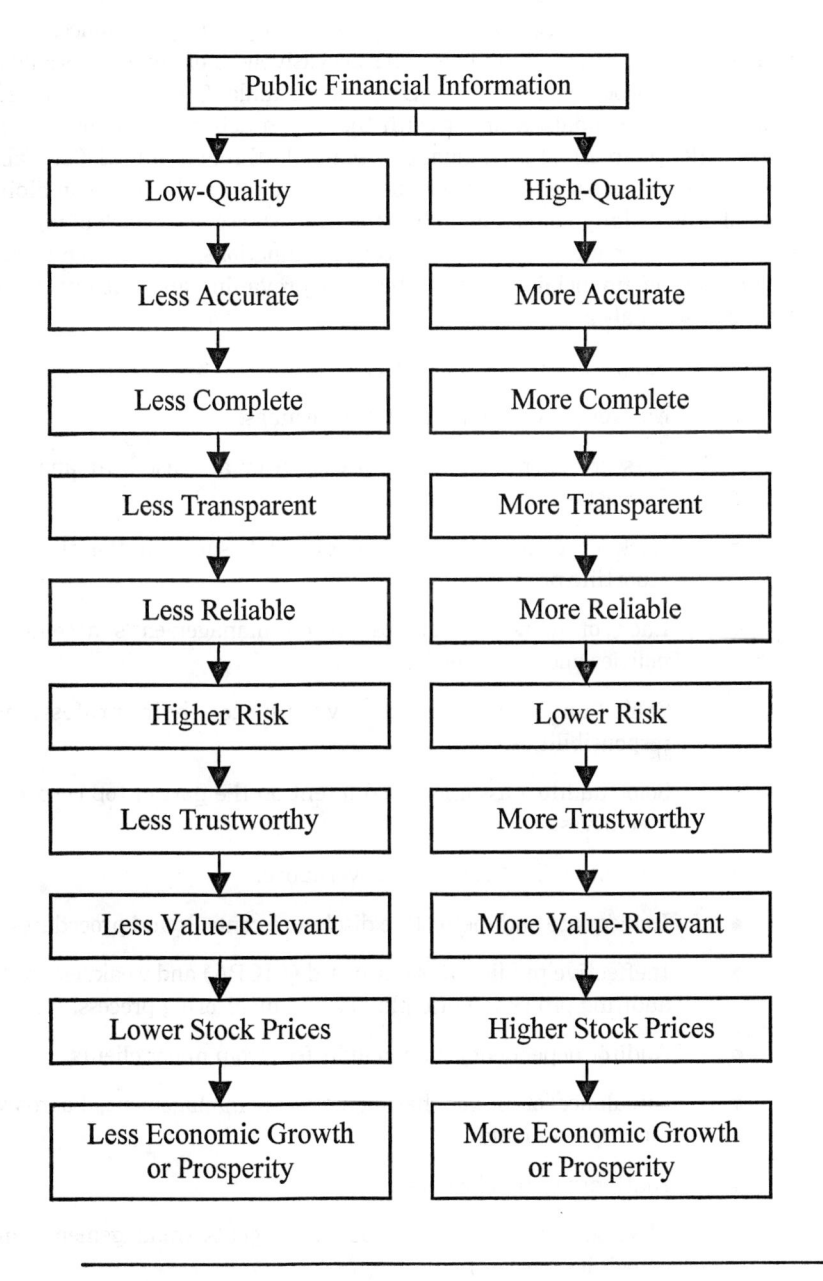

```
                    Public Financial Information
                    ↓                         ↓
            Low-Quality                High-Quality
                ↓                           ↓
            Less Accurate              More Accurate
                ↓                           ↓
            Less Complete              More Complete
                ↓                           ↓
            Less Transparent           More Transparent
                ↓                           ↓
            Less Reliable              More Reliable
                ↓                           ↓
            Higher Risk                Lower Risk
                ↓                           ↓
            Less Trustworthy           More Trustworthy
                ↓                           ↓
            Less Value-Relevant        More Value-Relevant
                ↓                           ↓
            Lower Stock Prices         Higher Stock Prices
                ↓                           ↓
            Less Economic Growth       More Economic Growth
            or Prosperity              or Prosperity
```

¶ 2604

¶ 2605 Causes and Effects of Financial Scandals

.01 Causes

The wave of corporate and accounting scandals during the early 2000s eroded investor confidence and public trust in corporate governance, financial reports, and audit functions. The pervasiveness of financial scandals encouraged Forbes to create "The Corporate Scandal Sheet" online to keep track of these scandals. Starting with the Enron debacle in October 2001, Forbes identified 21 alleged financial scandals through July 2002. Table 26.2 presents these scandals, their allegations, and reported dates in alphabetical order. Many factors, including the sluggish economy, lack of vigilant corporate governance, and ineffective audit functions, might have caused occurrences of financial scandals. The most prevailing and cited causes of financial scandals are:

- Simple greed and arrogance.
- Market pressure on short-term earnings.
- Pressure on management to exceed or at least beat analysts' forecast estimates.
- Lack of transparency or timely disclosures in the financial reporting process.
- Lack of mandated disclosures on management's accounting policies and practices.
- Some auditors did not live up to their professional responsibilities.
- Some auditors assumed good intent on the part of top corporate executives.
- Lack of vigilant corporate governance.
- Inadequate and ineffective disclosure controls and procedures.
- Ineffective public oversight board (AICPA) and weakness in the auditing profession disciplinary and monitoring process.
- Auditor dependency on nonaudit fees from major clients.
- Imbalance of power-sharing between management, boards of directors, and auditors.
- Inattentive shareholders.
- Misalignment of interests between agents (management) and principles (owners).
- Potential conflicts of interest between providers of financial information and users of financial information.

¶ 2605.01

Table 26.2

Reported Financial Statement Fraud

Company	Allegations	Reported Date
Adelphia Communications	Granted $3.1 billion in off-balance-sheet loans to its founder; overstated results by inflating capital expenses and hiding debt; used billions of dollars of company money for personal use.	April 2002
AES/Dennis W. Bakke	Used secured equity-linked loans to inflate revenues and bolster stock prices.	June 2002
AOL Time Warner	Inflated advertisement revenue to increase stock prices. Inflated sales by booking barter deals and ads it sold on behalf of others as revenue to keep its growth rate up and seal the deal.	July 2002
Anicom Inc.	A variety of accounting fraud charges including bank fraud, lying to the SEC, and making false statements.	October 23, 2003
Arthur Andersen	Shredded documents related to audit client Enron after the SEC launched an inquiry into Enron.	November 2001
Bristol-Myers Squibb	Inflated sales by offering incentives to wholesalers. Inflated its 2001 revenue by $1.5 billion by "channel stuffing," or forcing wholesalers to accept more inventory than they can sell to get it off the manufacturer's books.	July 2002
Citigroup	Assisted Enron Corp. and others to set up sham transactions to alter their finances.	October 2001
CMS Energy	Overstated revenues by about $4.4 billion in 2000 and in 2001 by using "round-trip" trades to artificially boost energy trading volume.	May 2002
Cutter & Buck, Inc.	A variety of criminal and civil charges pertaining to financial reporting fraud.	August 8, 2003
Duke Energy	Engaged in 23 "round-trip" trades to boost trading volumes and revenue.	July 2002
Dynegy	Inflated revenue and volume by executing "round-trip" trades to artificially boost energy trading volume and cash flow.	May 2002
El Paso	Used 125 "round-trip" trades to artificially boost energy trading volume.	May 2002
Enron	Boosted profits and hid debts totaling over $1 billion by improperly using off-the-books partnerships; manipulated the Texas power market; bribed foreign governments to win contracts abroad; manipulated California energy market.	October 2001

¶ 2605.01

Global Crossing	Engaged in network capacity "swaps" with other carriers to inflate revenue; shredded documents related to accounting practices.	February 2002
Halliburton	Improperly booked $100 million in annual construction cost overruns before customers agreed to pay for them.	May 2002
HPL Technology	Inflated stock prices by allowing executives following IPO to sell 85,500 shares at inflated prices.	October 2002
Homestore.com	Inflated sales by booking barter transactions as revenue.	January 2002
IMClone Systems	Charged with insider trading.	August 2002
JP Morgan Chase	Assisted Enron Corp. and others to set up sham transactions to change their financing.	October 2001
Kmart	Used accounting practices intended to mislead investors about its financial health by improperly accounting for vendor allowances.	January 2002
Merck	Recorded $12.4 billion in consumer-to-pharmacy co-payments that Merck never collected.	July 2002
Mirant	Overstated various assets and liabilities.	July 2002
Network Associates	Overstated revenues and understated expenses from 1998 to 2000.	July 2001
Nicor Energy, LLC, a joint venture between Nicor and Dynegy	Independent audit uncovered accounting problems that boosted revenue and underestimated expenses.	July 2002
Parmalat	Falsified bank statements by improperly claiming that it had $5 billion cash in a Bank of America account.	December 2003
Peregrine Systems	Overstated $100 million in sales by improperly recognizing revenue from third-party resellers.	May 2002
Qwest Communications International	Inflated revenue using network capacity "swaps" and improper accounting for long-term deals.	February 2002
Reliant Energy	Engaged in "round-trip" trades to boost trading volumes and revenue.	May 2002
Rite Aid	Inflated revenues by $1.6 billion from 1997-1999.	August 2002

¶ 2605.01

Tyco	Ex-CEO L. Dennis Kozlowski indicted for tax evasion. SEC investigating whether the company was aware of his actions, possible improper use of company funds and related-party transactions, as well as improper merger accounting practices by improperly creating cookie jar revenues.	May 2002
WorldCom	Overstated cash flow by booking $3.8 billion in operating expenses as capital expenses; gave founder Bernard Ebbers $400 million in off-the-books loans.	March 2002
Xerox	Falsified financial results for five years, boosting income by $1.5 billion.	June 2000

Sources:

CBS MarketWatch Scandal Sheet. Available at *http://cbs.marketwatch.com/news/features/scandal_sheet.asp.*

Citizen Works—Corporate Scandal Fact Sheet. Available at *http://www.citizanworks.org/enron/corp-scandal.php.*

Forbes. The Corporate Scandal Sheet (as of August 26, 2002). Available at *http://www.forbes.com/home/2002/07/25/accountingtracker-print.html.*

.02 Consequences

Consequences of reported financial scandals can be summarized as the following:

- Commission of financial statement fraud (cooking the books).
- Corporate and accounting scandals (e.g., Enron, WorldCom, Global Crossing, Qwest).
- Collapse of high-profile public companies (e.g., Enron, WorldCom).
- Substantial loss to investors and pensioners.
- Ineffective audit functions.
- Drastic declines in stock prices.
- Loss of investor confidence and public trust in financial reports.
- Frustrated investors and pensioners.
- Damage to auditors' credibility and reputation.
- Loss of executives' jobs.

.03 Responses

The wave of financial scandals encouraged lawmakers and regulators to argue that market-based correction mechanisms were not adequate and

¶ 2605.03

effective in preventing, detecting, and correcting further occurrences of financial scandals. Thus, in the absence of effective corporate governance, a volatile stock market, and a frustrated public, legislators, regulators, the business community, and the accounting profession responded to the crisis by undertaking the following initiatives:

- Lawmakers—Congress passed the Sarbanes-Oxley Act in July 2002.

- Regulators—The SEC issued more than 20 rules implementing corporate governance, financial reporting, and audit function provisions of the Act.

- National Stock Exchanges—Market-based correction mechanisms of corporate governance and financial reporting (NYSE, AMEX, NASDAQ, corporate governance principles).

- Regulation of auditing profession (Public Company Accounting Oversight Board).

- Accounting profession—AICPA issued SAS No. 99 and anti-fraud education and ethics courses.

- Academics—Forensic accounting, anti-fraud education, and ethics courses.

- Public companies—Initiatives to rebuild public confidence (management report on internal controls).

- Committee of Sponsoring Organizations of Treadway (COSO, AAA, AICPA, IMA, IIA, FEI)—Enterprise Risk Management Framework.

- Investor advocates—The Conference Board issued several reports on public trust, corporate governance, auditing, and accounting recommending specific best practice suggestions (benchmarks).

¶ 2606 Corporate Governance After the Sarbanes-Oxley Act

Traditionally, public companies in the United States have adopted voluntary corporate governance and codes of business conduct. Advocates of the agency theory argue that separation of ownership and control creates conflicts of interest between owners and management.[4] Thus, the role of corporate governance is to minimize the loss of value, and protect assets from loss or theft that may result from the separation of ownership and control. Corporate governance is viewed as a set of mechanisms to (1) protect assets from theft or loss; (2) monitor actions, policies, and decisions

---

[4] M. Jensen and W.M. Meckling. "Theory of the firm: Management behavior, agency costs, and ownership structures." *Journal of Financial Economics* (1976). 3: 305-360.

made by management in achieving organizational goals; and (3) induce management to make decisions that maximize shareholder value.

Table 26.3

Summary of Corporate Governance Under the Sarbanes-Oxley Act of 2002

1. Enhanced audit committee responsibility for hiring, firing, compensating, and overseeing auditors and pre-approval of nonaudit services.

2. Disclosure, in the periodic reports, whether the audit committee has at least one member who is a "financial expert" and if not, why not.

3. CEO and CFO certification of the accuracy and completeness of quarterly and annual reports.

4. Management assessment and reporting of the effectiveness of disclosure controls and procedures.

5. Ban on personal loans by companies to their directors or executives other than certain regular consumer loans.

6. Establishment of procedures by each audit committee for receiving, retaining, and handling complaints received by the company concerning accounting, internal controls, or auditing matters.

7. Review of each quarterly and annual report (forms 10-Q and 10-K) by officers.

8. Forfeiture by CEO or CFO of certain bonuses and profits when the company restates its financial statements due to its material noncompliance with any financial reporting requirements.

9. Improper influence on conduct of audits.

10. Insider trades during pension fund blackout periods.

11. Officers and directors bars and penalties for violations of securities laws or misconduct.

¶ 2606

Table 26.4

Guiding Principles, Requirements, and Recommendations for Improving Corporate Governance

New York Stock Exchange Recommendations	Business Roundtable	Financial Executives International	National Association of Corporate Directors	Conference Board
1. Require corporate boards to have a majority of independent directors.	1. Require stockholder approval of stock options.	1. All financial executives should adhere to a specialized code of ethical conduct.	1. Boards should be comprised of a substantial majority of "independent" directors.	1. The board should establish a structure that provides an appropriate balance between the powers of the CEO and those of the independent directors.
2. Tighten the definition of independent director.	2. Create and publish corporate governance principles.	2. Companies should actively promote ethical behavior.	2. Audit, compensation, and governance/nominating committees should be composed entirely of independent directors, and are free to hire independent advisors as necessary.	2. Each board of directors should adopt processes to ensure that the ability of the independent directors in fulfilling their oversight function is not compromised.
3. Require listed companies to have audit, compensation and nominating committees composed entirely of independent directors.	3. Provide employees with a way to alert management and the board to potential misconduct without fear of retribution.	3. Establish qualifications of the principal financial officer and principal accounting officer.	3. Each key committee should have a board approved written charter detailing its duties.	3. Every board should be composed of a substantial majority of independent directors.
4. Empower non-management directors to serve as a more effective check on management by meeting at regularly scheduled executive sessions without management.	4. Require that only independent directors serve on audit, corporate governance and compensation committees.	4. Create a new oversight body for the accounting profession staffed with finance and accounting professionals.	4. An independent director should be designated as chairman or lead director.	4. Every board should tailor the mix of directors' qualifications for its particular requirements.
5. The board must affirmatively determine that the director has no material relationship with the listed company.	5. Ensure that a substantial majority of the board of directors comprises independent directors both in fact and in appearance.	5. Place restrictions on certain non-audit services supplied by the independent auditor.	5. The performance of the CEO, other senior managers, the board as a whole, and individual directors should be evaluated.	5. Each board should develop a three-tier director evaluation mechanism.

¶ 2606

New York Stock Exchange Recommendations	Business Roundtable	Financial Executives International	National Association of Corporate Directors	Conference Board
6. Former employees or the independent auditor of the company—and their family members—may not be considered independent until five years after their employment ends.	6. Ensure prompt disclosure of significant developments.	6. Restrict the hiring of senior personnel from the external auditor.	6. Boards should review the adequacy of their companies' compliance and reporting systems at least annually.	6. Boards should be responsible for overseeing corporate ethics.
7. Director's compensation must be the sole remuneration from the listed company for audit-committee members.	7. Establish an appropriate management compensation structure that directly links the interests of management to the long-term interests of stockholders.	7. Reform the Financial Accounting Standards Board (FASB).	7. Boards should adopt a policy of holding periodic sessions of independent directors only.	7. The board and not management should retain special counsel for the necessary executives' investigation.
8. Increase the authority and responsibility of the audit committee, including the authority to hire and fire independent auditors, and to approve any significant non-audit services.	8. Require the audit committee to recommend the selection and tenure of the outside auditor.	8. Modernize financial reporting.	8. Audit committees should meet independently with both the internal and independent auditors.	8. Companies should formulate and communicate a strategy specifically designed to attract investors known to pursue long-term holding investment strategies.
9. Require listed companies to have an internal audit function.		9. Require continuous professional education for audit committee members.	9. Boards participate in companies' strategies.	9. Shareowners, particularly long-term shareowners, should act more like owners of the corporation.
10. Increase shareholder control over equity-compensation plans.		10. Periodic consideration of audit committee chair rotation.	10. Boards should provide new directors with a director orientation program.	10. Audit Committees should be vigorous in complying with applicable requirements and standards.
11. Require companies to adopt and disclose governance guidelines, codes of business conduct, and charters for their audit, compensation, and nominating committees.		11. Disclosure of corporate governance practices.		11. There should be an orientation program for each member of the Audit Committee.

¶ 2606

New York Stock Exchange Recommendations	Business Roundtable	Financial Executives International	National Association of Corporate Directors	Conference Board
12. Require foreign private issuers to disclose significant ways in which their governance practices differ from NYSE rules.				12. All companies should have an internal audit function.
13. Require CEO certification of the accuracy and completeness of financial information.				13. Audit Committees should consider rotating audit firms when there is a combination of circumstances that could call into question the audit firm's independence from management.
14. Allow the NYSE to issue a public reprimand letter to listed companies in violation of a corporate-governance standard.				14. The Audit Committee should, if necessary, retain professional advisors to assist it in carrying out its functions.
				15. Public accounting firms should limit their services to their clients to performing audits.
				16. The leadership of the Big Four accounting firms should each examine their business model to ensure that the model is consistent with the idea that quality audits is their number one priority.

Sources (from left to right):
1. New York Stock Exchange (NYSE). NYSE Approves Measures to Strengthen Corporate Accountability. (April 13, 2003). Available at *http://www.nyse.com/content/articles/1043269646468.html*.
2. Business Roundtable (BRT). Principles of Corporate Governance (May 2002). Available at *http://www.brtable.org/pdf/704.pdf*.
3. Financial Executives International (FEI). FEI Observations and Recommendations: Improving Financial Management, Financial Reporting, and Corporate Governance (2002). Available at *http://www.fei.org*.
4. National Association of Corporate Directors (NACD). 1999-2000 Public Company Governance Survey. Washington, D.C. (1999).
5. The Conference Board Commission on Public Trust and Private Enterprise. Findings and Recommendations Part 2: Corporate Governance: Principles, Recommendations and Specific Best Practice Suggestions. (January 9, 2003). Available at *http://www.conference-board.org/knowledge/governCommission.cfm*.

¶ 2606

Ethics and Corporate Governance

Table 26.5

SEC Final Rules

Act Section	SEC Final Rule	Description	Effective Date
302	Certification of disclosure in companies' quarterly and annual reports	CEOs and CFOs to certify: (1) the accuracy and completeness of both quarterly and annual reports; and (2) responsibility for establishing, maintaining, and assessing the effectiveness of internal controls. The first CEO and CFO fines levied under this rule were executives of RICO Foods, Inc., who signed on financial statements knowing they were not accurate.	8/29/2002
306	Filing guidance related to conditions for use of non-GAAP financial measures; and insider trades during pension fund blackout periods	The SEC issued interim guidance regarding the filing of information pursuant to new Items 11 and 12 of Form 8-K. Item 11 requires a registrant to provide public notice of a pension fund blackout period.	3/28/2003
501	Regulation analyst certification	Requires that brokers and dealers include in research reports certifications by the research analyst that the views expressed in the report accurately reflect his or her personal views, and disclose whether or not the analyst received compensation for recommendations.	4/14/2003
301 & 407	Standards relating to listed company audit committees	Directs the national securities exchanges and national securities associations to prohibit the listing of any security of an issuer that is not in compliance with the audit committee requirements mandated by the Sarbanes-Oxley Act of 2002.	4/25/2003
201, 203, 206, 208	Strengthening the commission's requirements regarding auditor independence	To enhance the independence of accountants who audit and review financial statements and prepare attestation reports filed with the SEC; prohibits non-audit services and requires the audit committee's pre-approval of all audit and non-audit services.	5/6/2003
303	Improper influence on conduct of audits	Prohibits officers and directors of an issuer, and persons acting under the direction of an officer or director, from taking any action to coerce, manipulate, mislead, or fraudulently influence the auditor of the issuer's financial statements.	6/27/2003
307	Standards for attorneys practicing before the SEC *ABA also requires corporate attorneys to report suspicions of fraud	Encourages lawyers to break their client confidentiality compact when clients are suspected of financial fraud. Inform corporate executives first of any violations of Securities laws and if continued, advise federal regulators (whistle-blowing by lawyers).	8/5/2003
404	Management's reports on internal control over financial reporting	The SEC adopted rules requiring public companies to include in their annual reports a report of management on the company's internal control over financial reporting.	8/14/2003

¶ 2606

Recent developments in corporate finance expand the aspect of corporate governance to cover all stakeholders and to define the balance of power among directors, executives, regulators, auditors, investors, and other stockholders (e.g., customers, creditors, employees). The stakeholder aspect of corporate governance has received considerable attention and support after the passage of the Sarbanes-Oxley Act of 2002. Table 26.3 lists corporate governance provisions of the Act. Table 26.4 summarizes guiding principles, recommendations, and requirements for improving corporate governance suggested by a number of organizations including the New York Stock Exchange (NYSE), Business Roundtable, Financial Executives International, National Association of Corporate Directors, and Conference Board. The SEC established more than 20 rules to implement provisions of the Act on corporate governance, financial reporting, and audit functions. Table 26.5 summarizes some of the important implementation rules established by the SEC.

Provisions of the Act, SEC-related implementation rules, and corporate governance guiding principles should provide benchmarks for establishing both internal and external mechanisms to (1) identify, manage, and possible reduce the potential conflicts of interest induced by the separation of ownership and control in corporations; and (2) promote corporate accountability and professional responsibility. These rules, regulations, and guiding principles have established a new framework of accountability for those who produce, certify, oversee, audit, analyze, and use public financial reports including the board of directors, the audit committee, and investment banks. Corporate governance provides both internal and external mechanisms for managing and monitoring corporate activities, and establishes a framework for professional interactions among all corporate governance participants as described in the following sections.

Table 26.6

Directors

Pre-Act	Post-Act
• Personal ties to company management	• The majority of directors should be independent
• Economic ties to the corporation (consulting fees, generous ownership pensions)	• Separate the roles of chairman of the board and CEO
• Personal and economic ties do not impair oversight function of directors	• Develop the knowledge and expertise to provide effective board oversight
• Personal and economic ties improve their working relationships with management	• Have resources to hire advisors and independent staff support
	• Set a "tone at the top" and a corporate culture that promotes ethical conduct
	• Periodic evaluation of the performance of the board of directors

¶ 2606

.01 Board of Directors

An ever-increasing interest in corporate governance underscores the importance of the board of directors as an internal mechanism for corporate governance in restoring investor confidence and public trust in the financial reporting process. Table 26.6 compares and contrasts the role of the board of directors pre- and post-Act. In the wake of the corporate scandals of Enron, WorldCom, Global Crossing, Qwest, and others, the board of directors was criticized for not fulfilling its oversight function by establishing personal and economic ties to management, which ultimately impaired the effectiveness of its oversight function. The role of the board of directors post-Act can be described as "a mechanism of (1) overseeing managerial plans, decisions, and actions; (2) safeguarding invested capital; (3) preventing the concentration of power in the hands of a small group of top executives; and (4) creating a system of checks and balances."[5] The success of the board of directors in fulfilling its oversight responsibility particularly its oversight role in the financial reporting process depends on its (1) structure, resources, and authority; and (2) working relationships with other participants in corporate governance including executives, auditors, regulators, standard-setting bodies, financial advisors, and legal counsel. The Sarbanes-Oxley Act and other initiatives by professional organizations (see Table 26.3 and 26.4) suggest the following recommendations for improving the effectiveness of the board of directors' corporate governance role:

- Separation of the position of CEO and the chairman of the board.
- Appointment of a lead, independent director who can convene the board without the CEO.
- Requirement that the majority of directors be independent.
- Assignment of directors to four committees of nominating, audit, executive, and compensation.
- Adoption of a code of conduct for directors and executives.
- Annual evaluation of the performance of the entire board, each of the assigned committees (e.g., nomination, audit, compensation) and individual directors.[6]

.02 Audit Committees

The audit committee is comprised of independent directors who oversee corporate governance, the financial reporting process, internal control, and the audit function. Table 26.7 compares and contrasts the role of the audit committee pre- and post-Act. Corporations have traditionally estab-

---

[5] Zabihollah Rezaee. Corporate governance role in financial reporting. Financial Research in Accounting Regulations. Forthcoming (2004). Vol. 17.

[6] Ibid.

lished voluntary audit committees as a liaison between management and external auditors to preserve auditors' independence. In the post-Act environment, public companies are required to establish audit committees that appoint, compensate, retain, and oversee independent auditors. The SEC and other initiatives (see Table 26.7) require that (1) the audit committee be composed of independent directors; (2) at least one member of the audit committee be designated as "financial expert"; and (3) a report by the audit committee be included annually in each proxy statement of publicly traded companies, which will ensure that financial statements are legitimate, the audit was thorough, and there was no conflict of interest that may jeopardize the auditors' objectivity, integrity, and independence. These new requirements placed on audit committees shift some of the management's financial reporting and audit involvements to the audit committee.

Table 26.7

Audit Committees

Pre-Act	Post-Act
• Voluntary audit committees	• Mandatory audit committees
• Personal and economic ties to management and corporation	• Independent members of audit committees
• Liaison between management and independent auditors	• Financial expertise
• Limited knowledge of financial reporting	• Appoint, compensate, retain, and oversee independent auditor
• Infrequent and short meetings	• Comply with new requirements for "independent" directors
• Lack of proper authority and resources	• Establish procedures for receipt, retention, and treatment of complaints relating to accounting, auditing, and internal control matters
	• Have authority to engage advisors
	• Be given appropriate funding, as determined by the audit committee, for external auditors and advisors
	• Disclosure of existence of at least one audit committee financial expert, if not, why not
	• Name of the audit committee financial expert and whether independent from management

.03 Management

Management is primarily responsible for the integrity, quality, transparency, and reliability of financial reports. As an important element of corporate governance, management is responsible for managing and monitoring business activities in achieving the goal of creating stockholder value. Management may be motivated to manipulate financial information, and if the opportunity is provided because of a lack of vigilant corporate governance, published financial statements will be misleading.

Table 26.8 compares and contrasts management's role in corporate governance and the financial reporting process pre- and post-Act. The Act's requirement of executive certifications of both financial statements and internal controls is expected to improve the reliability, quality, and transparency of public financial information. The Act has also changed the balance of power between management, the board of directors, and the auditors by requiring that the audit committee hire, fire, compensate, and oversee audit functions. The Act's requirements for reconciliation of pro forma statements with financial statements and disclosure of critical accounting estimates and accounting policies should also improve the quality of financial statements.

Table 26.8

Management

Pre-Act	Post-Act
• Information asymmetry between management and owners	• New certification requirements
• Management was given the opportunity to appoint the board of directors, the audit committee, and auditors, and offer monetary incentives for their continued employment	— Fair presentation of financial statements
• Potential conflict of interest existed in the sense that management could bend the board of directors, audit committee, and auditors at will	— Assessment of internal controls and procedures over financial reporting
• Management was motivated to use its discretion in choosing accounting practices that portray rosy earning projections in order to meet analysts' forecasts to sustain or boost stock prices	• Plan to comply with accelerated filing deadlines
	• Prepare for new disclosure requirements
	• Incorporate audit and non-audit service procedures
	• Enhance code of ethics for senior officers
	• Increase time and attention to governance activities

.04 Internal Auditors

Internal audit functions were not given proper attention prior to the passage of the Act. Public companies either established a voluntary internal audit function or outsourced their internal audit services. The Act has made it mandatory for public companies to establish internal audit functions. Furthermore, the revised definition of internal auditing, as discussed in Chapters 14 and 15, expands internal auditor activities to evaluating and improving the effectiveness of a company's corporate governance. Thus, internal auditing has become an integral part of corporate governance by focusing on a broad range of operating and financial activities. Internal auditors' activities after the passage of the Act (see Table 26.9) have been expanded to (1) assessing the effectiveness and efficiency of operational practice, (2) assisting management in the preparation of executive certifi-

¶ 2606.04

cations on financial statements and internal controls, and (3) ensuring responsible corporate governance.

Table 26.9

Internal Auditors

Pre-Act
- Voluntary internal audit functions
- Outsourcing internal audit functions
- Provide auditing services to the board and audit committee as consulting services to management

Post-Act
- Mandatory internal audit functions
- Independent internal auditors
- Oversight function of audit committee over internal audit function
- Internal controls over financial reporting (COSO)
- Enterprise Risk Management (COSO)

.05 External Auditors

The role of eternal auditors, as thoroughly discussed in Chapters 1–8, is to lend credibility to published financial statements. Investor confidence in audits of financial statements and auditor judgment plays an important role in considering audit functions as value-audit activities that make financial information useful, reliable, and relevant to investors. However, the wave of corporate and accounting scandals raised the important question: "Where were the auditors?" A substantial number of reported audit failures eroded public trust and investor confidence in audit functions and tremendously damaged auditors' reputations and image. Many factors have contributed to reported audit failures including the economic bond with management by performing consulting and other nonaudit services, an ineffective self-regulatory framework, the employment relationship with clients, and focusing more on audit growth and reducing audit costs than improving audit quality.

Table 26.10

Independent Auditors

Pre-Act
- Performance of non-audit services
- Quality of audit was improved by consulting services
- Auditors were influenced by economic pressures
- Management hires, compensates, and fires auditors
- No proper communication with audit committees

Post-Act
- Auditors are not immune from the economic pressures
- Regulatory framework for the auditing profession
- A five-member Public Company Accounting Oversight Board (PCAOB)
- PCAOB is empowered to register, inspect, and review registered public accounting firms and impose disciplinary actions
- PCAOB is responsible for issuing, auditing, quality controls, ethics standards

¶ 2606.05

- Do the minimum to meet GAAS

- Reduce the cost of audit
- Employment relationship

- Self-regulation of the auditing profession

- Partners' compensation was determined based on fees collected from clients
- Peer review evaluation of auditors' quality control system

- Nine non-audit services are prohibited (bookkeeping, financial information system design and implementation, actuarial services, appraisal, valuation services, internal audit outsourcing, management function, broker-dealer and investment advising, legal services, expert witness services)
- Attestation of and report on internal control over financial reporting.
- Inspections of the registered auditors by the PCAOB
- Rotation of lead partner or coordinating review partner every five years

Table 26.10 compares and contrasts audit functions pre- and post-Act. Several provisions of the Act have addressed ways to improve audit quality and effectiveness. First, the creation of the Public Company Accounting Oversight Board (PCAOB) has changed the perceived ineffective self-regulatory environment of auditors to a monitored regulatory framework. Second, public accounting forms that audit financial statements of public companies should register with the PCAOB and be annually inspected by the PCAOB. Third, the Act authorizes the PCAOB to issue auditing, quality control, and ethics standards for registered public accountants, which practically ended several decades of standard-setting authority by the AICPA. Fourth, the Act prohibits registered auditors to perform a number of nonaudit services to their clients contemporaneously with the audit of financial statements. Fifth, the lead partner or coordinating partner and the review partner of an audit engagement must be rotated every five years. Sixth, registered auditors must attest to and report on management's assessment of the effectiveness of their client's internal control over financial reports as an integral part of audit and financial statements. Finally, registered auditors should communicate their audit findings to management through the audit committee.

.06 Other Stakeholders

Other corporate governance participants that influence the effectiveness of corporate governance are regulators (e.g., SEC), standard-setting bodies (e.g., FASB, PCAOB), national stock exchanges (e.g., NYSE, AMEX, NASDAQ), financial analysts, institutional investors, investment banks, legal counsel, and users of financial information in general. The Act directs the SEC to issue rules to implement provisions of the Act pertaining to corporate governance, financial reports, and audit functions. The SEC has issued more than 20 implementation rules (see Table 26.5) in order to improve the timeliness, quality, reliability, usefulness, and transparency of published audited financial statements. The Act provides public funding for the FASB to continue issuing auditing standards for public companies. National stock exchanges have also established several corporate governance guiding principles to be observed by the listed companies (see Table 26.4). Security analysts play an important role in recommending stock and affecting stock prices by predicting earnings growth and quality and management incentives to meet these earnings forecasts. The Act directed the SEC to issue rules pertaining to financial analysts' conflicts of interest. The SEC issued the Regulation Analyst Certification (Regulation AC) that requires brokers and dealers to include certifications by the research analysts in their research reports that specify (1) their reports accurately reflect their personal views, and (2) whether or not they receive compensation or other payments in connection with their specific recommendations.

Corporate legal counsels are considered a part of corporate governance by providing advice to the board of directors, the audit committee, and management. The Act directed the SEC to establish rules setting minimum standards for the professional conduct of attorneys. The SEC has adopted its rule "Implementation of Standards of Professional Conduct for Attorneys" that requires attorneys to report evidence of a material violation of securities laws internally to the audit committee and if necessary to approach regulatory authorities.

The AICPA has taken several steps to assist public companies and their auditors to improve their performance toward the restoration of investor confidence and public trust. First, the AICPA has worked with the PCAOB to facilitate a smooth transition from the current self-regulatory environment to a regulatory framework for registered public accounting forms. Second, the AICPA has promoted anti-fraud controls and programs for certified public companies. Third, the AICPA has closely worked with the PCAOB to adopt or issue auditing standards for registered auditors. Finally, the AICPA has cooperated with business schools and accounting programs to incorporate anti-fraud education and forensic accounting into business and accounting curricula.

.07 Recommendations for Improving Corporate Governance

Corporate governance has recently received a considerable amount of attention. The Sarbanes-Oxley Act, the SEC, national stock exchanges, and professional organizations have taken several initiative to improve the effectiveness of corporate governance in creating stakeholder value. Tables 26.3 and 26.5 summarize these initiatives in corporate governance that require cooperation of all corporate governance participants examined in the previous paragraphs. Following are some suggestions for public companies, their board of directors, executives, and auditors to consider in ensuring responsible corporate governance, reliable financial reports, and credible audit functions:

¶ 2606.07

1. A dedicated long-term focus on "doing the right things and doing them right" starts at the top and filters down throughout the company.

2. Support senior executive certifications by continuously improving the underlying accounting process and internal controls that produce financial information.

3. Define and maintain director independence.

4. Conduct periodic self-evaluations of board performance and publicly disclose the results.

5. Position the audit committee to succeed with qualified independent directors.

6. Implement a meaningful code of conduct to promote responsible business practices.

7. Take a more conservative approach to accounting and reporting.

8. Increase effectiveness of the independent audit by creating a professional working relationship among the audit committee, external auditors, internal auditors, and management.

9. Establish an internal audit function and increase the focus on internal audit.

10. Improve accounting management (work-horse vs. show-horse CFOs); CFOs with hardcore accounting, financial reporting and risk-management skills not from the auditing firms vs. CFOs who excite analysts and drive share prices.

11. Establish close and continuous communications with directors and senior officers regarding functions, responsibility and value-adding activities of both internal and external audit functions.

12. Realign internal audit objectives with corporate governance missions.

13. Leverage technology in high-risk areas of real-time financial reporting (XBRL) and continuous auditing (electronic auditing).

14. Focus on enterprise risk management (ERM) capabilities in achieving organizations' goals.

15. Enhance the quality assurance process (internal and external quality assurance) to improve quality, reliability, and transparency of financial reports.

¶ 2606.07

¶ 2607 Future of the Accounting Profession

The 103rd American Assembly, consisting of leaders in the areas of accounting, finance, law, investment banking, journalism, regulatory officials, nongovernmental organizations, and academia, issued its special report on "The Future of the Accounting Profession" in November 2003.[7] This report addresses three broad areas of the accounting profession including its present state, its desired future state, and how it may reach the desired future state.

.01 Current State of the Accounting Profession

The current state of the accounting profession can be characterized by a low image caused by a lack of public trust in the profession. Several factors have caused the erosion in the public trust of the accounting profession. The report addresses some of the important factors as:

- Substantial failures in corporate governance.
- Significant audit failures.
- Ineffective regulation and oversight of the auditing profession.
- Decreasing value-relevance of financial statement audits.
- Non-response to structural challenges facing the accounting profession.

.02 Desired Future State

- Setting achievable goals.
- Resolving the debate over rules-based and principles-based accounting.
- Improving auditing and financial reporting standards.
- Encouraging more competition and less consolidation of the auditing industry.

.03 Reaching the Desired Goals

- Changing the current regime of relying less on specific rules and more on judgment in the future.
- Overseeing potentially problematic auditors by the PCAOB in order to ensure compliance with the highest possible standards.
- Adjusting auditing practices by changing the partners' compensation system that rewards top-quality audits rather than promoting "rainmakers" who bring in the most new business.

---

[7] The American Assembly Columbia University. The Future of the Accounting Profession. The 103rd American Assembly (November 13-15, 2003). Available at http://www.americanassembly.org.

- Reinvigorating audit committees to provide effective oversight functions over corporate governance, the financial reporting process, and audit functions.

- Preparing the next generation of professionals with a strong knowledge of business and finance.

- Development of directors to be financially literate and operationally effective with sufficient knowledge of the business.

¶ 2608 Summary

This chapter discusses ethical considerations and corporate governance characteristics that assist organizations' efforts toward restoration of investor confidence and public trust. Basically, ethics is good business. If management complies with applicable laws and regulations, pays the organization's taxes, produces safe products and services, develops new technologies, acts with awareness of social and environmental impacts, and reports its earnings fairly, the organization can avoid legal problems and better serve its shareholders.

A code of conduct is only as good as management's support of it. If employees see their managers acting ethically and upholding the code of conduct, they too will be encouraged to act ethically. Ethics must be enforced with a top-down approach. Infractions of the code should be dealt with in a manner that will let other employees know that unethical behavior is not tolerated in the company.

Ethics and corporate governance education in business schools is increasingly important, in order to sensitize the student to ethical concerns that he or she may meet on the job. In that first year of working, an accountant or businessperson is likely too busy attending to the daily job requirements to question the ethical implications of certain tasks assigned to them. That new accountant may just assume that his or her colleagues know better. Some unethical policies may become habit, and before long he or she may buckle under the pressure of colleagues to pursue profits at the expense of clients and shareholders. Ethics and corporate governance education will help a student determine what to do when faced with an ethical dilemma.

Many participants play a role in corporate governance. Recent developments in corporate finance have highlighted the balance of power split among directors, executive, regulators, auditors, investors, and other stakeholders (e.g., customers, creditors, employees); thus, the definition of corporate governance has been expanded to cover all stakeholders. Corporate governance is an interactive check and balance mechanism requiring cooperation of all corporate governance participants. The Sarbanes-Oxley Act, the SEC, national stock exchanges, and professional organizations have instigated several initiatives to improve the effectiveness of corporate governance in creating stakeholder value.

Appendix 1

Ethics Vocabulary

Attest engagement. An engagement that requires independence as defined in AICPA Professional Standards.

Attest engagement team. Individuals participating in the attest engagement, including those who perform concurring and second partner reviews. The attest engagement team includes all employees and contractors retained by the firm who participate in the attest engagement, irrespective of their functional classification (e.g., audit, tax, or management consulting services) except specialists as discussed in SAS No. 73, *Using the Work of a Specialist* (AICPA, *Professional Standards,* vol. 1, AU sec. 336) and individuals who perform only routine clerical functions, such as word processing and photocopying.

Client. Any person or entity, other than the member's employer, that engages a member or a member's firm to perform professional services or a person or entity with respect to which professional services are performed. [The SEC includes its parent, subsidiaries, and affiliates within the definition of client.]

Close relative. A parent, sibling, or nondependent child.

Covered member. A person who is:

    a.   An individual on the attest engagement team

    b.   An individual in a position to influence the attest engagement

    c.   A partner or manager who provides nonattest services to the attest client beginning once he or she provides 10 hours of nonattest services to the client within any fiscal year and ending on the later of the date (i) the firm signs the report on the financial statements for the fiscal year during which those services were provided or (ii) he or she no longer expects to provide 10 or more hours of nonattest services to the attest client on a recurring basis

    d.   A partner in the office in which the lead attest engagement partner primarily practices in connection with the attest engagement

e. The firm, including the firm's employee benefit plans or

f. An entity whose operating, financial, or accounting policies can be controlled (as defined by generally accepted accounting principles [GAAP] for consolidation purposes) by any of the individuals or entities described in (a) through (e) or by two or more such individuals or entities if they act together

Firm. Form of organization permitted by law or regulations whose characteristics conform to resolutions of the Council of the American Institute of Certified Public Accountants that is engaged in the practice of public accounting. Except for purposes of applying the Rule 101, *Independence,* the firm includes the individual partners thereof.

Holding out. Any action initiated by a member that informs others of his or her status as a CPA or AICPA-accredited specialist constitutes holding out as a CPA. This phrase includes, for example, any oral or written representation to another regarding CPA status, use of the CPA designation on business cards or letterhead, the display of a certificate evidencing a member's CPA designation, or listing as a CPA in local telephone directories.

Immediate family. A spouse, spousal equivalent, or dependent (whether or not related).

Individual in a position to influence the attest engagement. A person in a position to influence the attest engagement is one who:

a. Evaluates the performance or recommends the compensation of the attest engagement partner

b. Directly supervises or manages the attest engagement partner, including all successively senior levels above that individual through the firm's chief executive

c. Consults with the attest engagement team regarding technical or industry-specific issues related to the attest engagement or

d. Provides quality control or other oversight of the attest engagement (including internal monitoring)

Institute. The American Institute of Certified Public Accountants.

Joint closely held business investment. A business investment that is subject to control (as defined by GAAP for consolidation purposes) by the member, the client, the client's officers or directors, or any stockholder who has the ability to exercise significant influence over the client, individually or in any combination.

Appendix 1

Key position. A position in which an individual:

a. Has primary responsibility for accounting functions that support material components of the financial statements

b. Has primary responsibility for the preparation of the financial statements or

c. Has the ability to exercise influence over the board of directors or similar governing body, chief executive officer, president, chief financial officer, chief operating officer, general counsel, chief accounting officer, controller, director of internal audit, director of financial reporting, treasurer, or any equivalent position

Loan. A financial transaction, the characteristics of which generally include, but are not limited to, an agreement that provides for repayment terms and a rate of interest. A loan includes, but is not limited to, a guarantee of a loan, a letter of credit, a line of credit, or a loan commitment.

Manager. A professional employee of the firm who has either of the following responsibilities:

a. Continuing responsibility for the overall planning and supervision of engagements for specified clients or

b. Authority to determine that an engagement is complete, subject to the final partner's approval (if required).

Member. A member, associate member, or international associate of the American Institute of Certified Public Accountants.

Office. A reasonably distinct subgroup within a firm, whether constituted by formal organization or informal practice, where personnel who make up the subgroup generally serve the same group of clients or work on the same categories of matters. Substance should govern the office classification. For example, the expected regular personnel interactions and assigned reporting channels of an individual may well be more important than an individual's physical location.

Partner. A proprietor, shareholder, equity or non-equity partner or any individual who assumes the risks and benefits of firm ownership or who is otherwise held out by the firm to be the equivalent of any of the aforementioned.

Period of the professional engagement. Starts when a member begins to perform an attest engagement for a client. The period lasts for the entire duration of the professional relationship (which could cover many periods) and ends with the formal or informal notification (either by the member or the client) of the termination of the professional relationship or by the issuance of a report, whichever is later. Accordingly, the period does not end with the issuance of a report and recommence with the beginning of the following year's attest engagement.

Practice of public accounting. The performance for a client, by a member or a member's firm, while holding out as CPA(s), of the professional services of accounting—tax preparation, personal financial planning, litigation support services, and those professional services for which standards are promulgated by bodies designated by Council (e.g., statements of financial accounting standards).

Significant influence. An individual has significant influence over an entity if he or she meets the criteria established in Accounting Principles Board Opinion No. 18, The Equity Method of Accounting for Investments in Common Stock, and its interpretations [AC section 18] to determine the ability of an investor to exercise significant influence with respect to the entity.

Appendix 2

The Institute of Internal Auditors—Code of Ethics[1]

Introduction

The purpose of The Institute's *Code of Ethics* is to promote an ethical culture in the profession of internal auditing.

Internal auditing is an independent, objective assurance and consulting activity designed to add value and improve an organization's operations. It helps an organization accomplish its objectives by bringing a systematic, disciplined approach to evaluate and improve the effectiveness of risk management, control, and governance processes.

A code of ethics is necessary and appropriate for the profession of internal auditing, founded as it is on the trust placed in its objective assurance about risk management, control, and governance. The Institute's *Code of Ethics* extends beyond the definition of internal auditing to include two essential components:

1. Principles that are relevant to the profession and practice of internal auditing;

2. Rules of Conduct that describe behavior norms expected of internal auditors. These rules are an aid to interpreting the Principles into practical applications and are intended to guide the ethical conduct of internal auditors.

The *Code of Ethics* together with The Institute's *Professional Practices Framework* and other relevant Institute pronouncements provide guidance to internal auditors serving others. "Internal auditors" refers to Institute members, recipients of or candidates for IIA professional certifications, and those who provide internal auditing services within the definition of internal auditing.

Applicability and Enforcement

This *Code of Ethics* applies to both individuals and entities that provide internal auditing services.

---

[1] Adopted by The IIA Board of Directors, June 17, 2000. The Institute of Internal Auditors, 247 Maitland Avenue, Altamonte Springs, Florida 32701-4201 (2000). Reprinted with permission.

For Institute members and recipients of or candidates for IIA professional certifications, breaches of the *Code of Ethics* will be evaluated and administered according to The Institute's Bylaws and Administrative Guidelines. The fact that a particular conduct is not mentioned in the Rules of Conduct does not prevent it from being unacceptable or discreditable, and therefore, the member, certification holder, or candidate can be liable for disciplinary action.

Principles

Internal auditors are expected to apply and uphold the following principles:

Integrity—The integrity of internal auditors establishes trust and thus provides the basis for reliance on their judgment.

Objectivity—Internal auditors exhibit the highest level of professional objectivity in gathering, evaluating, and communicating information about the activity or process being examined. Internal auditors make a balanced assessment of all the relevant circumstances and are not unduly influenced by their own interests or by others in forming judgments.

Confidentiality—Internal auditors respect the value and ownership of information they receive and do not disclose information without appropriate authority unless there is a legal or professional obligation to do so.

Competency—Internal auditors apply the knowledge, skills, and experience needed in the performance of internal auditing services.

Rules of Conduct

1. **Integrity**

Internal auditors:

   1.1. Shall perform their work with honesty, diligence, and responsibility.
   1.2. Shall observe the law and make disclosures expected by the law and the profession.
   1.3. Shall not knowingly be a party to any illegal activity, or engage in acts that are discreditable to the profession of internal auditing or to the organization.
   1.4. Shall respect and contribute to the legitimate and ethical objectives of the organization.

2. **Objectivity**

Internal auditors:

   2.1. Shall not participate in any activity or relationship that may impair or be presumed to impair their unbiased assessment. This participation includes those activities or relationships that may be in conflict with the interests of the organization.

2.2 Shall not accept anything that may impair or be presumed to impair their professional judgment.

2.3 Shall disclose all material facts known to them that, if not disclosed, may distort the reporting of activities under review.

3. Confidentiality

Internal auditors:

3.1 Shall be prudent in the use and protection of information acquired in the course of their duties.

3.2 Shall not use information for any personal gain or in any manner that would be contrary to the law or detrimental to the legitimate and ethical objectives of the organization.

4. Competency

Internal auditors:

4.1. Shall engage only in those services for which they have the necessary knowledge, skills, and experience.

4.2 Shall perform internal auditing services in accordance with the *International Standards for the Professional Practice of Internal Auditing*.

4.3 Shall continually improve their proficiency and the effectiveness and quality of their services.

Appendix 3

International Standards for the Professional Practice of Internal Auditing[1]

Attribute Standards

Attribute Standard 1000	**Purpose, Authority, and Responsibility** The purpose, authority, and responsibility of the internal audit activity should be formally defined in a *charter*, consistent with the *Standards*, and approved by the *board*.
Implementation Standard 1000.A1 (Assurance Engagements)	The nature of assurance services provided to the organization should be defined in the audit charter. If assurances are to be provided to parties outside the organization, the nature of these assurances should also be defined in the charter.
Implementation Standard 1000.C1 (Consulting Engagements)	The nature of consulting services should be defined in the audit charter.
Attribute Standard 1100	**Independence and Objectivity** The internal audit activity should be independent, and internal auditors should be objective in performing their work.
Attribute Standard 1110	**Organizational Independence** The *chief audit executive* should report to a level within the organization that allows the internal audit activity to fulfill its responsibilities.
Implementation Standard 1110.A1 (Assurance Engagements)	The internal audit activity should be free from interference in determining the scope of internal auditing, performing work, and communicating results.
Attribute Standard 1120	**Individual Objectivity** Internal auditors should have an impartial, unbiased attitude and avoid conflicts of interest.
Attribute Standard 1130	**Impairments to Independence or Objectivity** If independence or *objectivity* is *impaired* in fact or appearance, the details of the impairment should be disclosed to appropriate parties. The nature of the disclosure will depend upon the impairment.
Implementation Standard 1130.A1(Assurance Engagements)	Internal auditors should refrain from assessing specific operations for which they were previously responsible. Objectivity is presumed to be impaired if an auditor provides assurance services for an activity for which the auditor had responsibility within the previous year.

---

[1] *International Standards for the Professional Practice of Internal Auditing*, copyright 2001 by the Institute of Internal Auditors, Inc., 247 Maitland Avenue, Altamonte Springs, Florida 32710-4201, U.S.A. Reprinted with permission.

Implementation Standard 1130.A2(Assurance Engagements)	Assurance *engagements* for functions over which the chief audit executive has responsibility should be overseen by a party outside the internal audit activity.
Implementation Standard 1130.C1(Consulting Engagements)	Internal auditors may provide consulting services relating to operations for which they had previous responsibilities.
Implementation Standard 1130.A2(Consulting Engagements)	If internal auditors have potential impairments to independence or objectivity relating to proposed consulting services, disclosure should be made to the engagement client prior to accepting the engagement.
Attribute Standard 1200	**Proficiency and Due Professional Care** Engagements should be performed with proficiency and due professional care.
Attribute Standard 1210	**Proficiency** Internal auditors should possess the knowledge, skills, and other competencies needed to perform their individual responsibilities. The internal audit activity collectively should possess or obtain the knowledge, skills, and other competencies needed to perform its responsibilities.
Implementation Standard 1210.A1(Assurance Engagements)	The chief audit executive should obtain competent advice and assistance if the internal audit staff lacks the knowledge, skills, or other competencies needed to perform all or part of the engagement.
Implementation Standard 1210.A2(Assurance Engagements)	The internal auditor should have sufficient knowledge to identify the indicators of *fraud* but is not expected to have the expertise of a person whose primary responsibility is detecting and investigating fraud.
Implementation Standard 1210.C1(Consulting Engagements)	The chief audit executive should decline the consulting engagement or obtain competent advice and assistance if the internal audit staff lacks the knowledge, skills, or other competencies needed to perform all or part of the engagement.
Attribute Standard 1220	**Due Professional Care** Internal auditors should apply the care and skill expected of a reasonably prudent and competent internal auditor. Due professional care does not imply infallibility.
Implementation Standard 1220.A1(Assurance Engagements)	The internal auditor should exercise due professional care by considering the: ● Extent of work needed to achieve the *engagement's objectives*. ● Relative complexity, materiality, or significance of matters to which assurance procedures are applied. ● Adequacy and effectiveness of risk management, *control*, and *governance processes*. ● Probability of significant errors, irregularities, or noncompliance. ● Cost of assurance in relation to potential benefits.
Implementation Standard 1220.A2(Assurance Engagements)	The internal auditor should be alert to the significant *risks* that might affect objectives, operations, or resources. However, assurance procedures alone, even when performed with due professional care, do not guarantee that all significant risks will be identified.
Implementation Standard 1220.C1(Consulting Engagements)	The internal auditor should exercise due professional care during a consulting engagement by considering the: ● Needs and expectations of clients, including the nature, timing, and communication of engagement results. ● Relative complexity and extent of work needed to achieve the engagement's objectives. ● Cost of the consulting engagement in relation to potential benefits.

Appendices **911**

Attribute Standard 1230	**Continuing Professional Development** Internal auditors should enhance their knowledge, skills, and other competencies through continuing professional development.
Attribute Standard 1300	**Quality Assurance and Improvement Program** The chief audit executive should develop and maintain a quality assurance and improvement program that covers all aspects of the internal audit activity and continuously monitors its effectiveness. The program should be designed to help the internal auditing activity *add value* and improve the organization's operations and to provide assurance that the internal audit activity is in conformity with the *Standards* and the *Code of Ethics*.
Attribute Standard 1310	**Quality Program Assessments** The internal audit activity should adopt a process to monitor and assess the overall effectiveness of the quality program. The process should include both internal and external assessments.
Attribute Standard 1311	**Internal Assessments** Internal assessments should include: ● Ongoing reviews of the performance of the internal audit activity; and ● Periodic reviews performed through self-assessment or by other persons within the organization, with knowledge of internal auditing practices and the *Standards*.
Attribute Standard 1312	**External Assessments** External assessments, such as quality assurance reviews, should be conducted at least once every five years by a qualified, independent reviewer or review team from outside the organization.
Attribute Standard 1320	**Reporting the Quality Program** The chief audit executive should communicate the results of external assessments to the board.
Attribute Standard 1330	**Use of "Conducted in Accordance with the Standards"** Internal auditors are encouraged to report that their activities are "conducted in accordance with the *International Standards for the Professional Practice of Internal Auditing*." However, internal auditors may use the statement only if assessments of the quality improvement program demonstrate that the internal audit activity is in *compliance* with the *Standards*.
Attribute Standard 1340	**Disclosure of Noncompliance** Although the internal audit activity should achieve full compliance with the *Standards* and internal auditors with the *Code of Ethics*, there may be instances in which full compliance is not achieved. When noncompliance impacts the overall scope or operation of the internal audit activity, disclosure should be made to senior management and the board.

Performance Standards

Performance Standard 2000	**Managing the Internal Audit Activity** The *chief audit executive* should effectively manage the internal audit activity to ensure it *adds value* to the organization.
Performance Standard 2010	**Planning** The chief audit executive should establish risk-based plans to determine the priorities of the internal audit activity, consistent with the organization's goals.
Implementation Standard 2010.A1(Assurance Engagements)	The internal audit activity's plan of *engagements* should be based on a *risk* assessment, undertaken at least annually. The input of senior management and the board should be considered in this process.

Appendix 3

Implementation Standard 2010.C1(Consulting Engagements)	The chief audit executive should consider accepting proposed consulting engagements based on the engagement's potential to improve management of risks, add value, and improve the organization's operations. Those engagements that have been accepted should be included in the plan.
Performance Standard 2020	**Communication and Approval** The chief audit executive should communicate the internal audit activity's plans and resource requirements, including significant interim changes, to senior management and to the board for review and approval. The chief audit executive should also communicate the impact of resource limitations.
Performance Standard 2030	**Resource Management** The chief audit executive should ensure that internal audit resources are appropriate, sufficient, and effectively deployed to achieve the approved plan.
Performance Standard 2040	**Policies and Procedures** The chief audit executive should establish policies and procedures to guide the internal audit activity.
Performance Standard 2050	**Coordination** The chief audit executive should share information and coordinate activities with other internal and *external providers* of relevant assurance and *consulting services* to ensure proper coverage and minimize duplication of efforts.
Performance Standard 2060	**Reporting to the Board and Senior Management** The chief audit executive should report periodically to the board and senior management on the internal audit activity's purpose, authority, responsibility, and performance relative to its plan. Reporting should also include significant risk exposures and *control* issues, corporate governance issues, and other matters needed or requested by the board and senior management.
Performance Standard 2100	**Nature of Work** The internal audit activity evaluates and contributes to the improvement of risk management, control and governance systems.
Performance Standard 2110	**Risk Management** The internal audit activity should assist the organization by identifying and evaluating significant exposures to risk and contributing to the improvement of risk management and control systems.
Implementation Standard 2110.A1(Assurance Engagements)	The internal audit activity should monitor and evaluate the effectiveness of the organization's risk management system.
Implementation Standard 2110.A2(Assurance Engagements)	The internal audit activity should evaluate risk exposures relating to the organization's governance, operations, and information systems regarding the ● Reliability and integrity of financial and operational information. ● Effectiveness and efficiency of operations. ● Safeguarding of assets. ● *Compliance* with laws, regulations, and contracts.
Implementation Standard 2110.C1(Consulting Engagements)	During consulting engagements, internal auditors should address risk consistent with the engagement's objectives and should be alert to the existence of other significant risks.
Implementation Standard 2110.C2(Consulting Engagements)	Internal auditors should incorporate knowledge of risks gained from consulting engagements into the process of identifying and evaluating significant risk exposures of the organization.
Performance Standard 2120	**Control** The internal audit activity should assist the organization in maintaining effective controls by evaluating their effectiveness and efficiency and by promoting continuous improvement.

Appendix 3

Appendices

Implementation Standard 2120.A1(Assurance Engagements)	Based on the results of the risk assessment, the internal audit activity should evaluate the adequacy and effectiveness of controls encompassing the organization's governance, operations, and information systems. This should include: • Reliability and integrity of financial and operational information. • Effectiveness and efficiency of operations. • Safeguarding of assets. • Compliance with laws, regulations, and contracts
Implementation Standard 2120.A2(Assurance Engagements)	Internal auditors should ascertain the extent to which operating and program goals and objectives have been established and conform to those of the organization.
Implementation Standard 2120.A3(Assurance Engagements)	Internal auditors should review operations and programs to ascertain the extent to which results are consistent with established goals and objectives to determine whether operations and programs are being implemented or performed as intended.
Implementation Standard 2120.A4(Assurance Engagements)	Adequate criteria are needed to evaluate controls. Internal auditors should ascertain the extent to which management has established adequate criteria to determine whether objectives and goals have been accomplished. If *adequate*, internal auditors should use such criteria in their evaluation. If inadequate, internal auditors should work with management to develop appropriate evaluation criteria.
Implementation Standard 2120.C1(Consulting Engagements)	During consulting engagements, internal auditors should address controls consistent with the engagement's objectives and should be alert to the existence of any significant control weaknesses.
Implementation Standard 2120.C2(Consulting Engagements)	Internal auditors should incorporate knowledge of controls gained from consulting engagements into the process of identifying and evaluating significant risk exposures of the organization.
Performance Standard 2130	**Governance** The internal audit activity should contribute to the organization's *governance process* by evaluating and improving the process through which (1) values and goals are established and communicated, (2) the accomplishment of goals is monitored, (3) accountability is ensured, and (4) values are preserved.
Implementation Standard 2130.A1(Assurance Engagements)	Internal auditors should review operations and programs to ensure consistency with organizational values.
Implementation Standard 2130.C1(Consulting Engagements)	Consulting engagement objectives should be consistent with the overall values and goals of the organization.
Performance Standard 2200	**Engagement Planning** Internal auditors should develop and record a plan for each engagement.
Performance Standard 2201	**Planning Considerations** In planning the engagement, internal auditors should consider: • The objectives of the activity being reviewed and the means by which the activity controls its performance. • The significant risks to the activity, its objectives, resources, and operations and the means by which the potential impact of risk is kept to an acceptable level. • The adequacy and effectiveness of the activity's risk management and control systems compared to a relevant control framework or model. • The opportunities for making significant improvements to the activity's risk management and control systems.

Appendix 3

Implementation Standard 2201.C1(Consulting Engagements)	Internal auditors should establish an understanding with consulting engagement clients about objectives, scope, respective responsibilities, and other client expectations. For significant engagements, this understanding should be documented.
Performance Standard 2210	**Engagement Objectives** The engagement's objectives should address the risks, controls, and governance processes associated with the activities under review.
Implementation Standard 2210.A1(Assurance Engagements)	When planning the engagement, the internal auditor should identify and assess risks relevant to the activity under review. The *engagement objectives* should reflect the results of the risk assessment.
Implementation Standard 2210.A2(Assurance Engagements)	The internal auditor should consider the probability of significant errors, irregularities, noncompliance, and other exposures when developing the engagement objectives.
Implementation Standard 2210.C1(Consulting Engagements)	Consulting engagement objectives should address risks, controls, and governance processes to the extent agreed upon with the client.
Performance Standard 2220	**Engagement Scope** The established scope should be sufficient to satisfy the objectives of the engagement.
Implementation Standard 2220.A1(Assurance Engagements)	The scope of the engagement should include consideration of relevant systems, records, personnel, and physical properties, including those under the control of third parties.
Implementation Standard 2220.C1(Consulting Engagements)	In performing consulting engagements, internal auditors should ensure that the scope of the engagement is sufficient to address the agreed-upon objectives. If internal auditors develop reservations about the scope during the engagement, these reservations should be discussed with the client to determine whether to continue with the engagement.
Performance Standard 2230	**Engagement Resource Allocation** Internal auditors should determine appropriate resources to achieve engagement objectives. Staffing should be based on an evaluation of the nature and complexity of each engagement, time constraints, and available resources.
Performance Standard 2240	**Engagement Work Program** Internal auditors should develop *work programs* that achieve the engagement objectives. These work programs should be recorded.
Implementation Standard 2240.A1(Assurance Engagements)	Work programs should establish the procedures for identifying, analyzing, evaluating, and recording information during the engagement. The work program should be approved prior to the commencement of work, and any adjustments approved promptly.
Implementation Standard 2240.C1(Consulting Engagements)	Work programs for consulting engagements may vary in form and content depending upon the nature of the engagement.
Performance Standard 2300	**Performing the Engagement** Internal auditors should identify, analyze, evaluate, and record sufficient information to achieve the engagement's objectives.
Performance Standard 2310	**Identifying Information** Internal auditors should identify sufficient, reliable, relevant, and useful information to achieve the engagement's objectives.
Performance Standard 2320	**Analysis and Evaluation** Internal auditors should base conclusions and engagement results on appropriate analyses and evaluations.
Performance Standard 2330	**Recording Information** Internal auditors should record relevant information to support the conclusions and engagement results.

Appendix 3

Implementation Standard 2330.A1(Assurance Engagements)	The chief audit executive should control access to engagement records. The chief audit executive should obtain the approval of senior management and/or legal counsel prior to releasing such records to external parties, as appropriate.
Implementation Standard 2330.A2(Assurance Engagements)	The chief audit executive should develop retention requirements for engagement records. These retention requirements should be consistent with the organization's guidelines and any pertinent regulatory or other requirements.
Implementation Standard 2330.C1(Consulting Engagements)	The chief audit executive should develop policies governing the custody and retention of engagement records, as well as their release to internal and external parties. These policies should be consistent with the organization's guidelines and any pertinent regulatory or other requirements.
Performance Standard 2340	**Engagement Supervision** Engagements should be properly supervised to ensure objectives are achieved, quality is assured, and staff is developed.
Performance Standard 2400	**Communicating Results** Internal auditors should communicate the engagement results promptly.
Performance Standard 2410	**Criteria for Communicating** Communications should include the engagement's objectives and scope as well as applicable conclusions, recommendations, and action plans.
Implementation Standard 2410.A1(Assurance Engagements)	The final communication of results should, where appropriate, contain the internal auditor's overall opinion.
Implementation Standard 2410.A2(Assurance Engagements)	Engagement communications should acknowledge satisfactory performance.
Implementation Standard 2410.C1(Consulting Engagements)	Communication of the progress and results of consulting engagements will vary in form and content depending upon the nature of the engagement and the needs of the client.
Performance Standard 2420	**Quality of Communications** Communications should be accurate, objective, clear, concise, constructive, complete, and timely.
Performance Standard 2421	**Errors and Omissions** If a final communication contains a significant error or omission, the chief audit executive should communicate corrected information to all individuals who received the original communication.
Performance Standard 2430	**Engagement Disclosure of Noncompliance with the** Standards When noncompliance with the *Standards* impacts a specific engagement, communication of the results should disclose the: ● *Standard(s)* with which full compliance was not achieved, ● Reason(s) for noncompliance, and ● Impact of noncompliance on the engagement.
Performance Standard 2440	**Disseminating Results** The chief audit executive should disseminate results to the appropriate individuals.
Implementation Standard 2440.A1(Assurance Engagements)	The chief audit executive is responsible for communicating the final results to individuals who can ensure that the results are given due consideration.
Implementation Standard 2440.C1(Consulting Engagements)	The chief audit executive is responsible for communicating the final results of consulting engagements to clients.
Implementation Standard 2440.C2(Consulting Engagements)	During consulting engagements, risk management, control, and governance issues may be identified. Whenever these issues are significant to the organization, they should be communicated to senior management and the board.

Performance Standard 2500	**Monitoring Progress** The chief audit executive should establish and maintain a system to monitor the disposition of results communicated to management.
Implementation Standard 2500.A1(Assurance Engagements)	The chief audit executive should establish a follow-up process to monitor and ensure that management actions have been effectively implemented or that senior management has accepted the risk of not taking action.
Implementation Standard 2500.C1(Consulting Engagements)	The internal audit activity should monitor the disposition of results of consulting engagements to the extent agreed upon with the client.
Performance Standard 2600	**Management's Acceptance of Risks** When the chief audit executive believes that senior management has accepted a level of residual risk that is unacceptable to the organization, the chief audit executive should discuss the matter with senior management. If the decision regarding residual risk is not resolved, the chief audit executive and senior management should report the matter to the board for resolution.

Appendix 3

Appendix 4

Possible Performance Measures

I. Overall Function Management:
    1. CAE Position Titles
    2. CAE Education/Certification
    3. CAE Year of Service
    4. CAE Reporting Relationships—Administrative
    5. CAE Reporting Relationships—Functional
    6. CAE and External Auditors Fees
    7. Involvement in ISO 9000
    8. Types of Audit Reviews
    9. Coordination With External Auditors
    10. Activities Audited
    11. Distribution of Time Within Audits
    12. Self-Assessment Activities
    13. Time Used by IT Auditors
    14. IT Integrated Auditing
    15. Annual Audit Plan
    16. Annual Plan Risk Factors
    17. Role of Internal Auditing Viewed by the Auditee
    18. Management Expectations of Internal Auditing
    19. Number of Management Requests
    20. External Quality Assurance Review
    21. Risk Assessment Factors
    22. Audit Committee Satisfaction Survey Results
    23. Role of Internal Auditing Viewed by the Audit Committee
    24. Percent of Board on Audit Committee
    25. Attendance at Audit Committee Meetings
    26. Frequency of Audit Committee Meetings

27. External Auditor Meets Privately with Audit Committee
28. CAE Meets Privately with Audit Committee
29. Audit Committee Agenda Items
30. Audit Committee Risk Concerns

II. Input:
1. Revenue Per Auditor
2. Assets Per Auditor
3. Employees Per Auditor
4. Percent of Staff Dedicated to IT Auditing
5. Internal Auditing Staff Profile
6. Salary Range
7. Auditor Hiring Mix
8. Auditor Education Levels
9. Staff Experience
10. Staff Turnover Rate
11. Percent of Certified Staff
12. Certification Mix
13. Percent of Time IT Auditing done by NON-IT Audit Staff
14. Average Years of Audit Experience
15. Staff Rotated to and from operations departments
16. Total Costs Per Auditor- Travel Included
17. Total Costs Per Auditor- Travel Excluded
18. Salaries as a percent of Total Costs
19. Travel as a Percent of Total Costs
20. Training as a Percent of Total Costs
21. Other Costs as a Percent of Total Costs
22. Reimbursement for Certification
23. Reimbursement for Professional Memberships/Meetings
24. Training Hours Per Internal Auditor
25. Internal Auditor Training by Type

Appendix 4

26. Internal Training As Percent of Total Training
27. Fieldwork—Respondents with Automated Work Papers
28. Dedicated Information Technology Auditing Staff
29. Personal Computer Availability- By Equipment Type
30. Personal Computer Availability- By Staff Size
31. PCs and Terminals
32. Operating Systems

III. Process
1. Customer Satisfaction Survey
2. Number of Complaints about audit
3. Level of Customer Satisfaction
4. Actual Hours versus Budgeted Hours
5. Completed versus Planned Audits

IV. Output
1. Number of Pages in Final Report
2. Number of Major Audit Findings/recommendations
3. Number of Repeat Findings
4. Number of Process Improvements
5. Number of Audit Reports Issued
6. Completed Audits per Auditor
7. Distribution of Audit Comments by Type
8. Importance of Audit Issue
9. Percent of Audit Recommendations Implemented
10. Amount of Audit Savings
11. Average Response time- Management Requests
12. Cost Savings as a Percent of Total Budget
13. Days from End of Field Work to Report Issuance
14. Target Completion Dates on Management Action Plans

Appendix 4

Appendix 5

Forensic Accounting and Expert Witness Vocabulary

Appellant (Petitioner) (Plaintiff). Person filing suit.

Respondent (Defendant). Person sued.

Pleadings. Formal written allegations of the parties—complaint and answer—stating their respective claims and defenses.

Complaint. Formal written pleading of the plaintiff setting forth his or her claims, allegations, and facts.

Answer. Formal written pleading of the defendant which denies, admits, or demurs the allegations in the complaint.

Demurrer. Statement of the defendant which takes exception to the sufficiency in the point of law of the plaintiff stating that the defendant does not have to answer or proceed with the dispute.

Stipulation. Voluntary agreement before trial between opposing parties concerning the disposition of certain points and/or facts to avoid the need for proof or to narrow the litigable issues.

Stare decisis. Doctrine of law that states that a case once decided will control. The doctrine of precedent states that when the court has laid down a principle of law as applicable to a certain set of facts, it will follow that principle in cases with same facts.

Judicial precedent. Judge not required to follow judicial precedent beyond own jurisdiction.

Res judicata (collateral estoppel). Once case or issue resolved, matter precluded from being litigated again.

Law of the case. Once issue decided one way, if not properly challenged, it will not be reconsidered.

Full Faith and Credit Clause. Court in one state must honor and enforce judgment of another state.

Venue. Judicial district where defendant resides.

Pro se. Party representing himself or herself.

Impeachment of witness. Question the veracity of a witness through evidence that the witness is not trustworthy (e.g., expert witness is not familiar with authoritative publications).

Motion in limine. Request before trial that evidence of the opposing side is inadmissible (e.g., exclude the testimony of an expert).

Surrebuttal. Explaining or contradicting rebuttal testimony.

Voir Dire. Preliminary questioning by the court (or attorney) of jurors, witnesses, or expert witness to determine competency.

Per curiam. Decision of the whole court.

En banc. Decision rendered by full court.

Concurring opinion. Agrees with court's conclusion, but for a different reason.

Dissenting opinion. Disagrees with majority.

Dicta (Dictum). Opinions of judge which go beyond the facts before the court and are not binding in subsequent cases as precedent.

Affirmed (Aff'd; Aff'g). Declares valid—to affirm a lower court's judgment.

Reversed (rev'd; rev'g). Disagrees with lower court.

Writ of Certiorari. Asks Supreme Court to hear your case.

Cert. Granted by Supreme Court.

Cert. Den. by Supreme Court.

Remand. Vacate the lower court decision and send back for further considerations

Overruling. Does not impact either party in the earlier case. Overrules a previous case.

Ad hoc. For one particular or special purpose (e.g., an ad hoc committee)

Ad valorem. According to value (e.g., in tax, assessment of taxes based on property value).

Bona fide. In good faith and without fraud and deceit.

Covenant. An agreement or promise to do *or* not to do something.

Dejure. In law or lawful; legitimate.

Deposition. A written statement of a witness under oath, often question/answer.

Enjoin. To command or instruct with authority (e.g., judge can enjoin someone to do or not to do something).

Appendix 5

Habeas corpus (writ of). Procedure to determine if authorities can hold a person in custody.

Nolo contendere. A party does not wish to fight or continue; person will not fight a charge.

Parol evidence. Renders any evidence of a prior understanding of a party to contract invalid if it contradicts the term of a written document.

Motion. Requests a rule or order in favor of the applicant.

Discovery. Process of getting information from the other party [Rule FRCP 26(b)(1)].

Best evidence rule. Historically required that original documents be produced, but today the rule is influenced by practicality and governed by statutes.

Demonstrative evidence. Consists of objects of just about any form (e.g., models, photos, videos, charts, etc.).

Authentication concept. A written instrument or object must be proven to be what it purports to be.

Three types of evidence. Testimony, writings, and objects.

Residium rule. No finding may be supported solely by hearsay evidence.

Hearsay. Evidence of a statement that was made out of court to prove the truth of the matter stated.

Subpoena duces tecum. A command to produce documents to a court that become evidence.

Subpoena ad testificandum. A command to a person to appear and testify as a witness.

Punitive damages. Intended to punish reprehensible conduct and defer future wrongdoers, in excess of actual damages sustained.

Compensatory damages. In a material breach of contract, a sum of money to make the plaintiff whole again.

Out-of-pocket loss. Referring to compensatory damages, the difference between the actual value received and the actual value conveyed, including no opportunity costs.

Benefit-of-the bargain measure. Difference between the actual value received and what the seller expected to receive.

But-for-loss. Reasonably foreseeable losses beyond out-of-pocket, including increased costs, loss profits, and decrease in value of the investment.

Alter ego. Removable of the corporate protection to obtain a judgment against the owners of a corporation.

Appendix 5

Liquidation damage clause. Clause in a contract specifying a dollar amount due on breach of a contract.

Consequential damage. Foreseeable damages caused by special circumstances.

Mitigation. Plaintiff must take steps to minimize the damages suffered.

Appendix 5

Index

References are to paragraph (¶) numbers.

A

AACSB Ethics Education Task Force, "Ethics Education in Business Schools" of 2603–2603.01, 2603.03–.04

Abnormal trends, analytics to identify 2202.02

Accounting firms. *See also* Public accounting firms
   audit committee responsibilities for 1507
   conflicts of interest for 102
   cooling off period for employment by clients of employees from 201.06
   PCAOB inspections of 401, 404
   peer or quality review requirement of AICPA for 401, 402.01–403
   public confidence in 503.05
   registration with PCAOB of . . 201.01–.02
   responsibility for actions of partners of 306.03
   SEC enforcement cases against . 308, 2050.01. *See also* individual firms
   selection of entity type to shield owners from liabilities of 205.06

Accounting principles
   country of origin of 903.04
   deliberate misapplication of 2005

Accounting Principles Board Opinion No. 18, Equity Method of Accounting for Investments in Common Stock 210

Accounting profession
   current state of 2607.01
   future of 2607, 2607.02–.03
   self-regulation of 2602, 2606.06

Accounts payable, analytical procedures for 2202.01

Accounts payable, auditing 704–704.04
   analytical procedures for substantive testing in 704.03
   for credit purchases 704.01
   issues specific to 704.04
   year-end detailed testing in 704.02
   year-end detailed testing in 704.02

Accounts receivable
   fictitious..................... 602
   positive and negative confirmation of............. 703.04

Accounts receivable, auditing . . 703–703.04
   for credit sales 703.01

Accounts receivable, auditing— *continued*
   issues specific to 703.04
   year-end analytical procedures in 703.03
   year-end detailed testing in 703.02

Accounts receivable fraud 2012.02

Accrual accounting method to express financial statements, GAAP requirement for . 109, 902.04, 1002

Actuarial services (with exceptions), independence impaired by providing audit client's ... 208.03, 210.06

Adverse opinion in financial audit report 108
   issued for condensed financial statements not included in document 804.06
   issued if financial statements are not fairly presented 803.03
   issued if going concern problem is inadequately disclosed 709

Adverse opinion in prospective financial statement report 1007.11

Adverse report, international standards for 2404

Advertising by auditing firms 205.04

Agency theory 2606

Air Force Inventory sample internal audit report................... 1706

Alternative dispute resolution (ADR) 112.04, 1215.01

American Accounting Association (AAA) joint research project with IIA 1404.03

American College of Forensic Examiners (ACFE) 1216, 2002.02

American Institute of Certified Public Accountants (AICPA)
   Accounting and Review Services Committee of 109, 402, 901, 902.01
   Code of Professional Conduct (Code) of 102, 112.02, 201.08–.09, 202.01, 205.06, 210.05, 303.01, 905.01, 1214
   formation in 1887 of........... 1203
   future role of 201
   Litigation and Dispute Resolution Services Subcommittee of ... 1202.01
   membership obligations for . 202.01, 402
   Peer Review Board of 401, 403.01
   Private Company Section of 402.01

AME

American Institute of Certified Public Accountants (AICPA)—continued
 Professional Ethics Executive Committee of 201.08, 209
 Quality Control Standards Committee of 402
 quality control standards of, focus of 401
 renamed in 1957 from American Association of Public Accountants 1203
 Rules of Conduct of ... 102, 112.02, 203, 2602
 SEC Practice Section of ... 207, 402.01
 Special Committee on Assurance Services (Elliott Committee) ... 111, 1101–1102, 1104, 1108
 task force to develop SysTrust of CICA and 122.03, 1105.02
 "Top Ten" information technology issues compiled annually by 2301
 transition to PCAOB regulatory framework from 2606.06
 web sites of 210.08
 WebTrust audits facilitated by .. 2305.09

American Management Association self-study course for forensic accountants 1212

American Society of Industrial Security 2002.02

Analytical procedures
 applied at final review stage of audit 710, 711, 804.05
 applying.............. 2202.03, 2202.05
 data quality of input to, controlling 2202.04
 defined..................... 2202
 employed during audit preparation stage............ .503.02
 expected results of 607
 follow-up of 2201
 general forms of 607
 importance of 2202.05
 integrated into audit tests . 121, 121.01, 2201–2202.05
 international standards for applying 2403.04
 not considered sampling 2203, 2205
 reasons for using.............. 2201
 in review engagement.......... .905.04
 for substantive testing 606–607, 620, 792.04, 703.03, 704.03
 technique included in 503.02
 types of 2202.01
 used during any phase of audit . 2202.02

Annual internal control report 1905

Annual report of environmental performance, percentage of companies producing 2110

Annual reports, management's verification of 115

Appellate courts.................. 1207

Application controls for IT system 2303.02

Appraisal services, independence impaired by providing audit client's 208.03, 210.06

Arbitration clause in engagement letter 502.02

Arbitration process 1215.01

Arthur Andersen
 allegations against 2605.01
 Deloitte & Touche peer-review report about 207
 demise of 1101, 2005
 double role of as Enron's independent and internal auditor of 208.05
 Enron as showing up on radar screen for fraud of 619
 negligence litigation by Baptist Foundation of Arizona against . .303.02
 SEC actions in 2001 against..... .206.01
 Texas Stadium Corporation's Jerry Jones as bringing malpractice claim against 302
 in WorldCom debacle 1201

Asset approach to risk-based audit planning................. 115.04, 1603

Assets, tracing 1307

Association of Certified Fraud Examiners (ACFE)
 credentials issued by 1216
 focus of 2002.02
 1993 survey by 2002

Association of Government Accountants (AGA)............. 2502

Assurance engagement, steps in preparing for SysTrust 1105.02

Assurance services 111, 1101–1110.01
 business risk 1103
 e-commerce ... 1106. *See also* WebTrust for electronic commerce
 eldercare 1108
 health care effectiveness 1107
 information systems .. 1105–1105.02. *See also* Information systems reliability
 new opportunities for internal auditing in.................. 1110.01
 other possible 1109

Attest engagement
 forms of 1102
 government...... 123.02, 123.05, 2504.03, 2504.06
 on management's quarterly report on disclosure controls .. 1905

Attorneys
 employing forensic accountant .. 1212
 inquiries of client's 706, 707
 opposing, approach of expert witness to 1212
 privileged matters of, as not subject to discovery 1207.02
 professional conduct standards set by SEC for 102, 2606.06
 reporting requirements under Sarbanes-Oxley Act for 102
 review of final contracts by 1907

Index—References are to paragraph (¶) numbers.

Attribute sampling test 2205–2206
   conditions for failure in 2206.02
   evaluating and documenting
     results of 2206.06
   sampling unit and population for
     .... 2206.03
   selecting and testing sample in . 2206.05
   setting sample size for 2206.04
   test objectives for 2206.01

**Audit and Accounting Manual
(AAM) (AICPA)** 303.01, 1007.03

Audit claims for malpractice 302

Audit committee of board of directors
   audit and non-audit services
     approved by 213.01
   audit plan submitted to 1602
   Blue Ribbon Committee's
     recommendations for
     improving 1207
   CAE's understanding with
     management and audit
     committee about 115, 1502, 1507
   charter of 1507
   charter of internal auditing
     department distributed to 1502
   communication with auditor
     about 618–619
   composition of 102, 115.02, 2606.02
   evaluation by auditor during pre-
     planning stage of composition
     of 502.01
   financial expert member of 102
   formats of internal audit reports
     given to 1703
   future improvements to 212
   independent directors on 2606.02
   inquiries about fraud risk to 503.05
   internal control audit findings
     communicated to 621
   oversight function of 2005, 2606.04,
                                    2607.03
   perpetrator of fraud in control of
     .... 2002.02
   rebutting auditee's response to
     internal audit report to 1702
   reportable conditions
     communicated to 610, 621
   risk-based audit assessment
     involving 1603
   roles before and after Sarbanes-
     Oxley Act of 2606.02
   Sarbanes-Oxley Act as expanding
     authority of 213.01
   Sarbanes-Oxley Act as mandating
     independence of 102, 115.02
   Sarbanes-Oxley Act as requiring
     timely reports by auditors to ... 102,
                                       201.06
   SEC regulations governing . 1404.06, 1507
   selection of performance
     measures for internal auditing
     department by management and
     1505
   support of CSA by 1903

Audit engagements. *See also* individual
types
   acceptance of 105, 501

Audit engagements. *See also* individual
types—continued
   audit preparation stage of
     financial audit planning phase
     begun upon acceptance of 501
   automation of 2306.03
   engagement letter as detailing
     objectives and time frame of ... 502.02
   permanent file of 503.08
   phases of 501
   pre-planning stage of 502.01
   process of 105
   risk of fraud requiring more
     experienced personnel on 605
   staffing of, consideration during
     pre-planning stage of 502.01
   staffing of, stipulation in
     engagement letter of 303.01
   timetable of, description in
     engagement letter of 303.01
   withdrawal from, reasons for. *See*
     Withdrawal from audit engagement

Audit evidence
   destruction of, as criminal
     misconduct 306.03
   evaluated for likelihood of
     financial misstatements 2004
   retention of 616.03
   sampling computer output to
     gather 2306.01

Audit fees, decline of 1201

**Audit findings, individual, for internal
audits**
   components of 1704.01
   order in audit report of
     components of 1704.02

Audit objectives
   for accounts payable 704.02
   for accounts receivable balance . 703.02
   achievement of, as evidence
     about management assertions . 617
   achievement of, due to
     ineffective internal controls 610
   communication of 504
   determining accomplishment of . 504
   developed and fulfilled during
     control testing phase 611
   for internal audit engagement ... 1604,
                                      1604.01
   internal controls and 610
   link between management
     assertions and 604–604.02
   for performance audit 1806
   for prospective financial
     statements 1007.03
   satisfying 607
   specialists to help auditor fulfill . 503.07,
                                        607

**Audit of Internal Control Over
Financial Reporting Performed in
Conjunction with an Audit of
Financial Statements, An
(PCAOB)** 1905

Audit plan ....
   for internal audit 1602
   international 2402, 2402.04

AUD

Audit planning, analytical procedures in 502.02
Audit planning conference with client 503.01
Audit planning for internal audit, risk-based 115.04, 1603
Audit planning for performance audit 1806
Audit program
    auditor preparation during financial audit of 106
    development of internal .. 1604, 1604.05
    steps in, recording names of audit team members performing 615
Audit report 801–802
    country of origin for accounting principles required in 903.04
    intended recipients stipulated in engagement letter for 303.01
    liability for negligence in 304.03
    negligent misrepresentation in incorrect 304.05
    opinion paragraphs in 803.01
    prepared or furnished by non-U.S. public accounting firm 2405
    sample, for independent registered public accounting firm use 907, 1008
    unqualified opinion report in 803.01
Audit report following financial audit
    auditing standards for 802
    categories of opinions in .... 108, 803–803.04. *See also* individual types
    dating 803.01, 2404
    evidence gathering for 108
    features of 116, 801
    impact of auditing process on 116.01
    international standards for 2404
    modified for scope limitation 706, 2404
    sample 805
    SEAI report in conjunction with .. 1003
    special dating issues for 804.02
    subsequent discovery of facts existing at date of 804.07
    unqualified opinion report based on another auditor's 803.01
    using OCBOA 1002
Audit report following internal audit 116, 1604.01, 1604.07–.08
    auditee response to 1702
    components of individual findings reported in 1704.01–.02
    draft prepared by in-charge auditor for 1702
    editing and proofreading 1705
    executive summary as beginning . 1703
    format of 1703
    as principal product of audit assignment 1701
    professional writer and/or artist used to enhance 1703
    quality assurance process for ... 1705
    as required to stand test of time, professional 1701

Audit report following internal audit—continued
    sample 1706
    submitted to CAE for issuance within organization 1702
Audit report following performance audit 1806
Audit results for financial statement audit, fraudulent implications arising during 618
Audit results for internal audit 116.02
    auditee response to 1604.08
    communication to appropriate parties of 1604, 1604.07
    internal review of 1604.06
    process for reporting 116.01, 1702
    reporting 1701–1706
    reviewing and assessing 1604
Audit risk. *See also* individual risk types
    components of 503.06, 2402.04
    defined 502.01
    materiality and 605, 2402.02
Audit scheduling, risk assessment and 118, 1602
Audit scope detailed in engagement letter 502.02
Audit staff supervision 504, 616.01
Audit team
    completing audit program steps, documenting names of 615
    composition of 616.01
    contradictions and discrepancies investigated by 1604.05
    as covered persons for SEC 208.07
    discussion of audit findings in 116.01
    documentation of steps completed by 106
    documentation review by 616.01
    meeting to discuss potential for material misstatement due to fraud required of 503.05
    planning memorandum documenting meeting about susceptibility of client to material misstatement of 503.09
    results of preliminary survey documented by 1604.02
    rotation of members of 201.06
Audit Technique Guides (ATGs) 1306.01
Audit tests. *See also* Attribute sampling test, Sampling, *and* Variable sampling test
    corroboration of 2202.02
    data patterns examined for 2208
    decisions to make for 121.04, 2205
    incorrect application of ...... '.. 2204
    integrating analytical procedures and sampling into 121, 121.01–.04
    international standards for substantive 2403.04
    objectivity and skepticism for ... 119, 2208
    in performance audit 1806
    poorly designed or irrelevant 2204

AUD

Audit tests. *See also* Attribute sampling test, Sampling, *and* Variable sampling test—continued
 unpredictable, SAS No. 99
  mandate for.............. 119, 2002

Auditing internal control standards by PCAOB . 201.07. *See also* individual standards

Auditing partner rotation
 audit committee enforcement of .213.01
 required by Sarbanes-Oxley Act. . 102, 201.06

Auditing procedures
 for accounts payable....... 704–704.04
 for accounts receivable..... 703–703.04
 for additional documents included with audited financial statements.................804.05
 additional financial audit....... 705
 analytical procedures and sampling integrated into... 2201–2208. *See also* Analytical procedures
 forensic-like.................. 2009
 implications of fraud for........ 618
 for internal audit............. 1604.04
 nature of 503.06
 to obtain evidence of contingent liabilities 706
 for related party transactions... 708
 substantive tests broken down into 607
 when illegal acts may have been perpetrated 619

Auditing Standards Board, governance of CPA services by SEC and...................... 901

Auditing standards, global convergence of................ 2405

Auditor
 compliance with standards of... 203, 204.05
 computer use during audits by 2306–2306.03
 credibility and reputation of... 2605.03
 defense strategies in securities suit used by.................305.05
 direct financial or material indirect financial interest in audit client of 208.02
 discreditable acts of 205.03
 due professional care of... 203, 204.02
 duties for clients prohibited under AICPA independence rule for 210.05
 as facilitator in CSA process.....118.01
 improper influence by officer or director on 102
 in-charge...... 1604.01–.06, 1604.08, 1702
 information technology and..... 122, 122.04, 2301–2308
 misconduct of, SEC Rule 102(e) addressing 206.01
 misstatements of interest to . 602. *See also* Material misstatement in financial statements
 as obtaining sufficient relevant data as basis for conclusions or recommendations 203, 204.04

Auditor—continued
 overall IT strategic planning efforts reviewed by 2303.01
 planning and supervision by..... 203, 204.03
 predecessor, successor auditor's inquiries of 502.01, 904.05, 906.03
 professional competence of..... 203, 204.01
 prohibition on double role of auditing and consulting by same 208.05
 responsibilities for detecting misstatements of 602
 services now prohibited for 201.06
 supervising 504
 technical training in client's industry for................503.01
 testimony in court of....... 307, 1212

Auditor responsibilities
 for detecting misstatements during financial audits 602, 618
 for identifying related party transactions 708

Auditor switching 2006

Auditor's opinion of conformity of financial statements to GAAP . 108, 802. *See also* individual opinion types

Audits of financial statements using OCBOA.... 1001, 1002. *See also* Financial audit

Automation of organizations, historical background of 2302

B

Balance sheet date
 events subsequent to, reviewing for 707
 substantive testing prior to 614

Balance sheet in financial statements 801, 904.06
 separate auditor opinion given for 803.04

Bank cutoff statement defined.....702.05

Bank deposit method of reconstructing income 1306.05

Basis of accounting, presentation prepared on non-GAAP or OCBOA 1005

Batch systems, early computer ... 2305.01

BDO Seidman, overstated receivables at 2006

Benchmarking as reality check for financial statements 2202.01

Benefit plan activities that do and do not impair auditor's independence.................210.06

Benefit-of-the-bargain theory for measuring damages............ 1213

Benford's Law 2010.01

Best evidence rule.............. 1207.04

BES

Billing and unpaid fee balances stipulated in auditor's engagement letter 303.01

Blue Ribbon Committee on Improving Effectiveness of Corporate Audit Committees 1507

Board of directors
approval of internal auditing department charter by 1502
approval of related party transactions by 708
autonomy of, auditor's evaluation during pre-planning stage of 502.01
CAE's understanding of internal auditing department's role with 115, 1502
checks and balances function of 2606.01
client's, independent auditor prohibited from reporting for management to 210.05
client's refusal to cooperate with revision of review or compilation report upon subsequent discovery of facts communicated to 804.07, 902.05
extension of credit prohibited for issuer to 102
independent members of 2606.02
management oversight duties of . 2005
responsibilities for enterprise risk management of 1904
roles before and after Sarbanes-Oxley Act of 2606–2606.01

Board of Environmental Auditing Roundtable, BEAC established by IIA and 114

Board of Environmental, Health & Safety Auditor Certifications (BEAC)
established by IIA and Board of Environmental Auditing Roundtable 114
14000 Plus certification program of 2107

Bookkeeping services, independence impaired by providing audit client's ... 208.03, 210.06

Breach of contract claims in client liability cases 103, 303

Breach of duty of care 303.02, 304.05

Burden of proof in civil cases 112.02, 1207.01

Business knowledge, obtaining ... 2402.01

Business performance measures
Elliott Committee development of business plan for 1101
services of CPAs for 1104

Business relationship between accountant and client, independence violated by 208.04

Business risk
combined effect of audit risk and 502.01
consulting activities that do and do not impair auditor's independence 210.06
defined 1103
types of 1103

Business Roundtable, corporate governance recommendations of . 2606

C

California Micro Services Corporation, auditors as missing accounting scam at 305, 2006

Canadian Institute of Chartered Accountants (CICA), SysTrust developed by task force of AICPA and 122.03, 1105.02

capital markets, improving efficiency and integrity of 2604

Case law, precedence of 1207

Cash account, auditing
for cash disbursements in general checking 702.03
for cash in general checking for . .702.01
for cash receipts in general checking 702.02
issues specific to 702.05
year-end testing of general checking for 702.04

Cash basis
financial statements prepared using 1002
financial statements prepared using, review report for 905.06
non-GAAP financial reporting using 902.04

Cash hoard, finding 1306.02

Cash on hand 1306.02

Cash schemes in misappropriation of assets 2012.01

Cash T (transaction account), preliminary and final 1306.02

Cendant Corporation civil suit settlement 305, 2006

Centennial fraud case 2006

Certificate in Control Self-Assessment (CCSA) specialty certification from IIA 1903

Certification in control self-assessment (CCSA) designation by IIA 114, 1403.04

Certified financial services auditor (CFSA) specialty certification ... 1403.04

Certified forensic accountant (CrFA) certificate (DABFA) 2002.02

Certified forensic accountants (Cr.FAs) 1216, 2001

**Certified Forensic Financial Analyst
(CFFA) credential** 1216

Certified fraud deterrence analysts . 2001

Certified fraud examiner (CFE)
designation of 1216, 1403.04
role in fraud detection of. . 2001, 2002.02

**Certified government auditing
professional (CGAP) designation
by IIA** 114, 1403.04, 2503

**Certified government financial
manager (CGFM)** 2503

**Certified information systems
auditor (CISA) designation by
ISACA** 122.05, 1403.04, 2307

**Certified information technology
professional (CITP) certification
by AICPA** 2307

**Certified internal auditor (CIA)
certification by IIA** 114, 1403.04

**Certified professional
environmental auditor (CPEA)
designation** 114, 1403.04, 2107

**Certified protection professional
(CPP) certificate from American
Society of Industrial Security** . . . 2002.02

Certified public accountant (CPA)
communication between
predecessor CPA and successor
compilation................904.05
for government auditor
performing financial audit 2504.04
independence of 202.04
internal auditor achieving
certification as 1403.04
membership obligations in AICPA of
...........................202.01
objectivity and integrity of . . . 202.02–.04
professional services performed
with due care by 202.05
risk assessment services
provided by, level of staff for . . . 1103
role of 202.02
as ultimately responsible for
services of auditing firm,
Council requirement for.......205.06

Charter for internal auditing group . 1502

Checks, theft or interception of. . . 2012.01

Chief auditing executive (CAE)
agreement on issues between in-
charge auditor and 1604.01
audit program and budget
approved by 1604.05
audit report appearance and
organization determined by . . . 116.02, 1703
audit units ranked by risk level by
.... 115.03, 1602
auditee's response reviewed by
in-charge and 1702
as authorizing and organizing
internal auditing function...... 1502
communication between in-
charge auditor and 1604.01

**Chief auditing executive (CAE)—
continued**
control self-assessment
implemented by 1903
cooperation with external auditor
of......................... 1504
as coordinating internal auditing
function with organizational
policies 1503
follow-up audit scheduled by ... 1604.08
in-charge auditor assigned to
auditable unit by 1604.01
influence on audit report of . 116.01, 1702
internal auditing function
managed by 115, 405, 1501
internal policies and procedures
of strategic importance
identified by 1902
knowledge, skills, and abilities of . 115
laws and regulations affecting
organization identified by 1906
organization divided into audit
units by 115.03, 1602
quality assurance process for
internal audit report established
by 116.02, 1505, 1705
responsibilities of 1501
risk factors used by............ 1602
staff internal auditing services
monitored by, to prevent
outsourcing of function 1506.01

Chief executive officers (CEOs)
certification of financial reports
required for 102, 306.03
internal controls responsibilities of
.... 102
signature on federal tax returns
required for................. 102

Chief Financial Officers Act of 1990
.... 2504.01

Chief financial officers (CFOs)
certification of financial reports
required for 102, 306.03
internal auditing department not
reportable to 1502
internal controls responsibilities of
.... 102

Chief information officer (CIO)
auditor as ensuring sensible
policies and procedures to
safeguard workers implemented by
.... 2303.01
to provide overall IT system
vision and governance....... 2303.01
strategic planning by 122.02

**Class action lawsuits involving
reported and whisper earnings** ... 305

Clean Air Act 2102
expenditures to meet
requirements of 2101

Clean Water Act 2102

Client
assistance provided for audit by,
engagement letter stipulation of
.........................303.01

CLI

Client—continued
  audit planning conference held with
    ....503.01
  contingent fees prohibited from .208.06
  employment relationship
    between accountant or family
    member and, independence violated
    by 208.03
  fraudulent acts by. *See* Fraud *and*
    Fraud detection
    with high versus low combined
    inherent and control risks 702.06
  illegal acts by 619
  investigated for good credit
    history before engagement . . . 303.03,
                                    502.01
  obtaining knowledge about 503.01
  obtaining understanding with....502.02
  resources required during
    engagement from, engagement
    letter detailing 502.02
  responsibilities of auditor to . 205–205.06
  warning signs of troublesome ...303.03

Client employees
  assistance during audit from 502.02
  independent auditor prohibited
    from supervising.............210.05

Client information, confidential,
Rule 301 for 205.01

Client-submitted document,
auditing procedures applied to ...804.05

Client's facilities, tour of 503.03

Client's legal representatives,
inquiries about pending litigation
made of 706, 707

Client's managers, inquiries
regarding subsequent events of .. 707

COBIT control framework (ISACA) . 122.03,
                                    2304

Code of ethics for senior financial
officers 102

Code of Professional Ethics (Code)
(AICPA). *See also* individual sections
  confidentiality requirement of ...502.02
  objectives of 201.09
  principles and rules sections of ..201.08
  rules promulgated by
    Professional Ethics Executive
    Committee for 201.08

Codes of ethical conduct of public
companies, focuses of 2602

Cohen Commission, Treadway
Commission evolution from 2002

Collusion
  auditor's degree of skepticism in
    presuming possibility of....... 2002
  creating material misstatement
    on financial statements 602
  detection of employee 2005.02, 2006

Commission of the European
Communities.............. 2401, 2405

Committee of Sponsoring Organizations
of Treadway Commission (COSO)
  assessment of information
    systems quality using 1105.01
  control model of......118.01, 1603, 1903
  enterprise risk management
    framework (ERMF) by 215, 1603,
                              1904, 1905, 2002, 2605.03
  Fraudulent Financial Reporting:
    1987–1997 report of 2002, 2005
  website of 2002

Competency Framework for
Internal Auditing (CFIA) (IIA
Research Foundation) 1403.01,
                              1404.04–1404.05–.06, 1501

Compilation engagements
  documenting client's verbal
    representations during 903.04
  engagement letter for..........903.01
  omit-disclosure 403.03
  standards for.................902.02

Compilation report
  discovery of facts existing at date
    of 902.05
  for financial statements compiled
    for comparative purposes 904.04
  format of, when all disclosures
    are omitted from financial
    statements 904.02
  format of, when CPA is not
    independent of client 904.03
  forms of 903.04, 904.01
  included in prescribed forms 904.07
  issued following compilation of
    prospective financial
    statements 1007.03–.04
  no opinion or assurance issued with
    ....902.02
  reasonableness of issuing.......904.10
  wording for standard 903.04

Compilation representation letter . 903.03,
                                    904.09

Compilations.............. 902.01–903.04
  change from audits or reviews to
    ....904.10
  defined.......................903.02
  with departure from GAAP or
    OCBOA 904.01
  developing understanding with
    client about services for 903.01
  of prior period review, current
    period with 906.02
  procedures for 903.02
  review of prior period, current
    period with 906.02
  SSARS requirements for........903.02

Completeness management
assertion 603.02
  correspondence to audit
    objectives of 604.02

Compliance audits............1901–1908
  auditable units for............. 1901
  control self-assessment (CSA) in . 1903
  differences between EMS audit and
    2109
  document review during 1604.02

Compliance audits—continued
  explained in terms of
    management assertions and
    established criteria........... 1802
  focus shift from conformity with
    to actual policies and
    procedures in....... 118, 1901, 1908
  by internal auditors, growth in
    incidence of......... 1402, 1901, 1903
  questions for preliminary survey in
    .... 1604.02
  reasons auditors perform....... 1901
  reporting results of............ 1902
  steps in...................... 1902

Compliance reports.............. 1004
  of past as "gotcha audits".. 1901, 1908

**Comprehensive Environmental
Response, Compensation, and
Liability Act (CERCLA)
(Superfund)**................... 2102

Comptronix Corp. fraud case..... 2005.02

**Computer, auditor's interactions
with**............... 122.04, 2306–2306.03

Computer forensics.............. 1209

**Computer-assisted audit
techniques, determining need for**
  .... 503.01

Computer-assisted audit tools.... 2306.03

**Concealed liabilities and expenses,
fraudulent**.................... 2006

**Conduct, levels of, compared with
rules of conduct**.............. 303.02

**Conference Board
recommendations for corporate
governance**................... 2606

**Confirmation letters of account
balance information**........... 107

Construction auditing........... 1907

**Continental Vending case of related
party transactions**............ 708

Contingent fees................. 205
  from audit clients as prohibited.. 208.06
  defined..................... 205.02

**Contingent liabilities in financial
audits, reviewing for**...... 706, 2403.02

Continuing professional education (CPE)
  to obtain industry knowledge for
    client's business............ 503.01
  requirements for.............. 205.06

Continuous (electronic) auditing.. 122.04, 2306.03

Contract auditing............... 1907
  external or internal auditors
    performing................. 118.03

**Contract disputes, elements for
forensic accountant in**......... 1206

Contracts
  controls for awarding...... 118.03, 1907

Contracts—continued
  requests for bids, diversity in
    distribution of.............. 1907
  sole-source.................. 1907
  types of, fixed-fee and cost-plus. 1907

Contractual agreements
  presentations prepared in
    compliance with............ 1005
  report on company compliance
    with...................... 1004

Control risk
  combined with inherent risk, high
    versus low................ 702.06
  as component of audit risk...... 503.06
  corroboration or revision of
    preliminary assessment of..... 613
  defined............. 106, 503.06, 605
  increased by computerized
    systems eliminating paper trail
    and segregation of duties..... 1208
  of internal audit.............. 610
  international standards addressing
    .... 2402.04
  inverse relation of detection risk
    and...................... 613

Control self-assessment (CSA)
  process.................. 118.01, 1903
  software for.................. 2109

Cooked books
  consequences of............ 2605.03
  detecting............... 119.02, 2006

Coopers and Lybrand
  failure to detect accounting scam
    at California Micro Services
    Corporation of.......... 305, 2006
  1999 SEC penalties against. 206.01, 2006

**Corporate accountability,
accounting scandals as increasing
focus on**..................... 2601

**Corporate codes of conduct, recent
attention to establish and disclose**
  2602

**Corporate finance activities that do
and do not impair auditor's
independence**................ 210.06

Corporate governance
  accounting scandals as
    increasing focus on....... 2601, 2603
  audit committee's roles in.... 2606.01, 2607.03
  checks and balances in....... 2606.05
  consequences of lack of effective
    2005
  defined..................... 2604
  directors' roles in........ 2606, 2606.01
  education in business schools for
    responsible.......... 2603.03, 2606.06
  external auditors' roles in..... 2606.05
  internal auditors' roles in...... 2606.04
  management's roles in........ 2606.03
  other stakeholders' roles in.... 2606.06
  recommendations for improving
    .... 2606.07

COR

Corporate governance—continued
 responsible and effective, intended financial statement fraud discovered by 2005
 roles in business of 2604, 2606
 SEC final rules for 2606
 summary of changes following Sarbanes-Oxley Act to 102, 2606

Cost-plus contracts 1907

Courtroom etiquette 307, 1212

Covered person defined 208.07

Crazy Eddie accounting scam, fraud methods in 2006

Credit purchases, auditing accounts payable for 704.01

Credit sales, auditing accounts receivable for 703.01

Criminal Investigation (CI) agent ... 113, 1301

Criteria of Control Board of Canadian Institute of Chartered Accountants (CoCo) control model 118.01, 1903

Current assets and liabilities, expected changes in proportion to sales of 2202.01

CVC International fraud case 2006

D

Damages
 laws aimed at preventing environmental 2102
 measuring 112.02, 120.06, 1213
 measuring environmental 2109

Data mining 1208, 2012.04, 2306.03

Data quality of input for analytical procedures 2202.04

Data warehousing
 to develop detailed view of business 2305.04
 to uncover inventory fraud 2012.04

Database systems, concerns with . 2305.03

Daubert **decision used to reject expert witnesses** 1210.03, 1211

DeAngelio, Anthony, fraud case of 2005.02

Debt factor, going concern issues focusing on 2006

Defalcation 304, 2003

Details of account balances, substantive tests of 606

Detection risk
 as component of audit risk...... .503.06
 defined............. 106, 503.06, 605
 international standards addressing 2402.04

Detection risk—continued
 inverse relation of control risk and 613
 planned, formula for 503.06, 606

Digital Analysis Tests and Statistics (DATAS) in ratio analysis....... 2010.02

Digital Equipment Corporation fraud case 2005.02

Digital signatures................ 1106

Diplomate American Board of Forensic Accountants (DABFA) . 2002.02

Direct (transaction) method of reconstructing income 1301

Disclaimed opinion in prospective financial statement report 1007.11

Disclaimer of opinion in financial audit report................ 108, 713
 for additional information included with audited financial statements 804.05
 international standards for 2404
 for non-public company when CPA has not performed services on financial statements 902.01
 stating that auditor does not express opinion on financial statements 803.04

Disclosures required by Sarbanes-Oxley Act 102, 2604

Discovery phase in litigation 112.02, 1207.02

Discrimination on basis on race, color, religion, sex, age, or national origin 205.04

Document shredding as crime 102

Dual dates for financial audit report 804.02

Due Professional Care Standard (IIA) 2002.01

E

Earnings management, legitimate and illegitimate 119.01, 2005–2007

Eco-labeling 2110

Economic Reality (Lifestyle) Audits . 1302, 1304, 1305

Economy and efficiency review in performance audit 1806

EITF Issues No. 89-13, 90-8, and 93-5 2104

Eldercare services
 defined.................... 1108

Electronic data in audits 2306.03
 Elliott Committee development of business plan for 1101
 table of direct, assurance, and consulting 1108

Electronic commerce (e-commerce)
.. 1106, 2305.09. *See also* WebTrust for electronic commerce

Electronic data processing (EDP) ... 2302

Electronic documents 1208, 1209

Electronic evidence 112.02, 1209

Embezzlement
cash schemes for 2012.01
as employee fraud 2001

Emerging Issues Task Force (EITF)
issues (FASB) 120.02

Employee benefit plans, audit of ...403.01

Employee fraud 2001

Employee lifestyles checked for fraud warnings 2013

Employee Retirement Income Security Act of 1974 (ERISA), audit engagement conducted pursuant to 403.02

Employment relationship between accountant and audit client, independence violated by 208.03

EMS audits. *See* Environmental audits

End-user systems for IT 2305.08

Engagement letter, compilation ... 903.01

Engagement letter, financial audit
contents of .. 204.02, 210.05, 303.01, 502.02
preparation of 502.02
sample 502.02
used in lawsuits against practitioner
.... 303.01

Engagement letter, review services .905.02

Engagement letter, SSARS review ..905.02

Engagement letter, SysTrust assurance 1105.02

Engagement review as type of AICPA peer review for small firms
.... 403.02

Engagement risk considered during pre-planning stage of audit 502.01

Enron
allegations against 2605.01
on Arthur Andersen's red alert for fraud radar screen 619
audit committee membership being examined following developments at............. 115.02
double role of Arthur Andersen as independent and internal auditor of 207, 208.05
fraudulent financial statements of
.... 2005, 2005.02
issuance of stock in exchange for notes receivable as material overstatement of shareholders' equity in 703.04
new accounting industry oversight organization formed as result of debacle of 207, 401

Enron—continued
off-balance sheet treatment of liabilities incurred by SPEs of .. 708
Special Committee of board of, related party transactions under investigation by 804.07
tax haven subsidiaries eliminating tax liability of 503.05

Enterprise resource planning (ERP) .122.03

Enterprise risk management
in achieving organization's goals, focus on 2606.07
components of 1904
COSO framework for ... 215, 1603, 1904
defined..................... 1904
implementation of............ 1603

Environmental auditing
organizational responsibilities for
.... 2111
origin of 2101
shift in social outlook changing audit objectives in 2113

Environmental auditing department, managing 2112

Environmental Auditing Roundtable (EAR), BEAC 14000 Plus certification program introduced by IIA and 2107

Environmental auditor, roles and operating areas of 120.05, 2108

Environmental audits
defined 120, 2101
differences between compliance audits and 2109
early....................... 2103

Environmental, health, and safety (EHS) auditing 2107

Environmental information needs .. 2110

Environmental laws, preventive and remedial 2102

Environmental management
defined 2105

Environmental management systems (EMSs)
components of successful 2111
design of 2103
principles of 120.03, 2105
purpose of 120.03
support offered by environmental auditor to 120.06, 2109
voluntary standards for 2105

Environmental Protection Agency (EPA)................... 120.01, 2103
criminal fines levied by 2101

Environmental risk, new approach systems for mitigating 120.06, 2109

Environmental statutes, terms of U.S. 2102

Equity Funding fraud case ... 2005.02, 2006

Ergonomics 122.02, 2303.01

ERG

Ernst & Young
　fraud study by 2005
　lawsuit for failure to detect CVC International accounting fraud against 2006

Ethical conduct
　accounting scandals increasing focus on 2601, 2602
　national trend toward improved . 2602

Ethical principles, auditor's adherence to 202–202.07

Ethical standard, breach of, civil liability claim for 303.02

Ethics education
　ethical decision-making in 2603.02
　ethical leadership in 2603.03
　need for 2603
　responsibility of business in society included in 2603.01

European Commission (EC) initiatives to globalize auditing standards 2405

European Federation of Accountants 2405

European Union (EU)
　desire for single set of standards of 2405
　promotion of economic progress by 2401

European Union (EU) Committee on Auditing 2401

Evidence
　analytical 1604.04
　competent 106, 609, 617
　computer equipment seized as criminal 1209
　computer technology and 1208
　destruction of 1209
　documentary 1604.04
　electronic 112.02, 1209
　evaluation of 617
　external and internal 609
　false 1215
　gathered when fraud risk factors are identified 503.05
　hearsay 1207.04
　internal audit 1604.04
　international auditing standards for 2403.01
　of performance of risk assessment, documenting 2004
　physical 1604.04
　real 112.02, 1207.01
　relevant 609, 1106, 1207.01, 1207.04
　of subsequent events 707
　sufficiency of 608, 803.04, 2403.01
　testimonial 1604.04
　timing of 604.02
　types of 112.02, 1207.01, 1207.04

Evidence gathering
　for financial audits . 106, 108, 802, 803.04
　by forensic accountant 1207.04
　for going concern problems 2403.09
　for revised financial statements 2403.08

Examination of prospective financial statements
　compilation versus 1007.03
　examination phase for 1007.08
　planning phase for 1007.06–.07
　preparing for 1007.07
　preplanning stage of 1007.06
　reporting phase for 1007.09

Executive or employee search activities that do and do not impair auditor's independence ... 210.06

Existence or occurrence
　management assertion 603.01
　correspondence to audit objectives of 604.02

Expectation gap between public expectation and auditor's stated responsibilities
　advice for overcoming 307
　for fraud detection ... 302, 303.02, 2002

Expenditure (source and application of funds) method of reconstructing income 1306.03

Expert witnessing. *See also* **Forensic accounting services**
　arbitration as driving force in England for 1205
　attacks against evidence of 1205
　compensation for 1211, 1212
　court appointments for 1211
　courtroom behavior for 1212
　exclusion of testimony in .. 1210.03, 1211
　by forensic accountant 112.01–.03
　growth in popularity of 1204
　liability in, risk management for .. 1215
　as one role of forensic accountant 1206
　opinion permitted in testimony for 112.02, 1210.03
　in trial court 112.02, 1207
　validation of reasoning and methodology used in 1210.03

Exposure Draft for a Proposed Statement on Standards for Accounting and Review Services (AICPA) 902.01, 904.05, 904.06, 906.03

eXtensible Business Reporting Language (XBRL) 2306.03

eXtensible Markup Language (XML) 2306.03

External environment approach to risk-based audit planning ... 115.04, 1603

External (independent) auditor
　adoption of financial research for external audit report by 612
　competence to audit technologies of 1208
　contract audits by 1907
　fraud risk assessment by, in audit planning 2004
　in-charge 1504
　interaction with internal auditors of 1504
　internal audit report reviewed by . 1703

Index—References are to paragraph (¶) numbers. **937**

External (independent) auditor—continued
  internal auditor assisting with
    evidence gathering by 1404.06
  role in corporate governance
    before and after Sarbanes-
    Oxley Act of 2606.05
  role in fraud detection and fraud
    examination of . . 119, 304, 502.02, 2002,
        2003, 2004
  use of internal auditor's work for
    financial statement audit by . . . 612,
        2002
  work of internal auditor used by
    . . . . 2403.11

F

Facilities tour by auditor 503.03

**Fact-finding interviews during
  internal audit** 1605

**Falsification of documents,
  auditor's degree of skepticism in
  presuming possibility of** 2002

FASB Exposure Draft 158-B 120.02

FDIC Improvement Act of 1991 . . . .403.01

Federal False Statements Statutes . .306.02

**Federal income tax basis, financial
  statements prepared using** 1002

**Federal income tax return, CEO
  signature of** 102

Federal Reserve Board, creation of . 1205

Federal Rules of Civil Procedures (FRCP)
  evidence under 1207.04
  governing district courts 112.02

**Federal Rules of Evidence governing
  expert witnesses** 1211

**Federal Trade Commission (FTC),
  creation of** 1205

**Federally insured depository
  institution, audit of** 403.01

Fees for audit
  auditor determination of
    potential client's willingness and
    ability to pay 502.01
  engagement letter describing
    basis of 303.01
  monitoring and controlling 303.03
  suing for client's failure to pay . . .303.03

**Fictitious revenues type of financial
  statement fraud, incidence of** 2006,
    2012.02–.03

Fieldwork 601–620
  analytics used during 2202.02
  auditing procedures performed during.
    See Auditing procedures
  auditor's report dated to last day
    of 803.01, 804.02
  documenting responses to fraud
    during 618
  for financial audit 106, 504, 601–620

Fieldwork—continued
  forensic 2002
  for internal audit 116.01, 1604.05
  for performance audit 1806
  substantive tests performed
    during 606–607
  two stages of 106, 601
  workpapers gathered during
    . . . . 616–616.02, 616.01

**Financial Accounting Standards
  Board (FASB)** 204.05
  Exposure Draft 158-B,
    *Accounting for Liabilities
    Related to Closure or Removal
    of Long-Lived Assets* 2104
  public funding of 2606.06
  Statement No. 5, *Accounting for
    Contingencies* 706
  supplementary information
    required in financial statements by
    . . . . .803.01

**Financial analysts, Sarbanes-Oxley
  Act reporting requirements for** . . 102,
    2606.06

Financial audit. *See also* Financial
  statement fraud
  audit program prepared and
    followed during 106
  audit report for. *See* Audit report
    following financial audit
  client restriction on scope of 803.04
  differences between fraud audit
    and 2003
  fieldwork for 106, 504, 601–620
  final analytical review of 711
  final review of 106, 620
  GAGAS standards for government
    . . . . 123.04, 2504.05
  integrated with operational and
    compliance auditing 1805
  internal auditor's work used by
    external auditor during 612, 2002
  international auditing standards for
    2402
  limited engagement for 804.01
  objective of 106, 601
  operational issues for areas of . . . 1805
  opinions in 108, 803–803.04
  other procedures in 705
  planning 105, 501–504, 2402
  questions for preliminary survey in
    . . . . 1604.02
  reaching conclusions about 107,
    701–713
  reporting considerations for 108
  risks associated with 503.06
  scope of 502.02, 2404
  special report dating issues for . .804.02
  submission of unaudited, for
    nonpublic companies 902.02
  subsequent events to, reviewing for
    . . . . 107, 707
  timing of 502.02
  trial balance versus 902.03

**Financial Executives International,
  corporate governance
  recommendations of** 2606

FIN

Financial information system design and implementation, independence impaired by providing audit client's 208.03

Financial institutions, confirmation letters sent to 107

Financial interest
of auditor in audit client, independence violated by.. 208.02, 210
of next of kin in client company, independence impaired by 210.02

Financial presentations........... 1005

Financial reporting
indicators of management engaging in fraudulent 2005, 2007
management report on internal control over........... 610, 1404.06
material weakness indicated by ineffective oversight of 1905
process of 2604
role of 2604
supply chain of 2604
timely 1210.02

Financial scandals of 2001–2002. See also individual companies
causes of.................. 2605.01
consequences of.... 501, 1210.02, 2005, 2605.02, 2606.01
"Corporate Scandal Sheet" tracking of................. 2005
responses to 2605.04

Financial statement fraud ... 2001–2005.02, 2006–2007, 2010.01
correction of committed . 1210, 1210.03, 2005
defined...................... 2005
as focus of auditing profession .. 2004
external auditor's responsibility to detect 2003
forensic accounting practices to prevent, detect, and correct 1210–1210.03
schemes common in........... 2005

Financial statements
adjusted for events subsequent to auditor report date 2403.08
attributes of trial balances versus 902.03
basic, list of 801, 804.05, 904.06
benchmarking and financial ratios used on 2202.01
client-prepared 902.02, 904.04
client-submitted documents included with audited........804.05
comparative . 803.01, 804.03, 904.04, 906.02
compiled 902.01, 902.02
compiled, reviewed, and audited, differences among 902.01
components of 801
condensed...................804.06
consistency of other documents and financial information in larger documents with 803.01
CPA responsibility for submitted . 109, 902.01

Financial statements—continued
determining overall reasonableness of 2202.03
draft.......................904.11
dual sets of, reporting on 804.04
Enron's restatement of 708, 804.07
of European company, sample of principles used in 2401
fair presentation for 2403.10
fraudulent 304, 2002, 2005–2005.02, 2006–2007, 2605.01
GAAP 1002
graphs accompanying 904.09
incomplete, report for financial presentation having 1005
information accompanying, reports on 804.05
limited reporting engagement for one of 804.01
material misstatement in.... 304, 602, 1905
material related party transactions disclosed in footnotes to.......................... 708
not prepared using GAAP or OCBOA, report on 1005
not to be used by third parties ...904.12
OCBOA methods for preparing .. 109, 902.04, 903.04, 905.06, 1002
prepared for use in another country 804.04
pro-forma 1007
prospective 1007–1007.11
public confidence in quality and reliability of 2005
of publicly held versus non-public company.................... 901
revision of 617
role of 2604
specified elements, accounts, or items of, for compilation report 904.08
submission of 902.02
unaudited, landmark case of auditor liability for preparing... 901
unaudited, limited-procedure, and audited, differences among 109
vertical analysis of 2008

Financial status audits, IRS........ 1305

Fixed fee contracts 1907

Follow-up internal audit 1604.08

Follow-up performance audit visit .. 1806

Forecasts as prospective financial statements. See also Prospective financial statements
compilation of............... 1007.03
content of 1007
examination of 1007.03, 1007.05–.11
format of 1007

Foreign Corrupt Practices Act (FCPA) 305.06

Forensic accountant
affidavits for summary judgment proceeding involving 1207.03
for computer-related audits 1208

Index—References are to paragraph (¶) numbers.

Forensic accountant—continued
    credentials of 1202
    damages measured by 112.02, 1213
    evidence admissible by 112.02
    as expert witness 112.01, 1212
    healthy skepticism of 119.02, 1202
    indirect methods of
      reconstructing income of .. 1301–1308
    IRS agent as 113, 1301
    lifestyle of employees examined by
      113
    motive considered by 1304
    role and services of 1206, 1212
    understanding of judicial
      procedure required for 112.02

Forensic Accountants Society of North America (FASNA),
    membership of 1216

Forensic accounting
    certifications in 1216
    coining of term 1206
    defined 1202

Forensic accounting practices
    .... 1210–1210.02

Forensic accounting services 112,
    1201–1215.01. *See also* Expert witnessing
    defining 1202
    evidence phase of 1205
    first book to explore 1212
    history of 1203
    in post-Enron era 503.05

Forensic audit, differences between GAAS audit and .. 2003. *See also* Fraud audit
    IRS agents as using approaches of
      1302

Forensic auditors, skepticism of ... 119.02, 2006

Forensic electronic imaging 1208

Foreseeability approach to auditor liability 304, 304.04

Former employee, influence on attest engagement of 210.01

Former practitioner, independence issues of 210.03

Fraud
    accounts receivable 2012.02
    as accumulation of circumstances
      618
    asset 304, 2003, 2010.01, 2011, 2012–2012.04
    audit malpractice claims involving
      302
    audit team meeting to discuss
      risks of material misstatement
      due to 503.05
    audit tests for 2002
    auditor's actions in response to.. 618
    auditor's responsibility for
      programs and controls to prevent
      713
    auditor's responsibility to consider
      .... 2403.12
    awareness of in-charge internal
      auditor to possibility of 1604.05

Fraud—continued
    behavioral considerations of 2003
    brought to attention of
      appropriate company management
      .... 305.06, 618
    common types of 2001, 2002
    conditions occurring in most 610
    definitions of 2001, 2002.01, 2402.03
    detection of. *See* Fraud detection
    disclosure of 713, 2004
    elements of concern for forensic
      accountant in 1206
    employee 2001, 2002.01
    expectation gap between public
      expectation and auditors'
      stated responsibilities for detecting
      .... 302, 303.02, 2002
    factors in, motive, opportunity,
      and lack of integrity as 2003
    financial statement 304, 1210
      2001–2005.02, 2006–2007, 2010.01
    heightened sensitivity toward ... 501
    high-profile cases of 2002, 2006
    impact on auditing procedures of
      618
    implications for audit of 605
    incidence of SEC filings for 2014
    indicia of, selected 2013
    internal auditing department
      investigation to recover lost
      assets following 115
    inventory 2006, 2012.04
    investment, avoiding 2008
    management .. 119.02, 2001, 2002.01, 2007
    material financial statement 2002, 2006, 2402.03
    prevalence of 1308
    recent studies of 2005
    red flags for 2006, 2008, 2010, 2011
    statistics of SEC alleged auditor
      deficiencies for 206.01
    statute of limitations for
      discovery of, new 306.03
    as type of misstatement 602

Fraud audit
    company employee interviews in . 2003
    differences between GAAS
      financial audit and 2003
    importance of 114
    time and fee requirements for
      conducting thorough 304

Fraud auditing 2001–2014
    behavioral aspects of 1304
    process of 2003
    reactive and proactive 2001

Fraud auditors
    as attacking financial statements
      like detective 2006
    backgrounds of 2001
    tests by 2011

Fraud detection
    for asset misappropriation fraud . 304, 2011, 2012, 2012.02
    data mining for vendor
      information used in 1208
    expansion of auditor's
      responsibility for, SAS No. 82 as
      providing 304

FRA

Fraud detection—continued
  forensic accountant as providing
    combination of litigation
    support and 1202
  guidelines, concepts, and
    requirements for 2004
  history of 2002–2002.02, 2004
  horizontal and vertical
    percentage analysis revealing red
    flags in 2008
  ratio analysis revealing red flags in
    2008
  as responsibility of all corporate
    governance participants 2005
  role of certified fraud examiners in
    .... 2002.02
  role of external (independent)
    auditor in .. 119, 304, 502.02, 2002, 2003, 2004
  role of internal auditor in ... 115, 1502, 2002.01, 2003

Fraud examination, certifications in
  1216

Fraud risk factors
  auditor's application of critical
    judgment to 2004
  impact on financial audit planning
    of 503.05
  misappropriation of assets 2011
  processes affected by 604.02
  types of financial statement 2007

Fraudulent financial reporting 119.01, 2005–2005.02

G

Generally accepted accounting procedures (GAAP)
  accrual basis of accounting
    required for financial statements by
    .... 109, 902.04, 1002
  applicable in client's industry,
    CPA understanding of ... 903.02, 905.04
  audit standards for 802, 2002
  auditor's opinion of conformity of
    financial statements to 108, 802
  condensed financial statements
    as not presenting fairly 804.06
  conformity of financial
    statements receiving unqualified
    opinion to 802, 803, 803.01
  departures from 803.01–.04, 804.04
  financial statement fraud as only
    type intended to be found
    under....................... 304
  financial statement titles under .. 109, 902.04, 1002
  footnote disclosures required by . 904.02
  government audits using 2504.03
  management assertions
    supported by proper application of
    .... 106, 604
  misapplication of, for prospective
    financial statements 1007.11
  reporting departures from 906.01

Generally accepted auditing standards (GAAS) (AICPA)
  audit design and limits described
    to client in terms of 303.01
  collusion impossible to detect
    according to 2006
  confirming accounts receivable
    under....................... 703.04
  engagement letter specifying
    accordance of audit with 303.01
  evidence gathering for auditor's
    report governed by 108, 802
  financial statement audits of non-
    public companies in
    accordance with............. 802
  followed in governmental audit .. 205.04
  GAGAS as incorporating fieldwork
    and reporting standards of
    .... 2504.01–.02
  independence requirement of ... 502.01
  insufficient evidence preventing
    auditor's compliance with 803.04
  negligence arising from failure to
    follow...................... 303.03
  quality control procedures to
    help ensure compliance with ... 104
  staff supervision required by 616.01
  wrong assumptions about
    evidence and internal controls
    despite application of......... 602

Generally accepted government auditing standards (GAGAS) 118.02, 123.01–.07, 403, 403.01, 1806
  applicability of............... 2504.02
  for attestation engagements ... 123.05, 2504.03, 2504.06
  compliance with Single Audit Act
    and 123.07, 2504.01
  for financial audits 123.04, 2504.05
  financial standards of 123.04
  fraud and violations reported to
    outside parties under 2504.05
  general standards of 123.03, 2504.04
  for internal control 2504.06
  organizations subject to 123.01
  for performance audits .. 123.06, 2504.07
  for single audit 2504.08
  as "The Yellow Book" 1806, 2504.01

Global Auditing Information Network (GAIN) program (IIA) ... 401, 1505

Going concern problems
  indications of 107, 709
  international standards for 2403.09

Government Accounting Standards Board (GASB)
  Concepts Statement No. 2 1807
  SEA performance measures of... 1807
  supplementary information
    required in financial statements by
    .... 803.01

Government attestation engagements 123.02, 123.05, 2504.03, 2504.06

Government auditors
  audit plans of 2504.07

Index—References are to paragraph (¶) numbers.

Government auditors—continued
  communication of engagement
    responsibilities by 2504.05
  as employees or contractors 2501
  evidence obtained by 2504.07
  nonaudit services of 2504.04
  professional organizations for ... 2502

Government audits . 123–123.07, 2501–2504.08
  deficiencies in internal control in
    .... 2504.05
  documentation for 2504.05
  fieldwork in 2504.05
  types of 123.02, 2504.03
  U.S. Generally Accepted Government
    Auditing Standards (GAGAS) for. *See*
    Generally accepted government
    auditing standards (GAGAS)

Government financial audit 2504.03, 2504.05

Government internal audit 2504.04

Government performance audit 117.01
  audit report for 2504.07
  GAGAS for 123.06, 2504.07
  objectives of 1806, 2504.03
  phases of 1806

Governmental unit, auditing 205.04

**Graphs, financial, as accompanying
financial statements** 904.09

Great Salad Oil Swindle fraud case
  .... 2005.02

**Gross receipts formula in bank
deposit method** 1306.05

H

**Hackers, denial-of-service attacks
by** 1105.02

**Handbook of International Auditing,
Assurance, and Ethics
Pronouncements 2003 Edition** ... 2401

**Health care providers, performance
measurement of**
  Elliott Committee development of
    business plan for 1101
  facilities using services in 1107

**Health South, fraudulent financial
statements of** 2005.02

Honorary director 210

Horizontal percentage analysis 119.03
  as analytical procedure
    performed during audit preparation
    .... 503.02
  red flags for fraud revealed by ... 2008

I

**IFAC web site about independence
issues** 210.08

**Illegal acts, engagement letter
covering auditor's intent to detect**
  .... 303.01

Illegitimate earnings management
  2005–2007

**Imaging technology for forensic
accounting** 1208

Improper disclosures, fraudulent .. 2006

In-charge auditor for internal audit .116.01

**Income statement in financial
statements** 801, 904.06

**Income tax basis, for financial
statements** 1002

Independence
  GAGAS general standard for ... 2504.04
  issues impairing CPA during
    review engagement for 905.01
  new rules for accounting firm
    services regarding .. 201.06, 213–213.03
  not required in preparing
    compilation reports 904.03
  required under GAAS 502.01
  services prohibited under
    Sarbanes-Oxley Act to preserve
    auditor's 102

**Independence rule of AICPA and its
interpretations** .. 210–210.07, 402.02, 905.01

Independence rules of SEC 208, 2006

**Independence Standards Board (ISB)
statements**
  1, *Independence Discussion with
    Audit Committee* 209
  2, *Certain Independence
    Implications of Audits of Mutual
    Funds* 209
  3, *Employment with Audit Clients*
    209

**Independence Standards Board
(ISB) website** 209

Independent auditor. *See* External
(independent) auditor

**Indirect methods of reconstructing
income** 113, 1301–1308
  five types of 1306.01–.05
  when to use 1306

**Industry conditions, fraud risk
factors associated with** 2007

**Information flows, external,
potential assurance services for** . 1110.01

**Information risk, financial
statement fraud addressed to reduce**
  2005

Information systems
  activities for, that do and do not
    impair auditor's independence . 210.06
  quality of, CPA services dealing
    with 1105.01

**Information Systems Audit and
Control Association (ISACA)** 122.03, 122.05, 2307, 2308

Information systems reliability
  Elliott Committee development of
    business plan for 1101

INF

Information systems reliability—
continued
  existing services of CPAs for ... 1105.01
  management and external
    services for 1105
  SysTrust for 1101, 1105.02

Information technology 2301–2308
  auditing organizations involved with
    2307
  auditor and 122, 2301–2308
  control frameworks for 215, 2304
  controls for, general and
    application 122.01–.03, 2303–2303.03
  internal control structure
    influenced by 1208
  personnel issues for 2303.01
  professional organizations for
    auditing 2307
  resources of, effective and
    efficient use of 2303.01
  system vision and governance for
    .... 2303.01
  "top ten" list published annually
    of issues in 2301

Information technology (IT) auditor
  academic preparation for
    becoming 2308
  certification of 2307
  demand and salary levels for 2308

Information technology (IT)
  steering committee 2303.01

Information technology (IT) systems
  access to, safeguarding 2303.01
  application controls for 2303.02
  auditing through the computer
    using 2306.02
  auditor's review of 122.01
  evaluating performance of 122.02
  failure of, ensuring business
    continuation following 2303.01
  internal controls built into 2303.01
  outsourced 2303.01, 2305.07
  performance measures for 2303.01
  privacy policy for 2303.01
  security of 2303.01
  self-auditing of, auditing through
    auditee's computer for 2306.02
  shared 2305.07
  staff for 122.02
  variety of 2305–2305.09

Information technology (IT) vision .122.02

Inherent risk
  as component of audit risk 503.06
  defined 503.06, 605
  increased by faster transaction
    processing of computerized
    systems................... 1208
  international standards addressing
    .... 2402.04

Inquiry by CPA of client's personnel
  .... .903.03

Inspection report by PCAOB, draft
  and final 404

Inspector General Act of 1978 .... 2504.01

Institute of Internal Auditors (IIA)
  activities of 1403–1403.05
  BEAC established by Board of
    Environmental Auditing
    Roundtable and 114, 1403.04
  BEAC 14000 Plus certification
    program introduced by EAR and
    2107
  certified government auditing
    professional (CGAP)
    certification program of....... 114,
      1403.04, 2503
  control self-assessment training
    and certification developed by . 1903
  education and training by 1403.05
  establishment in 1941 of 1403
  GAIN program of 401, 1505
  guidance on performance
    measures from 104
  Guidance Task Force of 1403.02
  internal auditing defined by 1402
  International Standards for the
    Professional Practice of Internal
    Auditing (ISPPIA) of 1403.03
  IT auditing designation in
    development by 2307
  member services of 114
  membership statistics for 1403
  mission statement of 1403
  professional certification
    maintained by............... 114
  professional standards issued by
    .... 1403.03
  standards of professional
    conduct issued by 102, 1403.03
  websites of 1403.04, 2307

Institute of Internal Auditors Research
Foundation
  fraud studied by 2005
  research project descriptions of
    .... 1403.01, 1501
  study of value-added assurance
    services 1110.01

Institute of Management and
Administration (IOMA) fraud
study 2005

Integrated test facility, auditor's
software installed on auditee's IT
system to create............. 2306.02

Intentional misrepresentation,
auditor's liability for 304.06

Interagency Corporate Fraud Task
Force 2014

Interbank transfer schedule in
auditing cash account 702.05

Internal audit
  audit plan for 115.03, 1602
  budget for 1604.04–.05
  fieldwork for 116.01, 1604.05
  follow-up procedures to 1604.08
  inability to detect fraud of 1502
  initial findings of, reporting
    process commencing with..... 1702
  preliminary survey conducted
    during 1604, 1604.02

Internal audit—continued
  reporting results of 116–116.02,
                     1604.06–.07, 1701–1706
  setting objectives for 1604.01

Internal audit staff assessment during pre-planning stage of audit
  . . . . .502.01

Internal auditing
  definition of 1402
  function of 1102
  future trends in 1404–1404.06
  globalization of 1404.01
  new assurance service
    opportunities for 1110.01
  outsourcing of 114, 115.01, 1404.02,
                          1506–1506.02
  paradigm shift to risk-based
    paradigm for 1404.04
  performance areas ranked for . . . 1505
  professional practices framework
    for 1403.02

Internal auditing department. *See*
Internal auditing function

Internal auditing engagement
  audit plan prepared for 1602
  audit program and budget
    developed for 1604.04
  audit report for. . 1604.07–.08. *See also* Audit
            report following internal audit
  budget for 1604
  estimate by CAE of resources for
    1602
  exit interview of 1702, 1703
  fact-finding interviews during 1605
  follow-up procedures for . . 1604, 1604.08
  identifying existence of internal
    controls in 1604.03
  independence impaired by
    performing audit client's 208.03
  meeting with auditee
    management during 1604.02
  objectives for 1604, 1604.01, 1604.04
  phases of 1604
  preliminary survey for 1604
  reporting process in . . . 116.01, 1701–1706
  risk assessment in 1604.03
  risk factors for 1602
  scheduling and performing 115.03,
                          1601–1605
  steps in typical 1604–1604.08
  unique findings of each 1701

Internal auditing function
  annual risk assessment and audit
    scheduling process of 1602, 1902
  audit committee oversight of . . 2606.04
  charter of 1502
  consulting engagements by 1502
  coordinating organizational
    policies with 1503
  environmental audits being
    performed by 2111
  independent contractors
    supplying specialized services to
    1506
  interactions with external auditor
    of 1504
  management of 115, 1501–1507
  mandates for 1404.06, 2606.04

Internal auditing function—continued
  marketing 1506.02
  objectives of 1502, 1505
  performance measurements for . 405,
                                      1505
  quality assurance program in 401
  reporting structure for 1502, 2111
  responsibilities for environmental
    auditing of 2111
  scope of audits prepared by 1502,
                                  1604.01
  services of 1401, 1404.02, 1506.02
  TQM approach to audit quality
    adopted by 405

Internal auditing profession . . 1401–1404.06
  impact of recent financial
    scandals on 1404.06

Internal auditor
  approaches to risk-based audit
    planning of 115.04, 1603
  compliance auditable units
    integrated into risk-assessment
    process of 1901
  continuing education for 1503
  contract audits by 1907
  essence of job of 1701
  external auditor using work of . . . 612,
                                      2002
  fact-finding interview tips for 1605
  fraud identification procedures by
    . . . . .503.05
  function in organization of 114
  impact of financial scandals on
    duties of 1404.06
  in-charge 1604.01–.06, 1604.08, 1702
  independence of 2606.04
  internal control process reviewed
    by 117.02
  international standards for 2403.11
  involvement in environmental
    areas of 2111
  job descriptions for all levels of . . 1503
  knowledge, skills, and abilities of
    future 1404.05, 2112
  new services offered by 111
  qualifications for 1503
  responsibilities for enterprise risk
    management of 1904
  role in EMS audit of 2112
  role in fraud detection of . 115, 2002.01,
                                      2003
  roles in corporate governance
    before and after Sarbanes-
    Oxley Act of 2606.04
  using work of 612

Internal control audit
  PCAOB proposed standard for . . . 1905
  steps in 201.07, 621

Internal control report required under Sarbanes-Oxley Act . 610, 1404.06

Internal control structure 1008

Internal control system in international auditing process . . 2402.04

Internal controls
  annual assessment of 1905

Internal controls—*continued*
  attestation by external auditors
    about 201.01, 621, 1905
  audit committee as setting
    organization's attitude toward .115.02
  audit objectives and 610, 1604
  audit team discussion of
    management override of 503.05
  auditor understanding required for
    610
  auditor's consideration of 611
  auditors' increased reliance on .. 1201
  client responsibility to establish
    and maintain................210.05
  components of............... 610, 1903
  compromise or override of...... 119,
    503.05, 602, 2002
  concepts vital to understanding . 1903
  documents created and used in .. 621
  engagement letter as detailing
    establishment and maintenance
    of.........................502.02
  evaluating effectiveness of .. 621, 1905
  in-charge auditor as ensuring
    existence of adequate 1604.03
  indicators of material
    weaknesses in 201.07, 610, 1905
  information technology as
    influencing 1208
  for information technology (IT)
    system 2303.01
  internal auditor as monitoring ... 612
  internal auditor reviews of .. 117.02, 1604
  knowledge obtained during client
    investigation of..............502.01
  management assessments of ... 102,
    201.07, 610, 1008, 2605.03
  management's attitude toward .. 2007
  material misstatements in
    financial statements not identified by
    1905
  operating effectiveness of 621
  testing 611

Internal Revenue Service agents as
  forensic accountants ... 113, 1301, 1307
  monitoring performance of 610
  reportable conditions
    representing significant
    deficiencies in client's 303.01
  responsibility shared between
    external and internal auditor for
    1504
  testing 106, 502.02, 611
  understanding of, during audit
    planning................503.06, 612

International Accounting
  Standards, adoption of 2401–2405

International Accounting Standards
  Board (IASB).................. 241

International Auditing and Assurance
  Standards Board (IAASB)
    formed by IFAC 2401
    international auditing
      requirements of 2405
    website of 2401

International Auditing Practice
  Statements (IAPS) 2401

International Federation of
  Accountants (IFAC) 2401

International Organization for
  Standardization (ISO)
    standards developed by ... 104, 120.04,
      406, 2105
    websites of 2106

International Organization of
  Securities Commissions (IOSCO) . 2401

International Standard on Quality
  Control (ISQC) No. 1 (IAASB) 2405

International Standards for the
  Professional Practice of Internal
  Auditing (ISPPIA)............. 1403.03

International Standards on Auditing
  (ISAs)...................... 2401
    ISA 200 .... 2403.12
    ISA 220 2405
    ISA 240 .... 2403.10, 2403.12
    ISA 300 2402
    ISA 310 .... 2402.01
    ISA 320 .... 2402.02
    ISA 400 .... 2402.04
    ISA 500 .... 2403.01
    ISA 501 .... 2403.02
    ISA 505 .... 2403.03
    ISA 520 .... 2403.04
    ISA 530 .... 2403.05
    ISA 550 .... 2403.06
    ISA 560 .... 2403.07
    ISA 570 .... 2403.09
    ISA 580 .... 2402.03, 2403.10
    ISA 610 .... 2403.11
    ISA 700 2404
    similarities between SAS No. 99
      and 2402.03

Internet
  business control issues for..... 2305.09
  business transactions on 2306.03

Internet service providers (ISPs),
  WebTrust engagements for
  entities using 1106

Interpretation No. 14 ....120.02

Interpretations of AICPA rules
  No. 101-1, "Interpretation of
    Rule 101" (Interpretation 101-1)
    .... 210–210.06
  No. 101-3 examples of non-attest
    services impairing
    independence..............210.06
  No. 302-1 examples of
    contingent fees..............205.02

Inventories
  fictitious 2012.04
  overvaluing of, fraudulent . 2006, 2012.04
  specialists to help auditors in
    valuing....................503.07

Inventory observation, planning .. 2403.02

Inventory, SEAI report relating to,
  for unaudited financial reports... 1003

Investment activities that do and do
  not impair auditor's
  independence..................210.06

INT

Investors, effects of financial
  scandals on 2605.02
IRS Form 4822, Statement of
  Annual Estimation of Personal
  and Family Expenses 1306.02
ISO 9000
  as management system standard
    . . . . 104, 406, 1803, 2106, 2107
  requirements for operational
    auditing of 1803
ISO 14000
  as environmental management
    system (EMS) standard . . . 120.04, 405,
                                       2107, 2112
  guidance in attesting information
    under 120.04
  niche practice for CPAs certifying
    and auditing EMSs under 2108
  obtaining certification under . . . 120.04,
                                              2106
  as voluntary 2105, 2106
ISO 14001 standards met for
  certification 2106
Issuers, public companies paying
  support fees as 201.03

J

Joint Committee on Internal
  Revenue Taxation 205.03
Joint Ethics Enforcement Program
  (JEEP) members 201.10
Judicial procedure 1207–1207.04
  forensic accountant as requiring
    knowledge of 112.02
Jump teams of IRS 1307
Jurors, expectations about
  accountants of 307

K

Kato, Yasuyoshi, off-book loans
  embezzlement case of . . 304, 1305, 2002
Kickbacks as employee fraud 2001,
                                           2005.02
Kiting
  cash schemes for 2012.01
  as employee fraud 2001
  uncovering 702.05
KPMG fraud study 2005

L

L.A. Gear fraud case 2005.02
Laws and regulations affecting
  organization identified and tested
  by CAE 1906
Leeson, Nick, financial statement
  fraud through derivatives trading
  by 2005.02
Legal liability of auditors 103, 301–308

Legislative law, precedence over
  case law of 1207
Liability of accountants 103, 301–308
  to clients 302–303.04
  fair share proportionate 305.03
  high-profile cases of 302
  joint and several 305.03
  statutory civil 302
  statutory criminal 302
  in SysTrust engagements
    because of dependence on
    SysTrust assurance reports . . 1105.02
  to third parties . . . 304–304.06, 305, 305.01
Liability of expert witnesses, risk
  management of 112.03, 1215
Liability of issuer of security 305.01
Lifestyle changes indicative of fraud
  and unreported income 1304
Lifestyle probes of unreported
  income 1302, 1304, 1305
Limited liability company (LLC)
  entities for accounting firms . . . 205.06,
                                              303.04
Limited liability partnership (LLP)
  entities
  advantages of 303.04
  national accounting firms
    organized as 103
Limited procedures used to review
  financial statements 109
Litigation between auditing firm
  and client, independence impaired by
    . . . . .210.07
Litigation, inquiries to client's legal
  representative about pending 706,
                                          707, 2403.02
Litigation risk, refusing clients
  having high 303.03
Litigation support by forensic
  accountant . 112.01. See also Expert witnessing
  combined with fraud detection . . 1202
  as management consulting
    specialty subject to AICPA's
    Statement on Standards for
    Consulting Services No. 1,
    Consulting Services: Definitions
    and Standards 1214
Litigation support counseling 1210.01
Litigation trend toward increased
  liability 301
Livent, Inc., fraud case 2005.02
Living expenses, determining
  IRS Form 4822 for 1306.02
  in net worth method 1306.04
Loan agreement, report on financial
  statements prepared pursuant to . 1005
Loans to or from client or client's
  officer or director, independence
  violated by 210, 210.04

LOA

M

McKesson & Robbins financial statement fraud case 2002, 2005.02

Mail and wire fraud, maximum penalty for 306.03

Malpractice insurance for CPAs 302

Malpractice suits. *See also* Liability of accountants
 as expensive to litigate 303.03
 from marketing claims of auditing firms 205.04
 statute of limitation for......... 303

Managed earnings 119.01, 2005–2007

Management
 incompetent 2005
 power-sharing with audit committee by 213.02
 responsibilities in corporate governance before and after Sarbanes-Oxley Act of 2606.03
 roles in fraudulent financial reporting of................. 2005

Management assertions. *See also* individual assertions
 applications of auditing procedures to. *See* Auditing procedures
 categories of 603–603.05
 defined..................... 603
 evidence to support........ 604.01, 617
 link between audit objectives and 106, 604–604.02
 proper application of GAAP as supporting 106

Management information systems (MIS) 2302

Management integrity, sources of information on client's 502.01

Management letter
 engagement letter stipulation of delivery by auditor of 303.01
 obtaining 713
 purposes of 713

Management representation letter
 obtaining 713, 2403.10
 requested in engagement letter . .303.01
 sample.................... 2403.10
 subsequent events addressed in . 707

Management responsibilities for enterprise risk management..... 1904

Management's plans reviewed if auditor doubts client company can remain going concern 709

Manufacturing plant, auditor as relating cost accumulation system to flow of materials and processes during 503.03

Market Segment Specialization Program 1306.01

Marketing of internal auditing services by outsourcers 1506.02

Material misstatement in financial statements
 of additional information included in financial statements 804.05
 assessment of control risk for ... 613
 auditing engagement with high degree of risk of 604.02
 auditor's adverse versus qualified opinion determined by 803.03
 auditor's responsibility for detecting 602, 2002, 2004
 collusion and fraudulent transactions creating......... 602
 correction of 502.02
 fieldwork assessment of 705, 710
 due to fraud ... 503.01, 503.05, 504, 604.02, 605, 610, 618, 705, 710, 2403.12
 forensic and fraud auditors as responsible for finding deliberate 1202
 immaterial versus 617
 internal controls designed to prevent and detect.......... 610
 tests of programs and controls for 611

Materiality, audit risk and ... 605, 2402.02

Mediation as form of ADR 1215.01

Minimum income probes 1303

Minutes of board of directors, auditor review of
 for discussions of subsequent events to balance sheet date... 707

Misappropriation of assets fraud
 risk factors for................ 2011
 schemes involving 2012–2012.04

Motion for summary judgment ... 1207.03

Motion *in limine* **challenging expert witness testimony** 1210.03, 1211

Multinational enterprises (MNEs) .. 2401

N

NASAA website links to regulatory agencies 2008

National Association of Certified Valuation Analysts (NACVA) 1216, 2002.02

National Association of Corporate Directors, corporate governance recommendations of 2606

National Association of Local Government Auditors (NALGA)... 1908
 audit summary database of . 1805, 1902, 1908
 state and local government accountants and auditors in ... 2502
 website of 1805, 1907, 1908

Near-privity approach to auditor liability 304, 304.02

Negative assurance in compliance reports 1004, 1902

Index—References are to paragraph (¶) numbers. **947**

Negligence
  in audit report, liability to third
    party for 304–304.06
  claims in client liability cases of .. 103, 303
  proving 303.02, 304
  types of, for auditor's actions ...303.02
  violation of Rule 501 by 205.04

Negligent misrepresentation by auditor 304.05

Negotiation as form of ADR 1215.01

Net worth method of reconstructing income 1306.04

Networks, computer 2305.05

New date for financial audit report for tests after last day of fieldwork 804.02

New York Stock Exchange (NYSE)
  corporate governance
    recommendations of 2606
  mandate for internal auditing
    function of 1404.06

Non-audit services, auditor providing specific, independence violated by 208.05, 210.05–.06

Notes to financial statements . 801, 904.06

O

Oklahoma City Federal Building bombing, IT system business continuation following 2303.01

OMB Circular A-133 .... 2504.08

Online systems, risks of 2305.02

Operating characteristics associated with fraud risk factors . 2007

Operating objectives for internal audit 1604.04

Operational audit
  audit tests for 117.02
  conclusion presented in draft
    audit report for..............117.02
  fieldwork for 117.02
  by internal auditors............ 1402
  phases of 117.02
  planning.....................117.02
  preliminary survey for 117.02
  users of 117

Operational audit engagement
  interviewing and observations in
    .... 1604.02
  questions for preliminary survey in
    .... 1604.02
  typical 1805

Operational auditing .... 1801–1807. *See also* Government performance audit
  cost savings and improvements
    in procedures identified by 1805
  defined 117, 1802
  demand for 1803
  examples of 1805

Operational auditing—continued
  as form of internal control review
    1806
  integrated with financial and
    compliance auditing 1805
  linked with TQM 1803
  measurement of effectiveness in . 1806
  nonaccountants performing 1804

Operational auditor, necessary knowledge, skills, and abilities and education for 1804

Operational issues for financial audit areas 1805

Opinion paragraph, unqualified opinion report 803.01

Organization charts of clients reviewed by auditors during audit preparation..................503.01

Other comprehensive bases of accounting (OCBOA)
  audits of financial statements
    prepared in conformity with ... 1001
  compilation reports for financial
    statements using 903.04
  non-GAAP financial statements
    using... 109, 902.04, 903.04, 905.06, 1002
  reports using 110, 1002

Out-of-pocket loss as theory for measuring damages............ 1213

Outside directors in organization's audit committee...............115.02

Outsourcing of internal auditing ... 113, 1506
  competition introduced by 1404.02
  marketing by independent
    contractors for 1506.02
  paradigm shift toward 1506.01

Oversight organization for accounting industry, new 207

P

Panel on Audit Effectiveness
  elements of financial reporting
    frauds described by 2006
  forensic-type procedures
    recommended for every audit
    by 304, 2003, 2011
  high-risk areas to audit identified
    by 2011
  peer review recommendations by
    ....403.04
  refusal to define illegitimate
    earnings management by 2005
  view of effectiveness of SAS No.
    82 of 2011

Partners, auditing firm
  compensation changes for 2607.03
  protection from liability of ... 103, 301, 303.04

Payroll and disbursements activities that do and do not impair auditor's independence.........210.06

PAY

Peer review program of AICPA . 402.02, 403
  assumed by PCAOB 401, 2602
Peer reviews of government auditors 2504.02, 2504.04
Pension fund blackout periods, insider trades during 102
Performance audit. *See* Government performance audit *and* Operational audit
Performance Measurement for Government website 1807
Performance measures
  categories of nonfinancial 1104
  developing 1807
  identifying relevant 1104
  IIA guidance on system for . . . 104.405
  information technology 2303.01
  operational audits emphasizing . . 1805
  potential services by CPAs for . . . 1104
  preferred by CAEs, IIA survey of . 1505
  tied to internal auditing department's mission and goals 405
  TQM approach to improvement on 1505
Permanent file of engagement, items included in 503.08
Personal computers (PCs)
  auditor's interactions with 122.04, 2306-2306.03
  evolution of 2302
  risks with 2305.06
Phar-Mor fraud case 2005.02
Physical inventory counting, international standards for 2403.02
Piecemeal opinions 1003
Pinez, Emanuel, fraud case against . 2006
Pitt, Harvey (SEC)
  improvements to address accounting problems suggested by 212
  new accounting oversight board proposed by 207, 401
Plains All-American Pipeline fraud case 2005.02
Planning financial audit 501-504
  audit staff supervision for 504
  benefits of 501
  impact of fraud risk factors on . . 503.05, 618
  judging risk during 503.06
  preparation stage of . . . 501, 503-503.08
  pre-planning stage of . . . 501, 502.01-.02
  time line for 501
Planning memo
  as evidence of financial audit planning 105, 503.08
  prepared at culmination of audit planning process 503.08
Pleadings in litigation 112.02, 1207.01

Preliminary judgment of materiality by auditor 503.04
Presentation and disclosure management assertion 603.05
  correspondence to audit objectives of 604.02
Price-level basis of accounting 902.04, 1002
PricewaterhouseCoopers
  actions by SEC against, for investments audit clients 2006
  alleged violation of SEC Rule 102(e) by 206.01
  client violations prompting "going concern" issues by 2006
Printer's proofs of financial statements reviewed and approved by auditing firm 303.01
Privacy law, IT system security following passage of stricter 2303.01
Private Securities Litigation Reform Act of 1995 (PSLRA) 305.03, 305.07
Professional conduct 201-212
Professional organizations, anti-fraud programs and recommendations of 1210.03
Professional skepticism
  of auditors 502.01, 503.05, 504, 2002
  defined in SAS No. 99 . . . . 502.01
  of forensic auditors 119.02, 2006
  of government auditors 2504.04
Professional Standards **(AICPA)**
  Interpretation No. 1, "System Reviews Performed at Location Other than Practitioner's Office" 403.01
  Rule 201, *General Standards* . . . 112.02, 1214
  Rule 202, *Compliance with Standards* 402
  Rule 301, *Confidential Client Information* 205-205.01
  Rule 302, *Contingent Fees* . 205, 205.02
  Rule 501, *Discreditable Acts* 205.03
  Rule 502, *Advertising and Other Forms of Solicitation* 205.04
  Rule 503, *Commissions and Referral Fees* 205.05
  Rule 505, *Form of Organization and Name* 205.06
Program review in performance audit 1806
Projections as prospective financial statements. *See also* Prospective financial statements
  assumptions made for 1007.02
  compilation of 1007.04
  content of 1007
  examination of 1007.05-.11
Proof of cash, preparing 702.05

PEE

Index—References are to paragraph (¶) numbers.

Prospective financial statements 1007–1007.11
   assumptions and disclosures
     about 1007.02, 1007.08, 1007.11
   compilation of 1007.03–.04
   conformity with AICPA
     presentation guidelines of 1007.08
   departure from AICPA guidelines
     prompting qualified or adverse
     opinion for 1007.11
   examination of 1007.05–.11
   minimum requirements for 1007.01
   other procedures performed on 1007.08
   report on 1007.09–.10
   responsible party for, determining 1007.03

Public accounting firms. *See also*
   Accounting firms
     consolidation of 102
     inspection by PCAOB of 402
     report of 805

**Public Company Accounting
Oversight Board (PCAOB)** 102, 701
   attestation standards being
     developed by 201.07, 212
   auditing internal control
     standards by .. 201.07, 212, 1905, 2606.05
   auditing standards established by .... 201.01. *See also* individual standards
   authority of 404, 501
   created by Sarbanes-Oxley Act
     .... 201–201, 201.01, 306.03, 401, 621
   direction of 2002
   disciplinary proceedings by 2602
   duties of 102, 2602
   final rules for............. 201.01, 2602
   funding rules and support fee of .201.03
   inspection of registered
     accounting firms overseen by .. 402, 2602
   interim rules for public
     companies of 201.04
   involved in developing ethical
     rules for accountants 201, 212
   members of 201.01, 404
   non-audit services curtailed by .. 1101
   oversight of non-U.S. public
     accounting firms by 2405
   in peer reviews 201.01
   powers of 201.01, 306.03, 2602
   pressure to look for fraud by 119
   quality control standards being
     developed by 212, 2606.05–.06
   registration system of .. 201.02, 404, 2405
   regulatory framework for
     auditing created by 2606.05
   sanctions of................. 306.03
   SEC oversight of 102.06
   self-regulation of accounting
     firms ended by 2602
   Standing Advisory Group (SAG)
     established to advise 201.01
   summary of competition,
     responsibility, and operating
     procedures of 404
   terms used by, definitions of 201.05

**Public Company Accounting Oversight
Board (PCAOB)**—continued
   work with European Commission
     (EC) on global auditing
     standards of 2405

**Public Company Accounting Oversight
Board (PCAOB) Auditing Standards**
   No. 1, References in Auditor's
     Reports to the Standards of the
     Public Company Accounting
     Oversight Board.... 108, 802, 805, 907
   No. 2, An Audit of Internal
     Control over Financial
     Reporting Performed in
     Conjunction with an Audit of
     Financial Services . 201.07, 501, 610, 621, 712, 1008
   No. 3, Audit Documentation and
     Amendment to Interim Auditing
     Standards 616.03

Public Oversight Board (POB)
   creation of................... 401
   as voting itself out of existence
     following Enron debacle 207, 401

**Public trust of accounting, financial
report and investment, and
management of public
corporations, crisis in** 119.01

Purchase Pro fraud case 2006

Purchases cutoff test 704.04

Q

**Qualified opinion in financial audit
report** 108
   auditor's reservations calling for .803.02
   international standards for issuing 2403.08
   issued if going concern problem
     is inadequately disclosed 709

**Qualified opinion in prospective
financial statement report** 1007.11

**Qualified report, international
standards for** 2404

Quality assurance
   AICPA efforts in 401, 402–402.02
   analytics used for 2202.02
   focus for corporate governance on 2606.07
   IIA GAIN program for benchmarking 401, 405
   for internal audit report, CAE as
     establishing process for .. 116.02, 1505
   ISO standards for. *See* ISO 9000 *and*
     ISO 14000
   peer review for small firms from
     AICPA for 403–403.04

**Quality assurance program in
internal auditing department** 401

**Quality control policies and
procedures of firm, factors for** ... 402

**Quality control standards for
auditing** 104, 210.05, 401–405

QUA

Query function in software,
 auditor's use of 2306.03
Questions for fact-finding
 interviews 1605
Questions for inventory that prompt
 red flags for fraud 2012.04
Questions for preliminary survey
 for all audit types............ 1604.02

R

Racketeer-Influenced and Corrupt
 Organization (RICO) statute,
 fraud types involving auditors under
 ....305.07
Ratio analysis
 as analytical procedure
  performed during audit preparation
  ....503.02
 Benford's Law in 2010.01
 DATAS in 2010.02
 defined 2010
 red flags for fraud revealed by ... 2008,
  2010
Reconstructing income.......... 113
Records, client, retention of 205.03
Red flags of financial manipulations
 .... 119.02–.03
Regression analysis as analytical
 procedure performed during
 audit preparation 503.02
Regulation S-K (SEC) 803.01
Regulatory agency
 presentations prepared in
  compliance with provisions of .. 1005
 report on company's compliance
  with 1004
 report on financial statements
  prepared using basis prescribed
  by 1002
Regulatory basis, financial
 statements prepared using 1002
Regulatory framework for auditors
 by PCAOB................ 401, 2602
Regulatory intervention, financial
 reporting fraud as encouraging .. 2005
Related-party transactions
 defined..................... 708
 in Enron, investigation by Special
  Committee of Board of
  Directors of................ .804.07
 international standards for 2403.06
 undisclosed recorded value
  greater than FMV due to 602
Remediation environmental laws... 2102
Rent-Way, Inc., accounting
 improprieties at 2002.01
Report review as type of AICPA peer
 review for small firms 403.03

Reportable conditions of
 deficiencies in internal controls . 303.01,
  610
Representation letter for SSARS
 review, sample client 905.05
Restatement Second approach to
 auditor liability 304, 304.03
Restatement Second of Torts § 531
 on intentional misrepresentation
 by auditor 304.06
Restricted use paragraph
 in financial presentation 1005
 in SEAI report 1003
Restrictive privity of relationship
 approach to auditor liability 304,
  304.01
Review engagements
 engagement letter for 905.02
 independence impaired during... .905.01
 standards for................. .902.02
Review procedures 905.04
Review report
 comparative 906.02
 form and language of SSARS 905.06
 on income tax basis 905.06
 reasons not to issue 905.01
 SSARS................. 905.06–906.01
 standard, for OCBOA financial
  statements 905.06
 subsequent discovery of facts
  existing at date of........... .902.05
Review representation letter 905.05
Reviews 905–905.06
 change from audit to 904.10
 with departure from GAAP or
  OCBOA 906.01
 planning for 905.03
 of prior period audit, current
  period with 906.02
 of prior period compilation,
  current period with 906.02
 prior period, current period with
  audit of 906.02
Rights and obligations management
 assertion 603.03
 correspondence to audit
  objectives of 604.02
Risk assessment
 analytics used during 2202.02
 compliance auditable units
  integrated into 1901
 as component of internal controls
  610
 documented in workpapers,
  evidence of performing.... 119, 2004
 during internal audit process 1602,
  1604.03
 Elliott Committee development of
  business plan for 1101
 focus of traditional 115.04, 1603
 internal policies and procedures
  of strategic importance
  identified during annual ... 118, 1902

Index—References are to paragraph (¶) numbers.

Risk assessment—continued
international auditing standards
for 2402.04
response to risk of material
misstatements during 2004
responsibilities for, internal and
external auditors sharing 1504
services included in 1103
types of risks addressed by 1103

Risk communication 1603

Risk factors for fraud . 503.01, 503.05, 604.02, 2004, 2007, 2011, 2403.12

Risk management
CAE as positioning internal
auditing function as key player
in enterprise 1603
enterprise. See Enterprise risk
management
environmental auditing seen as
tool of 2109
for expert witnesses 112.03, 1215
in risk-based audit planning 1603
for sampling 2208

**Risk officer, responsibilities for
enterprise risk management of** .. 1904

**Risks associated with financial
statement audits** 503.06

Rite Aid fraud case 2005.02

Rules of Conduct (AICPA)
101 Independence 203
102 Integrity and Objectivity 203
201 General Standards . 203, 204–204.04
202 Compliance with Standards.. 203, 204.05
203 Accounting Principles .. 203, 204.06
301 Confidential Client Information
.... 203
302 Contingent Fees 203
501 Acts Discreditable 203
502 Advertising and Other Forms
of Solicitation 203
503 Commissions and Referral Fees
.... 203
505 Form of Organization and
Name..................... 203

**Rules of conduct, levels of conduct
compared with** 303.02

S

Sales cutoff tests 703.04

Sampling
block or cluster 2203
classic variable (CVS) 2207, 2207.03
concepts of risk and exceptions in
.... 121.05
defined 121.02, 2203
extrapolation from 2203
integrated into audit tests . 121, 121.02
international standards for 2403.05
interval (systematic)........... 2203
probability proportional to size
(PPS) (dollar-unit).. 2205, 2207, 2207.03
risks of 121.03, 2204
setting sample size for .. 2206.04, 2207.03

Sampling—continued
statistical versus nonstatistical .. 2203, 2205
stop-and-go................. 2206.04
tests using. See Attribute sampling test
and Variable sample test
tips for accurate 2208
variable.................. 2205, 2207

Sarbanes-Oxley Act of 2002
attestation of internal controls by
management and external
auditor required by . 201.01, 621, 1404.06
authority to apply provisions to
non-U.S. public accounting firms of
.... 2405
corporate codes of conduct under
.... 2602
criminal misconduct under 306.03
eight non-audit services
prohibited under 111
fraud prevention efforts
increased in light of 112, 114
independence of auditors
mandated by 201.06
independence of audit committee
members mandated by 115.02
initiated to restore investor
confidence and public trust in
financial information 2601
internal control treatment under . 610, 712, 1905
management's verification of
annual reports mandated by ... 115
non-audit services curtailed by .. 102, 1101
Public Company Accounting
Oversight Board created by ... 201, 201.01, 306.03, 401, 621
SEC required to issue rules for
audit committees under 1507
summary of corporate
governance, accounting, and
auditing provisions of 102, 2606

Satisfaction surveys for auditors ... 1505

Scienter, proving 305.02

**Scope limitations in qualified
reports**...................... 803.02

**SEC Practice Section (SECPS) Peer
Review Committee** 403.04

Securities Act of 1933
auditor's civil liability under 305
civil liability penalties under 305.01
criminal penalties under 306.01
lawsuits for untrue statement of
material fact under 305.01
PSLRA as revising accounting
litigation provisions of 305.03
SEC enforcement of 206

**Securities analysts, conflicts of
interests of** 102

**Securities and Exchange Commission
(SEC)**
actions in 2001 against Arthur
Andersen of 206.01
assessing effectiveness of
internal control over financial
reporting required by 1905

SEC

Securities and Exchange Commission (SEC)—continued
audit committee regulations of 1404.06, 1507
Blue Ribbon Committee sponsored by stock exchanges and 1507
civil actions for infractions of securities laws brought by 305
direction of 2002
enforcement action statistics of . 2014
enforcement rules of 206–206.01
final rules for corporate governance by 2606
financial statement fraud being attacked by 2005.01
fraud deficiencies claimed by, breakdown by percentage of ...206.01
global financial reporting framework being developed by . 2401
governance of CPA services by Auditing Standards Board and . 901
prosecution of accounting fraud and increased enforcement cases brought by 308
rules for audit committees by ... 1507
rules to implement Sarbanes-Oxley provisions by . 102, 603.06, 2601, 2602, 2606.06
violations of independence of auditors' services being reexamined by 208–208.01
weak internal controls being attacked by 1905, 2005.01
web site for enforcement actions of 206.01
web site for independence issues 210.08

Securities and Exchange Commission (SEC) Enforcement Rules 102
Rule 102(e) 102, 206.01
Rule 2-01 revision mandating stricter auditor independence rules 208

Securities disputes, auditor's defense strategies in 305.05

Securities Exchange Act of 1934
auditor's civil liability under 305, 305.02
criminal penalties under 306.02
PSLRA as revising accounting litigation provisions of 305.03
SEC enforcement of 206

Securities fraud, new criminal category for 102

Securities Litigation Uniform Standards Act of 1998 ....305.04

Sequoia Systems fraud case 2005.02

Service bureaus for IT 2305.07

Service contracts for outsourced operations 1901

Service, Efforts, and Accomplishments (SEA) experiment of GASB 1807

SIAS No. 8 (IIA) 2009

Single Audit Act .. 118.02, 123.03, 2504.01–.02, 2504.08

Single audits, reports issued for .. 2504.08

Smarktalk TeleServices, SEC enforcement action against 306.03

Software
on computer system being examined, avoiding use of 1209
used by auditors 2306.02–.03

Source and application of funds (expenditure) method 1306.03

Source documents for client's transactions, auditor prohibited from preparing 210.05

Special Purpose Entities (SPEs), off-balance sheet treatment of liabilities incurred by Enron's 708

Special reports, categories of .. 110, 1001

Specialists
evidence gathering using 607
to help auditor fulfill audit objectives 503.07, 607
inventory valuation 503.07
objectivity of 607
verifying qualifications of 607

Specified elements, account, or items (SEAI) of financial statements, audits of 1003

SSARS review
client representation letter for, statements in 905.05
engagement letter for, sample ...905.02
review report for 905.06

Staff Accounting Bulletin (SAB)
No. 92, *Accounting and Disclosures Relating to Loss Contingencies* 120.02, 2104
No. 99 ....403.04

Standard Form to Confirm Account Balance Information with Financial Institutions 702.05

Standards for Professional Practice of Internal Auditing (SPPIA) (IIA) 2504.01, 2504.02

Stanford Securities Class Action Clearinghouse 305

State licensing rules for CPAs 201.10

Statement of cash flow in financial statements 801, 904.06

Statement of changes in stockholder equity 801

Statement of comprehensive income 801, 903.04, 905.06

Statement of Financial Accounting Standards (SFAS)
No. 5, *Accounting for Contingencies* 120.02, 2104
No. 19, *Financial Accounting and Reporting by Oil and Gas Producing Companies* 120.02, 2104

Index—References are to paragraph (¶) numbers.

Statement of Position (SOP) 96-1,
*Environmental Remediation
Liabilities*.................. 120.02, 2104

Statement of Position (SOP) 98-3,
*Audits of States, Local
Governments, and Not-for-Profit
Organizations Receiving Federal
Awards* 2504.08

**Statement of retained earnings in
financial statements** 801

Statement of Revenue and Expenses. *See*
Income statement in financial
statements

**Statements on Auditing Standards
(SAS)** 108, 403
No. 1, *Codification of Auditing
Standards and Procedures* 501,
503.06, 601, 803.02, 804.03 902.05
No. 12, *Inquiry of Client's
Lawyers Concerning Litigation,
Claims, and Assessments* 706
No. 25, *Relationship of Generally
Accepted Auditing Standards to
Quality Control Standards*..... 401
No. 31, *Evidential Matter* 603
No. 42, *Reporting on Condensed
Financial Statements and
Selected Financial Data* 804.06
No. 45, *Omnibus Statement on
Auditing Standards*........... 708
No. 51, *Reporting on Financial
Statements Prepared for Use in
Other Countries* 804.04
No. 54, *Illegal Acts by Clients* . . . 305.06,
1901
No. 56, *Analytical Procedures* ... 711,
2009, 2202.03
No. 58, *Reports on Audited
Financial Statements* 803.02
No. 59, *Auditor's Considerations
of Entity's Ability to Continue as
Going Concern* 709
No. 60, *Communication of
Internal Control Related
Matters Noted in Audit* 1105.01
No. 62, *Special Reports* 1002
No. 80, *Amendment to
Statement on Auditing
Standards No. 31, Evidential Matter*
.... 1209
No. 82, *Consideration of Fraud in
Financial Statement Audit*.. 103, 119,
304, 305.06, 602, 618, 2002, 2004, 2007, 2011
No. 84, *Communications
Between Predecessor and
Successor Auditor* 502.01
No. 85, *Management
Representations* 713
No. 89, *Audit Adjustments* 403.04
No. 96, *Audit Documentation* ... 607,
616.01
No. 99, *Consideration of Fraud in
a Financial Statement Audit* ... 103,
119, 204.02, 501, 502.01, 503.01, 503.05, 610,
613, 616.01, 618, 620, 711, 1202–1202.01,
2002, 2004, 2402.03, 2605.03

**Statements on Quality Control Standards
(SQCS)**
No. 1.................. 204.03, 402.02

**Statements on Quality Control Standards
(SQCS)**—continued
No. 2, *Systems of Quality Control
for CPA Firm's Accounting and
Auditing Practice* 402.01–.02
No. 3 .... 402.02
No. 5, *Personal Management
Element of Firm's System of
Quality Control, Competencies
Required by Practitioner in
Charge of Attest Engagement* . . 402.02

**Statements on Standards for
Accounting and Review Services
(SSARS) (AICPA)**......... 109, 403, 905
1, Compilation and Review of
Financial Statements 901, 904.12
2, Reporting on Comparative
Financial Statements 901
3, Compilation Reports on
Financial Statements Included
in Certain Prescribed Forms ... 901,
904.07
4, Communications Between
Predecessor and Successor
Accountants 901
5, Reporting on Compiled
Financial Statements 901
6, Reporting on Personal
Financial statements Included
in Written Personal Financial Plans
.... 901
7, Omnibus Statement on
Standards for Accounting and
Review Services—1992 901
8, Amendment to SSARS1 . 901, 904.12
Interpretation No. 15,
"Differentiating Financial
Statement Presentation from
Trial Balance".............. 902.03
Interpretation No. 16,
"Determining If Accountant Has
Submitted Financial Statements
Even When Not Engaged to
Compile or Review Financial
Statements"............... 904.11
review inquiry procedures under .905.04

**Statements on Standards for
Attestation Engagements (SSAEs)**
.... 403, 2504.04
No. 1, *Attestation Standards*... 1105.02
No. 2.................. 1008, 1105.01
No. 3 2111
No. 4 2111
No. 10, Attestation Standards:
Revision and Recodification ... 111,
1007–1007.04, 1007.07–.09, 1102

**Statements on Standards for
Consulting Services No.**
1, *Consulting Services: Definitions
and Standards*................ 1214

**StockDetective.com, SEC targets
listed by**..................... 2008

**Subsequent discovery of facts
existing at date of financial
statement audit report** 804.07

**Subsequent events to financial audits'
balance sheet date**
dating auditor's report for 804.02

SUB

Subsequent events to financial audits' balance sheet date—continued
  international standards for 2403.07
  reviewing for 707
Substantive tests
  applied prior to balance sheet date
  614
  applied to accounts payable audit
  .... 704–704.04
  applied to accounts receivable
  audit 703–703.04
  applied to cash account balance
  .... 702–702.05
  breakdown into procedures of ... 607
  defined 106, 606
  design of 610
  external auditor's use of internal
  auditor's 612
  interim 614
  for material account balances
  and classes of transactions in
  international auditing standards
  .... 2402.04
  risk of fraud requiring more 605
  timing of 614
  types of 606
  when fraud risk factors produce
  high degree of risk 604.02
Superfund. *See* Comprehensive Environmental Response, Compensation, and Liability Act (CERCLA) (Superfund)
Superfund Amendments and Reauthorization Act (SARA) 2102
Supervising auditor, role in financial audit of 504
System reviews as type of AICPA peer review for small firms 403.01
SysTrust engagement 1105.02
SysTrust for information systems reliability
  competency model of 2308
  as control framework for IT . 122.03, 2304
  in CPA attest engagement 1102
  developed by AICPA and CICA
  task force 1105.02
  Elliott Committee development of
  business plan for 1101
  principles and criteria for, table of
  .... 1105.02

T

Tax claims for malpractice 302
Tax compliance, current state of ... 1308
Tax services stipulated in auditor's engagement letter 303.01
Team, audit engagement. *See* Audit team
Technical Consulting Practice Aid 7: Litigation Services 1212
Technology issues in investigations and court cases 112.02
10 commandments for depositions
  .... 1207.02

Testimony of accountant. *See also* Evidence
  based on facts or opinion 112.02
  overcoming jurors' expectation
  gap during 307
Tests of controls 611
  applied to accounts payable audit
  .... 704.01–.04
  applied to accounts receivable
  audit 703–703.04
  applied to cash account balance
  .... 702–702.05
  external auditor's use of internal
  auditor's 612
Threat scenario approach to risk-based audit planning 115.04, 1603
Timing differences in financial statement fraud 2006
Total Quality Management (TQM) approach to audit quality 405, 1505
Transparency of financial statements, AICPA rules for 201.08
Treadway Commission report, *Internal Controls-Integrated Framework* 2002
Trend analysis 119
  as analytical procedure
  performed during audit preparation
  .... 503.02
  red flags for fraud revealed by ... 2008
Trial balance versus financial statements 902.03
Trial courts 1207, 1210.03
Tyco International fraud case 2005.02

U

Ultramares **approach to auditor liability** 304.02
U.S. General Accounting Office (GAO)
  report on IT investments 2303.01
  sample internal auditing report
  based on 1706
  Yellow Book published by . 1806, 2504.01
U.S. International Trade Commission (USITC), estimated Clean Air Act expenditures by 2101
U.S. Sentencing Commission guidelines 301
Unqualified opinion in financial audit report 108
  for additional documents
  included with audited financial
  statements 804.05
  for comparative financial
  statements 804.03
  contents of 803.01
  for financial statements prepared
  for use in another country 804.04
  issued for SEAI report 1003
  issued if going concern problem
  disclosure is adequate 709
  as most positive report 803–803.01
  situations allowing 803.01

SUB

Index—References are to paragraph (¶) numbers.

Unqualified report
    for condensed financial statements 804.06
    contents of 803.01
    for financial presentation 1005
    international standards for 2404
    for prospective financial statement 1007.09
    standard 803.01

Unrecorded liabilities, search during accounts payable audit for 704.04

Unreported income, reconstructing 113
    indirect methods of 113, 1301–1308

V

Validity of evidence, forms of upholding 609

Valuation
    of investments in precious metals and gems 503.07
    of pension plans 503.07
    of related party transactions 708

Valuation or allocation management assertion 603.04
    correspondence to audit objectives of 604.02

Valuation services, independence impaired by providing audit client's 208.03, 210.06

Variable sampling test
    for account balance testing 2207
    defining population for 2207.02
    documenting results of 2207.05
    sample selection for 2207.03
    setting sample size for 2207.03
    test objectives for............ 2207.01
    testing sample in............. 2207.04

Variance analysis 2202.01

Vendor information checked for inventory fraud 2012.04

Vendor performance, contract provisions for 1907

Vertical analysis to analyze income statements and margins 2202.01

Vertical percentage analysis 119.03
    red flags for fraud revealed by ... 2008

W

Waste Management case of exaggerated profits, Arthur Andersen fined by SEC for fraud in 206.01

WebTrust engagements 1106

WebTrust for electronic commerce in CPA attest engagement 1102

WebTrust for electronic commerce—continued
    Elliott Committee development of business plan for 1101
    online businesses "audited" using 2305.09
    risks of e-commerce sites addressed by 1106

Whisper earnings, class action lawsuits involving 305

Withdrawal from audit engagement
    delinquent client payments prompting 402.02
    fraudulent acts and fraud risk causing 618, 904
    inadequate managerial response to illegal acts prompting 619
    refusal to create management representation letter prompting 713

Workpapers, audit 616
    documentation of compilation services in................. 1007.03
    documentation of evidence of performing risk assessment in . 119, 2004
    documentation of preliminary assessment in 610, 1604.03
    features of 616.01
    retention of 102, 306.03, 616
    SAS 96 requirements for 616.01

Worksheets, characteristics of individual 616.02

Workshop, CSA 118.01, 1903

WorldCom
    collapse of 107, 501, 1201
    fraudulent financial statements of 2005, 2005.02, 2605.03

www.nasdr.com, broker disclosure information on 2008

X

Xerox, fraudulent financial statements of 2005.02, 2605.03

Y

Year-end testing procedures in financial statement audit
    for accounts payable balance ... 704.02
    for accounts receivable balance . 703.02
    for cash account balance, summary table of 702.04

Yellow Book. *See Generally accepted government auditing standards (GAGAS)*

Z

ZZZZ Best Carpet fraud case 2005.02, 2012.02